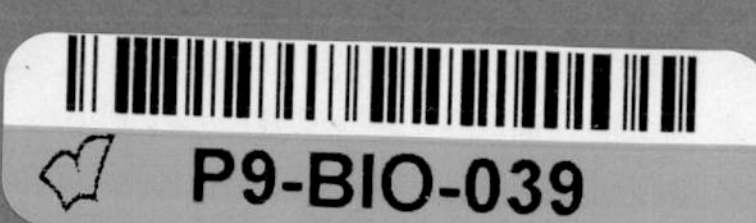

60984 81800

# EUROPEAN WRITERS

## The Twentieth Century

# EUROPEAN WRITERS
## The Twentieth Century

*GEORGE STADE*
*EDITOR IN CHIEF*

Volume 13

**JEAN ANOUILH**

**TO**

**MILAN KUNDERA**

Charles Scribner's Sons
NEW YORK

Collier Macmillan Canada
TORONTO

Maxwell Macmillan International
NEW YORK    OXFORD    SINGAPORE    SYDNEY

**Library of Congress Cataloging-in-Publication Data**
(Revised for volumes 10–11)

European writers.

Vols. 5– . Jacques Barzun, editor, George Stade, editor in chief.
Vols. 8– . George Stade, editor in chief.
Includes bibliographies.
Contents: v. 1–2. The Middle Ages and the Renaissance: Prudentius to Medieval Drama. Petrarch to Renaissance Short Fiction—v. 3–4. The Age of Reason and the Enlightenment: René Descartes to Montesquieu. Voltaire to André Chénier.—v. 5–7. The Romantic Century: Goethe to Pushkin. Hugo to Fontane. Baudelaire to the Well-Made Play—v. 8–9. The Twentieth Century: Sigmund Freud to Paul Valéry. Pío Baroja to Franz Kafka. v. 10–11. Yevgeny Zamyatin to Pär Lagerkvist. Walter Benjamin to Yuri Olesha. v. 12–13. George Seferis to Yannis Ritsos. Jean Anouilh to Milan Kundera.
1. European literature—History and criticism—Addresses, essays, lectures. I. Jackson, W. T. H. (William Thomas Hobdell), 1915–1983. II. Stade, George. III. Barzun, Jacques.
PN501.E9 1983 809'.894 83–16333

ISBN 0–684–16594–5 (v. 1–2)
ISBN 0–684–17914–8 (v. 3–4)
ISBN 0–684–17915–6 (v. 5–7)
ISBN 0–684–18923–2 (v. 8)
ISBN 0–684–18924–0 (v. 9)
ISBN 0–684–17916–4 (v. 10)
ISBN 0–684–18798–1 (v. 11)
ISBN 0–684–19158–X (v. 12)
ISBN 0–684–19159–8 (v. 13)

Charles Scribner's Sons
Macmillan Publishing Company
866 Third Ave.
New York, New York 10022

Collier Macmillan Canada, Inc.
1200 Eglington Ave. East
Suite 200
Don Mills, Ontario M3C 3N1



1 3 5 7 9 11 13 15 17 19 B/C 20 18 16 14 12 10 8 6 4 2

PRINTED IN THE UNITED STATES OF AMERICA

The paper in this book meets the guidelines for permanence and durability of the Committee on Production Guidelines for Book Longevity of the Council on Library Resources.

# ACKNOWLEDGMENTS

The following pamphlets in the Columbia University Press Series Columbia Essays on Modern Writers have been reprinted in this volume by special arrangement with Columbia University Press, the publisher:

Archer, Marguerite: *Jean Anouilh*
Copyright © 1971 Columbia University Press

Brée, Germaine: *Albert Camus*
Copyright © 1964 Columbia University Press

Roudiez, Leon S: *Michel Butor*
Copyright © 1965 Columbia University Press

# LIST OF SUBJECTS

## *Volume 12*

## *Volume 13*

# CONTRIBUTORS TO VOLUME 13


JAROSLAW ANDERS
Milan Kundera

MARGUERITE ARCHER †
*Lehman College, City University of New York*
Jean Anouilh

STANISLAW BARANCZAK
*Harvard University*
Czeslaw Milosz

GERMAINE BRÉE
*Vilas Professor Emerita, University of Wisconsin*
Albert Camus

ERIC BURNS
Michel Foucault

CARLA CAPPETTI
*City College of New York*
Natalia Ginzburg

ROBERT CONARD
*University of Dayton*
Heinrich Böll

MASON COOLEY
*Columbia University*
Roland Barthes

ROY C. COWEN
*University of Michigan*
Max Frisch

GORDON CUNLIFFE
*University of Wisconsin at Madison*
Günter Grass

DOROTHY M-T GREGORY
*Rutgers University*
Odysseus Elytis

ALEX KLIMOFF
*Vassar College*
Alexander Solzhenitsyn

GEORGE J. LEONARD
*San Francisco State University*
Claude Simon

JEANNINE P. PLOTTEL
*Hunter College*
Alain Robbe-Grillet

RANDOLPH D. POPE
*Washington University*
Camilo José Cela

AUSTIN QUIGLEY
*University of Virginia*
Jean Genet

LEON S. ROUDIEZ
*Columbia University*
Michel Butor

SAM TANENHAUS
Italo Calvino

GEORGE WELLWARTH
*State University of New York at Binghamton*
Friedrich Dürrenmatt

MATTHEW H. WIKANDER
*Columbia University*
Eugène Ionesco

# EUROPEAN WRITERS

## The Twentieth Century

# JEAN ANOUILH

## *(1910–1987)*

IN OCTOBER OF 1969, Jean Anouilh's play *Cher Antoine* (*Dear Antoine*) opened in Paris. The first-night audience was extremely enthusiastic; many clearly thought what several critics who attended the performance later wrote: that the play was a masterpiece and the author among the greatest of contemporary French playwrights. It was time for the curtain call, for the author to come forward to receive the audience's acclaim. But to the confusion of all, even the embarrassment of some, the author had left. Simply left, vanished into the Parisian night as though he had nothing to do with the play.

This refusal to acknowledge the plaudits of the audience baffled the spectators. It almost seemed to some as though the playwright was trying to prolong the spell he had cast on his audience. To the public, still caught up in the death of the leading character, Anouilh's double, the presence of Anouilh on stage would have seemed tantamount to a resurrection.

In the final scene the house of the now-defunct Antoine was being boarded up as a handful of acquaintances recalled his admiration for the ending of Chekhov's *The Cherry Orchard.* In that play, too, a house that once had sheltered a happy family is boarded up while its soul remains in it forever. The question left unanswered was whether it was Antoine or Anouilh who had chosen such a nostalgic finale. The presence of this doubt meant that Anouilh had reached the high point in the role of mystifier he had conceived for himself some forty years before. By playing on appearances, he had not intended to perform a dramatic unveiling of his soul but to lead the spectators up yet another rung of his ladder of pretending. Through a clever game of make-believe, which never ceased to be his first rule, he had achieved a fusion of illusion and reality in the spectators' minds. He had convinced them that, although he had formerly remained mute about private matters, he had stepped on stage that night to expose a large part of his emotional life.

Yet Anouilh was caught at his own game. The leitmotiv in *Dear Antoine* dealt with the solitude and disenchantment that overcame a playwright who, absorbed in his craft, let love pass him by. Like his greasepainted counterpart, Antoine de Saint-Flour, Anouilh felt too alienated to relieve his loneliness by accepting the acclaim of an excited crowd.

While delighting the spectators, who believed themselves to be in full command of the situation, the playwright was reveling in the ultimate theatrical trick. He had succeeded in enmeshing them in such a mixture of reality and dramatic fiction that they could not distinguish one from the other. Thus Anouilh had brilliantly resolved the essential polarity of his art and fulfilled his wish to "detheatricalize" the stage, that is, to reduce the distance between the spectator and the stage, so that the spectator becomes an integral part of the play and does not know the difference between make-believe and reality.

Ever since he set out to make the French theater his with *L'Hermine* (*The Ermine*) in 1931, Jean Anouilh has aroused great curiosity, and sometimes ire, among critics and public alike. The controversies that arise about his plays stem from the fact that he escapes clear-cut identification. This is due not to obscurity in his work or deviousness on his part but simply to the protean aspect of his plays. They are variations on given themes, and as such they give the impression that they constitute contradictions. This apparent inconsistency may originate in the ambiguous behavior of the protagonists. But it is simply a fact of life that ambiguity is an integral component of man's plight in relation to himself and to others; thus, to ask that an image of man be in clear and unambiguous focus is to ask for comforting falsehood. Besides, if man is a "disconsolate but gay animal," as Anouilh asserts, won't he be a paradox to himself?

The isolated works of some authors give evidence of those authors' characteristics, but a particular play of Anouilh's reveals at best only a few elements of his work, never his total makeup. Any one of his plays can be judged as only one hue in the spectrum of his work. It is interesting to discover that a reading of all of Anouilh's plays reveals a yearning on the author's part to treat each piece as a step in a progression. This interpretation is supported by the presence in newer plays of lines quoted from preceding plays. And as one notes in the novels of Balzac or Faulkner, mere names in earlier works by Anouilh appear as full-fledged characters in later plots.

Over the years Anouilh has been recognized as one of the world's leading dramatists: his works are among the most frequently performed everywhere. Theaters, repertory companies, drama schools, and avid readers constantly seek out his plays. He is best known in the United States for the success on Broadway of *L'Alouette* (*The Lark,* 1952) and *Beckett ou l'honneur de Dieu* (*Becket; or, The Honor of God,* 1959), and for the innumerable revivals of the irrepressible *Le bal des voleurs* (*Thieves' Carnival,* 1932), as well as *L'Invitation au château* (*Ring Round the Moon,* 1947) and *Antigone* (1942). *The Lark,* Anouilh's version of Joan of Arc's martrydom, received such acclaim that two English translations of it appeared the year it was performed. *Becket* has been transposed into a remarkable motion picture.

Throughout his long career Anouilh's fame was quite solid. Proclaimed a young avant-gardist in the 1930's, he showed great promise in competition for renown with a constellation of stage directors such as Georges Pitoëff, Charles Dullin, André Barsacq, Jacques Copeau, and Louis Jouvet, who were steering the French stage away from realism, toward stylization, classicism, and poetry. In the 1940's and early 1950's, the decades of the existentialist dramatists, Anouilh continued to attract audiences with the contemporary interpretation of a Greek theme in *Antigone* and the dramatization of man's sense of dedication in *Becket.* In 1959 he boldly endorsed the brash antiplays of Eugène Ionesco, Arthur Adamov, and Samuel Beckett. He went so far as to urge his public to go down the street from the theater where one of his plays was being performed to see Ionesco's *Les chaises* (*The Chairs*), and he unreservedly praised *Waiting for Godot* when Samuel Beckett was virtually unknown. Strangely enough, the birth of the antitheater may well be the reason for a six-year silence on his part. At any rate, he created nothing of his own between *L'Orchestre* (1962) and *Le boulanger, la boulangère et le petit mitron* (The Baker, His Wife, and His Apprentice, 1969), the success of which placed him again in the forefront of contemporary drama. Six years was a long silence for a man who in thirty-eight years had published thirty plays, had adapted works varying from Shakespeare to Oscar Wilde, had created scenarios, made records, written newspaper articles, and even produced a book of scathing fables. But between October 1969 and the following February, Anouilh presented two plays, *Dear Antoine* and *Les poissons rouges,* which provoked wild raves and renewed his love affair with his public. Thus time has shown that "The Great Anouilh," as he is called in France, who once said that a playwright is a gentleman who seduces a lady—the lady in question being the public—can lay claim to the place of Don Juan in the field of drama.

Jean Anouilh was born on 23 June 1910, in the Atlantic port of Bordeaux. His father was a tailor noted for the scrupulousness with which he exercised his skill. Stage directors who feel too restricted by Anouilh's minute descriptions of his characters' stances bemoan the fact that he inherited this particular trait. His mother, a violinist, often played in the orchestra of the casino of Arcachon, a seaside resort forty-five minutes from Bordeaux on the adorably lackadaisical shuttle train. It was in Arcachon that Anouilh's fascination for theatrics was nurtured, for as a little boy he had the privilege of gazing, baffled, at the operettas performed night after night for vacationers. If the actors were second-rate, they nevertheless mesmerized his imagination through their magic ability to play specific, well-defined roles. Orchestra members and struggling actors kept a unique place in his heart, appearing with various traits in *The Ermine, Eurydice* (*Legend of Lovers; Point of Departure,* 1941), *La sauvage* (*Restless Heart,* 1934), and *Le rendez-vous de Senlis* (*The Rendezvous at Senlis; Dinner with the Family,* 1941).

When he was nine, Anouilh moved to Paris with his parents; they lived in the Montmartre district, where some of his plays would be produced later on. At the age of thirteen he precociously wrote in verse what he calls "false plays" (or closet dramas) that he acted out for friends and relatives. After elementary schooling at the École Colbert, he pursued traditional studies at the Collège Chaptal. Jean-Louis Barrault, a classmate, recalled Anouilh as a distant, nattily attired young man, difficult to get to know. Thirty years later, in 1959, the two were to create *La petite Molière,* starring Anouilh's daughter Catherine. Going to law school after he finished at Chaptal must have seemed drab to the aspiring dramatist, especially after a balmy spring evening in 1928 when he was captivated by Jean Giraudoux's *Siegfried.* (It was from Giraudoux, Anouilh declared, that he learned the sense of stylization that characterized all his theater.) Soon after, he created *Mandarine* (1929). *Humulus le muet* (*Humulus the Mute,* 1929) was written the same year in collaboration with Jean Aurenche, whom Anouilh met when he gave up the law and started working in an advertising agency. The same pair wrote four film scenarios between 1936 and 1939. About his training in publicity Anouilh confides that, in lieu of poetic studies, slogans taught him the precision and timing essential to dialogue. In 1930, while awaiting the call to military service, he became Louis Jouvet's secretary general at the Comédie des Champs-Elysées, where most of his plays have been performed. Receiving, in effect, no guidance from the famous actor-director largely responsible for the success of the *Siegfried* he so idolized, Anouilh found the position disappointing and lonely. Still undaunted, he wrote *The Ermine,* which was presented at the Théâtre de l'Oeuvre by Pierre Fresnay in 1932. Acclaimed as a promising young dramatist, Anouilh resolved to dedicate his life to the theater. When in 1935 he sold to Metro-Goldwyn-Mayer the rights to *Y'avait un prisonnier* (*There Was a Prisoner,* 1935) he gained the financial independence that enabled him to start devoting his life to writing.

Although Anouilh's work seems effortless at times, it betrays the thirst for growth and renewal of a playwright acutely engaged in the present, a man of letters not likely to admit that he never forgot the classicist Nicolas Boileau's admonition to polish and repolish one's creations. His desire for constant improvement is illustrated by the various collections of his plays.

Anouilh said that his grouping of plays under the headings of *pièces noires, nouvelles pièces noires, pièces roses, pièces brillantes, pièces grinçantes,* and *pièces costumées* (black plays, new black plays, rosy plays, shining plays, grating plays, and costume plays) aimed to satisfy the public's need for classifications. As he indicates, we must consider such divisions to be somewhat arbitrary, since he did not write all the plays included in a collection at one time. But the groups nevertheless represent the different phases of his evolution.

The *Pièces noires* are not tragedies in the classical sense of the word, but they are dramas in the sense that they display the defeat of individuals in their quest to live within the framework of society and humanity, while at the same time preserving the self. The term "tragedy" would seem too formal to the unpretentious Anouilh, who at the outset of his vocation aspired to nothing more than the role of a man of the theater in the manner of Molière, the writer capable of distracting men from their cares. The volume of *pièces noires* includes *The Ermine, Restless Heart, Le voyageur sans bagage* (*Traveler Without Luggage,* 1936), and *Legend of Lovers.* These names evoke a gallery of portraits, for Anouilh intends to act as portraitist. Each painting represents the stylization of an individual with his past, his present dilemma, his interior climate. But while *The Ermine, Restless Heart,* and *Traveler Without Luggage* take place in a post–World War I setting, *Eurydice* moves in the timelessness of myth. Because all the characters have the same choice to make, they may be put into identical frames. In order to find serenity, each must decide whether to reject or acquiesce in his destiny, as it is assigned to him either by society or by more obscure forces.

Consider *The Ermine.* In a society dominated by the bourgeoisie, Frantz, a young man without money, loves the rich Monime. Her aunt opposes their marriage and a prosperous man thwarts Frantz's attempt to acquire the sum he needs. The young man must renounce Monime, or marry her and condemn her to a humiliating life of lowly prospects. Convinced that old women serve no purpose, he kills the rich aunt in order to use her money "to build an indestructible barrier around his love." Blind with rancor at seeing man's laws bar the way to his will to be happy, he defies those laws and stands alone as the monster-martyr born from the monetary shackles invented by man. He can survive only if he rejects the society that threatens to deprive him of the right to acquire happiness. His situation recalls Rousseau's image of man as enslaved by the merciless social organization men have devised.

Anouilh created Thérèse, the main character of *Restless Heart,* from his memories of the second-rate musicians who played in European cafés in the 1930's. His sympathy for these somewhat grotesque figures grew from an understanding of the tragedy inherent in their lives. They provided him with many a character for the *pièces noires,* since the gap between the life they led and the one to which they aspired was so wide. They lived under the illusion that because of their talent they deserved applause and the finer things of life, but in reality they received less and less of both each day. For Anouilh they symbolized in a stylized manner the fate of the common man, trying to find permanence in a world reduced to shambles by the financial depression of the early 1930's, a world moving inexorably toward World War II.

Thérèse is young, like all the principal characters in the *pièces noires,* and she represents the re-examination of accepted values to which the young have proceeded throughout history. Born to shabby musicians who are on the watch for the stroke of luck that will change their fate, she represses her love for Florent, a talented pianist with whom life would mean wealth and happiness. Her obstinate efforts to show him the sordidness of her background, so as to repel him, appear masochistic. In

Anouilh's terms, however, she accepts her true condition, which is one of suffering, deeming her action more worthy of a human being than giving in to happiness, which for her would be the same as to accept living a lie.

Gaston, in *Traveler Without Luggage,* betrays a yearning for the innocence of a child. He seeks the "noble savage" in himself. As a former amnesiac looking for his past, he is distressed to discover that his family created a jungle instead of a home and, worse yet, that he, too, behaved in a despicable manner. Destiny provides him with an escape from his family, but he has to kill his past, even in this escape, and killing anything is sad. Here the play intimates that a man must cut his ties with other human beings in order to acquire the freshness of spirit and nobility of character he desires.

The heroine in *Eurydice* moves within the pitiful circle of second-rate actors, attached to a mother for whom life is the series of clichés she has heard in bad plays. Like all the young heroines in Anouilh's theater, she emerges out of the playwright's boyish love affair with the ingenues he saw at Arcachon. Although his instinct taught him that they had been touched by many male hands, he has etched them throughout his work as abused but innocent females of the species whose hearts remain as pure as Iphigenia's. They receive nicknames such as "The Wild One" (La Sauvage), "The Dove" (Colombe), and "The Lark" (l'Alouette). With their strong libidos hidden by a rough beauty that nothing mars, they remain his porcelain dolls.

Eurydice's past takes the physical aspect of men's fingerprints left all over her body. She no longer remembers how they came to be there, but Orpheus sees them as so many disgusting tattoos. He knows they are part of her experience of life. When she slips confidently into the euphoria of love, and pictures her future relationship with Orpheus, she remembers that because of her past she lacks the virginity of soul she wishes she could offer to him. Unable to remove the marks, she chooses to die and thus redeem herself. Even Orpheus cannot save her, for when she is given a chance to return to life, he unwittingly lets her die again by indulging his own jealousy. Eventually he, too, chooses death, which seems to be the only realm where one may find gentle peace, beauty, pure love, and the cleansing of one's soul.

As we look at these plays as a whole, it is clear that the yearning for complete freedom and integrity drives all the protagonists to despair, although the circumstances vary. In Anouilh's vision every sight, every touch, every experience, every moment of time leave their imprint on the human soul and preclude any rebirth of interior freshness, of innocence. Man seems to resemble a sheet of blotting paper that can never be cleansed of its spots, even though he wishes to regain his purity.

In addition, according to their heredity, their past history of poverty or wealth, pain or pleasure, people are divided into two races that cannot communicate: as Charles Baudelaire expressed it, the race of Cain and the race of Abel. When the protagonists can be saved by redeemer-like characters who graciously give of themselves to prevent their beloveds' fate, they respond with a sardonic but melancholy refusal. In *Restless Heart,* for example, when Florent pleads with Thérèse to take his love and the serenity he promises, she refuses, and as he stands bewildered, she tells him that he must accept the role of a stranger on earth, the role of a king who possesses all without having suffered for it. Florent feels unjustly accused of some sort of crime, while Thérèse implies that she will remain in a brotherhood based on destitution. Neither of the two seems to have a real freedom of choice. Yet they must find a bearable stance in a world that holds them accountable for what is actually imposed on them by pure chaos.

As he developed the cycle of *pièces noires,* Anouilh was accused of treating only one subject. Actually, these four plays constitute variations on the dilemma of life. As such, they tend to show the pride, the yearnings, and the frustrations of certain characters rather than to expose the definitive philosophy of the dramatist. At this point in his career the young playwright was primarily concerned with the creation of characters, not with the growth of plot; hence the enigmatic quality of the characters' rejection. From the debates the characters engage in, however, one can deduce general trends of thought that Anouilh elaborates more fully in later plays. What mainly stands out in his early work is an interest in the complexity of human motives and the difficulty of making a lucid choice in the chaotic modern world, which pulls people in opposite directions.

Many interpretations of Anouilh's use of the money theme have been developed. Actually, his basic design, which is that of a moralist studying visible responses to social stimuli, is similar to that in works of fiction showing men adjusting to love, family, politics, and money. He explains that he observes men from the "moral" point of view, which to him means dealing with a choice of behavior that either does or does not conform to accepted standards, not only of ethics but also of custom and taste. He does not aim to create purely psychological or metaphysical plays, but attempts to hold a mirror up to his fellow men. However, even though he is not conscious of the fact, his astute studies of their conduct slip into meditations on the human psyche and the human condition, especially in the serious plays. For instance, the murder perpetrated by Frantz in *The Ermine* changes into a symbolic triumph over frustration. The old aunt, who personifies money, becomes the victim of Frantz's anxiety. He is afraid of his possible inability to love forever, of his desires, of his vulnerability. The girl he loves has the purity of a lily. To deserve her, he dreams of possessing a crystal-clear soul, cleansed of all the blemishes that living as a poor man has left.

Once the case of each hero in the *pièces noires* is examined, one realizes that the premise given at the very beginning of the play, involving only the way in which he will find serenity or happiness, becomes an academic question: Does the order of life, the makeup of humanity, the nature of the world, allow any one to achieve happiness or peace within oneself? In Anouilh's kaleidoscope, at this point, the answer is negative. For life transforms and erodes both the subject and the object of happiness in different degrees; it may be impossible for man to accept serenity, although he keeps thinking that he desires it above all things; at the same time society nullifies man's effort toward his own fulfillment by enslaving him through mass-produced rules. In *Antigone,* Anouilh will go so far as to advance the theory that happiness is only a human fabrication.

These dramas appeal by the fact that they enrich us with unconventional images of young individuals in search of a modus vivendi. The characters cannot be placed in neatly labeled boxes, for they fit into no system except the one created by their own identities and Anouilh's stylization. As he makes them define themselves in lucid, realistic dialogue ranging from the virulent to the pathetic, he puts us in the presence of men and women who manage to remain unforgettable. From their original expression of universal misery emanates a certain poetry associated with our vision of the young romantic making a stand in a harsh, absurd world. Finally, it is interesting to see how, while portraying the painful awakening of youth to the inequities brought by life lived among others, Anouilh casually slips into philosophical metaphors, refreshingly stripped of tendentious pronouncements.

The *nouvelles pièces noires* (new black plays) are *Jézabel* (1932), *Antigone* (1942), *Roméo et Jeannette* (*Romeo and Jeannette; Fading Mansions,* 1945), and *Médée* (*Medea,* 1946). It is logical that Anouilh, who avoided realism in his early plays, should turn to myth for the creation of two of these plays, *Antigone* and *Medea.* He was attracted by myth on several grounds. First, the successful modernization of myth accomplished by Giraudoux and Jean Cocteau proved justifiably inspiring. Second, the themes treated in myth fitted in with

Anouilh's penchant for examining the struggle to escape from social, psychological, or metaphysical bondage. Finally, the rejuvenation of mythical characters posed a challenge to Anouilh's capacity for developing the personalities of his protagonists, a development that must be carefully done if re-creation of myth is to be persuasive.

Although not literally mythical, *Jézabel* and *Romeo and Jeannette* fit into the *nouvelles pièces noires* because the fates of their title characters are as well known as those of Antigone and Medea: they are part of literary history. The fact that the shadow of death grows inexorably larger with each swing of the pendulum, while the spectator helplessly watches the hero or heroine being engulfed, gives these plays an atmosphere of tragedy. And the stylistic restraint in *Antigone, Romeo and Jeannette,* and *Medea* contributes to the timeless classical quality of their development and resolution.

As the generic title indicates, the *nouvelles pièces noires* are closely linked to the *pièces noires;* all the plays together form a progression, each gaining a larger degree of impact. In *The Ermine, Restless Heart,* and *Traveler Without Luggage* the prime origin of fate rests in the inflexibility of the characters. Though they represent extremes, they deserve understanding, even sympathy, for we share a slight kinship with them. Jézabel's fate arises from weakness, and it awakens fear that we, like her, may succumb to our own flaws; hence identification grows stronger. The fates of Frédéric and Jeannette fall upon them from unknown causes. We pity these lovers, who mysteriously disintegrate, as if eaten by a baffling disease of the mind. In the case of Antigone and Médée, destiny depends on the whims of the gods, regardless of the characters' own innocence or guilt. Their situation takes on awesome proportions, for it arbitrarily deprives the individual of the chance to save himself through any sort of ascetic withdrawal, no matter how hard the attempt may be. So we wonder whether our freedom, like theirs, is illusory, for we know that we, too, struggle and don't always succeed; complete empathy follows. In Anouilh's view our emotional reaction means that he has accomplished the feat of bringing the theater back to its essence, which is communion: he has succeeded in shocking the public out of its callous attitude toward its fellow beings. We see that as he has patiently humanized his characters to a greater extent with each play, the intensity of the impact on the audience has increased. All the while he continues to exploit the same general themes. Each play mixes the elements of choice and alienation; each plot develops within the narrow social confines of a couple or a family, except *Antigone,* which widens to include the political circle. Generally (*Jézabel* being the exception) the *nouvelles pièces noires* offer an ennobling picture of human courage.

*Jézabel,* a disturbing play, opens this collection, opposing its darkly grotesque atmosphere to the sublime beauty of the rest of the plays. As the title forecasts, the Jézabel of Anouilh, a counterpart of the one who slew the Lord's prophets, must indeed be eaten by dogs: she is an aging woman who poisons her husband to get his money and give it to her lover. Her son, Marc, is in love with a rich young lady from a good family. After he begs his mother to accept the fact of her age and to behave respectably so that he may marry Jacqueline, the play assumes naturalistic overtones. Jézabel vulgarly displays her drinking, her sexual urges, her slovenly appearance. Responding to criticism aimed at the appearance of this facile naturalism, Anouilh later defended the rightness of its use. On the occasion of his adaptation of Roger Vitrac's *Victor,* in 1962, he said that naturalism is actually "not a photograph of reality, but a careful reproduction of that accepted notion of life which has become life itself"; in other words, it is the stylization of an already stylized reproduction of life, and therefore not the result of facility. In truth, *Jézabel,* despite its unevenness, rises beyond its naturalistic level and deserves a reappraisal. Its central character, in all her pitifully abhorrent aspects, resembles many a human being in the courts, prisons, and drug rehabilitation centers. Her condition provokes meditation about the fall of humanity. Unlike Antigone or Medea, Jézabel lacks a personal identity and searches for it in men's arms, only to find herself completely bewildered by their animal responses. She rejects life in the sense that she cannot accept what it has done to her husband, now a man deprived of all enthusiasm. She recalls Eurydice and Antigone when she seems to say that death is indeed preferable to old age and the day-to-day deprivations entailed by the passing of time.

Written in 1932, this play has the obsessive quality and force of Sartre's *No Exit;* Jézabel and her son become each other's hell. He is her hell because no matter how she explains her sordidness, he judges her on his own terms; she is his hell because he knows he is like her and he tries desperately to change her image so that he can be saved.

Besides its philosophical implications *Jézabel* offers a somber comment on motherhood. It becomes a farce in which a woman requires a commitment from her husband and children on the ground that she is a mother, but then concerns herself solely with her beauty creams, her obsession with youth, and her lovers. Her husband, in this burlesque ballet, invariably retreats to the status of a nonentity, allowing himself to be overwhelmed by his wife's selfish recriminations. Instead of acting as the revered legendary head of the family, he turns out to be a beggar who hangs onto his children's coattails for sympathy and even for financial support.

In *Antigone,* as the Chorus remarks, we should enjoy a measure of serenity. We are told that we are among equals, for "we all are innocent." Our roles are interchangeable: one day we play the victim and another the spectator. When the Prologue takes us into the author's confidence by introducing the actors and explaining the casting, we feel like actors ourselves, taking a busman's holiday for the evening. As we settle back calmly into our seats to observe the unfolding of the action, we are quickly snapped out of our complacency by the reminder that we are so tranquil only because tonight it is not our turn to die. We are forced into the awareness that our death is but a question of time, and the play becomes not an individual story but a universal one. In this manner Anouilh, who states in *La grotte* (*The Cavern,* 1961) that the public makes the play and hence should be made to rehearse with the actors, legitimizes the presence of the Prologue in his modernization of the myth by using it to manipulate the spectator. Thus he provides the audience with the necessary distance to bear the sorrows they will witness and, at the same time, the closeness that will enable them to share in the catharsis.

*Antigone* is the masterpiece that brought international fame to Anouilh when it was first published. Written in 1942, and performed in 1944 during the Nazi occupation of France, it aroused the most heated controversy by its double aspect of myth and political satire, for Antigone clearly symbolizes the Resistance, whereas Créon's motives were interpreted by some as an approval of the Vichy government, and by others as a veiled satire of it. As an artist Anouilh did not have to choose sides. He meant to awaken people's consciousness to the concept of revolt. Were Créon's motives weaker than Antigone's, the play would become a clear-cut case of the triumph of good over evil, which would satisfy the emotions but not the intellect, for it would provide too simplistic a view of human dilemmas.

At the time it was particularly daring of Anouilh to modernize a myth embodying a political conflict. The French suffered daily from increasing restrictions that seemed the more arbitrary because they were dictated to the Vichy government by the Nazis. The nation was divided into a camp advocating revolt and a camp accepting the occupation as inevitable. By giving the tragedy an enigmatic meaning that does not exist in the original Sophocles play, Anouilh was offering the partisans in the Resistance the opportunity of interpreting Antigone's gesture as one of support for them, while the Nazis were unable to censure the play because Créon made such a good case for civic obedience. Nevertheless, the presence of this doubt resulted in strong abuse of Anouilh by those who misinterpreted his purpose. In *Pauvre Bitos* (*Poor Bitos,* 1956), published after the liberation, the playwright squelched those excessive and unfounded attacks.

Antigone, a skinny girl no one takes seriously, decides to challenge the so-called order of the world, knowing full well that she will be condemned to die for her boldness. In this she resembles her Greek counterpart but, unlike the classical Antigone, this young girl shows far more vulnerability and hardly conveys the notion that she is a heroic figure. After she attempts to bury Polynice, she runs promptly to her nurse's arms for warmth and security; she admits on several occasions that she is afraid; and while waiting to be entombed, she asks the guard what it is like to die.

As Antigone becomes increasingly shaken by Créon's arguments, she expresses her motives less and less clearly. Whereas she starts by asserting that she has to bury her brother out of fraternal love, she ends up sighing that she does not know anymore why she has chosen to die. This baffling response confers a seemingly insoluble ambiguity to the play. But the very evolution of her moral purpose eventually explains the mystery and removes some of its enigma.

As she talks to her sister, Ismène, at the outset of the action, Antigone appears to be a melancholy instrument of fate, regretting her role, saying that Créon's part is to decree her death, while hers is to bury her brother and accept that death as the consequence. Her action at this stage takes on the value of a clearly defined duty. Her disobedience stems from a fatal necessity dictated by the customs which advocate that the dead must be symbolically laid to rest by the living to escape the penalty of wandering forever in pain over the face of the earth.

When Ismène pleads for an "understanding" of the complexity of the situation and tries to explain the impossibility of making the right choice and the frightful consequences of disobedience, Antigone's anger flares up. The concept of "understanding" strikes Antigone as a cowardly escape from responsibility, as fear of unrestrained life. If Antigone chooses to die, does it mean that she does not feel like living? asks Ismène. Antigone answers by nostalgically reviewing her awareness of the value of life. She recalls the contemplation of a garden in the solitude of daybreak, the sense of wonder one has at the sight of millions of insects endowed with life, running through an incalculable number of living blades of grass. Later she indicates that living could also gain meaning through her love for Hémon, through procreation out of that love, through the relationship shared by members of a family. It becomes clear then that so complete is her knowledge of the value of life that the prospect of suffering or dying does not constitute enough of a deterrent to prevent her from living independently of any restriction, if only once, and even if the penalty for it is annihilation. At that point her original moral purpose is reinforced by her need to live in the absolute sense of the word, to commit herself completely to living.

Antigone's crucial confrontation with Créon takes her a step further. As he accuses her of being guilty of extreme pride, of making a display of personal pathos, of following in Oedipus' footsteps, of engaging in a contest with destiny and death—in a word, of showing "hubris"—he strengthens her decision to do "what she can" regardless of the consequences, as a simple human being, not a king's daughter, and because it is her duty to do so. At the beginning she was going to bury her brother because it was expected of her; now she wills it, as the one act that is in her power to perform, the act that gives her an identity.

When Créon describes the funeral rites as a sham, a series of pharisaical gestures that even she should be ashamed of, Antigone is submerged by a sudden awareness of the absurdity of customs. She resents the hodgepodge of fallacious constraints and the artificial, senseless, and arbitrary nature of any limitation that man allows to impede his right to live as he wants. She visualizes a complete revenge on this absurdity. Her act will be carried out in total freedom, as she desires. In the face of arbitrariness, there does not have to be any necessity to her act other than that which she imposes on it. She sarcastically tells Créon that she will accomplish her mission "for herself." In so doing she will commit an absurdity to limit the absurdity that limitations impose upon man; customs, rules, the state, the human condition will hem in life only so far as it wants to be hemmed in; she transcends the human condition, just as she decides to transcend pain when Créon twists her arm and she blurts out that it does not hurt, since for all intents and purposes she has no arm. Inasmuch as she chooses to impose her own rules and meaning on what happens to her, she can scorn Créon and declare that it is she who has become the queen, while he has become the slave of events. Antigone's solution is to impose her own absurdity on the universal absurdity as a means of conquering it.

Her moment of glory is temporarily reversed, however, when Créon discloses the sordidness of both brothers' characters and the consequent meaningless of his choice to bury one and desecrate the other. After this blow Antigone considers repudiating her decision; in a daze she mumbles, "Yes," when Créon tells her to go home and marry Hémon. But as the knot of the action tightens and Créon, on the threshold of victory, equates life and happiness, Antigone's moral purpose crystallizes in a flash. Men use "filthy happiness" to cover up their hypocrisy. Happiness serves to mask the lies, the compromises, the calculations that men cowardly accept so that they may go on living, so that they may avoid danger and death. Happiness is a masquerade of life itself, and she will not settle for living on those terms. She wants a full life even if it holds no hope of lasting. Therefore, she subscribes completely to her fate, proud to carry out the pursuit of truth begun by her father, Oedipus.

Yet Antigone becomes distraught despite her resolve. The world has turned into a void. As she dictates a letter to Hémon just before her death, she sighs that she does not know anymore why she dies. And neither do we. Her choice starts out as a moral necessity, changes into the rejection of the human condition, then to an endorsement of absurdity, and finally disintegrates into nothingness. In the end she is committing a totally gratuitous act, thereby illustrating the inexplicability of our actions. To the Chorus, which begs him not to let Antigone die, Créon answers that Polynice was a pretext for her and that, when she renounced her first premise, she found another, for what mattered was that she die. It appears that what actually mattered was that she act.

The Chorus concludes the play with a low-keyed wail over the scheme of humanity that augments our bewilderment. It chants that men get caught and die in the struggle of opposite beliefs, whether they themselves have strong beliefs or not. Once dead, their names are soon forgotten by the living. Occasionally one person creates havoc in the consciousness of some of his fellow men. They forgive him for it, as a sad lethargy overtakes them. As for the rest of men, they continue to play cards, oblivious to it all, suggesting that an act like Antigone's cannot change the machinelike indifference of life.

So this play ends with a disturbing lack of hope for the discovery of a rational meaning to our constant strife; yet it consoles us through its existence as a moving work of art. A brilliant handling of dramatic elements gives it a satisfying homogeneity that never falls into dullness. The character development and the organization of the plot impart complete plausibility to the action. The play maintains a smooth, dynamic rhythm thanks to the perfect balance of moods. The moments of intense emotion and those of banter or trivial discussion fit carefully together with the help of the classical restraint of the language. Whereas Sophocles' play is forbidding, Anouilh's work touches the whimsical at times, allowing the modern spectator necessary respite from its strong emotional content. In the scenes involving the nurse and the guards, the playwright not only aims at the comic relief often encountered in Shakespeare but also satirizes contemporary society by introducing the notions of pieces of toast and pensions. Anouilh is irrepressible at heart, and he admitted that he played such tricks to amuse himself.

He remains a master of dialogue by skillfully mixing humor with the poetic lines of Antigone as she evokes her childhood, her love for Hémon, her awe at disturbing the peace of the road in the morning light. As a result of these intricate combinations, Anouilh presents a very human though heroic Antigone who elicits curiosity, fear, pity, compassion, amusement, sorrow, and reflection; she provokes not only admiration but also attachment, as if she were a real person.

Continuing his voyage through man's tragic history, Anouilh turned next to the theme of the doomed lovers. To create *Romeo and Jeannette,* he grafted that theme onto the stifling situation displayed in the *pièces noires.* The plot does not appear very logical, for Frédéric's and Jeannette's characters make them unlikely lovers. But the plausibility of their love resides in its quality. Love befalls the two, as it befell Tristan and Isolde after they drank the love philter. When it has cast its spell, the lovers resemble two prisoners trapped in the same cage, desperately trying to understand why they are enslaved; at the same time they treasure gloomily what ties them, even in the face of a presentiment that it will cause their death.

This play offers a good occasion to examine Anouilh's ideas on love. Never did he present love as a salutary tie between man and woman. It can be sublime for a while, and then it leads to death; sometimes it appears to be a grotesque masquerade among caricatures; at other times it is what people talk about in make-believe, a kind of fairy tale resembling the *pièces roses;* in *Dear Antoine,* Anouilh presents it as a miracle, blessing very few chosen people. As Lucien, Jeannette's brother, warns, a promising love must be craftily hidden from "that one up there," who is jealous and will coldly steal it away. In other words, what we view as one of our few consolations on earth may be merely a myth.

The deaths of Frédéric and Jeannette in a purifying sea do not come as a surprise; this hero and heroine needs redemption for the sin of carnal knowledge as much as did Eurydice. The play, meant by its title to remind us of *Romeo and Juliet,* recalls more *Tristan and Isolde,* or better still Maurice Maeterlinck's *Pelléas et Mélisande,* simply because its rhythm plunges the spectator into the sort of mystic wasteland one finds in the Maeterlinck play. Inasmuch as the central characters keep groping for a way to express their predicament, they seem far removed from Romeo and Juliet, who can elucidate their situation so well.

While the style in *Antigone* showed the firmness befitting a grandiose subject, *Romeo and Jeannette* reveals a controlled poetic fluidity that testifies to Anouilh's amazing versatility. He explained that he first visualized a play before he captured it on paper. Like the later *Léocadia* (*Time Remembered,* 1939), this play has been invested with an aura of unreality. It offers the charms of an elegy, for the dialogue possesses a contemplative tone that puts one in a mood of gentle mourning.

Euripides emphasized a woman's potential for evil in his *Medea;* in his *Medea,* Anouilh redirected the Medea myth to his outlook, making it a confrontation of absolute love and life. As long as man and woman remain—according to Anouilh's favorite metaphor—two little soldiers fighting the battle of life side by side, love can last. Once circumstances transform the woman into a female unaware of the man's need to merge into the stream of life and compete with other men, he reverts to being a male, and the love act becomes a somber struggle in which each partner tries to subjugate the other. Médée does not escape Anouilh's rule of life; she is transformed by her blind passion and refuses to accept any limitation of her powers. Jason also has changed; he pleads for compromise with love, with life, with men, with the world. He is ready to find a purpose in the human condition such as other men have done and acquiesce in the form they have given the world around them. Quite often in Anouilh's work the characters who revolt against the inescapable barriers to their freedom and seem to think that courage lies in accepting death are enjoined to choose to live. For living takes a great deal of courage, too, says the author, the courage of the stoic, since every day brings new suffering. Jason knows this; however, he wants to go on living, to become a man who takes pride in being himself in his totality, not with complacency but with the recognition of his potential for humble acts as well as noble ones. Médée adheres to the identity of proud outcast she chose when she betrayed father, brother, and country to favor absolute love; she demands that commitment to her be absolute on Jason's part. At that point love is no longer possible between them; Médée can only choose death. She also needs to take revenge on a world that she rejects, so she kills her children. Yet we cannot help feeling pity for her, for she is a victim of fate.

The play marks an important step in Anouilh's development: for the first time in his work, the author paints in Jason a character who, having first rejected men's rules for the sake of an absolute, comes to terms with the imperfections inherent in man's condition.

To feel a moment of joy, the spectator of the *pièces roses* is invited to join Anouilh in unadulterated fantasy. In order to create vehicles for amusement, Anouilh delves into all the resources of his imagination as well as into his experience as a stage director, for the complicated physical activity in these plays necessitates a great deal of organization. In his comedies Anouilh resembles a cross between Molière choreographing ballet-comedies and Georges Feydeau compounding quid pro quos. For, like Molière when he had to provide entertainment for Louis XIV's court, Anouilh makes his comedy a spectacle, and like Feydeau he bases the laughter on multiple plots.

In *Humulus the Mute* he turns the tragic impediments of a mute young man and a deaf young girl into a hilariously funny skit. In *Thieves' Carnival* (1932) he enchants by showing the improbable gymnastics performed by thieves who try to hide their tricks from their benevolent victims. The antics executed by the characters have reminded many a critic of the spontaneity of the commedia dell'arte, although the apparent pell-mell of the action has been minutely timed by Anouilh. Had the play first been staged on this side of the Atlantic, *Thieves' Carnival* might well have evolved as a comedy in the manner of the Keystone cops. Anouilh, however, transforms his thieves into characters who move across the stage with the grace of ballet dancers. In this entertainment we again meet the familiar figure of the duchess, in this case Lady Hurf. Unlike her counterpart in *The Ermine,* however, she no longer represents the agent of evil fate, the obstacle to fulfillment; instead, continuing the generous work started by the Duchesse Dupont-Dufort in *Traveler Without Luggage,* she conducts herself as a benefactor bringing together the elements of happiness.

Lady Hurf, realizing that she has never really lived, amuses herself by assisting the thieves who intend to rob her. Though she penetrates their disguise as Spanish dukes, she pretends to recognize them as the real dukes. Everyone moves around her like amiable puppets, for she is the only character who seems to exist in a concrete way; since she is the real culprit of the situation, the action centers on her and she has to explain more forcefully than the other characters her system of values.

The action reveals Anouilh at his best as a showman manipulating the strings of his creations. As for the comedy, it goes beyond slapstick to elaborate a sort of intricate dance of pixielike but bungling thieves who at times steal from each other.

The decidedly tongue-in-cheek make-believe

of *Thieves' Carnival* bears no hint of the desperation that characterized the *pièces noires.* Gone is the need for the poor young man to commit a crime in order to deserve the rich girl he loves. The ludicrous Lord Edgar provides the hopeful suitor of the tale with the proper status by recognizing him as his once-stolen son. Quite a deus ex machina! In the *pièces roses* Anouilh seems to say that all is well that ends well. If man wants to be happy, he must accept all the rules of illusion; the best formula for survival may be to choose the rosiness of illusion instead of the blackness of reality.

*Time Remembered,* a *Sleeping Beauty* for grown-ups, is a glorious exercise in fantasy. In this fairy tale it is the girl Amanda, a little milliner portrayed as a variant of the Thérèse character in *Restless Heart,* who brings the prince to life and love after he has lost interest in both because of the death of his beloved diva. Though the theme is uncomplicated, the love story captivates, thanks to Anouilh's gift for characterization and plot construction. The happy ending of the story arises from the complementary attributes of the characters: with good-natured eccentricity the giddy duchess, hoping to create the atmosphere for love, reconstructs on her estate the setting of the prince's memories; at the same time the tenderness and goodwill of the girl interact perfectly with the ethereal romanticism of the prince.

As one considers the surrealistic decor that reproduces the park where Prince Troubiscoi had met the diva, one realizes how much of the freshness of the child remains in Anouilh. The juxtaposition of the ice-cream booth, the sleepy inn awakened by the sound of violins, and the legs hanging out of an old ivy-covered taxi now inhabited by rabbits seems to jumble together a series of adolescent dreams. One can understand why Anouilh's favorite characters remain Antigone, Eurydice, Thérèse—heroines possessing the qualities of children, marching to danger like child crusaders fiercely fighting the evil powers that threaten to tarnish their innocence.

In *Time Remembered,* as in all the *pièces roses,* Anouilh pleads with men to abandon their futile harshness: he shows them how easy it is to have fun and how, with a little laissez-faire, the world becomes a tenable place in which to live.

During the early part of his career, Anouilh alternated between writing *pièces noires* and *pièces roses.* Then, after effecting a kind of personal catharsis through the creation of three *nouvelles pièces noires* in a row, he immersed himself in art for art's sake with the *pièces brillantes,* and in black humor with the *pièces grinçantes.*

The collection of *pièces brillantes,* "brilliant" connoting brio, sophistication, and polish, includes *Ring Round the Moon* (1947), *Colombe* (*Mademoiselle Colombe,* 1951), *La répétition ou l'amour puni* (*The Rehearsal,* 1950), and *Cécile ou l'école des pères* (*Cécile; or, The School for Fathers,* 1954). *Ring Round the Moon* attests to one aspect of Anouilh's virtuosity that could easily occupy an entire article. In this play he accomplishes the feat of lending plausibility to the exits and entrances of identical twins played by the same actor. As a result of this achievement, he succeeds in so evenly distributing the action among the various characters that most of them spend an equal time on the stage. The result is that each character's situation is equally important and one cannot guess the outcome of the action. Here the ending is a happy one, achieved by Anouilh when he combines the themes previously exploited in the *pièces noires,* so that money and love can exist side by side in harmony. A delight for stage directors, *Ring Round the Moon* is the Anouilh work most performed throughout the world in drama schools and by amateur theater groups.

To further exercise his theatrical boldness, Anouilh turned to the eighteenth-century French dramatist Pierre de Marivaux, whose originality in plot construction and minute analysis of budding love is such that hardly any playwright has dared to imitate him. In *The Rehearsal* Anouilh superimposes the technique of the play-within-a-play, as in Luigi Pirandello, on the framework of Marivaux's love comedy *La double inconstance.* He makes the blasé aristocrat and the delicate young teacher who are falling in love rehearse scenes of the Marivaux play, so that it is Marivaux's dialogue that serves to explain their feelings. At the same time he weaves his own version of *La double inconstance* into the original in order to establish a striking contrast between the cruel monsters of cynicism who make their appearance in the *pièces brillantes* and the valiant, innocent young girls found in both his and Marivaux's works as symbols of idealistic love. The play was so unanimously acclaimed in France that it was published in the Classiques Larousse collection as an example of a dazzling replica of Marivaux's comedy.

To top it all, Anouilh tried his hand at a faithful pastiche of another psychological comedy of Marivaux's in *Cécile; or, The School for Fathers.* Called a jewel, this play was performed for the first time at the wedding of Anouilh's eldest daughter, Catherine. It deals with the relationship of a gracious father, as Anouilh was reputed to be, and his young daughter when she falls in love. As in previous *pièces brillantes,* here Anouilh is concerned with mastering yet another aspect of style. The play effortlessly re-creates the accents of the subtle manners and speech of the French classical era.

It is doubtful that these last two works would be enjoyed by a public outside France, for their charm originates in the very special tradition of the French theater in the seventeenth and eighteenth centuries, which even a Frenchman must have studied to appreciate fully.

The key to the cycle of *pièces grinçantes* lies in the scene in *La valse des toréadors* (*The Waltz of the Toreadors,* 1951) during which General Saint-Pé becomes desperate at the thought that life is not at all what he had believed it to be. Perplexed, he turns to the doctor and asks him the meaning of all he has read in books: the grandiose loves, the prodigious revelations, the tender young girls who love men forever, the joy one feels at having at one's side a little "brother in arms" who changes into a lovable woman at night. The doctor answers calmly that these things represent the dreams of authors who must have been poor devils just like the general, and they both agree that such authors should be prevented from spreading false notions of this kind. The fabrications enumerated by the general are obvious references to Anouilh's themes in the *pièces noires.* Anouilh suddenly seems to be turning his back on the idealism expressed in his earlier work.

In the *pièces grinçantes* he no longer divides the world between idealists and realists, but fills it with ludicrous puppets and cynical hypocrites. He once praised Molière for having written the blackest form of theater in a manner that made men laugh at their own misery and hideousness. As the use of the term "grinçantes" shows, Anouilh intended to do something similar in this new collection of plays. The word "grinçantes" implies, first, the interrupted motion of something that hits a snag. As such it can be applied to laughter interrupted by the awareness that one probably should cry. Second, it refers to the unpleasant sound of something that crushes or grinds, thus recalling the sound of things one does not really want to hear. It follows, then, that the laugh Anouilh wishes to extract must be brought about by a special brand of black humor. It is no surprise, therefore, that he introduces his first antihero, General Saint-Pé, in the first two *pièces grinçantes, Ardèle* (1948) and *The Waltz of the Toreadors.* As the first part of the general's name implies, he may wear the halo of the martyr, but as the second part ironically indicates, he will emerge from the plays as unwanted as a putrid bubble of human gas.

Although in *Ardèle* the action does not directly affect the general, it revolves around him. He starts out by leading a sort of burlesque ballet of people pursuing their personal visions of love. What they call love turns out to be an amalgam of infantile sexuality, pathological fixation, and insolent mimicry. For a time he thinks he is conducting a family council, gathered to decide the fate of an aunt who is a hunchback and is in love with another hunchback; in reality he is accepting with a disturbing complacency the monstrous pronouncements of caricatures who indulge in a ludicrous masquerade of love. Unfortunately, he is too flighty to recognize the pathology hidden in their decision that hunchbacks have no right to love, and he chatters away unaware of the urgency of the situation he has created. But Anouilh soon destroys the mood of light banter with a brutal cascade of bullets. The shock of the incident reminds everyone that human souls are at stake, but it is too late. The poor hunchbacks have been left only one escape, suicide. Not one person has really cared about them. The voice of the young man who encouraged his aunt Ardèle to love, despite her relatives' advice, has gone unheard. Only the cackle of the caricatures Anouilh has painted still rings in our ears. He evidently wants to convince us that idealism is destined to be drowned in the empty gibberish of the wicked and the futile. The general is totally inadequate to meet the responsibility he assumes when he locks up his sister, so he lets the hypocrites decide her fate. Thus he is just as guilty as they are of the ugly act that causes the death of the two innocents. And ugly acts have a way of propagating, as Anouilh points out in the last scene: the young children of the household are pretending to "be in love," so they imitate what they have seen their elders do; they fight like cats and dogs. With this conception of love, we can envision that some day they will also decide on someone's right to love. Somehow the scene is so ludicrous that we smile, but from embarrassment, at the mere sight of such illogical behavior. Our smile is "grinçant" (a gnashing of teeth) and cannot last long, for we realize that there is a serious lesson hidden in that spectacle.

*The Waltz of the Toreadors* sketches another episode in the life of General Saint-Pé. As it happens, he does not handle his own affairs any better than those of others. He continues to wait for someone or something, for "the right circumstances" to decide what he must do, for he is confused by the contradictions between what he is told and what he vaguely discovers to be true. But no one shows him the way. He is like Estragon and Vladimir waiting for Godot. He has not understood that man must jump at the slightest opportunity for fulfillment. Since life is a "ball that lasts only one night," he should dance as much as he can "before the colored lights go off." The moral of the play recalls the "Gather ye rosebuds while ye may" theme. But the general may have missed his chance out of fidelity to his wife; the moral may then be, as the doctor tells him, not to try to know "one's enemy, especially if it is a woman." The doctor implies that the general should not have postponed his happiness out of pity for his wife when he fell in love with Ghislaine, for, women being unpredictable, his sacrifice may prove to have been wasted. Although Anouilh exaggerates the play's cynicism for all its shock value, in reality he is asking whether it is worthwhile for the individual to cast aside his own happiness out of consideration for others who are themselves selfish. The general did not run away with Ghislaine the night he met her at the Saumure ball because he thought that his wife was deeply in love with him. Seventeen years later, while he still foolishly cherishes Ghislaine, his wife reveals to him that on that very night she left the ball and slept with a young officer. For having compromised and thought of others before reaching for his own happiness, General Saint-Pé ends up as a downtrodden buffoon who wears a shiny uniform as if he were ready for a gala but has to find pitiful solace in his kitchen maid's skirts. Anouilh has provided the forbidding answer to his own question: at this point in his plays, ethics have disappeared into the realm of dreams.

There is no obvious tie between *Ardèle* and *The Waltz of the Toreadors* other than the reappearance of General Saint-Pé. He emerges from both plays as an especially well-defined antihero who deserves close scrutiny. He represents especially the confused modern individual desperately trying to keep from drowning in the maze of contradictory forces that rule the world. He is made dizzy by the sweep of changing values in modern society, so he waits for a miraculous inspiration to move him in one direction or another. Since none materializes, he freezes into inaction. Face to face with evil, he does not recognize it or does not dare to acknowledge it. He struggles to find an ethic, although he is fallible enough to expect it to be easy to follow. A little cowardly, incredibly patient, he has been put on earth to be a victim, not a victor. He survives by sinking into sexual gratification and by wearing a uniform that becomes a kind of crutch. When he wears the uniform, others think he is strong and brave. He knows that deep inside he is a lonely, frightened man, but appearances are good enough for him. He is Anouilh's image of today's man.

Ornifle, in *Ornifle ou le courant d'air* (Ornifle; or, The Draft, 1955), is not a frightened man. He discovers, as does General Saint-Pé, that there can be no happy medium between honor and happiness. So he opts for happiness and then proceeds to laugh his way through life, often at the expense of those who are foolish enough to be gullible. Why should man, who does not ask to be born, spend his life surpassing himself? Society proves that any sort of self-denial is futile. Those who practice it are shy weaklings who deserve being used, or people who are possessed by an indecent brand of wickedness because they hide behind a mask of morality. So Ornifle will live for pleasure only.

This play succeeds in offering an interesting modern version of Molière's *Don Juan.* But Anouilh's motives when he created it were not entirely those of Molière. Whereas the action remains forbidding in both plays, Anouilh lends a more airy, flippant tone to his hero, the better to allow him to flaunt his views. Furthermore, when Ornifle collapses of a heart attack as he is about to betray another weakling, the suddenness of his death does not imply punishment, as it does in the Molière play, for Anouilh does not show that his death is inflicted by a mystic supernatural power stronger than he, as is the case with Don Juan. In this instance Ornifle falls dead as if struck by lightning; thus Anouilh bestows on him an almost painless death, such as we think only innocent creatures deserve. Anouilh is saying that Ornifle was an innocent creature, for he did not hide his wickedness.

*Ornifle* represented a first shot at a specific target, since Anouilh, who usually alternated writing at least two different types of plays, doggedly pursued his course, and the following year, with *Poor Bitos,* published what appears to be the sequel to *Ornifle.*

In truth, the political events that provoked his anger coincided with the point of development reached in his work that led him to write satires. In the early days of his vocation Anouilh had looked kindly upon idealism in play after play. Then, as years passed and he looked more closely at the world, he discovered after World War II that more often than not, idealism was a subterfuge used to cover the proverbial multitude of sins. He laughed in disenchantment at what might have been considered his naïveté. He was not certain whether it might not be that the world had changed so much that purity could no longer survive in it, so he seemed to ask those who had believed in his beautiful images of purity not to take him too seriously. At times it appeared that those who were pure enough to believe in tales of idealism were victimized either by life or by other men. Anouilh already knew the harsh rules of life; he now started to look at those who exploit men and distinguished two kinds of opportunists: the Don Juan type, who openly join the forces of evil but can be recognized, and the more dangerous variety, who wrap their wickedness in all sorts of beautiful trappings. In *Poor Bitos* the latter are the ones he pursues, while in *Ornifle* he shows how harmless openly wicked individuals actually may be.

After the liberation of France, a political purge took place. The entire odious episode was based on finger-pointing and summary accusations, and sometimes it led to the executions of those who appeared to have collaborated with the Germans. Naturally there were a number of unjust condemnations, and many people were revolted by the situation. Against this background Anouilh, who was already tormented by various forms of rampant hypocrisy and who had never wanted to judge others, wrote his first brilliant satire, *Poor Bitos.*

As might be expected, the play's strong impact derives from Anouilh's daring frankness and the clever device he chooses to denounce the true character of the *Épuration* (the Purge). By allowing the participants in the debate between Bitos and his tormentors to wear the headdresses of French Revolutionary leaders, he makes them express their motives more forcefully, for they can act safely behind what amount to masks. Since Anouilh wants to show the French their unfortunate tendency to repeat mistakes, the parallelism with the Terror initiated by Robespierre during the Revolution serves to concretize and reinforce his theory.

The indictment is a very severe one, for Anouilh lashes out not only at Bitos, the righteous self-appointed "defender of the people," but also at his tormentors. Bitos, the spokesman for those who hunted the "collaborators," turns out to be a narrow-minded little man for whom education is a dangerous thing. He retains only the cold theory of education, and resents those who teach him anything and those who exert any authority over him. He is a demagogue who hates men and who has been biding his time until he could revenge himself upon all those with more talent, more wealth, or more graciousness than he has. Because he has suffered, he has to make others suffer by submitting them to rigid rules that he can justify only in abstract terms. Most scathing of all is the fact that he will come to terms with those whose ideas he despises in order to serve his personal needs. The provocation of Bitos's obnoxious behavior shows Anouilh's irresistible urge to stylize the humiliating image of a man "caught with his pants down"; hence the scene when Bitos splits his pants and has to bend over to have them sewed up while still wearing them.

More repugnant than Bitos himself is the fact that such creatures have been used from time to time in France by government leaders who did not want to do the dirty work themselves but found a way to be accommodating to those who did. One of the characters, Brassac, points this out when he says that in France one can always find a general to sign a decree, and then add a retroactive clause if need be. The satire reaches its height when Anouilh turns the table on the tormentors of Bitos. They are rich bourgeois or aristocrats who think they belong to an elite that can sit in Olympian fashion and laugh at those who at least try to perform some social service; they do not possess courage enough to roll up their sleeves and serve their country. As Deschamps, the only moderate character in the play besides Victoire, gently reminds them, their motives are no more admirable than those of Bitos, for all they do is take from society and never give in return if they can help it.

Strangely enough, many critics reacted to *Poor Bitos* by lamenting that Anouilh hated humanity. But the play is precisely an indictment addressed to those who treat humanity with cold, mechanized methods instead of indulgence, compassion, and love. Anouilh enjoins those who see man as an abstraction to open their eyes and see that men are made of flesh and blood.

When asked in August 1969 what his favorite play was, Anouilh replied that it was *Poor Bitos:* first, because he had created a new character, which is always a "rosy" event in his life, and second, because he had dared to tell the French, at a time when it was unthinkable to do so, the things they needed to hear. What must be added is that satire was his natural medium of expression. The sweep of the discussion in *Poor Bitos* attests to that; so does the fact that in this form of drama his targets have no way of escaping his unrelenting scrutiny. Since he had the eye of Strindberg, the tongue of Shaw, and the aspirations of Molière, it has been hard for him not to choose exclusively to mock men for their weaknesses. There are signs that he may have come to acknowledge his talents in that field, for his widely acclaimed late plays, *Dear Antoine* and *Les poissons rouges ou mon père ce héros* (The Goldfish; or, My Father, That Hero, 1970), are primarily satires.

Anouilh's propensity for lampooning does not mean that he necessarily looks for objects to blame. If possible, he would just as soon encounter moral beauty of the quality seen in *The Lark* or *Becket*. These two *pièces costumées* are his only serious yet optimistic plays. (The third *pièce costumée* is *La foire d'empoigne* [*Catch as Catch Can,* 1962]).

*The Lark* retells the martyrdom of Joan of Arc. In the Anouilh play, however, "The Lark," as he calls Joan of Arc, remains in full control of her trial except in one instance of weakness, from which she quickly recovers. As for Becket, the archbishop of Canterbury, he forces Henry Plantagenet to reckon with the honor of the Church of England and the Saxons. Thus, as is expected of martyrs, both Joan and Becket emerge triumphant in death.

It would seem that at last, in these two plays, Anouilh found the pure idealism that he had searched for in his earlier plays. By contrast with the heroes of the *pièces noires,* the heroine and hero of *The Lark* and *Becket,* respectively, give their lives for a cause that goes beyond the self. They refuse the ways of materialism for definite reasons instead of ambiguous ones, as was the case with Gaston, Thérèse, and Antigone. Jeanne dies to protect the truth and to preserve the honor of the saints whose voices she heard. Becket accepts his own assassination in order to defend the honor of the Church of England, which he undertook to serve.

At the same time these champions of idealism remain human and accessible instead of becoming alienated from humanity, as did the protagonists of the *pièces noires.* Jeanne continues to sympathize with her soldiers and never answers her tormentors angrily. Becket never looks down on the King or speaks scornfully of anyone. As a matter of fact, the validity and the beauty of both plays emanate from the delicate balance that Anouilh establishes in the psychology of all the characters. He goes to great lengths to avoid opposing abstract "types" to his protagonists. In *The Lark,* although both Cauchon and Warwick represent the opposition of materialism to Jeanne's spiritualism, Cauchon conveys the devious thirst for power hidden in some prelates, while Warwick displays the callousness of political expediency. In *Becket* the king is a more defined individual than Créon in *Antigone.* He is coarse, but he admires and understands the value of Becket's subtlety. His ruthlessness does not preclude his continued love for his protégé; he lucidly plans the defeat of Becket but gallantly applauds him when he escapes the traps set for him. The King is a sympathetic mixture of roughness and tenderness.

As a result of this careful characterization, we feel that, although the characters do not share the ideals of their opponents, they still belong to the same "race." There is no need for two groups, the elect and the damned, as there was in the *pièces noires.* The protagonists' plight in the *pièces costumées* seems the more pathetic, since there should be a way for at least the men of the same group to live in harmony.

Although the two plays are similar insofar as meaning is concerned, the resemblance stops there. Each does more than conform to the patterned discussion of idealism that Anouilh started in his early plays. *Becket* unfurls the gripping history of a friendship that was meant to bring each partner lifelong comfort; it is the story of a mutual affection that lasts even through enmity. *The Lark* illustrates Anouilh's image of the lark that still sings in the sky while being shot at. It depicts the combination of strength and vulnerability that characterizes mankind. It is proof of the moral indestructibility of the man or the woman who is truly good.

Both excellent plays in which no aspect of dramatization has been neglected, *The Lark* and *Becket* had long runs on Broadway. The dialogue in each is a masterpiece of nuances. In *Becket* the strong, earthy language of the King and the barons is played against the measured, restrained language that Becket uses to seek understanding. In *The Lark,* Jeanne uses a language that seems rudimentary but that translates her acute common sense in such a way that what she says becomes irrefutable. At the same time Cauchon uses expressions filled with double meaning, while the short exclamations of the *promoteur* betray his lewdness in a hilarious manner. The pageantry one expects in a historical play is smoothly fitted into the plot so that one has the impression of witnessing an authentic yet modernized version of the story. In both plays Anouilh pushes the boldness of staging to the point of representing people on horseback. Finally, to stress the victory of the protagonists and to allow the spectator the satisfaction of a happy ending, he uses the flashback in various ways so that the last scene is one of triumph. The spectator leaves the theater not with the image of Jeanne being burned but with the sight of her radiant as she watches the consecration of the king of France. *Becket* ends not with the assassination of the archbishop but, as it had started, with the flogging of the repentant king in the church. Here the body of the play constitutes the flashback.

After the *pièces costumées* Anouilh concentrated on individual plays, including *La grotte* (*The Cavern*), published in book form in 1961. A clever mystery play of Pirandellian inspiration, supposedly written under the spectator's eyes, it introduces a long-awaited character in Anouilh's theater, "the author," who becomes Antoine de Saint-Flour in *Dear Antoine* and in *Les poissons rouges.*

In 1962 a one-act "concert play," *L'Orchestre,* appeared in *L'Avant-scène,* a literary journal. The same year Anouilh unknowingly took a major step in his development when he reproduced *Victor; ou, Les enfants au pouvoir* (Victor; or, The Children in Power),written by a longtime friend, the late Roger Vitrac. In this surrealistic play he found a technique that answered his own yearning to stylize the flow of human consciousness for the theater. Directed for the first time in 1928 by Antonin Artaud at the Théâtre Alfred Jarry, this work had been very poorly received by public and critics alike. When Anouilh saw *Victor* produced by the Michel de Ré Company in 1947, he was so impressed by it that, as he admitted, he slightly plagiarized it in *Ardèle.* His own production of *Victor* fifteen years later won wide acclaim. A subtly poetic "bourgeois drama," this play deals with Anouilh's favorite topic, the family circle; the plot focuses on the cruel fate of a child who suddenly realizes the true nature of the adult world and who accepts, along with this knowledge, his symbolic death. Anouilh was ready to investigate this particular subject; but, more important than its thematic value, *Victor* offered him an example of dialogue that follows the capricious meanderings of the consciousness of some of the characters.

*Le boulanger, la boulangère et le petit mitron* (The Baker, His Wife, and His Little Apprentice, 1969), the first play written by Anouilh in the six years following his production of *Victor,* shows the repercussions of his faithful efforts to vindicate Vitrac. In it a child becomes the central character and the play develops according to all the swirls and eddies of the stream of consciousness.

As far as children are concerned, Anouilh became preoccupied with their condition in the so-called family bosom quite early in his vocation, with *Humulus the Mute* and *Traveler Without Luggage.* Later he concentrated his attentions on adults. But after his exposure to *Victor,* he again gave a larger share of the limelight to children, reserving special treatment for the small boy Toto. In *Ardèle,* Toto is encountered as the child whose presence is overlooked by the family plunged into its petty problems. With Anouilh's delighted approval he unconsciously gets even with his family by mimicking its grotesque behavior at the most crucial moment. In *L'Hurluberlu* (*The Fighting Cock,* 1959), Toto becomes an incarnation of General Saint-Pé's childhood. When the general encourages him to eat a dose of magic "mininistafia," he is addressing not only his little boy but also the alter ego of his own youth, the vestiges of which are still visible in himself. In *Les poissons rouges* Toto attains a more complex status. He brings consolation to his father, the playwright Antoine de Saint-Flour; and to the extent that Anouilh can be identified with Antoine de Saint-Flour, one wonders how much of Toto is still a part of Anouilh.

In *Le boulanger, la boulangère et le petit mitron,* Toto represents all children. Writing this tragicomic bedroom farce in the aftermath of the "May events" (the student revolt in Paris of May 1968), Anouilh doggedly insists on showing the origins of the social troubles involving young people: in his view children are abandoned and lost in the average family, where Papa takes refuge from his wife and his boss in dreams of power and feminine conquests, while Maman either flies into dreams of passionate love or complains because she is not living in the grand style she feels she deserves. If the wife in this play is to be believed, had she married one of the glamorous suitors who lined up at her door before she condescended to marry her husband, she would have lived like a queen.

In a preface written in defense of young people, Anouilh points out that although children are neglected within their families, they must be psychoanalyzed and submitted to bewildering tests when they dare to revolt and ask for their rights in a society hopelessly oblivious to their existence and needs and primarily concerned with the rights of adults. The French public did not take too kindly to Anouilh's position and soon refrained from seeing the play, although it was hailed as a triumphant comeback on Anouilh's part.

The value of *Le boulanger, la boulangère et le petit mitron* lies especially in its surrealistic structure. Anouilh would object to the use of the term "surrealistic," for when he commented on Vitrac's *Victor* he purposely avoided it; he considered surrealism in the theater an evolution of the desire to represent the flow of consciousness, which, as he declared in an interview, was started by Aeschylus and was continued by Corneille, Shakespeare, and Pirandello. It is not surprising that Anouilh tried his hand at surrealism, for he steadily tore down the barriers between illusion and reality. In this play the dialogue exchanged on a conscious level by the protagonists matters little compared with the dialogue they use when they engage in their daydreaming, for it is then that their motives and their foolishness come to the fore, providing an explanation of their unreasonable behavior. Toto's dilemma also draws its emphasis from the impeccably timed intrusions of his daydreams into his parents' flight into fantasy. Peopled with storybook Indians and poetic historical figures, such as Louis XVI, Marie Antoinette, and their children facing danger as a family, Toto's dreams help us to measure the void in which he grows up. Though he should find warmth in the family nest, he must instead seek solace from his parents' bewildering quarrels in his books. And while he needs guidance and encouragement in the arduous process of getting an education, he must study his history lesson in utter loneliness, drawing conclusions as best he can.

Modern society has ceased to produce truly mature adults, and the children's problems stem from that fact, says Anouilh. It is significant that in his portrayal of the infantilism of present-day adults, some of the father's flights into illusion originate in the little boy's questions about American Indians (who still belong to the realm of fiction for the French). The father thus proves he stands just a step removed from the world of make-believe that his child lives in.

Begun as a bedroom farce, the play becomes a voyage into the inextricable mixture of reality and dream in which the characters are immersed, and it ends with Toto's nightmare about his parents being killed by Indians. Such an end is particularly effective, for within the play it serves to explain how Toto finds release from the mental torture caused by his parents' incessant arguments; outside of the play it satisfies somewhat the spectator's need to see the parents punished for their incorrigible thoughtlessness. Nevertheless, when the lieutenant kindly takes Toto under his protection and asks forgiveness for the parents, who have simply behaved like fallible human beings, the play closes on a compassionate note.

It was inevitable that Anouilh, indefatigable observer of men, would reach a point where he could not remain impassive at the sight of the excesses they commit, and would create a sort of spokesman. He did so in *Dear Antoine,* his first play of the 1969–1970 season, in which he introduced the playwright Antoine de Saint-Flour. After obtaining rave reviews for this play, Anouilh daringly presented a second play that season, *Les poissons rouges,* in which the same protagonist, seen at an earlier time, takes stock of himself. As he searches his past and present, he discovers that although he has tried to be a compassionate, fairly honorable human being, he is held responsible for every possible ill by the people around him. At home his wife nags him, his mother-in-law remains unconcerned at his being abused, his fifteen-year-old daughter declares she became pregnant out of wedlock so that she could leave home. In the outside world a childhood friend, who is a worker's son and whom he treats with unusual forbearance, insults him, morning, noon, and night, as if he had caused all the social ills the proletariat suffers from. Even his mistress is afflicted with a suicidal obsession and complicates his life no end. Plagued by all this, Antoine comes to feel at times that he should walk like a hunchback or even limp, in order to placate hunchbacks like his doctor (a frustrated literary critic), who chastises him for being healthy.

Permeated with the good-natured reactions of Antoine, opposed to the sourness and self-righteousness of others, the play greatly amuses by its wealth of impish repartee. In the exchange lies many a truth about the privileged and the not so privileged of our society. "Refreshing" is the epithet critics have used to describe this comedy, both *rose* and *noire.* Actually, Anouilh was never anything else.

## Selected Bibliography


### EDITIONS

#### COLLECTED PLAYS

*Pièces noires.* Paris, 1945, 1958 (*L'Hermine, La sauvage, Le voyageur sans bagage, Eurydice*).

*Nouvelles pièces noires.* Paris, 1946, 1958 (*Jézabel, Antigone, Roméo et Jeannette, Médée*).

*Pièces grinçantes.* Paris, 1956 (*Ardèle ou la marguerite, La valse des toréadors, Ornifle ou le courant d'air, Pauvre Bitos ou le dîner de têtes*).

*Pièces roses.* Paris, 1958 (*Humulus le muet, Le bal des voleurs, Le rendez-vous de Senlis, Léocadia*).

*Pièces brillantes.* Paris, 1960 (*L'Invitation au château, Colombe, La répétition ou l'amour puni, Cécile ou l'école des pères*).

*Pièces costumées.* Paris, 1960 (*L'Alouette, Becket ou l'honneur de Dieu, La foire d'empoigne*).

*Nouvelles pièces grinçantes.* Paris, 1970 (*L'Hurluberlu, La grotte, L'Orchestre, Le boulanger, la boulangère et le petit mitron, Poissons rouges*).

*Pieces baroques.* Paris, 1974 (*Cher Antoine, Ne reveillez pas Madame, Le directeur de l'opera*).

*Pièces farceuses.* Paris, 1984 (*Chers zoiseaux, La culotte, Episode de la vie d'un amateur, Le nombril*).

#### INDIVIDUAL PLAYS

*La petite Molière.* In *L'Avant-scene,* no. 210 (15 December 1959).

*L'Hurluberlu ou le réactionnaire amoureux.* Paris, 1959.

*La grotte.* Paris, 1961.

*Le boulanger, la boulangère et le petit mitron.* Paris, 1969.

*Cher Antoine ou l'amour raté.* Paris, 1969.

*Les poissons rouges ou mon père ce héros.* Paris, 1970.

*L'Orchestre.* In *Monsieur Barnett suivi de L'Orchestre.* Paris, 1975.

## TRANSLATIONS

### COLLECTED PLAYS

*Plays.* 4 vols. New York, 1958–1987. Vol. 1: *Antigone, Eurydice, The Ermine, The Rehearsal, Romeo and Jeannette.* Vol. 2: *Restless Heart, Time Remembered, Ardèle, Mademoiselle Colombe, The Lark.* Vol. 3: *Thieves' Carnival, Medea, Cecile, Traveler Without Luggage, The Orchestra, Episode in the Life of an Author, Catch as Catch Can.* Vol. 4: *Leocadia, Antigone, Waltz of the Toreadors, The Lark, Poor Bitos.*

*Collected Plays.* 2 vols. London, 1966–1967.

### INDIVIDUAL PLAYS

*Becket; or, The Honor of God.* Translated by Lucienne Hill. New York, 1960.

*The Cavern.* Translated by Lucienne Hill. New York, 1966.

*The Fighting Cock.* Adapted by Lucienne Hill. New York, 1960.

*Poor Bitos.* Translated by Lucienne Hill. New York and London, 1964.

*Ring Round the Moon.* Translated by Christopher Fry. New York, 1950; London, 1956.

*Thieves' Carnival.* Translated by Lucienne Hill. London, 1952.

*Traveller Without Luggage.* Translated by John Whiting. London, 1959.

*The Waltz of the Toreadors.* Translated by Lucienne Hill. New York, 1958.

## BIOGRAPHICAL AND CRITICAL STUDIES

An extensive bibliography of books and articles on Anouilh and his work is available in *French VII, Bibliography of Critical and Biographical References for the Study of Contemporary French Literature.* New York, 1949–. In 1969 the title was changed to *French XX, Bibliography: Critical and Biographical References for the Study of French Literature Since 1885.*

Borgal, Clément. *Anouilh: La peine de vivre.* Paris, 1966.

Comminges, Élie de. *Anouilh: Littérature et politique.* Paris, 1977.

Della Fazia, Alba Marie. *Jean Anouilh.* New York, 1969.

Didier, Jean. *À la rencontre de Jean Anouilh.* Liège, 1946.

Falb, Lewis W. *Jean Anouilh.* New York, 1977.

Gignoux, Hubert. *Jean Anouilh.* Paris, 1946.

Kelly, Kathleen White. *Jean Anouilh: An Annotated Bibliography.* Metuchen, N.J., 1973.

Lassale, Jean-Pierre. *Jean Anouilh, ou La vaine revolté.* Rodez, France, 1958.

Lenski, B. A. *Jean Anouilh: Stages in Rebellion.* Atlantic Highlands, N.J., 1975.

McIntyre, H. G. *The Theatre of Jean Anouilh.* Totowa, N.J., 1981.

Marcel, Gabriel. *L'Heure théâtrale de Giraudoux à Jean-Paul Sartre.* Paris, 1959.

Marsh, Edwin O. *Jean Anouilh: Poet of Pierrot and Pantaloon.* London, 1953; repr., New York, 1968.

Pronko, Leonard C. *The World of Jean Anouilh.* Berkeley and Los Angeles, 1961.

## INTERVIEWS

Ambrière, Francis. "Le secret de Jean Anouilh." *Les Annales* 15:45 (January 1952).

Archer, Marguerite. Paris, 25 August 1962, and Arcachon, 3 August 1969. Also present at the second interview was Roland Piétri, Anouilh's longtime codirector.

Delavèze, Jean. "Pour la première fois Jean Anouilh parle. . . . " *Les Nouvelles Littéraires,* 5 February 1959, pp. 1, 9.

Farrell, Isolde. "Anouilh Returns." *New York Times,* 3 January 1954, sec. 2, p. 3.

MARGUERITE ARCHER

# JEAN GENET

## *(1910–1986)*

JEAN GENET WAS born in Paris on 19 December 1910. His literary contributions include a large number of poems, four novels, and five plays. By common consent it is for the plays that he will be remembered most. But the plays are frequently bizarre, at times outrageous, and always rather complicated. It is tempting, therefore, to adopt a characteristic approach to puzzling literature and turn to the writer's life and historical milieu for assistance in explaining his work. This is particularly tempting in Genet's case, because he obligingly supplies us with a detailed autobiography (provocatively entitled *Journal du voleur* [*The Thief's Journal*], 1949). But there are problems with such an approach, not the least of which is Genet's tendency in the autobiography to treat the events of his life as if he were writing a novel rather than a history. His version of his past is as much an imagined story as a remembered sequence of events.

At first glance this might raise questions about Genet's right to distort the truth of his earlier life. But to Genet such imaginative rewriting of earlier events is not dishonesty. It is, instead, a higher form of honesty, one to be contrasted with the deceptive activity of pretending to recall events as they really were:

> If I attempt to recompose with words what my attitude was at the time, the reader will be no more taken in than I. We know that our language is incapable of recalling even the pale reflection of those bygone, foreign states. The same would be true of this entire journal if it were to be the notation of what I was. I shall therefore make clear that it is meant to indicate what I am today, as I write it. It is not a quest of time gone by, but a work of art whose pretext-subject is my former life. . . . Let the reader therefore understand that the facts were what I say they were, but the interpretation that I give them is what I am—now.
>
> (Frechtman trans., p. 71)

It is by no means easy, of course, for the reader to distinguish Genet's "facts" from his "interpretations," but that blurred line is only the first of several we will encounter as we explore Genet's life and art. Indeed, such blurring inevitably affects the clarity of that most important of lines, the one between life and art. When Genet concedes that his journal is a "work of art whose pretext-subject is [his] former life," he establishes an order of priority that reverses the one with which we are most familiar. Instead of art imitating or taking second place to life, the life seems to be subsumed in or to take second place to the art.

It is thus a dubious strategy to turn to the facts of Genet's life in order to elucidate his art. Indeed, if we are successfully to come to terms with that hybrid text *The Thief's Journal,* we would do well to try first to grasp his aesthetic principles. But there are important consequences of such an interpretative strategy, consequences of which Genet is fully aware and by means of which he hopes to achieve a great deal. As he provocatively points out: "In order [for the reader] to understand me, [his] complicity will be necessary" (p. 16). It will indeed, for Genet is constantly maneuvering his audience to his own advantage, and even as he bluntly indicates the role he has in mind for us to play, he remains much less blunt about what he hopes thereby to achieve, both for himself and for us.

If we are to do justice to Genet's work, however, we have little choice but to adopt the unusual stance he requires of us, one that may force us to do less than justice to people and principles we might otherwise view more favorably. The gain promises to be aesthetic: we will more easily come to grips with the work of a man who is justly regarded as one of the great writers of the twentieth century. The loss threatens to be moral: the characters and situations Genet depicts are often those likely to provoke sufficient moral disapprobation to deny them the benefit of our extended attention. The conflict between gain and loss that is thus precipitated in the reader/audience is symptomatic of a persistent tension in Genet's art between the aesthetic and the moral. The evolving interaction of the aesthetic and the moral is of central importance to Genet's life as we encounter in it his art, and its major manifestation is the pattern of aesthetic reconstruction he repeatedly tries to impose on an early life of apparent moral squalor. If we thus turn temporarily to that early life, it is less to find events that will explain his art than to locate events and attitudes that the art must help to explain.

So successful has Genet been at projecting stories of his life that it is very difficult indeed to distinguish the facts from the legends. What seems beyond dispute, however, is that he was born in Paris in 1910, the illegitimate son of Gabrielle Genet, who abandoned him soon after he was born. After a brief period in government care, he was handed over to foster parents and found himself living, as a child, with a peasant family in the Morvan region of France. His youthful behavior was such that he was subsequently sent, as a teenager, to a reformatory called Mettray. At this notorious institution near Tours, Genet found himself surrounded by the delinquent youth of his generation. The institution's goal was reform, and its major strategy was enforced hard labor. Reports of conditions at Mettray at this time stress the hunger, brutality, filth, and rampant homosexuality that characterized the lives of the inmates. The effect on Genet was not to reform him but to strengthen his commitment to the life of the criminal. He gained his release from Mettray by joining the army but found army life no more to his liking and soon deserted.

Genet spent the next twelve years wandering through Europe as a vagrant, thief, and prostitute. He served prison sentences in several countries and seemed destined to live the life of a convict until he discovered the activity of writing. During a period of incarceration in Fresnes prison, he wrote a poem called "Le condamné à mort" ("The Condemned Man," 1945) and began writing a novel, *Notre-Dame-des-Fleurs* (*Our Lady of the Flowers,* 1944), dedicating both to an executed prisoner, Maurice Pilorge. The novel was soon published through the financial assistance of a patron whose identity remains unknown. It is known, however, that the manuscript attracted the favorable attention of the noted author, actor, film director, and painter Jean Cocteau, who issued a dramatic appeal for clemency on Genet's behalf when Genet was next arrested: this time, ironically enough, for stealing books. Genet was subsequently adopted in French literary circles. When he was (unjustly) arrested again, in 1947, it took a combined appeal to the French president by several prominent writers, among them Jean-Paul Sartre and Cocteau, to avert a sentence of life imprisonment. Thereafter, Genet devoted himself to his writing and to political causes, never settling into a fixed pattern of life as a writer but always on the move until his death on 15 April 1986.

Although Genet appears to have ceased his criminal activities after his presidential pardon in 1948, it would be a mistake to conceive of him as a reformed convict. His work as a writer is a constant struggle to keep faith with a past for which he is ready to make no apology. Falling quickly under the influence of Sartre, whose acquaintance he made in 1944, Genet set about exploring his past as a repository of aesthetic possibilities rather than as a record of moral liabilities.

One of the chief contributors to the Genet legend was Sartre himself, whose book *Saint Genet: Comédien et martyr* (*Saint Genet: Actor and Martyr,* 1952) set out not so much to rehabilitate Genet as to justify him. Sartre, the renowned philosopher of existential choice, portrayed Genet as the heroic rejecter of a society that had rejected him. Condemned to the life of the criminal, Genet, in Sartre's terms, made not just a virtue but almost a religion of necessity by living to the full the criminal possibilities society had offered him. Sartre's argument—that Genet survived by converting his imposed image into a chosen emblem—is a brilliant one, and it earned the admiration of Genet himself. It is, however, Sartre's Genet: neither true nor false, but an imaginative reconstruction of a person and a world that Genet himself was to reconstruct with a more vital imagination for related but more complicated purposes.

Genet's first play, like his first poem and first novel, is about criminals. *Haute surveillance* (*Deathwatch,* 1949) explores the relationships among three criminals in a prison cell. One of them, known only as Green Eyes, is on trial for murder, and throughout the action his feet are chained together. Though it is evident that Genet is exploring his own prison experience through these three characters, we note that attention is devoted neither to issues of justice and injustice nor to possible plans for escape or pleas for clemency, but to the social status of the inmates within the prison society. And in Genet's hands social status is closely linked to social image and community aesthetics.

The curtain rises on a cell with a granite-block bed, heavy spiked bars, and walls of roughly hewed stone, the latter arranged, Genet indicates, in such a way as to suggest that the prison building is one with a complicated architectural structure. The complexity of the building's structure is indicative of the complex structure of the society it contains. As the play begins, Green Eyes is forcibly restraining Lefranc from killing the teenager Maurice. What has precipitated the violence is not some quarrel over property or territory, but a disagreement over the social reputation of Snowball, an incongruously named black convict in another cell.

> MAURICE (*pointing to Lefranc*): He's always trying to make trouble. There'll never be any peace with him around. For him, no one matters. Only Snowball.
>
> LEFRANC (*violently*): Yes, Snowball. You said it. He's got what it takes. Don't play around with him. He's a Negro, a savage. . . . He's out of this world. All the guys in his cell feel it. And in the cells around too, and the whole prison and all the prisons in France. He shines. He beams. He's black but he lights up the whole two thousand cells. No one'll ever get him down. He's the real boss of the prison. . . . All you've got to do is see him walk. . . .
>
> (Frechtman trans., pp. 105, 107; all subsequent quotations are from this translation)

Seeing Snowball walk involves seeing a man in chains struggling up the long stairways and narrow corridors invoked in the dialogue. But seeing also involves community perspective and community values, and the invoked picture of a proud man in chains is recapitulated in the rival image we have before us of Green Eyes, another candidate—indeed, Maurice's candidate—for the emblematic leadership of prison society.

This emerging concern for social image is both extended and revised by Green Eyes, who is less interested at this point in the image he presents to his peers inside the prison than in the one he presents to his girlfriend outside. Unable to read or write, he has enlisted the aid of Lefranc to compose letters to her and to read letters from her. As character interaction becomes more complicated, however, it becomes evident that he is now suspicious of the image Lefranc has incidentally projected of himself. Lefranc, in turn, blames that suspicion on Maurice: "Before you came, everything was fine. Green Eyes and I got along like two men. I didn't talk about him as if he were a bride" (p. 114).

Maurice's response is one of scorn, and it is accompanied by a recurring gesture designed to establish his own preferred image: he tosses back his head as if to relocate some stray locks of hair. The image he projects of submission to Green Eyes and defiance to Lefranc exhibits his complex attempts to establish a desired place in the social structure, and it is paralleled by Lefranc's similarly motivated manipulation of images. Trying not just to dominate Maurice but also to placate him and even woo him, Lefranc poses as a patron by supplying Maurice with extra food and extra blankets. Green Eyes, however, provides the most graphic display of attempted image control in the early action by baring his chest and displaying upon it a tattoo of his girlfriend's face.

Although all three convicts seem obsessed by the power of images, the picture on Green Eyes' chest registers most clearly the potential failure of attempts to control the world by appropriating its images. Green Eyes' girlfriend is not tied to that image and seems about to abandon him—or so, under the prompting of Lefranc, he is ready to believe. But what Green Eyes is actually doing is shifting from belief in the authenticity of one image (the faithful girlfriend) to belief in another (the unfaithful girlfriend), without receiving much evidence to justify either. The shift in his allegiance is no less strong for its lack of a clear justification, however, and the significance of her image seems to depend less on her actions than upon what others make of those actions: a point with large implications not just for their relationship but for the whole social structure depicted in the play.

This concern for the viability of images is, of course, as much an aesthetic as a pragmatic concern, and it serves to highlight the strange nature of the action we are witnessing. Though we are watching the interaction of convicts in a prison and though the action will culminate in a murder, there seems little here to suggest that Genet is employing images to depict in judgmental terms the life he used to lead. The banality of the criminal rather than the beauty or evil of criminality seems most prominently displayed. There is no attempt on the part of the prisoners to defy, threaten, or oppose the agents or the principles of the social system that has incarcerated them. Indeed, they seem supremely indifferent to the social world from which they are separated and equally indifferent to whether some more just society should take its place. Apart from their shared interest in Green Eyes' girlfriend, they register little concern for the life they led before they became criminals or for the life they might lead thereafter. The play's action and the characters' interests are restricted to the world of the common criminal. Or so it might seem. For steadily emerging in the action is a concern for the uncommon criminal, for the man who can transform being a criminal from a social condition into a social image, a man who can, without erasing the banality of evil, reveal its potential beauty.

In Genet's work in general, there is a strangely recurring mixture of triviality and lyricism, which is often embodied in a criminality whose tawdry unseemliness is somehow juxtaposed to, and even united with, a greater power and larger significance. But that larger significance is not to be sought in the defying of established moral codes nor in the assertion of alternative moral codes; rather, it is to be sought in an initial acceptance and subsequent reconstruction of community images that are first proffered and then projected. This is not an option for everyone, and it is not relevant to all criminal acts or criminal images. When Lefranc finally murders Maurice at the end of the play, for example, it is a murder whose moral repugnance is undermined by its aesthetic triviality—and it is a measure of the success of the dramatist that he can, by the end of the play, make his audience feel that the crime they have just witnessed is merely trite, that it is to be measured more by its aesthetic failure than by its moral significance.

To speak in such terms is, however, to retain our footing on the very terrain from which Genet wishes to dislodge us. The death is morally insignificant because the morality we live by has become, in this world, insignificant. What has taken its place is not another form of morality but another mode of social being, in terms of which social authenticity, not public morality, is the decisive factor.

The tensions in the prison cell focus primarily on the prison status and the internal strengths of Green Eyes. He is the dominant force in the cell and the potentially dominant force in the prison as a whole. He has, of course, a competitor in the fierce figure of Snowball, but the factor that weighs most strongly against Green Eyes' authenticity and authority seems to be his attachment to the girlfriend on the outside—an attachment under repeated review. Lefranc's love/hate relationship with Green Eyes is registered not only in his attempts to compete with Maurice for Green Eyes' attention and in his arguments for the superiority of Snowball, but also in his ongoing efforts to sever that relationship with the girlfriend.

> LEFRANC: I wanted to separate you from your girl, Green Eyes. I did all I could. I did what I could to isolate you from the world and to separate the cell, and even the prison, from the world. And I think I've succeeded. I wanted the whole world to know that we're here and that we're peaceful here. Among ourselves. I don't want a single breath of air to come from outside. And I'm working at it. More than anyone else. I wanted us to be brothers.
>
> (pp. 145–146)

It turns out that what Lefranc wants, however, is to be part of a brotherhood of kings. He wants to elevate Green Eyes into an authentic image by severing his lingering connection to the outside world and also to be seen by him as someone similarly separated and similarly elevated. As Maurice is quick to remind him, however, he doesn't belong; his crimes and his attitudes preclude him from membership in the peculiar elect that is emerging both before our eyes and before the eyes of the convicts, who seem more adept at recognizing it than they are at conceptualizing it.

To gain better understanding of the nature of that elect, we should explore further the one issue upon which both Maurice and Lefranc agree—the debilitating nature of the relationship with the girlfriend:

> MAURICE: To me, you're still Green Eyes. A terrific guy. But you've lost your force, your fine criminal force. You belong to your girl more than you realize.
>
> (p. 148)

That "criminal force" is the secret of the authentic image, and it is a force recognized and substantiated only by other prisoners, who are well tuned to the false alternatives that are manifest in the hollow stories of the self-impressed and socially aspiring:

> MAURICE: . . . the cells are full of the most terrific stories imaginable. There are times when it all hangs in the air, and the air gets so thick you feel like puking. And the worst of all are the ones they invent to make themselves look big. Racketeering, trafficking in gold, pearls, diamonds! It reeks. Phony dollars, cashboxes, furs! And galley slaves!
>
> (p. 150)

Though false stories abound, their very existence registers a recognition of the power exercised by similar stories that do not ring false. To captivate this audience is to invoke an important kind of social power and social being by standing in a peculiar relationship to the worlds inside and outside the prison. Further indication of this is supplied by the inconsistency in Lefranc's appeal to Green Eyes. On the one hand, he wishes to isolate the prison world from the outside world, but, on the other, he wants the whole world to know that they are there and at peace being there. And it is important to note that when Maurice seeks to substantiate the prestige of Green Eyes, he relies heavily upon the massive public attention the latter earned by his crime.

Green Eyes is in many ways an uncertain candidate for the role that is descending upon him, and not substantially more certain of its nature and genesis. He is more inclined to feel sorry for himself, for the likely loss of his girlfriend, and for his impending death. But without quite understanding why, he finds himself driven to adopt the role his fellow prisoners expect of him, just as he carried out the murder of a young woman without clear motive or conscious decision. With a fine flair for the picturesque, rather than a fine understanding of its significance, Green Eyes is often linked to the aesthetically pleasing. Before his recent crime he has been fond of posing with hands in pockets and a flower in his teeth; he leaves lilacs in the hair of the murdered woman; he carries the image of his girlfriend on his chest; and he regrets her impending loss not just personally but aesthetically: "She's going to let me down in cold blood without realizing that if she waited another two months she'd be a widow. She could have come and prayed at my grave and brought . . . [*he hesitates*] . . . flowers . . ." (p. 121).

This lost opportunity for striking a social pose seems to irk Green Eyes as much as the loss of a loving relationship. At one time nicknamed Paulo of the Flowery Teeth, Green Eyes is the stuff of which legends are made—as distinct from a man who makes legends. Though his actions are voluntary, what people make of them often comes as something of a surprise. But the key issue is how he responds to the expectations that he had not fully anticipated. As the action progresses, Green Eyes withdraws further and further from participation in events and moves steadily toward an abstract status. He suspends his personal intervention in the lives not only of his girlfriend but also of his cell mates; and when Lefranc tries again to murder Maurice, Green Eyes, this time, does not attempt to interfere. The image he is offered in the prison, and the one that he gradually adopts, is not that of a community agent but of a community emblem; he becomes the focus of the community's storytelling, the image of its aesthetic possibilities.

> GREEN EYES: I'm building myself up again. I'm healing. I'm making myself over. I'm getting stronger, more solid than a fortress. Stronger than the prison. You hear me, I *am* the prison! . . . I'm the prison and I'm alone in the world.
>
> (p. 137)

It is the personal isolation of the community emblem that allows Green Eyes to claim both that he includes everyone and that he is excluded from everyone. To play his community role he becomes, as Lefranc has argued, personally alone and individually inactive. The personal self is dissolved by solitude into the public image. The authenticity thus achieved is one that renders aesthetically inauthentic the deliberate murder Lefranc carries out in order to achieve (he hopes) the desired legendary status. Lefranc, poring over photographs of murderers and trying on Green Eyes' clothes, cannot find the key to converting his own notoriety into community legend. Green Eyes is more successful, but it is a matter of capacities whose significance he did not understand coinciding with possibilities whose existence he had not suspected. His image and his world are enacted into being rather than argued or enforced into being.

> GREEN EYES: You don't know the first thing about misfortune if you think you can choose it. I didn't want mine. It chose me. It fell on my shoulders and clung to me. I tried everything to shake it off. I struggled, I boxed, I danced, I even sang, and, odd as it may seem, I refused it

> at first. It was only when I saw that everything was irremediable that I quieted down. I've only just accepted it. It had to be total.
>
> (p. 162)

In the course of the action, Green Eyes moves from one aspiring to make fine phrases to one who becomes "a fine phrase" (p. 123). He learns the power of the stories he had earlier been prone to dismiss (p. 124). He learns the strength of images and the difficulty of constructing them: "A man doesn't have to strut. He knows he's a man and that's all that matters" (p. 143). He learns not to regard Snowball as a rival, nor to seek him as an ally, but to recognize him as one who carries the same community burdens he carries. In becoming less than individually human he also becomes larger than life, not just to himself but also to Lefranc: "You're radiant. You . . . you're beginning to be radiant" (p. 161). It is the radiance of one who has become the embodiment of the aesthetic possibilities of the criminal world, the embodiment of aspirations not for release or for reform, but for a link with a greatness that grows out of but does not supplant the sordid, the trivial, and the banal.

As Green Eyes learns some strange lessons, so do we. Genet is providing a perspective on the criminal community that is odd and unexpected. He focuses on the aesthetics of criminal society, and it is an aesthetics that does not supplant, but supplements, the reality of their everyday lives. Genet even suggests that the actors glide around on felt soles (p. 104) to register this linkage between everyday events and aesthetic significance.

This strange mixture of the aesthetically captivating and the morally marginal is one that has baffled many. But there is a logic to their interaction that works its way through all of the plays. In one way it is self-serving—it enables Genet to explore moral marginality in a context that draws attention to other aspects of such a life. But besides being self-serving, it is also artistically fruitful. The relationships between art and life, between fiction and truth, between illusion and reality that have fascinated many writers in the modern era are explored here from an oddly productive angle. Genet convincingly demonstrates what many theorists have proclaimed—that the art/life opposition is a false one and that the aesthetic is one perspective on life rather than something contrasting with life.

An aesthetic perspective on daily life is no more false or true than a psychological perspective, a sociological perspective, a historical perspective, or an economic perspective. Each offers a means of selectively abstracting certain elements from our world rather than a means of creating a false world. There is an aesthetics of ordinary life as well as of extraordinary life, and Genet's insistence upon the trivial and the transcendent in the realm of the criminal is an insistence that reveals and explores one of the complex sources of social power in every society. It means more to him, and should mean more to us, than an attempt to avoid taking responsibility for his criminal activities. For Genet is setting out on a process of exploration that will lead him and us to come to terms with aesthetic complexities of far-reaching consequence.

In his next play, *Les bonnes* (*The Maids*, 1947), Genet takes us beyond the world of the prison cell to the wealthy world of upper-class society. The possibility of a murder again pervades the action, but it is an action whose consequences are of larger social significance. The maids, like the prisoners in *Deathwatch*, struggle with their standing in the place where they live and work, but unlike the prisoners, they wish to play to a larger audience. The peculiar provenance of images that proved so central to the social world of the prison is of similar importance here, but Genet is extending rather than repeating his portrayal of them.

As the action begins, we encounter an elegant lady and a clumsy maid interacting in terms that emphasize the superiority of the former and the lowliness of the latter. The lady, in a bedroom full of lace and flowers, primps in front of the mirror, tries on various beautiful dresses, and compares her beauty to that of the Holy Virgin. The maid, in more homely garb and with "a face and body," she is told, not even adequate to the task of seducing the milkman, is treated as one both disdained and repulsive: "Avoid pawing me. You smell like an animal. You've brought those odors from some foul attic" (p. 40). But just as we begin to conceive of the action as a schematic exaggeration of social stereotypes, we discover that the lady of the house is, in fact, away from home, and that her two maids are acting out the mistress/maid relationship rather than living their usual role in her presence. The potentially hollow stereotypes enacted before us are supplied with a surprising authenticity by our recognition that they are in one sense fake—for we realize that the two maids are exploring the image the lady must have of them through the image they have of her.

In the hands of a lesser dramatist, a play of social propaganda might emerge in which exaggerated social stereotypes are displayed in order to establish an ideological point or to incite revolutionary action. Genet, however, is concerned both with the distortion social roles impose on the individual psyche and with the obsessive fascination these social roles seem to hold for the individual psyche. The point is embedded both in the overall structure of the play's action and in that evocative opening scene, which supplies an ironic answer to a question invited by the play's title: What do the maids do when they are not being maids? The answer is, of course, that they play at being maids—an answer that serves only to bring up the further question of which comes first, the social role or the individual psyche.

Genet is much too intelligent a writer to supply answers to "chicken and egg" questions, but it is important to understand why the naive question should be asked even if there is no justification for a similarly naive response. Genet is not about to lose us in a hall of mirrors in which life consists of nothing but social roles and public images. But he is concerned to display and explore the nature of lives lived in the context of such images. And the key to the action of the play is to be found in the dilemma that confronted Green Eyes in a narrower social context. To gain the power of the social image he had to give up his girlfriend, abandon Maurice, and withdraw from individual participation in social life. The two maids, Claire and Solange, however, are urgently committed to participating in a world they do not control. Their initial aim is not to create new images but to learn how to manipulate the images that have invidiously manipulated them. They want both individual power and the power of the inherited social image.

The aesthetic dimension of everyday life is once again the point of departure for a play seeking to explore the complexity of the relationship between the aesthetic and the pragmatic. Flowers are dispersed in great profusion about the room; Claire's rendition of Madame's role is acutely histrionic, with exaggerated gestures and melodramatic tones; and a repeated focus of attention is the choice of costume and jewelry for the evening's festivities. Solange (Claire) does indeed wish Claire (Madame) to be "lovely," to earn in full measure the admiration, envy, and hatred of the maid. But the aesthetic and the pragmatic are inextricably intertwined in a game that involves not only a repeated script but also one subject to variation and dislocation. The dialogue between maid and Madame is regularly interrupted by conversation between maid and maid as the latter allow their squabbles over status and lovers to mingle with the established script. The maid/Madame game provides an environment in which not only the maid/Madame relationship is subjected to scrutiny but also that between the two maids (who are rivals for and victims of the milkman's attentions).

> CLAIRE: I shall be lovely. Lovelier than you'll ever be. With a face and body like that, you'll never seduce Mario. [*dropping the tragic tone*] A ri-

diculous young milkman despises us, and if we're going to have a kid by him—

SOLANGE: Oh! I've never—

CLAIRE: [*resuming*] Be quiet, you fool. My dress!

SOLANGE: [*She looks in the closet, pushing aside a few dresses.*] The red dress. Madame will wear the red dress.

CLAIRE: I said the white dress, the one with spangles.

SOLANGE: [*firmly*] I'm sorry. Madame will wear the scarlet velvet dress this evening.

CLAIRE: [*naïvely*] Ah? Why?

SOLANGE: [*coldly*] It's impossible to forget Madame's bosom under the velvet folds. And the jet brooch, when Madame was sighing and telling Monsieur of my devotion! Your widowhood really requires that you be entirely in black.

CLAIRE: Eh?

SOLANGE: Need I say more? A word to the wise—

CLAIRE: Ah! So you want to talk. . . . Very well. Threaten me. Insult your mistress, Solange. You want to talk about Monsieur's misfortunes, don't you? Fool. It was hardly the moment to allude to him, but I can turn this matter to fine account!

(pp. 37–38)

Claire, who is not yet a widow in either of her roles, can and does "turn this [and other matters] to fine account" as the interpolations of Solange suggest new scenarios and precipitate reciprocal responses. The established script becomes a point of departure for two individuals seeking to explore and possibly transform not only the images they invoke and exploit, but also the selves so often exploited by them.

The latter is, of course, a very important point because the apparent foundation of the game-playing is the exploitation of the maids by the social system and by the people who assign them the role of maids. But within the game the maids appropriate both the images they are assigned and the images of those who assign them, and consequently put themselves in a position to exploit the very images that have exploited them. The irony is, however, that in order to appropriate authentic roles, they must play them to the full. And the danger is that in doing so they lose themselves in the very images they seek to control. It is the first of those points that drives them to play Madame and maid in terms that register in such an exaggerated way the beauty of the one and the loathsomeness of the other. And it is the second point that makes them struggle so much to bring to a transcendent conclusion or put to innovative use a game they have played many times before.

The alternating love and hatred the maids display for Madame and their similarly alternating urges toward mastery and submission are the underlying forces in a procedure that leads repeatedly toward, but never quite achieves, the murder of Madame. Their varied ways of playing the game and their alternation in the role of Madame are symptoms of an urge to use the aesthetically grounded game as a means of precipitating pragmatic change. But they seem unable to promote decisive change by employing stereotyped, mutually defining images. To usurp Madame's authority is not to eradicate it. The game-playing always goes on too long, it always fails to open up a route to decisive change, and it is always interrupted before Madame can be murdered.

Genet's interest in the aesthetics of everyday life has, by this point, begun to turn his characters into playwrights. But they are curiously limited playwrights. Although Claire accuses Solange of having stolen her "most fantastic stories" (p. 53), the two maids seem unable to generate a satisfactory script. They repeatedly find themselves lost in the midst of conventional images that provide the basis only for conventional fantasies. Using each other as audience, they seem not to share Green Eyes' need for extensive community corroboration. But the consequence of the limited community viability of their fantasies is that the aesthetic and pragmatic components of their lives can interact only in the context of this room. Their play within the play, though combining many traditional roles, has only a single stage set and a tiny audience. It is the larger play, containing theirs, that speaks of issues beyond those the maids can include in their games, and linkage between their play and the larger play is needed if the aesthetic is to be brought into fruitful conjunction with the pragmatic.

For this reason the crucial event in their current lives is Claire's betrayal of Madame's lover, Monsieur, to the police. In an anonymous letter (a fiction, of course) she has declared him to be a criminal and he has been arrested. Claire's indirect attack on Madame is matched by Solange's attempt to kill Madame while she is sleeping—an attempt thwarted by last-minute cowardice (p. 56). Such ignoble acts, like Lefranc's murder of Maurice, threaten to propel them, in the absence of some ennobling context, along the route to notoriety rather than toward transcendence. Only in a realm in which the aesthetically extreme links with the pragmatically disturbing can something authentically liberating and potentially transcendent be achieved. There is something about the extremity of crime that seems indispensable to significant change—change of the kind that has just, ironically enough, descended upon Madame.

> SOLANGE: Look, just look at how she suffers. How she suffers in beauty. Grief transfigures her, doesn't it. Beautifies her? When she learned that her lover was a thief, she stood up to the police. She exulted. Now she is forlorn and splendid, supported under each arm by two devoted servants whose hearts bleed to see her grief. Did you see it? Her grief sparkling with the glint of her jewels, with the satin of her gowns, in the glow of the chandelier! Claire, I wanted to make up for the poverty of my grief by the splendor of my crime.
>
> (pp. 56–57)

The splendor of an evocative crime constantly looms as the route to transcendence and transfiguration; but though the two maids acknowledge the possibility of glorious action, they seem incapable of conceiving an equivalent conclusion for their script. Attempts to strangle Madame and to poison her tea seem unlikely to meet the goal they set themselves: "The great thing is to end in beauty" (p. 88). Though the two sisters encounter considerable difficulty in achieving beautiful endings, they are, however, very skilled at creating beautiful beginnings. As impromptu playwrights they are adept at constructing exotic stage sets, luxurious costumes, imaginative plots, and striking images. When Madame stumbles unknowingly into the setting for their ceremony, she laughingly remarks, "You're trying to kill me with your tea and your flowers and your suggestions" (p. 78). Indeed they are, but those several components are collectively crucial and individually indispensable. The anticipated murder must emerge from and be grounded in an imaginative setting that is to give a potentially sordid crime a transcendent aesthetic stature.

As the ceremony begins again and is again in search of a novel ending, the maids switch out the lights, invoke God as the audience, and dress Claire in a dazzling white dress that doesn't quite cover her black maid's uniform (p. 85). The ceremony releases and enhances Claire's (Madame's) contempt for Solange (Claire) and Solange's (Claire's) hatred of Madame. The domination/submission roles are reversed as Solange (Claire) whips Claire (Madame), and the love/hate relationship between maid and Madame intersects with the love/hate relationship of the maids for each other. As Solange (Claire) strikes the kneeling Claire (Madame), she murmurs words of admiration as well as of anger.

> SOLANGE: Down on your knees! [*Claire hesitates and kneels*] Ah! Ah! You were so beautiful, the way you wrung your precious arms! Your tears, your petals oozed down your lovely face. Ah! Ah! Down! [*Claire does not move*] Down! [*Solange strikes her*] *Get Down*! [*Claire lies down*] Ah! You amuse me, my dear! Crawl! Crawl, I say, like a worm!
>
> (p. 87)

Claire, overcome by Solange's intensity in playing the role, retreats to the kitchen and leaves Solange to ponder the hopeless complexity of a situation that captivates and imprisons them.

Wearing the short black dress of a maid, Solange describes herself as "the monstrous soul of servantdom" (p. 93) and, in a new variation on an old script, addresses Madame and Monsieur as if she (Solange) had just strangled her sister. Melodramatically going out onto the balcony—(as Claire reportedly did earlier when imitating Marie Antoinette (p. 50)—Solange imagines Claire, as a dead servant, receiving a lady's funeral. Here, as in *Deathwatch,* we see how little of the maids' energies are directed toward reforming the social world. At Claire's imagined funeral Solange envisages traditional servants performing traditional ceremonial roles, even at a ceremony in which the aristocracy wears mourning for a maid and the heavens send a delegation to attend. The new fantasy and its ceremonial setting seem, once again, to have changed little of consequence. But when Claire re-enters, having overheard the final moments of Solange's fantasy on the balcony, she seems to have made a significant discovery.

Refusing to allow Solange to end the ceremony, Claire insists on being served a cup of the poisoned tea. Still wearing her white dress and still imitating Madame, she begins to rewrite the old script and bring it into line with one Solange has just imagined:

> SOLANGE: We're dead tired. We've got to stop. [*She sits down in an armchair.*]
>
> CLAIRE: Ah, by no means! Poor servant girl, you think you'll get out of it as easily as that? It would be too simple to conspire with the wind, to make the night one's accomplice. Solange, you will contain me within you. Now pay close attention.
>
> SOLANGE: Claire . . .
>
> CLAIRE: Do as I tell you. I'm going to help you. I've decided to take the lead. Your role is to keep me from backing out, nothing more.
>
> SOLANGE: What more do you want? We're at the end. . . .
>
> CLAIRE: We're at the very beginning.
>
> (p. 96)

Both maids are right. This is both an ending to a habitual ceremony and the beginning of a new one. Solange's fantasy on the balcony is not one in which Madame's death enables the maids to transcend their lot in life, but one in which the enabling death is that of Claire. And this is the key to a significant change that lies within their power. Though Solange is no more capable of killing Claire than she is of killing Madame, she is quite capable of publicly masquerading as one who murdered her sister to free her from bondage. If Claire can perform the grand gesture of suicide to allow her sister the grand role of murderer/liberator, perhaps the two can achieve that interaction between aesthetics and pragmatics which has eluded them for so long.

The game-playing is elevated from ceremony to ritual as Claire describes the flower-bedecked room as an "altar where one of the two maids is about to immolate herself" (p. 96). The transfiguration characteristic of religious ritual is invoked to substantiate the transfiguration the two sisters begin to envisage for each other. Describing her sister as "A staff! A standard!" Claire urges Solange (who is still playing the role of Claire) to "represent [her] in the world" (p. 97). The double role that Solange has played in the maid/Madame game now becomes the reality that she will carry forth into the world. Solange will "contain" Claire within her and "keep [them] both alive" (pp. 96–97) as she becomes, through an imagined crime, "immortal" (p. 98), like a sign.

Claire holds Solange by the wrists and forces her to repeat the appropriate lines and bring in the poisoned tea. The character as playwright becomes the character as prophet as the ritual she devises prompts first obedience from Solange (Claire) and then creative extrapolation. The image she offers her is first accepted and then projected, as the play cleverly conjoins the pragmatic and the aesthetic by concluding with Claire (Madame) drinking the poisoned tea while Solange (Claire) sets the stage, projects the future, and invokes the beauty of the new world they are jointly constructing.

> [(*Claire*) *takes the cup and drinks, while Solange, facing the audience, delivers the end of her speech.*]
>
> SOLANGE: The orchestra is playing brilliantly. The attendant is raising the red velvet curtain. He bows. Madame is descending the stairs. Her furs brush against the green plants. Madame steps into the car. Monsieur is whispering sweet nothings in her ear. She would like to smile, but she is dead. She rings the bell. The porter yawns. He opens the door. Madame goes up the stairs. She enters her apartment—but, Madame is dead. Her two maids are alive: they've just risen up, free, from Madame's icy form. All the maids were present at her side—not they themselves, but rather the hellish agony of their names. And all that remains of them to float about Madame's airy corpse is the delicate perfume of the holy maidens which they were in secret. We are beautiful, joyous, drunk, and free!
>
> (pp. 99–100)

Solange's verbal insistence on their beauty, joy, and freedom is juxtaposed to Claire's drinking the poisoned tea; the aesthetically transcendent and the morally marginal are thrust once more into disturbing interaction. Claire's earlier vision of the two sisters as "the eternal couple of the criminal and the saint" (p. 63) is brought to apparent fruition as each contributes one component to the other. Though neither has been able to transcend the role of maid sufficiently to bring about the actual death of Madame, they have located a mode of liberation, a domain in which they can act, a context in which the pragmatic and the aesthetic can combine to precipitate change. Madame, deprived of her maids, suffers a metaphoric death, while they themselves, escaped from Madame, gain a metaphoric freedom. But in a world in which signs saturate the reality of our lives, the metaphoric death and the metaphoric freedom are more than mere figments of the imagination, if a little less than the affirmed facts of history.

By invoking images in the context of religion, by implicating metaphor in the mystical, Genet extends fiction from the merely imagined to the incipiently pragmatic and potentially transcendent. The pragmatic and the aesthetic encounter each other on an "altar" upon which the real is ceremonially transformed by the pragmatics of sacrifice and the aesthetics of the holy. In Genet's world the morally blasphemous and the creatively transcendent are locked in the complicated coils of a symbiotic embrace.

There was a gap of several years between *The Maids* and Genet's next play, *Le balcon* (*The Balcony,* 1956). It is generally recognized that this and subsequent plays display an increased emphasis on the functional theatricality of the theater. Such an emphasis is already implicit in Genet's exploration of the relationship between the aesthetic and the pragmatic, and it had already become explicit in the two earlier plays. Attempts to have the actors glide around on felt soles in *Deathwatch* and efforts to depict characters as scriptwriters and roleplayers in *The Maids,* along with various strategies, visible in both plays, to highlight images, are all evidence of this concern. In *The Balcony,* however, the functional theatricality of the theater becomes not only the predominant concern but also a means of clarifying the complexities of the interaction between art and life that have preoccupied Genet as a writer.

The play's major setting is a brothel, "a house of illusions" (p. 36), a place where clients come to act out their own fantasies, write their own scripts, and distribute their chosen roles. As Irma, the madam of the brothel, puts it, "Each individual, when he rings the bell and enters, brings his own scenario, perfectly thought out. My job is merely to rent the hall and furnish the props, actors and actresses" (p. 36). She is also ready to accept the description of her establishment as a "sumptuous theatre" (p. 38) where people can come to escape from the world. But Genet is not interested in the dynamics of escape either in the brothel or in the theater. What fascinates him about this brothel/theater setting is its capacity to provide an emblematic location for the negotiation of power, power that repeatedly emerges from complex relationships between the aesthetic and the pragmatic. It is in *The Balcony* that Genet is able to explore the epistemological foundations and transfiguring possibilities of an interaction that has sometimes appeared merely quirky or self-serving.

When Claire, in her role as Madame in *The Maids,* begins to get so immersed in the role that it threatens to become reality, Solange points out, "There's no need to overdo it. Your eyes are ablaze," and she directs her to observe "limits, boundaries. . . . Frontiers are not conventions but laws. Here, my lands; there, your shore—" (p. 42). It is this attempt to establish boundary lines between the illusory and the real that provides the key manifestation in the play of Genet's recurring interest in the relationship between the aesthetic and the pragmatic. The image that dominates the play—the balcony that is both the title of the play and the name of the brothel—is an image of something poised between two domains. A balcony belongs partly to the building to which it is attached and partly to the world outside the building, where it remains supremely visible and precariously suspended.

In the brothel scenes we are repeatedly confronted with clients who come there to play the roles and violate the images of key public figures: the Bishop, the Judge, the General, the Virgin Mary, and so on. Sexual fantasies are acted out not in solely individual terms but in the context of powerful male and female images of the society. Each client is free to bring his own script, to select his own characters, to establish his own setting, and to rent his own private studio, but that privacy is always contaminated by the public images each fantasy includes. Further breaches of that privacy also occur, as the playing out of each fantasy is interrupted by screams, sudden noises, and even the sounds of machine-gun fire that intrude from outside. Whether "outside" means another studio or the world outside the brothel is not always clear. What is clear is that attempts to insulate one fantasy from another and fantasy in general from reality in general are doomed to inevitable failure: "Everything's padded, but some sounds always manage to filter through" (p. 89).

The point here is not, of course, that the brothel's soundproofing needs improvement (though Irma considers this as a possible option [p. 34]). The contamination of the studios by sounds from outside is reciprocal: "One can hear all that's going on in the street. Which means that from the street one can hear what's going on in the house" (p. 34). And it is this reciprocal contamination of illusion by reality and reality by illusion that is registered in the flow of sounds from studios to the outside and back again.

The point rendered so directly by the transfer of sounds from one domain to the other is one that is to be steadily extended and increasingly complicated by the emerging action. As we have already noted, the private fantasies of the brothel's clients include elements of the public world from which they have withdrawn in order to indulge their private imaginations. Yet those imaginations are saturated with the images that sustain the social world outside the brothel. And Genet is quick to extend the point further. Not only do individual fantasies include elements of reality, they depend on them for their very existence. In the studio scenes enacted before us, the client dressed up as the Bishop demands that the whore, who is playing the role of a sinner, have committed real sins for him to forgive. Otherwise his fantasy of playing the Bishop will not be authentic, will not be "real," and he will not be getting full value for money. Likewise, the client playing the role of the Judge insists that the thief have committed real crimes for him to judge, and the client playing the role of the General insists upon real blood and real military decorations.

Every script in every studio, it seems, requires "authentic detail" as well as "fake detail," the latter usually consisting of "black lace under the homespun skirt" (p. 35). And it is this dependence of the illusion upon real components (if it is to be persuasively authentic as an illusion) that begins to disturb our moorings in a world that assumes a safe and obvious dichotomy between illusion and reality.

What is most disturbing, of course, is our recognition that Genet is providing us with a reminder of something we already know: illusions, like the illusion of the theater, are indeed partly constituted by the real. There are usually real actors, real costumes, real lights, and real furniture up there on that stage, and we cannot but concede the point that persuasive illusions do indeed require elements of reality to support them. But Genet is quick to dramatize the converse: that reality is, in turn, partly constituted by the abstract, the illusory, the invented, and (particularly) the image.

When a new Bishop or new Judge presents himself for public approval, photographers are called in not just to capture how the new role-player really looks but also to tell him how to look. The Bishop is told to pray with "hands together. Head up. Eyes down. That's the classical pose," and the Judge is asked to exhibit "more severity" and to display "a pendulous lip" (p. 73). As the photographer puts it: "What I want is a shot of *the* Judge. A good photographer is one who gives a definitive image" (p. 73). The definitive image may, of course, be "born of a false spectacle," as another photographer concedes when using the General's monocle as a substitute Host and when recalling his staging of a picture of a rebel dying while trying to escape: "When some rebels were captured, we paid a militiaman to bump off a chap I'd just sent to buy me a packet of cigarettes. The photo shows a rebel shot down while trying to escape" (p. 75).

The reality we live by does indeed include a series of constructed and reconstructed images whose power is grounded not only in pragmatic achievements but also in aesthetic appearances. We dress for our own chosen roles, imitating (or imitating and violating) images that we have encountered before. Power in general, in our society, inheres not so much in particular individuals as in social institutions and social roles. And many of these roles seem, in one sense, more real than the individuals currently assigned to play them.

As rebellion breaks out in the world beyond the brothel, the attempt to kill the Queen founders on the recognition that while killing a particular queen is relatively easy, killing *the* Queen is almost impossible. In terms of a long tradition, the death of a monarch in the play is greeted with words of respect for her heir: ". . . if the Queen is dead. . . . Long live the Queen" (p. 65). And as the play reminds us in several ways, we respond to figures of authority not just because of their individual behavior but because of their abstract social status ceremonially displayed. Costumes, uniforms, ceremonies, and conventional scripts dominate our social lives and, indeed, make it possible for us to have social lives.

As the play progresses, Genet's efforts to dramatize the interpenetration of the real and the illusory become increasingly complicated and sophisticated. Carmen, one of the whores in the brothel, recalls the time she played the Immaculate Conception of Lourdes for a bank clerk, and the real effects that illusions can have: "I saw the effect I had on my bank-clerk. I saw his state of terror, how he'd break out in a sweat, I heard the rattle in his throat" (p. 32). She also recalls the real effect that playing this illusory role had on her: the "wild pounding of [her] heart" that always accompanied her efforts at impersonation (p. 38).

The peculiar reality status of images is also attested by one of the anecdotes about the play. It was initially banned in Paris, in part because it displays a bishop in a brothel—which it does not. It displays a client portraying the image of a bishop while in a brothel, but the very existence of the image of a bishop in such a context seems to implicate real bishops in ways that Genet is struggling to make us understand. For outside that brothel a rebellion is going on, a rebellion that seems at first directed against the major figureheads of society—

Queen, Judge, General, and so forth—but ultimately, and oddly, toward the brothel itself.

When the play first moves from the world inside the brothel to the world outside, it is to the domain of the rebellion, the arena from which the sound of machine-gun fire had earlier emanated. In the background of a public square the brothel looms large, and the rebels, dressed in black suits and black sweaters, have their machine guns trained on the balcony itself (p. 55). This striking image appears to confirm the fears of Irma, the madam of the brothel, that "the aim of the rebellion [isn't] to capture the Royal Palace, but to sack my studios" (pp. 31–32). Yet the scene depicting the opposition between rebellion and brothel also depicts, located between the two, a couple in close embrace. Roger, a rebel leader, and Chantal, formerly one of Irma's whores, embody the rebellion at its point of highest achievement and most agonized conflict. Their love registers the possibility of a new order, a new way of relating among social groups previously opposed.

Roger struggles to maintain a rebellion that is simply real, that is merely the aggregate of the individualities of its participants and uncontaminated by the power of images. But his fellow rebels feel the need to give the rebellion the unity and inspiration that only an emblem can provide. To battle the images of the old order they need an image of the new order, and they want Chantal to provide that image, to become their emblem, to "embody the Revolution" (p. 57). Only Roger is sharp enough to recognize that to do this is to convert the rebellion into a reflection of the very thing it is opposing:

> In order to fight against an image Chantal has frozen into an image. The fight is no longer taking place in reality, but in the lists. Field azure. It's the combat of allegories. None of us knows any longer why we revolted.
>
> (p. 57)

The battle between the new order and the old order has indeed become a "combat of allegories." In a brilliantly emblematic scene Genet portrays the images of the old order (Queen, Judge, and General) emerging onto the balcony of the brothel to uphold the claims of that order. Onto the same balcony walks Chantal. A beggar cries out, "Long live the Queen," a shot rings out, and Chantal is carried away, mortally wounded. The images of the old order demonstrate their power over the images of the new. As Roger later laments, in such a rebellion "no truth was possible" (p. 93).

The truth that Roger has in mind, however, is a truth that might be grounded in worlds beyond those constituted by the "combat of allegories." Genet, having displayed in many ways the interpenetration of reality and illusion, of fact and fancy, of public and private worlds, is not asking us to believe, with Roger, that the rebellion made a fatal mistake by seeking to envisage itself in terms of an emblem. What is at issue is not rejecting what cannot be rejected, but learning how to control the very signs we initially construct but that subsequently seem to end up reconstructing us. Genet is at pains to dramatize the complexity of their function because the aesthetic dimension of our lives has by now come to dominate its pragmatic element. His concern is not to alter that balance but to explore the power it makes available, for him and for us.

The key issue in this play, as in *The Maids,* is not only one of coming to understand the role of images in our lives but also of learning how to control them. The rebellion, whose guns were aimed at the Balcony, was employing the wrong weapons for the wrong war. At the end of the play, as at the beginning, the sound of machine guns firing registers not simply the strength of the old order or the demands of the new but the fact that "someone [is] dreaming" (p. 95), dreaming of new worlds as a consequence of living in the midst of old. But the emerging question is whether the old images can be dreamed of creatively, whether they can be used as a point of departure and not just as an inevitable destination. When the rebellion kills off a judge and a general and a queen, another judge, another general, and another queen emerge—but not always, and not always in the same way. We do not have to choose, as rebellious Roger suggests, between a world dominated by restricting images and a world without images. The key issue is how we might use images to produce change.

In *The Balcony* we see three such approaches to images. The first, the one we encounter in the brothel studios, is one in which established images are both invoked and violated. Such a use of images, though ending up reinforcing the very images employed, nevertheless enables a creative playing with images that can have therapeutic effects on individuals ("When it's over, their minds are clear. I can tell from their eyes. Suddenly they understand mathematics. They love their children and their country" [p. 35]). The second, which emerges when the apparently successful rebellion has killed off a judge, a general, and a queen, has new participants trying to play old roles in new ways. As the clients in the brothel move their studio roles into the real world, they remain conscious of the plasticity of their adopted roles and begin to battle for power among themselves. The third, the one that emerges at the end of the play, is the attempt to initiate power by developing a new social sign. As the Chief of Police moves from being a mere functionary to becoming a legendary figure (as a result of his success in defeating the rebellion), he makes available a new image whose importance is attested by its incorporation into brothel mythology. To add to the "nomenclature" is to enhance the possibility of creative social play.

It is the possibility of such creative play that fascinates Genet with all three options, for it is in this context that the aesthetic and the pragmatic can interact. The first client to imitate the Chief of Police is Roger, the former revolutionary, who, having discovered that outside "no truth was possible" (p. 93), and therefore no power was achievable, has now moved inside. What he discovers there is another kind of power—the power and creativity of sign use and image employment that is so often thwarted in the world outside. Out there, signs have their traditional social function, they are usually dominated by the very past that generated them. Inside, however, their status as imaginative emblems provides a starting point for creative employment. This creative use does not easily translate into a force of change in the world outside, and Roger struggles to find a way of violating the image into one under his own control.

> ROGER: If the brothel exists and if I've a right to go there, then I've a right to lead the character I've chosen to the very limit of his destiny . . . no, of mine . . . of merging his destiny with mine.
>
> (p. 93)

In a startling scene Roger castrates himself and violates, as others in the brothel have done before him, the very image that he is imitating. The castration registers both his own inability to bring about the revolution he had planned and his revenge on the Chief of Police for defeating him. But more important is its suggestion of the need to violate an image and thereby produce new meaning, to eliminate one source of its power in order to move toward another.

When Roger enters the brothel studio as Chief of Police, he is elevated on the high-heeled boots of the traditional tragedian and wearing shoulder pads, so that he seems both taller and wider than most human figures. He is, as the stage directions suggest (and as the stage directions for costuming the other figures in the brothel also suggest), "*larger than life*" (p. 7). In the brothel these figures from society's "nomenclature" are, indeed, larger than life. As the Bishop puts it, his power is the power of a "mode of being," not that of a functionary (p. 12). It is, indeed, the power Genet has struggled to capture before, the power of the image divorced from immediate practical use and displayed as an emblem of an aesthetic possibility that may be reconverted into pragmatic possibility. It is the sign encountered by the mind as something with a vivid history and a creatively imagined future, but without its usual fixity in a social and pragmatic context.

No longer limited to their traditional function but luminous because they have had such a function, these images generate aesthetic possibilities and invite creative consideration. They are indeed larger than life; they transcend individual lives, endure longer, and thus mean more. A queen can be killed, but the image of the Queen lives on to enrich or impoverish our lives, to enliven or to deaden our imaginations. In the context of such images we live, create, act, and dream.

When the Judge, the General, the Queen, and the Chief of Police confront one another after the revolution, the Bishop poses the key question of the new/old order: "Are you going to use what we represent, or are we . . . going to use you to serve what we represent?" (p. 79). What is missing is the use of representation to serve us as individuals. Is it indeed possible for "masquerade to change meaning" (p. 72), as he claims, and is it true that "everything beautiful on earth you owe to masks"? (p. 68). These issues of representation, change, and power are issues that invoke not only the outside world, in which reality is partly constituted by illusion, and not only the brothel, in which illusion is partly constituted by reality, but also the world of the theater, whose audience is now confronted by more questions than it can answer.

When the play begins, a mirror in the brothel studio appears to reflect an unmade bed that, in terms of the logic of visual relationships, ought to be located in the front rows of the audience. This puzzling image is retained for each of the first three scenes, until we discover in the fifth, the one set in Irma's room, the very bed that had formerly been reflected. The effect is to situate the audience at the beginning of the play in the center of the brothel, where it is surrounded by the moving and multiplying images of the brothel studios. At the end of the play Irma sends the audience home from both the brothel and the theater to a world that she proclaims is "falser than here" (p. 96). The action of the play serves both to complicate and to clarify the relationships among the three domains.

In the theater, as in the brothel, signs and images are demonstrably on the move. Their conventional pragmatic functions in the world outside are aesthetically contemplated, creatively reshaped, and imaginatively recombined. This is to do violence to existing paradigms for organizing our values and beliefs, and to change their mode of being in the world by changing our mode of conceiving of their being in the world. In the environment of the brothel and the theater, signs and images are transformed from the ontologically given to the socially constructed and the individually reconstructible. The world outside is indeed falser than the one inside, because from the inside perspective the world as we have imagined it into being is revealed as such, while outside that same world is taken as ontologically given and fundamentally real.

The audience leaves the theater building no longer seeing the theater in the light of its subordinate relationship to the world outside, but seeing the world outside in the light of its relationship to the world of the theater. Inside, the signs and images of the past are brought to terms with the creative play of the present; outside, the movement of signs is limited and evolving images have congealed into rigid sources of exploitation, coercion, and control. In the brothel, as in the theater, the possible worlds of signs constitute the privileged and power-giving reality. An aesthetic awareness of everyday life would reactivate their plasticity in the world outside and make revolutions against them not so much repeated as unnecessary. In this sense domains like the brothel and the theater convert the aesthetic into the pragmatic by making us aware of what happens to us when we live and act in a world dominated by signs. Such an awareness is a necessary component of any constructive force of change.

This attempt to implicate the audience in

the action, to render the theatricality of the theater both evident and instrumental, is an attempt that recurs throughout Genet's later plays. The theater, considered as the evocative site of image contemplation, image re-evaluation, and image creation, becomes the perfect location for Genet's exploration of social life through its aesthetic component, a component now revealed as a source of raw power. Genet's barely disguised attempt to manipulate the audience through the manipulation of images becomes not just a means to an end but an exemplification of a central thematic concern.

If *The Balcony* had been designed to make the audience critically aware of the complex function of a variety of socially sanctioned images, *Les nègres* (*The Blacks,* 1958) seems, at first glance, to take the opposite tack. Two major racial images, white and black, are graphically presented; and the audience, far from being asked to resist imposed images, is pressured to take on one role while the actors take on the other. The audience, to be precise, is offered a specific role in the play as Genet explores yet another way of combining the aesthetic and the pragmatic in the theater. In his prefatory note Genet remarks:

> This play, written . . . by a white man, is intended for a white audience, but if, which is unlikely, it is ever performed before a black audience, then a white person, male or female, should be invited every evening. The organizer of the show should welcome him formally, dress him in ceremonial costume and lead him to his seat, preferably in the front row of the orchestra. The actors will play for him. A spotlight should be focussed upon this symbolic white throughout the performance.
>
> (p. 4)

Genet is even prepared to have a black audience wear white masks or to use a white dummy, if necessary, but the key issue is that the audience must be offered a ceremonial role, a symbolic costume, and an incriminating appearance. all of which serves, among other things, to provide a white audience with the experience of being addressed in terms of a racial stereotype, an experience known only too well to the blacks who are about to perform their roles onstage.

The play, written for a white audience, is also written for a black cast, and the reductive stereotyping imposed on the white audience is one means of making it recognize the reductive stereotype it is inclined to impose on blacks. But this is only the first technique Genet employs for inducing a degree of slippage between individual selves and their public images. The black actors onstage are themselves playing the roles of blacks who are performing for a white onstage audience. That white audience (played by blacks in masks) is watching a re-enactment of the murder of a white woman by a black man. The white audience onstage consists of conventional images of the kind that provide the recurring basis for Genet's theater: the Queen, her Valet, the Governor, the Judge, and the Missionary. Their role is not only to watch the performance but also to judge the performers in both aesthetic and legal terms, and their readiness to judge partially anticipates and partially reflects that of the theater audience.

There is, however, an implicit and imposed critique of such behavior. The masked onstage audience registers the attitudes of the colonial era, and the white masks of the black actors serve to remind us of the limited and limiting nature of such white roles, of the potential gap between the actual and the possible.

Once again, this slippage between individuals and roles among the white characters is matched by a similar slippage among the black figures. The actors, it seems, are not quite black enough for the roles they are called upon to play. In order to represent to the full the black image imposed upon them by whites, they need to be very black indeed. A shoeshine box, containing black shoe polish, is prominently located onstage, and the black actors repair to it with some frequency to maintain the authenticity of their black appearance. And, as so often in Genet's plays, bouquets of flowers (here surrounding the catafalque) remind us of the aesthetic dimension of our world. The aesthetic appeal of the visual is a disturbing reminder of our tendency to judge by the visual, and of our readiness to judge by the visual alone—a readiness registered so dangerously in our habit of approaching reality in general and people in particular via classifying (and consequently distorting) images.

The distortion imposed by such images soon becomes apparent when the black actors indicate that they regard it as their (unwelcome) duty to perform the black roles in terms that a white audience would expect: "We embellish ourselves so as to please you. You are white. And spectators. This evening we shall perform for you" (p. 10). The distance between the actors and their roles, registered clearly in the very existence of this speech, is emphasized repeatedly as the actors, either as actors or as characters, step back from their roles to comment on their own lives, their own attitudes, their own rage, their own love, their own despair. Such distancing is a mocking denial of the audience's capacity for authentic empathy, for resisting the temptations of stage illusion, for being communicated with directly:

> In order that you may remain comfortably settled in your seats in the presence of the drama that is already unfolding here, in order that you be assured that there is no danger of such a drama's worming its way into your precious lives, we shall even have the decency—a decency learned from you—to make communication impossible. We shall increase the distance that separates us—a distance that is basic—by our pomp, our manners, our insolence—for we are also actors. (p. 12)

But the communication rejected at one level becomes a communication invoked at another, for the refusal of the black actors to merge with their roles operates also as a reminder of the provisionality of the roles of the whites. The masks, costumes, and roles adopted by actors, characters, onstage audience, and offstage audience alike speak of possibilities denied as well as possibilities engaged. The distance registered so graphically in the play between blacks and whites speaks also of the distance between all individuals and the social roles they have learned to adopt and accept.

In the historical moment of the play's action, however, at the height of the colonial era, the dominant masks are those of race, and these governing images compel the playing out of a governing ritual. We are reminded repeatedly that the action we are to witness is a recurring action, and the foregrounding of the imposed status of the script reminds us that the prescribed script is ideologically imposed but individually accepted. The repetition of a play in its performance run and of social events in an established era are cleverly run together, and with them comes a sense of an inevitability that was not inevitable.

In such a theatrical and social context events must run their course, and they do. But the danger of the performance that Archibald, with no little irony, had earlier dismissed turns out to be very real indeed. If the blacks play to the full the image the whites have of them, if they are indeed as black, as dangerous, as wild as the whites fear, it is only a matter of time until they rebel and kill not just the white woman of whose murder they are initially accused, but all the whites who oppress them. This is, indeed, what comes to pass as the blacks appropriate the power of images that had appropriated them. As the action progresses, the black roles the whites have created are played to their logical conclusion and the white audience, initially sitting in judgment on the blacks, is eventually eliminated in a ritual murder perpetrated by the blacks. The rehearsal of the earlier murder of one white by one black becomes a rehearsal of the eventual murder of all whites by blacks.

In the hands of an accomplished but lesser playwright, this brilliantly theatrical conception would suffice to make a narrowly ideological point. In the hands of someone with interests like those of Genet, this is but a play within the play. At a key point in the action we discover that this whole performance has been set up to distract the white audience from an action that has been going on backstage—an action setting not blacks against whites but blacks against other blacks, as they struggle with each other to construct and control the world that is to succeed the world of white power. But this world, like the world of the rebellion in *The Balcony,* is not the focus of Genet's concern. Both of those rebellious worlds suggest an interest in social power that is misplaced and misguided, for it merely reflects what it sets out to replace. Genet, as always, is in search of something else.

The conclusion of the play focuses not upon large social groups, emerging social institutions, or cultural ideologies but upon individuals. These individuals now just happen to be black, and they struggle to locate themselves and each other in the tiny, but infinitely complicated, relationship of two lovers trying to be just themselves:

> [*Village and Virtue remain alone on the stage. They seem to be arguing.*]
>
> VILLAGE: But if I take your hands in mine? If I put my arms around your shoulders—let me—if I hug you?
>
> VIRTUE: All men are like you: they imitate. Can't you invent something else?
>
> VILLAGE: For you I could invent anything: fruits, brighter words, a two-wheeled wheelbarrow, cherries without pits, a bed for three, a needle that doesn't prick. But gestures of love, that's harder . . . still, if you really want me to . . .
>
> VIRTUE: I'll help you. At least, there's one sure thing: you won't be able to wind your fingers in my long golden hair. . . .
>
> (p. 128)

This hesitant attempt to find gestures of love that hinge upon invention rather than imitation is the source of an alternative way of being that the play contemplates but cannot implement. The aesthetic and the pragmatic turn out to be interwoven in local as well as larger domains, and love seems inextricably intertwined with loveliness. But loveliness has a way of being largely visual, and the appealingly visual is, of course, partly traditional. The dilemma that confronts large social groups in the larger world also confronts the young couple in their private world. In domains dominated by images, yesterday's inventions have a way of becoming tomorrow's incentives to imitation. The loving gesture constructed locally has a way of becoming the emblem of tomorrow's global tyranny; the difficulty lies in getting beyond that dilemma.

At the end of the play Virtue, struggling desperately toward invention, can only characterize it in contrast with yesterday's imitation, and the image she uses to reject imitation is an image we now encounter, and they encounter, as worryingly attractive and disturbingly repulsive. The unavailable "long golden hair" is both desired and undesirable, and it has been the function of the play to install the latter in the audience's consciousness without removing the former. The white audience, its privileged image revealed as only an image, is likewise reminded of the ambivalent status of all its admired images. As agent and object of racist ideology, the white audience is also reminded of the dangers inherent in all available alternatives. New images, like old images, will also be implicated in power relationships, subject to distortion and open to abuse.

As the play concludes, the two young lovers walk back toward the social group from which they have emerged. Unable to find a realm of pure invention, they return to the company of black actors, who are surrounding a white-draped catafalque and dancing to the measures of a minuet from *Don Giovanni.* In a world of aesthetics and pragmatics, the verbal and visual images of the past continue to haunt the hearts and minds of those seeking desperately to find a way to reinvent the present.

In Genet's final play, *Les paravents* (*The Screens,* 1961), we again encounter the worlds of the brothel, the rebellion, and the colonial era; and they are again presented to us as worlds struggling to find a way beyond the images that constitute them. These socially derived images, which seemed so tangentially related to everyday life in *Deathwatch* and so rigidly in place in *The Maids,* have, in subsequent plays, become not only more powerful but also more mobile. The past that is codified in these social images dominates the present, but that domination becomes increasingly tenuous once awareness of it has been achieved. An increasing recognition of the aesthetic dimension of our daily lives has served not only to focus attention on the varied forms of beauty but also to help us understand the insidious social power of images whose authenticity we had taken for granted. To return the images to the status of images, to recognize their constructed status and their capacity to mislead, is to recognize the danger of our being taken for granted by what our culture has taken for granted. To acquiesce in this process is to allow the past to dominate the present instead of forcing it to function as a construction from which we begin to reconstruct the present.

In *The Balcony* the clients who dress up as Bishop, Judge, and General wear elevated shoes and shoulder pads. The images they depict are larger than life, larger than us. But Genet is at pains to dramatize not only the power of these images but also their multiplicity and mobility. Each studio is likely to contaminate another, each role is in precarious relationship with another, and, early in the play, each brothel scene ends by plunging into the wings of a moving stage, to be succeeded by another. The play displays in many ways the mobility of a sign once we have become aware of it as a sign, and it contrasts this with the unyielding inertia and inflexible power of any sign that has atrophied into reality. To recognize the masks imposed upon reality in general, and upon us in particular, is to rediscover the sign as a sign and to recover its mobility and ours. We thereby encounter in the aesthetic component of reality the concealed plasticity of a world that often seems too rigid to be susceptible to change.

In *The Screens* we are presented with a drama whose sets, costumes, structure, and characters are palpably mobile and bewilderingly multiple. The very title of the play focuses upon the screens Genet uses to depict multiple and mobile backdrops. These multiple and mobile settings coexist and compete before our eyes in the single location of the stage. The play employs ninety-six characters, with each member of the cast required to play five or six roles. Genet depicts a stage consisting of platforms of differing heights in an open-air theater whose rectangular arena is enclosed within a high wooden fence: "*There will thus be an extremely varied set of stages, levels, and surfaces*" (p. 9).

The screens, each about ten feet high, with objects and landscapes painted on them, enter and leave with the characters whose environment they depict. As the action progresses, characters begin to change their environments by drawing pictures on the screens. But to prevent any suggestion that we live only in psychological worlds and only in changing worlds, Genet insists that "*near the screen there must always be at least one real object (wheelbarrow, bucket, bicycle, etc.), the function of which is to establish a contrast between its own reality and the objects that are drawn*" (p. 10).

Once again, of course, the issue is not that the world of the image is independent of the world of the real, but that image and object, illusion and reality, psychological and social perspectives, are mutually dependent and mutually constitutive. The characters are likewise both real and masked, with "*excessive make-up contrasting with the realism of the costumes*" (p. 10). The costumes themselves are often gaudy, multicolored, and disturbing to the eye. Instead of converging and thus providing images of unity and conformity, the multicolored costumes keep the eye at work, reminding us of multiple possibilities of the character, no matter how narrow and limited the current role.

The major source of character roles at the beginning of the play is the colonial relationship between France and its Arab colonies. As was the case with the white and black races in *The Blacks,* the two sides in this conflict mutually define each other, perform roles for each other, and provide audiences for each other's performances. French flags are prominently on display, French colonial posture is assisted by appropriate padding, and the French Foreign Legion sums up (in aesthetic terms, of course) the superior culture of the governing class: "We represent a France clear and sharp. [*a pause*] And clean" (p. 116). The Arabs, by contrast, are portrayed as a race without glamour. As Sir Harold puts it, "According to a famous and eternal phrase: you're stinking jackals" (p. 95). The Arabs, following suit, straggle through much of the play as dirty, smelly, unreliable beings resigned to playing out the role that the colonials have assigned them: "The fact is that the dirtier they are the cleaner I am. They take upon themselves all the lice of the world" (p. 180).

These polarized sets of images gradually turn out to be oppressive to both groups of characters, a point registered early on by the central role that the brothel plays in colonial society. In a world of strongly defined and oppressive images, the brothel flourishes as one of the few places where images can be both idealized and violated. Only when the revolution gets under way does the brothel lose its status as a realm in which aesthetically grounded action provides an alternative mode of access to an aesthetically organized reality. As the brothel's status declines, so also does Warda's. The resident whore is forced to relinquish her commitment to extravagant costume, abandon her desire for a transcendent mode of being, and settle for a more trivial role as a sexual functionary.

> WARDA: Poor golden petticoats! I'd always hoped that one day, instead of being an adornment, you'd be, by yourselves, the whore in all her glory. A pipe dream. . . . Those gentlemen no longer have the strength to lift your leaded hem, and in order for them not to waste time I've had to cut a slit for them in front. . . . Bye-bye, my style! Men used to come from far away to see me, *me, Warda,* pick my teeth with my big hatpins. Now they come to fuck me.
>
> (pp. 129–130)

In the revolutionary world, Warda laments, "The brothel's no longer the brothel and, so to speak, we're fucking in the open" (p. 131). As the revolution progresses, however, and attains its victory, the new-world images replace the old, and the brothel regains its traditional role. The Arab fighters, now conceiving of themselves as "warriors" (p. 171), visit the brothel, which is again able to set its own prices and provide a daunting challenge to the wives of the town: "In short, all's well. The brothel is again the plague spot of the town. And our men are already what they were before the war" (p. 165).

The irony of this comment registers a dilemma that Genet has explored before. The revolution that changes the names of the leaders and the titles of the dominating images leaves too much intact. The urge toward change is repeatedly thwarted when change degenerates into a variation on what it replaces. In *The Blacks* the possibility (however tenuous) of authentic change is embodied in the young couple, Village and Virtue, seeking an inventive way of conceiving of love. In *The Screens* Genet searches for something even more local, something more free of the traditional, as a means of reaching beyond cultural constraints. The focus of attention is upon an aesthetics of the anti-aesthetic. As the colonials display their clarity, sharpness, and cleanliness; as they parade their costumes and wave their flags; as they admire the rose gardens and orange groves they have cultivated; and as they congratulate themselves on the improvements they have brought about in their colony, they confront a populace looking out of place in the new diversity of its own land, uncomfortable in the gaudy variety of Western clothing, and increasingly convinced of its own ugliness, slovenliness, smelliness, and dirtiness. The revolution is one response to the indignities suffered by the Arabs; another, and the one most central to the play, is that provided by two of the central characters: Saïd and his wife, Leila.

It is not easy for Saïd and Leila to distinguish between the images imposed by colonial, precolonial, or postcolonial worlds, for in any of these realms it remains the case that Saïd is regarded as (and conceives of himself as) a failure because he is desperately poor; it also remains the case that Leila feels a failure because she is remarkably ugly. The costume she wears is not a pretty dress to enhance her physical qualities but a black hood to hide them. The two marry not because of mutual love or mutual admiration but because, as Saïd's mother puts it: "She's left over because she's ugly. And you, because you're poor. She needs a husband, you a wife. She and you take what's left, you take each other" (p. 13). In a world organized in aesthetic terms, it matters little what the nature of the governing aesthetic is. There is no form of beauty they can conceive of that would elevate them to social prominence or increase their minimally surviving sense of self-worth. Take each other they do, but in the context of low expectations and mutual recrimination.

We encounter Saïd and Leila at the beginning of their marriage and we encounter them then, as subsequently, on journeys that continue throughout the play. As they move along on these journeys, as they move through their lives and through the play, things only get worse until Saïd, grimly pointing out to Leila how bad things are, ironically conceives of one way in which they could get worse—it turns out to be an aesthetic way, of course:

> SAÏD: There's not much more you lack: ugly, idiotic, a thief, a beggar, and now a cripple.
> LEILA: I can walk straight if I like. [*She walks straight for a few steps.*]
> SAÏD: [*hastily*] How would I look if all of a sudden you became beautiful, intelligent, honest, dignified, and you walked straight?
>
> (p. 107)

How indeed? Saïd and Leila walk not toward self-transformation but toward a vague possibility of social change that, instead of bringing them to the admired center of the world, might bring a world out to meet them on its margins. Advised early on by Saïd's mother that the way forward is the way of testing their own limits (p. 29), they move toward a promised land characterized as that of the shadow and the monster:

> LEILA: I want you to stop looking backward. I want you to lead me without flinching to the land of shadow and of the monster. I want you to plunge into irrevocable grief. I want you—it's my ugliness, earned minute by minute, that speaks—to be without hope. I want you to choose evil and always evil. I want you to know only hatred and never love.
>
> (pp.108–109)

Their fidelity to their own mode of being keeps them moving toward an anti-world, and it earns them neither oblivion nor fame but notoriety. As the major battle between colonials and natives runs its course, Saïd and Leila wander along the margins of the conflict with their eyes focused on other issues and their hearts preoccupied with other goals.

The public world, however, is not content to let them roam where they will and as they will. They are mentioned, in passing, by Sir Harold, who muses on "that Saïd, whose reputation keeps swelling" (p. 76), and their changing public images begin to be coveted both by the revolutionaries who obtain control of the living world and by the dead who retain an interest in it. As various groups attempt to transform Saïd into a flag, a song, or a sign, one of the combatants makes clear the nature of their quarrel over Saïd's emblematic status:

> THE COMBATANT: [*to the dead*] That'll do. You're not going to appropriate the victory or deter-

> mine the meaning it's to be given. That's for us the living to decide.
>
> (p. 196)

There is, however, one other source of authority on that decision: Saïd himself, who refuses the appeals of both groups and shares his mother's disdain for being synthesized into an image for posterity.

> The Mother: I brought *you* into the *world*. Make a getaway. Don't let yourself be conned by either the old girl or the soldiers. Don't serve either of them, don't serve any purpose whatever.
>
> (p. 199)

The latter appeal, the strident refusal to serve any purpose whatsoever, is the voice of major authenticity in a play riddled by an ever-multiplying array of false images, false goals, and false achievements. Saïd, turning as if to leave in the hope of exercising that option, is shot by soldiers unwilling to let him establish or achieve his own goals. Convinced that his wife has followed her own possibilities "to perfection" (p. 199), and that he has likewise been faithful to his own, he dies without reaching a new land of shadow and monster, and without having found either the desire or the means to change the society in which he lived. His commitment to a destiny he did not create but courageously chose remains as a testimony to something the play cannot articulate further.

Saïd remains a paradoxical emblem of an anti-aesthetic; he exits not so much as an achieved sign but as a possibility for a sign that registers an emphatic refusal to be converted into any pre-existing sign. A play replete with moving images and mobile signs focuses finally on the interrupted journey of an embryonic anti-sign. The play ends not with the brilliance of an extravagantly costumed emblem but with a bare stage; attention is finally drawn to the silence, emptiness, and uncertainty of a sign-deprived world that is fraught with the memory and the possibility of signs.

> The Mother: Saïd! . . . I'll simply have to wait for him. . . .
>
> Kadidja: [*laughing*] Don't bother. He'll no more be back than will Leila.
>
> The Mother: Then where is he? In a song? [*Kadidja extends her palms with a gesture expressive of doubt. During the last two or three speeches, the dead carried off their screens. The Mother leaves last, with her armchair. The stage is empty. It's all over.*]
>
> (p. 201)

In his reluctance to become an emblem of anything of which he can currently conceive, Saïd remains as a disturbing presence and a beguiling silence on a stage that is evocatively empty. One of the Arabs had earlier remarked that "things cease to belong to those who've been able to make them more beautiful" (p. 141), and the remark has implications for those colonials who felt they had improved the conquered land, for those who attempted to establish by costume and emblem their own or their country's importance, and for those who seek in any way to control a world dominated by images. This applies also to artists and audiences whose lives and art are saturated by images they might wish to transform or transcend. As the Academician in the play puts it when wryly contemplating the postcolonial world: "Can an art be born for the purpose of enshrining so many facts which they themselves would like to forget? And if there's no art, there's no culture. Are they therefore doomed to decay?" (p. 178). Are they, indeed? Are we?

As we gaze at the empty stage and the thwarted possibilities it represents, we encounter yet again the baffling questions that Genet's art forces us to ask. His aim is not to provide the answers but to find ways of posing the questions, to locate means by which we can comprehend what ordinarily we fail not only to comprehend but even to notice. In his sustained exploration of the aesthetics of everyday life, Genet finds ways to ask the previously unaskable, to explore the previously unexplored, to take us to limits previously beyond the limits of art. It is left to one of the whores of the brothel to ponder most explicitly her situation and, ironically, that of the audience at the end of the play:

> MALIKA: As for us, we returned at last to our solitude . . . and our . . . and our . . . and our truth. [*relieved*] It was hard. We had to invent. To discover by ourselves.
>
> (p. 183)

Such a process of invention and discovery is a process that involves individual beings struggling to hold onto an ill-defined individuality in a world of overdefined images. It is the process to which Genet as artist and as human being committed his life. And if we return now to the autobiographical fiction of *The Thief's Journal,* it is less with an aesthetic philosophy in mind than with a recognition of its unyielding complexity and precarious necessity.

In a text permeated with lyrical prose and gross detail, Genet emphasizes his own social images as traitor, thief, and homosexual. But Genet is clearly bent on challenging the status of these images. It is not enough, however, to argue that his life is an act of defiance, that he responds to being called a thief by playing out the socially codified possibilities of being a thief. His life is committed neither to defiance nor to rebellion but to possibilities in his assigned roles of which no one had previously dreamed. Praising the French Gestapo for its commitment to treason and theft, Genet notes that it lacked only the element of homosexuality to embrace the three theological virtues that seem to him most vital. Had it had all three virtues,

> what could be said against it? It was outside the world. It betrayed (betraying means breaking the laws of love). It engaged in pillage. And lastly, it banned itself from the world by homosexuality. It thus established itself in an indestructible solitude.
>
> (p. 149)

It is this solitude in the context of the social that is the precondition for Genet's own creativity and authenticity, and it is a solitude shared by many of his major characters. Such solitude is not the solitude of the exile. To be outside a world is not to be similarly independent of it or engaged with it. Genet notes than when truly outside of France, when living in another country, his transgressions were errors rather than sins, and that only a French penitentiary had the glamour of something worth sinning against (p. 143). The solitude he has in mind is the social site of a kind of freedom. Its origin is a socially codified status, one of being set in opposition to the accepted; but from that origin emerges the possibility of appropriating the very images society itself imposes. As Genet puts it, "If he has courage—please understand—the guilty man decides to be what crime has made him" (p. 242).

The key issue, however, is what the guilty man then makes of having been made into a criminal:

> I want to be guilty. Guilt makes for singularity (destroys confusion); and if the criminal has a hard heart (for it is not enough to have committed a crime; one must deserve it and deserve having committed it), he raises it upon a pedestal of solitude. Solitude is not given to me; I earn it. I am led to it by a concern for beauty. I want to define myself in it, delimit my contours, emerge from confusion, set myself in order.
>
> (p. 243)

Guilt, solitude, and beauty are the conditions that constitute the domain of freedom Genet carves out for himself. The guilty man who decides to be what crime has made him is using that acknowledgment not as a destination but as a point of departure. And the journey is from socially imposed solitude to chosen extremes of social isolation and social thinking. Only at the margins is it possible to recognize and grapple with the power of signs whose power at the center seems close to absolute.

Recognizing himself as limited by the very

world he opposes (p. 214), Genet seeks to carve out a domain of freedom predicated upon the belief that "acts must be carried through to their completion. Whatever their point of departure, the end will be beautiful. It is because an action has not been completed that it is vile" (p. 214). At this point of completion, at the margin of possibility, exist other possibilities: those of novelty, creativity, and beauty. On this margin the pragmatics of daily living and the pursuit of aesthetic possibility merge in the pursuit of the extreme: "If I cannot have the most brilliant destiny, I want the most wretched, not for the purpose of a sterile solitude, but in order to achieve something new with such rare matter" (p. 244).

Reflecting on the course of his life, Genet feels that his "courage consisted of destroying all the usual reasons for living and discovering others" (p. 175). And he is ready to acknowledge that "the discovery was made slowly" (p. 175). To readers of his prose it is clear that the process of discovery continues. As Genet points out, and as we noted earlier, *The Thief's Journal* "is not a quest of time gone by, but a work of art whose pretext-subject is my former life" (p. 71). This work of art, like the others Genet has produced, are not works that separate art from life but works in which the aesthetic and pragmatic components of social life are inextricably intertwined. It is Genet's achievement to demonstrate their interdependence in ways that are unexpected, illuminating, and disturbing. As Sartre has argued, Genet, in a sense, invents for us the meaning of betrayal and homosexuality. He appropriates our terms, for it is in his terms that they now "enter the human world; the reader sees them as his personal way out, the emergency exit that has been made for him" (*Saint Genet,* p. 589).

The effect on the reader of reading *The Thief's Journal* is like the effect of attending one of Genet's plays. It is not that we are reconciled with our world by being given a better understanding of how it is. Rather, we are forced to recognize how it might be for someone else and, consequently, how it might unexpectedly be for people like ourselves. As Sartre puts it: "What will remain when the book has been closed? A feeling of emptiness, of darkness and of horrible beauty, an 'eccentric' experience that we cannot incorporate into the web of our life and that will forever remain 'on the margin,' unassimilable . . . " (p. 589).

This possibility on the edge of our experience is not only unstable but also destabilizing. Genet's art offers a site that we can imaginatively occupy but cannot bring into harmony with what we already know. It establishes a site upon which aesthetic action and moral action discover their point of convergence. At such a location we can recognize both the reality posited by inherited modes of constructing the world and the reality of those modes of construction. We encounter a point at which we confront embryonic possibilities that must surely be incorporated into our aesthetic and moral perspectives but that have not yet disentangled themselves sufficiently to enable us to locate them in our social order. Nor do they offer means by which we can confidently include them in an alternative social order.

It is by shaking us loose from our conceptual moorings, by opening up a new world of aesthetic and pragmatic possibility, that Genet can make his notorious claim to saintliness—a claim that is at first glance not only startling but also staggering. Genet, however, argues that saintliness begins with the capacity to turn pain to good account (p. 205), that it is not a fixed state but a "moral procedure" (p. 215), and that it is a procedure in which he is persistently engaged. It involves the acceptance of isolation, the exploration of forbidden territory, the courage to commit sacrilege, the capacity to be creative, and the determination to be free. But at every point such saintliness must include the refusal to be finally categorized and definitively explained. It is a moral procedure that can be exemplified only in action, and in the kind of action whose claim to freedom is ambiguously situated in the midst of the forbidden, the aesthetic, and the moral. Without the pursuit of creative freedom, however, it is nothing, because it must be not only aesthetic and pragmatic but also genuinely capable of promoting change.

For Genet, whatever victory will be achievable in this quest is a victory that must fundamentally be verbal: "I want to rehabilitate this period [of my life] by writing of it with the names of things most noble. My victory is verbal and I owe it to the richness of the terms, but may the poverty that counsels such choices be blessed" (p. 59). The victory involves, as Sartre concisely puts it, not just "what people make of us but what we ourselves make of what they have made of us" (*Saint Genet,* p. 49). This procedure of reappropriating the sign that has appropriated us is the procedure that Genet—traitor, thief, homosexual, artist, and saint—has adopted and made his own. It is not just a matter of appropriating the signs that have been forced upon him but of appropriating those signs, like "saint," that we would be most reluctant to confer upon him. This is a task Genet explicitly sets himself, and one he constantly monitors. As he puts it in one self-critical comment, "Am I not, by this sentence, running the risk of restoring to saintliness the Christian meaning which I want to remove from it?" (p. 215).

As such comments suggest, Genet's is an art and life that situates itself on the margins of our world, advertises its iconoclastic presence, and invites us to come out to meet it (as we are invited to go out and meet Saïd); thereafter we must ponder it and go on as best we may. The exemplary life that appropriates our images invites us not to do the same thing in the same way, but to do something similar that each of us, in our solitude, can regard as our own.

> Though saintliness is my goal, I cannot tell what it is. My point of departure is the word itself, which indicates the state closest to moral perfection. Of which I know nothing, save that without it my life would be vain. Unable to give a definition of saintliness—no more than I can of beauty—I want at every moment to create it, that is, to act so that everything I do may lead me to it, though it is unknown to me, so that at every moment I may be guided by a will to saintliness until I am so luminous that people will say, "He is a saint," or, more likely, "He was a saint." I am being led to it by a constant groping. No method exists. . . . Like beauty—and poetry, with which I merge it—saintliness is individual. . . . But I wish to be a saint chiefly because the word indicates the loftiest human attitude, and I shall do everything to succeed.
>
> (pp. 208–209)

The "word" with which Genet grapples is both point of departure and unavoidable constraint. It invokes a traditional possibility to which Genet remains faithful even as he subverts the characteristics most closely associated with the term. In Genet's art and in his life tradition is the necessary point of departure as Genet converts a condition of knowledge into the problem of knowledge. The freedom Genet pursues is the freedom of someone seeking to escape the sign but uneasily settling for attempts to control the sign in a world that seems unavoidably constituted by signs. That is why the worlds he portrays and the life he lived exhibit struggles that inextricably mingle the aesthetic, the pragmatic, and the moral. His achievement is to make us aware of the nature of the struggle and of its importance to anyone who has ever judged an action or evaluated a book. The invitation to the reader to engage in the dangerous activity of reading and judging his books is an invitation to share the experience of an artist whose art and life are aesthetically committed and morally engaged.

Genet discovers and lays before us the aesthetic component of a reality in which neither art nor life can be definitively separated. "This book," he explicitly declares, "does not aim to be a work of art, an object detached from an author and from the world" (p. 267). Genet's is the work of an artist who seeks above all to engage us, who makes a deliberate and specific appeal to a reader who must choose a site of judgment—either where he began, at the center of a world securely constituted by social signs, or at the margin, at the point where judgment, though neither secure nor stable, is precariously necessary. The author is not indifferent to our judgment; he demands it, and we must take our stand. The author who has shocked us, disturbed us, and disoriented us concludes with an emphatic reminder that, as an embryonic saint, "I aspire to your recognition, your consecration" (p. 268).

## Selected Bibliography


### EDITIONS

#### INDIVIDUAL WORKS

POETRY

*Chants secrets.* Lyon, 1945. Contains "Le condamné à mort," "Dédicace" (to Maurice Pilorge), and "Marche funébre."

*La galère.* In *La table ronde,* cahier 3 (1945).

*Poèmes.* Lyons, 1948; 2d ed., Décines, 1962. Contains "Le condamné à mort," "Marche funébre," "La galère, "La parade," "Un chant d'amour," and "Le pêcheur du Suquet."

*Le condamné à mort; suivi de Poèmes, L'Enfant criminel, Le funambule.* Décines, 1966.

NOVELS

*Notre-Dame-des-Fleurs.* Monte Carlo, 1944. Revised version in *Oeuvres complètes,* vol. 2. Paris, 1951.

*Miracle de la rose.* Lyons, 1946. Revised version in *Oeuvres complètes,* vol. 2. Paris, 1951.

*Pompes funèbres.* "Bikini," 1947; rev. ed., Paris, 1948. Revised version in *Oeuvres complètes,* vol. 3. Paris, 1953.

*Querelle de Brest.* Milan, 1947. Revised version in *Oeuvres complètes,* vol. 3. Paris, 1953.

BALLET SCENARIO

*'Adame Miroir.* Paris, 1949.

PLAYS

*Haute surveillance.* Paris, 1949; rev. ed., Paris, 1965. Further slightly revised version in *Oeuvres complètes,* vol. 4. Paris, 1968.

*Les bonnes.* Lyons, 1947; rev. ed., Sceaux, 1954. Also in *Oeuvres complètes,* vol. 4. Paris, 1958.

*Le balcon.* Décines, 1956 (15 scenes); rev. ed. (9 scenes), Décines, 1960; definitive version (9 scenes), Décines, 1961.

*Les nègres.* Décines, 1958; rev. ed. (with minor variations), Décines, 1960.

*Les paravents.* Décines, 1961; revised version, Décines, 1976.

AUTOBIOGRAPHY

*Journal du voleur.* Paris, 1949.

#### COLLECTED WORKS

*Oeuvres complétes.* 5 vols. Paris, 1951–1979.

### TRANSLATIONS

*The Balcony.* Translated by Bernard Frechtman. New York [1958, 1960], 1966.

*The Blacks: A Clown Show.* Translated by Bernard Frechtman. New York, 1960, 1962.

*Deathwatch.* Translated by Bernard Frechtman. In *The Maids and Deathwatch.* New York [1954], 1962. Also published separately.

*Funeral Rites.* Translated by Bernard Frechtman. New York, 1969.

*The Maids.* Translated by Bernard Frechtman. In *The Maids and Deathwatch.* New York [1954], 1962. Also published separately.

*Miracle of the Rose.* Translated by Bernard Frechtman. New York, 1966.

*Our Lady of the Flowers.* Translated by Bernard Frechtman. Paris, 1949; New York, 1963.

*Querelle of Brest.* Translated by Gregory Streatham. New York, 1967. Also translated as *Querelle* by Anselm Hollo. London, 1966; New York, 1974. 1974.

*The Screens.* Translated by Bernard Frechtman. New York, 1962.

*The Thief's Journal.* Translated by Bernard Frechtman. Paris, 1954; rev. trans., New York, 1964, 1978.

*Treasures of the Night: The Collected Poems of Jean Genet.* Translated by Steven Finch. San Francisco, 1981.

### BIOGRAPHICAL AND CRITICAL STUDIES

Aslan, Odette. *Jean Genet.* Paris, 1973.

Bonnefoy, Claude. *Genet.* Paris, 1965.

Brooks, Peter, and Joseph Halpern, eds. *Genet: A*

*Collection of Critical Essays*. Englewood Cliffs, N.J., 1979.

Cetta, Lewis, T. *Profane Play, Ritual, and Jean Genet: A Study of His Drama*. University, Ala., 1974.

Chaudhuri, Una. *No Man's Stage: A Semiotic Study of Jean Genet's Major Plays*. Ann Arbor, Mich., 1986.

Coe, Richard N. *The Vision of Jean Genet*. London, 1968.

———, ed. *The Theater of Jean Genet: A Casebook*. New York, 1970.

Derrida, Jacques. *Glas*. Paris, 1974.

Driver, Tom F. *Jean Genet*. London and New York, 1966.

Grossvogel, David I. *Four Playwrights and a Postscript: Brecht, Ionesco, Beckett, Genet*. Ithaca, N.Y., 1962.

Hauptman, Robert. *The Pathological Vision: Jean Genet, Louis-Ferdinand Céline, and Tennessee Williams*. New York, 1984.

Jacobsen, Josephine, and William R. Mueller. *Ionesco and Genet: Playwrights of Silence*. New York, 1968.

Kleiss, Werner. *Genet*. Hannover, 1967.

Knapp, Bettina L. *Jean Genet*. New York, 1968; rev ed., Boston, 1989.

Laurent, Anne, ed. *Jean Genet aujourd'hui*. Amiens, 1976.

Magnan, Jean-Marie. *Pour un blason de Jean Genet*. Paris, 1966.

McMahon, Joseph H. *The Imagination of Jean Genet*. New Haven, 1963.

Morris, Kelly, ed. *Genet/Ionesco: The Theatre of the Double —A Critical Anthology*. New York, 1969.

Naish, Camille. *A Genetic Approach to Structures in the Work of Jean Genet*. Cambridge, Mass., 1978.

Sartre, Jean-Paul. *Saint Genet: Comédien et martyr*. Paris, 1952. Translated by Bernard Frechtman as *Saint Genet: Actor and Martyr*. New York 1963.

Savona, Jeannette L. *Jean Genet*. London, 1983.

Stewart, Henry E., and Rob Roy McGregor. *Jean Genet: A Biography of Deceit, 1910–1951*. New York, 1989.

Thody, Philip. *Jean Genet: A Study of His Novels and Plays*. London, 1968.

## BIBLIOGRAPHIES

Coe, Richard N. "Jean Genet: A Checklist of His Works in French, English, and German." *Australian Journal of French Studies*, 6 (1969), 113–130.

Webb, Richard C., and Suzanne A. Webb. *Jean Genet and His Critics: An Annotated Bibliography, 1943–1980*. Metuchen, N.J., and London, 1982.

AUSTIN E. QUIGLEY

# MAX FRISCH

## *(b. 1911)*

BY REACHING A broad international audience through his unique prose style and mastery of several approaches to drama, the Swiss writer Max Frisch has gained recognition as one of the outstanding literary figures not only of his homeland but also of the German-speaking countries in general. The inclusion of Frisch in any account of contemporary literature as a document of "modern" man's situation is likely to be questioned only by those who believe that "great" literature must portray our time primarily as one of mass movements, class struggle, and catastrophic changes. Although such aspects of modern life are indeed confronted by Frisch, both directly and indirectly, his starting point is always the individual as such.

In *Montauk* (1974–1975), which, albeit designated a "tale" (*Erzählung*), is really only one of Frisch's many patently and covertly autobiographical works, he asserts:

> I write for myself. The society, whichever it might be, is not my master; I am not its high priest or even its schoolmaster. The public as my partner? I can find more believable partners. Therefore, not because I think that I have to teach or convert the public, but rather because anyone, in order to recognize himself, needs an imaginary audience—that is the reason I publish. Ultimately, I am, however, writing for myself.
>
> (6.636)[1]

But what Frisch means goes beyond the merely personal or intimate. In his *Tagebuch 1966–1971* (*Sketchbook 1966–1971*), published in 1972, he asserts flatly that consigning a social function to literature is mere self-justification on the part of the author. He goes on to say:

> The domain of literature? I almost dare to say: the private. What sociology does not include [*erfassen*]; what biology does not include: the single being, the ego, not my ego but an ego, the person who experiences the world as an ego, who dies as an ego. It is the person who is included in the statistics but cannot express himself there and, as far as the whole is concerned, is irrelevant but has to live in the consciousness that he is irrelevant. The domain of literature: everything that human beings experience, sex, technology, politics, but, in contrast to science, seen from the viewpoint of the being that is doing the experiencing.
>
> (6.89)

[1] All quotations, unless otherwise noted, are translated by the present writer from the seven-volume edition of *Gesammelte Werke* (Frankfurt am Main, 1986).

In other words, Frisch is writing not as *the* individual but as *an* individual, and he is doing so not in the service of an idea or for a given audience, but for everyone and anyone who shares Frisch's conviction that he can see the world only as an individual.

## *EARLY LIFE AND RISE TO FAME*

Considering Frisch's publication of two sketchbooks and the salient autobiographical slant of his other writings, we might expect him to have led an extraordinary life himself. Some writers—one need think only of Ernest Hemingway—seek adventure and danger in order to write from immediate experience about individuals under such extreme circumstances. Others—and here the many exiled and persecuted writers of fascist and Communist countries come to mind—are themselves thrust into, or come in contact with, extraordinary ways of life. Still others look back on rather conventional, usually bourgeois lives and consequently emphasize stereotypical aspects of their class and environment. Frisch's life fits none of these patterns yet incorporates elements of all of them.

Frisch's experience is outlined in his sketchbooks, which deal with the periods 1946 to 1949 and 1966 to 1971 and with trips to France, Russia, the United States, and many other countries, as well as with many famous and obscure acquaintances, friends, and lovers. In particular, we must depend on the section "Autobiographie" in the sketchbook of 1946–1949 for most factual information on Frisch's life. His account begins as follows:

> I was born [on 15 May] in 1911 in Zurich. Our name is not of Swiss origin. It was brought there from neighboring Austria by a grandfather who had emigrated as a young saddler; in Zurich, which apparently pleased him, this grandfather married a local girl of simple stock with the name Naegeli. The maternal side is likewise mixed; her great-grandfather, Wildermuth by name, came from Württemberg, and with his son, i.e., my grandfather, it all began: he called himself a painter and wore an enormous cravat that was much bolder than his sketches and paintings. He then married a woman named Schulthess from Basel, who could never forget that her family had once owned a carriage, and directed the school of arts and crafts of our city. I do not know much more about my background.
>
> (2.584)

We note, of course, the somewhat ironic tone with which Frisch characterizes the beginnings of aesthetic activities in his family. This tone befits his tendency in his later works to downplay both the influence and the claims of art and the intellectual.

Moreover, a similar tone is applied to his family's aspirations in general and specifically to his brother's choice of a career in science. For after mentioning that his mother often told how she had worked as a governess in czarist Russia, Frisch talks about his father and his brother:

> Since as the son of a saddler he could not afford to study at a professional school, it was naturally his ambition to see his sons become academicians. Aside from that, we had a choice. My brother, who was older than I, chose chemistry, which had already filled our kitchen with the stench of magic during his entire youth. A book on the windowsill, retorts with their yellow fumes, Bunsen burners, tubes like glass intestines, the occasional explosion, intended or not—those were the Sunday afternoons, the rainy ones, when we could not possibly play soccer.
>
> (2.584)

All in all, Frisch treats his family's background in a casual, offhanded manner. Nor does he demonstrate any greater seriousness in describing his own path to literature. In fact, despite his subsequent preoccupation with the family relationships of his characters, Frisch, who uses his own relationship with his mother in portraying, for example, the mother of the title figure of the novel *Jürg Reinhart* (1934), says in the sketchbook covering 1966 to 1971 how a session with a New York psychiatrist revealed that he had suppressed, among other things, the memory of his father. And in *Montauk* he admits:

> I have kept silent to myself about my own life. I have served up stories for some audience or another. I have revealed myself in these stories, as I know, up to the point of being unrecognizable. I do not live with my own story, only with parts of it that I have been able to make into literature. Whole areas are missing: my father, my brother, my sister. Last year my sister died. I was moved by how much I know about her; but I have never written down any of it. It is not even correct that I have always only written about myself. I have never described myself. I have only betrayed myself.
>
> (6.720)

Instead of drawing on his childhood and family life, Frisch would concentrate on his experiences as a mature man with various women in his life.

"Autobiographie" also describes Frisch's early contacts with literature, which were modest and certainly not of an intellectual nature. Unlike most adolescents of his generation, he did not read the adventure novels of Karl May (1842–1912) about cowboys, Indians, sheiks, and so on. He reports having read only *Don Quixote* and *Uncle Tom's Cabin,* which he "liked a great deal," but which "were sufficient." Having thus emphasized his lack of interest in reading, he continues, "I had an insatiable enthusiasm for soccer and the theater" (2.584). The latter interest was awakened in Frisch—as in so many Germans before him—by Friedrich Schiller's rousing Sturm und Drang play *Die Räuber* (*The Robbers,* 1781). Two months later Frisch even sent the manuscript of a play entitled "Stahl" (Steel)—despite the ridicule of his father—to the prominent director Max Reinhardt in Berlin. Frisch remembers only the most salient details of this now long-lost manuscript, but he says about its return (after "seven long weeks"), "The manuscript came back . . . ; an exhaustive report was enclosed, which I did not understand."

Frisch did not abandon his youthful dramatic ambitions. His next inspiration came, however, from an entirely different direction: he discovered an inexpensive edition of the collected works of Henrik Ibsen. He continues in his autobiography:

> [Until finishing the *Realgymnasium* [technical school], which I naturally considered superfluous, ceremonious, ludicrous, and bourgeois and had to do only for my father's sake, I wrote another three or four plays, among them a comedy of marriage (I had not as yet even kissed a girl), as well as a farce about conquering the moon. The only activity that the world recognized was my completing school. The path to the university was inescapable.
>
> (2.585)

This was in 1930. Obviously Frisch could accept that he had not been a literary prodigy, but he did not look forward to an academic career.

Nonetheless, Frisch's account of his years at the University of Zurich (1930–1933) reveals that his poetic aspirations were still alive and his academic efforts were intended primarily to keep them alive. This is substantiated by the fact that his first publications fall into this period, beginning with his essay "Mimische Partitur?" (Mimic Score?; *Neue zürcher Zeitung,* 27 May 1931), which attests to his continued interest in the theater. Following this short essay about the artificiality of theatrical gestures, Frisch published twenty-nine essays and reviews in 1932 and twenty-four in 1933, only a few of which are reprinted in the collected works. Regarding his other activities at the university, we learn from Frisch: "I remember two peculiar years that I spent in lecture halls and almost as excitedly in the halls, always full of expectations, lonely, precipitous in my judgments, insecure, and usually entangled in some secret love about which the beloved knew nothing" (2.585f.). Almost as if he felt obliged to have written poems about such emotions, Frisch adds: "No poems were successful."

It is interesting to note that Frisch never published any poems, whatever he may have composed during these troubled, lonely years or in the subsequent ones. Although he was interested in "pure thought," his contact with it revealed only his own "lack of thinking power." Later he would admit his inability to think originally as a theoretician.

Furthermore, the names Frisch remembers in his sketchbook from these early years are not those of leading Germanists at the university. He says nothing about his readings or courses on literature, and in other fields as well he seems to have gleaned no values that would belie his assertion, "The growing feeling . . . that everything I am hearing is without a center, a warehouse-like alignment that calls itself a university—all this might have been a thoroughly genuine feeling, perhaps recognition; at the same time, however, it provided a welcome excuse for my own scientific inability" (2.586). Be that as it may, Frisch left the university in 1933—a step he related to the death of his father and his need to earn his own living.

Now Frisch increased his activity as a journalist, which took him to Czechoslovakia, Hungary, Serbia, Bosnia, Dalmatia, the Black Sea, and Istanbul, where he "learned about mosques and hunger," as well as to Greece. The direct artistic result of these travels was the "first, all-too-youthful novel" *Jürg Reinhart: Eine sommerliche Schicksalsfahrt* (Jürg Reinhart: A Fateful Trip in the Summer, 1934). Although a second novel, *Antwort aus der Stille* (Answer from the Silence, 1937), is not included in the collected works, Frisch permitted the inclusion of this first novel.

In 1935 Frisch also traveled to Germany, where he gathered impressions of the Nazi regime; but his written accounts, however much given to irony, are not especially outraged or particularly perceptive. Only after 1945 would Frisch offer a retrospective view of Hitler's Germany, and then obliquely, for he shows himself more concerned with Switzerland's own questionable actions than with Germany's guilt during World War II. As the 1949 essay "Kultur als Alibi" ("Culture as an Alibi") shows, the latter is more or less self-evident. Branding as "moral schizophrenia" any reference to "culture" as an excuse for political actions, Frisch comes to the following conclusion:

> Our preoccupation with the German question . . . seems to me to be a necessity, even though we have no hope at all of being able to offer the Germans fruitful assistance. It is necessary for us. We simply cannot overlook the fact there is no Switzerland without Germany. Not for long anyway. No more so than there is a Switzerland without France and Italy.
>
> (2.343)

Although Frisch eventually concerned himself with many questions in the realm of individual and national morality—for example, Vietnam, racial problems, and the waging of atomic war—here he accepts a pragmatic argument as such rather than trying to find any cultural justification for what is morally indefensible. The same attitude will underlie his opposition to atomic armament and war: there can be no moral excuse for what is obviously self-defeating and destructive.

In summing up his own gains from his journalistic activities, Frisch casually dismisses the field as a convenient one in which to earn money whenever needed. In retrospect, however, we recognize how indebted Frisch's prose narrative and sketchbook style is to the techniques he learned as a journalist and essayist. The subjectivity implied by the genre of the sketchbook and his concentration in novels on the thoughts and emotions of one person is frequently counterbalanced by his journalistic feeling for conciseness and objectivity.

In 1936, now twenty-five, Frisch was led by a combination of factors, as he says, "back to the school bench." A girlfriend whom he wanted to marry at the time thought that he should first have a fixed profession. At the same time, he was reading Gottfried Keller's novel *Der grüne Heinrich* (*Green Henry,* 1854–1855), a strongly autobiographical work that portrays the protagonist's failure as an artist in the bourgeois world of the mid nineteenth century. Finally, financial support for four years' study was provided by a friend. At this point Frisch, who had decided to study architecture and believed that he now had something tangible to work with, burned all his writings and set about studying. In 1941 he received his diploma as an architect from the Federal Technical University in Zurich.

The premature end of his career as a writer, however, lasted only two years. In 1938, convinced that Switzerland would not be spared by the coming war, Frisch began a diary about the Swiss mobilization. The diary would later appear as *Blätter aus dem Brotsack* (Leaves from the Knapsack, 1940). Frisch calculates that he spent about five hundred days in the uniform of his homeland, whose compulsory military service was extended in fear of a German invasion. (According to Frisch, an invasion was in fact planned for April 1943, but was called off just ten days before the deadline.) Although Frisch never did see combat, he later recounted episodes from this period in his *Dienstbüchlein* (Service Booklet, 1974), a collection of journal-like entries whose title is taken from the personal-data record booklet issued to each Swiss soldier. Here Frisch describes the military as a phenomenon that deprives one of one's "identity": "Don't stand out; remain interchangeable as a person—one learns that in a few weeks." And because the army does away with our personal freedom of choice ("entmündigte uns"), it undermines the very discipline that it wishes to instill in us. Instead, it employs punishment and achieves merely obedience. Frisch argues that

> discipline stems from our consciousness that we are our own masters, not the consciousness that we serve someone else. . . . Discipline begins with wanting to do something. . . . Discipline means that one demands something oneself. A mule does not do this. Neither does the gunner who is deprived of his freedom from the moment of rising to going to bed. . . . Discipline is a matter of conviction, with conscience; it is a matter of coming of age.
>
> (6.560)

We recognize how the military service contributed, if in a negative manner, to a prominent theme of Frisch's later works: the belief that a person must accept himself as a responsible being, must assume an "identity."

In 1942 Frisch married Gertrud Anna Constanze von Meyenburg; their first child was born in 1943. Frisch's attempt during these years to adjust to the role of a productive citizen is reflected in his acceptance of a position in an architectural firm in 1941 and, one year later, in his opening of his own office as an architect. The extent to which Frisch considered this occupation socially "useful" can be inferred from his lifelong interest in city planning as well as building houses. Having his own firm allowed him, as he says, to dispose more freely of his working hours.

By 1943 Frisch had found the time to write and publish his next novel, *J'adore ce qui me brûle; oder, Die Schwierigen* (I Adore Whatever Sets Me Afire; or, The Difficult Ones; reprinted in a second version with the French and German titles reversed, 1957). This continuation of the Jürg Reinhart novel ends with the suicide of Anton (i.e., Jürg) after he has, according to the narrator, "overcome the human homesickness to be understood." Anton has failed both as an artist and as an individual. Although certain of the characters and events are not without interest, the novel encountered a cool reception from critics and scholars. In 1944 Frisch wrote *Bin; oder, Die Reise nach Peking* (Bin; or, The Trip to Peking, 1945), which he described as a "daydream" (*eine Träumerei*). *Bin,* Frisch's first long narrative in the first person, also signals the introduction of a more humorous, ironic tone in his prose works, a tone that here offsets the central theme of "yearning" (one that easily lends itself to the overly reflective or sentimental).

In 1944 Frisch wrote his first published

drama, *Santa Cruz: Eine Romanze* (Santa Cruz: A Romance); it was first performed on 7 March 1946 in Zurich and appeared in print in 1947. Frisch had been encouraged to write a play by Kurt Hirschfeld, the dramatic consultant of the Zurich Theater, who had invited him to attend rehearsals of plays by Brecht, Sartre, García Lorca, Giraudoux, and Claudel. While the influence of one or more of these playwrights may be seen in this and subsequent plays by Frisch, it must be kept in mind that modern theater in general shows little regard for rigid interpretations of time and space, a tendency that can be traced back to many innovations made by the expressionists in plays and films. Much later, in his *Sketchbook 1966–1971,* he wrote:

> The sole reality on the stage consists of the fact that a "play" is taking place there. A play permits what life does not permit: we can dispense with the continuity of time; we can be in several places at once; a plot can be interrupted (songs, chorus, commentary, etc.) and not proceed until we have comprehended its causes and possible consequences; we eliminate what is mere repetition, etc. . . . Life is historical and definitive at every moment; it tolerates no variations. A play permits all this. Flight from reality?—the theater reflects it; it does not imitate it. Nothing is more pointless than the imitation of reality; there is already enough reality.
>
> (6.77f.)

Many of these insights are already incorporated into or implied by *Santa Cruz.* By calling it a "romance," Frisch not only suggests that the content concerns lovers; he also calls attention to the work's proximity to the ballad, which, of all storytelling genres, needs to pay the least attention to the constraints of time and space.

Quite simply, the setting of Santa Cruz forms the contrast to the snowed-in European castle of the cavalry captain and his wife, Elvira. Frisch's stage directions state that the action takes place in seven days and in seventeen years, for it shows the return of Pelegrin, whom Frisch calls a "Vagant" (a medieval traveling scholar), who left Elvira seventeen years earlier to sail to Hawaii, while the captain stayed by her, renouncing his dream of seeking adventure in Hawaii. Much is relived by Elvira and Pelegrin, but not merely in the sense of a flashback or a dream. The past becomes the present, and past places become present ones. Ultimately, however, one has made a choice, the captain for the solid, ordered life, and Pelegrin for one of adventure. The same applies to Elvira, who says to her husband in her last appearance onstage:

> Why could we not be more honest with one another? We were missing so little. We would have understood each other! You buried your yearning, as you write, for years in order not to frighten me. And I have been ashamed of my dreams for years because I knew they would frighten you. Neither of us wanted to disappoint the other . . . that is the comedy that we played for so long, for so long—until Pelegrin came.
>
> (2.73)

Despite all the new techniques Frisch employed, *Santa Cruz* centers on a problem reminiscent of Ibsen, a problem brought to the forefront by a figure out of the past. This figure is, of course, an overworked device of all naturalists after Ibsen. Despite his ability to create modern theater, Frisch was still writing about people whose situation is far from modern.

Shortly after *Santa Cruz,* which had been written in a very short time, Frisch turned to a more contemporary subject in *Nun singen sie wieder: Versuch eines Requiems* (*Now They Sing Again: Attempt at a Requiem,* 1946), which at Easter 1945 became Frisch's first play to be performed. This play combines not the past and present but the dead and living; its subject, the survivors and victims of the war, gives it a timeliness that Frisch had not previously attained. As a confrontation with the horrors of war, however, this play misses its mark. Frisch's own words in his preface to the published version seem to indicate that he had set himself other goals and had selected his techniques accordingly:

> The place where these scenes take place can be deduced from the spoken word. Sets should be present only to the extent that the actor needs them, and in no case may they simulate reality. For the impression of a "play" [*Spiel*] must be maintained so that no one will compare it with the true event, which is monstrous. We did not even see it with our own eyes, and one must ask whether a word about it is even proper for us. The sole circumstance that could justify our statement lies in the fact that we, who did not experience it personally, are free of the temptation to seek any vengeance. Yet the doubt remains. There are scenes that a remote sorrow must imagine over and over again, and even if it were under the involuntary force of dreams like those that haunt every contemporary, others will imagine others.
>
> (2.137)

This "attempted requiem" ends with the words of the priest, who has asserted that everything—death, life, the stars in heaven—is in vain. But when asked about love, he can only answer: "Love is beautiful, Benjamin, love above all. It alone knows that it is in vain, and it alone does not despair." And yet this appeal to love does not ring true, for it does not promise to prevent a repetition of the horrors that have preceded it.

Frisch's next work for the stage was *Die chinesische Mauer* (*The Chinese Wall,* 1947), which he wrote from November 1945 to May 1946. It was first performed on 10 October 1946 in Zurich. This was to be just the first of four versions, however. The second was written from February to July 1953 for a premiere in Berlin on 28 October of that year; the third version was first performed on 26 February 1965 in Hamburg; and the final and "official" version, which appears in *Collected Works,* is known as the "version for Paris," because it was undertaken for the Théâtre National de l'Odéon in Paris and performed by the Jeuve Théâtre National on 8 November 1972.

Obviously moved by the dropping of the first atomic bombs on Japan, Frisch tries to present in the form of "a farce" an essentially logical thought: in the era of atomic bombs, there is no place for a Napoleon or any of the other great individualists. As Frisch himself said in 1955:

> A present-day person, some average intellectual as a representative of today's consciousness, confronts those figures who populate our brains—Napoleon, Cleopatra, Philip of Spain, Brutus, Don Juan, l'Inconnue de la Seine, Columbus, Romeo and Juliet, and so on—in order to make clear to these figures that we can no longer afford to make history in their manner; to be sure, his knowledge, since it will not become history, remains impotent.
>
> (2.224f.)

In an earlier commentary to this work entitled "Wo spielt unser Stück?" (Where Does Our Piece Take Place?, 1946), Frisch calls attention to the use he had made of this same technique in *Santa Cruz,* but in the earlier play his juxtapositions of time and place are of more moderate proportions. Moreover, the problem underlying *The Chinese Wall* is modern, so totally modern that any thoughts of the past and its fictions that have formed our thinking must produce direct confrontations. We can no longer simply compromise with our previous manner of thinking. We cannot merely add this era to all of the previous ones and thereby imply a sense of continuity.

According to the author's 1955 comments (2.220–225), the first version of *The Chinese Wall* was performed in several countries, by amateur groups as well as by professional actors. Frisch even admits that the play's success encouraged him not to give up the theater. Nonetheless, he continued to write nondramatic prose. He had described the situation of wartime Switzerland after the occupation of France as a "prison." Now that the war was over, Frisch resumed his travels, recording many of his impressions in his *Sketchbook 1946–1949,* which appeared in September 1950. The first version of the diary had already been published in 1947 under the title *Tagebuch mit*

*Marion* and had covered 1946 and 1947. The final editing and expansion of this first version to form the final *Sketchbook* can be attributed to Frisch's encounter with Peter Suhrkamp on 25 November 1947 in Frankfurt, at the premiere of Carl Zuckmayer's play *Des Teufels General* (*The Devil's General,* 1946). Suhrkamp, who was later to become Frisch's sole publisher, encouraged the Swiss writer in this undertaking. The diary form now offered Frisch the opportunity to retreat to his journalistic experience and retrace his steps to prose fiction, steps that eventually led to the composition of his great novel *Stiller,* which was begun in 1951, interrupted for work on his drama on Don Juan, and finally published in 1954.

Frisch now worked concurrently on dramatic and nondramatic works. By July 1948 he had already finished his next play. It originally bore the title "Ihr Morgen ist die Finsternis" (Their Morning Is the Darkness), then "Judith" (after the biblical heroine), and finally *Als der Krieg zu Ende war* (*When the War Was Over*), under which title it was first performed on 8 January 1949 in Zurich. Although Frisch had met Brecht in 1947, this play does not show the influence of the latter's "epic theater" to any extent. Indeed, it not only remained the most conventional of Frisch's stage works but also occasioned criticism by Brecht himself, who wrote in a letter in July 1948:

> I have only one criticism, and it does not concern the subject matter and not the poetic intention; it concerns only one aspect of its execution: that considerably less is expected of the theater as an institution than has been the case with earlier playwrights with talent comparable to yours. . . . To put it crudely: I have the impression that you simply decline to analyze why your subject (in the treatment that you give it in the very beginning) seemed so fruitful to you.
>
> (2.766)

Brecht had much that was positive to say, but only later did Frisch write plays that satisfied Brecht's wish for more analysis of the situation in terms of its causes. Because *The Chinese Wall* could be performed by laypeople, one might have inferred the earlier influence of Brecht, who wrote several "teaching pieces" (*Lehrstücke*) especially for nonprofessional actors. But Frisch's play set the modern atomic era in pseudo-dialectical opposition to the past. Both new and old were considered as given factors without concern for how they came about, and no new synthesis was created from their opposition.

Quite aside from Brecht's criticism, *When the War Was Over* cannot be considered an unqualified success. Yet it remains important in terms of Frisch's development. On the one hand, it represents Frisch's last direct confrontation with the German situation after the loss of World War II. On the other hand, it has enjoyed continued attention by critics because here, for the first time, Frisch introduces his theme of the "graven image" (*Bildnis*). The incident on which the play is based is one that Frisch had heard about in Germany in 1947, when he recorded it in his diary (2.530ff., 536). A German woman is forced to wait on occupying Russian soldiers while her husband, who participated in the Warsaw Ghetto massacre, hides in the cellar (the Warsaw episode is also based on fact; see 2.280). Agnes Anders, the wife, falls in love with the Russian colonel, although neither can understand the language of the other. In the play's first version Agnes commits suicide when she learns about her husband's atrocities, but in the second version (1962) Frisch eliminates the third act and leaves Agnes and her husband only staring at each other in silence. Both Frisch and his critics saw this change as essential to the main motif of creating a "graven image" (Exodus 20:4—"Thou shalt not make unto thee any graven image, or any likeness of any thing that is in heaven above, or that is in the earth beneath, or that is in the water under the earth"). In his afterword to the play Frisch says:

> The commandment that we should not make a graven image of God does not lose its meaning if

> we understand God as the living part of every person, the inconceivable, the unnameable that we can only bear when we love; otherwise we always create for ourselves an image. Not prepared, not willing, and not in a position to face an individual, we stamp out entire peoples and cannot concede to them anything but the mask of our prejudice, which means a sin. An example of the latter is a historical one, the slaughter of the Jews in Warsaw, which is in the background of our story. In the foreground—and I hope that this polarity is clear enough—there is a love that, even though it could be called adultery, represents the exact opposite of a sin and is holy in so far as it overcomes the image.
>
> (2.279)

Frisch later applied to all interpersonal relationships what he says here about creating an image of entire nationalities or groups. In fact, the concept will even be applied to one's view of oneself.

Frisch's next drama, *Graf Öderland* (Count Öderland, 1951), which he called a "Moritat" (a ballad, usually about a murder, that is presented to the accompaniment of a hurdy-gurdy with pictures), combined motifs taken from his sketchbook: the newspaper account of a clairvoyant who assists the police in finding a professor's body (2.362), the story of a bank teller who kills his family without any apparent motive (2.403f.), the sketchbook episodes "Am See" (At the Lake, 2.404ff.) and "Skizze" (Sketch, 2.723–749). Many of his subsequent works also incorporate motifs that Frisch first "tested out," so to speak, in diary form. Naturally, the diary genre allows for a great variety of material and in Frisch's hands almost fulfills the eclectic function that the Romantics tried to force on the novel. This will be even more true of Frisch's second sketchbook (covering the years 1966–1971), in which "questionnaires" on various topics appear at intervals, along with the description, complete with rules for conduct, of a suicide club.

The extensive reworkings of *Öderland,* while typical for Frisch, stem mainly from his lack of satisfaction with this particular play, which in an interview in 1975 he himself called a "favorite" but a "failure" among his works. The premiere performance (February 1951 in Zurich) was a failure, and in 1956 Frisch offered a new version whose protagonist, because the material now had a contemporary political tone, was misunderstood by the audience as a caricature of Hitler. A third version in 1961 returned to the spirit of the original sketches by emphasizing the legendary aspects of this story about a district attorney who, seemingly without reason, has cast everything in his middle-class existence aside. To some he appears as Count Öderland, a legendary figure whose return is promised in various stories; then, almost capriciously, he commits murder and takes political control, only to find himself at the end both the master and the servant of the very "establishment" that he sought to escape. We recognize that the attorney's dissatisfaction with the tedium of real life has led to the "count's" escape into the violent life of legend and myth, but his outrageous acts merely plunge him back into tedium.

Perhaps Frisch's lack of satisfaction with his own artistic attempt to move back and forth between reality and legend (just as his works had already fluctuated between different realms in space and time as well as between life and death) explains his need to rework this play so often. Interestingly enough, each new version is paralleled by new variations in subsequent works on the underlying theme of "being someone else" in a world that constantly forces its "reality" and "senselessness" on us. Ultimately, in terms of Frisch's view of artistic creation and his professional background as an architect, one can also view his desire to reshape his material again and again as a substantiation of various statements by Frisch comparing an author to a sculptor:

> What is important: the unspeakable, the white space between the words, and these words always talk about incidental things that we do not really mean. . . . Language works like a sculptor with his chisel, for it too propels the emptiness,

> the speakable, toward the secret, the living. The danger always exists that one could shatter the secret; also the danger that one may stop too soon and leave everything only a shapeless mass, that one may not catch the secret, comprehend it, and free it from all that which would still be sayable, in short, that one does not penetrate to its last surface.
>
> (2.378f.)

Here Frisch likens writing to chipping away until only the secret that he wants to tell remains. Likewise, as we shall see, he came to see human life as "possibilities" and "variations" that must be tried out and discarded.

Although Frisch's *Biedermann und die Brandstifter* (*The Firebugs,* 1958) did not appear on the stage until 1958, the material had first been sketched in as a "burlesque" in the sketchbook for 1946–1949 (2.556f.) and then presented as a radio play in 1953 under the title *Herr Biedermann und die Brandstifter* (published in 1955). Like *Öderland,* it obviously had by then also gone through several transformations. *Biedermann* eventually became Frisch's first international success onstage, and Frisch, alluding to its protagonist, later said in an interview, "I never counted on being supported by this hair-tonic shyster."

As a stage work *Biedermann* is in the form of a political parable. But opinions have varied greatly concerning the author's intended target. In the final version of the play, the protagonist invites, one by one, three suspicious characters into his home during a rash of arson cases in his town. The three, who never really try to conceal their activities, ultimately burn down Biedermann's house. Since Biedermann himself symbolizes the worst aspects of capitalism, there is, morally and socially speaking, no little measure of poetic justice in his fate. The name "Biedermann," the word for an upstanding, honorable person, cannot help but evoke recollections of "Gottlieb Biedermeier," a figure invented by the nineteenth-century writer Ludwig Eichrodt to caricature the middle-class philistine of the time. Later the term *Biedermeier* came to designate the furniture and settings of the bourgeoisie during the first half of the nineteenth century in Germany. Such associations underscore the play's socially critical aspects from the very beginning. In the introductory remarks to the radio play Frisch himself said:

> I consciously chose a freely invented catastrophe, to wit, the burning of Seldwyla, in order not to evoke in the worthy listeners any shocks or personal feelings, which would only spoil for us the pleasure of casually and objectively observing with enjoyment that there are also catastrophes that did not need to take place.
>
> (4.277)

The ironic tone and the Brechtian "alienation effect" do not escape us, but we also note Frisch's use of the name "Seldwyla," a town invented by Gottfried Keller as the setting for a series of tales about mostly middle-class foibles and weaknesses. After the successful premiere of the stage version, Frisch commented in his short essay "Die Schweiz ist ein Land ohne Utopie" (Switzerland Is a Country Without Utopia, 1960):

> Both Dürrenmatt's *The Visit* [*Besuch der alten Dame*] and my *Biedermann and the Arsonists* could not have been written without the compact vis-à-vis of a bourgeoisie that was still mostly intact. The Swiss situation therefore also has its productive sides, certainly—if one bears it but gets away from it over and over again.
>
> (4.259)

Thus it is certainly no misinterpretation to see *Biedermann* as a humorous satire on Swiss society.

In 1959 the middle class and its growing prosperity were becoming an increasingly important social factor in West Germany. But this development would scarcely have explained the immediate success of Frisch's play. Correctly enough, audiences also recognized this play as a parable about Hitler's seizure of power and/or about the takeover of the Czechoslovakian government in 1948 by the Communists. What speaks for the last-named connection is the fact that Frisch's original material, which he presented with almost all the details of the final drama, first appeared immediately following a diary entry on Czechoslovakia. Yet whatever specific political disaster one wishes to see in *Biedermann,* the middle class must bear the responsibility.

The inability of the middle class to learn from its mistakes, either personally or as a group, in fact forms a thread connecting the steps to the play's final version. Because of the brevity of *Biedermann,* the first stage performance was filled out to an evening's length by the inclusion of Frisch's *Schwank* (farce) *Die grosse Wut des Philipp Hotz* (The Great Rage of Philipp Hotz, 1958), a piece that shows the comic efforts of the protagonist to escape his marriage and bourgeois existence:

> What is breaking up our marriage is not the few instances of adultery—they hurt, I admit, and as habitual behavior they are repulsive—but rather the fact, the simple and abysmally profound fact, Madam, that I am a man (albeit an intellectual), and my wife, if you will permit me to say so, is a woman.
>
> (4.122)

His attempt to dissolve the marriage consists in playing various enraged "roles"; but he then undermines these very roles because he does not really want to end the relationship after all. By putting *Hotz* on the same program as *Biedermann,* Frisch implies a connection between the two. We recognize, however, that the "farce" serves as a comic replay of the serious problems presented in the novel *Stiller* and has little in common with the themes of *Biedermann.* Realizing this, Frisch wrote an epilogue (Herr Biedermann Goes to Heaven), which reveals that the protagonist has really learned nothing.

Before returning to the Biedermann material and adapting it for the radio, Frisch had, in 1951, won a Rockefeller grant for drama and had spent a year in America and Mexico (1951–1952). On his return from New York, in the spring of 1952, Frisch brought with him the draft of his next play, *Don Juan; oder, Die Liebe zur Geometrie* (*Don Juan; or, The Love of Geometry,* 1953), which was first performed on 5 May 1953 in Zurich, less than two months after the first broadcast of the Biedermann radio play. Once again Frisch had returned to a subject that first appeared in his sketchbook for 1946–1949, albeit only briefly ("Arabesque" [2.628]). Don Juan also appears in the 1947 version of *The Chinese Wall* and, more prominently, in the version of 1955. In 1950 Frisch had been in Spain, an experience recorded in "Spanien—Im ersten Eindruck" (Spain—According to a First Impression, 3.179ff.); as he later said, the trip served as an inspiration.

Yet another influence on Frisch's decision to portray Don Juan in a drama goes back to the years of the sketchbooks. As he reports in his second sketchbook (1966–1971) in the section "Erinnerungen an Brecht" (Memories of Brecht, 6.26), the German playwright suggested in 1948 that Frisch, besides writing a play on Wilhelm Tell, should arrange the drama *La Celestina* (1499) by Fernando de Rojas for the actress Therese Giehse. Eventually the former suggestion led to the work *Wilhelm Tell für die Schule* (*Wilhelm Tell: A School Text,* 1971), which, although not a play, nevertheless serves, as Brecht proposed in 1948, to demythologize the Swiss national hero. Brecht's second idea, a stage work for which he declared himself prepared to write the songs, was realized only indirectly by Frisch in *Don Juan.* (Brecht himself reworked Rojas' play from 1948 to 1950, but his version remained unpublished; he also presented a new version of Molière's *Don Juan* in 1952 in East Berlin.)

As Frisch remarked in reference to his school years, he did not consider himself much of a reader. Speaking of *Don Juan,* one of his few encounters with a theme of truly worldwide distribution, Frisch said about his preparations for entering so well-populated a field:

> I experienced many more indirect influences than direct ones. . . . I wrote *Don Juan; or, The Love of*

> *Geometry* without being familiar with a single predecessor. The figure of Don Juan was known to me from general knowledge. Even Mozart's opera I did not hear until later. And even the literary examples, *Don Juan* by Tirso de Molina and the one by Molière, I read only later [i.e., in the summer of 1952].
>
> (3.862)

Nonetheless, we know that Frisch saw the following works on stage: José Zorilla y Moral's *Don Juan Tenoria* of 1844 (1951, in Spain), Christian Dietrich Grabbe's *Don Juan und Faust* of 1829 (1935, in Berlin), and George Bernard Shaw's *Man and Superman* of 1903 (1952, in New York.)

Frisch's "comedy," of course, has little in common with other works on the great Spanish lover. Instead, it becomes a vehicle for another character who reflects the problems inherent in Frisch's own view of man. Thus Frisch's Don Juan is the protagonist of a comedy, not a tragedy; loves geometry, not women; is an intellectual, not a swashbuckler; and—seduced rather than seducing—provides the world not with a public figure on which it can build a myth but rather with a myth about himself as a public figure in order to preserve his privacy. The play ends with Don Juan as a husband and expectant father. This end is typical for Frisch, who has the bishop comment:

> Truth cannot be shown, only invented. Let us imagine an audience that could see the real Don Juan: here, in this autumnal loggia in Ronda!—the ladies would boast and say on their way home: "You see!" And the husbands would rub their hands with malicious glee: a henpecked Don Juan! For there comes the point where the extraordinary bears a terrible resemblance to the ordinary. And where, my secretaries would call out, is the punishment? And some young dandy who likes to play the pessimist would explain: "Marriage, you understand, is truly hell!" And he would give us more platitudes. . . . No, it would be horrible to hear this audience that sees only reality.
>
> (3.165f.)

Don Juan achieves his "identity" by offering a lie that corresponds to the truth that society wants. In that sense the myth is truer than the reality that gave birth to it.

## *YEARS OF SUCCESS*

By 1953 Frisch had received various minor honors for his works, but he still maintained his architect's office. Then, in 1954, *Stiller* appeared. Looking back on the years immediately following the publication of this, his first truly successful novel, Frisch later said, "I can tell you that until my forty-sixth year of life I had earned enough to be able to ride a bicycle. At forty-eight I bought my first Volkswagen and found that I was, after all, starting to achieve something." These years of growing artistic recognition—including the Raabe Award, the Georg Büchner Award, and other German, French, and Swiss awards—were accompanied by decisive changes in Frisch's personal life. In 1954 he dissolved his architectural business and was separated from his wife. After travels to the United States, Mexico, and Cuba (1956) and Greece and the Arab states (1957), and the finalization of his divorce in 1959, Frisch finally settled (1960) in Rome with Ingeborg Bachmann, one of the most prominent lyricists of postwar Germany. Their relationship was to last for five years.

Frisch's emergence as an influential author resulted primarily from three works produced during this period: *Stiller; Homo faber: Ein* Bericht (*Homo faber: A Report,* 1957); and the stage version of *Biedermann,* which was followed by the more controversial *Andorra: Stück in zwölf Bildern* (*Andorra: A Play in Twelve Scenes,* 1961). Frisch's abandonment of his architect's office to devote himself to writing as a profession and relegation of architecture to a spare-time activity might lead one to believe that *Stiller* had been an immediate financial success as well as a critical breakthrough. This was not, however, the case. Frisch's obvious enjoyment in telling stories might have made this seemingly loose-knit volume popular with a large audience, but in fact the general public was slow to accept the work, perhaps because of the very characteristics that critics immediately recognized, namely a complexity and profundity that belied mere escapist storytelling. According to Frisch, *Stiller* had in any case an edition of only three thousand copies in its first year and two thousand in its second. Fifteen years had to pass before it reached annual editions of eight thousand to ten thousand.

"I'm not Stiller." So begins this novel, the first and major part of which consists of seven notebooks written by the protagonist during his imprisonment. These notebooks depict the prisoner's attempts to prove that he is Mr. White, not the Anatol Stiller whom he was arrested as at the Swiss border despite his American passport. He must convince not only the district attorney but also Stiller's wife, Julika, a dancer living in Paris, that he is not identical with the artist who disappeared six years earlier. This "proof" lies in Stiller-White's telling a variety of stories that draw not only on Frisch's own experiences but also on such events as the Spanish Civil War. In fact, the prisoner even confesses to several murders in America and elsewhere. Originally Frisch conceived of *Stiller* as a combination of five stories "that have the same persons in different combinations." Frisch later realized this same plan in several other works, especially in the novel *Mein Name sei Gantenbein* (Let My Name Be Gantenbein, 1964; translated as *A Wilderness of Mirrors*) and in the stage work *Biografie: Ein Spiel* (*Biography: A Game,* 1967–1985).

Frisch later admitted that he was most interested in telling the stories. As is the case with so many other works by Frisch, the final form of this novel was the result of an evolutionary process. During his stay in America, he had worked on a novel with the title "Was macht ihr mit der Liebe?" (What Are You Doing with Love?), and on 11 September 1951 he wrote to Peter Suhrkamp from Berkeley, California, "Much work on the novel; today I am packing up two hundred cleanly written pages, but aware that they will not remain fixed." Then Frisch put the novel aside to write *Don Juan.* On 23 August 1953 he wrote to Suhrkamp "about the work that now absorbs me again completely. . . . It is the theme that has occupied me again and again for a long time, but it has changed; stages have been added. . . . Thus: I am once again trying to write a prose work" (3.865).

In writing his notebooks, the prisoner presents us in essence with a diary and, because he is forced by circumstances to do so, thereby fulfills Frisch's dictum about his own writing: "We are being written. Writing means reading ourselves." Himself a writer of no mean proportions, with an eye to the elements of popular literature, Stiller-White includes among his tales of supposed murders and love affairs the story of Rip Van Winkle (which Frisch had already modernized for a radio play of that title, performed on the Bavarian Radio on 16 June 1953). But Stiller refuses to admit his identity and tells his stories as White. Nonetheless, neither character is an alter ego for Frisch himself.

Although the reader becomes increasingly certain that White is really Stiller, Frisch, by means of the various changes in narrative perspective, not only retains his own separation from both; he also maintains a strong element of mystery until the court's judgment at the end of the seventh notebook. The final shift in perspective occurs when the second part of the novel is narrated by the district attorney. Even after the resolution of the mystery to society's satisfaction, the ensuing story about Stiller's relationship with his wife and unsuccessful reintegration into society is no less interesting or illuminating, all the more so because it is told by the person who has come closest to understanding Stiller-White. Indeed, as in many other works, Frisch here shows "social" identity through a man's association with a woman rather than through his involvement with his family or sociopolitical institutions.

Obviously Stiller wants to become someone

else: his is the familiar symptom of an identity crisis. Stiller is Swiss. Nonetheless we note with interest that this attempt to reestablish one's identity coincides with the end of World War II. The events in Stiller's life that are covered by the novel can be divided into five periods: (1) the period before 1945, including not only his nine-year marriage to Julika but also his participation in the Spanish Civil War; (2) 1945, the year when the war ended in Europe and when Stiller experiences the marital crisis that causes him to disappear in January 1946; (3) 1946–1951, the period of Stiller's voluntary exile; (4) 1952, the year of Stiller-White's arrest and trial; (5) the last years of his life with Julika, her death, and Stiller's lapse into silence. What links *Stiller* with Frisch's previous work is a repetition of the "graven image" motif first introduced in *When the War Was Over,* which likewise portrays a situation at the end of the war. In *Stiller* it is introduced by a Jesuit priest whom Julika meets in the sanatorium. His words lead her to think about her relationship with Stiller:

> From this daily visitor, it seems, Julika also heard incidentally the scarcely unknown thought that it is a sign of not loving, therefore a sin, to form an image for oneself of one's neighbor or of any person at all and thereby say: "That's the way you are, and that's that!" This thought must have appealed to Julika directly. Was it not the case that Stiller, her husband, had made himself an image of Julika?
>
> (3.467)

And she later confronts him with this thought.

Stiller is also a sculptor; thus, as one might expect, this image becomes a multidimensional expression of his problem. Making an image can be done by a person to himself; he can form an image of the society in which he lives; and society can form an image of him as well. Obviously dissatisfied with his old image, Stiller writes about himself:

> One can tell everything, just not one's real life;—this impossibility is what condemns us to remain the way our companions see and mirror us. I mean those who claim to know me and who designate themselves as my friends and who never permit me to change myself and who destroy every miracle (that is, what I cannot tell, the unspeakable that I cannot prove)—they do all this in order to be able to say: "I know you."
>
> (3.416)

But society forces him back into this image, and in the end Stiller capitulates to society. He will become a part of the society that is governed by reproductions, that is, "images," which he describes as follows:

> We live in an age of reproduction. Most of what we have in our picture of the world we have never seen with our own eyes, or, to be more exact: with our own eyes but without actually being there; we are people who see, hear, and know from a distance.
>
> (3.535)

In the stories he tells, Stiller-White has seen a great deal of the world directly, but we do not know how much of what he relates is true. We do not know whether he could bear to experience events directly. Indeed, perhaps he could not do that very thing and for that reason has returned to Switzerland. (In fact we never learn for sure why he did return.) If this were true, then his attempt to become someone else by participating in events directly would have been condemned to failure from the beginning. Be that as it may: after his arrest he loses the personal sense of identity needed to tell his own story to the end. For he loses his wife, who could have given him a social identity, and he loses his artistic identity by becoming a maker of tourist items. He could not accept himself but finally has to. The rest can only be silence.

For all its concessions to the reader of popular fiction, *Stiller* remains a complex work, containing ever more levels of meaning. It should be noted, at least in terms of Frisch's confrontation with "modern" problems, that the novel's genesis coincided with that of several articles by Frisch on the future of Switzerland, especially in respect to planning for "human" needs. He speaks, of course, as an architect, as, that is, a builder and "maker." The problem of seeing the world exclusively as something to be understood and changed by technology then becomes the subject of his next novel, *Homo faber.*

Despite the demands presented by frequent juxtapositions of time and place in *Homo faber,* the new work was an immediate success, and we may assume that its instant acceptance by the public can be attributed to its being more contemporary and less "private." Although he is a well-educated and "thinking" person, the engineer Walter Faber (the "maker" of the title) is an exception to the long series of Frisch's intellectuals—Don Juan, Stiller, the Ph.D. in the stage version of *Biedermann,* Philipp Hotz, Professor Kürmann, "Bluebeard" Schaad—all of whom prove incapable of really accomplishing or making anything of importance. Admittedly, Faber also does not achieve his goals in the jungle, but his actions provide an almost conventional, recountable plot because they take place in the "real" world, not merely in his mind. In fact that is, to a large degree, Faber's existential error: he sees only the world that is "real" in the sense of sociology, biology, and the other sciences that Frisch denounced as incapable of revealing those aspects of life dealt with by literature. In turn, both "chance" and providence have been reduced by Faber to "probability." His bible is Norbert Wiener's *Cybernetics; or, Control and Communication in the Animal and the Machine* (1948).

To see *Homo faber* merely or even primarily as a parable about the encroachment of technology on myth in the modern world would be overly simplistic. Frisch has too little faith in the ability of technology and science to explain human life, and his narrator, who has excluded mythology from his thought, would scarcely represent its function as a positive pole.

Faber believes that he knows all the answers to life's questions. But he—or at least the reader—must learn that he has excluded too many questions about his own life, which is thrust into a mythic context when he discovers that Sabeth, the attractive young woman with whom he has been having an affair, is really his own daughter by Hanna Landsberg-Piper. Faber knew Hanna when they were both students in Zurich, and he wanted to marry her, but she was Jewish and felt that Faber really only wanted to save her from having to return to Nazi Germany. Faber's discovery of Sabeth's true identity is, however, only one of many "coincidences" that run through the book. For example, Faber's plane to South America is forced to make an emergency landing in Mexico; Faber meets the brother of Piper, the man whom Hanna married after she broke off with Faber but was still carrying his child. Faber and the brother then find Piper (whom Hanna has since divorced) in the jungle, where he has committed suicide. Further "chance" events and improbabilities propel the plot toward its final resolution in Greece, the birthplace of Western myth: there Faber meets Hanna again, is with Sabeth when she has a fatal "accident," and ends his account while waiting for a hopeless operation.

Faber's prewar affair corresponds—albeit without the birth of a child—to Frisch's own experience during his student days, and elsewhere throughout *Homo faber* Frisch drew on many personal experiences. In 1956 Frisch had traveled to America, and after giving a talk at the International Design Conference in Aspen, Colorado, he returned via San Francisco, Los Angeles, and Mexico, with an excursion to the jungles of Yucatán and to Cuba. Most of these places play a role in the novel, and—thanks to Frisch's journalistic talents—the descriptions give this "report" a high degree of authenticity in the very sense demanded by Faber. Faber's account convincingly reflects a technologist's narrow view of his environment, and to the extent of its exclusiveness his narrative becomes a document of "modern" man's patently inadequate view of his "identity."

Yet *Homo faber* is not an allegory: Faber's character is, although believable and consistent, in the end too extreme and too consistent. And what happens to him is simply too unique. Obviously, Frisch presents *one* modern man's struggle to gain a sense of "identity" through accomplishment in the modern age, with its overwhelming reliance on technology and science. In contrast with Stiller's situation, Faber's lack of identity has a tangible cause. Faber has created an "image" of everything and everybody, and in doing so, he has eliminated the unspeakable, the miracle. Thus Frisch explained in a 1975 interview:

> This man lives past himself because he is pursuing a generally offered image, that of technology. Basically speaking, "Homo faber," this man, is not a technician, but rather a crippled person who has created a graven image of himself, who has let a graven image be created for him that cripples him in coming to himself.
>
> ("Max Frisch," in *Jugend fragt—Prominente Antworten,* ed. Rudolf Ossowski [Berlin, 1975], p. 121)

If the written and printed words by Faber can be considered to constitute the "image" he makes of himself, then we have graphic evidence for his inability to achieve total clarity through his image-making. In *Homo faber*—as opposed to *Stiller*—Frisch retains his protagonist as the sole narrator, but here he not only interrupts the succession in the narrative but also has the narration printed in different typefaces. Thus the last account, written by hand just before Faber's operation, is printed in italics. (Although italics had been used earlier in the novel for various purposes, this section begins *They have taken away my Hermes-Baby.*) His ultimate reliance on his hand instead of a machine symbolizes the failure of the image he has pursued and the impossibility of true self-knowledge without recourse to the strictly human.

Following the eventual success of *Stiller* and the more immediate ones of *Homo faber* and *Biedermann,* Frisch wrote *Andorra,* the last work in his oeuvre that could be called *littérature engagée.* It continued Frisch's use of the "graven image" motif, which lent the early work *When the War Was Over* a timelessness not inherent in the subject of that play. *Andorra* also proved to be Frisch's last dramatic "parable," the form that provides the most tangible evidence for Brecht's influence on him. In his important correspondence with Walter Höllerer (*Dramaturgisches: Ein Briefwechsel mit Walter Höllerer* [Berlin, 1969]), Frisch explained his "discomfort" with the parable form. Earlier he had referred to *Biedermann* and *Andorra* as plays that attempt to save themselves through parable from the "theater of imitation," that is, the illusionary theater that reproduces reality. As he now wrote to Höllerer:

> The parable is a play of meaning [*Sinn-Spiel*]; a process is shown that could hardly take place in reality the way it is being shown. . . . That is the very point: the parable usually works out exactly. A tendency to meaning. It gives the illusion of being explicable, at least of being the result of necessity. At the same time, it claims its validity by remaining vague. The parable, because it forces a lesson on us, blocks me [*verbaut mich*].
>
> (pp. 18f.)

What Frisch has to say about the parable stems not only from his desire to explore new possibilities but also, we may assume, from the reception accorded *Andorra.*

Frisch asserts that the parable makes a claim to validity by remaining vague. In other words, we believe that we understand fully what Frisch is saying, but we do not know exactly about what or whom he is saying it. This point is especially significant because the parable supposedly provides us with a "lesson" about reality, not merely a fictional possibility. In the case of *Biedermann,* Frisch even tries to counteract the natural tendency to see a "lesson" here by adding the subtitle *Ein Lehrstück ohne Lehre* (*A Lesson Piece Without a Lesson*). And Frisch's later works, which likewise represent his reaction against the "theater of imitation," will in fact concentrate on nonbinding "possibilities," in both a dramaturgical and an existential sense.

The "vagueness" of a parable seems to be confirmed by the interpretations of *Andorra.* Once again Frisch, when called upon to write another drama, returned to an idea that had appeared earlier, first in "Du sollst die kein Bildnis machen" (Thou Shalt Not Make Any Graven Image, 1946), then as part of the original *Tagebuch mit Marion* in 1947, and finally as an entry in the *Sketchbook 1946–1949.* The title suggested in the sketchbook was "The Andorran Jew." Although the plot of the final stage version would—like that of *Biedermann* and the other "parable" works—remain exceptionally simple, Frisch first began to work on it in 1958, had to go through five (now-lost) versions, and did not complete it until 1961 (the first performance took place in November of that year). The character Andri, who has supposedly been saved by Andorra's schoolmaster from the Black Ones of the neighboring country, tries to fit into the "image" set for all members of the society. But the inhabitants of Andorra suspect him of being a Jew and thus gradually force him out of the customary course of social integration through marriage with the schoolmaster's daughter, apprenticeship as a cabinetmaker, and so on. In turn, Andri gradually accepts his new "identity" as a Jew. When the militarily stronger Black Ones conquer Andorra without opposition, the inhabitants submit to a "scientific" test for Jewishness and allow Andri to be put to death. In the meanwhile Andri has learned that he is not a Jewish refugee but rather the illegitimate son of the schoolmaster. Marriage to Barblin, the schoolmaster's daughter, would, in light of this revelation, have been incest, but Barblin has also been unfaithful to Andri, who simply accepts his fate as a "Jew." The parabolic nature of *Andorra* is stressed by the following note, which Frisch appended to the play: "The Andorra of this piece has nothing to do with the real little state of this name, neither is another real little state meant; Andorra is the name for a prototype [*Modell*]." Yet *Andorra* bears out how the very simplicity and—as Frisch stresses by rejecting specific counterparts in reality—deliberate vagueness of the parable can lead to varying interpretations.

For the reader familiar with Frisch's novels and earlier dramas, this parable continues his theme of the "graven image." The original sketchbook entry follows the section on the "graven image" by only a few pages, and in another section he writes, "The prerequisite for tolerance (in so far as it can exist) is the consciousness—a consciousness that we can hardly stand—that our thinking is always conditional" (2.522). Even at this time Frisch was thinking in generalities that obviated his linking existential truths to specific instances or places. And after the appearance of *Andorra,* Frisch wrote in a letter to Siegfried Unseld (October 1962): "The piece is not an allegorical illustration of history, but rather it reaches behind the history."

Yet the political implications were too obvious to be ignored so shortly after World War II and the Holocaust. Moreover, the behavior of the inhabitants, including the "heroic" action of the schoolmaster, corresponds patently to what Frisch elsewhere has critically described as typical Swiss behavior during the war. We recall as well that *Biedermann* revealed a strong bent toward criticism of Frisch's countrymen, albeit in a social context. Sensing perhaps a possible identification of Andorra with his homeland, Frisch even felt obligated in his short essay "Die Schweiz ist ein Land ohne Utopie" to assert in reference to the situation of a writer in Switzerland:

> In *Homo faber* I managed for the first time to separate myself completely from it, and today the "Andorra" of my next stage work is no more and no less than the prototype of a society that is not identical with itself—in no way, however, a parable [*Gleichnis*] of Switzerland.
>
> (4.258)

Nonetheless, neither this remark nor any other can conceal the fact that Andorra, by forcing an identity on Andri, does achieve, albeit in a negative manner, an "identity" of sorts for its inhabitants. This identity is, however, a false one, for it is attained by submission to the "graven image" created by the Black Ones and a corresponding loss of individuality. It may be recalled in this context that Frisch in 1953 published an essay entitled "Unsere Arroganz gegenüber Amerika" (Our Arrogance Toward America), whose content implies that Europe has made "graven images" of America and herself alike.

As we have seen, Frisch would certainly be the last person to accept, condone, or excuse what happened in Germany under Hitler. Yet *Andorra* was a controversial play, and some critics managed to see latent anti-Semitism in it. Both this view and the one that Frisch avoids the entire problem of anti-Semitism are based on the play's presentation of Andri's "Jewishness" as a "mistake." However, there is a precedent for Frisch's treatment of the subject. Andri's acceptance of his "Jewishness" parallels the change in Helene, the heroine of Ferdinand Bruckner's play *Die Rassen* (*Races,* 1934). Bruckner (Theodor Tagger), who had a Jewish father, fled Germany in 1933 and wrote this piece as a direct attack on the ideology of the new masters in his former homeland. Helene does not even think about her "Jewishness" until she is forced to do so by the "conversion" of her "Aryan" lover Karlanner to Nazism. Like Andri, she assumes a new identity as a "Jew." Since *Races* was first performed in Zurich in November 1933, Frisch might well have seen the play, which documented the Nazis' imposition of a new "identity" on Jewish Germans, who had previously felt themselves to be primarily Germans, not Jews. Nonetheless, the underlying tendency in Frisch's "parable" on coercion into a new racial identity is still the subject of debate.

The year 1961 also saw the third version of *Öderland,* and 1962 the second version of *Don Juan.* But Frisch's next major new publication was to be his novel *Let My Name Be Gantenbein,* which he had begun in 1960. A first version in manuscript form was finished in May 1963 under the title "Lila oder Ich bin blind" (Lila; or, I Am Blind); according to Frisch, it also contained operatic scenes featuring Hermes, a character mentioned in *Montauk.* There Frisch says that he wanted to write an opera about Hermes as the messenger of the gods but also as the inventor of the lyre and patron of both merchants and thieves. As Walter Schmitz has pointed out, Hermes is also important for Frisch (as well as for Thomas Mann) in his role as psychopomp.

Broadly speaking, this new novel, along with *Zürich-Transit: Skizze eines Films* (1966) and *Biography,* represents an entirely new direction for Frisch, one that has been called an "emigration into the private." While this new course seems to take Frisch away from further confrontation with political and social problems, it remains consistent with the recurring problem of "identity" in his works, a problem that in *When the War Was Over* and *Andorra* stemmed directly from contemporary events.

Not only does *Gantenbein* represent a formal experiment; Frisch's approach to its composition is also new. Most of his theoretical observations regarding his own work have up to this point been made post facto. Now, however, he outlines the theory underlying *Gantenbein* almost from its conception. Frisch's rejection of the "conventional" novel—if in the twentieth century one can still speak of such among serious writers—can be traced back to remarks such as his statement in the first sketchbook that Europe has no more prose narration (*epische Dichtung*) of the sort that America has and the Soviet Union could have:

> Areas of unknown life, unexperienced areas, a world that has not yet been portrayed and is worth mentioning as factual—that is the area of prose narration [*Epik*]. Europe has already portrayed itself often enough, well enough, and more than enough in almost all landscapes, but also in almost all social areas. . . . Our narrators no longer have a world to offer, a decidedly different one, a terra incognita that could change essentially our picture of the world.
>
> Epic is portrayal, communication, not discussion—the discussion of a world that can only be

> portrayed as one that cannot be discussed takes place in drama and there at its clearest; the novel that discusses itself is a late fruit of the conventional narrative [*epische Spätlese*]—the costumed essay-writing of Thomas Mann.
>
> (2.554)

And in his 1956 essay "Vom Umgang mit dem Einfall" (Dealing with Inspiration), Frisch repeats that "we are living in a late period, in a time for writing essays, and it cannot be denied that, at times, the observer surpasses the creator in spiritual power."

In 1960 Frisch published "Unsere Gier nach Geschichten" (Our Greed for Stories). In order to understand fully what moved Frisch to the theory he develops in this essay, one must recall the significance of "chance" in his thinking and work. For example, the last section of his first sketchbook is devoted to the subject of chance (*Zufall*). There Frisch states that we do not need to appeal to God for an explanation of chance events. Instead:

> It would suffice to imagine that always and everywhere we live, everything is present: for me, however, wherever I go and exist, not the totality of what exists determines my behavior but rather only that which is possible, i.e., that part of existence that I can see and hear. We simply live past everything else, even though it is present. . . . What is surprising and exciting in every chance event is that we recognize ourselves; chance shows me that for which I have eyes and ears, for which I have an antenna.
>
> (2.750)

According to Frisch, then, "chance" forces us to ask about reasons and therefore about our place in the scheme of things, but it also provides us with a measure of self-identity. In turn, the life of Walter Faber consists of one chance happening after another, and he, too, dismisses providence as the cause. For example, he says about his meeting his own daughter and becoming her lover: "It could just as well have happened that we simply passed each other by. How could it be providence! It could have come about completely differently." The irony of Faber's statement, however, lies in the implication that their meeting could have been different. He questions not the meeting but the circumstances, and by doing so, he denies himself the opportunity to "identify" himself in terms of the circumstances.

The question becomes one not of probabilities, as Faber maintains, but rather of possibilities. Faber himself, like several of Frisch's other characters, likes to play chess, the game that theoretically leaves no room for chance, and in "Unsere Gier nach Geschichten" Frisch develops his new theory of variations directly from chess. Anyone who follows the notation of a chess game knows that the outcome may be the result of chance or of strictly psychological, illogical factors. For example, Alexander Alekhine, the world champion from 1927 almost uninterruptedly until his death in 1946, was a master of psychological tricks, like Bobby Fischer in the 1960's. When famous games of chess are published, the record of the moves actually made is frequently complemented by discussion of alternative moves. The "variations"—the comments on—specific moves—pursue the logical results that would have stemmed from a different move, at least up to the point where another crucial decision would have to be made. But such "variations," because they exist solely as "possibilities" in the mind of the commentator, are not subject to illogical factors or "chance" happenings like illness that determine the "reality" of the historical game. In *Stiller,* the protagonist was described as having made a "graven image" of Julika, who describes his attitude with the words, "That's the way you are, and that's that!" In other words, he has deprived her of any new "possibilities." She is a game that has been played out and for which there are no more "variations." Now Frisch will carry this concept over to the artist, who, by portraying a person as a "real person" with an existence narrated in the past tense, makes in effect a "graven image" that has no more possibilities, no more "variations."

In "Unsere Gier nach Geschichten" Frisch speaks of how false it seems when a narrator gives details of a remotely past event. Ultimately, we cannot tell a story the way it happened but only as we would relive it today. In fact, he says, we are telling a story in the future rather than in the past tense. *Gantenbein* in turn reveals a predominance of the present tense, for the narrator will not even feign the reality implied by the past tense. In reliving an event in order to tell about it, we are in effect "experiencing ourselves." Consequently:

> By imagining how it could be, for example, if I were to be reborn, that is to say, by inventing what has never been and never will be, my experience [*Erfahrung*] appears purer than if I tried to report how it was at seven o'clock twenty-one years ago.
>
> (4.262)

Here, Frisch's further argument depends on the distinction in German between *Erlebnis* and *Erfahrung.* The former term designates an experience simply as an event in one's life, while the latter is an experience from which one has learned something. Only *Erfahrungen* are important, but they are without a "story" (*Geschichte*), just as the truth, because it has no beginning and no end, is not a story. Frisch continues:

> All stories are invented; they are games of imagination, rough drafts of an *Erfahrung;* and pictures [*Bilder*] are true only as pictures. Every person, not just the writer, invents his stories, but in opposition to the writer, he keeps them for his entire life. Otherwise we would not gain sight of our models for experience [*Erlebnismuster*], our experience of ourselves [*Ich-Erfahrung*].
>
> (4.263)

Thus an *Erfahrung* is an inspiration, not the result of incidents, yet one and the same incident can serve thousands of *Erfahrungen. Erfahrungen,* according to Frisch, do not stem from stories; we usually employ stories—preferably from the past—only to make an *Erfahrung* legible, that is, communicable. While most people have only one story for a lifetime, a writer distinguishes himself by realizing that "each story, regardless of how well it can be documented with facts, is still my invention." Having thus rejected the conventional approach to storytelling as one intended to have an audience draw conclusions from the story and having by implication also rejected the "parable" form of his preceding works, Frisch goes on:

> The *Erfahrung* is an inspiration; the inspiration is the real event; the past is an invention that does not admit to being an invention; it is a model pointing backward. I believe that the decisive turns in a life come from events that have never happened, from flights of imagination that are already there before a story seems to cause them.
>
> (4.264)

In other words, what is real and decisive in our lives are the inspirations, not the stories we make up to explain what we have learned from them. A person is defined by his inspirations; this becomes the basis for *Gantenbein,* for in this novel the only "real" person is the narrator of the stories about Gantenbein, who imagines himself in many situations yet remains the fiction of the narrator. From the narrator we hear only, "I imagine . . ." Over and over again, this narrator "imagines," but we learn nothing about him.

After the appearance of *Gantenbein,* Frisch offered further comments in the form of a fictitious interview, "Ich schreibe für Leser: Antworten auf vorgestellte Fragen" (I Write for Readers: Answers to Imagined Questions, 1964). There Frisch "answers":

> You therefore find that the book-"I" [*Buch-Ich*] is itself not a figure but rather remains a book-"I." Abstract. Or as you say: a white blank. That makes me uncommonly happy. I still remember how in the beginning, when a young friend asked

> me, I explained my intention: I wanted to show the reality of a person by letting him appear as a white blank, surrounded by the sum of fictions that this person is capable of producing. And this silhouette, as far as I was concerned, would be more precise than any biography, which, as we know, is based on suppositions. If you like, this is a negative process.
>
> (5.325)

Here, of course, one recalls Frisch's early sketchbook entry in which he likens himself to a sculptor who cuts away and continues to cut away until only "the white space between the words" is left. What he says about the book-"I" reflects the same view, applied this time to an individual. We are presented an "image" of the book-"I," not as a tangible likeness or "fact," but as the sum of possibilities. The extent to which a person is defined not by what he is but rather by what he could be—this is symbolized by the series of fictions invented by Gantenbein in which he imagines himself to be blind.

Frisch himself admitted that *Gantenbein* has no plot in the conventional sense but also conceded that he was tempted to impose one on the material. Instead, he goes from story to story by association, and even though he rejects chronology, he affirms "time" as important. "Without time," Frisch says, "there is no repetition." And only death terminates the repetition of "variation." The structure of *Gantenbein* has been effectively schematized by Walter Schmitz, who diagrams it as a symmetrical set of boxes, each one nesting within a larger one. In the center are the fables of Ali and Alil, of Philemon and Baucis, separated by an imaginary dividing line. The reader, as Frisch has pointed out, is led through Gantenbein's invented stories by key sentences and phrases: "I try on stories like clothing"; "Every ego that expresses itself with words is a role"; "Sooner or later everyone invents a story for himself that he keeps for his entire life"; "A man has experienced something and now he is looking for a story for it"; "I imagine to myself . . ." Even in the stories that purport to be historically "true" there remains the irony that they have been invented, not by the narrator of a story with a frame, and therefore by a narrator claiming the traditional reality of all fictional characters, but rather by a narrator who is himself a fiction, a character whose entire existence is expressed in the subjunctive mood.

Both with and without Frisch's help, many critics have attempted to ascertain literary and nonliterary sources for this "literature of variations." In some respects, *Gantenbein* represents Frisch's effort to apply Brecht's dramatic "alienation" to prose narration. The novel was written while Frisch was living with Ingeborg Bachmann; Bachmann had written her dissertation on Martin Heidegger, whose theory of "possibilities" as the basis of existence undoubtedly bears a resemblance to Frisch's approach. Pointing to another possible connection, Walter Schmitz says, "Max Frisch's narrative theory of 'stories' paraphrases the philosophy of stories by Wilhelm Schapp." Schapp's book, *In Geschichten verstrickt: Zum Sein von Mensch und Ding* (Entangled in Stories: On the Existence of Man and Thing), first appeared in 1953. An echo of Robert Musil's lengthy, uncompleted novel *Der Mann ohne Eigenschaften* (*The Man Without Qualities,* 1930–1942) can also be heard. And most certainly one cannot discount C. G. Jung's theories and the influence of the French existentialists, especially Sartre and Camus. In general, however, one does not need to go into such details to recognize that Frisch, for all his protests about not being a philosopher, placed himself right in the middle of postwar thinking and writing. He even claims to have gone farther than the French *nouveau roman* and says that many other names could be given as sources of inspiration: Uwe Johnson, Günter Grass, Martin Walser, J. D. Salinger.

In *Gantenbein,* Frisch is, of course, not writing about someone who seems to have existed within the conventions of fiction; he writes about the creation of stories about people (Lila,

Camilla, Enderlin, Svoboda) who all exist only in the imagination of someone else, and this someone else is arbitrarily called "Gantenbein" by a narrator whom we can discern by what he is not. *Gantenbein* is as much a discussion of literary reception as it is a novel itself. It does not surprise us that Frisch, rather than simply producing still more novels of this sort, now applies his new theory of "possibilities" to other media. That these media would be dramatic can be assumed from the predominance of the present, for drama knows only the present tense, even when dealing with past events. Everything is happening and being said at the same moment that the audience learns about it.

In his "Schillerpreis-Rede" (Talk on Receiving the Schiller Prize) in 1965, one year after the publication of *Gantenbein,* Frisch outlined his intentions. In this speech he rejects the classical *Dramaturgie der Fügung* (dramatic composition by arrangement), which shows events and situations to be the product of necessity. Remembering that Frisch was once inspired by Ibsen, we realize that here he is rejecting not only "classical" drama but also that of Ibsen and naturalism, as well as Brecht's "parable" form. All of these approaches, as different as they otherwise might be from one another, impute a "sense" [*Sinn*] to events. Now Frisch, following the "negative process" of *Gantenbein,* views events in terms of what has been eliminated, not what has survived. Regarding the "sense" of the factual world, or the dramatic world that implies factuality, Frisch says:

> We never experience [such a sense], and what we do experience is the opposite: something happens, while something else that would be just as possible does not happen, and this is never really a matter of a single action or omission. Wherever we reach a decision it proves to be the gesture of someone who is being manipulated but does not know by what he is being manipulated. We know only that everything following the gesture of deciding could proceed otherwise. What the last act shows us is not the necessary consequence of a dramatic climax but rather the result of a sum of chances. To be sure, necessity can be recognized for many events, but it still has only the value of probability, nothing more.
>
> (5.367f.)

Thus, according to Frisch, we could just as easily imagine that the attempted assassination of Hitler had succeeded. There are no plots with given, clear-cut climaxes or turning points in life. Therefore, Frisch seeks a dramaturgical approach "that accents the accidental nature of events [*Zufälligkeit*], if you like, a dramaturgy of disbelief, a drama of permutations." Obviously, Frisch's argument on discerning cause and effect in real events echoes that raised in the eighteenth century by the English empiricists. More important, however, is the fact that he calls his approach a "dramaturgy of disbelief" in contrast with the previous dramas of "arrangement" (*Fügung*), for the word *Fügung* also means "providence." In essence, Frisch is therefore calling upon the dramatist to stop playing God.

Frisch attempts his "drama of permutations" in *Biography,* which the subtitle identifies as a *Spiel,* or "game." Although the above remarks imply a theoretical link with *Gantenbein,* Frisch does not go directly from the novel to a stage work. The connections with *Gantenbein* are also of a practical nature that can be seen in *Zürich-Transit,* the "sketch for a film" that Frisch wrote in 1965. For the plot he uses a story told by Gantenbein to his friend Camilla Huber; here, once again, the protagonist tries out "variations," but this time in order to reach a decision. Despite support from Atlas-Filmproduktion, however, *Zürich-Transit* was never produced. As Frisch later wrote to Walter Höllerer, the entire concept of "variations" lends itself best to narrative fiction, because once filmed or presented on the stage, the "variations" take on too much of a real existence, that is, they lose their purely fictional quality.

If *Gantenbein* is an exercise in how to write narrative prose without committing oneself, then *Biography* is, in no small part, a treatise on how to dramatize without committing the characters to anything but their own imagination and the rules of the director. The protagonist, Dr. Hannes Kürmann (his name, a play on the German word *Kür,* means in essence "elector"), goes back in time repeatedly in order to make changes in his life, that is, his biography. The director, who has the files, also holds, one might say, the book of rules for this game. As in so many other works by Frisch, this work, too, primarily concerns the protagonist's relationship to a woman, Kürmann's wife, Antoinette, whom he needs but simultaneously rejects.

The words of the director to Kürmann are crucial to an understanding of Kürmann's "biography": "You see: you are not behaving according to the present but rather according to memory. That's it. You think that your memory allows you to know the future. For that reason it is always the same story" (5.492). This means in concrete terms, as the director says, "You consider yourself an expert on women because you commit the same mistakes with every woman." Kürmann tries to dispute this statement by changing his politics and other aspects of his previous life in order to prove that he is not a "cybernetic" person. Yet toward the end the director says:

> The same apartment. The same story with Antoinette. Only without a slap on the ear. You changed that. Moreover, you went to the party without becoming someone else. What else? You kept more or less to your diet. That's all you've changed, and we have put on this whole show just for that?
>
> (5.562)

Of course, a biography is usually written when its subject is dead. At the end of the play, which repeats the opening scene, the director says, "You are free—for another seven years." There has been no providence, no fate. Yet Kürmann has never really been free, nor will he be so now.

Although the style of this play, in which the characters are also self-consciously actors, may recall the "alienation effects" of Brecht, Frisch's "notes" include the following lines: "The piece does not prove anything. The director who directs the play represents no metaphysical power. He says what Kürmann himself knows or could know. Not a *conférencier,* he never addresses the audience but rather assists Kürmann by objectifying him" (5.579). Brecht wants his audience to "study" events on the stage and then apply the lessons learned to life. To this purpose he uses the theatrical device of addressing the audience, be it through a character, a song, or a placard. Frisch's approach remains psychological. As he says in his short comment of 1968 on *Biography* ("In My Own Defense"):

> It is played the way it could otherwise have happened. Thus not the biography of Herr Kürmann, which is "banal," but rather his relationship to the fact that a person after a certain time indisputably has one and only one single biography—that is the theme of the piece. I meant it as a comedy. The fact that someone has to die does not contradict the idea of a comedy; otherwise there would be no comedy with human beings. Our very consciousness that we are going to die gives rise to the question whether another biography would have been possible. The theater allows what reality does not: to repeat, to try out, to change . . .
>
> (5.582)

Even though Kürmann in one of his "variations" joins the Communist party in order to change his biography, we recognize that Frisch has indeed—and in direct opposition to Brecht—simply accepted the "facts" of our lives as unchangeable. They just do not prove anything.

This very eschewal of political lessons was praised when *Biography* first appeared on the stage. It became a popular success in the German theater season of 1967–1968. But as a play about playwriting it could have no sequel. Like *Zürich-Transit,* it would be the last of its kind, and for much the same reason that Frisch hints at above. In *Gantenbein,* which launches Frisch's series of works on "variations," the book-"I" exhausts all the stories he can invent without defining himself directly; the only thing left uninvented at the end of *Gantenbein* would be the introduction—as in *Stiller*—of a third-person narrator, and that would obviate the point of the novel. In *Biography,* Frisch, as a playwright, has nothing left to prove. For he is concerned not with a single biography but rather with "biography" itself (significantly, there is no article in the German title). *Gantenbein,* as its German title conveys, was conceived as a work in the subjunctive mood. But drama knows no subjunctive. Even when "imagining," Kürmann seems as real as any other stage character. Further biographies would lead only to more individuals like Kürmann, and each would himself tend to become a fictionally "historical" person and, by comparison, make his predecessors seem even more "historical."

Following the production of *Biography,* Frisch traveled to Russia in 1968, to Japan in 1969, and to the United States in 1970, 1971, 1972, and 1974. His main publications during these years were *Wilhelm Tell: A School Text, Sketchbook 1966–1971,* the fourth version of *The Chinese Wall,* and *Dienstbüchlein.* In 1975 he visited China with the delegation of the chancellor of West Germany, Helmut Schmidt, and in 1976 he published his impressions of that trip in *Der Spiegel.* In 1975 he also published *Montauk,* which he had written in the summer of 1974 and which has been called his "most private book."

In *Montauk* Frisch remarks that he "would like to narrate without inventing anything along the way." He calls this "a naive narrative perspective." What evolves is both autobiography and, as the subtitle proclaims, a "tale" (*Erzählung*). Consequently we have a plethora not only of details from Frisch's own life and of diary-like entries, but also of "stories." We also experience shifts in narration between the first and the third person. The narrator of *Stiller, Homo faber,* and *Gantenbein* is in each case an intellectual construct, and these works seem to be exercises in the art and limits of narration itself. Now Frisch, who prefixes *Montauk* with Montaigne's statement "I am the person I am portraying," remains true to his view of narration as self-revelation. Yet while he implies an approach as "naive" as that of Walter Faber, at the same time he produces a work of many levels and dimensions. Above all, it is a work that confronts death with the written word. In his second sketchbook Frisch invented and codified a suicide club; now, in the section of the novel entitled "Montauk Beach," he writes, "I have never undertaken a serious attempt at suicide, but also no unserious one. I have merely, at every age, thought often about it." Yet this is also a book of hope, for Frisch's own narration attests to the human imagination that is both fact and possibility.

Frisch returned once more to writing for the stage with *Triptychon: Drei szenische Bilder* (*Triptych: Three Scenic Panels,* 1978), the second scene of which he had begun in September 1976 and completed, in the first draft, in November 1977. There followed many revisions until, in January 1978, the twelfth and final version was completed. It is worth noting that the original title of the piece was "Styx," for in the central "panel" Frisch depicts, as he did in *Now They Sing Again,* the world of the dead. Despite extensive revisions, however, the path of this work onto the stage was marked by numerous hurdles, not the least of which were Frisch's own insecurity about it and the fact that theatrical groups expressed a negative opinion of it and declined to produce it. Although the text was published in 1978, the play was not performed until Easter 1979, and then merely as a radio play, a medium that ran patently counter to the generic implications of a title gleaned from the field of graphic art. Finally the work appeared on the stage on 9 October 1979, in a French translation for the Centre Dramatique de Lausanne. In December 1979 Frisch reworked the text (printed in September 1980), and the first production in German was on 1 February 1981 in Vienna. Obviously, this latest work was no repetition of the dramatic successes of previous years.

The reasons for the failure of *Triptych* are numerous. Alexander Stephan has listed many of the familiar motifs and themes that Frisch, to his own disadvantage, repeated here, most significant among them being the inability of man and woman to arrive at a lasting relationship. At many points in the play, Frisch simply seems to be quoting himself for the sake of the initiated (of whom there were, by now, a large number).

Lest these comments be interpreted as the reflection of a decline in Frisch's dramaturgical inventiveness, however, the experimental nature of *Triptych* and the problems inherent in Frisch's approach should be noted. The title deliberately implies that the stage work will have an essentially static quality, but the piece remains too static. The plot, if one can even speak of one, shows little progress, and any unity among the three scenes is mainly the result of the intellectual tensions created by the relationships among the various characters and the ideas they represent. A triptych is, of course, a group of three pictures that, by being joined together, provide both successive movement and a simultaneous impression for the eye. We would normally scan a triptych from left to right, and Frisch seems to imply such a movement by going from the first "scenic panel" (death) through the second (Hades) to the third (life). Yet these scenes remain scenes without actions. In the last scene Roger, who is supposedly still alive, confronts his lover, Francine, only to discover that he, too, is dead—an insight that, by returning to the theme of the first scene, is intended to impart to the audience the feeling that it has seen the entire work simultaneously. Frisch has abandoned the approach he used in *Biography,* yet the previous play came closer to achieving the mutual effect of simultaneousness and succession. Although the dramaturgy of permutations in *Biography,* as Frisch saw, cannot overcome certain problems that are produced by the very nature of drama as a genre, *Triptych,* which abandons completely the concept of "variations," for that very reason falls even shorter of achieving succession. By returning over and over again to the same starting point, Kürmann leaves us with the impression that all his "variations" are occurring simultaneously. Yet each one has a plot of sorts or at least leads us to believe that it has direction.

Some critics have seen in *Biography* the influence of Pirandello's *Sei personaggi in cerca d'autore* (*Six Characters in Search of an Author,* 1921). In the case of *Triptych,* comparisons have been made with Thornton Wilder, Sartre, and Giraudoux, as well as with the turn-of-the-century expressionistic dramas of Strindberg. The earlier work supports such a comparison, for Frisch did indeed study Pirandello's works intensively in Rome during the genesis of *Biography.* Of course, he goes far beyond—or stops short of—the Italian's six characters, for they are searching for a meaningful existence through art, while Kürmann wants only to free himself from a banal "biography" that he considers inadequate to describe his real self. In *Triptych,* on the other hand, Frisch simply has little to add that is new, in terms of either an effective technique or substantial ideas.

Almost simultaneously with his *Triptych,* Frisch created a long "tale" that most critics agree represents a major work for its author and for the 1970's, both in theme and in technique: *Der Mensch erscheint im Holozän* (*Man in the Holocene*). The first draft goes back to 1972, that is, to a time before the publication of *Dienstbüchlein* and *Montauk* as well as *Triptych.* In May 1974 a fragment with the title "Klima" (Climate) was published in which the narrator seems to be telling the protagonist the protagonist's own story. Between then and November 1977 twelve more versions evolved, and from August to November 1978 the final text was created (Frisch did not even formulate the work's ultimate title until October 1978). The book was published in March 1979.

At first many critics, albeit on slim evidence and despite the final shift to a third-person narration, wanted to see in *Man in the Holocene* yet another autobiographical work, but

Frisch puts such suggestions to rest in an interview with Fritz Raddatz (*Die Zeit,* 17 April 1981). To be sure, Frisch revealed in the interview that he did have a real-life model for Geiser, but added:

> Am I for that reason Herr Geiser? In the valley there was an old man by the name of Armand Schulthess, formerly a civil servant, a hermit who now, at an advanced age, suddenly wanted to know everything. Like *Bouvard and Peuchet,* the foolish encyclopedists. And like my Herr Geiser, who wallpapers his living room with incoherent bits of information from lexica. In order to feel at home in this world! Armand Schulthess went about it differently; he wrote everything on the lids of tin cans and nailed them to the trees on his property, Einstein's equation, literary quotations, statistics, and so forth.

Frisch is not Geiser, the seventy-three-year-old pensioner and widower who has let the picture of his dead wife fall down behind the mantelpiece, no more so than Geiser is Schulthess. Geiser becomes not a writer, not even an inscriber of tin-can lids, but a collector living under the threat of an impending natural catastrophe. Although this tale touches upon some of Frisch's main concerns in his earlier works as well as upon the theme of death, one of the main concerns of his later works, it is not specifically about either Frisch or an old eccentric he once knew. It shows man as man appeared in the Holocene.

If in *Triptych* Frisch was unable simultaneously to communicate a feeling of the passage of time and yet make time seem to stand still, then his accomplishment of this feat alone raises *Man in the Holocene* to an important position among his works. Aside from the jungle scenes in *Homo faber,* Frisch's previous work contains few descriptions of nature and no notable confrontations with it. Here, on the other hand, nature seems to stand still, yet stretches out as a symbol both of the infinite past and of what will destroy man while itself never ceasing to be. For that very reason, nature reminds man of his own death. Man is the only being with a sense of history. At the same time Geiser, a refugee from civilization and "progress," has withdrawn to a valley that, as he recognizes, has no future but apparently no past as well, for just as there is no hope that the valley will ever prosper, there is no indication that it has ever really prospered. Now the valley is being threatened by a summer storm. Eventually the road is washed out, the power lines disrupted. Inspired by the one great experience in his life, when he climbed a mountain, Geiser begins to climb out of the valley but returns to wait for death, which will follow soon.

A significant point is that the text of *Man in the Holocene* has the appearance of a collage. For one thing, we are told that Geiser is not content to copy articles out of the encyclopedia; instead, he cuts them out and saves them. Here Frisch realizes his description—and himself overcomes the "epic past" he despises—by literally cutting articles from reference works (he gives the sources in notes) and pasting them into the text. Some are in *Fraktur* (the old German typeface), others in modern print, arranged between passages that present the words of the narrator about Geiser, who is attempting to "fix" his own existence by saving the clippings (which represent the knowledge of mankind as a whole). At the same time Geiser is trying to save the Holocene as the period of human knowledge. As we know, man really appeared on earth in the Pleistocene, not the Holocene, and one of Geiser's clippings reads: "According to currently accepted view, man appeared first in the Pleistocene (Old Stone Age); the earth's historical present takes place in the Holocene." Man became man, it is said, when he became conscious of the past and, with it, the future; thus man did not become a significant factor until the Holocene. In other words, Geiser (or rather Frisch, as the one furnishing the clippings) is trying to achieve his modern identity among living things, not only in reference to geological formations and extinct species but also in reference to man as the sole representative of moral and cultural meaning in the world. Only man experiences catastrophes as such, and only man can impute moral significance to them. Geiser transcends the scientific thinking of Walter Faber, for included among the clippings are extracts from the Bible describing the Creation and the Flood, the latter seen as a punishment of man through nature. Another clipping presents a definition of eschatology. Then, at a point marking the near–geometric center of the tale, Frisch inserts a definition of man.

Yet Geiser realizes, about two-thirds of the way through the tale, "that there is a God even though there will someday be no more human beings who cannot imagine a creation without a creator—this is not proved by the Bible and the frescos of the Madonna. The Bible was written by human beings" (7.271). Ultimately, Geiser achieves consciousness of his humanity without God, and his clippings lose their significance. But even this achievement is unimportant in the face of the very things that led up to it:

> The ants that Herr Geiser recently observed under a dripping pine do not care whether man knows about them; neither do the dinosaurs, which died out even before man ever saw them. All the notes, whether they are on the wall or on the carpet, can disappear. What does *Holocene* mean! Nature needs no names. Herr Geiser knows that. The rock formations have no need of his memory.
>
> (7.296)

The tale closes with an idyllic description of the valley, which has been spared from catastrophe. Geiser is waiting for his death. There is no note of triumph of nature over Geiser, however, for nature is unfeeling and without memory—just as it has no moral intentions and is completely indifferent to man.

Frisch's next major work, *Blaubart: Eine Erzählung* (*Bluebeard: A Tale*), was written between October and December 1981. The story was published in serial form in *Frankfurter allgemeine Zeitung* in February and March 1982, and the book edition appeared in March 1982. In 1983 Frisch collaborated with Krzysztof Zanussi on the scenario for a television film of *Bluebeard,* which was broadcast in 1984, first in Switzerland, then in West Germany. The text was published in 1985.

In *Bluebeard,* as in *Stiller,* Frisch seems to make use of many ingredients from the genre of the mystery novel. This time, however, the tale begins with the verdict. Dr. Felix Schaad, a fifty-four-year-old physician, has earned his ominous-sounding nickname through his many divorces. The name "Bluebeard" thereby becomes an ironic comment on Schaad's banal bourgeois existence. Before the tale begins, one of Schaad's former wives, Rosalinde Zogg—now a successful prostitute with a Porsche—has been murdered, and Schaad's tie has been implicated as a murder weapon. Although his marriage to Rosalinde had been plagued by his jealousy, since the divorce he has been seeing her on a friendly basis. Now Schaad has been accused of the crime, but as the story opens, he has already been found innocent due to lack of evidence. In the course of the story, flashback scenes permit us to experience the trial along with Schaad, and we are also privy to Schaad's diary entries and dreams. What psychiatrists and others around Schaad provide in the way of information about this physician, husband of Rosalinde (and many other women), and respected citizen remains inadequate both as evidence of his legal guilt in the crime and as a revelation of his "identity." As the symbol of his social identity, his very name is just as ambiguous as is the appearance he makes to others: *Felix* means "happy" or "fortunate," and the name *Schaad* is a play on the German interjection *schade,* meaning "too bad" or "it's a pity."

As the story progresses, Schaad's rethinking of the evidence becomes a search for his identity, one that leads to "alternative" answers for the district attorney, to diary entries, and to dreams about his childhood and mother, all of which, as views of himself from within, help him arrive at a personal sense of guilt. Now he tries to confess to the murder, but in the meantime the police have found the "real" murderer. At the end of the tale, having tried to put an end to the ceaseless trial in his own mind by driving his Volvo into a tree, Schaad lies in the hospital, where a voice is telling him about his innocence. His seventh wife has left the modern "Bluebeard," whose guilt is no longer punishable (as was that of his predecessor). Society has judged him on the "facts," as it were, the "story" of the crime. Like so many other characters in Frisch's works, Schaad sees his guilt as an experience (*Erfahrung*) against which the real-life story is only incidental.

Schaad ends as a person whose recognition of his guilt—that is, his identity—is not based on the same criteria as the verdict of the "outside world." For the reader the former seems truer, but the same reader must accept the latter (within the realm of fiction) as the "historically real." Once again Frisch leaves his audience with the same question that he has posed all along, from *Öderland, Stiller, Homo faber,* and *Gantenbein* right on through *Man in the Holocene.* In each of these works the protagonist assumes a new role, invents stories about himself, creates "graven images" of himself and others, and even tries to test nature for a moral purpose that will confirm his identity. The stories and all other inventions of an individual's mind do indeed become a truer measure of his identity in the world than what really happens or has happened. Frisch frequently uses the phrase "to become identical with oneself." But if seen from this perspective, can the "truth" about oneself ever provide a person with the identity he seeks, or can it only make him all the more conscious of his inability to escape playing a role, albeit a cosmic one? Is the search for identity, like the need to invent stories, really terminated by death?

## *FRISCH AS A "MODERN" AUTHOR*

In respect to his ideas on literature and his techniques, Frisch seems to manifest the influence of, or at least an affinity with, many forerunners in German and world literature. Like Gottfried Keller, the great Swiss writer of the nineteenth century, he displays an obvious joy in simply telling stories in a personal tone. Yet he combines this bent with a self-conscious emphasis on complicated narrative technique for its own sake that recalls similar tendencies in the works of Keller's contemporary countryman Conrad Ferdinand Meyer. When Frisch extols the unlimited imagination and when he implies that only literature provides the truth, we sense a spiritual kinship especially with Novalis but also with other German Romantics. Yet such comparisons only substantiate that he, like any other writer, represents a continuation, in greater and lesser measure, of many conventions, traditions, and ideas. In order to understand the strictly "modern" appeal of Frisch's works, we must look at the problems he raises and at those figures of the past who, because they deal with similar problems, have just come into their own as "modern."

One might say that Frisch is writing for the "outsiders" in a world that consists only of "outsiders." His true theme is therefore one of "identity," both his own and that of others. In his first sketchbook, that covering the years 1946 to 1949, he compares the writer to a seismograph: "One holds the pen to paper like a needle in an earthquake observatory, and, properly speaking, we are not what is writing; instead, we are being written. Writing means reading ourselves." "Individuality" signifies what is peculiarly our own against a backdrop seen as homogeneously different. "Identity," on the other hand, describes our individuality as a part of a larger scheme. Our belief in our individuality must be retained if our identity is to have any meaning, for without individuality we would be completely described by sociology or biology. And Frisch, as we have seen, is unwilling to submit all of man's existence to the methods of either, which at best describe only class or race.

In the twentieth century, mass movements,

tyrannical ideologies, and world-changing events have either demanded the suppression of all feelings of individuality or forced many people to assume new identities. In either case individuals have been deprived of the social, political, or religious system according to which they had once had a sense of identity. At best, the people who still thought of themselves as individuals found themselves confronted by a different social and political order not of their making. At worst, they saw themselves living in a world that had simply discarded all their social and religious values. Under these circumstances the world, as Camus and others have pointed out, is an "unfamiliar" one. What happens in such an unfamiliar world seems like mere "chance," for it entails no discernibly higher purpose. When we, as individuals, can no longer identify our own role in either the new events or the circumstances brought about by them, we feel like "outsiders" and therefore bereft of an identity. Yet as individuals we necessarily seek an identity, however hopeless this search may be.

There have, of course, been periods in history when human beings had a strong feeling of identity, most notably during the Middle Ages. Identity in the medieval world was assured by a divinely ordained social hierarchy, and changes within this framework were not attributed to chance but subordinated to a divine plan. Since that time other alternatives have been advanced to explain "chance" events: in the eighteenth century, for example, one applied "reason"; in the nineteenth century one appealed to "scientific truth." But whenever authors—as often in the wake of social, political, or religious upheaval—have had to accept "chance" as the only explanation for both past and present events, there has been a corresponding concern with "identity." For example, Christian Dietrich Grabbe provides the hero of his play *Herzog Theodor von Gothland* (*Duke Theodor of Gothland,* 1827) with the following supposed insight: "Man himself reads the good into world history when he reads it because he is too cowardly to admit to himself its cruel truth" (act 2, scene 1). Almost all of Grabbe's heroes—Faust, Napoleon, Hannibal, and so on—have finally to concede that chance determines their lot. At the end of their respective dramas, they can only hope to live on as great individuals in other men's memories. The only one who manages to retain his identity is Don Juan, but he does so at a great sacrifice. At the end he asserts defiantly: "What I am, I remain. If I am Don Juan, then I am nothing, if I become someone else. I would prefer to remain Don Juan in the pit of brimstone than to become a saint in the light of paradise." Interestingly enough, Frisch's Don Juan accepts the argument that the world "needs" his legendary identity. Frisch knew Grabbe's play and on several occasions alluded to Grabbe's contemporary Georg Büchner, another writer for whom the issue of identity was important. In the latter's comedy *Leonce und Lena* (1836), in which two lovers try to escape their own planned wedding but encounter each other "by chance," Leonce, who suffers from "boredom" (i.e., from a lack of any belief that would give his actions purpose), asks why he cannot become someone else. And many of Frisch's works in turn—*Stiller* and *Gantenbein,* for example, as well as the comedies *Don Juan* and *The Great Rage of Philipp Hotz*—concern a person's need or desire to become someone else.

Both Grabbe and Büchner first gained acceptance in the twentieth century, particularly after the world wars. They had, of course, written their works shortly after the Napoleonic wars, which had—like any modern wars—destroyed the established political systems. Their works stem from a time when the idealistic explanations of existence, borne mainly by Romanticism, were losing their conviction. In other words, Grabbe and Büchner created their works when many of the old measures of individual identity had been destroyed or at least rendered questionable.

In a similar vein it has been correctly stressed by critics that Frisch started publishing during the 1930's. But Frisch gained popularity only after he and his readers had lived through the Spanish Civil War, World War II, and countless smaller wars and insurrections—quite aside from the periods of inflation, depression, and racial oppression that arose throughout Europe during this time. In trying to understand the appeal of Frisch as a "modern" writer, we must keep in mind how all these events caused individuals throughout the Western world to lose their confidence in the prevailing systems and values—social, religious, or economic—that had given them a sense of identity. All of these events had their most devastating effects in Germany. Naturally one can argue that Frisch lived in Switzerland, which never experienced the full impact of these catastrophes. Yet this does not alter the fact that, especially since World War II, the question of "identity" has come to be seen as "modern." One need only think of the emergence of existentialism in the postwar years.

Frisch's initial popularity stemmed from the West German reception of his works during the 1950's. To use Frisch's own "seismograph" image, anything located at the epicenter of an earthquake will be destroyed, much as in Germany itself, where in 1945 the writers could only speak of "the year zero." But an instrument situated as close as possible to the fault of an earthquake, yet left intact by the catastrophe, will give us the most accurate reading. While Frisch's works for the most part neither deal directly with the cataclysmic occurrences in Germany nor reflect the immediate bitterness, disappointment, and despair of many Germans, they do demonstrate a concern for the loss of identity of human beings in the modern world—regardless of the subject matter and Frisch's own motives for writing.

Ultimately the modernity of a writer's works has less to do with his nationality or even the intention of any specific piece than with his innate, instinctive, or even accidental ability to address a modern audience's deep-rooted general concerns; this applies to a Büchner as well as a Frisch. Regarding his own identity as a celebrated writer, Frisch writes in *Montauk:*

> [The famous writer] can, by the way, be a disappointment as a person, for example, if he is unhappy. If it turns out that he disavows a part or all of his oeuvre, then that is his business: his self-esteem is not binding on others; the name that he received at birth and has used his entire life denotes a public influence and has divorced itself from his person. . . . Fame does not produce the cessation of criticism. One only expects that the criticism will be directed not against the person and his work but against the fame. Society needs famous people. Whom does it, however, make into a celebrity? Criticism becomes criticism of society.
>
> (6.655f)

The many translations of Frisch's works clearly indicate that his audience is not limited to one country or group of countries. In that sense, he is not merely a Swiss author or a German-speaking author but a "modern" author. If we in turn, as Frisch says, "read ourselves" when we read his works, then we are doing so as modern individuals. And when we criticize them, we are criticizing the situation of modern society in general.

## Selected Bibliography

### EDITIONS

#### INDIVIDUAL WORKS

*Jürg Reinhart: Eine sommerliche Schicksalsfahrt, Roman.* Stuttgart, 1934.

*Antwort aus der Stille: Eine Erzählung aus den Bergen.* Stuttgart, 1937.

*Blätter aus dem Brotsack: Tagebuch eines Kanoniers.* Zurich, 1940.

*J'adore ce qui me brûle; oder, Die Schwierigen.* Zurich, 1943. Second version. *Die Schwierigen; oder, J'adore ce qui me brûle.* Zurich, 1957.

*Bin; oder, Die Reise nach Peking.* Zurich, 1945.

*Marion und die Marionetten: Ein Fragment.* Basel, 1946.

*Nun singen sie wieder: Versuch eines Requiems.* Basel, 1946.

*Die chinesische Mauer: Eine Farce.* Basel, 1947. Second version. Frankfurt, 1955. Third version. Unpublished. Fourth version. *Die chinesische Mauer: Eine Farce. Version für Paris, 1972.* Frankfurt, 1972.

*Santa Cruz: Eine Romanze.* Basel, 1947.

*Tagebuch mit Marion.* Zurich, 1947.

*Als der Krieg zu Ende war: Schauspiel.* Basel, 1949. Second version in *Stücke,* vol. 1. Frankfurt, 1962.

*Tagebuch 1946–1949.* Frankfurt, 1950.

*Graf Öderland: Ein Spiel in zehn Bildern.* Frankfurt, 1951. Second version. Unpublished. Third version. "Graf Öderland: Eine Moritat in zwölf Bildern." *Spectaculum 4.* Frankfurt, 1961.

*Don Juan; oder, Die Liebe zur Geometrie: Komödie in fünf Akten.* Frankfurt, 1953. Second version in *Stücke,* vol. 2. Frankfurt, 1962.

*Stiller.* Frankfurt, 1954.

*Herr Biedermann und die Brandstifter: Hörspiel.* Hamburg, 1955.

*achtung: Die Schweiz. Ein Gespräch über unsere Lage und ein Vorschlag zur Tat.* Basel, 1955. Written with Lucius Burckhardt and Markus Kutter.

*Die neue Stadt: Beiträge zur Diskussion.* Basel, 1956. Written with Lucius Burckhardt and Markus Kutter.

*Homo faber: Ein Bericht.* Frankfurt, 1957.

*Biedermann und die Brandstifter: Ein Lehrstück ohne Lehre; mit einem Nachspiel.* Frankfurt, 1958.

"Die grosse Wut des Philipp Hotz: Sketch." *Hortulus* (St. Gallen) 8 (2):34–50 (1958).

"Rip van Winkle: Hörspiel." In *Kreidestriche ins Ungewisse: Zwölf deutsche Hörspiele nach 1945.* Edited by Gerhard Prager. Darmstadt, 1960.

*Andorra: Stück in zwölf Bildern.* Frankfurt, 1961.

*Mein Name sei Gantenbein.* Frankfurt, 1964.

*Zürich-Transit: Skizze eines Films.* Frankfurt, 1966.

*Biografie: Ein Spiel.* Frankfurt, 1967. 2d, rev. ed.: 1968. New version, 1984: Frankfurt, 1985.

*Dramaturgisches: Ein Briefwechsel mit Walter Höllerer.* Berlin, 1969.

*Wilhelm Tell für die Schule.* Frankfurt, 1971.

*Tagebuch 1966–1971.* Frankfurt, 1972.

*Dienstbüchlein.* Frankfurt, 1974.

*Montauk: Eine Erzählung.* Frankfurt, 1975.

*Triptychon: Drei szenische Bilder.* Frankfurt, 1978. Revised version (1979) in *Spectaculum 33.* Frankfurt, 1980.

*Der Mensch erscheint im Holozän: Eine Erzählung.* Frankfurt, 1979.

*Blaubart: Eine Erzählung.* Frankfurt, 1982.

*Blaubart: Ein Buch zum Film von Krzysztof Zanussi.* Frankfurt, 1985.

*Schweiz ohne Armee? Ein Palaver.* Zurich, 1989.

COLLECTED WORKS

*Stücke.* 2 vols. Frankfurt, 1962.

*Öffentlichkeit als Partner.* Frankfurt, 1967. Contains "Festrede," "Kultur als Alibi," "Unsere Arroganz gegenüber Amerika," "Überfremdung 1," "Überfremdung 2," and "Endlich darf man es wieder sagen."

*Stücke.* 2 vols. Frankfurt, 1972–1973. The same as the 1962 *Stücke* with two exceptions: a new version of *Die chinesische Mauer* (Paris, 1972) and the inclusion of *Biografie: Ein Spiel.*

*Stich-Worte.* Edited by Uwe Johnson. Frankfurt, 1975.

*Gesammelte Werke in zeitlicher Folge.* 6 vols. Edited by Hans Mayer with Walter Schmitz. Frankfurt am Main, 1976. (Also in a 12-volume paper edition.)

*Gesammelte Werke in zeitlicher Folge: Jubiläumsausgabe in sieben Bänden, 1931–1985.* 1986. (The first six volumes are identical to the previous edition, which was checked for mistakes. Although no one collection includes all publications by Frisch, the seventh volume of this one has an updated bibliography, including newspaper articles and translations.)

TRANSLATIONS

*Andorra.* Translated by Michael Bullock. New York, 1964.

*Biography: A Game.* Translated by Michael Bullock. New York, 1969.

*Bluebeard: A Tale.* Translated by Geoffrey Skelton. New York, 1983.

*The Chinese Wall.* Translated by James L. Rosenberg. New York, 1961.

*The Firebugs: A Learning-Play Without a Lesson.* Translated by Mordecai Gorelik. New York, 1963.

*The Fire Raisers: A Morality Without a Moral, with an Afterpiece.* Translated by Michael Bullock. London, 1962.

*Four Plays: The Great Wall of China; Don Juan; or, The Love of Geometry; Philipp Hotz's Fury; Biography: A Game.* Translated by Michael Bullock. London, 1969.

*Gantenbein: A Novel.* Translated by Michael Bullock. London, 1982.

"The Great Fury of Philip Hotz." Translated by Michael Benedikt. In *Postwar German Theatre: An Anthology of Plays,* edited by Michael Benedikt and George E. Wellwarth. New York, 1967.

*Homo faber: A Report.* Translated by Michael Bullock. New York, 1959.

*I'm Not Stiller.* Translated by Michael Bullock. New York, 1958.

*Man in the Holocene: A Story.* Translated by Geoffrey Skelton. New York, 1980.

*Montauk.* Translated by Geoffrey Skelton. New York, 1976.

"Now They Sing Again." Translated by David Lommen. In *The Contemporary German Theater,* edited by Michael Roloff. New York, 1972.

*Sketchbook 1946–1949.* Translated by Geoffrey Skelton. New York, 1977.

*Sketchbook 1966–1971.* Translated by Geoffrey Skelton. New York, 1974.

*Three Plays: Don Juan; or, The Love of Geometry; The Great Rage of Philip Hotz; When the War Was Over.* Translated by James L. Rosenberg. New York, 1967.

*Three Plays: The Fire Raisers (with an Afterpiece); Count Oderland; Andorra.* Translated by Michael Bullock. London, 1962.

*Triptych: Three Scenic Panels.* Translated by Geoffrey Skelton. New York, 1981.

*A Wilderness of Mirrors* [*Mein Name sei Gantenbein*]. Translated by Michael Bullock. London, 1965.

"Wilhelm Tell: A School Text." Translated by Lore Segal and Paul Stern. *Fiction* 6 (1978).

BIOGRAPHICAL AND CRITICAL STUDIES

Arnold, Heinz Ludwig, ed. "Max Frisch." *Text und Kritik* 47/48 (1975). 2d, enl. ed. 1976.

Bänzinger, Hans. *Zwischen Protest und Traditionsbewusstsein: Arbeiten zum Werk und zur gesellschaftlichen Stellung Max Frischs.* Bern, 1975.

Beckermann, Thomas, ed. *Über Max Frisch.* Frankfurt, 1971.

Biedermann, Marianne. *Das politische Theater von Max Frisch.* Lampertheim, 1974.

Butler, Michael. *The Novels of Max Frisch.* London, 1976.

Durzak, Manfred. *Dürrenmatt, Frisch, Weiss: Deutsches Drama der Gegenwart zwischen Kritik und Utopie.* Stuttgart, 1972.

Frühwald, Wolfgang, and Walter Schmitz, eds. *Max Frisch: "Andorra"/"Wilhelm Tell." Materialien, Kommentare.* Munich, 1977.

Jurgensen, Manfred. *Max Frisch: Die Romane.* Bern, 1972.

———, ed. *Frisch: Kritik, Thesen, Analysen.* Bern, 1977.

Kieser, Rolf. *Max Frisch: Das literarische Tagebuch.* Frauenfeld, 1975.

Knapp, Gerhard P., ed. *Max Frisch: Aspekte des Prosawerks.* Bern, 1978.

———, ed. *Max Frisch: Aspekte des Bühnenwerks.* Bern, 1979.

Petersen, Jürgen H. *Max Frisch.* Stuttgart, 1978. Has extensive bibliography.

Picker, Gertrud Bauer. *The Dramatic Works of Max Frisch.* Bern, 1977.

———. "Hades Revisited: Max Frisch's *Tryptychon.*" *German Quarterly* 59: 52–64 (1986).

Probst, Gerhard F., and Jay F. Bodine, eds. *Perspectives on Max Frisch.* Lexington, Ky., 1982.

Schmitz, Walter, ed. *Über Max Frisch 2.* Frankfurt, 1976. Has extensive bibliography.

———, ed. *Materialien zu Max Frisch: "Stiller."* 2 vols. Frankfurt, 1977.

———, ed. *Max Frisch: "Homo faber." Materialien, Kommentar.* Munich, 1977.

———, ed. *Materialien zu Max Frisch: "Biedermann und die Brandstifter."* Frankfurt, 1979.

———. *Max Frisch: Das Spätwerk (1962–1982). Eine Einführung.* Tübingen, 1985.

Steinmetz, Horst. *Max Frisch: Tagebuch, Drama, Roman.* Göttingen, 1973.

Stephan, Alexander. *Max Frisch.* Munich, 1983. Has extensive list of published interviews.

de Vin, Daniel. *Max Frischs Tagebücher: Studien über "Blätter aus dem Brotsack" (1940), "Tagebuch 1946–1949" (1950) und "Tagebuch 1966–1971" (1972) im Rahmen des bisherigen Gesamtwerks (1932–1975).* Cologne, 1977.

Weisstein, Ulrich. *Max Frisch.* New York, 1967.

Wendt, Ernst, and Walter Schmitz, eds. *Materialien zu Max Frischs "Andorra."* Frankfurt, 1978.

White, Alfred D. "Max Frisch." In *The Modern German Novel,* Keith Bullivant, ed. Leamington Spa, England, 1987. Pp. 126–139.

*World Literature Today* 60 (4) (1986). Special issue devoted to Frisch.

ROY C. COWEN

# CZESLAW MILOSZ

## *(b. 1911)*

### *LIFE*

WHEN CZESLAW MILOSZ, the winner of the 1980 Nobel Prize for literature, was about to deliver his Stockholm lecture, he began with a surprising reminiscence. One of the favorite literary heroes of his childhood, he said, had been Nils Holgersson from Selma Lagerlöf's novel *Nils Holgerssons underbara resa* (*The Wonderful Adventures of Nils,* 1906–1907), a boy who takes flight with a flock of wild geese: "He is the one who flies above the earth and looks at it *from above* but at the same time sees it in every detail. This double vision may be a metaphor of the poet's vocation."

It may be a metaphor of Milosz's own development as a poet, too. His entire career can be seen as a process of steady ascension. In its course the poet's eye took in wider and wider horizons, sweeping over broader and broader thematic and problematic territories, up to the ideal point of an all-encompassing vision that does not care much about the traditional stylistic norms or generic restraints. According to the laws of real-life optics, this process of ascension should have had a negative side effect: the higher we go and the wider our horizons are, the fewer details we are able to perceive. Milosz, however, miraculously managed to render this rule invalid. One of the chief wonders of his poetry is that, while constantly widening its scope, he never loses sight of the minute details of reality. While searching for the absolute, he never gets lost in abstractions. His vision strives for completeness but also, at the same time, for utmost precision.

Milosz's complicated background made him, as it were, predestined to assume the role of a modern Nils Holgersson—a poet and thinker who, in his upward flight, became witness to more and more universal issues of earthly civilization. He was born on 30 June 1911 in Szetejnie, a village in Lithuania—a country that from the sixteenth to the end of the eighteenth century had been part of the Polish-Lithuanian Commonwealth and was incorporated into the Russian Empire after the final partition of Poland in 1795. The population of this territory was divided, roughly speaking, into Lithuanian or Belorussian peasants and Polish nobles, most of them petty squires living on small plots of land. Milosz's family belonged to the latter category. His father's career, however, reflected the ongoing transformation of a significant part of the landowning nobility into a modern intelligentsia. An engineer by profession, Aleksander Milosz in 1913 took his family to Siberia, where he had been offered a job; with the outbreak of World War I, he was mobilized into the Russian military service. The family returned to their Szetejnie estate only in 1918, the year of the rebirth of independent Poland, to which this part of Lithuania was to belong until 1939.

The larger part of Czeslaw Milosz's interwar years was spent in the city of Wilno (Lithuanian Vilna/Vilnius), the unofficial capital of Polish Lithuania. This was a city with rich historical and cultural traditions, the seat of the second-oldest Polish university, and a place famous for its monuments of baroque architecture. At the same time Wilno was characterized by a particularly diversified mix of very distinct ethnic groups—in its streets Polish could be heard along with Lithuanian, Yiddish, Belorussian, and German. This cultural diversity gave Wilno its unique flavor, but it also gave rise to a great deal of tension, which was to surface especially in the 1930's, when it was exacerbated by the economic crisis and growing radicalization of both the Left and the Right.

Milosz came to Wilno in 1921 to study at King Zygmunt August High School; in 1929 he was accepted by King Stefan Batory University, where he studied law for the next five years. The year 1930 marked his debut as a poet, in the student journal *Alma Mater Vilnensis.* The next year was especially consequential for Milosz's literary beginnings; he made his first trip to Paris, where he met his distant relative Oscar V. de L. Milosz, a French poet of Lithuanian descent, who greatly influenced his subsequent intellectual development. Also in 1931, before his Paris trip, Milosz and several fellow students founded a literary group called Żagary. (This name, in regional dialect, means charred pieces of wood that can be used to light a fire; it was a symbol of both the disappointments and the hopes of the generation of young people who had grown up in resurrected Poland but now were facing the crisis of the 1930's.) The group then began to publish its own periodical, also entitled *Żagary;* ironically, it was first issued as a supplement to the conservative Wilno daily *Słowo.*

Despite this affiliation the Żagary group consisted of poets and critics who were decidedly on the left, some of them quite radically. In subsequent decades one of the founders of the group, Teodor Bujnicki, was assassinated during the war by an anti-Communist guerrilla unit; another, Jerzy Putrament, became a gray eminence within the literary establishment of postwar Poland; and yet another, Stefan Jędrychowski, served for a number of years as a minister in the Communist regime. Milosz, even in his early years, never was as leftist as some of his friends, yet for a while he, too, was under the spell of Marxist ideology, which seemed to provide a ready answer to the troubling social and political questions of the day.

His sympathy to Marxism was perhaps most noticeable in the essays and articles Milosz wrote at this time, but it also was revealed in his first book of poems, *Poemat o czasie zastygłym* (Poem on Frozen Time, 1933). The book offered poetry of social protest with catastrophic undertones. Throughout the 1930's this catastrophic mood seized the poetry of Milosz and that of his contemporaries with increasing strength, so that finally the Żagary group was nicknamed "the Wilno Catastrophists." Meanwhile, Milosz graduated from university in 1934; in the same year he received an award for his poetry from the Wilno branch of the Polish Writers' Union. He spent the years 1934–1935 on a grant in Paris, and after his return to Poland he began to work as an editor in the Wilno office of the state-owned Polish Radio. In 1936 Milosz published his second, fully mature book of poems, *Trzy zimy* (Three Winters). The next year he lost his job at the radio station, fired for his allegedly leftist leanings; soon, however, he found shelter in the more liberal central office of the Polish Radio in Warsaw, where he moved in 1937. Despite the forced character of this move, it was an opportunity for him to be immersed in the literary life of the capital; in particular, he made friends with another excellent poet of this generation, Józef Czechowicz, who also was employed at the radio station.

The outbreak of World War II caught Milosz in Warsaw. He escaped from the German invasion by moving east, to Wilno. The city was taken by the Soviets in 1939 and annexed to Lithuania, which was incorporated into the USSR in 1940. After several months of futile attempts to leave for Sweden, he finally managed to cross the border between the Nazi and the Soviet parts of occupied Poland and to return to Warsaw in 1940. There he remained until the Warsaw Uprising in 1944, making a living by doing odd jobs while writing poems and essays, translating English poetry (from Shakespeare to T. S. Eliot's *The Waste Land*), and taking part in underground literary life. He clandestinely published a book of his poems, an important anthology of wartime poetry titled *Pieśń niepodległa* (The Invincible Song, 1942), and his translation of Jacques Maritain's essay against collaboration with the enemy.

After Communist rule was imposed on Poland in the wake of the war, Milosz initially lived for a while in Cracow, where he was editor of the newly established literary monthly *Twórczość;* soon, however, he joined the diplomatic service of the new regime. In the late 1940's he was a cultural attaché at Poland's embassy in Washington and its consulate in New York, then was transferred to Paris. Throughout that period his attitude toward the post-1945 political system was becoming increasingly critical. While his 1945 volume *Ocalenie* (Salvation/Survival) contained mostly his wartime poetry, the poems he wrote in the late 1940's dealt more and more often with the moral and political conflicts of the postwar era. An example is his long poem "Traktat moralny" (Treatise on Morals), published in 1948 in the monthly *Twórczość* through an apparent oversight by the censor. For the most part, however, these new poems never saw print until the 1953 publication of *Światło dzienne* (The Light of Day), Milosz's first book of poems published in exile.

Before that, however, a few highly dramatic incidents occurred in the poet's life. At the end of 1950 he was unexpectedly ordered by his superiors to return immediately to Warsaw, leaving his family behind (even though his wife was expecting their second child). After the plane had landed in Poland, Milosz learned that his passport had been revoked—a clear sign of political distrust—and, as a consequence, he was not allowed to leave the country. It took him weeks to obtain permission to leave. When boarding the plane bound for Paris, he knew he was leaving for good.

At the beginning of 1951 Milosz officially cut his ties with the Polish government by asking for political asylum in France. He also published in the émigré monthly *Kultura* an article titled "Nie" (No), in which he explained the motives behind his defection, underscoring first and foremost his inability to conform to the Stalinist spirit of postwar Polish culture. The subsequent months constituted one of the most difficult periods in his life. On the one hand, he became a target for rabid attacks in Poland's party-controlled media, some of them signed by well-known Polish writers and former friends of his; he was also treated with suspicion by the literary gurus of France, most of whom were openly pro-Communist at this time. On the other hand, he was far from being accepted by the Polish émigré community. Most of its leading representatives could not get over Milosz's previous allegiances; some of them went so far as to accuse him of serving as a Communist agent whose task was to infiltrate émigré circles. In this generally unfavorable atmosphere it was the émigré publishing house Institut Littéraire (the publisher of *Kultura*) that lent a helping hand to Milosz by offering him the chance to make his living by writing and translating. The poet was to maintain close ties with this publishing house for the next thirty-five years; practically all the first editions of his subsequent Polish books appeared through Institut Littéraire.

The ten years that Milosz spent in France with his wife and two young sons marked the beginning phase of his work in exile—a phase that produced numerous books of crucial significance: two volumes of poetry, *Światło dzienne* and the book-length poem *Traktat poetycki* (Treatise on Poetry, 1957); his only two novels, *Zdobycie władzy* (*The Seizure of Power,* 1953) and *Dolina Issy* (*The Issa Valley,* 1955); and several books of essays, among which *Zniewolony umysł* (*The Captive Mind,* 1953) and *Rodzinna Europa* (*Native Realm,* 1959) must be considered his best achievements. The early 1950's can be seen as a border-line in his career in yet another sense: very soon after his decision to stay in the West, Milosz consciously began to write books directed primarily to a Western audience. Very soon, too, these books were met with critical acclaim: the French version of *The Seizure of Power* won the prestigious Prix Littéraire Européen in 1953; and *The Captive Mind,* which appeared in the same year in English, French, and German editions (the latter two with a preface by the philosopher Karl Jaspers), was, despite the controversy it provoked, widely recognized as an instant classic of political literature. Throughout his French phase, however, Milosz was known in the West mostly as an essayist and novelist. His poetry remained confined to his relatively small Polish readership, both in the émigré community and in Poland, where *Ocalenie* was still read and remembered and where copies of his later books, mostly smuggled in by tourists, began to circulate in the late 1950's.

In 1960 Milosz arrived once again in the United States, to give a series of lectures at the University of California at Berkeley. The next year he settled there for good, as professor of Slavic literatures. Thus began the longest phase of his career—his American period. Again this was a period bewilderingly rich in artistic and intellectual achievements. While in America, Milosz published seven major collections of original poetry, nine books of essays (as of 1989), a textbook on the history of Polish literature, and numerous translations, particularly of the Bible and of Anglo-American poetry into Polish and of modern Polish poetry into English. The year 1973 marked the publication of Milosz's *Selected Poems,* his first collection in English translation, after which came four more, including his *Collected Poems, 1931–1987.* From the mid 1970's he was internationally recognized as a poet, winning a Guggenheim Fellowship in 1976, the Neustadt International Literary Prize in 1978, and finally the Nobel Prize for literature in 1980.

Milosz's Nobel Prize was wildly celebrated by thousands of his admirers in Poland, where the Communist authorities, albeit extremely grudgingly, agreed to lift the censorship ban on most of his books, which previously had circulated in smuggled-in émigré editions and underground reprints. His poetry's triumphant return to Polish readers culminated in Milosz's visit to Poland to receive an honorary degree from the Catholic University of Lublin in June 1981. This return, however, was not completely unobstructed. Especially after his public statements in support of the Solidarity movement and his condemnation of martial law imposed in Poland in December 1981, Milosz once again became a favorite target for attacks in the regime-controlled mass media. Even though his books had found their way to Polish readers, attempts were made by the censors in the 1980's to curtail their circulation and critical reception. These attempts ceased after Poland's dramatic return to parliamentary democracy in the summer of 1989. One of the most telling signs of the new government's policy in matters of censorship and culture was the unimpeded publication, in an edition of 100,000 copies, of Milosz's political classic, *The Captive Mind.*

## *THE TWO NOVELS*

There are writers whose lives have almost no relevance for the meaning of their work. Milosz certainly does not belong among them. His work can be understood only when we are aware of his location in both space and time. In other words, the reader has to keep in mind that he or she is dealing with a poet and thinker whose life coincided with, and who personally witnessed, some of the most crucial events of twentieth-century history, including the economic crisis of the 1930's, World War II, the reign of Stalinism in Eastern Europe and its influence in the West, and the protest movements of the late 1960's, as well as the birth of the democratic opposition in Eastern Europe in the mid 1970's and its long-delayed but spectacular triumph in 1989. It is equally important to realize that precisely because of the course history has taken, Milosz's life bridges extremely distant geographic areas. His life can be seen as a series of resettlements, farther and farther from his native Lithuania: first to Warsaw, then (after the defeat of the Warsaw Uprising) to Cracow, then to France, then to the United States. In particular the contrast between Wilno and California, with its bewildering differences in landscape, climate, language, and cultural atmosphere, often functions in Milosz's poetry and prose as a symbolic vehicle that introduces one of the central themes in his work, the theme of exile.

But the problem of exile is not merely a matter of geographical dislocation. In "Notes on Exile," published in *Books Abroad* (Spring 1976), Milosz defines the concept as both a state of mind and a destiny. An exiled writer finds himself in a particularly ironic situation: in his native land he was prohibited from speaking out, but people waited eagerly for his words; now he is free to say whatever he wishes, but no one wants to listen. All his previous experience, which, theoretically, could enrich the minds of his new readers, is rejected by them because it does not have much in common with their own experiences. The only use of exile, says Milosz, is that, when accepted as a destiny, it helps the writer to realize the nature of his own illusions.

In his own creative practice, however, Milosz was not always this pessimistic. On the contrary, after his deliberate choice of exile in 1951, he made numerous attempts to reach the Western audience, some of them instantly successful, some others (particularly poetry) successful over the long run, after many years of struggling. As noted above, his output can be roughly divided into works he wrote basically for himself and his Polish readers and works he undertook with the Western audience clearly in mind. While the first category of works (which includes his poetry, *The Issa Valley,* and certain essays) is lyrical, individualistic, and personal, the second one (*The Seizure of Power* and the greater part of the essays) is interpretative and explanatory. While in the first category Milosz employs the method of individual, self-centered reflection or meditation on his experience, the second is characterized by the presence of a reader-oriented description and interpretation of the experience. In both cases, however, it is still the experience of a man who lived for most of the twentieth century in parts of our globe as different as they could possibly be. What unifies the two perspectives is their common vantage point: the point of view of an individual whose personal and intellectual adventures can be seen as representative of the adventures of modern civilization, and whose own quest for identity reflects civilization's uncertainty about its true identity.

The difference between Milosz's two perspectives perhaps can be best illustrated by comparing his two novels, both written and published in the early 1950's, at the initial stage of his exile. *The Seizure of Power* is a political novel, directed primarily to the Western audience and seeking to transmit the realities of the Communist "seizure of power" in Poland in the years 1944–1950. In full accord with Milosz's usual creative method, it presents us not with generalities but with minute particulars of reality; not with a vast spectacle of historical events but with individual biographies, sparingly and randomly sketched. In fact, the novel can be read, at least in parts, as a roman à clef; many of its characters are fictionalizations of those who figured in Poland's history during the Nazi occupation and the Stalinist era.

But the device of a "novel with a key" by no means exhausts all the book's meanings. *The Seizure of Power* probes deeper, beyond superficial allusions to real people and events, to an analysis of the submerged processes at work in twentieth-century history. At the time it was the only Polish novel to brave a clear-sighted and dispassionate analysis of the tragedy then being perpetrated in Eastern Europe. In this respect it was a far cry both from the illusions of the writers inclined to believe in the blessings of the new system and from the illusions of those who, mostly from an émigré perspective, considered the Communist reality as a battleground of pure and absolute values (patriotism versus foreign aggression, freedom versus slavery, and so on). Milosz was one of the first Polish writers to perceive the great and intrinsic evil of totalitarianism: not only the abrogation and annihilation of all traditional values, but also the fact that individual survival very often depends on the fashioning of elegant rationalizations to justify the surrender of those values.

Milosz never doubted that Communism had been introduced into Poland at the point of a Soviet bayonet. But he also perceived in his characters' moral behavior a complexity of psychological motivation that compelled them, in one way or another, to bow to totalitarian power. In Milosz's eyes the Poland of 1944, no less than the whole of Western civilization, was unprepared to offer effective resistance to totalitarianism. It is significant that the novel has not a single character able to oppose "historical necessity" with a counter-ideology. His heroes are left with only the alternatives of death, isolation, escape, or collaboration with the system—acts that in themselves constitute defeat. There is a glimmer of hope, perhaps, only in the book's epilogue, in which an older professor—the bearer of humanist values but a recluse from public life, forced to earn his living by translating Thucydides—finds moral support in spite of his impotence. He finds it in a solidarity with common people, with those in whom an elementary sense of justice is preserved regardless of the triumph of lawlessness and mendacity.

In stark contrast with the political subject matter and polyphonic method of *The Seizure of Power, The Issa Valley* is a lyrical, apparently autobiographical novel about childhood. While employing seemingly the same kind of third-person narration, it nonetheless focuses more on the viewpoint of an individual protagonist, a young boy named Thomas. The world of history, so prominent in *The Seizure of Power,* seems to be absent here; Thomas' world is the world of nature, of the Lithuanian countryside years before it was trampled by marching armies and rolling tanks. Nature, however, is far from being idyllic and unequivocally harmonious. The story of Thomas' coming of age is actually the story of his awakening human consciousness, which exiles him from the world of nature and makes him aware that this is not a realm of innocence but a realm of sex, cruelty, and death. The feeling of the absurdity of such a world can be overcome by a search for metaphysical values; hence the supernatural elements of both pagan and Christian mysticism play a significant role in the plot.

But Thomas' process of maturing also means that sooner or later he will have to leave the enchanted world of his half-real, half-mythical valley, and enter the world of adult consciousness—and, by the same token, the world of History. Insofar as *The Seizure of Power* is one of the most "public" of Milosz's books, *The Issa Valley* can be seen as one of his most "private" ones. The distance between these two, however, is that between two sides of a coin; while apparently assuming diametrically opposed viewpoints, the two novels in fact shed light on the issue of human existence between the forces of Nature and History.

## *ESSAYS*

The same kind of range spanned by the extremes of the "public" and "private" perspectives is displayed in Milosz's rich and voluminous essays. Here, however, the more than thirty years that passed between *The Captive Mind* and his essays of the 1980's allow us to view the diversity of Milosz's approaches as a matter of his own creative evolution—as a process of his "ascension," the final result of which is his merging of individual and universal viewpoints into one all-encompassing vision. In fact, even Milosz's most "public," didactic, and reader-oriented early essays, such as *The Captive Mind* or *Native Realm,* could not have been conceived without the solid background of autobiographical experience and individual reflection. Likewise, his essays from the later period, such as *Widzenia nad zatoką San Francisco* (*Visions from San Francisco Bay,* 1969), *Ziema Ulro* (*The Land of Ulro,* 1977), and *Świadectwo poezji* (*The Witness of Poetry,* 1983), while seemingly centered on the author's search for his own identity, lead ultimately toward the most excruciating questions concerning the future of our global civilization.

A comparison between *The Captive Mind* and *The Land of Ulro*—to confine ourselves to two highlights of Milosz's output—may help us realize both the extent of inner differences and the degree of inner consistency within his essays. *The Captive Mind* was received as primarily a political book. As the author explains in the foreword to a 1981 edition, its subject is "the power of attraction exerted by totalitarian thinking," "the vulnerability of the twentieth-century mind to seduction by sociopolitical doctrines and its readiness to accept totalitarian terror for the sake of a hypothetical future." The setting is Eastern Europe, Poland in particular, in the late 1940's.

Contrary to prevailing opinion, Milosz views these countries at this point not merely as forced to accept the Soviet-backed Communist regimes but also as swept up in the progress of the Communist "New Faith." This attraction concerns, first and foremost, East European intellectuals whose conversion to the "New Faith" seems to Milosz to be a particularly ominous phenomenon. Using the cryptonyms Alpha, Beta, Gamma, and Delta, he describes the careers of four Polish writers (in reality, as every Polish reader was able to recognize, they were, respectively, Jerzy Andrzejewski, Tadeusz Borowski, Jerzy Putrament, and Konstanty Ildefons Gałczyński) as four exemplary paths—each of them different from the others but all of them concluding with the writer's slavish acceptance of Communist ideology. The common denominator of these four careers is the notion of the "New Faith" as a universal cure for doubts and perplexities stemming from the disasters brought about by recent history—as the magic "pill of Murti-Bing" (a metaphor borrowed by Milosz from the prewar catastrophic novel of Stanisław Ignacy Witkiewicz), the swallowing of which allows one to feel relieved from any individual responsibility.

The eager acceptance of the "New Faith" by East European intellectuals does not mean, however, their genuine and unequivocal belief in all its dogmas. What is most characteristic of totalitarian societies is, rather, a phenomenon that Milosz compares with the ancient Persian custom called Ketman—the art of secretly knowing the truth and, at the same time, publicly adhering to the official doctrine, even though these two sets of beliefs exclude each other.

For the reader of the 1980's, familiar with George Orwell's concept of "doublethink" and Erich Fromm's vision of "escape from freedom," Milosz's Ketman and "pill of Murti-Bing" seem highly convincing as metaphors for the mechanisms of both intellectual justification and subconscious acceptance of totalitarianism. In its time, however, *The Captive Mind* stirred up a great deal of controversy. Published, by an odd coincidence, in the year of Joseph Stalin's death, the book was met with virulent attacks from both Left and Right. The Western sympathizers of Stalinism labeled the essay as reactionary anti-Soviet slander. The anti-Communist émigré circles, on the other hand, criticized it as a perverse exculpation of the phenomenon of Stalinism, which, according to the critics, relied on the rule of terror rather than on any sophisticated ideology, just as its acceptance was based far less on intellectual hairsplitting than on ordinary fear or ruthless opportunism.

Yet it is enough to read Milosz's book closely and objectively to realize that his analysis of the intellectuals' "seduction" by totalitarianism is much more multifaceted than his critics would have had it. By no means does he lose sight of such primitive motivations as fear of persecution, greed for power, or craving for privileges and material goods. At the same time, however, he emphasizes that what interests him more are certain additional and more complex psychosocial mechanisms, those which are especially relevant for intellectuals; not because this group is the only one worthy of attention but rather because it is the intellectuals who are supposed to articulate and defend the system of humanist values—therefore, their surrender to this fundamentally antihuman ideology seems to be a particularly humiliating and disappointing case of failure. In addition, Milosz's analysis of, to borrow a later phrase from Jean-François Revel, "totalitarian temptation" transcends the spatial and historical limits of Eastern Europe and the Stalinist epoch. At its deeper levels the book offers Milosz's first essay attempting to deal with the problem that remained central to his work in later decades. It is the problem of the future of our civilization—civilization that, in the twentieth century, has all too often been inclined to relinquish the idea of the irreplaceable value of each and every individual and to trade it for the illusions of certainty supplied by ideologies and mass beliefs.

On the surface of genre and style it would be hard to imagine two essays more different than *The Captive Mind* and *The Land of Ulro.* The former is a sociopolitical analysis, rooted firmly in a specific external reality, while the latter can be roughly defined as an intellectual autobiography, dealing with both the author's personal experience and the inner world of his reflections. Moreover, *The Captive Mind*'s forte is its art of logical explanation, whereas in *The Land of Ulro* the manner of the presentation is ostensibly meandering and whimsical. After all, the genesis of these two books, divided by a quarter of a century, was quite different: the former was written with the contemporary Western audience clearly in mind, while the latter's American edition (published in 1984) is prefaced by a straightforward warning:

> Dear reader, this book was not intended for you. . . . When writing it, I indulged in a personal whim, dismissing in advance the idea of its publication in English. . . . I gave free rein to my meditations and didn't try to reach anybody in particular, except perhaps a few fastidious people able to read my Polish and belonging to the same circle of the literati.
>
> (p. v)

Indeed, the point of departure for *The Land of Ulro* is personal and autobiographical, even though the book deals with nothing less than problems in the intellectual history of Western civilization. By asking at the very beginning, "Who was I?" and "Who am I now, years later?" Milosz ostensibly tries to elucidate the reasons behind his own evolution; since it so happens, however, that the questions he constantly asks himself are questions that centuries of our civilization have tried to answer, his treatise on himself soon becomes a treatise on a certain current of thought, a certain neglected philosophical tradition.

This tradition's invisible thread, which in Milosz's book links such seemingly distant figures as Emanuel Swedenborg, William Blake, Feodor Dostoevsky, the Polish Romantic poet Adam Mickiewicz, and the French symbolist (and Milosz's relative) Oscar V. de L. Milosz, is the perennial question of *unde malum,* of the origins of evil. Even before Milosz began to search for an answer in the works of philosophers, ranging from the Manichaeans and Gnostics to Lev Shestov and Simone Weil, he had become obsessed by the irresolvable problem of how to reconcile the presence of evil with the notion of Providence. This obsession resulted in his lifelong attitude of paradoxical "ecstatic pessimism." But it also made him sensitive to the fact that Western civilization had for at least two centuries been bypassing the central paradoxes of human existence on Earth and simplifying the human world into what Blake had called the land of Ulro.

According to Milosz, Ulro is "the land of the disinherited," "a land where man is reduced to a supererogatory number, worse, where he becomes as much for himself, in his own eyes, in his own mind." Following Blake, Milosz sees the beginning of the process of such disinheritance in the Enlightenment, with its fundamentally wrong decision to put all of mankind's hopes in the triumph of science and reason. The period of Francis Bacon, John Locke, and Isaac Newton witnessed the first signs of a rapidly widening rift between the inner world of the human imagination and the outer world of science's abstract laws. The ensuing Romantic crisis of European culture, which has continued to our time, has been, in Milosz's view, a phenomenon contained within the walls of the land of Ulro; only a handful of prophetic seers have attempted, in both literature and philosophy, to seek some effective way out, usually at the risk of being perceived as "abnormal," incomprehensible, or excessively mystical.

But how do their efforts relate to the question of *unde malum*? One common denominator Milosz finds between these thinkers and his own intellectual inclinations is the notion of anthropocentrism combined with a "bias against Nature." In other words, those who try to bring down the walls of Ulro must consider humanity the center of the universe while being perfectly aware that there is no such thing as innate human goodness. Nature is not a harmoniously working mechanism, as the deists of the Enlightenment liked to imagine it, nor is it a refuge from the troubles of civilization, as post-Rousseau Romantics tended to think. On the contrary, Nature, including human nature, is branded by the unavoidable presence of evil.

Whoever realizes this must deem it impossible to create any system of ethics free of religious sanctions. The only way to create an intellectual space that a human society could inhabit is to reconcile the presence of evil with the notion of a providential plan by introducing the idea of "Godmanhood." Not deified man but just the opposite, humanized God, is the concept through which we can "assent to our existence on earth." Within such a vision Christ, as in Swedenborg, becomes identical with God the Father, and the moment of the Creation is simultaneous with that of the Crucifixion; the God who created the world, with all its evil and suffering, is the God who also agreed to participate in our pain, who "took on a human form and willingly died the death of a tortured prisoner."

Swedenborg, Blake, Mickiewicz, Dostoevsky, and Oscar Milosz were thinkers who, for all their human limitations and errors, had enough visionary power to give the notion of divine humanity or "Godmanhood" pride of place in their systems of thought—even to the point of, in Dostoevsky's radical phrase, "choosing Christ over truth" (that is, over the abstract truth of science). The twentieth century, on the other hand, is viewed by Milosz as living proof of "the utter failure of secular humanism, a failure sponsored by the very successes of that same humanism." Ours is a world disinherited of values, a world whose inner void can be—and is—too easily filled with worthless and often anti-human ideological substitutes of the sort that Milosz had dissected in *The Captive Mind.*

Such a diagnosis does not mean, though, that in *The Land of Ulro* Milosz readily dismisses every form of agnosticism or atheism as simply disguises for ethical relativism. On the contrary, his polemic with the twentieth-century Polish novelist Witold Gombrowicz—which makes extremely illuminating reading not just for the student of Polish literature—shows that he fully appreciates the kind of atheism that is "bound by the strictest ethical code" exactly because it does not admit the possibility of divine intervention or posthumous reparation: "Morally speaking, there is nothing, in my view, which argues either for Christians or against atheists. . . . I would even say that if someone can be an atheist, he ought to be one" (Iribarne trans., p. 262).

Would that mean, in turn, that religion can be reduced to a means of intellectual self-defense against an ethical void? Such a concept of religion, albeit theologically rather unorthodox, seems indeed to be quite close to Milosz's views. In fact, his book is a treatise on what Blake called "Divine Works of the Imagination"; it finds a possible remedy for the modern crisis of Christian civilization not merely in a re-animation of the religious spirit but, more demandingly, in broadening the sphere of imagination and thus reclaiming the abandoned space of the human world.

## *POETRY IN THE MODERN WORLD*

Milosz's defense of the imagination and its humanizing power, undertaken in *The Land of Ulro,* finds its direct extension and complement in his other essays (or poems, such as *Traktat poetycki*) that deal more specifically with the role of poetry in the modern world. This particular thematic thread stretches from his early collection of essays *Kontynenty* (The Continents, 1958), through the essays from *Prywatne obowiązki* (Private Obligations, 1972) and *Ogród nauk* (The Garden of Learning, 1979), up to *The Witness of Poetry* (1983), a series of six Charles Eliot Norton Lectures delivered at Harvard in 1981–1982 that contain the most consistent summarization of Milosz's ideas on poetry.

The underlying theme of the Norton Lectures is nothing less than hope, and poetry as a possible source of hope. Hope against hope, to be sure, since the author realizes that almost nothing in either contemporary poetry or the recent history of our civilization seems to justify such expectations. At least in Western societies, the reading public as well as poets have long been reconciled to a poetry reduced to confessing its own helplessness. Milosz begins by looking at the problem from a different perspective. His poetic credo has been shaped, after all, by his experience as an East European poet living in exile in the West. Accordingly, his introductory lecture, "Starting from My Europe" (which condenses the broad range of problems treated in his earlier essays, particularly in *Native Realm, Visions from San Francisco Bay,* and *The Land of Ulro*), presents the cultural experience of his youth. The remote Polish-Lithuanian corner of Europe where he lived was strangely situated: geographically between East and West, culturally between Rome and Byzantium, historically between past and future. There, people developed a keen sense of historical relativity. None of the disasters that swept over these crossroads of civilizations could seem final or irreversible; every vision of the future had to allow for some eschatology. In that country of historical cataclysms poetry became "a home for incorrigible hope."

For Milosz "the witness of poetry" means much more than the hackneyed formula "poetry as a testimony." A testimony can be wrung out of someone; a witness is born voluntarily, by someone who wants to help justice. If poetry is supposed to bear witness, that means it is considered a form of active participation in human affairs. But can poetry really, to reverse W. H. Auden's phrase, "make something happen"? If we leave Eastern Europe for a moment and consider poetry the world over, we will see that, instead of bearing witness, twentieth-century poetry more often than not "testifies to serious disturbances in our perception of the world." The second, third, and fourth of Milosz's lectures analyze three specific forms of such disturbances.

The first of them is sociological. The birth of artistic bohemias in the middle of the nineteenth century resulted in the poet's gradual alienation from "the great human family." Since then a schism between the poet and the rest of society has become accepted fact. Culture has been divided into pure art for the chosen few and entertainment or instruction for the despised philistines. The poet has deliberately chosen to become an outcast, and his work has turned from the pursuit of reality to various attempts to cultivate art for art's sake. But, as Milosz tries to show, the dichotomy of "reality" and "pure art" is, in fact, false. It is possible to conceive of a poetry that is at the same time mystical and yet immersed in history, artistically minded and yet responsive to social reality, individualist and yet not isolated from "the great human family."

Another cause of the twentieth-century crisis of poetry is what Milosz calls "the lesson of biology." In his view the progressive application of Darwinism to the social sciences has thoroughly refashioned our imagination: it has made us more and more disposed to interpret the human world within the categories of biological determinism. Moreover, the historical upheavals of our times have persuaded us that not only human beings but also human civilizations are mortal. All of this is totally at odds with the poet's natural tendency to look at the world, as it were, with the eyes of a child—a child who still believes in the criteria of good and evil. If the poet in our century retains such blessed naïveté, he is nevertheless constantly pressured by the cynical "adults" to respect "naked facts." Even though he may instinctively try to resist this pressure, he can no longer rely on old categories and ideals. As a result the poet of today is "ashamed of the child in himself": "the lesson of biology" teaches him, more often than not, to give up his childlike rectitude.

Finally, yet another reason for poetry's vitiated role is described by Milosz as a classicist temptation. The poet can trade in his social bonds for an attitude of haughty self-isolation; he can trade in his moral steadfastness for biological determinism; he can, finally, trade in his fidelity to the real world for compliance with ready-made conventions. Common to all three is the choosing of an easy, simple, undemanding solution. As far as the third choice is concerned, even though Milosz as a poet may occasionally have been attracted by classicism, he views it as a temptation that should be resisted. Poetry in our epoch is a battle between realism and classicism, faithfulness to the external world and adherence to the internal rules of art. The use of poetic convention makes contact with the reader possible, but at the same time it builds a glass wall separating the poet from reality. Thus, the division between the word and human experience grows continuously, separating mankind into "those who know but do not speak" and "those who speak but do not know."

After this general analysis of dangers hovering over contemporary poetry, Milosz turns again to the poetry of a specific place and time. His fifth lecture, "Ruins and Poetry," recounts the experiences of Polish poetry during World War II. Faced with the threat of physical extermination and the annihilation of culture, Polish authors were compelled to rethink the most essential questions concerning the tasks of poetry and its functions within a community. The apocalypse of the war had, ironically, one positive aftereffect in that it simplified everything: it created a need to give the new reality a name, to comprehend what seemed to be incomprehensible, to find hope in what was apparently hopeless. Paradoxically, the catastrophe of war restored some hierarchy of moral values and revived realism. It also proved to be a cure for poetry's isolation, since poets were facing the same dangers as other people. One of the unexpected results of the war and the disintegration of the European cultural tradition has been—at least for Polish poets and writers—the renewed belief that "the great schism in poetry is curable."

Milosz's last lecture, "On Hope," opens with a question: "What if the lament so widely spread in poetry today proves to be a prophetic response to the hopeless situation in which mankind has found itself?" (p. 101). What, in other words, if poetic catastrophism happens to be confirmed by some ultimate catastrophe? After all, Milosz himself—to mention only his prewar catastrophism and the bitter vision of mankind's prospects presented in his essays, from *The Captive Mind* through *The Land of Ulro*—has never been a thoughtless optimist. In fact, he discerns in contemporary history "a kind of race between the lifegiving and the destructive activity of civilization's bacteria," the final result of which is unknown and can be apprehended only vaguely by the prophetic imagination of poets. In Milosz's view, however, there is reason if not for optimism, then for the rejection of hopelessness. He sees humanity as having emerged as "an elemental force," which in our times replaces the anachronistic structures based on class distinctions and social hierarchies. Culturally this means that "Man is opening up to science and art on an unprecedented scale": there is a growing demand for culture as a source of knowledge about mankind's past. This enormous demand is still not fully realized and satisfied by culture itself. Nevertheless, such a demand offers new opportunities—especially to poetry, which in its function as "the witness" proves to be a particularly ample means of making the past an element of our present and relating universal problems of the human condition to a given place and time.

## *POETRY AS A WITNESS TO HISTORY*

Thus far we have looked at Milosz the poet from outside—from the vantage points of his biography and his prose, which, on one level, can be read as a series of more or less direct comments upon the nature of his own poetic art. *The Witness of Poetry* presents an especially valuable key to Milosz's work in that, by stating his opposition to certain tendencies in modern poetry, it clearly indicates the poet's own preferences. This book perhaps does nothing more than sum up the thoughts that were scattered throughout Milosz's earlier essays, but in so doing, it presents these thoughts as a highly consistent system. It is a system based on three fundamental premises—a metaphysical, an ethical, and an aesthetic one. Each of them boils down to a simple credo. First, in spite of the fallibility of our cognition, external reality does exist objectively, and its existence is a constant reason for our admiration of the world. Second, in spite of all relativistic theories and nihilistic ideologies, the borderline between good and evil does exist objectively, and the existence of evil is a constant reason for our abomination of the world. Third, the task of poetry is to bear witness to this irresolvable paradox and to find the means of expression that would be able to contain both admiration and abomination, both metaphysical rapture and ethical repulsion.

These three credos, extracted from Milosz's essays, seem to be simple enough; things, however, look more complicated if we try to discern and understand the coexistence of the metaphysical, ethical, and aesthetic concerns within the body of his poetry. After all, Milosz's poetry spans more than half a century, and it went through many changes. Despite the exceptionally high degree of consistency in his inner development as a poet, there were certain distinct phases in his career during which he seemed to be preoccupied with one of his creative roles—a poet-moralist, a metaphysical poet, a seeker of a "new diction"—more than with the others. Accordingly, there are readers who are fascinated by Milosz as a witness to our epoch and moralistic commentator on its evil; there are those who view him primarily as a poet obsessed with eternal paradoxes of existence and faith; and there are those for whom his place in twentieth-century poetry is secured by the revolutionary role he has played in broadening the sphere of lyrical expression. It is certainly important to be aware of the specific significance of each of these three roles. Nevertheless, Milosz's poetry can be fully understood only when the reader realizes that all three are intertwined, each being either a cause or a consequence of the others.

Chronologically speaking, Milosz's beginnings were dominated by his concept of poetry as a witness to History and a comment upon its moral aspect. In this respect his first book, *Poemat o czasie zastygłym* (Poem on Frozen Time, 1933), is quite characteristic of the attitudes prevailing among his poetic generation, the so-called Second Avant-Garde. What is particularly characteristic is not the book's social radicalism or catastrophic mood but, rather, its way of setting the poems squarely within a specific historical and geographic context. The reader of these early poems could have no doubts as to when and where the lyrical action took place; the time was the early 1930's—the years of the world economic crisis—and the poems were set "in the midst of a militarized country, in a city with streets / full of the shouts of nationalistic marches," that is, Poland and Wilno. The speaker's attitude toward the presented facts and events is that of indignation and protest; renouncing his individualist stance for the perspective of the oppressed, he views the established social order as one that is bound to be swept away by a violent mass rebellion.

If this can be considered an early form of Milosz's catastrophism, it must be noted that its one-dimensionality was overcome by the poet very soon. In his next book of poems, *Trzy zimy* (Three Winters, 1936), he emerges as a catastrophist in a much more profound sense. The notion of History is no longer meant as merely the course of political events, confined to a specific time and place; instead, the range of observation broadens to an almost cosmic dimension, and the images of the impending cataclysms have less to do with social revolutions or wars than with the eschatological categories of damnation and salvation of mankind. Likewise, the notion of evil is no longer narrowed down to the sphere of social injustice; rather, it is evil inherent in the very essence of the human world. As a consequence the impending catastrophe of this world is seen as a chance for its redemption:

> Three times must the wheel of blindness
> turn, before I look without fear at the power
> sleeping in my own hand, and recognize spring,
> the sky, the seas, and the dark, massed land.
> Three times will the liars have conquered
> before the great truth appears alive
> and in the splendor of one moment
> stand spring and the sky, the seas, the lands.
> ("Powolna rzeka" / "Slow River," SN[1])

The motif of salvation and redemption recurs with tremendous force in Milosz's wartime poems, collected in his 1945 volume *Ocalenie.* The title of this book is deliberately ambiguous: in Polish *ocalenie* means both physical survival (or escape) and rescue (or salvation). The difference between these two meanings is the basic ethical tenet of the book; it sounds as if the author is repeatedly asking: All right, we have survived, but have we been saved? And if not, where can we find salvation? Milosz views the reality of war not only in terms of extreme physical cruelty, destruction, and death but also, even more so, in terms of the collapse of traditional systems of values. The catastrophe, which in his prewar poetry was only a matter of vague premonitions, has now materialized; and instead of offering a chance for the world's redemption, it has materialized as the literal end of the world. The most pessimistic observation Milosz makes is that the scope of the actual catastrophe is inversely proportional to the world's reaction to it. The approaching "end of the world" is met with blind indifference on the part of both Nature and humans, who go about their everyday business as if nothing were going to happen:

> On the day the world ends
> A bee circles a clover,
> A fisherman mends a glimmering net.
> Happy porpoises jump in the sea,
> By the rainspout young sparrows are playing
> And the snake is gold-skinned as it should always
> be.
> . . . . . . . . . . . . . . . . . . . . . . .
> And those who expected lightning and thunder
> Are disappointed.
> And those who expected signs and archangels'
> trumps
> Do not believe it is happening now.
> As long as the sun and the moon are above,
> As long as the bumblebee visits a rose,
> As long as rosy infants are born
> No one believes it is happening now.

[1] Throughout the rest of the article, the following abbreviations are used to refer to Czeslaw Milosz's books of poems in English translation: BW—*Bells in Winter;* SN—*The Separate Notebooks;* SP—*Selected Poems;* UE—*Unattainable Earth.* These translations, cited in the bibliography, have all been made under the supervision of the poet.

Only a white-haired old man, who would be a
  prophet
Yet is not a prophet, for he's much too busy,
Repeats while he binds his tomatoes:
There will be no other end of the world,
There will be no other end of the world.

("Piosenka o końcu świata" /
"A Song on the End of the World," SP)

In other poems from the war period, the notion of indifference is more precisely identified with moral callousness. The atrocities of World War II had crossed a certain threshold of human receptivity, beyond which every new act of inhumanity—especially when directed against others—could meet with nothing but numbness. But, as Milosz points out, this kind of indifference to others' suffering was, in fact, nothing new in human history; rather, it was a perennial sign of the evil inherent in the human soul. Thus, in his "Campo dei Fiori" (in *Separate Notebooks*) he puts an equation mark between the indifference of the Roman crowd who surrounded the stake at which Giordano Bruno was burned and the indifference of the other people of Warsaw to the fate of the Jews as the ghetto was burned by the Nazis:

I thought of the Campo dei Fiori
in Warsaw by the carousel
one clear spring evening
to the strains of a carnival tune.
The bright melody drowned
the salvos from the ghetto wall,
and couples were flying
high in the cloudless sky.
. . . . . . . . . . .
Someone will read as moral
that the people of Rome and Warsaw
haggle, laugh, make love
as they pass by martyrs' pyres.
Someone else will read
of the passing of things human,
of the oblivion
born before the flames have died.

But that day I thought only
of the loneliness of the dying,
of how, when Giordano
climbed to his burning
he could not find
in any human tongue
words for mankind,
mankind who live on.

"The loneliness of the dying" is the same in Giordano Bruno's time and in our epoch. There is, however, a quantitative difference: World War II posed the problem of the ethics of the survivor on an incomparably larger scale. In those who witnessed the methodical destruction of cities and the annihilation of entire nations, only an ethical void remained with nothing to fill it. In his wartime poetry Milosz appears unable to fill this void with the authoritative voice of a moralist. Significantly, he often resorts (particularly in the excellent sequence "Głosy biednych ludzi" [The Voices of Poor People]) to the technique of the dramatic monologue, introducing someone else's voice and presenting someone else's predicament; in such poems he prefers to employ the device of ironic detachment and to let the character unmask himself in the course of his monologue rather than offering any moralistic comment from the author. In this way the technique becomes an indirect diagnosis: even the poet's moral authority can no longer be considered unquestionable.

The ethical void left by the experience of the war is, as we have said, the dominant theme of *Ocalenie.* While writing his wartime poems, however, Milosz was able to anticipate another kind of threat posed by the course of twentieth-century history. He understood the nature of modern mass societies well enough to realize that the ethical void demanded to be filled by something; and, since the old system of ethics could not really be restored, the void would probably be filled by a totalitarian "New Faith." Milosz's poem "Walc" (The Waltz), written in 1942, contains a nightmarish scene: in 1910 a young, beautiful woman, apparently pregnant, during a break in an elegant ball has a vision in which she sees her son, some thirty years later, marching in a convoy of slave workers "with an apish smirk"; he is "happy in slavery."

This vision of people "happy in slavery," people who have traded their freedom for the illusory sense of release from individual responsibility, was to haunt Milosz's poetry for years to come. This frightening vision is most vividly present in his poems written within the first five postwar years; for the most part, they remained in a drawer (for censorship reasons) until his emigration and the 1953 publication of *Światło dzienne.* The poem "Dziecię Europy" ("Child of Europe," SP), for instance, offers a portrait of an intellectual busy with inventing self-justifications for his decision to convert to the "New Faith," a decision based on quite cynical motivations. While similar to the portraits in *The Captive Mind,* this picture is even more devastating precisely because it is a self-portrait drawn by the character himself. The poem employs, once again, the technique of the dramatic monologue, fully utilizing the device of ironic distance this technique implies. As a result, in the course of the monologue the speaker's twisted mentality unmasks itself:

He who has power, has it by historical logic.
Respectfully bow to that logic.

Let your lips, proposing a hypothesis,
Not know about the hand faking the experiment.

Let your hand, faking the experiment,
Not know about the lips proposing a hypothesis.

Learn to predict a fire with unerring precision.
Then burn the house down to fulfill the prediction.

Even though in "Child of Europe" Milosz's use of irony allows him to withhold any direct, authoritative comment, the poems from *Światło dzienne* clearly represent the apex of a moralistic trend in his work. Many of them deliberately turn toward a certain tradition of poetic moralism, if not overt didacticism, namely, the tradition of the Enlightenment. The opening poem in the collection is, for instance, an epistle addressed to Jonathan Swift; some poems display an almost eighteenth-century stylization of language and verse. More important, at this stage Milosz's poetry is marked by a distinct predilection for such characteristic genres of the Enlightenment as the satire, epistle, ode, and poetic "treatise." In particular the role of the treatise cannot be overestimated, even though this generic term does not appear in Milosz's poetry very often. All in all, he wrote only two long poems that have the word "treatise" in their titles, but each of them is a work of crucial significance. "Traktat moralny" (Treatise on Morals, in *Światło dzienne*), a poem put deceivingly in comical-sounding verse, as if borrowed from children's poetry, is in fact a serious picture of the moral devastation created by the war and the postwar progress of the "New Faith." The poem once again poses the question of survival/salvation, and tries to answer it by pointing out that no ideology or "method" is able to fill the ethical void: "Salvation is in you alone." The only rescue possible is to return to the idea of individual responsibility for one's own words and actions, even though the individual's resistance against the overwhelming pressures of modern tyrannies seems to be doomed to failure: "The avalanche changes its course / Depending on the stones it rolls over."

*Traktat poetycki* (Treatise on Poetry, 1957), a book-length poem published during Milosz's stay in France, is a truly unique work in modern Polish literature; if it has any analogues, they belong to the Anglo-American tradition: for example, certain long poems by W. H. Auden and Karl Shapiro. Its subject matter, however, is thoroughly Polish: it is nothing less than the history of twentieth-century Polish poetry, with all its hopes, illusions, and mistakes, drawn as a series of brief, individual portraits of particular poets. This is, however, the main concern of approximately one-half of the poem; in the next half Milosz's vision broadens to encompass a more general problem of the modern poet's place between "the Spirit of Earth" (that is, all the antinomies inherent in the world of Nature) and "the Spirit of History" (that is, the Hegelian-Marxist concept of historical determinism).

As such, *Traktat poetycki* ushered in a new phase in Milosz's poetic evolution—a phase during which the metaphysical, ethical, and aesthetic concerns of his poetry ultimately became intertwined. It must be noted, however, that during the next thirty years of his career Milosz never shunned direct involvement in topical issues, nor did he give up his moralistic stance. On the contrary, some of his later poems can be considered more or less direct warnings against the course that our civilization has taken; others are reactions to particular acts of History's injustice. Milosz is perfectly aware that the demand for ethical involvement is, as a rule, at variance with the equally important demand for artistic perfection. In one of his poems from the 1980's he writes:

Still one more year of preparation.
Tomorrow at the latest I'll start working on a great
book
In which my century will appear as it really was.
. . . . . . . . . . . . . . . . . . . .
No, it won't happen tomorrow. In five or ten years.
I still think too much about the mothers
And ask what is man born of woman.
He curls himself up and protects his head
While he is kicked by heavy boots; on fire and
running,
He burns with bright flame; a bulldozer sweeps him
into a clay pit.
Her child. Embracing a teddy bear. Conceived in
ecstasy.

I haven't learned yet to speak as I should, calmly.
("Przygotowanie" / "Preparation," UE)

In other words, despite all the risks it entails, the formulation of poetry's tasks from the opening poem in Milosz's *Ocalenie* remains as valid for him as it was in 1945, even though it seems to demand the impossible from the poet:

What is poetry which does not save
Nations or people?
A connivance with official lies,
A song of drunkards whose throats will be cut in a
moment,
Readings for sophomore girls.
("Przedmowa" / "Dedication," SP)

## *METAPHYSICAL CONCERNS*

Milosz's writing from the 1950's on was also marked by his gradual shift from the ethical to the metaphysical and from a concern with History to a concern with Being. It would, however, be a gross oversimplification to date the poet's obsession with metaphysical paradoxes to this later period. Actually, the metaphysical strain in his poetry had originated much earlier. It is highly significant, for instance, that during the war years he wrote not only "Campo dei Fiori" but also "Świat" ("The World," SN), a poem of a completely different type, deliberately ahistorical and amoralistic. Subtitled "A Naive Poem," it is an attempt to reconstruct the metaphysical basis of the world's Being as seen through the eyes of a child:

*Hope* means that someone believes the earth
Is not a dream, that it is living flesh;
That sight, touch, hearing tell the truth;
And that all the things we have known here
Are like a garden, looked at from the gate.

You can't go in; but you can see it's there.
And if we could see clearly and more wisely
We know we'd find in the world's garden
Some new flower or undiscovered star.

Some people think our eyes deceive us; they say
That there is nothing but a pretty seeming:
And just these are the ones who don't have hope.
They think that when a person turns away
The whole world vanishes behind his back
As if a clever thief had snatched it up.

The war, or History in general, is absent here—or, rather, is present only insofar as it provides the unspoken reason why the world's foundations must be raised anew and why the preeminence of Being must be reconfirmed time and again. These two poems' proximity in time (both "Campo dei Fiori" and "The World" were written in 1943) offers an important clue to Milosz's poetry. In fact, what is most characteristic of his work is exactly this peculiar fusion of two perspectives—the poet always viewed human existence in both its historical and its metaphysical dimensions. Milosz's skill in blending these two dimensions culminates in his work from the 1970's and the 1980's, of which the long poems such as "Gdzie wschodzi słońce i kędy zapada" ("From the Rising of the Sun," BW) and "Osobny zeszyt" ("The Separate Notebooks," SN) are prime examples; the autobiographic content serves here to demonstrate how an individual life can be molded by the course of History while still being subject to the unchangeable laws of Existence.

Milosz's system of metaphysics is an extremely complex one, especially since it is inextricably linked with his system of ethics. In addition, neither of these two can be elucidated by referring to his poetry alone; as has already been noted, an indispensable key is provided by his essays, first of all by *The Land of Ulro.* To put it simply, we might begin by repeating the observation that the foundation for his overall poetic philosophy is the dissonance or antinomy created by the clash of two contrary convictions—the clash that results in what Milosz calls his "ecstatic pessimism." On the one hand, his poetry is a euphoric hymn to the beauty of objectively existing things, of everything that *is:*

> And so it befell me that after so many attempts at naming the world, I am able only to repeat, harping on one string, the highest, the unique avowal beyond which no power can attain: *I am, she is.* Shout, blow the trumpets, make thousand-strong marches, leap, rend your clothing, repeating only: *is!*
>
> ("Esse," SN)

Leaves glowing in the sun, zealous hum of bumble bees,
From afar, from somewhere beyond the river, echoes of lingering voices
And the unhurried sounds of a hammer gave joy not only to me.
Before the five senses were opened, and earlier than any beginning
They waited, ready, for all those who would call themselves mortals,
So that they might praise, as I do, life, that is, happiness.

("Godzina" / "An Hour," BW)

"What use are you? In your writings there is nothing except immense amazement," he addresses himself in his collection *Nieobjęta ziemia (Unattainable Earth,* 1984; the literal meaning of the title in the original Polish is "Earth too huge to be grasped"). Despite the ironic tone, there is much truth in this self-description. Milosz's constant, perpetually renewed "amazement" with the richness of "The Garden of Earthly Delights" (as he calls it in a poem that borrows its title from Hieronymus Bosch's famous triptych [UE]) can often attain the heights of an ecstatic hymn of praise and thankfulness. Many of his poems are defined by the critics as epiphanies—sudden illuminations that reveal a sacred truth of Being hidden behind the external appearance of an object, a landscape, or a human face. In such poems the ecstatic tone is not merely a matter of the speaker's emotional state of rapture; rather, it is motivated by his discovery of the "holiness of Being," which makes the poem a confession of religious faith. (Incidentally, this utter respect for the "holiness of Being" had, as we will see, tremendous consequences for Milosz's concept of poetic language, which strives for utter concreteness in naming things and reflects, by means of stylistic polyphony, the bewildering richness of various "voices" with which the world speaks.)

On the other hand, this ecstatic admiration of the world comes into conflict with Milosz's sober awareness that reality—not only the reality of History but also the reality of Nature—is tainted by the constant presence of evil. In this, he is clearly a modern version of a Manichaean heretic: evil is for him the ineffaceable shadow of all that exists, including, perhaps above all, the poet's own ego. As a religious poet and thinker he is able to note down, apparently with an approving nod, a statement by René La Senne: "For me the principal proof of the existence of God is the joy I experience anytime I think that God is." But, in the pages of the same book (*Unattainable Earth*), he is no less able to record this thought: "A decent man cannot believe that a good God wanted such a world." For Milosz, in other words, Earth is not "unattainable" only in the sense that the essence of its being cannot be grasped by our imperfect senses and intellect or reproduced by our imperfect language; it is also "unattainable" in that the coexistence of a good God and the indelible fact of unwarranted suffering is something beyond our comprehension.

Hence Milosz's "ecstatic pessimism," the unique tension produced in his poetry by the contrast between his ever-present fascination with the world's splendor and the equally ubiquitous tone of dissatisfaction, disappointment, or even bitterness. It is, first of all, the dissatisfaction of the speaker with himself; looking back at his own past (which happens with increasing frequency in Milosz's later poetry), he more often than not perceives it as an irritating accumulation of errors, violations of his own conscience, and manifestations of his shortcomings and weaknesses:

The history of my stupidity would fill many
  volumes.
. . . . . . . . . . . . . . . . . .
But all of them would have one subject, desire,
If only my own—but no, not at all; alas,
I was driven because I wanted to be like others.
I was afraid of what was wild and indecent in me.

The history of my stupidity will not be written.
For one thing, it's late. And the truth is laborious.
("Rachunek" / "Account," SN)

But even such self-accusatory poems indicate that evil does not necessarily have to be "my own" only. It can be, to quote another poem ("Separate Notebooks"), "my own and not my own"; it is not only the responsibility of the individual but also an inseparable constituent of what Milosz calls, in the same poem, "the truth of the Earth." In his consistent Manichaeism the poet is indeed very far from the Romantic myth of Nature's innocence; for him, as for Thomas in *The Issa Valley,* Nature is by no means a quiet and serene retreat but is rife with violence, brutality, and innate injustice.

However, Nature, although no less evil and sinful than Man, is at least stable and self-assured, devoid of any uncertainty or doubt. Compared with this, the human being stands out as a solitary example of ceaseless self-torment. The individual is constantly compelled to question not only the moral justness of his or her actions but also the very necessity of his or her existence. One needs only to see oneself against the background of the stable, solid Being of the outer world to ask the basic question: To what extent is my own existence necessary at all, since without it the world would exist anyway?

Under a starry sky I was taking a walk,
On a ridge overlooking neon cities,
With my companion, the spirit of desolation,
Who was running around and sermonizing,
Saying that I was not necessary, for if not I, then
  someone else
Would be walking here, trying to understand his
  age.
Had I died long ago nothing would have changed.
The same stars, cities and countries
Would have been seen with other eyes.
The world and its labors would go on as they do.

For Christ's sake, get away from me.
You've tormented me enough, I said.
It's not up to me to judge the calling of men.
And my merits, if any, I won't know anyway.
("Pokusa" / "Temptation," BW)

Even though this question is finally rejected by the speaker as an insinuation from "the spirit of desolation" (most probably synonymous with "the dark spirit" that appears in other poems), it leads naturally to another: Since my existence is a fact, why do I exist in this particular form, enclosed in this particular body and life? Why am I myself and what does it actually mean "to be oneself"? Milosz asks these questions with increasing frequency as his work progresses, and it is no accident that in his later phase—poems such as "Miasto bez imienia" ("City Without a Name," SN), "From the Rising of the Sun," and "The Separate Notebooks"—the issue of his own identity plays such a dominant role. First, it is consistent with a perspective he often assumed in the 1970's and 1980's—that of looking back on his own life's experience. Second, and more important, the question of the ratio between chance and necessity in one's own identity is absolutely crucial, because on it depends one's idea of the meaning of existence. If we imagine blind chance as the prevailing element, only a short step remains to nihilism and despair. On the surface Milosz seems to favor exactly such a vision of the human predicament; whatever he says about Man in the contexts of both Nature and History points toward the conclusion that an individual existence is not rationally justified and that human nature is inevitably branded by evil.

There is, though, a recurrent "however" in Milosz's work, a "however" that could be compared with Blaise Pascal's famous "wager." Milosz seems to be saying: Yes, our existence on earth is erratic, sinful, and senseless; *however,* there are individual acts of courage and virtue that defy this senselessness. Just as Christ assumed human form in order to suffer with human beings, Man is able—through acts of sacrifice—to go beyond the boundaries of human existence and imbue that existence with some kind of divine sense. Such is the meaning of Milosz's invoking specific, actual figures as heroes in his poems, from Giordano Bruno in "Campo dei Fiori" to the painter Mieczyslaw in "The Separate Notebooks," who during the Nazi occupation "used his workshop to help people / and hid Jews there, for which the penalty was death." Such is also the meaning of the poem "Zaklęcie" ("Incantation," SN), which is ostensibly an unconstrained hymn in praise of the triumph of human reason—and only the title indicates that the poem is not an assertive statement but, rather, a magical invocation of "what should be," despite all odds and all of our experience:

Human reason is beautiful and invincible.
No bars, no barbed wire, no pulping of books,
No sentence of banishment can prevail against it.
It establishes the universal ideas in language,
And guides our hand so we write Truth and Justice
With capital letters, lie and oppression with small.
It puts what should be above things as they are,
Is an enemy of despair and a friend of hope.

Milosz's unique stature among twentieth-century poets lies in more than the fact that he copes with metaphysical dilemmas in our rather anti-metaphysical age. Even more important, he has proved able to transfer philosophical problematics into the domain of private, personal, autobiographical experiences and reflections. Or perhaps the reverse is true: he has been able to elevate autobiographical material to the level of a universal vision of human existence. While speaking of the all-embracing problems of human nature, he never loses sight of the individual's simultaneous entanglement in various contexts—in bodily form, in surrounding space, in historical time, in society, in the world of Nature, in relation to God. Milosz's lyrical hero exists simultaneously in all these conflicting dimensions, and is perfectly aware of their mutual incompatibility. As a consequence Milosz's poetry offers no ready solutions, no comforting utopias. "My part is agony," he declares in the poem "To Raja Rao" (SP), in which he rejects the Buddhist ideal of peace of mind. "Sensing affliction every minute, in my flesh, by my touch, I tame it and do not ask God to avert it, for why should He avert it from me if He does not avert it from others?" he continues in the poem "Stan poetycki" ("A Poetic State," SN). This is a significant statement that leads in many directions at once. It implies the conviction that affliction is an unavoidable companion of human existence. It asserts that trying to avert affliction is somewhat immoral, since it involves demanding special rights for oneself. But it also states that it is possible to "tame" affliction, if not avert it.

One means of "taming affliction" is through poetry, through "searching for the Real" ("Haftki gorsetu" / "The Hooks of a Corset," UE) and trying to give the Real its true name. It is, at the same time, a means of coping with the dilemma of evil, since it results from the realization that "good is an ally of being and the mirror of evil is nothing" ("Poznanie dobra i zła" / "One More Day," UE), that what we call the devil or "the dark spirit" is actually "the Great Spirit of Nonbeing" ("Ksiądz Ch. po latach" / "Father Ch., Many Years Later," UE). As a consequence "searching for the Real," futile and unsatisfactory as it usually is, appears to be the only defense of good accessible to the poet. His affirmation of being through naming it has, by itself, an ethical dimension.

## *PHILOSOPHY OF LANGUAGE*

But to give the Real its true name is by no means a simple thing: for the poet, language is as much an obstacle as a tool. Milosz's generally antinomian philosophy includes his specific philosophy of language, likewise permeated with contradictions and paradoxes. Like many other poets he is tormented by the immutable shortcoming of language—its being out of proportion to reality:

> A word should be contained in every single thing
> But it is not. So what then of my vocation?
> ("From the Rising of the Sun," C.M. and Lillian Vallee trans., in *Collected Poems* [New York: Ecco Press, 1988])

On the one hand, language has many different names for the same thing; on the other, it is insufficient in relation to the abundance of the real world, the richness of "unattainable Earth." What makes Milosz's method of solving this perennial problem more specific is the basic premise of his philosophy: the preeminence of reality, of the general Being represented by many particular existences. All things of this world "participate in the universal, existing separately" ("Heraklit" / "Heraclitus," SP), but even their particular existence is unattainable to us, for we are separated from it by the threefold veil of our imperfect senses, memory, and language. The imperfection of language presents a special problem here, because language by its nature always more or less tends to generalization. What in a sensual experience—or even in a reminiscence—appears as a clear, concrete, substantial, and individual thing is, by receiving a name, automatically included in a superior class; it becomes not a thing but a representation of an idea of a thing. In Milosz's poetry this becomes another reason for his persistent feeling of disappointment, for the sense of Earth's "unattainability":

> Not a general one, a plenipotentiary of the idea of
> the fox, in his cloak lined with the universals.
> But he, from a coniferous forest near the village
> Zegary.
> . . . . . . . . . . . . . . . . . . .
> I wanted to describe this, not that, basket
> of vegetables with a redheaded doll of a leek laid
> across it.
> And a stocking on the arm of a chair, a dress
> crumpled as it was, this way, no other.
> . . . . . . . . . . . . . . . . .
> In vain I tried because what remains is the ever-
> recurring basket.
> And not she whose skin perhaps I, of all men, loved,
> but a grammatical form.
> ("Na trąbach i na cytrze" / "With Trumpets and Zithers," SP)

However, in the clause "In vain I tried" the second half is as important as the first; although the poet may be frustrated by language's slipperiness, he repeatedly *tries* to give things their exact names. Milosz's individual way of joining the centuries-old debate on universals ("Who would have guessed that, centuries later, / I would invent the question of universals?"—from the poem "Sroczość" ["Magpiety," SP]) consists of setting up a continuous struggle against the abstractness of language. The simplest way to do that is to search one's vocabulary in quest of words with an extremely particular meaning or special use:

> And the word revealed out of darkness was: *pear.*
> I hovered around it hopping or trying my wings.
> But whenever I was just about to drink its
> sweetness, it withdrew.
> So I tried Anjou—then a garden's corner,
> scaling white paint of wooden shutters,
> a dogwood bush and rustling of departed people.
> So I tried Comice—then right away fields
> beyond this (not another) palisade, a brook,
> countryside.
> So I tried Jargonelle, Bosc and Bergamot.
> ("Po ziemi naszej" / "Throughout Our Lands," SP)

Nevertheless, the whole operation is of no avail, for even such particular names as "Anjou" and "Comice" are nothing more than the names of classes or species, rather than individual things; and besides, the more concrete the word, the stronger its ties with "this, not another," setting, with an enveloping reality that separates the speaker from an object-in-itself. Therefore, the above-quoted poem ends with another expression of disappointment:

> No good. Between me and pear, equipages,
> countries.
> And so I have to live, with this spell on me.
> ("Throughout Our Lands," SP)

Milosz never gives up his lexical quest; as a rule he always tries to find the most concrete of all possible synonyms. His stylistic method of "searching for the Real," however, can be discerned not only within his vocabulary but also, even more clearly, within the field of figures of speech. Unlike most lyrical poets he almost completely rejects metaphors and symbols, strongly favoring the figure of *pars pro toto* instead. Stylistically Milosz strikes his reader as a poet of *pars pro toto,* one who offers a part instead of a whole:

> A hand with cards drops down
> on the hot sand.
> . . . . . .
> A broken shadow of a chimney. Thin grass.
> Farther on, the city opened with red brick.
> Brown heaps, barbed-wire tangled at stations.
> Dry rib of a rusty automobile.
> A claypit glitters.
> ("Przedmieście" / "Outskirts," SP)

The image—a landscape of a ruined city's outskirts—is shown here as a series of *partes pro toto,* almost like a sequence of film shots from a close-up to a panoramic view. This method is highly symptomatic of Milosz's philosophy of language. He would be able to say about himself what he says about the hero of the poem "Gucio zaczarowany" ("Bobo's Metamorphosis," SP):

> . . . he did not look for an ideal object.
> When he heard: "Only the object which does not exist
> Is perfect and pure," he blushed and turned away.
>
> In every pocket he carried pencils, pads of paper
> Together with crumbs of bread, the accidents of life.
> . . . . . . . . . . . . . . . . . . . . .
> How much he envied those who draw a tree with one
> line!
> But metaphor seemed to him something indecent.
>
> He would leave symbols to the proud busy with their
> cause.
> By looking he wanted to draw the name from the very
> thing.

Likewise, for Milosz "the accidents of life" are definitely more important than "the ideal object" that one tries to approach by means of metaphors and symbols; if we do not count the earliest phase of his work, he is a declared anti-Symbolist.

But although Milosz opposes the Symbolist idea of avoiding the direct denomination of an object, this does not mean that in his opinion one has easy access to the object-in-itself. On the contrary, as we have said, Milosz clearly sees numerous obstacles dividing us from the Real—natural limitations of our senses and intellect, semantic pitfalls inseparable from the nature of language, and the unreliability of human memory:

Does it matter that we long for things as they are in
themselves?
The knowledge of fiery years has scorched the
horses standing at the forge,
the little columns in the marketplace,
the wooden stairs and the wig of Mama Fliegeltaub.
("Elegia dla N. N." / "Elegy for N. N.," SP)

If even Milosz's poetic ontology accepts the object's being as its fundamental premise ("You can't go in; but you can see it's there," as the narrator of "The World" put it), his epistemology and theory of language are based on skepticism. We are not able to reach the essence of an object; at least we are not able to communicate it verbally to other people. Because of the unavoidable mediation of the system of language, every attempt at giving the Real its name causes a tension between the generality of the word and the concreteness of the object; the "question of universals" is unsolvable. What is left to the poet? Only the accumulation of details, of "accidents of life" that are imperfect representations of the whole of Being. Only the analytical crumbling of the Real into numerous *partes pro toto,* each of which seems to be another attempt to save the world from the tyranny of the "Great Spirit of Nonbeing," from the misery of transience, oblivion, and death:

There is so much death, and that is why
affection
for pigtails, bright-colored skirts in the wind,
for paper boats no more durable than we
are . . .
("Rady" / "Counsels," SP)

But there is another method left. To be fair to reality, one cannot multiply just its concrete fragments, "accidents of life"; one can also multiply various testimonies to the same reality, testimonies belonging to various points of view, value systems, voices. Both methods taken together resemble a court hearing, during which an objective truth has to be established by reporting as many details and summoning as many eyewitnesses as possible. The latter method helps to create a sort of lyrical polyphony, consisting in the frequent use of "someone else's voice" or "another person's point of view." Milosz began to apply this polyphonic technique in some of his poems written in the early 1940's and later he returned to it very often by subtly playing on the distance between the speaker and the author. He also realized very soon that one of the most useful effects of this technique is poetic irony. In Milosz's case, however, irony is just a side effect (incidentally, it tends to disappear in his poems written after the 1960's).

Even though the polyphonic technique helps create a self-ironic distance toward the poet's own ego, more important for Milosz is the fact that this technique allows him to augment complementary testimonies about reality. By doing so he declares that the poet's "searching for the Real," if it is to bring any result at all, cannot be done within the narrow limits of one mind, one place, one language, one epoch. It must consist of repeated attempts to "transcend [his] place and time" ("The Hooks of a Corset," UE), to multiply himself and "inhabit" objects and people, so that finally the voice of the poet speaks, as it were, on behalf of all the things of this world, all forms of being, both past and present, dead and alive.

This goal was at least partially achieved in two long poems from the 1970's and 1980's,

"From the Rising of the Sun" and "The Separate Notebooks," and particularly in his book *Unattainable Earth.* Each of the three reminds the reader of the *silva rerum,* "a forest of things," the seventeenth-century term for a fascicle containing loosely arranged notes, occasional poems, copies of letters, and memorable quotes. Likewise, each of these three works by Milosz consists only in part of his poetry; they also include his prose notes or aphorisms, translations, quotations of various sources (from philosophical treatises to old documents to children's books), and even (in *Unattainable Earth*) letters from his friends. It might seem that the ultimate point of Milosz's unique development as a poet has been, paradoxically, the ideal of dissolving his individual voice in an all-encompassing polyphony, in the immense dialogue of different voices, his own and not his own, the dialogue that resounds on the pages of his latest books.

At the same time, however, the evolution of his poetry also stems from his tireless search for a "new diction" of his own. He views modern poetry's language, including his own style, as constantly imperiled by the classicist "flaw of harmony"; consequently, he tries ever more seriously to get rid of everything that is superficially harmonious and "graceful":

What constitutes the training of the hand?
I shall tell what constitutes the training of the hand.
One suspects something is wrong with transcribing signs
But the hand transcribes only the signs it has learned.
Then it is sent to the school of blots and scrawls
Till it forgets what is graceful.
("Zdania" / "Sentences," SP)

The ultimate goal of this line of development is a lyrical utterance stylistically located somewhere between poetry and prose. In one of his later poems Milosz speaks about this in an almost programmatic way—though, let us note, not without a dash of irony:

I have always aspired to a more spacious form
that would be free from the claims of poetry or prose
and would let us understand each other without exposing
the author or reader to sublime agonies.
("Ars poetica?" BW)

From the point of view of a reader, the most outstanding among Milosz's poems are those which—apart from other merits—sustain the unstable balance between harmony and disharmony, regularity and irregularity (his Polish versification deserves a thorough analysis from this particular point of view), discipline and freedom, "high" and "low" style, "poetry" and "prose." Over the course of time Milosz has ever more decisively repudiated the dogma of a post-Symbolist tradition that separates poetic language from a supposedly "non-poetic" one, from all of the words, expressions, and styles that are prohibited to, or at least "not recommended" for, a poet because of their "prosiness."

However—and here we have another of Milosz's apparent contradictions—poetic language is endangered not only by the "flaw of harmony," by literary conventions that restrain its drifting toward undiscovered and unnamed territories. There is also peril from the other side: from the side of the language of contemporary life, of everyday communication. It presents itself to the poet as the tremendous pressure of a shapeless and senseless verbal pulp—and this pressure is particularly dangerous when we consider that modern History often persuades us: "Fashion your weapon from ambiguous words. / Consign clear words to lexical limbo" ("Child of Europe"). Only by considering all these factors can we fully understand the message of such concise but weighty poems as "Zadanie" ("A Task," SP):

In fear and trembling, I think I would fulfill my life
Only if I brought myself to make a public confession
Revealing a sham, my own and of my epoch:

We were permitted to shriek in the tongue of dwarfs
and demons
But pure and generous words were forbidden
Under so stiff a penalty that whoever dared to
pronounce one
Considered himself a lost man.

Milosz successfully overcomes the abovementioned contradiction every time he finds a way of steering between the Scylla of poetic convention (a language that is organized but limited) and the Charybdis of colloquial spontaneity (a language that is unlimited but also unorganized). He sympathizes neither with the former, which would mean another version of Neoclassicism, nor with the latter, which would mean a surrender to the linguistic chaos of contemporary life. He chooses a third way: the language of "austere and transparent phrases" ("Incantation"), which follows the unsurpassed example of the Bible with its "true dignity of speech" ("Lektury"/"Readings," BW). He wants a language open to every way of speaking, every recess of vocabulary, every possible style—as long as this language preserves the dignity of poetic speech that lies in its basic task: to give things their names, to search for the Real, to try to grasp "unattainable Earth."

## Selected Bibliography


EDITIONS

INDIVIDUAL WORKS

*Poemat o czasie zastygłym.* Wilno, 1933.
*Trzy zimy.* Warsaw and Wilno, 1936.
*Wiersze.* Warsaw, 1940. Written under the pseudonym Jan Syruć.
*Ocalenie.* Warsaw, 1945.
*Światło dzienne.* Paris, 1953.
*Zdobycie władzy.* Paris, 1953.
*Zniewolony umysł.* Paris, 1953.
*Dolina Issy.* Paris, 1955.
*Traktat poetycki.* Paris, 1957.
*Kontynenty.* Paris, 1958.
*Rodzinna Europa.* Paris, 1959.
*Człowiek wśród skorpionów.* Paris, 1962.
*Król Popiel i inne wiersze.* Paris, 1962.
*Gucio zaczarowany.* Paris, 1965.
*Miasto bez imienia.* Paris, 1969.
*Widzenia nad zatoką San Francisco.* Paris, 1969.
*Prywatne obowiązki.* Paris, 1972.
*Gdzie wschodzi słońce i kędy zapada.* Paris, 1974.
*Ziemia Ulro.* Paris, 1977.
*Ogród nauk.* Paris, 1979.
*Hymn o Perle.* Ann Arbor, Mich., 1982.
*Świadectwo poezji.* Paris, 1983.
*Nieobjęta zięmia.* Paris, 1984.
*Poszukiwania.* Warsaw, 1985.
*Zaczynając od moich ulic.* Paris, 1985.
*Mowa wiązana.* Warsaw, 1986.
*Kroniki.* Paris, 1987.
*Czesława Miłosza autoportret przekorny.* Cracow, 1988. Interviews with Aleksander Fiut.
*Metafizyczna pauza.* Cracow, 1989.

COLLECTED WORKS

*Wiersze.* London, 1967.
*Utwory poetyckie: Poems.* Ann Arbor, Mich., 1976.
*Poezje.* Warsaw, 1981.
*Dzieła zbiorowe.* 12 vols. Paris, 1980–1985.

TRANSLATIONS AND WORKS WRITTEN IN ENGLISH

*Bells in Winter.* Translated by the author and Lillian Vallee. New York, 1978.
*The Captive Mind.* Translated by Jane Zielonko. New York, 1953.
*Collected Poems, 1931–1987.* Translated by the author *et al.* New York, 1988.
*Emperor of the Earth: Modes of Eccentric Vision.* Berkeley, 1977.
*The History of Polish Literature.* New York, 1969.
*The Issa Valley.* Translated by Louis Iribarne. New York, 1981.
*The Land of Ulro.* Translated by Louis Iribarne. New York, 1984.
*Native Realm: A Search for Self-Definition.* Translated by Catherine S. Leach. Garden City, N.Y., 1968.
*Nobel Lecture.* New York, 1981.
*Postwar Polish Poetry: An Anthology.* Selected and translated by Czeslaw Milosz. Garden City, N.Y., 1965.
*The Seizure of Power.* Translated by Celina

Wieniewska. New York, 1955. Also published as *The Usurpers.* London, 1955.

*Selected Poems.* Translated by several hands. New York, 1973; rev. ed., 1980.

*The Separate Notebooks.* Translated by Robert Hass and Robert Pinsky, with the author and Renata Gorczynski. New York, 1984.

*Unattainable Earth.* Translated by the author and Robert Hass. New York, 1986.

*Visions from San Francisco Bay.* Translated by Richard Lourie. New York, 1982.

*The Witness of Poetry.* Cambridge, Mass., 1983.

## BIOGRAPHICAL AND CRITICAL WORKS

Birkerts, Sven. "Czeslaw Milosz." In his *The Electric Life: Essays on Modern Poetry.* New York, 1989.

Brooks, David. "Royal Messages: Some Notes on the Poetry of Czeslaw Milosz." *American Poetry Review* 11 (1) (1981).

Czarnecka, Ewa. *Podróżny świata.* New York, 1983. Czarnecka's book-length interview with Milosz plus her essays on his poetry.

Czarnecka, Ewa, and Aleksander Fiut. *Conversations with Cseslaw Milosz.* Translated by Richard Lourie. San Diego, 1987. A joint edition of English versions of Czarnecka's *Podróżny świata* and Fiut's *Rozmowy z Czesławem Miłoszem.*

Davie, Donald. *Czeslaw Milosz and the Insufficiency of Lyric.* Knoxville, Tenn., 1986.

Des Pres, Terrence. "Czeslaw Milosz: The Poetry of Aftermath." *Nation* 227 (30 December 1978).

Fiut, Aleksander. *Rozmowy z Czesławem Miłoszem.* Cracow, 1981. A book-length interview with Milosz.

———. *Moment wieczny.* Paris, 1987. The most extensive monographic study of Milosz's poetry. An English translation is forthcoming from the University of California Press.

Gorczyńska, R., and P. Kłoczowski, eds. *Czesław Miłosz: "Trzy zimy." Głosy o wierszach.* London, 1987.

Hoffman, Eva. "The Poet of the Polish Diaspora." *New York Times Magazine,* 17 January 1982.

Iribarne, Louis. "The Naming of Hell." *Times Literary Supplement,* 25 August 1978.

*Ironwood* 18 (1981). A special issue on Milosz.

Kwiatkowski, Józef, ed. *Poznawanie Miłosza.* Cracow, 1985. Contains the most important essays on Milosz written by Polish critics.

Łapiński, Zdzislaw. *Między polityką a metafizyką.* London, 1981. A popular presentation of Milosz's life and work.

*Poezja* 5/6 and 7 (1981). Special issues on Milosz.

Schenker, Alexander M. "Introduction." In Milosz's *Utwory poetyckie: Poems.*

*Teksty* 4–5 (1981). A special issue on Milosz.

*Twórczość* 6 (1981). A special issue on Milosz.

*Tygodnik Powszechny* 41 (1980). A special issue on Milosz.

Vendler, Helen H. "Czeslaw Milosz." In her *The Music of What Happens: Poems, Poets, Critics.* Cambridge, Mass., 1988.

*World Literature Today* 52, no. 3 (1978). A special issue on Milosz.

## BIBLIOGRAPHIES

Volynska-Bogert, Rimma, and Wojciech Zalewski. *Czesław Miłosz: An International Bibliography, 1930–1980.* Ann Arbor, Mich., 1983.

STANISLAW BARANCZAK

# ODYSSEUS ELYTIS

## *(b. 1911)*

### *BACKGROUND AND INFLUENCES*

ODYSSEUS ELYTIS IS one of the youngest members of the literary generation of the 1930's, the generation that will remain legendary in modern Greek letters for bringing prose to maturity and giving a new direction to poetry. The poetic renaissance that this generation achieved has transcended national boundaries and gained international recognition, as attested to by the Nobel prizes awarded to two members of that generation: George Seferis, Elytis' elder by eleven years, received the Nobel in 1963; Elytis, in 1979.

To understand the significance of the revitalization that these two poets—and others of their generation—brought about, the state of modern Greek poetry in the years just preceding the 1930's should be considered. But first it must be made clear that, although a need for revitalization presupposes that something has been moribund, it should not be assumed that important poetry had not appeared in modern Greece during the previous one hundred years of its existence. Greece was liberated from the Ottoman Empire only in 1830, but its language is thousands of years old. As the classical scholar Constantine Trypanis very accurately observes in his introduction to *The Penguin Book of Greek Verse,* which includes poets from Homer to Elytis, "poetry written in Greek constitutes the longest uninterrupted tradition in the Western world." In the four hundred years of Ottoman rule, Greek poetry remained alive and reached peaks of lyrical beauty and originality in its demotic songs (oral anonymous poetry), while in Cyprus and Crete, which fell to the Turks much later than the rest of Greece (Cyprus in 1571 and Crete in 1669), the influence of the Italian Renaissance helped produce works that have found a lasting place in Greek literature: the love poems of Cyprus; the dramas of seventeenth-century Crete and its great verse romance, *Erotokritos.*

After their liberation from the Turks, the Greeks faced, along with so many other problems, a "language question," namely whether the official language should be the vernacular (demotic) or the purified (katharevousa), an artificial compromise that aimed at "purifying" modern Greek of its foreign loanwords and bringing it closer to the grammatical system of classical Greek. But the fact remains that the Greek language possessed a fundamental richness and unity, that it was an instrument of infinite expressive possibilities, which new writers used with imagination and vigor. Among the many poets who wrote in the hundred years preceding the renaissance of the 1930's, brief mention should be made of three outstanding names: Dionysios Solomos (1798–1857), Kostis Palamas (1859–1943), and Angelos Sikelianos (1884–1951). (The great Alexandrian Greek poet Constantine Cavafy [1863–1933] is not considered an important pre-1930's poetic presence because recognition of his influence on modern Greek poetry came later. This is due partly to his modernity of expression and partly to his having lived in Alexandria, away from the mainstream of Greek life.)

Solomos, born in Zakynthos and educated in Italy, became the "Dante of Greece" by writing his poems in the vernacular while at the same time adapting a variety of Western meters to Greek versification. His poetic output was small in quantity but unsurpassed in quality. The much more prolific Palamas, with his extraordinary verbal virtuosity, continued Solomos' work and securely established the demotic as the language of poetry. And the poet-seer Sikelianos, with his lyrical power, reestablished for Greek poetry the lofty voice of the ancient rhapsodists. But in the decade of the 1920's, no true poetic renewal occurred in Greece.

In the rest of Europe in the aftermath of World War I, the 1920's were years of reorientation, and many writers and artists were already experimenting with new ways of expression. In the English language alone, 1922 is considered the annus mirabilis of modernism because it saw the publication of both T. S. Eliot's *The Waste Land* and James Joyce's *Ulysses.* But for the Greeks 1922 was a year of national disaster more devastating in its repercussions than World War I. Greece had fought during the war on the side of its English and French allies and had left its share of blood on the battlefield; but in the years just preceding and following World War I, the loss of life had been mitigated by the expansion of national frontiers, as Greece gradually acquired territories historically Greek but still under foreign rule. Yet in 1922, the ill-planned Asia Minor campaign led to the defeat of the Greek army by the Turks; thousands of civilians perished and the national dream of Greater Greece, whose crowning aspiration was the regaining of Constantinople, was shattered. Moreover, the following year, as a result of the Treaty of Lausanne, which stipulated the exchange of population between Greece and Turkey, one and a half million ethnic Greeks from Asia Minor and eastern Thrace were relocated to Greece. The economic problems that this abrupt demographic change created for a poor country, which until that time numbered a population of only five million, were staggering.

In a general mood of defeat and despondency, it is not surprising that the poets who first appeared in the 1920's express in their work a spirit of weariness and melancholy, an escapist and decadent attitude. Perhaps a major talent who could use national defeat and personal despair creatively did not exist among them. The most gifted of these poets, Kostas Karyotakis, committed suicide in 1928 at the age of thirty-two, bringing to a climax the defeatist attitude of his generation. It was left to the next generation to revitalize Greek poetry.

The first sign of change was given in 1931 by Seferis with the publication of a slim volume of poems, *Strophe.* Its ambiguous title, which means both "stanza" and "turning point," heralded a turning point in poetic expression. Seferis' diction has a frugality almost classical and, although his images reveal a profound sadness over some irreparable loss, there is neither self-pity nor self-indulgence in his poetry, only stoicism and tragic dignity. Seferis' first masters were the French symbolists, but his temperament prepared him for the assimilation of both Eliot's use of myth and Cavafy's mythical use of history. The publication of his next work, *Mythistorema,* in 1935, introduced modernism into Greek poetry.

The same year that established Seferis as a major poet also witnessed the emergence of Elytis with seven short poems that appeared in the November 1935 issue of *Nea Grammata,* a magazine founded earlier in the year by a group of young intellectuals. In their bright imagery and the repetition of such key words as "Aegean," "eros," "song," "dream," "life," "hope," these poems struck a different key from the somber tonality of Seferis' poetry. It seemed as if their poet had been born overnight. And in a sense, he was, for although his poems emerged from a long apprenticeship, the young law student about to abandon his studies to devote himself entirely to poetry christened himself "Elytis" to sign his first published poems. The choice of the euphoneous name was dictated by the poet's aesthetic and ethical ideal. The first two letters are the beginning letters of the Greek words for "Greece" (Ellas), "hope" (elpidha), "liberty" (eleftheria), and "Helen" (Eleni), the prototype of ideal female beauty. They are also the initial letters of "Éluard," the name of the French poet who had a decisive influence on Elytis' early years.

Elytis, the youngest of six children, was born Odysseus Alepoudhelis on 2 November 1911 on the island of Crete to a prosperous industrial family. Both his parents were from the island of Lesbos in the northeastern Aegean. When Elytis was three years old, his father moved the family business to Athens, where the young boy grew up and went to school.

Between Lesbos and Crete, the islands of Elytis' ancestry and of his birth, extends the Aegean archipelago, which the sensitive child came to know intimately during his summer vacations. In those islands, the nascent poet found the shapes of his splendid images and, naturally, when his first poetry appeared, he was hailed as "the poet of the Aegean." This characterization is accurate only if the presentation of the Aegean in Elytis' poetry is not viewed as merely descriptive. The ecstatic lyricism with which the young poet addresses the dazzling landscape of the Aegean had from the start an apocalyptic dimension. As he has indicated, the Aegean for him was not merely a part of nature but also "a signature" of the eternal; it was the mystery of the cosmos apprehended through the senses.

Another frequent characterization of Elytis that needs clarification is that of "optimist," which the poet finds misleading and for good reason. Optimism and pessimism are categories usually applied to a temperament in relation to its attitude to experience and to the outcome of such experience. For Elytis, however, whose poetry transcends the quotidian, such habitual distinctions are inaccurate.

In "To chronico mias dẹkaetias" (The Chronicle of a Decade), an essay describing his spiritual growth, Elytis mentions that as a sixteen-year-old adolescent living in a family that had had its share of mourning (his father and sister had died), he was yearning for a way of expression "which would be more difficult than simply the recording of despair." He was searching for a mode that would constitute "a personal analogue" to the inner sense of splendor and harmony he had often experienced as a child when he wandered barefoot on the shore of an island, a mixture of "brilliance" and "scintillation" that had made him feel at one with the world.

His search was answered one day when he was eighteen by a chance event, if the moments that stand out in a person's experience because they confirm an inner voice can be called "chance events." At a bookstore he happened on a book of poems by the French surrealist Paul Éluard and was immediately struck by a shock of recognition, to borrow the expression that Herman Melville used on first reading Nathaniel Hawthorne. But Elytis' shock of recognition was not prompted, as with Melville, by the "power of blackness" but by the power of light. Here in print was a world of water, sun, and color as he had imagined it and, again as he had imagined it, not rendered with photographic precision but through an array of bold images that appealed directly to the emotions. Elytis had spoken French fluently since childhood, but as he said, it was not the musicality of the words that captivated him but the combination of images that in their lack of obvious logical correlation produced a jolt in the soul; here were brevity and brilliance of expression in the service of the dream!

Eluard's poetry was Elytis' first encounter with surrealism. The next year, as planned, the young man enrolled in law school, but this did not prevent him from setting out painstakingly to find out more about surrealism, which seemed in many respects to spell out his own expectation from art. And when in the early 1930's, Andreas Embirikos, the first Greek psychoanalyst and surrealist poet, arrived in Greece from France, where he had spent several years in close contact with the leading surrealists, Elytis found an older friend "who had dined and drank with [his] gods."

To better understand the relation of Elytis' work to surrealism, it may be useful to state briefly the basic tenets of that movement. Surrealism was born in France in the aftermath of World War I. A movement of revolt against the forces that had led to the war carnage, it distrusted logic and affirmed the power of the imagination as a revelatory medium, a unifier of opposites. "I believe in the future resolution of these two states, dream and reality, into a kind of absolute reality, a surreality," declared André Breton, the movement's chief theoretician, in the "First Surrealist Manifesto" of 1924. The surrealists saw a connection between Sigmund Freud's exploration of the unconscious and "the psychic automatism" advocated by their theory. And, apparently, they considered automatic writing (with its fragmented images and abolition of traditional punctuation) as the equivalent in writing of Freud's method of free association. For them automatic writing was not merely a new literary technique but a new cognitive mode aiming at reuniting man's inner world: biological, emotional, spiritual.

If automatic writing is a necessary component of surrealism, then Elytis was never an orthodox surrealist. Although he wrote many surrealist poems in his exercise book, he used automatism mainly as a way of exploring freely all the resources of his lyrical inspiration; he never published any poems that had not also been subjected to the shaping process of the poetic imagination. Automatic writing, in any event, was only a means to an end; even its first fanatic practitioners gradually departed from it in varying degrees.

The more essential and lasting contribution of surrealism—the element that captivated Elytis when he first read Éluard—was that it opened man's consciousness to a new way of perception that embraced the irrational along with the rational, the sensual along with the spiritual, in the gestalt of the image. In this respect Elytis acknowledges a lasting debt to surrealism because it helped him, and others of his generation, to "find the true face of Greece" and link themselves "physiologically" with the Greek soil. "The Western world," the poet remarked in an interview with Ivar Ivask (published in *Odysseus Elytis: Analogies of Light*), "always conceives of Greece in the image created by the Renaissance. But this image is not true. Surrealism, with its antirationalistic character, helped us to make a sort of revolution by perceiving the Greek truth."

Elytis' perception of the "Greek truth" is a combination of sensuousness and idealism where natural and supernatural elements coexist. The perfect luminosity of the Greek landscape is for him also emblematic of moral perfection and transcendent truth, a measure of man's potential for aesthetic and spiritual fulfillment. And the poet becomes the initiator into this world of inner harmony. This physical metaphysic is for Elytis as profound and inexplicable as faith and, as such, remains constant in his poetry. At first an intuitive perception, it gradually deepens into a visionary understanding that he later formulates into a poetic theory. A chronological survey of his work will demonstrate both the constancy of his vision and the development of his art. One of the most unique characteristics of this art is its formal symmetry. Perceptible even in his early lyrics, in his mature work Elytis' regard for form develops into structures of intricate complexity where the voice of the lyricist joins the ordering intelligence of the mathematician.

## ORIENTATIONS

*Prosanatolismi* (*Orientations*), published early in 1940, is Elytis' first book of poetry. It includes several clusters of poems written in the 1930's, beginning with "Prota poiemata" ("First Poems"), seven of which introduced the poet to the reading public in 1935 through *Nea Grammata.* The book takes its title from one of its subsections, a group of fifteen poems that first appeared in 1936. This subsection is important because, as its title suggests, it shows in miniature Elytis' search for a mode of expression "more difficult than just the recording of despair." The cluster is made up of two sections of seven short poems each, flanking a longer central poem entitled "Epetios" ("Anniversary"). This poem (the title of which may allude to a birthday or another landmark event in the poet's life) is the first truly great poem by Elytis, one that Seferis singled out from the younger poet's early work. It sheds some light on a statement by Elytis that is pivotal to the understanding of his poetry:

> This is why I write. Because Poetry begins at the point where the last word does not belong to death. It is the end of a life and the beginning of another, which is the same as the first except that it goes much deeper, to the extreme point that the soul has managed to decipher, to the boundaries of opposites where the Sun and Hades touch each other. It is the never-ending movement toward the natural light which is the Word and the Uncreated light which is God.
>
> (*Anihta hartia* [Open Book], pp. 39/42[1])

Unlike its satellite poems, "Anniversary" has been translated into English and frequently anthologized:

> I brought my life this far
> To this spot which struggles
> Forever near the sea
> Youth upon the rocks, breast
> To breast against the wind
> Where is a man to go
> Who is nothing other than a man
> Reckoning with the coolness his green
> Moments, with waters the visions
> Of his hearing, with wings his remorse
> O Life
> Of a child who becomes a man
> Forever near the sea when the sun
> Teaches him to breathe there where the shadow
> Of a seagull vanishes.
>
> (Keeley and Sherrard trans.)

[1] Dual page numbers refer to the original 1974 edition and to that of 1987. Except where noted otherwise, all translations are by the present writer.

As the first stanza suggests, the poem is a meditation on man's mortality, described in a subsequent stanza as the "bitter furrow in the sand that will vanish." The power of the poem, apart from its vivid, unusual imagery, derives from a tension, which culminates in the final stanza, between the yearning for transcendence ("the sun's gain in a human heart") and a sense of futility ("the nets of doubt"). But Elytis' ultimate purpose in poetic expression was to move beyond the tension found in "Anniversary" to a vision of paradise, a charismatic moment of inner harmony that cancels out opposites and infuses one with a sense of eternity. When such transcendent vision is achieved, the inevitability of death becomes irrelevant. Poetry, the Word, has harmonized itself with the "Uncreated light."

It appears that both the poems preceding "Anniversary" (the seven short lyrics under the collective title "Orion") and the seven that follow it (under the collective title "Dionysus"), are exercise pieces in Elytis' quest toward a surreal, transcendent realm. Aiming at the same goal, these two clusters nevertheless differ in their imagery. The "Orion" poems—and we should not forget that Orion is a constellation of stars—use night and star imagery and, unlike Elytis after he has emerged from his orientation stage, they convey a somewhat bodiless ethereality. For example, in poem *a,* he writes:

> The night unburdened from noise and care
> is being transformed inside us
> and its new silence shines apocalyptic
> We find ourselves in the hands of God.

And in poem *c*:

> Descendants of ephemeral tears
> Oarsmen of aimless lakes
> We have left behind our earthly skins.
> . . . . . . . . . . . . . . . .
> Now our foreheads neighbor the stars.

In contrast, the "Dionysus" poems are full of bright and earthly imagery. Emotions are presented concretely: hopes are long-haired maidens; desires are swift schooners; dreams accept the sun's challenge to "a duel" of adventure. A very effective image that runs through most of the "Dionysus" pieces is the procession of the hours. These hours, "which have loved our own hours," appear to be a representation of eternity. As they move in complete harmony with "our own hours," a harmony achieved through both visual imagery and rhythmic diction, we feel that in these poems Elytis has achieved for the first time what becomes his most representative characteristic: transcendence through the senses.

"Orion" and "Dionysus" represent decisive moments in Elytis' poetic orientation. In both clusters there is an element of "meteorism," as Elytis has called that upward thrust of the soul that characterizes his poetry. But in "Orion" (as well as in "Epta nihterina eptastiha" ["Seven Nocturnals"], a preceding group of poems) that thrust is trying to fulfill itself through the pale light of a star-studded sky; in "Dionysus" it soars upward through the bright rays of the sun.

The resolution of the poet's orientation—the victory of light as the dominant image of his spirit—finds its clearest expression in the fourteen pieces (ten poems and four prose poems) that close the book. Their collective title, "I thitia tou kalokeriou" ("In the Service of Summer"), is apt indeed, since, in the summer months, the Greek landscape achieves its ultimate luminosity, sharing in the apotheosis of the sun. Compared to the surrealistic pyrotechnics of "Dionysus," these poems have a crystalline lucidity. In the "Dionysus" poems we are confronted with a flood of free-floating images, but "In the Service of Summer" the images spring from a center, a dominant image that often becomes the title of the individual poem as well. An example is the last poem of the cluster, "I treli rodia" ("The Mad Pomegranate Tree"), one of the loveliest lyric poems in the Greek language. Here the pomegranate tree in full bloom becomes the embodiment of a happy mood that has the power to combat "all the cloudy skies in the world." The whole poem is a series of bright questionings about the springs of joy. The questions—each dressed in a splendid image from the Greek countryside—radiate from and converge back to the pomegranate tree as it spreads its blossoms in the broad daylight. The poem leaves us breathless in its cascade of images; it intoxicates us with its lyrical power. Probably no translation can do justice to the word magic of the original, but the English-speaker can experience the enchantment of its imagery in either of two excellent translations, one by Kimon Friar, the other by Keeley and Sherrard.

*Orientations* enables us to experience the very birth of Elytis' images, written in the "alphabet" of the Greek countryside. It also helps us trace the influence of surrealism on the poet, not only in his use of imagery but also in more technical aspects such as free verse and the almost complete absence of punctuation; the most frequent punctuation sign in the early Elytis is the exclamation mark. But even more important, *Orientations* provides us with the first signs of the poet's preoccupation with formal symmetry and his mystical attraction to numbers, particularly the number 7, since most of the poems in the collection are arranged in clusters of seven or in multiples of seven. In the Pythagorean system of the interpretation of the world through numbers, seven is associated with justice, and we might wonder whether Elytis, consciously or unconsciously, has not attributed the same symbolic function to that number. This is quite possible since in his poetry justice or proportion (the perfect correspondence of the good and the beautiful) acquires paramount importance.

## SUN THE FIRST

On 28 October 1940 Italy sent an ultimatum to Greece demanding that the Italian army be permitted to cross the Greek frontier from Albania. Greece, which until that time had not become involved in World War II already raging in Europe, refused, and the Greek army fought a hero's war on the Albanian front, pushing the Italian forces sixty kilometers beyond the Albanian frontier. But six months later, after Germany (having crushed the Yugoslavian resistance) attacked Greece from its Macedonian frontier, the country succumbed to the enemy, and the hard years of the Italian-German occupation began.

Elytis served in the Albanian campaign with the rank of second lieutenant, and although he was not wounded in battle, he contracted a severe case of typhoid fever and only narrowly escaped death. Yet in 1943 in the middle of the occupation, he published his second book of poems, *Ilios o protos* (*Sun the First*), reaffirming the sun as the dominant image of his poetry. The majority of Athenians, starving and persecuted as they were under the Germans, were shocked by the sense of euphoria emanating from these poems. They thought that the poet had remained unscarred by the suffering of his country and his personal war experience. Little did they understand that Elytis, who does not believe in an art that competes with events in the recording of horror, was offering them a ray of hope, an antidote to darkness. In *Anihta hartia*, Elytis explains his philosophy by talking about Henri Matisse, an artist with whom he feels a profound affinity:

> In the years of Buchenwald and Auschwitz, Matisse painted the most juicy and fresh, the most enchanting flowers of fruit that were ever made as if the miracle of life itself had found a way to snuggle forever inside them. This is why they still talk to us today better than the most macabre description of cadavers of the period. [And this is so] because their creator refused to "bet for effect" . . . on the so-called "feeling" and its homeopathic qualities and preferred to obey not the phenomena but the reaction that such phenomena provoke in his conscience. (pp. 294/406–407)

Like Matisse's paintings, *Sun the First* was Elytis' way of counterbalancing a dark period in the history of his country.

The book is composed of two parts, a longer one of eighteen numbered poems and a shorter one of seven pieces under the general title "Paralayes pano se mian ahtida" ("Variations on a Sunbeam"). In their crispness and brightness, these poems have much in common with "In the Service of Summer" of *Orientations.* But the perceptive reader will find in them not only the culmination of a vision and of a technique toward which the poet had worked hard through his orientation years, but also his defiance of the powers that had subjugated his country. For Elytis the supreme force of resistance against foreign occupation is the Greek landscape, depicted as eternal, undaunted, related through bonds of kinship to its people:

> I lived the beloved name
> Under the shade of the grandmother olive-tree
> in the roaring of the perpetual sea.

Lines similar to these from poem VIII abound in the other poems, but in some of them we find a more definite, albeit subtle, invocation of liberty and justice for Greece. An illustration is poem III, offered here in its entirety:

Glittering day, conch of the voice that created me
Naked, to walk on my daily Sundays
Amid the welcoming cry of seashores
Blow on the first-known wind
Spread out an affectionate green meadow
On which the sun may roll his head
And light up poppies with his lips

Poppies that proud men will pluck
So there may be no other mark on their naked chests
Than the blood of carefree disdain that erased
  sorrow
Reaching as far as the memory of freedom

I spoke of love, of the rose's health, the sunray
That alone finds the heart straightway
Of Greece that walks the sea with surety
Of Greece that takes me on voyages always
To naked snow-glorious mountains

I give my hand to justice
Translucent fountain, spring on the mountain
  summit
My sky is deep and unchanging
Whatever I love is born unceasingly
Whatever I love is always at its beginning.

(Kimon Friar trans.)

(A more direct expression would certainly have been banned. The numbered poems in *Sun the First* were twenty-one when they went to print but three were banned by the German censorship. These three later became part of a seven-poem cluster with the inclusive title "I kalossini stis likopories" [Kindness in the Wolfpasses], which was published in the January 1947 issue of the little magazine *Tetradhio,* pp. 3–14.)

I have emphasized the element of resistance in *Sun the First* to show how unfair and superficial the estimation of the Greek public about Elytis was at the time of the publication of this collection. There are, however, other elements—constants in Elytis' poetry—that can best be singled out in *Sun the First.* One is the motif of childhood; the other, the mechanism of metamorphosis.

It has already been mentioned that Elytis aimed from the start at recreating the atmosphere of magic wonder he had experienced as a child on the Greek islands. That atmosphere already recaptured, in *Sun the First* he gives two detailed portraits of that child. Next to each other, poems X and XI present the little boy in absolute harmony with his surroundings, observing, perceiving, participating. In poem X, the "child with the skinned knee" watches "the wet pebbles," "the funny walk of the sea bream," the "hat of the little church." In poem XI, the "little sailor of the garden" climbs up to the clouds, steps on "the seaweed of the sky," and admonishes the angels to make room for the approaching boat, "The Lady of the Annunciation." These poems are reminiscent of Walt Whitman's "There Was a Child Went Forth," except that in Whitman there is more merging of the self and the landscape; in Elytis, it is the objects themselves that merge in a surreal landscape with which the child interacts.

There is a connection between the merging of objects—or more accurately the surreal extension of their properties—and Elytis' mechanism of metamorphosis. Explaining further how surrealism helped him find "the true face of Greece" Elytis mentions in his interview with Ivask that he consciously avoided introducing ancient Greek myths into his poetry because he found their use somewhat "facile" and adds: "Since my chief interest was to find the sources of the neo-Hellenic world, I kept the mechanism of mythmaking but not the figures of mythology." Metamorphosis is, of course, at the heart of mythmaking. In ancient Greek myths human beings become trees and birds, while the forces animating the earth and the sea are personified by the goddess Demeter and the god Poseidon. Elytis does something similar with fresh and original transformations, relating the imagination directly to nature without using ready-made myths as intermediaries. "Soma tou kalokeriou" ("Body of Summer") from *Sun the First* is a poem that he has discussed as an example of his technique. In that poem, the Greek landscape in the heart of summer is represented as a young man "smoking silver-colored olive leaves" as he lies stretched out on his back; while cicadas warm up familiarly in his ears, "lizards glide in the grass of his armpits," and the sea wave, sent by a little siren, rolls lightly through "the seaweed of his feet." There is something both seasonal and perennial in this personification that speaks directly to anyone who has experienced a Greek summer.

Another transformation (this one starting from the opposite direction: a human being assuming the properties of a tree) takes place in the central poem of "Variations on a Sunbeam," "I portokalenia" (The Orange-like Girl). In that poem a young girl, "inebriated" with the sap of the sun, consents to become the "small orange-like girl," a visual depiction of erotic fulfillment. It is important to note that in Elytis' work a metamorphosis always takes place by consent; it expresses a harmonious interaction between people and nature.

"Variations on a Sunbeam," with "I Portokalenia" at its center, is a remarkable group of lyrics in which a sunbeam is successively seen through each of the colors of the spectrum. The sequence of colors (and the title of each poem) goes as follows: "Kokino" ("Red"), "Prasino" ("Green"), "Kitrino" ("Yellow"), "I portokalenia" ("Orange"), "Anihto galazio" ("Light Blue"), "Vathi galazio" ("Dark-Blue"), and "Menexeli" ("Violet"). The seven colors of the spectrum seem to represent the movement of the day, the life cycle, and, more prominently, the stages of eros from "the first shudder in the body" to the evening of life. The imagery of each poem naturally centers around its predominant color.

The title "Variations on a Sunbeam," hinting at variations of perception, brings to mind "Thirteen Ways of Looking at a Blackbird" by Wallace Stevens, a poet with whom Elytis has sometimes been compared. But the similarity between the two poems, and the poets in general, is peripheral rather than essential. Both of them high priests of the imagination, these two poets differ in the role each ascribes to the imagination. For Stevens, the imagination is the creator of "a supreme fiction" that imposes beauty and order on a chaotic world; for Elytis, the imagination is the instrument of what by contrast we can call "a supreme vision," which perceives, through analogies between the seen and the unseen, the inherent beauty and order of the world. By dividing the sunbeam into its component colors Elytis seems to penetrate the layers of light and to achieve a translucence of perception that finds its full articulation in the poems of his maturity.

## *NEW APPRENTICESHIP AND FORMULATION OF A POETIC THEORY*

Contrary to the assumption of many, Elytis had been profoundly affected by the events of the Albanian front, and in 1943, the same year he published *Sun the First,* he also composed a heroic elegy dedicated to the unknown soldier who perished in the Albanian mountains defending liberty and justice. For obvious reasons, "Asma iroiko kai penthimo yia ton hameno anthipolohagho tis Alvanias" ("The Heroic and Elegiac Song for the Lost Second Lieutenant of the Albanian Campaign") was published only in 1945 after Greece had recovered its freedom. Concerning the genesis of the poem, Elytis wrote to Kimon Friar:

> The virtues I found embodied and living in my comrades formed in synthesis a brave young man of heroic stature, one whom I saw in every period of our history. They had killed him a thousand times, and a thousand times he had sprung up again, breathing and alive. He was no doubt the measure of our civilization, compounded of his love not of death but of life. It was with his love of Freedom that he re-created life out of the stuff of death.
>
> (*Odysseus Elytis: The Sovereign Sun,* pp. 16–17)

This heroic elegy, the longest single poem that Elytis had written up to that time, represented for him the keeping of a vow, a silent promise to his fallen comrades to recreate in poetry their composite greatness, the essence of the eternal Greek hero. That he identified closely with these comrades is evident from the fact that he made his unknown soldier a second lieutenant, giving him the rank with which Elytis himself had served in the war.

Abstractions are presented in Elytis' poetry through vivid, often unusual, metaphors. In this poem the violation of justice is viewed through the violation of the landscape: "There where the sun used to dwell . . . Now, as from the sigh of a God, a shadow grows larger . . . Winter enters the brain . . . something evil will flare up." In the fourteen sections of the poem, the imagery moves from winter to spring, from death through lament to resurrection, as the fallen hero "ascends . . . blazing with light" while far away "bells of crystal ring / Tomorrow, Tomorrow, Tomorrow, The Easter of God." Elytis connects his second lieutenant to the eternal Greek hero by incorporating into his verses motifs and cadences reminiscent of the Greek demotic songs: the hero's struggle with Charon "on the threshing floor" and the *miroloyi,* the traditional lament in which the good qualities of the mourned are extolled in metaphoric hyperbole commensurate to the enormity of the loss.

While the "Heroic and Elegiac Song" found an enthusiastic reception among the Greeks, for Elytis it was only a first step toward the poetic realization of the ordeal of his country during the war. In 1944 he composed the first sketch of a long poem in two voices, the *Albaniad* (a title that evokes the *Iliad*), which he never included in his official poetic canon most likely because its form did not measure up to his vision. The poet's vision was only realized after many years of fruitful silence in his masterpiece, *To Axion Esti* (*The Axion Esti,* 1959). (The liturgical phrase "axion esti," equivalent to the Latin "dignum est," may be translated literally as "worthy it is" or loosely as "praised be.")

During his years of poetic silence, however, Elytis accomplished many important things. Feeling that the times demanded the participation of everybody in the reconstruction of the country from the ruins of the war, he devoted his various talents to other artistic areas. In 1945, at the suggestion of Seferis, he served for a year as the director of programming for the newly founded Institute of National Broadcasting, while he also published various articles on literature and art and translated Federico García Lorca's poems into Greek. During the same period, he also turned to the service of his second vocation, painting, by becoming the art critic of the Athenian daily newspaper *Kathimerini.* Elytis is an accomplished painter and has produced a number of gouaches and collages. In fact, in 1948 he represented Greece in the Second International Gathering of Modern Painters in Geneva. The same year, feeling the need to get near "the sources of modern art," he left for Paris, where he stayed until the end of 1951 in close association with important French painters and poets. He also attended literature courses at the Sorbonne. In 1950 he participated in the First International Conference of Art Critics in Paris and was also elected a member of the International Union of Art Critics.

But as Elytis writes in *Anihta hartia,* his stay in Paris helped him most with rediscovering his true "beloved," who would always be poetry. This rediscovery did not come about through the influence of poetic movements but rather through his delving deeper into the essential elements of his Greekness, through the maturation of perceptions that had always existed in him in a somewhat inchoate form but which were now gradually transformed into illuminations. The distance from Greece gave him the proper perspective for this self-discovery by providing him with the clarifying advantages of a comparative approach.

Feeling somewhat out of place in the "existential" climate of postwar Paris, Elytis immersed himself in the study of Plato with the delight of a "thirsty man" who finds "a spring of clear water." Suddenly he was struck by an insight that had for him the apocalyptic power of a miracle: he perceived the organic relation between nature and language; he realized that things are born as the soul, responding to them, baptizes them in sound, which also means that language intrinsically conveys the ethos of a particular landscape. Elytis saw clearly the ethos of the Greek language (an ethos that could never vilify life) moving in a straight line from Plato to Solomos and felt privileged in his Greekness that enabled him to experience the sky and the sea, *ouranos* and *thalassa,* by addressing them with the very same words that Sappho, on the very same shores of Elytis' ancestral island, had used more than two thousand years earlier.

From his initial insight into the analogies among nature, language, and spirit, Elytis came gradually to the realization that technique in poetry—as in any form of art—had meaning only if it reached "the high point of *becoming part of the content.*" And for exactly this reason, "it should be *a personal invention, not a given method*" (the poet's emphasis). Ralph Waldo Emerson would have applauded such a concept of poetry.

When Elytis discussed his ideas with René Char and Albert Camus, they asked him to develop them in an article for a new magazine they were planning that would focus on Mediterranean values. The magazine, "Empedocles," never materialized, and consequently Elytis did not write the article. But the title he had planned for it, "Pour un lyrisme d'inventions architecturales et de metaphysique solaire" (Toward a Lyricism of Architectural Invention and Solar Metaphysics), contained his theory in a nutshell. By "architectural invention" he seemed to refer to the importance of form as an organic extension of the poem's content (the poet's vision); by "solar metaphysics," he was trying to convey his particular architectural invention in the sense that the sun becomes in his poetry a structural principle encompassing physical, ethical, and spiritual values. Later, Elytis referred to the kind of heightened perception he was trying to communicate through his theory of solar metaphysics as *diaphanea,* a term that has often been translated as "limpidity." Since *diaphanea,* however, provides the Greek root for our more familiar "diaphanous," retaining Elytis' term may help to convey his intended meaning, a limpidity of vision that can penetrate through the surface of things. Emerson's famous image of the "transparent eyeball" might help us visualize Elytis' *diaphanea.*

Both the word "metaphysics" and the fact that Elytis formulated his poetic theory after immersing himself in Plato have often raised the question as to whether there is metaphysical certainty in Elytis and whether he perceives the eternal forms as a Platonist. It appears that whereas in Plato's system of two ontological worlds the world of eternal forms is superior to the sensible one (the world of shadows), in Elytis the physical world itself is imbued with eternity. Whichever intangible world lies beyond the phenomena (and there are intimations in Elytis' poems that such a world exists), it is not superior to or more eternal than the physical one. Man may be a temporary dweller in this world but his "eternity" does not consist in the disembodied soul (which possibly preexists and survives after death) but in his potential to reach through the phenomena a moment of heightened awareness (a metaphysical illumination, a *diaphanea*), a perfect harmony of the physical, ethical, spiritual self. And in a country drenched with sunlight, the sun naturally becomes the agent of this inner transformation.

If Plato gave Elytis the insight that led to the formulation of his poetic theory, it was Pablo Picasso's living example that helped him move from theory to creation again. In the work of Picasso, who at that time lived and worked in a small house in Vallauris (near the villa of Elytis' friend and compatriot E. Teriade, the publisher of art books and the periodical *Verve*), Elytis saw the absolute convergence of natural landscape, artistic vision, and artistic form. After spending a day in Picasso's company, he was inspired to write in one sitting an essay entitled "Equivalences chez Picasso" (Equivalences in Picasso), which was published in the 1951 issue of *Verve,* dedicated to the artist:

> In the same way that the severe lines of a bare mountain, in their suggestion of simplicity and neatness, evoke equivalent actions on the moral plane, so do Picasso's lines, as they have developed across the amazing course of his work, teach us the adventure and the discovery of the world; they demand that we arrive at the realization of its poetic potential without any preconceived ideas.
>
> (*Anihta hartia,* pp. 436/593)

This article was Elytis' farewell to the world he was leaving behind. He felt that the time had come for him to return to Greece. In the aftermath of the civil war of 1946–1949, his country was still in ruins, but the poet had already shaped inside him both her passion and her deliverance in the form of *The Axion Esti.*

## THE AXION ESTI *AND* SIX AND ONE REMORSES FOR THE SKY

*The Axion Esti* came out in 1959, and it startled the literary world of Greece with its originality and complexity. Cautious critics were silent, while a few discerning ones hailed the reappearance of Elytis and declared him a major poet, a recognition that was sanctioned the following year by the state when Elytis was awarded the first national prize for poetry.

That same year (1960) also saw the publication of a small collection of superb lyrics entitled *Exi kai mia tipsis yia ton ourano* (*Six and One Remorses for the Sky*). Elytis had actually worked concurrently on the two books—in fact, some of the poems in *Remorses* were written before he started composing *The Axion Esti.* Both works are the product of the same frame of mind: confrontation with evil brought on by the impact of the war years (including the civil war) on the poet's consciousness. But whereas *The Axion Esti* is the lyrical epic of a country and its people, *Remorses* is (to use the title of one of its pieces) an "autopsy" of the poet's inner world after he was struck by evil. Thus, thematically, we can read *Remorses* as an introduction to *The Axion Esti.*

The general theme of *Remorses* is the poet's confrontation with evil and his assumption of a redemptive mission. "I aftopsia" ("The Autopsy"), the second poem, is a metaphor for the destruction of the poet's universe. In the dissection of his body, it was found that he had met evil "in the terrifying posture of the innocent," with nothing left in the brain but "a destroyed echo of the sky." "O ipnos ton yeneon" ("The Sleep of the Brave"), a poem in two versions (or rather two variant endings) presents those actually killed as they lie "face-down on a soil whose tiniest anemone would suffice to turn the air of Hades bitter."

In some respects "The Autopsy" and "The Sleep of the Brave" taken together recast the "Elegiac and Heroic Song for the Lost Second Lieutenant," where the fallen unknown soldier of the Albanian campaign is symbolically portrayed in the military rank with which Elytis had served in the war.

But in *Remorses,* both the poet (the "he" of "The Autopsy") and "the brave" have in addition an archetypal significance. Born out of specific historical circumstances, they nevertheless represent the innocent of any time and place. The ending of the first version of "The Sleep of the Brave" emphasizes the contamination of the formerly Edenic landscape by depicting vultures falling on the dead "to enjoy the clay of their guts and the blood." The second version, on the other hand, presents an image of redemption as "the brave," dwellers now of "the infinite azure," in their first effort to restore to things their true names transform a drop of clear water that had been hanging over the abyss into a young maiden whom they christen Arete (Virtue). Arete's task is to descend every morning from "the embrace of the Mountain" and labor to restore a landscape on which "men had inexplicably committed dark deeds."

The redemptive spirit with which this poem ends prepares us for "Lakonikon" ("Laconic"), characteristically entitled for its pithiness and brevity. In "Laconic," the poet, as a result of having been set on fire by the "burning grief"[2] of death, emits a radiance that "returns" him to the sun. The sun, in turn, sends the poet back into "the perfect correspondence of stone and air." In other words, the radiance of burning grief and the radiance of the sun ritualistically unite, and in that encounter the poet is entrusted with the mission of restoration. And, as he declares in the poem immediately following "Laconic," he decides to walk again in this world "without gods" (possibly meaning without illusions), "heavy with what by living [he has] snatched away from death." This heaviness is not only sorrow but also responsibility.

The poet's first ritualistic act of cleansing the polluted landscape begins in "O alos Noe" ("The Other Noah"), the penultimate poem of the collection: he whitewashes the horizons in order to build "the four walls" of his future, and he is joined in the "Arc of his asceticism" by the "rustling of woman," the most distanced and overlooked "brook," and the only bird left to him, "the sparrow." From the meager vocabulary of sorrow, he picks up only two or three words: "bread," *kaemos,* "love." (Elytis seems to use *kaemos* in its dual meaning of "burning grief" and "burning desire," intending probably to express both a profound sadness and the longing to overcome that sadness.) It is important to keep in mind that Elytis chooses his words very carefully to convey nuances of meaning. It is probable that the "rustling of woman" that joins the poet in the "Arc of his asceticism" is meant to suggest only the memory and not the presence of woman. The female figure in Elytis, particularly that of the young maiden, always signifies rebirth and resurrection. But resurrection and rebirth are still far away in *Six and One Remorses for the Sky.* In fact, the poet ends "The Other Noah" with a vision of the future in which woman as "bearer of things verdant" is seen ascending naked "the current of Time" and majestically opening her fingers to release "the bird" over mankind's toil. This redemptive vision is realized in *The Axion Esti.*

In *The Axion Esti* Elytis achieves the perfect balance of content and form for which he had been striving. The poem is divided into three parts, "I Genesis" ("The Genesis"), "Ta Pathi" ("The Passion"), and "To Doxastikon" ("The Gloria"), each one having its own subdivisions. The structural principle of this tripartite form, as several critics have observed, derives from the Greek Orthodox (or Byzantine) ecclesiastical tradition: the shape of the poem, in which "The Passion" occupies the longest and most important part, resembles the design of a church where the central nave is the largest; moreover, the language of *The Axion Esti* (although a diachronic synthesis of the main voices of the Greek experience) evokes primarily Byzantine hymnology. The very title of the poem is an immediate allusion to its central metaphor. "Axion Esti," which means "worthy is" and by implication "praised be," constitutes the beginning words of both an encomium to Christ sung in the Good Friday service and a celebratory hymn to the Virgin from the Sunday mass of the Orthodox liturgy.[3]

By evoking Byzantine hymnology in *The Axion Esti,* Elytis achieves three important things: he relates his poem to tradition; he

[2] The Greek word is *kaemos,* which, depending on the context, can mean either "burning grief" (anguish) or "burning desire" (longing). Antithetical as these two translations sound, they share the common denominator of "burning," etymologically inherent in the word's derivation from the Greek verb *kaio* (to burn). As a result of this ambiguity, in translations of "Laconic" the relevant phrase has been translated as both "ardor for death" (Friar) and "longing for death" (Keeley and Sherrard). But within the context of the poem and the general theme of *Remorses,* the word *kaemos* should be understood here as "burning grief," not a very poetic expression but one that indicates better than "anguish" or "sorrow" the linguistic relation in the Greek text between a sorrow that sets one aflame and the radiance one emits as a result.

[3] The first detailed discussion of the structure of the poem, with special reference to the symbolic function of number 7 in Elytis' poetry in general, was made by George Savidis

gives to the passion of Greece (and, by extension, to the passion of humanity) the significance of the passion of Christ; and he finds it possible to apply to his sensuous imagery Christianity's concept of sanctification. It should be made clear, however, that although the Greek Orthodox liturgy informs the overall shape of the poem, *The Axion Esti* is not a dogmatically religious work. The Greek Orthodox liturgy, which culturally and spiritually unites modern Greece to its Byzantine heritage, has a mythical significance in the poem; it provides the frame for both the passion and the glorification of a country and its people (and of humanity in general), as Greece, the microcosm of the poet's experience, becomes a representative symbol for both a geographical, horizontal macrocosm (every country and its people) and a vertical, transcendent one that unites the seen with the unseen, the physical with the ethical and the spiritual.

As several critics have noted, perhaps no other poem of the twentieth century compares in structural complexity to *The Axion Esti* (unless it is Elytis' subsequent work, *Maria Nephele* [1978]). Karl Malkoff convincingly points out thematic and structural parallels between T. S. Eliot's *Four Quartets* and *The Axion Esti.* But as Kimon Friar explains, "Eliot's *Four Quartets* has a complicated thematic counterpointing, a musical elaboration of ideas, but the architectural structure, in comparison with that of *The Axion Esti,* is relatively simple." Both George Savidis and Peter Greene have pointed out, as somewhat comparable in structure and "doxological allusions," David Jones's *The Anathemata,* but, as they rightly conclude, the structure of *The Axion Esti* is more intricate and its verbal achievement more astounding than Jones's work.

"Genesis," paralleling the biblical Genesis, is composed of seven sections or hymns in which the poet traces the stages of the creation of the cosmos as his developing consciousness perceives them from infancy to the full assumption of his poetic mission. The poet speaks about himself both in the first person and in the third. The first person refers to his mortal self; the third to an archetypal eternal entity of which the poet is a part, a larger self who acts as a guide in the poet's initiation into the small world—the landscape of his country—which also becomes representative of an eternal world.

The opening line of the first hymn, "IN THE BEGINNING THE LIGHT," recalls both the beginning of John's Gospel, "In the beginning was the Word" and God's command in the biblical Genesis, "Let there be light"—only here light assumes the significance of deity itself. It has always existed; it was not created. The sun, the agent of light and the subject of the first hymn, settles its axis inside the nascent poet and provides him with the power of communication between his two selves: the mortal one, still in the "cradle" and the eternal entity "of many centuries ago." In the second and third hymns appear the land and the sea sowed with the little worlds of the islands. After the plants and the birds are created in the fourth hymn, the Aegean landscape is presented in full splendor and, at the eternal self's command, it is received by the consciousness of the poet as holy communion.

Up to the fourth hymn, of all the senses sight is the predominant one. But in the fifth hearing is added as the growing consciousness "clears the silence to plant seeds of phonemes." And, at about the same time, woman—the consciousness of gender—is created, as young naked maidens appear by the sea uttering or spelling out words "strange and enigmatic": "ROES, ESA . . . NUS . . . ," anagrams for "eros," "sea," "sun," each anagram representing a primary value, not fully comprehended yet,

in his article "'Axion Esti' to poiema tou Elyti" (Praised Be Elytis' Poem), first published in December 1960 and also included in *Ekloyi,* an anthology of Elytis' poetry and critical commentary on his work (selected by the poet himself), published in 1979. A monumental structural and thematic analysis of *The Axion Esti* (a book-length philological study) is Tassos Lignadis' *To "Axion Esti" tou Elyti* (Elytis' "The Axion Esti"), published in 1971. In English, the most detailed discussion is Kimon Friar's in his introduction to *Odysseus Elytis: The Sovereign Sun.*

for the future poet. In the last two hymns, the sense of justice (or proportion), "a point of balance," and of responsibility toward others is created as the poet goes about the task of developing his "particular weapons," as he calls his poetic gift, so he can celebrate the marvel of creation that surrounds him, the microcosm that is also for him a macrocosm, celebrated in the exultant refrain with which each hymn ends: "THIS WORLD / this small world the great!"

"The Genesis" then is the spiritual autobiography of the young Elytis, who, as he says in the first psalm of "The Passion," had been created to sing the young maidens and the Aegean islands, but whom dark necessity compelled to use his weapons (both in the literal and poetic sense) to protect the "Fate of the innocent," which has become his own fate.

"The Passion" is composed of three absolutely symmetrical sections. Each section contains two prose readings flanked by two different kinds of poems: the psalms, designated by capital letters, and the odes, designated by lower-case letters. Within the liturgical atmosphere of "The Passion," the prose readings function as "Evangelia" (gospels) and constitute the epic narrative of the composition; the psalms, modeled on the psalms of the Old Testament, are written in free verse, and they are the "recitative" part of the composition, the poet's voice, which sometimes becomes the voice of his country; the odes evoke Byzantine troparia and have a choral function; they are the lyrical part par excellence of *The Axion Esti,* where Elytis' genius subtly evokes the hymns of Romanos the Melodist, the greatest of Byzantine religious poets, who lived in the sixth century. Each of the three sections is composed of six psalms, four odes, and two (prose) readings arranged in the following order: PPOROPPOROPP.

The polyphonic effect of "The Passion" is not limited to its masterful assimilation of ecclesiastical hymnology. In addition, Elytis harmoniously blends the long tradition of the Greek language from Homer to Solomos in his poem. As the philologist and critic D. Maronitis has observed, an invigorating synthesis of words from four millennia "supports" the poem "and this is not done through borrowings from older phases of the Greek tongue but with transformations or more accurately with graftings of older language forms upon the tree of contemporary poetry." This remarkable synthesis of tradition and living speech is also evident in the prose readings, where, while a certain loftiness of tone and particular expressions are meant to remind us of the Gospels, the style is reminiscent of the colorful demotic of General Yannis Makriyannis, one of the leaders of the Greek revolution of 1821 against the Turks, whose *Apomnimonevmata* (Memoirs) are considered the first important prose document of modern Greece written in the living language of the period.

In specific historical terms the theme of "The Passion" is the experience of Greece through the 1940's: in the first section Greece fights for its freedom in Albania; in the second it suffers the humiliation and deprivations of foreign rule; and in the third it goes through the agony of civil war and is finally delivered. But since the poem, like all great works of art, transcends specific national boundaries, we should also keep in mind Elytis' own thematic description of "The Passion": the first section depicts "consciousness facing tradition," the second, "consciousness facing danger," and the third, "consciousness surpassing danger."

Only a reading of the whole "Passion" can fully convey its complexity and harmony, as readings, psalms, and odes support each other not only thematically but also through the interweaving or the repetition of particular motifs; but some selected passages can serve as samples of the whole.

The second psalm, given here in its entirety, simultaneously exemplifies Elytis' understanding of the organic relationship between language, landscape, and ethos along with mores and his inclusion of the "diachronic" dimension of language within the "synchronic"—in other words, his presentation of the continuity of the Greek language from ancient times to the present not merely as a historical fact but as a living presence.

> GREEK the language they gave me;
> poor the house on Homer's shores.
> My only care my language on Homer's shores.
> There bream and perch
> windbeaten verbs,
> green sea currents in the blue,
> all I saw light up in my entrails,
> sponges, jellyfish
> with the first words of the Sirens,
> rosy shells with the first black shivers.
> My only care my language with the first black shivers.
> There pomegranates, quinces,
> swarthy gods, uncles and cousins
> emptying oil into giant jars;
> and breaths from the ravine fragrant
> with osier and terebinth
> broom and ginger root
> with the first chirping of finches,
> sweet psalms with the very first Glory Be to Thee.
> My only care my language with the very first Glory Be to Thee!
> There laurel and palm leaves
> censer and incense
> blessing the swords and muskets.
> On soil spread with vine-scarves.
> the smell of roasting lamb, Easter eggs cracking,
> and "Christ is Risen,"
> with the first salvos of the Greeks.
> Secret loves with the first words of the Hymn.
> My only care my language with the first words of the Hymn!
>
> (All quotations from *The Axion Esti* from Keeley and Savidis trans.)

The primacy of language ("my only care my language") for the growing young consciousness is repeatedly stressed as the poem moves from the intertwining of language and landscape to the intertwining of language and custom, language and Greek ethos, whether expressed as religious worship—"the sweet psalms of the very first Glory Be to Thee"—or as devotion to Fatherland—"with the very first words of the Hymn." The "Glory Be to Thee" in Greek attests to the linguistic continuity of the Greek Orthodox liturgy since Byzantine times, and the word "hymn" evokes for every Greek the "Imnos is tin Eleftheria" ("Hymn to Liberty") by Solomos, the first two stanzas of which became the national anthem of modern Greece.

The discussion of Elytis' masterful demonstration of the continuity of the Greek language from Homer to Solomos (and consequently to Elytis' own poetry) in the second psalm of "The Passion" would be incomplete if brief reference were not made to ode *a,* which follows the psalm. The diction and the imagery of the ode subtly evokes Solomos' "Hymn to Liberty" along with the very values that inspired it, values that the poet-to-be absorbed as a child while he was learning to articulate the word "liberty":

> MY MOUTH *still in clay, yet it named you—*
> *Rosy, newborn babe, mottled first dew—*
> *And since then, deep in daybreak, it shaped for you*
> *The line of lips, the smoke of hair,*
> *Gave you articulation, gave you the L and the Y,*
> *The airy infallible stride.*

In the second section psalm VII introduces the theme of "consciousness facing danger" as the poet becomes the voice of his country:

> THEY CAME
> dressed up as "friends,"
> came countless times my enemies
> trampling the primeval soil.
> And the soil never blended with their heel.

This theme, Greece threatened by enemies through its long history, is reiterated in the psalms that follow and becomes a choral lament in ode *e*:

> WITH THE STAR'S LAMP I *went out in the heavens.*
> *How in the frost of the meadows, the world's only shore,*
> *Can I find my soul, the four-leaf tear!*

In the poet's lament sadness is alleviated by a search for deliverance. In equating his soul with a four-leaf tear, the poet not only depicts the immensity of pain but also hints at the symbol of luck and hope, the four-leaf clover.

The title of the reading that follows is "I megali eksodos" ("The Great Sally"), alluding to the famous Sally of Missolonghi in 1826 in the war of independence against the Turks, but the particular event it commemorates happened on 25 March 1942. On that day the students of Athens, protesting against an order of the occupying authorities forbidding them to celebrate the national holiday, took to the streets of Athens and brought wreaths of laurel to the heroes of the war of independence. The Germans attacked them, and many young people were killed. Elytis, wishing to universalize his meaning, does not mention the specific enemy but simply refers to them as "the Others."

"The Passion" attains new intensity in the latter part of the second section—narrated in the fourth reading, "To ikopedo me tis tsouknides" ("The Vacant Lot with the Nettles")—and in the early parts of the third section that deal with the civil war, which is presented in the form of a parable in "I avli ton provaton" ("The Courtyard of Lambs"), the fifth reading. In ode *j* following the reading, the poet-shepherd dons the blood of his killed brothers, but at the same time he tries to redeem the blood with light as he summons to his help an ideal female figure, a composite of the Virgin Mary, Greece, and Liberty: "Mother far away, my Everlasting Rose." From this ode and through the psalms that follow, begins the rebirth of the spirit, which culminates in the last reading, "Prophitikon" ("Prophetic"). The tone of "Prophetic" is that of the Apocalypse: "Many years after Sin—which they called Virtue. . . . Turmoil will fall upon Hades, and the planking will sag under the sun's great pressure." Then the exiled poet "will return to stand among the beautiful ruins inside. And then the last of men will say his first word: that the grass shall grow tall and that woman shall rise at his side like a sun's ray." In the last psalm (XVIII) the poet-prophet leads the way to an ideal "unwrinkled" country, whose physical beauty is at the same time a register of the eternal and of moral commandment:

> I'm on my way to a far and unwrinkled country
> Now it is the hand of Death
> that grants the gift of Life
> and sleep does not exist.
> The noon bell chimes
> and slowly on the scorching stones letters are
> carved:
> NOW and FOREVER and PRAISED BE.
> Forever forever and now and now the birds sing
> PRAISED BE the price paid.

In the Greek text, the juxtaposition of *NYN* and *AIEN* (NOW and FOREVER) makes us practically hear the noon bells as they usher in the triumphant "Gloria."

It would be impossible to discuss here the complex stanzaic formations of "The Gloria." Suffice it to mention that it is formed of three parts, the central one of which is the longest. Each of the three parts culminates in a series of salutations: the first, to eternal womanhood in a style that echoes the salutations to the Holy Virgin in the splendid "Acathist Hymn" of the Greek Orthodox liturgy; the second, to the Poet, the poet-prophet of all ages who has the gift of seeing into the heart of things; and the last, to the twin entity of the NOW and the FOREVER whose interdependence makes worthy the price paid for this "small world the Great" that the poet presents with sensuous and sacred adoration.

In 1964 the Greek composer Mikis Theodorakis set parts of *The Axion Esti* to music and produced an oratorio as exhilarating and moving as the poem that inspired it. In this way *The Axion Esti,* reviving the tradition of the Homeric epics sung by ancient rhapsodists to their audiences, became accessible to all people.

## *FROM* THE AXION ESTI *TO THE NOBEL PRIZE: WORK OF TWO DECADES*

Again more than a decade went by before Elytis published any new poetry. But this silence, unlike the one that intervened between his early work and *The Axion Esti,* was not a new apprenticeship but a period of intense creativity. Shortly after he finished *The Axion Esti,* Elytis started working on *Maria Nephele,* a long poetic work published only in 1978. In the early 1960's he also visited the United States as the guest of the State Department, and Russia, at the invitation of the Soviet Union. Moreover, he was elected a member of the administrative board of the Greek National Theater, and he continued working on his essays and his translations of European poets and playwrights into Greek.

Elytis might have published some of the books he was working on earlier had not a historical event—a new ordeal for Greece and its people—intervened. On 21 April 1967, a military junta of the extreme Right seized power. The poet had never involved himself with party politics; therefore he was in no danger of being arrested. But as a sensitive artist, he felt acutely the anguish of those prosecuted and tortured; he also felt choked by the junta's censorship, which made all creative writers agree tacitly not to publish anything until the censorship was lifted. It was at about this time, according to Kimon Friar, that Elytis turned once again to "pictorial expression" and particularly "to collage as a way out of his impasse."

In 1969 the poet left secretly for France. At the villa of his friend Teriade, where he "sat to smoke his first free cigarette / Awkward in the midst of happiness," Elytis wrote "Villa Natacha" (1973), dedicating it to Teriade. This poem, which was later included in *Ta eterothale* (*The Siblings,* 1974), begins with the words "I have something to say, transparent and incomprehensible / like a bird's song in time of war." This mixture of "transparency and incomprehension" characterizes the magical poetry of his next collection, *To photodendro kai i dekati tetarti omorfia* (*The Light Tree and The Fourteenth Beauty*), published in 1971 after the poet's return to Greece. With the censorship lifted, Elytis published several works in the next few years: five books of poetry, his collected essays *Anihta hartia,* an anthology, and several translations. Two of these books are illustrated by the poet's own collages: *Ta Ro tou Erota* (The R's of Eros, 1972), a collection of lyrics to be set to music, and *Ekloyi* (Selections, 1979), the first anthology of his work, spanning the years from 1935 to 1978. Out of this rich harvest, three poetic works, *The Light Tree, To monogramma* (*The Monogram,* 1972), and *Maria Nephele* merit special attention.

More than any of his poetic collections, Elytis infuses *The Light Tree* with his "solar metaphysics," the creative imagination's diaphanous perception of the unseen through the seen. The poems, twenty-one in all (twenty-two if one counts separately the two variations entitled "Ta dio tou kosmou" or "The Two [Aspects] of the World"), are a series of epiphanies presented in the bright, concrete images that are both magical and enigmatic. These poems strike us emotionally and imaginatively, but we may find it hard to understand their magic. And this is as it should be because epiphanies are usually personal revelations, and the *diaphanea* that Elytis has achieved in these poems is not, as he has frequently stated, clarity of mind (the French *clarté*) but the raising of consciousness to a visionary state.

The book derives its title from its longest poem, which is placed fourteenth in order. In conversation with me, Elytis hinted at the significance of the title by mentioning that at the time he was composing *The Light Tree* in France, he was reading a book on Persian Islamic mysticism by Henri Corbin entitled *Spiritual Body and Celestial Earth.* In that book the number 14 refers to the "Fourteen Very-Pure," who in Islamic religion are considered theophanic incarnations of "precosmic eternal entities." Apparently, the concept of "the earth of vision" of Persian mysticism, a state of perception where spirit and body are seen as one, offered the poet an analogue to his own physical metaphysics.

The "light tree" and "the fourteenth beauty" of the title form more or less an equation in which the light tree represents *diaphanea,* the state of imaginative perception where earthly things become sacralized or transfigured; the fourteenth beauty, on the other hand, seems to represent the beatific vision itself, the transfiguration witnessed through the diaphanous state of imaginative perception.

More specifically, the poem "Light Tree" records a past visitation of the poet's consciousness by *diaphanea.* It starts with the memory of an adolescent yearning for death, a "nostalgia" for what lies on the other side. In this context, death is not presented (as most frequently in Elytis) as the grieved-for end of life, but rather as a mystical attraction, a means of merging with the beyond. Even within this context, however, a suicidal wish is acknowledged as an offense to life, as something "angry" and "unfortunate," from which the young man is saved by the sudden appearance of the light tree, which keeps walking "through the light like Jesus Christ or all people in love." Throughout the poem we find both the poet's awareness of the rarity of such diaphanous moments of the creative imagination and his unshakable belief in their possibility—in man's capacity to create his own paradise.

Unlike the "light tree," the "fourteenth beauty" of the title is not the title of a specific poem. The expression appears, however, in "The Two [Aspects] of the World." This poem, in both its variations, begins in a climate of despair, but it also asserts the poet's will "to disguise" himself into a happy man in order to deceive "the track of the Moon." (In Elytis, starlight, unlike sunlight, is often conducive to melancholy.) But this disguise is not exactly a faking but a preparation of the self for the anticipated epiphany that is announced by sounds of music and fresh scents from invisible rosebushes. The stage is set for a process of imaginative transformation through which everything will pass as it moves toward the attainment of "the celebrated fourteenth beauty," the ultimate epiphany.

Kimon Friar, in his discussion of *The Light Tree* (in *The Sovereign Sun*), reminds us that Yeats, in *A Vision,* also conceived of the number 14 (the fourteenth phase of the moon) as representing perfect human beauty, and he adds the valuable information that Elytis had not read this book. It is indeed remarkable that Yeats places in that phase Helen of Troy, Elytis' own special ideal of female beauty. Still more remarkable as an example of perfection in poetic expression, Yeats places in the same phase John Keats, in whom "thought is disappearing into image," something that could be said about Elytis himself. The mystical attraction of both Yeats and Elytis to the number 14—whether it derives from Pythagorean philosophy, Islamic mysticism, or, in the case of Yeats, from a revelation presented to him through the automatic writing of his wife—is astonishing.

In depicting his visionary experience in "The Two [Aspects] of the World," Elytis addresses the archangels Uriel and Gabriel, who "were holding the reins" when a "drop of the Globe" descended to him from the heights above. This annunciation motif is present in other poems as well, but for the most part its messengers are not traditional archangels but young maidens and birds. For example, "Ton Vaion" ("Palm Sunday"), the first poem, sets the tone of rare and perfect bliss, a childhood memory concretely presented through birds descending from the sky carrying green twigs in their beaks as a young girl with unbuttoned blouse is watching. At the same time, a mysterious figure, double the house in height, is discerned touching "the invisible door-knob." This image suggests the threshold of communication between the seen and the unseen, the "celestial earth" between the earth of ordinary sensory perception and the transcendent. In the second poem, "I kori pouferne o vorias" ("The Girl the North Wind Brought"), it is the girl who flies like a bird, her small breasts withstanding the wind, her open legs revealing "the place inside." Elytis' sanctification of the senses and the apocalyptic significance of sexual union is further reiterated in "Peri Politias" ("On the Republic") where a bearded man opens a cage to free a bird which, in turn, is transformed into a woman who invites the man to sexual union. And while in the background the four horses of the Apocalypse pass away without a rider or a saddle (a sign indicating, perhaps, that their day is over), the poet in a creative frenzy continues writing "On the Republic," affirming his own variant of Platonism. Finally, the short poem "Arhetipon" ("Archetype"), in which the poet reminisces about a seashore where he saw woman for the first time and found her to be "a dove," clearly explains his association of woman to the Spirit. She is a divine messenger, an initiator, a revealer of mysteries.

The space does not allow for a discussion of all the poems in *The Light Tree,* but the sample offered is representative of the whole. Most of the poems, whether starting with an epiphany as in "Palm Sunday" or with an "odor of despair" as in "The Two [Aspects] of the World," imagistically present suprasensory moments of intense limpidity. As Elytis has written in "Prota-Prota" (First of All), the introductory chapter to *Anihta hartia*, which can be read as a prose companion to *The Light Tree,* "with every new wave of poetry that returns to [him] after its having first struck [his] early youth [he] feel[s] closer to the light."

In more than one respect *The Light Tree* is reminiscent of *Sun the First.* In both works sunlight is the predominant symbol, except that in *The Light Tree* the light is much more abstract and metaphysical than in *Sun the First;* also, in both works the theme of childhood is evoked, with the difference that in *Sun the First* the "little sailor of the garden" was painted in more concrete physical detail, while in *The Light Tree* we witness the dream world of the child's mind. (Of the poems discussed, both "Palm Sunday" and "The Light Tree" start, respectively, with memories of childhood and adolescence, and so does another poem, "I Odissia" ["The Odyssey"], which offers the wealth of a child's imaginative journeys.) Finally, like *Sun the First, The Light Tree* was written during a dark period of Greek history. If the former included elements of resistance against foreign rule, the latter, written in voluntary exile in France during the years of the Greek junta, offers again a vision of redemption, a trust in the reappearance of justice. A whole essay could be written on the deliverance theme of these poems, beginning with the annunciation motif of the first two, in which the young girl can be perceived as liberty, justice, or Arete, and culminating with "Doro asimenio poiema" ("Silver Gift Poem"), the very last poem of the collection. But, since this particular poem is Elytis' special gift to his readers, we can let it speak instead. Its words are more suggestive than any commentary:

I know all this is nothing  and that the language I speak has no alphabet
Since even the sun and the waves are a syllabic script which can be deciphered only in times of exile and sorrow
And our country  a fresco covered by successive overlays Frankish or Slav  and should you try to restore it you are at once imprisoned and must render account
To a rabble of foreign Powers  always through the instrumentality of your own
As is the custom with disasters
And yet  let us imagine children playing  on an old threshing floor which could even be in a tenement  and that the loser
Must by the rules  speak and forfeit some truth to the others
So that at last they all find themselves holding in their hand a small
Silver gift poem.

(John Stathatos trans.)

With his "Silver Gift Poem," written in times of "exile and sorrow," Elytis was trying to offer a glimpse of paradise to his readers, to those at least who, like the poet, can transcend the adversities of everyday reality through the imagination. Elsewhere, recognizing that for every person there is a different possible paradise, Elytis has described his own in these words:

> Mine should irreparably be filled with trees of words that the wind adorns with silver like poplars, with people who see returning to them the rights they have been deprived of, and with birds which, even in the midst of the truth of death insist on singing in Greek and on saying "eros, eros, eros . . . "
>
> (*Anihta hartia,* pp. 38/41)

Elytis seems to be describing here the prerequisites of his poetic landscape. His paradise is inhabited by poetry, the beloved whom he has pursued since his youth "as if she were a woman" because he "could not bear" feeling incomplete ("half") in this world. His poetic paradise (trees of words and birds singing in Greek) offers him the "diaphanous vision" that for him is synonymous with beatitude.

Elytis' recognition of poetry as his other half might be helpful in our understanding *To monogramma* (*The Monogram,* 1971), a magnificent poem of love and paradise that bears on its front page an enigmatic epigram:

> I will always mourn for you—do you hear me?—
> alone, in Paradise.

One of the most beautiful love poems in the Greek language, *The Monogram,* as enigmatic as its epigraph, has elicited different interpretive speculations. Kimon Friar, for example, thinks that "although the poem receives its title from two reflecting monograms, 'M.K.,' it is written to the dearly beloved of all seasons." The late Greek critic Andreas Karandonis, who saw Elytis as the "archetypical and idealistic poet of eros," suggested that *The Monogram* might indeed be the only love poem by Elytis that "was born out of a specific person or situation," that the poet, having probably experienced in middle age a strong passion for a woman, mourns the fact that the time left to him is so short. Diametrically opposed to this interpretation is that of Maria Lampadaridou-Pothou, who in her study of Elytis stresses the metaphysical aspect of his poetry and consequently believes that *The Monogram* does not address any mortal woman but the "poet's own unknown soul, which inhabited his body bringing him messages from the Unknown."

Admittedly there is room for all these interpretations in this cryptic poem, for the enjoyment of which in the original it is worth learning the Greek language. Eugenios Aranitsis, a young critic whom Elytis considers one of the most astute readers of his poetry, has perceptively observed that the ambiguity of the feminine figure in Elytis relates to the fact that the poet's paradise (his diaphanous vision) is contingent on two mutually exclusive psychological states: loneliness and erotic happiness. The title of the poem itself seems to bear out Aranitsis' point. We usually think of the word "monogram" ("single letter," in Greek) as signifying the initials of a name and tend to forget that the "mono" part of the word means "alone" in Greek. By calling his poem "Monogram," which he also presents pictorially with the two reflecting initials of the title page, Elytis hints at its core: a hymn to the beloved cryptically alluded to through the two initials and, at the same time, the paradoxical admission that loneliness or separation from her is a price that has to be paid for the attainment of paradise.

The two inverted initials function as an ideogram for the whole poem, undoubtedly planned so by the poet, who considers the Chinese ideogram the "most poetic stamp of the ingenuity of the human spirit" in its "instant conversion of thought into image." The visual symmetry of the title is matched by the perfect symmetry of the poem itself. As most often in Elytis this symmetry is organized around the number 7, this time with extraordinary originality and complexity. The poem is composed of seven parts of which the first and the last consist of seven verses each, while the verses of the five parts in between are multiples of 7, in first ascending and then descending order: 7, 21, 35, 49, 35, 21, 7—For a total of 175 verses. (For a more detailed account of the stanzaic and metrical complexities of *The Monogram,* consult Friar's relevant section in *The Sovereign Sun.*) But, of course, on first reading *The Monogram* we are not aware of its structural complexity but only of its beauty and its mystery. Images of intense happiness are mingled with the anguish of imminent separation and reach a climactic point in part 4, the longest and central section.

Any attempt to pinpoint the meaning of the poem would be a reduction of its richness. It is possible, however, to suggest that the sections preceding section 4 may have encouraged the theory of the "specific beloved," whereas those that follow have possibly contributed to the "archetypical beloved" view. The first three sections of the poem present a succession of vivid images in which two lovers now embrace, now whisper somewhere in the Aegean, in a landscape concrete and recognizable in its whitewashed houses, its particular flowers, its waves and rocks. On the other hand, the sections following the central one, without ever abandoning the concrete imagery of an Aegean island, introduce more generalized and abstract expressions such as "About you have I talked in times of old with wise grannies and old rebels," or "For you alone, did God consent to guide my hand," an expression that could also be read as a reference to poetry.

In fact it is not hard to synthesize the two views. It may well be that a particular beloved or, along with her, the activated memory of other women deeply loved in the past, inspired the poem. But since loneliness (however painful the separation from the beloved) seems to be a prerequisite for Elytis' paradise, it is possible that through memory the various loved women from whom the poet needed to separate himself merge into the one archetypical beloved. It must be these intimations of the archetypical beloved in the poem that led Lampadaridou-Pothou to suggest that the poet's beloved is his own unknown soul. However, it seems more appropriate to equate the archetypical beloved with Poetry herself, whom by his own admission the poet pursued as "if she were a woman" and for whose sake probably he never married.

Poetry is for Elytis the only beloved who can share his paradise and to whose ministry all others have to be sacrificed. *The Monogram* orchestrates both the pain and the ecstasy of this sacrifice, an inner necessity it seems, which is expressed somewhat more directly in "The Leaf-Diviner," another deeply moving poem, which Elytis wrote in 1965 and later included in *The Siblings:*

> Alone but not alone; as always;
> As when I was young I advanced
> With the place on my right empty
> While from on high the star Vega followed me
> The Patron Saint of all my loves.

The initial conception of *Maria Nephele* goes back to the early 1960's. In his 1975 interview with Ivask, the poet explains that soon after he finished *The Axion Esti* he met a young woman, "a modern radical of our age," and "suddenly" wanted to write "something very different" that would present the young woman's "world-view," the world-view of the "young generation of today." But since more than fifteen years separate the conception of the work from its completion, it can be assumed (with support from the poem itself) that *Maria Nephele* incorporates not only the radicalism of the generation of the 1960's but also some of the disillusion of that generation in the more complacent and materialistic society of the 1970's.

In the United States the radicalism of the young, who demanded a more humane and just society, reached its peak in the university movements of 1967 and 1968; and in Europe the Parisian May of 1968 crystallized similar if not identical concerns. But in Greece the aspirations of the generation of the 1960's were abruptly jolted early in 1967 by the imposition of a military junta that suppressed all freedom of expression. The pent-up radicalism of the Greek youth surfaced again in the 1970's, and in *Maria Nephele* we see the interaction of that radicalism with some more recently developed cultural realities: increased cosmopolitanism (with its positive and negative aspects), technological advances, concern with material possessions.

The name of the heroine, the title of the poem, must have been chosen to represent her often contradictory qualities: a mixture of purity and sophistication, confusion and activism, pragmatism and idealism. "Maria," one of the most common names in the Christian world, is the Greek equivalent of "Mary" and brings to mind the Virgin Mary, a woman with a divine mission. As for "Nephele," it carries a host of linguistic and mythological associations. The word means "cloud" in Greek, and it alludes both to the heroine's clouded state of mind (her confusion) and the clouds on her horizon (her sadness). And, as Athan Anagnostopoulos reminds us in the introduction that precedes his translation of the poem into English, in Aristophanes' play *The Clouds* "the Nephelae represent the new natural deities, the new trends in educational, cultural and philosophical thought." In that connection the name is apt, since the heroine voices the ideas of the new generation. Moreover, in Greek mythology Nephele was a cloud formed by Zeus into the shape of Hera to protect the real Hera from the sexual advances of impious Ixion. In that sense "nephele" may be seen as the nonessential part of Maria, her semblance rather than her essence.

Since Elytis' heroine is the product of an urban environment, he sets the poem in the city; and in order to represent her generation he abandons for the most part the elevated tone of his other poetry and uses predominantly prosaic and colloquial diction. In the words of Andonis Decavalles, in *Maria Nephele* Elytis' colloquialism "includes jargon, profanity, technological neologisms, and trade terms . . . as well as foreign words, phrases and allusive quotations—all of which recall the practice of Eliot and Pound." There is indeed a "waste land" ambience in *Maria Nephele,* whose disoriented heroine seems to be drifting endlessly in a cosmopolitan metropolis that has lost its cultural cohesion. As a matter of fact, when asked whether he would agree that *Maria Nephele* is *The Waste Land* of his poetic canon, Elytis answered that such a parallel could apply only to a degree because his poem moves beyond despair to affirmation, particularly in "To eonio stihima" ("The Eternal Wager"), its final lyric. Of course, in the last two lines of *The Waste Land* there is a hope for redemption, but it is often missed in the overwhelming atmosphere of desolation of the whole poem. Probably, in comparing *Maria Nephele* to Eliot's poetry, it would be more accurate to say that *Maria Nephele* combines both the emptiness of *The Waste Land* and the redemptive promise of *The Four Quartets,* except that Elytis' redemptive message does not come from Christian faith, as in Eliot, but from his belief in the human potential for renewal.

Elytis, with his constant regard for form, orders his disparate collage of sounds and moods into a symmetrical structure. The basic principle of this symmetry is the twin poem: a series of dramatic monologues, spoken interchangeably by Maria Nephele and the Antiphonist (the poet's persona), and printed next to each other on facing pages. The most direct way to get an overview of the poem's structure is to glance at its table of contents. In the accompanying representation the bracketed phrases provide alternative meanings for ambiguous terms. The titles bearing asterisks are not translations but the poet's original non-Greek titles. (See following page.)

This table gives an idea of both the thematic richness and the structural symmetry of *Maria Nephele.* Each of its three main divisions contains seven pairs of poems, and each pair has a thematic connection. Moreover, as D. N. Maronitis has observed, there is also a broader thematic relation among all three pairs of poems designated by the same number in the three divisions. For example, the number 4 poems are short discourses: in the first division, on beauty; in the second, on purity; in the third, on justice.

*The Presence*

| MARIA NEPHELE SAYS | AND THE ANTIPHONIST |
| --- | --- |
| 1. The Forest of Mankind | 1. The Stigma (or The Fix) |
| 2. Nephele | 2. Nephelegeretes |
| 3. Patmos | 3. The Apocalypse |
| 4. Discourse on Beauty | 4. The Waterdrop |
| 5. Through the Mirror* | 5. Aegeis |
| 6. The Thunder Steers | 6. Hymn to Maria Nephele |
| 7. The Trojan War | 7. Helen |

*Maria Nephele's Song*

| THE ANTIPHONIST SAYS | AND MARIA NEPHELE |
| --- | --- |
| 1. Pax San Tropezana* | 1. The Planet Earth |
| 2. The Manual (or the Dagger) | 2. Each Moon Confesses |
| 3. The Ancestral Paradise | 3. The Paper Kite |
| 4. Eau de Verveine* | 4. Discourse on Purity |
| 5. The Upper Tarquinia | 5. The Eye of the Locust |
| 6. Hymn in Two Dimensions | 6. Official Declaration |
| 7. The Inquisition | 7. St. Francis of Assisi |

*The Poet's Song*

| MARIA NEPHELE SAYS | AND THE ANTIPHONIST |
| --- | --- |
| 1. Good Morning, Sadness | 1. Morning Exercise |
| 2. The Poets | 2. What Convinces |
| 3. The Twenty-four-Hour Life | 3. The Lifelong Moment |
| 4. Discourse on Justice | 4. Study of a Nude |
| 5. Electra Bar* | 5. Parthenogenesis |
| 6. Djenda* | 6. Ich sehe dich* |
| 7. Stalin | 7. The Hungarian Uprising |

*The Eternal Wager*

Another aspect of the poem that becomes apparent through the table of contents is that in the first and third divisions Maria Nephele speaks first, whereas in the middle section the Antiphonist (the respondent) precedes her. This juxtaposition has its thematic significance, which is rather complex. In general, in the first section Maria Nephele leads the Antiphonist into her world; in the second the Antiphonist, already there, comments on that world and juxtaposes it to an ideal one, while Maria Nephele in her own musings expresses a yearning for transcendence; in the third section Maria Nephele reaffirms her despondency while the Antiphonist reaffirms his belief in the eternal power of justice and beauty, which Maria Nephele personifies. An additional structural feature (which is not possible to present in the table of contents) is that each poem is followed by an epigram-like statement, a short maxim of one or two lines that functions in relation to the poem in a way analogous to the epigrammatic moral at the conclusion of a fable. In fact, the year before the publication of *Maria Nephele,* Elytis published these epigrammatic gems in a separate book with the title *Simatologion* (The Book of Signs), in which each epigram is accompanied with a small pictorial design, an ideogram of his thought.

*Maria Nephele* became an instant success, particularly among young readers, who felt that Elytis had captured both the spirit and the style of their times. Nikos Demou, a Greek man of letters broadly read in philosophy and literature, called *Maria Nephele* "as timely as a daily newspaper and as timeless as Homer," adding that Elytis' synthetic and assimilative power in this work can be compared only to Joyce's. Indeed, the complex thematic and structural correspondences among various parts of the work, the linguistic and metrical variety, the juxtaposition of playfulness and seriousness are comparable to Joyce's achievement in *Ulysses.* And understandably, several Greek critics, particularly of the younger generation, hailed *Maria Nephele* as Elytis' major work, surpassing even *The Axion Esti.* Still, *The Axion Esti* is the greater poem. There is no doubt that *Maria Nephele* is an important work and that its linguistic variety and structural ingenuity are extraordinary. But, probably because of its more prosaic language and the en face presentation of statement and response, when we read *Maria Nephele,* we remain aware (and in constant admiration) of the ingenuity of its construction, whereas the equally ingenious *Axion Esti* makes us forget the artist's craft in the organic harmony of the work.

The movement of *Maria Nephele* is that of a quest. For the heroine it is a circular quest without final resolution. For the Antiphonist it is a journey from his world to that of Maria Nephele and back to his own unshakable values. In his interview with Ivask, Elytis says that in this poem he comes to the conclusion that both the young woman and the Antiphonist (the poet himself) "search basically for the same things but along different routes." This realization, however, comes about gradually in the course of the poem.

In "I parusia" ("The Presence"), which describes their initial encounter, the Antiphonist is both attracted and puzzled by Maria Nephele, beautiful and sad, active but not really involved with whatever she is doing. In the garden of a museum, while they are both looking at the stele of an ancient grave depicting a young maiden holding a bird, the Antiphonist expresses his initial disapproval of Maria Nephele and the world she represents by telling her, "You will never hold a bird; you are not worthy." This is a significant statement in view of the association of woman and bird in the poetry of Elytis; but by the end of the poem, the Antiphonist has reversed this position by prophesying in "The Eternal Wager" that a time will come when "all the cruelty of the world will have turned to a stone" on which Maria Nephele, the archetypical seeker of freedom and justice, will sit majestically "holding a docile bird."

The initial rapprochement between the two speakers comes from the realization that they are both self-exiles. The Antiphonist has exiled himself into "the light and the sun" (the visionary world of *The Light Tree*), and Maria has exiled herself among people. In his first monologue, "To Stigma" ("The Stigma"), the poet of transcendence, asking forgiveness from "Poetry [his] Saint," places his hand in Maria Nephele's and accepts her invitation to initiate him into "To dasos ton anthropon" ("The Forest of Mankind"), which she describes in junglelike metaphors. (This is a reversal of Beatrice's leading Dante through the nine heavens.)

In the next pair of poems the interdependence between Maria Nephele and the Antiphonist is reaffirmed. Since she is seen as "Nephele," he is addressed as "Nephelegeretes" (the Cloudgatherer). The term is not Elytis' coinage but one of the many Homeric attributes of Zeus. In "Patmos" it becomes apparent that Maria Nephele does not feel quite at home in the milieu she claims as her own. Equipped with sleeping bags, maps, and other traveling conveniences, she finds herself on the pier of Mykonos—a Greek haven for tourists—but, as the title of her monologue suggests, deep inside she yearns for a Patmos (the Aegean island on which St. John the Divine lived and wrote his Apocalypse. In fact, her poignant cry, "Dear God, where can a person who has no destiny go?" makes clear her inner lack of direction. (The Greek word she uses is *moira,* literally "fate" or "destiny," which has also the metaphorical meaning of "hope" or "luck.") The Antiphonist understands this cry, which sounds like a variant of young Elytis' agonized question in his seminal poem "Anniversary": "Where is a man to go / Who is nothing other than a man?" The young Elytis was able to transcend pain and doubt through poetry, but the young woman, who has sought relevance in social commitment, finds herself empty, with only her body to claim as her own and give freely.

From this point on the Antiphonist begins to understand Maria Nephele, who again in "Through the Mirror" (an allusion to Lewis Carroll) yearns "to pass over the other side of things." In "Imnos sti Maria Nephele" ("A Hymn to Maria Nephele"), his sixth monologue, he addresses her also as "Iris," the young goddess of the rainbow and the winged messenger of Hera, relating her thus for the first time to the flying maidens of *The Light Tree.*

The fundamental convergence of the aspirations of Maria Nephele and the Antiphonist becomes clearer if we consider "The Trojan War" and "Helen," the seventh pair of poems in the first division, in conjunction with the pairs of the same number in the other two divisions. All three pairs of poems juxtapose a mythological or historical event of universal significance and a personage who, directly or indirectly, relates to that event. Thus, after "The Trojan War" and "Helen" (Ancient Greece) come "The Inquisition" and "Saint Francis of Assisi" (Medieval Western Europe) and, finally, "Stalin" and "The Hungarian Uprising" (Communist Eastern Europe).

In all three pairs of poems, an ideal is at stake—in the first, beauty or perfection; in the second, religious faith or conviction; in the third, justice or liberty. And in all three instances the road toward the attainment of these ideals is stained by violence. In the first two pairs, the ideal is presented through the figures of Helen and Saint Francis, while "The Trojan War" and "The Inquisition," the first spoken by Maria Nephele and the second by the Antiphonist, present their speakers' commentary on the universal significance of the particular events. If in the first pair Maria Nephele, the radical, is for Trojan wars and admonishes the "need for a tigress' leap into ideas," in the second pair she seems to echo the Antiphonist's views as she declares that we should not expect anything from "politics and science." To the Antiphonist's condemnation of any enforcement of ideology or faith in "The Inquisition" and his hope that "sooner or later the birds will tame us," she responds with the figure of Saint Francis, the true Christian, who loved all created things and who used to admonish the birds flocking around him to praise their creator. In the third pair, unlike the other two, the historical figure is not the embodiment of an ideal but the corruption of one. In her "Stalin," Maria Nephele, declaring that "the many corrupt the one," alludes to the ruthless dictators of all time, be they politically of the Left or of the Right.

In his essay on *Maria Nephele* (*Analogies of Light,* pp. 87–95), Byron Raizis convincingly suggests that some of the "rhyming couplets" interspersed through "Stalin" allude to "the 1967 slogans of the colonels in Greece." Very likely "Stalin" was inspired by the junta of the colonels who ruled Greece from 1967 to 1974. Concomitantly, "The Hungarian Uprising" (which literally refers to the Hungarian students' revolt against a totalitarian Communist regime in 1956) offers a suitable analogue for the Greek students' uprising against the junta in November 1973. That uprising, which signaled the downfall of the junta less than a year later, is known as "The Polytechneion" in reference to the Polytechnic University of Athens, which served as the headquarters of the revolt. All freedom-loving Greeks, irrespective of political persuasion, were in sympathy with the students. Elytis has kept himself away from politics, but in 1973 he also expressed his quiet defiance of the junta by firmly refusing their Great National Award for Literature. The "Hungarian Uprising," unlike "The Inquisition," endorses the Antiphonist's sympathy. Addressing Maria Nephele, the representative of many young women who participated in similar revolts, he exclaims, "O Maiden You Told me So"; and, concluding that "each era has its own Hungarian Uprising," at the end of the piece the poet appends an epigram that brings together sacrifice and resurrection: "Die if you must, but see that you become the first rooster in Hades."

The Antiphonist's affirmation, expressed most clearly in the concluding lyric, "The Eternal Wager," is a constant in Elytis' work, but in *Maria Nephele* he makes a connection between the transcendent vision of his poetry and the humane impulse that transforms "flower children" into fighting activists. "Each to his own weapons," he said twenty years earlier in *The Axion Esti.* And in a more recent statement, he makes it clear that he considers poetry, his own weapon, "a source of innocence full of revolutionary forces," which he tries to "direct against a world [his] conscience cannot accept." Elytis believes in poetry's potential for transforming consciousness. And unlike Plato, with whom he otherwise shares much, Elytis would entrust to poets the task of directing mankind to an ideal Republic that (to borrow a line from an early poem) can be "recreated beautiful from the beginning to the dimensions of the heart." This may be a utopian vision but, as he says in the epigram that concludes the Antiphonist's Revelation," "if you don't put one foot outside the earth, you will never be able to stand on it."

It was the year after the publication of *Maria Nephele* that Elytis received the Nobel Prize. *The Axion Esti,* for which the Swedish Academy especially praised him, prepared the way, and his publications of the 1970's strengthened the Greek poet's candidacy for the supreme literary prize.

## *THE 1980'S*

The award of the Nobel Prize imposed on Elytis obligations that to his distress forced him to devote less time to his poetry during the next three or four years. In 1982 he published *Tria poiemata me simea efkerias* (Three Poems Under a Flag of Convenience). But in 1984 he was able to complete both *O mikros naftilos* (*The Little Mariner*), a long work on which he had been working for several years, and *To imerologio enos atheatou Apriliou* (The Diary of an Invisible April), a shorter work. *To imerologio* was published in December 1984 while *The Little Mariner* came out in November 1985, marking the fiftieth anniversary of the poet's first appearance.

Concurrently, Elytis also completed two cherished projects of his: the translations of Sappho's poems and of the Apocalypse of St. John into modern Greek. The former, published in 1984, was a landmark event in Greek letters. Not simply a translation but a "resynthesis" with the ancient and modern Greek texts on facing pages, it includes not only the surviving fragments of Sappho's poetry but also its reconstructed missing parts inserted within brackets. The latter, published in 1985, was also received with considerable interest, in particular because it is the second rendition of the Apocalypse into modern Greek by a major poet after Seferis' version, his *metagraphe,* which was published in 1966. (Seferis introduced the word *metagraphe* for the rendition of a work from an older to a newer form of the same language to differentiate this task from that of translation between different languages.) In 1987, Elytis published his third *metagraphe,* the epigrams of Crinagoras, who, born and brought up in Lesbos in the first century B.C., lived most of his adult life in Rome at the court of Octavia, the sister of the Emperor Augustus. In Elytis' modern Greek, the verses of a mediocre epigrammatist like Crinagoras achieve a new poetic grace.

It has been customary to classify Elytis' poetry up to and including *Maria Nephele* into three periods: the early phase of *Orientations* and *Sun the First;* the period of greater historic awareness that centers around *The Axion Esti;* and the phase proper of "solar metaphysics," which begins with *The Light Tree* and ends with *Maria Nephele.* But such a division—although it neatly falls into three different chronological spans—is only approximately accurate with regard to the twin entity of content and form. The period of solar metaphysics has its intuitive birth in *Sun the First* (if not in *Orientations*), finds full expression in *The Axion Esti,* and culminates in *The Light Tree. Maria Nephele* probably relates no more to the *Light Tree* than it does to *Tria poiemata me simea efkerias,* which chronologically, at least, inaugurates a fourth period. And *The Little Mariner,* although published six years after *Maria Nephele,* has characteristics of the third period. If there is a common denominator in the three poetic works of the 1980's, it is that all three deal with the proximity of death. The focus that the poet gives to this subject is very different in each of the three works, which also differ from each other in their overall poetic invention.

*Tria poiemata me simea efkerias* is a meditation on the poet's values and the limited response that these values have found among his contemporaries. Rather prosaic and low-key in tone, these poems (each in seven sections) speak of the visionary moment as recollected rather than experienced. Doubt and despondency coexist with affirmation and hope. Expressions such as "the earth costs me a lot in despair" are counterbalanced by solacing assertions such as "there will always exist two or three brave people to see the world without expediency." It is as if under a "flag of convenience," which is not his usual habitat, the poet assumes the personae of both a doubting Maria Nephele and an encouraging Antiphonist.

Individually entitled "O kepos vlepi" (The Garden Sees), "To amygdalo tou kosmou" (The Almond of the World), and "Ad libitum," the three poems are thematically connected, but each one has its own thematic core. The first juxtaposes the visionary mode of perception to the pragmatic. The visionary perception, the poet seems to say, is not exclusively the domain of the artist, but of anyone who, in the manner of a "garden," can effect through the imagination a reversal of the process of decay. The second poem, whose title seems to symbolize the eternal and the immutable (which, however, lies in man's reach, "pulsating among the foliage" of the garden), raises the question of man's place of origin in verses reminiscent of both Plato's *Phaedo* and Wordsworth's "Intimations of Immortality":

> Man seems to have come from elsewhere
> this is why he sounds off-key
> with a memory fragmented but
> prone to miracles.

And the third poem speaks of the proximity of death (a subject that becomes more pervasive in *To imerologio enos atheatou Apriliou).* Using the metaphor of air travel in section 2, the poet visualizes himself lining up for "passport checking." As the poem progresses, he concentrates on images more specifically Greek, and finally ends with a pun on his first name, "Odysseus," as he projects himself on a raft, shouting out in Greek on behalf of "the other Odysseus" but receiving no response from his fellow man.

*Tria poiemata* is unusual in the Elytis canon because frustration and disenchantment dominate the poems. As such they do not transform our consciousness through lyrical magic, which is Elytis' unique and greatest gift. They do, however, impress us with their verbal dexterity—punning, anagrams, syntactical ambiguities (where the object of one sentence often serves as the subject of the next)—and with the subtle and masterful allusions to other poets, philosophers, or artists (Aeschylus and Heraclitus, Vivaldi and Mozart, Piero della Francesca, and many more).

*To imerologio enos atheatou Apriliou* is composed of forty-nine short poems and prose poems in the form of diary entries, preceded and followed by an introductory and a concluding couplet. The entries begin with Wednesday, 1 April, and conclude with Thursday, 7 May. The year that conforms to these dates could be 1981, but no year is mentioned. The poet's omission of the specific year gives the diary a representative character, making it a poetic inner landscape rather than a chronicle of events. Some dates have more than one entry, while a few are omitted altogether.

The unifying element of this "invisible diary" is the intimation of approaching death. The consciousness of death (or rather the canceling out of the power of death through the poetic experience) has always been central in Elytis, but now that the poet has reached seventy, that consciousness achieves a more personal urgency; it becomes "a daemonic pain."

One question raised by this work is, What were Elytis' aesthetic reasons (apart from any specific personal events) for choosing April as the framing month of his diary? The months that always stand out in his poetry—as months of enchantment, wonder, transformation—are July and August, the heart of the Greek summer. In "Laconic," the central poem of *Remorses,* in which reference is made to the seasons, spring is altogether omitted. Spring is of short duration in Greece. But all the same, this short season signals the rebirth of nature, and April, the quintessential month of spring, can be, as Eliot says, "the cruelest month" for those who cannot enter again the cycle of rejuvenation. Furthermore, April is the month of Easter, the most important religious holiday in Eastern Christian Orthodoxy, and it encompasses elements of both passion and resurrection.

The poet adorns his "daemonic pain" with "silver," evoking thus the silver icons of the mother of God. There are frequent references or allusions to the Virgin Mary in *To imerologio* as well as to the poet's mother, and sometimes the two images merge: "At the place where I first saw Holy Mary (or was she my Mother) there was a smell of burnt fir and of forgiveness." In many entries emerges an admission of disenchantment similar to that found in *Tria poiemata me simea efkerias.* The poet is unhappy for not having effected (at least to the extent he had hoped) the change of consciousness in others that he has envisioned as the key to man's paradise. But in *To imerologio* this disenchantment is expressed with sad acceptance and not with the tone of frustration frequently found in *Tria poiemata.*

The two works also differ stylistically. *Tria poiemata,* in long, prosaic, rarely punctuated sentences, comes across as philosophical, albeit cryptic, argument. *To imerologio,* written in short sentences of frugal lyricism, presents psychological states in a succession of concrete images filled with the memories of a lifetime, and thus it appeals more to the emotions. One of the two entries for Easter Sunday (26 April) admirably combines a vision of transcendence with an awareness of the proximity of death. As the poet gazes up at "the clear diaphanous day" above and at the sea "with its folded wings" below, he feels like flying up and from on high distributing his soul freely. After such a meteoric flight he would be ready to descend and "courageously take [his] place in the grave that belongs to [him]."

The concluding couplet epigrammatically sums up the work and the poet's hope in the generations to come: "—Everything vanishes. Each person's hour comes. / —Everything remains. I am leaving. Let's see what you will do." The enthusiastic response of the young to this book may very well be an indication that they have accepted the poet's challenge.

*The Little Mariner* is Elytis' third long work after *The Axion Esti* and *Maria Nephele,* and like the two earlier ones it is the product of many years' toil. It was basically composed between 1970 and 1974, and seven of its poems appeared in *Ekloyi* (the Elytis anthology published in 1979). But the poet continued revising parts of the work for years before deciding to publish it in its entirety. As intricately structured as any of Elytis' works, *The Little Mariner* consists of three main parts arranged in alternating clusters. Each of these three divisions has as its inclusive title a verse from a Greek poet, one ancient (Sappho), one medieval (Romanos the Melodist), and one modern (the nineteenth-century poet Andreas Kalvos), with all of whom Elytis has special affinities. Romanos' verse, "Myrisai to ariston" (To grace the feast with myrrh), is the title of the first main part, which includes, as the poet explained, "prose poems of a somewhat theoretical background." Each cluster of these prose poems is preceded by a shorter section entitled "Provoleas" (Projector) that presents quick scenes from Greek history. Kalvos' verse, "Kai me phos kai me thanaton" (With both light and death), is the title of the poems proper, the lyrical part of the composition. And Sappho's verse, "Otto tis eratai" (What one loves), is the title of three prose intermezzos that, following the poems, speak of what nourishes and sustains the poet's vision. In addition, the work is flanked by two short prose poems that serve as introduction and conclusion and are entitled "eisodos" (entry) and "exodos" (exit).

It will be helpful to glance at the structural outline of the work as it appears at the beginning of the book, bearing in mind that the parenthetical numbers refer to the pieces each cluster includes in sequential order:

*Entry*

THE LITTLE MARINER (*Projector a'*)
TO GRACE THE FEAST WITH MYRRH (I–VII)
WITH BOTH LIGHT AND DEATH (1–7)
WHAT ONE LOVES (The Traveling Bag)
THE LITTLE MARINER (*Projector b'*)
TO GRACE THE FEAST WITH MYRRH (VIII–XIV)
WITH BOTH LIGHT AND DEATH (8–14)
WHAT ONE LOVES (Aegean Port)
THE LITTLE MARINER (*Projector c'*)
TO GRACE THE FEAST WITH MYRRH (XV–XXI)
WITH BOTH LIGHT AND DEATH (15–21)
WHAT ONE LOVES (Snapshots)
THE LITTLE MARINER (*Projector d'*)
TO GRACE THE FEAST WITH MYRRH (XXII–XXVIII)

*Exit*

If we were to spell out the overall theme of *The Little Mariner,* it would be the poet's spiritual universe in juxtaposition with aspects of human conduct his conscience cannot accept. The projectors have picked up dark spots of Greek history (ancient, Byzantine, and modern) such as the condemnation of Socrates to death, Empress Irene's order to have her young son blinded, and the military junta's attempt to assassinate Makarios, the national and religious leader of Cyprus. The poet counteracts this ugliness by trying to restore "an innocence so powerful that can wash away the blood—the injustice." The task of the little mariner (the poet's persona) is "to grace" a defective world with the "myrrh" of an indestructible vision. Starting on a voyage of self-discovery, he takes along only his "traveling bag," his "guidebook," and his "camera." These three aids are alluded to in the subtitles of the "Otto tis eratai" intermezzos. The traveling bag is full of what the poet likes best in poetry, music, and art; the pages of the guidebook are filled with Greek words; and the "snapshots" that the camera has captured represent permanent imprints of supreme moments in the consciousness of the poet, moments emanating from the Greek landscape or from the grace of young maidens.

It is still early for a full assessment of this complex work, but we can expect it to occupy as important a position in the Elytis canon as *The Axion Esti* and *Maria Nephele.* The indisputable glory of the work is the poetry in "Kai me phos kai me thanaton." With magnificent imagery the poet faces his mortality and talks to his other self, whom he visualizes in different stages of life, now as a child, now as an adolescent (an *ephebe*) "kneeling in the diaphanous depth of the sea," now as a present companion of whom the poet asks hospitality in "the second fatherland of the upper world."

The backdrop of the poems is the poet's beloved Aegean, the natural milieu of the little mariner. The little mariner is still "the little sailor of the garden" of *Sun the First,* who in his familiarity with the sea cannot distinguish it from his garden; he is also the adult man, who in one of his essays wrote that the first time he had the chance to be on the deck of a boat, sailing south toward Santorini (Thíra), he "felt like a landowner who takes inventory of his ancestral estate, which [he is] about to inherit. Those expanses, curly with waves, were the arable lands where the only thing needed to be done was to plant cypress trees as boundaries." Gazing at this "unrepeatable sea" (in poem 18 of "Kai me phos kai me thanaton"), the poet expresses his gratitude by asking his other self to say "goodbye and thanks." His readers, in turn, express gratitude to the poet for the splendor he has bestowed on the Greek language.

Elytis' poetry has a secure place not only in Greek letters but in world literature. His work, little known outside Greece before he was awarded the Nobel Prize, has been widely translated in recent years. From the first translation of some of his poems into French by Robert Levesque in 1945 to this day, more than fifty translations have appeared in at least a dozen languages, among them English, French, German, Italian, Russian, Spanish, and Swedish. Most of the English translations are of high quality in spite of the fact that Elytis is not as easy to translate as Cavafy and Seferis. His lyrical genius and his unique language, lean and dazzling at the same time—the greatest delight for those who can read him in Greek—present a formidable task to his translators.

It is appropriate to conclude with the words of a non-native speaker of Greek, the British writer Lawrence Durrell, whose poetic sensitivity and command of modern Greek have enabled him to assess succinctly and accurately Elytis' contribution to poetry:

> Using the most up-to-date methods in technique, he has, at the same time, insisted that at bottom poetry is not simply a craft or a skill but an act of divination. His poems are spells, and they conjure up that eternal Greek world which has haunted and continues to haunt the European consciousness with its hints of a perfection that remains always a possibility. The Greek poet aims his heart and his gift directly at the sublime—for nothing else will do. That is why we respond with ardor and wonder when we see a poet like Elytis taking the same path as the ancients and, at his best, joining forces with them to affirm the eternal Mediterranean values of his land and tongue.
>
> (*Images of Light,* p. 43)

## Selected Bibliography

### EDITIONS

#### POETRY

*Note:* The early works designated by an asterisk have been republished in successive editions by Ikaros, Elytis' main publisher.

*Prosanatolismi.* Athens, 1940.*

*Ilios o protos.* Athens, 1943.*

"Asma iroiko kai penthimo yia ton hameno anthipolohagho tis Alvanias." First published in *Tetradhio.* Athens, August–September 1945.*

"I kalossini stis likopories." First published in *Tetradhio.* Athens, January 1947.

*To Axion Esti.* Athens, 1959.

*Exi kai mia tipsis yia ton ourano.* Athens, 1960.

*O ilios o iliatoras.* Athens, 1971.

*To photodendro kai i dekati tetarti omorfia.* Athens, 1971.

"Thanatos kai Anastasis tou Konstandinou Paleologhou." First published in *Tram.* Thessalonike, December 1971.

*To monogramma.* Famagusta, Cyprus, 1971. Special edition in the poet's handwriting. Reprinted Athens, 1972.

*Ta Ro tou Erota.* Athens, 1972; 1978; 1986 (expanded edition).

"Villa Natacha." First published in *Tram.* Thessalonike, June 1973. With an original sketch by Pablo Picasso.

"O fillomandis." Athens, 1973.

*Ta eterothale.* Athens, 1974.

*Simatologion.* Athens, 1977.

*Maria Nephele.* Athens, 1978.

*Tria poiemata me simea efkerias.* Athens, 1982.

*To imerologio enos atheatou Apriliou.* Athens, 1984.

*O mikros naftilos.* Athens, 1985.

PROSE

*O zographos Theophilos.* Athens, 1973.

*Anihta hartia.* Athens, 1974; 1982; 1987 (definitive edition).

*I magia tou Papadiamanti.* Athens, 1976.

*Anaphora ston Andrea Embiriko.* Thessalonike, 1978.

COLLAGE

*To domatio me tis ikones.* Athens, 1986. Collages by Elytis; text by Eugenios Aranitsis.

ANTHOLOGIES

*Ekloyi.* Athens, 1979. The first anthology of poetry and prose in Greek, selected by Elytis and illustrated with his collages; it also includes a selection of critical essays on Elytis by both Greek and non-Greek critics.

TRANSLATIONS BY ELYTIS

*Neraida.* Translation of Jean Giraudoux's *L'Ondine.* Athens, 1973.

*O kiklos me tin kimolia.* Translation of Bertolt Brecht's *Der kaukasische Kreidekreis.* Athens, 1974.

*Dhefteri ghrafi.* Translations of poems by Arthur Rimbaud, Lautréamont, Paul Éluard, Pierre Jouve, Giuseppe Ungaretti, Federico García Lorca, and Vladimir Mayakovsky. Athens, 1976.

*Sappho: Anasynthessi kai apodossi.* Resynthesis and rendition of the poems of Sappho into modern Greek. Athens, 1984.

*Ioannis: I apocalypsi.* Rendition into modern Greek of the Apocalypse of St. John. Athens, 1985.

*Krinagoras: Morphi sta nea ellinika.* Rendition into modern Greek of Crinagoras' Epigrams. Athens, 1987.

## TRANSLATIONS

INDIVIDUAL WORKS AND SELECTIONS

*The Axion Esti.* Translated by Edmund Keeley and George Savidis. Pittsburgh, 1974. A bilingual edition in the Pitt Poetry series, it was republished in 1979 in English only.

*The Little Mariner.* Translated by Olga Broumas. Port Townsend, Wash., 1988.

*Maria Nephele: A Poem in Two Voices.* Translated by Athan Anagnostopoulos. Boston, 1981.

*Odysseus Elytis: Selected Poems.* Edited and translated by Edmund Keeley and Philip Sherrard. Additional translations by George Savidis, John Stathatos, and Nanos Valaoritis. Includes excerpts from *Orientations, Maria Nephele,* etc.

*Odysseus Elytis: The Sovereign Sun.* Translated by Kimon Friar. Philadelphia, 1974. Includes selections from *Orientations, The Sovereign Sun,* and other works, as well as an excellent introductory essay and a bibliography.

"Selections from *Maria Nefeli.*" Translated by Kimon Friar and Andonis Decavalles. *Charioteer* 24–25 (1982–1983). Special issue on Elytis.

*Six and One Remorses for the Sky and Other Poems.* Translated by Jeffrey Carson. Helsinki, 1985.

*What I Love: Selected Poems of Odysseas Elytis, 1939–1978.* Translated by Olga Broumas. Port Townsend, Wash., 1986. A bilingual anthology.

IN ANTHOLOGY

*Four Greek Poets.* Translated by Edmund Keeley and Philip Sherrard. Harmondsworth, 1966.

*Introduction to Modern Greek Literature.* Edited by Mary Giannos. Poetry translated by Kimon Friar. New York, 1969.

*Little Treasury of World Poetry.* Edited by Hugh Creekmore and translated by Kimon Friar. New York, 1952.

*Modern European Poetry.* Edited by Willis Barnstone. Greek poems translated by Kimon Friar. New York, 1966.

*Modern Greek Poetry.* Translated by Rae Dalven. New York, 1971.

*Modern Greek Poetry: From Cavafis to Elytis.* Edited and translated by Kimon Friar. New York, 1973.

*The Penguin Book of Greek Verse.* Edited and introduced by Constantine Trypanis. Harmondsworth, 1971. Bilingual edition with prose translations.

*Six Poets of Modern Greece.* Edited and translated by Edmund Keeley and Philip Sherrard. New York and London, 1961.

*Voices of Modern Greece.* Edited and translated by

Edmund Keeley and Philip Sherrard. Princeton, N.J., 1981.

## CRITICAL STUDIES

### GREEK

*Aeolica Grammata* 43–44 (January–April 1978). Special issue on Elytis.

*ANTI* 146 (29 February 1980). Special issue on Elytis.

Aranitsis, Eugenios. "I Geographia tou Paradisou," "Mythos kai logotechnia stin Maria Nephele," "Odysseas Elytis: Simiosis yia mia monographia." In *To symplegma tou Kain*. Athens, 1980.

Argyriou, Alexis. *Dhiadhohikes anagnossis elinon iperealiston*. Athens, 1983.

Daniel, Anthoula. *Odysseas Elytis: Mia antistrophi poria; Apo "To imerologio enos atheatou Apriliou" stous "Prosanatolismous."* Athens, 1986.

Daniel, Iacov. *I archaeognossia tou Odyssea Elyti*. Athens, 1983.

Demou, Nikos. *Prossengissis: Elytis, Eliot, Skythinos, Seferis, Schultz*. Athens, 1982.

*Grammata kai technes* 43–44 (1985). Special issue on the fiftieth anniversary of Elytis' career.

*Hartis* 21–23 (November 1986). Special issue on Elytis.

Karandonis, Andreas. *Yia ton Odyssea Elyti*. Athens, 1980.

Lampadaridou-Pothou, Maria. *Odysseas Elytis: Ena orama tou kosmou*. Athens, 1981.

Lignadis, Tassos, *"To Axion Esti" tou Elyti: Isagoyi, scholiasmos, analysi*. Athens, 1971; expanded edition, 1977.

Lychnara, Lina. *I metaloghiki ton pragmaton: Odysseas Elytis*. Athens, 1980.

———. *To mesoghiako topio ston Seferi kai ton Elyti*. Athens, 1986.

Meraklis, M. G. *Decapende ermeneutikes dokimes ston Odyssea Elyti*. Athens, 1984.

Maronitis, Demetris. *Ori tou lyrismou ston Odyssea Elyti*. Athens, 1982.

Nisiotis, Vasilis (Panos Thasitis). "Odyssseas Elytis: I sinidisi tou Ellinikou mythou." *Kritiki* 1–18 (January–April 1961). Reprinted in Thassitis, Panos. *7 Dokimia yia tin poiessi*. Athens, 1979.

Papachristou-Papapanou, Evanghelia. *"Idou ego": 1 & 4 dokimia yia ton Odyssea Elyti*. Athens, 1980.

Papanicolaou, Mitsos. "O poietis Odysseas Elytis." *Neohellenica Grammata* 72 (1938). Reprinted in Elytis' *Ekloyi*.

Savidis, George. "'Axion Esti' to poiema tou Elyti." *Tachydromos* (10 October 1960). Reprinted in *Ekloyi*.

Vitti, Mario. *Odysseas Elytis*. Athens, 1984.

Zographou, Lili. *O iliopotis Elytis*. Athens, 1971; 1977.

### ENGLISH

Anagnostopoulos, Athan. "Introduction to *Maria Nephele*." In his translation of *Maria Nephele*. Boston, 1981.

Bien, Peter. "Elytis: Surrealism, Correspondence, Imagination, Greekness." *Western Humanities Review* 36: 345–349 (Winter 1982).

Decavalles, Andonis. "*Maria Nefeli* and the Changeful Sameness of Elytis." *Charioteer* 24–25: 23–57 (1982–1983).

———. "Time Versus Eternity: Odysseus Elytis in the 1980's." *World Literature Today* 621:22–32 (1988).

Friar, Kimon. Introduction to *Odysseus Elytis: The Sovereign Sun*. Philadelphia, 1974.

———, ed. *Odysseus Elytis: A Critical Mosaic. Charioteer* 2 (Autumn 1960). Essays by Mitsos Papanikolaou, Andreas Karandonis, Samuel Baud-Bovy, Nanos Valaoritis, Kimon Friar, and Nikos Gatsos.

Green, Peter. "The Poets' Greece." *New York Review of Books* (26 June 1980) 40–44.

Ivask, Ivar, ed. *Odysseus Elytis: Analogies of Light*. Norman, Okla., 1981. An expanded edition of the autumn 1975 issue of the quarterly *Books Abroad*, dedicated to Elytis, it includes, in addition to the poet's interview with Ivask, essays by Lawrence Durrell, Andonis Decavalles, Hans Rudolf Hilty, Christopher Robinson, Robert Jouanny, Vincenzo Rotolo, Edmund Keeley, Byron Raizis, Theophanis Stavrou, and Kimon Friar.

Keeley, Edmund. "The Voices of Elytis' *The Axion Esti*" and "Elytis and the Greek Tradition." In his *Modern Greek Poetry: Voice and Myth*. Princeton, N.J., 1983.

Malkoff, Karl. "Eliot and Elytis: Poet of Time, Poet of Space." *Comparative Literature* 36: 238–257 (Summer 1984).

Robinson, Christopher. "The Greekness of Modern Greek Surrealism." *Byzantine and Modern Greek Studies* 7:119–137 (1981).

Savidis, George. *Odysseus Elytis: Roes, Esa, Nus, and Miroltamity.* Athens, 1980. A monograph based on a lecture delivered at Harvard University in December 1979.

Sherrard, Philip. "Odysseus Elytis and the Discovery of Greece." *Journal of Modern Greek Studies* 1:271–293 (October 1983).

BIBLIOGRAPHIES

Vitti, Mario, with Angheliki Gavatha. *Odysseas Elytis: Bibliographia 1935–1971.* Athens, 1977.

DOROTHY M-T GREGORY

# EUGÈNE IONESCO

## *(b. 1912)*

ONE OF EUGÈNE Ionesco's exercises in French conversation for American students—published in the popular textbook *Miseentrain* (1969) but first staged in 1966 at the Théâtre de Poche—is called "Au théâtre" (At the Theater). In it Jean-Marie, the student, reports to his teacher on a visit to the theater in Paris. "What did you see on the stage?" asks the teacher, Philippe. "I saw nothing on the stage," replies Jean-Marie. "You didn't see the play?" asks Philippe. "What play?" Finally Jean-Marie describes what did happen during his visit to the theater:

> They knocked three times, very loudly, and the room went dark. Then they knocked three more times, very loudly. The chandelier could not resist. It fell from the ceiling onto the heads of the spectators sitting behind me. Luckily, the seats caught fire. Then I had a good view. It was really pretty, there were flames everywhere, lots of corpses. The firemen came. They made us take showers. I had a really good time. I applauded a lot. The next day, where the theater used to be, there was a little bit of ash.[1]

With its stilted phrase-book language and its wildly destructive vision, "Au théâtre" is reminiscent of Ionesco's first experimental dramas, "anti-plays" written in the early 1950's, Ionesco says, because of his loathing for contemporary commercial theater. More important, the motifs here of "lots of corpses" and a "little bit of ash" link up with an obsession with death and apocalypse that unites all of Ionesco's career. Ionesco's imagination fills the stage with things—corpses, eggs, coffee cups, chairs, gigantic dolls, rhinoceroses—as language disintegrates and the world collapses. Lavish scenic inventiveness and a profound responsiveness to light and dark are key elements of Ionesco's drama, from its beginnings in the tiny experimental theaters of the Left Bank to its regular appearances on the stages of the Comédie Française, London's West End, and Broadway.

The course from the avant-garde into the mainstream that Ionesco's career has taken may seem ironic; yet as Ionesco in his later plays reached more and more into a private language of fantasy and dream, the technical resources of big commercial playhouses became essential to the fulfillment of his vision. "The avant-garde," he said at the International Theatre Institute in Helsinki in 1959, "is freedom."[2] Ionesco's ideas of freedom led him from the championship of iconoclastic anti-theater to autobiographical dream plays requiring massive technical budgets, to election to the Académie Française, and to self-

[1] *Exercices de conversation et de diction françaises pour étudiants américains,* in *Théâtre,* 5. 297. All citations from Ionesco's plays are translated by the author from this Gallimard edition and appear in the text in this form.

[2] Eugène Ionesco, *Notes et contre-notes* (Paris, 1962), p. 37. All subsequent citations appear in the text as *Notes.*

portrayal in his polemical writings as a solitary voice crying out against a new "fascism of the Left" in contemporary European culture.

Born in Romania in 1912 and elected to the Académie Française in 1971, Ionesco did not disagree when an interviewer, Claude Bonnefoy, suggested that he might have grown up "doubly patriotic."[3] Ionesco's family moved to France when he was twelve months old; shortly thereafter his father returned to Romania to assist in the war effort. Because of his weak health the young Ionesco was sent to board at a farm, Le Moulin, in La Chapelle-Anthenaise, a small village near Le Mans. He has repeatedly described the time he spent there, from the ages of eight to ten, as a kind of paradise, an Eden from which he was snatched back to Paris. By the age of eleven, he had written his first memoirs; shortly there followed his first patriotic poems and plays. In 1925 his father, whom his mother had assumed to be lost in the war, summoned his family back to Romania, where they discovered that he had divorced his wife, remarried, and gained custody of the children.

Sent to school in Bucharest, Ionesco learned Romanian and wrote patriotic plays and poems in that language. In addition, he told Bonnefoy, he wrote his first comedy—a scenario for a film in which seven or eight children, after their meal, break their cups, break all the dishes, break the furniture, and throw their parents out the window. "Everything I have done," Ionesco wrote in his memoir, *Présent passé, passé présent* (*Present Past, Past Present,* 1968), "I did it in some way against him"—"him" being his father, who appears throughout his journals and memoirs as a figure of triumphant and complacent authoritarianism.[4] Ionesco's sister was driven out of the house by his stepmother; he himself eventually moved out, took his degree in French from the University of Bucharest (thus displeasing his father), and became a teacher of French literature and a regular contributor to anti-establishment literary journals (again to his father's displeasure). Horrified by the rise of fascism in Romania in the early and middle 1930's, Ionesco finally succeeded in moving back to France, described in his memoirs as his motherland, while Romania remains his fatherland. In 1936 his mother died and he married Rodica Burileano; he also began to publish in prestigious Romanian journals. Two years later he received a French government grant to write a thesis on sin and death in French poetry after Baudelaire, and he returned to Paris. His autobiographical writings are reticent on what he did during the German occupation of France.

In 1944 Marie-France, Ionesco's daughter, was born, and in 1945 the family moved from Marseilles to Paris, where they lived in a ground-floor flat in the Rue Claude-Terrasse. "I remember one day a pessimist came to visit me," Ionesco told Bonnefoy:

> My daughter was still a baby and we did not have very much room; we had put her diapers out to dry in the house. Well, my friend came and said this would never do, that life wasn't beautiful, that there was ugliness and misery and everything was sordid, and that our house was ugly and sad, etc. And I answered, "But I find all this beautiful, very beautiful; these diapers hanging from these lines in the middle of the room, it's very beautiful." He looked at me with astonishment and disgust. "Yes," I repeated, "you have to know how to look at it, you have to see. It's wonderful. Anything at all is a miracle; everything is a glorious epiphany; the least object is luminous."
>
> (Bonnefoy, pp. 30–31)

This sense of astonishment before the things of this world—a sense that in other places can be as grim as here it is exalted—is central to Ionesco's vision; again and again in his journals and memoirs he insists on seeing the world afresh, with equally intense euphoria and horror.

[3] Eugène Ionesco, *Entre la vie et le rêve: Entretiens avec Claude Bonnefoy* (Paris, 1977), p. 54. All subsequent citations appear in the text as Bonnefoy.
[4] *Présent passé, passé présent,* p. 24. All subsequent citations appear in the text as *Present.*

During this period Ionesco was working as a proofreader for a legal publishing firm; in 1948 he decided to learn English. "Trying to learn English does not necessarily lead to playwriting," he wrote in 1958. Copying out phrases from an introductory manual, he set to work. "Rereading them carefully," he recalled,

> I learned not English, but astonishing truths—that there are seven days in a week, for example, which I knew already, or that the floor is below and the ceiling above, a thing which I also probably knew, but which I had never really thought about or had forgotten, and which struck me instantly as both astounding and indisputably true.
>
> (*Notes,* pp. 155–156)

The textbook moved philosophically, Ionesco concluded, with a progression like that of Descartes, from universal, axiomatic truths to more complex and relative truths. " 'The country is more pleasant than the city,' assert some; 'Yes, but the population of the city is denser, therefore there are more shops,' reply the others, which is equally true and which proves, among other things, that conflicting truths can easily coexist" (*Notes,* pp. 156–157). Reading the English phrase book, as he read the diapers on the line, with a fresh eye, Ionesco found in it an essential principle of drama.

The result was *La cantatrice chauve* (*The Bald Soprano*), subtitled "Anti-play"; it was first performed before an audience of three at the Théâtre des Noctambules, directed by Nicolas Bataille, on 11 May 1950. "Abstract theater" is how Ionesco described the play in his journal: "Pure drama. Anti-thematic, anti-ideological, anti-social-realist, anti-philosophical, anti-boulevard-psychology, anti-bourgeois, rediscovery of a new theater" (*Notes,* p. 161). The play's first critics, too, had an easier time describing what the play was not rather than what it was. Even its title is misleading: there are no sopranos, bald or otherwise, in the play. Ionesco's first ideas for a title are of a different sort and point toward the play's genesis in the English phrasebook: *L'Anglais sans peine* (English Made Easy), *L'Heure anglaise* (The English Hour), *Big-Ben folies* (Big Ben Follies). But, he admits, "If I had tried and failed to learn Italian, Russian, or Turkish, it could just as easily be said that the play resulting from that vain effort was a satire on Italian, Russian, or Turkish society" (*Notes,* p. 154). English critics like Kenneth Tynan—who was an early champion of Ionesco and later repudiated him as a false messiah of the theater—first saw the play as a satire on middle-class British complacency.

It does begin that way: the description of the set leaves little doubt of a satiric intent. "English bourgeois interior, with English armchairs," it begins. "English evening. Mr. Smith, English, in his English armchair and his English slippers, smokes his English pipe and reads an English newspaper." Mrs. Smith, beside him in her chair, darns "English socks." "The English clock strikes seventeen English strokes." "Well, it's nine o'clock," says Mrs. Smith, and the anti-play is under way (1.21). The first interchanges between the Smiths are indeed reminiscent of language phrase books, as Mrs. Smith drones on, telling her husband what they had for dinner, where they live, and so on. Yet the universal truths of complacent middle-class life immediately become distorted: their daughter is named Helen and Peggy; she is a good housekeeper; she does not drink beer because she is two years old. "Yogurt is excellent for the stomach, the kidneys, appendicitis, and apotheosis," says Mrs. Smith (1.23), introducing into the play a metaphysical dimension that remains as elusive as the bald soprano herself.

"The progression of a passion without purpose" is one of Ionesco's descriptions of this play (*Notes,* p. 161). And the play is best understood in terms of its rhythmic development in time rather than in terms of satiric purpose or metaphysical theme. Punctuated by strokes of the English clock, the Smiths' purposeless conversation revolves around an attempt to distinguish among Bobby Watsons: Bobby Watson is dead, but whether this Bobby Watson is Bobby Watson's wife, mother, husband, uncle—all named Bobby Watson, and all traveling salesmen—leads to a disagreement, to a quarrel, and to a decision to "put out the lights and make dodo" (1.27). This first scene of the play thus contains a whole dramatic action, from exposition of the couple's Englishness, to complication arising from the Bobby Watson problem, to conflict, to denouement, to amorous resolution. What the first scene presents—as does the play as a whole—is the structure of a well-made play without traditional content.

Entrances and exits similarly function as structural elements without traditional grounding in plot and character. At the end of the first scene, the Maid enters and announces that the Martins, the Smiths' dinner guests, are waiting at the door. The Smiths exit to change their clothes, and the Martins enter and play out a recognition scene, at great length, discovering a series of coincidences—they live in the same house, in the same apartment, have the same children—that convince them they know each other. "Elizabeth, I've found you again!" cries Mr. Martin. The clock strikes, "loudly enough to make the audience jump." "Donald, darling, it's you!" exclaims Mrs. Martin. They embrace as the Maid steps forward to inform us that they think they are Donald and Elizabeth, but they are not the right Donald or the right Elizabeth. "While the child of Donald has a white right eye and a red left eye, the child of Elizabeth has a red right eye and a white left eye," she points out. "Thus Donald's whole system of argument collapses against this final obstacle that annihilates his entire theory" (1.33). The emotional drive toward recognition is subverted by a logic more rigorous than that of traditional dramatic construction.

"My real name is Sherlock Holmes," says the Maid as she exits, and in this line we see a hint of a linkage between the drama and the detective thriller that Ionesco will insist upon more explicitly later in his career. Drama, Ionesco says in his notes on *The Bald Soprano,* is a process leading to "the revelation of something monstrous" (*Notes,* p. 160). The failures of the Smiths' expository first scene and of the Martins' recognition scene to bring anything to light shows how far this play is from the compact systems of logical deduction that characterize the reasoning of Sherlock Holmes and the detective dramas in which he (and others like him) can be found.

Nonetheless, the movement of *The Bald Soprano* is toward a kind of revelation or apotheosis that defies logic in its pure theatricality. The disintegration of dramatic form into component parts—entrances, exits, exposition, recognition—does not prevent the anti-play from taking the emotional shape of a play. Changes of pace, punctuated by the clock, propel the play through moments of excitement and doldrums of boredom just as well-made plays must have peaks and valleys, highs and lows. New characters appear in order to salvage foundering action: the Fire Chief arrives and tells a series of stories that trail off, like the Bobby Watson discussion, into a mass of relationships. He and the Maid enact a recognition scene. "She put out my first fires," says the Fire Chief nostalgically (1.50), and the play reaches its lyrical center with the Maid's recitation of a poem, "The Fire":

> The polycanders were burning in the woods
> A rock caught fire
> The castle caught fire
> The forest caught fire
> The men caught fire
> The women caught fire
> The birds caught fire
> The fish caught fire
> The water caught fire
> The sky caught fire
> The ash caught fire
> The smoke caught fire
> The fire caught fire
> Everything caught fire
> Caught fire, caught fire.
>
> (1.51)

She is pushed off the stage by the Smiths, but this apocalyptic vision of mass conflagration (which also has been seen as an image of nuclear destruction) sets the tone for the accelerating pace of the play's final scene, in which the Smiths and the Martins hurl clichés and proverbs at each other in increasingly jumbled form and at increased volume until all four rise and shout syllables at each other in a sudden darkness. The play, like the world in the fire poem, hurtles toward destruction; the monstrous revelation is of inchoate but ferocious violence beneath the disintegrating social surface of language.

The final moments of the play show a return to the beginning, with the Martins in the armchairs speaking the Smiths' lines. This ending was not Ionesco's original idea; he was dissuaded from the latter by the considerable expense it would require. His first choice would have gone like this:

> Once the stage was empty, two or three audience plants would whistle, hiss, protest, and invade the stage. This would necessitate the arrival of the director of the theater with an official and the police; the rioting spectators would be shot, to set a good example. Then, while the official and the theater director congratulate each other for the good lesson they have given, the police, moving to the front of the stage, threatening, guns in hand, would order the audience to evacuate the room.
>
> (*Notes,* p. 164)

This ending, unlike the circular ending that Ionesco adopted, is in keeping with the play's dynamic of acceleration and disintegration. The revelation of the monstrous is turned against the audience itself.

Ionesco's next play, *La leçon* (*The Lesson*), performed at the Théâtre de Poche in February 1951, under the direction of Marcel Cuvelier, traces a crescendo into violence in a more compact and more sharply defined way. This play is in no way an "anti-play"; subtitled "comic drama," it is rigorously classical in its structure. A professor, meek, mild, unprepossessing, instructs a pretty, lively, self-assured girl in mathematics and philology. As the lesson begins, the Maid introduces a note of foreboding: "You'd do better not to start with arithmetic," she warns the Professor (1.69). The arithmetic lesson does begin to get out of control, as the Student can add and multiply without difficulty, but cannot subtract. Using the example of ears, the Professor attempts to make the principle clear: "You have two, I take one away, I eat one, how many are left?" (1.74).

As the Student loses self-assurance and energy, the Professor becomes increasingly voluble and emphatic. From arithmetic he moves on to linguistics. Again the Maid enters with a warning: "Above all, not philology; philology leads to worse . . ." (1.78). Indeed it does, as the Professor declaims wildly about the "neo-Spanish" language group, forcing the Student, now complaining feebly of a toothache, to translate the word "knife" into all these related tongues. "Knife! knife! knife!" he cries as the Student weakly enumerates the parts of her body that hurt: "Knife . . . my breasts . . . my belly . . ." (1.92). He falls upon her, wielding an imaginary knife; she tumbles dead into a chair, her legs open ("immodestly," says the stage direction); he gasps, shivers, sweats.

This is intellectual and physical rape; the play's drive to this moment is irresistible, and in its clarity and simplicity *The Lesson* has become a standard practice piece for actors. But the piece does not end here; summoned by the Professor, the Maid comes in, scolds him, and helps remove the corpse. We learn that this is the fortieth student he has killed today. "Arithmetic leads to philology, and philology leads to crime," intones the Maid. "You said 'to worse,' " objects the Professor. "I thought that 'Worse' was a city and that you meant that philology led to the city of Worse" (1.94). Concerned lest the neighbors complain about his conduct, the Professor frets; the Maid offers him an armband with a swastika. "If you're afraid, wear this," she says, "you'll have nothing to fear. It's political" (1.95). The play ends with the arrival of the forty-first student.

The introduction of the swastika here is disturbing; many of the play's critics have felt it to be unnecessary, a reduction of the play's abstract representation of rape to a specific political level. In his interviews with Bonnefoy, Ionesco discusses Dragomiresco, a professor under whom he studied in Romania, who claimed to be able to measure precisely the amount of "genius," "talent," or "virtuosity" in literary works, using quantitative methods.

> Other times, I had more profound disagreements with my professors, which were not simply the expression of adolescent rebellion. It was due to the fact that some of the professors had become nazified at that time; they were theoreticians of Racism, Nietzscheans, or sub-Nietzscheans, admirers of [Alfred] Rosenberg, or even of [Oswald] Spengler (who was not in favor with the Nazis but was all the same a pre-nazifier).
>
> (Bonnefoy, pp. 20–21)

The bullying Professor of *The Lesson,* then, has his origins in Ionesco's own university experiences. The progression from arithmetic to philology may indeed lead to crime; the Professor's diatribe on the "neo-Spanish languages" may in some way figure Nazi philology, with its insistence on the pure Aryan origin of the Indo-European languages. Intellectual bullying, rape, and fascism are all equated in the play.

If *The Lesson* enacts a rape, *Jacques, ou la soumission* (1955; published in the United States as *Jack; or, The Submission* and in Great Britain as *Jacques; or, Obedience*) enacts a seduction. This play is called a "naturalistic comedy"; it opens on a sordid, ill-kept room in which the Jacques family (all named Jacques) beg Jacques (sitting silent in a collapsed armchair) to make some unnamed concession. He refuses all blandishments and reproaches until his sister Jacqueline, alone with him, forces him to admit that he is "chronometrable" (1.107). This made-up word suggests mortality, living in measurable time; Jacques's excitement and anxiety in pronouncing it make him the first of Ionesco's heroes to find the idea of his impending death insupportable. (Ionesco, in his autobiographical writings, repeatedly insists upon the shock he felt when, at the age of four, he learned that his mother, and indeed everyone, was mortal.) Jacques, acknowledging his "chronometrability," makes the concession his family has begged for: "I adore home-fried potatoes," he declares, to the family's joy (1.109). Straightaway the Robert family enters with their daughter, Roberte, to whom Jacques is to be married: his embrace of greasy, "naturalistic" food leads to his full incorporation into bourgeois society. "I'm happy you adore home-fried potatoes," says his father. "I reintegrate you into your race. Into tradition. Into greasiness. Into everything" (1.109).

But Jacques continues to resist reintegration. Roberte, the proposed fiancée, is not ugly enough; he demands a wife with three noses. The Roberts recover from their mortification to announce that they have a daughter, Roberte II, who has three noses; she is brought on the scene, but Jacques continues to resist. Despite her three noses, she is beautiful. Left alone with Jacques, she begins to seduce him: "I understand, you're not like the others," she says, and she tells him a story:

> I wanted to take a bath. In the bathtub, full to the brim, I saw a guinea pig who had made himself at home. It was breathing underwater. . . . It raised its little head to me with its little eyes, without moving its body. Because the water was so clear, I could see two dark spots on its head, chestnut-colored, maybe. Looking more closely, I saw that they were swelling gently, two excrescences . . . two little guinea pigs, damp and soft, its babies growing there . . .
>
> (1.123)

"That's cancer," says Jacques coldly. "I know it," Roberte II responds. The dreamlike vision of the guinea pigs in the water weakens his resistance, though. "Come, don't be afraid," she woos him. "I am wet . . . my necklace is mud, my breasts dissolve, my pelvis is wet, I have water in my wrinkles" (1.127). Murmuring words containing the syllable "cat" to each other, the two wrap around each other erotically while the families watch.

Jacques's resistance to the idea of death, the dream of cancer, and the erotic lure of sinking in mud all anticipate Ionesco's autobiographical writings. More strikingly, the short story "La vase" ("The Mire," written in 1956) depicts a man succumbing to the lure of slime; Ionesco played that part himself when "La vase" was made into a film in 1970. With *Jacques,* Ionesco's own obsessions and dreams begin to enter into his drama.

The sequel to *Jacques, L'Avenir est dans les oeufs, ou Il faut de tout pour faire un monde* (The Future Is in Eggs; or, It Takes All Kinds to Make a World, 1957), rejoins the Jacques and the Robert families three years later. Jacques and Roberte II are still wrapped around each other, just as at the end of *Jacques,* making cat noises. Here Jacques must be persuaded of the need to propagate offspring and thereby continue the race. "The future of the white race is in your hands," asserts Jacques the father (1.146); the death of Jacques's grandfather, who appears onstage inside a picture frame, makes it necessary. While Roberte clucks loudly offstage, Jacques, groaning in his armchair, is brought basket after basket of eggs. Activity accelerates, as in *The Bald Soprano* and *The Lesson,* to a feverish pitch, as to a refrain of "Production" the relatives rush in and out with eggs, chant a whole roster of political types ("Nationalists . . . internationalists . . . revolutionaries . . . counter-revolutionaries"), and join in a chorus of "Omelets, lots of omelets" (1.155–156). "According to the technological possibilities," Ionesco suggests in the final stage direction, the whole crowd could disappear through a trapdoor.

Although they were written in 1950 and 1951, the *Jacques* plays were not performed until 1955 and 1957; by that time Ionesco was well established as an avant-garde dramatist, on the strength of performances in 1952 and 1953 of *Les chaises* (*The Chairs*), *Victimes du devoir* (*Victims of Duty*), and an especially popular presentation of *Sept petit sketches* (Seven Short Sketches). These all share with the *Jacques* plays the dramatic techniques of acceleration, proliferation, and crescendo. And like the *Jacques* plays they explore reality in images drawn from memory and dream.

First performed in April 1952 at the Théâtre Lancry, *The Chairs* joins the series of Ionesco's plays with subtitles expressing its relation to traditional dramatic forms: it is a "tragic farce." "It demands great tragedy and great sarcasm," Ionesco wrote to Sylvain Dhomme, its first director (*Notes,* p. 166). The play's action is, like that of *The Lesson,* a simple crescendo. An old man and an old woman are discovered alone on stage as the curtain rises, and as they share reminiscences and trade endearments (incongruously, the Old Woman appears to be named Semiramis), we learn that guests are expected. The Old Man has invited them to hear his "message"; to this end he has also invited the Orator, who will put the message into words.

As in *The Bald Soprano,* the doorbell rings and no one is there; nevertheless, the old couple welcome their first guest, apparently a woman, effusively. The Old Man brings her a chair, and they chat with the nonexistent woman for a while. The doorbell rings again; the invisible guest this time is a colonel. He, too, is brought a chair. The old couple's comments make it clear that the colonel is dropping cigarette butts on the floor, flirting with the woman, and generally misbehaving. As the play proceeds, the arrivals of invisible guests accelerate. More and more chairs must be brought in. The stage directions call for noises of arriving motorboats (the windows look out on a body of water) and for the frenzied distribution on stage of fifty chairs. "Don't reduce . . . the great number of chairs," Ionesco warned Dhomme (*Notes,* p. 166); in another note he writes, "We must feel the presence of the crowd" (p. 171).

The excitement peaks as the Emperor arrives; room must be made for him, and the old couple must show the surging and crushing crowd through physical reactions. There is one more surprise: the Orator appears. He is another actor, dressed in painter's smock and beret, exaggerated and conceited in his movements. In their ecstasy the old couple leap out the windows, tossing confetti and streamers at the Emperor. We hear the splash as they hit the water. The Orator turns to speak, but he is a mute. In the published version of the play he writes on the blackboard a series of random letters in which, tantalizingly, appears the word "DIEU" (GOD). In the production the Orator's mumblings were drowned out by the noises of the invisible crowd, and no blackboard was used.

"To explain the end of *The Chairs,*" Ionesco writes, " 'The world is a desert. Peopled by ghosts with plaintive voices, it murmurs love songs over the debris of my nothingness! But come back, sweet images' (Gérard de Nerval, *Promenades et Souvenirs*). That might be it, perhaps, without the sweetness" (*Notes,* p. 171). For the play to work properly, it is important that the old couple not appear to be senile. The crowd of invisible people, in their chairs, must be as real—or as unreal—as the audience in theirs.

*Victims of Duty,* first performed in February 1953 at the Théâtre du Quartier Latin, carries yet another self-conscious subtitle: "pseudodrama." This is the first of a group of five plays that Ionesco derived from short stories he published in 1962 in the volume *La photo du colonel* (*The Colonel's Photograph*). The story, "Une victime du devoir" ("A Victim of Duty"), is a first-person narrative; the drama opens, as is so often the case in Ionesco, on a bourgeois living room. Choubert, the protagonist of the story, sits in the armchair, reading his newspaper; Madeleine, his wife, darns socks. Unlike the reader of the story, the theater audience must be struck by this visual recollection of *The Bald Soprano.*

Reading from the paper, Choubert informs Madeleine that the government recommends a policy of "detachment": "It's the only way, they tell us, to remedy the economic crisis, the spiritual disequilibrium, and the embarrassment of existence" (1.163). Unlike the narrator of the story, Choubert is obsessed with theater. "All plays that have ever been written," he tells Madeleine, "from antiquity up to the present time, have never been anything but detective thrillers. Theater has never been anything but realistic and detective. Every play is an investigation brought to a successful conclusion" (1.165). Shortly after, they hear a knock on the concierge's door (this is the point at which the short story, with no discussion of "detachment" or detectives, begins)—and the Detective enters.

The rest of the play confirms, parodically, Choubert's theory of detective drama. The Detective is looking for the previous tenant of the apartment, Mallot with a "t" (or Mallod with a "d"); without hesitation Choubert says "Mallot with a 't' " (1.169). And in the logic of the play, the Detective must find him where he is lost in Choubert's memory. As Madeleine and the Detective watch, Choubert searches (in lyrical monologue and mime) through his mind; they, too, take on roles from his past. He sinks in mud: "We can still see your hair," says Madeleine. "Keep sinking. Stretch out your arms in the mud, spread your fingers, swim in the thickness, get to Mallot, at all costs" (1.179). Shifting lights, alterations of voice and posture by Choubert and Madeleine, and menacing and clownish behavior by the Detective serve to heighten an audience's sense of irreality and dream.

Choubert is unsuccessful in finding Mallot; again a pair of entrances work to accelerate the action. A Lady appears, without speaking, to watch over the final third of the play; Nicholas d'Eu, a poet, also arrives. The Detective, eager to do his duty and find Mallot, forces Choubert (whose exertions have not made him hungry) to eat crust after crust of dry bread. Like the Old Woman in *The Chairs* or the relatives in *The Future Is in Eggs,* Madeleine rushes in and out, bringing coffee cups onstage; heaps of them mount up. Possessed with a sudden hatred for the Detective, Nicholas falls upon him with a knife. "Long live the white race," the Detective cries as he dies, "I am . . . a victim . . . of duty!" (1.211). So that he will not have died in vain, Nicholas and Madeleine decide to find Mallot; to that end they turn upon Choubert, forcing him to eat, in order to fill the holes in his memory. "Chew! Swallow! Chew! Swallow!" they shout. The rhythm mounts; the silent Lady joins in the chant, as does the gagging Choubert; the curtain falls.

"I have a dream of an irrationalist theater," Nicholas explains to the Detective earlier in the play. "We will abandon the principle of identity and unity of character in favor of movement, a dynamic psychology. . . . We are not ourselves. . . . Personality doesn't exist. There is nothing in us but contradictory or noncontradictory forces" (1.204–205). *Victims of Duty* takes shape as an old-style detective drama operating under these new rules. "Surrealistic theater?" asks the Detective. "Insofar as surrealism is oneiric," replies Nicholas (1.204). "Oneiric"—derived from the Greek word for dream—is a favorite word in Ionesco's discussion of his own theater. Detective-like probing into memory and dream is the source of his artistic production.

*La rhume onirique* (The Oneiric Cold) is the title of one of the seven short sketches performed as an "Ionesco Spectacle" at the Théâtre de la Huchette in August 1953. The manuscript has been lost, but one critic quoted by Richard Coe remembers the play as a spectacle of "one or more players 'sneezing and miaowing' " (Coe, p. 159). Among the sketches that do survive are *Le salon d'automobile* (*The Motor Show*), in which a customer seems to expect the attributes of a wife from a car and ends up marrying a salesgirl; *Jeune fille à marier* (*Maid to Marry*), in which the maid turns out to be a heavily mustached man; and *Le maître* (*The Leader*), in which a crowd of devotees gathers to greet a leader who is never seen. *The Motor Show* had previously been performed as a radio play; the other two were published in anti-establishment journals. Richard Coe tracked down another of these sketches, *La nièce-épouse* (*The Niece-Wife*), and published it in translation as an appendix to his book. In it a viscount proposes to his wife that she become his niece. Full of puns and discontinuities, the sketches fit Nicholas d'Eu's vision of "irrationalist theater" to perfection. At the same time, however, Ionesco was at work on his first full-length play, a traditional three-act "comedy" (as the subtitle announces) based upon his short story "Oriflamme."

*Amédée, ou Comment s'en débarasser* (*Amédée; or, How to Get Rid of It*) was performed in April 1954 at the Théâtre de Babylone, under the direction of Jean-Marie Serreau. The "it" of the title is a corpse; the short story makes it clear that Amédée killed his wife's lover some years ago, but in the play the identity of the corpse is not so certain. What is certain is that the corpse must be got rid of because it keeps growing and mushrooms keep sprouting because of its influence. In the first act Amédée and Madeleine, his wife, try to avoid looking at it but remain fascinated by its growth. But the corpse's gigantic feet burst onto the stage, shattering the door. "It isn't human any more, no, it isn't human . . . human . . . human," sobs Madeleine as the feet take over the room. "And my plays," says Amédée, who has been trying throughout the first act to write a dialogue between an old man and an old woman, "I'll never be able to write now. . . . We're finished" (1.244).

In the second act Amédée and Madeleine decide to do something about the corpse, which now grows visibly onstage. In the process they must, like Choubert, descend into their memories: youthful doubles for them appear (either the same actors or young actors who look like them). The lyricism of Amédée II meets opposition from Madeleine II: "We drift on the limpid lake. Our bark a bed of flowers . . . cradle. . . . The waves carry us . . . we slide. . . ." "I'm sliding!" she cries. "What bark? Tell me what bark you're talking about! What bark can you be thinking of? Where do you see any ba-arks? Hee hee hee! Barks in the mud, in the desert sand, is that possible?"

(1.265). Amédée's vision remains his own as they emerge from the dream sequence to tug the body into position by the window. He looks out. "The light is silken," he effuses, gazing at the Milky Way. "Bouquets of flowered snow, trees in the sky, gardens, fields, domes, capitals, columns, temples. . . . And space, space, infinite space!" (1.275).

In the third act Amédée does not get rid of the corpse; rather, he gets rid of this world. As he drags the gigantic body across the stage (now, after the first two acts indoors, representing the public square), he meets an American soldier; the neighbors wake up; and the corpse, like a huge kite, takes flight, Amédée rising with it. Scenically extravagant as it is, the ending reflects an interest by Ionesco in dreams of flight that would become fully expressed in *Le piéton de l'air* (*A Stroll in the Air,* 1962) later in his career. The corpse means original sin, growing in time, to Ionesco; its taking flight is a kind of transcendence, leaving behind the grim apartment of Amédée and Madeleine with its crop of mushrooms. "The couple is the world itself," Ionesco told Bonnefoy, "they are man and woman, Adam and Eve; the two halves of humanity who love each other, rediscover each other, cannot love each other any more; who, in spite of everything, cannot not love each other, cannot live one without the other" (Bonnefoy, p. 83). This play, then, more than any of the other early plays, reaches out toward a religious and metaphysical plane of significance, and uses a scenic language of dreams to do so.

As a three-act play *Amédée* has a structural problem, in that the third act is extremely short. All that happens dramatically is the levitation of Amédée, a levitation that in the short story sounds exalted but on stage runs the risk of looking ludicrous. In addition, a host of actors is required to play the bit parts of American soldiers, prostitutes, neighbors, and other witnesses to Amédée's flight.

In *Le nouveau locataire* (*The New Tenant*) Ionesco returned to the short-play format. *The New Tenant* was first performed in Finland in a Swedish version in 1955 directed by Viveca Bandler. Despite the volubility of the Concierge in the play—she chatters mindlessly while the Tenant examines his empty apartment—the play is not as dependent upon puns and language games as most early Ionesco. Once again acceleration and proliferation are the keys to the action, as two movers surround the Tenant with furniture. First they bring in small objects, laboriously, with great effort; as the play proceeds, the movers bring in larger and larger pieces of furniture at a faster and faster pace. Yet the more they bring in, the more there seems to be outside. "You have lots of furniture!" says the Second Mover. "You're blocking the whole country." Traffic in the city streets is jammed; the subways cannot move. "The Seine cannot flow," intones the Tenant, "blocked too. No more water" (2.199).

The image of the traffic jam or bottleneck will appear again in Ionesco's drama; here this suggestion of massive urban congestion is confirmed by the clutter on stage. The Tenant protects himself from the incursion of the furniture with a chalk circle inscribed on the floor. There he sits in his armchair as the movers begin to lower more things from the ceiling. At the end of the play, the stage is completely filled and the Tenant is completely enclosed in his circle, invisible to the audience.

This is a powerful image of willful isolation, and it is reminiscent of the resistance to incorporation into the world that Jacques attempts and of Amédée's flight into the Milky Way. In fact, by this time Ionesco found himself under attack by critics who, invoking against him the name of Bertolt Brecht, chided him for his lack of social responsibility. Kenneth Tynan, who had introduced Ionesco to British audiences with his lavish praise of the social satire in *The Bald Soprano,* would soon turn against what he called a cult of Ionesco and his world populated by "solitary robots" (*Notes,* p. 70). Tynan's repudiation of Ionesco would come in 1958; in February 1956 Ionesco tackled his severest French critics in *L'Impromptu de l'Alma, ou Le caméléon du berger* (The Impromptu of Alma; or, The Shepherd's Chameleon). As the title makes plain, the play models itself upon Molière's *Impromptu de Versailles,* in which the playwright placed his critics on stage and answered them. Here Ionesco snores at his desk as the curtain rises; he is interrupted by the entrances of three critics, Bartholomeus I, II, and III. They are dressed in scholars' robes, and each has an ax to grind. The three represent aspects of "Brechtian tyranny," as Ionesco calls it (Bonnefoy, p. 149). Specifically, their objections to Ionesco's works were culled from the criticism of Roland Barthes, Bernard Dort, and Jean-Jacques Gautier. As their robes indicate, they demand a pedagogical and didactic theater.

"Every play is, for me, an adventure, a chase, a discovery of a universe revealing itself in me at whose existence I am the first to be surprised," mumbles Ionesco as Bartholomeus I asks about his next play (2.13). He is eager to present it using the most modern, "ultra-scientific" methods. To Bartholomeus I the proposed play, *The Shepherd's Chameleon,* represents a reconciliation of self and other. "If you would," Ionesco hesitantly says, "I myself am the shepherd, the theater being a chameleon, because I have taken on a theatrical career, and theater is always changing, because theater is life. It is changeable, like life. . . . The chameleon therefore is life!" "That formulation is almost a thought," Bartholomeus I notes. "You are not enough of a sociologist for that" (2.15). The imposition of sociological rigidities upon Ionesco's uncertainties and hesitancies continues as the other Bartholomeuses, with their dogmatisms, arrive. Consulting the "Book of Bertholus," the critics decide to "historicize" Ionesco, while his maid, Marie, knocks on the door. Placards and signs appear, declaring the beginning of "Century B"; Ionesco's costume is "historicized" as his pants drop and he is given a dunce cap. At last Marie manages to enter and rescue him. "Criticism must be descriptive, not normative," Ionesco declares in his final speech:

> If criticism has any right at all to judge, it must judge only according to . . . the mythology of the work itself, entering into its own universe. . . . Theater is, for me, the projection onto the stage of the interior world; in my dreams, my anxieties, my hidden desires, my internal contradictions, I reserve the right to find my own theatrical material.
>
> (2.56–57)

Despite the clownery of the *Impromptu,* this sounds quite serious, and it is in fact a straightforward expression of Ionesco's artistic credo. But as the speech continues, Ionesco himself becomes incoherently pedantic; the maid dresses him in a scholar's robe, and the curtain falls.

"The artistic process, which is creation and exploration, cannot be limited to the expression of a thesis," Ionesco told Bonnefoy in discussing the *Impromptu* (Bonnefoy, p. 149). What Ionesco finds disturbing in Brechtianism is its rigidity, but he also rejects Brecht's Marxist perspective. In a 1971 article entitled "Je n'aime pas Brecht" (I Do Not Like Brecht), he wrote:

> Brechtian man is flat, he has only two dimensions, those of the surface; he is only social. What he lacks is the dimension of depth, the metaphysical dimension. . . . There can be no theater without the revelation of secrets; there can be no art without metaphysics, there is no society without an extra-social background.
>
> (*Antidotes,* p. 193)

To Ionesco, Brecht's ideas are threatening because they suggest that the world of dreams is the product of social conditioning and that theater therefore should function as critique rather than as creation.

Thus, the radiant city in which Bérenger finds himself at the beginning of *Tueur sans gages* (*The Killer,* 1959) is not to be understood in terms of utopian social planning, but rather in terms of a personal, quasi-mystical experience:

> It is light, the city of light. Light is the world transfigured. For example, in spring, it is the glorious metamorphosis of the muddy roads of my childhood. All of a sudden, the world takes on an inexplicable beauty. When I was young, I had luminous reserves. It's beginning to diminish with age . . . I'm heading toward the mud.
>
> (Bonnefoy, p. 30)

*The Killer* is the first of four plays in which Bérenger, Ionesco's semi-autobiographical everyman, appears as hero. Like *Victims of Duty* and *Amédée,* it is based upon a first-person short story; in this instance it follows its original, "La photo du colonel" ("The Colonel's Photograph") quite closely. The play opens with a lighting effect; from gray tones ("like an overcast afternoon in November or February," reads the stage direction [2.63]), the stage suddenly is brilliantly lit. Amazed, Bérenger enters into the radiant city at the end of every tramway.

But from the first there are troubling signs. Although Bérenger had no idea he would come here today, he is greeted by the Architect, who seems also to be some sort of policeman with access to personal dossiers. Bérenger suddenly sees a pool, which the Architect is reluctant to show him. "I was, I became aware that I had existed forever, that I was never going to die," Bérenger rhapsodizes. "A little leap, I would have started to fly . . . I'm sure of it" (2.78). At the same time, in counterpoint, the Architect pleads on the phone with his secretary not to resign from the Administration: "With us, you have a sure future, and life . . . and life!" (2.78). But the secretary, the lovely Dany (whom Bérenger immediately decides to marry), resigns anyway; by the end of the act she, too, has been murdered by the Killer of the title, a homicidal maniac who spares only civil servants. The Killer in the radiant city figures the Fall, Ionesco says (Bonnefoy, p. 31). He meets his victims at the tramway terminus, where the radiant city begins. None can resist his blandishments. Beside the pool he offers to show the colonel's photograph; the victim succumbs to the temptation and, caught off guard, is thrown into the pool and drowned. The first act ends with the news of Dany's death; Bérenger rushes out, crying "Something must be done!" while the Architect complacently declares the case closed (2.98).

As the first act opens in light, so the second act opens in darkness. Bérenger's room remains dark for quite some time while the audience hears the voices of the concierge and the neighbors in the hallway and the sounds of traffic in the street. Well into the act Bérenger arrives, turns on the light, and finds his friend Édouard waiting for him in the dark. They discuss the Killer. Much to Bérenger's surprise, Édouard's briefcase is full of trinkets and photographs of the Colonel, as well as a detailed journal of past and future crimes. Curiously vague, Édouard remembers receiving the materials for publication in a literary journal. The two men rush out to deliver the briefcase to the authorities; Édouard returns to turn out the light and leaves the briefcase behind.

The third act presents us with a political rally and a traffic jam. Under a green flag with a white goose on it, Mother Pipe addresses the crowd. Sounding like one of the Bartholomeuses, she offers a program of "demystification": "If ideology does not fit with real life, we will prove that it does, and that will be perfect. The good intellectuals support us. Against the old myths they will give us anti-myths. We will replace myths . . . with slogans!" (2.142). As the speech continues, Bérenger accosts passersby who have briefcases, hoping to find the one Édouard has lost. There is a huge traffic jam; the police insult Bérenger as he attempts to tell them about the Killer. He walks off alone. "The director, the set-designer, and the lighting-designer must make us feel the solitude of Bérenger, the emptiness of this road between the city and the country," reads the stage direction (2.158). Here Bérenger faces the Killer.

Or not. Ionesco leaves it optional whether

the audience will see the Killer (who in this case is not Édouard) or merely hear his quiet chuckles as Bérenger attempts to communicate with him. He tries to figure out why the Killer does what he does: "You want to destroy the world because you believe the world is doomed to unhappiness?" Bérenger suggests. "You are a pessimist?" The Killer snickers. "You are a nihilist?" The Killer snickers. "An anarchist?" The Killer snickers. (2.163–164). Enraged by the Killer's refusal to respond, Bérenger finally pulls two pistols from his pockets: "I'll kill you, you're going to pay, I'll keep on shooting, then I'll hang you, cut you into a thousand pieces, throw your ashes into hell with the excrement you came from, you vomit of Satan's mangy dog, cretinous criminal" (2.171). But Bérenger's anger has no power against the Killer's "cold determination," his "cruelty without mercy." "My God, nothing can be done!" Bérenger babbles, sinking to his knees as the Killer strokes the blade of his knife. "What can be done? what can be done?" This final line of the play is a grim answer to Bérenger's final line in the first act and his futile but purposeful exit at the end of the second. From light the play plunges into darkness, and the fall is complete.

Mother Pipe and her goose-stepping geese suggest a political dimension to the collapse of the radiant city. *Rhinocéros* (1959), Ionesco's next Bérenger play, draws its central image from his experience of the rise of fascism in Romania. "In this play," Ionesco said in an interview in 1970, "I wanted quite simply to tell the story of an ideological epidemic. I had lived through one, a first time, in Romania, when the intelligentsia became, little by little, Nazi, anti-Semitic, 'Iron Guards' " (*Antidotes,* p. 94). In his private journal in the 1930's, Ionesco used the image of the rhinoceros to characterize the "new race" of "new men," to which he felt acutely that he did not belong. "The new man seems to me to be not only psychologically but physically different from man. I am not a new man. I am a man. Imagine one beautiful morning you notice that rhinoceroses have taken power" (*Present,* p. 97).

The play *Rhinoceros* and the short story on which it is based are attempts to realize this nightmare. The play's world premiere, at Düsseldorf in late 1959, grimly stressed the play's applicability to Nazism; Jean-Louis Barrault, on the other hand, staged the play as "terrible farce and fantastic fable" in its first performances in France in January 1960. "Both interpretations are worthwhile," said Ionesco (*Notes,* p. 184). He was less enthusiastic about the Broadway production of *Rhinoceros* a year later: "Stage directions should be taken as seriously as the text," he complained, "they are necessary and they are also sufficient" (*Notes,* p. 185). The play is not a satire on "conformism," he continued, "but it is the objective description of the process of fanaticization, of the birth of a totalitarianism that grows, propagates, conquers, transforms the world, transforms it totally, of course, because it is totalitarianism" (*Notes,* p. 186). Once again we find in Ionesco's description of his drama the idea of the revelation of something monstrous, an aesthetic at odds with the commercial imperatives of the Broadway stage.

Like *The Killer, Rhinoceros* begins in a world of light. It is near noon on a Sunday; tables are set up outside a café in a little village square. Church bells ring; a housewife goes shopping. Bérenger, disheveled and dusty after a hard night's drinking, meets his friend Jean at the café. Meticulous, tidy, boasting of the strength of his will, Jean scolds his friend but is interrupted by the sounds of a rhinoceros passing by. Things quickly return to normal; Jean continues to chide Bérenger, suggesting that he improve his mind by going to see a play of Ionesco's, while in counterpoint the Logician and the Old Gentleman discuss the nature of syllogism. "All cats are mortal. Socrates is mortal. Therefore Socrates is a cat," the Logician intones. The Old Gentleman agrees: "I have a cat named Socrates." Jean directs philosophical reproaches at Bérenger: "You don't exist, my friend, because you don't think. Think, and you will be" (3.25). Rationalism becomes further baffled as the sounds of a rhinoceros rushing by are heard once more. "He crushed my cat," mourns the Housewife, bringing in the bloody remains (3.32). "What do you expect?" says the Logician. "All cats are mortal" (3.33). The dead cat suggests the ruthlessness of the rhinoceros; the giant beast's logic is impervious to the cat's life.

Trying to hide from Daisy, with whom he is in love, Bérenger is drawn into an argument with Jean about whether the two manifestations of rhinoceros are two appearances of the same rhinoceros or of different rhinoceroses, and whether the Asian or the African rhinoceros has two horns. Losing control, Jean turns on Bérenger: "Two horns, you've got two horns, you Asiatic!" "Asiatics are men like everybody else," says Bérenger. "They are yellow!" screams Jean, beside himself (3.36). It is significant that the dispute over the first appearances of the rhinoceros leads to this racist outburst and that logic is confounded by the riddle of the rhinoceros' horn. "It may be logical," says the Grocer at the end of the act, "but should we allow our cats to be crushed before our eyes by a rhinoceros with one horn, or two horns, whether they be Asiatic or African?" (3.42). In counterpoint to this grandiose humanistic statement, Bérenger, immediately contrite about quarreling with Jean, orders a double cognac.

The first act identifies the crushing of the cat with both the rhinoceros' inexorable charge and the Logician's nonsensical reformulations of philosophical clichés. In addition, Jean's racist refusal to allow that Asiatics are "like everybody else" because they are yellow takes place as the Housewife mourns a cat who was "so sweet, he was just like one of us" (3.36). Thus we are prepared for Jean's onstage transformation into a rhinoceros in the second act and for the news of the Logician's transformation in the third. The crushing of the cat insists that an essential aspect of rhinoceros is cruelty. "I was looking for a terrible animal, small-minded, crushing everything that got in its way," Ionesco said in 1970 (*Antidotes,* p. 95). In the first act the Logician and Jean already seem to possess these qualities.

The first scene of the second act takes place at the office. Daisy's co-workers, Botard and Dudard—their names suggest a comic interchangeability—argue fiercely about the previous day's sightings of rhinoceroses. "Is it a question of a male cat or a female cat?" asks Botard, skeptically perusing the newspaper report of the crushing of a cat by a pachyderm. "What color? What race? I'm not racist myself, I am anti-racist" (3.47). Racism again intrudes into the discussion of the rhinoceros. Bérenger arrives and confirms Daisy's story: "Collective psychosis," snorts Botard, "like religion, the opiate of the people!" (3.52). Boeuf, who has failed to show up for work, arrives in the shape of a rhinoceros (his wife recognizes him) and destroys the stairs in attempting to ascend to the office. The firemen are summoned to help the workers out. Botard suggests there is a conspiracy afoot. Bérenger decides to visit Jean and apologize.

But it seems to be too late: in the next scene Jean, coughing on his bed in the dark, has begun to change. The transformation is at first psychological. Bérenger tries to apologize for the affair of the "miserable rhinoceros." "Who told you those two rhinoceroses were miserable?" asks Jean (3.67). Jean goes in and out of the bathroom; with each entrance his skin is greener and the horn on his head grows larger. Bérenger suggests that he see a doctor. "I only trust veterinarians," Jean grunts (3.71). When Bérenger invokes the idea of friendship, Jean rejects him: "Friendship doesn't exist. I don't believe in your friendship. . . . If anyone gets in my way, I crush him" (3.72). "Man . . . Don't say that word," he grumbles. "Humanism is all finished. You're a sentimental old fool" (3.76). Finally, bellowing "the swamps, the swamps," Jean becomes wholly rhinoceros; his horn smashes through the door of the bathroom as Bérenger flees. But the neighbors he attempts to warn have turned into rhinoceroses as well.

The third act begins in Bérenger's room—

strikingly similar to Jean's. Dudard comes to visit; he claims he will never become a rhinoceros, but there are disturbing signs. "I'm not ambitious," says Bérenger, wondering about Jean's transformation. "I'm happy with who I am." "Maybe he liked the fresh air, the country. . . . Maybe he needed to relax," Dudard replies. "I'm not saying this to excuse him" (3.84). Dudard urges Bérenger to be realistic. "You think it's natural?" exclaims Bérenger. "What could be more natural than a rhinoceros?" Dudard replies (3.93). Discussion of natural and unnatural, normal and abnormal, becomes contorted. Bérenger wishes for the help of the Logician, only to be told that he, too, has become a rhinoceros. Daisy arrives; her obvious affection for Bérenger and her familiarity with his apartment provoke Dudard's jealousy. "It's better to criticize from within," he declares, and departs to join the pachyderms, whose noises swell throughout the rest of the act.

Bérenger and Daisy are left alone. They will read to each other, they promise, take long walks. "Yes," says Bérenger, "on the banks of the Seine, in the Luxembourg Gardens. . . ." "At the zoo," Daisy sighs (3.107). From vowing to be a new Adam and Eve (3.112), they quickly come to quarrel. "I am a little ashamed," Daisy says, "of what you call love, this morbid sentiment, this weakness of man. And woman. It can't compare with the ardor, the extraordinary energy that animates all the beings that surround us." "You want energy?" shouts Bérenger. "Here's energy for you!" And he slaps her (3.113). After this explosion Daisy decides to go. "It is no longer possible for us to live together," she says, in a shocking reprise of Nora's famous exit line from Ibsen's *A Doll's House,* and she leaves (3.114). Surrounded by heads of rhinoceroses (which, according to the stage directions, become more and more beautiful), Bérenger struggles on alone: "I will not capitulate!" he exclaims as the curtain falls.

Bérenger's refusal is less attributable to heroism or lucidity than to what Ionesco calls his immunity to the contagion, his "allergy to the epidemic of rhinoceritis" (*Notes,* p. 185). The rhinoceroses' attack on humanism extends even to historical celebrities: Cardinal de Retz has made the change, we learn, along with Mazarin and the Duc de Saint-Simon. "Our classics!" cries Bérenger (3.99). Neither the Logician's discipline nor Dudard's lucidity and detachment can resist the headlong drive of the rhinoceros. What seems to make Bérenger immune is his incoherent, inarticulate, and confused trust in his own emotions. The thick green skin that Jean develops as he changes into a rhinoceros epitomizes his repudiation of Bérenger's friendship. Dudard retreats from the possibility of a love triangle with Daisy and Bérenger into the unfeeling herd. Daisy's last words, as she leaves Bérenger, are "He isn't really nice, he isn't nice" (3.115). This is ironic in one way—Daisy thinks that the rhinoceroses are "nice"—but also poignant, in that "niceness" is central to Bérenger's character, yet he has quarreled with Jean, hurt Dudard's feelings, and slapped Daisy. In the unheroic muddle of his isolation at the end, Bérenger epitomizes an emotional vulnerability that is utterly human.

The rhinoceros, Ionesco said in 1970, may have been the wrong animal for his purposes. "The rhinoceros is a solitary animal," he pointed out. "I ought to have said 'ferocious sheep.' My rhinoceroses are sheep that have gone mad" (*Antidotes,* p. 95). But the play is more subtle than this. In rejecting their humanity, Ionesco's rhinoceroses join a mass of solitary animals: the paradox of herds of rhinoceroses suggests that there is a kind of ruthless egotism involved in joining mass movements. The tough skin, the nearsightedness, the irresistible onward progress of the rhinoceros represent the attractiveness not just of fanaticism but, more profoundly, the lure of the idea of invulnerability. Life is fragile. The rhinoceros is tough.

The similarity between the rhinoceros-like "new man," who believes in the authority of the state, and Ionesco's characterizations of his father is hard to miss. "For him," Ionesco wrote, "when a party took power, that party was right. Hence he was an Iron Guard, a democratic Freemason, a nationalist, a Stalinist. For him, all opposition parties were wrong" (*Present,* p. 26). The complexity of response to rhinoceroses in the play is in part due to the complexity of Ionesco's feelings about his father and about Romania. Much later in Ionesco's career he actually brought his father onstage.

Of equal importance to the genesis of the rhinoceros-man is a clearer literary influence: Alfred Jarry's Ubu. "Simplified to the point of becoming an archetype, embodying the value and truth of myth," Ionesco said to Bonnefoy, Ubu represents "the worst, the lowest" kind of humanity (Bonnefoy, p. 188). Ionesco was a member of the "Academy of Pataphysics," a group of Jarry's admirers. Many of his early self-interviews and manifestos first appeared in the *Journal* of that society. The rhinoceros, like Ubu, provides a powerful image of human inhumanity.

After the appearance of *Rhinoceros* in 1959, Ionesco produced some short pieces, but his next full-length plays were not performed until 1962. On the same day, 15 December 1962, *Le piéton de l'air* (*A Stroll in the Air*) received its world premiere in Düsseldorf—like *Rhinoceros,* in a German version—and *Le roi se meurt* (*Exit the King*) was first performed in Paris, at the Théâtre de l'Alliance Française. *Apprendre à marcher* (*Learning to Walk*) is a scenario for a ballet that was performed in 1960; in it appear images that these two final Bérenger plays will explore at greater length. A young man who appears to be paralyzed is brought to his feet by a nurse. They dance together; then alone he ascends a staircase that appears upstage, "luminous and without end" (4.246). In *A Stroll in the Air,* Bérenger will actually fly into the heavens; in *Exit the King* he will be helped out of his wheelchair as he learns not how to dance but how to die.

*A Stroll in the Air* is based upon another of the short stories in *The Colonel's Photograph.* Ionesco noticed the "anti-theatrical" quality of the story, but he nonetheless felt that he had "found" an appropriate image for the play (Bonnefoy, p. 85). Most critics do not agree, finding the Bérenger of the story less preachy and garrulous than the Bérenger of the play.

This Bérenger is a successful author on holiday in England (where Ionesco had gone to rest after achieving international fame with *Rhinoceros*). The Journalist hounds him for an interview. "Give us a message," he begs Bérenger. Sounding more than a little like the Ionesco of his polemical writings, Bérenger refuses. "Nothing is simpler than the automatic message," he declares, and we are reminded of Ionesco's strictures against Brecht and Brechtians (3.128). Warming to his topic, Bérenger, who had earlier refused to speak to the Journalist, offers a speech about death. "We could stand all of it if only we were immortal. I am paralyzed because I know that I am going to die. It isn't a new truth. It's a truth we forget . . . in order to be able to do anything. But I can't do anything any more; I want to cure death" (3.128).

He retires into his cottage. The scene that immediately follows is baffling. Josephine, Bérenger's wife, is accosted by the Mortician and her uncle, the Doctor, who inform her that her father, whom she thought was dead, is alive. The Mortician is enraged by such inappropriate behavior. Josephine cannot see her father (although the Uncle says he is right there), and as she wistfully reaches out for him, a huge explosion leaves the cottage in ruins. These events are separate in the short story: Josephine tells her husband her dream about her father after he has emerged from the bombed house. Throughout the short story there is the sense that the narrator himself might be revived from the dead; in the play Bérenger emerges from the wreckage slightly discommoded. The English pedestrians, out for a stroll, are unimpressed. "You couldn't have asked for a better excuse not to work," says Josephine. The little English girl begins to sing, like a mechanical lark; the little boy snatches off her wig. "Oh yes," says the second Englishwoman, "our little daughter, she's the little bald soprano" (3.134–135). The joke falls flat.

Bérenger's problem as a blocked writer troubled by the question of death seems to be Ionesco's problem as well; the play has trouble getting under way. Bérenger explains Josephine's dream to her as they stroll in front of a revolving panorama with Marthe, their daughter, while the English pedestrians, moving in the opposite direction, do not notice its astonishing beauty. Marthe sees a man her parents cannot see; Bérenger explains that it is a visitor from the anti-world. There are many universes, "an indeterminate number of quantities. These worlds interpenetrate, superimpose themselves on each other, without touching, for they coexist in the same space" (3.146). Parts of the visitor appear and disappear; a pink column emerges and disappears. "What's nothingness?" Josephine asks (3.151). "You can't say it exists, because if it existed, it wouldn't be nothing," Bérenger explains (3.152). Marthe picks flowers.

In the distance a silver bridge appears. "You're the only one who understands yourself," Josephine tells Bérenger. "I understand him," says Marthe. "There it is, there's the reason," cries Bérenger, pointing to the bridge. It is so beautiful that he begins to fly. This is the same feeling that the Bérenger of *The Killer* had when he first saw the radiant city. Dreams show that people still have the instinct of flight; the skill has simply been forgotten.

While Bérenger flies to the limits of the universe, Josephine is put on trial by a gigantic judge. Marthe explains to her that it is only a nightmare, but this is no consolation. There is no consolation in the heavens either, Bérenger returns to report. "What did you see?" ask the English. "Geese," says Bérenger, "I saw men with the heads of geese. . . . Men licking the asses of monkeys, drinking the piss of sows." "Sir, sir, that's indecent," complains the Journalist (3.195). Bérenger goes on to describe a world that is explicitly apocalyptic ("He read that in the book of Apocalypse," says the Journalist). Instead of other anti-worlds at the end of the time-space arch, Bérenger has found only more of the same horrors—the horrors of war, blood, and mud that had sent him into retirement. "There's nothing more," he groans, "nothing but unlimited abysses, abysses." An English fireworks display begins in the distance. "Maybe the flames will go out . . . maybe the ice will melt . . . maybe the abysses will fill up . . . maybe . . . gardens . . . gardens . . .," muses Marthe as the play ends (3.198). In terms of the interview at the beginning of the play, flying is not the cure for death that Bérenger sought. Marthe voices some hope, but for Bérenger there is only despair.

The apocalyptic vision of fire and ice here is also found in two short pieces written in the same year as *Stroll* (1961). *La colère* (*Anger,* a screenplay for the film *Les sept péchés capitaux* [The Seven Deadly Sins], directed by Sylvain Dhomme) begins, like *Rhinoceros,* with a pleasant village scene. A newlywed husband returns home to his loving wife. They exchange affectionate clichés, and she serves him soup with a fly in it. Intercut with this are episodes of other husbands and wives enacting the same scene, including the discovery of the fly in the soup. A quarrel develops—many quarrels—and the police are called out. In the final image of the film, the planet Earth is destroyed by exploding atomic bombs. In *Délire à deux* (*Frenzy for Two*) two no-longer-young lovers are arguing whether "snail" and "turtle" are the same animal. Offstage, sounds of fighting are heard. Shells and grenades fly into the room; walls collapse; revolutionaries enter. The squabble continues. Both of these short pieces illustrate the point that Bérenger tries to make to the Journalist at the beginning of *A Stroll in the Air:*

> We are living in a terrible nightmare; literature has never had the power, the clarity, the force of life: today even less. To be equal to life, literature must be a thousand times more atrocious. But as atrocious as it can be, literature can only present

the most feeble and attenuated images of real atrocities; just as of real miracles.

(3.127)

In these two short pieces and in *A Stroll in the Air,* Ionesco pushes his scenic imagination to extremes to express both miracle and horror. And the realization of the miracle of flight is indeed "feeble and attenuated."

*Exit the King,* the final Bérenger play, does not require flying harnesses or cycloramas for its staging, nor does it invite comparison with a more successful short story. Rather, it is a ruthlessly classical play with a single simple action. *Exit the King* is based on a scenario for a ballet; like *The Bald Soprano,* and unlike the first Bérenger plays, *The Killer* and *Rhinoceros,* it is rhythmic and musical in its development. Ionesco's description of the play's genesis is also marked by a meticulous awareness of time:

> *Exit the King* was written in twenty days. First I wrote for ten days. I had just been sick and I had been very afraid. Then, after ten days, I had a relapse, and I was sick again for fifteen days. After fifteen days I started to work again. Ten days later I had finished. Only when I reread the play did I discover—and later on when it was performed—that the rhythm of the first part was not the same in the second. It was a different rhythm, a different breath, as though there were two distinct pieces stuck together. You could feel a break right in the middle.
>
> (Bonnefoy, pp. 77–78)

The turning point comes when the King declares, "I could decide not to die" (4.57), when it appears that his resistance to death is exhausted; the mood of the play shifts from tragic farce to something more lyrical.

The play's parodic relationship to traditional tragedies—"sad stories of the death of kings," as Shakespeare's Richard II puts it—is signaled from the very beginning. Like a classical French tragedy it obeys the unities of time, place, and action. "You are going to die in an hour and a half," Marguerite tells the King. "You are going to die at the end of the show" (4.22). A few pages later she reminds him, "You are going to die in an hour and twenty-five minutes." "Yes, sire," chimes in the Doctor (who is also the court executioner and astrologer), "in one hour twenty-four minutes and fifty seconds" (4.29). Unity of place matches unity of time: the entire action, as befits classical tragedy, is played out in the throne room. And the plot is classically simple: the King dies.

The King's death is tragic not only in formal terms but also in its political and cosmic resonances. As in Shakespearean tragedy, the world of this play is "out of joint," and the tragic plot is also a restoration of order. "Snow is falling on the north pole of the sun," says the Doctor. "The Milky Way looks as though it's curdling. The comet is worn out with fatigue, chasing its own tail, turning on itself like a dying dog" (4.17). "This is what always happens in cases like this," Marguerite points out a bit later, whereupon the Guard announces the arrival of the King (4.18).

The rest of the play is devoted to setting the world right by persuading the King (like Jacques) to accept the fact of his mortality. Marguerite, his first wife, and the Doctor work to this end; Marie, the King's young second wife, resists. The action is punctuated by announcements from the Guard, as in this episode, in which the King attempts to prove that he can stand up:

> King: I can stand up by myself.
> [*He stands up by himself, but with difficulty.*]
> Guard: Long live the king. [*The king collapses.*] The king is dying.
> Marie: Long live the king.
> [*The king stands with difficulty, with the aid of his scepter.*]
> Guard: Long live the king. [*The king collapses.*] The king is dead.
> Marie: Long live the king! Long live the king!
> Marguerite: What a comedy.
>
> (4.25)

"Tragic puppet-show" is the style of the scene as described in the stage direction.

"Like an actor who doesn't know his part on opening night, who has gaps, gaps, gaps," the King describes himself (with one hour left). "Like an orator pushed before a tribunal who doesn't know the first word of his speech, who has no idea who he's addressing. I don't know this audience. I don't want to know it, I've got nothing to say to it." He refuses to play his part. "Your majesty," the Doctor pleads, "think of the death of Louis XIV, of Philip II, of Charles V who slept twenty years in his coffin. The duty of your majesty is to die with dignity." "Die with dignity?" exclaims the King, and he shouts out the window, "Help! Your king is going to die!" (4:32–33).

Nor is Marie, with her invocations of light and joy (which gave the Bérenger of *The Killer* temporary feelings of immortality), any help. "Let yourself be flooded with joy, with light, be astonished, be dazzled," she urges. "Bedazzlement pierces flesh and bone like a flood, like a river of overwhelming light. If you want it to." "I don't understand," mumbles the King (4.42). As in *A Stroll in the Air,* exaltation is no cure for death.

The second movement of the play is a process of divestment; the king loses his history, his language, his sense of self. His achievements are all the great achievements of humanity: he invented gunpowder, wrote the *Iliad* and the *Odyssey* and the plays of Shakespeare, invented the automobile, the telephone, and, "not long ago, he invented atomic fission," announces the Guard. "Now he doesn't know how to light or put out a lamp," says Juliette, the housekeeper and nurse (4.58). The grandiose identification of king with realm and cosmos becomes a subsumption of self into nothingness. Left alone at the end, with Marguerite as his guide, the King still clings to the idea of self: "Me," he stammers. "Oh, no," says Marguerite, "he imagines he is everything. He thinks his being is all being." Death is instead a kind of dissolving: "The grain of salt that melts in the water doesn't disappear, because it makes the water salty" (4.71). Out of his wheelchair, he slowly mounts the steps to his throne; she disappears, he sits. "This scenic effect is very important," announce the stage directions. "The disappearance of the windows, door, walls, king, and throne must happen slowly, progressively, very distinctly. The king, sitting on his throne, must remain visible for a few moments before disappearing in a kind of fog" (4.74). The tragic farce of the first part of the play is annihilated in the final triumph of death.

"We are alive in order to die," Ionesco wrote in his *Journal en miettes* (*Fragments of a Journal,* 1967):

> Death is the real end of existence; that is a very ordinary truth, one would say. But sometimes through the used-up language, the banal disappears and truth swells up again, renewed. I am in one of those moments when it seems to me that life has no other end but death. One can do nothing. One can do nothing. One can do nothing. One can do nothing. What is this condition of being a marionette on a string? By what right am I being made ridiculous?
>
> (p. 39)

The puppet-show tragedy of *Exit the King* illuminates the sense in the journal that the mere fact of death makes life ridiculous, erases all human history and achievement. "All men are mortal; Socrates is a man; Socrates is mortal," Ionesco recalls in the *Journal:* "I woke up tonight and thought about that. Not in a long time have I experienced an anxiety so clear, so present, so glacial" (p. 40). After *A Stroll in the Air* and *Exit the King,* all of Ionesco's literary production becomes not Bérenger's search for a cure for death, nor King Bérenger's ridiculous clinging to life, but an exploration, through memory and dream, of the fragile bonds that tie humans to life and to each other.

The shift to a more personal direction that the Bérenger plays suggest is confirmed by the publication in the early and middle 1960's of memoirs and discussions of his work by Ionesco. *The Colonel's Photograph,* published in 1962, includes, in addition to the source stories for *Amédée* and the first three Bérenger plays, the long story "The Mire," which Ionesco rewrote in the form of a screenplay in 1970. In the film's final scene the narrator—played by Ionesco—is completely engulfed in mud. More important at this point, *The Colonel's Photograph* concludes with a section entitled "Spring 1939," subtitled "Rubbish of Memory." Here Ionesco intersperses observations from his visit to La Chapelle-Anthenaise in 1939 with memories of his childhood there. This technique of juxtaposition animates his full-length memoir, *Présent passé, passé présent* (*Present Past, Past Present*), published in 1968. In 1962 Ionesco also published *Notes et contre-notes* (*Notes and Counter Notes*), a collection of occasional and polemical writings on theater, and in 1966, Claude Bonnefoy published the first edition of his interviews with Ionesco. *Fragments of a Journal* appeared in 1967. Indispensable as these materials are for the understanding of Ionesco's art, it is worth pointing out that they are themselves works of art and subject to interpretation. We have already noticed, for example, Ionesco's tendency to oversimplify the symbol of the rhinoceros in his later discussions of that play. Thus, while the nondramatic works provide what Ionesco in the *Impromptu* calls the author's "mythology," the images in the plays frequently take on lives of their own.

*La soif et la faim* (*Hunger and Thirst*) represents, like *A Stroll in the Air* and *Exit the King,* a highly personal journey through memory and dream. It was first performed in German at Düsseldorf in 1964; it received its first French performance in February 1966 at the Comédie Française under the direction of Jean-Marie Serreau. There is nothing of the anti-play in its structure; *Hunger and Thirst* is made up of three related one-act plays, *La fuite* (*The Flight*), *Le rendez-vous,* and *Les messes noires de La Bonne Auberge* (*Black Masses of the Good Inn*). They trace a simple story: Jean, the protagonist, oppressed by guilt and gloomy thoughts, leaves his wife and infant child. In the second play he waits for an unnamed woman who does not arrive. In the third he finds himself at an inn run by an order of monks who entertain travelers with didactic plays. Marie-Madeleine, his wife, and Marthe, his daughter, appear in the distance, but he cannot join them until he has paid his bill. The monks chant a figure that never ends, and the play ends as, in counterpoint, Marie-Madeleine promises to wait.

Like so many of Ionesco's protagonists, Jean is seeking light. *The Flight* begins in a dark room; Jean complains of moving from a spacious apartment to this grim ground-floor flat. "I know quite well," Ionesco confided to Simone Benmussa, "where I got this image; it represents my mother's apartment. . . . She did not have time to live there, she died just before moving day. So this memory of an apartment which Jean comes back to in the first act is at the same time, for me, my mother's apartment and her tomb" (*Eugène Ionesco,* p. 10). "I will light it with the light of my eyes," Marie-Madeleine offers, but Jean continues to complain (4.81). The ghost of his Aunt Adelaide comes to visit, and Jean vows to leave this morbid place. "I need a healthy ambience," he declares. "Fresh air will revive me, give me back my strength. I need mountain air, somewhere like Switzerland, a hygienic country where no one dies. A country where the law forbids you to die" (4.96–97). "Bonds, I untie them," he vows, "knots, I undo them. So they won't bury me, I bury my memories. I reject memory. I am keeping only what I need to know who I am, I forget everything except this: I am nothing other than myself, I need only be myself" (4.97–98).

"Could you really pull up the roots, my love? Could you really pull up the roots of love, the love you have for us, could you?" chants Marie-Madeleine as the play transforms itself into a game of hide-and-seek (4.98). Jean is not to be found wherever she seeks him. She gets her answer in a striking scenic image: "Jean appears. He tears from his heart a branch of eglantine, very long; without expression, with an elaborate gesture he wipes the drops of blood on his shirt, on his fingers, leaves the branch on the table, carefully buttons his vest, and tiptoes out" (4.102). Marie-Madeleine, left alone with the baby, grieves for him. The back wall disappears, revealing an exquisite, bright garden. At the left appears a beautiful silver ladder. "If he could have seen it, if he could have known," says Marie-Madeleine as the curtain falls, "if he had had a little patience . . ." (4.103).

*The Rendezvous* begins in a mountain landscape, illuminated by a light without shadow and without sun. "What light," Jean effuses, "I've never seen any light so pure. These mountains might look severe to someone who doesn't like cleanliness" (4.105). As he waits at the door of the museum for a woman, he tells the two guards about her. "Do you remember her last words to you?" one asks. " 'I love you, my love, I love you madly, my poor dear, don't upset yourself,' " Jean replies. "On these words, she left me. She turned around in her blue dress, a smile of love on her lips. Ah, if the image of her grace could leave me; she could not tear the love out of her heart, out of her heart she could not tear the love" (4.113). The refrain is Marie-Madeleine's. No woman appears, so Jean sets off to find her: "Show me, in my night, you, living, dazzling, sweet, intense, ardent, soothing" (4.118). "Aren't you hungry?" says the second guard to the first. "I smell soup." "I can already taste the wine in my mouth," replies the first. "Bon appétit" (4.119).

At the beginning of the third play the hungry Jean arrives at the Good Inn. He eats and drinks unconscionable amounts. The monks ask for an account of his travels; like Choubert in *Victims of Duty,* he eats and drinks to fill the gaps in his memory, and speaks of deserted plains, fogs, and mud. The Brother Pedagogue presents a play. Two clowns in cages, Tripp and Brechtoll, appear in a drama of re-education; they must be trained to believe the opposite of what they believe. As Jean presides and the monks, wearing red or black hoods to indicate which side they support, applaud, Tripp is forced to deny his belief in God and Brechtoll is forced to deny his atheism. When the reversal is achieved, the clowns get bowls of good hot soup. But they do not get their freedom. Neither does Jean. As Marie-Madeleine and Marthe (now fifteen) appear in the background, in the garden from the end of the first play, he receives a monk's robe and must serve food to the monks at the table. The monks chant in chorus the numbers put on the blackboard by the Brother Accountant; the figure never ends. Jean serves them faster and faster as Marie-Madeleine waits.

"Have you always been devoured by insatiable thirst, by a hunger you could never assuage?" Brother Tarabas asks Jean before the appearance of his loved ones. "Yes . . . no . . . ," he replies (4.165). Having torn from the heart the love that could have lit up the gloomy house of the first play, Jean has been led by his desires to recognize the existence of the garden that he could not see before. His journeys have been in vain; the failure of his faith has led to his imprisonment in a Brechtian nightmare of didactic theater.

Tripp and Brechtoll in their cages represent for Ionesco the extremes of dogmatism. The right-wing Tripp and the left-wing Brechtoll are interchangeable; what characterizes their belief is its rigidity, not its ideology. Ionesco himself refuses to be pinned down on the matter of belief in God: "I don't know whether I'm Christian or not," he told Benmussa:

> . . . religious or not, a believer or not, mystical or not, but I had a Christian upbringing. *Hunger and Thirst* is in fact a biblical title. We are all hungry, we are all thirsty. We have many hungers and many thirsts: for earthly foods, for water, for whiskey, for bread; we hunger for love, for the absolute. The bread, the wine, the meat that Jean, the hero, thirsts for are merely substitutes for what could satisfy a hunger and thirst for the absolute.
>
> (Benmussa, pp. 8–9)

"Blessed are they who hunger and thirst after righteousness, for they shall be filled," reads the Sermon on the Mount. The names of the wife and the child and the description of the woman in the blue dress in *The Rendezvous* suggest, along with the title, a complex of traditional Christian symbols for the play, in which case Jean's accelerating service of plates in the Good Inn seems to be an allegory of Purgatory. Some critics have read the play this way. "I'm happy for them and congratulate them," Ionesco said (Benmussa, p. 39). But for him any single system of belief can too easily turn into a prison of dogma.

Ionesco's next play after *Hunger and Thirst* was *Jeux de massacre* (*Killing Game*), which had its world premiere in German at Düsseldorf on 24 January 1970. Based upon Defoe's *Journal of the Plague Year,* no play could be less like the mystical pilgrimage of *Hunger and Thirst.* In structure *Killing Game* is a series of nineteen vignettes; it has no central or even continuing characters except a Black Monk who silently haunts the scene. The pace is fast, the mood is comic, the stage is littered with corpses.

The formal inspiration for this return to the anti-play might well have been the Ionesco spectacle *Mêlées et démêlées* (Mixed-up Mixups), a series of ten short sketches performed in 1966 at the Théâtre de la Bruyère in Paris under the direction of Georges Vitaly. These included some early pieces, such as *The Motor Show, Maid to Marry,* and *Le tableau* (*The Painting,* first performed with *Jacques* in 1955), a selection from the French conversational exercises for American students; and a dramatization of the screenplay *Pour préparer un oeuf dur* (How to Cook a Hard-boiled Egg). Like the conversation exercise "Au théâtre," this last piece explodes in an image of universal destruction. *Pour préparer un oeuf dur* begins as a parody of a home economics film. A pretty housewife purchases an egg and instructs us in how to cook it. "Hold the match next to the openings on the burners, through which the gas, after traveling through the pipes, emerges in the form of little flames," she says as we see on the screen the following sequence of images:

> Close-up, greatly magnified, of pipes, of burner openings, of the little flames, which become much larger. Forest fire, light glowing in the sky over the forest. A river catches fire. Fish on fire. A house on fire; in the middle of the flames an old woman whose clothes catch fire. A young man rushes to pull her from the fire, does not succeed, silent struggles; the woman disappears, reaching out her arms from a thick cloud of smoke; the anguished face of the young man, his necktie on fire. Herd of sheep on fire rushing through meadows where the grass is on fire. Back to a shot of the river. Sound of boiling water, close-up of the pot on the stove with boiling water. Gracious and serene smile from the young woman in the kitchen.
>
> (4.212–213)

This hallucinatory sequence brings together the fire poem from *The Bald Soprano* and Jean's vision of guilt in *Hunger and Thirst.* "Always, after reaching out her arms the same way, she disappears into the flames," he says. "I didn't have the courage to throw myself into the flames" (4.93). The night before his mother died in 1936, Ionesco reports, he had a premonitory dream: "I dream that my mother was surrounded by flames. She looked at me, poor woman, with terrified eyes. She asked me to save her. I tried, many times. I couldn't take her in my arms, touch her, because of the fire. I hated myself. I felt infinitely guilty" (*Un homme en question,* pp. 145–146). The appearance of this key personal image in *Hunger and Thirst* is not surprising; its appearance in *Comment préparer un oeuf dur* may suggest the savage blend of comedy and horror in *Killing Game.*

In the first scene of *Killing Game,* characters stroll through a village square—the stage should be full of people, the stage directions suggest, or if actors are not available in sufficient numbers, huge dolls. The Black Monk passes by. After a series of random interchanges about disease and death, the Fourth Man discovers that his twins are dead in their baby carriage. "Mother-in-law, you killed them," he cries, attacking her; she drops dead. "I didn't touch her," he mutters as the Sixth Man turns on him. "That woman was my benefactor," the Sixth Man says, pulling a knife; the Fourth Man drops dead. "I missed him," says the Sixth Man as the Third Man attacks him, "he fell down all by himself" (5.20–21). The comedy of death continues until everyone on stage is dead.

In the next scene a city official announces that the city is quarantined. "People are dying at random," he explains (5.26). This is both the comedy and the horror of the play. "I am impenetrable. I am untouchable," announces the Master of the House in the third scene, and falls face down among his dishes. Like the growing corpse in *Amédée,* the bodies multiply in geometric progression. "When I left my friends' house, there were two of them," says one passerby to another in a short street scene. "I went to buy a paper, and I came right back. I went upstairs and opened the door and there were eleven corpses stretched out. . . . What we ought to know, what we should establish, is this: did they multiply while they were alive or afterwards?" (5.54). In split staging, simultaneous deaths occur, victims and survivors uncannily echoing each other. Government and opposition politicians propose solutions, shout slogans, only to die.

Reminiscent of the lyricism of *Hunger and Thirst* is the scene between the Old Man and the Old Woman near the end of *Killing Game.* "At first, the world filled me with wonder," says the Old Man. "I looked at myself, too: 'What is all this?' and then, awakening from my stupor: 'What was I?' and I was in a new stupor looking at myself" (5.89). Gently the Old Woman contradicts him. "I was happy with the mysterious presence of the world, everything around me, and the consciousness of being alive. I never felt the need to know more. Every question stabs at existence, wounds it" (5.91). This scene replays the debate between the guilt-ridden Jean and the unself-conscious Marie-Madeleine of *Flight.* "If only you knew what you were looking for! You've never known," croaks the Old Woman (the stage directions insist upon cracked elderly voices for her and the Old Man's speeches of love and rebellion). "My love. The trouble you give me" (5.93). She almost collapses as the Old Man continues to inveigh against the quarantine and against the world. She dies, and he staggers off with her body. The Black Monk enters, followed by two undertakers with a cart drawn by actors dressed like horses. The undertakers fetch the bodies of the old couple; four women loot their shop; a fifth woman enters, and the scene ends as they fight wildly among the brightly colored feathers and dresses.

The play closes with an image that is both historical and personal. With the plague stamped out, the city is destroyed by fire. This is the fate of London in Defoe's narrative; the Great Fire of 1666 did indeed follow the plague of 1665. In *Killing Game,* Ionesco makes the plague more threatening and random by, in effect, de-historicizing it. Because the play is set in a generalized city, rather than in Defoe's seventeenth-century London, the effect of such authentic details as the killing of plague victims by their nurses, the sequestering of survivors in the houses of plague victims, and the traveler who orders in French a "pinte" of beer all work to heighten the play's sense of gratuitousness.

The *Impromptu* makes clear enough Ionesco's distaste for the Brechtian techniques of "historicization"; what he does in *Killing Game* is de-historicize Defoe's plague into an image of the human condition. We are all sentenced to random death. "There is a truth in history," Ionesco writes in *Découvertes* (Discoveries), a memoir illustrated with drawings by the author published in 1970. "History is not totally stripped of value; the *truth* of history and its *value* exist to the extent that they are extrahistorical. What is valuable is that which, still remaining historical, exists outside history. I am speaking of archetypes, of myths that history and ideologies have not succeeded in disfiguring" (*Découvertes,* p. 115). The plague becomes myth; the Black Monk is the archetype of death.

"Every revolutionary becomes in time a tyrant," Ionesco continues (*Découvertes,* p. 115). This is the central argument of *Macbett,* Ionesco's adaptation of Shakespeare's *Macbeth,* which was presented in January 1972 at the Théâtre de la Rive Gauche in Paris under the direction of Jacques Mauclair. Like *Killing Game, Macbett* is a systematic de-historicization of its original. Ionesco came to the play inspired by Jan Kott's essay "*Macbeth;* or, Death-Infected" in his book *Shakespeare Our Contemporary*: for Kott, Shakespeare's play depicts history as nightmare. "What can the 'high' metaphysics of Shakespeare be reduced to?" Ionesco asks rhetorically. "It is simple and banal: the world is sound and fury" (*Antidotes,* p. 260). Banal, nightmarish, loud, and furious: all these qualities are attributes of *Macbett.*

Kott concludes his essay on *Macbeth* by wondering why Shakespeare spends so much time discussing Cawdor's death at the beginning of the play. Ionesco begins *Macbett* with a conversation between Candor and Glamiss, two disaffected lords. The transmutations of the names are deliberate puns, reminiscent of Alfred Jarry's systematic, coarse, frequently nonsensical punning not only in the Ubu plays but also on social occasions. The uprising of Candor and Glamiss is staged as an offstage battle: "The lighting effects and noises must not, especially toward the end, be comparable with reality. The roles of lighting designer and sound-effects engineer are here of great importance," read the stage directions (5.124). What we see is a spoof of a battle scene, as a lemonade vendor hawks his wares: "Lemonade to cure wounds, lemonade against fear, lemonade for soldiers," he cries (5.124). Macbett enters and speaks:

> The blade of my sword is dyed red with blood. I've killed dozens and dozens, with my own hand. Twelve dozen officers and soldiers who never did anything to me. I've had others shot, hundreds and hundreds, by firing squads. Thousands of others are dead, burned alive when I set fire to the forests where they had hidden.
>
> (5.127)

The speech goes on and on; the numbers of the dead mount into the tens of millions. As in *Exit the King* the hyperbolic language of high tragedy is pushed to the limits. The joke reaches its peak of exaggeration when Banco appears and utters the same long speech as his opening soliloquy.

Repetition is the key to Ionesco's mythic idea of history. In *Macbett* everything repeats. Banco is indistinguishable from Macbett. When the two voice their disaffection with Duncan, they repeat the dialogue of Glamiss and Candor from the beginning of the play. The bloody sergeant of Shakespeare's play, bringing the news from the battle, becomes here a wounded conscript, forced to fight on the rebel side, then taken prisoner and forced to fight against the rebels. "He left the battle right in the middle," Duncan says, "like walking out of a play he didn't like" (5.132). There is no Lady Macbeth in *Macbett;* instead, Macbett is seduced into assassinating Duncan by Lady Duncan, who is one of the witches. All roles multiply wildly in history's nightmare.

Finally, Macbett meets Macol in single combat at the end. "No man of woman born can defeat me," he cries. "You've been cheated, Macbett!" replies Macol. "Sung or spoken," reads the stage direction, "Wagnerian" (5.199). The witches' show of the descendants of Banquo in *Macbeth* becomes a clown show here. As adopted son of Duncan and real son of Banco and a gazelle (a witch turned her into a woman), Macol will take the name of Banco, and he shows the heads of a series of famous clowns to Macbett. Banco VI is "the head of the author of this play, laughing, mouth wide open." "Never, since the days of Oedipus, has destiny so greatly and so well made mock of a man," declaims Macbett (5.200). On Macbett's death Macol ascends the throne. His coronation speech sounds familiar: "I know all the vices so well grafted in me that, when they shall be opened, black Macbett will seem as pure as snow, and the poor state esteem him as a lamb, being compared with my confineless harms" (5.203). As the lines continue, we recognize with a shock the play's only direct quotation from Shakespeare. In the English scene in *Macbeth,* Malcolm tests Macduff's loyalty by portraying himself as a worse tyrant than Macbeth. When Macduff turns on him in rage, Malcolm is assured of the thane's loyalty to Scotland rather than to any particular man. In *Macbett* this heavily ironic speech is given straight—just as so much of the tragedy is ironically parodied. Macol is a monster. Guillotines appear before the backdrop. A man with a butterfly net crosses the empty stage. The tragic clown show is over.

In *Macbeth* we hear of, but do not see, the English king's ability to cure disease with his touch. Ionesco devotes a long scene to Duncan's curative abilities in *Macbett,* and among his patients is one whose symptoms would seem resistant to cure. "What is your ailment?" asks Duncan. The Second Patient replies:

> My lord, I can't live and I can't die. I can't stay seated and I can't stay in bed, can't stand without moving or running. I've got burning and itching from my head to my feet. I can't stand a house or a street. The universe for me is a prison or a chain gang. . . . I can't stand light, I can't endure darkness, I'm terrified of human beings and I'm afraid of being alone. I turn my eyes away from trees and sheep, dogs or grass, stars or stones. I'm not happy for even a moment. I would like to be able to cry, my lord, and to know joy.
>
> (5.177–178)

"Forget that you exist," says Duncan. "Remember that you *are.*" Duncan is able to cure this malaise with a touch.

Ionesco's first novel, *Le solitaire* (*The Hermit*), published in 1973, is an extended exploration of a similar kind of anxiety. The novel serves as source for Ionesco's next play, *Ce formidable bordel!* (*A Hell of a Mess!*); first performed in 1973, it draws its inspiration from Ionesco's dreams and journals, especially the published *Fragments of a Journal* and *Present Past, Past Present.* Like the Old Man in *Killing Game,* like the Second Patient in *Macbett,* and like Ionesco's self-portrayals, the narrator of the novel is possessed by anxiety, obsessed by death, incapable of accommodating himself to the world.

After inheriting a small fortune from his uncle, the novel's narrator leaves his job and takes an apartment in a good neighborhood. There he sits in a state of detachment, watching the world with a confusion that sometimes turns into astonishment or despair. He locates a nearby restaurant, where he eats and drinks to excess; when anxiety awakens him at night, he dulls it with cognac. The waitress from the restaurant moves in with him, but when she moves out, he cannot remember her name. The city is destroyed by a series of revolutions and counterrevolutions of which he takes little notice. "When I feel alone," he thinks while sitting at the restaurant, "cosmically alone, as though I were my own creator, my own God, master of appearances, that's when I feel out of danger" (*Le solitaire,* p. 61). Yet he finds himself less and less capable of maintaining this kind of isolation. "What was lacking?" he asks himself near the end. "What was lacking in me? I would have wanted to know everything. That's what was lacking. Not knowing. Not knowing everything. I was ignorant but not ignorant enough not to know it" (p. 187). Like Jean he hungers and thirsts; and, as in *Hunger and Thirst,* the answer comes in the form of a silver ladder. "Instead of the wall, images formed, slowly. It became luminous. A tree crowned with flowers and leaves appeared. . . . For whom, this field, this garden, this light? . . . On the right of the tree, to my left, a silver ladder, hanging one meter above the ground, disappeared in the blue sky" (p. 190). The vision vanishes: "I took it for a sign" (p. 191).

"I'll begin again, I'll begin again," says the voice of the Character (played by Ionesco) at the end of the screenplay of *The Mire.* As he sinks deeper, we see only his eye; then the fogs dissipate, and we see blue sky. Blue skies, gardens, light: these images all speak to the mythology of Ionesco. "There is a golden age," he wrote, "the age of childhood, of ignorance; once you know you're going to die, childhood is finished" (*Journal,* p. 31). The recovery of childlike astonishment at the world is a recovery of Eden. "In order to talk about this light, to talk about this astonishment, of a light, of a sky, of an astonishment more powerful than anxiety, dominant over anxiety, that's why I write literature," Ionesco says in *Découvertes* (p. 60). The experience of light, the silver ladder, at the end of *The Hermit* is a vision of paradise regained.

It is not a political vision, Ionesco is ready to point out. The utopian politics of Left or Right, figured in the meaningless seizures of power in *Macbett* and in the street fighting in *The Hermit,* leads nowhere. "In *The Hermit* I gave the power of speech to a character who is in conflict with history, or rather who lives parallel to history," Ionesco told Bonnefoy.

> History and politics attempt in vain to resolve or conceal the fundamental problem of our condition, because they cannot answer these questions: What am I doing here? Why do I exist? What is this world around me? These are the elementary questions that history ignores, but we cannot not ask them: we cannot lose consciousness of our selves.
>
> (Bonnefoy, p. 165)

"I fall upon the newspaper and I enjoy myself morosely, but it's still a kind of enjoyment, as I read the headlines that talk about wars, atrocities, fires, floods, the pollution building up, that will perhaps suffocate us," says the Narrator (*Solitaire,* p. 102). Against a background of gratuitous violence and impending apocalypse, the silver ladder leads to another, better world.

"Despite my apocalyptic sense of history," Ionesco said, "I think I've never completely lost my sense of humor. I still have the notion that history, such as it is, that is to say, terrible, tragic, unacceptable, is a sort of farce that God plays with humanity" (Bonnefoy, p. 163). The comedy is more apparent in the play *A Hell of a Mess!* than in the novel. Ionesco recognized that the form of the novel—the internal monologue of a man isolated from the world—was inherently undramatic. In adapting *The Hermit* for the stage, he reversed the strategy: everyone but the Character, as he is called, talks incessantly. He is monosyllabic, noncommittal in his responses, inarticulate. The play opens as his colleagues at the office discuss his new legacy, and the comedy is simple. Before he arrives, they malign him; when he is present, they protest friendship. In the bar his former lover, Lucienne, reminds him of their affair; he does not answer her. "Poor Lucienne," says the narrator in the novel, "who thinks that under other conditions it could have worked. There are no objective conditions" (*Solitaire,* p. 13). Each of his new neighbors addresses the Character with a lengthy harangue to which he (somewhat like the New Tenant) does not respond. Drawn to such length, the unresponsiveness of the Character becomes comic, as does his inertness when the Revolutionaries take over the stage, exclaiming slogans.

The ending of the play differs in emphasis from that of the novel. "Thank you. Turn off the lights," says the Character as the new concierge brings him his dinner (the line is the same as the final line of *The New Tenant*). The action repeats and accelerates, punctuated by partial blackouts. Between the entrances and exits of the Concierge, the dead appear and speak to the Character. Their speeches are brief, and their message is the same: We loved you. His mother, Lucienne, his old schoolteacher, even neighbors we have glimpsed only fleetingly repeat the refrain. The Character drinks cognac after cognac as the short visits accelerate. Finally a Woman (no more specifically defined than that) appears: "Oh, Monsieur, I loved you. I never dared tell you. We could have been happy. I never dared tell you how much I adored you from afar." All the characters reappear. "You were loved," they say, extending their arms. He hurls the bottle at them, shouting insults (6.198).

Now the Character finds himself alone. The Concierge does not answer his calls. "I'm going to die of hunger!" he cries, "I'm going to die of thirst!" The stage is flooded with a bright light, the walls have disappeared, and the final vision, as in the novel, begins. The tree with its leaves and flowers appears. But there is no silver ladder in the play. In place of the sense of a luminous sign with which the novel concludes, the play ends in laughter: "You joker!" the Character cries, making an obscene gesture to the sky. "I should have known all along. What a farce! It's outrageous! What a joke! What a huge joke! What a huge joke! And I took it seriously," he shouts with laughter. Still laughing, he turns to the audience. "What a joke, my children! What a joke, ladies and gentlemen!" (6.199). For the transfiguration, the glimpse of a better world elsewhere, at the end of the novel the play substitutes derisive despair.

The sequence in which figures from the Character's past materialize and tell him of their love anticipates Ionesco's two latest plays, *L'Homme aux valises* (*Man with Bags*), first performed in 1975 at the Théâtre de l'Atelier, under the direction of Jacques Mauclair, and *Voyages chez les morts: Themes et variations* (*Journeys Among the Dead: Themes and Variations*), first performed at the Guggenheim Museum in New York in September 1980. As their titles suggest, the two are journey plays, quests along the lines of August Strindberg's *To Damascus,* in which an unnamed traveler meets the dreams and memories of his past.

*Man with Bags* begins on the bank of a river. "Hire a boat; get across. . . . " "That's the Seine," says the Painter to the Man with two suitcases. The Man hears the sounds of fighting. "You've got it wrong," says the Painter. "We're in 1938; you think it's still the Revolution. People still feel the big wind of 1789" (6.9–10). At the other side of the river is France, but it is also the past; *Man with Bags* is a journey to the land of the dead. In the second scene the Man approaches a house, its windows illuminated by flames inside: "This is the house where I was born," he tells the young man. His mother used to live there. "The ground floor was below ground level; the bedroom and the living-room were on the ground floor" (6.13). From *Hunger and Thirst* we recall these details of Ionesco's personal mythology: the flames speak of his premonitory dream of his mother's death; the ground-floor flat is her last apartment. The Man's quest after his mother is infused with feelings of guilt. In the third scene the Old Woman in a Wheelchair claims to be his mother, and she turns on him with violent reproaches: "I dedicated my life to you, to you and your father! And you deny me! You've been preparing me for that a long time. I never would have believed it. You've killed me, the two of you! Your father sunk a dagger in my heart. Now you're going to finish me off" (6.17). Generations jumble; in the next scene the Old Woman is wheeled about by a young woman—her mother.

In the midst of a traffic jam of people (if we recall *The Killer,* another of Ionesco's most important images), the Man with Bags finds his Father, still middle-aged. "You haven't killed any children," says the Old Woman to the Man with Bags. "I'm not afraid," says the Father, "I acknowledge my crimes. I'll kill more if they don't stop me." "But I can't live with the burden of my guilt," says the Man with Bags. "At least I never killed any children. So why this incurable remorse?" "We've all killed children," replies a Woman, "but not on purpose" (6.26).

This episode is based on a dream that Ionesco recorded in *Fragments of a Journal.* In the dream the father's part is played by Samuel Beckett:

> I am a murderer, I've killed children. I'm not the only defendant. Beckett also has been arrested as well as a third playwright, Pinter maybe, or Genet, who melts, whom I see literally melt and vanish into a gray sky with no clouds. Beckett acknowledges his guilt . . . he will keep on kill-

> ing children unless he is stopped. I am seized with remorse, ravaged by an ineluctable sense of guilt. Yet I haven't killed any children. Or I haven't done it on purpose. Or maybe I wanted to kill them, because who hasn't wanted to kill children? But I never fulfilled my plans. The proof is that every time I tried to kill children or killed them by mistake, I called the police myself. In fact, here it is again, coming in response to my call, the police car. . . .
>
> (*Journal,* pp. 202–203)

The story of the dream in the journal helps to make some sense of the scene in the play; the Man's sense of the crowds of 1789 in the first scene and his observation of his father's big shoes in this scene also are derived from *Fragments of a Journal.* The transformation of the Beckett of the dream into the Father of the play creates in the reader of both a confusion of the professional and the personal spheres of reference. Such complex interrelatedness is characteristic of the later work of Ionesco.

"I am staging there the conflict that I had with my father and his second wife, against my father and his brothers-in-law," Ionesco says of *Man with Bags.* "The search that propels the play is the search for the identity of my mother and my grandparents, the search for my own identity" (Bonnefoy, p. 169). The police who torment the Man throughout the play, challenging his nationality, forbidding citizens to speak to him, threatening to jail him, also reflect this personal content.

> *Man with Bags* is a nightmare of the country I was born in, where, after spending my childhood in France, I lived through my adolescence and part of my youth. I have often had the nightmare of returning to this country that I left—that I escaped from—for political reasons, because at that time the extreme right was coming to power. But I also left because of my father and his family. All this: the conflict with my family, the search for the identity of my relations, the presence of totalitarianism, can be found in the play.
>
> (Bonnefoy, pp. 169–170)

The play reaches out to a system of private reference already published in *Present Past, Past Present* and *Fragments of a Journal.*

In this way *Man with Bags* follows logically from the progression of plays that began with *Victims of Duty,* plays based upon dreams and memories that had previously been written down in nondramatic form. Its immediate predecessors—*Killing Game, Macbett,* and *A Hell of a Mess!*—all rely heavily upon their narrative sources. In the case of *A Hell of a* Mess! the relationship with the novel is virtually symbiotic—the play supplies the comic interaction that the novel lacks, and the novel provides the sense of the inner life of the hermit that the play lacks. Neither functions satisfactorily without the other. Likewise, *Man with Bags* fully takes shape only in light of the narrative accounts of the dreams it dramatizes, and in light of Ionesco's own explanations of its sphere of reference.

Formally, Ionesco's late plays, with their episodic structures and discontinuities, are reminiscent of Strindberg's post-*Inferno* dramas—especially *To Damascus* (1898–1904; like these a quest play through a nameless protagonist's guilt-ridden past) and *The Dream Play* (1902). Whereas Beckett, with whom Ionesco's name has often been linked, has moved through his career in the direction of stripping away the hardware of staging in his later minimalist plays, Ionesco has created a drama that is confessional, lyrical, and personal, and that relies heavily upon scenic effects to work its magic.

In the early 1960's the phrase "theater of the absurd" was coined by Martin Esslin as a way of emphasizing the connection he saw between the experimental drama of those years and continental existentialist philosophy, especially the philosophies of Albert Camus and Jean-Paul Sartre. Both Beckett and Ionesco have suffered from the indiscriminate application of the term "absurdist" to their work, both in its technical sense as a philosophical category and in its less formal sense as suggesting an extreme playfulness. For Ionesco, Beckett, like himself, is a metaphysical playwright: "For the moment," he writes in "À propos de Beckett," "Beckett teaches us yet again that man is a metaphysical or religious animal. Without metaphysics, we would be nothing" (*Antidotes,* p. 209).

Ionesco's emphasis on the religious dimension of his work—a dimension most openly apparent in *Hunger and Thirst,* but always present—is at variance with the existentialist rejection of faith, just as Ionesco repeatedly finds himself at daggers drawn with Sartre in matters of politics. In Ionesco's development the cheerful nihilism of the early anti-plays has been left behind. It is not coincidental that he sees Robert Wilson, whose spectacular dreamlike performance pieces require the facilities of opera houses for their staging, and the Stanley Kubrick of *2001: A Space Odyssey* as exemplars of a new "cosmitude" of spirit that he admires (Bonnefoy, p. 198). In its lavish spectacle, its explicitly autobiographical dream content, *Man with Bags* seems antithetical to Ionesco's early aesthetic of anti-theater.

But central to Ionesco's earliest pronouncements on theater is the idea that theater is a process of revelation, and writing plays, a process of discovery. The late dream plays fit this idea without difficulty, just as Ionesco's anti-Communist polemics of the 1960's and 1970's are made comprehensible in light of his anti-fascism in the 1940's. Sometimes his efforts to achieve an effect of seamlessness for his career strike a jarring note; in program notes for Jean-Louis Barrault's revival of *Rhinoceros* in 1978, he stridently insists upon the play's political message. By making the rhinoceros stand exclusively for totalitarianism, he strips the image of much of its power.

In the issue of the *Cahiers de la Compagnie Jean-Louis Barrault–Madeleine Renaud* that accompanied the 1978 revival of *Rhinoceros,* Ionesco published narrative and dramatized versions of the dreams that would constitute the source of his latest play, *Journeys Among the Dead.* Here the central character is a famous writer, who has long lived away from his native country, in search of his mother. Before he can find her, he stumbles upon his father. Like Ionesco's own father, the Father in this play was a lawyer who survived a revolution: "Because I was obedient, they recycled me," he tells Jean, the protagonist. "They recycled you in the police?" Jean asks. "No, they recycled me in the novel, in the realistic novel," the Father replies, revealing himself to be an author like his son. "We belonged to the Ministry of Police, we were subsidized by the Ministry of Police, but we weren't detectives" (7.17). For Choubert, in *Victims of Duty,* all plays that have ever been written are detective stories; here Jean tracks his memories through terrain that is both strange and familiar. He finds his mother in a grim ground-floor apartment that he has to stoop to enter. The mill at La Chapelle-Anthenaise, where Ionesco spent his childhood, appears in Jean's memories as a castle; the Rue Claude-Terrasse, and the ground-floor flat in which Ionesco lived in the late 1940's, are invoked for Jean by a Friend. "The real houses are those we remember," Jean says, "but also, and above all, they are those we remember in dreams, that we rediscover and enter in our dreams" (7.117). Although Jean's journey ends with the play's final words, "I do not know" (7.134), the play's act of recovery is complete.

The motif of the journey is central to Ionesco's most recent work, *La quête intermittente* (The Intermittent Quest, 1987), an autobiographical meditation similar in form to the *Fragments of a Journal.* Here he portrays himself as a retired writer who spends most of his time painting while bits and pieces of his past life occur to him in memories and dreams. Ionesco complains of exclusion from the honors and fame justly due to him as a prime mover of the theater of the absurd. Why, he wonders, do the critics minimize his contributions to the avant-garde theater of the 1950's? "Because they don't like me. Why not? Because

I wasn't a Communist at a time when it was in bad taste not to be one. They have never pardoned me for being anti-Communist in public" (*Quête,* p. 46). Angrily he points out the diminution of his importance in successive editions of Esslin's book.

But the rage, as befits part of an intermittent quest, is passing. In a section entitled "Exercises de style (?) ou Prières pour des morts?" (Stylistic Exercises [?] or Prayers for the Dead?) the comedy of proliferation returns as Ionesco imagines sixty-six deaths, ranging from the heroic to the ridiculous. Augustine's *Confessions* figure self-consciously as a model for *Quête* because of their special focus on the relationship between memory and the search for God. Again, Ionesco shares his dreams with his readers, and the dreams are familiar. One in particular is arresting for its combination of elements; in it both Ionesco's obsession with his parents and with his art figure:

> I dream of my mother tonight. I dream of her so rarely, but she was in the company of my father . . . whom she wanted to marry.
>
> She had to give her name. She concealed the real spelling of her name; she was called, she said, wrote, Artaux or Arteaux with an *x.* Why not simply spell it like the great man of the theater? What was troubling her? Such a beautiful name.
>
> (*Quête,* pp. 155–156)

In this vision of the unhappy union that gave birth to him, Ionesco also sees the artist with whom he has most in common in the modern theater, Antonin Artaud.

Artaud's idea of a theater of "cruelty," engulfing an audience in an experience of unsettling sounds, meaningless and violent actions, grotesque and threatening effects of light, was never fully realized in his lifetime. But Ionesco's drama, from the earliest antiplays to the latest autobiographical dream visions, not only uses much of the hardware that Artaud prescribed—gigantic dummies, for example—but also seems to share Artaud's desire to return theater to its origins in sacred ritual. In a way, Ionesco's anger at Beckett as a darling of leftist critics meets a kind of answer as his mother, in a dream, identifies herself with the theoretician who preceded both playwrights and whose work was the necessary precondition for all of the avant-garde theatrical activity of 1950's Paris. The quest, however intermittent, is a quest for origins.

In the 1974 essay "Pourquoi est-ce que j'écris?" (Why Do I Write?) Ionesco characterizes his art as a search to rediscover the Eden of childhood:

> I am in search of a world that has become virginal again, of the paradisiacal light of childhood, of the glory of the first day, an untarnished glory, the intact universe that looks as though it had just been born. It's as though I wanted to be present at the moment of the world's creation before the Fall, and I search for this moment in myself, as though I wanted to turn back the course of history, or in my characters, who are other than myself or like others who resemble me, in search, consciously or not, of an absolute light.
>
> (*Antidotes,* p. 316)

Each work of Ionesco's is thus part of a quest, and a quest in itself. The self-absorption of the later plays places Ionesco clearly in the tradition of French thinkers and writers, like Montaigne or Descartes, who have created a whole world through the contemplation of the self. With the publication of *The Colonel's Photograph* in 1962, Ionesco laid the groundwork for this project. After its appearance the plays could no longer be treated in isolation as theatrical experiments but had to be linked with their source stories and with those stories' sources in memory and dream. Ionesco's prose works—the journal, the memoirs, the polemical writings—all function to assure the unity and integrity of his achievement as an artist. The result is a seamless and complex personal mythology that finds its most compelling expression in the scenic language of the stage.

## Selected Bibliography


EDITIONS

PLAYS

The standard edition of Ionesco's plays is that published by Gallimard in seven volumes. Play titles are followed by the date of first production.

*Théâtre I* (1954, 1975): *La cantatrice chauve* (1950), *La leçon* (1951), *Jacques, ou La soumission* (1955), *Les chaises* (1952), *Victimes du devoir* (1953), *Amédée, ou Comment s'en débarasser* (1954). In the revised edition *Les chaises* is replaced by *L'Avenir est dans les oeufs* (1957). All quotations from volume 1 are from the revised edition.

*Théâtre II* (1958, 1975): *L'Impromptu de l'Alma, ou Le caméléon du berger* (1956), *Tueur sans gages* (1959), *Le nouveau locataire* (1955), *L'Avenir est dans les oeufs* (1957), *Le maître* (1953), *Jeune fille à marier* (1953). In the revised edition *Les chaises* replaces *L'Avenir est dans les oeufs.* All quotations from volume 2 are from the first edition.

*Théâtre III* (1963, 1975): *Rhinocéros* (1959), *Le piéton de l'air* (1962), *Délire à deux* (1962), *Le tableau* (1955), *Scéne à quatre* (1959), *Les salutations* (unperformed), *La colère* (screenplay for film *Les sept péchés capitaux* [1961, released 1962]).

*Théâtre IV* (1966, 1975): *Le roi se meurt* (1962), *La soif et la faim* (1964), *La lacune* (1966), *Le salon de l'automobile* (1966), *L'oeuf dur* (unproduced screenplay), *Pour préparer un oeuf dur* (1966), *Le jeune homme à marier* (ballet for Danish television, 1965), *Apprendre à marcher* (ballet, 1960).

*Théâtre V* (1973): *Jeux de massacre* (1970), *Macbett* (1972), *La vase* (film, released 1972), *Exercices de conversation et de diction françaises pour étudiants américains* (1966).

*L'Homme aux valises: Théâtre* [VI] (1975): *L'Homme aux valises* (1975), *Ce formidable bordel!* (1973).

*Théâtre VII* (1981): *Voyages chez les morts: Thèmes et variations* (1980).

NONDRAMATIC WORKS

*Notes et contre-notes.* Paris, 1962; rev. ed., 1966.

*La photo du colonel: Récits.* Paris, 1962, 1964.

*Journal en miettes.* Paris, 1967.

*Présent passé, passé présent.* Paris, 1968.

*Mise en train: Premier année de français.* New York, 1969. With Michel Benamou.

*Découvertes.* Geneva, 1969.

*Discours de réception à l'Académie française et la réponse du Professeur Jean Delay.* Paris, 1971.

*Les murs canadiens de Joseph Iliu.* Paris, 1973.

*Le solitaire.* Paris, 1973.

*Contes pour enfants de moins de trois ans.* 4 vols. 1976.

*Antidotes.* Paris, 1977. Collection of articles.

*Un homme en question.* Paris, 1979. Collection of articles.

*Pour la culture, contre la politique.* Paris, 1979.

*Hugoliade.* Paris, 1982.

*Le blanc et le noir.* Paris, 1985. Essay and lithographs.

*Non.* Translated by Marie-France Ionesco. Paris, 1986.

*La quête intermittente.* Paris, 1987.

WORKS IN ROMANIAN

*Elegii pentru fiinte mici.* Craiova, Romania, 1931.

*Nu!* Bucharest, 1934. Essays.

TRANSLATIONS

PLAYS

Most of Ionesco's plays are available in English translations by Donald Watson, and are published in London by J. Calder as *Plays,* 12 vols. (1958–1985). Vol. 4 is translated by Derek Prouse; vol. 11, by Donald Watson and C. Williams; and vol. 12, by Barbara Wright. In the United States, the following translations have been published in New York by Grove Press:

*Exit the King.* Translated by Donald Watson. 1967.

*Four Plays.* Translated by Donald M. Allen. 1958. (*The Bald Soprano, The Lesson, The Chairs, Jack; or, The Submission*)

*Hunger and Thirst and Other Plays.* Translated by Donald Watson. 1969. (*The Picture, Anger, Salutations*)

*Journeys Among the Dead: A Play with Lithographs.* Translated by Barbara Wright. 1987.

*The Killer and Other Plays.* Translated by Donald Watson. 1960. (*Improvisation, Maid to Marry*)

*Killing Game.* Translated by Helen Gary Bishop. 1974.

*Macbett.* Translated by Charles Marowitz. 1973.

*Man with Bags.* Adapted by Israel Horovitz from a translation by Marie-France Ionesco. 1977.

*Rhinoceros and Other Plays.* Translated by Derek Prouse. 1960. (*The Leader, The Future Is in Eggs*)

*A Stroll in the Air and Frenzy for Two or More: Two Plays.* Translated by Donald Watson. 1968.

*Three Plays.* Translated by Donald Watson. 1958. (*Amédée, The New Tenant, Victims of Duty*)

NONDRAMATIC WORKS

*The Colonel's Photograph and Other Stories.* Translated by Jean Stewart and John Russell. New York, 1969; repr. 1970.

*Fragments of a Journal.* Translated by Jean Pace. New York, 1968.

*The Hermit.* Translated by Richard Seaver. New York, 1974.

*Hugoliad; or, The Grotesque and Tragic Life of Victor Hugo.* With a postscript by Gelu Ionesu. Translated from the Romanian into French by Dragomir Costineanu with the participation of Marie-France Ionesco; translated from the French by Yara Milos. New York, 1987.

*Notes and Counter Notes.* Translated by Donald Watson. New York, 1964.

*Present Past, Past Present.* Translated by Helen R. Lane. New York, 1971.

*Stories for Children Under Three. Story Number 1,* translated by Calvin K. Towle. London, 1968. *Story Number 2,* translated by Calvin K. Towle. New York, 1970. *Story Number 3,* translated by Oiba Vaughan. New York, 1971.

## BIOGRAPHICAL AND CRITICAL STUDIES


Benmussa, Simone. *Ionesco.* Paris, 1966.

Bonnefoy, Claude. *Entretiens avec Eugène Ionesco.* Translated by Jan Dawson as *Conversations with Eugène Ionesco.* New York, 1971. These interviews, with additional material, are in Eugène Ionesco, *Entre la vie et le rêve: Entretiens avec Claude Bonnefoy.* Paris, 1977. With detailed bibliography.

Bradescu, Faust. *Le monde étrange de Ionesco.* Paris, 1967.

Coe, Richard N. *Eugène Ionesco: A Study of His Plays,* rev. ed. London, 1971. With detailed bibliography.

Dobrez, Livio. *The Existential and Its Exits.* London, 1986.

Esslin, Martin. *The Theatre of the Absurd.* Garden City, N.Y., 1961.

Grossvogel, David I. *The Blasphemers: The Theatre of Brecht, Ionesco, Beckett, Genet.* Ithaca, N.Y., 1965.

Hayman, Ronald. *Eugene Ionesco.* New York, 1976.

Hughes, Griffith Rees, and Ruth Bury. *Eugene Ionesco: A Bibliography.* Cardiff, Wales, 1974.

*Ionesco: Situation et perspectives.* Colloque de Cerisy. Paris, 1980.

Jacobsen, Josephine, and William R. Mueller. *Ionesco and Genet: Playwrights of Silence.* New York, 1968.

Lamont, Rosette C., ed. *Ionesco: A Collection of Critical Essays.* Englewood Cliffs, N.J., 1973.

Lamont, Rosette C., and Melvin J. Friedman. *The Two Faces of Ionesco.* Troy, N.Y., 1978.

Laubraux, Raymond. *Les critiques de notre temps et Ionesco.* Paris, 1973.

Lazar, Moshe, ed. *The Dream and the Play: Ionesco's Theatrical Quest. Interplay 1: Proceedings of Colloquia in Comparative Literature and the Arts.* Malibu, Calif., 1982. Includes three unpublished dream scenes by Ionesco.

Leiner, Wolfgang, with Marianne Bailey et al. *Bibliographie et index thématique des études sur Eugène Ionesco.* Fribourg, 1980.

Lewis, Allan. *Ionesco.* New York, 1972.

Pronko, Leonard C. *Eugène Ionesco.* New York, 1965.

Wellwarth, George. *The Theater of Protest and Paradox.* New York, 1964, 1971.


MATTHEW H. WIKANDER

# CLAUDE SIMON

## *(b. 1913)*

THE CONTEMPORARY READER, taking Claude Simon's works down from the library shelf for the first time, realizes that he has found a dozen novels, each more demanding than *Ulysses* (no "plot," no paragraphs, frequently no sentences, parentheses inside parentheses), and considers swiftly putting the novels back. Courage! Claude Simon is no obscurantist; he is not hard for hardness' sake. In the best works, William York Tindall used to say, form *is* content. In Claude Simon's best works, extreme forms give the experience of extreme states: war, jealousy, obsessive lust. Simon's works include one of the best novels about World War II and, amazingly, one of the best novels about the quality of American urban life. Simon has rightly been called a classic French novelist who makes use of the "New Novel's" forms for classic humanist ends.

One may read Dickens for a lifetime and never feel tempted to open a book like this, but Simon's readers, like Joyce's, need help. Seeking that help, the reader should discriminate between works about Simon's books and works that use Simon's books to illustrate something else. One may legitimately illustrate essays about phenomenology, Freud, Marx, or anything else with quotations from Simon (or from Homer or Dante); but one risks giving the impression that those were Simon's interests as well as the essayist's. Worse, some critics give the impression that Simon wrote his novels as sustained illustrations of phenomenology, Freud, Marx, "the New Novel," or whatever. Simon has vocally resisted such co-optation. In particular, though greatly honored that the famous French phenomenologist philosopher Maurice Merleau-Ponty used his works for illustrations, Simon has often carefully remarked how little influence on him Merleau-Ponty exerted.

### *LIFE*

Since Simon has said that "most of" his books "are autobiographical . . . notably *L'Herbe, La route des Flandres,* and *Le palace,*" we naturally turn to his biography with increased attention. Lately critics have begun to read Simon's novels as if their greatest value were as symptoms with which to psychoanalyze Claude Simon. What would it mean, however, for the reader to conclude that fictional events in certain of Simon's novels "really" happened? Do we care what Picasso's wife "really" looked like? The picture is what counts. Yet we undeniably learn something about art while watching a fine artist like Simon convert the world around him into art.

It is also reassuring to know that the mountains of detailed "facts" that conspicuously fill Simon's mature novels are based closely on his experiences. (Madame Bovary read Balzac to learn facts about life in Paris; we can be forgiven for taking that kind of pleasure in Simon's work.) Simon's great war novel *La route des Flandres* (*The Flanders Road,* 1960) is more interesting when we know that Simon, like his novel's hero, served in one of the last horse cavalry troops in World War II, was a prisoner of war, and successfully escaped. Like John Updike, Simon originally trained to be a painter; like Updike, Simon has a painter's memory for visual detail. A New Yorker reading Simon's *Les corps conducteurs* (*Conducting Bodies,* 1971) can even, from Simon's precise description, guess the exact subway station the protagonist stands in.

The endless flow of faithfully recorded sights, sounds, even smells in Simon's works makes us aware of his general preoccupation with giving us experiences, making us taste what it is really like to lie exposed to enemy shells, to be a prisoner of war, to be silently, hopelessly in love. Simon is a difficult novelist but no audience-be-damned obscurantist: his most difficult techniques result from an eagerness to communicate extreme emotional states to the reader.

Claude Eugène Henri Simon was born a French citizen on 10 October 1913 in Tananarive, on the island of Madagascar off the coast of Africa (Madagascar was then a French colony). Both his father (Louis) and mother (Suzanne Danamiel Simon) were French. The family returned to France when Simon was nine months old and then Louis, a career cavalry officer, went to fight in World War I. He was killed. Simon never knew him. The death of the aristocratic Baron de Reixach, a cavalry officer, is a recurring episode in Simon's novels.

Claude and his mother were taken in by her family. His mother fell ill. Simon was raised primarily by his uncle, whose good-humored fictional counterpart we meet in the novel *Histoire* (1967), mismanaging the family estate, translating *The Golden Ass,* writing unpublished poetry, and having affairs. Simon grew up in Perpignan, the windy, dusty, provincial place he has lived in, off and on, for most of his life. At seven, like most boys of his social class, he was sent to a private Paris Catholic school, the Collège Stanislas. Simon's mother died when he was eleven.

Simon later based the private school in his novel *Histoire* on the Collège Stanislas, which was as brutal as it was devout. In *Histoire* the "rat-like" priests compete with each other in devising physical punishments for the boys, and Latin seems to be the principal subject taught. Enforced, regimented worship turns many of the boys rebelliously toward atheism and leftist politics.

Perhaps in reaction to the Collège, Simon decided against attending a university. Instead, he studied to be a painter with André Lhôte. Lhôte, a respected cubist, was then the most famous French teacher of a kind of methodized cubism (a style whose novelty already lay nearly thirty years in the past). Though Simon says he quit because he lacked the painter's hand, most readers notice Simon has the painter's eye—the superhumanly sharp perception and trained visual memory we find in Updike. Many of Simon's novels' scenes are extended still lifes, Postimpressionistic word-paintings. Even cubist word-paintings.

Simon, then, had just left school when the Great Depression struck. Like many, he became interested in left-wing politics (an interest he has maintained). In his mid twenties, Simon even ran off to Barcelona to help in the Spanish Civil War: memories of this time recur in many of his novels, including *Le palace* (*The Palace,* 1962), *Histoire,* and *Les géorgiques* (*The Georgics,* 1981). Brigades of leftists and, indeed, Communists, came to Spain from all over the world to try—unsuccessfully—to stop General Franco's fascist forces from overthrowing the government. Though by French standards Simon is a moderate, and *Conducting Bodies* even contains dead-on satire of left-wing literary politics, the Reagan administration almost tried to stop Nobel laureate Simon from entering the United States to attend a 1985 writers' conference.

In September 1939, the Germans invaded

Poland and World War II began. Twenty-six-year-old Simon was drafted and, like his father, assigned to the cavalry (31st Dragoons). In 1940, during the French military disaster, Simon lived through a series of experiences that lie at the core of his novels and his later attitudes to life.

In May 1940 Simon rode with the French cavalry to the northeastern front, where Generals Guderian, Huntziger, and Rommel were leading a blitzkrieg of planes and panzer tanks. The French government was attempting to turn back this blitzkrieg with men mounted on horses—rearing, terrified horses. For France (then a modern world power arguably greater than the United States) to have put its soldiers in this suicidal position was inexcusable. The government had placed its trust in networks of fixed defenses facing Germany (such as the notorious "Maginot Line"): the Germans simply flew over the defenses in airplanes, dropped paratroopers behind them, and raced around them in a variety of fast tanks called panzers.

What happened to Simon's unit on a road in Flanders, near the Belgian border in northeast France, he later reproduced faithfully in *The Flanders Road* and in many other of his novels about which former comrades in arms wrote him "to compliment him on the accuracy of the descriptions"—particularly the central episode, in which one Captain de Reixach is killed by a German paratrooper-sniper. (See the section "The de Reixach Family.")

This battle (the Battle of the Meuse River) figures so often in Simon's work that contemporary readers should be aware how truly historic it was—not only for France but for subsequent world history as well. The Germans, revenging themselves on France for the punitive Treaty of Versailles that the French, principally, had imposed on the German nation—a treaty with provisions so humiliating that it made the German middle class ripe for Hitler's chauvinist backlash—crushed and slaughtered the French army so quickly that the British, stunned, could not get back across the Channel in time, and were pinned down on the Dunkirk beach. Hitler gained the English Channel as a protecting moat and the French coast as a launching place for the London blitz. Years of deaths and the entire Normandy invasion on D-Day, 1944, merely returned the Allies to the position they were in before the French defeat. During those years Hitler had time to exterminate additional millions of people and (perhaps an even more lasting effect) permanently damage Western culture's opinion of mankind.

For Simon and for French readers, this battle also has the kind of imaginative significance that the defeat at Gettysburg had for the American South. The year 1940 was the real end of France as a great power.

The prisoner-of-war scenes that recur throughout Simon's novels are based on Simon's stay in prisoner-of-war camps in Germany and France from May 1940 to November 1940, when he escaped and made his way home to Perpignan in the south. France is a large country, and the Germans could not spare the manpower to occupy it: they negotiated a peace with a French puppet government (headed by Pétain and Laval at Vichy) to administer the southern two-thirds of the country, which in return was spared an occupation by the Germans. In his childhood home, during the German rule of France, Simon worked for the French Resistance and wrote, but made no attempt to publish, a first novel, *Le tricheur* (The Cheat). It appeared in 1945, after France was liberated. *La corde raide* (The Taut Rope, 1947), *Gulliver* (1952), and *Le sacre du printemps* (The Rite of Spring, 1954), all still untranslated, concern either the Spanish Civil War or the German occupation. While writing, Simon took over the family vineyard, a setting for many of the later novels.

*Le vent* (*The Wind,* 1957) was followed the next year by what most critics consider Simon's first masterwork, his sixth book, *L'Herbe* (*The Grass*).

Literary prizes and wide recognition began for Simon in 1960 when he won the Prix de

L'Express for *The Flanders Road,* followed by the Prix Médicis in 1967 for *Histoire.* (In its English translation *Histoire* retains its French title.) After the Prix Médicis, Simon, like *Conducting Bodies'* internationally known author-protagonist, began receiving honorary degrees and invitations to speak all over the world. He was still the least known of the "New Novelists" and was almost totally unknown to the general public when he received the Nobel Prize in 1985. A mystified radio announcer, Leon Roudiez reports, said that the Nobel had gone "to a seventy-two-year-old French wine grower."

## *STYLE*

After Simon's *The Grass* (1958) critics began associating him with Alain Robbe-Grillet, Michel Butor, Nathalie Sarraute, and others supposedly writing *le nouveau roman,* the "New Novel"—a term Robbe-Grillet used in several much-discussed tracts (collected as *Pour un nouveau roman* [For a New Novel] in 1963). Placing authors in "schools" or fixing names on "periods" is more convenient than accurate, but there is justice in associating Simon with these writers. The New Novelists, Serge Doubrovsky tells us, were "no longer satisfied with describing to us *what* happens" but were instead interested in "showing us how what takes place is *perceived* and *reflected upon* by a particular consciousness."

How *nouveau* is Simon's *nouveau roman?* Certainly there are antecedents. Joyce's and Faulkner's great examples are usually acknowledged. The English-speaking reader who enjoys Molly's poetic "stream of consciousness" at the end of *Ulysses* (1922) has all the skills needed to follow Simon's narratives. The reader who already enjoys T. S. Eliot's *Waste Land* (1922), sensing the emotional logic behind the sudden changes of topic and tone, will have little trouble sensing the emotional logic behind the leaps in Simon's protagonists' consciousnesses. In fact, Simon's joy in dense, playful, poetic language is markedly closer to these great modernists' than to the stripped-down language of other New Novelists.

It's interesting that calling attention to the familiarity of Simon's techniques would probably be taken today as negative criticism. Yet no one thinks less of Milton or Shakespeare for following in great predecessors' footsteps. Must modernists always innovate? Can't great modernists have ancestors? Simon is, artistically, an heir—a point often made.

Interestingly, Simon's protagonist in many of the novels, Georges (a figure whose life shares incidents with Simon's), is himself very much the heir, a man living surrounded by portraits of ancestors in a decayed mansion on a failing vineyard. How easy to draw parallels with Simon the artist living in the oversized mansion of modernism, picking grapes from the vines planted by Joyce, Proust, and Faulkner. Simon's books, however, are too good for that cheap shot: he brilliantly uses modernist methods to explore new situations. Yet the sense of Simon as a worthy heir, as a true successor to those who planted the vineyard, is an accurate one.

Although in matters of style Proust, Faulkner, and Joyce are Simon's ancestors, it is useful to think of Eliot's poem when first approaching Simon's novels. *The Waste Land,* like Simon's novels, relies heavily on the power of montage, in the cinematic sense of the term. Montage is an artistic technique which rests on the awareness that, in the human mind, one and one makes three. In a famous example, a Russian silent film director filmed a man's hand holding a kitchen knife and, at another time, took some footage of a baby. When he spliced the two clips together and showed an audience first the baby, then the knife, the audience gasped. Placing the two ordinary images together, the director created a dreadful third image in their mind.

Similarly, Eliot's poem juxtaposes a number of previously unrelated scenes and conversations—"fragments I have shored against my ruins"—to create a sense of a collapsing world.

Simon's novels work that way: in *Histoire,* for instance, the violent juxtapositions of scenes from old postcards, fragments of remembered Latin poems, memories of the beautiful Corinne, Simon's cousin, as a child sitting in a cherry tree—all expertly create a mood of mute longing, of sadness too deep to be spoken. Simon's cubist training with Lhôte undoubtedly predisposed him to montage, which works in time the way collage works in space.

The reader will discover that he must trust Simon as he first trusted Eliot, must start at page 1 and begin assimilating the apparently unrelated images, letting the the book play on the screen of his mind's eye as if it were a film. Before long characters and then meanings emerge from the montage: in *Histoire* we slowly realize that the thoughts of the beautiful childhood playmate sitting in a cherry tree are playing in the mind of a failing middle-aged businessman as he walks home to sell his furniture after begging for a bank loan to save himself. The way he keeps fleeing from the ghastly present back to that childhood memory—remembering more and more details, lingering over them—conveys his mental state better than any omniscient narrator could. Simon never intrudes into the text to say something like "Crushed, broken, he withdrew from the present and fled back to that moment in his mind." Simon presents the thoughts and lets us decide. Sharing the man's actual thoughts ourselves, we share his experience more deeply than if we were merely informed of it by a narrator. It is the difference between being told about an event and actually experiencing it.

Yet Eliot's poem does not take one twentieth of the reading time needed for a Simon novel, and this matters: Simon's montage in *Histoire* rarely works as well as Eliot's. Montage needs speed to work, much as film itself depends on speed and persistence of vision. Project a film too slowly, and the eye cannot blend the still pictures into the illusion of motion. Separate two Simon images by thirty pages of text, and they simply do not montage as if they were separated by three pages of Eliot's poetry. Montage is a persistence of mental vision, and a novel can run too slowly and too long.

Worse yet, the beginning reader, baffled by Simon's difficulty, will slow down even more and try to untangle the text. But you mustn't untangle montage; the "tangle" makes it work. Simon's books actually become clearer if they are read quickly and in as few sittings as possible.

The authors just mentioned are Simon's artistic, but in no way his philosophical or spiritual, ancestors. Simon must loathe Eliot's addiction to formal religion and his right-wing politics. The Faulkner who thought that man would not only "endure" but "prevail," the Joyce of the joyous epiphanic visions—this optimism is foreign to Simon. Even in Simon's first novels, when he was still interested in Dostoevsky and Camus, an older philosophy keeps showing beneath the existential clothes: pessimism, "the vanity of human wishes," man as the victim of his own ceaseless desiring. When critics speak (as they invariably do) of Simon as a "pessimist," they mean something more specific than hopelessness or gloom.

In the German philosopher Arthur Schopenhauer's classic exposition of pessimism, *The World as Will and Idea* (1818), which was important to one of Simon's masters, Proust, man's unhappiness stems from his inability to control the desires that send him perpetually sucking for milk at the universe's dead rock breast. Schopenhauer calls man's hungers for food, for love, for meaning—for all of it—man's "will." In Schopenhauer's usage, man is the victim of his own unstoppable "willing." (I do not mean to suggest that Simon studied Schopenhauer; pessimism is not a conviction one needs to learn from books.)

Pessimism is *not* existentialism. We may take postwar French existentialism's essence to be captured in Camus's image of Sisyphus, "happily," even heroically, rolling his rock up the hill. Though he knows it will come bouncing down, Camus's Sisyphus does not care. It is his familiar rock, his familiar hill, his work in the world: "We must picture Sisyphus happy," Camus assures us (*The Myth of Sisyphus,* 1942).

No philosophy would repel a pessimist more. Camus might as well ask us to admire Tantalus, pessimists would say, or Samuel Beckett's little clown in *Act Without Words I* (1956), who has objects placed within his reach only so they can be yanked away. Simon's work often reminds one of Beckett, who has spoken of how important Schopenhauer was for him and who studded his book on Proust with references to Schopenhauer. Simon is like Beckett without the sense of humor.

Pessimism, on the other hand, is not negativism: Schopenhauer wrote that once we recognize that we are all in the same boat, we can be kinder to each other. We should address each other as "companion in misery," should offer each other the kind of sympathy and fraternity that lightens for many of us the bums' lot in *Waiting for Godot.* If there were not so much real charity and sympathy in Simon's books, the sadness would be unbearable. His usual protagonist, Georges, comes through as a deeply decent, caring person, a man more sinned against than sinning. *King Lear,* after all, is not a cheerful or optimistic play. Optimism offers us inspiration, but pessimism offers us commiseration, and each of the two sects appeals to us at different moments in our lives.

Pessimists look not for happiness but for surcease, peace. Pessimism has always had a special fondness for the aesthetic experience, for the detached contemplation of sunlight on surfaces, the tranced postponement of our besetting desires. Simon had not accidentally studied to be a painter. His novels are filled with word-paintings and aesthetic admirations. The later novels are, in fact, fictions generated from the contemplation of favorite paintings, above all (significantly) Nicolas Poussin's study of the frustrated will, *The Blind Orion Searching for the Dawn.* The blinded Orion stands to Simon's work as the "happy" Sisyphus stands to Camus's. To take the blind Orion searching for something he lacks the faculties to find is to repudiate Camus.

In Simon's work the quest for peace in aesthetic contemplation regularly evolves into a kind of self-forgetful sex. Here, I think, is the explanation for the particular kind of long, detailed sexual scenes that fill Simon's work. His protagonists notice the way waves rip apart and scatter sunlight, notice every wind ripple in the grass, and finally, notice each other as objects of aesthetic, then physical, delight. As Tristan took refuge from the world by going to live with Isolde in the Venus grotto, so Simon's tormented intellectuals constantly escape into sex. In Simon's books sex seems not an act of willing but a step beyond self into a kind of ultimate aesthetic delight, a savoring of the texture of skin, the beautiful "apricot" soles of Corinne's feet, the flowerlike folds of her labiae, the gastronomic savoring of kisses, salt sweat, and cunnilingus. (If there is any significant change in American "pornography" laws, Americans will not be permitted to read Simon's novels: "Corinne took it first between her lips then the whole thing in her mouth like a greedy child it was as if we were drinking each other" [*The Flanders Road,* 259].)

Schopenhauer believed that all pleasures of this sort are just the alms thrown a beggar, sustaining him in his misery for one more day. Similarly, Simon's books unfailingly balance the moments of sexual pleasure against years of tormenting sexual jealousy, rejection, and humiliating cuckoldry. Sex is no solution. Life offers no hope and only temporary escape. Everything human is conquered and destroyed by history and time. Simon's best-known novel, *The Flanders Road,* ends with a vision of "the world stopped cold exhausted crumbling into dust caving in bit by bit to pieces like an abandoned hut, used up, left to the incoherent, casual, impersonal and destructive work of time."

Simon has protested the "pessimist" epithet. Soon after publishing the passage above, he complained to the newspaper interviewer Madeleine Chapsal, "I'm in love with everything,

everything, with a woman, a grass blade, a pebble." Questioned about that statement sixteen years later, Simon swore that he had meant it and that the feeling had only grown stronger with age. This from a man whose novels' usual protagonists are shown jealous, near bankruptcy, cuckolded, drinking, and ill.

Critics have a term, "the intentional fallacy," for the error of reducing a novel to the intention of its novelist—accepting his description of the novel he claims he has written for a description of the novel he actually wrote. But although there is no way around the fact that Simon's novels deal with life's horrors, in war or in peace, Simon's protest that he is "in love with everything" should be heeded: his pessimism is not a hatred for life but a mourning over the good things of this world as he watches it "exhausted crumbling into dust" before the "incoherent, casual, impersonal" onslaught of time.

## *THE DE REIXACH FAMILY*

Simon's most discussed novels involve characters connected in some way with the fictional aristocratic de Reixach family. (Reixach rhymes with "eye shack," Simon has had to explain even to French readers.) More specifically, the novels concern a few characters whose lives are changed in some way by cavalry Captain de Reixach's death during the 1940 French debacle. By the later works Simon either has become so tired of explaining the de Reixach story or so confident that his early novels have been read that he includes de Reixach material without explanation. Many Simon novels, therefore, will be much easier to read once one knows the outlines of the de Reixach story. Simon has been careful to leave the full interpretation of "what happens" up to each reader, so the following outline is not definitive, just a head start.

The reader should be careful, however, not to connect the books too closely. They are not sequels to each other in any traditional sense, but independent novels; the reader will even find that important details of the characters' lives change from book to book. And, for reasons I will explain later, *Histoire,* though a de Reixach novel, must be considered separately.

Georges is the protagonist of most of the de Reixach novels. If he is not quite a fictional stand-in for Claude Simon, his life certainly shares many events with Simon's. Georges, born around 1913, like Simon, grows up in a "good family" (wealthy, minor aristocracy by marriage) on a vineyard near a provincial city similar to Simon's Perpignan. Though his artistry is more implied than apparent, Georges belongs to a familiar tradition in post-1800 world literature: the portrait of the artist as a sensitive young man.

Georges's father, Pierre, a grossly fat and respected professor, is a Rousseauean rationalist and optimist in the tradition of the Enlightenment, the eighteenth-century French Age of Reason. "Being the son of illiterate peasants, he's so proud of having been able to learn to read that he's profoundly convinced there's no problem, in particular that of human happiness, that can't be solved by reading good authors" (*The Flanders Road,* p. 222). This could almost be a comment about the French eighteenth-century rationalists, whom the father personifies. Such certainty about being able to solve life's problems—"in particular . . . human happiness"!—is, to someone of Simon's persuasion, not only true ignorance but also almost unbearable self-satisfaction and ludicrous pride. Georges's father has filled his library with Enlightenment books capped by a conspicuous edition of Rousseau. By the time of World War II the father (like the tradition, Simon implies) is old, grotesque, "mountainous," lumbering—as unable to comprehend the horrifying, irrational world outside as he is out of touch with his disillusioned twentieth-century son.

Sabine is Georges's mother. Georges's paternal grandfather was a peasant, but on Sabine's side the family has tenuous connections with the aristocratic de Reixach family. Moreover, through the complications of legacies and property divisions, Sabine has acquired the ancestral mansion in which they now live. Perhaps because her connection with the de Reixach line is so marginal, Sabine exalts herself into the guardian of family traditions and legends, chattering endlessly, weaving strange romantic stories about the great leaky pile she and Georges live in.

Obviously, Georges is Simon's portrait of the twentieth-century French artist. It is hard not to see Sabine as personifying the nineteenth-century French Romantic tradition, much as her husband is the last eighteenth-century philosophe. Just as the latter tradition has ended in this "pachyderm," so the Romantics Victor Hugo and Eugène Delacroix have dwindled into a chattering old gossip telling preposterous stories to aggrandize her link with a romantic past. Sabine affects coquettish ways and coats herself with makeup, an absurd caricature of romantic beauty. Georges, the modern artist, lives in the leaky, oversized, ghost-filled mansion of French literature with these two relics.

Sabine has the artistic impulse, at least, and one of the stories she weaves around an ancestral portrait fascinates Georges. Sabine turns a reddish crack in the canvas into the blood-stained reminder of that de Reixach ancestor's suicide. (In many of Simon's books, too, either Georges or a narrator will use Sabine's method of meditating on a picture until a narrative grows from it.)

The "Ancestor," as some critics appropriately call him, plays an important role in Georges's mental life and in Simon's novels. In Sabine's version, the Ancestor, though a nobleman, was converted by Rousseau's works and joined the Revolution. He cast his vote for the king's death, then served Napoleon as a general in Spain, which at first seemed a war of liberation. Disillusioned, he came home to Perpignan and blew his brains out with a pistol Sabine now preserves downstairs in a display case. Simon has such an ancestor himself and is plainly inspired by the story of the aristocrat who sides with the people against his class. His *The Georgics* is the book most preoccupied with the Ancestor to date.

Georges rebels against both traditions his parents represent by trying to become, like his paternal grandfather, a worker, a peasant on the land. Both Pierre and Sabine are disappointed in him—though, Simon is ironically aware, Georges proves their paternity through his Rousseauean, Romantic decision to go "back to the land," so to speak. Georges discovers that he is no longer even capable of being a good, productive peasant, and there the situation stands for several of the novels: the three of them living together in the leaky mansion, his father preferring the rational world of his books to the post-occupation France outside, Georges's mother babbling her dreams and legends, Georges trying to work the land and falling ever deeper into debt and drink.

When Georges is drafted into the cavalry at the start of World War II, Sabine writes to his commanding officer, Captain de Reixach, to introduce Georges as a distant cousin—so distant, plainly, that de Reixach had never heard of Georges until that moment.

The fullest version of Captain de Reixach's death comes in *The Flanders Road.* Throughout Georges's boyhood, as he had listened to Sabine, the de Reixach name and family had come to symbolize a highly romanticized version of France's glorious aristocratic past. From the dawn of modern European history France had been a great power, the country of Charlemagne, of Louis XIV, of Napoleon—of the de Reixachs. As Captain de Reixach rides proudly on his horse at the start of World War II, disdaining to take cover, "the epitome of elegance and chic," we are meant to remember that "chevalier" and "chivalry" originally referred to the horsemen and their code. De Reixach is a figure from a heroic equestrian statue in a public square.

And when (in novel after novel) he is shot down by a humble paratrooper-sniper hiding unchivalrously behind a hedge, when Baron de Reixach topples with his horse "like an equestrian statue," we are meant to see the statues of Charlemagne, Louis, and Napoleon falling finally into the twentieth-century mud with him. The France that had lasted a thousand years goes with him.

As discussed earlier, de Reixach's death is elaborated out of a very similar incident Simon witnessed. Could his imagination have been triggered by the name of the officer he saw ambushed—Rey—which actually means "king" in Spanish? No novelist would dare be as baldly symbolic as life sometimes is. The unusual name "de Reixach" combines memories of "Rey" and "reich."

Someone in John Le Carré's much underrated *Tinker, Tailor, Soldier, Spy* (1974) laments of Claude Simon's English counterparts, "Poor loves! Trained to Empire, trained to rule the waves!" Despite Simon's sincerely anticolonial, left-wing politics, part of the malaise that hovers over Simon's novels is the haunting sense of a France diminished from the France that he, the child born to a cavalry officer in a French colony, was educated to expect. The anticolonial French Left is often as uncomfortable with Simon's novels (particularly *The Palace*) as the common French regicides must have been with the noble Ancestor that Simon identifies with.

Simon is generally hostile to or contemptuous of the aristocracy, but his attitude toward the chivalric code is much more complex. The fall of the chivalric values—however ambivalent he is about them—represents for Simon the victory of a bourgeois world given only to opportunism and respecting nothing but money. Simon is hardly the first to choose this theme. We could complain that de Reixach's death could as easily have come from an English commoner's longbow at Agincourt (1415), which spelled the end of the armored knight on horseback. Nineteenth-century medieval romanticism in England and France was often a reaction to the perceived victory of Scrooge-like utilitarians who cared for nothing but money; generations of nineteenth-century artists combined contempt for the current aristocracy with respect for the chivalric ideal; English "radical Tories" pioneered in anticapitalist politics (and notice the fusion of anticapitalism and chivalry in the name of the first American labor union [1869], the Knights of Labor); Proust's epic concerned (he thought) the end of aristocracy and loss of respect for anything but wealth (the childhood fascination of Proust's narrator, Marcel, with the Guermantes is much like Georges's childhood fascination with the de Reixachs); and Faulkner chronicled the gradual fall of Colonel Sartoris' values and the takeover of the Snopeses.

Here, as so often, Simon is heir to a tradition; and, as so often, he seems to have improved on the tradition, written a climactic last chapter to it. The historical moment Simon selects for his version of the Fall rings truer than those before: for a thousand years aristocratic French horsemen had ridden out to battle, but this was the last time. De Reixach dies at the hands of a paratrooper, next to an overturned truck, amid the stink of burning tires. As Georges and his comrades wander dazed during the debacle, they encounter over and over again his dead horse, dissolving beneath the rain into the mud, like the chivalric world to which the horse lent its name. The historical moment Simon chooses is the end of old France and indeed of old Europe, divided between French and English power since Charlemagne's coronation in A.D. 800.

Did de Reixach *know* his world had already ended, did he ride to his chivalric death as a kind of suicide? Later, in prison camp, Georges associates the Ancestor's suicide with de Reixach's. Sabine had claimed that the Ancestor knew himself to be cuckolded when he died, and Georges believes that de Reixach knew that his wife, Corinne, had deceived him with their racing stable's jockey, Iglesia.

Corinne, de Reixach's fabulously beautiful, lustful wife, a girl young enough to be his daughter, is the most important player in the de Reixach material. The reader will recognize references to Corinne throughout the novels when memories surface of a childlike woman in a gauzy, cherry-red, almost indecently transparent dress, or naked in bed (the narrator often remembers her "cherry" lipstick and the "apricot" soles of her bare feet).

Captain de Reixach arranges for Corinne's supposed lover, Iglesia, de Reixach's jockey during the glamorous days of their racing stable, to follow de Reixach into the cavalry as an orderly. Iglesia is a tiny man, ugly as "a carnival mask" with a great nose "like a lobster claw." Georges becomes obsessed with Corinne through the stories Iglesia tells about her when he and Georges are captured and put in a prisoner-of-war camp together.

Remembering these few characters will help the reader immeasurably when he or she plunges into the whirl of thoughts that make up Simon novels written after *The Wind*. We need only mention, in closing, Louise, Georges's wife, who betrays him in *The Grass*. Louise, however, appears much less often than Corinne.

The 1967 novel *Histoire* must be considered totally apart. In *Histoire* Simon made the bold move of taking the by-then-famous de Reixach material and altering it, reworking it. (See the *Histoire* section of this essay.) Even so, the broad outlines sketched here will help when one enters *Histoire*.

## *INVENTING HIS NOVEL: THE FIRST WORKS*

Simon's first novels are now considered apprentice work and remain untranslated. Simon disparages them; only scholars read them. Their interest lies in watching a fine novelist make first, often unsuccessful, attempts to invent his novel—for there is no such thing as "the" novel, only "novels" that disparate novelists have created to suit their disparate visions and talents. Certainly by Simon's day the term "novel" was an "open" category, as the philosopher Ludwig Wittgenstein once claimed the word "game" was.

Simon has often protested that his evolution as novelist is insufficiently understood as a response to the problems that a working novelist, not a philosopher, faces. In the 1972 conference at Cérisy, when Simon listened to papers on his works and joined in roundtable discussions with his critics, he was forced repeatedly to make remarks like "As I've said, I'm not a philosopher and I've never read Derrida . . . the theory [about my work you propose] is in a field completely outside my competence." He even reminded the critics, irritably, "You make me repeat: one must above all notice that (it's written on the cover) *Le palace* is a novel . . . which means . . . *before all else* . . . [it has to obey] *literary* . . . considerations" (Simon's emphasis). The present essay tries to give Simon the sort of reading he has suggested would most clarify his work.

Simon has been engagingly candid about the way his own assortment of talents altered the form of the novel he created. He is frank about how bad he was at inventing characters and "plot," limitations that ruled out what he calls the "traditional" novel. Simon's first novels offer a good chance to watch a novelist find out what he can do, what he cannot do, and then (the hard part) invent a form that lets him do what he can and avoid what he can't—yet embodies his philosophic content. It is a triple challenge. Few bring it off. Critics underestimate the accomplishment when they write as if the last part of the challenge were the whole of it.

If novel criticism has a general fault, it is ignorance of the conditions of production. Historians of medieval art know better than to speculate about the philosophic motives behind Cimabue's choice of a gold background: all that was specified by the commissioning church in a contract, down to the amount of gold leaf the church would provide. Novel critics—Simon's critics—generally exaggerate the amount of freedom novelists have, as if, despite all evidence to the contrary, novelists have the power to write any way they choose. The limits of one's talents bind one more tightly than any medieval church ever did. What different "novels" Proust, Dickens, Hemingway, and Claude Simon have cobbled together to suit their different powers while expressing their different visions!

*Le tricheur* is the title of the novel Simon wrote in Perpignan during the period 1941–1945, after escaping from the prisoner-of-war camp. In *Le tricheur* (The Cheat) we watch the youthful Simon try his hand at some Camus, some Faulkner, some Sartre and Dostoevsky—the French literary idols of the day.

When critics notice that Simon's first protagonist, Louis, is a Stephen Dedalus–like figure, they are really noticing that a sensitive boy in a turn-of-the-century Catholic school in France, as well as in Ireland, could become a violently anticlerical writer. Simon's rage surpasses Joyce's, and Simon did not need Joyce to teach him about such rage. Simon's protagonist, Louis, now grown, hunts down a priest to murder him. Indeed, in the priest's presence Louis becomes so rabid that he forgets the revolver in his pocket and beats in the priest's head with a brick. Some twenty-five years later, in *Histoire,* Simon's hatred for the scene of his childhood humiliations, and by extension his childhood's religion, has not lessened. The Collège Stanislas can probably take credit for training a young aristocrat to detest established power for the rest of his life.

Critics have remembered Gide's and Camus's philosophic murderers as possible models, but Dostoevsky is a more likely antecedent. Simon has admitted that *The Wind* is a French update of Dostoevsky's *The Idiot* (1871) and that *La corde raide* is much like Dostoevsky's *Diary of a Writer* (1876–1877), with elements of *The House of the Dead* (1862). Dostoevsky wrote *House* about his stay in prison camp, and Simon began *Le tricheur* after his own stay in one. For years afterward Simon seems to have felt a special affinity for his fellow ex-inmate: we find Dostoevskian "idiots," "doubles," and freedom-thirsting murderers in Simon's early novels. I should add that during the 1940's Simon also would have seen Dostoevsky through a cloud of critical interpretations (going back to Gide) which turned that authoritarian Russian Orthodox Christian into a forerunner of French existentialism.

Dostoevsky's blundering Raskolnikov, in *Crime and Punishment* (1866), seems particularly close to *Le tricheur*'s Louis. Raskolnikov is, like Louis, a sensitive, "injured" young man, a half-baked philosopher who decides to prove his freedom to himself with a murder; his inability to control events turns Raskolnikov, like Louis, into a mere head-basher. Man doesn't control history; it controls him. The "cheater" Simon's title refers to is Louis, who tries to cheat destiny, "correct chance," prove his freedom with a willful act (Louis calls his revolver the "solid form" his "will" has taken). Simon always argues that the individual has no chance against life's overwhelming forces.

"Disoriented by the critical reception of *Le tricheur,*" Simon later told Ludovic Janvier, "unsure of myself, I then tried to prove—*enterprise absurde!*—that I could write a novel in the traditional form. An excellent and fruitful error, as it turned out. The result was edifying: I couldn't!" The "fruitful error" was Simon's second novel, *Gulliver,* written in 1952 after the Dostoevskian meditations of *La corde raide.* If Simon needed added proof of how radically he would have to redesign his novel to fit himself, *Gulliver* supplied it.

In an atmosphere of Faulknerian melodrama, the children of a degenerate provincial French family clash after the war. Jo had fought for France, his twin brother Loulou had collaborated with the Nazis, and their sister Eliane has had a child by the dissolute, disillusioned, bisexual Max. Once again Simon's theme is the vanity of human wishes, the futility of man's attempts to control life. Max had once been an idealist, but his war experiences have turned him into the casual corruptor of Eliane and others. Loulou, the Nazi collaborator, spends the book conning a Jew, Herzog, into thinking that Loulou can find his wife and daughter, who vanished in the Holocaust. Max has abandoned Eliane for Bobby. Bobby abandons Max, only to be accidentally killed by Loulou. Max kills himself. Herzog realizes that he has been taken but finds no sympathy from the embittered postwar French. Bert, a reporter in love with Eliane, tries to make sense of it all but cannot. Bert is a stand-in, perhaps, for the reader, who cannot make sense of it either.

The "error" of trying to write *Gulliver* was, however, "excellent and fruitful," as Simon said. He turned his back on what he called the "traditional" novel and returned to the form he had experimented with unsuccessfully in *Le tricheur:* the interior monologue. At this point the future Nobelist was forty-one, had been writing seriously for thirteen years, and was still an awkward beginner. Simon's fourth novel, *Le sacre du printemps,* still contains melodramatic elements, but far fewer of them. Simon uses a smaller palette of characters and we learn about them through only three interior monologues. *Sacre* is under much better control. Here Simon explores themes he later developed in his best works and creates his first genuinely successful character, Bernard Mallet.

Bernard, a haughty teenage engineering student, despises his undistinguished mother and stepfather and thinks that he will order his life as if it were mathematics. It is a youthful idea: Bernard is still ignorant of love or sex, of all the primitive "rites of spring" to which the book's title refers. (*Le sacre du printemps* is also the title of Igor Stravinsky's famous 1913 modernist ballet score, whose savage discords and primitive pounding rhythms caused scandalized French audiences to riot when it premiered.)

Bernard obtains a position as a mathematics tutor, and his student's sister, the beautiful Edith, awakens Bernard's humanity. Before long the would-be logician is helping Edith sell a ring she has stolen to pay for (we discover later) an abortion. Bernard, as a rite of passage, voyages like a mythic hero into the underworld in two senses: he enters a moral underworld where the hoodlums Abel and Jacky can sell the stolen ring, and he enters a physical underworld of Paris subways and even sewers where Jacky's bunch hangs out. Bernard makes love to Jacky's whore, Josie. After she leaves, he cannot find the ring and, hunting her, he confronts Jacky, who beats him up. In a moving image, Bernard washes his wounds in the Seine and, ceremonially initiated into and educated about parts of man's character that the conscious will has never controlled, he goes home.

Edith is struck by a car. Bernard encounters his despised, unglamorous stepfather in the hospital. As they talk, Bernard begins to realize how his experiences echo his stepfather's initiation and disillusion during the Spanish Civil War. Worse, to further the identity, they both have been infatuated with the same woman: Edith carries the stepfather's child. Finally Bernard takes out his handkerchief and discovers, buried in it, the ring. So even the beating was pointless—as, perhaps, was the Spanish Civil War, which his stepfather's side had lost to Franco.

Schopenhauer said that someone who lives too long feels as if he has sat through the same play twice. Pessimists have always insisted (as Simon does) on the monotonous unoriginality of human experiences—a conviction that leads Simon to embrace such virtues as humility and compassion for others (who are after all as sad as oneself). J. A. E. Loubère points out that the student Bernard's profession in French is *répétiteur,* literally "repeater," and the middleman stepfather's is *revendeur,* "reseller." The ring itself is the book's emblem of circularity, futility, and repetition. It is impossible to avoid noticing that Simon repeated his father's service in the French cavalry and came close to repeating his death during the military collapse.

*Sacre* received little attention. Three years later, in 1957, Simon published *The Wind,* his fifth book and the last novel of what he calls his "first period." He was forty-four and had been a novelist for sixteen years.

"An idiot, nothing more," the town notary is telling the narrator at the start of *The Wind.* He refers to Antoine Montès, a character strongly reminiscent of Dostoevsky's saintly Prince

Mishkin in his *The Idiot* (1871). Simon has candidly described the book as a French "remake" of the Russian novel. Labeling Montès an "idiot" in the first sentence is the novelist's way of providing a footnote, calling attention to the debt and acknowledging it cheerfully.

Dostoevsky had written, in a letter, that the greatest challenge in literature was creating a "*positively* good" man: he admired Don Quixote and Mr. Pickwick. Deeply good, even Christ-like, characters almost always repel an audience (because we have so little in common with them?); Dostoevsky thought Pickwick and Quixote do not estrange us because they are "also ridiculous and succeed by virtue of that fact." The good character could be "ridiculous," an "idiot," a foolish innocent. (Indeed, there was a surprising medieval tradition of Christ as an innocent clown.) Dostoevsky's Mishkin was cast in that mold and was, of course, a great success.

On *The Wind*'s first page we learn that Simon's Antoine Montès is an idiot because he acts against his "self-interest." Sane people, the village notary tells the narrator, have "one . . . motive and only one . . . self-interest." Here we recognize Scrooge's philosophy, utilitarian capitalism.

In the later novel *The Flanders Road,* Captain de Reixach knows that his world is over and invites death; in *The Wind,* Montès, who also acts for greater motives than his own petty self-interest, lives on, out of place in modern France, but only as "an idiot, nothing more." Simon links Montès to the "Idiotic family tree," inviting our comparison: Don Quixote lives a life we would have to call valuable, Mr. Pickwick triumphs, and Prince Mishkin comes only to personal grief—but Montès' goodness devastates everyone around him. There are a few episodes in *Don Quixote* (1605) in which the hero's intervention leaves everyone worse off than they were before, but Montès' goodness destroys both of the women who are inspired by it, killing one of them and thus orphaning two children.

Montès comes to the windy vineyard town to claim his dead father's estate: he is one of many Simonian heirs. The estate's bailiff quarrels with him, and during the ensuing litigation Montès takes rooms in a cheap hotel. A serving woman there, Rose, and her two small daughters are uplifted by his Christ-like nature. Rose entrusts some jewelry to him. Montès' cousin, Cécile—a haughty, nervous type familiar to us from Dostoevsky novels—gradually falls in love with the saint. For the first half of the novel Montès' goodness gentles and transforms those around him (less like *Don Quixote* than like the popular musical *Man of La Mancha*). The only ominous note is the wind.

Then a gypsy, who is Rose's daughters' natural father, kills Rose for giving to Montès the stolen jewelry she had been holding for him. The police then kill the gypsy, and the little girls are sent to an orphanage. The cousin's trusting, too-revealing letter to Montès is stolen from the simpleton by a salesman, who, like a good entrepreneur, uses it to blackmail her. The bailiff wins the lawsuit and Montès has to sell what little he has and leave town. "Monasteries . . . were invented," the narrator tells Montès at the end, to keep "people like you . . . from doing harm. . . ." The world is so bad that positive goodness makes it worse. Don Quixote no longer inspires, he destroys.

At the novel's close the relentless fall wind "rips the last red leaves off the vines" and bends the trees, "its strength without pause, without purpose, doomed to exhaust itself without end," the wind "envying the men sleeping," envying "their chance at . . . peace: the privilege of dying." It would be hard to call this anything but pessimism. It is not optimism.

*The Wind* was Simon's most praised work to date, probably because the least adventurous. It seems, like Renoir paintings of the late 1880's, to come from a middle-aged artist's temporary exhaustion with a lifetime of unappreciated experiment. *The Wind* could have been written anytime in the twentieth century: the characters are Dostoevskian, the narrative technique almost too indebted to another modernist ancestor Simon has acknowledged,

Joseph Conrad. (Conrad's narrator Marlowe, long-winded, philosophizing, often implausibly omniscient, tells such stories as *Lord Jim* [1900].) To *The Wind* alone Simon affixed a pretentious, oddly irrelevant subtitle, *Tentative de restitution d'un retable baroque* (Attempted Restoration of a Baroque Retable [altarpiece]), perhaps to hint at some novelty for his book. We value *The Wind* anyway for Simon's first sharp fictional portrait of windy, provincial Perpignan, masterfully rendered.

Perhaps encouraged by *The Wind*'s relative success, Simon got his own wind back and the very next year published his boldest experiment yet, *The Grass. The Grass,* the first work in Simon's mature style, begins the series of novels he calls his "second period," the books on which his reputation will probably continue to rest.

## *FINDING HIS NOVEL: THE WORKS OF SIMON'S MATURITY*

*The Grass* is both Simon's first de Reixach novel and the first novel written in his mature manner, which plunges the reader into a character's consciousness—not into the character's mind alone (expect no clinical verisimilitude) but into everything of which the character is aware, often poetically augmented by the author. These novels are widely available in English and are much discussed; we will consider each at length.

As we read *The Grass,* we gradually understand that the consciousness we have entered is that of Georges's wife, Louise, a vital young woman for the first time forced into an intense awareness of death. Marie, Georges's father's spinster aunt, has come to Georges's family's estate to die with dreadful slowness in a room upstairs. Aunt Marie wastes away day after day to an inhuman shape, and her death rattle, regular as a bellows, grows so loud that there is no escape from it in the house. Georges (whose artistic "back to the land" scheme to work the family estate like some romanticized peasant has predictably been failing) flees from the sound of death in the house and the smell of acres of rotting pear trees outside to spend his time drinking and gambling in town, leaving his young wife alone with the dying woman and Georges's parents, themselves old and grotesque.

Not surprisingly, Louise has been approached by an unnamed would-be lover, and—not surprisingly—during the novel she takes refuge in forgetful sex with him in the grass.

Helping sort through the dying woman's pitiful souvenirs, Louise is forced into an awareness of life's futility. Simon usually calls such awareness a sense of "the triumph of Time": the sun beating through the edges of the closed shutters opposite the old lady's deathbed seems, to Louise, to form a huge capital "T," a burning symbol of Time's victory over human life. She can see disquieting parallels between her bad marriage and that of Georges's parents; Georges's painted, lonely old mother and the breathing "mummy" upstairs forecast to Louise how little life holds in store for her.

In Beckett's plays situations this grim will suddenly erupt into comedy, as with the couple in *All That Fall* (1957), who are reduced to hysterical laughter upon hearing a cheerful sermon title: "The Lord upholdeth all that fall."

Simon's pessimism lacks Beckett's "black comic" depth—but Beckett's pessimism lacks Simon's compensating consciousness of the earth's beauty. Louise's new awareness of death shocks her, and the reader, into the corresponding awareness of life's frailty, its beauty, which seizes us as we leave a hospital or stand in a cemetery. Aunt Marie's last days lift Louise—and Simon's prose—to achingly beautiful, grateful perceptions of the ordinary natural world around her—perceptions of "little girls sprawled in chairs, bare elbows on the chair arms too high for them," of the "tiger-striped spot" of a cat among the "dazzling jumble of shadows" in a garden, of the "mad unconscious sunflowers, their long stems crossing, jostling, tangling . . . against the black background of the blackberries humming with insects." Louise's mental state gives Simon, the ex-painter, the chance finally to let his painter's eye energize his prose. We read Conrad for such moments of piercing sensation (not to abstract his "philosophy"). In *The Grass,* Simon has visions that often equal Conrad's.

*The Grass,* above all, is the first book in which Simon stops trying to tell a story and starts trying to present an experience. His own experience in war had long made him skeptical of anyone's ability to tell stories about what "really" happens. Simon has written of how he was impressed with Conrad's preface to *The Nigger of the Narcissus* (1897), in which Conrad rested fiction's merit on its ability to "reach the secret spring of responsive emotions." Fiction reaches us "through the senses" and should "aspire . . . to the colour of painting, to the magic suggestiveness of music."

Fiction gives not only explanations but also sensations, emotions, experiences. From *The Grass* onward Simon has had enough of telling stories. He has no further interest in narrative coherence; he had always been "struck," he told Janvier, by the "opposition, even the incompatibility" of the world's chaotic "discontinuity" and literature's neat "continuity." Starting with *The Grass,* Simon organizes his novels to "magically suggest" the discontinuity of experiences.

The reader, understandably unfamiliar with so radical a decision, tends to make *The Grass* harder than it is. Even sophisticated critics have assumed that Simon takes a plot (coherent story with beginning, middle, and end), cuts it up like a jigsaw puzzle, and requires the reader to put it back together. But what would be the point of that? Such a belief perhaps betrays an academic's conditioned idea of novels as problems to be solved in papers and on finals. Simon's novels are, at their best, magical Conradian suggestions of human experience.

Of course, Conrad never said you must choose stories *or* experiences. We have seen how telling stories had never come naturally to Simon. Having learned what he could not do (novels like *Gulliver,* the "fruitful" failure) and what he could do, Simon at last fashioned what he could do into a form that embodied his weltanschauung, his "worldview." Having watched Simon spend sixteen hard years developing his vision, we can better appreciate how, though the New Novelists (or any novelists) may resemble each other, the roads to their creations are painfully solitary.

*The Grass* is the first book in which Simon almost entirely replaces personal names with "he" and "she." If the success of the novel depended on the reader sorting out who "he" and "she" are in each line, the reader would be properly exasperated. If *Waiting for Godot* (1952) depended on figuring out who Godot is (with Beckett knowing all along, like Agatha Christie, but for some reason coyly refusing to tell), the reader might very well complain. Beckett assures us that if he knew who Godot was, he would have put it in the play.

The reader who goes ahead and reads *The Grass* will find all the seemingly unique individuals in the novel collapsing, from time to time, into a nameless "he" and a "she," unoriginal, repetitious, eternal, loving, betraying, quarreling, inventing nothing, and getting nowhere. Conrad—in the preface Simon liked—had asked for a novel that was "the perfect blending of form and substance," and Simon's aggregate "he" and "she" blend perfectly with his message: the pessimist's moral that we are in no way as unique as we think. As in FitzGerald's *Rubáiyát,* the eternal Saki from his bowl has poured millions of bubbles like us, and will pour. Aunt Marie gives Louise a cookie tin on which is depicted a girl lying on the grass (just like Louise) looking at a cookie tin on which there is a picture of a girl lying on the grass looking at a cookie tin on which there is a picture of a girl . . . and so forth. Louise's awareness of repetition and unoriginality even causes her to fear that the phallus, the seed transferrer, is what Life really cares about, not us, and that all our brains and senses have been provided merely to sustain the phallus, like providing so much good "loam" for a plant to root in. *The Grass* is a lesson in humility.

Two years later, in 1960, Simon followed *The Grass* with his greatest book, *The Flanders Road,* in which Louise's husband, Georges, appears as narrator for the first time. We have already considered in some detail its central episode, Georges's witnessing the death of Captain de Reixach. *The Flanders Road* material had been on Simon's hands for twenty years, but not until *The Grass* did Simon finally discover the technical vocabulary to express his experience of the debacle.

*The Flanders Road* is, among war novels, the one that best satisfies Conrad's desire for a novel that is a "perfect blending of form and substance." Had Joyce or Eliot written of war, the result might have been like this. Here again, the reader who thinks that his duty is to construct a coherent novel from Simon's fragments will miss the point. Incoherence, chaos, disorder, partial and confused knowledge are the very points about war that Simon makes. One of the most famous war scenes in French literature, Fabrizio's experience of the Battle of Waterloo in Stendhal's *Charterhouse of Parma* (1839), made that point about war.

Compare *The Flanders Road* with *Charterhouse,* or with Norman Mailer's *The Naked and the Dead* (1948), and see, though Stendhal and Mailer talk of war's confusion, how linear, clear, and logical they make war seem! The supposed disorder unfolds in a tidy succession of numbered chapters and rationally organized paragraphs. Sentences and actions have clear beginnings and ends. Reading *The Flanders Road* makes one realize how falsely rational an experience of war even the best war novels give—important information to have. Mailer argues the unknowability of the campaign's events while his form makes them seem as transparent as the events in most novels seem, when seen through the eyes of an omniscient narrator who enters all minds effortlessly and reports to us all thoughts, feelings, and motives, even those of which the characters are unaware.

That transparency, superior to life, is one of the pleasures for which we read novels; nowhere is it written that artworks must be identical to ordinary events or things. *The Flanders Road* lasts too long and often exasperates. However, veterans have long insisted that we must grasp the chaos, confusion, and illogic of what happens during wars before we can understand anything else about them or morally judge what happens during them. Experiencing *The Flanders Road,* a contemporary American may recall, with fuller understanding, much of what has been said about Vietnam. Even as we struggle through the text, we realize that the form becomes extreme as Simon follows the track of an extreme experience.

To read *The Flanders Road,* picture Georges lying in bed, having just violently seduced Corinne, Captain de Reixach's widow, right after the war. Just as one of the American prisoners in Vietnam survived by building an entire house in his head, so Georges has stayed alive in a German labor camp by elaborating with his friend Blum on how he will escape and make love to Corinne. (It seems that none of his comrades—Blum, Wack, Iglesia—survive.) Telling stories "to keep ourselves alive," Georges gradually raises Corinne's beauty and fierce carnality to goddess-like proportions. Those stories—of Corinne's infidelity with Iglesia, of the glamorous world of prewar racing stables, of an aristocracy so associated with horses that they were kinds of "centaurs," half man, half horse—these stories fade in and out of Georges's memories of de Reixach's death and his own wanderings during the fall of France. When he finds Corinne after the war, he seems to release all the violence at last in the ecstasy of sex. The war is over. Some critics believe the sexual experience transforms him and unlocks the memories that will make him an artist.

*The Flanders Road* forced Simon to unusual techniques. We have spoken of the reader's difficulty of sustaining so long a montage (dozens of times longer than *The Waste Land*) in the mind. The compositional difficulties—Simon mentally shuffling hundreds of written and possible fragments in his mind—are correspondingly great. For relief, Simon created a visual *plan de montage* of *The Flanders Road* by assigning each character or theme a certain color. He made a "little résumé" of what would happen in each possible fragment and crayoned on the appropriate color. Tacking the colored résumé papers in a great line along his walls, Simon the ex-painter worked with the colored line as if it were a painting, adding "certain passages because I needed a little green or a little red at this or that spot." "Some of the best" passages in *The Flanders Road* were added to balance the colored painting his book had generated. Oddly enough, Faulkner originally wanted the various voices of *The Sound and the Fury* to be printed in different colors.

Armed with his new techniques, Simon quickly turned to another experience he had never been able to do justice to, the Spanish Civil War. *The Palace* is written with such confidence that critics who think of Simon's novels as puzzles to fit back together have resented this cascade of experiences. Simon splashes on the paint with assurance, like Willem de Kooning painting his monster-women. Reading *The Palace* makes one realize that Hemingway's admirable *For Whom the Bell Tolls* (1940) imposes logical conventions (even best-seller conventions) on the Spanish Civil War.

Fifteen years after the war, a man who had fought against Franco sits again in a café across the street from the former revolutionary headquarters, his mind being tossed back to that time by the inimitable sounds and smells: the whir of pigeons; the background stink from the public urinals; clipped, formal Spanish; and the smell of café shellfish starting to spoil in the Spanish sun. For Simon, as for Hemingway, Spain is a country of primal smells: "ORINA—ESPUTOS—SANGRE," advertises a giant neon (!) pharmacist's sign—chemical analyses of urine, spit, and blood. But the sign "would make a good motto for the . . . country itself," a sarcastic American comrade says. Simon's painterly eye is usually praised, but in *The Palace* he somehow makes you *smell* revolutionary Spain.

The narrator has asked the waiter a question about the Palace across the street (which had been a "millionaires' hotel," then revolutionary headquarters, then burned in the fighting). From this question the waiter realizes that the narrator fought for the revolution. The waiter shuns him. Like the whore waiting patiently nearby, the waiter is one of "the dead," unwilling to awaken the memories of pre-Franco hopes. The professions Simon chooses for his male and female postwar Franco Spaniards seem significant. It is 1951: Franco has ruled for ten years, and the waiter and the whore would serve him docilely for another thirty. Simon, whose home is so near Spain, has had a love-hate relationship with the Spanish culture all his life. Long before the war his mother seems to have had a wide circle of friendships in Spain.

*The Palace* drew a mixed reception in France partly because it flouted the French tendency to romanticize the Spanish Civil War and lionize its fighters—such as Simon himself. Whatever Simon's conscious beliefs, D. H. Lawrence used to say, "You can't fool a novel." Though Camus told us that we must picture Sisyphus happy, Camus's novels' heroes show even less concern for their lives than Hemingway's or Simon's. *The Palace*'s 1930's Spanish are too primitive and xenophobic to sustain a revolution. Simon has even chosen a bitter, un-Marxist dictionary definition of a "revolution" for his novel's epigraph: movement of a body in a closed curve through the same points—futile, pointless. Looking back at the idealistic "student" who went to help the Spanish fifteen years ago, the man sees someone so ridiculous that he thinks, "That: me?" And yet, he calls his present burned-out self little more than the "excrement" left from that idealistic young man.

Those Americans who now remember with a wince their idealistic 1960's selves will identify with him.

The man remembers his disillusioning. His memories are not counterrevolutionary; rather, they are of a revolution betrayed, aborted, stillborn like (one frequent image) a "microcephalic" infant flushed into the sewers to become part of the pervading stink. He remembers himself as the "student," standing in the Palace headquarters with four other revolutionaries, men the very "condensation" of violence, able to kill without remorse.

They examine newspapers headlined, Who Has Killed General Santiago? The sarcastic American, whom the student likes, drinks, laughs, and jokes about it. Gradually we realize that the American is baiting the revolutionary in command, whom the student thinks of as a grim, small-town "schoolteacher." Slowly we understand that it was the "schoolteacher" who had Santiago done in. The revolution is dividing into murderous factions. The American suspects that he is next to die and is goading the "schoolteacher" into showing his hand.

A memory comes of the day before, when the student had met the Italian he calls "the Rifleman." A professional assassin, the Italian uses the obviously innocent young man to confess, as to a priest. The gunman's story, a tour de force that takes up almost a fifth of the book, is a second-by-second account of how it feels the first time you murder a man. The way time lengthens and expands with the flashbulb intensity of the experience is unforgettable, and only André Malraux's account of Ch'en's first assassination in *Man's Fate* (1933) comes close to Simon's for psychological tension.

A bald, military-seeming man hears the American's joke about "Orina—Esputos—Sangre" being a good motto for the country and takes deep offense. He wonders out loud if the American is a "radish"—red outside but white (royalist) inside, one of Franco's "fifth column," that is, a spy. The revolution is being used to settle personal grudges, national grudges. Nothing has really changed. It begins to seem that the Italian gunman has been summoned to take care of the American.

That night the student sits up, watching his friend's window. Sometime during the night he dozes off, then hears noises, wakes, and miscounts the windows so that he thinks he sees a whore in the American's room. In the morning the American has vanished. The student has to struggle past the sentries to confront the "schoolteacher" and the bald man. They claim that the American left suddenly for the front. The Italian assassin, we notice, also seems to have gone. The student summons his nerve and asks questions until the Spanish give him the look they gave the American. Deeply scared, disillusioned, the student makes his way out of the headquarters, now fittingly called the Palace, and goes to the underground urinal. There, at the heart of the stink, confronted by starving shoeshine boys carrying boxes like children's coffins, the student throws up.

Simon followed *The Palace* with *Histoire.* Imagine Joyce, after *Portrait* and *Ulysses,* writing a second version of Stephen Dedalus' boyhood, giving him a new set of parents, making the bird-girl of Stephen's vision into Stephen's cousin, and moving her into Stephen's house as a child. In the earlier *Flanders Road,* Georges sees Corinne only once, from afar, before he finds her and seduces her. By 1967 Simon apparently saw greater dramatic possibilities for this relationship: in *Histoire* Georges and Corinne are cousins who grow up in the same house, so that his passion for her grows from childhood.

This bold revision preserves the Corinne and de Reixach characters and, above all, the legend of Captain de Reixach's fall, which has such significance in Simon's cosmology. (Even there the reader will be startled to notice that Simon changes familiar details of the shooting.) To move Georges to Corinne's home as a child, Simon throws out Sabine and Pierre, giving Georges a new mother and father more closely based on Simon's real parents. After their deaths Georges is raised by his kindly, ineffectual Uncle Charles, a gentleman winemaker who writes unpublished poetry. Later Georges has a different wife, Hélène; though Louise may very well have left him at the end of *The Grass,* there is no memory of her.

Now a caution: though, like many critics, I approach *Histoire*'s main character as if he were Georges, Simon never gives him a first name. Simon has told A. C. Pugh that he is not even sure himself who the "I" in *Histoire* is. In any event, *Histoire*'s narrator could not be a totally new character, since he has Georges's memories of de Reixach's death. Simon has admitted how hard he finds it to invent characters. He did not want to give up two of his best, Corinne and de Reixach, just because he wanted to handle Georges differently. Revising the de Reixach material in *Histoire* was a daring move, and it reminds us that the only rule in the novel—even the New Novel—is whatever works.

*Histoire* works: Corinne is more human than before; it is a joy to meet her as a tyrannical child and as an adolescent becoming aware of how useful her new beauty might be. Her newly acquired brother, Paulou, is one of Simon's best creations. Simon knows that we know that these are fictions ("It says so on the cover," he once reminded a critic), and we have no more difficulty making believe a second biography for Georges than we had making believe a first.

*Histoire* makes one think of John Cheever's work: the restrained hopelessness, the sensitive man from a "good family" facing failure, the ecstatic, almost feverish, visions of the natural world, and the flights into forgetful sex. *Histoire* shows a side to Simon's anticapitalist politics that we had suspected. The group originally most opposed to the bourgeoisie was not the Communists but the aristocrats, and in *Histoire* Simon's hatred for the bourgeoisie seems less a fury at class oppressors than a lordly disgust for people "in trade"—a phrase that appears in *Histoire.* The portrait of the woman who comes to buy Georges's furniture is so harsh that we begin to rebel against it. There are long, loathing aristocratic fantasies about bankers and loan officers—even Lord Rothschild making book, as it were, on the French dying at Waterloo.

What exactly has happened to Georges's wife we cannot know, but we can reconstruct the nature of it. It is so bad that everyone who meets him, even those who barely know him, want to ask him about it, but do not dare. They halt in mid sentence in ways that indicate that mentioning what had happened would embarrass him. Even Georges cannot bring himself to think of it. Whenever his mind approaches it, his thoughts skirt off to another subject.

There are indications that Hélène had lost her mind, and Georges seems obsessed by a headline that describes a woman's suicide. He also constantly thinks about his uncle's wife, who apparently killed herself after discovering Uncle Charles's affair with a model. Georges so strongly identifies with Uncle Charles that late in the book the narrator's "I" frequently refers to Uncle Charles, not to Georges. Simon's comments about the resulting confusion suggest to me that he tried a gambit about the nature of identity but did not bring it off.

Georges is contrasted with three childhood friends who have become representative successes in contemporary France. We watch Corinne coldly learning to use her beauty, then social-climbing upward to become Baronne de Reixach. The quality of Georges's memories indicates the loss this was for him: he keeps fleeing the present to remember a haughty little girl sitting in a cherry tree, hanging the cherries over her ears as precocious earrings. Corinne, like a sunflower to the sun, turns Right: those on the Right have status, and that is what she wants. Georges very likely runs off to fight in the Spanish Civil War partly in the hope of at least annoying her into noticing him.

During the long bad day described in *Histoire,* Georges has to drive to the seashore to ask for a signature from Corinne's brother Paul so that Georges can mortgage some property. Paul (called Paulou as a boy) is moderately intelligent, without emotions or imagination, and almost without speech: he is exactly suited, Simon suggests, for financial success in bourgeois society. Corinne has achieved status, Paulou has gotten rich. The beauty of the Paulou portrait is Simon's honesty with himself. Artists, in portraits of characters so foreign to their own, usually hint that these creatures hide a secret unhappiness. Simon's Paulou is, by contrast, entirely contented with good food to eat, holidays by the sea, a beautiful wife, and lively children. He wants nothing more—he could imagine nothing more.

While a campus sports star, the hulking Paulou had somehow known intuitively where to move to block a (rugby) football; as a man he knows intuitively when to pick up a telephone and sell a piece of real estate for ten times what he paid for it. He is quite happy. In contrast, Paulou's sensitive, intellectual cousin Georges, who needs to read, think, and make sense of the world, has therefore neglected to make money. The life of the mind has led to a life of ceaseless financial anxiety and humiliation.

Simon will not let us dismiss Paulou, the satisfied bourgeois, as somehow evil or unkind. When Georges, late on this terrible day, has to drive to see Paulou on vacation at the seashore to request his signature on the mortgage, Paulou signs without inquiry, advice, or condescension. Paulou never looks at Georges with any expression harsher than mild concern that Georges may be about to fly off the handle. Paulou is attentive to his family; he has, with family piety, named his daughter after his sister Corinne. Georges waits for the signature while Paulou, his Greek business friend, and an M.D./investor (a knowing touch!) sit stolidly with their beautiful, bikini-clad wives. The women "chatter" over a new diamond Paul has given his wife. The scene picks up themes from a monologue overheard earlier at a restaurant in which a chatty woman had explained frankly that what mattered to her was "a man's ability" to pick up a check. Covered with tiny gleaming drops of water and sweat, the women seem like jewelry themselves, objects purchasable for the price of a diamond. Corinne, too, has sold herself to de Reixach, a man twice her age. The ease and frankness with which women vend themselves in *Histoire* is unnerving.

Georges's world offers no hope from the Left, either. His third childhood friend who is now a success is Bernard Lambert, grown up to be a famous Communist or Socialist politician. Georges's memories show Lambert as the poor boy on scholarship at the priests' school, developing scorn and irony to mask his consuming envy. We see the famous revolutionary as just the boy no one would pick when choosing up sides for games, the one who stood by himself and yelled "You idiots!" because they would not let him play. That seems the heart of his politics even now. What used to be called the "counterculture" or "alternate politics" seems only an alternate ladder up for those unable to social-climb like Corinne or make money like Paulou.

That morning Georges, in his desperation, had emptied out an heirloom chest of drawers to sell it. He had found the cards and letters his mother had saved from the days when she was a girl and his father courted her. His father had been an officer stationed at various posts in the French colonies, and the pictures on his father's ancient postcards send Georges's mind escaping from the dismal present back to a vanished imperial world. His mother is dead, his father is dead, the French empire is dead, and Georges (like France?) is on his hands and knees emptying out the heirlooms to sell them to the furniture dealers, thinking himself a "failure, both as a revolutionary and as a bourgeois." In his final image he pictures himself inside his mother as a fetus while she wrote one of the cards. In his mind Georges has finally retreated back inside her womb.

Simon followed *Histoire* with *La bataille de Pharsale* (*The Battle of Pharsalus,* 1969), the book that he says began his "third period." I want to skip forward, however, to a more successful book, *Conducting Bodies.*

*Conducting Bodies* is, unexpectedly, a great

novel of American city life and a great New York City novel—a populous genre in its own right. The important question *Conducting Bodies* addresses, over and over, is, What is the artist's moral responsibility?

In the course of answering this question, the novel also captures the spirit of its time, the late 1960's. The American government's escalation of the widely unpopular Vietnam War, being fought by draftees, set off worldwide student protests, riots, and street fighting. A student revolution at Columbia University triggered violent riots in Paris. For several years thereafter, in Western intellectual circles the triumphant "New Left" called every art before the bar and demanded that it explain what it was doing to further "the revolution," or at least to end human exploitation. In *Conducting Bodies,* while the protagonist watches wearily, New Left radicals scornfully disrupt a conference given by Old Left, Spanish Civil War–era artists like Claude Simon. Led by a young writer "with the flabby good looks of a young male lead," they demand to know what these old artists have done about human suffering *lately.*

At the book's start, a man slumps for support against a fire hydrant on a steaming Manhattan street. As *Conducting Bodies* progresses, we realize we are inside the perceptions of an internationally respected French author, the kind of man who gets invited to conferences in South America on *el deber del escritor,* the duty of the writer. He is alone in New York, a stranger, seriously ill (perhaps dying), jilted by his lover. During the novel "the sick man" (Simon's curt identification) pushes himself off the hydrant and tries to walk to his hotel room nearby. Drinking has damaged his liver. He has not walked a block before he dives into a bar and orders a beer—but the pain in his liver has him throwing up in the bathroom before he can touch it. Hallucinating that a kind of tide is rising around him, catching at his feet (a withdrawal symptom?), he starts out again, and from there on, he reminds one of Ray Milland's great portrait of an alcoholic writer stumbling through New York in *The Lost Weekend* (1945).

But Simon's version derives added power from the facts that Simon's protagonist is a great European writer and that we see New York freshly through his eyes, his artist's vision sharpened by his pain and fear. The writer's mind keeps flying back to the South American city he was in for the conference: what strikes one is how impossible it is to tell those scenes from the ones in New York. Seeing through these European eyes, we realize that New York is a mighty Spanish and African city. Simon's montage technique makes the effect even more telling: since he only seems to report facts, we think we draw our conclusions for ourselves.

To a man in this weakened state, a trip down Manhattan Island becomes an epic, life-threatening journey. Memories of paintings of Spanish soldiers lost in jungles drift through his mind, as do glimpses he has had of jungle rivers. He looks at, and forces one to see, the street population of the homeless and the mentally ill that the American city dweller learns, for emotional survival, to exclude from his or her consciousness. The veteran New Yorker will know that Simon is not stacking the deck: in the course of a midsummer trek down Broadway near Macy's (whose sign, The World's Largest Store, comes to seem a symbol for New York), anyone would encounter figures like the ragged junkie living on a bench, his body "collapsing slowly bit by bit like a snowman in the sun."

Thomas Carlyle is supposed to have taken Ralph Waldo Emerson through London to convince him that there is a hell. The human misery the writer sees returns his mind again and again to the question asked at the writer's conference: What is the artist to do? Art is a form of power; power brings responsibility. In the face of the urgent suffering Simon's writer sees as he drags himself through the masses of New York, is there any excuse for writing anything but agitprop? Tolstoy did not think so. The question must have been weighing on Simon in

1969: after a lifetime of politically aware and humanistic writing, he found himself increasingly fascinated by pure style.

This novel was his reply. In *Conducting Bodies* Simon's principal irony is that this artist being asked to save the world is scarcely capable of getting himself home to his hotel room and has plainly made a mess of his life. The other high-minded writers at the conference he has attended spend most of the book trying to adjourn for dinner, and at last prove incapable of it. The artist has the power to speak, but does he know what to say?

Simon compounds that picture with a second, beautiful irony: even while the hapless artist staggers home, even as he asks himself what an artist is to do, he keeps performing—almost unconsciously, from a lifetime's habit—art's invaluable social role of bearing witness: "dando testimonio," as a speaker phrases it at the conference, to the world's suffering, and through his vision giving a voice, "dando una voz," to those who suffer. In *Conducting Bodies* Simon paints a powerful, unsentimental Portrait of the Artist: sick, jilted, exhausted, he still keeps on seeing the life around him and, with a lifetime's power, keeps storing it up so that others may later experience it through him. Therein, not in propaganda, Simon replies, lies the true *deber del escritor.* The writer is a "conducting body" for experience, as are books, pictures, and words: experience flows through to us through him as through them.

## *SIMON'S "THIRD PERIOD"*

*Conducting Bodies* is Simon's farewell to humanism, his last great novel. The novels of what he calls his "third period" are read primarily by Simon specialists interested in fine questions of technique and style. This essay will treat them only briefly.

The process of change had actually begun two years before *Conducting Bodies,* in *The Battle of Pharsalus,* a book that smells of the laboratory. The first eighty-odd pages of *Conducting Bodies* were originally published separately as *Orion aveugle* (The Blind Orion, 1970); this volume includes some of the paintings the protagonist thinks about as well as a preface in which Simon explains some of the compositional questions that had begun to interest him.

In the essay collection *Orion Blinded,* Randi Birn, a critic friendly to Simon, has attempted to defend Simon's "third period," saying that "gradually and painfully" Simon "liberated himself from an obsession with the problems of human existence, those questions of time, space, nature, war, and love." Simon replaced "the passion to know" with "a need to investigate the possibilities of language," says Birn (p. 289).

Such praise is the harshest criticism of Claude Simon that one could make. Time, space, nature, war, and love do indeed drain from his later works; like the aging Joyce, he becomes preoccupied with techniques for their own sake, with the ways a writer can use images or words themselves to "generate" a text. Richard Kuhns once remarked on how Dickens, that critic of industry, had become an industry for scholars; so has Simon. After 1972 Simon's novels increasingly talk theoretical shop with those who (like this writer) earn part of their salary studying him. In the last part of *The Battle of Pharsalus* the characters are replaced by "O," which can be understood to mean "Observer" or "zero," as you wish. Characters from Simon novels replay certain short scenes with O and passages within the text repeat themselves, with modifications. *The Battle of Pharsalus* is one of the few works in which Simon seems influenced by other New Novelists. Long passages describing the objects within O's field of vision provide much for a scholar to decipher, but little reason for a reader to care about the answer.

Perhaps Simon's heightened interest in style came about partly because his matter had gone while his method remained. It is no harsh criticism to say that after harvesting his experiences in ten novels, Simon, in his sixties, at last was down to gleaning behind himself. He had even harvested the de Reixach characters twice, in two different ways. Few writers have emulated E. M. Forster, who said he stopped writing because he had nothing more to say.

*Triptyque* (*Triptych*, 1973) is a succession of the word-paintings and descriptions of pictures we are familiar with from *Histoire* and *Conducting Bodies.* A triptych is a painting in three panels. The images normally relate to each other, but this time Simon's text insists that the images do not, and one of the characters, Brown, is pointedly shown knocking a jigsaw puzzle off a table. Scenes we think we see turn out to exist only in a script, a person we think we met turns out to be a picture on a poster. The images are sometimes joined by slender, punning plays on words. If, as critics hesitantly aver, Simon is making some point about the nature of representation, he has lowered his sights a great deal from the days of *The Flanders Road.* The Communist politician-opportunist Lambert from *Histoire* and an aging Corinne reappear.

When, in *Leçon de choses* (literally "Lesson of Things"; inexplicably translated as *The World About Us,* 1975), Simon tried writing the shooting of Captain de Reixach yet again—this time from the point of view of a slangy "dog-face" soldier, as in a bad Hemingway short story—there were general cries of déjà vu. Those already steeped in Simon like *The Georgics* better, for we learn infinitely more about the Ancestor in it than we had known before. Simon is a master at retroactively enriching an earlier novel with a later one, knowing that we project our knowledge backward. A narrator reads through papers relating to the Ancestor while memories arise of his own and others' war experiences. "Cross-cutting" between the French army in the heroic days of the Ancestor and the dispirited French army during the debacle in 1940 seems like nostalgia for French military *gloire.* We sense afresh Simon's identification with the old aristocrat and the aristocratic roots of Simon's anticapitalism.

*The Georgics* also cuts away to material about the Spanish Civil War filtered through the consciousness of an English writer (George Orwell?) and to long sections in which the narrator goes through the seasonal routines of working the land—images of peace, in this context. Vergil called his own Latin poem about the land *The Georgics.* If the narrator is, as one suspects, Georges, there may be a further pun. One must admit that the *The Georgics* plows extremely familiar ground.

Simon has almost no American heirs. Serge Doubrovsky's "auto-fiction" may be related to Simon's manner of fictionalizing his life; American phenomenologist Charles Calitri's *The Goliath Head* (1972) uses that Caravaggio painting to generate a text the way Simon has used Poussin's *The Blind Orion Searching for the Dawn.*

Simon's 1985 Nobel came at a time when his works—just becoming known—were no longer considered avant-garde. Umberto Eco, John Barth, and others had long been interested in fiction that was not, as Leslie Fiedler said, "*about* myth, but which *was* myth." Writers seeking contemporary myths that could serve us as the Oedipus legend did the Greeks began looking to popular genres and subgenres for plots as if they were Sophocles rewriting familiar old legends or Shakespeare reworking popular melodramas like Thomas Kyd's *Hamlet.* Truman Capote tried writing murder trial journalism as serious art (nervously calling his new form "the non-fiction novel"); Norman Mailer tried "history as a novel, the novel as history"; William S. Burroughs, Kurt Vonnegut, and Thomas Pynchon looked into whether science fiction could carry serious literature's weight. Others experimented with subgenres like the American screen thriller or the murderer's True Confession.

We have interpreted Simon's journey as his long struggle to invent the forms that would embody experiences like the fall of France and the Spanish Civil War. Form must embody content, not undercut it like a love song set to a

Sousa march. If, however, some perfect form is already at hand (a "readymade," David Antin calls it) it is otiose to invent a new one. Rather, like Marcel Duchamp calmly choosing a bicycle wheel to be what he called a "readymade" sculpture, these writers take up the "readymade" genre and use it.

The New Novelists were not opposed to such genre appropriation—novelists are rarely as harsh with each other as their critical partisans are. Alain Robbe-Grillet told me in 1978 that he liked the idea of appropriating traditional plot devices to use "with derision," and Claude Simon has gone beyond Robbe-Grillet to acclaim Balzac's "novelistic forms" as perfect for Balzacian content. He probably enjoyed Tom Wolfe's self-conscious attempt to bring Balzac to New York, *The Bonfire of the Vanities.*

As for Fiedler's request for modern myths, Simon himself created a potent one, the death of Captain de Reixach. He has given international readers novels of World War II and the Spanish Civil War that make conventional war novels seem stylized, falsely rational, and tame. His maelstrom style may be the best-suited to capturing the quality of life in modern urban America. Simon is a gambler. He takes great chances, and he does not always win. Nevertheless, like the other great modernists, he has permanently enlarged the vocabulary of forms that novelists may draw on to present experiences, as they continue, like Simon's wandering artist, *dando testimonio,* bearing witness.

## Selected Bibliography


### EDITIONS

#### INDIVIDUAL WORKS

*Le tricheur.* Paris, 1945.

*La corde raide.* Paris, 1947.

*Gulliver.* Paris, 1952.

*Le sacre du printemps.* Paris, 1954.

*Le vent: Tentative de restitution d'un retable baroque.* Paris, 1957.

*L'Herbe.* Paris, 1958.

*La route des Flandres.* Paris, 1960.

*Le palace.* Paris, 1962.

*Femmes (sur vingt-trois peintures de Joan Miró).* Paris, 1966. A very free prose poem related loosely to the pictures.

*Histoire.* Paris, 1967.

*La bataille de Pharsale.* Paris, 1969.

*Orion aveugle.* Geneva, 1970. Contains the much-quoted preface Simon wrote about his "third period" method. *Orion aveugle* is a penultimate draft of the first quarter of *Les corps conducteurs,* with the pictures that text was "generated" by.

*Les corps conducteurs.* Paris, 1971.

*Triptyque.* Paris, 1973.

*Leçon de choses.* Paris, 1975.

*Les géorgiques.* Paris, 1981.

*Le chevelure de Bérénice.* Paris, 1983. The prose poem that accompanied the Mirós in *Femmes,* printed by itself.

### INTERVIEWS AND ARTICLES

"Qu'est-ce que l'avant-garde en 1958?" In *Les lettres françaises,* no. 717 (24–30 April 1958).

"Réponse à une enquête: Pensez-vous avoir un don d'écrivain?" In *Tel quel* (Spring 1960):38–43.

"La fiction mot à mot." In *Nouveau roman: Hier, aujourd'hui.* Paris, 1972. Pp. 73–97. Important statement in an important collection. See also pp. 99–116.

"Hugo et moi." In *Quinzaine litteraire,* no. 448:7 (1985).

### TRANSLATIONS

*The Battle of Pharsalus.* Translated by Richard Howard. New York, 1971.

*Conducting Bodies.* Translated by Helen R. Lane. New York, 1974.

*The Flanders Road.* Translated by Richard Howard. New York, 1961.

*The Georgics.* Translated by Beryl and John Fletcher. New York, 1989.

*The Grass.* Translated by Richard Howard. New York, 1960.

*Histoire.* Translated by Richard Howard. New York, 1967.

*The Palace.* Translated by Richard Howard. New York, 1963.

*Triptych.* Translated by Helen R. Lane. New York, 1976.

*The Wind.* Translated by Richard Howard. New York, 1959.

*The World About Us* [*Leçon de choses*]. Translated by Daniel Weissbort. Princeton, N.J., 1983.

## BIOGRAPHICAL AND CRITICAL STUDIES

Alphant, Marianne. "Claude Simon: *Leçon de choses." Les cahiers du chemin,* no. 26:137–144 (1976).

Anex, Georges. "Les feuilles de l'acacia. . . . " In *Les critiques de notre temps et le nouveau roman.* Edited by Réal Ouellet. Paris, 1972. Pp. 82–85.

Apeldoorn, J. V. "Bibliographie selective." *Critique* 37:1244–1252 (1981).

Baetens, Jan. "Passages images." *Littérature,* no. 61:118–128 (1986).

Berger, Yves. "L'Enfer, le temps." *La nouvelle revue française* 97:95–109 (January 1961).

Birn, Randi. "Proust, Claude Simon, and the Art of the Novel." *Papers on Language and Literature* 13, no. 2:168–186 (1977).

———. "From Sign to Sage: Dynamic Description in Two Texts by Claude Simon." *Australian Journal of French Studies* 21, no. 2:148–160 (1984).

Birn, Randi, and Karen Gould, eds. *Orion Blinded: Essays on Claude Simon.* Lewisburg, Pa., 1981. Important collection.

Bishop, Thomas. "Fusion of Then and Now." *Saturday Review* (30 March 1968):28.

———. "La vue d'Orion ou le processus da la création." *Entretiens,* no. 31:35–39 (1972).

———. "L'Image de la création chez Claude Simon. In *Nouveau roman: Hier, aujourd'hui,* vol. 2. Paris, 1972. Pp. 61–71.

Bjurström, C. G. "Dimensions du temps chez Claude Simon." *Entretiens,* no. 31:141–158 (1972).

Bourdet, Denise, *Brèves recontres.* Paris, 1963. Pp. 215–224.

Brewer, Maria Minich, (guest) ed. "Claude Simon." *L'Esprit Créateur* 27, no. 4 (1987). An important issue that includes essays on all aspects of Simon by such leading critics as David Carroll.

Brosman, Catharine Savage. "Man's Animal Condition in Claude Simon's *La Route des Flandres." Symposium* 29:57–68 (Spring-Summer 1975).

Caminade, Pierre. "Déjeuner avec l'herbe." *Entretiens,* no. 31:117–119 (1972).

Carroll, David. *The Subject in Question: The Languages of Theory and the Strategies of Fiction.* Chicago, 1982.

Chapsal, Madeleine. "Le jeune roman." *Paris: L'Express* (12 January 1961):32.

———. *Quinze écrivains.* Paris, 1963. Pp. 163–171.

Christ, Ronald. "The Translator's Voice: An Interview with Helen R. Lane." *Translation Review,* no. 5:6–18, (1980).

Conte, Rafael. "Claude Simon: Pintura, música, memoria." *Insula* 41, no. 470:8–9 (1986).

Deguy, Michel. "Claude Simon et la représentation." *Critique* 187:1009–1032 (1962).

Descaves, Pierre. "Réalités du roman." *La Table Ronde* 157:163–172 (January 1961).

Doubrovsky, Serge. "Notes sur la genèse d'une écriture." *Entretiens,* no. 31:51–64 (1972).

Duncan, Alastair B. "Claude Simon and William Faulkner." *Forum for Modern Language Studies* 9:235–252 (1973).

———, ed. *Claude Simon, New Directions: Collected Papers.* Edinburgh, 1985.

Duranteau, J. "Claude Simon: 'Le roman se fait, je le fais et il me fait.'" *Les lettres françaises,* no. 1178 (13–19 April 1967). Important Simon statement of method for the later works.

Du Verlie, Claud. "The Novel as Textual Wandering: An Interview with Claude Simon." *Contemporary Literature* 28:1–13 (1987).

Evans, Michael. "Two Uses of Intertextuality: References to Impressionist Painting and 'Madame Bovary' in Claude Simon's *Leçon de choses." Nottingham French Studies* 19, no. 1:33–45 (1980).

———. *Claude Simon and the Transgressions of Modern Art.* London, 1987.

Fitch, Brian. "Participe présent et procédés narratifs chez Claude Simon." *Revue des lettres modernes* 94–99:199–216 (1964).

Fletcher, John. "Claude Simon and the Memory Enigma." In *New Directions in Literature.* Edited by John Fletcher. London, 1968. Pp. 116–128.

———. "Érotisme et création ou la mort en sursis." *Entretiens,* no. 31:131–140 (1972).

———. *Claude Simon and Fiction Now.* London, 1975. Important book on Simon's affinities with contemporary novelists.

Frohock. W. M. "Continuities in the New Novel." In *Style and Temper.* Cambridge, Mass., 1967. Pp. 122–127.

Gould, Karen. "Mythologizing in the *Nouveau Roman:* Claude Simon's Archetypal City." In French Literature Series, vol. 3, *Mythology in French Literature.* Edited by Phillip A. Crant. Columbia, S.C., 1976. Pp. 118–128.

———. *Claude Simon's Mythic Muse.* Columbia, S.C., 1979.

Guicharnaud, Jacques. "Remembrance of Things Passing: Claude Simon." *Yale French Studies* 24:101–108 (Summer 1959).

Heath, Stephen. *The Nouveau Roman: A Study in the Practice of Writing.* Philadelphia, 1972. Pp. 153–178.

Higgins, Lynn A. "Language, the Uncanny, and the Shapes of History in Claude Simon's *The Flanders Road." Studies in Twentieth Century Literature* 10, no. 1:117–140 (1985). Contains a good introduction to *The Flanders Road.*

Hollenbeck, Josette. *Éléments baroques dan les romans de Claude Simon.* Paris, 1982.

Howlett, J. "La route des Flandres." *Les lettres nouvelles* (December 1960):178–181.

Janvier, Ludovic. *Une parole exigeante: Le nouveau roman.* Paris, 1964. Pp. 89–110.

———. "Sur le trajet de ces corps." *Entretiens,* no. 31:69–80 (1972).

———. "Réponses de Claude Simon à quelques questions écrites de Ludovic Janvier." *Entretiens,* no. 31:15–29 (1972). Exceptionally informative interview with Simon.

Jean, Raymond. "Pour saluer *La route des Flandres.*" In *La littérature et le réel: De Diderot au nouveau roman.* Paris, 1965. Pp. 214–218.

———. "Les signes de l'éros." *Entretiens,* no. 31: 121–129 (1972).

Jiménez-Fajardo, Salvador. *Claude Simon.* Boston, 1975. Includes detailed introductions to the most discussed novels.

Jost, François. "Claude Simon: Topographies de la description et du texte." *Critique* 30, no. 330: 1031–1040 (1974).

———. "Les aventures du lecteur." *Poétique* 8, no. 29:77–89 (1977).

Kreiter, Janine A. "Perception et réflexion dans *La route des Flandres*: Signes et sémantique." *Romanic Review* 72, no. 4:489–494 (1981).

Lanceraux, Dominique. "Modalités de la narration dans *La route des Flandres." Poétique* 4, no. 14:235–249 (1973).

———. "Modalités de la narration dan *Le palace* de Claude Simon." *Littérature,* no. 16:3–18 (December 1974).

Léonard, Martine. "Photographie et littérature: Zola, Breton, Simon: Hommage à Roland Barthes." *Études françaises* 18, no. 3:93–108 (1983).

Lesage, Laurent. "Claude Simon et l'ecclésiaste." *Revue des lettres modernes* 94–99:217–223 (1964).

Levitt, Morton P. "The Burden of History." *Kenyon Review* 31:128–134 (1969).

———. "Disillusionment and Epiphany: The Novels of Claude Simon." *Critique: Studies in Modern Fiction* 12, no. 1:43–71 (1970).

Loubère, J. A. E. *The Novels of Claude Simon.* Ithaca, N.Y., 1975. Includes general introductions to each book up to *Triptyque.*

Mauriac, Claude. *L'Alittérature contemporaine.* Paris, 1969. Pp. 292–305.

Mercier, Vivian. "Claude Simon: Order and Disorder." *Shenandoah* 17, no. 4:79–92 (Summer 1966).

———. "James Joyce and the French New Novel." *TriQuarterly* 8:205–219 (1967). Important essay by a supporter of the New Novelists who is both Irish and an expert on Joyce and Beckett.

——— *The New Novel: From Queneau to Pinget.* New York, 1971. Pp. 266–314. A much-needed international perspective.

Merleau-Ponty, Maurice. "Cinq notes sur Claude Simon." *Médiations* 4:5–9 (Winter 1961–1962). Reprinted in *Entretiens,* no. 31:41–46 (1972); and in *Esprit,* no. 6:64–66 (1982).

Morrissette, Bruce. "The New Novel in France." *Chicago Review* 15, no. 3:1–19 (1962).

Mortier, Roland. "Discontinu et rupture dans *La bataille de Pharsale." Degrés,* no. 2:c–c6 (April 1973).

O'Donnell, Thomas D. "Claude Simon's *Leçon de choses.* Myth and Ritual Displaced." *International Fiction Review* 5:134–142 (1978).

Pellegrin, Jean. "Du mouvement et de l'immobilité de Reixach." *Revue d'Esthétique* 25:335–349 (1972).

Pingaud, Bernard. "Sur *La route des Flandres." Les Temps Modernes* 178:1026–1037 (February 1961).

———. *Écrivains d'aujourd'hui.* Paris, 1961. Pp. 471–477.

Pugh, Anthony C. "Simon: The Narrator and His Double." In *Direction in the Nouveau Roman.* Canterbury, 1971. Pp. 30–40.

———. "Du *Tricheur* à *Triptyque,* et inversement." *Études littéraires* 9, no. 1:137–160 (April 1976).

———. *Simon: Histoire.* London, 1982. The best introduction to *Histoire.*

———. "Defeat, May 1940: Claude Simon, Marc Bloch, and the Writing of Disaster." *Forum for Modern Language Studies* 21, no. 1:59–70 (1985).

Raillard, Georges. "*Triptyque.*" *Les cahiers du chemin* 18:96–106 (15 April 1973).

———. "Femmes: Claude Simon dans les marges de Miró." In *Cahiers du 20e Siècle,* no. 4:123–137 (1975). Also in Ricardou, *Claude Simon* (below).

Raillon, Jean-Claude. "Propositions d'une théorie de la fiction." *Études littéraires* 9, no. 7:81–123 (April 1976).

Ricardou, Jean. *Problèmes du nouveau roman.* Paris, 1967.

———. *Pour une théorie du nouveau roman.* Paris, 1971. Pp. 118–158, 200–210.

———. "Un ordre dans la débâcle." *Critique* 16:1011–1024 (1960). Also in *Les critiques de notre temps et le Nouveau Roman.* Edited by Réal Ouellet. Paris, 1972. Pp. 85–88.

———. *Le nouveau roman.* Paris, 1973.

———, ed. *Claude Simon: Analyse, Théorie.* Colloque de Cérisy. Paris, 1975. Simon took part in this conference on his work.

———. "Le dispositif osiriaque." *Études littéraires* 9, no. 7:9–79 (1976).

———. "Le texte survit à l'excité (réponse à Michael Holland)." *Texte* 2:193–215 (1983).

Riffaterre, Michael. "Orion voyeur: L'Écriture intertextuelle de Claude Simon." *MLN* 103, no. 4:711–735 (1988). In the same issue, see Lucien Dällenbach, "L'Archive simonienne," pp. 736–750; Roger Dragonetti, "Leçon de choses et Le son de choses," pp. 751–768; Gerard Prince, "How to Redo Things with Words: La route des Flandres," pp. 769–781.

Rogers, Michelle, "Fonction des quatre photographies publiées dans l'*Orion aveugle* de Claude Simon." *French Review* 59, no. 1:74–83 (1985).

Rossum-Guyon, Françoise van. "De Claude Simon à Proust: Un exemple d'intertextualité." *Les Lettres Nouvelles* 4:107–137 (September 1972).

———. "Ut pictura poesis: Une lecture de *La bataille de Pharsale.*" *Degrés,* no. 3:k1-k15 (July 1973).

Roubichou, Gérard. "Continu et discontinu ou l'hérétique alinéa." *Études littéraires* 9, no. 7: 125–136 (1976).

———. *Lecture de "L'Herbe" de Claude Simon.* Lausanne, 1976.

Roudiez, Léon S. *French Fiction Today: A New Direction.* New Brunswick, N. J., 1972. Pp. 152–182. Contains many good introductions to Simon and all the New Novelists.

———. "The 1985 Nobel Laureate: Claude Simon." *World Literature Today* 60, no. 1:5–8 (1986).

Rousseaux, André. "L'Impressionisme de Claude Simon." In *Littérature du vingtième siècle,* vol. 7. Edited by André Rousseaux. Paris, 1961. Pp. 173–179.

Rousset, Jean. "Trois romans de la mémoire: Butor, Pinget, Simon." *Formalisme et signification. Cahiers Internationaux du Symbolisme* 9–10:70–81 (1965–1966). Also in *Les critiques de notre temps et le nouveau roman.* Edited by Réal Ouellet. Paris, 1972. Pp. 27–35.

Séguier, Marcel. "Proposition en lieu et place d'un avant-propos à une réflexion collective." *Entretiens,* no. 31:9–13 (1972).

———. "Le langage à la casse." *Entretiens,* no. 31:81–95 (1972).

Seylaz, Jean-Luc. "Du *Vent* à *La route des Flandres:* La conquête d'une forme romanesque." *Revue des lettres modernes* 94–99:225–240 (1964).

Simon, John K. "Perception and Metaphor in the 'New Novel': Notes on Robbe-Grillet, Claude Simon, and Butor." *TriQuarterly* 4:153–182 (1965).

Sims, Robert. "The Myths of Revolution and the City in Claude Simon's *Le Palace.*" *Studies in the Twentieth Century,* no. 16:53–87 (1975).

Solomon, Philip H. "Claude Simon's *La route des Flandres:* A Horse of a Different Colour?" *Australian Journal of French Studies* 9:190–201 (1972).

———. "Flights of Time Lost: Bird Imagery in Claude Simon's *Le Palace.*" In *Twentieth Century Fiction: Essays for Germaine Bree.* Edited by George Stambolian. New Brunswick, N.J., 1975. Pp. 166–183.

Storrs, Neal. *Liquid: A Source of Meaning and Structure in Claude Simon's "La bataille de Pharsale."* New York, 1983.

Sturrock, John. *The French New Novel: Claude Simon, Michel Butor, Alain Robbe-Grillet.* London, 1969. Pp. 43–103.

Suleiman, Susan Rubin. *Authoritarian Fictions: The Ideological Novel as a Literary Genre.* New York, 1983.

Sykes, Stuart W. "'Mise en abyme' in the Novels of Claude Simon." *Forum for Modern Language Studies* 9:333–345 (1973).

———. "Claude Simon: Visions of Life in Microcosm." *Modern Language Review* 71, no. 7:42–50 (1976).

———. "Ternary Form in Three Novels by Claude Simon." *Symposium* 32, no. 1:25–40 (1978).

———. *Les romans de Claude Simon.* Paris, 1979.

"La terre et la guerre dans l'oeuvre de Claude Simon." Special issue of *Critique* 37:1147–1243 (1981).

Vidal, Jean-Pierre. "*Le palace:* Palais des mirages intestins ou l'auberge espagnole." *Études littéraires* 9, no. 7:189–214 (April 1976).

Weinstein, Arnold L. *Vision and Response in Modern Fiction.* Ithaca, N.Y., 1974. Pp. 215–256.

GEORGE J. LEONARD

# ALBERT CAMUS

## *(1913–1960)*

"ABOUT CAMUS, THE writer, what can I say that has not been said, and said so aptly, so beautifully, that it debars one from adding any further cliché?" A little over a quarter of a century after Camus's death on 4 January 1960, the flow of critical studies, of books, articles, and colloquia confirms and challenges this statement, so modestly proffered by A. Noureddine. After a brief decline, since the late 1970's interest in Camus has again been on the rise. The span of years that distance us from Camus is brief. But in that interim the intellectual climate, notably in France, has shifted more than once. And so too has the map of the world and its areas of conflict. For Camus's contemporaries, his work punctuated a brief and momentous period between 1942, when *L'Étranger* (*The Stranger*), a short novel by an unknown young Algerian, was published in Paris under German occupation, bringing its author quasi-instant celebrity, and 1957, when *L'Exil et le royaume* (*Exile and the Kingdom,* 1957), a collection of short stories, came out as France and Algeria were about to plunge into the worst phase of a war that would end only in 1962, two years after Camus's death. Today, thanks to the work of many dedicated scholars, we know more about Camus than did his contemporaries—in fact, in some instances, more than he knew about himself. We can also better grasp the sociopolitical forces that transformed the Algeria of his youth from a colonial French territory, administered as a group of three French departments, to the independent Republic of Algeria.

### *A MANY-FACETED LIFE*

Actually, Camus's three-pronged career as journalist, man of the theater, and writer began not in 1942 with his first published work, but ten years earlier, far from Paris, when he was a student in Algiers. In 1960, when he died in an automobile accident in France, he was carrying the first draft of a new novel *Le premier homme* (The First Man). "I have turned down all engagements for 1960," he had written a friend. "It will be the year of my novel. It will require a lot of time, but I'll get it done." He was on his way to Paris to start on another venture, the direction of an experimental theater. Camus at forty-six still felt he could draw on what he once described humorously as a "consternating vitality." It was his death that cut short his writing, not as Patrick McCarthy has suggested, his death that saved him from the anguish of a "burnt-out" creativity. His whole career, to be sure, developed in times of war, revolutions, conflicting ideologies, and concentration camps. Passions ran high—passions that have not yet subsided. But where Camus is concerned we can by now disentangle his personality and accomplishments from the masks and distortions, the legends, misinformation, and gossip of the hour.

"At various times and in various countries," wrote Alexander Solzhenitsyn, the anti-Stalinist Russian writer who had corresponded with Camus, "there have arisen heated, angry and exquisite debates as to whether art and the artist should be free to live for themselves or whether they should be forever mindful of their duty toward society, albeit in an unprejudiced way." For himself, he added in his Nobel Prize acceptance speech (1970), there was "no dilemma." For Camus there was one, however. That dilemma underlies much of his writing. "As artists," he wrote at the time of his own Nobel Prize award in "Création et liberté" (Creation and Liberty),

> perhaps we do not need to intervene in the affairs of our time, but as men, yes. . . . From the time of my first articles to my latest book, I wrote a lot, perhaps too much, but because I cannot help being drawn to everyday concerns, on the side of those, whoever they may be, who are humiliated and downtrodden."
>
> (*Actuelles II: Chroniques 1948–1953,* in *Essais,* pp. 802–803)

Camus placed himself within a tradition that saw art as serving the needs of human beings, not human beings as serving the needs of art. He took no answers comfortably for granted but rather sought to reframe basic questions concerning human existence and commitments in the world, as truthfully as possible, in terms of the situation in the contemporary world as he knew it. What were the possible human answers to these questions? It is characteristic of Camus's work that in an age given to absolutes he, from the outset, thought in terms of diverse possibilities. The writer, he felt, could project such possibilities, leaving it up to readers to select among them and reach their own conclusions. The question of the artist's role was hotly debated by the European intelligentsia between the 1920's and the 1970's, fueled by the doctrinaire tenets of Marxist-Leninist thought. Camus's basic positions did not change over the years; what touched him deeply, rather than ideologies or aesthetic theories, was what he called "the human face," certainly not the allegedly inevitable "march of history."

Of all European writers of his generation, Sartre among them, Camus was, during his lifetime, the writer who commanded the widest international attention. A journalist by profession, he had started his career in uneven combat against the inequities suffered by the Muslim population under French colonial rule in Algeria. Later, during the years of clandestine warfare in Nazi-occupied France, he found himself at the hub of the ideological warfare that sharply divided that country through the climactic mid century years into the early 1970's. He could hardly have avoided becoming enmeshed in what seems to us today the obsessive, often specious, political argumentation of intellectual infighting. The Algerian war of independence was not calculated to ease the tensions and hostilities that his meteoric fame inspired among those rivals he had outdistanced, or those who disagreed with his stance. Yet his critics, momentarily disarmed by his death, registered dismay in the face of the double loss: of the man himself and the anticipated work he would have produced. "Whatever he did or decided in the future," wrote Sartre, "he could never have ceased to be one of the major forces in our cultural field, nor in his way could he have ceased to represent the history of France and our century."

Admirers of Camus tended to represent an idealized, often sentimentalized, image of the man; opponents tended to distort and to diminish the character, scope, and accomplishments of the complex human being he was. His contemporaries tended to cast Camus in the role of "representative man," often reproaching him, then, with the image. Camus did not cherish the role. His ambition had never been to "represent the history of France" or that of the century, but only to produce a literary work of intrinsic worth that would truthfully reflect his own experience. Such works, he often repeated, alone allowed him to integrate, reconcile, and discipline the violent feelings and contradictions that characterized his own passionate and basically unruly personality. His writing expressed his feelings, struggles, perplexities, and development—transmuted into objective literary works by the severe discipline he imposed upon himself. That is perhaps why Camus's work elicited so wide and immediate a response from far beyond the boundaries of France. Already in 1968 a complete bibliography, prepared by Robert Roeming, of articles dealing with Camus listed some three thousand items from almost every part of the world, including, in addition to the countries of Western Europe, Scandinavia, Poland, Hungary, Turkey, Israel; the United States, Puerto Rico, Mexico; the nations of South America and of Africa; Japan, Formosa, and India. According to a UNESCO survey made in the 1960's, Camus's work had been translated by then into thirty-two foreign languages.

### *Origins*

Albert Camus was born on 7 November 1913 in the small town of Mondovi (now called Drean), south of Bone (now Annaba) in what was then French Algeria, which the French considered not a colony, but a "department" of France. Camus did not live to see the change that in 1962, with the end of the Algerian war for independence, made Algeria a fully autonomous republic. There, as noted above, French place-names were soon replaced by Arabic or Berber ones. Camus's forebears, according to a legend in the family, had supposedly come to Algeria from Alsace after the Franco-Prussian War. Actually, as Camus's biographer Herbert Lottman has proved, they had come to Algeria much earlier, probably soon after the 1830 conquest by the French. They came from the Bordeaux region and the Massif Central, the very heart of France. Camus on his father's side was thus a fourth-generation French Algerian. His maternal ancestors came from the island of Minorca, a Spanish possession with an ancient culture and character of its own. In a sense, then, Camus was indeed justified when he claimed a "Mediterranean" rather than a French inheritance. His was a family of poor, illiterate, hardworking people. Lucien Camus, the father, was employed in a wine-making enterprise and had learned to read and write; his wife, Catherine Camus, like the rest of the family, had not. Drafted in 1914, Lucien was badly wounded at the battle of the Marne and died in France of his wounds.

Shortly before Albert's first birthday, Catherine moved into her mother's two-room apartment in the working-class section of Algiers with her two sons. She worked first in a munitions factory, then, after the war, as a cleaning woman. Camus was brought up in stringent circumstances. Five people were crowded into the apartment: a harsh grandmother, an infirm uncle, Camus's almost deaf, silent, and strangely undemonstrative mother, and the two boys. The younger boy, Albert, was deeply though mutely attached to his mother, whose presence haunts many of his books. His childhood world laid the foundation for his lifelong commitment to the nonprivileged and the manner in which he related to them; he always saw them as individuals, with their human idiosyncrasies, foibles, and needs, never under collective categorizations such as "the proletariat" or "the masses." This is the human world that marks his first books.

Of a family that "lacked almost everything and envied almost nothing," Camus spoke retrospectively with gratitude: "Merely by its silence, its reserve, its natural and restrained pride, these people, who could not even read, gave me the highest teaching." He enjoyed, besides, the freedom of the working-class boy, in a world devoid of television and, for him at first, empty of books. He roamed the beaches and the busy port and silently absorbed the sensuous beauty of the Mediterranean coast. It was shaping his vision of the world, his sense of his physical bond with his environment long before it became a concept and a personal myth. "Poverty was never a misfortune for me," he wrote of those childhood years, "for it was flooded with light." Many years later he linked together in a single sentence the "two or three great and simple images" that defined his sensitivity—the silent, uncomplaining mother, the light, the beauty of the world. Unlike the childhood of many of France's prominent writers, his predecessors or contemporaries—notably Proust, Gide, and Sartre—his was not a childhood turned in on itself. He was an active, outgoing child who participated in the physical pleasures of his peers—swimming, football, and later, as a spectator, boxing.

Camus was ten years old when an intervention from outside gave a new impetus to his life. His grade-school teacher, Louis Germain, noticed his unusual potentialities, tutored the child, and persuaded his somewhat recalcitrant family to let him pursue his education, first as a scholarship student at the lycée, to which he was admitted in 1924, and then, with the help of another great master, the writer-philosopher Jean Grenier, at the University of Algiers (1933). Louis Germain was a stern disciplinarian who shaped Camus's meticulous attention to the rigors of "classical" French as codified in the rules and examples taught in the French academic system. Camus, who was a born mimic, could use and enjoy the popular Algerian street idiom, the "Cagayous," as it was called. But as a writer he remained faithful to the established literary patterns of the French language; this at a time when in France, under the impetus of Dada and surrealism, writers like Raymond Queneau, Louis-Ferdinand Céline, and (to a lesser degree) Sartre were attempting to bridge the gap between spoken and literary French. In part it may have been the combination of Camus's fresh lyrical sense, his vision of a world steeped in light, and a literary style stripped of all irrelevancies that contributed to his initial success.

### *Beginnings*

At twenty, Camus had come a long way from the austere world of his childhood, yet not without some setbacks. At seventeen he had suffered the first virulent attack (very nearly fatal) of the pulmonary tuberculosis that was to plague him all his life. After a period of despair he reacted with typical energy. He left home, worked at various jobs, and began his studies in philosophy at the University of Algiers.

The University of Algiers was a good place for a talented young man to be and it had a decisive influence on his career. There he was soon one of a group of friends, some of them lifelong, who shared his enthusiasms and with whom he came to know a freedom and range of thought and speech new to him. The group, in the liberal context of the university, voiced its disagreements with the sociopolitical attitudes and institutions of colonial society and with the optimism of youth set out to challenge them. Its members were not popular with the local colonial authorities. They were eager too to keep abreast of Paris, proud of their "Mediterranean" heritage, and determined to put North Africa on the literary map. They were of varying origins: French, Italian, Spanish, and in the case of a few—very few—Muslim. In the early 1930's there was a feeling of excitement and hope abroad before the upsurge of fascism, the hope that a new world was in the making, the utopian world of official Marxism. Far from the European scene, in the happier, more relaxed atmosphere of prewar Algiers, Camus and his group shared this optimism. These were happy days for the young man who, off and on, shared the communal life of student friends living in what he called "the house facing the world," a starkly furnished villa overlooking the bay of Algiers. These friendships certainly softened the emotional disaster of his marriage at age 21 to a brilliant, much sought-after young woman who had charmed him by her fanciful turn of mind, which was in large part due to her addiction to drugs. Two years later they separated, when Camus discovered she was not given to marital fidelity.

In 1935, Camus joined the Communist party, though rather unenthusiastically. He soon became restive under the constraints imposed on him and was excluded from the party, or—according to his version—resigned. This brief association had positive consequences. Under the aegis of the Communist party leadership, anxious to develop a sense of cultural solidarity with the working class, cultural centers were being organized. For a while Camus directed the cultural center in Algiers and realized one of his dreams: the creation of a theater group. His "workers' theater," launched in 1935, outlived his commitment to the party. It became a "group theater," was renamed Le Théâtre de l'Équipe, and ran successfully until the outbreak of World War II. It presented an eclectic program ranging from an adaptation of Aeschylus' *Prometheus Bound* to the adaptation of a recent André Malraux novel, *Le temps du mépris* (*Days of Wrath,* 1935) and included works by Synge, Gide, Gorky, Pushkin, and Rojas. Camus, director, adaptor, actor, and publicity manager, was at the center of all the activity. A collectively written play of immediate sociopolitical relevance, *Révolte dans les Asturies* (Revolt in the Asturias), based on a 1934 miner's strike in Spain, was scheduled for production in 1936 but was banned by the administrative authorities: the outbreak of the Spanish Civil War had served to reinforce the reactionary tendencies of the local colonial authorities. Camus was by now skirmishing on two fronts: against the PCA (the Communist Party of Algeria) on the Left, and against the local colonial authorities on the Right. He had begun to write around 1932, and from 1935 on—as shown by the notebooks he kept until his death (published as *Carnets* in 1962 and 1964)—he was determined to become a writer. In those early years he was working simultaneously on a novel, on a play already entitled *Caligula,* and on an essay. Two slim books of essays came out in Algiers—*L'Envers et l'endroit* (*The Wrong Side and the Right Side,* 1937) and *Noces* (*Nuptials at Típasa,* 1939).

The year 1938 was a crucial one. Camus had intended to become a professor, but he could not pass the medical examination required by the government. He then turned to journalism, writing for a liberal left-wing paper, *Alger Républicain.* Reporting on scandalous instances of the miscarriage of justice, then on the desperate plight of the Berber peasants in Kabylia, Camus began to show unsuspected strengths.

### *The Years in Europe*

Literature, philosophy, theater, journalism, a deep concern with social justice—by 1938 the main lines of Camus's activity and interests were established. With the outbreak of World War II, events beyond his control were to project him out of Algeria and onto the European scene. Although Camus was released from the obligation to serve in the military for reasons of health, his paper was suppressed by the Algerian authorities because of its openly pro-peace and pro-Arab sentiments, and he himself was requested to leave; Camus consequently moved to Paris in March 1940 to work on the staff of the daily *Paris-Soir.* He married again in Lyons in December 1940 and returned to Oran in January 1941. From that time until the end of 1943 or early 1944, the date to which his activity in the clandestine underground network Combat can be traced, Camus led a somewhat disjointed life. Without a job, he first taught in a private institution for Jewish children who had been crassly expelled from the Oran lycée. His health deteriorated, however, and in 1942 he returned to France, moving to the Cévennes mountains for therapeutic treatment. The Allied landing in Casablanca cut him off from his wife and Algerian friends; he would be able to return only in 1945. Meanwhile in Paris, *The Stranger* and *Le mythe de Sisyphe* (*The Myth of Sisyphus,* 1942) brought him immediate recognition. He left for Paris in the spring of 1943 to work as a reader for the publishing firm of Gallimard. In the fall of that year, under the name of Beauchard, he assumed the responsibility for the publication and diffusion of the news sheet *Combat* (organ of the network of the same name)—a dangerous task. Camus also wrote under the name of Albert Mahé. He narrowly escaped from the

Gestapo when arrested while carrying a layout for an issue of *Combat.* When, with the liberation of Paris on 24 August 1944, *Combat* came out in the open, Camus, at thirty-one, enjoyed a double fame. He was awarded the Medal of the Liberation, a rare honor.

From 1944 on, Camus's public life reflects the agitations and the almost unbearable disappointments that followed the Liberation. After 1954 the savage Algerian conflict that he had predicted tore at his heart. Of the many editorials and articles he wrote during that decade, only a few are available in English—unfortunately, for they present a chronicle of the swiftly changing atmosphere and the startling events of those years. They show the evolution of a thought that was to lead, in 1951, to the publication of *L'Homme révolté* (*The Rebel*), an essay that sparked a bitter controversy and consecrated the rift that had been growing between Sartre and Camus. Four plays, produced with varying success—*Le malentendu* (*The Misunderstanding,* 1944), *Caligula* (1944), *L'État de siège* (*State of Siege,* 1948), and *Les justes* (*The Just Assassins,* 1949)—had been accompanied by a long novel, *La peste* (*The Plague,* 1947). *The Rebel* marked a new point of departure, which *La chute* (*The Fall,* 1956) emphasized. New themes and new techniques characterized his volume of short stories *Exile and the Kingdom* (1957). Once again Camus became involved with the stage, adapting and directing a half dozen plays, two with success—Faulkner's *Requiem for a Nun* (1956) and Dostoevsky's *The Possessed* (1959).

A merely factual account of Camus's life leaves out the essential. Camus belonged to a generation deeply affected by historical circumstances. He recalled in his Nobel Prize acceptance speech in Stockholm the "more than twenty years of absolutely insane history," when he had felt "lost hopelessly like all of [his] age in the convulsions of the epoch." He had been twenty when Hitler came to power in the politically agitated 1930's. He had seen the rise of several great totalitarian states, the collapse of the socialist and liberal movements in Europe, the purges in Russia, police terrorism and torture spreading over Europe, total war, and concentration camps. The Algerian conflict was at its height when he died. It was an era not calculated to inspire serenity. Besides the toll taken in time, energy, and health, Camus felt that the times had also imposed on his work an orientation it might not otherwise have had.

Like many young intellectuals—even more than most, perhaps, because he came from an inarticulate proletarian group—he felt the need to rethink the world, to make sense of what he, along with millions of others, was witnessing and experiencing. The ideas he developed in his essays, the themes that patterned his work, were not abstract exercises in theoretical logic or literary games. He was accustomed to harsh realities, and with these he grappled intellectually, convinced that thought must be welded to action, that there are more fundamental elements involved in human conduct than the niceties of theoretical verbal argumentation.

Brutal as they were, the years between the two world wars in France were rich in artistic achievement and intellectual ferment. There were undoubtedly two sides to the coin: a sense of doom, but also a restless, exciting sense of a new world in the making. Both were reflected in the arts and the violence of the ideological conflicts that kept the French outside totalitarianism but took them instead to the brink of civil war. Algeria as Camus knew it was, at first, the coastal city of Algiers on the periphery of all the European agitation, more stable in appearance, gayer, more confident in the future. In his first essays, with a keen eye for the shortcomings of his compatriots and a sense of humor all the freer because it was directed at himself as well, Camus described the typical North African attitudes—the elementary ethics, the reliance on immediate, uncomplicated physical satisfactions in a land that lavishly proffered them, the religious and metaphysical void, a mute accord with the natural elements and the beauty of the Mediterranean homeland, and an equally mute horror of death—attitudes of a people he described as gay and resigned, without traditions, "without questions." Camus's illness seemed to have awakened his mind to questions he might otherwise have ignored, questions that dominated post–World War I philosophical debate. He explored the many avenues of secular philosophy, the Greeks, the philosophers of history—G. W. F. Hegel, Karl Marx, and Oswald Spengler—and the existential and phenomenological thinkers who were rapidly replacing Kant in the minds of the young: Søren Kierkegaard, Friedrich Nietzsche, Edmund Husserl, Karl Jaspers, Martin Heidegger.

But unlike his brilliant French predecessors and contemporaries Gabriel Marcel, Maurice Merleau-Ponty, Jean-Paul Sartre, and Simone de Beauvoir, Camus did not think of himself as a professional philosopher. He was not interested in building a coherent, systematic, philosophical explanation of man's situation in the world. In fact, he had a rational aversion toward all such systems. He never wished to speak as a specialist. Perhaps because of his background he was much more interested in becoming, in a Socratic sense, a man with an ethic. On ethical grounds he had rejected an ideology that in the Stalin-dominated 1930's was, he had come to feel, merely a facade cynically masking political opportunism and the repressive mechanisms of a police state. What he diagnosed as the dominant mood of his time was the widespread existence of a fundamental nihilism, whether latent or carefully reasoned. The intellectual skepticism born of political experience and philosophical eclecticism; the onslaught against the various forms of rationalism inherited from the Enlightenment; Nietzsche's attacks on Western values; Spengler's prophecies of doom, grafted on prevalent notions concerning the predetermined course of history—these merely gave that nihilism its arguments.

With literature, Camus was thoroughly at home. His early book reviews in *Alger Républicain,* two of them of Sartre's first fictional works; the critical essays he wrote throughout his career, the two earliest of which (on Dostoevsky and Kafka) he later included in *The Myth of Sisyphus;* the notes he jotted down and the prefaces he wrote—all give a fair account of his tastes. He shared the predilection of his generation for Dostoevsky, Kafka, Faulkner, and Hemingway. But he also made his own choice among the "greats" in literature, a classical choice—the Greeks, Shakespeare, and the French classics, along with Herman Melville (according to Camus, one of those truly great writers). Of the brilliant group of French writers during the 1920's and 1930's, three gained his sympathetic attention: Henry de Montherlant, whose haughty isolation and aristocratic ethic he admired; Jean Giono, whose love of the elemental beauty of the world he shared; and André Malraux, whose tense and dramatic investigation of modern man's "fate," as it was being molded in the great revolutionary movements of the Far East, raised questions that echoed in Camus's own mind. But to no one of the moderns did he give his full allegiance.

In these prewar years, still bathed for him in Mediterranean light and vibrant with energy, Camus wrote his first series of works. A novel, *The Stranger,* a play, *Caligula;* and an essay, *The Myth of Sisyphus,* developed almost simultaneously. In his *Notebooks* he later grouped them together under a single label—"Sisyphus: Cycle of the Absurd." A fourth work, belonging to the same group, *The Misunderstanding,* was in an embryonic state in 1939. It serves as a kind of transition to the second group of Camus's works, the Promethean cycle.

Although, toward the end of his career, the lyrical essays collected in *L'Été* (*Summer,* 1954) and the short stories of *Exile and the Kingdom* seem unrelated to any preconceived design, the pattern of this first series of works was maintained by Camus. In the postwar years he produced a novel, *The Plague;* two plays, *The Just Assassins* and *State of Siege;* and an essay, *The Rebel.* He grouped these under the label—"Prometheus: Cycle of Revolt." His *Notebooks* show that he had projected further developments: a cycle of Nemesis, or measure; a cycle dealing with love or compassion. In each case he projected a novel, plays, an essay. To a question that concerned the relationship of his essays to his novels and plays, Camus answered:

> I write on different levels precisely to avoid mixing genres. So I wrote plays in the language of action, essays in the rational form, novels about the heart's obscurity. True, these different kinds of books say the same thing. But, after all, they were written by the same author and, together, form a single work.
>
> ("A Final Interview" [with Robert Spector], *Venture* 3–4:35–38 [1960])

A single work, a single author, but the "cycles" of Camus's work reflect in turn different atmospheres: prewar Algiers, with its predictable routines and enjoyments; the tense dreary days of occupation, with their regimentation and dull horror; the intellectual confusion and frustrated political idealism of the fifties; the slow return to the rhythm and concerns of private living. Camus seems to have been exceptionally sensitive to the complex emotional, political, and intellectual currents of his time.

## *THE WRITING*

### *Early Work: The Writer as Reporter*

Readers of *The Stranger,* the first of Camus's works to reach a wide audience, were tempted to identify the narrator's point of view with Camus's own, so persuasive was the author's use of first-person narration. The facts belie any such simple identification. During the years when he was working on the novel Camus was at work on other projects, including his writing as a journalist—one of a small team of men, French, French-Algerian, and Muslim—who labored to keep afloat an "independent" local paper, dedicated to the defense of the working class and to "the political and social emancipation of the Algerian people," while maintaining high standards of accuracy in reporting. The wave of reaction against the social reforms of the Socialist "popular government" was running strong in Algeria. The intent of the paper was to counteract that reaction by informing its readers as to the implications of both local and metropolitan policies. *Alger Républicain,* a daily morning paper, under ever-closer surveillance by police forces as international tensions increased, became *Soir Républicain,* an afternoon sheet reduced in format, until it was suspended early in 1940. Both papers were judged locally as highly subversive.

Camus's contributions to the paper, largely unknown in France, were later collected and published in toto under the apt title *Fragments d'un combat* (Fragments of a Combat, 1978), though perhaps "skirmish" would be a better term; they are "fragments" because taken together they furnish a kind of running commentary on the local Algerian situation as it developed from day to day in those years. "Algeria" at the time designated a vast territory, comprising a variety of regions, from the rich coastal Sahel to arid stretches of desert. Tribes and villages, widely scattered as one moved south, offered different modes of social organization, the single bond betweeen them being Islam. Algerian nationalism was to grow and define itself only in the coming years. Young Camus's Algeria was essentially the coastal Algiers in which he lived. It was his work as a reporter that took him farther afield and broadened his Algiers-centered point of view, one that the disastrous French situation between 1940 and 1945 was temporarily to eclipse. In the following years Camus joined forces in another combat. World War II had strengthened his aversion to the use of violence for resolving power conflicts in the world. One of his major concerns in the next years would be the battle for peace. But in the prewar years Camus's commitment was simpler, within a complex and sometimes contradictory situation. For him the inequities suffered by the Muslim population under the colonial regime were intolerable and in contradiction with the principles of a democratic regime. This position never changed; rather, as the political climate degenerated, the proposals he put forward as a political solution to the problem were changed.

Camus's reports and investigations are concerned with specific events in clearly defined conditions, and they aim at achieving practical results. He had been active for a couple of years in the local Communist party cell and was familiar with the infighting among the Muslim factions dissatisfied with the colonial regime. However, his articles are aimed not at them, but at his European-Algerian readers: his targets were the arrogant, high-handed local administrators, more particularly the notoriously reactionary mayor of Algiers.

A reporter is, in essence, an observer. As narrator of what he was observing, Camus often wrote in the first person singular. The "I" brought into play the rhetoric of a detached "cool" witness. But Camus also used pseudonyms: Zaks, Demos, Vincent Capable, Irenaeus, Jean Meursault. Camus devolved functions to these "I's" and to each an elementary personality defined by a style: tongue-in-cheek candor, deadly irony, earnest puzzlement, and bland self-righteousness. These stylistic games open the text to laughter and allow a distancing of the reader from the text that encourages critical readings: satire, irony, parody, caricature enter into play, creating complicity between readers and writer; "everyday" modes of behavior and opinion take on the aura of patent absurdity. An example in the realm of parody is "The Manifesto of Integral Conformism," presented as a solemn declaration of unconditional support for administrative policies by a group of "conscious and determined conformists." Their earnest endorsements of current slogans, regardless of consistency, builds up to a deadpan phantasmagoria of absurdity. Behind the masquerades of language, Camus was tilting at the masquerades of power. More serious are his attacks against the "regrettable" mayor of Algiers and the "puppet show" of city council meetings at which the mayor is described as making a mockery of the rules of democratic representation by blatantly manipulating the procedure in order to reduce the legally elected Muslim delegates to a humiliating silence. Masks and masquerades, "voices" rising in dialogue or confrontation within a common situation, are inherent to Camus's literary creations. Consciously used, they illustrate Camus's refusal to deal in verbal absolutes or the dialectics so popular with intellectuals at the time.

When, in contrast, Camus comes face to face with the reality of human degradation within the system, masks are discarded, and the "I" speaks in the voice of Camus himself, as in his reportage on the plight of the Berbers in the famine-stricken mountain community of Kabylia. The report is accompanied by photographs. Shame, pity, horror, outrage, and revolt accompany Camus's "itinerary" through the lands of famine, where the degradation of individual human beings is inseparable from the disintegration of a community. Famine is a plague. The famine in Africa in the mid 1980's recorded on our television screens, has made those images of extreme deprivation familiar to us. The young reporter's reaction is not far removed from the popular upsurge of emotion that triggered the flow of help to aid the victims of famine in Ethiopia in 1984. Camus's urgent appeal for immediate practical forms of help, beyond all political or ideological concerns, came up short against that other reality—a European war and then, a world war, which for a short while made of North Africa an adjunct to France. But ideological conflicts had definitely given way in Camus's vision of reality to a concern for the devastations wrought by political powers under whatever language they were officially justified.

The Kabylian episode seems to have been an important stage on Camus's way in search of his own "voice," a voice that would account for his experience in the world. Camus had left behind for good the temptation to accept doctrinaire systems of meaning such as Marxism offered. He was an agnostic, but also a philosophy student. The unexamined life of the working-class men and women among whom he lived as a child could not satisfy him. He shared the human need to make sense of the world and alongside his craft as journalist had turned to other forms of writing.

### *The Cycle of the Absurd*

In 1937 and 1939 two small, very different, autobiographical volumes of essays by Camus, *The Wrong Side and the Right Side* and *Nuptials at Típasa,* were printed locally in Algiers. Meanwhile he was working on a more ambitious project, a three-pronged group of connected works: novel, play, essay. All three dealt with a single theme, a theme that had become familiar to the post–World War I generation of intellectuals attuned to the "anti-Kantian–anti-Hegelian" philosophical trend represented by Kierkegaard and Nietzsche: the confrontation between the human need to make sense of the world and the human perception of the world's silence and opacity. This was the experience of what he called "the absurd." Camus's trilogy deals with alternative ways of confronting it, of construing a lived experience in an attempt to give it significance, if not meaning. The *Notebooks* indicate that he worked on the trilogy for many years; preliminary versions were completed while he was living in Algeria and were later revised considerably, no doubt under the impact of the historical conjuncture.

The five essays in *The Wrong Side and the Right Side*—"Irony," "Between Yes and No," "Death in the Soul," "Love of Life," and the title essay—combined brief vignettes of the Algerian working-class milieu with an orchestration of two fundamental and contradictory themes: the "nothingness" that lies at the heart of human life and the glory of life itself. *Nuptials at Típasa* develops with lyrical eloquence the two themes of life and death against the background of the Mediterranean landscape: the glory of life in "the morning sun" of Típasa and the "great joy" filling the vast space of sky and sea; the certainty of death voiced by the "arid splendor" of the dead city of Djémila; life, savored on the burning Algerian beaches in the heart of the summer; the reconciliation with death glimpsed among the gentle hills of Italy. In no immediate sense was young Camus a stranger among men or to this earth. "I am happy, on this earth," he wrote in his *Notebooks,* "for my kingdom is of this earth." And Patrice, his first fictional hero, reiterates: "I shall speak of nothing but my love of life."

It has become customary, when discussing *The Stranger,* to see the story not as fiction but as the fictionalization of an abstract philosophy of the "absurd." Camus perhaps is partly responsible for the misunderstanding, having himself launched the term. But the preface to the *Myth of Sisyphus* expressly states that a philosophy of the absurd is precisely what we lack, and it was not Camus's intent to furnish that philosophy. Through the *Notebooks* we can follow the adventures the novel underwent between 1935 and May 1940, when it was finished. Publication was delayed until 1942 amid the chaos of the French defeat.

Camus had envisaged a quite different book, *La vie heureuse* (A Happy Life), as a semiautobiographical novel to be presented through a third-person hero, a would-be writer, Patrice Mersault. Camus wrote a first and then a second version, in the course of which the title shifted to *La mort heureuse* (*A Happy Death,* 1971). As he worked, certain themes of *The Stranger* appeared, sometimes separately, sometimes connected with the story but lost in a maze of other themes. *The Stranger* took shape slowly, through trial and error, the result of a long circuitous search. The book that emerged was strikingly different from the one Camus had planned.

*The Stranger.* The story of *The Stranger* is uncomplicated, on the surface at least. Meursault, an office clerk in Algiers, receives a telegram announcing the death of his mother in an old people's home. He asks for a two-day leave, attends the funeral, and then comes back to Algiers. He goes to the beach, picks up a girlfriend, Marie, and takes her to the movies. They then go to his apartment and make love. By chance, he becomes involved in the unsavory affairs of a neighbor, Raymond, a pimp who starts a dangerous feud with some Arabs. One Sunday, Raymond, Meursault, and Marie go off together for an outing. The Arabs follow them. Raymond gets into a fight. Later, Meursault, who prudently had taken Raymond's revolver, encounters one of the Arabs. A knife flashes in the sun, Meursault pulls the trigger. . . . He is arrested, tried, and condemned to death.

Although *A Happy Death* had little in common with *The Stranger,* two of its themes point to the two centers of tension in the later novel: a mother-son estrangement and a man sentenced to death. It is only little by little that the estranged son became the man sentenced to death and that Camus provided him with an act—a murder—justifying the sentence. Whatever interpretations *The Stranger* may suggest, and they are many, one should not forget that his novels, as Camus said, speak of the "obscurity" of the human heart. It was the voice of the man sentenced to death that had spoken first, though not alone, in the heart of the young Camus, who as an adolescent had almost died in complete solitude, faced with the surprising indifference of the world, an indifference which seems to have long echoed in his own empty heart. Meursault's fundamental trait, his indifference, seems to be—in part at least—a reflection of that initial experience: hence the power this singular hero derived over his creator's imagination.

"Today Mother died, or perhaps yesterday. . . ." So begins the novel. Camus, after much experimentation, adopted for *The Stranger* a form of the widely used first-person narrative technique. Meursault tells his own story as it evolves. Attempts have been made to discover a definite point in time from which Meursault views the events he recalls, but they have all been unsuccessful. Questionable if discussed on realistic grounds, the device was obviously chosen for aesthetic reasons and proved to be remarkably persuasive. Because of the shifting perspective of his story, the controlling point of view is not entirely Meursault's. He is unaware of the future ramifications of his acts, himself advancing blindly toward a trap carefully laid for him by the circumstances he notes. His position is curiously analogous to what happens in a dream, where the dreamer both evolves the dream and lives in it; yet, unlike the nightmarish world of Kafka, the world of Meursault is a brilliantly lighted, clearly delineated, everyday world—that of Algiers.

The narrative device chosen by Camus has advantages: the persuasive immediacy of the situations described, the creation of a climate of chance, suspense, and yet inevitability, and for Camus the freedom to create sharp fluctuations in the reader's emotional reaction to Meursault. The first pages are told in a low-keyed, matter-of-fact tone, and the reader views the funeral and the old people's home and its inhabitants through Meursault's eyes. But as Meursault proceeds, telling of his return, his involvement with Marie and then with Raymond, the reader becomes alarmed. He finds himself obliged to view and judge from the outside, even though he is entirely dependent upon Meursault for the facts and atmosphere of the story itself. A first distancing is created, but strictly within the confines of Meursault's self-contained world. The novel ends in uncertainty, so far as Meursault's immediate fate is concerned. The appeal on his behalf submitted by his lawyer has not been acted upon, a loophole is left. The voice of Meursault therefore is the voice of a living man, a man sentenced to death to be sure, but one who, within the limits of the novel, unlike us, will never die. Begun as the most ordinary of anecdotes concerning the most indistinguishable of men, the novel thus moves toward myth. Set apart from all men because he killed a man, judged and condemned to the guillotine, Meursault, speaking to us as a "man sentenced to death" exemplifies the most universally shared human situation that exists. Thence, no doubt, the enigmatic quality of the character.

The story falls into two parts: the account of the events that lead Meursault from his mother's funeral to the murder on the beach and the events that concern Meursault's imprisonment and trial. They stop just short of his execution. Factual in appearance, the first part describes a routine life, lived among ordinary people, carrying with it a flavor of sun and sea, the sense of a direct semiconscious, nonverbalized enjoyment of simple physical things—swimming, sunshine, the softness and charm of a young girl's presence. The second part of the story brings no new events, only a judgment. It takes place indoors—whether prison or courthouse—and in solitude or, as during the trial, moral solitude. But the young man who in the opening pages of the book had asked his boss for leave to attend his mother's funeral has traveled a long way by the time he reaches the end of his tale.

Behind Meursault there is, of course, Camus the novelist, who controls both Meursault's changing experience and the reader's reactions, invisibly manipulating a situation that seems to move inexorably of its own momentum. He can thus charge it indirectly with a dramatic irony that is not always apparent at the first reading. It underlies the focal situation—murder, however unintentional—and the focal problem: the relation of Meursault to his act. The events that lead to Meursault's fatal encounter with the Arab on the beach are set up with great care. At first they do not concern Meursault at all. The Arabs' anger is directed at Raymond, Meursault's neighbor, for his blatantly brutal treatment of his Arab mistress. Meursault is involved only indirectly, by association. Even the revolver he holds at the time of the shooting is not his. He had taken it from Raymond as a precaution against violence. When he pulls the trigger, in the heat of the midday sun, his gesture is irrational, unforeseen, unmotivated.

Implicated in a quarrel not his own, driven by the violent pressure of outer elemental circumstances—the pitiless glare and heat of the sun—a man has killed another man. There is no going back on the act. Excluding all ordinary "psychological" motivations for the crime, Camus carefully designed Meursault's situation so that the mechanisms of chance and outer pressure would lead to this brief loss of control.

Meursault is obviously not a "criminal" type. There is little to distinguish him except his tendency to say nothing and a kind of passive gentleness: he is friendly, sympathetic to others, apparently content with a life he sees no reason to change. He is scrupulous in the expression of his feelings, but apparently far more indifferent with regard to his acts. He likes to make love to Marie, but he will not say he loves her. Yet he acquiesces when she suggests marriage. He acquiesces too soon when Raymond involves him in his plan of vengeance, and thereby supports Raymond's primitive ethical code. Behind the character's seemingly disconnected acts one begins to see a constant: Meursault is a man who acquiesces in what is. His inertia leads to the irrevocable last acquiescence, the finger on the trigger, and the forcible transformation of his life.

At no time does Meursault plead innocence, nor does Camus at any time suggest that he is innocent. That with the shooting something has gone irrevocably wrong, Meursault knows immediately, though he understands neither what nor why. After the murder is committed, we move away from the deceptively realistic tone of the narrative toward a far more stylized treatment of Meursault's situation.

The second part of the novel is concerned with the enigmatic problem of Meursault's act, a problem as puzzling to Meursault as to the reader. Camus makes short shrift of the usual interpretations, presenting them ironically in Meursault's semiburlesque interviews with the prosecutor, magistrate, and lawyer, and in his account of his trial. The first-person narrative now establishes a strange dissociation between the facts and feelings Meursault had previously described and the attempts made by others to interpret these coherently. A definite shift in perspective is introduced: the reader finds himself in the position of judge, jury, and privileged witness. He and Meursault alone know the facts. Camus has thereby put upon the reader the burden of providing an explanation Meursault is unable to furnish. Self-critical and self-correcting, the novel rapidly moves toward its end.

The official characters Meursault encounters during his imprisonment and trial are little more than subtly wrought masks, incarnating and deliberately satirizing interpretations that Camus rejects as irrelevant—guilt, remorse, atonement, conversion. The trial itself, seen from the outside, is little more than a grotesque preview of the many possible arguments for or against Meursault, his character and motivations. They leave Meursault intact and the problem of his act unsolved.

Meanwhile, in his prison Meursault awakens to a new dimension of life, an inner awareness that he had totally lacked. The death sentence, after an initial shock, finally sets him on the path of an epiphany that reaches back to the beginning of the novel, wrenches Meursault out of his passive state, and prepares him to counter the terror of death with the concentration of all the forces of life. His apparent indifference to his mother's death, to Marie's love, drops from him like a cloak as he confronts the chaplain who comes to speak to him of compensation in an afterlife. In the solitude of his prison, what Meursault reaches for goes deeper than guilt and remorse. He had acquiesced to the "natural death" of his mother and was indifferent to the rituals with which society surrounded it; he had himself participated in the death of another human being, indifferent to the interpretations society put upon his act.

The awakening that follows his death sentence alone can bring into focus those two moments unifying the pattern of his experience. Meursault sees, at last, that to exist is happiness. His indifference to the sights and smells of the world turns into a conscious love; his passive acquiescence to the violence done to human beings turns into a passionate revolt against death and a sense of human fraternity. He can now understand the small joys that filled the last days of his mother's humble life. The revolver shot that precipitated him from his semiconscious existence into the closed universe of his mind has, as its counterpoint, the violent act of consciousness whereby Meursault emerges from his isolation to assume his identity as a human being, the full responsibility for his life in its beauty and incomprehensible strangeness. Camus leaves Meursault on the threshold of a new awareness and a new passion, suspended between life and death. But this change does not account for the two most dramatic passages in the book—the murder itself and Meursault's last imaginary bid for the hatred of the crowd, should his execution take place.

Twelve years after the publication of *The Stranger,* Camus wrote a semi-ironic and typically paradoxical preface that has been widely quoted, often without a glint of humor and out of context. "From my point of view," he remarked,

> Meursault is not a human wreck, but a poor and naked man, in love with the sun that leaves no shadows. Far from lacking sensitivity, he is animated by an intense, because stubborn, passion, a passion for the absolute and for truth. It is still negative truth, the truth of being and feeling, but without it there can be no conquest of oneself or of the world.
>
> (*L'Étranger,* p. vi)

This, then, would be the unexpressed inner compulsion that drives Meursault: the refusal to conclude without evidence, to rely on words, to go beyond what he thinks is true, to strike attitudes, to "plead innocent" or "plead guilty." In Camus's eyes this makes of him a man who, in a sense, accepts death for the sake of truth. "I have sometimes said, albeit paradoxically," Camus concludes, "that in the person of my character I have tried to create the only Christ we deserve." It is a challenging statement, obviously sarcastic.

However we wish to interpret *The Stranger,* it is clear that we cannot be satisfied to read it merely as a story. Camus obviously intended to create an autonomous, exemplary figure. At one time in his *Notebooks* he had envisaged a novel centering on a character conceived as "L'Indifférent" ("The indifferent man"). Meursault's shattering adventure has its source in characteristic indifference, and its significance seems to lie in the revelation of the basic and dangerous inadequacy of this attitude. It leads him into a trap where his initially imperceptible inadequacies are fully revealed and then, in a reverse moment, transcended. This method of creation is typical of Camus's writing, and reminiscent of André Gide, but in Camus's case it would seem more obviously connected with Plato.

*Caligula.* When a revised version of *Caligula* was produced on the Paris stage in 1945, it was an indubitable success, the greatest that Camus was ever to enjoy as a playwright. For each new production of the play—in 1950, 1957, and 1958—he reworked his text, modifying it quite considerably. But by and large it remained the play Camus had written in his twenty-fifth year, Caligula's age in the first version of the play.

If, of the twelve ferocious emperors described by Suetonius, it was Caligula who caught Camus's fancy, this was no doubt because of that emperor's youth and of the peculiar forms his madness took. Camus provided a motivation that transformed the emperor from a historical into a contemporary, though imaginary, figure. In those years Camus was preoccupied with death. The "man sentenced to death"—his double, in a sense—had appeared in the *Notebooks* approximately a year before. At the root of Caligula's adventure is an emotional and intellectual confrontation with the finality and inevitability of death.

The first act of the play sets the stage for the developments that take place in the subsequent acts, three years later. Its purpose is to establish the inner climate of distress that gives coherence to Caligula's fantastic external acts and to set up the outer circumstances that give these acts their dramatic plausibility. Caligula, a "relatively attractive prince," has been absent for three days, since the death of Drusilla, his beloved sister and mistress. The curtain rises, just before his return, on a group of more or less anxious patricians. Four people in the emperor's entourage stand out: Caesonia, his mistress; Cherea, an older, thoughtful, and reserved man; Scipio, a young poet; and Helicon, a former slave freed by Caligula, now his henchman. They sound the note of concern that prepares Caligula's intensely dramatic entry. Distraught, and like Hamlet, proffering strange and incongruous words, Caligula spreads consternation around him. Camus attempts to reveal the emperor's state of mind through gestures and acts and by words that emanate from it but do not explicate it. Violently striking a gong to alert the palace, Caligula effaces from a mirror the image of the "relatively attractive prince," thus announcing the advent of a new Caligula. It is clear to the audience that Caligula's "descent into hell" has sent him back transformed.

When the curtain rises on the second act, three years have gone by and Caligula has become an "impossible" character, a monster, a ferocious tyrant, isolated in his court, attended only by Caesonia and Helicon. Reluctantly, his former friends Scipio and Cherea have been forced to abandon him. As a revolt gains momentum, Caligula accumulates grimly burlesque masquerades that mock, humiliate, kill, and devastate. In a last powerful scene, completely isolated now, Caligula breaks the mirror, confronts his assassins in whose plot he had deliberately acquiesced, and dies with a wild last cry: "I am still alive."

Brilliant in conception, and richly executed in a vibrant lyrical language that moves with ease from irony through pathos to tragic intensity, the play has, nevertheless, certain weaknesses. The first act raises the question of the connection between Caligula's confrontation with death and the crisis heralded by the strokes on the gong. The suspense it creates should be slowly resolved in the successive acts. But the young dramatist has eluded the problem. The three-year lapse between acts 1 and 2 does not bring about a transformation in depth of character or situation. In the next stage, the inner coherence of the play is somewhat sacrificed to the spectacular masquerades that seem to have tempted the stage director in Camus; their arbitrariness detracts from their plausibility. The significance of the main character is overshadowed by the horrifying stage business that accompanies Caligula's ferocious appearances. The primary theme of the play, Caligula's self-destruction, is obscured.

Caligula's inner development, suggested in the first act, has its source in his discovery of a simple yet startling truism: "Men die, and they are not happy." Hence his violent revolt, his intolerable sense that all life is a futile masquerade, his need, as a compensation, to achieve something "impossible"—change the world, possess the moon, reverse the seasons, conquer death itself, assert his absolute freedom. Concomitantly he wants to spread his gospel and communicate his own stark revelation. All-powerful, he decides to impersonate cold fate. Logical to an extreme, he consistently identifies himself with the arbitrary, derisive, or cruel forces that destroy human security. But in the course of this identification, of necessity he destroys his human self. His murder, accepted by him, is a "superior suicide," brought about by the tragic realization that he has miserably failed. *Caligula,* as Camus conceived it, "is the story of the most human and tragic of errors," an error whose nature Caligula recognizes just before he dies. "My freedom was not of the right kind."

*The Misunderstanding.* A tragic human error, implacably carried to its logical limit, is also at the dynamic core of *The Misunderstanding,* a three-act play produced a year before *Caligula* but written some years later. The play reaches back in setting and mood to 1936, to a dismal night of solitude Camus had spent in Prague. Written in the atmosphere of occupation, "in the middle of a country encircled and occupied," it is heavily charged with a gloom and "claustrophobia" that are entirely new in Camus's work. The story of *The Misunderstanding* is a variant of an old folkloric tale whose components are simple: an isolated inn run by an innkeeper who assassinates travelers in order to rob them. The variations on the pattern are innumerable, and its symbolic potentialities are evident. Camus tightened the plot so as to create, he said, an "impossible situation." In his play the inn, situated in the heart of Czechoslovakia, is run by two women, an old mother and her daughter, Martha. When the curtain rises, they are discussing the arrival of a traveler, whom they are to drug and drown in the weir that night, like others before him, but with a difference: he is to be the last, for their ultimate purpose will now be achieved. They will have the money that will bring them freedom and allow Martha at last to reach the sunny beaches of the south. The traveler appears, and the trap closes. He reveals—but only to the audience—both his purpose and his identity. A prodigal son who had left home twenty years before, now a wealthy man living in the warm southern land to which Martha aspires, he has come to help his mother and sister. But he plans to remain incognito until he is recognized. The play moves grimly to its end in a kind of nightmarish tug-of-war between the inflexible mechanism of murder set off by the traveler's arrival and the repressed emotions and hesitations of mother, daughter, and son fumbling unsuccessfully toward its arrest. Jan, the son, will be recognized, but only after he has been killed. His mother will join him in the weir. His sister commits suicide, but only after she sees and denounces the horror of the trap into which she has fallen. Maria, Jan's wife, is left in moral torture to face the bitter uselessness of it all. Her anguished cry for help elicits from the old, enigmatic, and seemingly mute waiter who haunts the inn, only a single syllable: "No." "A son who expects to be recognized without having to declare his name and who is killed by his mother and sister as a result of the misunderstanding—this is the subject of the play"; yet the whole design of the plot points to an underlying, hidden meaning.

Camus admittedly was interested in only one form of drama—tragedy. In this he was not alone. Eugene O'Neill in America; T. S. Eliot in England; Jean Giraudoux, Jean Anouilh, and Henry de Montherlant in France, to mention only a few contemporary names, all experimented in that form. One of the more tempting paths Camus's predecessors had explored was the reinterpretation in modern times of well-known Greek themes. In his own experiments as a dramatist, Camus seems to have deliberately attempted to free his plays from dependency on the ready-made tragic characters and conflicts so often reinterpreted by his contemporaries. He wanted to find a "modern" design that could disclose the particular forms the tragic conflict assumes at the present time.

In its structure, *The Misunderstanding* harks back to the Greeks: the rigid masklike quality of the two women, the fatal chain of crime engendering crime, the murder within the family group, the inflexible working out of an initial purpose, and the recognition theme. *Caligula* is more closely related to the Molière technique of unleashing a Tartuffe or Don Juan to wreak havoc within a relatively "normal" world; but here the nature of the havoc wrought is different and at first eludes the mind. Camus outlined his idea of the "tragic conflict" (partly derived from Nietzsche) as the coexistence of two equally necessary, equally valid but irreconcilable principles or orders that place individuals in "impossible," hence incomprehensible, situations where the irrational prevails. He thus conceived his theater as a "theater of the impossible," presenting in *Caligula* an "impossible character" and in *The Misunderstanding* an "impossible situation." The restless, impatient surge of human beings to transcend their limitations seemed to him the very essence of the modern tragic situation. The "impossible" figuration on stage therefore has a significance beyond itself, not explicated by the characters. The spectator or reader must make his way back to the initial feeling and thought that animates the play. Camus's purpose is to awaken the consciousness—rather than, like Hamlet's, to "catch the conscience"—of his audience.

For *Caligula* the pattern, though somewhat obscured, is clear: Caligula's initial revolt is thoroughly human, involving a sense of the poignancy of living. He cannot accept the haphazard game that nature plays with human life. Since he cannot attach the metaphysical, social, political ordering of human existence to a universal frame of reference, he sees it as a derisory sham. He embodies thereby a tragic conflict: his revolt negates his logical conclusions. This "impossible" position is mirrored in his passionate desire to impose his vision on all about him, while using a method that makes communication impossible. It is mirrored, too, in a sense of moral freedom that leads him only to the dead end of despair. If Caligula embodies one of the latent tendencies of our thinking, it is from Caligula that the play wants to free us.

*The Misunderstanding* is more obscure. Martha and her brother are committed to the same very human project: to transform the bleak situation at the inn, to achieve happiness. Jan, secure in his own happiness and love, vaguely takes for granted a situation where things "work out," a natural order in which a mother will always recognize her son; he walks confidently into the mechanical, abstract pattern of crime set up in the inn by Martha, whose "right" to achieve happiness justifies the means automatically employed. The two approaches, inflexibly pursued by brother and sister, each with the same goal in view, blind them to the recognition of their real situation: the brother and son is not recognized; he does not even glimpse the nature of the situation he came to remedy. It was Camus's contention that, grim though it was, *The Misunderstanding* suggested a perspective beyond itself.

> If a man wants to be recognized, he must simply say who he is. If he is silent or lies, he will die alone, and everything around him will be condemned to disaster. But if he speaks the truth, he will die undoubtedly, but after having helped others and himself to live.
>
> (preface to *Le Malentendu*)

Like *Caligula, The Misunderstanding* is concerned with the passion for an absolute, with human happiness as an absolute in a human world that engenders crime upon crime. The question raised takes us full circle back to *The Stranger* and the enigma of Meursault's relation to an act that he seems not to be troubled about, though he is ready to accept its consequences. In the plays no fatality is involved. The burden of the disaster rests squarely on the decisions of the protagonists. All that outer circumstances offer is blind chance, and it was also blind chance, symbolized by the chain of incidents that led him to the beach, that triggered Meursault's gun. Camus, in his short novel, seems to have wanted to describe "a man," to say "who he is." His hero experiences the full range of a man's possibilities, stopping at none until, face to face with death, he grasps them in their totality: violence and compassion; beauty and death; solidarity and solitude. He is a man, that is, a "stranger"—unique, impossible, and real. Caligula discovers the violence and rejects the beauty and compassion; Martha knows the infinite nostalgia and rejects the present possibilities; Jan believes in innocence and ignores the horror. The hero in each play has only one fragment of the total awareness to which Meursault eventually accedes. Hence the conflict, the mutilation, and the self-destruction that make these people tragic figures in Camus's eyes.

*The Myth of Sisyphus.* Underlying all three works is the same pervasive feeling of moral distress engendered by a human society that can no longer reach outside itself for a coherent system of ethical values. The hubris that sets off the infernal machine of fate is thus bred in the stubborn decisions of distraught human minds. Camus insisted, with some measure of reason, that although they expressed mental conflicts or attitudes, his plays did not involve an abstract philosophy. *The Myth of Sisyphus,* an essay which developed in the same years, and which he defines as a personal testimony, intellectualizes the mood that gave substance to his first fictional works.

The "absurd"—a word that was to hypnotize Camus's readers and critics, somewhat to his distress—seems to have begun to fascinate Camus in the summer of 1938, when both *Caligula* and *The Stranger* were being written. He was not the first to use it. The word was in the air, a part of the restless, anxious mood of the time. It was used in a wide variety of contexts to designate the incomprehensible, the unpredictable, the purposeless, incongruous, "impossible" aspects of life. For Camus as for Sartre, although not to the same extent, the basic mood had been conceptualized through contact with existential and phenomenological approaches to philosophy. Analysis of the failure of the intellect to encompass the complex reality of human existence was common to Pascal, Kierkegaard, and Nietzsche as well as to Husserl, Jaspers, and Heidegger. Unlike Sartre, though, Camus, when he wrote the *Myth of Sisyphus,* was not concerned with a "philosophy of the absurd" but rather, given a "sense" of the absurd, with how profitably to live with it, transforming it into a positive incentive "to live lucidly and to create." The heavy abstract superstructure that has been imposed by critics on his short essay has tended to obscure its essential feature, its lyrical emphasis on the exhilarating reality of a life that transcends the intellect. Life is incomprehensible, to be sure, but in young Camus's eyes its existence is not open to question.

The *Myth of Sisyphus* is a clarification of the problem of "the absurd," valid only within a given mental framework of reference and experience, Camus's own. It is addressed to those who have no religious, metaphysical, or philosophical system of belief to which they can relate their acts, and whose acts thereby lose their relevance. Intellectual indifference and moral irresponsibility, Camus observed, are the price they tend to pay for a freedom that takes the form of an infinite array of equally irrelevant decisions; living tends, then, to become a senseless mechanism pervaded by a paralyzing sense of its nothingness. Without reaching outside his nihilism, one of the essential elements in the problem he had set himself, Camus proposed in his essay to "find a means to go beyond it."

"The fundamental subject of *The Myth of Sisyphus* is this: it is legitimate and necessary to wonder whether life has a meaning; therefore it is legitimate to meet the problem of suicide face to face." From this classical problem, Camus rapidly moved to the equally classical situation in which, in an apparently stable social world, the question of meaning arises, and with it metaphysical anxiety with regard to the whole of existence. Camus briefly enumerated the "walls" that bring rational answers to a halt, then turned to the existential philosophers, only to reject them all for the same reason. Having faced the fundamental relativity of all rational systems of explanation in a nonrational world, these philosophers, Camus charges, "make a leap"; they arbitrarily and irrationally derive from the nonrational a principle of explanation.

Camus's purpose was different—different, too, from that of Sartre, who from the same vision of man's moral freedom and consequent responsibility in a purposeless universe drew his terrifying ethic of a perpetual and anguished creation of the self. According to Camus, the basic limitations of human living cannot be changed, nor the contradictions resolved. If once the mechanism of routine living is stopped, if the shot rings out on the beach and awareness starts, we shall always find the same human creature in the same role: judge, accuser, witness, advocate, accused, a "stranger," whose being must remain forever incomprehensible.

In the first section of *The Myth of Sisyphus* the age-old paradoxes are briefly summarized: the love of life, the inevitable death; the need for coherence, the basic incomprehensibility; the surge toward happiness, the evidence of pain. Camus proposes a lucid acceptance of the situation: to love life, and to live with the knowledge that life is incomprehensible; to multiply all the chances for happiness, knowing its impossibility; to explore the infinite possibilities of life within the narrow limits of a life. That the full reality of experience transcends the intellect was, he felt, an insufficient statement; he defined man's metaphysical existence by the refusal of human reason to accept definition in terms of the irrational.

*The Myth of Sisyphus* proposes to seek in this paradoxical and inescapable situation the source of man's unique and peculiar value, his creativity. To the destructive transgressors—Caligula, Jan, and Maria—it opposes a gallery of truly "absurd" heroes: the actor, the Don Juan, the conqueror, the creative artist, and finally, subsuming them all, Sisyphus. Camus's Sisyphus is a man wedded to his limitations, living out a role assigned to him, each conflicting part of which is integral and must be lucidly confronted.

With *Sisyphus,* the cycle of the absurd can be seen as a whole. Meursault, Caligula, Jan, Martha, and Sisyphus are all objectified, intensely personal projections of certain inner moods. The four works are related by the resurgence of recognizable images, concrete and at the same time symbolic: light (the light that suffuses Meursault's Algiers), but also an inner light, whether the cruel light of evidence, the burning light of violence, the quiet light of beauty, or the soft light of acquiescence; sea, stone, and desert; human faces that appear, merge, and become autonomous, observable by others—judge, jury, or horrified witnesses. It is not by chance that the "creator" is one of the four "absurd men." It is clear that for

Camus in the 1930's, artistic creation was not a solution to a situation that he had diagnosed as insoluble, but rather a confrontation with himself, a way of existing in harmony with himself. The aesthetic urge was already so strong in him that it freed him from the Marxist dogma of "social realism," although in *The Stranger* and *Caligula,* young Camus's antagonism to established society, its institutions and representatives—so clear in his first journalistic writings—comes through in a grotesque satirical lampooning: in the novel, of the court of justice and its clownlike functionaries; and in the plays, of the patricians. In comparison, the murderous actions of a Caligula or a Martha are so violent an expression of revolt against the limitations of reality that one cannot but see in them a deeper anguish and protest whose only check is the creative act itself.

Between the years when Camus conceived the first set of works and the years when they were published, momentous events had transformed the climate of France. The 1930's had been years of social problems, political discussions, ideological battles. Camus had taken a stand on all these; yet his creative works rose as a block, beyond them. His heroes, conscious of the contingency of their existence, all invent an "impossible" existence, based on the full expansion of one part only of the self. At the time they were created they stood outside the mainstream of literary preoccupations. In the 1940's, they reached a disconcerted audience living in a Caligula-like world of insecurity. It was the "absurd" view of man's situation, inherent in the structure, character, and action of Camus's fictional works, that struck his readers. The underlying protest, the ambivalence of the whole, the upsurge of vital force, and the imaginative power that defined the aesthetic unity of the work tended to pass unnoticed. Artist though he was, Camus was disguised as a philosopher. But the foundations of his work were laid. Its basic language, forms, conflicts, and themes were not to vary greatly in the coming years.

### *The Mid-Century Years*

One of Camus's preoccupations, clearly evidenced in his first essays, was a tragic sense of human suffering—as seen, for example, in Caligula's downfall. His first works, concentrating on the discovery and creation of the self, sidestep the theme. The war was to bring Camus face to face with the problem. He had not eluded the question in his personal life, but it had not been an essential source of inner tension and hence of creativity. A Marxist first, then a non-Marxist socialist, he had, it seems, settled the question of human suffering in his own mind. War and occupation, liberation, and the political no-man's-land of postwar Europe imposed on Camus new concepts involving the relation of the artist to the human community. The basic theme underlying the second, "Promethean," cycle of Camus's work is the conflict between an obsessive, collective situation involving large-scale injustice, mass murder, enslavement, and torture, and a no less obsessive longing for the freedom to breathe and to create a harmonious work of art. In his articles and speeches throughout this period, Camus dwells on the inroads that political action makes on an artist's creative powers.

Opposed to Sartre's theory of political commitment, as well as to the Marxist view of the artist, he defined solidarity with the oppressed as one of the sources of the artist's integrity. The artist could not, in certain circumstances, avoid being militant. In the political arena for better or worse, he could not, however, change his language in the interests of a party. He could not let his writing serve in dubious ways, for this would betray his art, corrupting his use of the language itself.

Camus's speeches and works illustrate how deeply he felt the disruptive pull of these two factors in his life during the 1950's. To be free from the harrowing obsession with horror and the petty disputes of politics—to write as he wished—was the nostalgic aspiration of these years. *The Plague, The Just Assassins,* and *The*

*Rebel* constitute a statement and a working out of his conflict. The countermyths that Camus created, incarnating the force of his reaction to the concrete, oppressive world around him, express his claim to something other.

*The Plague.* A first version of *The Plague* was finished in 1943. The plague had appeared early in Camus's personal imagery as a symbol, perhaps first striking his attention in a strange essay, "The Theater and the Plague," written by a former surrealist, Antonin Artaud. The symbol is already at work in *Caligula*—Caligula is the plague—and up to its last appearance, in *State of Siege,* is was to prowl in the background of Camus's imagination as the most representative image of the calamities that can befall a human society. In 1941 he jotted down a title for a novel: "The Plague or Adventure." It was no longer a question of describing a subjective Caligula-like adventure. The plague, by then, had taken on a specific form, so eloquent that retrospectively it was to give *Caligula* and *The Misunderstanding* levels of meaning that Camus had not anticipated. With these topical meanings the new novel originated. "*The Plague,*" Camus wrote a friend, "which I wanted to have read at several levels, has nonetheless as its evident content the struggle of the European resistance against Nazism."

For several years Camus read extensively, plunging into the vast literature extant on the scourge—memoirs, chronicles, treatises, biblical descriptions, and works of fiction—Boccaccio, Kleist, Pushkin, Manzoni, and Defoe. In the course of the writing the novel changed. The fragments of a first draft are charged with savage irony. But by 1943, irony had given way to a bleak and desperate seriousness. Camus was in France, ill and ever more deeply involved in the struggle against the German occupation. He could measure the ruthlessness of the machinery of oppression grinding millions of human beings to death. The plague, which he had first cast in the guise of a grotesque, outrageous bureaucrat, now became a killer, invisible but all pervasive, regulating, tabulating, insulating, dehumanizing, and silencing.

For quite a while Camus searched for a mode and tone for his narrative that would transmit the atmosphere he wanted. A first-person narrative, centering interest in one individual, would not give a sense of the collective nature of the "adventure." Camus did not want the narrator to become an epic hero, but a completely objective recording would lack the immediacy of testimony—the narrator had to be "one of us." The solution was suggested to him by the opening chapter of Dostoevsky's *The Possessed* (1871–1872). The chronicle of the plague is written by Bernard Rieux, a citizen of Oran who in the last pages gives his reasons for undertaking the task and so reveals his identity. His social position is functional: he is a doctor. He writes for several reasons: first, "so that he should not be one of those who hold their peace, but should bear witness in favor of those plague-stricken people"; second, "to state quite simply what we learn in a time of pestilence: that there are more things to admire in men than despise"; and third, because

> he knew that the tale he had to tell could not be one of final victory. It could only be the record of what had to be done, and what assuredly would have to be done again in the never ending fight against terror and its onslaughts, despite their personal afflictions, by all who, while unable to be saints but refusing to bow down to pestilences, strive their utmost to be healers.
>
> (Gilbert trans., p.287)

Rieux knows that the plague bacillus never dies and that the day could come when "it would raise up its rats again and send them to die in a happy city."

Critics have objected both to the symbol Camus chose and the mode of narration, more on realistic or even political grounds than on aesthetic ones. For the socially "committed," the plague as an invisible evil abstracted from human beings—that is, from the Nazis—smacked of "bourgeois idealism," of a conscience "situated outside history," of the refusal politically to accept the "dirty hands" involved in the action. For others, the symbol itself—its appearance and development, the closing-off of the quarantined city—seemed too far removed from the actual medical process, too obsolete to be credible. The deceptiveness of the third-person chronicle, and the carefully controlled factual, "descriptive-diagnostic" tone, seemed to others to circumscribe too rigorously the effectiveness of the book, while the combination of symbol and testimony in the eyes of some turned the novel too obviously into an allegory. Nonetheless, it has remained one of the most widely read novels of our time.

Camus had answered these objections for himself. He had carefully chosen his terrain: the atmosphere of collective suffering, the inner tensions, the gradual snuffing out of individual aspirations, the sense of impotence and frustration. He was dealing with a struggle in which he had proved his own capacity for action, recording rather the price paid in the process. It was not the black and white, the right and wrong of world war, political parties, and their ethics that he wanted to describe and endorse; heroic postures seemed to him irrelevant and inappropriate in the impersonal atmosphere of modern warfare.

Against the terrifying description of the rise, rule, and decline of the plague, what he threw into the balance may seem flimsy: the stubborn, weary, unglamorous struggle of a few men; the deep joy of a night swim outside a pestilence-ridden city. It was a confession, Camus said, but also the creation of a counterimage to liberate him from the grip of his experience—perhaps, too, the book worked to tunnel a way out for others as deeply oppressed as himself. In response to the great plumes of smoke rising from the collective funeral pyres, the inner flame of comradeship rises in the service of human survival, marking the limits of the plague's dehumanizing power.

*The Plague* develops at an even tempo, relentlessly, in five parts, each concerned with a certain phase in an overall movement. The narrator first evokes an everyday existence that the plague, remorseless and compelling, transforms into a fantastic, visionary hell. Each phase in the siege of the city has a countertheme: the muffled orchestration of human voices exchanging views, attempting to elucidate a position with regard to the unthinkable reality. Rieux, Tarrou, Rambert, Grand, Paneloux, and Cottard propose variations of the human answer to the plague, their voices as persistent as the whistling of the scourge over the sun-baked city. What perhaps explains the impact of this most widely read of Camus's works, despite the critics, is the eerie blend of stark realism and poetic vision that characterizes it. A gloomy but courageous book, *The Plague* was an effort in detachment from the tangle of historical and sociological interpretation, so that the reader could be made aware of the affective impact of the experience on the behavior of a social group and of the appalling power of the revelation of the scourge itself.

*State of Siege,* a play Camus wrote in collaboration with Jean-Louis Barrault (who staged it), is a kind of exuberant final exorcism. Camus attempted to give it an epic quality, using a medley of music, mime, and dance. Unsuccessful, so far, at least in performance, the play expresses the great burst of joy and hope that came with the Liberation. Simone de Beauvoir's *La force des choses* (*Force of Circumstance,* 1963) shows how widely this hope and exaltation were shared by other intellectuals. *The Just Assassins* and *The Rebel* now completed an itinerary that had led Camus gradually to counterbalance the constricting demands for public commitments by a new affirmation of *joie de vivre* as the source that he could no longer deny of hope and creativity.

*The Rebel.* In much the same way as *The Myth of Sisyphus* had posed the problem of suicide in order to conclude with a "lucid invitation to live and create," *The Rebel* posed the question of "logical," "legalized," ideologically justified murder in order to conclude with a leap of faith, expressing belief in the value of free, affirmative, individual creativity in the present-day world as it is, "beyond nihilism." But in the politically charged atmosphere of literary Paris in the early 1950's, the book had unforeseen and, viewed from the outside, inexplicable repercussions. The violence of the militant Communist press is hard to take seriously. *The Rebel* was denounced as an "ignoble" book whose purpose was to "justify anti-Communist repression, anti-Soviet war, and the assassination of the leaders of the proletariat." In the ever more "committed" *Les temps modernes,* Sartre's periodical, Camus was soundly taken to task by one of Sartre's then-close friends, Francis Jeanson, sparking a bitter dispute such as periodically shakes the French literary world.

Clearly Camus had touched on a burning issue. Yet he claimed that his essay was a personal exploration in impersonal form of the implications of tendencies apparent in an intellectual climate that was carefully situated in postwar Europe. He presented it as an attempt to clarify his own position in order, "the world being what it is, to know how to live in it." It would be idle to summarize the movement of the essay, entirely directed toward the exposure of the paradox whereby revolt in the name of freedom and justice, a generous, creative, and Promethean impulse, flounders and collapses in police states, Prometheus ending inevitably as Caesar. Whatever the alleged shortcomings of Camus's documentation and point of view, the fact remains that all of his opponents saw his essay as a direct attack on Stalinist Russia and the reduction of the Marxist credo to, in Camus's own words, "a gigantic myth." This no doubt was the case, but only within the framework of one of Camus's persistent themes, the equivocal dynamism whereby, in the human mind, aspirations are rationalized into logical imperatives and then used as justifications for a machinery of action that brooks no opposition: a catastrophic dialectic. With *The Rebel,* Camus was merely carrying this view into the realm of political ideology and action. The more specific criticism of the Marxist "leap," its consequent justification of the means by a hypothetical end, disguised as inevitable, predictable, and concrete—though it could hardly be missed—was a secondary, not a primary, objective. Recently the question of Camus's significance as a thinker, long downplayed by his critics, has begun to be reconsidered. In relation to a general investigation of the function and formal characteristics of the essay in the movement of literature, Édouard Morot-Sir, in *Lettres modernes,* vol. 12 (1985), has detected in *The Rebel* an innovative and modern epistemology.

*The Just Assassins.* Produced in 1949, *The Just Assassins* had created no such stir, yet the themes and conflicts of the play are organically linked to the essay. In those years, justice in relation to politics was a live issue. For Camus it was a disturbing issue that the Liberation and the Stalinist repression in Russia had posed in all its ambiguity. Once again he used the theater to explore the problem—to illuminate it from within, as a problem that by now permeates our society. The play is a dramatization of the tragic human dilemma lived by terrorists, whose actions are motivated by a deep revulsion to blatant social injustice as well as by a hopelessness in regard to the power structure's ability to deal with it.

An austere play, *The Just Assassins* borrows its cast and external design from the history of a small terrorist group who in 1905 had assassinated the Grand Duke Sergei, Russian Minister of Justice. Camus unified the action by dramatizing the internal conflicts and tragic repercussions the assassination itself seems to have created in the tightly knit group of terrorists. The play concentrates on the tragic awareness of the two idealistic central figures, Kalayiev, the thrower of the bomb, and Dora, in love with him. The play, begun in a climate of eager heroism, ends in a disturbing atmosphere of ambiguity and doubt. It has no thesis; it merely shows the irreconcilable disparity between the generous initial impulse, its ideological justification, and the suffering endured by the flesh-and-blood people involved in an act like Kalayiev's. Kalayiev and Dora confront the tragic paradox of their action in its unforeseen personal consequence, the mutilation of their lives. "Scrupulous murderers" in Camus's eyes, they reach the extreme limit of the permissible. The play, again, is a counterimage set up in protest against the vicious cycle of violence whereby complacent "bureaucratic" murderers engaged in mass repression set off the deadly mechanisms of terrorism.

*Camus as journalist.* In the four years between the Nazi victory over France and the liberation of Paris, Camus's activity as journalist was of necessity minimal. From 1944 on, as communications were reestablished and his reputation grew, articles, interviews, and lectures followed one another in quick succession; transient and scattered as such "occasional" texts are bound to be, they were eventually collected in three volumes entitled *Actuelles: Chroniques* (1950, 1953, 1958). These volumes cover, with some overlap, the period between 1944 and 1958. Only a few of these texts have been translated into English. "Actuelles," "Chronicles"—the title designates their function: they are records of contemporary historical events as lived, day by day, by the chronicler-witness Albert Camus.

Like his early articles, these pieces might be described as "fragments of a combat" fought against the fast-changing historical events of the day. But the freewheeling irony and verbal play of the brash young reporter of the prewar days have all but disappeared here. Events were not reassuring: the concentration camps, the atomic bomb, the Berlin Wall; the spread of Soviet power in Eastern Europe, the Korean war, the Algerian war, and the bitter polemics those conflicts generated.

These articles and a number of occasional speeches highlight the writer's basic concerns and are closely linked to his creative work. The texts most often discussed are the Algerian chronicles that punctuate the rapidly deteriorating Algerian situation from 1945 to 1958. They give us many insights into the genesis of Camus's more specific literary work. Camus's detractors have criticized what they call his moralism, and it is true that from article to broader reportage, to lecture or debate, Camus raises the same basic question, the relation of collective to individual morality, a question that—almost a half century later—is one of the crucial issues of the times. In disagreement with critics such as Conor Cruise O'Brien and Simone de Beauvoir, who see in these pieces (the Algerian group more particularly) little more than the hollow rhetoric of abstract moralism, Michael Walzer writes in "Commitment and Social Criticism: Camus's Algerian War":

> Rereading *Actuelles III* . . . it is hard to see the bad faith. Moral anxiety lies right on the surface of the reprinted articles and speeches; universalism and particularism, justice and love, are equally in evidence; nothing is concealed. These are essays in negotiation, the work of a social critic continually aware of the on-the-ground obstacles that the map of right and wrong only inadequately represents.
>
> (*Dissent* 31:425 [Fall 1984])

Camus was antidogmatic and opposed to a rhetoric that defined political solutions only in terms of confrontation, of right versus wrong. He sought other alternatives: conciliation via some form of negotiation. He had hoped that France and Algeria might have avoided the appalling seven and a half years of war with its escalating cycle of vicious terrorism and repression. "By the end of the war," writes David Caute in his *Frantz Fanon,* "the FLN [Algerian Liberation Front] estimated Algerian deaths, including victims of starvation, at over one million out of a population of nine million." The majority of Europeans fled, and by the end of 1962 Algerian industry was at a standstill: two million were unemployed, and four million others were declared "without means of subsistence"; the Algerian government had no alternative but to remain dependent upon French financial and technical aid. And, in fact, peace was brought about in 1962 not by a military victory but by careful negotiations and mutual concessions. As Camus had foreseen, France and Algeria would remain closely bound by economic and cultural ties. Perhaps, as Walzer notes, even though Camus described his reports as "the record of a failure," "that is not to say that he was wrong to try."

### *New Thresholds*

"There are writers, it seems to me," Camus once remarked, "whose works form a whole, each throwing light on the others, and which all look toward one another." Critics accustomed to viewing a writer's work chronologically and seeking to draw simple connections between the writer's "real" world and his imaginary world have often failed to take into account Camus's experiments with simultaneous but separate modes of elaboration of coexistent contradictory moods or drives. The recognition of these contradictory impulses and their inclusion within configurations transcending the previously sacrosanct concepts of unity and noncontradiction define, in Édouard Morot-Sir's analysis of the rhetoric of *The Rebel,* Camus's break with obsolete rules of unilinear discourse. When, in 1952, Camus spoke of the correlation between all his works, he was drawing attention to a pattern clearly present from the start within any one work and from work to work. Indeed, the workaday world of *The Right and the Wrong Side,* the lyrical celebration of the Mediterranean earth in *Nuptials,* and Mersault's itinerary and human relationships in *A Happy Death* are textual projections of a complex experience of reality, no aspect of which excludes the others. Their juxtaposition signals to the reader how resistant experience can be to the exigencies of language, which can never circumscribe it in its entirety. That in the 1950's Camus's life was overshadowed by personal and political events has been underscored. But little attention has been given to the essays collected in *Summer.* "La mer au plus près" ("The Sea Close By"), with its intimations of new departures and vast horizons, counters the darker shades of Camus's writing in the 1950's, with its powerful interweaving of dream and desire:

> At midnight alone on the shore. A moment more, and I shall set sail. The sky itself has weighed anchor, with all its stars like the ships covered with lights which at this very hour throughout the world illuminate dark harbours. Space and silence weigh equally upon the heart. . . . I have always felt I lived on the high seas, threatened, at the heart of a royal happiness.
>
> (*Lyrical and Critical Essays,* p.181)

In the last years of his life, Camus was, it seems, feeling his way toward a work that would encompass more fully in a single structure the contradictory, conflicting "intimations" concerning human life with which human beings live.

More deeply than *The Rebel, The Just Assassins* had underscored the basic theme of the Promethean cycle: the extreme predicament of the artist faced with extreme injustice. What Kalayiev and Dora eventually lose is their flesh-and-blood vitality, the richness of their sensuous relation to the world, to one another. It is the poet who dies, and with him Dora's power to love. With the creation of Kalayiev, Camus was laying aside the heroic romanticism of the war, freeing himself from the obsession with political responsibility that had been characteristic of the Resistance years. The secret inner itinerary he had been following can be traced in those eight lyrical essays, written between 1939 and 1953, that he collected in *Summer.* They revolve around a few central images woven into the fabric of his language: the sea, the desert, the "immense African nights," the "black, buried sun" burning at the heart of the artist's work. Thematically, the essays show an ever more persistent emphasis on beauty, happiness, art; on light as opposed to darkness, night as opposed to black despair; on the great sweep and freedom of the sea as opposed to the closed prisons of men. These themes express an increasingly confident joy in life and serve to qualify the somber atmosphere of the Promethean cycle. That the artist cannot serve the political designs of those who "make" history was by now Camus's firm conviction. He had come to terms with the problem of Sartrean sociopolitical "commitment"; now he was definitely committed to the difficult path of individual integrity, free from doctrinaire imperatives. But before he moved to more personal concerns, Camus fired a parting shot. With *The Fall* he unleashed that most histrionic, equivocal, and sardonic of creatures, Jean-Baptiste Clamence, self-appointed "judge-penitent," "hero of our time," and any conscious man's double.

*The Fall.* Jean-Baptiste Clamence is not an individual but a voice, reminiscent of the demon who spoke with Ivan Karamazov and the one who reveled in Job's torment. *The Fall* is a short novel in the form of an impassioned monologue or "implied dialogue," such as that used by Feodor Dostoevsky in his *Notes from the Underground* (1864) and James Hogg in *Private Memoirs and Confessions of a Justified Sinner* (1824). The speaker is a seedy lawyer who encounters his silent interlocutor in a bar in Holland. Clamence's inspired rhetoric, disguised as a confession, spirals around his interlocutor, apparently at random. But it has design and derives its momentum from a secret, fixed, inner purpose. The patterning of the disconnected facts revealed by Clamence in his specious confession gives *The Fall* the appearance of an irrefutable demonstration, but one whose conclusion is always elided. Clamence's "fall," or so he insinuates, is linked to a leap that he failed to make, a leap over a bridge to save a slim girl in black.

A perfect individual according to the generally accepted nineteenth-century bourgeois ideal, Clamence, one night hearing laughter that rings sardonically behind him, discovers the delights of self-questioning, anxiety, and then guilt. So he runs the full gamut of twentieth-century consciousness, eagerly examining his most ordinary gestures, carrying even further the disintegration of his formerly "noble image" of himself. Vanity, insincerity, and eroticism finally lead through a variety of sins to sacrilege. And all lead back to one reiterated proposition: self-knowledge leads to the contempt of self, and of all men. Carefully selecting his data, Clamence repeatedly follows through to the brink of his indictment and stops, leaving it to the interlocutor to leap, to admit that there is only one remedy to personal perversity—the abdication of freedom. Clamence, fully enjoying his shame, will never leap; he is the Saint John the Baptist of an anti-Enlightment.

The diversity of interpretations proposed for *The Fall* underscores its ambiguity. It has been read as an admission of guilt on Camus's part, as a retraction of his former statements, more particularly in *The Stranger.* Yet the satiric, diabolical figure of Clamence hardly seems to warrant so flat a reading. As we leave the judge-pentitent shivering with fever on his bed, in solitary tête-à-tête with a stolen painting, *The Just Judges* (a panel of van Eyck's *Adoration of the Lamb*), we would be hard put to think of him as a "straight" character. A virtuoso with words, a consummate actor, aggressive, fawning, sure of his ultimate mastery, Jean-Baptiste Clamence is in truth the inspired perpetrator of a colossal fraud; and he is also a man frustrated, shut in upon himself, who cannot break the charmed circle of his isolation. The caricature of the artist as Camus conceived him, a caricature and a perversion, Clamence reveals at last his basic impulse toward self-destruction. Clamence, as Camus indicated, is an "aggregate of the vices of our time," and Camus has fused them all into his hero's fraudulently disguised project.

Perhaps, as it has been suggested, Camus was expulsing Clamence from himself, or attempting to counter the image of himself as a "good man." But these seem banal and very partial explanations. There is something gleefully Swiftian about *The Fall* that savors of vengeance. The battle of *The Rebel* was not far distant, nor were the bitter polemics with Sartre. Even the writing and method of exposition in *The Fall* take on the semblance of the Sartrean dialectic. And there are closer connections. In 1952, Sartre had published his extensive psychoanalytical work on Jean Genet, *Saint Genet, comédien et martyr* (*Saint Genet, Actor and Martyr*)—a characterization that fit Jean-Baptiste Clamence perfectly. A thief and jailbird, and a writer to boot, Genet, Sartre suggested, is a kind of scapegoat, virtually thrown out of the city walls with the secret evils of society magically heaped upon him; it is a thoroughly Sartrean interpretation. Genet became thereby, in Sartre's eye, "one of the heroes of our time," in fact an image and symbol of what we are fated to be, denizens of an impotent society, incapable of "the leap" that would put us on the "right side" of history. Clamence's hollow voice seems curiously to echo Sartre's as Camus leaves him in his rhetorically built "cell of little ease," on the brink of a leap he will never take, free to accumulate the sterile guilt with which he inoculates others.

Whatever the "figure in the carpet," *The Fall* revealed new potentialities, perhaps even to Camus himself. A short novel like *The Stranger,* it had originally been designed as one of a series of short stories that Camus had begun to work on.

*Exile and the Kingdom and The Possessed.* The six short stories of *Exile and the Kingdom* present considerable variety in theme and form, from the quasi naturalism of "L'Hôte" ("The Host") to the elusive symbolism of "La pierre qui pousse" ("The Growing Stone") and the allegorical suggestiveness of "Le renégat" ("The Renegade"). In each story a situation is carefully delineated in concrete terms and presented with apparently complete objectivity and great attention to plausibility. The situations are potentially dramatic and build up to a crucial moment of decision, free and open in its possibility. An insight is reached, experienced, and acted upon—though not verbalized. The resolution turns on a simple impulse, a movement toward greater understanding that casts an aura of nobility on the quite ordinary protagonists. The impulse that "goes wrong" and eventually ends in disaster—so fundamental a theme of Camus's previous work—is fashioned only in "The Renegade," a monologue and lament closely related to *The Fall.* "Jonas; ou, L'Artiste au travail" ("Jonas, or, The Artist at Work"), in contrast, is an ironic variation on the theme of the artist as scapegoat. The painter Jonas, a public figure besieged on all sides by obligations, finally takes refuge in a hideout, where one day he collapses, leaving a single unfinished word scrawled across his empty canvas. Whether the word is "solitude" or "solidarity," who can tell? Somewhere between these two conflicting exigencies, the modern artist has to find his equilibrium. The story is an ironic commentary on one of the most crucial problems of Camus's own existence, one that was operative even in his death; but yet it touches on a fundamental theme: life as a perpetual act of equilibrium between extremes.

It would be impossible to read Camus without noting the prominent place of Algeria in his work. After *The Stranger,* a number of works—*The Plague,* the lyrical essays, and four of the five other short stories of *Exile and the Kingdom*—are set in Algeria, and it is from the use Camus makes of the Algerian landscapes, its coast, its high plateaus, its oases, that they draw their power. The characters are humble people: Janine, a middle-aged woman, travelling with her husband Marcel from the coast to the oases of the south, to seek new opportunities in their small dry-goods business, now suffering from the post–World War II economic slump; the "renegade," originally a peasant from the harsh Massif Central in France; Yvars, an employee in a small cooper's shop in Algiers; Daru, a schoolmaster in an isolated school on the high plateaus. It would be idle to try to analyze these stories or point to their "meaning." Numerous, varied, and often contradictory decodings have been suggested in each case, particularly for the last story, that of d'Arrast, a French engineer in Brazil who is commissioned to build a barrage against the seasonal flooding of estuary lands. The title of each story, like the diversity of the narrative techniques, situations, and *décors,* points to underlying meanings that are never proffered. But it is clear that each adventure is lived from within an initial "climate," a closed world of feeling, which breaks down under the impact of unexpected circumstances. The individual then once again faces life in all its ambiguity. "Symbolic," some critics have suggested; "allegorical," others have said; yet others have spoken of "parables." The metaphors of the overall title *Exile and the Kingdom* are familiar ones, suggesting a close interweaving of joy and suffering in human experience, neither excluding the other. What perspective this title opens on each story and finally onto the volume considered as a unity are questions that are still being widely discussed. *Exile and the Kingdom* is proving to be one of the most resilient of Camus's works.

After *Exile and the Kingdom* only one more work is crucial—*Les possédés* (1959), the stage adaptation of Dostoevsky's *The Possessed,* a novel that had deeply impressed itself on Camus's imagination when he read it as a youth. Dostoevsky's restless cast of men driven by a passion for destruction—"possessed"—are the very embodiment of the enemy Camus had been fighting. This enemy Dostoevsky had defined as "the spirit of negation and death" in all its forms and varieties, from the most frivolous to the most insidious, compounded in the mysterious figure of Stavrogin, on whose secret crime, evolution, and fate Camus centered his play. Moving from "satirical comedy, to drama, to tragedy," Camus's adaptation sets up as a counterimage to the "dead souls" of the nihilists, the poignancy of human love, manifest in Chatov, the victim of a senseless murder. *The Possessed* is a synthesis, a grand orchestration of Camus's previous work, a kind of catharsis before Camus's move to a projected new cycle with *Le premier homme,* a cycle dealing with "a certain kind of love" that the car accident on the road to Paris was to cut short.

Camus's work shows a marked inner coherence and unity. He is not a wide-ranging writer, drawing his power rather from deliberate self-limitation. Like most of his contemporaries, he gave much thought to the relationship between art and the specific circumstances, social and historical, in which he found himself, and to what might truly characterize the modern consciousness. He thereby touched upon some of the crucial issues of the period—in politics, philosophy, and religion.

In his own daily living, in the decisions he made and the actions he carried out, he attempted to achieve and maintain some kind of balance between thought and act, a difficult enterprise that he considered with a rather wry and ironic stoicism. In public affairs he was heir to the reasoned though qualified optimism of the Enlightenment and was opposed to any fanatical cult, whether of the rational or the irrational. He was an advocate of "dialogue," of the open mind and the scrupulous act. He shared with the existentialist philosophers a sense of the contingency of human life and the gratuitous nature of human aspirations and values. But he accepted the situation as fundamental, man as present with his characteristics and limitations. "The absurd" and "revolt" are the two terms he chose for expressing the insoluble paradox of the human situation as he saw it. It was not his purpose to conclude, expound, or dictate, but to live and to write. He was not, he claimed, a philosopher, but an artist. His essays merely define the self-chosen limits of his art. In his 1954 preface to the reissue of his first book of essays, *The Wrong Side and the Right Side,* he compared the artist's career to a tightrope walker's performance—a traditional image that illustrates the aesthetic urge to achieve an apparently harmonious equilibrium by a hard-won control over conflicting forces. Some of the disruptive forces at work at mid century were ostensibly social; but there were, too, personal disruptive impulses in Camus's own personality that furnished the more fundamental substance for his art: the Meursault-like urge to give free rein to a sensuous enjoyment of life, indifferent to the rest; and the equally strong urge to achieve a Caligula-like nihilism in lucidity. To keep both impulses in check, without plunging into one extreme or the other, Camus needed his art. His often-repeated statement that he could not live without it is not merely rhetorical. It also explains each work's ambiguity. Camus is never absent from his work, nor is he on one side or the other in conflicts he describes; he is affiliated with all his characters, examining and recognizing them all. But only with *Exile and the Kingdom* does he seem to have replaced the ultimate criticism and rejection of his "impossible" characters by the creation of "possible" and acceptable ones. Camus's rejection of extremes, in an age given to excesses, is a powerful factor of originality.

His work clearly belongs to one of the main currents of modern Western literature, which he himself has designated by his references to Melville, Dostoevsky, Proust, and Kafka. For these writers, the external patterns of the narrative, concrete and specific, lead to a central inner meaning, which initially organized them. Camus's narratives and plays combine a surface simplicity and apparent realism with a consistent design. The titles he gives his works, some of which have biblical echoes, all have a concealed relation to the theme developed therein. Camus's intent, like those of the writers to whom he refers, is carefully delineated through fiction and by means of situations and characters to illuminate an aspect of experience, an illumination that is *experienced* within the narrative and not demonstrated. The integrity of the work and its force of conviction depended, Camus felt, on the artist's effort to "sacrifice" nothing. Hence Camus's power to reach his readers, even if such concepts as "the absurd" and "revolt" seem to some unpersuasive.

What characterizes his own techniques as a writer is formal control, a natural consequence of his preference for the Greek ideal of beauty, an effect, too, of his fierce drive for coherence. The clarity of outline, the sharpness and precision of the details observed, the overall effect of detached objectivity transmit a sense of formality, even of constraint, that runs counter to the more powerful trends in contemporary art. The human content and significance run counter to others in that they are more abstract.

The recurrence of images, figures, themes, and patterns within each work and from one work to another; the rhetorical texture of the language, its range of tempo and rhythm—these give Camus's writing an enigmatic intensity, in direct relation to the restraint he imposed on his expression. The limitations inherent in this combination of clarity and controlled design very much concerned Camus. He wanted to overcome them, envisaging for the future a greater freedom of expression. But he belongs to the tradition of conscious thinking and hard discipline in art. His control of his medium, coupled with his conception of art as the illumination of an individual experience that has been communicated and universalized, sometimes pushed the work to the border of parable. Wherever the tension in the quality of Camus's writing slackens and rigor of thought shades off into truism, or emotion into pathos, a certain moralism tends to overshadow the deeper underlying theme. This occurs more particularly in the works of the Promethean cycle, which deals with conflicts that were less deeply rooted in Camus's own complex personality and in fact were hostile to what he felt impelled to say. Camus defined his own realm quite early and explored it with sustained intellectual and artistic integrity, thus achieving a difficult balance between the erotic and the critical, between the solitude of the self and the claims of society. There are, of course, other works, other expressions just as valid as his, but his writing seems to have the decisive resonance that we associate with durable works of literature.

## Selected Bibliography


### EDITIONS

#### INDIVIDUAL WORKS

FICTION

*L'Étranger.* Paris, 1942.
*La peste.* Paris, 1947.
*La chute.* Paris, 1956.
*L'Exil et le royaume.* Paris, 1957.
*La mort heureuse.* Paris, 1971.

PLAYS

*Caligula.* Paris, 1944.
*Le malentendu.* Paris, 1944.
*L'État de siège.* Paris, 1948.
*Les justes.* Paris, 1949.
*Les possédés.* Paris, 1959.
*Caligula.* (1941 version.) Paris, 1984.

ESSAYS

*L'Envers et l'endroit.* Paris, 1937.
*Noces.* Paris, 1939.
*Le mythe de Sisyphe.* Paris, 1943.
*Actuelles I: Chroniques, 1944–1948.* Paris, 1950.
*L'Homme révolté.* Paris, 1951.
*Actuelles II; Chroniques, 1948–1953.* Paris, 1953.
*L'Été.* Paris, 1954.
*Actuelles III: Chronique algérienne.* Paris, 1958.
*Écrits de jeunesse.* Paris, 1973.
*Fragments d'un combat.* Paris, 1978.
*Journaux de voyage.* Paris, 1978.

#### COLLECTED WORKS

*Carnets, 1939–1958.* 2 vols. Paris, 1962, 1964.
*Théâtre, récits, nouvelles.* Edited by Roger Quillot. Paris, 1962.
*Essais.* Edited by Roger Quillot and Louis Faucon. Paris, 1965.

### TRANSLATIONS

*Albert Camus: The Essential Writings.* Edited with interpretive essays by Robert E. Meagher. New York, 1979.
*Caligula and Three Other Plays: The Misunderstanding, The Just Assassins, State of Siege.* Translated by Stuart Gilbert. New York, 1958.
*Exile and the Kingdom.* Translated by Justin O'Brien. New York, 1958.
*The Fall.* Translated by Justin O'Brien. New York, 1957.
*A Happy Death.* Translated by Richard Howard. New York, 1972.
*Lyrical and Critical Essays.* Translated by Ellen Conroy Kennedy. New York, 1968.
*The Myth of Sisyphus and Other Essays.* Translated by Justin O'Brien. New York, 1955.
*Neither Victims nor Executioners.* Translated by Dwight Macdonald. Berkeley, Calif., 1968.
*Notebooks 1935–1942.* Translated by Philip Thody. New York, 1963.
*Notebooks 1942–1951.* Translated by Justin O'Brien. New York, 1965.
*The Plague.* Translated by Stuart Gilbert. New York, 1948.
*The Possessed.* Translated by Justin O'Brien. New York, 1960.
*The Rebel.* Translated by Anthony Bower. New York, 1954.
*Resistance, Rebellion, and Death.* Translated by Justin O'Brien. New York, 1961.
*The Stranger.* Translated by Stuart Gilbert. New York, 1946.
*Youthful Writings.* Translated by Ellen Conroy Kennedy. New York, 1976.

### BIOGRAPHICAL AND CRITICAL STUDIES

*À Albert Camus, ses amis du livre.* Paris, 1962.
Brée, Germaine. *Camus.* Rutgers, N.J., 1959.
———. *Camus and Sartre: Crisis and Commitment.* New York, 1972.
Brisville, Jean-Claude. *Camus.* Paris, 1950.
Coombs, Ilone. *Camus, homme de théâtre.* Paris, 1968.
Costes, Alain. *Albert Camus et la parole manquante.* Paris, 1973.
Cruikshank, John. *Albert Camus and the Literature of Revolt.* New York, 1959.
Gay-Crosier, Raymond. *Les envers d'un échec: Étude sur le théâtre d'Albert Camus.* Paris, 1967.
———. ed. *Camus 1980.* Gainesville, Fla., 1980.
Grenier, Jean. *Albert Camus: Souvenirs.* Paris, 1968.
Lazere, Donald. *The Unique Creation of Albert Camus.* New Haven, Conn., 1973.

Lottman, Herbert R. *Albert Camus: A Biography.* Garden City, N.Y., 1979.

McCarthy, Patrick. *Camus.* New York, 1982.

Onimus, Jean. *Camus.* Bruges, 1965.

Parker, Emmett. *Albert Camus: The Artist in the Arena.* Madison, Wis., 1965.

Quillot, Roger. *The Sea and Prisons: A Commentary on the Life and Thought of Albert Camus.* Translated by Emmett Parker. University, Ala., 1970.

Rizzuto, Anthony. *Camus' Imperial Vision.* Carbondale, Ill., 1981.

Sarocchi, Jean. *Camus.* Paris, 1968.

Sprintzen, David. *Camus: A Critical Examination.* Philadelphia, 1988.

Sutter, Judith D., ed. *Essays on Camus's Exile and the Kingdom.* University, Miss., 1981.

Tarrow, Susan. *Exile from the Kingdom: A Political Rereading of Albert Camus.* University, Ala., 1985.

Thody, Philip. *Albert Camus.* New York, 1962.

Treil, Claude. *L'Indifférence dans l'oeuvre d'Albert Camus.* Montreal, 1971.

Weis, Marcia. *The Lyrical Essays of Albert Camus.* Ottawa, 1976.

Willhoite, Fred H. *Beyond Nihilism: Albert Camus' Contribution to Political Thought.* Baton Rouge, La., 1968.

## BIBLIOGRAPHY

A bibliography of writings on Camus would fill a volume. For a bibliography of Camus criticism, see *Albert Camus,* edited by Brian T. Fitch and Peter C. Hoy (Paris, 1972). This list has been updated periodically in Peter C. Hoy's *Carnet bibliographique* in the Albert Camus series of the *Revue des lettres modernes,* nos. 2–12 (Paris, 1968–).

GERMAINE BRÉE

# ROLAND BARTHES

## *(1915–1980)*

IN HIS EXCELLENT short book on Roland Barthes, Jonathan Culler writes:

> When Roland Barthes died in 1980 at the age of sixty-five, he was a professor at the Collège de France, the highest position in the French academic system. He had become famous for incisive and irreverent analyses of French culture but was now himself a cultural institution. His lectures attracted huge, diverse crowds, from foreign tourists and retired schoolteachers to eminent academics. . . . Outside France, Barthes seemed to have succeeded Sartre as the leading French intellectual.
>
> (*Roland Barthes,* p. 9)

Like Sartre before him, Barthes, a literary man, acquired a fame that in countries other than France is accorded only to motion picture stars and sports figures. He first became widely known as one of a number of innovative thinkers grouped together under the name of structuralism. Structuralism, which dominated French intellectual life in the 1960's, was a many-sided movement; however, all the structuralists working in France during this period acknowledged certain common influences. They all drew ideas from Marxism and from psychoanalysis; indeed, their work changed psychoanalysis from a minor to a major enterprise on the French intellectual scene. In addition, linguistic analysis was of primary importance to all of them. They drew much of their methodology from the linguistics of Ferdinand de Saussure, a Swiss linguist whose *Cours de linguistique générale* (*Course in General Linguistics,* 1916) was decisively important in the founding of modern linguistics.

The leaders of the movement were Claude Lévi-Strauss in anthropology, Jacques Lacan in psychoanalysis, Michel Foucault in history and the structure of knowledge, and Barthes in literary criticism and the analysis of contemporary cultural artifacts. The work of this group, and of younger associates such as Jacques Derrida and Julia Kristeva, has been a dominant force in French intellectual life since the 1960's. Their theoretical and critical work has attracted more attention than the traditionally "creative" work going on in poetry, the novel, and drama.

These writers have produced books on such obscure subjects as semiology, kinship systems, and the rise of the medical clinic; their prose systematically and on principle is an attack on classical ideals of clarity and completeness. They wanted to disrupt the compact between the reader and the writer imposed by traditional French prose—to disallow appeals to common sense and received ideas about what constitutes "the natural order of things." As a result, these authors have often been charged with being unreadable. Their writings are full of neologisms, inconclusive, fragmented, abstract, and outrageous to good taste and common sense. In short, like many avant-garde works of the twentieth century, these structuralist works are hard on the reader, exploding received ideas into unrecognizable fragments and willfully disappointing stylistic and logical expectations.

Yet structuralist works have an intellectual vigor and excitement, a bravura and air of adventure that has brought them readers and acclaim. Initially these writers may have been read because of the intellectual scandals they were so adept at creating, but the range and power of their speculative thought have continued to attract readers even after they have ceased to provoke fashionable excitement.

Barthes, in particular, has been growing in popularity since his death, not despite the oddity of his style but because of it, and perhaps because of his fundamentally aesthetic attitude toward the various theoretical languages available to him. Helen Vendler puts the matter thus in speaking of Barthes's prose:

> That texture—delightful to many of us—is composed of the mutual jostling of many (often mutually incompatible) registers of discourse. Linguistics, literature, philosophy, anthropology, mythology, art history, economics, politics, information theory, psychoanalysis, sociology, history, semantics, Marxism—these are only the commonest of the many categories that organize Barthes' thinking. Insofar as Barthes' medley is his message, one can say he exemplifies his own definition of a human person—a consciousness constituted by the available languages of its social and historical era. . . . The play of differences is for Barthes the definition of linguistic Utopia.
>
> ("The Medley Is the Message," *New York Review of Books,* 33: [8 May 1986])

To arrive at this extraordinary position as a kind of living summa of modern culture, Barthes followed a familiar path for a French left-wing intellectual. After early years marred by comparative poverty and protracted illness, Barthes recovered to make his intellectual fortune by the time-honored route of opposition to the official canons of his culture. He went from being a marginal figure on the fringes of the French academic system to the ultimate academic prestige of a chair at the Collège de France.

Barthes's childhood and youth were characterized by experiences that often seem to go into the making of a writer: loneliness, genteel poverty, and illness. On 12 November 1915 Barthes was born into a middle-class Protestant family in Cherbourg, a small city on the Atlantic coast in northwestern France. A year later his father was killed in a naval battle in the North Sea, with the result that Barthes grew up without a father and his family had a much reduced income that left them close to poverty.

Sartre and Camus also lost their fathers early. They wrote at length about the impact of that loss on their lives, but Barthes, in contrast, has comparatively little to say about his fatherless state. Philip Thody summarizes two episodes that cast light on how Barthes made up for his half-orphaned condition:

> When, during his later schooldays at the Lycée Louis-le-Grand, in Paris, his form-master solemnly inscribed on the blackboard the names of the boys whose relatives had died for their country, Barthes felt no pride at being the only one able to claim a father. All he felt was an emptiness, a lack of social anchorage, the absence of a father whom he might, like Oedipus, oppose and kill—a frustration, in fact, as he later observed, at not being able to live out a Freudian childhood to the full. In an interview in 1973, however, he also made a remark which confirmed what critical readers of his work had long since suspected: that an Oedipus with no Laius to kill will invent one; and that in Barthes's case his Laius was what he calls the *Doxa,* the stifling set of received and ready-made opinions, of stereotypes and fixed ideas, that he sees as characterising the bourgeoisie.
>
> (*Roland Barthes: A Conservative Estimate,* p. 1)

Barthes spent his childhood in Bayonne with his mother and maternal grandmother; an aunt who gave piano lessons for a living taught him how to play, and he was composing short musical pieces before he learned how to read. In later life, he often returned to Bayonne to spend vacations with his provincial relatives. His ideological hostility to the bourgeoisie did not extend to his hometown or to members of his family.

When Barthes was nine, he, his mother, and his elder brother (mentioned only once in Barthes's writings) moved to Paris, where his mother supported the family by working as a bookbinder. They settled in the sixth arrondissement, where Barthes lived for the rest of his life. The loneliness of his early years there is beautifully rendered in a parenthetical sentence in *Fragments d'un discours amoureux* (*A Lover's Discourse: Fragments,* 1977): ". . . interminable days, abandoned days, when Mother was working far away; I would go, evenings, to wait for her at the U^bis bus stop, Sèvres-Babylone; the buses would pass one after the other, she wasn't in any of them." He did brilliantly in school until he had an attack of pulmonary tuberculosis in 1934 that left him unable to compete for entry into the École Normale Supérieure, which would virtually have assured him a privileged academic post. Instead he studied French, Greek, and Latin at the Sorbonne from 1935 to 1939 and helped found the Groupe de Théâtre Antique.

In 1937, Barthes was found unfit for military duty. After teaching at lycées in Biarritz and Paris for two years, he had a relapse of tuberculosis in 1941 and spent the years up to early 1947 in and out of sanatoriums. Thus Barthes was excluded from the decisive experience of his generation, participation in World War II. He had been brought up a Protestant in a Catholic country, he had not gotten the credentials that would have brought him a secure place in the university system, he was a (discreetly) avowed homosexual in a family-dominated culture. No wonder he asked ironically toward the end of his life, "Who does not feel how *natural* it is in France to be Catholic, married, and well qualified academically?"

Although he was not pronounced cured until 1947, Barthes was well enough to be able in 1942 to take his *licence* in grammar and philology and to publish his first essay in *Existences,* the review of the Sanatorium des Étudiants. Called "Note sur André Gide et son Journal" ("On Gide and His Journal"), the piece is a remarkable performance for a young man of twenty-seven just launching his career. In it, Barthes is already formed as a writer: he has found his literary voice—suggestive, resonant, polite, already showing a taste for unusual turns of thought and expression.

As the piece shows, Barthes was already strongly attracted to the fragmentary, an attraction that as his career progressed won out over his equally strong attraction to systematic discourse. He is fascinated by literary personality but also skeptical about it, half-convinced that there is no such entity, only a loose agglomeration of traits. He already recognizes his own skeptical, urbane, and above all paradoxical, cast of mind in Montaigne and Gide. The first paragraph reads:

> Reluctant to enclose Gide in a system I knew would never content me, I was vainly trying to find some connection among these notes. Finally I decided it would be better to offer them as such—notes—and not try to disguise their lack of continuity. Incoherence seems to me preferable to a distorting order.
>
> ("On Gide and His Journal," in *A Barthes Reader,* p. 3)

The discussion of Gide's criticism sounds uncannily like one part of Barthes's future strictures on his own writings:

> Gide's work is a net of which no mesh can be dropped. I believe it is quite futile to divide it up by chronological or methodological slices. It almost requires to be read in the fashion of certain Bibles, with a synoptic table of references, or even like those pages of the *Encylopedia* where marginal notes gave the text its explosive value. Gide is often his own scholiast. This was necessary in order to permit the work to retain its gratuitousness, its freedom. Gide's version of the work of art is deliberately evasive; it escapes—God be

> thanked—any annexation of parties or dogmas, even if they were revolutionary. . . . But from this to infer that Gide's *thought* is evasive is a mistake.
>
> (p.11)

While he was in the sanatorium from 1943 to 1945, Barthes spent several months in premedical study with the intention of becoming a psychiatrist. But when he returned as a convalescent to Paris, he published an essay in 1947 in *Combat* (a journal closely associated with Albert Camus) that later became the first part of his first book, *Le degré zéro de l'écriture* (*Writing Degree Zero,* 1953). From this point onward, Barthes without pause followed the career of a writer; he published steadily for the next quarter of a century, producing fourteen books and numerous essays, reviews, and interviews.

*Writing Degree Zero* was well received in France, and has been translated into more languages than any other book by Barthes: Spanish, Dutch, Japanese, Italian, Swedish, Czech, Portuguese, Catalan, German, and English. Although Barthes does not explicitly say so, Susan Sontag persuasively argues that the book is an answer to Sartre's *Qu'est-ce que la littérature?* (*What Is Literature?,* 1946). In that work Sartre argues for an engaged literature ethically sanctioned by the aim of bringing liberation to all people. He takes a relatively unsympathetic view of experimental and modernist writers who produce hermetic works of art directed at an elite audience. Sartre argues that "literature is in essence a taking of positions" and that "art has never been on the side of the purists."

Barthes's political position during this period was close to Sartre's, and he does not set out to refute Sartre's wealth of arguments; instead, he seeks to dissolve them in a more subtle and complex view of writing. To do this, in *Writing Degree Zero* Barthes introduces a threefold distinction. First there is language, which "enfolds the whole of literary creation" and is "unified and complete in the manner of a natural order." Language is social and historical. Style, on the other hand, turns away from the social and the historical toward the body and the biography of the writer; it reflects his peculiar bodily rhythms and his individual experiences. It is the "transmutation of a humor," private and personal. Neither language nor style, the first a "given" from history, the second a "given" from the body, is constitutive of a literary work.

A third term occupies a middle ground between language and style—*écriture.* By it, Barthes means personal utterance and the process of writing through which the writer shapes his work. It gives the writer his freedom and is responsible for "form considered as human intention." Thus *écriture* is the exercise of choice between two necessities, language and style, and the exercise of choice creates form, which makes it possible for a piece of discourse to be part of literature. (This three-part distinction is a precursor of later structural analysis.)

In the second part of *Writing Degree Zero,* Barthes proposes a very general historical scheme for understanding the varying fortunes of *écriture.* Until about 1650 there is

> a fairly lavish profusion of literary languages because men are still engaged in the task of getting to know Nature, and not yet in that of giving expression to man's essence. . . . This is what gives to this pre-classical writing the genuine appearance of many-sidedness, and the euphoria which comes from freedom.
>
> (p.55)

In addition, the French language had not yet "fully settled on the character of its syntax or the laws governing the increase of its vocabulary."

With the rise of the classical form of the French language, genuine diversity was virtually banished:

> The diversity of the "genres" and the varying rhythms of styles within the framework of classical dogma are aesthetic, not structural, data. . . .

> there was indeed one and only one mode of writing, both instrumental and ornamental, at the disposal of French society during the whole period when bourgeois ideology conquered and triumphed.
>
> (*Writing Degree Zero,* p. 56)

The function of this mode of writing is always rhetorical and instrumental—to persuade; it always bears the marks of its class origin; and it supposes itself to be the work of universal human reason expressing universal human nature.

This classical writing preserves its ascendancy until the revolution of 1848, which revealed that society was split into warring classes and also unmasked the class basis of classical writing. From Gustave Flaubert onward, writing becomes increasingly difficult and problematic. The writer may, like Camus in *L'Étranger* (*The Stranger,* 1942) attempt "white writing," that is, the scrupulous neutrality of "writing degree zero." Or he may resort to the "splendid but useless" language of the past. Hence the proliferation of the many modes of writing in modernism and the impossibility of a writing simply and unequivocally "engaged."

> Like modern art in its entirety, literary writing carries at the same time the alienation of History and the dream of History; as a Necessity, it testifies to the division of languages which is inseparable from the division of classes; as Freedom, it is the consciousness of this division and the very effort which seeks to surmount it.
>
> (*Writing Degree Zero,* pp. 87–88)

Sartre's call for a simple, urgent rhetorical style of persuasion is shown to be a historical impossibility. Modernism is not a mere bohemian caprice.

Barthes's first book, then, focuses on the interaction of language, style, history, and the act of writing (*écriture*). The choices of the writer are limited by his moment in history, and not all kinds of writing are available at all points in time. The work is a foreshadowing of the underlying concerns with language, art, and history that are evident beneath all the changes that occur as Barthes's work develops. Whatever his ostensible subject matter, language, art, and history are never far from his thoughts and they largely determine the direction of his arguments.

If *Writing Degree Zero* studies the impact of history on modes of writing, *Michelet par lui-même* (*Michelet,* 1954) studies the impact of Jules Michelet's "organized network of obsessions" on his historical writings. Possibly following some hints in Sartre's *L'Être et le néant* (*Being and Nothingness,* 1943) about "existential thematics," Barthes ignores Michelet's linear narrative and argumentative procedures and looks instead at his pervading metaphors to find the underlying themes of his work. Barthes says, "Take away his existential thematics, and all that is left of Michelet is a petit bourgeois." Michelet's ideas are said to be commonplaces, and his narrative power is insufficient to keep his work alive. Its vitality springs from his fascination with smoothness, fatness, appetite, and blood. Barthes says, "He reverted to the few essential movements of matter: liquefaction, stickiness, dryness, electricity."

From his study of Michelet's writings, Barthes concluded (to his critics, outrageously) that for Michelet

> femininity is therefore total only at the menstrual moment. Which is to say that love's object is less to possess Woman than to discover her. "Love's sharpest goad is not so much beauty as passion." Michelet's erotics evidently takes no account of the pleasures of orgasm, whereas it attributes a considerable importance to Woman in crisis, i.e., to Woman humiliated. This is an erotics of seeing, not of possession, and Michelet in love, Michelet fulfilled, is none other than Michelet-as-voyeur.
>
> (*Michelet,* pp. 149–150)

Barthes trusted the accuracy of his analysis of Michelet's work sufficiently to predict that

Michelet's then-unpublished *Journal* (written between 1820 and 1874, but published from 1959 to 1976) would bear witness to the truth of these speculations. The editors who were then preparing an edition of the *Journal* for publication wrote an essay for *Combat* showing that the *Journal* did in fact bear out Barthes's theory. Thus *Michelet* is a demonstration of the predictive powers of structural analysis, at least in one instance.

In addition to writing two books, during this period Barthes was becoming a well-established essayist for the literary press. From 1952 to 1959, he worked at the Centre National de Recherche Scientifique, doing research first in lexicology and then in sociology. These studies led to his famous series of "mythologies," essays of a few pages each in which he did witty analyses of contemporary "myths"—Garbo's face, Einstein's brain, wine and milk, wrestling, striptease, soap powders, and so on. Most of the essays originally appeared in *Les lettres nouvelles* and later in book form in 1957 under the title *Mythologies.*

In his studies of myth Barthes has nothing to say about the myths of primitive cultures; his are the myths found in newspaper stories, magazine articles, advertisements, photographs, cabarets, sports arenas. His main thesis, to which he returns again and again, is that myth always serves to transform history into "nature." An oft-cited example is a picture of a young black man on a cover of *Paris-Match.* He is dressed in a French military uniform and looking up while he salutes a French flag that is located outside the picture frame. The message of this image, Barthes says, is "that France is a great Empire, that all her sons, without any colour discrimination, faithfully serve under her flag, and that there is no better answer to the detractors of an alleged colonialism than the zeal shown by this Negro in serving his so-called oppressors." What inspires Barthes's "nausea" in such instances is the way myth tries to pass off political ideology as "natural," "obvious," and "what goes without saying."

Barthes does not think of myth as merely a strategy of bourgeois ideology. The Left, too, has its myths, and indeed mythologizing comes into play in any discourse where values are at stake. Myth is as inevitable as metaphor. What Barthes objects to is the effort to deny and conceal the mythologizing activity. He is under no illusion that it is possible to break out of artifice and return to some "natural" discourse. What he does call for, however, is the acknowledgment of artifice. He proposes as a way of overcoming the duplicity of myth the Cartesian formula "Larvatus prodeo" (I advance pointing to my mask). Myth acknowledged as myth loses its harmfulness (and perhaps most of its power?).

During this period Barthes also began to be known as an advocate for writers of the avant-garde. Of particular note are his writings on Alain Robbe-Grillet and Bertolt Brecht: his first essays on both were written in 1954 (these essays, along with many others, are collected in *Essais critiques* [*Critical Essays,* 1964]). Both writers helped him to define and extend his sense of what constituted an authentic modernist art.

Alain Robbe-Grillet's *Les gommes* (*The Erasers,* 1953), an early novel, attracted Barthes chiefly as a particular kind of "writing degree zero." The book confines itself to describing the visual surfaces of objects, refusing to seek their inner meaning, their significance for the characters, their place in the development of the plot. Robbe-Grillet was attempting to "erase" psychology, interiority, and story from the novel. In his essay "Littérature objective" ("Objective Literature," 1954) Barthes writes:

> This slice of tomato in an automat sandwich, described according to Robbe-Grillet's method, constitutes an object without heredity, without associations and without references, a stubborn object rigorously enclosed within the order of its particles, suggestive of nothing but itself, and not involving its reader in a functional or substantial *elsewhere.*
>
> (*Critical Essays,* p. 15)

Barthes is fascinated by Robbe-Grillet's (almost impossible) project of cleansing objects of their accumulated meanings and thus freeing them from traditional associations, from canons of bourgeois art and psychology, from all the trammels, in short, with which language has endowed them. As he writes in "Objective Literature":

> Robbe-Grillet's scrupulosity of description has nothing in common with the artisanal application of the naturalistic novelist. Traditional realism accumulates qualities as a function of an implicit judgment: its objects have shapes, but also odors, tactile properties, memories, analogies, in short they swarm with significations; they have a thousand modes of being perceived, and never with impunity, since they involve a human movement of disgust or appetite. Instead of this sensorial syncretism, at once anarchic and oriented, Robbe-Grillet imposes a unique order of apprehension: the sense of sight. The object is no longer a center of correspondences, a welter of sensations and symbols: it is merely an optical resistance.
>
> (*Critical Essays,* p. 14)

Barthes's motive for championing this flat, noncommittal mode of description is what he considers its power of disrupting our inherited way of turning all our experiences into "stories," of assuming that stories are the natural and inevitable way of organizing experience. In "Littérature littérale" ("Literal Literature," 1955) Barthes notes:

> A story . . . is a typical product of our civilizations of the soul. Consider Ombredane's ethnological experiment: the film *Underwater Hunt* is shown to black students in the Congo and to Belgian students; the former offer a purely descriptive summary of what they have seen, precise, concrete, without *affabulation;* the latter, on the contrary, betray a great visual indigence, they have difficulty recalling details, they make up a story, seek certain literary effects, try to produce affective states. It is precisely this spontaneous birth of drama which Robbe-Grillet's optical system aborts at each moment.
>
> (*Critical Essays,* pp. 52–53)

By 1962, Barthes's views on Robbe-Grillet had been modified. *L'Année dernière à Marienbad (Last Year at Marienbad*), a film for which Robbe-Grillet wrote the script, appeared in 1961 and provoked a major outbreak of interpretations from puzzled critics. There are now *two* Robbe-Grillets, as Barthes suggests in "Le point sur Robbe-Grillet?" ("The Last Word on Robbe-Grillet?"): "on the one hand the Robbe-Grillet of immediate things, destroyer of meaning, sketched chiefly by the earlier criticism; and the other, the Robbe-Grillet of mediate things, creator of meaning . . ." (*Critical Essays,* p. 198).

In "The Last Word on Robbe-Grillet?" Barthes accepts the swing back toward (largely conjectural) meaning in an equable, playful spirit:

> Yet these empty forms irresistibly invite a content, and we gradually see—in criticism, in the author's own work—certain temptations of feelings, returns of archetypes, fragments of symbols, in short, everything that belongs to the realm of the adjective, creeping back into the splendid *Dasein* of things. In this sense, there is an evolution of Robbe-Grillet's *oeuvre,* an evolution produced simultaneously by the author, by criticism, and by the public: we are all part of Robbe-Grillet, insofar as we are all busy relaunching the meaning of things, as soon as we open one of his books.
>
> (*Critical Essays,* p. 204)

At the end of this essay Barthes appears to take some comfort from the fact that "everyone has explained *Marienbad,* but each explanation was a meaning immediately contested by the next one: meaning is no longer disappointed, but it remains suspended." If meaning cannot be avoided altogether, the next best thing is to suspend it.

Susan Sontag argues that Barthes's championing of Robbe-Grillet is not to be understood as part of his desire to further the cause of modernism, but rather as a consequence of his stance as an aesthete and dandy. She says that he found in Robbe-Grillet

> a new, high-tech version of the dandy writer; what he hailed in Robbe-Grillet was the desire "to establish a novel of the surface," thereby frustrating our desire to "fall back on a psychology." The idea that depths are obfuscating, demagogic, that no human essence stirs at the bottom of things, and that freedom lies in staying on the surface, the large glass on which desire circulates—this is the central argument of the aesthete position.
>
> ("Writing Itself: On Roland Barthes," in *A Barthes Reader,* pp. xxvii–xxviii)

Robbe-Grillet, as he appears in the works of Barthes, is a compelling figure, but those who decide to investigate his novels for themselves may find themselves agreeing with the American critic Robert Alter that "none of Robbe-Grillet's novels really equals in fascination Roland Barthes's brilliant description of them."

Barthes once commented that when he saw the Berliner Ensemble production of Brecht's *Mutter Courage* (*Mother Courage*) in Paris in 1954, he was "literally set on fire" by the play and by an excerpt from Brecht's writings on the theater that was printed in the program. From the beginning, Brecht, the astute critic and theoretician of drama, was as important to Barthes as Brecht the dramatist. In 1971, Barthes wrote:

> Brecht is still extremely important to me, the more so since he is not fashionable and has not yet succeeded in becoming part of the avant-garde one takes for granted. What makes him exemplary for me is neither his Marxism nor his aesthetic . . . but the conjunction of the two: namely of Marxist analysis and thinking about meaning. He was a Marxist who had reflected upon *the effects of the sign:* a very rare thing.
>
> (Quoted in Culler [1983], p. 51)

As a further indication of Brecht's importance, Susan Sontag reports that Barthes frequently cited Brecht's prose writings as exemplary in his seminars during the 1970's.

According to Culler's presentation, Barthes seems to have drawn three chief points from Brecht's work. First, theater should be intellectual rather than emotive, calling attention to the machinery of signification rather than to feelings. Sets and costumes should signify rather than represent. Better to indicate an army with a few banners than to bring on the troops.

The second point, a corollary of the first, is that theater should emphasize its own artificiality rather than attempt to conceal it. Verse should be spoken as verse, not disguised as prose. A theater that plays down interiority and emphasizes surfaces has a potential to demystify political disguises.

Third, Brecht creates meanings but does not fill them in or complete them. His theater asks questions, but leaves the final answer to the audience. His aim is to increase awareness in the audience, not to enforce solutions. In writing on the theater, Culler says, Barthes articulates his views "in language sustained by some fundamental contrasts: surface versus depth, outside versus inside, lightness versus heaviness, critical distance versus empathetic identification, mask versus character, sign versus reality, discontinuity versus continuity. . . . Can political efficacy have a light touch? This is the possibility Brecht seems to offer."

For all his insistence on detachment and artifice, Barthes's reaction to Brecht's theater was profoundly ethical and emotional. In the last paragraph of "Mère Courage aveugle" ("Mother Courage Blind," 1955) Barthes drops his ironic qualifications and intellectual preoccupations and writes with unqualified enthusiasm:

> Others will describe the concrete—and triumphant—efforts of this dramaturgy to achieve a revolutionary idea, which can alone justify the theater today. In conclusion, let us merely reaffirm the intensity of our response to the Berliner Ensemble's *Mutter Courage:* like every great work, Brecht's is a radical criticism of the evil which precedes it: we are therefore profoundly *edified* by *Mutter Courage.* But this edification is matched by delight: the performance proved to us that this profound criticism has created that theater without alienation which we had dreamed of

> and which has been discovered before our eyes in a single day, in its adult and already perfected form.
>
> (*Critical Essays*, pp. 35–36)

The theater of Brecht fascinated Barthes enough to make him employ the language of delight, a language he was not to make freely his own until more than fifteen years had passed.

Procedures that would later be identified with semiology appear in *Mythologies* and in *Critical Essays,* but when Barthes wrote the essays he had not yet read Saussure's *Course in General Linguistics.* But in 1970, writing a preface to the second edition of *Mythologies,* he announced he had "just read Saussure" and hoped as a result to move past the "pious show of unmasking" to "account *in detail* for the mystification which transforms . . . culture into a universal nature."

With or without Saussure, Barthes was already eager to undertake a work that would show the power of structural analysis. In 1957 he began work on *Système de la mode* (*The Fashion System*), a detailed analysis of the "vestimentary code," that is, the language system of the fashion magazines. This is his most exhaustive piece of research, and was intended to be a definitive illustration of structuralist method. The book was not completed and published until 1967. In an interview that year (republished in *Le grain de la voix* [*The Grain of the Voice,* 1981]), Barthes explained the genesis of the book. It came at a time

> when I had discovered—or thought I had discovered—the possibility of an immanent analysis of sign systems other than language. From that moment on, I wanted to reconstruct one of those systems step by step. . . . And so I chose clothing. Writers like Balzac, Proust, and Michelet had already postulated the existence of a kind of language of apparel, but it remained to give a technical, not just a metaphorical, content to what are too loosely called "languages". . . . From this point of view, clothing is one of those objects of communication—like food, gestures, behavior, conversation—which I have always profoundly enjoyed investigating because, on the one hand, they possess a daily existence and represent to me an opportunity for self-knowledge on the most immediate level (since I invest myself in my own life), and because, on the other hand, these objects possess an intellectual existence, offering themselves to systematic analysis by formal means.
>
> (*The Grain of the Voice,* p. 43)

The project, then, was attractive to both the theoretical and the novelistic aspects of Barthes's interests, presenting an opportunity to combine the phenomena of daily life with the pursuit of theory. Barthes's method was to study and classify the captions under the photographs in a year's issues of two fashion magazines, following out the theoretical ramifications of such statements as "Prints win at the races" and "Slim piping is striking." The book is instructive in its demonstration of structuralist methods of analysis, but the first two-thirds make laborious reading. The last third, beginning with chapter 16, treats the rhetoric of fashion and has some of Barthes's liveliest and wittiest writing. Here is an instance from the chapter entitled "The Rhetoric of the Signifier: The Poetics of Clothing":

> There are four great eponymous themes: nature (*flower-dress, cloud-dress, hats in bloom,* etc.); geography, acculturated under the theme of the exotic (*a Russian blouse, Cherkess ornaments, a samurai tunic, pagoda sleeve, toreador tie, California shirt, Greek summer tints*); history, which primarily provides models for an entire ensemble ("lines"), as opposed to geography, which inspires "details" (*Fashion 1900, a 1916 flavor, Empire line*); and last, art (painting, sculpture, literature, film), the richest of inspirational themes, marked in the rhetoric of Fashion by total eclecticism, provided the references themselves are familiar (*the new Tanagra line, Watteau's déshabillés, Picasso colors*). Naturally—this is the characteristic of connotation—the signified of all these rhetorical signifiers is not, strictly speaking, the model, even if it is conceived in a generic manner (nature, art, etc.): it is the very

> idea of culture which is intended to signify, and by its own categories this culture is a "worldly" culture, i.e., ultimately, academic: history, geography, art, natural history, the divisions of a high-school girl's learning; the models Fashion proposes pell-mell are borrowed from the intellectual baggage of a young girl who is *"on the go and in the know"* (as Fashion would say).
>
> (p. 240.)

A less laborious way to see how structuralism works than reading *The Fashion System* is to take a careful look at "La Tour Eiffel" ("The Eiffel Tower," 1964) one of Barthes's most famous essays, and one that gives a particularly clear illustration of Barthes's structuralist way of looking at the world. The essay is a meditation on the role of the Eiffel Tower in Parisian life:

> And it's true that you must take endless precautions, in Paris, not to see the Eiffel Tower; whatever the season, through mist and cloud, on overcast days or in sunshine, in rain—wherever you are, whatever the landscape of roofs, domes, or branches separating you from it, *the Tower is there;* incorporated into daily life . . . determined merely to persist, like a rock or the river, it is as literal as a phenomenon of nature whose meaning can be questioned to infinity but whose existence is incontestable. There is virtually no Parisian glance it fails to *touch* at some time of day. . . . All this night, too, it will be there, connecting me above Paris to each of my friends that I know are seeing it: with it we all comprise a shifting figure of which it is the steady center: the Tower is friendly.
>
> The Tower is also present to the entire world. . . . As a universal symbol of Paris, it is everywhere on the globe where Paris is to be stated as an image. . . .
>
> (*The Eiffel Tower and Other Mythologies* [1979], p. 3)

The Tower is always there, yet it wavers in the mind, an object of uncertain status, like nature but not part of it. It is both flatly present and a disturbing metaphysical provocation. It is the center of things, but it has no function. It is even hard, once one is at the Tower, to distinguish clearly between the inside and the outside.

From praise of the Tower as seen, Barthes moves to praise of the Tower as seer: "An object when we look at it, it becomes a lookout in its turn when we visit it, and now constitutes as an object . . . that Paris which just now was looking at it." A little later he says that "the world ordinarily produces either purely functional organisms (camera or eye) intended to see things but which then afford nothing to sight, what *sees* being mythically linked to what remains *hidden* (this is the theme of the voyeur), or else spectacles which themselves are blind and are left in the pure passivity of the visible." At this point we get hints about the erotics and metaphysics of seeing and being seen, scopophilia and exhibitionism, secrecy and revelation, the element of desire in every gaze, the element of unresponding blindness in what is seen.

A little later Barthes begins to transform the Tower into an emblem of the "structure" of the structuralists—that empty, meaningless form hospitable to infinite interpretations:

> The Tower . . . transgresses this separation, this habitual divorce of *seeing* and *being seen;* it achieves a sovereign circulation between the two functions; it is a complete object which has, if one may say so, both sexes of sight. This radiant position in the order of perception gives it a prodigious propensity to meaning: the Tower attracts meaning the way a lightning rod attracts thunderbolts; for all lovers of signification, it plays a glamorous part, that of a pure signifier, i.e., of a form in which men unceasingly put *meaning* (which they extract at will from their knowledge, their dreams, their history) without this meaning thereby being finite and fixed.
>
> (p.5)

The essay is a prose hymn to the joys of intellection and the joys of sensation. For Barthes, perception is just a special kind of sensation; sight is touched by sensations, as the skin is touched by the winds. The Eiffel

Tower affords a principle of organization and a locus for transformations. It is an empty monument, a physical reality, a center of civic life, a pole to hang a meaning on, a line drawn from bottom to top, from earth to heaven, an object lesson in the workings of the structuralist imagination. A close analogue to the essay is Wallace Stevens' "Anecdote of the Jar," the first stanza of which reads thus:

> I placed a jar in Tennessee,
> And round it was, upon a hill.
> It made the slovenly wilderness
> Surround that hill.
>
> (*The Collected Poems of Wallace Stevens* [1954], p. 76)

The second and third stanzas extend the metaphor of the "gray and bare" jar as the organizing principle of the wilderness that takes "dominion everywhere."

The 1960's were a busy, productive period for Barthes. In 1960, while he was working on *The Fashion System* and still writing his mythologies, he went to the École Pratique des Hautes Études as chairman of the sixth section, which was concerned with the social and economic sciences. In 1962, he was appointed director of studies. At last he had a secure academic post, even though it was on the fringes of the university system. He was well-known as a critic, but he had not written the massive dissertation needed to advance a university career. From his new vantage point in the École Pratique, he launched an attack on traditional university-based criticism.

In 1963, Barthes published in the *Times Literary Supplement* and *Modern Language Notes* two articles that draw a contrast between the boring, pseudo-positivist criticism written in the universities and the sprightly, ideologically varied criticism written by the "new critics" working mostly outside the university system. Both of the articles—"Qu'est-ce que la critique?" ("What Is Criticism?") and "Les deux critiques" ("The Two Criticisms")—were reissued the next year in *Critical Essays.* According to Jonathan Culler, Barthes's attack on academic criticism in these essays involves two chief points. First,

> academic criticism . . . pretends to have no ideology. Without theoretical argument it claims to know the essential nature of literature, and eclectically accepts or rejects, in the name of common sense, everything offered by ideologically committed criticism. It will reject Freudian or Marxist interpretations as exaggerated or farfetched . . . without granting that this rejection implies an alternative psychology or theory of society.
>
> (*Roland Barthes,* p. 62)

The second objection is that, because of its penchant for causal explanations rather than immanent analysis, academic criticism loses itself in pursuing the bearing of the author's life on his work and on the chimera of "influence."

These two articles were the beginning of a literary quarrel that made Barthes famous with a large public outside the limited readership of the literary reviews. Such re-enactments of the storming of the Bastille are a regular feature of French intellectual life, and this type of spectacle is always popular with the public. Literary controversies between the Left and the Right provide fireworks without the danger of subsequent real gunfire. Commentators at the time compared the controversy to the quarrel between the "ancients" and "moderns" in the seventeenth century, which involved a dispute between those who advocated a literary style based on ancient texts and those who sought to innovate. The twentieth-century ancients were the university scholars with their claims to scrupulous objectivity and scientific rigor. The moderns were mostly non-university critics, practitioners of what came to be known as *la nouvelle critique,* who wrote about literature from an expressly ideological point of view, basing much of their work on theoretical innovations and iconoclastic doctrines.

In "What Is Criticism?" Barthes says that the four major ideological positions of this modern criticism are existentialism, Marxism, psychoanalysis, and structuralism. Barthes wrote in the language of each of these ideological systems, and in the essay he comments parenthetically that "in a certain sense I subscribe to each of them at the same time." Thus Barthes could speak on behalf of criticism originating in any of the chief ideological camps, and of course he was the ideal target for attacks on ideological criticism in general.

Barthes's chief opponent in this dispute was Raymond Picard, a distinguished Racine scholar and a professor at the Sorbonne. He first attacked Barthes for writing two essays "irresponsibly" belittling French academic criticism before an English-speaking audience. The controversy deepened and spread with the publication of Barthes's *Sur Racine* (*On Racine,* 1963). Barthes later described the work as one that provided "an anthropology of Racinian man" in a "mildly psychoanalytic language." To English-speaking readers hardened by the extravagances of Shakespearean criticism, Barthes's rough handling of Racine might have passed with no more than a few murmurs. But to the proponents of French academic criticism it was a declaration of war.

Barthes's method was to superimpose all the tragedies of Racine on one another to find the underlying structure out of which the individual characters and typical dramatic situations arose. What he discovered were fundamental relations of authority, rivalry, and love. These are just the motifs of the myth of the primal horde analyzed by Freud in *Totem and Taboo* (1913). In this archetypal account, the brothers band together to murder the father, who has ruled over them and prevented them from finding wives by maintaining a monopoly on the women. After the death of the father, the sons feel blood-guilt, eventually found a social order to control their dissension, and establish an incest taboo. Barthes says, "the archaic bedrock is there, close at hand." To attribute the underlying structure of the most decorous and supposedly "pure" of French tragedies to this violent sexual myth was no doubt a calculated outrage. Equally provocative was Barthes's calling plays revered for their verbal beauty "an empty site eternally open to signification."

By such measures Barthes roused Racinian criticism from its dogmatic slumbers and joined battle with academic criticism on fundamental issues. In 1965 Picard published *Nouvelle critique ou nouvelle imposture?* (New Criticism or New Fraud?), using Barthes's book as a point of departure. He launched a general attack on the *nouvelle critique* for its unhistorical and subjective absolutism. Barthes in turn accused academic criticism of always locating the meaning of a work in an "elsewhere" outside the work—in the biography of the author or in the literary sources—or outside of history altogether in an eternal essence. In defense of the new critics, he argued that they were taking up the works of the past and describing them in order to discover what could be done with them in the present age. In a 1965 interview in *Le Figaro* Barthes defended his critical practice:

> I am the one, in fact, who believes Racine may still be read today, I am the real guardian of national values. Modern criticism, in fact, asks a vital question: Can modern man read the classics? My *Racine* is a meditation on infidelity, and it is thus in no way cut off from problems which concern us today.
>
> (*The Grain of the Voice,* p. 41)

In this interview Barthes answers Picard's criticisms with more heat and less irony than he would permit himself in the numerous interviews he gave later in life. After he became famous, he discussed attacks on his work with Olympian urbanity and wit. Defending his positions—when he did not rather casually announce that he had abandoned them—became a form of entertainment hedged about with courtesy and humor.

Before the Barthes-Picard controversy ended, it generated a half-dozen books by French intellectuals in addition to dozens of essays and commentaries in newspapers and periodicals. The end result was to make Barthes famous, to stir up Racine studies by making Racine seem modern and problematic, and to put a fascinating example of structural analysis before the public.

At the same time these spirited polemics were going on, Barthes brought out *Éléments de sémiologie* (*Elements of Semiology,* 1964), his most deeply pondered and comprehensive discourse on method. This hundred-page monograph is an elaboration of the ideas of Saussure, and in form it is a series of expanded definitions of four sets of binary terms: language (*langue*) and speech (*parole*); signifier and signified; syntagm and system; denotation and connotation. Commenting on this arrangement of contrasting pairs in the introduction, Barthes writes:

> It will be seen that these headings appear in dichotomic form; the reader will also notice that the binary classification of concepts seems frequent in structural thought, as if the metalanguage of the linguist reproduced, like a mirror, the binary structure of the system it is describing. . . . It would probably be very instructive to study the pre-eminence of binary classification in the discourse of contemporary social sciences. The taxonomy of these sciences, if it were well known, would undoubtedly provide a great deal of information on what might be called the field of intellectual imagination in our time.
>
> (*Elements of Semiology,* p. 12)

The most important of these pairs is the first. By *langue* Barthes (following Saussure) means the general nature of a language as a whole at any given time. By *parole* he means individual acts of speech and writing. Much of structural analysis arises from the study of the interplay of these two aspects of language. This analysis can make use of synchronic linguistics to study the state of a language at a given moment, or it can use diachronic linguistics to study the changing state of a language over time.

The signifier and the signified involve difficult problems of definition, but to put the matter very simply, the signifier is the phonetic, alphabetic token of a signifier, which is not a "thing" but a mental representation of some kind. The relationship of a sign to its signification is a matter of arbitrary linguistic convention.

The syntagm is

> a combination of signs, which has space as a support. In the articulated language, this space is linear and irreversible . . . two elements cannot be pronounced at the same time . . . : each term here derives its value from its opposition to what precedes and what follows. . . . the analytical activity which applies to the syntagm is that of carving out.
>
> (*Elements of Semiology,* p. 58)

*S/Z* (1970), Barthes's book-length study of a Balzac short story, derives its method from the syntagm: Barthes divides the story into 581 *lexia* (fragments of the text, usually brief) that he analyzes in terms of their difference from what precedes and what follows.

Barthes exemplifies the contrast between "syntagm" and "system" in a table that illustrates the distinction between the two. In the "food system," "system" is a "set of foodstuffs which have affinities or differences, within which one chooses a dish in view of a certain meaning: the types of entrée, roast, or sweet." The "syntagm" is the "real sequence of dishes chosen during a meal." In the "furniture system," the "system" is a "set of stylistic varieties of a single piece of furniture (a bed)." The "syntagm" is the "juxtaposition of the different pieces of furniture in the same space: bed—wardrobe—table, etc."

The section on denotation and connotation begins with showing how the signs of the denoted system make up the signifiers of connotation. Barthes then moves to a consideration of "metalanguage," that language which "takes over" another language in order to describe it.

As Barthes once told a questioner, a reader

who finds any or all of these terms in a piece of writing can be fairly certain that he is dealing with structuralist discourse. But these terms mean little unless one has some sense of the *goals* toward which structuralist analysis is directed and the intellectual context in which it arose as a practice among French intellectuals.

As to the intellectual situation that led up to the structuralist movement, its chief feature was the decay in the mid 1950's of faith in the Stalinist brand of Marxism and an associated decline in the intellectual fortunes of existentialism. History was ceasing to seem a reliable guide to action, and the "committed" stance of existentialism was tainted by its association with Stalinism. In 1955, Claude Lévi-Strauss published *Tristes Tropiques,* a combination of anthropology and autobiography that made use of structuralist principles to analyze anthropological materials. *Anthropologie structurale* (*Structural Anthropology*) followed in 1958, and these two widely influential books mark the beginning of the decade from the mid 1950's to the mid 1960's in which structuralism was at the center of French intellectual life. As H. Stuart Hughes said, "French social thought of the desperate years began with history and ended with anthropology."

Lévi-Strauss, sometimes called "the father of French structuralism," explained the value of structural linguistics in this way: "First, structural linguistics shifts from the study of *conscious* linguistic phenomena to the study of their unconscious infrastructure: second, it does not treat *terms* as independent entities, taking instead as its basis of analysis the *relations* among terms: third, it introduces the concept of *system.* (quoted in Kurzweil, p. 16).

This "structure," then, is quite distinct from the other kinds of structure connected with language that an English-speaking reader is likely to be familiar with. It is not akin to the deep structure of Noam Chomsky's American linguistics, by which people know how to generate grammatical discourse in their own language. Nor is it like the structure of traditional literary analysis—that is, study of the concatenations of plot, of the dovetailing of images in the service of a theme, the parallels and contrasts among characters, and so on. French structuralism seeks the unconscious patterns of thought as they are implicit in language but never stated. The goal is nothing less than uncovering the buried foundations of discourse, the silent but operative logic of its combinations and distinctions.

Lévi-Strauss' studies of myth in primitive societies provide the earliest and clearest example of this project. He sought to study every version of every myth in the tribes among whom he had done fieldwork. He broke down each version into short sentences and then grouped the sentences into categories. He attempted to "read" their structure as a reflection of a series of cultural transformations, using such Freudian concepts as defense mechanisms, repression, reaction formations, and blocking. For Lévi-Strauss the versions of myth do not represent historical developments, but a complex interplay of mental forces at a given moment. Lévi-Strauss' grand design was never really fulfilled, but it exerted a compelling influence over the French intellectuals of the period, including Barthes. Surely his *On Racine* and *The Fashion System* follow the pattern laid down by Lévi-Strauss in his study of myth, and a more diffuse influence runs through two later books—*S/Z* and *Sade, Fourier, Loyola* (1971).

*S/Z* is a virtuoso feat of reading. Focusing on Balzac's "Sarrasine" (1830), Barthes examines each segment of the short story to discover the "codes" buried in it, the way it incorporates meanings from literary tradition and from "intertextuality." He also shows how each segment establishes itself through its "difference" from its immediate neighbors. The five codes that Barthes employs in *S/Z* have caused a good deal of critical discussion. Critics have gone astray in trying to elicit a useful analytic system from the codes and their derivatives. In an interview in 1970, Barthes summarized the codes thus:

1. *The code of narrative actions* (or proairetic code, a term borrowed from Aristotelian rhetoric), which ensures that we read the novella as a story, a succession of actions.

2. *The semantic code* gathers together signifieds which are more or less psychological, atmospheric, pertaining to character. It's the world of connotations in the current sense of the term. For example, when a character's portrait is meant to transmit the message "He is irritable," but without ever pronouncing the word "irritability," then irritability becomes signified in the portrait.

3. *The cultural codes,* broadly understood; i.e., the set of references and the general knowledge of a period which support the discourse. For example, psychological, sociological, medical knowledge, etc. These codes are often very strong, especially in Balzac.

4. *The hermeneutic code* covers the setting into place of an enigma and the discovery of the truth it conceals. In a general fashion, this code governs all intrigues modeled on the detective novel.

5. *The symbolic field.* As we know, *its logic differs* radically from the logic of reasoning or of experience. It is defined, like the logic of dreams, by elements of intemporality, substitution, and reversibility.

(*The Grain of the Voice,* pp. 74–75)

Barthes warned that there was no hierarchy among the codes and that they were useful primarily as *topoi* (points of departure) for following out the activities of structuration in Balzac's text. He emphasized the loose and unsystematic character of his strategy:

> Hence we use *Code* here not in the sense of a list, a paradigm that must be reconstituted. The code is a perspective of quotations, a mirage of structures; we know only its departures and returns; the units which have resulted from it (those we inventory) are themselves, always, ventures out of the text, the mark, the sign of a virtual digression toward the remainder of a catalogue. . . . They are so many fragments of something that has always been *already* read, seen, done, experienced; the code is the wake of that *already.*
>
> (*S/Z,* p. 20)

Barthes's analysis in *S/Z* shows how ambiguous, tantalizing, and rich in suggestion is this seemingly straightforward, traditional melodramatic tale of Balzac. Its codes look to the past, but the surprising uses to which some of them are put hint at the modernist future.

Balzac's story is told by an anonymous narrator to the Marquise de Rochefide, who has seen a mysterious old man come briefly to the party they were at and leave a jewel with the daughter of the house. The Marquise is curious about the old man's relations with the Lantres and implies that she will sleep with the narrator if he will tell her the story of the old man. The tale he then tells is about a young French sculptor, Sarrasine, who visits Rome and falls in love with a famous singer known as La Zambinella. He goes back to the theater to see her night after night and begins a statue of her. The sculptor abducts La Zambinella, but at last discovers that she is not a woman but a castrato. La Zambinella's protector has Sarrasine killed and orders a marble copy of the statue Sarrasine was working on. This statue is ultimately the model for the statue of Adonis in the garden of the house where the narrator and the Marquise attended the party. The mysterious old man is La Zambinella.

By the time Barthes has finished dissolving "Sarrasine" into its overtones and implications, he has done an impressive job of complicating and modernizing it. He insists that he is not writing an *explication de texte.* If he were, he would be working toward a clear central meaning. But, in fact, he is working in the opposite direction, to open up the meaning, to unbraid it and let it float out wide. Here is part of what Barthes does with the first sentence of the tale, "I was deep in one of those daydreams":

> There will be nothing wayward about the daydream introduced here: it will be solidly constructed along the most familiar rhetorical lines, in a series of antitheses: garden and salon, life and death, cold and heat, outside and interior. The lexia thus lays the groundwork, in an introductory form, for a vast symbolic structure, since it can lend itself to many substitutions, variations, which will lead us from the garden to the

castrato, from the salon to the girl with whom the narrator is in love, by way of the mysterious old man, the full-bosomed Mme de Lanty, or Vien's moonlit Adonis. Thus, on the symbolic level, an immense province appears, the province of the antithesis, of which this forms the first unit, linking at the start its two adversative terms (A/B) in the word *daydream.*

(*S/Z,* pp. 17–18)

*L'Empire des signes* (*Empire of Signs,* 1970) was published at the same time as *S/Z* and can be regarded as a companion piece to it. *S/Z* is a speculative reading of a classical literary text; *Empire of Signs* is a speculative celebration of the unreadability of Japanese civilization. Barthes has nothing to say about Japan as a powerful modern industrialized society; his Japan is a rarefied affair. *Empire of Signs* is the semiotician's delighted vacation from meaning in a half-fictive land where he does not speak the language and where customs seem to present a perfected surface rather than to reveal something beneath.

Barthes generally had stayed inside the confines of French literature and the French language, seldom writing on authors in other languages. For all his urbanity, he has a certain provincialism of Frenchness. Japan, his imagined land, was an escape from that. In *Empire of Signs* he writes:

> The dream: to know a foreign (alien) language and yet not to understand it: to perceive the difference in it without that difference ever being recuperated by the superficial sociality of discourse, communication or vulgarity; to know, positively refracted in a new language, the impossibilities of our own; to learn the systematics of the inconceivable; to undo our own "reality" under the effect of other formulations, other syntaxes . . . to descend into the untranslatable, to experience its shock without ever muffling it, until everything Occidental in us totters and the rights of the "father tongue" vacillate. . . . How beneficial it would be . . . to gain a vision of the irreducible differences which a very remote language can, by glimmerings, suggest to us.
>
> (p. 6)

The very great distance of Japanese from French was what delighted Barthes. He was also, somewhat surprisingly, delighted by the sprawling, unplanned Japanese towns without centers, so unlike the Paris organized around the Eiffel Tower; they reflected his aesthetic preference for loose and indefinite organization over the centralization evident in every aspect of French life.

Barthes chooses the Japanese art of packaging as an instance of the elaboration of surface and the indifference to what is concealed inside:

> Without even regarding as emblematic the famous set of Japanese boxes, one inside the other down to emptiness, you can already see a true semantic meditation in the merest Japanese package. Geometric, rigorously drawn, and yet always signed somewhere with an asymmetrical fold or knot, by the care, the very technique of its making, the interplay of cardboard, wood, paper, ribbon, it is no longer the temporary accessory of the object to be transported, but itself becomes an object; the envelope, in itself, is consecrated as a precious though gratuitous thing; the package is a thought. . . .
>
> Yet, by its very perfection, this envelope, often repeated (you can be unwrapping a package forever), postpones the discovery of the object it contains—one which is often insignificant, for it is precisely a speciality of the Japanese package that the triviality of the thing be disproportionate to the luxury of the envelope: a sweet, a bit of sugared bean paste, a vulgar "souvenir" (as Japan is unfortunately so expert at producing) are wrapped with as much sumptuousness as a jewel: . . . hordes of schoolboys, on a day's outing, bring back to their parents a splendid package containing no one knows what, as if they had gone very far away and this was an occasion for them to devote themselves in troops to the ecstasy of the package. . . . but the very thing it encloses and signifies is for a very long time put off until later, as if the package's function were not to protect in space but to postpone in time; it is in the envelope that the labor of the confection (of the making) seems to be invested, but thereby the object loses its existence, becomes a mirage: from envelope to envelope, the signified flees, and

> when you finally have it (there is always a little *something* in the package), it appears insignificant, laughable, vile.
>
> (pp. 45–46)

Barthes speaks of feeling happy and at home in the strangeness of Japan—both intellectually and sensuously. The reason is probably that there was much that was familiar in the midst of the strangeness. Sometimes called the France of Asia, Japan is the *other* country that has long appealed to aesthetes as a utopia. The elegance and reticence of Japanese culture are matched by the same qualities in French culture. In addition, Barthes found in Japan support for his own values. As Susan Sontag says, "To be both impassive and fantastic, inane and profound, unselfconscious and supremely sensuous—these qualities that Barthes discerned in various facets of Japanese civilization project an ideal of taste and deportment, the ideal of the aesthete in its larger meaning." This most hedonistic of Barthes's books points forward to the final period of his career, when pleasure became a central value.

In *S/Z* Barthes pursues differentiating structure down to individual syllables in single words. In *Sade, Fourier, Loyola* he examines the universal classification systems of the sadist, the socialist, and the saint. Each of these "logothetes" tried to create an exhaustive system: Sade of narratives of sexual activity, Fourier of a socialist utopia, Loyola of Christian spiritual exercises. Here is part of Barthes's account of Sade's units and rules of combination:

> These rules may readily permit a formalization of the erotic language, analogous to the diagrammatic "trees" proposed by our linguists. . . . In Sadian grammar there are two principal rules of action: they are, we might say, the regular procedures by which the narrator mobilizes the units of his "lexicon" (postures, figures, episodes). The first is a rule of exhaustiveness: in an "operation," the greatest number of postures must be simultaneously achieved. . . . The second rule of action is the rule of reciprocity. . . . All functions can be interchanged, everyone can and must be in turn agent and patient, whipper and whipped, coprophagist and coprophagee, etc. This is a cardinal rule, first because it assimilates Sadian eroticism into a truly formal language, where there are only classes of actions, not groups of individuals, which enormously simplifies its grammar . . . [and] second, because it keeps us from basing the grouping of Sadian society on the particularity of sexual practices.
>
> (*Sade, Fourier, Loyola,* pp. 29–30)

By the time he finished this book, Barthes had exhausted his interest in such overarching "grammatical" structures. By 1971 he was far enough away from structuralism to call it a "euphoric dream of scientificity." Even during the period of his most intense involvement he had written critical pieces that were not notably structuralist in intention. He continued to champion modernist works and to comment on the literary and political scene. At no time did theoretical work claim all of his attention.

By the last decade of his life, Barthes had become a French cultural institution. But by then he also had turned away from the kind of theoretical and critical writing that had gained him that august status. He moved away from theory and toward meditative and novelistic forms of writing. His style was as fresh and full of surprises as ever, and his opposition to convention as determined as it ever was. But he adopted something of the stance of the nineteenth-century man of letters—personal, pleasure loving, cultivated, attracted to the arts of living, almost completely aesthetic in his interests and judgments.

Barthes wrote no more connected exposition and argument. Rather, he composed artful fragments that were suggestive, seductive, and resonant rather than argumentatively persuasive. These fragments are full of novelistic or personal elements—imaginary dialogues, scenes of daily life, presentations of moods and perceptions, lyric evocations of melancholy and joy. Analysis is braided into passages that also have elements of narrative, of natural description, and of strong emotional coloring.

The writer who had devoted his career to attacking *doxa,* demolishing received opinions, and making questionable what had been taken for granted now wrote about pleasure, the body, memory, romantic love, daily life—traditional themes of the bourgeois literary man. If in this final period he was still attacking *doxa,* they were the *doxa* of the literary Left, with its puritanical contempt for pleasure and the arts of living. This Barthes was easier for the reading public to assimilate than the left-wing mandarin who wrote difficult, elliptical books of semiological theory and was best known for his essays unmasking bourgeois mythologies.

The chief works of this period are *Le plaisir du texte* (*The Pleasure of the Text,* 1973), an aphoristic defense of reading and writing that shows them to be erotic and subversively asocial; *Roland Barthes par Roland Barthes* (*Roland Barthes by Roland Barthes,* 1975), an autobiography that avoids a narration of the author's life and denies the existence of a knowable self; *A Lover's Discourse: Fragments,* a defense of amorous passion that presents it as largely composed of madness and misery; and *La chambre claire: Note sur la photographie* (*Camera Lucida: Reflections on Photography,* 1980), a meditation on photography that turns into a moving elegy on the death of the author's mother. Barthes may be pursuing traditional themes in these works, but he is still centrally concerned with transforming every form of discourse he adopts into something new and strange.

*The Pleasure of the Text* explicitly rejects literary works as objects of knowledge and proposes instead that they are objects of pleasure. Barthes makes a distinction between works of pleasure and works of bliss ("bliss" is the English translation for *jouissance,* which can mean "coming"):

> Here moreover, drawn from psychoanalysis, is an indirect way of establishing the opposition between the text of pleasure and the text of bliss: pleasure can be expressed in words, bliss cannot. Bliss is unspeakable, interdicted. . . .
>
> The writer of pleasure (and his reader) accepts the letter; renouncing bliss, he has the right and the power to express it: the letter is his pleasure; he is obsessed by it, as are all those who love language (and not speech), logophiles, authors, letter writers, linguists: about texts of pleasure, therefore, it is possible to speak (no argument with the annihilation of bliss): *criticism always deals with the texts of pleasure, never the texts of bliss:* Flaubert, Proust, Stendhal are discussed inexhaustibly: this criticism speaks the futile bliss of the tutor text, its *past or future* bliss: *you are about to read. I have read:* criticism is always historical or prospective: the constatory present, the *presentation* of bliss, is forbidden it; its preferred material is thus culture, which is everything in us except our present.
>
> (pp. 21–22)

Barthes is subtle and surprising, coming at pleasure in an oblique way that verges on the outrageous. His discussion has nothing of the coziness that usually goes with talk of "the pleasures of reading." Bliss is associated with modernist works, pleasure with the works of the past. Bliss comes from disjunctions and gaps in reading and occurs in those texts that require the reader to become "writerly" himself to put the text together. Pleasure comes from the "readerly" texts that permit the reader to take in the text by referring to the traditional shapes and codes of literature. In this process, the author is no longer necessary:

> As institution, the author is dead: his civil status, his biographical person have disappeared; dispossessed, they no longer exercise over his work the formidable paternity whose account literary history, teaching, and public opinion had the responsibility of establishing and renewing; but in the text, in a way, *I desire* the author: I need his figure (which is neither his representation nor his projection), as he needs mine.
>
> (p. 27)

The author as the ultimate authority on the text, by reference to whom its puzzles may be solved, is destroyed. But he is immediately restored as a figure desired by the reader, a creation of the reader's imagination and desire. Barthes's replacement of the writer by the reader as the central figure, the one who "writes" the text as he reads it, is very thoroughgoing. And this centrally located reader turns out to be more a "body" than a "character" or repository of cultural knowledge and themes. As Barthes writes in *The Pleasure of the Text,* "Whenever I attempt to 'analyze' a text which has given me pleasure, it is not my 'subjectivity' I encounter but my 'individuality,' the given which makes my body separate from other bodies and appropriates its suffering or its pleasure: it is my body of bliss I encounter" (p. 62).

Barthes in this last period attempts to anchor both writing and reading more and more in an erotically conceived body. Pleasure, especially the orgasmic part of pleasure that he calls *jouissance,* seems to offer a refuge from history and culture, something anchored in nature rather than society and language. Increasingly he wrote of writing itself as arising out of the body, passing out through the fingers into the interweaving braids of the emerging text. He wrote pieces about calligraphy, about Cy Twombley's scrawled notations in his paintings, about Erté's drawings of women as letters of the alphabet. In doing so, Barthes was trying to locate a source for reading and writing outside the endless circulations of meaning. He might be accused of the same maneuver that he so relentlessly exposed in the myths of the bourgeoisie: that of attempting to disguise a piece of ideology as something given, a part of nature. Barthes concluded *The Pleasure of the Text* with an analogy drawn from films to exemplify what he means by "bliss":

> In fact, it suffices that the cinema capture the sound of speech *close up* (this is, in fact, the generalized definition of the "grain" of writing) and make us hear in their materiality, their sensuality, the breath, the gutturals, the fleshiness of the lips, a whole presence of the human muzzle (that the voice, that writing, be as fresh, supple, lubricated, delicately granular and vibrant as an animal's muzzle), to succeed in shifting the signified a great distance and in throwing, so to speak, the anonymous body of the actor into my ear: it granulates, it crackles, it caresses, it grates, it cuts, it comes: that is bliss.
>
> (p. 67)

Compared with the idea of God or natural law, the grain of the voice may be a very slight representative of what is left outside the ceaseless transformations of history and language. But for Barthes, such a residue, however minimal, is a saving residue. If Barthes does not quite manage to persuade us that he has gotten outside language, he at least succeeds in "shifting the signified a great distance." And if he is still inside language, he is nevertheless able to elude final formulations and closure. Even when he was writing works of theory, he held back from the final "scientific" summing up of a text or a topic. But to theorize at all is to move toward conclusive formulations, and that is what Barthes's strategies of writing are meant to avoid in his last books.

In 1975, Barthes published *Roland Barthes by Roland Barthes* in the same series that had brought out his *Michelet* twenty-one years earlier. The epigraph at the beginning counsels, "It must all be considered as if spoken by a character in a novel." Characteristically, Barthes wants to place a distance between his actual life and person and his discourse, even in his autobiography. Then follow some forty unnumbered pages of photographs with Barthes's accompanying commentary. There are photographs of the author's parents and grandparents, of the author himself as a child and youth, of the streets and parks of Bayonne, of himself and his beloved mother. The only obviously ideological photograph is one of Barthes as an infant looking at himself in a mirror. The caption reads, "That's you," and thus the picture illustrates Lacan's notion of the "mirror stage" in the formation of a sense of identity.

There are comparatively few photographs

from the author's adult life—the life he began to live at the age of twenty-seven, when he was at last cured of tuberculosis and began his life as an author. Barthes writes:

> So you will find here, mingled with the "family romance," only the figurations of the body's prehistory—of that body making its way toward labor and the pleasure of writing. For such is the theoretical meaning of this limitation: to show the time of the narrative (of the imagery) ends with the subject's youth: the only biography is of the unproductive life. . . . Another repertoire will then be constituted: that of writing.
>
> (*Roland Barthes by Roland Barthes,* pp. 2–3)

The photographs themselves are like all family photographs, both commonplace and touching, blurred and poignant. The parents and grandparents stand stiffly at attention for the camera in formal dress. Barthes himself is represented as a solemn child; a pensive, gangling youth; a young man with a cigarette always in his hand, wearing a sultry look that combines boredom and intensity. The portrait of the writer in childhood and youth follows the outline of the bildungsroman faithfully—solitude, maternal love, living in fantasy and in books, undergoing the discipline of protracted illness, arriving at the capital to write and be famous. The picture is unified and self-consistent, more literary and predictable than we expect any actual life to be.

But when the reader turns from the photographs to the written text, he finds that Barthes is determined to dissipate any impression of unity and self-consistency that the reader may attempt to form. Barthes generally refers to himself as "R. B." or "he." There is no story, no account of the events of the author's life, no reminiscences about friends and enemies. Rather, there is a series of alphabetically arranged entries from a paragraph to several pages in length. Their typical subject matter is a discussion of the workings of the author's mind in dealing with intellectual matters. Here is what Barthes has to say under the entry "En fait" (In fact):

> You suppose that the goal of the wrestling match is to win? No, it is to understand. You suppose that the theater is fictive, ideal, in relation to life? No, in the photogeny of the d'Harcourt studios it is the stage which is trivial and the city which is dreamed. Athens is not a mythical city; it must be described in realistic terms, without reference to humanist discourse. The Martians? They are not invoked to stage the Other (the Alien) but the Same. The gangster film is not emotive, as might be supposed, but intellectual. Jules Verne a travel writer? Quite the contrary, a writer of claustration. Astrology is not predictive but descriptive (it describes very realistically certain social conditions). Racine's theater is not a theater of erotic passion but of authoritarian relations, etc. . . .
>
> Such figures of Paradox are countless; they have their logical operator: the expression "*in fact*": striptease is not an erotic solicitation: *in fact,* it desexualizes Woman, etc.
>
> (p. 83)

Barthes represents one of his own favorite figures of thought—the statement of a received opinion, immediately followed by its overthrow and restatement as its opposite. He does not say anything about the content of these paradoxes drawn from his earlier writings. Rather, he is interested in their form—the structure of transformation that is located in the logical operator "in fact." Another writer would be interested in what he had to say; Barthes is interested in the form of his opinions, almost as if that form brought into being the opinions themselves.

He is also interested in the form of his own existence, though he treats the very existence of such a form as highly problematic. To illustrate the way naming gives a continuity that is otherwise lacking, he uses the image of the ship of the Argonauts, "each piece of which the Argonauts gradually replaced, so that they ended with an entirely new ship, without having to alter either its name or its form." He says the *Argo* is the product of two operations—substitution (where one part replaces another) and nomination (where the name is in no way dependent on the continued existence of the same parts). "*Argo* is an object with no other cause than its name, no other identity than its form."

Barthes's autobiography is an extended illustration of his love of paradox, almost as if it were written to show that the writing of autobiography is not really possible. He sets out to show that there is no consistent, essential self whose being can be revealed through narrative. We receive personal details; Barthes likes "too-cold beer, flat pillows . . . all kinds of writing pens . . . realistic novels . . . Pollock . . . all romantic music . . . the Marx Brothers." But his likes and dislikes, his oddities, mean only that "*my body is not the same as yours.*" The thesis of his book is that "R. B." the subject is, like all subjects, not a stability but a process, a sequence of changes, an unfolding in no way obligated to be consistent with itself or to add up to some meaning that can be summarized. The demonstration of the subject's free-floating lack of unity is carried out in a thoroughgoing and consistent fashion.

The epigraph at the end of the book reads, "*And afterward? / —What to write now? /Can you still write anything? / —One writes with one's desire, and I am not through desiring.*" At the beginning Barthes tells us that what we are going to read is the speech of a character. At the end he tells us that writing, like living and desiring, is unpredictable. To respond in a Barthesian spirit, one can say that Barthes never reveals himself more vividly than when he assumes the mask of a character, and that the unpredictability of his writing arises out of his unwavering determination to avoid the predictable.

*A Lover's Discourse* has been the most popular of all Barthes's books; it became a best-seller in France and was even adapted for the stage. In its representation of the tense moments, inner monologues, and circular ponderings of the lover, the book is like a novel, but it has no plot and no characters. In its power of analysis and generalization, the book is like a critical work, but it avoids as much as possible the metalanguage of critical discourse—the language about language.

As with all of Barthes's works, there is something of a polemical intent behind *A Lover's Discourse.* Sex, he believes, has ousted amorous passion from serious discourse, and the lover has become a marginal figure, ignored by high culture and alive only in films, popular songs, and women's magazines. In his preface Barthes writes:

> The necessity for this book is to be found in the following consideration: that the lover's discourse is today *of an extreme solitude.* This discourse is spoken, perhaps, by thousands of subjects (who knows?), but warranted by no one; it is completely forsaken by the surrounding languages: ignored, disparaged, or derided by them. . . . Once a discourse is thus driven by its own momentum into the backwater of the "unreal," exiled from all gregarity, it has no recourse but to become the site, however exiguous, of an *affirmation.*
>
> (p.1)

In an interview in *Art Press* in 1977, Barthes explained that the book grew out of one of his seminars in which the topic was "amorous discourse" and the "tutor text" was Goethe's *Die Lieden des jungen Werthers* (*The Sorrows of Young Werther,* 1774). Both he and his students were surprised at what strong emotional reactions they had to the extravagant elations and despairs of this very old-fashioned love story with its hero who prided himself on his "sensibility." Barthes undertook to resurrect the intense inner drama that embodies the joys and torments of love. Commenting on his method in the *Art Press* interview, Barthes said, "Since *The Pleasure of the Text* I have not been able to put up with 'dissertating' on a topic. So I fabricated, feigned the discourse of a lover." Barthes did not give an unqualified answer to the interviewer's question about the identity of the "I" who speaks in *A Lover's Discourse.* He said, "You see, the one who says 'I' in the book is the *I* of writing. . . . Naturally, I can be lured into saying that I'm the subject—but then I offer Flaubert's reply: it's me, and it isn't me" (*The Grain of the Voice,* p. 285).

The lover of *A Lover's Discourse* is the somewhat disembodied speaker of the various codes that make up the "love talk" with which he talks to himself or to his imagined beloved. The eighty-two alphabetically arranged fragments that compose the book neither tell a consecutive story nor present a rounded personality. Nevertheless, a portrait, a literary personality, emerges—anguished, sometimes comic, ironic and self-observant, prone to hysteria, despair, and exaltation, and supremely literary in his sensibility. Again and again the lover launches into monologues in which he tries to establish the meaning, the lack of meaning, or the ambiguity of the beloved's silence or absence. As Barthes noted in a 1977 *Playboy* interview:

> The lover is the natural semiologist in the pure state! He spends his time reading signs—he does nothing else: signs of happiness, signs of unhappiness. On the face of the other, in his behavior. He is truly a prey to signs. . . . Love is not blind. On the contrary, it has an unbelievable power to decipher things, which is related to the paranoid element in every lover. You know, a lover combines bits of neurosis and psychosis: he's tormented and crazed. . . . He deciphers perfectly, but he's unable to arrive at a definite interpretation, and he's swept away by a perpetual circus, where he'll never find peace.
>
> (*The Grain of the Voice,* p. 303)

The lover is also a virtuoso in self-torment and in finding means of self-victimization. This quality is evident in the following passage from a section of *A Lover's Discourse* called "Dependency." The notations Barthes had printed in the left-hand column call our attention to Renaissance ideas of *cortezia,* reverence and service to the beloved, and to the discussion in Plato's *Symposium* of the service the lover gives to the beloved:

> The mechanics of amorous vassalage require a fathomless futility. For, in order that dependency be manifest in all its purity, it must burst forth in the most trivial circumstances and become inadmissible by dint of cowardice: waiting for a phone call is somehow too crude a dependency; I must improve upon it, without limits: hence I shall exasperate myself with the chatter of the women in the drugstore who are delaying my return to the instrument to which I am subjugated; and since this call, which I don't want to miss, will bring me some new occasion for subjugation, it is as if I were energetically behaving in order to permit this dependency to function.
>
> (p. 82)

The lover's self-observation in no way lessens the sway of his compulsions; indeed, his lucidity seems only to show him how to make his abasement more complete. Unlike a real madman, the lover is clear-headed enough to recognize the extent of his devastation. The lover does not conceive of himself as living through an unfolding drama. Rather, he is hurled first here and then there by imperious obsessions, overwhelming moods of sadness or elation. While they are going on, they seem to have no beginning and no end. Barthes said in the *Art Press* interview, "My vision of the lover's discourse is essentially fragmented, discontinuous, fluttering. These are episodes of language swirling around in the mind of the enamoured, impassioned subject. . . . I was careful to preserve the radical discontinuity of this linguistic torment unfolding in the lover's head." A little later in the interview Barthes speaks of *A Lover's Discourse* as a protest against the love story:

> I'm convinced that the well-constructed love story, with a beginning, an end, and a crisis in the middle, is the way society hopes to persuade the lover to be reconciled with the language of the Other. . . . I feel the unhappy lover is not even

> able to benefit from this reconciliation, and that he is not, paradoxically, within a love story; he's in something else that closely resembles madness, because it's not for nothing that we say someone is madly in love, and the story is simply impossible from the lover's point of view.
>
> (*The Grain of the Voice,* p. 286)

Barthes's strategy, then, is to write always from within the lover's perspective and to present his utterance with complete immediacy, without the softening and rationalizing effect of hindsight or foresight. Thus the lover's voice is protected from ironic undercutting and from absurdity. Rendered at the moment in the inner drama when it is conceived and uttered, even the reflective, generalizing dimension of the lover's speeches becomes urgent and filled with passion. Amorous passion is shown to be above all a form of inner theater—a drama of meeting, separation, and reunion. It is performed for the benefit of the imagined beloved, and at once mourns the absence of the beloved and hallucinates the presence of the beloved as the auditor of the mourning caused by his absence.

Barthes's treatment of the language of love is full of lover's stratagems: twisting speech to fit his somewhat mad purposes, doubling back on himself, and seeking quixotic remedies for imaginary despairs and lyric expression for momentary joys. The love depicted by Barthes is in the great tradition of self-destroying romantic passion, the tradition represented by Paris and Helen, Hippolytus and Phaedra, Dido and Aeneas, Tristan and Isolde, Romeo and Juliet, Anna Karenina and Vronsky, Swann and Odette. Barthes's lover suffers and swoons, fears and waits, abandons himself to his passion, considers suicide. But, comedian that he is, he outlives his passion (unlike most of his distinguished predecessors) and goes looking for another one. Barthes' lover posits love as a value, not a sickness, and when he recovers from one passion, he eventually goes out into the world to seek another one. What love has to offer is not happiness or sexual gratification or personal intimacy but a quasi-religious exaltation.

Perhaps the semiotician in Barthes (and that was a very important part of him) was especially attracted to the subject of amorous love because this passion exerts a magnetic attraction on language, especially poetic language. Yet amorous passion is also deaf to language, plunging along its course oblivious to praise, irony, warnings, threats, and elegies, impervious to words amid all the words it inspires.

*Camera Lucida* was published in the month of Barthes's death, March 1980. On 25 February he was hit by a laundry truck as he was crossing the rue des Écoles in front of the Sorbonne, after having lunch with the philosopher-historian Michel Foucault and the leader of the Socialist party, François Mitterrand. At the time of his death a month later there was speculation that he might have survived his injuries had it not been for his intense grief over the death of his mother, Henriette Barthes, in October 1978.

The second half of *Camera Lucida* is a meditation on a photograph of Barthes's mother taken in her childhood. It speaks movingly of Barthes's feeling of loss, and establishes the connection for him of photography with death:

> It is always maintained that I should suffer more because I have spent my whole life with her; but my suffering proceeds from *who she was:* and it is because she was who she was that I lived with her. To the Mother-as-Good, she had added that grace of being an individual soul. I might say, like the Proustian Narrator at his grandmother's death: "I did not insist only upon suffering, but upon respecting the originality of my suffering"; for this originality was the reflection of what was absolutely irreducible in her, and thereby lost forever. It is said that mourning, by its gradual labor, slowly erases pain; I could not, I cannot believe this; because for me, Time eliminates the emotion of loss (I do not weep), that is all. For the rest, everything has remained motionless. For what I have lost is not a Figure (the Mother) but a being; and not a being, but a *quality* (a soul): not the indispensable but the irreplaceable. I could

> live without the Mother (as we all do, sooner or later); but what life remained would be absolutely and entirely *unqualifiable* (without quality).
>
> (*Camera Lucida,* p. 175)

This passage is remarkable for its depth of feeling and also for Barthes's sense of the absolute character of his loss. His mother had a worth beyond all language and all categories, and that unique worth perished with her. Death is indeed outside language and outside history. Also, the individual is the bearer of value, and when a loved individual perishes, a value perishes that cannot in any way be compensated or replaced. Here Barthes confronts what is beyond irony, linguistic mediation, and intellectual stratagem. In both feeling and language, he is adequate to the occasion when no signifier, no circulation of meaning, is of any use to him.

In the first part of the book, before the powerful lyricism of his meditation on the death of his mother, Barthes does some deliberately informal theorizing about the nature of photography. Barthes said to an interviewer:

> The world has existed for hundreds of thousands of years, there have been images for thousands of years, since the cave paintings. . . . And then, all at once, around 1822, a new type of image appears, a new iconic phenomenon, entirely, anthropologically new.
>
> It's this newness that I try to examine, and I place myself in the situation of a naïve man, outside culture, someone untutored who would be constantly astonished at photography.
>
> (*The Grain of the Voice,* p. 357)

This assumed simplicity on the part of Barthes leads him to pay little attention to sophisticated art photographs and to concentrate on news photographs and private snapshots. He denies to photography the status of an art because it is so much at the mercy of the given, so comparatively barren of codes.

Characteristically, Barthes creates binary terms to deal with his subject. First there is the aspect of photography that he calls *studium:*

> It has the extension of a field, which I perceive quite familiarly as a consequence of my knowledge, my culture . . . it always refers to a classical body of information: rebellion, Nicaragua, and all the signs of both: wretched un-uniformed soldiers, ruined streets, corpses, grief, the sun, and the heavy-lidded Indian eyes. . . . my emotion requires the intermediary of a rational and emotional culture.
>
> (*Camera Lucida,* pp. 25–26)

In contrast with this culturally mediated reading of the record of what has been, what was actually there, is the experience of the *punctum,* the unexpected point in the photograph that pierces the viewer's attention. The *punctum* is, roughly, what jumps out of the photograph because it doesn't fit. An artificial *punctum* rigged by a photographer does not interest Barthes. It has to be there, somehow, in the "natural" field of the photograph. The *punctum* is a sign of intractable reality.

In the final reversal in a career of reversals, Barthes makes clear his preference for photography as a form of absolute realism, "obliging the loving and terrified consciousness to return to the very letter of Time: a strictly revulsive movement which reverses the course of the thing, and which I shall call, in conclusion, the photographic *ecstasy.*" In contrast, photography as an art subjects "its spectacle to the civilized code of perfect illusions" and is by comparison an impoverished and banal affair.

Looked at as a whole, Barthes's career gives an impression both of constant change and of extraordinary consistency. The variety is suggested by the chapter headings in Jonathan Culler's *Roland Barthes:* "Man of Parts," "Literary Historian," "Mythologist," "Critic," "Polemicist," "Semiologist," "Structuralist," "Hedonist," "Writer," and "Man of Letters." Every time Barthes felt one of his stances hardening into a doctrine, he moved away toward something new. Established truths were for him something to be abandoned: hence he always positioned himself on the cutting edge of thought.

Although Barthes first became famous as a theorist and critic, he was always primarily a writer seeking things to write about. He had at least as much regard for style as for ideas. Even at his most controversial and argumentative, he stays away from the "terrorist" style of Parisian intellectual controversy, with the result that his controversial works still read freshly because they are free of stale polemics. His discourse represents a highly idiosyncratic art form full of artifice and formal daring. He is the most attractive and accessible, the most readable, of the leaders of the "new" French thought. His style is supple, witty, and full of verbal novelty; his neologisms and obscurities yield up their meaning without undue labor of thought. Even at his most outrageous, he has an urbanity and sweetness of temper that disarm the reader.

Barthes's primary commitment was to writing; his primary subject matter was language. He had many secondary subjects—advertising, fashion, politics, art, wrestling, striptease, patriotism, photography, and so on—but his focus was always on the language of whatever subject he was dealing with: its connotations and its rhetorical strategies. Like much of radical French thought since World War II, Barthes's works tend to convert psychological issues into linguistic issues. For him, linguistics (in the most comprehensive sense) replaces psychology as the master subject, so that he looks at every facet of the world from the point of view of its vesture of words. The author is displaced from his former position at the center of a literary work by literary codes. The very self is treated as an invention of nomination. Amorous passion is examined as a rhetorical phenomenon.

In a profound way Barthes is a comic writer, a writer in love with irony, paradox, and contradiction. He approaches tragic issues and overwhelming melancholy, but in the spirit of comedy eludes them at the last moment. As a writer he sought surprise and joy, a blissful rather than a sour irony. Barthes appreciated best of all shifts, gaps, sharp turns of thought, and syncopations off the beat of ordinary thinking. The comedian as theorist and literary critic requires some adjustment of our ideas, perhaps a more playful and less solemn attitude toward the life of the mind than is customary. The Wallace Stevens of *Harmonium* (1923), especially of "Le monocle de mon oncle" and "The Comedian as the Letter C," would have recognized in Barthes a sensibility much like his own—one that was able to hold a humor and a theory together in a single thought.

## Selected Bibliography

### EDITIONS

*Le degré zéro de l'écriture.* Paris, 1953.

*Michelet par lui-même.* Paris, 1954.

*Mythologies.* Paris, 1957.

*Sur Racine.* Paris, 1963.

*Éléments de sémiologie.* Paris, 1964.

*Essais critiques.* Paris, 1964.

*La tour Eiffel.* Paris, 1964. With photographs by André Martin.

*Critique et vérité.* Paris, 1966.

*Système de la mode.* Paris, 1967.

*L'Empire des signes.* Geneva, 1970.

*S/Z.* Paris, 1970.

*Sade, Fourier, Loyola.* Paris, 1971.

*Le degré zéro de l'écriture. Suivi de Nouveaux essais critiques.* Paris, 1972.

*Le plaisir du texte.* Paris, 1973.

*Roland Barthes par Roland Barthes.* Paris, 1975.

*Fragments d'un discours amoureux.* Paris, 1977.

*Sollers écrivain.* Paris, 1979.

*La chambre claire: Note sur la photographie.* Paris, 1980.

*Le grain de la voix: Entretiens 1962–1980.* Paris, 1981.

*L'Obvie et l'obtus: Essais critiques III.* Paris, 1982.

*Le bruissement de la langue.* Paris, 1984.

*L'Aventure sémiologique.* Paris, 1985.

## ROLAND BARTHES


### TRANSLATIONS

*A Barthes Reader.* Edited with an introduction by Susan Sontag. New York, 1982.

*Camera Lucida: Reflections on Photography.* Translated by Richard Howard. New York, 1981.

*Critical Essays.* Translated by Richard Howard. Evanston, Ill., 1972.

*Criticism and Truth.* Edited and translated by Katrine P. Keuneman. London, 1987.

*The Eiffel Tower and Other Mythologies.* Translated by Richard Howard. New York, 1979.

*Elements of Semiology.* Translated by Annette Lavers and Colin Smith. London, 1967; New York, 1968.

*Empire of Signs.* Translated by Richard Howard. New York, 1982.

*The Fashion System.* Translated by Matthew Ward and Richard Howard. New York, 1983.

*The Grain of the Voice: Interviews 1962–1980.* Translated by Linda Coverdale. New York, 1985.

*Image, Music, Text.* Selected and translated by Stephen Heath. New York, 1977.

*A Lover's Discourse: Fragments.* Translated by Richard Howard. New York, 1978.

*Michelet.* Translated by Richard Howard. New York, 1980.

*Mythologies.* Selected and translated by Annette Lavers. New York, 1972.

*New Critical Essays.* Translated by Richard Howard. New York, 1980.

*On Racine.* Translated by Richard Howard. New York, 1964.

*The Pleasure of the Text.* Translated by Richard Miller. New York, 1975.

*The Responsibility of Forms: Critical Essays on Music, Art, and Representation.* Translated by Richard Howard. New York, 1985.

*Roland Barthes by Roland Barthes.* Translated by Richard Howard. New York, 1977.

*The Rustle of Language.* Translated by Richard Howard. New York, 1986.

*Sade, Fourier, Loyola.* Translated by Richard Miller. New York, 1976.

*The Semiotic Challenge.* Translated by Richard Howard. New York, 1988.

*Sollers Writer.* Translated by Philip Thody. Minneapolis, 1987.

*S/Z.* Translated by Richard Miller. New York, 1974.

*Writing Degree Zero.* Translated by Annette Lavers and Colin Smith. London, 1967; New York, 1968.

### BIOGRAPHICAL AND CRITICAL STUDIES

Burnier, Michel-Antoine, and Patrick Rambaud. *Le Roland-Barthes sans peine.* Paris, 1978.

Compagnon, Antoine, ed. *Prétexte: Roland Barthes.* Paris, 1978.

Culler, Jonathan. *Roland Barthes.* New York, 1983.

——— . *Structuralist Poetics.* Ithaca, N. Y., 1975.

Fages, J.-B. *Comprendre Roland Barthes.* Toulouse, 1979.

Hawkes, Terrence. *Structuralism and Semiotics.* London, 1977.

Kurzweil, Edith. *The Age of Structuralism: Lévi-Strauss to Foucault.* New York, 1980.

Lavers, Annette. *Roland Barthes: Structuralism and After.* London, 1982.

Norris, Christopher. *Deconstruction: Theory and Practice.* London, 1982.

Scholes, Robert. *Structuralism in Literature: An Introduction.* New Haven, 1974.

*Studies in Twentieth Century Literature* 5 (Spring 1981). A special issue on Barthes.

Thody, Philip. *Roland Barthes: A Conservative Estimate.* London, 1977.

Ungar, Steven. *Roland Barthes: The Professor of Desire.* Lincoln, Neb., 1983.

Wasserman, George R. *Roland Barthes.* Boston. 1981.

Wiseman, Mary B. *The Ecstasies of Roland Barthes.* London. 1989.

Wood, Michael. "The Rules of the Game." *New York Review of Books,* 4 March 1976, pp. 31–34.

### BIBLIOGRAPHY

Freeman, Sanford, and Carole Anne Taylor. *Roland Barthes: A Bibliographical Reader's Guide.* New York, 1983.


MASON COOLEY

# CAMILO JOSÉ CELA

## *(b. 1916)*

THE STYLE OF the winner of the 1989 Nobel Prize in literature, Camilo José Cela, is rough, down-to-earth, musical, and surprising, shot through with bitter yet compassionate irony. With unequaled genius he delves into the deeper complexities of Spanish life and expresses them in a forceful and always avant-garde way. A writer of considerable versatility and breadth, Cela has written novels, short stories, travel books, poems, plays, and journalistic essays mostly concerned with describing the language and people of Spain.

Born in Iria-Flavia, a small village of La Coruña in northern Galicia, on 11 May 1916, Cela used to his advantage the international background of his family, an English mother and an Italian grandmother, to develop an amused view of the idiosyncrasies of his country. He attended schools run by religious orders in Vigo and in Madrid; and then, for the academic year 1934–1935 he registered at the University of Madrid in the School of Medicine. However, he showed greater interest in the humanities than in becoming a physician. Having left medical school, he attended classes of the poet Pedro Salinas while preparing for examinations to qualify for employment as a customs official.

The Spanish Civil War (1936–1939) interrupted Cela's haphazard formal education, and he fought on the Nationalist side that had rebelled against the Republican government. He had spent fourteen months in Republican Madrid, exempted from military service because of a previous bout with tuberculosis, before he decided to join the Nationalist army by crossing the fighting lines through Valencia. He was wounded in 1938 and was inactive for the rest of the war. From 1939 to 1942 he studied law while he sought to establish himself as a writer.

After Franco's victory in 1939, literature was as devastated as Spain itself. Many important writers, such as Federico García Lorca, Ramiro de Maeztu, Antonio Machado, and Miguel de Unamuno, had died or been murdered during the war, while many others, such as Francisco Ayala, Jorge Guillén, and Pedro Salinas, were in exile. Miguel Hernández, today considered one of the best poets of a brilliant generation, died in jail in 1942. Censorship was erratic but strict; the general scarcity of paper restricted publications; and lack of buying power reduced the reading public. A flood of inferior translations of second-rate books could not replace works banned by the censors. Past masters such as Federico García Lorca, Machado de Assis, and Ramón del Valle-Inclán were frowned upon for their leftist leanings, and the production of their plays or the publication of their writings was forbidden. Spain was thus isolated both politically and culturally during World War II because it had sided with Hitler and Mussolini, even if it had never actually joined them militarily, and the isolation lasted until the early 1950's.

After the war Cela, like many who had fought in the Nationalist army, became critical of the harsh economic conditions everyone had to endure and of the vicious persecution by the authorities of anyone remotely suspected of having been a Republican or harboring any criticism of the Franco regime. Repression, hunger, and the rhetoric of fascism are the background of the publication in 1942 of Cela's *La familia de Pascual Duarte* (*The Family of the Pascual Duarte*), written while he was working as a clerk at the Textile Union in Madrid. The novel starts out with a framing device: the *transcriptor* (transcriber) says that he has found Pascual Duarte's manuscript in a drugstore in Almendralejo, a town in Badajoz, in the middle months of 1939, that is, just as the Civil War ended. He claims to have transcribed it faithfully, but he acknowledges that he has corrected the spelling, ordered the unnumbered pages, and cut out some passages he considered too crude. These references to censorship and the distancing of the protagonist's true voice, which is overlaid with the transcriber's voice, work as a muffling surface that runs through the whole novel, effectively reflecting the situation of all writing in Spain during the 1940's.

Readers at that time became distrustful practitioners of advanced hermeneutics and could find a hidden meaning even in a blank space, or perhaps especially there, where a cut would have left a gap. News of China was interpreted as a thinly veiled reference to what was happening in Madrid. The place where the manuscript of Pascual Duarte was said to have been found is not without significance: in Spain the drugstore is often a meeting place for intellectuals in small towns, Pascual's manuscript can also be compared to bitter medicine that sickens some readers with its gruesome details of violence, ignorance, and poverty in the Spanish countryside, but brings new vitality to others who are not afraid to face the sordid side of reality.

In the prologue to the first edition of his later novel, *La colmena* (*The Hive,* 1951), Cela wrote: "Life is what lives—in us or outside of us—we are nothing else than its carrier, its excipient, as pharmacists say" (*Obra completa,* 7.957).[1] The inert substance, the observing writer busy with living his private life, is just a device to convey the medicine, to reach and affect the reader with the text. Conceding the floor to Pascual is more than a simple structural device; it is part of Cela's consistent poetics: life must be searched for outside, in the tumult of life, in the other; in this case, the refined intellectual turns over the narration to a poor peasant who is about to be executed for murdering a rich man.

The note from the transcriber is followed by a letter from Pascual, dated 15 February 1937, explaining to a Mr. Barrera why he is sending the manuscript to him. Pascual clarifies here that the book is an apologetic description of his own ill-fated life led astray by the wrong education, his own bad instincts, and an unfavorable providence. He entrusts his writings to the rich and religious Mr. Barrera (Mr. Obstacle), as he had to trust before in the priest of the town, the director of the prison, and other representatives of authority. The date of Pascual's letter, the fifteenth, coincides with the day of Passover on which the Jews eat the Paschal lamb, and the identification of the criminal with a victim is carefully etched in as the manuscript progresses. It must not be forgotten that Pascual is attempting to justify his actions, perhaps even hoping to obtain a last-minute reprieve of the execution he is awaiting as a consequence of having killed don Jesús González de la Riva, count of Torremejía, the rich man in town.

Does Cela support Pascual's contention that he is innocent, or does he show how clever ideology may try to explain away bloody and brutal crimes? These questions are matters of debate. What Cela clearly presents is the opaque nature of language, as he eliminates any objective evidence—we have only Pas-

[1] All quotations from Cela have been translated by the present writer from the editions cited in the bibliography.

cual's version of events—that would nail down the meaning of the text. According to Mr. Barrera's testament that follows Pascual's letter, he condemned the manuscript to the flames, recommending to whoever found it in a drawer of his writing desk not to read it because it was immoral and contrary to the good order of life. He allowed, nevertheless, that if the manuscript was not destroyed in eighteen months (twice the gestation period of a human being?), whoever found it could do whatever he wished with it. The reader can suppose, therefore, that by special dispensation of heavenly grace the manuscript was saved from the flames, like the *Aeneid,* and considered worth publishing.

The reference to Vergil's foundational epic is probably not accidental, since Aeneas had to leave home in order to create for himself a new country, after his own had been annihilated by the Trojan War, and Pascual will have to leave behind his family in order to reach the paradoxical freedom of his prison cell. This presentation also stresses two possible opposing views about Pascual's memoirs: as upsetting the commonly held values in conventional society (Mr. Barrera's opinion) or as a valuable example of a model not to follow (the transcriber's view).

The core of the book is the autobiographical manuscript of Pascual, the son of a Portuguese immigrant, a poor peasant in a small southern town, reminiscing in jail about the conditions and events that brought him to face a death sentence. The first chapter accumulates stark symbols in the description of the town where the drama takes place. In the lovely plaza, the ground covered with tiles and surrounded by houses so white that Pascual's eyes hurt even now when he remembers the sun reverberating upon them, a fountain sticks out its three dry spouts, while the rich don Jesús has enough water to keep many flowers in his garden. The clock of the town hall is broken, blank, and as indifferent as a white consecrated host. The reference is clearly to the feudal conditions that have kept Spanish peasants frozen in time, exploited by a coalition of the aristocracy and the church. At the start of the Civil War, Pascual participated in the murder of don Jesús González de la Riva, count of Torremejía, who recognized him before receiving the last blow and called Pascual by an affectionate diminutive.

This patronizing attitude shows that don Jesús is Pascual's superior. By being involved in don Jesús' murder, Pascual has at last committed a crime that will not be pardoned, as were those originating only in personal quarrels but not in class struggle. Pascual's manuscript will not address the events of the Civil War, conveniently avoided. His defense will consist instead in a description of the conditions of brutality and marginality in which he grew up, which did not educate him to control his instincts. While before the Civil War he was only a common criminal, his acts during the uprising would necessarily have been interpreted by his captors as politically motivated. It must not be forgotten that he is writing from the jail of Badajoz, six months after the town has been taken over by the Nationalist army. Therefore, he decides to keep his explanations close to home. His mother's drinking and love affairs, his sister's prostitution, his younger brother's death—a retarded child who drowns in a vat of olive oil—the accidental abortion of Pascual and Lola's first child, the death by sickness of their second, all conspire to frustrate an introverted man who finds only late and on paper the capacity to express himself adequately.

Gruesome details accumulate: his father dies from rabies, a pig eats his younger brother's ears, Pascual shoots his favorite hunting dog, stabs a friend during a bar brawl, kills a horse, frightens his first wife to death, kills her lover, and in an especially brutal scene, stabs his mother to death. This last scene opens the text to at least two interpretations: one could see Pascual as an Orestes figure, come back to avenge his father, who suffered at the hands of an adulterous wife; or one could see Pascual as a man who had always been in search of the mother figure promised by his culture, in which the Virgin Mary is the paragon of all women, but who found only a miserable woman intent on satisfying her own desire for drinking and sex, in which case the murder becomes a desperate attempt to make real contact with her at last. In any case, it is clear that Cela made this last embrace between mother and son an instant in which birth and death, and sex and violence, merge into one encounter that alludes to the passion of Christ and the redemption obtained by removing the sinful origin.

Pascual approaches his mother, asleep in her bed, while he muses about his situation, sunk in the clay of his human condition, which threatens to suffocate him:

> At that point then there was no other solution. I sprung on her and pinned her down. She struggled, wiggled away. . . . for a moment she had me by the neck. She was shouting as a madwoman. We fought; it was the most awful fight you could imagine. We roared like beasts, spit came out of our mouths. . . . I came to have my clothes torn, the chest exposed. The damned woman had more strength than a devil. I had to use all my manhood to keep her from moving. If I caught her fifteen times, fifteen times she got away. She scratched me, she kicked me and punched me, she bit me. There was a moment in which she caught one of my nipples in her mouth—the left one—and she tore it out from its root. At that same instant I stabbed her in the neck. . . . Blood ran as a runaway horse and it hit my face. It was warm as a womb and it tasted just like the blood of a lamb.
>
> (chap. 19)

In Pascual's text the story emerges with temporal displacements as the memory fights to clarify this misunderstood and partly repressed past. The womb, the house, and the prison cell are successive encroachments on Pascual's development, and they are superseded only when he attempts to retrace his steps in the scribblings on the blank page. Pascual will be his own creator, once his mother and society have failed him. Yet he has been framed, and he is entrapped, cocoon-like, by his own complex text, as well as by the note of the transcriber at the beginning, and the letters of the prison chaplain and a prison guard at the end, both telling their versions of Pascual's inglorious death, his neck triturated by the garrote, his voice silenced by this primitive execution method.

This is a somber text structure, in which all that is left is recollection, a revision of a censored past. Pascual's cell is surrounded by the representatives of Order, Grammar (the transcriber), the Church, and the Police. The first sentence in Pascual's confession becomes a persistent question for the reader, who is forced to take the judge's bench: "I, Sir, am not a bad man, even if I did not lack motives to be one" (chap. 1). For Pascual, who declares himself innocent, every detail becomes a dark exterior motivation, a justification of his actions that therefore do not spring from his inner self. We are in the presence of a paranoid text, bent on proving the complicity of elements, circumstance, and history in the undoing of a Pascual who could have been a better man.

A vivid example is Pascual's memory of the day his sister Rosario was born: "Nothing moved in the countryside, scorched by the sun, and the crickets with their saws seemed to want to file away the bones of the earth; people and animals were under cover and the sun, way up above, like the lord of everything, illuminating all, burning all" (chap. 2). For the fire of lust, hate, and anger, the Duarte family is dry kindling unable to endure and survive.

But even in descriptions of the greatest violence, Pascual's writing adds the lyric dimension that becomes his saving grace; this lyricism also emerges in his expressions of concern for the bones of the earth, for his sister Rosario, for what he sees just outside the window of his cell: "Walking down the road—how well I could see them from my window—some persons went by. Probably they weren't even thinking that I was looking at them, they acted so naturally. They were two men, a woman, and a child; they seemed happy walking down the road" (chap. 6). Here there is a perceived harmony, in which two men can walk naturally with a woman and not engage in battle over her. Pascual also notices how in Madrid people are able to resolve their conflicts by venting their anger in words, and he dreams of emigrating to America, as did so many others during the harsh 1940's. He grows and develops through his travels in Spain and by means of his illusions of a different life, as can be seen when one compares the peasant who acted with the prisoner who wrote.

As Pascual writes in his cell about how, at the funeral of his little brother, he raped Lola over the recently removed earth of the grave (she provoked him to it and later became his first wife), his pen prefigures events that the peasant could not foresee as he acted, but that the prisoner discovered during his meditations in jail:

> It was a brutal fight. Thrown to the ground, pinned down, she was more beautiful than ever. . . . Her breasts went up and down faster and faster as she breathed. I grabbed her by the hair and held her close to the ground. She struggled, wiggled away. . . . I bit her until I tasted blood, until she gave in and was tame as a young mare.
>
> (chap. 5)

Pascual praises Lola, comparing her to a young mare, a valuable and most useful possession in his agrarian society. But just as he cannot control the women in his life, the image of life—the mare—will bring death: the son begotten at the encounter on the grave will be aborted when Lola is thrown to the ground by a young mare as they return from their honeymoon. Pascual will then stab the mare repeatedly until she dies, closing the cycle of death underlying the apparently innocent image, in the rape scene, of a peasant in control of his animals: nature turns against Pascual, and tricks him into blind alleys.

After the rape, Pascual observes six drops of blood on the ground, like six poppies. They prognosticate his six acts of bloody violence, but in a significant irony they reappear in the chapel, in the form of the poppies that Pascual orders to decorate it when he marries Lola. At the time, he was blind to the teasing symbols of his condition, where the beauty of a mare and poppies concealed violence and death, where possessing his wife prefigured killing his mother. Yet, what Pascual the peasant could not then see, Pascual the writer now clearly understands.

This forceful story, framed by explanations of how the manuscript was found and by letters of the chaplain and the prison guard who saw Pascual executed, dragged away in terror to the garrote, was an immediate success in Spain and abroad for several disparate reasons. It was seen by some as a confirmation of the brutality of the populace, as a testimony in writing to the monstrous and evil spirit that had been exorcised by Franco's victory. Others, who could not accept the narration as accurate in respect to the conditions of peasants, coined the term *tremendismo,* rejected by Cela himself, to safely explain away the rough edges of the narrative as mere literary exaggeration. Still others saw a sociological explanation for the pent-up violence that led to the Civil War and that could recur at any moment.

The text is cleverly ambiguous and eludes a univocal interpretation. It is clear today that it contains two elements perhaps not sufficiently understood at the time of its publication, but that nevertheless had a strong effect on the reading public. First, it debunks the myth of the family, a myth that was central to the paternal rhetoric and image of the Caudillo Franco and to the fascist replacement of class struggle with family unity. Pascual's family was nothing to brag about, and in fact it is only by murdering his mother that Pascual can attain any feeling of freedom. The second element is the tension between Pascual's brutal actions and his writing, lyrical yet precise, riddled with effective symbols, meticulous and breathless, a tour de force of dazzling craft. The language wins the reader over, even if conscience may reject Pascual's rationalizations for his crimes.

The murderer appears, with a face and a voice, in the full contradiction of life.

The censors, always vigilant, briefly suppressed the second edition of this lucid nightmare, but once respected critics adopted the book, under the taming label of *tremendismo* as an early masterpiece of post–Civil War Spain, it was allowed again into circulation; and it brought new life into an almost dead literary establishment. Official Spain began to tolerate Cela mainly because he was one of the very few writers it could present to challenge the accusation of the writers in exile that culture had left Spain with them. *The Family of Pascual Duarte* and Carmen Laforet's *Nada* (Nothing, 1945), also the story of a lurid family scarred by the Civil War, share the undisputed distinction of being considered both by the general public and by the critics as the two most important Spanish novels of the 1940's.

A film based on *Pascual Duarte* (1976), directed by Ricardo Franco, portrays in detail the harsh conditions of peasant life while it intensifies the sociological implications of Pascual's violence. But the film fails on two accounts: first, the novel thrives precisely because of its ambiguity; it is as if the manifest fear results from the fist of the clenched writing hand enclosing what it is unable or unwilling to denounce openly. Second, the description of Pascual's brutal actions is blurred in the novel by the first-person narrative into a tortured, numb passion that the screen image is unable to duplicate.

A novel successful in Spain and abroad, soon translated into most major languages, was all the more welcome because the two previous important groups of writers, the generations of 1898 and 1927, had excelled in poetry and the essay but had been less fortunate in the narrative, with the possible exception of Pío Baroja, who could be claimed as an important inspiration for Cela. In fact, Cela asked Pío Baroja to write a prologue for *The Family of Pascual Duarte,* but Baroja, already quite old, told him that he did not wish to go to jail and that the younger writer could face that danger alone. This anecdote conveys some of the uniqueness and courage of Cela's writing, qualities that may have become obscured as the 1940's receded into the past.

Cela's second novel, *Pabellón de reposo* (*Rest Home*), published in 1943, presents the writings of seven tuberculosis patients identified only by the numbers of their rooms. In the first part of the novel they optimistically examine their life histories and their futures, while in the second part they confront the reality of their unavoidable deaths. The image of a wheelbarrow used to cart coffins away returns constantly to remind patients of their true condition as transitory occupants of the waiting room of death. The authorities of the institution are considered cruel by the patients, who invent small and ineffective substitutes for rebellion, consoling themselves with their writings and private lives: "The director may be in charge of the sanatorium, but he has no power over my heart," writes one of the patients (chap. 5). It becomes progressively clear that the true enemy is the body, and that nature continues its course without taking notice of the individual's disintegration:

> It is cruel and bitter, this indifference of what is alive and in full health toward what dies slowly, withered and downtrodden. The innocent bird of the morning, flying happily over the sowed fields does not waste even a second to look at the sky lark wounded by the cruel hunter, the sad sky lark dragging herself on the ground as if she were a woodchuck, since all her grace was lifted away by that shot that went on bouncing off from rock to rock on the hill.
>
> (chap. 6)

The questions asked by the pastoral novel are posed here under a drab surface, not of ardent shepherds consumed by unrequited love but of feverish, secluded men and women whose spirits soar as their bodies weaken: Why are human beings so imperfect, why do they inflict so much pain on each other, why can't they control their destinies, and why have they lost the harmony that the rest of nature seems to have kept? The repetitions found in the quoted passage are characteristic of Cela's prose; they evoke the cadences of spoken language and the sententiousness of the country folk. But this literary device also represents the constant return of the same situations, the repetition of life itself, in which even heroes are not unique. A note by the author interrupts the characters' writings, claiming that a doctor has asked him not to continue the publication of the text as a newspaper serial because some patients he knows are depressed by what they consider the public revelation of their own stories. But fiction, for Cela, is at the same time the affirmation of the value of human beings and the mocking of individuality: "No one who is sick should believe himself the world's belly button. No one should believe that their troubles are truly exemplary. No one should identify with these not too fortunate characters of my fiction" ("Note of the Author").

This Spanish contribution to situations and techniques, amply explored by Thomas Mann and Virginia Woolf, shows, despite the possible unfavorable comparison with Mann's *The Magic Mountain* (1924), Cela's knack for interpreting his period. Not only was tuberculosis a frequent illness, ransacking a society debilitated by real and widespread hunger, but it also masterfully represented the isolation and hopelessness into which citizens had been led by an effective machinery of repression. A young student in *Rest Home* examines his social life harshly: "Liberty does not exist for me. It never existed" (chap. 3). The symbolic implications do not thin the text into abstraction, but instead are conveyed in a thoroughly realistic presentation. Cela could give chilling details of the daily life of his characters, having experienced tuberculosis himself and having been forced to spend periods in a sanatorium in 1931 and 1942.

The constant experimentation that characterizes Cela and his astonishing knowledge of Spanish classical literature revealed themselves in his next book, *Nuevas andanzas y desventuras de Lazarillo de Tormes* (New Wanderings and Misadventures of Lazarillo of Tormes, 1944). In this novel he attempted a contemporary version of the adventures of a boy who discovers the harshness and corruption of the world while in the service of different masters, on the model of the anonymous *Lazarillo de Tormes* (*Lazarus of Tormes,* 1554). Even if the experience of growing up in the Spain of the 1940's was better described later, realistically by Miguel Delibes in *La sombra del ciprés es alargada* (The Shadow of the Cypress Tree Is Elongated, 1948), and allegorically in Rafael Sánchez Ferlosio's masterpiece *Industrias y andanzas de Alfanhuí* (*Alfanhui,* 1951), Cela's attempt is not altogether a failed one: his delight in archaisms, in rescuing from kitchens and roads the creative expressions of the poor, smoldering with an acid brutality, gives the *Nuevas andanzas* a mystifying, almost solemn, tone.

Cela's choice as a model of a classic book of the Spanish Golden Age, an age that was elevated as a paradigm by the Franco regime and contemplated with nostalgia by many intellectuals of the period, was double-edged, since *Lazarus of Tormes* revealed that under the clouds of gold the lining was one of poverty, blindness, deceit, and violence. The worry underlying all actions of the young Lazarus in 1554 is hunger, and nothing seems to have changed in Cela's novel, nor indeed in the time in which it was published, the 1940's, a time that has come to be known as "the years of hunger."

In the prologue to *Nuevas andanzas* José María de Cossío, a highly respected critic of the period and a scholar who had studied Golden Age literature, stressed the immediate relevance of Cela's apparently anachronistic novel:

> Our feelings have changed radically and the most important theme of the picaresque novel, hunger, that could then be treated with a smile . . . today is nothing less than the central worry of politics.

> A picaresque novel that followed today the model of the old ones would have as its theme a truly crucial problem of our society.

And this was precisely what Cela did, turning on its head the nostalgia for the imperial past by showing its rags and the continuance of Spain's unresolved problems.

Cela, like most writers of the Generation of 1898 before him (Unamuno, Baroja, Machado), was an avid traveler in his own land and wrote several books and many newspaper articles based on these local expeditions. Three volumes (4–6) of his *Obra completa* (Complete Works) contain accounts of some of his trips in Spain. *Viaje a la Alcarria* (*Journey to the Alcarria,* 1948) is the first and the best, imitated later by other writers and by Cela himself, who never again attained such a concise, graphic description of an impoverished countryside as in this compact text, in which small towns and their inhabitants are portrayed with the irony of the city dweller but warmed by a charity comparable to that of Fellini's classic films and the best of Italian neorealism.

As the traveler leaves Madrid in the early morning, he encounters a silent city, reeking of death, wherein "the mysterious black streetcars of the night carry in all directions their scaffolding on wheels; the conductors are men without uniform, men with a beret, silent as corpses, hiding their faces with scarves" (chap. 2). The reference to the frequent disappearance of citizens at night during and after the Civil War is clear, and is reiterated in other seemingly innocent passages: "On their way to the slaughterhouse, sheep pass by, sheared, dirty, and with a red *B* painted on their backs" (chap. 2). The locomotives at the train station look like horses killed in battle.

Leaving the city and setting himself on the road with no specific goal, the traveler tastes freedom: "No one forces me to do anything . . . what I have to do is done equally well a quarter of an hour earlier than later; it is of no consequence at all" (chap. 2). In his walk from the sixth to the fifteenth of June 1946, he rediscovers in the resilience and grace of the country folk the complex fabric of Spanish history that persists untouched at a short distance from Madrid. On the other hand, the traveler observes that even though seven years have gone by since the Civil War ended, the ruins remain and there are no signs of modernization in rural Spain. His conclusion is that "past glories are a heavy weight that, worst of all, sap the will; and without a strong will, as can be clearly observed, and with people given over to the contemplation of past greatness, everyday problems are left to fester" (chap. 11). But even with his scalding observations the narrator is grateful for the freedom that his walk has granted him: "The traveler, back on the road, feeling rested from his recent nap, thinks about things he hasn't thought about for many years, and he feels as if a slight breeze made his heart light" (chap. 3).

The traveler meets a gallery of characters who with magical economy and grace come to life under his pen: the sad red-headed boy, the traveling salesman, the schoolteacher, all limited in their horizons but occupying with dignity their marginal spaces in life, much like the peasants Goya had painted a century earlier. He also notices, without comment, the hardships of primitive industrial production:

> Near Valdenoches some laborers are cutting stones. They are black as soot and wear handkerchiefs under their caps to soak up the sweat. They work slowly and wearily, and protect their eyes with a small piece of wire screen tied at the back of the neck with strings. When the cart goes by they do not raise their heads.
>
> (chap. 3)

But mostly the traveler enjoys his trip, even to the point of becoming worried by the pain this happiness will bring him later, when he has lost it, or by the restlessness this taste of freedom may bring to the routine of his daily life. The trip must end, and the traveler returns to the city in a bus, to reintegrate himself with his humdrum reality, in which most people are anonymous and lack the roots and vigorous tradition he has found in the countryside.

The writing of the book and its publication by the most intellectual journal of the period, the *Revista de Occidente,* was an act of restoration of realistic vision, or at least a successful attempt to demonstrate that a gap existed between literature and historical reality in Spain. In the next decades many novelists followed Cela's lead and tried to fill the vacuum left by a bland and blind press, notably Delibes and Juan Goytisolo with brilliant examples of the travel genre.

In 1951, correctly anticipating problems with censorship, Cela published in Buenos Aires *The Hive,* a novel that had been five years in the making and had gone through five versions (the first version had been rejected by the censors in 1946). The authorities were not pleased with Cela's bleak portrayal of Spain and of the sordid lives of most protagonists of *The Hive.* As an immediate consequence, Cela was expelled from the Spanish Press Association, and his name was banned from Spanish newspapers. *The Hive* marked the start of a new period in Iberian literature. Even if at a first reading the text resembles a collection of anecdotes loosely thrown together, reminding the reader of John Dos Passos' *Manhattan Transfer* (1925), its structure is complex and extremely tight. Cela has compared it to the mechanism in a watch, and the comparison is apt, for a conception of time as circular and meaningless is one of the clues to this verbal puzzle in which no piece is idle.

The novel is divided into six chapters and an epilogue, entitled in Cela's typical deadpan manner "Final" (Ending). The action spans five or six days in Madrid during 1942 or 1943, but the chapters do not follow a chronological sequence; the material would be ordered consecutively only if the chapters were rearranged I, II, IV, VI, III, V, and Ending. Many of the brief glimpses of life in a café, in the streets of Madrid, and in middle-class apartments, as lived by around 350 characters, are like tiles that overlap each other and reappear in different chapters, while some of the chapters are interlocking and not just sequential.

What made this novel surprising in the Spanish context of the early 1950's was that almost all previous postwar novels had been concerned with the plight of a single character or at most of a family, while here a large segment of Madrid's society becomes the multitudinous "character." Also, the experimental nature of the time sequences opened up new possibilities. As a structuring device, most anecdotes can be related to the experience of Martín Marco (Marco means Frame), an out-of-luck, jobless, mediocre intellectual who is afraid that his past connections with liberal causes, while he was a university student before the Civil War, may come back to hurt him. Martín's portrait is characteristic of Cela's irony:

> The man is not run of the mill, not just anyone, he is not a common man, a man of the masses, an undistinguishable being; he has a tattoo on his left arm and a scar in the loin. He has studied a few years and he translates some French. He has followed carefully the comings and goings of literary and intellectual movements, and there are some literary supplements of *El Sol* that he could still repeat almost by heart. As a young man he had a Swiss sweetheart and he wrote ultraist poems.
>
> (chap. 1)

His claims for uniqueness are slim indeed. Martín follows literary and intellectual movements but does not initiate change, and he *almost* remembers some articles from the liberal newspaper *El Sol.*

We first meet Martín when he wanders into doña Rosa's café, where most of the first chapter takes place, and he is sent away in shame when he can't pay for his cup of coffee. His moment of glory will come when he is able to return and pay not only for his coffee but also for a shoeshine and cigarettes. Martín's crowning pleasure is to reject the coffee he could not pay for before, in an attempt to return to the owner doña Rosa the humiliation she had inflicted upon him. The other characters in this café, controlled by a dominant and cruel woman who hopes that Hitler will win the war, are numb survivors of everyday life: the aging prostitute, the failed, halfhearted entrepreneur, a woman whose son recently died just as he was about to become a mailman, a famished poet, a vain printer, and many others. Such an enumeration does not do justice to the quick, deft scalpel of Cela's prose, which with few words creates grotesque characters and then elevates them to human beings who struggle, surrounded by mirrors, in this constricting society in order to satisfy their basic urges for food, sex, and power:

> Reclining over the old marble surfaces of the tables covered with a film of dirt, the clients see the owner go by, almost without noticing her now, while they foggily meditate about this world that—alas!—turned out to be not what it could have been, about this world in which everything has been failing little by little, perhaps due to an insignificant detail, without anyone offering a good explanation.
>
> (chap. 1)

In the next sentence the reader discovers that many of the marble table surfaces were previously used as tombstones and that a blind man would still be able to read on their hidden surfaces the inscriptions, one of them in memory of the death of a young woman called Esperanza Redondo (Round Hope), and another of a man who was in charge of the National Office for Development. Such juxtaposition, with no connecting comment, of important tiles in the mosaic of the novel allows criticism to seep through without being explicit—which was part of the necessary encoding of literature under a repressive censorship. This made *The Hive* a provocative novel to read in Spain, but obscured its full import elsewhere.

In the novel itself there is an example of the fear that a writer can feel when confronted by authority. Martín, wandering through the city at night, is asked for his identity papers by a policeman. He claims to have left them at home, but he identifies himself as a writer who publishes in the official press, his latest effort being an article entitled "Reasons for the Spiritual Permanence of Isabella the Catholic." He hurries away and the narrator observes that "he harbors in his body a terrible fright that he can't possibly explain" (chap. 4). A few lines later he is running, "sweating like a calf, like a gladiator in the arena, like a pig being slaughtered." Then he starts off in a runaway stream of anxious thoughts:

> What am I afraid of? Ha, ha! What am I afraid of? Of what, of what? He had a gold tooth. Ha, ha! What could I be afraid of? What of, what of? I could use a gold tooth. It would look good! I am not involved in anything! In anything! What can they do to me if I don't get involved in anything?

Of course, the implied thought is that if he does get involved, say by writing a novel such as *The Hive,* he can expect "them" to do something to him.

Cela chose differently than Martín Marco. For a citizen of Madrid, the conclusion of the previously quoted description of clients oblivious to the despotic presence of the owner, lost in thought about the undetectable origin of their failed lives while leaning on tombstones, could not have gone undetected as a condemnation of a guilty official indifference that refused to consider the collective and political determination of each human life: "The clients of the cafés are people who believe that things happen just because, and that there is nothing you can do about anything" (chap. 1). Each client is submerged in his own private problem, like a helpless fish in the artificial and illuminated environment of a fishbowl. The reader is gently prodded to notice the contrast between the isolation in which the characters believe they live and the social network of which they form part, a part not very different from any other.

Money is the honey in this hive, and it is common to all, passing from hand to hand, exchanged for coffee, self-esteem, or human bodies. The bride of a man afflicted by tuberculosis sells herself in order to buy food and medicine for her future husband. A woman who was Martín's girlfriend at the university gives him some money, most of which he loses in the restroom of doña Rosa's café, where it is found by a musician who happily buys fancy eyeglasses for his wife.

The brothel in which Martín takes refuge from the vastness of life in an indifferent city is a place, as is the text itself, in which the same acts are repeated with different characters. Yet, in the recognition of the common needs of the body, a principle of solidarity gradually emerges, and it breaks down the distinctions that are used to justify the humiliation of those human beings branded as inferior.

The "Ending" segments present Martín's visit to his mother's grave on 20 December. He carries a newspaper that he reads from the first to the last page, but he misses the one section that his friends are reading in different parts of the city, a section also hidden from the view of the reader. It appears that there is a warrant for Martín's arrest, perhaps as a suspect in the strangling of a woman who was murdered a few days before, while he was in the neighborhood, perhaps for some other actions in his probable Republican past. The newspaper emerges as a form of literature parallel to *The Hive,* since in it items are brought together by contiguity and chance; thus history is reduced to snippets of anecdotes awaiting further development. On the other hand, the newspaper brings together, to the same text, hundreds of thousands of readers in the city, constituting a prefiguration of a deeper possible solidarity, superior to the caustic web of money. The generous reaction of Martín's friends, all worried by his destiny and willing to take risks in order to help him, indicates their emergence from the previous state of inaction and aimless vagrancy.

The text has many threads, besides the main storyline, that imbricate disparate elements into a deeper unity. In the first chapter the reader encounters a cat at doña Rosa's café: "Among the tables runs a fat cat, with a shining coat; a cat full of health and well-being." The poignancy of these observations becomes apparent only later, when the full misery of the clients of the café is revealed and we notice that, unlike the clients, the cat is well fed, sleeps well, does what he wishes. A cat, a tiger, or a lion is frequently mentioned in *The Hive* in relation to power and sexual satisfaction. They are symbols of the energy of desire that binds all animals, including human beings. The wilted old prostitute, Miss Elvira, has a delightful dream, after a wasted night, in which she is possessed by a cat who grows into a tiger; her dream illuminates retrospectively the importance of that cat seen running among the tables of the café at the very beginning, a symbol of the desire and passion that can still glow warmly even in the worst of conditions.

In the excellent film version of 1983, directed by Mario Camus, the ending was modified, and Martín is seen in the last images of the film walking away from the police station after he has been cleared of all suspicion. More than just an adulteration of the original text to make the plot more palatable to the public of the 1980's, this movie ending is an indication of how strongly the novel's conclusion reflected the general hope placed in solidarity during the early 1950's, in the face of a strong, repressive police and the lingering memory of the Civil War dead. In a new, democratic Spain, Martín is allowed to go free, alone, in search of his chance for a life of his own.

This novel was conceived as the first in a series of novels to be called *Caminos inciertos* (Uncertain Paths), but the series was never completed. The distorted echo of Sartre's *Les chemins de la liberté* (*The Roads to Freedom,* 1945–1949) reveals the close connection of Cela's values and ideas to those of existentialism. *The Family of Pascual Duarte* bears a resemblance to Albert Camus's *L'Étranger* (*The Stranger,* 1942), but the common preoccupation with the desolate condition of the individual in the twentieth century seems more a parallel interest than a direct influence. In his dialogue with existentialism Cela takes advantage of centuries of stark Spanish realism and disenchantment with heroic and transcendent projects.

In 1945 Cela published a collection of his early poems under the title *Pisando la dudosa luz del día* (Walking on the Hesitant Light of Day), a phrase from Luis de Góngora and a reference to the emptiness discovered at the center of the Spanish Baroque. Cela shares Góngora's pleasure in the texture of words and the turn of a phrase, all that is left in a world where higher values are spurned and God has receded out of sight. With the other master of Spanish Baroque, Francisco de Quevedo, he has in common a delight in scatological terms and in revealing the unredeemed insignificance, cruelty, and meanness of human beings, loved nevertheless for their folly and persistence in inventing transcendent justifications for mediocre lives. These surrealistic poems are of minor importance, especially when compared with the work being done in the same years by other poets, but Cela's "Himno a la Muerte" (Hymn to Death), written in Madrid between 1 and 11 November 1936, is a striking and painful portrait of a young man who believes that the world into which he is about to be plunged will be so repellent that death is a better alternative. One can anticipate here the bitter root of Cela's outsider stance, his fierce independence, and his daredevil attitude.

In 1953 Cela published a novel inspired by surrealism, *Mrs. Caldwell habla con su hijo* (*Mrs. Caldwell Speaks to Her Son*), an experiment that was not well received at the time but that acquired increasing significance later on. It reveals Cela's creative restlessness and his search to move out from the stagnant Spanish cultural atmosphere of his time by reestablishing relationships with García Lorca, Rafael Alberti, and other surrealist poets of the 1920's; it also shows his desire to reveal the hidden recesses of the mind, in an introspective method seldom practiced in Spanish narrative. In the prologue to *Mrs. Caldwell* that Cela added for the *Obra Completa,* he maps out his territory:

> The mind of human beings is very confused and bitter; it is full of mysterious keys, of unexamined echoes, and of registers of cadenced or desperate sounds that are never quite understood: neither in peace nor in war, neither in orgasm nor abstinence, nor in madness, nor when a man cautiously turns in a friend to the police
>
> (*Obra completa,* 7.363)

This fragmentation and fundamental opacity of the mind is studied microscopically by Cela through the relationship of a mother, Mrs. Caldwell, to her son, Eliacim, in a series of 215 brief chapters (two are presented in two versions). At times the novel reads like a prose poem, as Mrs. Caldwell jots down the passion of her progressively deranged mind. Her last entries, after the death of her son, are made at the Royal Hospital for the Insane in London. There is a curious and attractive counterpoint of an openly expressed acceptance of desire and its rejection, of self-knowledge and self-deceit, of revelation and concealment: "I never failed you, my son, because I never asked you even a single question about which I had any doubt as to its answer. We women, Eliacim, when we don't need it anymore for anything, experience the birth of a strange instinct in our heart, an instinct warm and heavy as the mouth of a hot oven" (chap. 135).

The superficially blunt humor of this book embraces a radical desolation, for example, in the fragment that starts out with Mrs. Caldwell's musings about how to feed her son: "Should we drink soup? Or rather, should one not drink soup?" Faced with her lack of knowledge in such minor matters, she discovers her own insufficiency and wasted existence: "The fondness I have for your memory is great, is it not? Nevertheless, in spite of my love I can't tell you anything useful about soups" (chap. 29).

The narrative voice in the different stages of Mrs. Caldwell's progressive madness continuously borders on enlightened self-knowledge, but ends by steering away in a reticence that avoids the almost evident, yet missed, explanations. Cela is not the only one in this novel who is creating a world of fiction: Mrs. Caldwell mirrors the creative artist as she repeatedly rewrites her past according to her wishes in order to make acceptable sense out of her life. These attempts leave behind only words swirling in a vast stream of uncontrollable imagination working in the unknowable recesses of her mind: "The pale, small pebbles that the water carries away, Eliacim, are the image of fiction, the luminous shadow of fiction" (chap. 62).

At times, she expresses herself with harsh exactitude: "I do not want you as an angel, my son. Nor do I want you as the dweller of a white cloud, a gray cloud, or a black cloud. I desire you in a way that is much more simple and impossible" (chap. 87). The double distance brought about by the prohibition of incest and the death of Eliacim has left only a vacuum filled by an incessant writing that cannot recover the totality of the presence of the loved body:

> I am horrified by the thought that your lips, my son, may have already dissolved in the sea and that they swim scattered into thousands and thousands of minuscule fragments in the cold wasteland of sirens, those insatiable phantoms of immense and virtuous lips, of immense and wisely virtuous lips.
>
> (chap. 134)

The mother's fear of losing her son in another woman's arms is intensified by the thought that Eliacim is disappearing for her even as a memory. The vase that unaccountably explodes on the occasion of Eliacim's first birthday can represent his mother's incapacity to contain him, as well as the failure of the text itself to reconstitute a homogeneous and complete portrait of the irrevocably absent object of desire, Eliacim.

On 31 December 1952, as a consequence of the publication of *The Hive,* the secretary of the Press Association barred Cela from practicing journalism in Spain. Cela then left for several trips to Latin America between 1952 and 1955, visiting Colombia, Ecuador, Chile, Argentina, and Venezuela, trips that he chronicled in *La rueda de los ocios* (The Wheel of Idle Moments, 1957). He also moved permanently from Madrid to Majorca in 1954. It was in this new domicile in the Balearic Islands that Cela started editing his independent literary journal, *Papeles de Son Armadans.* From 1956 to 1979 the small pages of this Spanish journal celebrated such diverse cultural figures as Picasso and Baroja, anathemas to the governmental establishment, and each month introduced much of the best and the newest from abroad into the mainstream of Spanish culture.

During Cela's stay in Venezuela he accepted a commission to write a novel about that country, but the resulting product, *La Catira* (The Blonde, 1955), did not please most critics on either side of the Atlantic, even though it received the prestigious Prize of Literary Critics in 1956, which probably honored the totality of Cela's work rather than his most recent novel. *La Catira* is an adventure novel in which a domineering woman takes over a large estate in the uncivilized Venezuelan countryside. It reads like a remake of the classic Venezuelan novel by Rómulo Gallegos, *Doña Bárbara* (1929), but it does not reach the complexity and poetic force of Gallegos' masterpiece. A glossary at the end of the novel includes 896 "exotic" words, seemingly as an appendix to help the reader understand the peculiar aspects of Venezuelan Spanish as portrayed by Cela. The Venezuelan Royal Academy of Language considered his attempts to reproduce the Spanish spoken in Venezuela linguistically inexact. Most probably Cela started where the reader ends, with a list of unusual words and expressions that he stuck into his narrative wherever he could, most of the time being satisfied with just one example of usage. This is arguably Cela's weakest novel: he was led astray by his fascination with language, and he was also betrayed by his ironic bent, which undercut the attempt to write a narrative adventure of epic proportions and heroic gestures.

Censorship and other sanctions did not prevent Cela from becoming by the mid 1950's one of the best-known and most read Spanish writers. He had many admirers and friends among the writers of the older generation, and he was careful to let them know that even if he appeared to be a rebellious outsider, he would be pleased to be considered for one of the Royal Spanish Academy's vacancies. On 26 May 1957, Cela was inducted as the youngest member of the academy, the highest honor conferred by Spain on her writers. At the time Cela's profane and somber view of Spain was considered less dangerous by the authorities than the new brand of social realism that could be seen in novels of younger writers, such as Rafael Sánchez Ferlosio and Juan Goytisolo, and there had been intermittent, brief periods of relaxation in the rigid governmental control of cultural affairs. Also, by then Cela was considered a master of style, and his novels, essays, short narrations, and newspaper columns were received with great interest both by the general readers and by the critics. His talent as a storyteller, not unlike that of Gabriel García Márquez, managed to create texts that could be consumed with pleasure as simple anecdotes but also could be read with continuous surprise at the unexpected sparkling of the language and the originality of the author's vision of reality.

In an article titled "El escritor, su conciencia y el mundo en torno" (The Writer, His Conscience, and the World Around Him), included in *Los vasos comunicantes* (Communicating Vessels, 1981), Cela writes: "The Spain I have known can be found in my books as a conditioning background and as the originating place, and I have never avoided confronting her problems" (p. 145). Indeed, Cela saw more of Spain than most people, and he recorded in his writings a great variety of Spaniards, their language, their environment, their eccentricities. Like Cervantes, Shakespeare, and García Márquez, Cela was an extraverted writer who allowed himself to disappear with an illusion of transparency, not speaking about his own self but powerfully impressing on everything he wrote his own unmistakable style. Even in his autobiographical writings, published under the general title *La cucaña* (The Greased Pole, 1959), his attention was always diverted from himself toward the surrounding atmosphere and the anecdote.

As an example, there is an amusing story at the very beginning of his memoirs, a recollection of the occasion on which his relative Fray Juan Jacobo Fernández was beatified by Pope Pius XI in 1926:

> I remember that day very well. It was very hot in the atrium of St. Mary of Carballeda and I was being suffocated by the scarf they had put on me as an ornament. All of us, the relatives of the blessed, entered into the church under a canopy and according to rank. The ceremony promised to be quite splendid and edifying, but it ended badly, because the relatives, who were many more than could be accommodated under the canopy, shoved and kicked each other not to be left out. My uncle don Claudio Montenegro sent a servant to get his dog—a mastiff used to hunt wolves, of fierce appearance, called, paradoxically, *Wilson*—and when he brought it to him my uncle let it loose of its chain and sicked it against all the relatives who had come from out of town, except my father and myself. Thanks to the wise decision of my uncle Claudio the matter now stood better, because some of the relatives ran away.
>
> (p. 27)

We are left with a colorful and memorable scene, with the name of the uncle and the dog, but we are not told about the emotions of the boy confronted with the scandalous behavior of his relatives. Certainly, even if perhaps frightened, he was taking in all the details and would be able to reproduce them later with prodigious memory.

It is public life that concerns Cela, the gatherings in church, the marketplace, the coffeehouses—places in which his own emotions had to be held at bay in order to allow the others to express themselves clearly. He was very much the city dweller, amused by the constant activity in the street just outside his window, snapping portraits of passersby before they disappeared forever. Among the many texts populated with overflowing cities, towns, and roads, the short novel *El ciudadano Iscariote Reclús* (Citizen Iscariote Reclús, 1965) can be singled out as one of the best examples of Cela's writing. It tells its story through a narrative voice of the town gossip, titillated by the pleasure of scandal and the joy of observing someone else's misfortunes. The reader can feel himself transported to Cela's living room in Majorca, where he listens to a series of anecdotes that conjure up an ordinary but rather eccentric man, Iscariote Reclús, who inhabits the fringes of society as a naturist, anarchist, believer in the transmigration of souls, and advocate of Esperanto. He also dresses in mourning for the crimes of those who are in power. Then he dies in a traffic accident as he pedals his bicycle in his continuing search for a healthy and natural life. This loving spoof of Spanish anarchists and hippies is brilliant, taut, and evocative.

A long period passed before the publication of another major novel. Cela traveled to France in 1958 and 1959 and became a friend of Picasso's, who illustrated *Gavilla de fábulas sin amor* (Sheaf of Fables Without Love, 1962). In 1965 Cela served as a juror for the literary prize of Casa de las Américas in Cuba. He visited the United States in 1964 and 1965. He continued to publish many articles and numerous minor delightful narratives.

In 1969 Cela published his long-awaited novel on the Spanish Civil War, *Vísperas, festividad y octava de San Camilo del año 1936 en Madrid* (Eve, Festivity, and Octave of Saint Camillus in the Year 1936 in Madrid). The book is made up of long paragraphs sorted into three sections and an epilogue. Throughout, myriad voices are deflected from their private obsessions by the whirlpool set in motion by the beginning of the conflict in 1936. Individual characters in the novel can hardly comprehend the significance of events, which are experienced primarily through the mediation of contradictory gossip, muddled news, and opinionated commentary. The dominant narrative voice has no stability and constantly gives way to other voices. His mind is contaminated and overwhelmed by publicity, radio announcements, graffiti, political propaganda, popular songs, leaflets, and the polylingual jabber of mass media intruding into his private psyche. The main character wants to know who he is and insists on looking at himself in a mirror, but what he sees there is the interference of others. All that he can manage to find out is that he is not any of a series of famous historical people—he is just a member of the chorus, a follower, someone taken for a ride by collective life.

Since the novel implies that the people of Spain have been led unawares into a tragic situation, the suggestion that there was no serious motivation for the Civil War is far from accidental. But Cela's analysis of the Spanish political circumstance in 1936, which many critics have considered insufficient and even immoral, stems from his reverence for human life and simple pleasures, which should not be subordinated to any ideology. His total and corrosive irreverence does not take seriously any profound and coherent justification offered for a civil strife that counted its dead in hundreds of thousands.

In contrast with the darkness of the historical events, there is a joyful and detailed description of most of the houses of prostitution in Madrid, as if the narrator, bewildered by the approaching unknown, were concentrating on a feasible task—classifying the well known.

The epilogue is a paean to free love as a force not affected by superficial change, an open manifestation of an instinct that resists suppression or domination by social norms of propriety:

> You that are twenty years old it is enough to defend your heart from the ice, make an effort to believe in something that is not history, that great fallacy, you must believe in the theological virtues and in love, in life and in death, you can see I don't ask too much from you, love is never a torment and in any case it is always love, in spite of what people assume I assure you that love is never a tyrant and on the contrary it is always a companion for our uncertain voyage through life, life is a tunnel through which we walk sowing and harvesting love or giving and receiving a blind beating, there is no other alternative, open wide the doors of your soul and let love inhabit you, invade you as the tide, do not defend yourself with bullets and bites, give yourself completely, become food for love, the food for life and the food for death are already parceled out for you by the law of the world, only your becoming or not becoming food for love depends on you and your mettle.

Twenty-seven years later, Cela is thus replying to Pascual Duarte's actions, his bullets and bites, but he still holds fast to his notion that the course of history (if it does exist at all) lies beyond the grasp and control of the individual.

At the center of *San Camilo,* a receding and never clearly perceived center, lies the violence of war, in contrast with the delight in sex. The feast of Saint Camillus takes place on 18 July, two days after Franco and the Nationalist forces began their uprising in Morocco against the Republican government. On the day of the feast, arms are distributed to the people in Madrid and the war begins. In a prelude to it, Lieutenant Castillo, of the mainly socialist paramilitary riot police, is assassinated on 12 July. He has been implicated in the killing of a cousin of José Antonio Primo de Rivera, the founder of the Falange, a fascist group that will provide the ideological backbone for the Franco regime. On 13 July one of the leaders of the conservative opposition, Calvo Sotelo, is taken from his house in the early hours of the morning by friends of Lieutenant Castillo and is later found murdered. These brutal acts of violence shock the Spanish people and precipitate the uprising.

The narrator, caught in the escalating chain of violence without being a participant, but also without claiming complete innocence, cannot stop this vicious circle:

> Blood calls for blood, blood is the echo of blood, the shadow of blood and its trail, there has never been a criminal who was satisfied with only one crime and at times one breathes in the air something like the floating fragrance of crime and it makes more than one person drunk, no, you do not necessarily have to be a criminal but it is quite possible that you will not be able to deprive yourself of the old pleasures, ask for the taste of blood, no one will answer, the taste of blood is a sensation that is guarded as jealously as bedroom secrets, almost no one speaks about his bedroom's dirt but no one is free from his own bedroom's dirt, almost no one can strangle it, man is afraid of truth.
>
> (chap. 3, part 1)

In such passages Cela forcefully establishes a relationship between speaking out about sexual pleasure, stripping from it the varnish of courtly love rhetoric, and revealing the base and befuddled motivations that have been gilded by politicians but then have laid the land waste. Cela is never afraid of telling his own truth, even if it may seem blunt and excessively unheroic to some of his readers.

The Alfaguara Spanish edition of this novel has, opposite the title page, a haunting portrait of the young Cela in 1936, his head tilted slightly toward the right, his clothes elegant but his shirt collar sticking out, his hair almost standing on end, his dark and brooding eyes contemplating a life over which he is about to lose control as the mightier currents of the national conflict take over and transform the adolescent into a soldier. The novel is dedicated to the men who were drafted in 1937, "all losers of something: life, liberty, illusion, hope, decency."

The loud chatter of the many speakers in this novel delineates a world of corruption and misery where "the mirror does not have a frame, it does not begin or end" (chap. 1, part 1), and therefore it becomes impossible to have a complete, clear, and final image of personal and social history. In its brilliant ramblings the text offers an intriguing model of how the mind perceives the complexities of reality and of how language can wander off to become more an obstruction than a path, more a mask than a mirror.

In the history of the Spanish novel, 1962 was a crucial year because of the publication of Luis Martín Santos' *Tiempo de silencio* (Time of Silence). Most novels of the 1950's had attempted to portray objectively the social conditions that were studiously avoided by the official press. The catchwords were social responsibility, behaviorism, a collective hero, the camera's point of view, and the necessity of providing a voice for the workers who had been marginal in literature. On the one hand there were detailed descriptions of the drudgery and danger involved in constructing a dam or in working in a mine, while on the other hand there were descriptions of the upper bourgeoisie that showed it as decadent, irresponsible, sexually perverted, drowned in alcohol, and condemned always to repeat the same routines. Cela never allowed himself to be drawn completely into this movement; his wit, for one thing, was an anomaly among the intentionally muted tones of other writers. His lack of confidence in altruistic motives and his refusal to see workers as a morally superior class prevented him from adopting the simplistic dichotomy that informed many novels of that period. A few masterpieces by Sánchez Ferlosio, Jesús Fernández Santos, and Carmen Martín Gaite, it is true, proved that any approach is amenable to talent. But with Luis Martín Santos' *Tiempo de silencio* the thesis that animated the novelists of social and realist description was radically undermined.

In this novel the narrator presides over an intricate text that continuously flaunts its specific literary quality. The simple story of a medical student who falls into disgrace for taking part in an illegal abortion is only a pretext for a brilliant, learned, humorous dialogue with the whole of western literary tradition. This novel is as much about language as about the city of Madrid, and is directed more to intellectuals than to an average reader. A succession of other important novels by established writers reinforced this pattern of difficult texts that present almost insurmountable problems to readers but at the same time provoke complex thoughts and give free rein to an ostentation of novelistic craft. The French *nouveau roman* (New Novel), the greater permeability of Spanish cultural life to European and North American literary experiments (especially a belated but strong influence by Faulkner), and above all the example of the Latin American Boom affected the course of the Spanish novel. A few examples are Juan Benet's *Volverás a Región* (*Return to Region,* 1967), Juan Goytisolo's *Reivindicación del conde don Julián* (*Count Julian,* 1970), Luis Goytisolo's *Recuento* (Recount, 1973), Juan Marsé's *Si te dicen que caí* (*The Fallen,* 1973), and Miguel Delibes' *Parábola del náufrago* (*The Hedge,* 1969).

Cela, although he was already sixty-two years old, showed that he was still ahead of the game and produced probably the most enigmatic text of the period, *Oficio de tinieblas 5* (Tenebrae Service 5, 1973). The complete title anticipates the overflowing and baroque quality of the 1,194 numbered paragraphs that follow, designated as "monads," with almost no punctuation or capital letters:

> *tenebrae service 5 or thesis novel written to be sung by a choir of ailing singers as ornament of the liturgy that celebrates the triumph of the blessed and the circumstances of the bliss as is told: the torture of saint theodore the martyrdom of saint venancio the banishment of saint*

> *macario the solitude of saint hugh whose passing took place under a shower of abject smiles of gratitude and is commemorated on the first day of april.*

The reader is off to a perplexing start when he finds, right after this title page designating the text as a "thesis novel," a contradictory epigraph: "Naturally, this is not a novel but a cleansing of my heart."

The ambiguity can be reduced by claiming that it is not a traditional novel (there are no clear story lines or rounded characters or evocations of settings), but that it corresponds to what the postmodern novel has become: a desultory, even desperate, exploration of the rubbish heap of language, with no confidence in the referential capacity of words to describe anything that could be conventionally designated as historical reality. In fact, history is seen as just another mode of fiction constantly modified to serve the purposes of each generation or interest group. In Cela's novel there are constant references to the death of the narrator's father, whose name must never be pronounced. This prohibition can be interpreted in terms of the prohibition against the naming of God in a kaddish, where God is the unnameable at the origin of existence whose presence would be reduced to a fragment, to a tag, to fallacious knowledge if replaced by a word.

Around the absence of the deceased father the unpunctuated monads stop and go, accumulating irrelevant thoughts: the sexual activities of someone called "yourcousin" and his masochistic lover, the life of a hangman and his family, the licentious life of the narrator's grandmother, and myriad references to all sorts of sexual aberrations found in the footnotes of history books, drawn here briefly to center stage under a cruel light that shows the universal debasement of human beings. *Oficio de tinieblas 5* is more obscene than erotic, always amusing, intelligent; and in its many modulations it resembles a kaleidoscope of vivid and sensuous colors.

As in the novels of the same period by Juan Goytisolo, there is in Cela's text a violent attack on conventions and a rejection of the sacredness of filial obligations. Part of monad 1,104 may serve as an example:

> sit facing the black wall of your coffin inside your fake coffin dressed in mourning where night after night day after day you punish yourself and you enjoy sudden erections and you confess and listen what you are about to tell yourself try not to move the muscles of your face remember that impassive features is what is proper or do just the opposite do not listen because your process is irreversible shudder if you wish and as much as you want no one will give a damn: the time you have to live in makes you sick and time past your country and all other countries your family and all other families paternalism and filialism laws and institutions make you sick also the order of nature and the dirty chaos of minerals food makes you sick and drink and tobacco and opium of the people and herbivorous and carnivorous animals stones that pretend to be sculptures trees passing off as friends or relatives and the green blade of grass humble very humble the jagged face you see in the mirror makes you sick and your name heard thousands of times your purpose is encouraging but there is no way no one could ever start out again it would be wonderful if you were called benjamin nipple count liweinstein.

The text is as much a coffin as his father's, where all the dreams are found wanting, and only the death of the old man (the father and the old self) can bring about change, a new name, the life-giving nipple.

As in Carlos Fuentes' *La muerte de Artemio Cruz* (*The Death of Artemio Cruz,* 1962), certainly a presence in Cela's *Oficio,* the narrator has been defeated by life and its vulgarity; he seeks an escape by excavating through the stops and gaps of repressed memory, destroying the idols that buttress the corrupted personality: "the appropriate path is not to give up in the beheadings not even for one instant" (monad 738). Even if the text reveals the common malaise of Spanish intellectuals who could not embrace their past or present, falsified and rarefied into inanity, it also expresses the general frustration of any man approaching old age without having realized his own dreams. It is as much a litany for the dead father as for the wasted lifetime of the son.

In *Oficio* there is as much Boccaccio as Kafka, as much Petronius as Beckett, made one and new by the sheer force of Cela's writing:

> play hard play the card of insolence jack knight and king and take note that something is being demolished around you even if you do not know for sure what it is your world your country your family your house your person and all that justifies your world your country your family your house your person the weight at the end of the line does not fall any longer at a right angle with the horizon and the air bubble in the level refuses to settle between the two small lines of harmony all that presented itself as solid as granite and immutable like a quartz crystal is collapsing in a blinding cloud of dust all that served for years and years as a guidance for life as model of conducts as mirror of exemplary minds.
>
> (monad 975)

The richness of Cela's culture, his brutal humor, his characteristic disrespect for all authority is what makes of this unsettling and blinding, shattered mirror of words an extremely interesting text, among the very best of this period in Spanish literature.

In this period Cela wrote the text of a cantata, *María Sabina,* which he called a symphonic tragedy. It was first presented, with music by Leonardo Balada, at Carnegie Hall in New York on 17 April 1970 and was recorded by the Louisville Orchestra in 1973. This incantatory work is the portrait of a Mexican woman with magical powers, who knows and uses drugs, especially peyote. Branded an evil witch by the authorities, she is, like Pascual Duarte, about to be hanged. She represents all of humanity and speaks to all, and through her voice Cela attempts to restore the unity of clarity and darkness, the wholeness of life that the authorities negate in order to keep their power. In the third section of the cantata, María Sabina sings:

> I declare I am Nero in the bonfire
> I declare I am the martyr Sebastian pierced
> by arrows
> I declare I am the rose from Alexandria
> I declare I am the woman who sleeps with the devil
> I declare I am the caterpillar in the apple of Paradise
> I declare I am Adam and Eve
> I declare I am the fishing gull.

She goes on to thirty further identities. Here again Cela opens up to the marginal and forbidden—in this case black magic—that authorities try to reject and repress but cannot uproot from society. Life and humankind, implies Cela once and again, can be understood only when the heart of darkness is considered not alien but an integral part of all of us. Those present at the Spanish premiere in the Teatro de la Zarzuela in Madrid, on 28 May 1970 thought otherwise, and repeatedly interrupted the performance, stomping and shouting to show their displeasure.

After the death of Franco in 1975, during the transitional period to democracy, Cela took a prominent position in political life. He was named a senator by King Juan Carlos in June 1977, and he served in this capacity until January 1979, participating actively in the drafting of the new constitution of 1978. In 1983 Cela published a masterful, playful, intricate novel, *Mazurca para dos muertos* (Mazurka for Two Dead Men), for which he received Spain's National Prize of Literature in 1984. The story takes place in the author's native Galicia, a rainy region of small hamlets and long memories, where the news from abroad or even from the national scene has no significance. The manuscript is supposedly written by Robín Lebozán, a reader of Cervantes and of the novelists of the nineteenth century. He structures the story as if it were made up of the many conversations motivated by the visit of a Mr. Cela, who has come to find out more about his family, since he is related to the Celas, the Moranes, and the Guxindes, who dominate the region.

The narration starts out with Lebozán's memory of the death of Lázaro Codesal, a young man well known for his sexual prowess and his dexterity in fighting with a long stick, who died during the dictator Primo de Rivera's African campaign in the 1920's. He was shot by a Moor while masturbating under a fig tree; as a sign of sorrow it has rained since then in Galicia, and the rain has erased the line of the horizon. It is a death that can't be avenged, and is an indication of the loss of control these peasants experience over their own lives.

The novel progresses like a musical score; it returns once and again to the same motifs, slightly modified, in the incessant reiteration of memory. The countryside, in which sex, food, and conversation are the principal motivating pleasures, is disjointed by the Civil War. An outsider, Fabián Minguela, takes over and is responsible for many brutal deaths of persons considered possible sympathizers with the opposition. He kills two members of the narrator's powerful clan, and after the death of one of them, in 1936, the blind musician of the town's most famous house of prostitution plays the mazurka "Ma petite Marianne" all night long. It is not played again until 1949, when the clan avenges the deaths and slays Fabián Minguela. The novel closes with a forensic report on the death that blames it on wolves and declares it accidental.

The uninterrupted conversations, the same stories repeated by different voices, the litany of violence and desire, the porousness of collective memory, find their symbol in the continuous rain with which the novel begins:

> It is raining softly and without pause, it rains not with great conviction but with infinite patience, like all life, it rains over the land that is the same color as the sky, not quite pale green not quite light, ashen gray, and the line of the mountains has not been seen for a very long time.

The indefiniteness of life and its blurry borders make language the Seeing Eye dog of perplexed people who constantly try to make sense of their own meaningless lives—just as the blind accordionist plays his mazurka to ritualize deaths that would otherwise simply remain unnoticed among the hundreds of thousands dead during and after the Civil War.

> We are in the midst of everything, the beginning is the center of everything, and no one knows how much we have left until the end. Two dogs have just made love under the rain and they wait now, one looking toward the east, the other toward the west, until the blood in their organism returns to its normal state.
>
> (p. 36)

The sexual energy of the universe, its fertilizing rain, acquires a history in the family tree: "Families are like the sea, boundless, with neither beginning nor end" (p. 76). The novel reads like the transcript of a very large family meeting, where under all the dissension and bittersweet memories a common lineage establishes a covenant that gives the family enough strength to face the world outside and its continual, indifferent rain.

Throughout the text Cela intersperses 325 Galician words that are translated in a glossary added at the end of the book, but in contrast to the exotic terms in *La Catira,* the vivid, lively, and frequently used Galician expressions in *Mazurca* seem to emerge naturally from the atmosphere of the narration.

Cela's irony shows how the minds of his protagonists are submerged in superstition and pride and constantly shore up a facade to resist the unknown:

> The sexton from Torcela began to tell stories of will-o'-the-wisp, of the souls of purgatory, and of dead men that had resurrected after having been for over a century in their graves; the corporal from the Guardia Civil did not believe him. "That

is not possible, after a month no one can resurrect and before that, very few, no one will tell me any stories!"

(p. 138)

The novel winds down to a stop, but the laws governing life in the mountains demand continuation: the expansion of the family, the accumulation and retelling of stories, the search for food and pleasure, the necessity of avenging a dead man: "The last man has not died yet, there is always a dead man outstanding in this never ending account, as a conveyor belt carrying corpses and moved by inertia" (p. 246).

In 1988, Cela published *Cristo versus Arizona* (Christ Versus Arizona), a novel that describes life in the North American West from the turn of the century to around 1920. The text is a single monologue by a man called Wendel Liverpool Espana, or Span, or Aspen. The missing tilde over the *n* and the different versions of the name could indicate how the memory of Spain (*España*) has been weakened for the sons of the immigrants by the span between Europe and America. Abandoned as a child, Wendel Espana has only fragmented images of his father's life; but he does meet his mother, a prostitute, and makes love to her in the typical carefree manner that characterizes the novel. Espana endlessly remembers the same events that show the brutal side of life in a frontier town. While *Cristo versus Arizona* is at times witty and funny, the proliferation of brief anecdotes of violence, sexual exploitation, racism, and vulgarity wears thin, and it may bore or disgust some readers.

Cela's opinions of culture and human beings are well summarized in this paragraph of "Gayola de grajos y vencejos" (Cage of Rooks and Pallid Swifts, 1964):

> A human being is mostly a hesitant animal, thoughtful, idealistic, hysterical, and tricky; one has a rather precarious idea of man, that miserable small creature obsessed in obstructing the generous pace of nature. Among the serious animals—the lion, the donkey, the goat—there are no public employees, no state attorneys, no priests, no policemen, no businessmen, and life flows with greater ease and good sense. It is clear that the so-called civilization is the patrimony of vocational prisoners, of recluses that love and caress—and even polish, on Sunday mornings, for greater pleasure—the cage that constrains them and cuts the wings of their freedom
>
> (*Obra completa,* 3.9)

Cela was consistent in these views: he found life in the dark recesses of a world that seems devoid of culture, the lower middle class and the peasants; and he also became an enfant terrible of the Spanish language, a writer who spattered the printed page with words that are quite often heard but seldom written.

In fact, Cela compiled a *Diccionario secreto* (Secret Dictionary, 1968–1971), in which the meanings of many profanities are explained, and in which examples of their use by some of the most highly reputed Spanish writers prove that the "literary" vocabulary has been formed by a process of purification, by a rejection of the popular, vulgar, and intimate verbal forms offensive to academic ears—forms that Cela knows how to salvage and offer in all their striking force and beauty. The *Enciclopedia del erotismo* (Encyclopedia of Eroticism, 1976–1977), written by a team under his general editorship and contained in volumes 14–17 of his *Obra completa,* is part of this project of amplifying the realm of the expressible in Spanish literature. His long labor was successful in part because the political changes in Spain produced a considerable revolution in sexual mores, but Cela's deconstruction of literary Spanish was his great personal achievement; it can be compared to the revolution against academic Spanish conducted by the writers of the Latin American boom on the other side of the Atlantic.

Cela did believe in the social responsibility of authors and expressed his belief in numerous ways. In *Al servicio de algo* (At the Service of Something, 1969), a collection of articles previously published in *Papeles de Son Armadans,* he writes: "It is the duty of literature to support, with the lance of words, reason, and to resist, with the shield of that same word, the attacks of force that just because it is force demands that all call it reasonable . . . all else is graphomania" (p. 12). In the prologue to a series of concatenated texts, more a collection of vignettes than a real novel, *Tobogán de hambrientos* (The Hungry People's Slide, 1962), he describes his concept of writing:

> Literature is life itself, not just its artistic or heartfelt chronicle, and I can fathom only one thing more to say: to dress literature with a jacket and designer pants—and even with very expensive jackets and pants cut to size—is an absurd goal, because literature ends by coming up with the arbitrary register of bad manners and it lowers its trousers unexpectedly or it shows up, no shame at all, with the jacket over her shoulder and with a bare bottom.

The seventeen volumes of his *Obra completa* published as of 1989 attest to Cela's massive production in a variety of forms in which he perfected the art of presenting an anecdote or landscape description with amenity and an always surprisingly fresh vocabulary. This edition is also of great documentary value for an understanding of how strict the censorship was during the years in which Cela wrote most of his work. For example, in the 1940's the censors deemed offensive the mention of possibly adulterous Spanish wives and struck it out (while they retained the sentence referring to adulterous husbands), and they did not allow the publication of an open letter to the king of Sweden on the subject of Baroja and the Nobel Prize because this novelist from the Generation of 1898, very close to Cela in his dark, anarchic, and satiric view of life, was considered an undesirable model for Spanish writers.

One of the remarkable aspects of Cela's art is his instinct for sensing the permissible limits at a time when novelistic discourse was constrained by irrational, frivolous, and very strict censors who did not allow any offense against the government, the church, or traditional moral standards. As a last selection, Cela included in *Mis páginas preferidas* (My Favorite Pages, 1956) a lecture called "La galera de la literatura" (The Galley of Literature). He states there that to be an author in Spain is a difficult task, with little economic recompense. "Life is not good; man isn't either" (p. 395). The task of the writer is to unmask this truth, but it is also a compulsion, comparable to madness or the fertility of nature: the obligation of a writer is to keep on writing. Cela has been a writer conscious of his craft, of language, but also alert to social responsibility. He sees his way of fulfilling his mission in terms of a special attitude that he describes with his usual tendency to make a universal, provocative statement out of what is only an excellent description of his own literary practice:

> The writer is the notary public of the conscience of his age and world, and one must feel the pulse of conscience where it is, close to the earth, glued to the crust of the earth, that resonating box where one can hear, isochronous and bitter, the savage beating of the hearts. It is forbidden, in accordance with the rules of the game of the writer, to desire to adopt a perspective that beautifies characters, situations, and passions by making them smaller. All has its proportion, good or bad, exact and cruelly inflexible.
>
> (p. 399)

Did he measure up to his own program? Certainly: one can read in Cela the intimate history of Spain, and his standing is assured as the most important Spanish writer of the postwar period.

## Selected Bibliography

### EDITIONS

#### INDIVIDUAL WORKS

NOVELS

*La familia de Pascual Duarte.* Madrid and Burgos, 1942.

*Pabellón de reposo.* Madrid, 1943.
*Nuevas andanzas y desventuras de Lazarillo de Tormes.* Madrid, 1944.
*La colmena.* Buenos Aires, 1951.
*Mrs. Caldwell habla con su hijo.* Barcelona, 1953.
*La catira.* Barcelona, 1955.
*Vísperas, festividad y octava de San Camilo del año 1936 en Madrid.* Madrid, 1969.
*Oficio de tinieblas 5.* Barcelona, 1973.
*Mazurca para dos muertos.* Barcelona, 1983.
*Cristo versus Arizona.* Barcelona, 1988.

SHORT NOVELS

*Timoteo, el incomprendido.* Madrid, 1952.
*Santa Balbina, 37, gas en cada piso.* Melilla, 1952.
*Café de artistas.* Madrid, 1953.
*El molino de viento y otras novelas cortas.* Barcelona, 1956.
*El ciudadano Iscariote Reclús.* Madrid, 1965.
*La familia del héroe.* Madrid, 1965.
*El tacatá oxidado: Florilegio de carpetovetonismos y otras lindezas.* Barcelona, 1973.

SHORT STORIES AND OTHER BRIEF NARRATIVES

*Esas nubes que pasan.* Madrid, 1945.
*El bonito crimen del carabinero y otras invenciones.* Barcelona, 1947.
*Baraja de invenciones.* Valencia, 1953.
*Nuevo retablo de don Cristobita: Invenciones, figuraciones y alucinaciones.* Barcelona, 1957.
*Historias de España. Los ciegos. Los tontos.* Madrid, 1958.
*Los viejos amigos.* 2 vols. Barcelona, 1960–1961.
*Gavilla de fábulas sin amor.* Palma de Mallorca, 1962.
*Tobogán de hambrientos.* Barcelona, 1962.
*Las compañías convenientes y otros fingimientos y cegueras.* Barcelona, 1963.
*Garito de hospicianos.* Barcelona, 1963.
*Once cuentos de fútbol.* Madrid, 1963.
*El solitario y los sueños de Quesada.* Palma de Mallorca, 1963.
*Toreo de salón: Farsa con acompañamiento de clamor y murga.* Barcelona, 1963.
*Izas, rabizas y colipoterras: Drama con acompañamiento de cachondeo y dolor de corazón.* Barcelona, 1964.
*Café de artistas y otros cuentos.* Madrid, 1969.
*La bandada de palomas.* Barcelona, 1970.
*Cinco glosas a otras tantas verdades de la silueta que un hombre trazó de sí mismo.* Madrid, 1971.
*La bola del mundo: Escenas cotidianas.* Madrid, 1972.
*Fotografías al minuto.* Madrid, 1972.
*Balada del vagabundo sin suerte.* Madrid, 1973.
*Cuentos para leer después del baño.* Barcelona, 1974.
*Crónica del cipote de Archidona.* Madrid, 1977.
*Los sueños vanos. Los ángeles curiosos.* Barcelona, 1979.
*El espejo y otros cuentos.* Madrid, 1981.
*El juego de los tres madroños.* Barcelona, 1983.

TRAVEL BOOKS

*Viaje a la Alcarria.* Madrid, 1948.
*El gallego y su cuadrilla, y otros apuntes carpetovetónicos.* Madrid, 1949.
*Avila.* Barcelona, 1952.
*Del Miño al Bidasoa: Notas de un vagabundaje.* Barcelona, 1952.
*Judíos, moros y cristianos.* Barcelona, 1956.
*Cuaderno del Guadarrama.* Madrid, 1959.
*Primer viaje andaluz.* Barcelona, 1959.
*Madrid.* Madrid, 1965.
*Nuevas escenas matritenses.* 7 vols. Madrid, 1965–1966.
*Páginas de geografía errabunda.* Madrid, 1965.
*Viaje al Pirineo de Lérida.* Madrid, 1965.
*Viaje a U.S.A.; o, El que la sigue la mata.* Madrid, 1967.
*Barcelona.* Madrid, 1970.
*La Mancha en el corazón y los ojos.* Barcelona, 1971.
*Nuevo viaje a la Alcarria.* Madrid, 1986.

POETRY

*Pisando la dudosa luz del día.* Barcelona, 1945.
*Cancionero de la Alcarria.* San Sebastián, 1948.
*Dos romances de ciego.* Málaga, 1966.

DRAMA

*María Sabina.* Madrid and Palma de Mallorca, 1967.
*El carro de heno; o, El inventor de la guillotina.* Palma de Mallorca, 1969.

ESSAYS

*Mesa revuelta.* Madrid, 1945.
*Ensueños y figuraciones.* Barcelona, 1954.
*Cajón de sastre.* Madrid, 1957.

*La obra literaria del pintor Solana.* Madrid, 1957.
*Recuerdo de don Pío Baroja.* Palma de Mallorca, 1957.
*La rueda de los ocios.* Barcelona, 1957.
*Cuatro figuras del 98: Unamuno, Valle-Inclán, Baroja, Azorín y otros retratos y ensayos españoles.* Barcelona, 1961.
*Diez artistas de la escuela de Mallorca.* Madrid, 1963.
*Marañón, el hombre.* Alicante, 1963.
*Al servicio de algo.* Madrid, 1969.
*A vueltas con España.* Madrid, 1973.
*Los vasos comunicantes.* Barcelona, 1981.
*Vuelta de hoja.* Barcelona, 1981.
*De genes, dioses y tiranos.* Madrid, 1985.
*Conversaciones españolas.* Barcelona, 1987.

### ANTHOLOGY

*Mis páginas preferidas.* Madrid, 1956.

### OTHER

*Diccionario secreto.* 2 vols. Madrid, 1968–1971.
*Enciclopedia del erotismo.* 4 vols. Madrid, 1976–1977.
*Rol de cornudos.* Barcelona, 1976.

### COLLECTED WORKS

*Obra completa.* 17 vols. Barcelona, 1962–1986.

## MEMOIRS

*La cucaña: Memorias. Libro primero: La rosa.* Barcelona, 1959.

## TRANSLATIONS

*Avila.* Translated by John Forrester. Barcelona, 1956.
*The Family of Pascual Duarte.* Translated by Anthony Kerrigan. Boston, 1964.
*The Hive.* Translated by J. M. Cohen in consultation with Arturo Barea. Introduction by Arturo Barea. New York, 1953.
*Journey to the Alcarria.* Translated by Frances M. López-Morillas. Introduction by Paul Ilie. Madison, Wis., 1964.
*Mrs. Caldwell Speaks to her Son.* Translated by J. S. Bernstein. Ithaca, N.Y., 1968.
*Pascual Duarte and His Family.* Translated by Herma Briffault. Bilingual edition. New York, 1965.
*Rest Home.* Translated by Herma Briffault. Bilingual edition. New York, 1961.

## BIOGRAPHICAL AND CRITICAL STUDIES

This selection stresses what is available in English. The entire Fall 1984 issue of the *Review of Contemporary Fiction* is devoted to Cela and contains excellent articles in English on most aspects of Cela's work.

Asún, Raquel. "Introducción" to her edition of *La colmena.* Madrid, 1984. Pp. 7–85.
Bernstein, J. S. "The Matricide of Pascual Duarte." In *Homenaje a Rodríguez-Moñino.* Madrid, 1966. Vol. 1, pp. 75–82.
———. "Pascual Duarte and Orestes." *Symposium* 22:301–318 (1968).
———. "Confession and Inaction in *San Camilo.*" *Hispanófila* 51:47–63 (1974).
Cela Conde, Camilo José. *Cela, mi padre.* Madrid, 1989.
Díaz, Janet W., and Ricardo L. Landeira. "The Novelist as Poet: The Literary Evolution of Camilo José Cela," *Anales de la narrativa española contemporánea* 4:21–43 (1979).
Foster, David W. *Forms of the Novel in the Work of Camilo José Cela.* Columbia, Mo., 1967.
Gullón, Germán. "Contexto ideológico y forma narrativa en *La familia de Pascual Duarte.*" *Hispania* 68:1–8 (1985).
Henn, David. *C. J. Cela: La colmena.* London, 1974.
Ilie, Paul. *La novelística de Camilo José Cela.* Madrid, 1963.
———. "The Politics of Obscenity in *San Camilo, 1936.*" *Anales de la novela de posguerra* 1:25–63 (1976).
Kirsner, Robert. *The Novels and Travels of Camilo José Cela.* Chapel Hill, N.C., 1963.
Livingstone, Leon. "Ambivalence and Ambiguity in *La familia de Pascual Duarte.*" In *Studies in Honor of José Rubia Barcia,* edited by Roberta Johnson and Paul C. Smith. Lincoln, Neb., 1982. Pp. 95–107.
McPheeters, D. W. *Camilo José Cela.* New York, 1969.
Penuel, Arnold M. "The Psychology of Cultural Disintegration in Cela's *La familia de Pascual*

*Duarte." Revista de estudios hispánicos* 16:361–378 (1982).

Polansky, Susan G. "Narrators and Fragmentation in Cela's *Mrs. Caldwell habla con su hijo." Revista de estudios hispánicos* 21:21–31 (1987).

Sobejano, Gonzalo. *Novela española de nuestro tiempo.* 2nd ed. Madrid, 1975. Pp. 89–141.

Spires, Robert. "Systematic Doubt: The Moral Art of *La familia de Pasucal Duarte." Hispanic Review* 40:238–302 (1972).

Thomas, Michael. "Narrative Tension and Structural Unity in Cela's *La familia de Pascual Duarte." Symposium* 31:165–178 (1977).

Urrutia, Jorge. "Introducción" to his edition of *La familia de Pascual Duarte.* Barcelona, 1977. Pp. ix–xcvii.

RANDOLPH D. POPE

# NATALIA GINZBURG

## *(b. 1916)*

IN 1986 THE Italian publisher Arnoldo Mondadori published the collected works (*Opere*) of Natalia Ginzburg, one of the most prolific and able among contemporary Italian authors. Each of the two attractively bound volumes displays a black-and-white photograph. The first is a portrait of Ginzburg in her early forties. Her face has the solid beauty of a handsome woman: dark, short hair parted not quite in the middle, high cheekbones, slightly Arabic eyes, and a large smile showing square, straight teeth. Her features are both Mediterranean and Jewish, and she smiles at the camera with confidence and cordiality. Surrounded not by bookshelves but by trees, she wears a flowery shirt and a simple light cardigan, and she looks like the women in an old De Sica or Fellini movie. Absolutely nothing in this picture suggests the shy, naive, inept, often incompetent autobiographical heroines of Ginzburg's works: not the insecure and antisocial adolescents and young women of *Tutti i nostri ieri* (*A Light for Fools,* 1952) or *Le voci della sera* (*Voices in the Evening,* 1961), nor the bewildered child who recounts the events of Fascism and the war in her autobiography, *Lessico famigliare* (*Family Sayings,* 1963). This is the portrait of a mature artist who observes the world with a detached, ironic, and penetrating eye.

The photograph in the second volume portrays an old woman looking away from the camera, her gaze wandering vaguely in the distance. A dark background enfolds her and highlights the few visible lines: the wood of the chair, her gray hair, the wrinkles on her face. The contradictory image that emerges from the two portraits is perhaps more emblematic of Ginzburg's work than either portrait taken by itself. One picture emphasizes irony; the other, nostalgia, and the best of her work skillfully balances these elements. Her nostalgia is less an invocation of the past than an alienation from the present, and her irony is less a biting rejection than an affectionate rebuke.

If we include the period that was central to her parents' lives, and consequently to the cultural milieu in which she grew up, we can say that the biography of Ginzburg stretches through most of the nodal points of both Italian and European recent history. And just as her portraits belie the naive innocence of her speakers, so her own history belies her frequently proclaimed lack of intellectual knowledge and her ignorance of politics, history, and art.

Ginzburg was born Natalia Levi on 14 July 1916, the youngest of five children. Her parents, Giuseppe Levi and Lidia Tanzi, were by birth Jewish and Catholic, respectively, although by choice they were socialist and atheist. Natalia's paternal grandmother had opposed the mixed marriage because "someone had told her that my mother was a very devout Catholic, and that at every church she saw she would conspicuously bow and cross herself. It wasn't true at all" (*Opere,* 1.918).[1] More important than the different religions of the families were their political, social, and cultural affinities.

Lidia Tanzi's father, Carlo, had been a prominent socialist lawyer in mid-nineteenth-century Milan, and a close friend of the socialist leader Filippo Turati and his companion Anna Kulischov. Lidia therefore grew up surrounded by socialists and anarchists who were fighting for the unification of Italy, and she maintained close friendships with representatives of that world throughout her life. Giuseppe Levi, a biologist and a professor of comparative anatomy, was a representative of the typical nineteenth-century alliance between positivism and socialism. He had been active in the Irredentist movement in his youth—the political movement for the annexation of Italian territories left out of the unification—and later, with his whole family, an active anti-Fascist.

The economic background of Ginzburg's parents and grandparents represented a second important point of affinity. Giuseppe Levi was descended from a "lineage of bankers," which, to his youngest daughter, made his own and his brother's poor sense of business rather inexplicable. Natalia's paternal grandmother had been very wealthy until World War I. At that time,

> because she did not believe that Italy was going to win, and she had total faith in Francis Joseph, she insisted on keeping some Austrian bonds that she owned, and so she lost a lot of money; my father, Irredentist, tried with no success to convince her to sell those Austrian bonds. My grandmother used to say "my disgrace" when she alluded to that loss of money; and she would despair over it in the morning, as she paced up and down the room wringing her hands.
>
> (*Opere,* 1.907)

In her granddaughter's affectionate and comic recollection, "she wasn't that poor," only poorer.

Natalia's maternal family was economically less well off. The grandmother had been an actress in her youth and had subsequently married a young lawyer. To her great chagrin her husband "threw himself into socialist politics" and kept bringing home people she considered less than appropriate company for her young daughter, whose marriage prospects worried her more than did the political destiny of Italy. Eventually, many from the Tanzis' social circle became prominent figures in Italian politics after the unification.

The geographic background of Natalia Ginzburg's parents provided a third important point of cultural kinship. That both Giuseppe Levi's and Lidia Tanzi's families should be from Trieste, the important seaport at the head of the Adriatic Sea, was of consequence in the second half of the nineteenth century. The mother was "Milanese, but of Triestine origins. . . . She had married, along with my father, many Triestine expressions; Milanese would permeate her talk whenever she recounted memories of her childhood" (*Opere,* 1.914). Only recently unified, Italy was at the time of her parents' marriage (and to a large extent remains today) divided into regions and provinces distinguished by different dialects. The Triestine origin of Ginzburg's parents affected not just the linguistic atmosphere of her home but the cultural one as well. As the only port of the Austro-Hungarian Empire, and therefore its door onto the Mediterranean, Trieste had enjoyed great prosperity. Its ethnically mixed population included Italians, Slovenes, Croats, Austrians, Germans, Jews, and the usual large number of foreigners who settle in commercial seaports. Politically, geographically, and culturally, Trieste was both central European and Mediterranean, Austrian and Italian, all of which, besides its being a center of Irredentism, made it an intellectual center of international stature. Ironically, by virtue of the Austrian oppression, Trieste, more than

[1] All quotations from Ginzburg's works are translated by the present author from the two-volume *Opere* (Milan, 1986).

any other Italian city in the late nineteenth century, had the privilege of being in contact with most of the modern cultural ferment of Europe. That Italo Svevo, whose real name was Ettore Schmitz and who was German-Jewish on one side and Italian on the other, and James Joyce should come together in Trieste was far from accidental. Especially through Lidia Tanzi, the influence of modern European culture (Verlaine, Wagner, Proust) was central to the Levi household and permeated Ginzburg's childhood.

To the cultural and linguistic cosmopolitanism of the family was added their geographic mobility. By the time young Natalia was three, they were living in Turin and had already lived in Trieste, Milan, Florence, Sassari, and Palermo. This must have been the equivalent of having moved nowadays between the main cities of Europe. Thus, even though the provincialism and cultural isolation of Italy worsened as a result of the nationalistic emphases of Fascism, Ginzburg's family was a rare exception to this trend. This milieu formed an important breeding ground for both the fluidity of hybrid dialects in her prose—an element that eludes translation—and her many allusions to modern European culture.

Representative of nineteenth-century positivism, of early-twentieth-century art, and of the politically engaged bourgeois intelligentsia, the family emerges from Ginzburg's recollections as a crossroad of European culture and history. If this was true of the period that preceded Ginzburg's birth, it became even more vivid by the time she was a young child.

In 1919, when her father was assigned to teach at the University of Turin, Ginzburg was only three years old. The family moved to industrial, working-class, and socialist Turin at a time of widespread political unrest: workers were striking for the eight-hour day, collective bargaining, and higher wages. It was in Turin that the left wing of the Socialist party had some of its strongest leaders. Among these was Antonio Gramsci, at the time a student in his mid twenties who had come from Sardinia to study philology and linguistics at the University of Turin. As the Levis were getting settled in Turin, Gramsci started to publish the newspaper *L'Ordine Nuovo* (1919–1922), which became the focal point for left-wing socialists intent on challenging the conservative and reformist tendencies of the party. A year after the Levis' arrival, a powerful wave of strikes and factory takeovers swept a number of industrial centers, Turin foremost among them. This culminated in a historical defeat of the movement on the one hand and in the foundation of the Italian Communist party in 1921 on the other.

Ginzburg was too young to be aware of these events, but the controversies recorded in *Family Sayings* attest that both her parents and her siblings followed the developments avidly. She was no longer a child by the time Mussolini seized total power in 1928. Behind him were large numbers of industrialists and landowners, as well as the king himself, who had perceived quite correctly in the revolutionary activities of the late 1910's and early 1920's an imminent threat to private property. In 1922 Mussolini had been "hired" by the ruling elite to do the dirty work, to clean up the factories and the fields of agitators; he was then expected to step down and obediently return power to the industrialists and landowners and their political representative, the king. Things went differently, however, and Mussolini remined in power for two decades.

Ginzburg's growth from child to adolescent to young woman kept pace with the transformation of Fascism into a harsh dictatorship. Although life provided her copious material, in her work Ginzburg refused to indulge in easy drama and offered few personal details. This reticence led one critic to state:

> It appears to be a paradox that Natalia Ginzburg, who in her books has said so much about herself, has never told us anything of herself. What do we know about her? All and nothing. . . . About herself, in her own words, N. Ginzburg has never told us and never tells us anything. . . . Nothing is ever said of the childhood of the character who

> says "I" [in *Family Sayings*]. . . . That face hides in the shade. It withdraws from view. It is reduced to two eyes, dark and piercing, very mobile, affectionate and impassioned . . . [but] as soon as the story of her family verges toward her own personal destiny, N. Ginzburg suddenly stops talking. . . . The problem is that while saying "I" all the time, N. Ginzburg can only talk about other people.
>
> (Garboli, pp. 7629–7630)

In general, Ginzburg preferred to let the people and events around her come to the fore; when she did allow herself personal reminiscence, she frequently evoked her sense of being "different," of being in "exile" within her social class. In an ironic recollection, the political views of her socialist family are evoked as a source of chagrin to the child, thirsty for uniformity and sameness with the world:

> And I was, as a child, rhetorical, conformist, and full of petit bourgeois ideals. . . . I wanted a mother who at night would sew under a lamp. My mother did not sew, or not enough for my taste. I wanted to hear about the motherland. At home it was never mentioned. I wanted to hear about the king. They would refer to him as a fool. . . . I wanted us to have, on the national holidays, a flag on the porch. We had no flag.
>
> (*Opere,* 2.106)

Her father's obsessive fear of bacterial infections provided another cause of alienation. As was common for children of wealthy families, but less so for children of the petit bourgeoisie, Ginzburg was tutored at home. This fact, coupled with her family's Jewish identity and atheistic views, practically isolated her from the two main sources of socialization in childhood:

> I went through all grammar school at home because my father insisted that in the public schools children became sick. . . . I developed, in that solitude, a number of strange ideas, like the idea that poor people went to school, and rich people studied at home with a teacher; therefore I was perhaps rich, which, however, seemed strange to me, since I frequently would hear at home that we had "no money." . . . Going to school, much like going to church, was a privilege of other people; the poor maybe; those who, at any rate, were "like everyone else"; whereas we were maybe like no one. We went neither to church nor, like some of my father's relatives, to temple; we were "nothing," my brothers had explained to me; we were "mixed," in other words half Jewish and half Catholic; but, after all, neither the one nor the other; nothing.
>
> This being "nothing" in the religion of my family seemed to me to envelop our whole existence: after all, we were neither truly rich nor truly poor: excluded from each world, we were exiled to a neutral, amorphous, limitless, and nameless region.
>
> (*Opere,* 2.55–56)

Finally, and most important, the language spoken at home was yet another emblem of Ginzburg's "difference." When she was taken to the regular public school at the end of each year in order to pass the state examination and be admitted to the next grade, Natalia met a social class and a linguistic universe to which she did not belong:

> Curious and shy, the children would surround me. I too was very curious about them and intractably shy; they wore closely cropped hair, light blue bows, and white smocks; they spoke Piedmontese, a language that I understood little and that I loved and hated since it appeared to me as the sublime and blessed language of the poor, of those who could go to school and to church, of those who had the immense fortune of being all that I was not.
>
> (*Opere,* 2.56)

The end of childhood and the beginning of adolescence coincided for Ginzburg with the passing in 1926 of Mussolini's Special Laws, which barred all political opposition and led many anti-Fascist intellectuals either to exile or to jail. The Levi household became a center of underground activities; there the Socialist leader Filippo Turati found clandestine shelter on his way to France; and some of the main figures of northern Italian anti-Fascism appeared as well. Among these was Leone Ginzburg, a friend of Natalia's brothers, the man who was to become her husband. At the end of a period that saw the arrest of her three brothers, her father, and Leone, she noted the linguistic changes that bore witness to the dramatic political swing:

> My mother had given up Russian, since she could no longer be tutored by Ginzburg's sister, because it would be compromising. New words had entered our home.—We can't invite Salvatorelli! It's compromising!—we would say.—We can't have this book in the house! It could be compromising! They could search the house! And Paola would say that the building was under "surveillance," that there was always someone with a trenchcoat standing there, and that she felt she was being "tailed" whenever she went for a walk.
>
> (*Opere,* 1.1002)

When Leone was eventually released (in 1938), he and Natalia were married. Leone had been born in Russia, and with his family had moved to Italy when he was still a child; they continued to speak Russian at home. He was a professor of Russian literature at the University of Turin, a well-known name within both the intellectual and the political circles of that city. Like many others, he was fired when he refused to swear allegiance to the Fascist regime, and he then began to work for the newly formed publishing house of Einaudi. The political climate inevitably darkened the life of the newly married Natalia:

> Fascism did not seem about to end any time soon. On the contrary, it seemed it would never end.
>
> In Bagnole de l'Orne, the Rosselli brothers had been killed.
>
> For years Turin had been full of German Jews who had fled from Germany. My father too had a few of them in his laboratory working as assistants.
>
> They were exiles. Perhaps in a short while we also were going to be exiles, forced to travel from town to town, from police office to police office, with no job, no roots, no family, no home.
>
> (*Opere,* 1.1029)

The German exiles soon had to flee from Italy, since there, too, the "racial campaigns" were put into effect. Otherwise, the picture was an accurate foreshadowing of what would soon happen to Natalia and her family.

At first, while everyone who could fled to France and Switzerland, the Ginzburgs and their two children could not leave because Leone's citizenship and passport had been revoked. As soon as Mussolini declared war (in 1940), Leone—like many other political activists—was sent away to the *confino,* a combination of forced residence and internal exile whereby politically and racially "undesirable" or "dangerous" persons were sent to live in the poorest and most isolated villages of southern Italy. Natalia and the children soon joined him. There they remained for three years, during which time a third child was born. This period later provided the material for quite a few of Natalia's early stories. The contrast between the backward rural world and the sophisticated urban world remained a lifelong theme of hers.

The false quiet of this pastoral interlude ended abruptly when Leone was arrested in Rome, where he went in 1943 after the Allies invaded Sicily. Natalia's recollections of these bleak moments are even more austere than her generally unadorned style:

> Then came the 25 of July, and Leone left the village and went to Rome. I remained there. . . . My heart was full of the darkest presentiments. . . . Except for Leone, all the exiles had remained there because they did not know where to go.
>
> Then came the armistice, the short exultation and the frenzy of the armistice; and then, two days later, the Germans. The German trucks were running along the road; the hills and the village were full of soldiers. There were soldiers in the hotel, on the porch, under the pergola, in the kitchen. The village was petrified with fear. . . .

> I left the town on the first day of November. I had received a letter from Leone, brought by hand by someone who had come from Rome, in which he told me I must leave the village immediately, because it was difficult to hide there and the Germans would identify us and take us away. . . .
>
> When I arrived in Rome, I took a breath and I imagined that a happier time was about to begin for us. I had few reasons to believe it, but I believed it. . . . Leone was the director of an underground newspaper and was always out. They arrested him twenty days after our arrival; and I never saw him again.
>
> (*Opere,* 1.1059–1061)

The causes of Leone's death were never officially revealed, and Natalia never directly discussed it in her essays, fiction, or autobiography. "Leone died in prison," she wrote with her usual parsimony, "in the German wing of the Regina Coeli jail, in Rome, during the German invasion, in an icy February" (*Opere,* 1.1054). Apparently, Leone became seriously ill after being beaten during an interrogation. He improved after receiving a shot but died of a stroke during the night.

Natalia Ginzburg found herself alone in occupied Rome, a widow at twenty-seven, with three small children. She wrote of that terrifying period with an uncharacteristically epic voice:

> There has been a war and people have seen many houses come crushing down, and they no longer feel secure in the home that was once quiet and secure. There are things one can never be cured of and many years will go by but we will never recover. . . . Those of us who have been persecuted will never again find peace. A ring at the door at night can only mean for us the word "police." . . . When I look at my children as they sleep, I think with relief that I will not have to wake them up at night to escape. But this relief is neither full nor deep. I still imagine that one of these days we will once again have to get up in the middle of the night to escape and leave everything behind, quiet rooms, letters, memories, clothes. . . . We will never recover from this war. It is hopeless.
>
> (*Opere,* 1.835–836)

By this time Natalia had returned to Turin, where she was reunited with her family and friends. She resumed working for the publisher Einaudi, who gathered around himself many prominent intellectuals and writers engaged in the arduous task of revitalizing Italian culture after two decades of all but total hibernation.

When Ginzburg was barely seventeen, her first two short stories were accepted for publication by *Solaria* and *Letteratura,* two important if small literary magazines. But her true literary debut took place in 1942, during that dramatic period of her own life and of Italian history. *La strada che va in città* (*The Road to the City*), Ginzburg's first novel, came out under the pseudonym Alessandra Tornimparte in order to hide the Jewish identity of its author. From 1945 onward, Ginzburg turned out an uninterrupted and rich list of publications that included narrative, theater, literary, and journalistic essays, as well as translations. After two short novels, *È stato così* (*The Dry Heart,* 1947) and *La madre* (Mother, 1948), she published her famous novel *A Light for Fools,* for which she received the Veillon Prize and which gained her great acclaim. In 1957 she published two novellas under the title *Valentino,*[1] which brought her the Viareggio Prize. In 1961 and 1962, respectively, she published the novel *Voices in the Evening* and the collection of essays *Le piccole virtù* (*The Little Virtues*). In 1963 she received the prestigious Strega Prize for her autobiography, *Family Sayings.*

During the next two decades Ginzburg turned to the theater and to essays. In 1966 she published *Ti ho sposato per allegria* (*I Married You for Fun*), and in 1973 another collection of plays came out under the title *Paese di mare* (*Seaside Resort*). During this period she also wrote regularly for the third page—the cultural page—of several Italian daily newspapers, which eventually resulted in two collections of

[1] Consisting of *Valentino* (first published in 1951), *Sagittario,* and the short story "La madre."

essays, *Mai devi domandarmi* (*Never Must You Ask Me,* 1970) and *Vita immaginaria* (Imaginary Life, 1974). After 1973 Ginzburg returned to writing novels, almost exclusively in the epistolary form. She published *Caro Michele* (*Dear Michael,* 1973; also translated as *No Way,* 1974); two short stories, and the only straight (non-epistolary) narratives *Famiglia* and *Borghesia* (*Family* and *Bourgeoisie* 1977); the nonfiction novel *La famiglia Manzoni* (*The Manzoni Family,* 1983); and *La città e la casa* (*The City and the House,* 1984). In 1985 she received the Pirandello Prize.

To this intense literary production Ginzburg then added her work in Parliament: in 1983 she was elected on a leftist independent ticket sponsored by the Italian Communist party.

Ginzburg's early work does not dramatically depart from the aesthetic conventions and the ideological underpinnings of neorealism, the literary current predominant during the 1930's and the 1940's among Italian anti-Fascist and (later) progressive authors. Broadly speaking, the onset of neorealism in Italy and in Europe generally coincided with the end of the aesthetic experimentation that had dominated the cultural scene during the first two decades of the century; the end, that is, of futurism, expressionism, and the whole phase that goes by the name of the avant-garde. The generation of writers to which Ginzburg belonged came of age too late really to be part of that exciting period. Rather, it found itself constrained between the nationalistic, provincial, anti-experimental aesthetic imperatives of Fascism and the boldness in subject matter but tameness in form of neorealism. Alberto Moravia's famous novel *Gli indifferenti* (1929) ushered in the new phase and remains to this day its most emblematic product. Equally representative are the names of Cesare Pavese, Vasco Pratolini, Carlo Levi, and Elio Vittorini—all contemporaries of Ginzburg, and like her caught in different forms of what the critic J. A. Gatt-Rutter identified as the "escapisms" of neorealism: documentarism on the one hand and exoticism—its complementary opposite—on the other.

The first phase of Ginzburg's work bears all the scars of these historically constrained contradictions. Her early short stories are all marked by the effort to avoid authorial interpolation, to let the closely observed detail carry the burden of the narrative. Yet this extreme attention to details is accompanied by a remarkable lack of specificity at the level of locale. The two apparently contradictory elements of specificity and abstractness in fact complement each other; they express the alienation from the historical world that Ginzburg shared with other contemporary progressive authors. The most useful comments for understanding this first phase of her career came from the author herself; she recalled that much of her early work had been informed by a profound alienation from her identity as a female writer, as a Piedmontese writer, and as a petit-bourgeois writer: "At the time I had a strong desire to write like a man; I was terrified that someone might realize from my writing that I was a woman" (*Opere,* 1.847). It is very revealing that the desire to write "like a man" is associated with the fear of autobiography and with the attraction for an aesthetic of male coldness and detachment: "I was horrified by autobiography. It horrified and terrified me: because the autobiographical temptation was very strong, as I knew easily happens to women: and my life, my own self, banished and hated, could break in suddenly in the forbidden land of my writing" (*Opere,* 1.1121).

Ginzburg's alienation from themes and forms perceived as "female" specifically impeded her as a female author. Writing at a time when the dominant aesthetic aims were coldness, detachment, and a generally hard-boiled style—in other words, the style of modern American novels, banished by the Fascists and hungrily read by young intellectuals—she shared the alienation from place and class with many other authors: "I felt sorry for myself for being born in Italy and for living in Turin, because in my books I wanted to describe the

Nevskii Prospect, whereas I was forced to describe the Po Riverside. And this I felt was a great humiliation" (*Opere,* 1.1118–1119). The escapist impulse toward faraway and exotic places complements the escapism from a class and social background perceived as prosaic and uninteresting.

> I did not like my social background. I was the daughter of a university professor. My father's profession seemed to me, I don't know why, unacceptable: it seemed, among the professions, the most unlikely to generate a writer. I wanted my father to be either a prince or a peasant; that we should be either very rich or very poor. And instead my family was neither very rich nor very poor: we were, alas, bourgeois. And on top of that, we were Jewish, which also seemed to exile me very far from the world of poetry, because I knew of no writer who was at once Jewish, bourgeois, the child of a professor, and brought up in Piedmont.
>
> (*Opere,* 1.1119–1120)

What is most original in Ginzburg's early work and saves many pieces from being just the first experiments of a gifted but immature writer is her honest and genuine confrontation with such troubling impulses. Her early work can be read as the record of her eventual discovery of the aesthetic merits of the female voice.

If most of Ginzburg's later production had its social center in the family and its emotional center in women, this first phase focused more closely on lonely and unhappy young women who are unable either to challenge or to satisfy the restrictive codes of behavior that define what is proper for a marriageable woman or a wife or a mother.

"Un'assenza" (An Absence, 1933), one of the early pieces republished in the collected edition, is a short story written in the third person, a form Ginzburg was to discover uncongenial. It is the portrait of a wealthy man whose wife is vacationing on the Riviera and is probably betraying him. He is Ginzburg's first exploration of a certain type of man: apathetic, mediocre, indifferent, empty, inept. The man's puny impulse for revenge against his wife's adultery is consumed in the decision, which closes the story, to visit a prostitute.

The man in "Un'assenza" is the first in a series of Ginzburg's portrayals of the most reprehensible types of a decadent high bourgeoisie, individuals whose decisions or indecisions in the face of personal crises read at times as an allegory of Fascism. The vapid and effete inaction of these bourgeois types proved in fact to be as important for the vigor of the Fascist regime as the violent squads of Mussolini's Black Shirts—who were recruited by and large from a petit bourgeoisie impoverished by post–World War I economic recession and later by the Depression.

"Casa al mare" (House by the Sea, 1937), another of these early pieces, is recounted in the first person by a male protagonist. At the beginning of a very thin plot the narrator is asked by Walter, a friend he has not seen in many years, to join him and his family at a sea resort where they are vacationing and to help in some vaguely mentioned "difficulties." The narrator's arrival brings no help to what appear to be marital problems. He is unable to break the silence that envelops Walter to such a point that no help is ever openly asked for nor is the situation ever discussed: "During our interminable walks he would be silent most of the time" (*Opere,* 1.183); "I gave no advice and no one asked me for it" (*Opere,* 1.182). This is only partly true. Vilma, the wife of Walter, confesses to the visitor her attachment to another man. Behind the adultery, the reader can infer, is a marriage surviving only on inertia and for the sake of the child, on whom the woman seems to concentrate an inordinate amount of unsublimated energy. More central to the story is what happens to the detached and vaguely perplexed narrator. Very quickly Vilma loses interest in the other man and becomes infatuated with the narrator. "I should have left immediately. But I couldn't do it" (*Opere,* 1.183), he admits. With this turn the story is transformed into a confession, the soliloquy of a man retracing the steps that have led to his seduction by the woman and to the betrayal of his friend.

Recalling this story, Ginzburg commented:

> When I wrote "Casa al mare" I felt that I had reached the height of coldness and detachment. I only dreamed of coldness and detachment, and that story seemed admirable: and yet something in all that detachment disgusted me. In order to write like a man I had even pretended in that story that I was a man: which I never did, and will never do, again. I had, however, discovered the first person, the great pleasure of writing in the first person, a pleasure until that day unknown to me.
>
> (*Opere,* 1.1123–1124)

What separates "Casa al mare" from "Un'assenza" is not just the use of the first person. More important, the story challenges a narrator whose tone and style proclaim him outside the scene but who ultimately finds himself immersed in it. The story inaugurates Ginzburg's lifelong distrust of detachment and her effort to bring the subjectivity of a narrator into open view.

Only four years separate "Casa al mare" from "Mio marito" (My Husband, 1941). During this time, however, much happened in Ginzburg's life and in the surrounding world that drastically altered her aesthetic and thematic priorities. "Mio marito" marks the author's first openly embraced commitment to social, historical, and gender specificity. That it should take place at a moment of intense personal drama must have been far from accidental. She recalled her ambivalence toward both the village of her exile and the city she had left behind:

> I wrote "Mio marito" in May 1941, in Pizzoli, a village of the Abruzzi countryside. I had never in my life lived in the country. I had spent time in the country but only on holidays. Pizzoli was an exile village and I went there when Italy entered the war. I remained there for three years. . . . The women with their black shawls in "Mio marito" are those who would pass by, back and forth, on the donkeys, along paths that climbed toward the hills or that descended among the vineyards, and down to the river. . . . That town I both loved and hated. I would always feel a stinging nostalgia for Turin, the city in which I grew up, which had always seemed to me foolish and dull; and now I imagined it beautiful in my memory, with its wide boulevards traveled by swinging and chiming trolleys.
>
> (*Opere,* 1.1124–1125)

The narrator of "Mio marito" is a young woman of twenty-five who has just married an older man, a village doctor, and has thus dispelled the threat of spinsterhood. The story is in the form of a confession by a person driven by the need to relieve an overburdened memory. After a short engagement and a quick marriage, the narrator moves from her small town to begin a new life as the wife of the village doctor. Estrangement at finding herself in a new place and disillusion with her romantic ideas about marriage mark the first period of her new life. The estrangement reaches its climax when her husband confesses that for a number of years he has had a secret relationship with a young and very poor local peasant. He had cured her when she was fifteen and brought food to help her recover, since the family was too poor to do anything for the girl. Their meetings eventually became sexual encounters, and he found himself the prisoner of this illicit passion. His marriage, he admits with sincerity, was prompted by the hope that his wife would help him free himself from Mariuccia. The accidental discovery that her husband still sees Mariuccia proclaims to the narrator the failed redemption of her husband. In a second and most revealing confession the husband finally acknowledges how much more than just adultery the passion for Mariuccia represents:

> —What do I care about you?—he said.—You mean nothing new to me, you have nothing I care for. You resemble my mother and mother's mother, and all the women who have lived in this house. You, you have not been beaten as a child. You did not starve. You were not forced to work in

> the fields from morning until night, under a sun that breaks your back.
>
> (*Opere,* 1.197)

For the man, both the wife and the girl are forbidden objects: by marrying a woman who is like his mother and his sister he has broken the taboo of incest, and by coupling with a girl who belongs to a different class he has broken the taboo of something like miscegenation.

With great skill Ginzburg brings together, in this simple story, two opposites: on the one hand the bourgeois woman, mature, educated, clean, understanding; on the other, the peasant girl, childish, poor, wild, dirty, enigmatic. The story lucidly depicts the dichotomies in which the wife becomes caught—poles that are at once bourgeois-proletarian, urban-peasant, male-female, young-old—and vaguely posits the moment of labor as the one time when the polarity is briefly overcome by virtue of an experience that is beyond class distinctions. In the southern village where the story was written, hundreds of miles from the educated, bourgeois, industrialized world of northern Italy, Ginzburg—somewhat like the husband in the story—acknowledged and accepted her own class and gender identity, at the moment when she discovered the identity of the "other."

The dichotomy between country and city, first tentatively explored in "Mio marito," is the main theme of *The Road to the City* (1942), Ginzburg's first novel.

> I started to write *The Road to the City* in September 1941. Floating in my mind was September, September in the Abruzzi countryside, which is not rainy but warm and clear, and the dirt turns red, the hills turn red, and floating in my mind was nostalgia for Turin, and perhaps also *Tobacco Road,* which I had read, I think, around that time and liked a little, not much.
>
> (*Opere,* 1.1125)

Here, as in the previous story, feelings of nostalgia and separation made stronger by the season and by the changing landscape appear as an important poetic source. The distant city of the author and the village of her present exile merge to produce a landscape that is vague—it is neither the city of Turin, nor the village of Pizzoli, nor the nearby town of Aquila—and yet is also specific, being recognizably all these places at once.

The novel revolves around Delia, a seventeen-year-old who lives in a small town a few miles from a large city, and specifically around her movements between the town and the city, one the one hand, and the town and a remote mountain village, on the other. This first-person narrative unfolds as if by inertia, as if motivated by the simple pleasure of telling and retelling. We follow Delia's lackadaisical affair with Giulio, the son of the town doctor, and her infatuation with Nini, an orphan cousin who was brought up in her house and is now a factory worker in the nearby city. Delia is a childish, egotistical, and sincere young woman. She is also a restless, rebellious poor girl who exhibits none of the modesty required of women from a wealthier class. As a result of her promenades in the woods with Giulio, Delia becomes pregnant, and the two families engage in maledictions first, and then negotiations. It is finally agreed that the two young people will be married in a few months, after Giulio has finished his courses at the university. For the time being Delia is sent to a nearby mountain village to keep her out of sight. After the wedding the young couple moves to the city, where the baby is born and Delia is transformed into the citified wife of a doctor. Nini, meanwhile, has died of pneumonia and alcohol. The story closes with Delia trying not to think of him and leading the modern life she has been longing for.

Although the novel is spun of material fit for melodrama—a seduced girl, the amending marriage, the death of the true lover—it is remarkably empty of all melodramatic effects. The complexity of this moving first novel derives mainly from the depth of Delia's world. Her town is not the rural wilderness of "Mio marito" nor the anonymous Riviera of "Casa al mare," but a sociologically hybrid space between country and city where boredom and poverty provide the main motives for the young people's escape to the city. The city is culturally and sociologically a well-defined space. Neither enchanted nor critical, Delia goes there with a naive, curious, and childish desire for ice cream, clothes, windows, perfumes. Nini, who also escapes the town, represents other aspects of the city—the factory, a job, politics, books, newspapers. The mountain village where Delia is sent during her pregnancy represents yet another locale. Here the girl lives in a house filled with sacks of corn and chestnuts, the local staples; there is no electricity or running water; the children are always dirty and the air smells of manure. The village, the town, and the city represent the cultural horizons of Delia, an aged child and a childish woman, a village girl and a city girl. They are also in some respect the horizons of Italy just before the war, and for a while after it, until the economic boom of the 1950's and 1960's transformed the country more deeply than did the worst wartime bombings.

How exotic the worlds that provide the setting for "Mio marito" and *The Road to the City* must have appeared to Ginzburg becomes clear from a passage written years later, in which she states that the village of her exile was as "far away and remote as India or China" (*Opere,* 1.1128). The dominant atmosphere, in both "Mio marito" and *The Road,* is marked by the attraction and repulsion of the strange, primitive village where the two narrators find themselves. It is this same ambivalence that marks the recollection of Ginzburg's exile:

> At a time now distant of my life, I lived in the country for a few years. I had not chosen that village; others had chosen it for me. In fact it was a village of exile. And yet having slowly started to love it, I never forgot, during the time of my residence there, that I had not chosen it and I never stopped dreaming of other more remote villages. . . . There was, not far from the village, a hamlet called Cavallari, five or six houses scattered around a swamp, and I would imagine my life there. . . . Walking through the fields toward Cavallari one would sink in the mud to the knee, and in the alleys among the black ruined houses one would sink in manure.
>
> (*Opere,* 2.120)

*Cristo si e fermato a Eboli* (*Christ Stopped at Eboli,* 1945) by Carlo Levi bears the same marks of ambivalence and is the by-product of the same politically and racially motivated exile. As one critic noted, Cesare Pavese's mythical-mystical attraction for the Piedmontese peasants and the vine-covered hills of his youth, while the product of migration and distance rather than of exile, is also part of the same context. The *confino* threw Ginzburg, an intellectual, northern Italian, bourgeois woman, into close touch with the world of poor mountain peasants, of illiteracy and high infant mortality, a rural world that was neither idyllic nor pastoral and that with the German invasion became another spot in the infernal and war-torn landscape of central Italy.

The next three stories by Ginzburg continue in different ways the theme of *The Road to the City.* Written between 1947 and 1951, after the writer had returned to Turin, they take place within a predominantly petit-bourgeois milieu and portray the existential despair of a woman—a wife, a mother, a sister. Here one discovers that Ginzburg's gift for dialogues and monologues extends in fact to silence, to the quiet, almost wild, acquiescence that masks despair and sometimes explodes into tragedy.

*È stato così* (*The Dry Heart,* 1947) is the story of yet another woman who has escaped the village for the city and spinsterhood for marriage. Like one in shock, she recounts the events that have led to the act to which the title—"it happened like this"—alludes. "I shot him in the eyes," she announces at the start. She then plunges into a long confession, at the end of which we realize that the story we have just read was written by a woman on the point of committing suicide. If the homicide-suicide that frames the story, the mystery and denouement that sustain it, and the confessional tone of the narrative all promise the lure of drama, the story actually develops as a long, subdued monologue. Through flashbacks we encounter the protagonist as a young high school teacher, a middle-class young woman who fantasizes about engagement and marriage and who, in spite of the town's perception of her as one of the "modern girls," is in fact modest, shy, reserved, and fully acquiescent to the proprieties of her class and culture.

The turning point in her life comes when she meets Alberto—forty years old, white trenchcoat, briefcase, small, slender hands—a familiar type of aged boy in Ginzburg's fiction. The pale romance of their engagement is followed by marriage and this, in turn, by the discovery that the man has a lover. When a child is born, the couple seems to grow closer, but it is a false impression. Alberto soon resumes his adultery, while the woman begins to perceive the abyss of despair in which she is trapped. The story—as in "Mio marito"—is more concerned with adultery as a symptom than as a cause of spiritual and existential malaise. The adultery is simply the catalyst of an explosion caused by an unstable mixture: a passive, cowardly man and a romantic young woman.

After Ginzburg's "pleasant" discovery of and devotion to the first person, "La madre" (1948), the next short story, represents a return to the third person. The mother of the title is—somewhat like the author herself at the time—a lonely widow who lives with her two small children and her old parents. Very young, small, and thin, she is a chain smoker who leaves chaos wherever she puts her hands, does not know how to cook, has no authority, sleeps out—in other words, fails to conform to the standards that define a woman and mother. With an admirable touch Ginzburg shifts to the point of view of the children in order to characterize her further:

> The mother was not important. Important were grandmother, grandfather, aunt Clementina, who lived in the country and would arrive every once in a while with chestnuts and cornmeal; important was Diomira, the maid; important was Giovanni, the tuberculous super. . . . All these people were important for the two boys because they were strong people that one could trust, strong people in saying yes and no, very good in all that they did and always full of wisdom and strength; people who could defend someone from the storm and from the robbers. But if they were alone with the mother, the boys were scared as if they had been alone.
>
> (*Opere,* 1.204)

During a temporary absence of the grandparents the mother becomes involved with a man who comes to the house, befriends the children, and then disappears. The return of the grandparents is a great relief for the boys:

> Once again there was a tablecloth on the table at lunch, and glasses and everything; again there was the grandmother sitting in the rocking chair with her docile body, with her smell: grandmother could not run away, she was too old and too fat, it was nice to have someone who stayed home and could never run away.
>
> (*Opere,* 1.212)

Deserted by the man, the mother becomes more and more desperate, smokes more than ever, cries in bed at night until, one day, she fails to return home and the boys discover that she has committed suicide:

> The mother was brought home and the boys went to see her after she had been laid on the bed: Diomira had dressed her with the patent leather shoes and the red silk dress that she had on for her wedding; she was little, as little as a dead doll.
>
> (*Opere,* 1.213)

The boys' last view of their dead mother is the picture of a child observing another child, one who becomes a mother before she became a woman. Without ever sentimentalizing the woman or the children, and with great sensitivity for the ambivalence of motherhood, Ginzburg has recorded the despair of a lonely young mother, in a story that delicately balances itself between an objective but compassionate narrator and the perplexed, egotistical, but ultimately nonjudgmental, point of view of the boys.

In 1951 Ginzburg published the short novel *Valentino,* according to several critics the most accomplished work of this early phase in her career. The story is told by Caterina, the sister of the title character. She is in her early twenties, lives at home, works to help her family, and leads a secluded and uninteresting life with few expectations for either marriage or economic improvement. She belongs to a petit-bourgeois family, decorously but unmistakably poor. The father is a retired teacher, the mother a private music teacher, Caterina is studying to become an elementary school teacher while her brother Valentino goes to medical school. He is, as the only son, the focus of his parents' attentions and ambitions. From Valentino, the father dreams, will come professional success and economic advancement for the family. In her characteristic flat tone, the narrator explains:

> My father thought that [my brother] was going to become a great man: there was, perhaps, no reason to believe it but he believed it. . . . He imagined that Valentino would become a famous doctor and would go to conferences in the main European capitals and would discover new drugs and diseases. Valentino, instead, did not seem to care about becoming a great man: at home, usually he played with the kitten; and he made toys for the children of the super . . . or he would dress up in a skiing outfit and watch himself in the mirror. . . . He found himself very handsome wearing that outfit and he would walk in front of the mirror first with a scarf around his neck and then without; and then he would appear on the porch so as to let the children of the super see him.
>
> (*Opere,* 1.219–220)

The two men in the family thus both live in fairyland—one imagines the most successful career for his unambitious son, and the son still indulges himself with childhood toys or adolescent narcissism. Vain, indolent, weak, infantile, like many other male characters drawn by Ginzburg, Valentino suddenly announces his engagement. The fiancée is not one of the many high school girls to whom he has engaged and disengaged himself many times before. Instead, she is a very wealthy, older, unattractive woman. Against the will of his family and to their surprise, given his whimsical record, Valentino marries Maddalena and begins a new life with her: an elegant villa, summer resorts, extravagant furs, expensive furniture, and a car. This provides the occasion for one of Ginzburg's favorite themes, the contrast between the mean circumstances of the poorer petit-bourgeois strata and the extravagant life-style of the high bourgeoisie. The historical context of the publication of *Valentino* was the new and highly visible consumerism slowly spreading within Italian society, the herald, after the Depression and wartime poverty, of a new economic phase.

The death of her parents is a turning point in Caterina's life. She joins the household of Valentino and Maddalena, and a new and more affluent existence begins for her. Maddalena, meanwhile, emerges as a strong woman, unsentimental but generous and gentle beneath the harsh surface. She is the antithesis of the self-centered Valentino, who is now, as ever, a pampered child whose main devotion is to his appearance and to Kit, a cousin of Maddalena's with whom he spends most of his time. Kit proposes to Caterina but immediately withdraws the proposal. When, shortly thereafter, Kit commits suicide, the causes of his behavior are discovered in the homosexual relationship he has carried on with Valentino. Maddalena and Valentino separate, and Valentino and Caterina move in together. Brother and sister at the end of the story are not too different from the many estranged couples that populate Ginzburg's fiction. They avoid tension by avoiding words and memory.

Except for "Un'assenza," all of these early works remain as valuable testimonies of Ginzburg's obstinate search for a female voice, one that could at once be her own—that of a novelist, an intellectual, and a bourgeois woman—and that of the many less articulate women whose confusion, rebellion, solitude, and ambivalence she shared and wished to capture. They all deserve to be read, for few contemporary authors have recorded such a range of emotional responses and so many cries of existential anguish of young women at that turning point in their lives called marriage.

Between 1952 and 1963 Ginzburg's work reached what critics consider its peak. During this period she published two novels, *A Light for Fools* and *Voices in the Evening;* her autobiography, *Family Sayings;* the novella *Sagittario* (*Sagittarius,* 1957); and the collection of essays *Le piccole virtú* (*The Little Virtues,* 1962). By Ginzburg's own acknowledgment, much of this writing is distinguished by a surrender to memory, to a source of creativity she had banned in youth as impure: "I reached the pure memory like a wolf, by taking the back trails, by telling myself that the springs of memory were those I should never taste, the one place on earth I should never go to" (*Opere,* 1.1133).

The dominant trait of Ginzburg's fiction during this period, her "surrender" to memory and to the past, stands at the crossroad between her biographical departure from Turin and the country's historical departure from a rural and small industrial economy. Just as Ginzburg's exile to a poor southern village was a turning point in her early literary career, so her move from Turin to Rome in 1952, following her remarriage, was an important turning point for her later writing. The move took her from the industrial to the political capital of Italy, from an introverted, homogeneous northern city to an extraverted, heterogeneous, and truly Mediterranean city, from a politically radical but culturally conservative city to its opposite. During the decade following this move Ginzburg followed two very different directions. First, she directed her attention toward the past, toward her parents' generation as well as her own, as if her departure from Turin had brought to the surface those early experiences and had freed the desire to confront them and give them artistic form. Second, she focused her attention on the contemporary world, recording the dramatic changes that were transforming the once gray, oppressive, provincial world of the 1930's and 1940's into an extravagant, vacuous world that lacked any sense of time, memory, and history.

What justifies the critics' selection of these novels as Ginzburg's masterpieces is their greater historical and social scope. The poetics of "little things" that had been so recognizably hers from the beginning translated during this period into a more complex vision of the relationship between private and public, story and history, the individual and society. Ginzburg's attempt to reproduce in her early stories the uneventful and barely audible flow of everyday life now became integrated with the convulsive rhythms of history. Finally, her alienation from her personal and social identity gave way to a rediscovery of her roots and a specific delineation of time, class, and space.

If the rediscovery of the past was motivated by Ginzburg's separation from the world of her youth, it must also be understood as an expression of the period between the mid 1940's and the late 1950's. Historically, this period was marked by the cold war on the international stage and by conservative political trends on several domestic fronts. The renewed hegemony of the right-wing Christian Democrats ratified the end of the resistance and its postwar ideals and found expression in widespread repression in the factories, as well as in very conservative policies within the government, policies that guaranteed a decade of capitalist expansion, technological advances, and large industrial investments. These policies prepared the ground for what Italian sociologists came to label the Second Industrial Revolution or the Economic Miracle. Thanks to the high profits made possible by a conservative government, thousands of people abandoned the countryside throughout Italy, especially in the south, and moved to the industrial cities of northern Italy and northern Europe. Fascism, the resistance, the war, the invasions, and the bombings all seemed tame compared with the massive social and economic upheavals of this period. These changes must have seemed particularly momentous to Ginzburg's generation, many of whose members had lived through the coercive stability of the Fascist regime and had survived the ravages of war, only to discover that the return to peace would not bring back "their" time. As one critic noted, Carlo Cassola's novel *La ragazza di Bube* (*Bebo's Girl,* 1960), Giorgio Bassani's *Il giardino dei Finzi-Contini* (*The Garden of the Finzi-Continis,* 1962), Tomasi di Lampedusa's *Il gattopardo* (*The Leopard,* 1958), and Ginzburg's novels of these years all share the same unease and nostalgia. Time, which had moved too slowly for them during Fascism, was now spinning too fast. In an essay entitled "Vecchiaia" (Old Age), Ginzburg wrote an epitaph for this period:

> Now we are becoming what we wanted never to become, and that is old. . . . The slow pace of our becoming old contrasts with the whirling pace of the world that rotates around us, the rapid transformation of places, and the rapid growth of children and youth; within such vortex we alone are slow, changing our looks and habits with the speed of a caterpillar. . . . The world that rotates and changes around us maintains but a few traces of the world that has been ours. . . . Except for these tenuous traces, the present appears dark to us, and we do not know how to become accustomed to such obscurity.
>
> (*Opere,* 2.23–26)

*A Light for Fools* differs from other Ginzburg novels: it is long; it is written in the third person; it is both epic and historical. Yet it is also emblematic of her work in that it subordinates the historical material to the priorities of the bildungsroman.

Two neighboring families provide the main plot for this story, which takes place during the years of Fascism and is set in Turin, at that time a small, provincial, industrial city. The families represent two different strata of the Italian bourgeoisie, the one modestly wealthy, of intellectual and socialist orientations, the other very wealthy and conspicuously consumerist. The story centers on Anna, the youngest of the children (in the intellectual and socialist family), and on her development from childhood through adolescence to young womanhood. The book opens with a description of Anna's dead mother, whose portrait hangs on the wall of the dining room, and with a reference to the dead grandmother, whose lady-in-waiting, old Signora Maria, acts as maid, aunt, and surrogate mother. Anna's family is thus characterized by the absence of a mother figure. The old generation is represented by two fathers. One, the father of Anna, is an old socialist who lives in the seclusion of his study, writing his "memoirs," in which he promises to reveal "all the truth" about Fascism and its converts; the other, the father of Emanuele, Amalia, and Giuma, is senile and oblivious to the adulterous affairs of his young wife. The young generation includes the solitary and alienated Ippolito, the fatuous and love-torn Concettina, as well as Giustino and Anna herself, children at the beginning of the novel and young adults by the end. Across the street are the politically engaged Emanuele, Amalia (who is also in the midst of love conflicts), and Giuma, who is the same age as Giustino. Early in the novel both fathers die, making official what was apparent even before: the young people who come of age during the dark days of Fascism are orphans, lacking both emotional and political guidance.

The deaths of the two old fathers alter the rhythms of the young people's lives and the atmosphere of the households:

> There was a great deal of freedom in the house. But it was a type of freedom that made one

scared. There was no one left who was in command. Every once in a while Ippolito would try to give orders, just a few, but no one listened, and he would shrug his shoulders.

(*Opere,* 1.287)

More important, the two deaths open the doors between the two houses and coincide with the beginning of the friendship and political involvement of Emanuele, Ippolito, and Danilo, an unsuccessful suitor of Concettina:

> Anna asked what Danilo had in mind. Giustino turned up his nose and pursed his lips, came closer to her face, becoming more and more ugly.—Po–li–tics—he whispered in her ear and ran away. . . .
>
> "Po–li–tics," she repeated softly, and now suddenly she felt she understood. . . . They wanted to overthrow the Fascists, to start a revolution. . . . Now Anna would imagine herself on the barricades, on the day of the revolution . . . with Ippolito and Danilo, shooting with rifles and singing.
>
> (*Opere,* 1.297)

Ginzburg uses the point of view of Anna and Giustino—at this time in the novel, children in their teens—both to characterize the activities of the young men as mysterious and conspiratorial and as a subtle way to make light of the romantic passion inspiring these young bourgeois activists.

The arrival of Cenzo Rena at the country house adds the perspective of a true outsider. Rena sees Italy and Fascism from a broader perspective than the young men, as if through a reversed telescope:

> Cenzo Rena often took walks with Ippolito and Emanuele through the countryside, and would go hunting with them. . . . When they returned home Cenzo Rena was tired and disappointed; he would throw himself on a chair under the pergola and shake his head; for a long time he would shake his head and say to Ippolito and Emanuele that the two of them were full of smoke and fog, and considered themselves who knows what, but then they did not even know how to shoot a bird. Two little provincial intellectuals, that's what they were, the saddest and strangest thing that can exist on earth. They had never seen anything, he—Cenzo Rena—had been in America, Constantinople, and London, and he knew what Italy looked like when seen from Mexico or London, like a black flea Italy looked, Mussolini the flea's shit. And instead Emanuele and Ippolito did not even know Italy, had never seen anything besides this little city, and they imagined that all of Italy was like their little city, and full of professors and white collars, with a few workers; but even the workers and the white collars looked like professors in their imagination. And they had forgotten that Italy was also the priests and the peasants . . . that Italy was the South, Cenzo Rena would shout. . . . They did not know what the South is, and what are the southern peasants, who have only a few beans to eat.
>
> (*Opere,* 1.317)

Cenzo Rena's tirade is an unblinking analysis of the northern intellectuals, of their shallow understanding of the world they plan to change; the speech also prepares the ground for the change of locale of the second half of the novel, and for the forthcoming complex view of Italy and Fascism.

The departure of Cenzo Rena and the return of the family to the city at the end of the summer are accompanied by the first signs of the approaching war, at first with the German invasion of Poland, and then with the declaration of war against Germany by France and England. Against this menacing setting Anna and Giuma meet again as adolescents. Giuma has become an elegant, sophisticated young man whose main objections to Fascism are that it is "ugly" and "provincial." He thinks that it is not worthwhile for one to fight and risk going to jail, because Fascism will disappear by itself.

In time the renewed friendship between Anna and Giuma melts some of the arrogance of the spoiled young man. Their afternoons along the river, at the movies, or in a café give way to a sexual relationship. These are rare pages because they record the confusion, ambivalence, and guilt of a sixteen-year-old who has just broken a taboo and become a woman:

> At home she sat benumbed at the desk of her room, and saw again, feeling a painful pull at her heart, the face of Giuma, that face so immersed in a wrathful and private sleep, with his eyelids tightly shut, that face that had neither words nor thoughts left for her. . . . She wanted someone to come and scold her for not doing her homework, and to tell her never again to go on walks with Giuma among the bushes along the river. But no one was coming to say anything, no one was coming even to see if she was back.
>
> (*Opere,* 1.375)

Anna's anguish is that of the girl who has left her adolescence behind and whose first steps as a young woman are rendered insignificant by Giuma's lack of love and by the approaching war. The first bombing of Turin coincides with Anna's realization that she is pregnant and that the only help Giuma has to offer is in the form of money for an abortion. Only to Cenzo Rena, who visits once more, is Anna able to confess that she is pregnant and that she wants to have an abortion:

> Anna asked what else she could do . . . she had done everything wrong and therefore what would that baby have when it came into the world, only a mother who had done everything wrong and who had no courage. Cenzo Rena said that no one found courage ready-made, courage must be made little by little; it was a long story that lasted almost all one's life. . . . He told her that until that day she had lived as an insect, an insect that knows nothing besides the leaf on which it lives suspended.
>
> (*Opere,* 1.417)

These words contribute to a larger theme that is embedded in the novel. Beneath the argument over the difficult choices available to a young woman hides a critical analysis of the motivations of the intellectuals who became involved in the resistance.

Cenzo Rena's proposal to marry Anna and adopt the baby closes the first part of the novel. The northern Italian industrial and intellectual bourgeoisie fades as the young bride finds herself in a small rural village with one main street and no train. The turning point of Anna's life, like that of Ginzburg's, thus coincides with her move to a culturally and economically foreign region. At the point when she stops being a child and becomes an adult, Anna is once more an outsider—it is her point of view that the author closely follows.

Central to the second part is the abyss that separates North and South. This is dramatized comically in the encounter between Signora Maria and Maschiona, the housekeeper of Cenzo Rena, and tragically in the encounter of Signora Maria and the village:

> [Signora Maria] had gotten into her head to teach Maschiona a great deal of things; she wanted her to wash the dishes with soap and Maschiona kept explaining that if she washed the dishes with soap she could not give that nice fatty water from the dishes to the hogs, and Signora Maria still did not understand and continued to throw soap in the vat, and Maschiona would become desperate for all the wasted rinse. Finally Cenzo Rena prohibited Signora Maria from interfering with the rinse of the dishes. Signora Maria started to visit the houses of the peasants, and she would see the children and come home in shock, saying that all the children had scabs and fleas in their scalps. . . . The fleas were the least of the problems, [Cenzo Rena] said; the fleas do not cause death, and there were other things that cause death, pneumonia, and dysentery. Dysentery was the worst of all problems, every summer many children became sick, and he would go in the houses to explain the diet, and he would bring the doctor along, and he would even leave money for the rice. But the peasants did not buy rice and hid the money in the mattress, and the children dragged themselves through the alleys, sucking pieces of cabbage and figs, and they cried . . . and then one night they died, and were taken to the cemetery in a little box.
>
> (*Opere,* 1.454–455)

It is not very often that one finds in the many descriptions of "others" such compassion and sensitivity, such freedom from patronizing and chauvinistic overtones. Characteristically, these passages by Ginzburg transform into prose poems, sounding an even lower depth of grief while reaching the highest pitches of emotion.

The abyss between North and South is also articulated through the different meaning that the word "politics" has in a world where revolution means bare survival and heroism is as strange a concept as electricity. Actively involved in the small, humble, everyday work of using his knowledge to help the illiterate peasants, Cenzo Rena represents a way of being politically engaged that is concrete and practical, in a world that leaves no room for vain heroisms or purely existential motivations. The complexity of vision and the depth of understanding that make *A Light for Fools* Ginzburg's masterpiece are inseparable from her own experience in the South as an exile. No wonder she could so well deride the pretensions of the urban northerners without idealizing or minimizing the tragic realities of the poor southern peasants.

Anna's growth into a woman, not just physically but also emotionally and intellectually, provides the other main theme. Anna's estrangement from an older and still unfamiliar husband, her perception of her rapidly changing body, and later of her new baby girl, all contribute to the unidealized and deromanticized representation of marriage and motherhood already sketched by Ginzburg in her first short stories:

> She had become very big and heavy, and would spend the days sitting with her hands in her lap, letting the baby grow inside. She would sit next to the fireplace and rummage in the fire with the tongs, thinking of the child and imagining it with blue eyes and sharp teeth, she imagined it as a newborn with a mouth full of teeth like a fox.
>
> (*Opere,* 1.438)

> Anna would climb up to the pinewood with the baby girl. . . . [She] would sit and place the baby on a pillow, her feet wrapped in a blanket; the baby would kick the blanket, lift her red, skinny feet . . . Anna would stare at her and find nothing to say to her because she did not know how to whisper with babies as Signora Maria did. As soon as the baby fell asleep, she would start to unravel her thoughts, collecting all the scattered threads of her life and weaving them together . . . of the baby who had been for a long time only a bit of dark space inside of her, and then suddenly had become a real baby.
>
> (*Opere,* 1.464)

The shaking of the cinders and the unraveling of the thoughts show us the side of Anna that most closely personifies Ginzburg herself and her poetics. Moreover, the two actions signal Anna's growth into a mature adult who reflects about herself and the world around her, who is no longer living "as an insect."

Against the slow and uneventful rhythms of village life the political events become increasingly tumultuous, at first with Germany's declaration of war against Russia, then with the entrance of Italy into the war, and finally with the soldiers' arrival at the village: "Soldiers and soldiers started marching on the road of San Costanzo, and they sang *Lili Marlene,* a song that Cenzo Rena had learned and that seemed to him very sad; he said the song was about the wreckage of the earth" (*Opere,* 1.496).

Following the fall of Mussolini and the invasion by the Germans, the absurd, antiheroic death of Cenzo Rena occurs. Anna's return to the North brings the novel to its close on a note of nostalgia and hope:

> And they laughed a little and felt very close, the three of them together, Anna, Emanuele, and Giustino, and they were happy to be together thinking of all who had died, and the long war, the pain and the clamor and the long difficult life that lay ahead of them and was full of things they did not know how to do.
>
> (*Opere,* 1.574)

The ignorance and perplexity here described mark the growth of a generation of northern Italian bourgeois youth, their transformation from cartoon revolutionaries to mature individuals who have escaped the claustrophobic shell of their class and culture.

Unjustly criticized by orthodox leftist critics for what they saw as a subordination of history and politics to memory and subjectivity, *A Light for Fools* was vindicated by the post-1968 feminist challenges to those distinctions. What superficially appears as a circumvention of history and politics does not here, and never did in any of Ginzburg's works, serve the cause of political relativism or agnosticism but attests instead to a lifelong search for the ways the private and public come together. Rejecting easy sentimentality and melodrama, Ginzburg added her own version to both the resistance novel tradition and the modernist portrait-of-the-artist tradition.

Between *A Light for Fools* and *Voices in the Evening,* the next important novel, Ginzburg wrote the novella *Sagittarius* (1957), a story less concerned with history and the past than with a fully modern present.

The narrator is an egocentric, ambitious, and naively entrepreneurial woman. Eager to find in the city, where she has just moved, a sophisticated and intellectual world, she forms a partnership with an equally pretentious woman, who swindles her out of her savings. Ginzburg herself criticized this short novel as contrived. The affectionate irony, which is her trademark, here became a cutting irony, one that beneath the comic surface hid a bitter sense of loss and alienation.

*Voices in the Evening* (1961), Ginzburg's next novel, is a combination of family chronicle, personal journal, ethnographic record, and dramatic monologue. The framing narrative captures the world of the protagonist narrator, a young woman on the verge of spinsterhood; her middle-class family; her intrusive and chattering mother; her provincial and gossipy town; and her pallid romance. Along with her story the novel presents, in the form of an internal narrative, two generations of the De Francisci family, who own a small textile mill and are the main employers in the town. Formally, the internal narrative consists largely of the life histories of the De Francisci children, self-contained pieces loosely strung together, individual destinies whose common thread is their inability to overcome the paralysis imposed on them by their class. In a fragmented and disjointed manner the two main narratives form a historical continuum that stretches backward to the first Industrial Revolution and to the socialist ideals of that period, and forward to the economic boom of the postwar years.

The love affair of the narrator with Tommasino, the youngest of the De Franciscis, links the two narrative levels but does not alter their formal discontinuity. Tommasino represents the connecting link between the family of the narrator and his own, between the external and the internal narrative, between the prewar and postwar years. Tommasino and Elsa are involved in a secret love affair that takes place in the nearby city, away from the eyes and ears of the town and their families. From the beginning their relationship is presented in the laconic tone characteristic of the narrator and premonitory of the relationship's doom:

> We meet, Tommasino and I, every Wednesday in the city. . . .
>
> We see each other only in the city. In the town we avoid meeting. He wants it that way. For months and months now, we have been meeting like this, on Wednesday, often also on Saturday, at that street corner; and we always do the same things. We exchange the books at the "Selecta" library, buy oatmeal cookies, buy, for my mother, fifteen centimeters of black grosgrain.
>
> And we go to a room that he rents, in Gorizia Street, on the top floor.
>
> It's a room with a round table in the middle, covered with a green cloth, and on the table is a glass bell that covers some coral twigs. There is also a hot plate behind a curtain where we can, if we want, make some coffee.
>
> (*Opere,* 1.737)

Tommasino's refusal publicly to acknowledge his relationship with Elsa expresses his desire to protect it from the invasive curiosity of the town as well as his inability to choose and to commit himself. Finally brought into the open with an official engagement, wedding plans, and family dinners, the relationship collapses. Surrounded by chaperones and relatives for whom a wedding is a matter of rules, appearances, and rituals, Tommasino begins to fantasize about a woman from a faraway place and unknown background. The publicity of the relationship has finally forced Tommasino from the inability to choose to a situation that exemplifies the impossibility of choosing. It is a predicament that resonates with the existential arguments over the political engagement of intellectuals in the postwar period. At the end of the novel, the engagement has been broken and the narrator is again promenading with her mother through the town.

Ginzburg explained that the novel was written in London, where she lived between 1959 and 1961:

> I started writing *Voices in the Evening* with the idea of writing a short story of two or three pages. . . . Suddenly I saw emerging from that story, uninvited, the landscape of my childhood. Here was the countryside of Piedmont and the streets of Turin. All my life I had been ashamed of those places, I had banished them from my writings as my unacceptable origins. . . . And now, instead, I found them again there, in London.
>
> (*Opere,* 1.1132)

*Family Sayings* (1963), Ginzburg's autobiography and the last work of this period, is not a typical autobiography because its focus is less the author than her family. Ginzburg readily admitted that to be the case: "I had little desire to talk about myself. This in fact is not my story but rather, blanks and gaps notwithstanding, the story of my family" (*Opere,* 1.899). More specifically, *Family Sayings* is the portrait of her family through its words, dialogues, monologues, and recitations; it is history in the form of a collective memory. The narrative revolves around the accumulation of words and phrases that develop and grow within families in the course of time and that remain, after the family itself has dissolved, as a lifelong treasure of each member:

> We are five siblings. We live in different cities, some of us live abroad: and we don't write to each other often; when we meet we might happen to be, with one another, indifferent or careless. But one word is enough among us, one word, one phrase is enough: one of those old phrases, heard and repeated hundreds of times, in the times of our childhood. . . . And we rediscover our old ties, and our childhood and youth, bound forever to those phrases, to those words. One of those phrases or words would allow us to recognize one another in the darkness of a cave, among millions of people. Those phrases are our Latin, the vocabulary of our old days; they are like the hieroglyphic of the Egyptians or the Assyro-Babylonians, evidence of a live core that has ceased to exist but survives in its texts, salvaged from the fury of the waters, and the corrosion of time.
>
> (*Opere,* 1.920–921)

The reference to those ancient cultures, far from being insignificant, indirectly suggests how archaic that type of family, or maybe the institution itself, has become. More than just an account of the author's old-fashioned family, the book is in fact the story of a representative family of the Italian anti-Fascist intelligentsia, of a generation, and of an epoch.

Emblematic of the autobiography's overall enterprise is a description of the mother's perception of geography and space:

> My mother could only imagine places in relation to the people she knew who lived there. For her in all of Belgium, only Chèvremont lived there. When something happened in Belgium, floods or political changes, my mother would say:
>
> —What will Chèvremont say about this!
>
> In France . . . for her there was only a Mr. Polikar, that she and my father had met at a conference. She would always say:
>
> —And what about Polikar!
>
> In Spain she knew a man whose name was Di

> Castro. If she read about a thunderstorm or a seastorm in Spain she would say:
>
> —And what about Di Castro! . . .
>
> Then came Franco, then the World War, and we never heard from him again. . . . The war also swallowed Mr. Polikar. We never heard again from Ms. Grassi, who lived in Freiburg in Germany. . . .
>
> Her geography was totally out of order after the war. One could no longer easily evoke Ms. Grassi and Mr. Polikar. Once, they had had the power to transform, in my mother's eyes, faraway and foreign countries into something familiar, ordinary, friendly, to make the world into a village or into a street that one could travel through in one's thought, following the footsteps of those few familiar and reassuring names.
>
> (*Opere,* 1.1063–1064)

The task of *Family Sayings* is nothing less than to salvage a time that, like the mother's geography, has been torn apart not merely by the war but also by the profound economic changes that followed. Just as places exist for the mother only if attached to real people, so the past exists for the narrator only through her collection of its words and phrases.

The narrative follows both the events of the family—marked by the monotonous rhythms of schooling, deaths, marriages, and births—and the political history of Italy during Fascism, the war, and its aftermath, a history kept at the margins of the narrative, as if extraneous to the chronicle, but in fact consistently present throughout.

The narrative opens with the portrait of Ginzburg's intellectual, half-Jewish and half-Catholic, but wholly atheistic, parents, at once typical of the lower bourgeois strata of Italy at the turn of the century, yet also atypical and strongly idiosyncratic, personal, and intimate. The household, as re-created by the youngest of the children, is polarized between the cheerful and artistic temperament of the mother and the impetuous and bearish temperament of the father. The mother's favorites are Verlaine, Wagner, Proust; she likes modern painting and modern drama; and it is her great pleasure to tell stories:

> She would start telling a story around the dinner table, addressing one of us: and . . . she would become animated with joy and it was always as if she were telling that story for the first time, to ears that had never heard it. "I had an uncle"—she would begin—"who was called Barbison." And if someone said:—This story I already know! I have heard it so many times!—then she would turn to someone else and softly go on with her story.—How many times have I heard this story!—my father would roar.
>
> (*Opere,* 1.919–920)

The father, on the other hand, is a representative of science and rationality; he likes "socialism, England, Zola's novels; the Rockefeller Foundation; mountain climbing and the mountain guides of Val D'Aosta" (*Opere,* 1.914). His antipathy is undisguised when he is confronted with the hypocrisy of those complacent toward Fascism:

> My father always came home furious because he had met, in the street, processions of Black Shirts; or because he had discovered, during a faculty meeting, new fascists among his acquaintances.—Clowns! Rascals! Buffooneries!—he would say as he sat at the dinner table; he would shake the napkin, the plate, the glass and huff full of contempt. He was used to expressing his thoughts aloud in the street, walking home with his acquaintances; and they would look around frightened.—Cowards! Slaves!—my father roared at home, as he described the fear of his acquaintances; and he enjoyed, I believe, frightening them.
>
> (*Opere,* 1.928)

In time, the storytelling and recitations are taken over by political discussions, which become more and more tense as the situation worsens. Around the dinner table we see reproduced in microcosm some of the tensions that split the anti-Fascist opposition between liberals and leftists, or the Left between reformers, radicals, and revolutionaries. These arguments eventually give way to more dramatic confrontations with the outside world. The beginning of the most severe political persecutions and of the "racial campaigns," with the exile and incarceration of political activists, Jews, and foreigners, marks the beginning of adulthood for the narrator. It also marks the dissolution of the family by marriage, exile, or arrest of the children.

In the central section of the autobiography the chronological order gives way to a more erratic shuttling back and forth between past and present, the chronology constantly broken as the narrator confronts the most tragic events of her life and of that period. The domestic scene fades to make room for the insistent intrusion of history. The "lexicon," so pivotal an element in the first part of the narrative, is more rarely present in the second part. Like art, it suffers the derangement of the times, a derangement that destroys the conditions out of which it can grow. Instead we are left with a few graphic images that seem to resist the narrative form altogether:

> The war, we thought, would immediately subvert and overturn everyone's life. Instead, for years many people remained undisturbed in their homes, doing what they had always done. When, at last, people thought that after all they had gotten away cheaply and there would be no chaos whatsoever, no houses destroyed, no escapes or persecutions, suddenly the bombs began to explode, and mines were everywhere, and the houses collapsed, and the streets were full of ruins, soldiers, and refugees. And now no one could ignore it, close his eyes and shut his ears and hide his head under a pillow, no one. In Italy the war was like that.
>
> (*Opere,* 1.1046)

Although the narrative suddenly moves to 1945, the painful events of the war keep reappearing in the shape of discontinuous flashbacks. That her husband has died in jail will come up much later, after the narrator sees his portrait in the office of Einaudi, the publisher for whom she is then working:

> The publisher had hung on the wall in his office a small portrait of Leone, his head bent a little, his glasses hanging low on the nose, his thick black head of hair, the deep dimple on his cheek, his feminine hands. Leone had died in prison, in the German wing of the Regina Coeli jail during the Nazi invasion, in an icy February.
>
> (*Opere,* 1.1054)

Central to the third section of the autobiography, Ginzburg's work as reader, editor, and translator for the publisher Einaudi structurally reproduces in surrogate form the intimate family of the first part. Here the personalities of Cesare Pavese, Felice Balbo, Giulio Einaudi, and other important intellectuals emerge through Ginzburg's shrewd, ironic, but always affectionate gaze. Like *Voices in the Evening, Family Sayings* closes on a theatrical scene: the old mother and father, now alone, sit around as they shuttle back and forth between past and present, glorifying the past at every recollection until it becomes something altogether new, something that, like the book itself, is as much the product of imagination as of memory.

The most incisive comment on Ginzburg's justly famous autobiography comes from Cesare Garboli, a literary critic and longtime friend of hers: "The generations change but Natalia Ginzburg continues to tell us about . . . her family: as if the world were the infinitely ramified extension of one tree, one kinship group, one primordial tribe that reproduces itself through the same blood" (Garboli, p. 7629). *Family Sayings* is in fact a monument to a dying institution, the bourgeois family. Some critics saw in Ginzburg's work a cult of the "tribal family" and traced it back to her Jewish identity and to a biblical view of the family and the tribal father. It is at least as important to acknowledge the family as Ginzburg's emblem of all that was rotten about the past and of what is even more rotten about the present. The nostalgia that undeniably colors her writing should not mislead one to take her for an apologist of an idyllic past. She is first and foremost a pessimist whose apocalyptic view is of a present caught between a dark past and a darker future.

That Ginzburg should suddenly give up the novel and for a decade devote herself exclusively to writing plays or essays is testimony to a changed relationship between the author and the world. The transition to the theater, and later to the epistolary novel, immediately followed the proliferation of dialogues and monologues at the expense of narrative, a change already noticed in *Voices in the Evening* and *Family Sayings.* Paradoxically, far from resulting in greater communication, the proliferation of words that ultimately leads to the writing of plays also accompanies a regime of greater silence and isolation, and reveals a world wrapped in deaf sounds, not unlike a deceptively silent landscape newly covered by snow.

Ginzburg's theatrical production consists of the two collections, *I Married You for Fun* (1966) and *Seaside Resort* (1973). As she herself admitted, nothing much happens in her plays. There are no dramatic events, few social or geographic specifics. Casual encounters trigger long personal stories that combine gossip and confession. The lack of action in fact serves to emphasize the quantity of words that these women pour on their captive audiences. Confused, circular, digressive, their stories produce the impression that something is being worked out on stage, in front of our very eyes. On stage, in every one of the eight plays, is the existential condition of a middle-aged woman, her relationship with a man, her family, and ultimately the world. The women of the plays, however, represent a new type for Ginzburg. Like the female narrators of her early short stories, they cannot repress the impulse to tell, but they are driven to the confessional monologue by darker and more threatening impulses. Their narratives resemble an embankment on the verge of bursting after a long season of rains. Ginzburg's plays put on stage either the moment just prior to the explosion or that of the bursting and its immediate consequences.

*L'inserzione* (*The Advertisement*), *Dialogo* (Dialogue), *La segretaria* (The Secretary), and *La parrucca* (The Wig) all dramatize intense moments of confession that climax or come close to climaxing in tragedy and death. *The Advertisement* is typical in this respect. Originally performed at the National Theatre of London under the direction of Laurence Olivier (in 1968) and the next year at the Arti Theater of Rome under the direction of Luchino Visconti, it was one of Ginzburg's most popular productions. It dramatizes the encounter between Elena, a young student who is looking for a room, and Teresa, an older divorced woman who is looking for a roommate. The encounter becomes the occasion for a long monologue in which Teresa recounts her life history: one of Ginzburg's familiar stories of a country girl who comes to the city to escape the oppression of her family and village, marries a wealthy man, and finds herself alone and desperate. The tense separation that followed the marriage has now shifted to what appears to be a more friendly routine of visits between Teresa and her ex-husband Lorenzo, a routine that Teresa proudly characterizes as free of emotional excesses.

The arrival of Lorenzo in the second act, after Elena has taken up residence with Teresa, is the occasion for his version of their marriage, a story that reveals their very different motivations and personalities. The third act opens a few months later. Elena confesses to Teresa that she and Lorenzo are in love and are going to live together, and expresses her happiness at seeing that Teresa is not jealous. They then move offstage to get Elena's luggage ready. On an empty stage we hear a shot. Teresa, who for three acts has convinced us that she was past the pains of love, and for whom

Elena had become an adopted daughter, has killed Elena. We are left with the chilling sensation of having witnessed the workings of an insanely lucid mind, a mind ravaged by solitude and despair.

Like *The Advertisement,* the plays *I Married You for Fun, Dialogo, La parrucca, Fragola e panna* (Strawberry [Ice Cream] Cone), and *La segretaria* all revolve around an estranged couple whose members belong to different classes or to different generations. In *I Married You for Fun* the wife comes from a poor rural village and the husband belongs to a wealthy family; these backgrounds are reversed in *Seaside Resort.*

In *I Married You for Fun* Giuliana and Pietro are recently married, but seem still strangers: neither has any insight into the other's personality or motivations for getting married. A hybrid of soap opera and theater of the absurd, the dialogue is regularly interrupted by Giuliana's insistent questions about why they got married at all.

In the first act Giuliana finds in her maid Victoria a willing listener to her life history. Giuliana came to Rome from a poor rural village with the fantasy of becoming an actress—only to be seduced and made pregnant. When she met Pietro at a party she was desperate and, she honestly admits, she would have married anyone. The dialogue between Giuliana and Victoria is a thinly disguised psychoanalytic session, a therapeutic monologue encouraged by Victoria's perfunctory remarks "And then?" "And so?" "And you?" It is soon quite evident that Giuliana is a candidate for the shrink and that Ginzburg has a critical view of this sort of therapy. Shortly after this dialogue Giuliana recounts to her bourgeois mother-in-law, who has come to visit, how her friend Topazia had taken her to see a psychoanalyst in the moment of greatest disaster in her life in order to cure her of her "inferiority complex," which, according to Topazia, was the original cause of all her misfortunes. In contrast with Giuliana, who projects confusion from every word, Pietro appears as the image of stability and inner clarity. This, however, emerges as a thin disguise. He has been on the verge of marriage eighteen times already. As the play makes increasingly clear, he hides his confusion under a thin cover, which the troubled Giuliana is quick to detect. The ending suggests that the confusion they share might, paradoxically, be a sound basis for this strange marriage.

In *La segretaria* the emphasis shifts from the couple to the family. On stage is the living room of a family, one of Ginzburg's favorite symbols of modern life. Here people meet, talk about private and intimate matters, and then move into their own private solitudes. Members of the family here are Nino, the father, who is concerned only about his horse; Titina, his neurotic wife; Sofia, his unhappy sister; and, from time to time, Enrico, the family doctor. They are a typical modern household, as defined by Ginzburg: there is no privacy, no true intimacy, no solid relationships, and no sense of what separates a home from the world outside. All boundaries have dissolved, leaving the family members in a state of existential nomadism, an authorial concept recurrent in Ginzburg's essays and here expressed by Titina:

> TITINA: Once upon a time there was the family.
> SOFIA: What family?
> TITINA: Yes, the family. Each family was like a closed shell. Now there are no families left, someone comes and someone goes, the doors are always open for everyone, you have to take care of every stranger as if he was a close relative, strangers come into your house and make their nest there.
>
> (*Opere,* 1.1340–1341)

In this amorphous household nothing goes right. The sister translates books for someone who does not return her love nor pay her for her work; the young wife has no milk for her baby, and because she refuses to use contraceptives, she thinks she might be pregnant with her third child in two years; the horse is defecating blood; the coffee machine is out of order; the car works only sporadically. A young hippie soon joins this disjointed family; she is welcomed by Nino's fantasy that she will set things straight:

> NINO: That girl will be a great help. She will solve all our problems. She will take care of the children, of the house. She will go shopping in the village, with her motorcycle. . . . She will type all my notes, remarks, travel notes, thoughts. She will bring some order in our life.
>
> (*Opere,* 1.1328)

She quickly dispels any such illusion. The newcomer is a stereotype of the modern girl who has no skills and simply adds to the level of confusion. By the end, one of the characters has committed suicide, another has tried to, and the proclaimed love of yet another has been revealed as false.

This is the most pessimistic of Ginzburg's plays. It suggests that the condition of the household is not so different from that of the outside world, a world where love is ephemeral, marriage is erratic, relationships are empty, children are in the care of immature adults. The chaos within, we infer, is simply a reflection of the infinitely worse chaos without. It is also the play most consistently void of positive characters. Titina, who seems reasonable in her feelings about the state of disrepair of the household and in her plea for a family, is also the most neurotic character; Nino, the only one who feels some sympathy for the girl, has no credibility largely because he has more affection for his horse than for any human being; furthermore, we suspect that his sympathy is mediated through his perception of her as a poor little lost "pet." At the end of the play, in spite of the monologues, the confessions, the occasional intimate dialogues, we are left with no one who can speak for the author, as alone in the audience as the characters are on stage.

*Caro Michele* (*Dear Michael,* 1973) represents Ginzburg's return to the novel after almost a decade of theater. To state that it is an epistolary novel is to describe its form but to leave out the more important fact that much of it consists of staged scenes. This is to say that Ginzburg's return to the novel is in fact spurious and is marked not by confidence in authorship but by the need to overcome the claustrophobia of the stage, as created by her plays. The authorial persona who introduces the letters, orders them, records the dialogues, and disappears during most of the novel hides behind a dry, factual prose that suggests a playwright more than a novelist. Her task is never to interpret and rarely to describe; rather, it is to order the letters so as to preserve some long-lost traces of emotions.

Michele, the young son of a bourgeois family from Rome, has been politically active in the extra-parliamentary Left of the early 1970's. As the novel opens, he has just left for England for fear of being arrested. There he works as a dishwasher in London, then as a butler in Sussex, and afterward moves to Leeds, where he marries an older American woman who is divorced, has two children, and is an alcoholic. He dies in Bruges, Belgium, during a demonstration, stabbed by a fascist.

This modern-day picaresque story provides the opportunity for the epistolary exchanges, which make up the greater part of the novel: between Michele and his family; between Michele and friends; between family and friends. Michele thus becomes a hub of a network of relationships among family, friends, and acquaintances. In the fluid confusion that characterizes all these relationships one sees the once well-defined and self-sufficient family as an archaic, anachronistic institution. The new family—if a new one it is—resembles a kaleidoscope, mixing and separating, forming new colors, in permanent flux. Those who are divorced are never clearly separated and can neither live together nor apart, because of children or personal disposition. Those who are married live as if they were divorced and carry on independent lives. Friends are sometimes more involved and generous than relatives.

The narrative depicts a younger generation—the generation of hippies and student militants of the late 1960's and early 1970's—that is unable to stop and remember, caught as if in a storm that moves too fast. An oddball as a homosexual and an old-fashioned seller of old books, Osvaldo, a friend of Michele's, is one of the very few who still believes in memory and to whom, therefore, is entrusted the task of bringing the story to a close. The last letter is written by him to one of Michele's sisters; it is written from Leeds, where he has gone to look for some relic of Michele, in a pilgrimage of sorts:

> Of Michele I have found nothing. . . . I believe that it is useless to save the objects of the dead, after they have been touched by strangers and their identity has faded. . . .
>
> From this friendly youth Ermanno Giustiniani, with whom I will have dinner tonight, I am unable to learn much about Michele, because he saw him little or remembers him little. He is a youth. Today's youth have no memory, and mostly they do not cultivate it, and you know that Michele too had no memory, or rather he never stopped to inhale it and cultivate it. The only ones left who cultivate memory are you, your mother, and I; in your case it is temperament; for your mother and me probably it is because our lives contain nothing worth the places and times we have encountered on the way. Those places and times, as I lived and observed them, were enfolded by an intense brilliance, but it was because I knew that I would later kneel to remember them. I have always suffered deeply that Michele would not or could not know this brilliance, and that he always moved onward without ever turning back to look.
>
> (*Opere,* 2.495–496)

"The youth who have no memory"—the verdict that closes the narrative—is also a diagnosis of the form of the novel in an age of "no memory." Few passages express with such clarity Ginzburg's distance from what Michele represents: a generation that took over the streets to prosecute the past and all the authority that such past sustained. The generation of the 1960's is one to which Ginzburg has been unable to bring the full measure of her sympathy. "The youth who have no memory" is in fact also a verdict on Ginzburg herself. A main source for her imagination in her novels of the 1950's, memory here returns with a vengeance, not merely as a source of creativity but becoming the self-conscious spiritual object of this late novel. Perhaps as an inevitable development in times of crisis, Ginzburg's early valiant assault on a narrow definition of the historical novel that suppressed all that is fragmentary, private, and episodic, ironically here became an apologia of memory conceived as the antithesis of history. Ginzburg's earlier successful challenge against the polarization of memory and history resulted in yet another narrative theory—a theory of pure subjectivity and private memory—one apparently antithetical but in fact complementary to that of the historical novel.

The two short novels *Famiglia* and *Borghesia* (*Family* and *Bourgeoisie,* 1977) are variations on the themes confronted in *Dear Michael.* Both revolve around death and the memory such an event produces, death of the two main protagonists but no less of the two institutions embodied in the titles, and inevitably of the novel, the literary form most closely associated with those two institutions.

"A man and a woman one afternoon went to see a movie. It was Sunday and it was summer. With them were a young girl of fourteen and two children of seven or so" (*Opere,* 2.689). In this fairy-tale style *Family,* the more successful of the two, opens. What the reader takes for a family walking the summer streets of a city is in fact a group of people from different relationships, affairs, and marriages. Carmine, the man, is not married to Ivana, the woman, but to Ninetta, who is away on vacation. Dodo, one of the children, is his son; Daniele, the other one, belongs to a neighbor of Ivana's who wanted to stay home and sleep. Angelica, the teenager, is the daughter of Ivana, who is a single mother. The impression of family fragmentation that this opening produces is a leading motif of the narrative, which develops as a long flashback framed at both ends by the group's promenade through the deserted streets.

Carmine and Ivana had lived together and had discussed marriage every so often, without ever quite deciding for or against it. The death of their baby girl ended a relationship that in fact had been dead for a while. Ivana then escaped to England and was involved with Joachim, with whom she had a second baby—the now fourteen-year-old Angelica. Joachim had never learned of Angelica, for at the time of her birth he was in a clinic with one more nervous breakdown, one from which he never recovered. Ivana and Carmine meet again ten years after their separation. Carmine is now married to Ninetta, who has recently given birth to Dodo. The flashback here briefly expands to depict the social worlds of the two different families. On the one hand is the bourgeois world of Carmine and Ninetta, of her aristocratic mother who lives downstairs, of their maids and baby-sitters; on the other hand is the hippie life-style of Ivana and Angelica, whose home has few schedules and even fewer rules. The contrast stands out in sharp relief in Carmine's eyes:

> Carmine arrived home late in the afternoon. It was Sunday. Ninetta was wearing a new red cardigan that day, Dodo was playing with his cars on the rug, Evelina had brought up a cake, they were drinking tea; Ciaccia Oppi was sewing, on Ninetta's request, a big half-moon on the magician costume that Dodo was to wear in a few days at a costume party given by Ciaccia Oppi's mother at her villa in Velletri. Evelina's large head dominated the room, with her light blue feathery hair, her majestic and prosperous height and her smile, much like Ninetta's, offered as a jewel, but accompanied by a secret self-satisfaction for being, in old age, so tall, erect, and attractive. She stood there, a monument to elegant, wise, cautiously healthy and wealthy old age. Carmine felt he hated her. He also hated the other two with her. He felt horrible at seeing Dodo associated with that hate. He hated everyone in that room, and the room also. He said he wanted to take Dodo for a walk. They discouraged him. Dodo was about to eat his cereal, and moreover, he had to be measured for his magician costume.
>
> (*Opere,* 2.713–714)

From the outside, Ninetta's living room represents just such a solid and extended family as Ginzburg had eulogized in the past: the grandmother, the maids, the neighbor, the overwhelming presence of female figures, regular meals, a tranquil domestic atmosphere, a child who is closely supervised and taken care of. And yet over this domestic picture hangs a cloud: the alienation of husband and wife, and father and child; the intrusions of Evelina and of Ciaccia Oppi; the excessive pampering of Dodo, who is treated as a delicate, exotic plant.

Ivana's living room is the antithesis of Ninetta's. Again we observe the scene through Carmine's eyes:

> Isa Meli was sitting next to Ivana's bed and was knitting, Matteo Tramonti was playing chess with Angelica; Daniele, Isa Meli's son, watched and made suggestions, since he was, in spite of his age, very skilled at chess. The dog was asleep. Carmine thought that Daniele was very precocious. Not only did Dodo know nothing of chess but he moved so unsteadily and awkwardly, and he wasn't very quick, he thought; he was behind for his age. He was fat. They shouldn't give cereal to fat children. They should ask the pediatrician for a new diet. What did Daniele eat? He asked him what he ate for dinner. Daniele said he ate cauliflower. "With vinegar?" he asked. Yes, sure. Dodo was not allowed to have vinegar. He had never tasted a drop of vinegar in his life. He remembered the dinners of his childhood, they weren't even dinners, they were pieces of leftover bread.
>
> (*Opere,* 2.716)

The flashback picks up speed again to recount two adulteries, first of Ninetta and then of Carmine, and closes with a picture of false rapprochement; the "hours of quiet" that "produced no real quiet" and the "quarrels" that "produced no real anger" stand as epitaphs on the tombstone of the so-called solid and stable family.

The novel does not end here, however, but moves on to reveal how the framing scene was itself part of a larger flashback. Soon after that summer Sunday in the city, Carmine had become sick while both families—his own and Ivana's—were away on vacation. The illness was eventually diagnosed as cancer, and Carmine had died after only a few months. In the last paragraph of the novel we realize that we have watched the reels of a dying man's memory, and that the logic of that memory has been the hidden motor of the story. Death and memory, more self-consciously and programmatically than ever before, emerge as the two agents that can bring the flux of time and experience into some kind of shape and order that the author can hope to capture.

With *La famiglia Manzoni* (*The Manzoni Family,* 1983), Ginzburg takes her dialogue with the novel and the family to the very border between fiction and history. Out of documentary material—the letters of the Manzoni family over the course of three generations—she composes a text that is at once a documentary and a novel.

That such iconoclastic operation should take place over the dead body of Alessandro Manzoni—the Walter Scott of Italian literature—in other words, over the most important monument of the Italian bourgeois novel, is of course not irrelevant. A family journal recomposed a posteriori through the letters that three generations of Manzonis wrote to each other and to a few close friends, the novel is itself a monument of sorts to the man literary history has consecrated as the founder of the Italian national novel. The editor who composes this family mosaic, however, does not deify him. She gives us not Manzoni the public man surrounded by the aura of his fame, but the private man, with his ailments, egocentricity, pettiness, family quarrels; a man no more reprehensible than anyone else in his time and class, but no better either.

Of the book Ginzburg stated:

> I have tried to restore the story of the Manzoni family. I wanted to reconstruct, to recompose it, to align it neatly in time. I had some letters and some books. I did not want to comment, but to limit myself to a simple and naked succession of facts. I wanted to let the facts speak for themselves. I wanted the letters, sad or cold, formal or frank, openly false or undoubtedly sincere, to speak for themselves. . . . I did not want Alessandro Manzoni to be the protagonist of this long family story. Family stories do not have a protagonist; each member is from time to time brought to light and then left in the shadow again. I did not want him to have more space than anyone else; I wanted him to be seen sideways and in perspective, and in the midst of everybody, confused in the dust of daily life.
>
> (Clementelli [1986], p. 95)

The first part of the novel—1762 to 1836—stretches between the Bastille takeover and the fall of the Napoleonic Empire; the second—1836 to 1907—overlaps with the monarchic restorations of Europe, the bourgeois revolutions, and the unification of Italy. Each part is subdivided into chapters that are roughly chronological but are specifically devoted to different members of the family, all but two of them to the Manzoni women: Giulia Beccaria, mother of Alessandro and daughter of Cesare Beccaria, the author of a famous treatise against capital punishment; Enrichetta Blondel, married at sixteen to Alessandro and who, in the course of twenty-two years, becomes pregnant twelve times, gives birth to nine children, and dies, not surprisingly, given the reproductive rhythm, at forty-two years of age; Giulietta, Manzoni's oldest daughter, unhappily married and dead soon after, at twenty-eight; Teresa Borri, Alessandro's second wife, hypochondriac and egocentric; and Vittoria and Matilde, the two youngest daughters of this numerous brood, placed in boarding school at an early age after their father's remarriage. In the tradition of family chronicles, the extended epistolary exchange finds its primary material in the biological and economic records, that is, births, deaths, illnesses, contracts of marriage and sales, and testaments.

Considering how recent these events are, one wonders at the abyss that separates us from this world where marriages are arranged, daughters are married off before they turn eighteen—sons not much later; where even among the well-off classes women's bodies are wrecked by constant childbearing; medical practice resembles the methods of witches; children are frequently in the care of servants, relatives, and older siblings and for long periods are separated from their parents; and where lawsuits between family members over the terms of a will are a matter of routine.

But along with these profound ethnographic differences, some things never change. Perhaps we are just reading an allegory—well disguised by the historical records—of our own world, as Ginzburg represented it in her fiction. The mythical solid patriarchal family presided over by the paterfamilias turns out to be a scattered institution even two centuries ago, with a father often too busy with his own work and egocentric worries, with parents who devote more energy to taking good care of their souls than to caring for their children's bodies and minds.

On some level *The Manzoni Family* is a personal or subjective memory, the primary basis of Ginzburg's late fiction. However, beneath the apparent shift from first-person memory to third-person memory this is a work of historical memory nevertheless, on the irrationality and capriciousness that personal memory and the historical record share.

*La città e la casa* (*The City and the House,* 1984), Ginzburg's next work, is also an epistolary novel. It consists of the letters written by an extended group of friends, relatives, and lovers, occasioned—much as in *Dear Michael*—by the departure of one of them, Giuseppe. Unlike the previous ones, this novel relies exclusively on letters. The absence of an internal editor-narrator results in a greater sense of immediacy and lets the reader feel he or she is following the events as they are occurring rather than at a later date and as reconstructed by someone. Moreover, this choice heightens the tension around the final outcome of the story because—the narrative choice implies—such outcome is neither foreclosed nor in the past.

Two narrative levels intersect in the letters. On the one hand they record the present events, at whose center are Giuseppe and Lucrezia. Giuseppe has just sold his apartment in Rome and is preparing to move to Princeton, the home of his older brother, under whose protective wing he imagines himself spending the rest of his life. As Giuseppe makes clear about himself—"We are all a brood of children" (*Opere,* 2.1394)—but as is equally true of many other characters, he is an aged child forever searching for a father figure. Likewise, when another character, Lucrezia, stops being completely dependent on her friend Roberta, the latter describes the event by stating that "apparently she has learned to be an orphan" (*Opere,* 2.1546). Lucrezia, the ex-lover of Giuseppe, is the lady of the title country house, a former retreat for a large group of friends that has long since lost its charm and social function. It has become instead another of Ginzburg's open houses, without doors, schedules, or boundaries to distinguish between private and public, friends and strangers, day and night: another center of chaos rather than intimacy. By the end of the novel three marriages have fallen apart; at least a dozen people have fallen in and out of love; three children have been born without a family; five people have died.

The convulsions of these events, strangely enough, do not produce a dramatic narrative; they are muffled in part by the epistolary form of the novel and by the physical distance that separates people and events. More important, the dramatic tension is softened by the analytic and self-reflexive nature of the letters. When Giuseppe recounts to Lucrezia the details of his first marriage, their love affair, her children, and his son, we are disoriented: Why should he tell her these things? Why now? She must know them all by heart. This is true of several other characters who indulge in long reminiscences about the past. The inability to answer these questions led Ann Cornelisen to criticize Ginzburg for burdening the narrative with material not justified by the context (*New York Times Book Review,* 13 September 1987, p. 30). The truth, however, is more complex than fictional plausibility. These letters—and this is the originality of otherwise familiar Ginzburg themes—read as monologues addressed to an absent shrink or to oneself. The dialogue between reminiscence and contemporary chronicle is precisely what endows the novel with psychological depth. The letters—this cumbersome, archaic form in an age of high technology—allow people to talk as they have never done in person in the past, or by telephone in the present. This is true not only of the characters but also of the author herself, whose narratorial absence complements her heavy-handed presence in many letters. To use an expression Ginzburg herself used once in reference to Emily Dickinson's poems, they come to resemble the letters of an individual to a world that ignores her—but the individual does not give up and goes on writing the letters anyway.

The pictures of Ginzburg that accompanied the reviews of her work in the *New York Times* in the late 1980's were quite different from those in the two volumes of her collected works in Italian. The *Times* photos portray an old woman casting a skeptical and severe glance at the world. The closely cropped frame and sharp contrasts heighten that impression. The short gray hair and the wrinkles on her face bring out the cutting edge that was Ginzburg's most characteristic trait during the 1970's and 1980's. In contrast with the Italian pictures, there is no softness on her face or haziness in her gaze, and her expression is rather hard and edgy. If she seems to waver between mild disapproval and undisguised censure, she still keeps her gaze fastened on the world around her. Hardened by Fascism and war in youth and by the excessively rapid changes in her mature years, she now faces the world—in her old age—with the estrangement and skepticism of an exile:

> I believe that everyone in every time has had, upon reaching old age, to suffer this destiny: to kneel and behold the ruins and the remains of a world on which he had spent pride, vanity, and love. But those of our generation have suffered this destiny so cruelly and violently that when we look out over the time of our youth we feel we are gazing over an abyss.
>
> (*Opere,* 2.612)

The onset of Fascism coincided for Ginzburg with the beginning of childhood, the onset of open political persecution with the beginning of adolescence, the war with adult life. History conferred upon her generation a most fraudulent bequest. The experiences of these tragic years molded her outlook, formed the basis of her material, and provided the elements of her aesthetics, one that stretches between the estrangement of the child and the alienation of the old woman.

Central to Ginzburg's work from the very beginning was the privileged perception of the child as a naive and candid observer of a world that is surprising and strange, ineffable and marvelous even in the presence of tragedy. "The secret of Natalia's simplicity is this," Italo Calvino wrote in this respect:

> The voice that says "I" is always confronted with characters whom she considers superior to herself, situations that appear too complex for her power, and so the conceptual and linguistic tools that she adopts in order to represent them are always just below what is required. And it is out of this disproportion that the poetic tension is generated. Poetry has always been this: to pour

> the sea through a funnel; to impose on oneself a most limited number of expressive tools and to try expressing with it something extremely complex.
>
> (p. 134)

Calvino also characterized Ginzburg's prose as "stubborn and fierce" on the one hand, as "frightened and desperate" on the other, or as being "courteously savage"—an oxymoron that captures better than most critics have done the most salient trait of her later work. For Calvino this mixture of yearning and cruelty was the inevitable outcome of Ginzburg's lifelong commitment to the genre of "family chronicle." "But," he warns,

> One must not believe that writing family chronicles for Natalia can be the same as for the nineteenth-century author. Her beloved masters are indeed the lesser Tolstoy and Chekhov, and to Jane Austen she is closest in spirit. And yet the firm stable family that the nineteenth-century author could represent as a reality of nature is now something that can only be evoked through a nostalgia imbued with cruelty.
>
> (p. 136)

Few statements better express the spirit of Ginzburg's work. If in her early work she eloquently spoke as a protagonist, in her late work she became a tenacious witness of the emotional chasm that had opened for her generation, a chasm that had left many in an existential vestibule of sorts, where neither sorrowful nostalgia nor jubilant acceptance of the present would do:

> To deny oneself to the present, to surround oneself with regret for a dead past, is to refuse to think.
>
> It seems, however, even more fatuous to have the opposite attitude: to force ourselves to love and pursue all the new things that appear around us. This . . . means to be afraid of showing ourselves as we are, in other words, tired, bitter, at last paralyzed and old.
>
> (*Opere*, 2.108–109))

Far from an inevitable biological destiny, the alienation and bitterness of old age as Ginzburg experienced and poetically appropriated them are yet another powerful metaphor of the willed homelessness and exile that have been so central to modern literature. This is what the pictures of Ginzburg as an old woman in the *New York Times* most truthfully capture: the commitment of an author who, in spite of her personal alienation and the widespread cynicism of the later twentieth century, refused to give up, look away, turn inward, and who most emphatically turned down the easy consolation of self-proclaimed and self-willed impotence.

## Selected Bibliography


EDITIONS

INDIVIDUAL WORKS

FICTION

*La strada che va in città.* Turin, 1942. Published under the pseudonym Allessandra Tornimparte.

*La strada che va in città e altri racconti.* Turin, 1945. Includes the title novel as well as "Un'assenza," "Casa al mare," and "Mio marito."

*È stato così.* Turin, 1947.

*Tutti i nostri ieri.* Turin, 1952.

*Valentino.* Turin, 1957. Includes the title novel as well as the short story "La madre" and the short novel *Sagittario.*

*Le voci della sera.* Turin, 1961.

*Lessico famigliare.* Turin, 1963.

*Caro Michele.* Milan, 1973.

*Famiglia.* Turin, 1977. Includes the title novel as well as *Borghesia.*

*La famiglia Manzoni.* Turin, 1983.

*La città e la casa.* Turin, 1984.

PLAYS

*Ti ho sposato per allegria e altre commedie.* Turin, 1966. Includes the title play as well as *L'inserzione, Fragola e panna,* and *La segretaria.*

*Paese di mare.* Milan, 1973. Includes the title play as well as *Dialogo, La porta sbagliata,* and *La parrucca.*

ESSAYS

*Le piccole virtù.* Turin, 1962.
*Mai devi domandarmi.* Milan, 1970.
*Vita immaginaria.* Milan, 1974.

COLLECTED WORKS

*Opere.* 2 vols. Milan, 1986.

## TRANSLATIONS BY GINZBURG

*Riflessioni e pensieri inediti.* By Charles-Louis de Montesquieu. Turin, 1942. Translated with Leone Ginzburg.
*Il silenzio del mare.* By Vercors, pseudonym of Jean Bruller. Turin, 1945.
*La strada di Swann.* By Marcel Proust. Turin, 1947.
*Le armi della notte.* By Vercors, pseudonym of Jean Bruller. Turin, 1948.
*Madame Bovary.* By Gustave Flaubert. Turin, 1983.

## TRANSLATIONS

*The Advertisement.* Translated by Henry Reed. London, 1969.
*All Our Yesteryears.* Translated by Angus Davidson. London, 1956.
*The City and the House.* Translated by Dick Davis. Manchester, 1986.
*The Dry Heart.* Translated by Frances Frenaye. London, 1952.
*Family: Two Novellas.* Translated by Beryl Stockman. Manchester, 1988.
*Family Sayings.* Translated by D. M. Low. New York, 1967.
*A Light for Fools.* Translated by Angus Davidson. London, 1957. Also published under the title *Dead Yesterdays.* London, 1956.
*The Little Virtues.* Translated by Dick Davis. Manchester, 1985; New York, 1986.
*The Manzoni Family.* Translated by Marie Evans. New York, 1987.
*Never Must You Ask Me.* Translated by Isabel Quigly. London, 1973.
*No Way.* Translated by Sheila Cudahy. New York, 1974. Published in England under the title *Dear Michael.* London, 1975.
*The Road to the City.* Translated by Frances Frenaye. Garden City, N.Y., 1949.
*The Road to the City and The Dry Heart.* Translated by Frances Frenaye. Boston, 1990.
*Valentino; and Sagittarius.* Translated by Avril Bardoni. Manchester, 1987; New York, 1988.
*Voices in the Evening.* Translated by D. M. Low. New York, 1963.

## BIOGRAPHICAL AND CRITICAL STUDIES

Bàrberi Squarotti, Giorgio. *La narrativa italiana del dopoguerra.* Bologna, 1968. Pp. 94–96.
Bowe, Clotilda Soave. "The Narrative Strategy of Natalia Ginzburg." *Modern Language Review* 68 (4):788–795 (1973).
Bullock Alan. "Natalia Ginzburg and Ivy Compton-Burnett." *Rivista di letterature moderne e comparate* 30 (3):203–227 (September 1977).
———. "Uomini o topi? Vincitori e vinti nei *Cinque romanzi brevi di Natalia Ginzburg." Italica* 60 (1):38–54 (Spring 1983).
Calvino, Italo. "Natalia Ginzburg o le possibilità del romanzo borghese." *L'Europa letteraria* 2 (9–12):130–138 (June–August 1961).
Clementelli, Elana. *Invito alla lettura di Natalia Ginzburg.* Milan, 1972, 1986.
Crescenzi, Lilia. *Narratrici d'oggi.* Cremona, 1966.
De Tommaso, Piero. "Natalia Ginzburg." In *Letteratura italiana.* Vol. 3. Milan, 1970. Pp. 817–833.
Gatt-Rutter, J. A. *Writers and Politics in Modern Italy.* London, 1978.
Garboli, Cesare. "Il piccolo mondo famigliare di N. Ginzburg." In *Novecento.* Edited by Gianni Grana. Vol. 8. Milan, 1980. Pp. 7627–7633.
———. "Fortuna critica," in Ginzburg's *Opere* (cited above), 2.1577–1591.
Heiney, Donald. "Natalia Ginzburg: The Fabric of Voices." *Iowa Review* 9 (4):87–93 (1970).
Lombardi, Olga. *Narratori neorealisti.* Pisa, 1967.
———. "Natalia Ginzburg." In *Novecento.* Edited by Gianni Grana. Vol. 8. Milan, 1980. Pp. 7606–7627.
Luperini, Romano. *Il novecento,* Vol. 1. Turin, 1981.
Manacorda, Giuliano. *Storia della letteratura italiana contemporanea, 1940–1965.* Rome, 1967.
———. "Natalia Ginzburg." In his *Vent'anni di pazienza.* Florence, 1972. Pp. 375–380.
Marchionne Picchione, Luciana. *Natalia Ginzburg. Il Castoro* 137 (May 1978).
Montale, Eugenio. "Vite quasi inutili." *Il Corriere della Sera,* 20 June 1961.
———. "Lessico famigliare: Crudele con dolcezza." *Il Corriere della Sera,* 7 July 1963, p. 7.

O'Healy, Anne-Marie. "Natalia Ginzburg and the Family." *Canadian Journal of Italian Studies* 9 (32):21–36 (1986).

Pacifici, Sergio. *A Guide to Contemporary Italian Literature: From Futurism to Neorealism.* Cleveland and New York, 1962. Pp. 135–143.

Piclardi, Rosetta D. "Forms and Figures in the Novels of Natalia Ginzburg." *World Literature Today* 53:585–589 (1979).

Russi, Antonio. *Gli anni dell'antialienazione: Dall'ermetismo al neorealismo.* Milan, 1967.

———. "Natalia Ginzburg." In *Letteratura italiana contemporanea.* Edited by Gaetano Marianni and Mario Petrucciani. Rome, 1982. Pp. 429–441.

Salinari, Carlo. *Preludio e fine del neorealismo in Italia.* Naples, 1967.

Spagnoletti, Giancinto. "Natalia Ginzburg." *Belgafor,* 39 (1):41–54 (January 1984).

Varese, Claudio. "Natalia Ginzburg." In his *Occasioni e valori della letteratura contemporanea.* Rocca San Casciano, 1967. Pp. 365–378.

CARLA CAPPETTI

# HEINRICH BÖLL

## *(1917–1985)*

### *LIFE*

BECAUSE HEINRICH BÖLL was born in Cologne on 21 December 1917, his early life was inevitably shaped in part by war and the social upheaval produced by war. Yet the effects on his life of international crisis and national economic disaster were counteracted by a home life marked by unusual love, kindness, and wisdom. Böll's childhood belies the often-heard assumption that artists come from unhappy families.

Heinrich was the youngest of five children born to Viktor and Maria (née Hermanns) Böll. From a previous marriage between Viktor Böll and Katharina Giessen, which ended with Katharina's death in 1901, one of three children had survived as well, making a total of six children in the family. At the time of Heinrich's birth, his father was a master furniture-maker with his own workshop in a densely populated quarter of Cologne. In this city, Heinrich Böll went to elementary school, attended the gymnasium, and lived most of his life. Many of his novels and short stories take Cologne as their background, and when the setting is not specifically Cologne, it is usually the Rhineland area between Bonn and Cologne.

Böll's family was Catholic, and the Catholic education that he received at home and in school influenced his thinking so completely that Catholic values became an integral part of his work, earning him at times the narrow label he so hated of "Catholic writer," much as Bernard Malamud would dislike the label "Jewish writer." Since Böll's religious attitude is essential to understanding his writing, however, it is important to define its nature. It was a remarkably liberal Catholicism that Böll practiced. When, between the ages of fourteen and eighteen, Heinrich Böll stopped going to church, he was not harassed at home for his decision. In 1933, when the Nazis came to power, the Catholic teachers at the gymnasium Böll attended were thorough antifascists. Böll grew up steeped in a faith practiced by family and close friends that was humane, liberal, and undoctrinaire, providing the young Heinrich with an effective defense against the seductive propaganda of Nazism. This humanistic Catholicism formed his conscience and determined the person and writer Böll became. Böll's faith often gave him the inner strength he needed to oppose injustice, whether it came from the Catholic church itself, from the fascist society of the Hitler period, or from the perversions of German democracy that he so harshly criticized after World War II.

Next to the religious faith to which he adhered his life long, Böll's family provided the greatest influence on his system of values. In the 1965 essay "Interview mit mir selbst" (Interview with Myself), Böll spoke of his mother as a "wonderful great woman" who offered a cup of coffee to anyone who came to the door, Nazi and anti-Nazi alike. This gesture of hospitality that so impressed Böll became characteristic of his own attitude to people and determined his later respect for all persons as human beings, whether friend or enemy. All of the positive characters in his stories and plays possess this naive goodness, a resistance to prejudice and an inability to attack the human dignity of another person.

Besides religion and family, a third force molded Böll's character and personality: the social conditions into which he was born. Böll traced his earliest memory back to the year 1919, when he claimed to have seen General Hindenburg's defeated army march through Cologne. Whether Böll actually remembered this event (he would have been only two) or whether he later created the recollection for effect is unimportant. Important is its indication that historic events gave meaning to his life. The end of World War I, the inflation of the 1920's, the depression of the 1930's, the Second World War, the liberation from fascism in 1945, the hunger years of the late 1940's, the economic recovery of the 1950's, the affluence of the 1960's, the terrorism of the 1970's, the missile crisis of the early 1980's—these are the touchstones that mark the development of Böll's life and work. Böll's concern focused on stages in history represented by specific historical developments. Thus, with the years his work unintentionally became a running account of the history of Germany during his lifetime, earning for him, as had the work of Dickens and Balzac in the previous century for them, the label "chronicler of the nation."

In 1924, Böll began his formal education at a Catholic elementary school in Cologne, which he attended for four years. In 1928 he left the elementary school for the gymnasium. Böll described these years in the autobiographical essay "Raderberg, Raderthal" (1965). His recollections were happy ones despite the inflation that brought ruin to his father's business and forced the family to move from the city. The essay praises his parents for their political and religious convictions that permitted him to associate with the children of socialists and atheists and to play with the "Reds," and contrasts his parents' liberality with the narrow-mindedness of the parents of many of his friends, who did not allow their children this free association. The open atmosphere of his home, although his family was threatened by imminent financial ruin, permitted the young Böll to judge people by their character rather than by shibboleths. The essay recalls the strong affiliation of his father with the Catholic Center party, but more important, his father's fairness and his mother's unideological socialist thinking. Looking back in 1965, he could see her as a "real Catholic leftist in comparison to whom all other Catholic leftists paled."

From 1928 to 1937, Böll attended the Kaiser-Wilhelm-Gymnasium in Cologne. These years, especially from the beginning of the Hitler period in 1933 to his graduation, are recounted in the autobiographical work *Was soll aus dem Jungen bloss werden?* (*What's to Become of the Boy?,* 1981). Böll was only one of three in the school who did not belong to a Nazi organization, although the school's teachers were remarkably anti-Nazi. His teacher of German had his pupils practice their critical faculty by rewriting passages of *Mein Kampf* for clarity and precision—an exercise that permitted the pupils to expose the content of Hitler's ideology through stylistic analysis, as well as to improve their own writing. Böll attributed the ease with which he avoided the taint of Nazism not only to a native aversion to racism but also to his teachers, friends, and family. Still, to protect the family business, someone in the family had to belong to a Nazi organization. After some discussion Alois, Heinrich's older brother (born 1911), was chosen to join the storm troopers.

In 1933 the concordat between the Third Reich and the Vatican presented the Böll family with a religious crisis. They might have left the church in protest against what they considered its "sellout" of good faith, because to the Bölls then (as many historians would later agree) the Vatican's accord with the Hitler government conferred an element of respectability on the new government that furthered the interests of fascism. Yet the Bölls remained in the church, because they did not want to appear to be adding to the already large number who had deserted the ranks to join the Nazi party.

During these years as a student at the gymnasium Böll began to read Jack London, Georg Trakl, and the Catholic writers Léon Bloy, Georges Bernanos, Henri Barbusse, Evelyn Waugh, and G. K. Chesterton. The most important of these writers for Böll was the radical Catholic Bloy, whose love of the poor and hatred of the rich as expressed in his novel *Le sang du pauvre* (*The Blood of The Poor,* 1909) wielded a profound influence on Böll long after he turned against the French writer's contradictory extremism.

In these years, as Germany succumbed to Nazism, Böll's family, his teachers, his loyal friends helped him to survive the period. The protective framework of eccentric Catholicism, gentle humanism, common sense, and calculated behavior brought him and the family through these dangerous years.

After graduation in 1937, Böll had difficulty choosing his direction in life. He knew only that he wanted to be a writer. From the age of seventeen, this profession had called him. He had, in fact, already started writing poetry and had completed possibly six novels before the war. All of these early writings were later destroyed in the bombings of Cologne. In 1938, Böll accepted an apprentice position to a book dealer in Bonn. This experience is fictionally recounted in the pages of *Gruppenbild mit Dame* (*Group Portrait with Lady,* 1971). In the winter of 1938–1939, after only a few months as an apprentice, Böll was called to compulsory labor service and required to dig irrigation ditches and to do forestry work in the interest of the nation. After completion of his labor service he wanted to study German philology and literature at the University of Cologne, but his refusal to join the Nazi party made enrollment difficult. He finally managed to enroll in June 1939, but that July, two months before the war began, he was inducted into the *Wehrmacht* as an infantryman. His military service lasted the full six years of the war. Through this entire period Böll never stopped hoping for the defeat of his country and liberation from National Socialism.

In 1940 he was garrisoned in Poland, where for the first time he witnessed the cruelty of the SS to the oppressed people in the occupied territories. At the end of June 1940 he was sent to France, where the war was already over. There he came down with dysentery and had to be returned to Germany. After recovering, he was assigned to guard supply depots in and around Cologne. In 1942 he was returned to France and stationed on the Atlantic Wall between Abbeville and Dieppe. In France he continued to read Léon Bloy.

On leave in 1942, Böll married Annemarie Cech, a young teacher of English whom he knew from the Catholic discussion group that met in the Böll home while he was still a student at the gymnasium. After the war she became a prominent translator of English, Irish, and American literature. She and Böll later worked as collaborators on translations of George Bernard Shaw, Brendan Behan, and J. D. Salinger. They had four sons: Christoph, who died shortly after his birth in 1945; Raimund, born 1947, died 1982; René, born 1948; and Vincent, born 1950.

In 1943, Böll was sent to the eastern front, but before crossing the French frontier the train struck a mine laid by the Maquis. Böll was injured in the right hand and again returned to Germany. This reprieve from the terror of the war in the east lasted only two weeks, however. He was next sent to the Crimea, where he was wounded in the leg. Shortly afterward a grenade fragment struck Böll in the head and necessitated his being sent to a field hospital in Odessa. When he recovered, the front was approaching the city. He was transferred to Iasi (Jassy) in Romania, where eight days later he was wounded again, this time seriously, in the back. Until August 1944 he remained in a field hospital in Hungary. Since the war was rapidly coming to an end, Böll, who had often tried to avoid military service by malingering, now made more serious attempts to escape danger. He returned to Germany with forged papers, and by claiming a death in the family managed to obtain a legitimate pass to visit his home. His mother had, in fact, died during an air raid in 1942.

On this visit home, Böll and his wife conspired to keep him out of the war by administering injections to him of a serum used against syphilis. The resulting high fever kept him hospitalized until February 1945, after which time they abandoned the injections as being too dangerous. Böll now deserted and took his wife to a small village outside Cologne. Recognizing that desertion would be too dangerous, however, he managed to return to his regiment near Mannheim, hoping for a speedy liberation by the Allies. As the front approached, he surrendered on 9 April 1945. On 15 September 1945, after five months of Allied internment, he was released. In 1964, he wrote of this day in the essay "Stichworte" (Catchwords) as his final release from "German imprisonment."

Although Böll readily acknowledged the crimes of the German nation, he never accepted the idea of "collective guilt." He had witnessed too many individual acts of humaneness by Germans to condemn his compatriots en masse and knew many Germans like his own family and friends who had been enemies of National Socialism from the outset. Still, throughout his work, Böll never tired of calling his fellow countrymen to account. His work is a constant reminder of crimes that should never be forgotten. His first novel, *Wo warst du, Adam* (*And Where Were You, Adam?* 1951), contains a description of a commandant of a concentration camp who murders all his Jewish prisoners. With this novel, Böll became one of the first German writers to acknowledge the Holocaust in literature.

In 1945, at the age of 28, Böll returned with his wife to the bombed-out city of Cologne to begin writing, to start the only career he had ever envisioned for himself. His first job after the war was in the family furniture shop, now run by his brother Alois. He soon found employment in the statistical office of the city of Cologne, but the main source of family income was his wife's salary as teacher. Böll also reenrolled at the University of Cologne, but only to obtain a legal ration card. His sole serious occupation was writing. Not until 1947 did his first short stories begin to appear in magazines. By 1950 about sixty stories had appeared in several periodicals and newspapers, but his name was still unknown to the public. Böll's first book, a novella entitled *Der Zug war pünktlich* (*The Train Was on Time*), was published in 1949, and the following year the same publisher, Middlehauve, brought out a collection of twenty-five stories under the title *Wanderer kommst du nach Spa . . .* (*Traveller, If You Come to Spa . . .*; also translated as *Stranger, Bear Word to the Spartans We . . .*). (These stories are available in the American edition of selected stories, *The Stories of Heinrich Böll.*) This book was followed in 1951 by the novel *Adam.*

While all three books were well received by critics, they were not financially successful, even though Böll's reputation was enhanced by his nomination for the 1951 literary award of Group 47 (a group of German writers founded in 1947 by Hans Werner Richter) for his short story "Die schwarzen Schafe" ("Black Sheep"). Because he had proved to be an unprofitable author and Middlehauve now decided to concentrate on scientific publishing, Böll was released from his contract. Yet although Böll was not known to a broad public, within literary circles his talent was recognized. The Cologne-based publisher Kiepenheuer & Witsch picked up his contract in 1952 and published all of his major works from that time forth.

Because Kiepenheuer & Witsch had a better grasp of book marketing, Böll's next novel was made into a financial and literary success.

This novel, *Und sagte kein einziges Wort* (*And Never Said a Word,* 1953; first translated under the title *Acquainted with the Night,* 1954), established Böll's reputation, gave him a secure income, and allowed him to begin to live entirely from his writing. From this time on, at regular intervals, novels, stories, essays, plays, and poems appeared, winning for Böll one honor after the other. Most important was the Nobel Prize for literature in 1972, but he received as well honorary doctorates in England and Ireland; an honorary title of professor from the state of North Rhine–Westphalia, and an honorary citizenship of the city of Cologne; became an honorary member of the American Academy of Arts and Letters; and was elected president of International PEN. All in all, Böll became one of Germany's best-known literary figures and the best-known German writer around the world.

Böll's oeuvre through the years has become large by any standard. In 1977 his collected *Romane und Erzählungen* (Novels and Stories) appeared in five volumes of some five to six hundred pages each. In 1978 three equally bulky volumes of *Essayistische Schriften und Reden* (Essayistic Writings and Speeches) appeared. After the publication of these collected works, further novels, stories, essays, autobiographical writings, continued to appear, of which the most important are the collection of stories *Du fährst zu oft nach Heidelberg und andere Erzählungen* (You Go to Heidelberg Too Often and Other Stories, 1979), the novel *Fürsorgliche Belagerung* (*The Safety Net,* 1979), and a posthumous novel, *Frauen vor Flusslandschaft* (*Women in a River Landscape,* 1985).

When Böll died on 16 July 1985, the whole German nation mourned, including his enemies, who respected him not only for his literary accomplishments but also for his legendary fairness. The funeral was attended by the president of the Federal Republic, prominent writers carried his casket, and hundreds of mourners appeared at the funeral site in Bornheim. Around the world the front pages of major newspapers announced his death, and tributes continued to appear in Germany and abroad over the next several months.

## *WORKS*

### *The Essays*

Böll's essays are most readily accessible in the volumes *Werke: Essayistische Schriften und Reden* and *Interviews* (vol. 1, 1978) and in three separate volumes that appeared after 1978: *Vermintes Gelände* (Mined Terrain, 1982), *Ein- und Zusprüche* (Objections and Exhortations, 1984), and a final volume, published after Böll's death, *Die Fähigkeit zu trauern* (The Ability to Mourn, 1986). None of these volumes has been translated, but a collection of selected essays entitled *Missing Persons and Other Essays* (1977) contains several important essays originally published between 1952 and 1974.

Böll's essays are important for three reasons. By revealing his aesthetic principles and defining his *engagement* as a writer, they provide readers with the best standards by which to judge his stories; they clarify Böll's position in relation to the events of West German history that form the background of his novels; and in sheer quantity they represent about half of Böll's oeuvre. Böll himself considered the essays as no different from his other work; they were simply part of the ongoing process of his *Fortschreibung,* his "continuous writing." He made often the latter point in his life, but most succinctly in 1983, in his acceptance speech for the honorary citizenship of the city of Cologne. In this address, "Ich han dem Mädche nix jedonn . . ." (I Didn't Do Anything to the Girl), he argued against viewing his work in separate categories: "What I have not understood . . . was the attempt to separate the storyteller from the writer who on occasion wrote essays, reviews, and whom you have heard on occasion give a speech. The point is that essays, reviews, and speeches are literature too" (in *Ein- und Zusprüche*).

Almost everything we know about Böll's life comes to us from his essayistic writings, because he often argued from his own experiences. Essays such as "Brief an einen jungen Katholiken" (Letter to a Young Catholic, 1958), "Über mich selbst" (About Myself, 1958), "Hierzulande" (In This Country, 1960), and "Raderberg, Raderthal" (1965) are good examples of his personal, informal autobiographical style. Böll's essays are unique in that they are not argumentative in the formal sense. They are never formulated in the language of cool, rational discourse, but rather in the warm, intimate language of dialogue. They make their appeal to the reader's conscience by emotive means—directed, certainly, to the mind, but through the heart. Pathos controls Böll's logos. The essays often substitute the anecdotal method for objective, rational discourse. The writer speaks in uncomplicated language to a friend willing to listen, or as one would talk to a concerned neighbor. In Böll's essays one perceives a development of postwar German democracy, an intrinsic respect for people.

This high regard for the individual does not mean the essays do not contain hard words or harsh judgments. In fact they often do; witness, for example, Böll's criticism of *Bild-Zeitung,* West Germany's most widely read tabloid newspaper, in the essay "Will Ulrike Meinhof Gnade oder freies Geleit?" (Does Ulrike Meinhof Want Mercy or Free Passage? 1972). Böll accused the newspaper outright of being "no longer crypto-fascistic, no longer fascistoid, [but] naked fascism. Persecution, lies, crap." Nor did he hesitate to mention the publishing magnate Alex Springer, *Bild*'s owner, by name and wish that he would choke on the bones of his Christmas fish.

Böll's essay on *Bild-Zeitung,* which appeared originally in *Der Spiegel* (10 January 1972), is the most notorious article of its kind in West German journalistic history. For months following its publication repercussions were felt throughout the media, dividing the country into Böll's supporters and Böll's critics. What is interesting is that the debate did not center on Böll's main point, which was the undemocratic journalistic practices of *Bild-Zeitung.* Instead, the national debate focused on Böll's language, his use of archaic legal terms, especially in the title of the article—*Gnade* (grace, mercy) and *freies Geleit* (free passage, safe-conduct)—and on his alleged support of terrorism. Böll's critics, almost all of whom were in the pay of the Springer Press, the largest press conglomerate in West Germany, missed the point that Böll was simply demanding for the suspected terrorist and symbolic outsider Ulrike Meinhof—as for anyone else—democratic legal protection under the law. For his defense of democracy, Böll was himself accused of sympathizing with terrorism.

In brief, the background of the episode was *Bild*'s reporting of a bank robbery on 23 December 1971 and its headline "Baader-Meinhof-Gruppe mordet weiter" (Baader-Meinhof Group Continues to Murder). In fact there had been no evidence at that time that the group in question had committed the crime, which the article in *Bild* actually admitted in smaller print. No one had been arrested or charged, and no conviction was ever obtained.

Böll's main attack was against *Bild*'s consistently inhuman, inaccurate, politically motivated reporting of the news in a way that aroused its readers to lynch justice by creating a climate of hatred and fear reminiscent of Nazi Germany. Like the anti-Semitic periodical *Der Stürmer* of the Nazi years, which created an atmosphere for public acceptance of the "final solution," in Böll's opinion, *Bild-Zeitung* was now systematically creating conditions in which any critic of West German democracy or West German capitalism could be accused of supporting terrorism. Böll's article put the responsibility for this demagoguery squarely on Alex Springer's shoulders.

The Meinhof article reveals much about Böll as a person, his style, his way of thinking. In it he showed his concern for the future of

West German democracy and his willingness to defend true democracy against all undemocratic practices. To Böll undemocratic social tendencies always produced fascistic practices. It was impossible for him to reconcile the systematic denunciation of human beings with any concept of political fairness. In addition, the article shows how quickly Böll came to the defense of persons unable to defend themselves; thus, in Böll every victim of injustice found an advocate.

In most cases Böll's causes were unpopular, but he saw in small things the larger failings of society. If *Bild* was permitted to practice its style of journalism, then no one, in Böll's mind, was safe from denunciation, neither prominent persons nor unknown individuals. Böll's attack against *Bild* was entirely consistent with his permanent literary effort to create a more humane society through constant vigilance.

Typical of Böll's essayistic method is a strong predilection for the narrative form. This technique is evident in passages of the Meinhof article, but it is more pronounced in essays like "Suchanzeigen" ("Missing Person," 1971) and "Die Moskauer Schuhputzer" ("The Moscow Shoeshiners," 1970). In fact, several of Böll's essays can pass as both stories and essays. Böll's most pronounced talent was his skill in narration, and even in the essays it manifests itself fully. His reaction to what he read in the newspapers, heard on the radio, or saw on television usually found expression in the essays. The style he developed can best be called democratic because it draws the reader into a circle of intimacy with its conversational tone. The tone wins the goodwill of the reader, who is drawn into the dialogue by the ethos of the speaker and is won over by the humanity of the writer and the common sense he manifests. Böll's essays always appeal to the reader's sense of morality, to the goodness that the writer assumes is in everyone. They take for granted that a sense of fairness and decency is the common heritage of all men and women.

In "Hierzulande" (In This Country) Böll tells of accompanying a visitor to catch a midnight train. The visitor is a German who had left in 1937 and now, in 1960, has returned for a visit. The evening has gone badly. Böll and his guest have never found the right words with one another. The essay now recounts the final minutes before the guest leaves. The guest asks, "What distinguishes the people here from 1933?" Böll replies, "Nothing, naturally," then adds, "Economically they're a little better off." The guest asks, "Are there still Nazis in this country?" "Naturally," Böll replies. "Did you expect the mere date of 8 May 1945 to change people?" They sit and wait for the train. Böll thinks about German history from 1917 to 1933, 1933 to 1960, about what has happened to Germany in the years from the war to the currency reform of 1948, and the economic miracle that it produced. Then he thinks of the trains that carried prisoners away and Jews to their death, of all the tears that have been shed on German train platforms, of what it is like to be a German in 1960, of what the Germans have forgotten, what they try not to remember.

When the train leaves, Böll says, "I wanted to tell the visitor all that, but could not find the words in conversation." Thus, the reader becomes the substitute for the guest; the essay replaces the failed conversation of that evening. Because the essay deals with guilt, it treats the single most important topic in postwar German life and letters. But there is in the essays no "argument" in the formal sense. There is instead a "story," an anecdote, a narrative. The recounted events themselves may not even be true; the episode of the visit, the failed evening, the ride to the station, the wait for the train may never have taken place. The whole work may be a fiction related in the first person, a short story like any other with a beginning, middle, and end, with characters and events. But, whether essay or story, it contains a strong indictment of Germany, fifteen years after World War II, as a nation without a memory, succumbing to the opiate of consumerism.

"Hierzulande" can serve as a model of many of Böll's most successful essays because it employs a pattern he frequently used. For example, in "Brief an einen jungen Katholiken" (Letter to a Young Catholic, 1958), Böll does much the same thing. The "letter" is addressed to a fictitious young Catholic about to begin a religious retreat in preparation for his military service in the newly established *Bundeswehr.* Böll tells the young man about his own similar experience in 1939; as he does so, the letter becomes a devastating critique of the Catholic church for its indirect cooperation with fascism and the military during the Nazi period. The letter recounts how the retreat master in 1939 insisted that Catholic soldiers remain loyal to authority, demonstrate the virtues of obedience and hard work, and avoid the dangers to chastity that the military life offered. Instead of explaining the importance of the primary virtues of faith, hope, and charity in time of war, he instilled in his young charges dubious secondary virtues that could serve any cause. Thus, the church, the letter regrets, taught Catholics to follow orders rather than their consciences. The letter concludes that the Catholic church is making the same mistakes again by supporting Germany's rearmament and finds the church failing again to give moral leadership in all forms of conscientious objection.

The letter caused a furor. It was banned from broadcast over the station WDR (West German Radio) and provoked harsh attacks from the Catholic press after it appeared in the Düsseldorf periodical *Christ und Bürger heute und morgen* (Christian and Citizen Today and Tomorrow). This letter was again typical of Böll's essayistic method: narrative rather than argument, dialogue instead of discourse, and characters representing ideas: the retreat master standing for the authority of the church and the recruit for young Catholics eager to receive principles of faith but instead offered rules of obedience.

The essay "Der Zeitgenosse und die Wirklichkeit" (The Contemporary and Reality, 1953) is essential to an understanding of Böll's work. In it he makes the simple distinction between "reality" and "actuality." The latter he calls a mere fact of history, such as the announcement that Japanese fishermen were contaminated by atomic tests set off in the Pacific. Reality, he insists in the essay, is what lies behind actuality: in the case of the Japanese fishermen, it is the effect of the radiation on their personal lives and the lives of members of their families, and the effect of radiation in the air on all living things. The essay describes reality as an obligatory letter addressed to all contemporaries. To decipher the letter, however, the reader must possess the faculty of imagination (*Phantasie*), that is, possess the natural ability to comprehend the message that lies behind the surface of actuality. Implied in Böll's essay is the belief that it is the task of the writer to help provide his contemporaries with the imagination they need to read the letter of reality composed by actuality. The essay's final words refer to the need for each person to comprehend the reality of his age as "a matter of life and death."

Böll's theory is in essence an accepted socialist understanding of realism, similar to that presented by Bertolt Brecht in the 1930's or by Martin Walser in the 1960's. In 1964, Walser spoke of the difference between what is *wirklich* and what is *realistisch. Wirklichkeit,* according to Walser, is that which simply exists, but reality is what lies behind *Wirklichkeit* and needs to be exposed. Writers who merely describe the surface of things without penetrating the veneer merely polish and maintain the furniture of society. The task of a writer, Walser wrote, is to remove the veneer and reveal the structure. Hence, the goal of writers with a socialist bent like Walser or Böll is the enlightenment of the reader by a process of exposure in order to improve the condition of society.

Essential to this concept of realism is the belief that the writer is committed to his own times, to write about and explain his own age by treating the ordinary things of daily life. Böll began his "Frankfurter Vorlesungen" (Frankfurt Lectures, 1966), given at the University of Frankfurt in 1964, with these words: "In the following hours I want to try to develop, by discussing individual books, themes, and theses, an aesthetic of the humane." What Böll meant by an "aesthetic of the humane" he made clear. It was nothing abstract. It was writing about how people lived in a neighborhood, how they ate together, how they created *Heimat* (homeland), and how money, love, and religion affected their lives. These themes put in a political context make up the essence of Böll's oeuvre.

In the third lecture Böll summarized his aesthetic in the following sentence: "Literature obviously can only choose as its subject matter what society has declared to be garbage (*Abfall*) or valueless." Böll's aesthetic principle challenged the ruling acquisitiveness of Germany's postwar affluent society. In his opinion, West Germans had buried their recent past under the pleasures of capitalist materialism. The "garbage" Böll had in mind as the fit subject matter of literature was the poor, the outsider, the traditional Christian concept of suffering that Germans had now declared valueless, an obstacle to consumption.

In 1959, Böll received the Edward von der Heydt Prize of the city of Wuppertal. His acceptance speech is entitled "Die Sprache als Hort der Freiheit" (Language as the Bulwark of Freedom). The substance of this speech is an effective manifesto of Böll's artistic commitment. The theme of the speech is the relationship of conscience to writing. The speech is Böll's clearest expression of his view of the relationship of aesthetic and moral principles:

> Whoever is accustomed to using words in a passionate way, as I confess I do, will become increasingly aware, the longer he works with words—because nothing can save him from this recognition—what a split nature words have in our world. Scarcely spoken or written down, they change themselves, and burden him who spoke or wrote them with a responsibility whose full burden he can seldom bear. Whoever writes or speaks the word *bread,* does not know what events he may put in motion. Wars are fought for the sake of this word, murders committed. It carries a powerful heritage, and whoever writes it or speaks it should know what this heritage is and which transformations it is capable of. . . . Behind every word stands a world, and whoever uses words, as everyone does who writes a newspaper report or composes a poem, should know that he is putting worlds in movement, is releasing split natures: what may comfort one, can cause the death of another.
>
> (*Werke: Essayistische Schriften und Reden,* 1.301–302)

Böll saw the responsibility of the writer in even a broader context than the individual's responsibility to his own conscience, for, he claimed, the writer who separates language from conscience commits not just a personal act of bad faith but treason as well because he "betrays everyone who speaks his language." Böll envisioned in this speech terrible possibilities for a man to be robbed of his dignity—such as by being beaten or tortured—but, he concluded, for him the worst possibility he could imagine would be "to write a sentence that could not stand up in the court that constituted the conscience of a free writer." Böll's writing has always possessed this high moral purpose without descending to the level of cheap edification. For that reason, when he died in 1985, many commentators saw in his death not only the passing of a great man but also the diminution of the nation's conscience.

### *The Short Stories*

Böll's short stories are most readily available in the first five volumes of his collected works (1977), in *Du fährst zu oft nach Heidelberg und andere Erzählungen* (You Go to Heidelberg Too Often and Other Stories, 1979), and in *Die Verwundung und andere frühe Erzählungen* (*The Casualty and Other Early Stories,* 1983). The last collection contains twenty-two stories, written between 1946 and 1952, which appeared after the war in various local newpapers and obscure journals. If one considers (as most critics do) Böll's *Irisches Tagebuch* (*Irish Journal,* 1957) to constitute a collection of eighteen stories about Ireland rather than a travel diary, then Böll's collected short stories total well over one hundred. About half of the short stories are available in English in the collection *The Stories of Heinrich Böll* (1986).

Many of Böll's short stories have become acknowledged postwar classics; indeed, had he written nothing but his stories, his place in German literature would be secure. His first collection, *Traveller, If You Come to Spa . . .*, established him in this genre. Böll very early on solved the language problem confronting German writers after the war. With artistic sensitivity he conquered the corrupted idiom of Nazi propagandists and the destructive jargon of bureaucracy that had paved the way for the Holocaust and the war. German writers found it impossible after the war to write so much as a simple sentence without using words that conjured up visions of horror or produced involuntary recollection of the crimes of the Third Reich. Böll summed up this problem in a single sentence in his 1976 essay "Jahrgang 1922" (The Class of 1922): "It was difficult to begin writing in 1945," he said, "considering the depravity and untruthfulness of the German language at that time." In the 1964 Frankfurt Lectures, too, Böll had maintained that "German postwar literature as a whole had been the literature of finding language." He also insisted in these lectures that "people have not yet understood what it meant in 1945 to write just half a page of German prose" and to work through the "darkness that our language had entered in the course of history."

To solve the linguistic problems that they faced, two ways were open to German authors: a return to the rudiments of vocabulary and syntax, to the power of primitive expression; and a conscious playing on the now perverted meaning of German tradition. Böll used both of these methods. Any story from *Traveller, If You Come to Spa . . .* serves to illustrate his technique of the early years. The opening lines of "An der Angel" ("On the Hook," 1950) can serve as a model of the first method:

> I know it's all foolish. I shouldn't go there anymore; it's so senseless, and still I live from going there. It is one minute of hope and twenty-three hours and fifty-nine minutes of despair. But I live from it. It's not much, there is almost no substance in it at all. I shouldn't go there anymore. It's killing me, that's what it's doing: killing me. But I must, I must, I must go there. . . .
>
> (*Werke: Romane und Erzählungen,* 1.261)

All the stories in *Traveller, If You Come to Spa . . .* manifest this linguistic minimalism: simple vocabulary, elemental syntax, and unorthodox punctuation to simulate the patterns of speech. Typical also is the first-person narration (twenty-two of the twenty-five stories in the book have this point of view); also pervasive are the passive heroes in rebellion against the system, as is the sympathy the author expresses for the suffering of people on the margin of society.

The story "On the Hook" concerns a man who goes to the train station every afternoon at 1:20 to meet a train from which he expects his girlfriend to alight. Three months and four days previously he received a telegram saying she was coming on the 1:20 train; however, the telegram gave no date of arrival. Thus he has been going faithfully since then to the station and living for the minute it takes the train to pull into the station. Because he has given up his job in order to meet the train, he has been forced to sell all he owns to maintain himself. On the day the narrative takes place, he possesses nothing more than the clothes on his back.

Böll presents in this fictional situation what he had learned in the war and from the immediate postwar period to be the universal social estate of the poor and the powerless who had no control over the conditions of their own lives. These wretched martyrs who can neither understand nor influence what controls their lives represent for Böll a typical condition of the mass of mankind. Such helpless people have, throughout Böll's oeuvre, the author's total sympathy. Böll's existential view of suffering comes from his experience during the war, where soldiers and civilians alike were victims of the decisions made by faceless people whose commands moved forces that destroyed life. In "On the Hook" the narrator acknowledges the absurd by identifying the enemy as an anonymous "they":

> These people, they have more in their power than just us. They control everything. This clique has power and security, while we, we who wait, we have nothing; we live on the knife's cutting edge, we balance ourselves from one minute of hope to the next minute of hope; for twenty-three hours and fifty-nine minutes we balance ourselves on the edge of the knife, for a single moment we get to rest.
>
> (*Werke: Romane und Erzählungen,* 1.262)

On this last day of waiting, when the narrator has absolutely nothing left, not even his hope, and has decided to commit suicide if his loved one does not come, she steps from the train and rushes into his waiting arms. Yet despite the narrator's sense of ecstatic fulfillment, the last lines of the story express a strange sense of helplessness: "She lies against my breast . . . and I possess nothing but her and a platform ticket, just her and a canceled platform ticket."

Here the irony—another element characteristic of Böll's early stories—is twofold. In contrast with the tone of the narrative, the story concludes with a "happy ending." But this pleasing irony is undercut by the narrator's miserable social condition, which has not changed. The existential feeling of powerlessness, of being at the mercy of the anonymous "they," remains the same. Hope in this world, Böll's story says, promises much but delivers little.

Böll's existentialism is, however, not of the typical French kind. The message of the collection is that hope and comfort derive not from accepting the absurd, but from ordinary love of the most simple kind, from the natural bond between men and women.

Of the collection about half the stories treat the suffering and despair of war and the other half the helplessness and suffering of the immediate postwar period. Many of the war stories feature narrators who tell their tales from beyond the grave, where they have finally found peace, or from a station this side of the tomb, where they are about to die. The title story, "Traveler, If You Come to Spa . . . ," demonstrates this narrative perspective and reflects the pacifism that was Böll's response to his six years of military service. A wounded and delirious soldier is carried into a school building whose corridors are lined with the busts and statues of antiquity: Caesar next to Cicero, Marcus Aurelius next to Nietzsche—history, art, militarism, the philosophy of the superman side by side. When the soldier awakes from his operation in the school's art room (now an emergency hospital), he realizes that he is back in his own school, the one he left only a few weeks ago to become a soldier. As he looks down at his body on the bed, he sees that his arms and one leg are missing; simultaneously he recognizes on the blackboard the remains of a sentence that he himself had written: "Stranger, bear word to the Spartans we . . ." With this recognition is implied a realization that the classical tradition as taught in the Hitler period had perverted the European tradition of humanism.

The stories Böll wrote between 1950 and 1960 were for the most part satiric. From this period date the masterpieces "Nicht nur zur Weihnachtszeit" (Christmas Not Just Once a Year, 1951), "Doktor Murkes gesammeltes Schweigen" ("Murke's Collected Silences," 1955), and "Der Wegwerfer" ("The Thrower-Away," 1957). These three satires have been acclaimed by such diverse German critics as Walter Jens, Hans Magnus Enzensberger, and Erhard Friedrichsmeyer as the high point of Böll's work and the best of Germany's satiric literature since 1945.

"Christmas Not Just Once a Year," set in 1947, tells how Aunt Milla wants to celebrate Christmas continuously, and forces the members of her family to yield to her bizarre, destructive demand. The target of Böll's satiric attack has been variously identified as false piety, Christians who wish to cling to empty ritual, the commercialization and sentimentalization of Christmas in a secular world, the state of religion in postwar Germany, and the new bourgeoisie. While each of these interpretations can be supported by the text, the work attacks first and foremost a dual target: West Germany's desire after the war to avoid coming to terms with the Hitler years, and the nation's failure to learn from its most recent historical experience. Most remarkable about "Christmas Not Just Once a Year" is the way it presents this message with objectivity and cool detachment in a genre not noted for either of these virtues. In contrast to the very idea of Christmas every day, itself a form of hyperbole, the work consistently presents a tone of matter-of-factness and deliberate indirectness that results in a thorough indictment of Germany's postwar social sickness.

The opening sentences of the story suggest Böll's intention:

> Symptoms of decline have become evident in our family. For a time we were at pains to disregard them, but now we have resolved to face the danger. I dare not as yet use the word *breakdown,* but disturbing facts are piling up at such a rate as to constitute a menace and compel me to report things that will sound disagreeable to my contemporaries; no one, however, can dispute their reality. The fungi of destruction have found lodgement beneath the hard, thick crust of respectability; colonies of deadly parasites that proclaim the end of a whole tribe's irreproachable correctness.
>
> (*Werke: Romane und Erzählungen,* 2.11)

The key words of the opening lines suggest that the story is about the German family and a sickness that is destroying it, and that this illness, if not faced up to, will ruin the nation (the "whole tribe"). The disease is compared to a deadly fungus spreading below the surface of respectability. But coupled with this metaphor of the nation and its cancer is the leitmotif of "the good old days." This often-repeated longing of Aunt Milla to return to the past is, however, not a wish for the days before Hitler, but merely a desire for the days before the war. Thus, Böll hints at Germany's acceptance of Hitler's fascism coupled with the wish simply to have severed itself from the unfortunate war.

If this satire were merely to be read as a critique of Germany of the 1950's, it would not be counted among the recent classics of world literature. But the tale has much more than parochial significance. It can be read with equal validity as an attack upon those of any nation who try to cover up their national crimes and who refuse to deal with the immoral acts of their own history. In truth, the satire points out that all countries would like to escape their past by celebrating Christmas every day.

The Italian critic Cesare Cases regards "Murke's Collected Silences" as "one of the finest works of European literature since World War II." In this story Böll attacks opportunistic Christians and the religious attitude in West Germany as it changed from the sincere piety of the hunger years into the empty ritual of the "economic miracle." At the same time, as is usual in Böll's satires, the story features more than one satiric object. Besides religion, the culture industry comes under attack. In fact, Böll's work implies that religion and culture in West Germany go hand in hand, that to attack one is to implicate the other.

The story focuses on Bur-Malottke, a celebrated guru of media-religion and art. He hosts two popular weekly radio programs, most often about "God" and "Rilke"; 2.3 million copies of his philosophico-religio-historico-cultural books are in print; he edits three periodicals and two newspapers and serves as the chief reader for a major publishing house. This high priest of refined taste in large measure determines what is culturally acceptable for his countrymen. He is the infallible weathervane of his nation's changing fashions. Bur-Malottke's adversary in the satire, Dr. Murke, is a young psychologist, recently hired by the radio station that broadcasts Bur-Malottke's cultural programs. Murke secretly rebels against all the commercialism that Bur-Malottke represents. His symbolic demonstration against the general vapidity of the station's programming is to collect the snips of dead air cut from tapes of edited radio broadcasts. The open confrontation between the two comes when Bur-Malottke decides to replace the word "God" in his taped broadcasts with the currently more suitable, pompous phrase "that higher Being Whom we revere." Murke, who has been given the task of carrying out this editing job, destroys his adversary in the process, but proves to be himself a ruthless achiever. Böll created in Murke a new type of sympathetic hero, one who is no longer a victim but a dominant type desirous of power and willing to use it. Böll's double irony reaches its high point when Murke forces his girlfriend to record silences for him; thus, Murke's own willfulness negates his symbolic protest of Bur-Malottke's tyranny.

Through the years a consistent target for Böll's satire has been the absurd world of technology. In "Murke's Collected Silences" this intention is inherent in the detailed descriptions of the operations of the radio station. But in the satire "The Thrower-Away," the direct object of Böll's criticism is the social role of technology. Here the first-person narrator relentlessly applies rational means to minimize work and save labor. To achieve this end, he ruthlessly reduces all actions to the element of time, undisturbed that his blind rationalization is dehumanizing.

In "The Thrower-Away" Böll exaggerates his protagonist and his occupation in the extreme. The anonymous narrator has created for himself a well-paying job with an insurance company by developing methods of sorting and destroying the company's junk mail. After systematically destroying the work of compositors, printers, artists, writers, and packers according to scientifically developed time-study methods, the thrower-away returns home to his apartment-cum-laboratory to refine his theories. Here he contemplates opening a chain of schools for throwers-away and to place his pupils in post offices to save postage. Eventually, he plans even to save the labor of compositors, printers, artists, and the writers who produce junk mail by eliminating their work before it even exists. When at the conclusion of the story the narrator confesses to being an asocial madman who has managed to adjust himself perfectly to contemporary norms, Böll reveals his own view of the dangerous, growing use of technology to eliminate jobs for the sake of increasing profit.

In the 1960's Böll wrote few short stories, explaining later that he found them too easy to write. His most successful satiric stories of the 1950's were, indeed, formulaic in nature; each presented a plausible situation exaggerated to absurdity, narrated by a sympathetic, half-mad rogue. After the 1950's, many of the stories Böll wrote leaned toward experimentation and were, in effect, attempts to find a new style or formula. Although he was never as successful with these as he had been earlier with the tales, two of his later stories are nonetheless outstanding. "Du fährst zu oft nach Heidelberg" ("Too Many Trips to Heidelberg," 1977), about a young man who ruins his chances for a teaching career by traveling to Heidelberg to visit Chilean refugees (thus making himself suspect of harboring leftist sympathies), is an effective attack on Germany's political paranoia in the late 1970's. The story "Zundhölzer" (Matches, 1982) shows again Böll's lifelong sympathy for the marginal members of society, as he depicts with loving restraint an old widower in a rest home whose daily concern is to account for his disappearing matches and to figure out who is taking them. Both these stories are less experimental than most of the later tales which may suggest that Böll wrote his best when he stayed within the limits of traditional realistic fiction.

### *The Novels*

The two novellas *The Train Was on Time* (1949) and *Das Vermächtnis* (*A Soldier's Legacy,* 1982 [written 1948]) and the episodic novel *Wo warst du, Adam? (And Where Were You, Adam?* 1951) represent Böll's longer treatment of the war. While they differ from one another in plot and structure, they share with Böll's war stories the fatalistic earthly view that death is bigger than life and the optimistic Christian one that heavenly consolation is greater than suffering. Thus, all the war narratives acknowledge that God is still in his heaven although all is not right with the world.

*The Train Was on Time* tells in the first person the story of Andreas, a soldier who knows he is going to die when his troop train reaches the front. He even picks out on a map the place where he will be killed. This tale of inevitability, lightened only by the love Andreas finds with Olina, a Polish prostitute, just hours before he dies exactly in the place he predicted, is a tour de force of tragic perfection.

*A Soldier's Legacy* presents a more complicated perspective. In 1948 the narrator, Wenk, a former soldier, happens upon his former commanding officer, Captain Schnecker, celebrating the latter's graduation from law school and overhears Schnecker and his fiancée planning their optimistic future. The occasion causes the narrator to recall how Schnecker had murdered Wenk's friend Lieutenant Schnelling while they were fighting in Russia. The story by Wenk, written in the form of a long-overdue letter to Schnelling's brother, tells him the truth of his brother's death. The novella focuses on Wenk's dealing with the past and his recognition that by 1948 ruthless, unconscionable men like Schnecker were beginning to dominate the new Germany with their values of success at any price.

The novel *Adam* is a third-person, episodic story of Feinhals, a soldier in Hungary in 1944–1945 who falls in love with Ilona, a Jewish schoolteacher. The episode of Ilona's death in a concentration camp is one of the most outstanding episodes in Böll's early fiction. This novel, like all of Böll's fiction about the war, concludes on a note of tragic irony as Feinhals dies on his own doorstep from an exploding German grenade as he returns to his mother's home in the last days of the war.

The epigraph Böll chose for the novel *Adam* (taken from Antoine de Saint-Exupéry's *Pilote de guerre* [*Flight to Arras,* 1942]) can stand as an epigraph for all his war stories from this period: "When I was younger, I took part in real adventures: establishing postal air routes across the Sahara and South America. But war is no true adventure; it is only a substitute for adventure. War is a disease just like typhus." Alan Bance has pointed out that this apolitical perspective on the war was typical of German literature in the 1940's and 1950's. He even sees a kind of "realism" in this political vagueness because, as he says, "war is not conducive to clear thinking." In Böll's case this unanalytic response to the war (the interpretation of international conflict as a natural illness) was compounded by his feeling of being a lucky survivor, for only one out of four German men in Böll's age group returned from battle.

His sense of survival as fate led Böll to deal subjectively rather than objectively with the suffering of the Hitler years. This narrow perspective manifests itself in Böll's simplistic division of characters into two groups: victims and executioners, with the victims often being the Germans themselves. Such a dichotomous view of World War II is understandable and indeed accurate for someone who was himself an antifascist and a sufferer of twelve prolonged years of oppression. Still, the consequence of this view is that the war stories cannot reveal in depth what the war was about; the limited categories of suffering innocents and brutal henchmen are too unrefined to do the job. This kind of dualism, as Walter Sokel has called it, which is characteristic of Böll's work in this period, is missing in the later stories, which become more sophisticated in their characterizations. Günter Wirth's indictment of Böll's war stories as "timeless irrationalism" is to the point: certainly war is not like typhus or any other sickness that stems from biological causes. War is not of nature's making; it is made by human beings with political and economic interests.

But the novel *Adam* has a second epigraph as well, one taken from the wartime diaries of the Catholic writer Theodor Haecker: "A world catastrophe can serve many ends, one of which is to find an alibi before God. Where were you, Adam? 'I was in the World War.'" Of these two epigraphs, the one from Haecker is clearly the more important, for Böll takes the title of his novel from it. Clear also is Haecker's irony, which informs Böll's novel: war is no excuse before God. Ultimately people are responsible for what they do. This message goes far to undercut the metaphor that war is like typhus, especially since the main chapter of the novel describes the Nazi commandant of a concentration camp as he murders all his Jewish prisoners. Clear also in the way the novel recounts the circumstances surrounding this episode is that all who cooperated with the Nazi system of extermination are guilty, from those who transported the victims to those who ordered and did the killing. The excuse that "we did not intend what happened" finds no support within the economy of the novel.

This boldly honest attitude casts an undiminished moral light throughout Böll's writing. Though he may have viewed the world unhistorically in the 1940's and early 1950's under the influence of Christian existentialism, he learned quickly in the 1950's that without recognizing the forces of history he could not understand what was going on in Europe around him. Böll's literary development from ahistoricity to historicity, from presenting only men and women suffering to presenting and analyzing the causes of their suffering by giving the historical background of events represents a fundamental change in his work.

Beginning with the novel *Und sagte kein einziges Wort* (*And Never Said a Word,* 1953), Böll evolved a method for dealing with contemporary reality. He began choosing themes, drawing characters, and selecting events tied directly to current developments in Germany. For this reason, one of the best histories of the Federal Republic is Böll's collected work. When his works are read chronologically, the reader goes through every significant phase in West German history from its establishment in 1949 to the mid 1980's. His themes form a running chronicle of the first thirty-five years of the Second Republic, including the hunger period after the war, the restoration of German capitalism, the period of rearmament, the years of prosperity, the terrorist response to the social and political inequities produced by Germany's "economic miracle" up to the soul-searching of the 1980's. Other topics are the role of the Catholic church in West German politics; the problems of love and marriage amidst poverty and plenty; the shortcomings of the press in a free and democratic society; and the possibility of finding a humane social alternative to the ruthless competition, militant profit-taking, and demand for ever more production with inequitable distribution that are so characteristic of modern Western society. Böll treats all these aspects of West German history not as isolated phenomena of the postwar era, but in light of the Hitler years and German history since the turn of the century. His oeuvre thus contributes not only to the establishment of postwar West German literature but also to the political and social understanding of German development in this century. The young man who began in his late twenties and early thirties by publishing realistic, pathetic accounts of the misery of war developed into an astute chronicler of his nation's history.

Because the novel *And Never Said a Word* develops a method of dramatic intensification that Böll started in the early stories and continued throughout his work, this novel can serve as a paradigm of his fiction. The method is simply to set a moral person in an immoral situation and record what happens. In this novel Fred Bogner, his wife, and their three children are forced to live in a single rented room. They find that their lives are determined by the pressures of these harsh circumstances.

The Bogners' poverty and the oppressive closeness of their living conditions produce the episodes of the novel, which in turn give rise to a strong criticism of institutional Catholicism's role in Germany's economic revival. The church is shown to be indifferent to the existential needs of its members while it concerns itself with social and political power in a developing free-market economy that is actually creating two classes of West German citizens: the privileged and the underprivileged.

The bishop of Cologne and the Bogners' Catholic landlady are the figures through which the novel chastises the church and reveals the ecclesiastical institution's disregard of social justice. The Catholic Bogners, on the other hand, demonstrate how religion can still be the source of a Christian piety that enables them to practice an actual love of neighbor.

The novel is paradigmatic in a second way in that it is Böll's first experiment with changing narrative perspective, a technique used in several later novels: *Haus ohne Hüter* (*The Unguarded House,* 1954), *Billard um halbzehn* (*Billiards at Half-Past Nine,* 1959), *Fürsorgliche Belagerung* (*The Safety Net,* 1979), and *Frauen vor Flusslandschaft* (*Women in a River Landscape,* 1985). In *And Never Said a Word* the Bogners' story is told in alternating first-person narratives by husband and wife. The history of the family is revealed slowly and fragmentarily in flashbacks, interior monologues, and conversations.

Finally, the book demonstrates a third paradigm typical of Böll's later work. The actual time frame of the novel is quite short; it describes a period from Saturday before noon to before noon on the following Monday, over the weekend of Saint Jerome's Day (30 September) 1951. In the course of the novel the reader learns about fifteen years of the Bogners' married life during war and peace. This technique of reducing the narrated time and expanding the time within the narration allows Böll to show how the past affects the present.

For example, *The Unguarded House* takes place during a single week in the summer of 1953 while presenting events from the war years up to the time of the narrative present (the early 1950's). The novel *Billiards at Half-Past Nine* takes place on the single day of 6 September 1958, on the eightieth birthday of the revered architect Heinrich Fähmel, but covers fifty years of German history, from 1907 to 1958. The novel *Ansichten eines Clowns* (*The Clown,* 1963) tells the life story of the mime Hans Schnier through one evening of phone calls and reminiscences in his apartment. The novel *The Safety Net* presents the history of West German economic development since 1945 before a backdrop of terrorism in the late 1970's during the brief time span between the election of the protagonist Fritz Tolm to the presidency of the National Association of Entrepreneurs up to his resignation the next day. And *Women in a River Landscape* exposes in just twenty-four hours the political development of West Germany through the Adenauer years up to the mid 1980's by presenting the machinations behind the scenes of leading figures in the Christian Democratic party as they replace a minister and choose a new head of state.

Böll himself referred to this kind of structure (reducing the narrative present while broadening the novel's historical horizon) that in an ideal form would describe in a single minute of narrative time all the forces of history that might affect a character's life and determine his or her decisions. This method permitted him to examine how actions and thoughts are actually conditioned by past political and economic events and to show how people and events have become who and what they are, while at the same time it allowed him to state that those in responsible positions are answerable to history.

In Böll's work, little people become the objects of social forces or victims of the decisions of others. This philosophical position, which lies at the heart of Böll's work, surprises no one aware of what Böll considered important in his own formation as an individual: two world wars, inflation, depression, and economic restoration.

In *Die verlorene Ehre der Katharina Blum* (*The Lost Honor of Katharina Blum,* 1974), which again takes place in a few days—this time four days during the Carnival festival in Cologne—Böll used this method to show how an apolitical, law-abiding young woman could be turned into a vengeful murderer by society's toleration of social injustice. Katharina Blum becomes a "dangerous" woman because she finds herself a victim of character assassination perpetrated by those institutions most responsible for a just democratic society: the press, the police, the law.

The philosophical position implied in Böll's assumption that a person is a product of social forces could be called Marxist, except that it is thoroughly religious, lacks the happy dimension of Marxist optimism, and never recommends the introduction of social change through political organization. Social solutions are not found in Böll's work. Implied, however, is the belief that if people in power acted with more concern for those subject to their power or practiced more compassion in the execution of their offices, society would be more just. His heroes and heroines always make important decisions regarding their own lives. They are not completely passive; they do not yield to or reluctantly accept injustice. Their decisions affirm their individual human dignity and assert a militant humanism. Although their actions may be vain in effecting significant social change and merely permit the characters to live with their consciences, their decisiveness functions as symbolic opposition to an unjust world and, as such, suggests that social awareness and conscious opposition are the way to a better future. The story of Katharina Blum's vengeance neither recommends nor condones murder, but merely illustrates the simple truth that the toleration of injustice often engenders social violence.

This tendency to decisiveness and action on the part of individuals is a prevailing pattern in Böll's work. At the conclusion of *And Never Said a Word,* Fred Bogner chooses to return to his wife and children despite the crowded conditions of their single room because he is determined to try to save his marriage and his family. In *Billiards at Half-Past Nine* the father and son both alter their lives. Old Heinrich Fähmel accepts his son's destruction of the abbey of Saint Anthony because he understands his son's motivation as a moral protestation of the church's collusion with the Nazis. When Old Fähmel refuses to attend the dedication of his restored architectural masterpiece, he asserts that individual lives can be made happier with moral decisions even if these decisions cannot immediately change society. His reclusive son Robert in turn chooses to reintegrate himself into society by adopting an orphan in order to give the boy a better life and to revitalize his own life.

In *The Unguarded House,* the father figure "Uncle" Albert decides to marry the widowed Mrs. Brielach because it means a better life for himself, for her, and for her young son. In *The Clown,* Hans Schnier chooses to become a white-faced beggar in the train station at Bonn because he believes that his desperate performances there may prick the consciences of at least some of his friends who see him. In *The Safety Net,* Fritz Tolm rejects the prestigious presidency of a national organization in order to show solidarity with the antimaterialist values of his children. And in *Women in a River Landscape,* after a day of political intrigue, the intellectual, proletarian speech writer Grobsch decides to change over from the Christian Democratic to the Social Democratic party, and the septuagenarian Count Heinrich von Kreyl decides to reject the offer of the nation's presidency to retire to his *Heimat* in the north.

While such decisions do not alter the course of West German history, they do show that individuals can be courageous and virtuous. Moreover, the decisions made at the end of Böll's novels frequently involve more than one person. They are often group decisions, made by members of a family or by a circle of friends. These small groups who decide to put their own moral lives in order represent Böll's model for a more humane society.

When the Swedish Academy awarded Böll the Nobel Prize in 1972, it singled out the novel *Gruppenbild mit Dame* (*Group Portrait with Lady,* 1971) for special praise, calling that work the summation of Böll's oeuvre. Although Böll continued to publish novels, stories, poems, plays, and essays regularly after 1971, *Group Portrait* maintained its unique place in his writing as the single work that came closest to representing the whole of Heinrich Böll. The book was both summary and summation in that it recapitulated his major themes and culminated their formulation.

In an interview with Dieter Wellershoff, Böll stated the aim of *Group Portrait:* "I tried to describe or to write the story of a German woman in her late forties who had taken upon herself the burden of history from 1922 to 1970." In this story of Leni Gruyten-Pfeiffer and her family and friends, Böll challenged the norms of West German society with a model of radical socialism and religious humanism.

The heroine Leni synthesizes a number of seeming contradictions. Although she is a simple person, she confounds any attempt at simple explanation. She is a materialist who delights in the senses and a mystic who penetrates the mystery of the Virgin Birth; an innocent at heart and a tramp in the eyes of society; a Communist by intuition and an embodiment of the Nazi ideal of *das deutsche Mädel.* In Leni; her Russian lover, Boris; and their son, Lev, Böll has created a holy family that proclaims an undogmatic Christian socialism as a gospel for our time.

Around Leni are grouped more than 125 characters representing all classes of society and various nations. They are communists and capitalists, industrialists and proletarians, fascists and antifascists, Jews and Muslims, Turks and Germans, rich and poor, saints and sinners—the whole spectrum of German society between 1922 and 1970.

To hold the various levels of the story together and to keep Leni in the center of the novel, the work employs two narrative techniques. In the first half of the novel an unnamed narrator scrupulously relates the events of Leni's life. This half of the book consists of the narrator's meticulous research on Leni and his comments on the accuracy and validity of his findings. Leni's story proceeds chronologically from her birth to 2 March 1945, the day of a nine-hour Allied raid on Cologne, the day World War II effectively came to an end for the people of that city. After this event, midway through the novel, the narrator relinquishes this role to assume one as a member of Leni's circle of friends; that is, he becomes an actor in the events of the novel. At this point various characters tell their life stories from the day of the terrible bombing up to 1970. Since these people all have contact with Leni, their stories also reveal, from various perspectives, Leni's own life during this twenty-five year period. Again Böll found a structure to suit his purpose of coming to terms with recent German history and postwar developments.

Politically the novel condemns the system of communism as strongly as it does capitalist society. Because the work criticizes specific actions of the Communist party in the period between the Russo-German nonaggression pact of 1939 and the Warsaw Pact invasion of Czechoslovakia in 1968, the novel has appeared in the Soviet Union only in an abridged form that omits all criticism of the Communist party as well as some sensitive sexual passages. Despite a political evenhandedness in the novel, Böll's criticism of the Western and Eastern systems differs. The former is depicted as a society based on production for profit instead of human needs, one that lacks compassion and justice. The practice of capitalism as presented in the novel is that of a philosophy of greed run amok. Böll's criticism of communism, in contrast, is not of its ideals but of its failure to live up to its precepts. From this point of view the novel's criticism of established socialism parallels its criticism of the institutional church. Through Leni, and especially through her son, Lev, Böll demonstrates that socialist and religious principles go hand in hand as partners of a shared humanism. The novel is, indeed, the summation of Böll's writing, for it crystallizes the radical message that runs through all of his work beginning with *And Never Said a Word:* Christianity and capitalism are incompatible with each other; their long-standing marriage survives only because organized religion continually sacrifices its humanistic values to the demands of economics and politics.

## Selected Bibliography

Several primary and secondary bibliographies on Böll exist. One of the most useful of the former type, because of its intelligent organization (which makes it easy to find isolated translations in anthologies and periodicals), is Werner Martin, *Heinrich Böll: Eine Bibliographie seiner Werke* (Hildesheim, 1975). More comprehensive, however, containing information not available elsewhere on performances and recordings of Böll's work and a thorough list of secondary literature, all periodically brought up to date, is Werner Lengning's *Der Schriftsteller Heinrich Böll: Ein biographisch-bibliographischer Abriss* (Munich, 1977).

### EDITIONS

#### INDIVIDUAL WORKS


PROSE

*Der Zug war pünktlich.* Opladen, 1949.
*Wanderer kommst du nach Spa . . .* Opladen, 1950.
*Wo warst du, Adam?* Opladen, 1951.
*Und sagte kein einziges Wort.* Cologne, 1953.
*Haus ohne Hüter.* Cologne, 1954.
*Das Brot der frühen Jahre.* Cologne, 1955.
*Irisches Tagebuch.* Cologne, 1957.
*Doktor Murkes gesammeltes Schweigen und andere Erzählungen.* Cologne, 1958.
*Billard um halbzehn.* Cologne, 1959.
*Entfernung von der Truppe.* Cologne, 1961.
*Ansichten eines Clowns.* Cologne, 1963.
*Ende einer Dienstfahrt.* Cologne, 1966.
*Gruppenbild mit Dame.* Cologne, 1971.
*Erzählungen 1950–1970.* Cologne, 1972.
*Die verlorene Ehre der Katharina Blum; oder, Wie Gewalt entstehen und wohin sie führen kann.* Cologne, 1974.
*Du fährst zu oft nach Heidelberg und andere Erzählungen.* Bornheim, 1979.
*Fürsorgliche Belagerung.* Cologne, 1979.
*Was soll aus dem Jungen bloss werden? oder, Irgendwas mit Büchern.* Bornheim, 1981.
*Das Vermächtnis.* Bornheim, 1982.
*Die Verwundung und andere frühe Erzählungen.* Bornheim, 1983.
*Frauen vor Flusslandschaft.* Cologne, 1985.

DRAMA

"Ein Schluck Erde." In *Homo viator: Modernes christliches Theater.* Cologne, 1962.
*Hausfriedensbruch: Ein Hörspiel / Aussatz: Ein Schauspiel.* Cologne, 1969.

ESSAYS AND SPEECHES

*Frankfurter Vorlesungen.* Cologne, 1966.
*Aufsätze, Kritiken, Reden.* Cologne, 1967.
*Neue politische und literarische Schriften.* Cologne, 1973.
*Berichte zur Gesinnungslage der Nation.* Cologne, 1975.
*Einmischung erwünscht: Schriften zur Zeit.* Cologne, 1977.
*Querschnitte aus Interviews, Aufsätze und Reden von Heinrich Böll.* Edited by Viktor Böll and Renate Matthaei. Cologne, 1977.
*Vermintes Gelände: Essayistische Schriften, 1977–1981.* Cologne, 1982.
*Bild, Bonn, Boenisch.* Bornheim, 1984.
*Ein- und Zusprüche: Schriften, Reden und Prosa 1981–1983.* Cologne, 1984.
*Die Fähigkeit zu trauern: Schriften und Reden, 1983–1985.* Bornheim, 1986.
*Rom auf den ersten Blick: Landschaften, Städte, Reisen.* Bornheim, 1987.

COLLECTED WORKS

*Werke.* Edited by Bernd Balzer. 10 vols. Cologne, 1977–1978. The first five volumes, which appeared in 1977, make up the most complete collection of Böll's novels and stories. The second five volumes, which appeared in 1978, contain the most complete collection of Böll's radio plays, dramas, film texts, poems, essays, reviews, speeches, commentaries, interviews, and sundry writings.

TRANSLATIONS

*Absent Without Leave, and Other Stories.* Translated by Leila Vennewitz. New York, 1965.

*Acquainted with the Night.* Translated by Richard Graves. New York, 1954.

*Adam, and the Train: Two Novels.* Translated by Leila Vennewitz. New York, 1970.

*Adam, Where Art Thou?* Translated by Mervyn Savill. New York, 1955.

*And Never Said a Word.* Translated by Leila Vennewitz. New York, 1978.

*Billiards at Half-Past Nine.* Translated by Patrick Bowles. London, 1961.

*The Bread of Those Early Years.* Translated by Leila Vennewitz. New York, 1976.

*The Casualty.* Translated by Leila Vennewitz. New York, 1986.

*Children Are Civilians Too.* Translated by Leila Vennewitz. New York, 1970.

*The Clown.* Translated by Leila Vennewitz. New York, 1965.

*Eighteen Stories.* Translated by Leila Vennewitz. New York, 1966.

*End of a Mission.* Translated by Leila Vennewitz. New York, 1968.

*Group Portrait with Lady.* Translated by Leila Vennewitz. New York, 1973.

*Irish Journal.* Translated by Leila Vennewitz. New York, 1967.

*The Lost Honor of Katharina Blum; or, How Violence Develops and Where It Can Lead.* Translated by Leila Vennewitz. New York, 1975.

*Missing Persons and Other Essays.* Translated by Leila Vennewitz. New York, 1977.

"Poetry to 1972." Translated by Robert C. Conard in collaboration with Ralph Ley. *University of Dayton Review* 13, no. 1:23–44. (Winter 1976).

"Poetry from 1972–1984." Translated by Robert C. Conard in collaboration with Ralph Ley. *University of Dayton Review* 17, no. 2:5–14 (Summer 1985).

*The Safety Net.* Translated by Leila Vennewitz. New York, 1982.

*A Soldier's Legacy.* Translated by Leila Vennewitz. New York, 1985.

*The Stories of Heinrich Böll.* Translated by Leila Vennewitz. New York, 1986.

*Tomorrow and Yesterday.* Translated by Leila Vennewitz. New York, 1957.

*The Train Was on Time.* Translated by Richard Graves. New York, 1956. Translated by Leila Vennewitz. New York, 1970.

*Traveller, If You Come to Spa . . .* Translated by Mervyn Savill. London, 1956.

*The Unguarded House.* Translated by Mervyn Savill. London, 1957.

*What's to Become of the Boy? or, Something to Do with Books.* Translated by Leila Vennewitz. New York, 1984.

*Women in a River Landscape: A Novel in Dialogues and Soliloquies.* Translated by David McLintock. New York, 1988.

BIOGRAPHICAL AND CRITICAL STUDIES

Armster, Charlotte. "Katharina Blum: Violence and the Exploitation of Sexuality." In *Women in German Yearbook,* vol. 4, edited by Marianna Burkhard Jeanette Clausen. Lanham, Md., 1988.

Arnold, Heinz Ludwig. "Im Gespräch." (Interview with Böll.) In *Edition Text und Kritik* (1971).

Beck, Evelyn T. "A Feminist Critique of Böll's *Ansichten eines Clowns." University of Dayton Review* 12, no. 2:19–24 (1976).

Bernhard, Hans Joachim. *Die Romane Heinrich Bölls: Gesellschaftskritik und Gemeinschaftsutopie.* 2nd ed. Berlin, 1973.

Beth, Hanno, ed. *Heinrich Böll: Eine Einführung in das Gesellschaftskritik und Gemeinschaftsutopie.* 2nd ed. Berlin, 1973.

Bienek, Horst. *Werkstattgespräche mit Schriftstellern.* Munich, 1962.

Carlson, Ingeborg L. "Heinrich Bölls *Gruppenbild mit Dame* als frohe Botschaft der Weltverbrüderung." *University of Dayton Review* 11, no. 2:51–64 (1974).

Cases, Cesare. "'Der Waage der Baleks,' dreimal gelesen." In *In Sachen Böll,* edited by Marcel Reich-Ranicki. 3d ed. Cologne, 1970.

Conard, Robert C. "The Humanity of Heinrich Böll: Love and Religion." *Boston University Journal* 21, no. 2:35–42 (1973).

———."The Relationship of Heinrich Böll's Satire

'The Thrower-away' to Jonathan Swift's 'A Modest Proposal.'" *Michigan Academician* 10, no. 1:37–46 (1977).

———. *Heinrich Böll.* Boston, 1981.

———. "Heinrich Böll's Political Reevaluation of Adalbert Stifter: An Interpretation of Böll's 'Epilog zu Stifters *Nachsommer*.'" *Michigan Academician* 14, no. 1:31–39 (1981).

———. "Heinrich Böll's 'Nicht nur zur Weihnachtszeit': A Satire for All Ages." *Germanic Review* 59, no. 3:97–103 (1984).

Deschner, Margareta. "Böll's 'Lady': A New Eve." *University of Dayton Review* 11, no. 2:11–24 (1974).

———. "Heinrich Böll's Utopian Feminism." *University of Dayton Review* 17, no. 2:119–128 (1985).

Durzak, Manfred. *Der deutsche Roman der Gegenwart.* Stuttgart, 1971.

———. "Heinrich Bölls epische Summe? Zur Analyse und Wirkung seines Romans 'Gruppenbild mit Dame.'" In *Basis: Jahrbuch für deutsche Gegenwarts literatur,* vol. 3, edited by Reinhold Grimm and Jost Hermand. Frankfurt am Main, 1972.

———, ed. *Gespräche über den Roman.* Frankfurt am Main, 1976.

Fetzer, John. "The Scales of Injustice: Comments on Heinrich Böll's *Die Waage der Baleks.*" *German Quarterly* 45:472–479 (1972).

Friedrichsmeyer, Erhard. "Böll's Satires." *University of Dayton Review* 10, no. 2:5–10 (1973).

———. *Die satirische Kurzprosa Heinrich Bölls.* Chapel Hill, N.C., 1981.

———. "Böll's Short Stories Since 1977." *University of Dayton Review* 17, no. 2:63–70 (1985).

Ghurye, Charlotte W. "Heinrich Böll's *Fürsorgliche Belagerung:* A Bloodless Novel of Terrorism?" *University of Dayton Review* 17, no. 2:77–82 (1985).

Grothmann, Wilhelm H. "Zur Struktur des Humors in Heinrich Bölls *Gruppenbild mit Dame.*" *German Quarterly* 50:150–160 (1977).

Grützbach, Frank, ed. *Heinrich Böll: Freies Geleit für Ulrike Meinhof. Ein Artikel und seine Folgen.* Cologne, 1972.

Haase, Horst. "Charakter und Funktion der zentralen Symbolik in Heinrich Bölls Roman *Billard um halbzehn.*" *Weimarer Beiträge* 10:219–226 (1964).

Hoffmann, Christine Gabriele. *Heinrich Böll.* Hamburg, 1976; Bornheim, 1986.

Jeziorkowski, Klaus. *Rhythmus und Figur. Zur Technik der epischen Konstruktion in Heinrich Bölls "Der Wegwerfer" und "Billard um halbzehn."* Bad Homburg, 1968.

Jurgensen, Manfred, ed. *Böll: Untersuchung zum Werk.* Bern, 1975.

Kurz, Paul Konrad. "Heinrich Böll: Die Renunziation des Krieges und der Katholiken." *Stimmen der Zeit* 96:17–30 (1971).

———. "Heinrich Böll: Nicht versöhnt." *Stimmen der Zeit* 96:88–97 (1971).

Kuschel, Karl-Josef. "The Christianity of Heinrich Böll." *Cross Currents* (Dobbs Ferry, N.Y.) 39 (1):21–36 (Spring 1989).

Ley, Ralph. *Böll für Zeitgenossen: Ein kulturgeschichtliches Lesebuch.* New York, 1970.

———. "Compassion, Catholicism, and Communism: Reflections on Böll's *Gruppenbild mit Dame.*" *University of Dayton Review* 10, no. 2:25–40 (1973).

MacPherson, Enid. *A Student's Guide to Böll.* London, 1972.

Matthaei, Renate, ed. *Die subversive Madonna: Ein Schlüssel zum Werk Heinrich Bölls.* Cologne, 1975.

Murray, Anne Louise. "Satirical Elements in the Narrative Prose of Heinrich Böll." Ph. D. diss., Indiana University, 1972.

Myers, David. "Heinrich Böll's *Gruppenbild mit Dame:* Aesthetic Play and Ethnical Seriousness." *Seminar* 13:189–198 (1977).

Nägele, Rainer. *Heinrich Böll: Einführung in das Werk und in die Forschung.* Frankfurt am Main, 1976.

Nahrgang, W. Lee, "Heinrich Böll's Pacifism: Its Roots and Nature." *University of Dayton Review* 17, no. 2:107–118 (1985).

Parent, David. "Böll's 'Wanderer kommst du nach Spa . . .': A Reply to Schiller's 'Der Spaziergang.'" *Essays in Literature* 1:109–117 (1974).

Pickar, Gertrud B. "The Impact of Narrative Perspective on Character Portrayal in Three Novels of Heinrich Böll." *University of Dayton Review* 11, no. 2:25–40 (1974).

———. "The Symbolic Use of Color in Heinrich Böll's *Billard um halbzehn.*" *University of Dayton* Review 12, no. 2:41–50 (1976).

———. "Game Playing, Re-entry, and Withdrawal:

Patterns of Societal Interaction in *Billard um halbzehn* and *Fürsorgliche Belagerung.*" *University of Dayton Review* 17, no. 2:83–106 (1985).

Poser, Therese. "Billard um halbzehn." In *Möglichkeiten des deutschen Romans: Analysen und Interpretationsgrundlagen zu Romanen von Thomas Mann, Alfred Döblin, Hermann Broch, Gerd Gaiser, Max Frisch, Alfred Andersch und Heinrich Böll,* edited by Rolf Geissler. Frankfurt, 1962.

Rectanus, Mark W. "*The Lost Honor of Katharina Blum:* The Reception of a German Best-Seller in the USA." *German Quarterly* 59:252–269 (1986).

Reich-Ranicki, Marcel. *Deutsche Literatur in West und Ost.* Munich, 1963.

———, ed. *In Sachen Böll.* 3rd ed. Cologne, 1970.

Reid, James Henderson. *Heinrich Böll; Withdrawal and Reemergence.* London, 1973.

———. "Böll's Names." *Modern Language Review* 69:575–583 (1974).

———. *Heinrich Böll: A German for His Time.* Oxford, 1988.

Schwarz, Wilhelm Johannes. *Heinrich Böll, Teller of Tales: A Study of His Work and Characters.* Translated by Alexander Henderson and Elizabeth Henderson. New York, 1969.

Schröter, Klaus. *Heinrich Böll in Selbstzeugnissen und Bilddokumenten.* Reinbek, 1982.

Wirth, Günter. *Heinrich Böll. Essayistische Studie über religiöse und gesellschaftliche Motive im Prosawerk des Dichters.* Berlin, 1967.

Ziolkowski, Theodore. "Heinrich Böll: Conscience and Craft." *Books Abroad* 34:213–222 (1960).

———. "Albert Camus and Heinrich Böll." *Modern Language Notes* 7:282–291 (1962).

———. "The Author as *Advocatus Dei* in Heinrich Böll's *Group Portrait with Lady.*" *University of Dayton Review* 12, no. 2:7–18 (1976).

ROBERT C. CONARD

# ALEKSANDR SOLZHENITSYN

## *(b. 1918)*

### *LIFE*

BY THE TIMING of his birth on 11 December, 1918, Aleksandr Solzhenitsyn automatically earned the designation of "October child." This was a Soviet term for youngsters born soon after the 1917 October Revolution who were expected, as members of an entirely new generation, to complete the glorious social structure projected by the architects of communism. These expectations proved completely inaccurate, and in Solzhenitsyn's case particularly so. He was destined to experience at first hand the nightmare reality lurking behind the facade of lofty slogans, and by the power of his pen to do more than any other human being to demolish the mendacious myths on which the Soviet system is based.

Aleksandr Isaevich Solzhenitsyn was born in Kislovodsk, a small town in the Caucasus mountains that was about to be engulfed in the Russian Civil War. Both parents were of peasant stock, but their ties to the traditional way of life had been loosened by extensive schooling. The future writer's father, Isaaki Solzhenitsyn, had left the family farm to pursue an education and was enrolled at Moscow University at the outbreak of World War I. Despite pacifist leanings inspired by the teachings of Tolstoy, he dropped out of college to enlist in the military, serving with distinction as an artillery officer. The writer's mother (née Taissia Shcherbak), the daughter of a prosperous Ukrainian farmer, had graduated from an exclusive girls' school and was studying at an agricultural academy in Moscow when she met Isaaki Solzhenitsyn. The pair were married in 1917, but Solzhenitsyn's father did not live to see his firstborn: he died as a result of a hunting accident several months before Aleksandr's birth.

After the untimely death of her husband and the expropriation of her father's land and possessions by the Bolsheviks, Taissia Solzhenitsyn had no choice but to seek employment, a task made difficult by the new regime's policy of deliberate discrimination against relatives of former landowners and officers. The meager earnings brought in by sporadic work as typist and stenographer in Rostov-on-Don were barely enough to sustain mother and son, and Solzhenitsyn's childhood was a time of severe and continuous deprivation. Yet despite these hardships, and despite the lack of sympathy for the Soviet regime among the family's closest circle of friends, we have the writer's recollection that he soon began to be swayed by the ideological fervor of the time. Soviet education was winning him over, and by the late 1930's Solzhenitsyn had become a committed disciple of Marx and Lenin.

The same years also marked the beginning of persistent literary experimentation in both prose and verse. Solzhenitsyn dismissed these early writings as "the usual adolescent nonsense," but with one significant exception: during his last year in high school and first year at university, Solzhenitsyn had undertaken extensive research into the Russian army's ill-conceived invasion of Eastern Prussia in August of 1914, his ultimate purpose being to incorporate an account of the ensuing Russian defeat into a large epic devoted to the Russian Revolution. We can easily recognize Solzhenitsyn's *Avgust chetyrnadtsatogo* (*August 1914,* 1971; complete text, 1983) and its sequels in this early design, even though in the intervening decades the author's views of the Revolution itself were to undergo a radical transformation.

Solzhenitsyn entered Rostov University in 1937, specializing in mathematics and physics despite his growing interest in literature. His choice was in large part determined by concern for his ailing mother, who had developed tuberculosis and was by now too ill to move from Rostov or to be left behind if he were to enroll in an institution where literature was taught at a level more sophisticated than that available in Rostov. (In later years Solzhenitsyn came to regard this decision as providential, since it was precisely his diploma in mathematics that would bring about his removal from labor camp—at a time when his physical survival was at risk—to the relative security of a closed prison institute.)

In any event, Solzhenitsyn was outstandingly successful in his university career, an excellent academic record being matched by his enthusiastic involvement in activities such as the editorship of a student newspaper. He also managed to undertake a systematic study of literature through a correspondence course offered by the prestigious Moscow Institute of Philosophy, Literature, and History (MIFLI). His manifold activities did not prevent him from striking out in other directions as well. He met and courted Natalia Reshetovskaia, a fellow student at the university who, just like himself, was studying science but in addition had extensive interests in music. They were married in 1940.

Solzhenitsyn graduated with distinction in the spring of 1941, but instead of looking for a position in science or mathematics, he resolved to take up the full-time study of literature in Moscow. As he arrived in the capital in June of that year, the Nazi attack on the Soviet Union made shambles of all his plans. Solzhenitsyn immediately tried to enlist, but to his great chagrin was disqualified on medical grounds. Four months later, however, he was called up for service in a horse-drawn transport unit. Frustrated by the unfamiliar task of dealing with horses, Solzhenitsyn wrote incessant appeals to be transferred to the front. At last his luck changed and he was admitted to a wartime training course for artillery officers. His skill in mathematics determined the rest: Solzhenitsyn came to specialize in sound ranging, a technique whereby the location of an enemy battery is determined by means of dispersed microphones.

Commissioned in 1942, Solzhenitsyn soon received command of his own battery, and from mid 1943 until 1945 was involved in major action at the front. In military terms his record was excellent: his unit won top ranking for discipline and battle effectiveness, while he himself was twice decorated for personal heroism and promoted to captain. He was brought low by a lack of political caution. For some months he had carried on a correspondence with a fellow officer in another unit, a good friend from Rostov who, like Solzhenitsyn, had developed serious reservations about Stalin and his policies. Assuming that personal mail would be subjected to merely superficial censorship, the two friends had exchanged views on this subject in only slightly veiled fashion.

They were quite mistaken. Solzhenitsyn was arrested at the front in February 1945, brought to Moscow for interrogation, and sentenced to eight years in corrective labor camps for "anti-Soviet agitation" and "malicious slander." The most important phase of his education was about to begin.

Solzhenitsyn served the first part of his sentence in labor camps in the outskirts of Moscow and inside the city itself. In volume 2 of *Arkhipelag GULag* (*The Gulag Archipelago,*

1973–1975), the writer gives an unsparing account of himself during this period, when naiveté and a complete lack of psychological preparation led him to humiliating compromises with his conscience. He was also reaching the point of physical collapse and almost certainly would not have survived had he not attracted the regime's attention with his background in mathematics. It was common practice at the time to put prisoners with specialized training to work in prison research institutes (referred to as *sharashkas*), and in mid 1947 Solzhenitsyn was pulled out of camp and assigned to Marfino, an institute that was charged with designing and producing a telephone scrambler. Apart from a marked improvement of living conditions—there was no exhausting physical labor and the diet was more substantial—the three years he spent there were for Solzhenitsyn a time of great intellectual growth. His Marxist faith had already been shaken to its roots by his earlier labor camp experiences; and at the Marfino *sharashka* he was able to test and realign his evolving views in the process of endless philosophical debates with several friends. In the novel *V kruge pervom* (*The First Circle,* 1968; full version, 1978), Solzhenitsyn's ideological and spiritual odyssey is ascribed to Gleb Nerzhin, a fictional character whose fate has many points in common with Solzhenitsyn's own experience in Marfino.

In 1950, on account of a conflict with the authorities, Solzhenitsyn was expelled from the prison institute and transported to a newly organized camp for political prisoners in Ekibastuz, part of an immense forced-labor empire sprawled over the plains of Soviet Central Asia. The three years at this camp were eventually to provide Solzhenitsyn with rich material for his future work. By turns a common laborer, a bricklayer, and a foundryman, Solzhenitsyn also witnessed a major protest strike by the prisoners and came into contact with numerous individuals who had long histories of incarceration in various Soviet prisons and camps. The implacable routine of the camp system and its effect on a representative cross-section of the inmate population is depicted in Solzhenitsyn's *Odin den' Ivana Denisovicha* (*One Day in the Life of Ivan Denisovich,* 1962), while many of the accounts he heard from his new acquaintances were later incorporated into *The Gulag Archipelago.*

In 1952 Solzhenitsyn underwent surgery in the camp hospital for the removal of a large cancerous swelling. The procedure was deemed a success at the time, and Solzhenitsyn later related that at a certain point during his convalescence he felt the need to rededicate himself to the Christian faith of his childhood. That same year brought him the depressing news that his wife, who had earlier filed divorce papers for the semblance of dissociating herself from an "enemy of the people," had now finalized the divorce proceeding and was living with another man.

Solzhenitsyn was released from camp in March 1953, shortly after his eight-year sentence had expired. But instead of being granted full freedom, former political prisoners were routinely confined "in perpetuity" to places of internal exile determined by the authorities. In Solzhenitsyn's case this was Kok-Terek, a tiny hamlet on the southern border of Kazakhstan, where the writer eventually received a job as a teacher of mathematics and physics at the local school. All his spare time was now taken up by a feverish haste to record on paper the prodigious amount of verse he had composed in the preceding years. Camp regulations had strictly forbidden inmates from keeping any notes, but Solzhenitsyn had hit upon a method of preserving his thoughts: he cast them in poetic form and committed them to memory, using an elaborate ritual to review the growing text at regular intervals. The major product of this activity was the narrative poem "Dorozhenka" (The way), which allegedly contained over 10,000 lines of verse. Solzhenitsyn later expressed reservations about the poetic quality of this text, and for this reason allowed only small sections to be published, but "Dorozhenka" served him as a repository of his thoughts and feelings during the time of his imprisonment. The title itself is clearly a metaphor for the intellectual and spiritual odyssey of the autobiographical protagonist, set against the kaleidoscopic background of events that he had witnessed. The poem, prefigured in a fundamental manner much of Solzhenitsyn's later work, reflecting both his extraordinary drive to record past experience, and his constant attempt to draw meaning from the raw data of life by subjecting it to the discipline of literary form.

Other works composed and memorized in camp, but recorded in full written form only in Kok-Terek, are *Prusskie nochi* (*Prussian Nights,* 1974), *Pir pobeditelei* (*Victory Celebrations,* 1981) and *Plenniki* (*Prisoners,* 1981). The first two were in fact originally part of "Dorozhenka," but then evolved into independent works. All three are based on the author's experiences in early 1945, at first as an officer in the victoriously advancing Soviet army and then as a prisoner of Soviet counterintelligence.

Some months after settling in Kok-Terek, Solzhenitsyn's ambitious literary plans suddenly appeared to turn moot. He had developed acute abdominal pains that were diagnosed as cancer and probably stemmed from a metastasis of the cancerous growth excised in camp. By late 1953 he was desperately ill and was given only a few weeks to live. Racked by pain and filled with despair that his writings would now be lost, Solzhenitsyn buried them in his garden and undertook an arduous journey to a cancer clinic in Tashkent; his stay there later found reflection in the novel *Rakovyi korpus* (*Cancer Ward,* 1968).

Massive radiation treatment succeeded in shrinking Solzhenitsyn's tumor substantially, and in 1954 he was able to resume his duties as a teacher in Kok-Terek, while continuing to dedicate all his spare time to writing. His next work was another play on the labor-camp theme, ironically entitled *Respublika truda* (Republic of labor, 1981). (The version of this text published under the title *Olen' i shalashovka* [*The Love-Girl and the Innocent,* 1969] was prepared in 1962 in the hope of a Soviet theatrical performance; it represents an abridged and "softened" variant in which Solzhenitsyn also changed the names of many characters.) And in 1955 he began work on what was to become the masterly novel *The First Circle.*

The liberalization that followed Stalin's demise in 1953 had direct consequences for Solzhenitsyn. His sentence of "perpetual exile" was annulled in 1956, and Solzhenitsyn was permitted to return to the European part of Russia. He first took up residence in Miltsevo, a small village about a hundred miles east of Moscow, where he resumed teaching school and using all his spare time to write. The first draft of *The First Circle* was completed here, and Miltsevo became the setting of his famous short story entitled "Matrenin dvor" ("Matryona's Home," 1963).

In the following year the criminal charges that had originally led to Solzhenitsyn's arrest in 1945 were reviewed by one of Nikita Khrushchev's "rehabilitation tribunals" and declared invalid; Solzhenitsyn was issued an official certificate clearing his record. In 1957 he also reinstated his marriage to Natalia Reshetovskaia, moving with her to Ryazan, a provincial town southeast of Moscow, where he soon settled into his by now familiar routine of teaching physics and writing in secret.

The next three years were representative of the astonishing productivity that marked Solzhenitsyn's entire career as a writer. He undertook a fundamental revision of *The First Circle,* laid the groundwork for the project that would eventually grow into *The Gulag Archipelago,* completed a cycle of contemplative prose sketches, composed a screenplay about a camp uprising (*Znaiut istinu tanki* [Tanks Know the Truth], 1981), tried his hand at a play deliberately set outside any specific historical context (*Svecha na vetru* [*A Candle in the Wind,* 1969]), and wrote three prose works of great significance: the narrative that later acquired the title *One Day in the Life of Ivan Denisovich,* and two short stories of more conventional length, "Matryona's Home" and "Pravaia kist'" ("The Right Hand," 1968). All of these works, it must be noted, were written "for the drawer," that is, without the hope of having them appear in print during the author's lifetime.

*One Day* was the text that was destined to change all that. Following the Twenty-Second Congress of the Soviet Communist Party in October 1961, at which Stalinism had been ringingly denounced, Solzhenitsyn decided to risk submitting his manuscript to *Novyi mir,* the Soviet Union's most respected literary monthly. In *Bodalsia telenok s dubom* (*The Oak and the Calf,* 1975), Solzhenitsyn's account of his uneven struggle with the regime, the writer relates with great verve how clever planning by intermediaries got the text directly into the hands of Aleksandr Tvardovsky, the chief editor, who expressed enthusiasm but had to undertake extraordinary further maneuvers to see the story into print.

The appearance of *One Day* in the November 1962 issue of *Novyi mir* was immediately recognized as an event of great significance. While the West treated it primarily as a political bombshell, the official Soviet interpretation sought to present the story as an excoriation of the abuses of the Stalinist past, now safely and irrevocably gone. For the many millions of ordinary citizens who had come face-to-face with the reality of the camps, however, the impact of the text was of a different order entirely. *One Day* was the first "legitimate" publication to address the camp theme honestly—this after decades of official evasions or outright denials concerning the very existence of the labor camp system. In such a context the story represented a powerful reaffirmation of objective reality, a public acknowledgement that the suffering inflicted—but long denied recognition—had indeed taken place. It was perceived as a restoration of the past and a redemption of lost time, for this reason evoking an emotional response of great intensity. At the same time those who preferred to erase this terrible period of Soviet history from their memory were also profoundly disturbed by *One Day.*

As a result of this publication Solzhenitsyn was inundated with letters. The majority of correspondents expressed fervent approval and gratitude; many described their own camp experiences or offered to do so. A few years earlier Solzhenitsyn had begun sketching out plans for a historical survey of the Soviet penal system, but had abandoned the project as too ambitious. But now fate itself seemed to be summoning him to this task, and in the course of 1963 and 1964 he met privately with many of his correspondents in order to record their accounts in as much detail as possible. Most of this data was eventually incorporated into *The Gulag Archipelago.*

Meanwhile, the wave of liberalization in the Soviet Union that had made the publication of *One Day* possible was already beginning to recede, with immediate consequences for Solzhenitsyn. Increasingly hostile criticism was levelled at his prose works published in *Novyi mir* in the months following the appearance of *One Day* (especially "Matryona's Home"), and his nomination for the Lenin Prize in 1964 was sabotaged at the last moment by floating the shameless allegation that Solzhenitsyn had been a Nazi collaborator during the war. The atmosphere deteriorated further after the late-1964 coup that removed Khrushchev from power. Under the circumstances, Solzhenitsyn's attempts to get a revised and toned-down version of *The First Circle* published in *Novyi mir* were doomed to failure, and the writer decided to have a microfilm of the manuscript spirited abroad in 1964.

Things took another sharp turn for the worse in 1965 when KGB raids on the apartments of two friends resulted in the confiscation of a large volume of Solzhenitsyn's notes, files, and manuscripts of unpublished works. Apart from *The First Circle,* the latter included early plays like *Victory Celebrations,* where the unmistakable expressions of hostility toward the regime could easily serve as grounds for arrest. In fact the authorities soon began making selective use of the confiscated material in an effort to discredit the writer. This development, and

Solzhenitsyn's inability to get his major new work, *Cancer Ward* (written during 1963–1966), into print, seems to have precipitated the writer's resolve to reach his readers in ways defined by himself. In the Soviet Union of the 1960's this meant releasing a copy of the manuscript into the so-called samizdat network, an informal system whereby texts that had not received (or could not receive) official sanction for publication were manually retyped in several copies and distributed chain-letter fashion among like-minded individuals.

In general Solzhenitsyn became increasingly bold in his actions and outspoken in his expression of antipathy for the authorities; the image of him as the tough infighter and master strategist in the struggle with the Soviet regime dates primarily from the post-1965 period. In sharp contrast to his previous tendency to withdraw from the public eye, Solzhenitsyn now made a point of being noticed, firing off eloquent protests, agreeing to give public readings from his works, and even granting interviews to foreign correspondents. His most conspicuous act of defiance at the time was the 1967 open letter to the Soviet Writers' Union in which he bitterly rebuked the organization for its craven acceptance of everything the regime had dished out over the years, from the heavy-handed censorship of literary works to the physical persecution of hundreds of writers. The letter was individually sent to some 250 delegates attending the Fourth Congress of Soviet Writers, but discussion of the topics it raised was blocked by the union's leadership.

Apart from such highly visible activities Solzhenitsyn was moving with even greater resolve behind the scenes. In conditions of utmost secrecy he undertook the gargantuan task of weaving together the data contained in the testimonies he had collected from hundreds of former inmates of Soviet camps and prisons into an 1800-page-long historical overview of the entire system entitled *The Gulag Archipelago.* In 1968 he microfilmed the completed study and had the film smuggled abroad for safekeeping. And a year earlier he had given a signal to proceed with the publication of *The First Circle* in the West. Meanwhile, *Cancer Ward* had crossed the border of its own accord (such was the typical result of samizdat distribution) and in 1968 Solzhenitsyn had the satisfaction of seeing the virtually simultaneous appearance of these two major works in the leading Western countries. The critical reception was overwhelmingly positive, and from now on Solzhenitsyn's formidable international reputation could not but inhibit the Soviet regime from undertaking any extreme actions against him.

But the writer had no intention of resting on the laurels of these victories. With his customary energy he next turned to the vastly ambitious project that he described as the "principal task" of his life. This was the multipart historical epic centered on the Russian Revolution, collectively known as *Krasnoe koleso* (*The Red Wheel*), in which *August 1914* represented the first installment or "knot" (*uzel*). Working with intense concentration in 1969 and 1970, Solzhenitsyn completed the version of this volume that appeared in Paris in 1971. (A substantially expanded edition was published in two volumes in 1983.)

In the meantime there had been new developments in the ongoing duel between the writer and the authorities. In late 1969 Solzhenitsyn was summarily expelled from the Union of Soviet Writers for "antisocial behavior" and views judged to be "radically in conflict with the aims and purposes" of the organization. In the Soviet context this action could be a damaging blow, since it formally closed access to "legitimate" publication and rendered the writer technically unemployed (a punishable offense under Soviet law). In this particular instance, however, Soviet journals were already closed to Solzhenitsyn, and the regime must have been painfully surprised by the outpouring of protest from Western writers and literary associations that followed the expulsion. Moreover, the action of the Writers'

Union apparently played a role in Solzhenitsyn's decision in 1970 to retain a Swiss lawyer in order to look after his interests abroad, which was by Soviet standards an unprecedented arrangement.

In October 1970 the Nobel Prize for literature was awarded to Solzhenitsyn "for the ethical force with which he has pursued the indispensable traditions of Russian literature." In the eight short years since the appearance of *One Day,* Solzhenitsyn had risen to the pinnacle of international fame and had without question become the world's most celebrated living author.

The writer accepted the prize gratefully and expressed the intention of attending the award ceremonies, but a furious campaign launched against him in the Soviet press forced a change of plans, since it seemed likely that he would be barred from returning to his homeland. A further shadow was cast on the event by the refusal of the Swedish government to allow an alternative award ceremony to take place in their embassy building in Moscow, evidently for fear of offending Soviet sensibilities. (No mutually satisfactory procedure could be worked out at the time, and the Nobel insignia were presented to Solzhenitsyn four years later, when the writer was already living in the West.)

At the very time of the Nobel Prize announcement and its aftermath, Solzhenitsyn was in the midst of a painful crisis in his relationship with Natalia Reshetovskaia. He and Reshetovskaia had been steadily drifting apart during the preceding several years, but now matters had come to a head when Solzhenitsyn revealed his relationship with another woman, one that he had no intention of terminating. The distraught Reshetovskaia made an attempt to commit suicide. Her life was saved, but Solzhenitsyn now resolved to press for a divorce, and despite Reshetovskaia's opposition and her appeal to a Soviet court, the break was finalized in early 1973. Shortly thereafter Solzhenitsyn married Natalia Svetlova, a mathematician by training, who in due course became his irreplaceable assistant and confidante, the trusted editor of his works, and the mother of his three sons.

Although the press campaign against Solzhenitsyn occasioned by the Nobel Prize soon began to abate, there were signs that the regime was preparing more serious moves. In August 1971 the summer cottage Solzhenitsyn had been using as a retreat was ransacked by a group of KGB operatives during his absence, and a friend who happened to stumble onto the scene was savagely beaten and threatened. Meanwhile, another group of agents was dispatched to Solzhenitsyn's birthplace in the hope of uncovering damaging information about his background. And with the same goal in mind, the Soviet press agency Novosti approached Reshetovskaia, offering to publish her reminiscences of Solzhenitsyn. She agreed, and the Russian version of her heavily doctored text appeared in 1975.

But by far the most ominous development was the mid-1973 arrest of Elizaveta Voronianskaia, a Leningrad woman who had helped Solzhenitsyn in the typing of his manuscripts. After days of relentless interrogation by the KGB, Voronianskaia had revealed the hiding place of a manuscript copy of *The Gulag Archipelago*; soon thereafter she was either murdered or committed suicide. Solzhenitsyn reacted to this tragic news with the only response he considered appropriate: *The Gulag Archipelago* now needed to be published without delay and in its entirety. The corresponding instructions were sent to Solzhenitsyn's Swiss lawyer, and the first volume of the Russian edition appeared in Paris at the very end of 1973, making front-page news around the world.

The impact of *The Gulag Archipelago* in the West can be compared only to the seismic shock produced by *One Day* upon Soviet readers. The facts laid out in Solzhenitsyn's history of Soviet prisons and camps were in themselves not really new, since both specialist studies and numerous memoirs by former inmates had been available in the West for many years. Yet despite this, and despite the de-Stalinization campaign waged by Khrushchev a decade earlier, Western public opinion had to a large degree retained a visceral distrust of information of this sort. It was therefore a measure of Solzhenitsyn's skill as a writer that by the force of his narrative he was able to break this pattern of automatic skepticism, and to convince millions of readers of the stark reality of his portrayal. In this sense *The Gulag Archipelago* will undoubtedly remain the most shattering blow ever delivered to the image of the Soviet Union.

Predictably enough, the Soviet regime reacted to the appearance of *The Gulag Archipelago* with torrents of vituperation. Journalists vied with milkmaids and lathe operators (who had of course not laid eyes on the work in question) in denouncing the author in essays and outraged letters to the editor. Solzhenitsyn was called a psychotic renegade choking with hatred for the country of his birth, a corrupt offspring of embittered class enemies, a despicable Judas dancing to the tune of Western warmongers and Red-baiters, a Nazi sympathizer, a slimy reptile, and so on. There were also threatening phone calls to his Moscow apartment and leering notes in the mail.

Unpleasant as this orchestrated eruption of hatred must have been, Solzhenitsyn was inclined to believe that the storm would blow over, just as the earlier press campaign against him had not led to any further action. This time he was wrong. On 12 February 1974 a large party of KGB agents showed up at his door with an order for his arrest. Solzhenitsyn was taken to Lefortovo prison, subjected to all the humiliating procedures for incoming prisoners, charged with treason, stripped of his Soviet citizenship, and on the next day expelled to West Germany on a plane specially reserved for this purpose. In *The Oak and the Calf* the writer gives an extraordinarily vivid account of these two days and of the inner tumult to which they gave rise.

Solzhenitsyn first set up residence in Zurich (where his wife and family joined him after being allowed to leave the USSR), but soon began to look for a place more suited to his need for privacy, and in mid 1976 he relocated to the United States, settling in Cavendish, a village in a sparsely populated area of southern Vermont.

During his initial years in the West, Solzhenitsyn travelled widely, consenting to a number of appearances and interviews. Some of these became major public events, as for example his television discussion with several short-tempered French intellectuals (April 1975), his blunt remarks in Washington and New York about the illusions of détente (June and July 1975), his speeches to the British on television and radio (February 1976), and his celebrated commencement address at Harvard University (June 1978).

While the interest generated by each of these occasions was considerable—in some cases it was enormous—Solzhenitsyn's public pronouncements did not meet with unanimous approval in the West. Rather, there rose an ever-increasing chorus of dissent, much of it based on genuine disagreement with Solzhenitsyn's message. The writer's belief in the irredeemably evil and hence "unreformable" nature of communism collided with deeply ingrained Marxist sympathies, while his sharp rebuke of the West for what he considered its loss of moral fortitude was deemed shrill and offensive by some. It was charged that the writer's public statements lacked the nuance and complexity that distinguished his literary work. Solzhenitsyn was also assailed by angry critics for his alleged hostility to democracy and to the principle of free speech, for supposedly harboring theocratic and monarchist sympathies, and for willfully ignoring the defects of prerevolutionary Russia while exaggerating those of the contemporary West. Solzhenitsyn's many essays and interviews are a large subject in themselves; suffice it to say here that most of the charges listed above could be substantiated only by wrenching the writer's words out of context. The fact remains, nevertheless, that Solzhenitsyn's hitherto unassailable public image in the West sustained damage from these attacks and innuendos. And this, in turn, seems to have contributed to his increasing tendency to abstain from commenting on public issues. Turning his prodigious energies inward, Solzhenitsyn began to concentrate on his own work: in 1978 he launched his authorized collected works, and he immersed himself in the historical cycle initiated by *August 1914.*

Solzhenitsyn nevertheless got involved in one other major project. In 1977 he announced the formation of the Russian Memoir Library, an entity visualized both as a repository for unpublished materials bearing on twentieth-century Russia and as a research facility. He appealed to Russian emigrés to submit manuscripts, letters, and photographs in their possession, urged them to write their own reminiscences, and promised to publish the most interesting of the materials received. By 1988, eight volumes of the memoir series had appeared in print. Solzhenitsyn also sponsored a series of scholarly studies on modern Russian history, and several important titles had been published by the late 1980's. The aim of this undertaking was of course consistent with Solzhenitsyn's entire oeuvre and expressed his overwhelming desire to preserve and rescue from oblivion the true contours of Russian twentieth-century history.

The late 1980's brought promising developments. As the winds of *glasnost* (openness) began sweeping away taboos in Mikhail Gorbachev's Soviet Union, the long-forbidden name of Solzhenitsyn started to crop up in Soviet publications in various positive contexts. In mid 1988 a Moscow periodical called for an annullment of the 1974 charges against Solzhenitsyn and the restoration of his citizenship; the response from readers indicated strong support for the proposal. Meanwhile, *Novyi mir,* the journal on the pages of which Solzhenitsyn had begun his public career as a writer, had succeeded in working out an agreement with him whereby selections from *The Gulag Archipelago* were to appear in early 1989, with the novels *The First Circle* and *Cancer Ward* to follow at a later point. The process of returning Solzhenitsyn to readers in the Soviet Union was due to begin even earlier, with several literary meetings scheduled to coincide with the writer's seventieth birthday on 11 December 1988 and a promised publication of his Nobel Lecture.

But these plans were disrupted at the last moment by the direct intervention of the Politburo. Some of the literary gatherings honoring Solzhenitsyn were cancelled outright, those allowed to proceed were denied press or media coverage. More important, the publication of *Gulag* in *Novyi mir* was officially pronounced to be out of the question. In what was a startling acknowledgement of the power of Solzhenitsyn's writings, the party's chief ideologist declared that to publish such works in the USSR would be "to undermine the foundations on which our present [Soviet] life rests" (*The New York Times,* 30 November 1988).

Absolute as this ban seemed to be, it was breached within only a few months. By mid summer of 1989, Solzhenitsyn's essay entitled "Zhit' ne po Izhi" ("Live Not By Lies," written in 1972–1973 and first published by the London *Daily Express* on 18 February 1974 and then in Russian in Paris the next year) had appeared in a number of Soviet periodicals, the classic short story "Matryona's Home" had been republished in the mass-circulation journal *Ogonyok* (June 1989), an Estonian-language monthly had printed a chapter from *The Gulag Archipelago, Novyi mir* had published the "Nobel Lecture" (July 1989) and was once again announcing plans to serialize substantial portions of *The Gulag Archipelago* on its pages, two large publishing houses were speaking of bringing out editions of selected works, and the leadership of the Writers' Union was said to have voted unanimously for allowing the full text of *Gulag* to be published in the Soviet Union. And thus, despite restrictions and prohibitions the works of Aleksandr Solzhenitsyn began to return to the country for which they were always intended.

## *WORKS*

The study of Solzhenitsyn's works presents certain methodological difficulties. The most fundamental one concerns the textual corpus itself. From 1978 onward Solzhenitsyn oversaw the publication of the authorized *Sobranie sochinenii* (Collected works)[1], but the texts issued in this series often diverge from earlier editions, at times in significant ways. To mention only the most notable examples, *August 1914* grew to almost twice the length of the version published in 1971, *The First Circle* features a completely different plot line in its 1978 edition, and the authorized versions of key works like *One Day* and "Matryona's Home," which were both published in *Novyi mir,* contain passages that could not have appeared on the pages of a Soviet journal in the 1960's.

Some of these changes are simply restorations of texts that had earlier been cut or "toned down" by the author himself as a way of accommodating—or anticipating—the demands of Soviet censorship, others reflect later emendations, still others exhibit a mixture of the two. Any scholarly study should take these variants into account, and there is the further consideration that the extant critical literature is largely based on the earlier editions and could in some cases be textually unsound.

The problem is unfortunately compounded for readers who know no Russian, since beyond the fact that most translators worked with Russian texts that became superseded in the late 1970's and 1980's, the various translated renditions are frequently inadequate, and some contain an inadmissable number of errors.

One other aspect of tangled textual history of Solzhenitsyn's works deserves mention here. The sequence in which Solzhenitsyn's works first appeared in print did not at all correspond to the order in which they were written. The actual chronology became known only later, well after the launching of some spurious notions about the evolution of his thought. Due to the political furor surrounding Solzhenitsyn's name in the 1960's and 1970's, the writer was the subject of much hasty theorizing based on incomplete and erroneous data.

Any approach to Solzhenitsyn must also take into account the literary tradition to which he belongs, since the Russian writer relies on certain assumptions that may not always be familiar to Western readers. Chief among these is the view that literature must not withdraw from the world in quest of aesthetic purity. Together with such predecessors as Tolstoy, Dostoevsky, and Turgenev, Solzhenitsyn believed that the writer must confront issues of great social concern, even if this means coming into conflict with fashionable views or reigning ideologies. In fact it is the writer's moral duty to speak out on such questions, because his special gift of insight gives him the power to discern aspects of reality inaccessible to others. It is unnatural for literature to be artificially separated from the pains and worries of the world.

For the same reason, the Russian literary tradition also rejects any preconceived restriction on what constitutes appropriate form. This point was best articulated by Tolstoy in remarks defending the unusual structure of *War and Peace.* Writing in 1868, Tolstoy claimed that in all of Russian literature "there is not a single artistic prose work, rising at all above mediocrity, which quite fits into the form of a novel, epic, or short story" (*L. N. Tolstoi o literature* [Moscow, 1955], p. 115).

Solzhenitsyn had a similarly unorthodox view of genre conventions, and his prose gravitated toward autobiographical, historical, and

[1] Page references will be to this edition (abbreviated *SS* for *Sobranie sochinenii*) except for items that Solzhenitsyn did not include in the Collected Works series. All translations are by present author.

other nonfictional modes. At the same time those of his works that would seem to be "nonfictional" by design—*The Gulag Archipelago* and *The Oak and the Calf*—were conceived in terms usually associated with aesthetic goals. Such a deliberate confluence of art and reality was a central feature of Solzhenitsyn's writing. Although it had obvious roots in the Russian nineteenth-century tradition, Solzhenitsyn carried it to greater lengths than his predecessors, perplexing critics used to seeing their fiction and nonfiction served in separate, conventionally shaped containers.

### *Early Works*

The earliest work by Solzhenitsyn that has so far appeared in print is *Prussian Nights,* a 1,200-line narrative poem composed in labor camp in 1950. Driving, breathless rhythms usher in a description of the Red Army's tumultuous advance into East Prussia in early 1945, then accompany the portrayal of the looting, arson, rape, and murder that was visited upon the local civilian population with the tacit approval of the Soviet high command.

In *Prussian Nights* the writer traces and effectively dramatizes the painful birth of moral awareness in the first-person narrator who is a witness and participant of these events. At the outset of the poem the narrative voice is not individualized, and we are aware only of the undifferentiated mass of soldiers carried away by their cruelly cheerful savagery ("Let's torch those houses, lads!" [*Prusskie nochi,* p. 7]). Only gradually does a narrator with a separate consciousness emerge, an officer who has deliberately chosen to be an uninvolved observer ("like Pilate" [p. 15]) amid the chaos and destruction that swirl around him. But as the poem progresses, the focus shifts to the growing discord in his mind. He becomes an increasingly willing participant in the injustices committed on all sides, yielding to instincts of greed and sensuality, and drowning out the reproving voice of conscience he makes appeal to facile slogans like "carpe diem" (p. 55). This is not a solution, however, and the dissonance reaches a crescendo in two episodes that form the heart of the narrative. In the first of these, the narrator is shocked to find himself indirectly responsible for a wanton murder he should have, and easily could have, prevented. Shortly thereafter he sets in motion a squalid plan to trap a timid and quietly attractive German woman into having sex with him. The moral ugliness of this act is manifested with searing force as the narrator dwells on the contrast between his own rapacious yet cowardly scheme and the woman's poignantly meek resignation. His revulsion at himself and the moral awakening to which it leads anticipates the intense focus on ethical values that marks all of Solzhenitsyn's subsequent writings.

After the narrative poem, Solzhenitsyn turned to the genre of the drama, and in the next four years composed a trilogy with the collective title *1945.* It consists of *Victory Celebrations,* a verse play labelled a "comedy" by the author and committed to memory in 1951, *Prisoners,* a play identified as a "tragedy" and containing a mixture of prose and verse (also composed in camp in 1952), and the prose drama *Respublika truda* (completed in exile in 1954).

Technically and stylistically, the plays document the writer's experimentation with literary forms that would best serve as vehicles for expressing his thought, among other things reflecting his distinct movement toward prose. Thematically, the plays exhibit numerous motifs elaborated in the writer's later work. A strong autobiographical basis is evident throughout, with the setting and time in each play related fairly closely to Solzhenitsyn's actual experiences in 1945: a banquet on newly overrun East Prussian territory (*Victory Celebrations*), eye-opening conversations among inmates of a jail operated by Soviet counterintelligence (*Prisoners*), and the abysmally corrupt environment of a labor camp (*Respublika truda*). All three plays also feature an important character who is clearly meant as a version of the real Solzhenitsyn. A conscientious and well-meaning individual, this character is depicted as naively unfamiliar with the new realities he needs to face. But he is also a man determined to learn, and, like later autobiographical heroes of Solzhenitsyn's, a stubborn seeker after truth.

The understandably bitter tone of these early plays is to some extent suggested by their titles. *Victory Celebrations* ostensibly takes its name from a lavish banquet organized to mark a Soviet military victory, yet the battle-hardened veterans who gather there are easily cowed by the insinuating remarks of a rookie officer from SMERSH (the Soviet counterespionage service). Solzhenitsyn is sarcastically pointing out who the true victors are. *Prisoners* is more bitter still, since the incarcerated men in this play have no inhibitions about speaking their minds, and we are treated to a series of devastating critiques of the Soviet regime and of communist ideology. The title also draws attention to the paradox that the majority of the prisoners are actually much freer—intellectually, psychologically, and spiritually—than their ideology-bound captors. The title *Respublika truda* (Republic of Labor), finally, refers ironically to the contrast between the professed goals of the forced-labor camps and their grossly inefficient, graft-ridden, and murderous reality.

While it is probably fair to say that the dramatic trilogy does not measure up to the standards of literary excellence achieved in Solzhenitsyn's later prose, it exhibits considerable flair as well as some very inventive language. But perhaps the trilogy's greatest significance was in serving as a sort of workshop in which Solzhenitsyn could test ideas and images on which he then drew later. One obvious continuity involves characters from the trilogy who resurface under the same or a similar name in a work of prose. Thus Gleb Nerzhin, the author's *porte parole* in the novel *The First Circle,* had made earlier appearances in both *Victory Celebrations* and *Respublika truda.* And Lev Rubin, the voluble true believer in communism ever at odds with himself and perhaps the most interesting character in *The First Circle,* has a virtually identical predecessor by the same name in *Prisoners.* But the most surprising migratory figure of this kind is Georgi Vorotyntsev, formerly a colonel in the Imperial Russian Army, who is sentenced to death in the soviet jail depicted in *Prisoners.* Since this is clearly the same character who emerges as a central figure in *August 1914* (written almost two decades later) and then reappears in its sequels, we here get an inkling of the complex interrelationships in Solzhenitsyn's vast artistic world.

In 1955 Solzhenitsyn began work on his first novel, *The First Circle,* a text that underwent several revisions, with the definitive ninety-six-chapter version published only in 1978. All the translations into Western languages, however, are based on a substantially different version containing eighty-seven chapters and published in the West in 1968. This odd state of affairs is the result of rapidly changing official attitudes toward Solzhenitsyn in the mid 1960's. In 1962 the novel (in its ninety-six-chapter form) was considered complete by the author, but Solzhenitsyn was then still an obscure physics teacher who could not seriously contemplate publication of his work. Facing an entirely new situation after the appearance of *One Day,* Solzhenitsyn decided that the novel could be made publishable by cutting and altering certain sections that were too politically explosive to appear in a Soviet journal. The result of this pruning and "softening" was an eighty-seven-chapter version of *The First Circle* that was accepted for publication by the editors of *Novyi mir* in 1964, but blocked by the censors. After some further emendations, Solzhenitsyn released this text for publication abroad, where it appeared in 1968. The ninety-six-chapter version, published ten years later in the *Sobranie sochinenii,* basically restores the 1962 text, but also introduces an unknown number of further changes. The complex textual history of the novel thus spans twenty-three years.

*The First Circle* is based on Solzhenitsyn's experiences during the three years he spent in the prison research institute on the outskirts of Moscow. The title is drawn from Dante's *Inferno,* in which the various circles of hell are enumerated and described. In Dante's scheme the first circle is the region of hell where one finds the souls of virtuous pagans and others who do not deserve the punishment meted out to ordinary sinners. Solzhenitsyn is suggesting an analogy between Dante's idea of a "privileged" section of hell and the special status of the *sharashka* within the Soviet penal system. (Inmates are not forced to engage in physical labor, they are fed reasonably well, and have access to books.)

An enormous cast of characters and a complex narrative structure containing subplots and flashbacks serve two principal goals. The first is to dramatize the quest for moral criteria undertaken by Gleb Nerzhin, an inmate with obvious similarity to Solzhenitsyn himself, as he struggles to find his bearings amid conflicting ideologies and ethical quandaries. The second goal, linked at many levels to the first, is to depict the moral climate of a cross-section of Soviet society during the period of "high Stalinism" (the action is set in late 1949).

The plot connecting these two thematic axes shows substantial differences between the "softened" eighty-seven-chapter version of the novel and the "restored" ninety-six-chapter redaction. In the version familiar from existing translations, a Soviet diplomat named Innokenti Volodin tries to warn a doctor acquaintance against sharing a sample of a Soviet experimental drug with French colleagues at a medical convention: in the paranoid atmosphere of the late 1940's this would be construed as an act of treason. The doctor's telephone is tapped, Volodin's call is recorded, and the hunt for the caller in due course involves the inmates of the *sharashka,* whose work on a voice scrambler gives them some expertise in voice analysis. In this redaction Volodin's call is motivated by pity, and the psychological background that leads to this act is not elucidated at great length. Since the act is primarily an impulse of simple human decency, perhaps no great build-up is required.

The situation is very different in the ninety-six-chapter version. Volodin here telephones the American Embassy in Moscow to warn of an impending Soviet espionage operation involving nuclear bomb technology. Several chapters in this redaction are accordingly devoted to tracing Volodin's evolution from a privileged and jaded servant of the Soviet regime to an active opponent who is sufficiently moved by hatred of the system to try to foil Stalin's plans of acquiring weapons of mass destruction.

We know from the published memoirs of Lev Kopelev, Solzhenitsyn's fellow inmate in the *sharashka,* that a call to the U.S. Embassy of the type described by Solzhenitsyn did in fact take place, although the personality of the diplomat involved seems to have been quite different. One must assume that the Volodin of the novel gives voice to the author's own disgust at the devastation visited upon the Russian countryside by Soviet policies, and at the string of cynical deceptions that have marked the regime's behavior from the beginning. In this connection one should add that Solzhenitsyn also drew on his own experience in depicting Volodin's initiation into the prison system (shown in both versions of the novel).

Although there are further interesting differences between the two versions of *The First Circle,* the core chapters detailing the complex interrelationships among the prisoners of the *sharashka* are essentially the same in both. Center stage is occupied by Nerzhin and his two fellow inmates, the proud and brilliant elitist Dmitri Sologdin and his ideological antipode, the engaging communist true believer, Lev Rubin. To the extent that Nerzhin is a fictionalized portrayal of Solzhenitsyn himself, Rubin and Sologdin are also based on the real-life prototypes, Lev Kopelev and Dimitri Panin. Both these men wrote memoirs describing their stay in the *sharashka* and their friendship with Solzhenitsyn, thus providing a unique insight into Solzhenitsyn's manner of creating literary worlds from actual experience.

Nerzhin's stance vis-à-vis his two strong-minded friends is one of skeptical independence and committed eclecticism. He learns a great deal from both but refuses to accept their ideological premises. And he is constantly open to insights from other quarters, including such unlikely individuals as the humble, barely literate, but steadfast janitor.

The novel sweeps outward from this central core, pursuing various links between the men inside the *sharashka* and the world outside its walls, and we have the opportunity to glimpse the life of a wide range of Soviet citizens, from impoverished graduate students to members of the elite. We are also given a detailed portrait of Stalin. The aging tyrant is shown as the supreme jailmaster of a system in which he is paradoxically the ultimate prisoner. The ninety-six-chapter version dwells at some length on the suspicion long held by a number of historians that Stalin had been a paid police informer in tsarist Russia.

One interesting aspect of *The First Circle* is the constant attention that is given to the problem of communication in all its forms. Language itself is a theme, and one notes the curious way in which language is shown to resist rational analysis. The inmates of the *sharashka* are hard at work on the design of a voice scrambler (but they have not gotten very far), and they are studying the acoustic features of human speech (but are only beginning to scratch the surface of the subject). Sologdin strains to invent new lexical items so as to avoid using words of foreign origin. (The result is awkward and unintentionally funny.) Rubin struggles to confirm Marxist theory through comparative etymology. (The idea is far-fetched and entirely unpersuasive.) And Stalin labors as hard as his failing mind permits to produce an essay on language. (It is hopelessly muddled.)

But the principal focus is on communications that have been disrupted by force or ideology. Examples are too numerous to list, but the categories include rules forbidding or restricting normal human contact, lies of every description, and ideologically induced false decoding of information. A brilliantly sardonic play on all of these themes is "Buddha's Smile," a chapter presented as a tongue-in-cheek oral account of a mythical visit by Mrs. Roosevelt (referred to as "Mrs. R." in the eighty-seven-chapter version) to a Moscow prison. Everyone in this fable fulfills his role to perfection: the jailers with their preposterously elaborate plan based on the suppression of all truth about the prison and its inmates, the prisoners reduced to naive docility by their utter lack of information about the proceedings, and the visitors in their blind eagerness to believe the Soviet lies. In this instance the lack of communication is of course caricatured, and the theme is more typically presented in bitter and tragic terms.

*The First Circle* was the first of Solzhenitsyn's works to feature what he called the "polyphonic" principle of construction. (Although the term itself was drawn from the writings of the literary scholar Mikhail Bakhtin, in Solzhenitsyn's usage it refers only to a particular compositional device; certain critics to the contrary, no further link can be demonstrated to the complex theories associated with Bakhtin's name.) As the author defined it, this principle is a means to assure that "each character, as soon as the plot touches him, becomes the main hero" (quoted in Michael Scammell, *Solzhenitsyn,* p. 582). The effect is achieved by shifting the point of view while formally preserving the third-person narrative. In a given section of text (usually a chapter) we become privy to the unuttered thoughts of one particular protagonist, together with his or her subjective vision of the world. In technical terms Solzhenitsyn offers a montage of "authorial" third-person narrative interspersed with interior monologue. It is a remarkably powerful tool for characterization, and in *The First Circle* it is used with great effect to render psychological portraits of Volodin, Rubin, Stalin, and many others. In this connection it is useful to recall that the earliest redaction of the ninety-six-chapter version of the novel was completed in 1957, and that *The First Circle* was thus the first major work undertaken by Solzhenitsyn after the completion of his dramatic trilogy. It therefore seems legitimate to postulate a continuity between the polyphonic method and the dramatic form, with each character in the prose work allowed the equivalent of a chance to deliver a dramatic monologue from center stage.

In the late 1950's and early 1960's Solzhenitsyn turned to short prose, with the most important work from this period being *One Day in the Life of Ivan Denisovich.* Written in 1959, *One Day* demonstrates the method of subjective third-person narrative developed in *The First Circle* but here applied to only one individual, Ivan Denisovich Shukhov. He is a man of peasant origin and no formal education who is currently being held in a Soviet forced-labor camp on the charge of having spied for the Germans. (In reality he has simply escaped from a German POW camp.) The story traces the events of a single day from Shukhov's perspective, beginning with the moment he emerges from sleep at the sound of camp reveille, and ending as he retires to his bunk at night. Nothing particularly dramatic occurs in between these times, and nothing, in fact, is capable of disrupting the relentless camp routine that makes every day alike. But the low-keyed narrative serves only to increase the impact, for the story shocks by understatement, as for example in Shukhov's closing thought that the day just past had been an "almost happy one" (*SS,* vol. 3, p. 120).

A philosophical issue of some import is involved here. Solzhenitsyn's narrator faces the flagrant injustices perpetrated by the camp system without retreating into despair or otherwise giving voice to the alleged meaninglessness of the world that one might expect from a modern work on this theme. Instead of that Shukhov—tough and wily survivor though he is—retains an indestructible sense of moral perspective that informs all his actions. He is, to begin with, stubbornly unreconciled to victimhood, and not for a moment is he deceived about the true essence of the system that has incarcerated him. As a result he never hesitates to cheat the authorities if he can do so without great risk, while at the same time maintaining completely honest dealings with fellow prisoners. He appreciates and respects manifestations of human goodness, as in the case of a pious Baptist prisoner, but he is not ready to accept this creed or anyone else's. Shukhov's guiding principle here and throughout the story is the desire to protect his independence. This also explains why he insists on clinging to certain mannerisms that have no practical importance in a camp, such as making a point of removing his hat during meals.

Other manifestations of this spirit, however, have very explicit significance. Perhaps the most interesting example is the celebrated episode where Shukhov is building a brick wall together with other members of his work brigade. Almost despite themselves, the men begin to put forth their best effort, and Shukhov becomes so caught up in the process that he risks punishment to finish laying a row of bricks after quitting time. Although it is late, he steps back to admire his handiwork: "It was fine. He ran up to take a look over the top of the wall, glancing right and left. Ah, his eye was as true as a level! The wall was perfectly even, his hands had not yet lost their touch!" (*SS,* vol.3, p. 77).

Nikita Khrushchev is said to have admired this scene greatly (thus facilitating the printing of *One Day*), presumably because he believed it to reflect "labor enthusiasm" of the type routinely offered in works of socialist realism. As the above quote makes clear, however, Shukhov is moved not by the desire to contribute to a collective project, but by the need to assert his continuing worth as an individual human being. It is one of the ways in which he resists being reduced to a faceless slave.

Of Solzhenitsyn's other short prose works, the best known by far is "Matryona's Home." Written in 1959, the story is described by Solzhenitsyn as "completely autobiographical and authentic" in that it presents a true account of the writer's stay in the village of Miltsevo in 1956–1957. Since this work is also considered by a number of commentators to be Solzhenitsyn's most perfect literary creation, "Matryona's Home" is a particularly instructive example of the way "art" is not equated to "fiction" by writers of the Russian literary tradition. No necessary link is seen between literary craftsmanship and invention per se; artistry is demonstrated, rather, by the writer's skill in selecting, shaping, and presenting the data of reality within a coherent structure, and by the ability to perceive patterns and analogies.

"Matryona's Home" manifests these principles in many ways, and the opening passage is a good example. We are told in the very first sentence that trains used to slow down at a certain point "for a good six months after it happened" (*SS,* vol. 3, p. 123). What the "it" refers to here is not explained until midway through the story, and the comment lingers in our memory as a troubling and unresolved note. When we eventually do learn that Matryona was killed in an accident at a railroad crossing, the earlier comment takes on the resonance of foreknowledge. The impact of the work is produced by an accumulation of such details of organization.

The story also exhibits a thematic pattern that is repeated frequently in Solzhenitsyn's writings. This is the motif of a quest or mission that ends in failure, but during which something more valuable is acquired by virtue of defeat. In the case of "Matryona's Home," the first-person narrator emerges from his compulsory stay in Central Asia full of yearning for the elusive quality he associates with traditional Russia ("I wanted to efface myself, to lose myself in deepest Russia—if it was still anywhere to be found" [p. 123]). But the superficial trappings of this entity do not result in satisfaction: a beautiful village with a melodious name turns out to be unfit for habitation, the landscape of "deepest Russia" is scarred and disfigured by industrial blight, a handsome and dignified village elder is a monster of greed behind his imposing appearance, and the traditional funeral laments performed by the villagers after Matryona's death serve as a convenient front for perpetuating mean-spirited quarrels and jealousies. The ideal Russia the narrator has been seeking so assiduously seems nowhere to be found. Only at the end of the story does he realize, in a flash of illumination, that the qualities he has been looking for have no visible "ethnographic" form: they are moral, spiritual, and transcendent, and they were incarnated in the humble, selfless, and ever-suffering Matryona. She was that "righteous one without whom, as the proverb says, no village can stand" (p. 159).

A similar twist occurs in "Sluchai na stantsii Kochetovka" ("Incident at Krechetovka Station," 1963; the place name was changed from "Krechetovka" to "Kochetovka" in *Sobranie sochinenii,* with the latter form corresponding to a real geographical location). The protagonist in this story, Lieutenant Zotov, is a well-meaning and fundamentally decent man who earnestly desires to understand the precepts of Marxism-Leninism as he tries to subordinate his life to these principles. As a result he uncritically accepts propaganda clichés about the need to be "ever vigilant" against lurking enemy agents and saboteurs, and commits the irreparable blunder of turning over a completely innocent man to the NKVD. (This is a recently drafted actor separated from his unit by the chaos of war.) But even as he lures the alleged infiltrator into the guardroom by a false promise of food—a deceptive little play staged to trap an actor who does not suspect the role he has been assigned—Zotov is stung by the perversity of his own behavior. But the deed cannot be undone, and when Zotov's growing guilt feelings eventually prompt him to inquire about the man he has had arrested, he is more troubled than ever to receive a reply in which the actor's name is badly garbled, followed immediately by the assurance that "we [that is, the NKVD] never make mistakes" (*SS,* vol. 3, p. 255).

This grimly ironic punchline precedes the closing sentence of the story, where we learn of Zotov's inability to drive the painful memory of this incident from his mind "for the rest of his life." The clear implication is that Zotov has failed in his attempt to think and act in terms of orthodox Marxism-Leninism. He has been "corrupted" by having recognized the unbridgeable gap between moral reality and ideological cliché. But this failure is of course a victory in human terms, and the unremitting pain of remorse that Zotov experiences is the assurance of a permanently awakened conscience.

Mention must also be made of Solzhenitsyn's series of seventeen brief sketches written in 1958–1960. The author referred to them collectively as "Krokhotki" (miniature stories) and also characterized them as "poems in prose." The latter designation seems to fit particularly well, since apart from the extreme brevity of these texts (the length ranges from slightly more than a page down to a dozen lines), they exhibit meticulous attention to rhythmic structure, and resemble contemplative poetry in their manner of deriving broad philosophical statements from a single episode or observation. Many of the themes touched upon are familiar from other works of Solzhenitsyn's: a marked distaste for modern secular and mechanical civilization, a love of nature and a particular attachment to the Russian rural landscape, and an acute distress at the desecration of the Russian land by its current masters. At the same time Solzhenitsyn's vision of the past is by no means idyllic. Thus the narrator wanders through a wretched village where the peasant poet Sergei Esenin (1895–1925) had spent his childhood, and reflects on the mystery of the "divine fire" that had come down upon the poet, enabling him to recognize beauty in these depressing surroundings (*SS,* vol. 3, p. 177). And in another piece he broods mournfully about the mute human cost that stands behind the spectacular beauties of St. Petersburg (p. 172).

Other works of short prose include "Pravaia kist'" ("The Right Hand," 1968), another story with a pointed reversal in the ending, "Dlia pol'zy dela" ("For the Good of the Cause," 1963), a longish tale that Solzhenitsyn himself does not consider particularly successful, "Zakhar-Kalita" ("Zakhar-the-Pouch," 1966), about the selfless keeper of a monument on a Russian battlefield, and "Paskhal'nyi krestnyi khod" ("The Easter Procession," 1969), a wrathful denunciation of the barely human mob of gawkers who surround a Russian Orthodox church during the Easter midnight service.

Solzhenitsyn's second major work, *Cancer Ward,* was produced in the years 1963–1966. Although the book is more than 500 pages long, the author insisted on designating it a "tale" (*povest'*) rather than a novel (*roman*), arguing that the latter must treat a larger number of characters in more depth. (*The First Circle* is the only one of Solzhenitsyn's works to which he referred as a novel.) The setting is a cancer clinic in Tashkent in early 1955, and the events described reflect many aspects of Solzhenitsyn's own treatment for an abdominal tumor under similar circumstances. The chief protagonist is Oleg Kostoglotov, a tough, prickly, and assertive former prisoner whose iconoclastic views on politics are matched by his lack of deference for accepted medical procedures.

Beyond the hospital grounds, meanwhile, the attempts of the party leadership to distance itself from the Stalinist legacy are sending shock waves through the system. As this information filters into the ward, Kostoglotov is increasingly drawn into conflict with another patient, a self-important party functionary named Pavel Rusanov. The "Rusanov line" in *Cancer Ward* is quite substantial, with the first chapter describing Rusanov's arrival at the clinic (as seen from his perspective) and several others devoted largely or entirely to him and his relatives. Together with his articulate and aggressive daughter, Rusanov emerges as a sinister representative of the Stalinist past. This explicitly political strand in *Cancer Ward,* taken together with other sections in which political ideology is discussed at some length, led some critics to read the entire work as an allegory about figurative "cancers" on the Russian body politic. While some associations of this type are perfectly appropriate, since every significant work of art is capable of supporting a multitude of symbolic meanings, it would be a gross error to approach *Cancer Ward* on that level alone. The paramount focus of Solzhenitsyn's book is both simpler and more fundamental: it is the drama of human consciousness confronting death. Speaking more broadly, *Cancer Ward* explores the ways in which the proximity or threat of death tests the hierarchy of values that each person brings to the experience. Hence the debates on "ultimate questions" among the patients of the ward, debates in which ideological commitments naturally play a part, but in which most of these commitments offer no answer to the problem of mortality. Physical torment and the fear of death humbles them all alike—earnest Communists, cheerful cynics, grasping careerists, and committed hedonists—and there are moments when we can see even the despicable Rusanov as a suffering fellow human being.

Kostoglotov is the only person in the ward who tries to grapple with the philosophical issues involved. Throughout the text he holds to the belief that "survival at any price" cannot be a goal worthy of a human being. But this position (instinctively held by Ivan Denisovich) does not solve the question of just how high the price can go before it becomes unacceptable, since *some* degree of compromise is inevitable. (Thus Kostoglotov convinces a fearful teenager to go through with an amputation.) Kostoglotov's approach is to keep as well-informed as possible about the treatment he is receiving so as to be able to judge its potential negative effects. To the considerable annoyance of his doctors he tries to monitor their every move and is shocked to discover that the hormone shots that have been prescribed for him will wipe out his virility. Such a sacrifice appears entirely unreasonable to a man starved for feminine companionship after years of enforced bachelorhood—at the front, in prison camp, and in exile. Nor is the problem an academic one, since Kostoglotov is greatly attracted to Zoya, a lively young nurse, while at the same time falling in love with Vera, a high-minded and luminously feminine doctor in the clinic. Fate could not have been more cruel: just as he begins to recover from his primary affliction and as the two women respond positively to his advances, Kostoglotov has to face this new trial. It is a powerful reinforcement of the theme of inescapable physicality that runs through the book. Human beings are in a real sense prisoners of their bodies, and victims of an inscrutable fate.

Yet *Cancer Ward* does not end on this note. With great pain and uncertainty Kostoglotov gropes his way toward a means of overcoming the dark vision of ultimate hopelessness that would otherwise emerge from the text. He chooses the path of renunciation. In what are among the most memorable pages of the book, Kostoglotov decides to return directly to his place of exile upon his release from the hospital, rather than taking advantage of the invitation offered by Vera to stay over at her apartment. (Zoya had made a similar offer.) To depart is the only honest thing to do, he concludes, since he has been warned by the chief doctor that for physical reasons he should not contemplate marriage for some years. Spiritual and ethereal though Vera is, it would be unrealistic, and unfair to her, to place hopes in a purely platonic relationship. Kostoglotov's departure is therefore a conscious act of self-sacrifice, which, however, is not presented in terms of any mystical epiphany. On the contrary, the overwhelming cost of this renunciation is emphasized, but as a free expression of Kostoglotov's moral will it moves him beyond despair toward spiritual liberation.

The years in which this book was being written coincide with the most active phase of Solzhenitsyn's work on *The Gulag Archipelago,* and this proximity has left deep traces in *Cancer Ward.* Oleg Kostoglotov is a former *zek* (labor-camp prisoner), and all his views of life have been irreversibly affected by the harsh experience of life in extremis. This is presented as a mixed blessing at best: while Kostoglotov may have a clearer understanding than others of what really matters in life, the oppressive memories of his past pursue him like a curse, constantly reminding him of a life ruined by unmotivated evil. It is a motif that echoes, and merges with, the equally tragic theme of illness and mortality, reinforcing the somber vision which Kostoglotov struggles to overcome.

## The Gulag Archipelago

*Gulag:* the word is as alien-sounding in Russian as it is in English. Solzhenitsyn combined this acronym, which stands for "Main Administration of Corrective-Labor Camps," with the metaphor of a chain of islands to produce his most famous work, a guided tour of the world of Soviet prisons and camps between 1918 and 1956. While the image of a large body of islands surrounded by sea has an obvious spatial analogy in the network of penal institutions dotting the map of the Soviet Union, the writer is also implying that the contrast between land and water is as great as that between the world of common experience and the special universe of Soviet prisons and camps. The "archipelago" seems to represent an entirely separate dimension of reality, a point that is stressed in the opening of part 1:

> How does one get to this mysterious Archipelago? Not an hour goes by without airplanes taking off, ships putting out to sea, and trains rumbling away, all headed in that direction, yet not a single sign on any of them indicates their destination. Ticket agents or the employees of Soviet travel bureaus will be astonished if you ask them for a ticket there. They know nothing either of the Archipelago as a whole nor of any of its innumerable islands; they've never heard of it.
>
> Those who are sent to run the Archipelago enter via the training schools of the Ministry of Internal Affairs.
>
> Those who are sent to guard the Archipelago are inducted through the military conscription centers.
>
> And those who are sent there to die—like you and me, dear reader—enter exclusively and necessarily through the procedure of arrest.
>
> (*SS,* vol. 5, p. 15)

The mythical overtones are unmistakable, for the Archipelago is being compared to the nether world of classical literature: it is a space inaccessible to the ordinary traveller, invisible to common humanity, and, for the average person, attainable only via the ritual of arrest—the death of the former self. (One notes the continuity of this image with the vision of the Soviet penal system as hell that is reflected in the title of Solzhenitsyn's novel *The First Circle.*)

Yet to acknowledge the "otherness" of the Gulag universe, as Solzhenitsyn does here, is not to be reconciled with the deliberate policy of concealment that is associated with it, and the whole thrust of the book is in fact directed toward exposing the ugly secrets of this hidden world. For *The Gulag Archipelago* is above all an act of witness to the reality of the camp system, a monumental effort to reveal an entity the very existence of which had been strenuously denied for decades. To this end Solzhenitsyn marshalled the testimony of over 200 former *zeks,* drawing also on his own experience and on the available literature. Taken as a whole the book stands as an overwhelming "case" brought against the state—and the ideology—that nurtured a monstrous institution behind a facade of enforced silence and mendacious propaganda.

Yet Solzhenitsyn recognized that even a massive collaborative effort of this kind could not do justice to the dimensions of the human tragedy that needed to be brought to light. The subject is too vast even for the combined memories of the hundreds of witnesses that Solzhenitsyn assembled. Indeed, the writer was convinced that no conventional history of Soviet prisons and camps can ever be written, because too much documentary evidence was systematically destroyed, and too many of the victims were silenced forever.

It was in awareness of this problem that Solzhenitsyn turned to the method proclaimed in the subtitle of his work: *Opyt khudozhestvennogo issledovaniia (An Experiment in Literary Investigation*; an alternative translation of the subtitle might be: *Essay in artistic inquiry*). As the adjective in this phrase makes clear, Solzhenitsyn deliberately set out to enlist the devices of literary art in the service of a cognitive goal. To begin with, the narrative exhibits the literary craftsmanship of the author: it has the evocative power that only masterful prose can possess. But Solzhenitsyn's method involves the very specific further step of relying on aesthetic intuition to generalize from what the writer acknowledges to be an incomplete set of facts. Overarching metaphors and clusters of images provide a frame of reference for the events portrayed, thereby infusing seemingly disparate facts with significance. For example, Solzhenitsyn repeatedly likens the Gulag system to a sewer designed to accumulate, channel, and dispose of the "human refuse" that needs to be covertly drained from the surface of "Soviet reality" (part 1, chap. 2). Solzhenitsyn never pretended that this was more than a metaphor, yet it is one that tallies perfectly both with the degrading conditions in which *zeks* were routinely kept (the excremental theme is prominent throughout) and with the squeamish disdain that the authorities displayed toward the prisoners.

*The Gulag Archipelago* consists of seven parts divided into three volumes and totalling almost 1,800 pages. The text is a complex interweaving of historical exposition with individual case histories (including vividly presented episodes from Solzhenitsyn's own experience), everywhere interspersed with comments, exhortations, questions, and objections that are by turns ironic, bitter, despairing, or melancholy. This running commentary is the most striking stylistic feature of the book, since it assures that the material cannot be read in any "neutral" and detached manner.

Parody is one of the devices Solzhenitsyn uses here with great effect, as when he mimics the phraseology of a communist ideologue who would be expected to voice approval for acts of barbarity described in the text. For example, when a religious community is rounded up for not wishing to join a collective farm, and individual members try to flee from the rafts on which they are being transported to their place of exile, the convoy troops methodically machine-gun them all. The description of this episode ends with a mock exhortation: "Warriors of the Soviet Army! Tirelessly consolidate your combat training!" (*SS*, vol. 7, p. 368).

At other times the subversive edge of the commentary is turned against the author himself, setting up a sort of "interior dialogue" that turns expository prose into drama and demonstrates Solzhenitsyn's continuing affinity for the polyphonic mode. In part IV of *The Gulag Archipelago,* for example, the writer examines the moral and spiritual consequences of incarceration. The first chapter ends with the author making the paradoxical declaration that he is grateful to prison for opening his eyes to moral reality: "Bless you, prison, for having occurred in my life." But this seeming apotheosis is followed immediately by a radical qualification, delivered in sotto voce manner by being enclosed in parentheses: "(But from the burial pits I hear a response: 'It's very well for you to say that—you who've come through alive.')" (*SS*, vol. 6, p. 571).

*The Gulag Archipelago* is undoubtedly the least "acceptable" of Solzhenitsyn's books from the traditional Soviet point of view, and the reason is not difficult to identify, for Solzhenitsyn was not content to lay the blame for the Gulag system on Stalin alone. While he fully agreed that Stalin had presided over the "flowering" of the murderous system, he cited abundant evidence to show that the roots of the slave-labor empire—both institutionally and in terms of philosophical rationale—went back to the sacrosanct early years of the Revolution when Lenin was at the helm. Fierce intolerance was a central ingredient of Bolshevik ideology from the beginning, and Solzhenitsyn's work documents the inevitable way in which this trait became embodied in the laws and institutions of the new revolutionary regime. For this reason *The Gulag Archipelago* represents nothing less than an attack on the legitimacy of the entire Soviet system. In the words of George Kennan of March 1974, the book is "the greatest and most powerful single indictment of a political regime ever to be leveled in modern times" (quoted in Scammell, *Solzhenitsyn,* p. 878).

### The Red Wheel

Solzhenitsyn stated repeatedly that he looked upon his writings on the camp theme as a fulfillment of a solemn moral obligation to the millions who disappeared forever into the abyss of the Gulag world. Immense as this responsibility was, the writer nevertheless regarded it as finite, and in *The Oak and the Calf* he spoke metaphorically of *The Gulag Archipelago* (and the works that preceded it) as a huge boulder that he was able to roll aside in order to get on with the "main task" of his life: a fundamental re-examination of the Russian Revolution.

The original conception for an epic cycle on the theme of the Revolution goes back to 1937, a time when the young Solzhenitsyn was brimming with Marxist enthusiasm. War, arrest, long years of imprisonment, and a near-fatal bout with cancer followed, all contributing to a radical change in Solzhenitsyn's views, but only increasing his desire to delve into the history of this fateful event. Even though he was able to give the subject a great deal of thought over the years (thus Gleb Nerzhin, the author's alter ego in *The First Circle,* compiles voluminous notes on Russian history), other concerns and obligations always seemed to take precedence, and it was only after the spring of 1968—when Solzhenitsyn received word that a microfilm of *The Gulag Archipelago* had been safely carried across the border to the West—that he felt free to devote his full energy to this project.

The cycle is collectively called *Krasnoe koleso* (*The Red Wheel*) and subtitled *Povestvovanie v otmerennykh srokakh,* a phrase that was translated as "A Narrative in Discrete Periods of Time." As was also the case with the subtitle in *The Gulag Archipelago,* Solzhenitsyn's wording here points very explicitly to the method adopted by the writer in this particular work. The key principle involves rejecting any attempt to encompass the full sequence of historical events. Instead, Solzhenitsyn focused, in extraordinary detail, on relatively brief and sharply demarcated segments of historical time, making no effort to fill in the gaps between these discrete periods. The text allocated to each segment is referred to as a "knot" (*uzel*), a term taken from the mathematical concept of "nodal point," and meant to suggest a moment in history when the central issues of the day had become intertwined in a manner that offered a particularly clear view of the underlying conflicts which were nudging Russia toward the precipice.

The initial plan for the cycle envisaged twenty "knots," each with a separate title corresponding to the time frame covered. "Knot I" is named *August 1914,* and the two immediately following "knots" are *Oktiabr' shestnadtsatogo* (October 1916) and *Mart semnadtsatogo* (March 1917). (It should be noted that Solzhenitsyn's Russian titles refer to dates in the Julian calendar, used in Russia before 1918, which was thirteen days behind the calendar used in the West at this time.) "Knot XX" was to be set in the spring of 1922, and five epilogues were to bring the story up to 1945. This highly ambitious plan had to undergo considerable revision in the course of Solzhenitsyn's work. *August 1914* was first published in 1971, but after the author was expelled to the West in 1974 he came upon new data that begged to be inserted into his cycle, even though most of it predated the time frame of what he had announced to be his first installment. Solzhenitsyn's solution to this problem was to publish a much expanded version of *August 1914* with the title unchanged, but with the added materials prefaced by an internal title page that reads "From Previous Knots." With the starting point of his cycle thus pushed back considerably, and with the burgeoning size of the early "knots" (in *Sobranie sochinenii* edition, Knot I contains just under 1,000 pages, Knot II has almost 1,200, and Knot III has more than 2,800), Solzhenitsyn realized that he would have to cut off his narrative well before the end point he had originally aimed for. Indeed he decided to stop short even of the October Revolution, and according to a statement made in 1987, "Knot IV" (*Aprel' semnadtsatogo* [April 1917]) was to be the final installment in the cycle.

*The Red Wheel,* like *The Gulag Archipelago* before it, is a troublesome work to define in terms of genre, but the difficulty is here compounded by the substantial change in mode that seems to have occurred after the project had already gotten under way. Thus while the early version of *August 1914* (published in 1971 but reflecting plans conceived many years before) fits the general pattern of the historical novel, the expanded "knot" can no longer be easily accommodated within the novelistic tradition. This is so because the balance between fictional and historical aspects that held in the first edition is sharply altered in the direction of "pure history" by the addition of a 350-page-long insert with no fictional intent whatever. Even more telling is the fact that in the massive four-volume Knot III (published in 1986–1988), the fictional characters introduced in the earlier "knots" become virtually peripheral to the narrative. The general movement away from all fictional constructs and toward dramatized history could not have been more clearly indicated. It should be added that this shift is consistent with the approach stated in Solzhenitsyn's subtitle, for the unbridged gaps in time between the various "knots" are in fundamental conflict with the literary demands of character development. Since the writer set himself the goal of tracing the ill-starred convolutions that had shaped twentieth-century Russian history, the focus of Solzhenitsyn's narrative is not on individual fates but on the greater tragedy that engulfed the entire nation.

In stylistic terms *The Red Wheel* exhibits the characteristic features developed in Solzhenitsyn's earlier work as well as a number of new literary devices. A prominent example of the former is the "polyphonic" technique (initially elaborated in *The First Circle*), whereby individual characters are given the opportunity to carry the narrative point of view in the section of the text where they are the principal actors. This device is used throughout Solzhenitsyn's historical cycle, with an entire chapter typically being given over to a particular character. In Knot III this creates an unexpected effect due to the extreme brevity of the chapters: the frequent shifts of perspective that result serve to accentuate the sense of disruption and chaos that is central to Solzhenitsyn's description of revolutionary turmoil.

Among the stylistic innovations in *The Red Wheel* the most significant is the manner in which the writer interspersed his prose with diverse materials that are visually set off from the main text: documents in boldface, historical retrospectives in 8-point font, collages of excerpts from the press of the time set in a variety of styles and sizes, "screen sequences" arranged in columns of brief phrases intended to mimic actual cinematic effects, and Russian proverbs printed entirely in capital letters.

The last-named item deserves a special word of explanation. Solzhenitsyn always had the highest regard for Russian proverbial expressions, admiring them as much for their verbal compactness as for their wry wisdom. (In *The Oak and the Calf* the writer relates how he regained composure in times of difficulty by reading collections of Russian folk sayings.) Proverbs appear as independent entries at the conclusion of some chapters in *The Red Wheel,* offering a succinct commentary on the preceding text. For example, at the end of a chapter where Solzhenitsyn describes the public reaction to the news that Prime Minister Stolypin had been seriously wounded in an assassination attempt, the writer gives us a long list of organizations and institutions that rushed to arrange special church services [*molebny*] to be offered for Stolypin's recovery. The bitter irony is that many of these same organizations had earlier been cool or hostile to Stolypin's valiant efforts to restore health and balance to the Russian body politic. The reproach is tersely summed up in the following saying: PRAYERS WERE OFFERED, BUT ALL TO NO PROFIT. (This translation attempts to render the partial rhyme of the Russian original: I MOLEBNY PETY, DA POL'ZY NETU [*SS,* vol. 12, p. 283].)

It is clear that proverbs have a privileged position among the many voices that make up Solzhenitsyn's work: they represent an authoritative "folk judgment," serving a function akin to that of the chorus in Greek tragedy. Together with the cinematic sequences, they provide evidence of the deep mark that the principles of drama have made on the writer's prose.

It should be added that all the proverbs cited by Solzhenitsyn are culled from the glossary of Vladimir Dal, a nineteenth-century lexicographer whose massive compilation of the Russian popular idiom was the writer's principal source and model in his campaign to revitalize the Russian language. It was Solzhenitsyn's belief that the ubiquitous ideological clichés that all too often typified Soviet speech and writing were both a cause and a symptom of the radical impoverishment of the Russian language: the rich linguistic legacy of the past was in danger of being lost forever, together with the nation's historical memory and cultural tradition. The damage could be undone, he believed, by reintroducing the half-forgotten lexical and syntactic structures that had been characteristic of peasant speech. And this was exactly what Solzhenitsyn attempted to do in *The Red Wheel,* with results that caused considerable controversy among Russian readers, many of whom find this experimentation unpalatable.

The major thematic concerns of *The Red Wheel* are not difficult to identify. The central one involves the opposition of those individuals in whom a love of Russia prompts efforts to achieve constructive changes, to those who are blinded by ideology-induced hatred or obsessed by self-interest. In Knot I, the principal bearers of the positive impulse are two historical characters, Prime Minister Petr Stolypin and General Aleksandr Samsonov, commander of the Russian forces invading East Prussia in 1914. The assassination of the former by a revolutionary fanatic in 1911 and the betrayal of the latter by highly placed bunglers and cowards at the battle of Tannenberg are the two tragedies that make up the twin core of Knot I, and they become symbolic of the unreconcilable conflicts tearing Russia apart as well as of the ineluctable way in which the best people in the land seem doomed to fail or perish. The further we progress into the cycle, the less resistance there seems to remain to the surging forces of chaos and destruction, forces that Solzhenitsyn chose to associate with the image of a wheel rolling or rotating in an unnatural way. In one of the early screen sequences, a Prussian windmill is engulfed by flame during a battle, and the heat of the fire causes the vanes to begin turning, providing us with the first emblematic vision of a "red wheel":

> The radial framework, glowing in red and gold,
> is turning mysteriously,
> as though it were a fiery wheel rolling through the air.
> And then it disintegrates,
> crumbling into a shower
> of blazing fragments.
>
> (*SS,* vol. 11, p. 264)

The image is developed in another screen sequence, where a wheel tears loose from a field ambulance that is careening over a road littered with abandoned equipment:

The wheel rolls on by itself, overtaking the carriage.
It seems to grow bigger all the time,
and bigger still!
It fills the entire screen!
THE WHEEL!—rolls onward, lit by the
  conflagration,
unrestrained,
unstoppable,
crushing everything in its path.

(*SS*, vol. 11, p. 322)

The Revolution is seen as a similarly furious release of energy, at once spectacular, destructive—and self-destructive. Certainly this is Solzhenitsyn's view of the irresponsible political frenzy that preceded and accompanied the abdication of the tsar. It does not mean, however, that the lack of movement which is a central feature in the depiction of Nicholas is presented as a positive alternative. For Nicholas is shown to reside in what is almost a different plane of reality, a world of static calm barely in touch with the ever-quickening vortex forming around him. Indeed, the tsar seems to relate only to the orderly status quo, and is pathetically incapable of escaping the narrow roles prescribed by court tradition and family obligations. The portrait is at once generous and pitiless, and must be counted among Solzhenitsyn's greatest artistic achievements.

The vision of the tsar imprisoned in patterns of behavior above which he cannot seem to rise brings us to the unresolved—and unspoken—philosophical problem that is present just below the surface of the entire cycle: the issue of inevitability. Since Solzhenitsyn is depicting real events that he obviously deplores, he is at pains to note the many purely accidental occurrences which have contributed to the unfortunate outcome. Yet at the same time his descriptions are so compelling that it is not easy to imagine a result different from the one provided by history. If only the tsar had greater vision and more strength of will to resist psychological pressures, if only military headquarters could have been rid of certain bemedaled incompetents, if only. . . . Such sentiments fairly cry out from Solzhenitsyn's text, but the scrupulously historical intent of the narrative keeps the writer from indulging in any tempting fantasies. On the contrary, he uses his fictional apparatus to validate the actual sequence of events instead of exploring lost opportunities. Thus Colonel Vorotyntsev, the principal fictional character of *The Red Wheel* and a man of powerful will and luminous intelligence, in Knot II finds himself immobilized by a marital crisis, thereby echoing the psychological paralysis of the tsar. The tension between what did happen and what might have happened remains painfully clear to every reader, and it is perhaps this quality more than any other that energizes Solzhenitsyn's cycle and provides its tragic coloration.

It is always difficult to sort out the mass of conflicting judgments to which contemporary writers are subjected. Excessive proximity to a subject tends to obscure more than it reveals, and only historical distance allows us to distinguish the true proportions of literary phenomena. Thus few Russians living in the 1820's and 1830's could have guessed that this period in the country's cultural history would eventually come to be known as the Age of Pushkin. And certainly the pompous tsarist ministers who, together with sneering critics and high-society drones, had treated Pushkin with distrust and disdain, could never have imagined that they were destined to shrink in historical memory to their unsavory roles in the great poet's biography.

It is therefore too early to speculate whether the pattern might be repeated, and the decades that have echoed with raucous attacks on Aleksandr Solzhenitsyn's beliefs, credibility, and literary competence might yet be recorded as the Age of Solzhenitsyn.

The perspective of the early 1990's nevertheless permits us to say several things about the writer with a considerable degree of certainty. Aleksandr Solzhenitsyn was without question a major figure in the history of Russian literature. The most powerful talent in the field of Russian prose to emerge in the post–World War II period, Solzhenitsyn must also be regarded as the most formidable single adversary ever to confront the Soviet regime. For that reason he was also an immensely influential figure in the intellectual history of the twentieth century, a writer whose works (especially *The Gulag Archipelago*) modified the political climate in Western countries like France, and whose monumental *The Red Wheel* was clearly destined to affect Russia proper in an equally profound manner. It must also be emphasized that the writer's great impact cannot be dismissed as a fact irrelevant to literature, since the only source of his influence lay precisely in the eloquence of his writing and in the utter persuasiveness of the world he created—or re-created—for his readers. In an age when literature has frequently come to be viewed with cynical disinterest, the works of Aleksandr Solzhenitsyn testify to the explosive power of high art.

## Selected Bibliography


### EDITIONS

#### FIRST EDITIONS PUBLISHED IN THE SOVIET UNION

"Odin den' Ivana Denisovicha." *Novyi mir* 11:9–74 (1962).
"Sluchai na stantsii Krechetovka." *Novyi mir* 1:9–42 (1963).
"Matrenin dvor." *Novyi mir* 1:42–63 (1963).
"Dlia pol'zy dela." *Novyi mir* 7:58–90 (1963).
"Zakhar-Kalita." *Novyi mir* 1:69–76 (1966).

#### FIRST MAJOR EDITIONS PUBLISHED IN THE WEST

*V kruge pervom.* New York, 1968. (The eighty-seven-chapter version.)
*Rakovyi korpus.* London, 1968.
"Pravaia kist'." *Grani* (Frankfurt) 69: I–X (1968).
*Svecha na vetru.* Frankfurt, 1969. *Student: Zhurnal avangarda Sovetskoi literatury* (London) 11/12: 1–80 (1968), has marginal textual significance.
*Olen' i shalashovka.* London, 1969. (An earlier edition [1968] is textually corrupt.)
*Avgust chetyrnadtsatogo.* Paris, 1971. (The early version of Knot I of *Krasnoe koleso,* superseded by the much-enlarged edition of 1983 in the collected works.)
*Arkhipelag GULag.* 3 vols. Paris, 1973–1975.
*Prusskie nochi.* Paris, 1974.
*Lenin v Tsiurikhe.* Paris, 1975. (A compendium of the chapters dealing with Lenin and drawn from Knots I–IV of *Krasnoe koleso.*)
*Bodalsia telenok s dubom.* Paris, 1975.
*Skvoz' chad.* Paris, 1979. (A polemical addendum to *Bodalsia telenok s dubom.*)

#### COLLECTED WORKS

*Sobranie sochinenii.* Vermont and Paris, 1978–. (By 1989, eighteen volumes had been published. This edition contains the only complete and authorized texts of the works listed below.)
Vols. 1–2 (1978). *V kruge pervom.* (The ninety-six-chapter version.)
Vol. 3 (1978). *Rasskazy.* (Contains: "Odin den'," "Matrenin dvor," the prose "miniatures," "Pravaia kist'," "Sluchai na stantsii Kochetovka," "Dlia pol'zy dela," "Zakhar-Kalita," "Kak zhal'," "Paskhal'nyi krestnyi khod."
Vol. 4 (1979). *Rakovyi korpus.*
Vols. 5–7 (1980). *Arkhipelag GULag.* (A corrected and augmented version of the work first published in 1973–1975.)
Vol. 8 (1981). *P'esy i kinostsenarii.* (Contains: *Pir pobeditelei, Plenniki, Svecha na vetru, Respublika truda, Znaiut istinu tanki, Tuneiadets.*
Vol. 9 (1981). *Publitsistika: Stat'i i rechi.*
Vol. 10 (1983). *Publitsistika: Obshchestvennye zaiavleniia, interv'iu, presskonferentsii.*
Vols. 11–12 (1983). *Avgust chetyrnadtsatogo.* (This is the expanded version of Knot I of *Krasnoe koleso;* the earlier version was published in 1971.)
Vols. 13–14 (1984). *Oktiabr' shestnadtsatogo.* (Knot II of *Krasnoe koleso*).
Vols. 15–18 (1986–1988). *Mart semnadtsatogo.* (Knot III of *Krasnoe koleso*).

### TRANSLATIONS

Translations marked with an asterisk (*) are based on textually dated originals.
———. Knot I of *The Red Wheel.* Translated by

Harry T. Willetts. New York, 1989. [Translation of the enlarged Russian edition of 1983.]

August 1914.* Translated by Michael Glenny. New York, 1972. [Translation of the superseded Russian edition of 1971.]

*The Cancer Ward.* Translated by Rebecca Frank. New York, 1968.

*Cancer Ward.* 2 vols. Translated by Nicholas Bethell and David Burg. New York, 1969.

*Candle in the Wind.* Translated by Keith Armes. Minneapolis, 1973.

*East & West.* New York, 1980. (Contains the Nobel Lecture, the Harvard commencement address, *Letter to the Soviet Leaders,* and a 1979 BBC interview.)

*The First Circle.** Translated by Thomas Whitney, New York, 1968. (87 chapters).

———.* Translated by Michael Guybon. London, 1968. (87 chapters).

*The Gulag Archipelago.* Vol. 1* Translated by Thomas Whitney. New York, 1974.

———. Vol. 2* Translated by Thomas Whitney. New York, 1975.

———. Vol. 3* Translated by Harry T. Willetts. New York, 1978.

———.* Edited by Edward E. Ericson, Jr. New York, 1985. (A one-volume authorized abridgment of the above three volumes.)

*Lenin in Zurich.* Translated by Harry T. Willetts. New York, 1976.

*The Love-Girl and the Innocent.** Translated by Nicholas Bethell and David Burg. New York, 1969.

*The Mortal Danger: How Misconceptions About Russia Imperil America.* Translated by Michael Nicholson and Alexis Klimoff. New York, 1980; 2nd ed., New York, 1981. (The second edition contains Solzhenitsyn's lengthy reply to his critics.)

*The Oak and the Calf.* Translated by Harry T. Willetts. New York, 1979.

*One Day in the Life of Ivan Denisovich.** Translated by Max Hayward and Ronald Hingley. New York, 1963.

———.* Translated by Ralph Parker. New York, 1963.

———. Translated by Harry T. Willetts from the authorized text. New York, forthcoming.

*Prussian Nights: A Poem.* Translated by Robert Conquest. New York, 1977.

*Stories and Prose Poems.** Translated by Michael Glenny. New York, 1971. (Contains "Matryona's House," "For the Good of the Cause," "The Easter Procession," "Zakhar-the-Pouch," "An Incident at Krechetovka Station," and short prose poems.)

*Victory Celebrations. Prisoners. The Love-Girl and the Innocent: Three Plays.* Translated by Helen Rapp, Nancy Thomas, Nicholas Bethell, and David Burg. London, 1983; New York, 1986. (The translation of the third play is based on an outdated text.)

*Warning to the West.* New York, 1976. (Contains texts of speeches to the AFL-CIO, to the U.S. Congress, and to British television and radio audiences.)

*A World Split Apart.* Translated by Irina Alberti. New York, 1978. (The Harvard address.)

## BIOGRAPHICAL AND CRITICAL STUDIES

*"Avgust chetyrnadtsatogo" chitaiut na rodine.* Paris, 1973. (A collection of Soviet samizdat reactions to the early edition of *August 1914.*)

Barker, Francis. *Solzhenitsyn: Politics and Form.* New York, 1977.

Berman, Ronald, ed. *Solzhenitsyn at Harvard: The Address, Twelve Early Responses, and Six Later Reflections.* Washington, 1980.

Carpovich, Vera. *Solzhenitsyn's Peculiar Vocabulary: Russian-English Glossary.* New York, 1976.

Dunlop, John B., et al., eds. *Aleksandr Solzhenitsyn: Critical Essays and Documentary Materials.* Enl. ed. New York, 1975.

Dunlop, John B., et al., eds. *Solzhenitsyn in Exile: Critical Essays and Documentary Materials.* Stanford, 1985.

Feuer, Kathryn, ed. *Solzhenitsyn: A Collection of Critical Essays.* Englewood Cliffs, N.J., 1976.

Gul', Roman Borisovich. *Solzhenitsyn: Stat'i.* New York, 1976.

Hegge, Per Emil. *Mellommann i Moskva.* Oslo, 1971.

Kopelev, Lev. *Ease My Sorrows.* Translated by Antonina W. Bouis. New York, 1983.

Labedz, Leopold, ed. *Solzhenitsyn: A Documentary Record.* 2d ed. Harmondsworth, 1973.

Lakshin, Vladimir. *Solzhenitsyn, Tvardovsky, and "Novy Mir".* Translated by Michael Glenny. Cambridge, Mass., 1980.

Markstein, Elisabeth, and Felix Philipp Ingold, eds. *Über Solschenizyn: Aufsätze, Berichte, Materialen.* Neuwied and Darmstadt, 1973.

Medvedev, Zhores. *Ten Years After Ivan Denisovich.* Translated by Hilary Sternberg. New York, 1974.

Moody, Christopher. *Solzhenitsyn.* Enl. ed. New York, 1976.

Nivat, Georges, and Michel Aucouturier, eds. *Soljénitsyne.* Paris, 1971.

Nivat, Georges, *Soljénitsyne.* Paris, 1980. (This French-language study is the best general introduction to Solzhenitsyn written to date. A Russian translation exists: *Solzhenitsyn.* Translated by Simon Markish. London, 1984.)

Nowikowa, Irene, ed. *Seminarbeiträge zum Werk Aleksandr Solženicyns.* Hamburg, 1972.

Ozerov, N. "Po povodu 'Pis'ma' Solzhenitsyna." *Russkaia mysl'* (Paris), 13 June 1974.

Panin, Dimitri. *The Notebooks of Sologdin.* Translated by John Moore. New York, 1976.

Reshetovskaia, N. *V spore so vremenem.* Moscow, 1975. Translated into English by Elena Ivanoff as *Sanya: My Life with Aleksandr Solzhenitsyn.* Indianapolis, 1975. (This memoir by Solzhenitsyn's first wife, and the equally, but somewhat differently, doctored English version, were coauthored [that is, rewritten] by the Soviet press agency Novosti.)

Scammell, Michael. *Solzhenitsyn: A Biography.* New York, 1984.

*Solzhenitsyn: A Pictorial Autobiography.* New York, 1974.

Vinokur, T. G. "O iazyke i stile povesti A. I. Solzhenitsyna 'Odin den' Ivana Denisovicha'." *Voprosy kul'tury rechi* (Moscow), 1965, no. 6, pp. 16–32.

## BIBLIOGRAPHY

Fiene, Donald M. *Alexander Solzhenitsyn: An International Bibliography of Writings By and About Him.* Ann Arbor, 1973. (For bibliographic guides covering a later period, see the bibliographic sections in the two Dunlop volumes listed above.)

ALEXIS KLIMOFF

# FRIEDRICH DÜRRENMATT

## *(b. 1921)*

FRIEDRICH DÜRRENMATT WAS born on 5 January 1921 in Konolfingen, a small town in the canton of Bern, not far from the Swiss capital. His father was the town's pastor. These two bare facts need to be noted particularly in any attempt to understand Dürrenmatt's work and thought. As with every European, the experience of World War II, which broke out when Dürrenmatt was just eighteen, was decisive, all the more so in his case because the war encompassed his intellectually formative years. As a native and resident of neutral Switzerland, Dürrenmatt was on the sidelines during the war, a young man whose violently anti-Nazi feelings were tempered with relief at not being directly involved, guilt at being safe, and fear that the safety would end. In the event, Germany did not invade Switzerland, and Dürrenmatt endured nothing worse than a period of rationing. The experience, however, was the primary cause of the sardonic and detached observation that pervades his writings. His father's profession as a Protestant minister also, and equally inevitably, marked his attitude to life indelibly. That attitude—strong rejection of his religious upbringing—places Dürrenmatt squarely in the mainstream of modern philosophical thought.

Although Dürrenmatt is by no means exclusively a dramatist, he is internationally known primarily for his plays; and while some of his novels and short stories will be referred to in this essay, I shall concentrate on explicating Dürrenmatt's works in the context of dramatic literature.

It is necessary first to sketch the cultural and intellectual context in which Dürrenmatt's works have become meaningful. A writer, whether he be a minor commercial hack or a great artist, always reflects his times. This may mean any one of several things. It may mean that he reflects his audiences as they like to think of themselves (the commercial hack), or as they are (the sincere but uninspired writer), or as they should be but are not (the great artist). Put another way, the commercial hack snuffles along behind the crowd, licking boot heels; the sincere but uninspired writer is in the midst of the crowd, reporting as accurately as he can what he sees; and the great artist is in front of the crowd, attempting to lead it in what he considers to be the right direction. George Bernard Shaw put it very well in his extended essay on Ibsen when he said that the ordinary writer marches forward with his eyes in the back of his head, recording the past and what little present his peripheral vision reveals to him, while the great writer marches forward with his eyes in the usual place, peering into the future. Dürrenmatt, a great writer by any definition (for an artist should have the privilege of being judged by his best works), is of the latter breed.

By a curious coincidence—if, indeed, it is one—Dürrenmatt is a prominent amateur astronomer. A more than casual interest in astronomy is peculiarly appropriate to a modern writer, for there can be little doubt that modern times began with an astronomical event. The replacement of the geocentric theory of the universe with the heliocentric was the turning point of human history. Copernicus' discovery that the earth revolves around the sun and is therefore not the center of the universe ripped humanity from the comfortable womb of certainty and cast it out into the era of doubt. It is hard for us who have had to become accustomed to living in a spatial and temporal infinity to imagine the state of mind of those who lived before and who believed space to be finite and spherical and time to have a beginning and an end. Most people even today still cling desperately to the old beliefs while realizing that they are clutching at a spar of illusory solidity. For this reason a large part of popular religion has transformed itself into a classic example of a crisis cult.

The confusion between a frantically adhered to belief and an equally frantically suppressed, yet ever burgeoning, doubt is a conflict that provides the basic material for the plots elaborated by those dramatists most closely attuned to the trends of modern philosophical thought. For Dürrenmatt, brought up in a minister's household, the problem of doubt has been of particular significance.

It is in the setting of this background of the conflict between doubt and belief—not only with respect to religion but also with respect to the meaninglessness of all other aspects of life—that Dürrenmatt's work must be understood.

Dürrenmatt is not the first thinker, nor the first literary artist, whose perception of the impossibility of belief has caused him to retreat to the opposite extreme. It is a curious fact that serious thought about belief and non-belief leads to extremes; but to believe partially requires a degree of mental agility that appears to be incompatible with the structure of the human brain. The loss of belief—the realization of its impossibility—brings about a feeling of disillusionment and helplessness that shows itself in the impersonal, satiric mordancy that may be said to be the hallmark of Dürrenmatt's style. Like Franz Kafka, who was undoubtedly one of his spiritual masters, Dürrenmatt feels "the predicament of a man who, endowed with an insatiable appetite for transcendental certainty, finds himself in a world robbed of all spiritual possessions" (Erich Heller, *The Disinherited Mind* [New York, 1957], p. 218). One might almost say that Kafka is the god of spiritual despair and Dürrenmatt is his prophet.

The theme of spiritual despair shows itself early in Dürrenmatt's work and remains the ground theme on which he plays seemingly endless variations. In an early story, "Der Tunnel" (1952), the protagonist is a young student with an uncanny physical resemblance to Dürrenmatt himself. The student habitually takes the train from Bern to Zurich and back as he travels to and fro between home and college—another autobiographical touch. He is thoroughly familiar with the route and thus is not surprised when the train enters a tunnel right on schedule. But the tunnel stretches on endlessly—long after the train should have emerged, it is still rushing through darkness—and, furthermore, going downhill. The student runs through the train in a panic, but to his amazement, everybody is acting as if the situation were completely normal. Only the conductor will admit that something unusual is happening. He and the student risk their lives clambering over the couplings to the engine. The train is now plunging downward at an unheard-of speed, the angle of descent so sharp that it is almost impossible to remain standing. The engine cab is empty, and none of the controls work. The train, constantly gathering speed, now appears to be heading toward the center of the earth—and it cannot be stopped.

The controls are delusive. The conductor is the only clear-sighted human being on the train. He reveals that he has been aware all along that the engineer and the rest of the train crew jumped off within five minutes of the train's entering the tunnel. When asked why he had not jumped off as well, the conductor answers, "I have always lived without hope."[1] Hearing this, the student repeats, "Without hope" and thinks, "We sat in our compartments and didn't know that everything was already lost." As the story ends, the student and the conductor sit helplessly pressed against the front of the engine cab, rushing to oblivion. The conductor, panic-stricken at last, screams, "What shall we do?" The student, who has understood at last, and faces a life that, like the onrushing and descending train, is merely a prelude to death (or, perhaps better, an intermezzo between two oblivions), answers, "with unearthly cheerfulness, 'Nothing.'" A fitting ending for one who, at the very beginning of the story, is described as a person who senses "the horror in the wings."

In the course of the story, which is clearly not so much an allegory of human life as a symbolic depiction of an awakening to reality, the student learns the painful truth, which he cynically accepts at the end, that, as Orestes puts it in Sartre's *The Flies,* "human life begins on the far side of despair." Life is valuable, Dürrenmatt tells us, only insofar as it is understood and accepted as being an inexplicable interlude of consciousness between two voids, impersonally cruel: a joke without a joker.

In the original version of the story, written in 1952, the student's last words were "Nothing. God let us fall and thus we are rushing up to him." This led to the usual outpourings by romantic critics (critics whose "criticism" transforms the work of art into a mirror image of their own wishes) about Dürrenmatt's belief in religion, in a Christian world order, in a God who is there but interveneth not, and so forth. Probably it was to counteract this nonsense that Dürrenmatt cut the last sentence in the 1978 version and ended the story with the starkly uncompromising and flatly unambiguous "Nothing." A clearer statement in literary terms of the meaninglessness and incomprehensibility of life, of the supremacy of chance as a deciding factor in life, and of loss of belief could hardly have been written.

Loss of belief in religion or, indeed, in any possibility of understanding the conditions of our existence can easily be shown to be the principal theme of modern times. With the exception of a very small number of writers whose work is less an honest and objective attempt to depict and interpret reality than a nostalgic and subjective yearning for a symmetrical whole, it is regularly reflected in one guise or another in modern literature. For a writer like Dürrenmatt, brought up in a strict pastoral household, the crossover from childhood belief to adult disillusionment was particularly difficult and painful; and the struggle can be followed quite clearly in his works.

Before we examine Dürrenmatt's treatment of his principal theme in some depth, however, it might be useful to discuss some of his stylistic attitudes. The first thing a reader or viewer of a Dürrenmatt work will be likely to notice is that while the setting, the characters, and the action appear realistic, the realism is deceptive and superficial. The setting and the characters usually can quite easily be discerned as symbolic; the action, as schematic. Like all serious writers, Dürrenmatt strives for universality, and that quality always lurks just below the surface textual level, not infrequently breaking through the crust of verisimilitude to show the archetypes or generalizations beneath.

According to Dürrenmatt, this type of writing is virtually forced on a writer like himself because of sociopolitical pressures. Writers are necessarily divided between what Dürrenmatt calls "great state" and "small state" writers. "Great state" writers are able to take as their subject matter the minutiae of daily life in their societies; they are able to write true, realistic drama. The reason is that the mid-twentieth-century world political situation consists of two great powers facing each other, with all other countries—whatever they might delude themselves into thinking and however

[1] All translations of Dürrenmatt, unless otherwise noted, are by the present writer.

much they might preen themselves on their historical traditions—occupying essentially subsidiary positions. What goes on in those two great powers, including the daily life of the citizens, necessarily is of interest to anyone, since everything done in either of them automatically affects the rest of the world. In effect, of course, there is only one great power from this point of view, since Russian literature is censored and, consequently, unless the literature has been smuggled out of the country, it is of significance only as an obliquely written political position paper and not as a sincere cultural expression.

"Small state" literature, on the other hand, is of no interest to anyone except, possibly, the comparatively small number of people living in that particular country. Thus, a play about American family life by Arthur Miller or Tennessee Williams becomes a play of universal interest by virtue of America's political position in the world, whereas a play about Swiss family life by Dürrenmatt would barely manage to interest the Swiss theatergoing public, who would probably be more interested in one of the American plays, and in any case is not large enough to support a writer all by itself. Because of this, according to Dürrenmatt, "small state" writers like himself are obliged to write symbolically and without psychological empathy.

Another thread that runs through all of Dürrenmatt's work is his refusal to write in traditional tragic form. Given his orientation to reality, Dürrenmatt's plots are inevitably tragic in theme; yet they are invariably comic in form and tone. The reason is that Dürrenmatt believes that tragedy is no longer possible as an art form. In the twentieth century we *live* tragedy—and we live it as we have never lived it before. Tragedy in real life now is different from tragedy in real life in pre-modern times, both in kind and in degree.

That it differs in degree is easy to see: with the invention in theory and the elaboration in practice of the ultimate weapon—a weapon capable of destroying humanity, if not in a cataclysmic, fiery immolation then gradually, through wasting and scabrous diseases and mutation into subhuman life forms—mankind has the possibility of a real-life tragedy that paralyzes the resources of even the most originally imaginative artistic minds. Nothing, in other words, can be invented that can stand comparison with the horror that now lurks permanently in the collective subconscious of humanity: the horror of both personal and genetic extinction.

That modern tragedy differs from pre-modern tragedy in kind as well is perhaps not quite as easy to see. Traditional tragedy had as its purpose—a purpose that was both artistic and moralistic—the purification of the spectator's emotions and fears, for the tragedy had in it elements of an optimistic and mystical spiritual apotheosis. Indeed, the older tragedy offered us hope for the future and balm for our fears. Suffering was believed to have a purifying effect and to prepare us for the eternal salvation that emanates from a supernal fount of mercy and forgiveness. That is no longer possible; and tragedy no longer can be invented because it *is.*

For Dürrenmatt, then, tragedy can be approached on the stage only through comedy: tragedy becomes a sardonic and self-lacerating mockery of the human condition. Dürrenmatt illustrates this by giving four examples of how different authors might treat a particular tragic subject ("Dramaturgische überlegungen zu den Wiedertäufen," in *Die Wiedertufer,* p. 101). He takes as an example of a real-life tragedy the death of Captain Robert Falcon Scott and his companions on their return from their abortive expedition to the South Pole in 1912. Scott and his party, already overcome with a sense of disappointment and futility as a result of finding the Norwegian flag at the South Pole when they got there, froze to death in a blizzard on their way back.

Shakespeare, according to Dürrenmatt, would have treated the story in such a way as to make it seem that the great explorer's fall was due to defects in his character, such as unjustified pride in his abilities; jealousy and betrayal on the part of his companions would have done the rest of the damage. Bertolt Brecht would have caused the tragedy to come about through sociological factors and faulty class feelings. Scott's upbringing as a member of the English upper class would have prevented him from lowering himself to the extent of permitting himself to be seen drawn around by dogs, and he would have insisted on purchasing ponies instead. Ponies being considerably more expensive than sled dogs, this decision would have forced him to skimp on the purchase of other equipment, with the foreseeable tragic consequences. In Samuel Beckett's treatment the tragedy would already have happened. The whole action would be reduced to the ending. Scott and his companions would be encased in separate blocks of ice, speaking into the void, unanswered and unaware of being heard.

Finally there is Dürrenmatt's way. Scott, as in Brecht's version, may be imagined back at base, purchasing provisions for the expedition. He is locked in a freezer room by mistake, presumably while purchasing meat, and there—as the result of an idiotic oversight—meets the same death by freezing that in actual fact befell him in the Antarctic wastes; but this time it happens in the middle of a city, a few feet from a busy street.

Dürrenmatt rightly points out that there is a radical difference between Scott dying among the Antarctic glaciers, hopelessly far from any help, as if he were stranded on another planet, and Scott dying in a freezer in the midst of civilization, the victim of someone's absentmindedness. In the first case his death is tragic in the classical sense; in the second his death is comic. In both cases the death is the same, death by freezing; but the incongruity, unexpectedness, and senselessness inherent in the "comic" death make it more tragic. A death that is the result of chance may truly be described as tragic, whereas the real Scott's real death, the result of freely willed risk taking, may best be described as exquisitely appropriate. As Dürrenmatt puts it, the "worst turn" that a story can take is the turn toward comedy.

Dürrenmatt's "worst turn" theory implies two things: that the worst turn a story can take is also the most exemplary and that only comedy—not tragedy—can lead us to that worst turn. The worst turn is always "comic" because it is something at which we can only laugh—but the laughter manifests itself as the despairing rictus of mental self-laceration. The "manly lachrymosity" of which Sir Richard Steele spoke in the early eighteenth century is no longer pertinent to the contemplation of reality. Lachrymosity, in any case, can now be seen as a self-indulgent appeal for sympathy not only to one's fellow beings but also to the Almighty. It is the introduction of theater, with all its attendant insincerity, into life. Laughter, on the other hand, is *real:* it is instinctive, and so one cannot laugh and think at the same time. To think is to rationalize, to explain away, to bring about a transference from reality to a mental icon. The worst turn a story can take is also the most exemplary, because if the worst possible outcome of a situation is not presented and dissected, we have an appreciably smaller chance of avoiding it.

With these principal attitudes and techniques of Dürrenmatt's in mind, we can turn to an examination of the works that illustrate his most important theme, the loss of belief in a transcendental order and the consequent supremacy of chance—a synonym for meaninglessness in human life.

To recognize the utter meaninglessness of the individual human life and to acknowledge that life itself *and everything else* are the result of a virtually infinite series of fortuities is to accept the fact that we, as well as everything we perceive, are effects without a cause. It is to accept logic as a purely human artifact. Religion, too, accepted logic as a purely human artifact when it found itself obliged to resort to the concept of an Unmoved Mover to define God. An Unmoved Mover is not so different from a Causeless Cause that we need worry about the difference; and a Causeless Cause implies the supremacy of chance in the creation of the world and in human affairs. If logic is a purely human artifact, thinking becomes a game; if chance is the governing principle in everything, all human volition becomes as significant and meaningful as a throw of the dice. No one who accepts these discoveries can accept them with equanimity, but their acceptance necessarily is particularly painful for a person who, like Dürrenmatt, was brought up in a strict religious home by a professional in the field.

Dürrenmatt's crisis of belief can best be seen in *Der Meteor* (1966). The play's protagonist, Wolfgang Schwitter, is a Nobel Prize-winning author who appears to be dying. It is necessary to stress that he *appears* to be dying—at first glance. In fact he is not dying; he is dead. When the play opens, he has just been resurrected in the traditional religious sense. During the course of the play he dies again and is again resurrected. Try as he will, he cannot die—or at least cannot stay dead. He is like a meteor, flaring up to be the center of attention and destroying everyone who comes too close. In the course of the play four people who come near him die unexpectedly and seven others have their lives ruined.

Dürrenmatt said that the idea on which he based the play was the resurrection of a man who does not believe in resurrection. He emphasized that Schwitter really is resurrected. This is not a case of a quack making a false diagnosis. Dürrenmatt makes a point of characterizing the doctor as being particularly distinguished. His purpose in inventing this rather bizarre situation was, he said, to test the extent to which religion is still valid in modern times: "Christians believe in the resurrection of the human being at the Last Judgment—the question is only to what extent Christians still really believe this today."

What does Dürrenmatt mean by this? Is his insistence that Schwitter experiences a real, Lazarus-like resurrection from death an expression of belief, as some critics have alleged? It is clearly a confusing situation, which is certainly not helped by Dürrenmatt's insistence that an actual resurrection must be understood to have taken place. Nevertheless, on Dürrenmatt's own evidence the play is not an affirmation of religious faith. To the question of whether he is a believer, Dürrenmatt has flatly stated that to him doubt is as important as belief, that belief cannot exist without doubt, and that whatever one's belief, it must remain purely subjective. The moment belief is externalized and made objective, it becomes dogma, which has nothing to do with belief. The church (that is, organized religion), according to Dürrenmatt, is totally useless and one of the worst things that one encounters in life because it forces on people a belief, a religion, and a Christianity that are unreal.

Dürrenmatt's conviction that organized religion is essentially a sham explains the real significance of Schwitter's resurrection. The play is set in a fantasy world where resurrections are possible. Schwitter, a nonbeliever, refuses to believe that he has been dead. Resurrection, Dürrenmatt tells us, is possible only through belief, and belief is subjective. Resurrection and all other aspects of religion exist for the believer; they do not exist in their traditional religious forms because in those forms they are objectivized and become dogma, that is, a prescribed system of thought that does not have to be understood in order to be believed.

Dürrenmatt's point in *The Meteor* is the same as Sartre's in *The Flies*: religion ceases to exist the moment it ceases to be believed in. Just as for Orestes the Furies and Zeus cease to exist the moment he ceases to believe in them, so for Schwitter resurrection does not, and cannot, exist because he considers it and all the other appurtenances of religion nonsensical. Religion thus is seen as an abstraction without concrete referents that some people happen to believe in.

Twelve years earlier Dürrenmatt had written another play that touched directly on the validity of religion in modern times. *Ein Engel kommt nach Babylon* (*An Angel Comes to Bab-*

*ylon,* 1954) is a play that makes no pretense at reality, as *The Meteor* does, but is placed in a timeless setting peopled by symbolic characters. The scene is ostensibly ancient Babylon, but there are bicycles, streetcars, and "an old-Babylonian gas-lamp." The ruler is the biblical Nebuchadnezzar, who has just become king again after serving for 900 years as King Nimrod's footstool. Nimrod is currently occupying that position, and the two men are clearly symbols of the eternal and mindless interchange of power: political power is self-perpetuating and benefits nothing but itself.

The hero of the play is Akki, the symbol of individualistic independence. Akki is a beggar, the last one left in Babylon because Nebuchadnezzar has outlawed begging and ordered all beggars to become servants of the state. The other main characters are an Angel and a young girl named Kurrubi. The latter is only a few minutes old, having been created by God and handed over to the Angel with instructions that she be given to the lowliest of men. Kurrubi, who represents selfless love, is given to Nebuchadnezzar by mistake because the king has disguised himself as a beggar in order to make a last-ditch try at recruiting Akki for the civil service. He and Akki have a begging contest, which Nebuchadnezzar loses, leading the Angel to take him for the lowest man on earth.

Nebuchadnezzar, vexed at being taken for the lowest man on earth, gives Kurrubi to Akki. She becomes the beggar's companion for ten days, and the whole city falls in love with her because of the selfless love that radiates from her. The people insist that she marry the king, and thus she learns that the lowest and the highest of mortals are one. She refuses to marry the king unless he becomes a beggar again, which he refuses to do. Nobody else will do it either, and the populace's "love" turns to hate when they realize that Kurrubi is serious about loving only the lowest of mortals. She is handed over to the hangman, but the fairy tale ends in the traditional manner when it turns out that the hangman is really Akki in disguise. They escape happily into the desert, where they can be safe from the corruption of "civilized" society.

Dürrenmatt is dealing with two parallel symbolic themes here: the ultimate triumph of the type of human being represented by Akki, the self-reliant man who is independent of both society and religion, and the inability of human beings who accept values that are imposed on them to accept selfless love. The Angel is one of Dürrenmatt's most amusing creations. His character throughout is that of an absentminded professor. He bears a strong resemblance to the equally bumbling Angel in Shaw's *The Simpleton of the Unexpected Isles* (1934), but his function in the play is much closer to that of the three gods in Brecht's *The Good Woman of Setzuan* (1938–1941). In that play the three gods descend to earth with a traditional religious function in view: they wish to find an honest person in the general morass of immorality that they feel their domain has become. When they do find such a person, they reward her for her honesty and then abandon her when her honesty brings her into difficulties. Brecht clearly intends them to represent the uselessness of religion in the modern world and to show that its separation from the practicalities of everyday life and its insistence on the supremacy of abstract qualities bring about a combination that is lethally cruel to those who take its teaching literally.

The Angel who comes to Babylon is just as cruel in his impersonal way. When Kurrubi expresses amazement at human cruelty, he replies, "Be calm, my child. A simple accident only, which has no effect on the harmony of things." Everything becomes simple from the religious point of view, in other words, since it is a point of view from the aspect of eternity. From that aspect, of course, everything is necessarily insignificant. When Kurrubi suggests that the lowest of men must surely be unhappy, the Angel replies, "Whatever is created is good, and whatever is good is happy. In my extended travels throughout creation I have never seen the smallest atom of unhappiness." The evil that the Angel is unable to see is the evil of human institutions, the means by which the power possessors coerce the helpless majority.

Akki is by far the most dignified and exemplary character in the play. He preserves his dignity by refusing to have anything to do with the things that might tend to associate him with those he despises: all the money that he begs each day he throws away in the evening. The only thing he keeps is food: "The culinary art, properly practiced, is the only aspect of human endeavor about which nothing bad can be said." Dürrenmatt looks upon Akki and his kind as a sort of dike holding back the impatient floods of ignorance: "We are secret teachers . . . of the people. . . . We obey no laws in order to celebrate freedom."

That Dürrenmatt, brought up in a professionally religious atmosphere, had difficulty in rejecting his upbringing is not surprising. Nor can it be said to be surprising that he made attempts in his writing to reconcile his disillusionment with his former belief. These attempts may be said to be corollaries to, rather than contradictions of, plays like *An Angel Comes to Babylon* and *The Meteor.* The themes of this group of writings are wish fulfillment (expressing a nostalgia for a world that makes sense) and an attempt to explain the classic religious problem of the existence of unalloyed evil. Both of these themes are exemplified in two of Dürrenmatt's detective novels, *Der Richter und sein Henker* (*The Judge and His Hangman,* 1952) and *Der Verdacht* (The Suspicion, translated as *The Quarry,* 1953). Dürrenmatt's attraction to the detective novel is in itself interesting. He wrote three—the other is *Das Versprechen* (*The Pledge,* 1958)—and each in its own way is a masterpiece of the genre.

The detective story is an essentially religious genre. It promises solutions to problems and the ultimate—but not too long delayed—triumph of good over evil; and it provides a suprahuman emissary to bring about these desirable ends. And the emissary *never* fails. In short, the detective genre makes exactly the same promises that religion makes. It is a microcosmic mirror image of religion that produces Judgment Day in the compass of a novel.

Near the beginning of his *Victims of Duty* (1954), Eugène Ionesco has his leading character, Choubert, discuss the history of drama:

> All the plays that have ever been written, from Ancient Greece to the present day, have never been anything but thrillers. Drama's always been realistic and there's always been a detective about. Every play's an investigation brought to a successful conclusion. There's a riddle, and it's solved in the final scene. Sometimes earlier. You seek and then you find. Might as well give the game away at the start. . . . The police arrive, there's an investigation and the criminal is unmasked.
>
> (Ionesco, *Plays,* vol. 2, trans. Donald Watson [London, 1958], 269–270)

Dramas of this sort are extremely comforting, of course. They constitute a closed world that is entirely sufficient unto itself and symmetrical in form, with a corresponding solution to every problem. A welcome relief from the open-ended world of reality where everything is asymmetrical and solutions, if they exist at all, rarely correspond to the problems with which they are linked.

It is thus no surprise that a desperate nostalgia for meaning would lead a writer to compose detective novels. In both *The Judge and His Hangman* and *The Quarry,* Dürrenmatt indulges in this sort of wish fulfillment as well as in his attempt to explain the problem of evil. In both books the detective is a senior officer of the Bern Police Department named Bärlach. Bärlach has all the attributes of the traditional fictional detective: he despises modern, impersonal scientific methods of detection and works on hunches derived from immersing himself in the situation, and he has a finely honed and barely concealed contempt for his superiors. Bärlach has one peculiarity that he does not share with the traditional fictional detective: he has cancer and knows that he has only a year to live.

The story of *The Judge and His Hangman* is not in itself remarkable. What matters for our purposes is that when the murderer is revealed at the end, it turns out that Bärlach knew his identity from the start—that is, he had solved the mystery almost as soon as he started investigating it: the magical solution by the all-knowing mythic figure of the heaven-sent detective, as it were. All through the novel Bärlach plays a cat-and-mouse game with the murderer so as to manipulate him into a situation where he murders again. This time he murders the real villain, a powerful, highly respected, wealthy man whom Bärlach has known since his youth and who represents the quality of absolute evil. This man is evil on principle, because he enjoys it, and in order to oppose the meaninglessness of virtue. At this point in his career Dürrenmatt can see no other way to solve the problem of evil than to kill the evil person, as if he were a disease carrier who must be eliminated before he can infect anyone.

In *The Quarry,* which takes place immediately after *The Judge and His Hangman,* Bärlach is recuperating in the hospital from the operation that is designed to give him another year of life. While reading a copy of *Life* magazine dating from 1945 (the story takes place in 1948), Bärlach runs across a picture of a Nazi concentration camp doctor who has disappeared. The picture, secretly taken in the camp by an inmate, shows the doctor at his favorite pastime, operating without anesthesia. Bärlach's surgeon, an old personal friend, is reminded by the picture of a Swiss physician named Emmenberger, who is reputed to have spent the war in Chile and is now running a clinic for rich people in the hills near Zurich.

Bärlach, his traditional magical detecting powers failing him momentarily, perhaps because of his debilitating illness, has himself admitted to Emmenberger's clinic, where he interrogates his quarry so clumsily that the surgeon's suspicions are instantly aroused. Emmenberger injects Bärlach with a sedative that puts him to sleep for five days, and when he awakes, he finds himself in a prisonlike room adjacent to the operating room. His nurse, a totally crazed Christian religious fanatic, calmly informs him that no one ever comes out of this room alive. In addition, since he has just retired as commissioner of the Bern city police, his picture is all over the papers. It is as if the hitherto infallible detective's powers are being sapped as he nears his own demise, just as the powers of nature are sapped as the cold death grip of winter approaches. And death is approaching rather more rapidly than had been anticipated, since Emmenberger tells Bärlach that he will kill him that day by operating on him without anesthesia unless Bärlach can convince him of his own moral rectitude.

Dürrenmatt tries to explain the problem of absolute evil in human character by having Emmenberger argue that nothing means anything, that the flow of human affairs is controlled by chance—an aimless and unpredictable drifting. From this doctrine he has the doctor conclude that there is no such thing as justice, whence it follows that human "justice" is an arbitrary artifact, which is true; that man is therefore free, which is also true; and that this freedom is demonstrated by the willingness to commit crimes, which is so ridiculous that it is hardly worthwhile to point out that it is not true. To all this Dürrenmatt rather effectively has Bärlach unable to give an answer, for indeed good cannot argue with evil, since all argument between total opposites that have no point of contact whatsoever (for instance, God exists versus God does not exist) is merely futile puerility.

Dürrenmatt presents here what is essentially a mirror image of the last scene of Ionesco's *The Killer* (1958), in which Bérenger tries to argue the cause of good against the silent and sinister dwarfish killer. In Ionesco the symbol of evil triumphs also, but far more effectively, by not saying anything: evil is self-explanatory, good is not. The bent toward evil is either (as in Ionesco's killer or Dürrenmatt's doctor) a genetic predisposition toward socially aberrant behavior, probably caused by a minimally different pattern of cortical convolution, or (as with the rank-and-file concentration camp personnel) a normal predisposition to abrogate responsibility for one's acts and seek refuge in the comforting camaraderie paradoxically composed of self-enslavement and the feelings of superiority that the mob grants its members.

In the event, Bärlach is saved. Good triumphs, but it triumphs magically. Dürrenmatt breaks the deadlock he has set up with the triumph of evil as the only possible solution by introducing a mysterious, ghostly, almost supernatural figure: a gigantic Jew named Gulliver who had been operated on without anesthesia by Emmenberger in the concentration camp. Despite his size, Gulliver has the ability to move silently through the night—he never appears by day—and squeeze through small spaces. He is scarred all over and seems to nourish himself exclusively with enormous drafts of hard liquor, bottles of which, together with glasses, he carries concealed in his ragged caftan without compromising the silence of his movements. In short, Gulliver is a magical myth figure with elements of the Wandering Jew, here transformed into an apostle of revenge on the enemies of the Jews. Gulliver forces Emmenberger to commit suicide, and so the story ends. The problem of unalloyed evil continues to baffle us, not least because it is the only position that can be defended logically; and justice triumphs through magical wish fulfillment.

Emmenberger's argument about the supremacy of chance makes no sense as a "logical" justification of evil, but that chance is the supreme—indeed, the only—element in the world is Dürrenmatt's second principal theme. Linked to this are three subsidiary themes: the futility of trying to control human events, the futility of attempting to impose reason on reality, and the inevitability of the worst possible outcome. This last is, of course, a purely Dürrenmattian idea used for dramatic effect.

The best way to lead into a consideration of Dürrenmatt's view of chance is to continue our examination of his detective novels with his third and last one, *The Pledge,* significantly subtitled *Requiem for the Detective Story.* Dürrenmatt's subtitle indicates that for him the detective story is dead, and that neither amusement nor nostalgia can any longer justify writing it. The funeral dirge that he chooses to sing over the grave of the genre is particularly effective because he changes nothing about the mythic, infallible figure of the detective himself. Inspector Matthäi is the mainstay of the Zurich cantonal police. Although only fifty, he is about to retire and take a temporary job reorganizing the Jordanian police. He is the ascetic-cerebral type of detective. For all his years on the force Matthäi has lived in the same furnished room and taken his meals in the same restaurant. He does not drink or smoke, and appears wholly uninterested in sex. His colleagues, while in awe of his ability, call him "Matt the Automat." In short, he is the Sherlock Holmes thinking-machine type of detective.

On Matthäi's last day at the office a report comes in: the horribly mutilated body of a young girl has been found in the woods near a remote village in the mountains near Zurich. There are no clues, but the man who found the body, an itinerant peddler with a record of child molestation, is suspected. Matthäi just manages to save the man from being lynched and takes him to the city, having first given his word to the mother of the murdered child that he will bring the killer to justice. The prisoner, after being subjected to rigorous interrogation by Matthäi's assistant, hangs himself in his cell. The case is closed. Matthäi prepares to take off for Jordan. At the airport, just as he is about to board his plane, he turns around and goes back. A combination of seeing a crowd of schoolchildren, the nagging memory of his promise, and the hunch, so characteristic of the infallible detective, that something was not quite right with the solution causes him to give up everything and devote himself to solving the case.

Matthäi is now alone. He is no longer a member of the police, and he has let his new employers down. Like most of the magical and ultimately omniscient detectives of literature, he is now a loner attached only marginally to the fabric of society. It is not clear whether he is acting a part or whether he really is transformed; but having, so to speak, left society—which it was formerly his duty to protect—he becomes an outcast. He moves to a seedy hotel room, starts to drink and smoke, stops shaving regularly, and generally lets himself deteriorate. Pretty soon he disappears altogether, only to surface as the proprietor of a run-down gas station and roadhouse on one of the highways leading to Zurich. He himself is more run-down than ever and seems to live in a permanent alcoholic stupor. He has married a former prostitute with a young daughter, and in her slatternly way she helps him run the place.

The great detective is, in fact, solving the mystery. He has found out that the murder he promised to solve was the third murder in the past several years involving the mutilation and murder of a blonde girl dressed in red. He has figured out, by drawing a diagram of the locations of the murders, that the killer must in each case have passed the gas station he has purchased. He therefore has set a trap, keeping his blonde stepdaughter dressed in red and playing in front of the building. The plan works. After a considerable time he notices signs that the stepdaughter has been seeing someone secretly. A police trap is set: Matthäi is about to be vindicated. But the killer does not fall into the trap, and Matthäi is disgraced again, this time irrevocably. He vegetates in his gas station and, totally obsessed with his crusade to find the murderer and fulfill his promise, becomes a sodden alcoholic, still waiting for the killer to show up and still convinced that both his deductions and his method were right.

And here Dürrenmatt produces his "kicker": Matthäi *was* right. The great detective did not fail; as always, he had analyzed the situation correctly and correctly had set about laying a trap for his quarry. Matthäi, despite his run-down appearance, had followed a rigidly logical line of reasoning and had arrived at the correct solution of the mystery.

But Dürrenmatt has written a "requiem" for the mystery novel: logic and reason applied by a superior brain are not enough. Humans, despite their superior minds and understanding, despite their ratiocinative powers, cannot control reality, which is random and unpredictable. Human reason is powerless against chance. Despite the correctness of his conclusions, Matthäi foundered because he put his faith in his own ability to understand reality, which cannot be understood. The attempt to impose reason upon reality is like trying to paint an infinite number of randomly changing shapes at once. Years later it is discovered that the murderer was on his way to the rendezvous with the girl, was about to fall into Matthäi's carefully laid trap, when he was killed instantly in a traffic accident.

Dürrenmatt's point, which he repeats in several of his plays, is that chance is the governing principle in human affairs because we are the by-products of random chance, as is the universe. The tragedy of human striving is thus to a great extent comic because what happens is beyond our comprehension and our control. Tragedy in the traditional sense is self-created by human beings who destroy themselves or others through their own errors or evil intentions, or it is visited upon human beings by greater powers for reasons of their own, the nature of which can only remain presumptive (as in the very similar cases of Oedipus and Job). But when nothing makes sense, when chance governs all, one can only laugh, perhaps bitterly. Captain Scott freezing to death in the meat cooler in the middle of a large city because someone has been absentminded is just as tragic as Captain Scott freezing to death heroically in the Antarctic blizzard—but the latter is not funny.

The supremacy of chance has a number of corollaries in Dürrenmatt's work. Chief of these is his demonstration of the futility of trying to improve the world and the inevitability of the worst possible outcome.

The world improvers and their futility are the subject of three of Dürrenmatt's best plays: *Romulus der Grosse* (*Romulus the Great,* 1956), *Die Ehe des Herrn Mississippi* (*The Marriage of Mr. Mississippi,* 1952), and *Die Physiker* (*The Physicists,* 1962). In the first of these plays he deals with the end of the West Roman Empire in the year 476. In place of the actual Romulus Augustulus, who was only about fifteen years old, Dürrenmatt creates a fictional Romulus the "Great" (the honorific is Dürrenmatt's, and it is sardonic), a man in late middle age whose urbanity nicely combines culture with cynicism. Romulus has been on the throne for about twenty years, an extraordinarily long reign for a late Roman emperor. He has managed to "rule" for so long by the simple expedient of not ruling. For twenty years he has lived in his crumbling country villa raising chickens, which seems to be the only practical thing that interests him.

But Romulus does have one other practical interest: the final and definitive destruction of the Roman Empire. Underneath his urbanity and detached amusement Romulus is a moral fanatic. As a historical scholar he has seen that the history of the Roman Empire is a history of conquest, oppression, war, and rapine. He has therefore married the daughter of the previous emperor in order to ascend the throne and because, as he puts it, he considers himself Rome's judge. His decision is that the Roman Empire must be destroyed in order to expiate its sins, and he pursues this end with the moral fervor of a Puritan divine.

When the play opens, Romulus is at the apex of his career, as he sees it. His twenty years of doing nothing have rendered Rome powerless, and it is now crumbling before the onslaught of the barbarian Germanic hordes. His conscience is clear because, with the typical fanatic's logic, he plans to expiate his deed with his own life; he will await the arrival of the Germans, who will, he feels sure, kill him.

It is here, with Dürrenmatt's characteristic sardonic humor, that chance intervenes and not only spoils Romulus' plan but also makes it ridiculous. Instead of beheading Romulus on the spot, Odoacer, the leader of the Germans, prostrates himself before the emperor. He, it turns out, is also urbane and highly cultured—and a devoted chicken breeder. Aware that the innate barbarism of his people will break out and wreak havoc everywhere the moment his nephew Theodoric takes over, he has come to surrender to what he imagines to be the indestructible might of the Roman Empire, so that his people will be civilized in the Roman manner. Theodoric, he surmises, will soon kill him and take over, since he is displaying all the most dangerous symptoms: he isn't interested in girls, is a teetotaler, sleeps on the bare ground, practices fighting daily, and does calisthenics at every spare moment.

Odoacer and Romulus recognize that chance has ruined their plans. Each has judged his people and planned carefully, and each is made to look—and be—a ridiculous failure. Romulus becomes "Great" only at the end of the play, when, defeated in all his plans, he accepts his fate: to mark time while Odoacer rules until Theodoric feels secure enough to kill them and speed civilization on its way back to barbarism—the worst possible solution. In this case, however, one that really happened.

In *The Marriage of Mr. Mississippi,* Dürrenmatt introduces us to two more "world betterers." This time they are religious improvers. Mississippi and St. Claude, boyhood companions in the gutters of a great city, have become fanatical adherents of rival religious philosophies as a result of having read books they picked up by chance. Mississippi read the Old Testament; St. Claude, *Das Kapital.* Inspired by serendipitous chance, they have clawed their way out of the gutter. Mississippi has studied law with a view to reinstituting absolute justice in the world in the form of the Mosaic law. In pursuit of this ideal he has already succeeded in forcing through 200 death sentences in his capacity as public prosecutor at the time the play opens. By the end of the play he has more than 350 death sentences in thirty years as public prosecutor to his credit. St. Claude, on the other hand, having read Marx, has become a professional revolutionary, Russian citizen, colonel in the Red Army, and member of the Cominform Politburo.

They meet again in the symbolic room in the house now occupied by Mississippi and his wife, Anastasia. The room is symbolic because it represents the ordinary, everyday world in which people live. The room is depersonalized: tastelessly furnished with bric-a-brac from various periods and showing a northern bucolic view out of one window and a southern one out of the other. In short, the room is a hodgepodge suspended in space and representing the Western world in its most quotidian aspects. In Dürrenmatt's words, "it stinks to high heaven," and it is what the play is about. That is, the play is about the modern world, which is too diverse to be saved by any one ideology and which has perhaps become so tasteless and depersonalized that it is no longer worth saving.

The details of the plot are too complex and fantastic to be summarized here; but, clearly, in Dürrenmatt's scheme both Mississippi and St. Claude must die because they are attempting to impose their individual wills upon the amorphousness of chance. As fanatical idealists, Mississippi and St. Claude are predictable; but the intrinsically unpredictable cannot be controlled by the predictable. The unpredictable here is Anastasia, the eternal femme fatale, the individual without morals who lives only to satisfy her own desires. Anastasia had murdered her previous husband for having an affair with Mississippi's wife; Mississippi had murdered his wife for her infidelity—although he calls it an execution in accordance with the Mosaic law. He then forced Anastasia to marry him for purposes of mutual punishment and expiation. Meanwhile Anastasia, ever without principles, has affairs with St. Claude in case his revolution succeeds and with Diego, a high government official, in case it doesn't. At the end Mississippi, suspecting all this, poisons Anastasia and is himself poisoned when he drinks a cup of coffee with which Anastasia intended to kill St. Claude, who is shot for failing to bring about the revolution. Diego, the eternal opportunist, as unprincipled as Anastasia, comes out on top.

Throughout the play the figure of Count Bodo von Überlohe-Zabernsee is present either in spirit or in person. Bodo is a direct contrast to Mississippi and St. Claude, for he is the type of altruistic idealist whose principle is to see the world as composed of individuals to be helped. Like Mississippi, St. Claude, and Romulus, Bodo lives by a prescribed system. The fact that he does good instead of the evil inherent in believing that everyone must be bent to fit an arbitrary concept of conduct makes no difference. To try to impose order upon chaos is futile. In a perverse way it is the closest we can come to sinning.

The futility of trying to impose order upon chaos is nowhere better illustrated than in *The Physicists,* Dürrenmatt's central work. *The Physicists* not only incorporates in its highly ingenious plot all the aspects of the supremacy-of-chance theme, but also leads us into Dürrenmatt's third main theme: the triumph of human mechanization.

*The Physicists* is about the fate of the world and takes place, appropriately for such a subject, in a lunatic asylum that is more like an extremely luxurious rest home. It is run by a hunchbacked psychiatrist who makes a point of emphasizing her virginity. Resident in the particular section that we see is Möbius, who has been there for fifteen years. "Möbius" is an interestingly subtle label that Dürrenmatt has invented to indicate that its bearer inevitably gets nowhere, like the Möbius curve that twists about itself, always dizzyingly returning the bewildered traveler along it to his starting point.

It is significant that Dürrenmatt gives his protagonist this ominous name despite the fact that Möbius is the most profound thinker *and* the most selflessly moral man who has ever lived. Some twenty years previously, when Möbius was still a student, he solved the problem of gravity and the unified field theory, and by now he has worked out the equation for the "principle of universal discovery." Most of this is just scientific-sounding jargon, of course. The point is that Möbius is a myth figure representing the apex of human striving and the perfection of human knowledge. He is the man who possesses the formula for knowing everything, for whom the universe can hold no secrets, either actually or potentially. He also represents the culmination of human goodness and selflessness.

Realizing that the publication of his discoveries would be fatal to humanity because it is not yet ready—and perhaps may never be—to bear the burden of ultimate knowledge, Möbius passes up the chance to become the most famous and admired man of all time, for he realizes that knowledge is power, that power tends to corrupt, and that absolute power tends to corrupt absolutely. And absolute power is what his discoveries offer to humanity. Instead, Möbius pretends to be insane, announcing that King Solomon appears to him in visions, and has himself committed for life to the asylum. As he puts it, physicists—that is, searchers for the ultimate nature of reality—are "wild beasts" who must never be unleashed on mankind again.

Möbius shares his quarters with two recently arrived inmates, also physicists; one of them thinks he is Sir Isaac Newton, and the other is under the impression that he is Albert Einstein. Actually all three are completely sane. Möbius, as we have already seen, is deliberately pretending to be insane in order to save humanity. Einstein and Newton are pretending to be insane for precisely the opposite reason. Both are eminent physicists who, having run across the traces of Möbius' early work, have been able to see its potential although they do not have his ability, and therefore have not been able to work out his conclusions. Newton and Einstein are agents for the secret services of the West and the East, respectively, and have been sent by their governments to bring Möbius back so that the destructive potential of his discoveries may be used to bring about the supremacy of their own governments.

What happens next is the culmination of humanistic idealism. Möbius, the myth figure of both mental and moral perfection, persuades his fellow physicists to follow his example. He convinces them that they are "wild beasts" whose knowledge will only be used for harm by lesser minds. He persuades them, in short, to give up fame, fortune, family, and freedom, and remain with him in the asylum for the rest of their lives so that mankind may be saved from itself:

> Only in the mental hospital can we still be free. Only in the mental hospital can we still think. Out there our thoughts are dynamite. . . . Either we remain in this lunatic asylum or the world becomes one. Either we extinguish ourselves in the memory of men or mankind itself is extinguished.
> (*Werkausgabe,* vol. 7, pp 75–76)

Then, heroically, the three physicists resign themselves to their fate:

> NEWTON: Lunatic, yet wiser than before.
> EINSTEIN: Caged, yet freer than before.
> MÖBIUS: Physicists, yet guiltless.

Their sense of self-satisfaction is only momentary, however. It is here that Möbius' name becomes significant. He is back where he started from. The world cannot be saved by the goodness and self-abnegation of a few. In trying to save the world by burying their superiority, Möbius and his two disciples are guilty of hubris—quite possibly the most monumental case of hubris on record. As Möbius had remarked earlier, what has once been thought can never be unthought. The three sublime moral heroes suddenly become ridiculous when they discover that they are prisoners, their nurses replaced by guards who are professional thugs. The hunchbacked psychiatrist who runs the place really is mad and really does think that King Solomon appears to her with instructions to conquer the world. She has stolen Möbius' notes and taken over the universe by means of his formula for attaining the key to all knowledge.

Three things need to be noted about the way in which *The Physicists* is written. First, it illustrates Dürrenmatt's thesis that a play must show the inevitability of the worst possible outcome of the action even if that outcome is a grotesque exaggeration and is not realistic. The point is that it might become realistic at some point in the future and must therefore be warned against. The worst possible outcome is the inevitable and logical conclusion of a series of events that, like the speeding train in the downsloping tunnel of Dürrenmatt's short story, is started on a trajectory toward doom. We do not always arrive at the worst possible outcome in life because the trajectory is occasionally stopped, if only temporarily, either by stopgap human intervention or, most often, by chance.

Second, *The Physicists* shows Dürrenmatt's use of the grotesque—another anti-realistic device to illustrate the core of reality. Two kinds of grotesques meander through Dürrenmatt's works, showing up under various guises in almost every one of his plays. The grotesque is the distortion of the human character so as to bring to the fore what the author sees as the central quality of the character or of the segment of humanity that the character is intended to represent. Typically, the grotesquerie consists in the display either of the central moral warp of a type of humanity or of an insensitive naïveté masquerading in a self-induced stupor of idealism as profound moral responsibility: the world rescuer complex, in other words. We can see the latter type clearly in Möbius, Romulus, Mississippi, and St. Claude, in whom the single-minded, self-sacrificing pursuit of an exalted idealism aimed at reforming some or all of the ills of humanity transforms the character into almost the opposite: either, as with Möbius, into a guileless fool unwittingly stripped of all power by the forces he has tried to thwart or, as with Romulus, Mississippi, and St. Claude, into a ruthless fanatic at the mercy of his own theory.

The other type of grotesque, the one that displays a central moral warp of humanity, is well illustrated in *The Physicists* by Dr. von Zahnd, the owner and director of the lunatic asylum and the only really insane person in the play. In her the lust for power is reflected in the grotesquerie of the human body's distortion. The doctor is hunchbacked and insane, and her insistence on her virginity raises denial of life to the level of a principle. Claire Zachanassian, "the richest woman in the world," who is the protagonist of *Der Besuch der alten Dame* (*The Visit,* 1956), has become obsessed and corrupted by power (in the form of money rather than equations), and it has dehumanized her, as shown symbolically by her being almost as much artifact as flesh and blood.

The dehumanization of people is Dürrenmatt's third main theme. It is a quintessentially twentieth-century theme, closely related to the loss of belief. Much can legitimately be said against religion and much can be said for a life free from religious beliefs, but there is one essential advantage to the religious life: it necessarily treats—or gives the impression of treating—each human being as a separate and unique individual. The purely secular life, despite its manifold superiorities, does not necessarily protect the uniqueness of the individual.

Dürrenmatt was not the first writer to discover the phenomenon of secular dehumanization. That dubious honor belongs to Franz Kafka, who symbolically robbed characters of their identity by depriving them of their names (though a nominal label is in itself a pitiful form of identity) and by turning them into animals. Jean Giraudoux has the Ragpicker in *The Madwoman of Chaillot* (1945) describe the new dehumanized breed as faceless, with gelatinous eyes.

In Dürrenmatt we see dehumanization in the form of the mechanization of the human being. In *The Physicists,* the play in which virtually all of his important themes are summed up, Dr. von Zahnd becomes a personification of the formulas she has stolen from Möbius. Her control of the world through those formulas is impersonal and inhuman, visually concretized in the robotized thugs she uses to carry out her orders. To treat human beings in accordance with formulas is literally to turn them into machines.

Some people, however, do not need to turn themselves or be turned into machines; they seem to have been born as part of the machine that society has become. In *Frank V* (1960) Dürrenmatt shows us a "natural" progression from old-fashioned individualistic "free enterprise" evil to evil as a matter-of-course characterological appendage of personality. Frank V is the president of a private bank founded by his great-great-grandfather, Frank I. Ever since its founding the bank has operated on two inflexible business principles: "Never make an honest deal" and "Never pay back any money."

The play relates how the bank became one of the richest in Europe by faithfully following these two rules. Nowadays, however, freewheeling individualistic crookedness no longer works because it can work only by outsmarting other individuals. It is powerless against the enormous and impersonal megamachine that society has become in the secular and overpopulated times in which Frank V lives. The firm is in such a desperate position—virtually on the brink of bankruptcy—as the play opens that Frank has to fake his own death so as to save the business temporarily by putting his life insurance money into it. Things get worse and worse, and in the end the bank is unexpectedly taken over by the younger generation, Frank VI and his sister, who lead the enterprise into "honesty" for the first time in its history—that is, they transform it into an entity that is even more ruthless and evil but performs its financial depredations in open and perfect conformity to the laws of the machine that society has become. In short, Dürrenmatt tells us the story of the transformation of the heads of pickpocketing, mugging, and racketeering gangs into "respectable" big-business executives.

In *Der Mitmacher* (The Conformist, translated as *The Sell-out,* 1976) Dürrenmatt writes about a man degraded by economic difficulties from wealth and professional prominence to being a cog in a machine without any will but the desire to stay alive at any cost. Doc is an intellectual, a prominent scientist, who gives up his university teaching position to take a job in industry. He becomes wealthy beyond the modest dreams of a university professor, but discovers that there are no tenured positions in industry. During a recession he loses his job and is impoverished (university positions in his field, he discovers, have meanwhile been filled by people with more modest financial ambitions). His family deserts him and he becomes a cab driver. In this job he meets Boss, a caricature of the gangster chief, who runs a murder-for-hire business. Killing is no problem for Boss—he has plenty of people who can do that efficiently enough—but getting rid of the bodies is.

Doc agrees to work for him and invents a process whereby bodies can be dissolved without trace. Boss's business flourishes, and Doc is installed in a cellar five floors below street level that he almost never leaves and where he installs his flesh-dissolving machine. In the course of the play Doc is obliged to dissolve the bodies of the woman he loves and of his son—and to deny that he knows them. At the end the Murder, Inc., gang for which Doc opted to work has passed from Boss's ruthless hands into the hands of the Establishment: the police, the mayor, the judiciary, and the governor now absorb the structure of the murderous gang into the greater and more complex structure of the state; and Doc becomes a smaller and totally insignificant cog in the social megamachine.

What Dürrenmatt is showing us in this play is that Doc as an intellectual or a rich man or a cab driver was in a very real sense outside and independent of society—not wholly, of course, but sufficiently so as to be able to have the feeling that he could make existential decisions about his life. As soon as he joins a group, as Dürrenmatt sees it, Doc gives up the modicum of freedom possessed by an intellectual, a plutocrat, or an independently contracting worker and becomes part of a machine. Doc's self-abasements—denying his mistress and his son and dissolving their bodies—are to prevent his being cast out of the machine, that is, killed; and since he has no belief, having started out as an intellectual, he is obligated to cling to life under any circumstances, since for him that is all that there is.

The mechanization of the human being that Dürrenmatt has shown us in the persons of Dr. von Zahnd and her robotized cohorts, in Doc, and in the sleekly modern Establishment figures of Frank V's children would never have been possible without what Dürrenmatt sees as the innate weakness and corruptibility of the human being. It is ultimately that point—that the human being is innately weak and corruptible—which crystallizes Dürrenmatt's basic philosophical belief. He has dramatized that belief in three of his most powerful plays, one of them the play that made him internationally famous, the other two comparatively obscure radio plays.

*Der Besuch der alten Dame* (The Visit of the Old Lady, translated as *The Visit,* 1956) takes Dürrenmatt's view of the world to a sardonic level equaled only by the ending of *The Physicists* and the parable about the various approaches to tragedy using Captain Scott as an example. The play is set in Güllen, a down-at-heels town somewhere in the German-speaking part of Europe. The town used to be quite prosperous, but in recent years it has become virtually derelict. The prevailing gloom has lifted a little lately with the news that Güllen's most illustrious native, the world's richest woman, Claire Zachanassian, is coming to visit the town for the first time since being drummed out of it forty-five years earlier as a woman of unsavory reputation. Claire, at that time Klara Wäscher, became pregnant as a result of a youthful affair with Alfred Ill, now the rundown and harried keeper of the general store. Ill, not wishing to marry the town's poorest girl, caused false evidence to be presented indicating that Klara was lying when she accused him of being the father. As a result she fled from the town and became a prostitute in Hamburg, where one of her clients, Zachanassian, the world's richest man, fell in love with her, married her, and promptly died, leaving her everything.

Now, dazzled by her money and totally forgetful of the distant past, the town fathers can only surmise that Claire is returning in order to save the town; and they depute Ill, as her old heartthrob, to romance her with memories of love in order to ease along the process of financial extraction that will rescue their town and them with it. In fact, they have been finessed by Claire. She has no desire to regenerate her native town, which is in its current straits because she has secretly bought all the industries and shut them down. Claire's desire is solely for revenge, and she is prepared to spend as much of the world's greatest fortune as necessary to get it.

During the welcoming banquet given by the town, she rises and offers the town a billion—half for the town and half to be divided equally among all its families—if in return they will at last grant her justice: "A billion for Güllen—if someone kills Alfred Ill." The citizens are horrified, of course, and rally loyally around their respected fellow townsman. Claire waits, confidently. Indeed, very soon Ill's friends and fellow citizens, starved for so long of all the good things of life—consumer goods—begin almost imperceptibly to get deeper and deeper into debt, justifying their actions by pretending that it is Ill's shameless crime that has been depriving them for all these years. Eventually, Ill realizes that even his family wants him to die (his son has a new car, his wife a new fur coat—on credit), and he loses his will to live. In one of the peaks of Dürrenmatt's stagecraft he is murdered as his "friends" crowd around him, ostensibly congratulating him for being of such material help in obtaining the money that saved the town.

Claire Zachanassian is another of Dürrenmatt's dehumanized monsters. In her case the condition is signified by the fact that much of her body consists of prostheses, as Ill discovers in his ludicrous attempts to recall their long-past lovemaking. The real protagonist of the play, however, is the population of Güllen. Dürrenmatt's portrayal not only of the gradual erosion of morality under the influence of economic pressure but also of the simultaneous process of imperceptible, unconscious, and perfectly sincere self-justification is unequaled in literature, outside Jonathan Swift, as a mordantly sardonic description of human nature. Economic self-interest determines morality, Dürrenmatt is saying in this play; and history backs him up.

*The Visit* is a straightforward play whose point is not really original. The idea that economics determines morality may be found as early as the 1830's in the opening scene of Georg Büchner's *Woyzeck.* It appears again in Shaw's *Mrs. Warren's Profession* (1895) and is the basis of Bertolt Brecht's best work. The only difference between Dürrenmatt and his predecessors is that he does not take the matter seriously and assumes a derisory rather than a reformist attitude to humanity.

In his two best radio plays, *Das Unternehmen der Wega* (Operation Vega, 1958) and *Abendstunde im Spätherbst* (translated as *Incident at Twilight,* 1957), Dürrenmatt has developed his attitude much further. Human character is no longer seen as something corrupted by outside influences, as in *The Visit,* but as something that has undergone an intrinsic change as a result of which the ethical restraints imposed upon human behavior, initially by religion and secondarily by society, have been paralyzed and are no longer operative or have disappeared altogether. Dürrenmatt attributes this state to the experience of scientifically organized genocide and of the creation and use of the Bomb. In his view these have given birth to a new power class consisting of moral mutants: people who accept the abnormal as normal, to whom enslavement to an emblematic way of life masquerades as freedom, and for whom moral responsibility is equated with personal safety and conformity.

In *Das Unternehmen der Wega,* Dürrenmatt introduces us to the new moral mutants. The *Wega* is a spaceship on the way to Venus in the year 2255. Venus has been used for years by both Russia and the Western powers as a dumping ground for undesirables—a sort of New Australia. Now each side wishes to enlist the help of the inhabitants in order to use Venus as a base from which to attack the other. The *Wega's* mission is, therefore, either to enlist the Venusians or to destroy them with the cobalt bombs it has on board. Sir Horace Wood, the head of the mission, finds it hard to negotiate because the Venusians live in an environment in which they constantly have to fight to survive. There is too much heat, too much humidity, too much radiation, poisonous bacteria, burrowing parasitic worms, deadly viruses, swamps, seas of boiling oil, volcanoes, monstrous hostile life forms. Every day the negotiating representative is whoever is free at the moment.

Finally Sir Horace, the well-read, urbane man of culture to whom killing is abhorrent, gives up and orders the genocidal bombing:

> Now the bombs have dropped and soon they'll drop on the earth. Thank goodness, I have a bombproof shelter as a public official. . . . I'll read the classics. T. S. Eliot, preferably. He's the most soothing of them all. There's nothing unhealthier than exciting reading.
>
> (*Werkausgabe,* vol. 17, p. 124)

Just as *The Physicists* showed that absolute goodness is derisively played with by absolute evil, *Das Unternehmen der Wega* shows the vanity of the hope placed by most men in the humanizing effects of culture—unless, of course, Dürrenmatt's reference to Sir Horace's perusal of Eliot is ironic, which it may well be.

In *Incident at Twilight,* Dürrenmatt reaches the acme of his cynicism. Maximilian Korbes is a peripatetic writer living in an apparently endless series of luxurious hotels where he has written twenty-two novels, all of them detailed accounts of thrill murders whose perpetrator is never caught. Some ominous notes are introduced when we learn that the murderer is always described as looking exactly like the author and when we learn that Korbes is the winner of the Nobel Prize for literature for his series of novels.

Korbes is visited by a timid little retired bookkeeper named Feargod Hofer. As his Christian name indicates, Hofer is an innocent, a misfit in the modern world, though not, as we shall see, an uncorrupted one. For the past ten years, ever since his retirement, Hofer has been following Korbes, living hand-to-mouth in the luxury resorts the writer frequents and ruining himself in the process. He has become, he tells Korbes, a private detective specializing in literature as a result of an ontological theory he has formed: "Whatever exists in the world of fiction . . . must also exist in reality because it seems to me impossible to invent something that does not exist somewhere in reality."

Blissfully unaware that this is bad logic, that bad logic leads to bad philosophy, and that bad philosophy leads to fatal behavior, Hofer has set out to prove that all the murders described in Korbes' novels actually occurred exactly as described and that they were all committed by the author. Korbes admits the truth of the accusation and asks Hofer whether he intends to turn him in. But Hofer has sipped the drug of excitement. He proposes to give up the fame and fortune that he thinks would be his if he made his sensational discovery public. Instead he asks for the privilege of becoming a secret part of Korbes' entourage and being paid a small sum each month to supplement his pension. Korbes informs him that his persistent and brilliant detective work was unnecessary: the whole world already knows what Hofer has discovered. Nobody would pay a penny for his novels if they were not known to be true accounts. He is protected by the authorities and has become a public cultural institution.

Korbes is a symbol of the media violence that pervades our lives and enables the majority of the populace to sublimate their sadomasochistic instincts. We live, in other words, in a society where lawlessness is the accepted norm—as long as the fact is not admitted. Hofer's problem is that he comes from a small town in Switzerland, Korbes informs him. "Don't underestimate the place," Hofer tells him, "Ennetwyl . . . has an active cultural life." "That's exactly what I mean," answers Korbes. "Nowadays places that have an 'active cultural life' are on the other side of the moon, so to speak—otherwise you would have been aware of the senselessness of your investigations" (George E. Wellwarth, ed., *Themes of Drama* [New York, 1973], p. 169).

Korbes is the successor to that other Nobel Prize winner, Wolfgang Schwitter of *The Meteor.* Schwitter got his Nobel legitimately, but his son tells him that his books are no longer earning royalties because people are tired of literature and only want sensation. Along comes Korbes and supplies that need. Korbes is not an artist like Schwitter: he is a crystallization of people's basest needs. As for Hofer, he resembles Möbius of *The Physicists* in that he believes, in all innocence, that all is well with the world as long as decent, cultured people are around to act as moral guides. But, unlike Möbius, Hofer himself becomes morally tainted. As he investigates Korbes, he becomes more and more fascinated by him and finally wants to become a part of the evil he has uncovered, to travel with the great man and become his confidant, to participate in Korbes' thrill murders by proxy. But he discovers that Korbes himself commits his thrill murders by proxy, so to speak: as a murderer Korbes acts only as a surrogate for the sublimated wishes of the whole world.

Korbes and Hofer are both puppet figures in what Dürrenmatt so aptly calls "the Punch and

Judy show of our century," that show of which he is so quintessentially the chronicler:

> Tragedy emphasizes guilt, despair, moderation, an all-encompassing vision, and a sense of responsibility. In the Punch and Judy show of our century there are no longer people who are guilty or people who have responsibility. It wasn't anybody's fault, and nobody wanted it. Everything really did happen without anyone's doing anything about it. Everyone was swept along and caught somewhere. We are collectively guilty, collectively enmeshed in the sins of our fathers and of our fathers' fathers. We are simply the children of other children. This is not our guilt: it is our misfortune. Guilt exists only as a result of personal effort, as a religious deed. Comedy alone is suitable for us.
>
> (*Theaterprobleme* [Zurich, 1955], pp. 47–48)

## Selected Bibliography


EDITIONS

INDIVIDUAL WORKS

PLAYS

*Es steht geschrieben.* Basel, 1947.
*Die Ehe des Herrn Mississippi.* Zurich, 1952.
*Stranitzky und der Nationalheld.* In *Hörspielbuch 1953.* Frankfurt am Main, 1953.
*Ein Engel kommt nach Babylon.* Zurich, 1954.
*Herkules und der Stall des Augias.* Zurich, 1954.
*Der Besuch der alten Dame.* Zurich, 1956.
*Romulus der Grosse.* Basel, 1956. 2nd version, Zurich, 1958.
*Abendstunde im Spätherbst.* In *Akzente,* June 1957. Pp. 194–216.
*Nächtliches Gespräch mit einem verachteten Menschen.* Zurich, 1957.
*Der Prozess um des Esels Schatten.* Zurich, 1958.
*Das Unternehmen der Wega.* Zurich, 1958.
*Der Blinde.* Zurich, 1960.
*Der Doppelgänger.* Zurich, 1960.
*Frank V.* Zurich, 1960.
*Die Panne.* Radio version, Zurich, 1961. Stage version, Zurich, 1979.
*Die Physiker.* Zurich, 1962.
*Der Meteor.* Zurich, 1966.
*Die Wiedertäufer.* Zurich, 1967.
*Porträt eines Planeten.* Zurich, 1971.
*Der Mitmacher.* Zurich, 1976.
*Die Frist.* Zurich, 1977.
*Dichterdämmerung.* Zurich, 1980.
*Achterloo.* Zurich, 1983.

FICTION

*Der Richter und sein Henker.* Einsiedeln, 1952.
*Die Stadt. Prosa I–IV.* Zurich, 1952.
*Der Verdacht.* Einsiedeln, 1953.
*Grieche sucht Griechin.* Zurich, 1955.
*Die Panne.* Zurich, 1956.
*Das Versprechen.* Zurich, 1958.
*Der Sturz.* Zurich, 1971.
*Justiz.* Zurich, 1985.
*Minotaurus.* Zurich, 1985.
*Der Auftrag.* Zurich, 1986.

ADAPTATIONS

*König Johann: Nach Shakespeare.* Zurich, 1968.
*Play Strindberg.* Zurich, 1969. (Strindberg's *Dance of Death*).
*Titus Andronicus: Eine Komödie nach Shakespeare.* Zurich, 1970.
*Urfaust.* Zurich, 1980. (Goethe).
*Woyzeck.* Zurich, 1980. (Büchner).

ESSAYS

*Theaterprobleme.* Zurich, 1955.
*Monstervortrag über Gerechtigkeit und Recht.* Zurich, 1969.
*Rollenspiele* (with Charlotte Kerr). Zurich, 1986.

COLLECTED WORKS

*Werkausgabe,* 29 vols. Zurich, 1980.

TRANSLATIONS

*An Angel Comes to Babylon.* Translated by William McElwee in *Four Plays.* London, 1964; New York, 1965.
*The Assignment* (*Der Auftrag*). Translated by Joel Agee. New York, 1988.
*A Dangerous Game.* Translated by Richard Winston and Clara Winston. London, 1960. Also translated as *Traps.* New York, 1960.
*The Execution of Justice* (*Justiz*). Translated by John E. Woods. New York, 1989.

*Incident at Twilight.* Translated by George E. Wellwarth in *Themes of Drama,* edited by George E. Wellwarth. New York, 1973.

*The Judge and His Hangman.* Translated by Cyrus Brooks. London, 1954.

*The Marriage of Mr. Mississippi.* Translated by Michael Bullock in *Four Plays.* London, 1964; New York, 1965.

*Once a Greek.* Translated by Richard Winston and Clara Winston. New York, 1965; London, 1966.

*The Physicists.* Translated by James Kirkup in *Four Plays.* London, 1964; New York, 1965.

*Play Strindberg.* Translated by James Kirkup. London, 1972.

*The Pledge.* Translated by Richard Winston and Clara Winston. New York and London, 1959.

*The Quarry.* Translated by Eva H. Morreale. London and Greenwich, Conn., 1962.

*Romulus the Great.* Translated by Gerhard Nellhaus in *Four Plays.* London, 1964; New York, 1965.

*The Sell-out.* Translated by William Elwood in *Modern International Drama* 19, no. 1 (1985).

*The Visit.* Translated by Patrick Bowles. London, 1962.

## BIOGRAPHICAL AND CRITICAL STUDIES

Arnold, Armin. *Friedrich Dürrenmatt.* Translated by Armin Arnold with Sheila Johnson. New York, 1972.

Fritzen, Bodo, and Heimtraut F. Taylor, eds. *Friedrich Dürrenmatt: A Collection of Critical Essays.* Normal, Ill., 1979.

Jenny, Urs. *Dürrenmatt: A Study of His Plays.* Translated by Keith Hammett and Hugh Rorrison. London, 1978.

Lazar, Moshe, ed. *Play Dürrenmatt.* Malibu, Calif., 1983.

Peppard, Murray B. *Friedrich Dürrenmatt.* New York, 1969.

Sander, Volkmar, ed. *Friedrich Dürrenmatt: Plays and Essays.* New York, 1982.

Tiusanen, Timo. *Dürrenmatt: A Study in Plays, Prose, Theory.* Princeton, N.J., 1977.

Whitton, Kenneth S. *The Theatre of Friedrich Dürrenmatt: A Study in the Possibility of Freedom.* London and Atlantic Highlands, N.J., 1980.

## BIBLIOGRAPHY

Knapp, Gerhard P. *Friedrich Dürrenmatt.* Stuttgart, 1980.

GEORGE WELLWARTH

# ALAIN ROBBE-GRILLET

## *(b. 1922)*

A PHOTOGRAPH TAKEN in the 1950's in front of Éditions de Minuit, a publishing house founded by Jérôme Lindon during the Nazi occupation in order to print and distribute "subversive" material of the French Resistance, shows Alain Robbe-Grillet in the foreground, Robert Pinget and Samuel Beckett slightly to the back, Nathalie Sarraute and Claude Ollier to the side facing him, and on the other side, behind him, Claude Mauriac and Claude Simon. The group was about to dethrone the existentialists reigning in nearby Saint-Germain-des-Prés. These writers' names were not linked to any "isms" so typical of the Paris scene: surrealism, personalism, and structuralism. Nor would they be identified with any café, restaurant, or bistro. Neither the Café Flore, nor the Deux Magots (where it is said that Jean Giraudoux used to take his coffee and talk with the friends who could not otherwise reach him), nor the Brasserie Lipp (linked with Pablo Picasso, Louis Aragon, Gertrude Stein, and Rainer Maria Rilke) served as their headquarters. Instead, the writers published by Minuit came to be identified with an abstract act of perception that seemed to constitute their novelty at the time. They were soon labeled "romanciers du regard," novelists of the glance. When the accuracy of this term came to be questioned and the diversity of these writers became more and more obvious, their novels more and more puzzling, the adjective "nouveau" was affixed to both product and producer. "Nouveau roman" and "nouveaux romanciers" replaced the former more explicitly descriptive label.

The stage for popularizing the *nouveau roman* (New Novel) was set not in Paris, but at the Centre Universitaire de Cérisy-la-Salle, a small castle in southern Normandy, where Mme Heurgon-Desjardins re-established the *decades,* or ten-day conferences, continuing the tradition of les Entretiens de Pontigny. These famous conferences, attended by many leading intellectuals, including André Gide, Thomas Mann, Paul Valéry, and Roger Martin du Gard, were established in 1910 by her father, Paul Desjardins (1859–1940), who was also the founder of the Union pour la vérité (Union for Truth, 1906) at a twelfth-century Cistercian abbey in order to encourage international cooperation in literary, social, aesthetic, political, and religious realms. The *decade* in 1970 firmly established the New Novel in the mainstream of contemporary French literature, with Alain Robbe-Grillet at the helm. Robbe-Grillet's prominent position was further reinforced in 1975, when ten days were devoted to examining his novels and films. Yet until he was thirty years old—long after he had completed his education—literature, film, and painting were far from the core of his professional endeavors.

Alain Robbe-Grillet was born on 18 August 1922 in Saint-Pierre-Quilbignon, a municipality that is now part of Brest in Brittany. He was the second child and the only son of the former Yvonne Canu, who had married Alain's father, Gaston, a graduate engineer of the *arts et métiers* at Cluny after the war. Although the socioeconomic status of his parents was fairly modest, they were particularly arrogant, convinced that they were more intelligent, capable, and talented than the world-at-large. Filled with contempt and hatred for French democratic institutions, they were anarchists of the extreme Right, free-thinking followers of Charles Maurras's Action Française, the royalist movement founded at the height of the Dreyfus affair in order to rally support for the army against Captain Dreyfus and his supporters, who were led by Georges Clemenceau, Jean Jaurès, and Émile Zola.

In spite of the fact that the goal of Action Française was a stable society founded on nationalism, the monarchy, and the church, its publications were placed on the Index on 29 December 1926 by the Roman Catholic church, where they remained for about a dozen years. While this upset many of the group's Catholic followers, it delighted the secular Robbe-Grillet household, which included two anticlerical grandfathers, partisans of Captain Dreyfus. Although Robbe-Grillet's parents believed that Catholicism as a state religion was in the best interest of the people, the excommunication of Action Française's members was perceived as another sign of corruption in the Third French Republic led by Aristide Briand, whom they called the "blessed pimp." During the war his parents were followers of Marshal Pétain and retained their convictions long after the war ended.

Unlike the ultranationalist Maurras, Gaston Robbe-Grillet—a lieutenant who had been wounded during World War I after four years of combat duty during which he had been awarded the Croix de guerre and several other citations—was a passionate antimilitarist. According to his son he remained slightly unhinged forever after the war. For instance, every night after drinking his coffee with milk, he would sit at his desk absorbed in translating Schiller's dramatic works, quickly writing pages and pages in a tiny hand without ever looking up any words in the dictionary. His children eventually realized that their father had never learned German and that the product of his diligent work was totally devoid of sense. Robbe-Grillet's pseudo-autobiography, *Le miroir qui revient* (*Ghosts in the Mirror,* 1984), lovingly describes his father's legacy: how he taught him skiing and ice skating as well as enjoyment of manual labor and the outdoors.

Gaston's wife, Yvonne, claimed that when this madness was handed down to Alain, it changed into genius. Along with his father's quirkiness, Alain inherited his mother's enormous intelligence. She taught her children reading and writing before they were old enough to go to school. Alain especially liked Lewis Carroll, but also was fond of Rudyard Kipling, in particular his tales about India, "specifically the ones where morbid visions terrify soldiers." Thirty or forty years later, he remembered vividly the story of the legionnaire lost in the night who meets another British patrol and the legend of Colonel Gadsby. Mme Robbe-Grillet seems to have been a mother who lived mostly for her children and who was immensely proud of all their accomplishments. Both of them were excellent students, at the very top of their class, always eager to study and learn, giving their parents complete satisfaction.

The 1940 debacle of the French army had less of an impact on Alain, who graduated from the Lycée Buffon just as the war was breaking out, than did the unconditional surrender of the Nazi Reich in 1945. Like many men and women of his background and class, he had been educated to believe that everything was rotten and corrupt in France and that defeat was a sort of retribution for the decadence of its institutions. Families who believed that the League of Nations should not have censured Mussolini for invading Ethiopia in 1935, that

Franco should have been supported in his crusade, and that England was to blame for World War II were not unhappy to see the fall of the Third Republic. The Robbe-Grillet family did not actively collaborate with the German invaders, choosing instead to mind their own business and live one day at a time without supporting the Resistance in any way.

After the defeat, going about his life as best as he could, Alain began to prepare for the competitive entrance examination to the National Institute of Agronomy at the Lycée Saint-Louis. He was admitted to the school and entered in the fall of 1942 just as it began to appear that Germany might not win the war after all. The battle of El Alamein, the siege of Stalingrad, and the scuttling of the French fleet in Toulon by its crews in order to avoid capture were some of the events providing the historical backdrop to that autumn. In the spring of 1943, along with all young men born in 1922, Alain was advised that instead of being drafted, as would have been the case under the Third Republic, he was required instead to report for work in Germany in order to contribute to the war against the Allies.

Many of Robbe-Grillet's contemporaries refused to comply with this Service de travail obligatoire (Service of Required Work, or STO). He went willingly. In fact, it would have been difficult for him to do otherwise. While young men living in small towns or country villages found it possible to avoid compliance, Robbe-Grillet claims that in Paris it was very dangerous to do so. Current evidence shows that this was so, and furthermore that men born in 1922 were the hardest hit. Every male born in that year had to carry a *carte de travail,* a work card that had to be shown whenever an identity check was required and for all administrative formalities, including obtaining rationing coupons. It is likely also that at the age of twenty-one he still clung to his family's ideology, one that held England to be far more noxious than Hitler's Reich.

A distinction must be drawn, and Robbe-Grillet does so objectively, between those who were drafted for work in Germany and those who were deported. There is no doubt that the future author of *Dans le labyrinthe* (*In the Labyrinth,* 1959) endured many hardships during the eighteen months he spent at the Maschinenfabrik-Augsburg-Nürnberg factory (MAN), but they were of an order and kind that matched the ordeal of the German people in the face of defeat. They were not comparable to the fate of even the most fortunate inmate of Buchenwald, Ravensbrück, or Auschwitz. In fact, until they died the senior Robbe-Grillets held steadfastly to their beliefs that crematoriums and the extermination of Jews, Gypsies, and the mentally ill were fabrications of one sort or another.

When Robbe-Grillet returned home in 1944 after having been hospitalized for an acute rheumatic episode, one can imagine that he met much the same reception that greeted the Vietnam veterans returning to the United States. He himself has never suggested it, but perhaps he was not unhappy to work "abroad" in Martinique after graduating from the National Institute of Agronomy in 1945. Although he no longer shared his family's political views, what was considered an inglorious past would not embitter everyday life as long as one remained far away in a colonial outpost. By 1952, when he decided to quit his profession and remain in Paris in order to write a novel, the climate was very different: what amounted to a less than glorious civil war under the Vichy regime was "forgotten" or repressed whenever possible. The general pretense was that almost everyone had participated in the Resistance. Conflicts in Indochina and Algeria were now at the forefront of the political arena. Robbe-Grillet took up his pen, but he refused to inject politics overtly into his work. He sought to write from the perspective of modernity. The revolution he wanted had to be expressed in the shape and texture of the work itself and not in the expression of partisan politics. While the prestige of a writer or an artist might lend weight to his stand on a particular issue, this was best accomplished through political gestures such as signing a manifesto or demonstrating in the streets. Nothing would be gained by molding these statements in an aesthetic format.

In order to support his writing of a first novel, *Un régicide,* in 1948 Robbe-Grillet abandoned his career as an agronomist and began working in a biological laboratory performing various procedures on animal organs. When the manuscript was finished, he sent it off to Gallimard, which rejected it. Undaunted, he set the work aside and began working on a second novel, *Les gommes* (*The Erasers*), a novel published in 1953 that won the Fénéon prize the following year. At about this time, he also began writing articles about literature that appeared in *L'Express,* which was then published as a daily newspaper by Servan-Schreiber; François Mauriac's "Bloc Notes" were a regular feature. Robbe-Grillet developed these into several other essays published in *Critique,* a journal founded in 1946 by Georges Bataille and Eric Weil. Eventually, most of these pieces were reprinted with revisions in *Pour un nouveau roman* (translated as *Towards a New Novel* and *For a New Novel,* 1963).

His next novel, *Le voyeur* (*The Voyeur*), published in 1955, won the Prix des Critiques and ignited a controversy of sorts between those who favored Robbe-Grillet's technique of stripping the novel form bare and others who found the enterprise completely outrageous. Among the former was Roland Barthes, whose essay on *Le voyeur,* "Littérature objective" ("Objective Literature"), attracted as much attention as the novel itself. His famous sentence defined the New Novel for almost a decade: "Robbe-Grillet's writing is without alibi, without thickness, and without depth: it remains on the surface of the object and covers it evenly without favoring any of its attributes: it is therefore the exact opposite of writing as poetry." Robbe-Grillet's next two books, *La jalousie* (*Jealousy,* 1957) and *In the Labyrinth,* secured his position as one of the leading novelists in postwar France, ranking with Jean-Paul Sartre and Albert Camus as well as with his fellow New Novelists. He had also become literary adviser to Editions de Minuit, and his generosity toward the fellow novelists he admired, Robert Pinget for instance, should be noted.

In 1957 Robbe-Grillet married Catherine Rstakian, who, under the name Catherine Robbe-Grillet and with the guidance of her husband, has herself written at least one novel, *L'Image* (1956). Robbe-Grillet has taught film and literature at New York University and Washington University in St. Louis, Missouri, and lectured extensively throughout the United States.

Beginning in 1960, Robbe-Grillet's career alternates from novels to films, films to novels. He has written three ciné-novels: *L'Année dernière à Marienbad* (*Last Year at Marienbad,* 1961), which was directed by Alain Resnais when it was made into a film; *L'Immortelle* (*The Immortal One,* 1963); and *Glissements progressifs du plaisir* (*Slow Slide into Pleasure,* 1974). Besides *The Immortal One* and *Glissements progressifs du plaisir,* he has also written and directed the following films: *Trans-Europ-Express* (1966), *L'Homme qui ment* (The Liar, 1968), *L'Eden et après* (Eden and Afterward, 1970), *Le jeu avec le feu* (Fire Games, 1975), and *La belle captive* (The Beautiful Captive, 1983).

In these and in his novels beginning with *La maison de rendez-vous* (translated in the United States with the French title; in Britain as *The House of Assignation,* 1965), Robbe-Grillet's motifs have become more and more erotic and violent and his writings have many components of sadomasochistic pornography. They are, however, always sustained by a self-reflexive awareness tinged with irony and humor—a kind of verbal rendering of the comic-strip mode. Titles express stereotypes of postmodernity: *Instantanés* (*Snapshots,* 1962), a volume of short fiction; *La maison de rendez-vous; Project pour une révolution à New York* (*Project for a Revolution in New York,* 1970);

*Topologie d'une cité fantôme* (*Topology of a Phantom City*, 1976); and *Souvenirs du triangle d'or* (*Recollections of the Golden Triangle*, 1978).

*Ghosts in the Mirror* is a reluctant autobiography spiced with a romance narrative about a certain Count Henri de Corinthe, a fictional doubling of Robbe-Grillet's father. It also includes a composite pseudofictional character with traits of famous Frenchmen of the period: Henri de Kerillis, a deputy of the Right who voted against Munich; François de la Rocque, the head of the Croix de Feu (a nationalistic, anticapitalist, and anti-Marxist league composed largely of war veterans), and Count Henri de Paris, the leading legitimist contender for the French crown should the monarchy be restored. This superb account was followed by *Angélique ou L'Enchantement* (Angélique; or, Being Enchanted, 1987), a sequel turning all the author's previous books on their heads and undermining many of his former theories about writing, literature, and the New Novel itself. Not unlike Salvador Dali's undermining of his early associations with surrealism, these two books put into question many of Robbe-Grillet's earlier pronouncements about aesthetics and point out many current misconceptions about his practice of writing. Because his novels are so enigmatic—bare plot lines, silhouette-like characters, careful manic-seeming descriptions, pointless explanations undermining traditional techniques of realist writers—the analytic pieces in *For a New Novel* seemed designed to allow readers to get a handle on these texts.

According to Robbe-Grillet, almost everyone was taken in. More attention was devoted to the so-called underlying theory and to the various critical studies about them than to the works themselves. Fashion moves on, and much of this criticism now seems dated. The works under scrutiny have turned out to be not as different from other novels as early readers were led to believe. The works of Robbe-Grillet, following the great realist tradition he sometimes deplored and often admired (Honoré de Balzac, James Joyce, and Samuel Beckett), are imaginative reconstructions of his own life. In his words, "I have never talked about anything but me."

In one of his first published pieces, writing in the newspaper *L'Express* in 1956, Robbe-Grillet made clear his belief that the substance of novels coincides with life itself:

> The very stuff of novels, whatever their category, seems to deal with all of humanity: love and fear, space and time, silence and death, etc. They are the elements of any life whatsoever. Becoming aware of this concerns awareness itself, and this act is not restricted only to novelists. Techniques of the novel are but the form they have invented embodying and giving consistence and order to something that initially seemed to defy analysis.
> (*L'Express*, 21 February 1956, p. 11)[1]

Love, fear, space, time, silence, and death are the themes of Robbe-Grillet's works, and the techniques he uses are but instruments at his disposal for implementing his being. Many tools that served gardeners well in the time of Balzac and Stendhal have been superseded today. Others are still in use. And who will argue that the gardens of the twentieth century are more beautiful than those of the past? Likewise, if some of the novel's traditional techniques are no longer used by Robbe-Grillet and his peers, this is not to say that the gardens they cultivate are inferior to those of their predecessors.

When the New Novel was at the peak of its popularity, some of the Paris intelligentsia discussed the theory but did not read any of the novels. One might suppose that the novels were meant to illustrate the theory. Nothing could be further from the truth. Now that the values of the New Novel have been widely accepted, Robbe-Grillet, true anarchist that he is, determined it was time to call everything into question. The narrow-minded pawns who championed its theories were to return to the

[1] All translations of Robbe-Grillet's writings are by the present author.

beginning; writing itself was to retract to its origins.

*The Erasers,* the author's first published novel, is a pseudo-detective thriller with a Homeric correspondence, reminiscent of the process used by James Joyce in *Ulysses.* Here is a summary of the plot compiled by Robbe-Grillet himself and included in the publisher's blurb attached to copies of the book:

> It is about an event that is precise, concrete, essential: man's death. It is an event with the component of a mystery thriller—that is to say there is a murderer, a detective, a victim. In a way their roles are respected: the murderer shoots the victim, the detective solves the problem, the victim dies. But the relationships linking them are not quite as simple, or rather they are simple only when the last chapter is finished. Because the book is actually the tale of the twenty-four hours between this pistol shot and this death, the time taken by the bullet to go three or four meters—twenty-four hours too much.

An attentive reader, having made a note of the "exergue" attributed to Sophocles, "Time that watches over everything has provided the solution in spite of yourself," may note correspondences with classical archetypes from the very beginning of the novel.

Following ancient models, *The Erasers* opens with a prologue set at dawn, at precisely 6:00 A.M., in early winter. The title of the book sets forth its theme: the rubbing out or removing of something from the physical universe as well as from life and from memory. If we consider the etymology of the word *theme* (from the Greek *tithenai,* to place, set, lay down), we understand that when the nameless proprietor takes down twelve chairs from the table tops of imitation marble he is literally laying down the themes of the novel. Erasure is suggested throughout the prologue. Not only is the lighting obscured, but the proprietor himself barely emerges from the limbo of sleep. Time is thus suspended. The purity of its absolute blankness exists only insofar as the scene is devoid of any actual events of the past or future. In this context, the immediate instant is stripped of everything that came before and everything that may follow. It is the perfect blank that erasure seeks to emulate.

Shaded by the dimness, the proprietor restores order in his realm. One of the tables has a funny little spot on it that looks like blood. He tries to wipe it off, but it will not disappear. The original stain remains, barely visible but never completely removed. The trace of the impression announces and generates the tale, its interpretation and its meaning. The underlying paradox is how to achieve total elimination while ensuring complete restoration at the same time. Can we forget and yet remember? In other words, how can the dead be killed and, though murdered, also remain alive?

Putting aside this ontological perspective, the underlying mystery story follows the tradition of its Anglo-American counterparts. As the proprietor halfheartedly tries to wipe the stain, he recalls events from the night before: "Daniel Dupont last night; two steps from here. A fishy story: a burglar wouldn't have entered the lighted room on purpose, the guy wanted to kill him, that's obvious. Personal revenge, or what? Clumsy, in any case. It happened yesterday. Look for it later in the paper." And a few pages later, when he has more time, he reads the following item: "Tuesday, October 27.—At nightfall a daring burglar entered the residence of M. Daniel Dupont, 2 rue des Arpenteurs. Interrupted in his task by the owner, the thug fled, firing a number of shots at Mr. Dupont."

What makes this narrative different from a story by Raymond Chandler is that the plot is constituted by a puzzle generated by a static pattern, the Oedipal topos of erasure, rather than by the interplay of dynamic forces. At first, the events recounted in the prologue and the objects described seem disconnected and often pointless. We learn, for instance, that for the last seventeen years two letters—we don't know which ones—have been missing from the sign "Furnished Rooms" (*chambres meublées*) on the café's glass front. On a narrative level, the existence of the sign itself rationalizes the inconsistency of an honest citizen's decision to rent a room in such a shabby café. The important point, however, is that part of the sign is erased. Perhaps this is why the man who came to this bar the night before and asked to rent its only room has a name, Wallas, with two double letters, *a* and *l*, perhaps the very same letters missing from the sign. When the proprietor notices that it is 6:30 A.M., time for him to wake up his boarder, he finds that Wallas is already gone, that is, that he has been erased. A few minutes later a man comes looking for Wallas, thereby suggesting a possible restoration of what seems to be gone. Almost every item here is related to this theme of absence and presence, being and nothingness, fullness and void. There is no coffee in the café; the lamps are put out when daylight erases darkness; wine obscures sight; the boss is surrounded by debris—he absentmindedly wipes off his bottles and is perpetually trying to reconstitute what remains of his tattered intelligence.

One could go on. Yet one must not suppose that these motifs are mere variations on a theme. They are part of the transcendental puzzle underlying this novel. Fragments of it are formulated several times by one of the café's regular clients, who is always shown quite drunk. At the beginning of the prologue, this drunk tells the proprietor and his friend Antoine that he has a funny riddle for them: "What is the animal that in the morning . . . ?" With skillful irony, the narrator hints at the solution: "He is funny, of course, but the two others don't have the heart for joking when the life of a man is at stake between them." At the end of the novel, several men in the café are shown in a discussion about walking straight ahead on an oblique path. This time, the enigma is the following: "Tell me a little what is the animal who is a parricide in the morning, incestuous at noon, and blind at night."

Robbe-Grillet told Bruce Morrissette, the American author of the first full-length study about him, that Samuel Beckett was the only one among his early readers to notice the Oedipal reference. Today, much has been written about this aspect of *The Erasers,* and readers cannot help but read this book while recalling the Greek myth, just as readers of James Joyce's *Ulysses* read it bearing in mind the Homeric structure. Just as *Ulysses* recounts twenty-four hours in the life of Bloom, so the ostensible story here is twenty-four hours in the life of Wallas, a special agent sent to investigate the murder of Professor Daniel Dupont.

All the facts about the murder are set forth in the prologue. Although various newspapers have confirmed the murder of the fifty-two-year-old law-school professor and author of books on the organization of production (*Labor and Organization, The Phenomenology of the Crisis* [1929], *Contribution to the Study of Economic Cycles*), no corpse has been found. It seems that a certain Garinati, hired by Bona and his gang to shoot Dupont through the heart, merely grazed his arm. Another scene suggests that the wound might have been the consequence of the professor's unsuccessful attempt at self-destruction. In any case, Daniel Dupont is very much alive, and he has enlisted the help of a gynecologist, Dr. Juard, who is the proprietor of a clinic suspected of performing illegal medical procedures. Encouraged by a mysterious political faction supported by several members of the government, whose purpose is to uncover the leaders of an anarchist organization, Juard has agreed to cooperate. He will help Dupont get away, and he will invent an explanation so that the case will be closed. The local police have been relieved of the case, and the great Fabius himself, a blend of Fantomas and Maigret, is put in charge of the investigation.

As the reader follows Wallas, whom Fabius has dispatched from Paris, all the facts and all the characters rotate around this narrative bait. For instance, Wallas wears the secret-agent uniform: he is a tall man in a raincoat with a soft pale-gray hat over his face. One cannot tell exactly who in the story wears this costume, nor whether Wallas is always Wallas. It is possible, for example, that Fabius has disguised himself as Wallas. In the ministry, everyone is familiar with the caricature that shows him dressed as a loiterer, with huge dark glasses and an outrageously false beard. Wallas's identity card also shows a photograph of someone with glasses and a beard. It is also possible that Wallas and Garinati, the killer hired by Bona and his gang to kill Dupont, may be one and the same. The drunkard who tells riddles saw a man wearing a raincoat wandering around Dupont's house at the time of the shooting. He is sure that Wallas was the man he saw although the reader has been led to think that Garinati was the prowler.

A number of games are going on here. Stereotypes of mystery stories are presented in an exuberant carnival of techniques. Identities are blurred, and murderers and victims may seem interchangeable. If we compare *The Erasers* to Graham Greene's *Brighton Rock* (1938), a novel with a seaside setting that Robbe-Grillet knew well, we see that the various rivalries of occult political factions, Garinati and Roy-Dauzet, parody the competition of warring factions of the English novel's mobs, the feud between Colleoni's gang and the one led by Pinkie, the Boy. Graham Greene's police sergeant is as inept as the authorities in the French book and he resembles Wallas insofar as he fails to protect the victims. This is not to say, however, that the atmosphere of the two novels is the same.

According to the blurb on the American Grove Press edition, the setting of *The Erasers* is an unidentified Flemish town. Although it has been generally assumed that the town in question is located somewhere in northern Europe, I doubt that we can be sure that it is indeed Flemish. The sea nearby is identified as the Northern Sea, and many of the street names—Avenue Christian-Charles, Rue Joseph Janeck, Rue de Copenhague—suggest northern Europe. But the geography here cannot always be found in an atlas. For example, the name of the street of the Café des Alliés, the Rue des Arpenteurs, is a homage to Kafka's *The Castle* (1926). The French word *arpenteur* means land surveyor, and the street name probably refers to l'Arpenteur K., the land surveyor who is the protagonist of *The Castle.* The cafés in *The Erasers* have the same narrative function as the various inns in Kafka's tale. In both works they are abstract backdrops against which abstract characters expressing widely shared opinions act as counterparts for the central characters. One cannot determine whether Rue de Corinthe is meant to refer to the ancient or modern city of the Peloponnesus in Greece or to the American city in Mississippi. The publication of *Ghosts in the Mirror* and *Angélique* confirms the importance of the name Corinthe in Robbe-Grillet's personal mythology. His fictional hero, Comte Henri, was supposed to be related to Lovis Corinth (1858–1925), a German painter known for his landscapes of the Walchensee who trained in Paris and led the Sezession movement with Max Slevogt and Max Liebermann. If his name is added to the other Corinths celebrated here, then it may be that the locus of the landscape may have to be shifted slightly. The Boulevard Circulaire, the Place de la Préfecture, the Rue de la Charte, and the Boulevard de la Reine cannot be specifically localized.

The difference between *The Erasers* and other suspense thrillers can be seen in the handling of the theme of the secret agent, who is himself the murderer. There are stories by Maupassant and Poe in which the reader gradually comes to perceive that the criminal or madman has been put in charge of the inquest. The novelty here lies in the integration of this structure with the Oedipal motif of the son who kills his father. Indeed, although one cannot be absolutely certain, there is a lot of circumstantial evidence that suggests Dupont may be Wallas's father. Many years before, Wallas visited the same town with his mother. He begins to recall that they were looking for a female relative, but later in a flash he recalls that the relative in question was a male relative, his father. The café's proprietor has already told the police inspector that, twenty years before, Dupont had a "relationship" with a woman who gave birth to a boy, but whom he refused to marry. This son had visited Dupont several times and asked him for funds. Neighbors had heard the two men quarrel. There are many hints throughout the book that this boy might have been taken to Dr. Juard's clinic, 11 rue de Corinthe, just as the shepherd took Oedipus from Mount Cithaeron to Corinth, where he was adopted by King Polybus and his wife. But the most compelling evidence is to be found in the scene in which Wallas sees an arrow pointing to the Victor Hugo stationery shop. The symbol is obvious: it is in this ultramodern, recently opened boutique on a rather isolated street near the center that the author of this New Novel will find material for the book he is writing. What French writer would not want to be like Victor Hugo? And what does the author have his hero buy in this store? An eraser with two missing letters—all the better to wipe out the anxiety provoked by this father of French letters. The book in which this illustration appears is itself a riddle elaborating narrative structures generated by the picture in the window, the picture of Dupont's house on the Kafkaesque Street of the Land Surveyor, set against the ruins of Thebes, whose king, Laius, was killed by his son Oedipus. In other words, it represents a modernist Oedipal folktale.

Oedipus is present everywhere here, even when he does not appear to be. For instance, Wallas spends a good part of his twenty-four hours walking around the town. "Wallas likes walking. In the cold air of the early winter he likes walking straight ahead in this unknown city. He looks, he listens, he feels; this contact in perpetual renewal gives him the soft impression of continuity: he walks and he unfolds little by little the uninterrupted line of his own passage." Although this is surely an autobiographical passage—Robbe-Grillet has confided that Wallas is in many ways a self-portrait—the act of walking itself is relevant to the Oedipus legend. When Laius exposed his baby son on Mount Cithaeron, he pinned his ankles together, hence the name Oedipus, meaning swell-foot.

While *The Erasers* is a story with twenty-four hours too many, *The Voyeur,* the first novel by Robbe-Grillet to be translated into English, is a tale in which an hour is missing. Mathias, the protagonist, a traveling watch salesman, sails to the island of his birth, a small place with barely two thousand inhabitants where all the houses look alike. As Robbe-Grillet wrote in *Ghosts in the Mirror,* the decor is a transposition of the Kerangoff landscape of his childhood, images of the "sea cliffs, the moors, the heaths, the dunes, the sandy beaches between the rocks." Nothing there attracts Mathias, neither old friendships nor early memory. Because it is his birthplace, he figures that by pretending to be personally acquainted with various relatives of the inhabitants, he will be able to sell all his watches to them in just a few hours. The novel follows him as he walks from one house to another in the village and then bicycles around the countryside (the route of his journey forms the outline of a figure eight) peddling his "bracelet watches." Detailed and minute descriptions of houses, furniture, landscape, perceptions, still-life objects, and movements unfold together with the thoughts and visions present in Mathias' consciousness.

In the first part of the novel, a novel in three parts, nothing seems to be actually happening. All at once, Mathias who has been allowed to come into the last house of the village, a house belonging to Mme Dulac, is startled by the photograph of a young girl on the dining room sideboard, "a photograph of Violette as a young girl." Only it is not Violette, of course, but Jacqueline. Violette is the name of someone from Mathias' past. Jacqueline, who looks like her, is the young girl who lives on the island. Less than an hour earlier, gossip overheard in the café alluded to this precocious and perverse thirteen-year-old girl, who has the devil inside her, "a wild animal" and "a real curse." Mathias is told that she is tending her sheep at the edge of the cliffs. At this point there seems to be a void in the narrative, a void that the reader's imagination fills paying close attention to time and to the topology of the road. This road will come to a fork. In order to reach the spot where Jacqueline/Violette is tending sheep, one must continue straight ahead on the road toward the right to the lighthouse. The road forking to the left leads past the mill toward the Marek farm. Mathias, who has known the Marek family for a long time, is ostensibly heading there. But when he comes to the fork in the road, at about 11:25 A.M., he takes the path to the right, toward the girl and her sheep by the sea.

As the reader turns the page, part 2 of the novel opens with a view of Mathias standing in the middle of the fork in the road, one hand holding the handlebars of his bicycle and the other grasping his suitcase. The crushed corpse of a tiny frog lies across the road, and a hundred yards beyond a country woman, who turns out to be Mrs. Marek, comes toward him. She cannot see whether he has reached the fork from the left or from the right, that is to say from the lighthouse where Jacqueline is tending her sheep or from the farm. Mathias stops the old woman and begins to talk to her and tells her about his visit to the empty farm. Except that the attentive reader realizes that if his account had been truthful, the meeting with Mrs. Marek would have taken place at 11:40 A.M. at the most, more likely 11:35 A.M., fully an hour earlier than was actually the case.

In other words, an hour has gone by, and Mathias may be fibbing about what he did during that time. How did Mathias really spend the hour that he will later reconstruct as the approximate time from 11:25 A.M. to 12:25 P.M., give or take five or ten minutes each way? Did he go back and forth to the empty farm, first on his bicycle and then on foot when his bicycle chain broke? Or did he spend his time by the Black Rocks lighthouse one mile away, where Jacqueline was tending her sheep? From this point on, the narrative is centered around its own void, that is to say the missing hour, and all of Mathias' utterances, expressed through dialogue, interior monologue, and stream of consciousness, are engaged in constructing an alibi. When the reader discovers that the thirteen-year-old girl has been raped and murdered, several innocuous details emerge from memory generated by what has been previously narrated and repeated. One is made aware that the bland voyager is also a homicidal maniac.

The novel is inhabited by obsessional motifs that confirm this suspicion. The repetition of the figure-eight shape throughout the novel is particularly characteristic. Mathias saves pieces of string rolled into two circles, and throughout this tale he carries these in his pocket and feels the double circles with his hand. His suitcase also contains a piece of cord rolled into a figure eight on top of a pile of cardboard strips. He rolls up candy wrappers into little balls. At the beginning of the novel the blue pack of Gauloise cigarettes that is thrown overboard into the sea rises and falls and its position in the water has the shape of a figure eight. On the same page, two rings fixed into the embankment form a design shaped like another figure eight. The door of the last house on the road to the lighthouse has wood fibers in the shape of two round knots, which look like two big eyes or a pair of glasses. The island's roads are in the shape of a figure eight, and Mathias' trajectory is itself a double circuit, a mirror of the narrative itself. In fact, there are two pairs of voyeuristic eyes: the eyes of Mathias, who, if he is innocent, might be the voyeur of the title (the novel was first called *Le Voyageur,* "The Voyager") and those of Julien Marek, a retarded boy who seems to have witnessed the crime.

Other clusters of anxiety reinforce the nightmarish mood pervading this narrative: the little girl standing on the deck of the ferry who foreshadows the other young girl in the book; the billboard of the movie house depicting a man dressed in a costume of the Renaissance holding the wrists of a young girl in a nightgown while he is strangling her. Then there is the newspaper clipping about the murder of a girl, written in the conversational and veiled language of the press, that Mathias carries with him; the torture scene Mathias witnesses or imagines; the dozen identical little knives in the window of the hardware store; his own abnormally long pointed nails; the mutilated mannequin without limbs displayed in a store window; the pun on the name Violette (in French *viol* means "rape").

Less obviously, Mathias utters stereotyped phrases that seem empty and meaningless, but that can be read into, giving them new meaning. When he hears complaints about the thirteen-year-old Jacqueline, he repeats the commonplace "On a du mal avec les enfants" ("Children are a lot of trouble" or, more colloquially, "Children are a pain"). On the surface, this sentence suggests that he is sympathetic to the fact that a child can be a lot of trouble. But one cannot help but infer that he himself has a lot of trouble with children, that is to say with doing whatever he does to them, particularly to young girls. Literally the sentence also can be interpreted to link children, pain, evil, and finally the squashed corpse of the flattened frog that turns out to be a toad. One can readily understand the reaction of Robbe-Grillet's mother when she read the novel. He confides in *Ghosts in the Mirror,* "As for all the manuscripts at the beginning of my career, my mother was the *Voyeur*'s first reader. After having finished, she said to me: 'I think it is a remarkable book, but I would have preferred it not to have been written by my son.'"

Gradually Mathias' alibi appears more and more improbable, and he is seized with panic. Little by little he incriminates himself, but the islanders don't seem to care. When the body is found, the concern shown is the same as it might have been for a stuffed doll thrown over the cliff. Everyone accepts the fact that there was an accident: the girl tripped and plunged over the cliff. The attitude is that she was such a devil that her fate was not undeserved. In other words, in the American vernacular, she had it coming to her. At least three persons, including her sister and her married female lover, know there must have been foul play. Julien Marek undoubtedly watched the crime, and there is no ostensible reason for him to keep his information to himself. Mathias fully expects to be turned in and he imagines that the police are about to arrest him. But everyone remains silent. Mathias returns to the mainland as if nothing had happened.

The irony here is that the victim, not the murderer, is blamed for the crime. The islanders, that is to say society, believe that Jacqueline is guilty, not Mathias. Following traditions of folktale and legend, the devil has entered her soul. She is the reincarnation of the archetypal sorceress who pollutes everyone with whom she comes into contact. Her murderer will not be held accountable in any way. An anxious night filled with nightmares will be his only punishment.

In *Angélique ou l'enchantement,* Robbe-Grillet recounts that he once told Jérôme Lindon, the publisher of Editions de Minuit, that the little girl of *The Voyeur* had actually existed. Her name was neither Violette nor Jacqueline, but Angélique. Her ancestors were called Arno and they had once lived in the ancient Venice ghetto. Alain met her one summer in Morbihan when she was twelve and he was thirteen. They experimented in the kinds of love games many adolescents play at this age, although their games were perhaps a trifle more perverse than is the norm. For instance, Angélique liked to make her companion tie her up. After a dramatic scene in which she casts a magic spell over her partner, humiliating him and warning him that she has caused him to be eternally impotent, she disappears forever:

> I did not see her the next day, nor the day after that. Nor ever again. Was she sick? Had they brought her to the Sister's hospital at Saint-Paul-de-Léon? It would have been convenient to believe this. But, deep inside myself, I knew right away where she was hidden.

> They found her body at the foot of the cliffs, at low tide, in a dangerous point where we weren't allowed to play. She floated between two tides, a pale Ophelia, in a deep and bright hole between dark, rounded, and slippery rocks. Long red algae nodulated around her, oarweeds and sea-tangles, as if they were trying to hold her back by her graceful, indolently spread out limbs. A seaweed gatherer brought her back on his cart that was already full. He wasn't going to make an extra trip, with his old horse and a hill to go up, for some Parisian kid, who to top it all was a devil, and so probably was her mother.
>
> It was already cold, past the equinox and its storms. The adolescent was naked. They thought the waves had undressed her. Nobody noticed the black woolen sweater hanging on top of the precipice, way above marks left by the highest tides.
>
> (*Angélique ou l'enchantement,* pp. 245–246)

Upon being questioned, Alain said that he hadn't seen his friend for a few days and knew nothing. A perfunctory inquest concluded that it had been an accident.

One cannot tell whether this version is really the true story. The question is whether the true story will ever be told. In both versions the young girl is a sorceress. Perhaps the reason Jacqueline was considered wicked is that she played the same games with her friends that Angélique played with Alain. The girls differ insofar as Angélique is "Parisian," that is to say a stranger whose forebears were born in the ancient Venetian ghetto, whereas Jacqueline is a local peasant girl. The inference can be made that a crime perpetrated upon a witch does not really count. This is how one can rationalize the fact that in many instances the population at large remains indifferent to assaults by natives against little girls, witches, victims, that is to say outsiders and foreigners.

*Jealousy,* perhaps the most "modern" of Robbe-Grillet's novels, is marked by a center that cannot be located. In a dedication written for a copy of the book belonging to Professor Artine Artinian, the author described it as "a plotless narration" having "minutes without days, windows without windowpanes, a house without mystery, a passion without a person." While these words convey the reader's general impression, in fact the novel does have a plot, there is a day and even a night, some of the windows have panes, the house is full of mystery, and the passion is that of a husband without a name. The sense of void does not come from the emptiness of these various artifacts. The blank focus is generated by the organizing principle underlying the novel itself. More than twenty years after *Jealousy* was published Robbe-Grillet explained:

> The absent narrator of *Jealousy* is himself the blind point in a text based on objects that his glance desperately tries to order and hold in hand against the conspiracy incessantly threatening the delicate scaffolding of his collapsing colonialism: the proliferating vegetation of the tropics, the ravaging sexuality attributed to blacks, the bottomless eyes of his own wife, and a parallel unnameable universe, constituted by the noises surrounding the house.
>
> (*Ghosts in the Mirror,* pp. 39–40)

It is significant that the author bemoans the fact that while his critics have been sensitive to visual perceptions in his novels, almost nobody seems to have mentioned auditory phenomena.

This lack of attention to sounds can be explained by the fact that in the 1960's and 1970's readers were guided by the theoretical propositions advanced by Roland Barthes and by Robbe-Grillet's essays in *For a New Novel.* They failed to perceive that the theories were protective armor against the demons within. Appearances misled them just as their forebears had misunderstood the apparent frivolity of dadaism and surrealism. In the 1920's and 1930's the public failed to perceive that, above all, Tristan Tzara, Philippe Soupault, Louis Aragon, and André Breton were undermining the rhetoric of those who continued to believe and preach the virtues of nationalism and patriotism. Their productions inverted the nihilism of habits and customs that went on as though the war that had killed and maimed millions had not taken place. Likewise, the *nouveau roman* and the *nouvelle critique* represented nostalgia for and a rebellion against values that remained sometimes unscathed and often repressed by the cataclysm of World War II, the defeat of France and of Germany, the dropping of atomic bombs on Hiroshima and Nagasaki, the destruction of European Jewry, the French Indochina War (1946–1954), and the Algerian War (1954–1962). How could one confess longing for the ecstasy of desire and death in the abyss of universal cataclysm? At the same time, was it possible to continue expressing the precariousness of one's state in traditional modes of writing? There are hidden facets in *Jealousy,* and in all of Robbe-Grillet's previous and future fictions, to which readers were impervious. They failed to see that the jealous husband in *Jealousy,* for instance, is on the verge of losing control and collapsing. His endless recollections of a few persistent scenes constitute the substance of this novel.

While there is no actual plot, a story emerges from the repetition of moving images. Four chairs are set up for a drink on the porch of a colonial dwelling held up by pillars and set in a banana grove in the Antilles. According to Robbe-Grillet (whose specialty as an agronomist was the illness of banana plants), although the banana plantation in *Jealousy* is set on an island purporting to be in the Antilles, the vegetation described suggests Africa, more specifically the Canary Islands. Everything returns several times. For instance, in one version, at noon, there may be four persons on the porch, the narrator, his wife A., Franck, and his wife Christiane. The same porch is seen at night, and the narrator is called upon to bring ice from the pantry inside the house. He leaves his wife alone on the porch with Franck and enters the pantry as the servant is about to bring out the ice. The ice scene is repeated, as is the scene of A. in her bedroom in which the husband presumably sees her writing a letter on blue stationery, a letter he thinks he sees her give to Franck.

The recurrence of these scenes constitutes the plot of the novel. A vision that shifts over and over presents the three characters seated on the veranda having drinks. A. notices there is no ice. The presumed husband goes to fetch some, and as he goes through his study he looks through the slats of the venetian blinds, the *jalousies,* and observes Franck and A. When he comes to the pantry, it turns out the houseboy knows the ice is missing, but the reader has no information about the instructions A. has given him.

Franck's car breaks down quite frequently. He decides to buy a new one, and A. asks whether she can come with him and take advantage of the lift to do a number of errands. Several versions are given of the planning of this outing: they will leave at 6:00 A.M., meet for lunch, and return the same evening. When the trip is recounted—again there are several flashforwards and/or flashbacks—it turns out that the car has been put out of commission so that Franck and A. could spend the night in a hotel. Did the car really stop working? Is this a subterfuge made up by an adulterous couple who wanted to spend a night together? Or does the malfunction allude to Franck's own body machine rather than to the engine of his car? Did any of this actually happen or is it all a figment of the imagination of a jealous husband?

There are a number of passages in *Jealousy* that guide the reader. For example, both A. and Franck are reading an African novel, perhaps Graham Greene's *The Heart of the Matter* (1948). A footnote in Bruce Morissette's *The Novels of Robbe-Grillet* lists the similarities between the two books: the post office calendar, the wife's photograph on the husband's desk, the game of squashing the lizard and the cockroaches on the wall, and Scobie's reaction when he sees Wilson kissing his wife.

When the narrator summarizes A. and Franck's discussions about this novel, his recapitulation serves as a guide for how to approach *Jealousy* itself; or at the very least we are led to consider the poetics underlying this novel. The two readers utter no judgments as to the various values expressed. They talk and seem to remember places, events, and characters as if they were real. Their conversation gives equal weight to knowledge gained through direct participation in events and to experience that merely reflects a story one has been told. They talk about the characters in the novel and about the Africa depicted as if they had personally encountered them. But they never consider the likelihood or the probability of any of the events in the tale. Its coherence is never put into question. Arbitrariness of plot, however, is bemoaned, and one of the common utterances is: "What bad luck!" They also like to imagine different endings: "Variants are quite numerous; variants of variants even more so. They seem to multiply them on purpose, exchanging smiles, finding excitement in the game, and made dizzy by this proliferation."

The best example of Robbe-Grillet's use of variations is the novel's most disturbing episode, a scene that provides the key to *Jealousy*—assuming there really is a key—that is to say, the killing of a creature (described variously as a centipede or millipede) in the dining room. Minute variations centering on the millipede's size and its movements suggest the anxious intrusion of obsessive concerns beyond mere centipedes, arthropods, and scutigera. In the initial version, the insect is already dead and a spot remains, the image of a crushed, fragmented millipede whose organs can be seen as though they were printed on an anatomical table in a scientific book, the partial shape of a body convulsed in a question mark. In the first flashback of how this spot came to be, what is presented is a scutigera of average size, about the length of a finger; it does not shift its position and can be seen quite clearly. A few pages later, the small creature is still seen clearly but now it is not just a matter of a pause in movement, but of motionlessness. There is but an infinitesimal difference, but it is this very infinitesimal quality that gives resonance to the text.

Eventually the millipede and its motion are not described at all: Franck simply takes his napkin, comes close to the wall, and crushes it, first against the wall and then on the floor. The French word for "napkin" is *serviette,* and this word can mean both hand towel and table napkin. It also can refer to "briefcase," suggesting the testes, the glands that define maleness. A close-up of Franck's phalanxes next to the blade of a knife insinuates the sadomasochistic component of jealousy, a component underlying the various relationships of the characters in this book. This is reinforced in still another version, a purely imaginary one, in which the millipede is "gigantic, one of the largest to be found in this climate"; no longer the size of a finger, it fills the entire plate. A precise description of its anatomy in motion implies that this beast is an objective correlative of sexual body parts in action. The reader senses that the repetitions are arranged so as to convey a gradual crescendo of force and intensity. Suddenly the beast writhes on the floor, moving in spasms as if trying to vomit. It emits a crackling noise that sounds like the electricity generated by the tortoise teeth of the comb in A.'s freshly washed hair. The animal stops, but the noise is heard in spite of the general silence. The climax is aborted when Franck rolls his *serviette* into a ball and squashes the beast as before, first against the wall and then against the floor. Only this time it is a bedroom floor and the *serviette* is not a napkin but a towel, which Franck will hang on a metal rack near the wash bowl on his way toward the bed, where the mosquito net falls all around, "interposing the opaque veil of its innumerable strands, where rectangular patches reinforce the torn places." The desire at the root of the observer's gaze cannot be satisfied any further. The primal scene will forever elude him, but he has come as close to it as is possible.

There is, however, a penalty for transgressing the prohibitions of society. While there is little hint here of any moral or ethical stance about the substance of what is forbidden and proscribed, the narrative voice artfully and delicately insinuates that violations of the law (for instance, the killing of the millipede by Franck) are punished by the bestowal of hysteria and impotence upon the perpetrators.

On one level, colonialism is itself a transgression. A careful reading of *Jealousy* reveals some of the problems. Franck's wife, Christiane, cannot cope with malaria, the heat, or the general environment. Although she is suffering from a variety of physical ailments, the phrase "c'est mental" dismisses the organic component of her illness. In *Ghosts in the Mirror,* Robbe-Grillet explains that Christiane is suffering from the illness that plagued him when he worked at Fort-de-France and forced him to return to France.

When Robbe-Grillet was an agronomist working in Fort-de-France, in a house very much like the one described in *Jealousy,* a local director had shown him an example of a local bulletin published by a French regional station in Africa. "The next day," writes the author,

> I told my hierarchical superior that all this research didn't ever lead to any concrete results whatsoever, that one could consider that these reports were exercises of the imagination. Keeping a straight face, I proposed drafting a comparable monthly bulletin in a few days completely by myself, under several pseudonyms if need be.
>
> He didn't laugh. But a few months later when I found myself in a Guadeloupe clinic with a multiplicity of tropical illnesses certified by all kinds of analysis and examinations, this honest man, who also had a certain kind of insight—and who I think liked me a lot and appreciated the many good points that I displayed in spite of everything, even on the professional level—in his official report to the central administration that was concerned about my state, declared without any hesitation whatsoever that in his opinion everything in my case was "mental." It was a judgment one could not appeal (probably one that was less unfair than I had felt at the time), and one that is found intact seven years later in *Jealousy,* about the colonial malaise undermining the health of the invisible Christiane, my chief having left some of his more gross traits (including this sentence) in the character of Franck, the plantation neighbor who always comes to dinner without his far too delicate wife.
>
> (*Ghosts in the Mirror,* p. 62)

In *Ghosts in the Mirror,* Robbe-Grillet wrote that the fall of the Third Reich left a much greater mark on him than the defeat of France in 1940. What he does not say is that *In the Labyrinth* chronicles this experience. The enigmatic foreword to the novel is an invitation to read it against the contemporary historical background transfigured by the artist's imagination.

"This story is a work of fiction, not a testimonial." This very first sentence recalls Freud's observation in his essay "The Unconscious" that "negation is a substitute, at a higher level, for repression." But *In the Labyrinth* does seem to be a testimonial. The rest of the preface lends itself to similar insights.

"The reality described isn't necessarily the one experienced by the reader: thus, in the French infantry the regimental number isn't worn on cloak collars. Likewise, recent western European history fails to record any important battle at Reichenfels or its vicinity. However, the reality depicted here is a strictly material reality, that is to say it doesn't aspire to any allegorical values." If we continue following Freud's model in his famous 1925 essay "Die Verneinung" ("Negation"), the conclusion is that many readers have experienced the reality depicted here, including the writer, who was himself the very first reader of his own work. The regimental number in the French infantry may not actually have been worn on cloak collars, but the significance of a number affixed to an article of clothing serves as a reminder that identification numbers of soldiers weren't imprinted on the flesh as were the numbers assigned Jews in extermination camps at Auschwitz, Treblinka, and Buchenwald. *Ghosts in the Mirror* even reproduces the slogan written just beneath the roof of the entrance of the factory at Nuremberg where the author was forced to work during the war: *Du bist ein Nummer und dieses Nummer ist nul*

("You are a number, and this number is nothing"). The battle of Reichenfels may not have taken place in the Reichenfels one finds on a map for a very good reason: it may be intended to be a reference to the battle of the fall of the Third Reich itself. Finally, the word "labyrinth" suggests an allegory through its reference to the maze constructed by Daedalus for Minos, king of Crete, in which the Minotaur was confined.

The conclusion of the preface is an invitation to read this piece of fiction much the way one reads any historical work: "The reader is therefore invited to see only the things, gestures, words, events that are reported without attempting to give them either more or less significance than in his own life, or his own death."

The characters and events of *In the Labyrinth* are products of the imagination insofar as one cannot identify them with any real persons or events. They are real nonetheless, not symbolic expressions of such topics as the futility of war or the tentativeness of human life. One might compare this genre to that of paintings in which figures convey a story or message based on history. In fact, the organizing principle of this book is painting, or rather a black-and-white engraving or reproduction of the last century, perhaps one of the illustrations of the famous *La petite illustration,* which Robbe-Grillet never tired of looking at when he was a child.

On the left of the etching, that is to say at the center of the scene, a bald fat "patron" of a cabaret filled with customers, some seated and others standing, is seen with his shoulders curved toward a group of bourgeois wearing waistcoats. One cannot help but read into this figure an allusion to the "patron" of *The Erasers,* perhaps an indirect tribute to Robbe-Grillet as the young writer of a first published novel. The significance of this allusion is uncertain, but so is the meaning of all the gestures and words of all the characters in the etching. It is as if language has been absorbed by a "thick glass pane." At the extreme right—left and right are not merely spatial references, but also are political entities—a group of workers is looking at a poster or announcement posted on the wall. A boy is seated on the ground among the heavy shoes, his two legs folded under his body, closing his arms around something that might be a shoe box. Is he the young boy that will guide the soldier through the streets in the novel? Or is this boy a self-portrait of the child Alain Robbe-Grillet growing up in a family of extreme Right "petit bourgeois" anarchists depicted also in *Ghosts in the Mirror* and *Angélique*?

Apart from the crowd surrounding them, three soldiers are seated at a small table, sitting perfectly still and rigid, their stiffness in contrast to the mobility of the civilians filling the room. They are the only ones to have their heads covered, with short pointed police caps. At the back, people are standing, and the drawing is quite indistinct. Underneath the painting, the title is given in English: "The Defeat of Reichenfels." The mention of English writing, rather than Gothic German script, is a subtle reminder that this etching should be attributed to someone on the side of the winners, not the losers. Waterloo was a victory for the English, but merely a battle for the French.

Just like the characters in Lewis Carroll's *Through the Looking Glass* (1872), one of the soldiers will walk right out of the picture into this novel. The face that is presented from the front, a tired thin face, made even thinner by the growth of a beard a few days old, with shining eyes, is the face of the wandering soldier who is the protagonist of the novel. Befriended by a young boy, who may or may not be the boy in the picture, this soldier roams through the town, where snow is falling, searching for a man who is supposed to receive a package containing the few remaining belongings of a fallen comrade. Simulating the effects of dreams and memory, characters and events undergo doubling processes as one soldier turns into another; present and past fuse in flashbacks and flashforwards; the result is a maze that is a correlative of the ultimate debacle, in which one of the soldiers dies in the apartment of the young mother of the boy, suggesting that this boy may be another part of the soldier himself rather than a separate individual. For this is the story of the life and death of someone, and following the author's wish, nothing else should be read into the tale except that, just as Flaubert once wrote, "Madame Bovary c'est moi," so here it might be said, "I am *In the Labyrinth*."

Beginning with *Instantanés,* a volume of short fiction, Robbe-Grillet seemed to veer toward one of the major literary traditions of France, the tradition of literary lewdness. The novels of the Marquis de Sade, for example *Justine* (1791) and *Philosophy in the Bedroom* (1795), mark an important moment in the history of ideas. Many modern French writers, among them Georges Bataille, Jean Paulhan, and Pierre Klossowski, have written commentaries about the "divine" Marquis and have themselves also contributed to the genre. The *Encyclopaedia Britannica* notes that in Chinese literature tales such as *Jou pu tuan* (*The Prayer Mat of Flesh*), which appear to be nothing more than pornography to westerners, express ethical and religious truths. Many of Robbe-Grillet's novels and films (*La maison de rendez-vous, Project for a Revolution in New York, Recollections of the Golden Triangle,* and *Topology of a Phantom City*) belong to this tradition.

The fact that Robbe-Grillet writes pornographic literature does not mean that he disapproves of the censorship of such material. In France, he writes, the Left opposes censorship on principle, but because of its own principles, that is to say inherited regard for virtues, leftists quickly "find themselves against pornographers on the side of censors" and of virtue. "I hate virtue," he continues in a short article, "Histoire de rats ou La vertu c'est ce qui mène au crime" (A Story of Rats; or, Virtue Leads to Crime"), published in *Obliques* 16–17, a special Robbe-Grillet issue:

> I hate it not out of principle, but because I have encountered it much too often and because historically I know where it leads: let us never forget that most of all Hitler and Stalin were virtuous, and that they made virtue (socialist, bourgeois, or "aryan" what difference does it make?) the backbone of their political constructs and the justification of their massacres; because, of course, he who speaks Virtue also speaks Repression: if one believes in it, one has to see to it that it be respected. And everyone can see all around that the rigid moralist is fairly often (this is a litotes) a swine.
>
> (pp. 170–171)

Robbe-Grillet believes that pornography has a Socratic function insofar as it allows us free access to our hidden self, transforming into liberty, into a game, into pleasure what was formerly alienation and could easily become crime or madness. "What virtue cannot stand, in reality, is not really this supposed danger (which nobody really believes) in letting some simple soul be perverted, what it cannot stand is pleasure . . . especially if it is intellectualized." The real question is why looking at the representation of a given erotic image gives more pleasure than the erotic act itself:

> We have here the problem of the imagination—and the word "imagination" itself suggests it—endlessly creating images and needing to be nourished by them; this is one of the highest faculties of the human species, I should even say that it is almost its most fascinating characteristic. Because a bull, even a loveless one, will never let his glance wander on the ass of a cow. Man, on the other hand, is fully a man only if everything functions through his head, even (and above all) sexuality. The famous sentence of the mathematician Henri Poincaré is well known: "An adult needs pornography in the same way as the child fairytales." Let us say, in a more general way, that at every stage, man is a consumer and a producer of myths, be they images or stories. As far as the

> spectator [in a New York City porno shop] who observes at such length the full size reproduction of a vulva in bloom—like a marine animal, all pink, soft, and dangerous, ajar and drowning under algae—one understands that he is more of a man than all men, the one who has pushed all possibilities to their ultimate consequences: that is to say an intellectual.
>
> (p. 172)

The conclusion is that such motifs are part of the society that one carries within, and that it is dangerous not to be aware of it.

From this "know thyself" perspective the pseudolicentious novel and film have a pedagogic purpose. Their function will be to undermine the noxious stereotypes of modern society that we carry in our heads by bringing them into full view. These works are criticized for being filled with depraved scenes of drug-induced violence, perversity, pedophilia, and sadomasochistic crimes, but there is an aesthetic redemption in the kind of eroticism that educates us to what is in our unconscious; it ensures that all of it will remain there rather than be acted out.

*La maison de rendez-vous* may be the author's most successful attempt in this category. The cliché of the opening sentence sets the tone: "Flesh of women has always taken up, no doubt, a lot of room in my dreams." The novel is set in Hong Kong, but the "author wants to specify that this novel should in no way be taken for a document about life in the British territory of Hong Kong. Any resemblance, whether of setting or situation, would only be the effect of chance, objective or not." Another note explains that, nevertheless, the places described depict a reality of the Orient: "Should any reader, habitual traveler to Far Eastern ports, be led to think that the places described here do not correspond to reality, the author, who has himself spent the greater part of his life there, would advise him to come back and take a better look: things change quickly in these climes." This apparent paradox can be resolved when we realize that in the first note, the author is talking about actual *life* in the Hong Kong of today, linked with an allusion to André Breton and the surrealist's notion of "objective" chance; in the second note, he is referring to *reality,* a metaphysical entity that to the surrealists was more real than life itself. This author and other authors spend the greater part of their lives in such climes. The Hong Kong of his imagination, the Hong Kong "everyone knows," with its harbor and the hundreds of small islands; its junks and ferryboats from Kowloon and Victoria; its office buildings and sugarloaf hills; the double-decker London buses; the pagoda-shaped sentry boxes at the intersections where policemen direct traffic; the large-wheeled red rickshaws with green hoods that shield the passengers without actually sheltering them from sudden torrential rains; its Eurasian women wearing white silk split skirts, is also like the Orient of filmmakers. Its center is the Blue Villa, an upper-class brothel with Eurasian servants named Kim, as if they belonged in a Rudyard Kipling novel. Its characters are stereotypes from American movies and comic books, with names to match. The hostess who organizes special entertainment for her intimate acquaintances is called Lady Ava, or perhaps Eva Bergmann. It is possible that she has never been to China, and that the deluxe bordello in Hong Kong may only be a story people have told her. Except that it actually might have been in Shanghai, a huge baroque palace called "Le Grand Monde" (The Great World), "or something of the sort," with gaming rooms, all kinds of prostitutes, gourmet restaurants, theaters with erotic spectacles, and opium dens. In fact, "she is born in Belleville, near the church, her name is neither Ava nor Eve, but Jacqueline, and she was not married to an English lord."

There is an everlasting American, who may also be English, named Johnson (like the heroes of the film *Blazing Saddles*) or Sir Ralph, or Sir Ralph Johnson. He seems to have settled in the New Territories, where he is living in a suite in a former luxury hotel in Kowloon that is now out of fashion. His money may come from growing Indian hemp and white poppies and Erythroxylum, and also from selling all kinds of remedies, poisons, youth potions, love philters, and aphrodisiacs to the Chinatowns all over the world, from the Indian Ocean to San Francisco. He may also be a Communist agent concealing his true identity by pretending to be manufacturing and/or trafficking in various drugs. He falls in love with a prostitute named Lauren (Laureen, Loraine), who has several names, all starting with L; she is a victim of the white slave trade, and he wants her to go away with him.

The most intriguing story in the book is that of Édouard Manneret, a spoof of Édouard Manet's painting of Stéphane Mallarmé, "a fat man with the red face" who is murdered several times and seems to be already dead at the beginning of the novel. There are several accounts of his death throughout, one more fanciful than the next, exemplifying the many possibilities of murder one finds in spy thrillers and murder mysteries, until finally, in a manner reminiscent of the ending of *The Erasers,* he is murdered by Johnson himself:

> Without thinking about taking the elevator, he walks up the seven flights. The door of the apartment is ajar, the door of the apartment is wide open in spite of the late hour, the door of the apartment is closed—what's the difference?—and Manneret himself comes to open it; or perhaps a Chinese servant, or a young sleepy Eurasian who has been called out of bed by the ringing of a bell, or perhaps by an insistent electric buzzer, or fist blows against the door. What importance is all this? What importance? Anyway, Édouard Manneret hasn't gone to bed yet. He never goes to bed. He sleeps fully dressed in his rocking chair. He hasn't been able to sleep for a long time now, even the strongest sleeping pills have stopped having the slightest effect upon him. He is sleeping quietly in his bed, but Johnson insists that he be awakened, and he himself waits in the living room, he shoves aside the terrified servants and enters the bedroom by force; all this is all the same. Manneret first takes Johnson for his son, he takes him for Georges Marchat, or Marchant, he takes him for Mr. Tchang, he takes him for Sir Ralph, he takes him for King Boris. It's all the same, because ultimately he refuses. The American insists. The American threatens. The American begs. Édouard Manneret refuses. Then the American calmly takes out his pistol from the inside right pocket (or left?) from his tuxedo, the pistol he had taken a little while ago (when?) from the closet or the chest of his hotel room, under the starched, well-ironed, very white shirts. . . . Manneret watches him and remains impassive, still smiling and slowly rocking in his chair to a regular rhythm. Johnson removes the safety catch. Édouard Manneret remains smiling, without moving a fold of his face. He looks like a wax figure in a museum. And his head goes up and down at the same cadence.
>
> (pp. 210–211)

Johnson finally leans on the trigger and "shoots five times in a row: down, up, down, up, down. All the shots have reached their target."

There is nothing bloody or gory about this crime. Everything is smooth, amiable, and agreeable. It is as though an attempt is made to minimize and to palliate the significance of what is about to take place. In fact, the only suggestion of death is the lifelessness of the murder itself. After all the games, all the fun, all the clichés, all the whimsy, it appears that the secret underlying Robbe-Grillet's works is the desire to displace and deny death. *Project for a Revolution in New York, Topology of a Phantom City,* and *Recollections of the Golden Triangle,* to my mind not entirely successful works, bring this theme to the ultimate, apocalyptic vision of the end of all things.

The essay by Sigmund Freud, "Our Attitude Towards Death," written in 1915 after the outbreak of World War I, may help to explain the meaning, or at least the significance, of these obsessions in Robbe-Grillet:

> It is an inevitable result . . . that we should seek in the world of fiction, in literature and in the theatre compensation for what has been lost in life. There we still find people who know how to die—who, indeed, even manage to kill someone

else. There alone too the condition can be fulfilled which makes it possible for us to reconcile ourselves with death: namely, that behind all the vicissitudes of life we should still be able to preserve a life intact. For it is really too sad that in life it should be as it is in chess, where one false move may force us to resign the game, but with the difference that we can start no second game, no return-match. In the realm of fiction we find the plurality of lives which we need. We die with the hero with whom we have identified ourselves; yet we survive him, and are ready to die again just as safely with another hero.

(*Standard Edition of the Complete Psychological Works of Sigmund Freud*, vol. 14, p. 291)

Robbe-Grillet's fascinating autobiographical works, *Ghosts in the Mirror* and *Angélique*, are written in a distinctive postmodern style blending fact and fiction and confirm that he shared the mutilated life of the generation injured by the events of World War II. One senses that in the face of what happened, be it a consequence of the war or of more private concerns, he was unable to maintain the integrity of his own existence. Perhaps that is why in the prime of his life, when he was thirty years old, after devoting years to the study of science and agronomy, he turned to writing. It is essential that the standard view of the author as a mannered stylist be counteracted. Like all storytellers, Robbe-Grillet's fictions give life a second chance.

## Selected Bibliography


### EDITIONS

#### INDIVIDUAL WORKS

NOVELS

*Les gommes.* Paris, 1953.
*Le voyeur.* Paris, 1955.
*La jalousie.* Paris, 1957.
*Dans le labyrinthe.* Paris, 1959.
*Instantanés.* Paris, 1962.
*La maison de rendez-vous.* Paris, 1965.
*Projet pour une révolution à New York.* Paris, 1970.
*Topologie d'une cité fantôme.* Paris, 1976.
*Un régicide.* Paris, 1978.
*Souvenirs du triangle d'or.* Paris, 1978.
*Djinn: Un trou rouge entre les pavés disjoints.* Paris, 1981.

CINÉ-NOVELS

*L'Année dernière à Marienbad, ciné-roman.* Paris, 1961.
*L'Immortelle.* Paris, 1963.
*Glissements progressifs du plaisir.* Paris, 1974.

ESSAYS AND CRITICISM

*Pour un nouveau roman.* Paris, 1963.

### AUTOBIOGRAPHICAL WORKS

*Angélique ou L'enchantement.* Paris, 1987.
*Le miroir qui revient.* Paris, 1984.

### TRANSLATIONS

*Djinn.* Translated by Yvone Lenard and Walter Wells. New York, 1982.
*The Erasers.* Translated by Richard Howard. New York, 1964.
*For a New Novel.* Translated by Richard Howard. New York, 1966.
*Ghosts in the Mirror.* Translated by Jo Levy. New York, 1988.
*The House of Assignation.* Translated by A. M. Sheridan Smith. London, 1970.
*The Immortal One.* Translated by A. M. Sheridan Smith. London, 1971.
*In the Labyrinth.* Translated by Richard Howard. New York, 1960; translated by Christine Brooke-Rose. London, 1967.
*Jealousy.* Translated by Richard Howard. New York, 1959.
*Last Year at Marienbad.* Translated by Richard Howard. New York, 1962.
*La maison de rendez-vous.* Translated by Richard Howard. New York, 1966.
*Project for a Revolution in New York.* Translated by Richard Howard. New York, 1972.
*Recollections of the Golden Triangle.* Translated by J. A. Underwood. London, 1984.
*Snapshots.* Translated by Bruce Morrissette. New York, 1968.

*Snapshots and Towards a New Novel.* Translated by Barbara Wright. London, 1965.

*Topology of a Phantom City.* Translated by J. A. Underwood. New York, 1977.

*The Voyeur.* Translated by Richard Howard. New York, 1958.

## BIOGRAPHICAL AND CRITICAL STUDIES

Alter, Jean. *La vision du monde d'Alain Robbe-Grillet.* Geneva, 1966.

Armes, Roy. *The Films of Alain Robbe-Grillet.* Amsterdam, 1981.

Bernal, Olga. *Alain Robbe-Grillet: Le roman de l'absence.* Paris, 1964.

Fletcher, John. *New Directions in Literature.* London, 1968.

———. *Alain Robbe-Grillet.* New York, 1983.

Heath, Stephen. *The Nouveau Roman: A Study in the Practice of Writing.* Philadelphia, 1972.

Jefferson, Ann. *The Nouveau Roman and the Poetics of Fiction.* Cambridge, 1980.

Leenhardt, Jacques. *Lecture politique du roman: "La jalousie" d'Alain Robbe-Grillet.* Paris, 1973.

Le Sage, Laurent. *The French New Novel.* University Park, Pa., 1962.

Mercier, Vivian. *The New Novel from Queneau to Pinget.* New York, 1971.

Miesch, Jean. *Robbe-Grillet.* Paris, 1965.

Morrissette, Bruce. *Alain Robbe-Grillet.* New York, 1965.

———. *The Novels of Robbe-Grillet.* Ithaca, N.Y., 1975.

Ricardou, Jean. *Pour une théorie du nouveau roman.* Paris, 1971.

Ricardou, Jean, ed. *Robbe-Grillet.* 2 vols. Paris, 1976.

"Robbe-Grillet." *Obliques* 16–17 (1978). Edited by François Jost.

Roudiez, Leon. *French Fiction Today: A New Direction.* New Brunswick, N.J., 1972.

Stoltzfus, Ben F. *Alain Robbe-Grillet and the New French Novel.* Carbondale, Ill., 1964.

———. *Alain Robbe-Grillet: The Body of the Text.* Rutherford, N.J., 1985.

Sturrock, John. *The French New Novel.* London, 1969.

Zants, Emily. *The Aesthetics of the New Novel in France.* Boulder, Colo., 1968.

## BIBLIOGRAPHIES

Fraizer, Dale Watson. *Alain Robbe-Grillet: An Annotated Bibliography of Critical Studies, 1953–1972.* Metuchen, N.J., 1973.

Rybalka, Michel. "Bibliographie." In *Obliques* 16–17:263–283 (1978).

JEANINE P. PLOTTEL

# ITALO CALVINO

## *(1923–1985)*

ITALO CALVINO'S SUDDEN death on 19 September 1985 cut short one of the most opulent careers in late-twentieth-century literature. In his final years he had become a major replenisher of fiction, at once ingenious and accessible, unique in his fusion of avant-garde technique with the primitive enchantment of storytelling. Even in America, habitually suspicious of European imports, especially those labeled "experimental," Calvino had a dedicated following that included Mary McCarthy, John Updike, and Gore Vidal; he died polishing lectures he was to have delivered at Harvard.

Cosmopolitanism put Calvino in the line of the great modernists. Like James Joyce, Vladimir Nabokov, and Samuel Beckett, this Italian citizen spent many years outside his homeland, primarily in Paris; and although he was not an émigré in the conventional sense, with its connotation of deportation, protest, or disillusionment, he seemed a passing stranger amid Italy's contemporary writers, a fugitive from an earlier age—the Renaissance springs to mind. Calvino inherited its capacious humanism, its polymathy, its easy mingling of the intuitive and the logical.

Calvino's uniqueness began with his upbringing. His father was an agronomist by profession and by conviction an "anticlerical, masonic republican, an anarchic Krapotkinian in his youth, and then a reform Socialist"—wholly at odds with Italy's Catholic tradition. In his early manhood he forsook San Remo, a lovely town on the Ligurian coast in the far northwest, near France, for a long, fruitful exile in Mexico and Cuba, alone and then with his wife, a Sardinian "raised in the religion of civic and scientific duty" (*Italo Calvino,* 1985). She had earlier been a botanist at the University of Pavia and like her husband exhibited the passion for scientific reason that constituted a heterodox faith during the early years of this century, when Charles Darwin and Albert Einstein seemed twin apostles of a liberating truth.

The Calvinos were unusually old—he forty-eight, she thirty-seven—when Italo was born, in Santiago di Las Vegas, outside Havana, on 15 October 1923. Two years later the family returned to San Remo and inhabited an ancestral farm, which became an outdoor laboratory for the couple's plant experiments (inventors and tinkerers recur in Calvino's fiction) as well as an island of enlightened refuge from the Fascist dictatorship of Benito Mussolini. While *il Duce* hypnotized his countrymen with wild invocations of Italy's glorious past and with deluded dreams of military conquest, the freethinking Calvinos inculcated in their son a calm skepticism that eventually lent piquancy to his fiction but created extreme anguish for him as an adolescent. The few boyhood reminiscences in his stories and interviews compositely yield a shy, awkward youth, uneasy with his fellows, miserable around girls, his unhappiness hidden behind a mask of ironic jesting. And loneliness is an essential condition of his fictional universe, which yields very little satisfying love, or even lasting friendship; Calvino's characters often seem transients in a world of Others.

Solitude so resounding must be chosen to some extent, and the young Calvino stood willfully apart; he took pride in being excused from religious instruction at his *liceo* (high school) and barely concealed his contempt for the Fascist youth group to which he compulsorily belonged. In his memory story "Gli avangardisti a Mentone" (The Vanguardists in Menton, 1953) he confesses that his repugnance was aesthetic as well as moral: the Fascists, with their epaulets, their bluster, their clubbiness, were not only thugs but philistines who so soured him on institutional authority that when he was drafted in 1943, after Mussolini had been ousted and Italy had taken up the Allied cause, he deserted the national army and joined a Resistance cadre in the Maritime Alps, an experience that haunted him the rest of his life in violent nightmares.

But the war also had a salutary effect; it gave Calvino the courage to rebel against his parents, a rebellion most difficult, perhaps, for the child reared in an iconoclastic home. Since boyhood he had preferred San Remo's unruly pine forests to the regulated environment of the greenhouse and had escaped his parents' strict rationalism by reading "novels of adventure and fantasy, romances full of action" (*New York Times Magazine,* 10 July 1983, p. 33); yet in 1941, when he enrolled in the University of Turin, he halfheartedly undertook agronomy studies, "hiding my literary ambitions even from my best friends and almost from myself"—not to mention his father, who sat on the university's science faculty. It would take the crucible of war—the long months of peril, rough living, and the earthy comradeship of partisan peasants—to enflame his passion for literature. In 1945 he resumed his studies in Turin but switched his major to English literature. More important, he took up the bohemian life of the novice artist, renting an unheated garret and producing his first fiction, mostly about his war experiences.

The reader of Calvino's World War II stories is immediately struck by their narrow focus. "Fascist," "partisan," "Nazi," "Allies," and other signposts of the era seldom appear, and when they do they are shorn of their customary associations. It helps to know that for Italy the war had been all along a murky enterprise; a pact with Adolf Hitler, formalized in 1939, dismayed even loyal followers of Mussolini; after he was deposed, the nation, rather than joining the Allies by public consensus, was simply surrendered over to them by its king, Victor Emmanuel III. As Calvino later wrote, "For many of my contemporaries chance alone had chosen sides for them; frequently, they suddenly changed allegiances—from Fascists they became partisans, or vice versa. Either way they shot or were shot at; only death gave to their choice an irrevocable sign" (*Il sentiero dei nidi di ragno* [*The Path to the Nest of Spiders,* 1947]). The young author's distrust of ideology corroborates the wider skepticism of a specific moment in history, but his reticence goes even further. He refuses to gaze past immediate events into the larger dimensions of the partisan battles—their historical, political, and social contexts. Instead Calvino limits himself to psychological studies of individual soldiers. He isolates the bacillus of fear that invades even the tranquil moments of armed conflict, examines hysteria as a heightened state of mind, locates the instant in which trauma opens the way to revelation. These early vignettes feel authentic because they distill the terrible absurdity of war.

"Campo di Mine" ("Mine Field," 1946) in *Gli amori difficili* (*Difficult Loves,* 1970) is set just after the Liberation. An unnamed young man, either a partisan or a Fascist (probably the latter since he hopes to escape the country), climbs a mountain slope he knows is mined, confident he can avoid a misstep. He proceeds with methodical care, surveying the brush for clues—"earth moved, rocks placed purposely, newer grass"—but he is gradually unnerved; he can't be sure of picking up every clue and, worse, days of near starvation have left him so hungry that he begins to hallucinate. He imagines the mines lying in wait for him like "enormous marmots crouched in underground lairs, with one keeping watch from the top of a stone, as marmots do, hissing an alarm" (p. 159).[1] Images of the rodents assail him—their teeth, their smell, their squeals—until, when at last he reaches the valley where a safe crossing should be possible, he is gripped by a combination of amazement and terror: the area is blanketed "by rhododendrons, a uniform and impenetrable sea from which jutted only the humps of gray rocks." This, we realize, is no hallucination: he has stumbled into the place where the mines must be buried, beneath the vast expanse of blooms. He feels "a strange craving, made of hunger and fear, that he could not satisfy" (p. 162), as he plods knowingly, almost gratefully, toward death.

Equally dreamlike is "Ultimo viene il corvo" ("The Crow Comes Last," 1946). The protagonist is again unnamed, "a mountain child, with a face like an apple" (p. 133), who is so gifted a marksman that he effortlessly shoots trout out of the water, hawks out of the sky, and squirrels out of the trees. Here too the action is simple, the emphasis falling on the magical ease with which the boy kills and on his own detached wonder at his power: "It was strange, thinking about it, to be encircled so by air, separated by meters of air from other things. But if he pointed the rifle, the air became a line, direct and invisible and taut, from the muzzle to the object, to the hawk that moved in the sky with motionless wings" (p. 134).

The boy soon progresses to human targets, no less alluring—"the glint of the soldiers' arms, the gray and the shine of their uniforms" (p. 136)—and finally, on his first mission, he sights a German soldier from whose point of view the concluding paragraphs are told. Again we inhabit the mind of a man transfixed by the prospect of his own death. The soldier first marvels at the young marksman's extraordinary prowess—birds drop from the sky, pine cones explode on branches; then he grows confused, for the child has evidently overlooked a crow that has wheeled into view:

> Perhaps the crow did not exist, and was only a hallucination. Perhaps someone about to die sees every kind of bird pass before his eyes, and when he sees the crow it means that the time has come. But he must warn the boy, who continued to fire at the pines. So the soldier rose to his feet and indicated the black bird with his finger. "There it is, the crow!" he shouted, in his own language. The bullet hit directly in the middle of the spread-winged eagle embroidered on his jacket. The crow slowly circled down.
>
> (p. 139)

Is there actually a bird overhead or is it a premonitory death-glimpse sparked by the insignia on the victim's own tunic? It scarcely matters; in any case the vision has accurately foretold his demise, an almost supernatural occurrence. Like his counterpart in "Mine Field," the German stares through the distortive lens of fear, yet what he discerns really exists, for his tautened senses open the way to apocalyptic insight. "If there are mysterious forces around," says one of Saul Bellow's characters, "only exaggeration can help us to see them."

Calvino was doubtless aware that by probing the membrane that joins the imaginary to the real he had joined issue with some of the leading Italian writers of the day, two of whom lived in or near Turin and adopted Calvino as their protégé. Elio Vittorini was an acclaimed anti-Fascist novelist, the author of *Uomini e no* (*Men and Not Men,* 1945), and a champion of American realism. He translated William Faulkner, F. Scott Fitzgerald, and Ernest Hemingway. He also edited the Communist weekly *Il Politecnico,* where some of Calvino's apprentice fiction ran. Cesare Pavese (who committed

[1] Unless indicated otherwise, citations of quoted material refer to the Italian editions, translated by the present author.

suicide in 1950) was probably the most admired novelist of the preceding generation. He held an editorial post at Giulio Einaudi editore, an anti-Fascist publishing house founded in Turin in the 1930's (the novelist Natalia Ginzburg, another formative friend, was also on its staff, as Vittorini had been some years before). These writers, somewhat older than Calvino, spearheaded a literary movement, "neorealism," that had emerged in the buoyant wake of Mussolini's defeat and defined a generation of Italian fiction.

"Neorealism" is a chameleon term. Calvino himself viewed it as a belated outburst of expressionism (banned by Mussolini in the 1920's), and described it as a

> collection of voices, mostly peripheral, a manifold discovery of different Italys, also—or especially—of the Italys until then mostly unknown to literature. . . . Local characterization was meant to give a truthful flavor to a representation in which the whole vast world would be recognizable. Therefore language, style, and rhythm mattered greatly to this realism of ours that must be as distant as possible from naturalism.
>
> (*Il sentiero dei nidi di ragno,* p. 9)

Neorealists, in other words, were less concerned with documenting the visible than with giving shape to the unseen. They wanted to wrest the mythic from the commonplace, as Calvino himself had done in "Mine Field" and "The Crow Comes Last."

Encouraged by Pavese and Ginzburg (who, according to legend, had wearied of their protégé dumping stories in their laps), Calvino began his first novel. He hoped to conjure up the landscape he had known both as child and soldier, to plumb the psychology of the partisans, and to articulate the mood of a rising generation that had endured a civil war, conquered Fascism, and now exulted in the belief that history had rewarded it with a blank slate on which to inscribe the future.

*Il sentiero dei nidi di ragno* (*The Path to the Nest of Spiders*), completed at the end of 1946, met the deadline for a contest sponsored by Oscar Mondadori, a Milan publishing house. It did not impress the selection panel, so Calvino showed it to Pavese at Einaudi, which released it in November 1947 to modest sales, critical praise, and a prize, the Premio Riccione. The author was vindicated, but one sympathizes with the unpersuaded Mondadori panel—for all its many virtues, this first novel is an anomalous, rather than original, performance.

It is set in an old Ligurian city, presumably San Remo, where the orphan Pin and his sister Rina, a prostitute, inhabit a few shabby rooms in a dingy back alley. Pin is pathetically streetwise for his age (about thirteen). He spends his days in a tavern frequented by adult roughnecks whom he detests but who are his only companions. They enjoy hearing him sing folk songs in his crabbed, tortured voice, and incite him to vicious barbs by taunting him about his sister, the mistress of a German sailor. The action opens when Pin is challenged to steal the German's pistol, a feat he manages that same night, slipping into his sister's room while she and the sailor sleep. But the next day, when Pin arrives with his trophy, the men have forgotten the dare and start in with their witless needling. Confused and humiliated, Pin flees to his hideout on the riverbank outside town and buries the weapon in a secluded place where he fantasizes that "among the grass, the spiders make their dens, tunnels compacted of dry grass . . . with a little round door that can be opened and closed" (p. 51). Evening falls and Pin, on his way home, is nabbed by a German patrol rounding up curfew violators; he is beaten and tossed into jail. He contrives an implausible escape, then wanders aimlessly until he happens upon a genial partisan named Cugino, who leads him on a hilly climb to the farmhouse where his detachment is holed up.

Abruptly, with a gnashing of gears, a child's adventure story becomes an episodic chronicle of the motley partisans, castoffs from more disciplined units, with comic-book nicknames and infantile fixations. Dritto (Crafty), the demonic commander, sends the others off to battle while he stays behind romancing the cook's slatternly wife; the viperish Pelle (Skin) resembles an older, dissolute Pin, with his runny nose and fever for sex and weapons; Zena il lungo (Long Zena) keeps his nose buried in a trashy thriller called *Supergiallo;* even the amiable Cugino (Cousin), with his unshakable conviction that women are the root of all evil (he is himself a cuckold), seems a child; in fact he becomes Pin's confidant, initiated into the secret of the spiders' nests. They are unlikely heroes.

In his preface to the 1964 reissue of *Path,* Calvino explained that he programmatically overdid the coarseness of Dritto's unit in order to affront two opposed but equally smug factions: the left-wing literary establishment, which clamored for uplifting hymns to the Resistance, and the high-minded middle class, which had sat out the fighting but emerged when the smoke cleared to snipe at the partisan victors. To the first faction Calvino's message is, Yes, these men were heroes, but hardly saints; and to the second, Yes, they were knaves, but you owe them your freedom (for in Italy, as in France, the middle class willingly collaborated with their oppressors in World War II). The message comes through—at a price. The novel does not wear its politics lightly, particularly in chapter 9 when the author stops the narrative in its tracks with a watered-down Marxist analysis (delivered by a thoroughly extraneous character) of the partisans' historical roles. Calvino's mentors pleaded with him to drop these pages, but he was adamant; as he notes disarmingly in the 1964 preface, the interpolation was appropriate because it was of a piece with the "composite and spurious" quality that characterizes the entire novel (p. 11).

"Spurious" is severe, "composite" apt. But then how many novels, let alone first novels by twenty-three-year-olds, are entirely convincing? *The Path to the Nest of Spiders,* after all, scores many local triumphs: the stolen pistol is an excellent device for triggering the plot; the fanciful spiders' nests linger in the mind as an emblem of vestigial innocence; and Pin—crude, mocking, witheringly misanthropic, but underneath a sad and friendless child—seems truly imagined, unlike the thinly disguised self-portraits usually foisted on us by young authors. And Calvino's verbal strategies are inspired. The present-tense narrative captures the immediacy of the events it describes. It also conveys the daily improvisations of the Resistance struggle, as do the mystifying neologisms scattered throughout the book, such as the military acronyms "gap" and "sim"; these also particularize the partisan war and enable us to see it, through Pin's eyes, as a malignant adult game. Finally, the harsh bantering dialogue—spoken in the tavern, the prison, the hills, the few exchanges between Pin and his sister—permanently added to neorealism's "collection of voices" a music that Calvino alone recorded, the echo of evenings when he had huddled with his comrades around the evening campfire, listening to anecdotes swapped in "a style, a language, a humor akin to boasting . . . [a] new oral tradition" (p. 8).

With the publication of *Path,* the shy loner who had hidden his literary ambitions as he slunk off to the Turin science faculty was propelled into Italy's intellectual vanguard, in his middle twenties an acclaimed novelist and short-story writer (a collection, *Ultimo viene il corvo* [The Crow Comes Last, partially translated as *Adam, One Afternoon, and Other Stories*] appeared in 1949). Einaudi, which would remain his lifelong publisher, gave him a desk in its publicity department (he later was promoted to editor, then editorial director, and actively served the company as an adviser until his death). As a rule, writers accept publishing jobs only out of necessity, but in the *dopoguerra* (postwar era) Einaudi was an especially exciting place to be, transformed by Pavese and Ginzburg into a neorealist nerve center. Calvino profited from daily interaction with his mentors and from lusty debate about literature, culture, and politics—topics clothed in newness after two decades of Fascist censorship.

And nearby was Vittorini, asserting in the pages of *Il Politecnico* that to protect against future outbreaks of totalitarianism writers must be politically engaged (*impegnato*). Calvino took this advice seriously. He had already joined the Communist party, in the last months of the war, and had strengthened the nexus at the outset of the Liberation by enrolling in Turin University's Communist sect and by contributing polemical articles to *Il Politecnico*. He served on the staff of *L'Unità*, Italy's official Communist newspaper, in 1948–1949 and subsequently appeared in its pages as editorialist, commentator, and analyst. Even after Vittorini broke with the party over the direction of *Il Politecnico* (he balked at turning it into a propaganda sheet), Calvino held firm, largely because he had never swallowed Communist orthodoxies; to him the party offered only a "realistic program for opposing a resurgence of Fascism and for rehabilitating Italy."

This political activity coincided with a brief creative drought. *The Path to the Nest of Spiders* behind him, Calvino set out to produce a second novel along the same lines, a sociopolitical treatment of World War II. It was natural that he do so: Fascism was far from exhausted as a subject, and the partisan war, beyond being a crucial episode of recent history, offered a fresh allegory of Italy's political fate. Yet as much as there remained to tell, he could squeeze out only three thin stories, dead-end installments in a fictionalized memoir, eventually released in 1954 as a triptych, *L'Entrata in guerra* (Entering the War). These stories, which have not been translated into English, are interesting mainly for the light they shed on the author's adolescent years.

More fruitfully, he revisited the fabular region he had tentatively explored in his apprentice stories. This time, he ventured deeper. Heretofore he had planted magical features in solidly realistic soil; he now tried a reverse tactic. In a succession of novels and tales, he devised an impossible, even preposterous premise, fitted it into a rigorously formal design, then fleshed it out with details that were scrupulously observed and sorted, even classified, like his parents' plant specimens. The consequence was a complete unlocking of Calvino's imagination. In a single decade, the 1950's, as much good prose poured out of him as issues from some writers in a lifetime. The superabundance can be roughly separated into two groupings. One includes the historical fantasies *Il visconte dimezzato* (*The Cloven Viscount,* 1952), *Il barone rampante* (*The Baron in the Trees,* 1957), and *Il cavaliere inesistente* (*The Nonexistent Knight,* 1959)—later released as the trilogy *I nostri antenati* (Our Ancestors, 1960). The other includes the contemporary fables "La formica argentina" ("The Argentine Ant," 1952) and "La nuvola di smog" ("Smog," 1958), the satirical novella *La speculazione edilizia* (Building Speculation, 1957), and the short stories, some of them brilliant, collected in *I racconti* (Stories, 1958). At the same time, Calvino researched, edited, and revised the two hundred *Fiabe italiane* (*Italian Folktales,* 1956) and produced essays, polemics, and reviews. It is an astonishing, almost daunting output for a man not yet forty, particularly one who seems to have worked for pleasure rather than to exorcise demons or quench some desperate need, who was possibly less a "hunger artist" than any great writer of his time.

The breakthrough came with *I nostri antenati,* usually referred to as a trilogy though none of the novels is actually linked—no characters overlap, each book has a unique time and setting, and the themes differ. *The Cloven Viscount* is the most overtly allegorical of these novels, with its hero split literally in two, one half irredeemably evil, the other purely virtuous. *The Baron in the Trees,* an adventure story like *Robinson Crusoe,* comments on the modern temperament and its eighteenth-century origins. And *The Nonexistent Knight,* fusing existential comedy with literary parody, treats the distant past as an ironic mirror of the present.

The most remarkable of these historical

romps may be *The Cloven Viscount,* not because it is the best of the three—in fact it is the most schematic—but because it represents an incalculable advance over the author's previous work. Reading Calvino's first two novels in succession, it is difficult to believe that they were produced by the same mind and only five years apart. *Viscount* is not only a confident work but, what we never would have guessed, an elegant one as well.

Set in the late seventeenth century, it begins like an arch version of *Don Quixote.* Its hero is a starry-eyed nobleman, Medardo di Terralba, who, accompanied by his Sancho Panza, a sardonic squire named Curzio, arrives at an Austrian encampment the night before the resumption of a bloody battle against Turkey. After a restless night in which he imagines the glories that await him, the soldier plunges into the fray and immediately sustains an injury both macabre and preposterous: a cannonball splits him in two. Half of him is left for dead, but doctors patch up the rest—one arm, one leg, "an eye, an ear, a cheek, half a nose, half a mouth, half a chin, and half a forehead" (p. 18)—and return it, draped in a black cloak and hood, to Terralba, where the viscount receives a hero's welcome. It soon becomes apparent, however, that he has been split more than physically; he is half a man morally as well—the evil half, intent on bringing misery to all those around him. He hangs peasants for petty offenses, sets fire to the abodes of blameless citizens, banishes his aged wet nurse to a leper colony. Matters complicate when his other half, left for dead amid a heap of corpses, unexpectedly appears after a journey "for months and years through the Christian nations . . . astonishing people along the way with his acts of goodness" (p. 73). As the first viscount is unregenerately wicked, so is Medardo impossibly kind, reminiscent of St. Francis as he traipses through the countryside leading lost children out of the woods, succoring hurt animals, and straightening bent trees.

This hundred-page novella is, in sum, an extended lark about duality, and its pleasures derive from the author's witty expansion of his initial premise. Calvino created a group portrait of partisan roughnecks in *The Path to the Nest of Spiders.* Here he depicts an entire world rent in two, filled with characters as fissured as Medardo, though less sensationally. The maiden Pamela, pursued by both viscounts, is at once virginal and lusty; Dr. Trelawney, an English physician, ignores his patients in order to comb the countryside for will-o'-the-wisps; Mastro Pietrochiodo, the local carpenter, sweats to build a mobile contraption that is simultaneously a pipe organ, mill, bakery, and well, but has better luck perfecting gibbets and racks; and the narrator, Medardo's young nephew, the bastard offspring of a misalliance between a noblewoman and a poacher, hovers on the margins of two opposed social worlds. Most strikingly, two groups of outcasts, lepers and Huguenots, offer contrasting examples of communal excess: the lepers sprig their hair with flowers and conduct orgies; the Huguenots dourly toil from dawn to dusk and glower at everyone, including one another.

As Calvino nimbly works out the algebra of his premise we marvel at his tact, for he manages to fashion a world of self-contradictory types without straining our credulity; even the knight's injury seems a reasonable metaphor for the familiar condition of inner dividedness, no more outlandish than the alter egos in Feodor Dostoevksy's *The Double* or Joseph Conrad's "The Secret Sharer" (Conrad had been the subject of Calvino's undergraduate thesis). Similarly, the contest between the two adversaries reverberates with overtones of that ancient, unfrolicsome subject, the war between good and evil. The contrast between the two viscounts puts the reader in mind of William Butler Yeats's "The Second Coming" and its description of moral anarchy: "The best lack all conviction, while the worst / Are full of passionate intensity." The good viscount does not precisely lack conviction, but, unlike the bad one, he seems deficient in intensity, that is, in the energy needed to convert sentiment into action. "The good thing about being halved," he explains in a somber moment, is "understanding that every person and thing in the world knows the sorrow of incompleteness. I was whole and I didn't understand, and moved deaf and dumb amid the sadness and suffering all around me" (p. 74). Yet, having arrived at this understanding, having been awakened to the reality of sadness and suffering, he fails in the effort to dispel them because, like many saintly people, he tragically underestimates the dark forces ranged against him and rather smugly overestimates the sheer power of virtue. Calvino adds a powerful irony: Medardo does as much harm as good because his ministrations only drive his opponent to further atrocities. Not until the good viscount himself resorts to violence, meeting his evil half in a swordfight that accidentally mortises them into a single body, is balance restored.

The second panel of *I nostri antenati, The Baron in the Trees,* unites fancy and intellect with even greater skill; moreover, it stays entirely within the bounds of possibility. Here the premise is the notion that, as Thomas Mann puts it in *Dr. Faustus,* "flight from mankind sometimes only involves the more with humanity the man who flees." The fleer is twelve-year-old Cosimo Piovasco di Rondo, who, one spring day in 1767, defies his stuffy father, a minor nobleman, by leaving the dinner table, climbing up an oak outside his house, and vowing never to touch soil again. As in *Viscount* the narrator is kin to the hero, in this case his worshipful younger brother, Biagio, who narrates the baron's adventures as he skips from branch to branch clothed in animal furs, devising clever ways to nourish, clean, entertain, and educate himself; and again we meet an eccentric cast of characters whose dilemmas echo the hero's, though in this case loneliness, or estrangement, seems the general malady. Cosimo's parents, for instance, have nothing in common but their incurable dissatisfaction—his mother, the daughter of an Austrian general, pines for the excitement of the military life she knew as a girl, while his father schemes idly for an unattainable duchy. The narrator, Biagio, equally disaffected, simmers with filial resentment but remains till the end the dutiful son. Only Cosimo, with his impetuous leap, gains control over his life. At one point, in conversation with his *grand amour* (he manages a number of trysts), he breathlessly summarizes his accomplishments:

> I've hunted, even boar, but mostly fox, hare, marten and, you know, thrush and blackbird; and then the Turkish pirates—there was a great battle, my uncle died in it; and I have read many books, for myself and for a friend, a brigand who was hanged; and I've got the whole *Encyclopedia* of Diderot and I even wrote to him and he replied, from Paris, and I've done a lot of work, pruned trees, saved a forest from fire.
>
> (p. 181)

The novel is a paean to human ingenuity. It also dramatizes a seismic event whose tremors are still being felt today—the birth of Romanticism, the revolution of thought and feeling that erased the waning traces of European feudalism and ushered in a social order founded on the notion of complete personal liberty. The baron himself is part civilized man, part noble savage. He is so marinated in high culture that he evolves an idiom of pan-European polyglot ("Il y a un pre where the grass grows toda de oro / Take me away, take me away, che io ci moro!" [p. 188]). And he declaims this while he swings on the limb of an ash, his head crowned with feathers, "like the American aborigines."

For all his public involvement—he joins numerous guilds, becomes a freemason, even proposes an "Ideal State" confined to the trees—Cosimo remains apart from the conventional community and, at bottom, its enemy. His affection for humanity does not extend to its institutions. Behind *The Baron in the Trees* lie the antinomian reforms of Charles Fourier and Robert Owen, whose planned communities radically protested bourgeois society; and Calvino may have based his hero on the documented case of Victor, the Wild Boy of Aveyron, who reputedly lived as a human beast in the forests of southern France before he was captured in 1799 by a physician who tutored him in civilized conduct—with disastrous consequences. At a dinner party Victor pounced on a female guest and, when he was rebuffed, fled into the garden and scaled the nearest tree trunk. The baron's climb is equally impulsive, and, though from his perch he benefits his fellow humans, he remains as aloof as a Syrian tree monk. He feels no temptation to descend, even after he has grown old and infirm and incapable of caring for himself. On the brink of death and in danger of returning to the soil for good, he grabs hold of a passing balloon. It drops him into the sea, and his vow is preserved to the very end.

Nearer to a full-blown hero than any character Calvino subsequently created, Cosimo seems an idealization of his author, who was himself a humane renouncer of humanity, a skeptic, but also a hopeful visionary (fascinated by Fourier, whom he later edited and explicated). Just as Cosimo earns our admiration by resourcefully fashioning an arboreal existence that seems an apotheosis of the life ideally available on the ground, so Calvino dazzles us by giving us a new vantage point on the *terra firma* of familiar experience. Author and hero become one in Biagio's assessment of the anecdotes his brother loves to narrate and embroider:

> In sum, he was taken by that mania of the story teller who never knows which stories are more beautiful, those that actually happened and whose evocation recalls the swell of distant hours, of sentiments, boredom, happiness, doubt, vainglory, of self-disgust, or those that are sheerly invented, in which he cuts along a pattern, and everything seems easy, but then varies it as he realizes that he has spoken, after all, of things that really happened or are really living. (p. 142)

*The Nonexistent Knight* hurls us back much further in time, to the eighth century and an encampment outside the walls of Paris where the army of Charlemagne is bivouacked on the eve of a battle against the Muslims. Among the troops is a paladin named "Agilulfo Emo Bertrandino of the Guildiverni and of the Others of Corbrentraz and Sura, Knight of Selimpia Citeriore and Fez." He is a model warrior in every way but one: he does not exist, at least not physically. He is an empty suit of gleaming white armor; outfitted in breastplate and metal pants, his visor shut, he looks and sounds like his fellows. Yet inside he is irremediably different.

Once more the secondary characters suffer from more or less plausible versions of the hero's exaggerated debility: his squire, Gurdulu, is schizophrenically incapable of distinguishing himself from external objects—he repeatedly plunges his head into steaming soup tureens; the female warrior Bradamante is part Amazon, part wench; the young knight Torrismondo, unhinged by the prospect that he is not, as he had long thought, the illegitimate son of the Knights of the Holy Grail, complains that "I don't know who I am"; and even the narrator has variable identities.

The novel is enriched by strategic borrowings from Ludovico Ariosto's epic poem, *Orlando Furioso,* written at the turn of the sixteenth century to satisfy popular nostalgia for chivalric romances featuring chaste knights, amorous princesses, sage kings, and festive battles—all diametrically opposed to the gory realities of the time, as Ariosto well knew. For even as *Orlando* capitulated to fashion, it made light of it: the author contrasts the characters' grandiloquent gestures with their crass deeds, deflates suspenseful moments with windy digressions, and contorts the plot wildly.

Calvino's debts to Ariosto are legion. He reproduces *Orlando*'s time and locale, mocks the pomp of the Holy War, and steals a major character, the female warrior Bradamante. In Ariosto's poem she weathers harrowing escapes in her search for her pagan lover. In *Knight* she pines for Agilulfo, who, though bodiless, alone measures up to her exacting standards of manhood—an irony typical of the novel. On a more antic level, Calvino hilariously updates his source's Renaissance skepticism about the Age of Chivalry, presenting it as an early incarnation of modern bureaucracy: the jaded knights approach each day's joust with the bored indifference of workers punching a time clock; elaborate codes of military honor are shown to prefigure the circumventions of institutional red tape; and the impeccable Agilulfo is portrayed as an infuriating fussbudget who at one point officiously directs Rambaldo, an inexperienced Hotspur itching to avenge his slain father, to the "Superintendancy of Duels, Vendettas, and of Stained Honor," where "it will be determined how best to put you in a position to achieve the desired satisfaction" (p. 20).

In a contemporary story, it would come as no surprise to see Rambaldo's naive heroism squelched in this way; but placed in the alien context of the Middle Ages the lunacy of the "system" strikes us as if for the first time. This strange world disorients us through familiarity. *Knight,* more directly than either *Viscount* or *Baron,* clarifies that what Calvino relishes about the past is that it enables us to look anew at the present. Early on, we are pointedly reminded that "the state of the world was still confused in the era in which this story takes place. It was not rare to run into names and ideas and forms and institutions which did not correspond to anything in existence" (p. 37). It was a time, in short, much like our own.

In one of the loveliest scenes in all of Calvino, a sumptuous banquet at which Agilulfo, who has no need or desire for food, punctiliously manipulates cutlery and crockery and even harries waiters, the hero is suddenly denounced by the young and tormented Torrismondo, who accuses him of building his reputation on false pretenses, since a girl he once rescued was not properly a maiden, having already been robbed of her chastity. Insofar as Agilulfo exists at all, it is by virtue of his interior standard of probity; he has no choice but to establish the girl's virginity, and toward this end he embarks on a transcontinental quest that parodies the sacral journeys of the Arthurian heroes. He is followed by the adoring Bradamante, who is pursued in turn by Rambaldo, whom she has smitten, while Torrismondo heads off on a quest of his own to locate his true patrimony. *Knight* now becomes a kind of *On the Road* set in the age of chivalry, flavored with magic, mysticism, and maidens—all mordantly lampooned, as when Torrismondo at last locates the Knights of the Round Table only to find that these sainted men extort provender from defenseless peasants.

All this activity is related in a curious manner that recalls the authorial intrusions of Ariosto. *Knight* is the first of Calvino's novels to use an unreliable narrator. In the third chapter the omniscient author suddenly reveals herself as "Sister Teodora, nun of the order of San Columbano," who, even while she writes, assembles her story "from old papers, from chatter heard in our parlor and from some rare testimony of people that were there." We've known from the outset that everything—character, incident, setting—has been fabricated, as with any story, but it is disconcerting to be reminded of this by the narrator herself and further to learn that it is all meant to divert not only us but also herself, steeped in the gloom of the convent refectory with its clatter of pots and pans and its stink of cooked cabbage. We participate in yet another quest as Sister Teodora reports her struggle to sew all these adventures into a tight web while simultaneously pushing the plot forward and evoking on the flat page the changing landscape traversed by her improbable characters. The true protagonist of this tale turns out to be its teller.

The trilogy *I nostri antenati* caused an international sensation (in the Soviet Union *The Baron in the Trees* sold fifty thousand copies in one week), and the novellas remain among the most scintillating intellectual comedies of the 1950's. They also ignited considerable debate. Were they trifles, or worse, trifles veneered with portentous themes (the divided self, the noble savage, the man without qualities)? Had a dedicated neorealist relaxed into foppish escapism? Today such questions seem irrelevant for several reasons. First, Calvino as historical novelist peers obliquely at the crises of modern culture; second, even his early "engaged" work evinced a fabular quality; third, by straying from dowdy realism he drew closer to the elusive truth of his time, as testified by the continued freshness of these glorious jeux d'esprit a generation after their composition.

Yet there is immediate evidence that Calvino still clung to his neorealist vision; in the intervals between the three panels of *I nostri antenati* he produced a quantity of fiction set resolutely in the present: in 1963 he published *Marcovaldo; ovvero, Le stagioni in città* (*Marcovaldo; or, The Seasons in the City*), a story sequence about urban blight; "Smog," a long story, appeared in Alberto Moravia's journal *Nuovi argomenti* in 1958, a year after the publication of *La speculazione edilizia,* a satirical novella about the spoliation of the Italian Riviera; and in 1952—the same year *The Cloven Viscount* appeared—the journal *Botteghe oscure* ran "The Argentine Ant."

These might all be termed civic parables; in fantastic terms they evoke the postindustrial climate and dramatize the fate of the ordinary citizen shaped by it. "The Argentine Ant" and "Smog," the most successful of these works, exquisitely balance the plausible and the absurd, the nightmarish and the comic, the visionary and the ironic. "Ant" is set in a small town on the Riviera. The working-class narrator, homeless and jobless, has moved with his wife and their infant son to the Riviera and rented a tiny house, which they soon discover is infested with ants. Like any good horror writer, Calvino establishes his premise quickly and through an accretion of convincing details. The couple first see ants on their washstand, then their bedroom, and then in the baby's crib, crawling into his ear. The next morning a mass of ants forms a scab on an open milk bottle, and tiny armies resolutely crisscross the little house and its scraggly fringe of barren garden. By virtue of exaggeration that remains carefully within the bounds of the credible, Calvino makes this quite harmless foe assume terrifying proportions. The ants do not crudely "stand for" any particular evil, yet they ultimately embody something new in the world, discipline raised to the power of anarchy.

The ants are always described in realistic terms, but the various people in the story take on absurd dimensions. The couple's neighbors, whom we meet in brief episodes, have all been victimized by the ants, against whom they devise elaborate defenses. Some openly challenge the enemy: the elderly Reginaudis, for instance, possess an arsenal of useless insecticides; and Captain Brauni, a tireless inventor, has a backyard crammed full of Rube Goldberg contraptions that mechanically and uselessly slaughter ants by the thousands. Others resort to humbler strategies, such as getting drunk at the local tavern or, like the narrator's stoical landlady, refusing to acknowledge the ants' existence, even when they appear to be wriggling under her clothes. And the only person with any hope of combating the ants, the local exterminator, actually fattens them with mild doses of molasses. Moreover, he physically resembles an ant with his squat body, black hair, and lips that quiver like antennae (shades of Kafka's *Metamorphosis*).

The point is that the townspeople have surrendered to the ants by virtue of their own obsession with them, an obsession that climaxes when they assemble to confront the exterminator. Even as they vent their anger—shouting "Ants in our beds, ants on our plates, every day, every night. Already we have little to eat and we must feed them too!" (p. 124)—the narrator hears something odd in their rage, a kind of pride or bravado that leads him to suspect they secretly identify with the ants and that without them their days would be purposeless. He decides that although he may never escape the ants, he will refuse to become fixated on them to the exclusion of everything else. He leads his besieged young family on a stroll to the huge and quiet sea, where he contemplates the distant-reaching water and "the infinite grains of soft sand down on the bottom, where the current lays down white shells washed clean by the waves" (p. 127).

A similarly irresolute ending occurs in "Smog," regarded by Calvino as a companion piece to "Ant" (a volume containing the two was issued in 1965). In "Smog" the implacable enemy is an entirely human creation—urban filth, rendered in cunning images: dust films the elegant office where the narrator works and the pages of his books, which he must wipe with a rag; his shirt collars are embossed with the paw prints of his landlady's cat. These images fill the story's corners much as dirt invades actual surfaces. Here filth acquires an eerie beauty, as Calvino evokes through it shadows, clouds, mist, night, secrets, silence, death—all the dark forces that unaccountably attract us.

Like the narrator in "Ant," the nameless protagonist of "Smog" has recently arrived in an alien environment, a large northern city (probably Turin). A rootless, affectless intellectual, he has just been hired as managing editor of *La Purificazione* (Purification), a trade magazine dealing with industrial pollution and published by an institute whose fastidious president, *l'ingegner* (engineer) Corda, has gotten rich at the head of corporations responsible for the dangerous exhaust his journal reports on and inveighs against. A similar irresoluteness defines other characters in the story. The narrator's landlady, who rents him a room in her large house, never tidies up for her tenants but keeps her own quarters immaculate, except for the kitchen, the only room she inhabits. Dottor Avandero, an editor for *La Purificazione,* impersonates the ideal company drone, glued to his desk, but secretly fobs off his work on the narrator and subsides into depression between weekend ski trips. And the narrator's lover, Claudia, a glamorous jet-setter who phones him at inconvenient hours, always from a different city, chirps enthusiastically about each new place only to tire of it overnight and fly off to the next. The only character free of ambivalence is Omar Basaluzzi, a factory hand and union organizer who "did not seek to escape from all the smoky gray that surrounded him but transformed it into a moral value, an interior standard" (p. 62)—a standard so opposed to capitalist exploitation that it ironically depends on it and its symbol, smog. Like the neighbors in "The Argentine Ant," these characters owe their identity to the very force that threatens them. Even the narrator, when he writes an essay alerting *La Purificazione*'s readers to the perils of overindustrialization, ends up composing a lyric to urban decay:

> I began to write one of the usual harangues but little by little, word by word, I found myself describing the cloud of smog as I had seen it rubbed on to the city, and the life that could be realized behind that cloud, the aged facades, full of juttings, of indentations, where it thickened with a black deposit, and the modern facades, smooth, monochrome, square, over which crept the obscure shadows, as on the white collars of clerks, dirtied in half a day. And I wrote that there still were those who lived outside the cloud of smog, and perhaps there always would be, those who could pass through the cloud, linger there, and exit, their bodies unsoiled by the slightest puff of smoke or granule of carbon, their different rhythm, the beauty of the other world, never upset; but that what mattered above all was all that was inside the smog, not outside it: only by immersing ourselves in the heart of the cloud, breathing the foggy air of these mornings (already winter had blotted out all life in an indistinct mist), could we touch the depth of the truth and perhaps then free ourselves.
>
> (p. 54)

Like his counterpart in "Ant," the narrator achieves momentary relief. He trails a cleaners' cart into the periphery of the city, a district populated by laundries where teams of women scrub sheets in a canal and pluck sparkling linen from clotheslines; in this paradise "the field in the sun bestowed greenness upon the white, and the water flowed away swollen with bluish bubbles. It was not much, but for me who was searching only for lasting images, it was perhaps enough" (p. 81).

Extraordinary as this is, it leaves one uneasy. Do lovely images really compensate for our squalid lives—for anyone but an artist? And if the lone solution is unblinking acceptance, a refusal to slump into neurotic defensiveness, where do we go from there—once we have given evil a hard unflinching look? Do we then retreat into our old befuddlement? We sense that Calvino has tricked us in "Smog" and also in "Ant"—that his satire, aimed superficially at our defeatism, is meant instead to unmask our vestigial delusions of social improvement. It is no mistake that public authority in these stories accrues only to the most insidious characters—the ant exterminator and the corporateer Corda—for they alone have an innate gift for bureaucratic double-dealing. Everyone else sinks into quietism. Then again, Calvino may want us to protest his heroes' complaisance. He may want, above all, to deny us the comfort of detachment, for it, too, can become a mere reflex, no better than Claudia's city-hopping. If there is an exit from our plight it is the tireless activity of examining it, which may prime us for the insight that vaults us into new awareness. This verges on a religious argument, and, though these stories hardly endorse orthodox beliefs, they consciously extend the visionary line that can be traced back to Romantic poets such as William Blake and William Wordsworth and that reached its modern fruition in the perceptual revelations of Marcel Proust, in the secular "epiphanies" of Joyce, and in what Mann called the "religious humor" of Kafka.

Two other works written at this time succeed less unequivocally, but thematically are of a piece with "The Argentine Ant" and "Smog." *La speculazione edilizia* is the only Calvino novella not yet translated into English. Like "Smog" it satirizes a specific development in contemporary Italy, the building boom of the 1950's when parvenus rushed en masse to acquire vacation apartments on the Riviera. The protagonist, Quinto, a bourgeois fallen on hard times, decides to spruce up and sell his family's summer place with the assistance of Caisotti, an entrepreneurial scalawag who boasts crucial contacts in government and industry. As the project proceeds, retarded at every stage by Caisotti's bungling chicanery, Quinto flirts with corruption, shamelessly excited by the allure of commerce though he fatally lacks the swindling instincts of the successful businessman. Meanwhile he estranges his cool-headed brother, a university chemist; and their mother, deeply attached to the house and its lush garden, beholds her small paradise first trampled into ruins and then entombed in concrete. It is all very neat and unfolds with admirable economy, but the antitheses between characters are overdrawn, the contrast between manmade ugliness and natural beauty borders on the schematic, and the outcome feels foreordained.

More successful is *Marcovaldo; or, the Seasons in the City,* a whimsical story sequence begun in the 1950's and completed in the early 1960's. Here the hero is an unskilled factory worker, a transplanted peasant with a wife and six children he can barely feed. Disoriented by the noise, the stench, the anonymity, and the hectic pace of urban life, Marcovaldo plots to brighten his life by finding the crevices where he supposes nature to be hiding. One night he tries sleeping on a park bench in the open air, only to be disturbed by quarreling lovers, the "false moon" of a stoplight, and then by a fire hydrant, which drenches him. He sets about curing his neighbors' rheumatism with wasp stings but winds up beside them in the hospital, tattooed with bruises. One winter day his children, on a search for kindling, wander out to a highway lined with billboards that they mistake for a forest and tote home branches plastered with ads for toothpaste, cheese, and razors. Not all the episodes work—at times the whimsy seems sugared—but at its best *Marcovaldo* testifies to Calvino's marvelous affinity for the visible world and the sudden small miracles it continually offers to unjaded eyes. On a deeper level the stories comment on our psychic hunger for nature, a need so intense that when we cannot see trees and the moon we feel driven to invent them. Of equal interest is the book's organization: there are twenty stories in all (none more than twelve pages long and many only five or six), each assigned to a season. A spring episode opens the volume, followed by a summer, then an autumn, and by the end we have been through a five-year cycle, a design that anticipates Calvino's metropolitan masterpiece, *Le città invisibili* (*Invisible Cities,* 1972).

"The Argentine Ant," "Smog," *La speculazione edilizia,* and the first *Marcovaldo* vignettes appeared in the omnibus volume *I racconti* (Stories, 1958) along with all the short fiction Calvino had published in the decade following his earlier collection, *Ultimo viene il corvo. I racconti,* including so much, reminds us that Calvino conceived most of his work on a small scale; even his longest novels, *The Baron in the Trees* and *Se una notte d'inverno un viaggiatore* (*If on a winter's night a traveler,* 1979) barely top 250 pages. This does not mean Calvino was a miniaturist who lacked the ambition or concentration necessary for full-blown fictions, but rather that his large intelligence sought always to hone and elide, on the order of a theoretical physicist who distills an ambitious theory into a single elegant axiom. Thus "The Argentine Ant" and "Smog" have the texture of much lengthier works. They also assimilate and sum up a vast literary tradition. Similarly, the best of his "L'Avventura" (Adventure) tales in *I racconti,* later issued as *Gli amori difficili* (*Difficult Loves,* 1970), slight as they are, send us back to the grander fiction of an earlier age and seem retrospectively to irradiate it.

One such story, the sublime "L'Avventura di un miope" ("The Adventure of a Nearsighted Man," 1958), deserves special mention. Only eight pages long, this epigrammatic tale opens in the classic manner of nineteenth-century short fiction. A young salesman, Amilcare Carruga, suddenly finds that life has grown inexplicably dull and blurred; things that once gave him pleasure—movies, pretty women on the street, the shape and color of new cities—now seem "faint, flat, anonymous" (p. 71) and excite not even his passing interest. The author's grave prose leads us to believe that Amilcare's problem stems from an interior malaise, the harrowing ennui depicted most famously by Leo Tolstoy in "The Death of Ivan Ilyich" and by Anton Chekhov in "The Lady and the Pet Dog." But then, a paragraph into the story, it seems we've been had: we are informed that the hero's crisis has nothing to do with the state of his soul—the world looks dim because he needs glasses. Having overreacted to what is, in fact, a slight physical maladjustment, easily rectified, Amilcare feels sheepish, and so do we, who have also overreacted, by projecting an existential crisis onto a commonplace occurrence. The hero visits an oculist, who prescribes the correct lenses, and, as we would expect, the world around Amilcare suddenly burgeons anew with marvels, only they are so many and so distracting that he finds it as difficult to get around as before, when he couldn't make out tram numbers. Familiar sights, which he now views clearly for the first time, assume utterly foreign appearances, confusing him so thoroughly that he begins to doubt his own reality. He wonders if the whole orbit of his experience is "purely accidental, capable of transformation, [for it seems] you could be completely different and it wouldn't matter, which leads you to think that what you are or aren't is all the same anyway, and from there it is a small step to the threshold of despair" (p. 73). By this time Amilcare feels himself in the grip of a genuine spiritual crisis, and we realize, with amazement, that Calvino has fooled us again and indeed created a contemporary analogue to the condition introduced in his opening paragraphs. He has turned our skepticism against us and reminded us that, even at this late date, revelation is still possible. Amilcare's myopia is, in sum, a metaphor for all perceptual uncertainty, including the uncertainty of readers. There is no more ingenious example of postmodernist storytelling than "Adventure of a Nearsighted Man," with its binding of reader and hero, its subversion of familiar narrative practices, and its sly effort to rescue an old-fashioned humanism.

In 1958, at the same time that *I racconti* was published, Calvino quit the Communist party, disgusted with the Soviet Union's incursions into Czechoslovakia and Hungary, and renounced all politics. The decision ratified a disillusionment that had been growing through the 1950's and that found fictional expression in "Smog," with its benighted unionist, and in *La speculazione edilizia,* whose protagonist is a lapsed Communist dilettante of the sort so common a generation ago. But we must not exaggerate Calvino's previous commitment. True, for more than ten years he had been a card-carrying party member (during the reign of Stalin, let us admit) and as a journalist lent his name to the cause; as an artist, however, he held his ground, and instinctively shied away from putting art to ideological uses. In 1955, for example, while still a Communist, he announced in his most famous essay, "Il Midollo del leone" (The Lion's Medulla) that "political engagement, participation, even compromise are, beyond a duty, a necessity for today's writer, and not only for the writer, for modern man." But, in the same breath, he chastised the writer who "aims to repeat the deeds of political leaders and mimic their habits of thought, and to do so not in the world but on the page . . . and thus delude himself that he has dispensed lessons, performed a service somehow equal to the political act" (*Una pietra sopra,* pp. 12–13).

This ambivalence informs Calvino's one attempt to deal explicitly with politics in fiction, his magnificent novella, *La giornata d'uno scrutatore* (*The Watcher,* published in *The Watcher and Other Stories,* 1963), which exposes the futility of shaping an adequate worldview out of sheerly political assumptions. For the first time Calvino sets his story in an actual place—Turin's Cottolengo Hospital, an enormous Catholic institution for the retarded, deformed, and disabled—and also focuses on a specific moment in Italian history, the election year of 1953, when the Communist party, on the strength of the 1948 parliamentary constitution, seemed on the verge of making substantial inroads into the political establishment. A major obstacle the party faced was election fraud, practiced widely at election sites such as Cottolengo, reservoirs of illegal votes for the church-allied Christian Democrats—the hospital's administrators and staff shamelessly exploited a provision that gave mentally incompetent inmates the status of responsible voters: "each election instances were discovered of idiots being led to vote, or dying old women, or men paralyzed with arteriosclerosis, in any case, people unable to make logical distinctions" (p. 6).

Yet Calvino does not simply denounce Cottolengo for cynically manipulating the democratic process: How can anyone accuse a place of corruption when it selflessly observes codes that transcend mere political honesty? Hospitals, after all, are monuments to self-sacrifice, utility, and charity, sheltering and ministering to humanity's damaged goods. A more forward-looking society, founded on inflexible laws of utility and justice, might well abandon the very souls kept alive by medieval anachronisms such as Cottolengo. In its way Cottolengo is nothing less than a utopian community.

As the election day wears on, this conundrum obsesses Amerigo Ormea, a representative of the Communist party assigned to monitor the balloting at the huge hospital. Amerigo—whose name hints of mental exploration and democratic passion—may be Calvino's most convincingly portrayed intellectual, someone for whom every opinion, explanation, or idea acts as a pivot, swinging its opposite into view. His boring task as a poll-watcher and the parade of suffering humans who pass before him give rise to many troubling thoughts. The more he thinks, the cloudier things seem; even evident truths grade into uncertainty. He protests the hypocrisy of Cottolengo's nuns, who illegally mark the ballots of incompetent inmates, until it occurs to him that this infraction pales beside their daily sacrifices, which eloquently advance the socialist ideal of human fraternity. This discovery is reminiscent of the one made by Joseph, the narrator of Saul Bellow's *Dangling Man,* who proposes that "any hospital nurse did more with one bedpan for *le genre humain* than they [the Communists] did with their entire organization." So, too, Christ may offer a redemption more radical than any election returns, until Amerigo remembers that Catholicism provides only a few enclaves of charity whereas a Communist victory will guide the entire community toward selflessness and the public good. But then this point of view gives way to another, his sudden perception that the party, with its maniacal insistence on discipline and loyalty, harks back to the feudalism of a bygone era.

Thus *The Watcher* unspools, a series of ideas beautifully pondered and lucidly propounded against the squalid backdrop of the voting room, into which file idiots, dwarfs, and cripples, each exposing by his solid presence the flimsiness of Amerigo's tortured intellection. Like *The Cloven Viscount, The Watcher* rests on an axis of juxtaposed opposites: Cottolengo is both sacred and corrupt; Amerigo is both serious thinker and inept apparatchik; the inmates are scarcely human yet somehow divine. But *The Watcher*'s subject is not dualism; it is, rather, an effort to analyze the reasoning method of Marxism—dialectical materialism—by testing its viability as a narrative device. Here, perhaps, we can take the full measure of Calvino's new skepticism about politics. He seems to be saying that for a political outlook to be truly universal it must offer solutions not only to problems of society but to problems of narrative and it must accommodate the individual imagination as well as the collective utilitarian good. This is a far cry from the dualism of *The Cloven Viscount.* That novella splits humanity into two self-sufficient compartments; every character has twin identities, blithely ignorant of each other. In *The Watcher* opposites openly interact. Evil begets goodness; hope, despair; corruption, ideals. Even Calvino's coiled sentences, with their numerous parenthetical asides, advance by a kind of friction.

Election day ends with Amerigo torn between pity and ire, with Cottolengo portrayed as charitable and fraudulent, with the election viewed as both meaningless and crucial. Hope glimmers for Amerigo when the final inmate miraculously proves himself a responsible voter; though he has no hands, he deftly manipulates pencil and paper, carefully folds his ballot, all with great pride and discernible intelligence; yet his triumph is to be ordinary, to merge into the undifferentiated norm, and we have no doubt that he has cast his lot with the retrograde Christian Democrats, as did the majority of the Italian electorate in 1953. Calvino in 1963 reminds his readers of something they have long known, that this election brought about no social revolution. He reminds them also that politics itself offers no lasting solutions, that its form of enlightenment is narrow and ambiguous, that it must be continually embarrassed by the larger requirements of *le genre humain.* But, like its two great predecessors "The Argentine Ant" and "Smog," *The Watcher* passes no adverse judgment on the event it describes, and like them it closes with a benevolent image, of Cottolengo bathed in dwindling sunlight, "the ultimate city of imperfection [at] its perfect hour" (p. 73).

*The Watcher* concluded nearly two decades of writing that was impressively various yet governed by a consistent vision. Certain preoccupations carry over from work to work in Calvino's early fiction: the mingling of logic and lunacy, the ironic approach to moral questions, the collision of realism and magic. Perhaps nothing conveys the synthesizing rigor of his early art more effectively than the device of the synoptic catalogue—of infantilism in *The Path to the Nest of Spiders,* spiritual debilities in *I nostri antenati,* neuroses in "The Argentine Ant" and "Smog," and physical deformities in *The Watcher.*

Calvino's urge to classify, to sort things out, betokens the subtle influence of his scientific parents, chiefly his mother, a trained botanist; and his penchant for recasting moral issues into fabular molds seems to stem from a surprisingly literal mentality intrigued by pure specimens, first causes, and teleological designs. Imagine a cloistered scientist emerging into the fog of postwar angst, puzzling out its opaque crises: "What do you mean by a divided self—split in two? Existentially nil—you mean he doesn't exist? How do you escape society—live in a tree?" This is not to suggest that Calvino was reared in a vacuum; his father had been a reform socialist, his mother had been nurtured in the "religion of civic duty," the author himself was a partisan guerrilla, *impegnato* neorealist, and Marxist journalist. The point is that Calvino borrowed the calculated neutrality of the scientific outlook and sharpened it into an attitude of willed wonder, a blend of innocence and skepticism that enabled him to approach even ancient questions with unjaded interest. Seldom has a writer so knowing managed to seem, as John Updike has said, so "benignly curious" about the world.

Yet it is a benignity somehow remote, at any rate dispassionate. There is not much fervor in the early Calvino. Even the work most charged with feeling—*Path*—seems emotionally blocked, its anti-Fascism canalized into a studied point of view, an argument. And there are few hints of Eros: "Smog" and *The Watcher* include a sustained love interest but limit it mostly to telephone spats, bursts of fury and apology that sound too familiar, too "Italian"—reminiscent, in fact, of the movies. *The Nonexistent Knight* inverts passion: Bradamante lusts after a bodiless suit of armor who himself desires only honor; the narrator, after first concealing her gender, cloaks her sexuality in a nun's habit, then sublimates it in commentary on the ecstasies and disappointments of storytelling. Only *The Baron in the Trees* describes a believable love affair, and it discomfits Cosimo more than all his other ordeals combined—addicted to reason, he repeatedly misreads the intentions of his mercurial mistress, who finally departs in fury. Often Calvino's women are abstractions, embodiments of feminine principles—the elusive Pamela in *The Cloven Viscount* (part Artemis, part Aphrodite), the shrewish wife in "The Argentine Ant." And they baffle men cut from the Prufrock mold, hesitant, dithering, panicky.

Pleasure in Calvino is an aesthetic rather than physical concern; he is interested in the coupling not of bodies but of mind and matter, idea and image. Still, the harmonies in his later fiction generate an exultant warmth, even heat, by fitting opulent phenomena—real or imagined—into exact and exacting formal schemes. As one of his narrators confesses: "In me the idea of a world absolutely regular, symmetrical, methodical, corresponds to that first impulse and bloom of nature, to the amorous tension you call Eros" (*t zero,* p. 40). In all his works from the 1960's through the 1980's—in the evolutionary and genetic processes explored in *Le cosmicomiche* (*Cosmicomics,* 1965) and *Ti con zero* (*t zero,* 1967); in the chivalric retellings in *Il castello dei destini incrociati* (*The Castle of Crossed Destinies,* 1969; expanded in 1973); in the lapidary inventions of *Invisible Cities;* in the multiplying parodies of *If on a winter's night a traveler;* and in the exponential epiphanies of *Palomar* (*Mr. Palomar,* 1983)—the dominant motif is no longer the catalogue but the serial.

The best point of entry to Calvino's next phase is his move in 1964 to Paris, where he stayed until 1980 except for brief sojourns, including several to the United States (a country he had first visited in 1959 for six months at the invitation of universities in New York and California). It is not precisely clear why he stayed in Paris so long. It seems not to have been a renunciative act, for he remained in the employ of Einaudi (becoming, in absentia, its editorial director), published with Vittorini the journal *Menabò,* and through the 1970's flung essays, like loose change, into the Milanese newspaper *Il Corriere della Sera.* Perhaps he preferred the cultural centrality of Paris to relatively out-of-the-way Turin and the diffuse southern energies of Rome, his home for a time in the 1950's; perhaps, like other Italians from the extreme northwest, he felt drawn to France by an ancestral tropism.

In any case expatriation released the cosmopolitan that had long lurked inside him. In 1964 he married Chichita Singer, an Argentine translator for UNESCO. They had a daughter, their only child, the following year. *En famille* the Calvinos spoke Spanish and Italian interchangeably, and according to Gore Vidal, a close friend of Calvino's, the author spoke French "perfectly." (His languages also included English, which he read with ease but had slight difficulty speaking.) In Paris he met major intellectuals such as the anthropologist Claude Lévi-Strauss and the structuralist nuncios Roland Barthes and A. J. Greimas, and belonged to a circle that met monthly to bandy theories of the novel. All his fiction from this time is tinted with French intellectual discourse: frequent references to "signs"; refractory musings on the trinity of author, text, and audience; a touch of deadpan pointillism borrowed from the *nouveau roman.*

The surest mark of the cosmopolitan writer is his eager, even greedy, appropriation of languages and knowledges. Moving amid strangers, he annexes new traditions, like Nabokov, or evolves a rarefied polyglot, like Joyce. As for Calvino, while still in Italy, he had evinced a taste for bravura displays of erudition, most obviously when he dusted off Ariosto's *Orlando Furioso* but also in his other historical fantasies. A more ambitious excavation was *Italian Folktales,* commissioned by Einaudi and published after the author spent two strenuous years burrowing through Europe's oldest folk tradition, a vast literature that ranges over one hundred and fifty years, from the sixteenth century to the eighteenth, and comprises many hundreds of tales in almost numberless versions. Calvino culled two hundred samples, representing every major region and dialect, sifted through variants, braided them into single narratives, standardized the grammar and diction, appended bibliographical notes, and then prefaced the results with an introduction that lauds the whole enterprise as Italy's answer to the Brothers Grimm. Many readers concur; indeed a large segment of Calvino's audience knows him chiefly through *Italian Folktales.* To me they seem stilted, though the fault lies less with their scribe (his emendations notwithstanding) than with the material itself. For all the suggestiveness of the subtexts—an array of metamorphoses, symbolic journeys, rites of passage, trials of character—the narratives themselves lack the compelling interest of the Grimms' or Hans Christian Andersen's.

Calvino, however, reveled in this labor of assemblage and collation, probably because of the stimulus it gave to his own inventions. He remarks in his introduction that folktales, originating in an oral or preliterate tradition "must be recreated every time, so that at the center of the customary tale is the persona, remarkable in every village or town, of the storyteller, male or female, with his own style, his own appeal [*fascino*]. And it is through this person that the timeless story is given a renewed bond with the world of his listeners, with history" (p. 28). To which it may be added that a village storyteller functions like a banker, hoarding the local verbal capital, and also like a shaman, intoning the spell that animates old memories, linking the living to the dead and transmitting cherished lore, as suggested by a synonym for *fascino, incanto* (charm), cognate with our own "incantation."

And this quality now enters Calvino's writing. *I nostri antenati* and his Kafkaesque stories turned naturalism inside out in order to evoke the absurd realities of the postwar climate; now he fits abstruse subjects into archaic narrative forms.

The very title *Cosmicomics* mates primitiveness and sophistication; its epigraph could be Robert Musil's assertion, in *The Man Without Qualities,* that "In science the way things happen is as vigorous and matter-of-fact and glorious as a fairy tale." Calvino's topic embraces nothing less than the evolution of the universe, from the Big Bang to the present. And he chooses a form based on the comic strip, modernity's answer to the ancient saga, with its hero made into a character who, in Northrop Frye's phrase, "persists for years in a state of refrigerated deathlessness." The joke in *Cosmicomics* outrageously magnifies this notion: we are given a protagonist—he doubles as narrator—literally as old, or ageless, as the universe itself. Palindromically named, or not named, Qfwfq (a tongue twister in English, but in Italian unpronounceable), this evolutionary agent has witnessed the universe's cataclysmic growing pains from the point of view of a particle of light, a vertebrate crawling out of the aquatic broth, a dinosaur about to become extinct, and a mollusk secreting its striped shell. He is monad and nomad; consciousness in perpetual search of a shape. But from the outset we know that Qfwfq, even as he molts identities, is really human. When, as one of the first amphibians, he dolefully recollects how his sweetheart deceived him with his uncle (a fish nearing extinction), or when, as the last surviving dinosaur he prepares for doom, his tone vibrates with the richness of a complex inner life.

Each story has a headnote that summarizes a scientific fact or theory that, in turn, occasions a tongue-in-cheek reminiscence by Qfwfq: for example, the proposition that at one time the moon hung very close to the earth introduces his account of his family rowing out to the moon with a ladder, then climbing up with a bucket and spoon to collect "moon milk [which was] very thick, like a kind of ricotta." An episode about the first appearance of solid matter implies that snobbishness may have its origins in something more primal—pride of species: Qfwfq admits dryly that his backward brother Rwzfs, the family's black sheep, eloped when very young with "an alga, one of the first, and we heard nothing more of him" (p. 30), and that his sister G'd(w)$^n$, after being swallowed up by the condensing earth, resurfaced at last "at Canberra, in 1912, married to a certain Sullivan, a retired railroad worker, so changed I scarcely recognized her" (p. 37).

The tinge of a boast in "one of the first alga" and of hauteur in "a certain Sullivan" lofts *Cosmicomics* out of the realm of science fiction and into the crystalline galaxy of Calvino's ironic art. "The more the world changes the more it stays the same" is a cliché, but taken to this extreme, which telescopes billions of years, it becomes high comedy, worthy of Jonathan Swift. Indeed, like some of Swift, these stories seem meant on one level for children. Their world recalls the intuitive Darwinism of fairy tales wherein metamorphosis correlates to growing up, growing big, growing old, growing different. And their Pop Art picture of space-time reminds us that Einstein's theory, with its unaging galactic travelers, slowed clocks, and elongated measuring rods, is itself a kind of myth, a stepchild of the primitive imagination. The reductio ad absurdum of *Cosmicomics* camouflages serious questions: Are time and space anything more than sheer inventions, concepts that can be bent to fit arbitrary purposes? Does scientific investigation lead anywhere but into the recesses of our fantasying minds?

There is another sort of make-believe in *Cosmicomics,* equally antic but highly cerebral, like the systematic lunacy of *I nostri antenati.* It is most pronounced in stories like "Quanto scommettiamo" ("How Much Shall We Bet?"), about the logic of randomness, or "Un segno nello spazio" ("A Sign in Space"), in which Qfwfq makes a nick in the universe to mark the spot the sun will have passed after completing its 200-million-year revolution of the Milky Way. How can Qfwfq manage this? He is a disembodied consciousness afloat in nothingness, lacking tools and hands, in a time when even the thought of hands and tools lies in the almost infinite future. Through telepathy, a willing-into-being similar to the mental exertions of Agilulfo, the nonexistent knight. As Qfwfq explains, "I had the intention of making a sign, or rather the intention of labeling as a sign anything that it occurred to me to make, and thus, in that point of space and not another, having made something meant to be a sign, the result was that I had made a sign after all" (p. 31).

This preoccupation with signs points to the influence of fashionable postmodernist French writers, particularly Barthes. A more palpable influence is the twentieth-century master of metaphysical doubletalk, Jorge Luis Borges. It is tempting to credit Calvino's Argentine wife for introducing him to the *ficciones* of her illustrious compatriot, but he had probably discovered Borges earlier at Einaudi, which published many foreign writers. In any case, a Borgesian nimbus hangs above the companion book to *Cosmicomics, t zero,* a tripartite story collection. This is most evident in part 3, which includes two extended meditations on the geometry of moving automobiles—"L'inseguimento" ("The Chase") and "Il guidatore notturno" ("The Night Driver")—and a brilliant closing story, "Il conte di Montecristo" ("The Count of Monte Cristo"). This last is an attempt, light-years beyond the apprentice efforts of *Ultimo viene il corvo,* to demonstrate that external reality can be molded into conformity with our secret visions. Calvino uses Alexandre Dumas's novel as the springboard for a monologue delivered by its hero, Edmond Dantès, who through ingenious sophistry argues first that the Chateau d'If, where he is imprisoned, must be constructed so perfectly as to preclude escape, and second that his fellow inmate, the Abbé Faria, must be at work on an opposite proof disclosing an inevitable flaw in the chateau's design. Dantès concludes that these two imaginary constructs, opposite extremes of a single idea, will inevitably converge at a place contiguous to the actual chateau and thereby liberate both prisoners, if only they can "identify and locate the exact point where the invented fortress does not meet the real one." Behind the apparent irony—no one can think himself out of a fortress—lies hope. The imagination introduces, at least, its possibility. Dreams give birth to the actual.

This parable is preceded by the continued episodes of Qfwfq, more time-scrambled than ever; for instance, in "La molle Luna" ("The Soft Moon") he commutes between an office on Madison Avenue and his house in New Jersey, where his wife, an astronomer, trains her telescope on the moon as it is about to be sucked into the earth's gravitational field. His adventures end with "Priscilla," a three-part exploration of the biochemical analogue to the expanding universe, cell division, which Calvino grafts onto the narrator's wistful remembrances of his hopeless love for the eponymous heroine. She is "an individual of my same species and of the opposite sex" who appears variously as a microorganism, a camel, a freckled Briton sojourning in Paris, and an electronic charge. In each incarnation she defies Qfwfq's efforts to define and thus possess her. In this last tale the narrator's bemusement ripens into sorrow as he broods, like Proust, above the abyss of thwarted desire.

*Cosmicomics* and *t zero* sent small ripples of interest to the United States, and Europe's canniest fabulist became, like Kurt Vonnegut, the special property of college students. Yet, although these psychedelically titled volumes seem knowingly glossed in 1960's chic, they make no explicit appeal to a countercultural audience (unlike Vonnegut's cartoonish books). Calvino reveres tradition, perhaps to his detriment: his violations of the plausible—so formal, bookish, and tactful—serve no anarchic cause, affront no inherited literary values. An original, he is drawn to origins and advances by looking over his shoulder—at the folktale, at the mock epic, at nineteenth-century realism.

A phrase in "The Count of Monte Cristo" helps situate Calvino's last fiction along the continuum of his career. The narrator, Dantès, uncertain whether his alter ego, the Abbè, hopes to dig a path into the sea or into a cave filled with gold, at last concludes that "in either case, seen optimally, he tends toward a single point of arrival: the place of the *multiplicity of possible things*" (p. 159, my emphasis). The same can be said of Calvino. Multiplicity, or plurality, shapes his ideal fictive universe: just as *I nostri antenati* populates whole epochs with variations on a single human type, and his "science fiction" novels constellate the empty wastes of space-time, so do his four final works fit the multiplicity of possible things into intricately ordered designs.

The first of these experiments is *The Castle of Crossed Destinies,* a variation on Boccaccio's medieval masterwork, the *Decameron.* In it, storytelling becomes at once aleatoric and highly regulated, an organized randomness contained within a simple frame device (far simpler, at any rate, than Boccaccio's). At an unspecified time and place in the Middle Ages, overnight travelers, all strangers, assemble around a large dinner table (first in a castle, then a tavern) and are mysteriously robbed of speech. A tarot deck is placed before them, and its seventy-eight pictures and symbols become their medium of communication. The first player, a handsome youth, lays down cards that summarize his life and also describe, with mythological overtones, the comeuppance of a scapegrace—or so the sequence is interpreted by the narrator, himself one of the mute guests, who goes on to translate the tales related by the other guests as they, in turn, lay down cards. This goes on until the deck is exhausted. The game has two rules: first, each player must lay down the cards in the order in which they have already been arranged in the dwindling deck; second, the successive storytellers are allowed to build on the rows already formed, appropriating and sometimes altering the meanings established by previous players. The reader is also included in the game; on the margins of each page, alongside the written commentary explaining the tales, appear the corresponding cards, reproduced in miniature. And at the end of both sections each configuration is depicted for us whole, two roughly rectangular tapestries that—when read up, down, across, and back—interweave the various stories.

*The Castle of Crossed Destinies* is physically an elegant book; the tarot cards handsomely adorn the text, and the elaborate symbolism of their printed images rewards close scrutiny. The relation of the visual texts to the verbal, however, never seems truly symbiotic, and as fiction *Castle* falls curiously flat. Once we have deciphered the remarkable stratagem of the narrative, there is little to nourish us. Calvino, unfortunately, translates the tarot pictures—of a throned king, crossed swords, seven goblets, a naked goddess, and others—into characters and objects either predictable or gratuitous; and the extrapolated tales tediously rattle the old skeletons of Greek tragedy, medieval romance, and Elizabethan drama. The author evidently anticipates our disappointment. He makes numerous dry asides about the blind alleys of narration and encourages us to conclude that *The Castle of Crossed Destinies* is less a celebration of fiction's plenitude than an alarming confession of its ultimate monotony, an attempt, even, to expose the bedrock poverty of the literary imagination, with its archetypes overdrawn from an exiguous fund. This instrument for storytelling, like computer models of the brain, has a touching ungainliness. Its logic is somehow naive, so open to permutation that it precludes the purely accidental leaps that create true suspense and that make narrative a legitimate analogue of actual experience. Indeed, the hidden purpose of *Castle* may be to warn us against the danger of overrationalizing the process of telling a story.

Calvino's next work, the great *Invisible Cities,* also involves characters forced into silent dialogue: the thirteenth-century Mongol emperor Kublai Khan and his emissary Marco Polo. Back from a tour of China's cities, the Venetian, who speaks no Tatar, reports what he has seen by "extracting objects from his suitcase: drums, salt fish, necklaces of warthogs' teeth, and pointing to them with gestures, leaps, shouts of joy or horror, or imitating the bark of the jackal and the hoot of the owl" (p. 45). As the khan ponders these objects and effusions they ramify into dazzling prose poems about different cities—fifty-five in all, named Diomira, Anastasia, Maurilia, Cloe, Adelma, and Sibilla, among others. None exists, as the emperor gradually discerns, but each evokes places that do. The conspicuous consumption practiced in Leonia, for instance, might be observed in any overstocked city:

> On its sidewalks, wrapped up in clear plastic bags, the remains of yesterday's Leonia await the garbage truck. Not only squeezed tubes of toothpaste, burned-out lightbulbs, newspapers, containers, packing material, but also boilers, encyclopedias, pianos, porcelain services: Leonia's opulence is measured less by the things that daily are produced, bought, and sold than by the things discarded daily to make room for the new. And you ask yourself if the true passion of Leonia is really, as they insist, the enjoyment of new and different things, and not rather the thrill of expelling and expunging, cleansing itself of a recurrent impurity.
>
> (p. 119)

Leonia is a "continuous" city, one of eleven poetic classifications that enable Calvino to range far and wide in his evocations of urbanity. They include cities and memory, cities and desire, cities and signs, thin cities, trading cities, cities and eyes, cities and names, cities and the dead, cities and the sky, and hidden cities. The book has nine chapters. The middle seven each proceed cyclically through five categories and each chapter introduces a new type and phases out an old—a total of thirty-five distinct places. The remaining twenty cities are divided equally between the longer first and final chapters. It is a more harmonious pattern than *Castle*'s and more felicitous; like certain interlocking rhyme schemes it tumbles the narrative forward. The cyclical progression highlights a Spenglerian drama of cultural collapse, as the cities evolve from the quaint to the surreal, as gold domes, sea-shelled staircases, and crystal globes give way to airports, high-rises, and sprawling suburbs.

This advancement, or decline, haunts Kublai Khan's gathering awareness that Marco Polo is spinning a cautionary riddle about his own empire, imperiled by relentless growth, its armies receding into disorderly regions, its populace spoiled by luxury. There is, moreover, a philosophical drift: all these places are, in the end, versions of the same city—any city—fifty-five spokes radiating from the hub of an idea, "the invisible order that regulates cities . . . the rules that determine how they rise, take shape, prosper, and adjust to the seasons, and then wilt and fall into ruin" (p. 128). Yet even as it sounds this final lament, *Invisible Cities* sustains the author's utopian pluralism, his ideal of a "multiplicity of possible things," and culminates the many cityscapes in his fiction: the dank twisty alleys of *The Path to the Nest of Spiders;* the begrimed Turin of "Smog"; the paved-over mysteries of *Marcovaldo;* and Cottolengo, the city of the damned. *Invisible Cities* even offers a tentative exit from the dilemma of seeing-to-no-purpose, the burden of impotent knowledge that often traps Calvino's urban explorers. In Ipazia, Marco Polo is taught that "signs form a language but not the one you think you know." If he can master the real language he will see past "the images that up till then had announced to me the things I sought"—see past the images, perhaps, that falsely comforted the narrators of "The Argentine Ant" and "Smog" and Amerigo Ormea in *The Watcher* and kept them from breaking through to new modes of thought, new categories. As Calvino notes in another context, the 1977 essay "Gli dei della citta" (in *Una pietra sopra*),

> To see a city correctly it is not enough to open your eyes. You must first discard everything that impedes your view, every received idea, the preconceived images that occlude your field of vi-

> sion and your understanding. Next you must simplify, reduce to their essentials the vast numbers of elements thrust before your eyes every moment by the city, and then collect the scattered fragments into a design both analytic and unitary, like the explanatory diagram of an engine.
>
> (p. 282)

In 1979 Calvino published his penultimate novel, *If on a winter's night a traveler.* This tour de force resumes the experiments of its two predecessors, although in it narrative permutation, hitherto a method, now becomes the author's subject. He dispenses with substitutive fictions—cards and cities—and invents the first chapter of a novel, itself called *If on a winter's night a traveler,* which he tells a total of ten times. Each version has a different title and introduces different characters, plots, and themes. And each, incredibly, parodies a different contemporary literary style, ranging over Italy, France, Germany, Poland, Japan, Ireland, Latin America, and murkier regions, like the extinct, quasi-fabular land of Cimmeria and the completely fanciful Cimbria. Parody is perhaps a misleading term, for as Calvino himself explained in an interview, his intention was not to mimic particular authors or literatures, but to evoke current narrative fashions, "examples of which can be found in one country as well as in another or which may even bounce back and forth from one continent to another."

And bounce they do, in a kind of literary globe-hopping, a high-comic *Around the World in Eighty Days.* The tone is set by the famous first paragraph, which lightly chides the presumptive geniality of postmodernist fiction:

> You are about to begin Italo Calvino's new novel, *If on a winter's night a traveler.* Relax. Concentrate. Banish every other thought. Let the outside world fade. Better close the door; no doubt the television is flickering nearby. Tell the others, "No, I don't want to watch television!" Raise your voice, if they don't hear you. "I'm reading! I don't want to be disturbed!" Perhaps they haven't heard you, with all that racket. Announce it louder, shout: "I'm starting to read the new book by Italo Calvino!" Or if you don't want to say it, don't; we'll hope they leave you in peace.
>
> (p. 3)

After further instructions (we should stretch our legs, adjust the light), Calvino eases us into the opening pages of a novel related by a solitary traveler in a railway station who is aware that we are reading about him and so steps off the page to help us along. He cautions us that the author's monochromatic prose, conjuring up a psychological "no-man's land of experience reduced to the least common denominator . . . is a strategy for involving us little by little, snaring us in the action without our realizing it: a trap" (p. 13). It is the kind of trap we relish, the stuff of good storytelling, but we are not allowed to enjoy it; the tale abruptly breaks off at a point of high tension—the typesetter, we are told, has omitted the second chapter.

Calvino again adopts the second-person address and hurries the Reader (or us) to a bookstore, where he learns that the whole edition is defective and, even more improbably, that the thirty pages he has read are not the opening to *If on a winter's night a traveler* but the mislaid signature of a novel called *Fuori dell'abitato di Malbork* (Outside the town of Malbork) by Tazio Bazakbal, a factitious Pole. Intrigued by his accidental sampling, the Reader eagerly starts in on this new writer's book, which has nothing to do with the chapter he (we) just read, and which foils him (us) again by abruptly breaking off at a crucial moment. Thus the pattern is established, as fragment follows fragment, spoof follows spoof: *Senza temere il vento e la vertigine* (Without Fear of Wind and Vertigo) has the ferocious hilarity of an Eastern European writer like Milan Kundera; the chic nihilism of *Guarda in basso dove l'ombra s'addensa* (Looking Down Where the Shadow Thickens) echoes contemporary French novelists such as Claude Simon and Alain Robbe-Grillet; *Sul tappeto di foglie illuminate dalle luna* (On the Carpet of Leaves Illuminated by the Moon) pastiches the erotic longueurs of Japanese novelists, like Yukio Mishima; *Intorno a una fossa vuota* (Around an Empty Ditch) glances at "magical realism," made famous by Gabriel García Marquez.

Dissimilar as these chapters are, an adhesive self-consciousness binds them together as their narrators, mostly writing in the first person, theatrically bemoan the pain of literary parturition, rather like Sister Teodora in *The Nonexistent Knight.* The diarist in *Sporgendosi dalla costa scoscesa* (Leaning from the Steep Hill) records his struggles to decode the cross-signals of that most baffling text, daily life; another diarist, a best-selling Irish recluse named Silas Flannery, dithers hopelessly between two theories of fiction, one that sees it as "the equivalent of the unwritten world translated into writing," the other as "the written counterpart of the unwritten world, its subject . . . what is not and what cannot be, unless written" (pp. 171–172). And Calvino himself splices in similarly self-referential remarks, informing us at one point that all literary invention grasps hopelessly after the world's one meaningful fiction—the collective life of the actual human race with its entangled characters, incidents, and implications.

As if these competing voices did not confuse us enough, *If on a winter's night a traveler* (not the chapter within the novel, but the novel itself [how it all complicates!]) is mounted on another story, this time continuous, indeed ludicrously so, about the Reader's search for a completion to the ten stalled openings. It involves us (or him) with Ludmilla, a lovely, dimpled female Reader who, with her twin sister, Lotaria, introduces us to a pair of bickering scholars but sends us alone to a publishing house where we uncover the source of the faked chapters, Ermes Marana, a shadowy translator or literary counterfeiter who is also an operative of the Organizzazione per la produzione elettronica d'opere letterarie omogeneizzate (Organization for the Electronic Production of Homogenized Literary Works) whose multinational tentacles reach from a Latin American police state (where we are briefly imprisoned) to the Soviet Union (where we are sent on an obscure mission). But again, as in the embedded novels, the action, just as its excesses reach a frenzied peak, suddenly collapses like a mistimed soufflé. In the final pages we marry Ludmilla, who lounges beside us in bed as we finish "*If on a winter's night a traveler,* by Italo Calvino" (p. 263).

Calvino pilots us blithely through this resistant material, but, as in *The Castle of Crossed Destinies,* our arrival slightly disappoints: the parodies proceed arbitrarily—their order could be switched to no ill effect and their subjects and at times even their styles, though often delectable, finally grade into a mannered, quizzical sameness. There is something desperate, almost mad, about this creation, as if Calvino, like the carpenter in *The Cloven Viscount,* has fallen victim to his own heroic intentions—aiming to devise a machine that will tirelessly provide the primitive thrill of storytelling, he has instead given birth to a grotesque apparatus that, like a rack, stretches his original premise into shapelessness and, like a gibbet, dangles it to death. Still we are won over by the author's geniality, his knowingness, and his sympathy—for his exaggerated effort to thwart our desire for an ending paradoxically exalts "that privileged rapport with books that is the reader's alone: the power to consider the written work as something finished and definitive, in need of no addition or subtraction."

*If on a winter's night a traveler* remains among Calvino's most crucial works because it forcefully reminds us, even as it playfully frustrates our expectations, that its author has a surpassingly serious, critical mind. His genial ventriloquism dramatizes a genuine crisis, the late-twentieth-century writer's paralysis before a proliferation of forms and a deadening banality of experience. Calvino's pretend novels—for instance, "Without Fear of Wind and Vertigo," with its food shortages, striking workers, ubiquitous military vehicles; or "Looking Down

Where the Shadow Thickens," with its murderers coupling excitedly under the glassy stare of a corpse—not only mimic current modes of fiction but also define the affectless tenor of our age. Parody is imitation and imitation, according to the hallowed precept, is where art begins. In other words, it may be that the writer intent on interpreting contemporary reality must begin by replicating the clues spewed forth daily by our cultural assembly line—the cryptic images, names, and novels that in the information age not only appeal to our tastes but subtly direct them.

In any age, the objects we create acquire a strange separateness from ourselves, and threaten to veer off into a world of their own, like the blameless items summoned to nightmarish life by the sorcerer's apprentice. The need to demystify those frightening identities, to discover in that alien world something consonant with our original dream of it, has never been more evident than it is today. Calvino provides a glimmer of hope in the preposterous frame story, the search for an ending. The Reader, alone in Ludmilla's apartment, which he is visiting for the first time, inspects its furnishings, appliances, potted plants, photographs, and books, looking for clues to their owner. At first her identity seems obscured by the ordinariness of this consumer display; these could be anybody's possessions. "But," says the author, now addressing a female Reader, "every object proves special, in an unexpected way. Your relationship with them is confidential and selective: only the things that feel like yours become yours: it is a relationship with the physicality of things, not with an intellectual or affective idea that substitutes for the act of seeing and touching them" (p. 144). The very physicality of the objects, their dense interaction, composes a unique text, as do the ten overlaid narratives; taken as a simple entity, it is a text that, for all its self-reference, ultimately peers beyond itself, to Ludmilla, the Reader, the reader, and the universe that contains them.

In 1980, as if beckoned home by the huge international success of *If on a winter's night a traveler,* Calvino returned to Italy. He took a flat in central Rome near the Pantheon and near his friend Gore Vidal. Three years later he published *Mr. Palomar,* also a return, this time to nonliterary experience. Its serial vignettes spell out a mathematical operation—the number three raised to the third power. There are three parts—"Le vacanze di Palomar" ("Palomar's Vacation"); "Palomar in città" ("Palomar in Town"); and "I silenzi di Palomar" ("The Silences of Palomar"). Each is divided into three subparts—"Palomar sulla spiaggia" ("Mr. Palomar on the Beach"); "Palomar fa la spesa ("Palomar Does the Shopping"); "Le meditazioni di Palomar" ("The Meditations of Mr. Palomar"), and so on—and the subparts themselves split thrice, yielding a total of twenty-seven (or $3^3$) terse episodes. An index sorts them out and places alongside each a tag, a permutation of the numbers 1, 2, 3; their order signifies, for every episode, its proportional correlation to three "thematic areas, types of experience and investigation that . . . appear in every part of the book." The first area is visual, the second "anthropological, cultural in a wide sense," the third "more speculative, regarding the cosmos, time, infinity, the relationship between the self and the world" (index).

For the first time we sense that Calvino's irony is directed at his own formal schemata. Never before has he trumpeted a pompous metaphysic ("the cosmos, time, infinity")—and thereby deflated it; never before has his structural wizardry impinged less on the act of reading. These Mendelian diagrams make a difference, but only because they wittily implicate the author in the quixotic mission of his eponymous hero, himself a relentless pigeonholer of experience. Wherever he happens to be—shopping, at the zoo, touring Mexican ruins, gazing out from his apartment terrace—Mr. Palomar, like the California observatory he is named for, acts as a great rapt eye. He zeroes in on the minutiae of the external world, then tries to fit them all into a comprehensible order, all the while wondering, "Is there a single and absolute principle from which all forms and actions proceed? Or a limited number of distinct principles, lines of force intersecting to give the world a form that appears, singly, instant by instant?" (p. 18).

Here, as occurs so often in the autumnal works of masters, Calvino pares his foliate art down to its philosophical nub and asserts, gently but explicitly, that the effort to gather up the "multiplicity of possible forms" must result in failure, for the transcendent wholeness apprehended in the psyche exists nowhere outside it. Moving through the world in a pensive cloud, the monkish hero, a "nervous man who lives in a frenetic and congested world," brims with exquisite perceptions: that to a gull the roofs of Rome seem a "dry, tiled sea"; that cheeses in a Parisian shop resemble the paintings in the Louvre because "behind each object [is] revealed the presence of the culture that has given it form and that takes form from it"; that "silence can be considered a type of discourse, because it refutes the uses to which others put words." But these aperçus, even as they heighten Palomar's experience, spoil his visionary project: the plenitude of forms defeats all summary, exhausts all categories. Like Edmond Dantès he dreams of an exit from the labyrinth of phenonema but is doomed never to find it.

Palomar has a literary ancestor, Monsieur Teste, Paul Valéry's ferocious truth-seeker, created in the 1890's; his precursors also include earlier Calvino characters, who huddle like fraternal ghosts around this last hero: Dantès; the poll watcher Amerigo Ormea; the anonymous narrators of "The Argentine Ant" and "Smog"; the nearsighted Amil Carruga; even the ecstatic dying soldiers of the war stories. Palomar's inquiries into first causes hark back to the bemusement of Qfwfq, and the book's present-tense narration eerily recalls *The Path to the Nest of Spiders.* But in one important sense Palomar travels alone; his tranquil passage seems cloaked in newfound serenity, in terminal bliss.

The book concludes with its hero reconciled to death, then suddenly dying, and it is comforting to infer that Calvino, the cosmic comic, intuited his own approaching end. In fact, his health had been good when he suffered a cerebral hemorrhage in September 1985 at his summer home outside Siena. He was working, as we might expect, finishing the lectures he had agreed to deliver as Harvard's Charles Eliot Norton Professor of Poetry. News of his stroke sent out a worldwide alarm; in America you could roughly follow his final days—the six hours of brain surgery, his strong recovery, the doctors' guarded optimism, and then on 19 September, a month shy of his sixty-second birthday, his sad death. The epitaph he wrote for Cosimo some thirty years before will do for himself: "Lived in the trees—always loved the earth—rose in the sky."

Calvino's crystalline art is light, deft, elegant, and, in both senses of the word, true: he seldom misses his target, and he engages the large concerns of his time with brave fidelity. He looms as the most inviting of the postwar experimenters because he is the most benedictory: he gives us astonishment, rapture, release, and above all deliverance. The further his fiction strays into unfamiliar places the more it re-situates us in the here and now, the quotidian zone where our vexed and luminous lives unfold.

## Selected Bibliography

### EDITIONS

#### INDIVIDUAL WORKS

##### FICTION

*Il sentiero dei nidi di ragno.* Turin, 1947.
*Ultimo viene il corvo.* Turin, 1949.
*Il visconte dimezzato.* Turin, 1952.
*L'Entrata in guerra.* Turin, 1954.
*Il barone rampante.* Turin, 1957.
*La speculazione edilizia.* Turin, 1957.
*I racconti.* Turin, 1958.
*Il cavaliere inesistente.* Turin, 1959.

*I nostri antenati.* Turin, 1960.
*La giornata d'uno scrutatore.* Turin, 1963.
*Marcovaldo; overro, Le stagioni in città.* Turin, 1963.
*Le cosmicomiche.* Turin, 1965.
*Ti con zero.* Turin, 1967.
*Il castello dei destini incrociati.* Milan, 1969; expanded version, Turin, 1973.
*Gli amori difficili.* Turin, 1970.
*Le città invisibili.* Turin, 1972.
*Se una notte d'inverno un viaggiatore.* Turin, 1979.
*Palomar.* Turin, 1983.

COLLECTED ESSAYS

*Una pietra sopra: Discorsi di letteratura e societa.* Turin, 1980.
*Collezione di sabbia.* Rome, 1984.

WORKS EDITED BY CALVINO

*Fiabe italiane; raccolte dalla tradizione popolare durante gli ultimi cento anni e trascritte in lingua dai vari dialetti.* Turin, 1956.
*Orlando furioso di Ludovico Ariosto raccontato da Italo Calvino.* Turin, 1970.

## TRANSLATIONS

FICTION

*Adam, One Afternoon, and Other Stories.* Translated by Archibald Colquhoun and Peggy Wright. London, 1983.
*The Baron in the Trees.* Translated by Archibald Colquhoun. New York, 1959.
*The Castle of Crossed Destinies.* Translated by William Weaver. New York, 1977.
*Cosmicomics.* Translated by William Weaver. New York, 1968.
*Difficult Loves.* Translated by Archibald Colquhoun, Peggy Wright, and William Weaver. New York, 1984. Not identical to the Italian edition; it includes selections from *Ultimo viene il corvo* and *I racconti.*
*If on a winter's night a traveler.* Translated by William Weaver. New York, 1981.
*Invisible Cities.* Translated by William Weaver. New York, 1974.
*Italian Folktales.* Selected and retold by Italo Calvino. Translated by George Martin. New York, 1980.
*Marcovaldo; or, The Seasons in the City.* Translated by William Weaver. San Diego, 1983.
*Mr. Palomar.* Translated by William Weaver. San Diego, 1985.
*The Nonexistent Knight and The Cloven Viscount.* Translated by Archibald Colquhoun. New York, 1962.
*The Path to the Nest of Spiders.* Translated by Archibald Colquhoun. New York, 1976.
*t zero.* Translated by William Weaver. New York, 1969.
*The Watcher and Other Stories.* Translated by William Weaver and Archibald Colquhoun. New York, 1971. Includes "Smog" and "The Argentine Ant".

NONFICTION

"The Written and the Unwritten Word." Translated by William Weaver. *New York Review of Books,* 12 May 1983, 38–39.

## BIOGRAPHICAL AND CRITICAL STUDIES

Adler, Sara Maria. *Calvino: The Writer as Fablemaker.* Potomac, Md., 1979.
Bernardini Napoletano, Francesca. *I segni nuovi di Italo Calvino.* Rome, 1977.
Bonura, G. *Invito alla lettura di Calvino.* Milan, 1972.
Calligaris, Contardo. *Italo Calvino.* Milan, 1985.
Du Plessix Gray, Francine. "Visiting Italo Calvino." *New York Times Book Review,* 6 June 1981, 1. An interview.
Heaney, Seamus. "The Sensual Philosopher." *New York Times Book Review,* 29 September 1985, 1, 60. Review of *Mr. Palomar.*
Lucente, Gregory L. "An Interview with Italo Calvino." *Contemporary Literature* 26:245–253 (1985).
MacShane, Frank. "The Fantasy World of Italo Calvino." *New York Times Magazine,* 10 July 1983, 22–23ff. An interview and biography.
McCarthy, Mary. "Acts of Love." In *Occasional Prose.* San Diego, 1985.
Mitgang, Herbert. "Italo Calvino, the Novelist, Dead at 61." *New York Times,* 20 September 1985, A20.
Manacorda, Giuliano. *Storia della letteratura italiana contemporanea (1940–1975).* Rome, 1977.
Olken, I. T. *With Pleated Eye and Garnet Wing: Symmetries of Italo Calvino.* Ann Arbor, Mich., 1984.
Pazzaglia, Mario. *Antologia della letteratura italiana. Con lineamenti di stora letteraria,* vol. 3. Bologna, 1972. Pp. 1269–1280.

Pescio Bottino, G. *Calvino.* Firenze, 1967.

"Talk of the Town." *The New Yorker,* 28 October 1985, 26–27. Anonymous reminiscence of Calvino's last visit to New York.

Updike, John. Reviews of *Invisible Cities, The Castle of Crossed Destinies, Italian Folktales,* and *If on a winter's night a traveler.* Originally in *The New Yorker;* collected in *Hugging the Shore: Essays and Criticism.* New York, 1983.

———. "Italo Calvino." *Granta,* no. 17:241–243 (Autumn 1985). An obituary.

Vidal, Gore. "Fabulous Calvino." *New York Review of Books,* 30 May 1974, 13–21.

———. "On Italo Calvino." *New York Review of Books,* 21 November 1985, 3–10. An obituary and reminiscence.

Woodhouse, J. R. *Italo Calvino: A Reappraisal and an Appreciation of the Trilogy.* Hull, Eng., 1968.

SAM TANENHAUS

# MICHEL BUTOR

## *(b. 1926)*

### *LIFE*

THERE IS HARDLY a literary genre that Michel Butor has left untouched. He gained early, worldwide recognition primarily as a novelist, but his fiction soon transcended the boundaries of what is commonly called the novel. He has also written critical essays and poetry, and many of his books cannot easily be defined. Much as one may like to classify authors (a modicum of respect for genres does have limited but undeniable usefulness), we shall understand and appreciate his works the more as we discard conventional academic preconceptions. In fact, undermining the very notion of genre is what characterizes Butor's literary production after 1960.

Michel Butor was born on 14 September 1926 at Mons-en-Baroeul, a suburb of the industrial center of Lille, in northern France. He was the eldest son and the third of seven children of a white-collar employee of the private railroad company serving the area. His father, who was less fond of trains than of drawings, watercolors, and woodcuts (all of which he practiced with a fair degree of competence), was transferred to Paris in 1929. Michel was soon sent to Catholic schools in the metropolitan area. Not yet thirteen at the outbreak of World War II, he was moved from Paris to the relative safety of Évreux, in Normandy. In May 1940 his family joined the exodus of refugees fleeing before the oncoming German army, finally reaching Tarbes, in the southwest, where they had relatives. Michel was familiar with the area, but neither then nor on previous visits did he see the shores of the Mediterranean. Not until after the war did he see those lands that play so important a part in his early works.

Michel was back in Paris in July 1940, and the subsequent fall he entered the Lycée Louis-le-Grand, where he studied for four years. He passed his *baccalauréat* examinations in 1942 and 1943 and remained an additional year in preparation for the École Normale Supérieure. These were not particularly happy years; he did not do well in his courses, nor was he impressed with the quality of his teachers. As a consequence he changed his orientation from the École Normale to what was then called the Sorbonne—the Faculty of Letters of the University of Paris—but the university could not undo the harm inflicted at the lycée, and Butor failed two out of three examinations for the *licence* in literature. With his literary studies getting nowhere, philosophy attracted him and, effecting a second change of direction, he obtained his degree in philosophy in 1946. It really looked as though he had found his calling at last, for he proceeded to complete his *diplôme d'études supérieures* in 1947, writing a thesis called "Mathematics and the Idea of Necessity" under the direction of Gaston Bachelard. Something went wrong again, however, and he failed to qualify in the very stiff competitive examinations for the *agrégation* in 1948 and 1949.

Butor had matured when existential philosophies were sweeping Europe and was nonconsciously molded by them before taking his *licence.* Jean-Paul Sartre's thought was the natural intellectual context of Butor's development, but at the same time it was anathema to many university professors. His interests in contemporary ideas prompted him to go beyond the familiar texts by Sartre to explore the writings of Edmund Husserl—where he found much to disagree with—and of Martin Heidegger. These philosophers, too, were personae non gratae at the university. Consequently most professors at the Faculty of Letters stood rather low in Butor's esteem, except for Bachelard (whom Butor termed an "extraordinary teacher" and admired especially for his writings on science), Maurice Merleau-Ponty, and Jean Wahl, who obtained for him, among other things, a few odd jobs at the Collège Philosophique, thus ensuring his material survival. Through an uncle, Édouard Leroy, who had held a chair in philosophy at the Collège de France, Butor was invited to colloquia held at the Château de la Fortelle, where he met a number of intellectuals—among them Jacques Lacan and Michel Carrouges.

Although constituting a passport to the choicest positions, the *agrégation* is not a requirement for teachers. In 1949 Butor obtained a temporary assignment to the lycée of Sens, and for most of the ensuing eight years he taught at various schools, nearly all of them outside of France. He spent the year 1950–1951 at Al-Minya, Egypt, and the next two years at the University of Manchester. While in England he wrote his first novel, *Passage de Milan,* completed in 1953 and published in 1954. He held no teaching post in the year 1953–1954 but was busy in Paris translating Aron Gurwitsch's *The Field of Consciousness,* a study in phenomenology, which appeared in 1957 as *Théorie du champ de la conscience.* The following year Butor was at the Lycée Français in Salonika, Greece; after that, replacing Roland Barthes at a school that trained French teachers for service abroad, he was back in Paris for another year. By then, however, his second novel, *L'Emploi du temps* (*Passing Time,* 1956), was nearing completion, and the year 1956–1957, which he spent at the École Internationale in Geneva, marked the beginning of a pause in his regular teaching career. For a while Butor applied the bulk of his energies to literary activities. In 1958 he became an advisory editor with the house of Gallimard, a not uncommon activity for a writer in France since, as he himself explained it, it is nearly impossible to earn a living by writing respectable books alone. In Butor's case "living" meant supporting a family: he married Marie-Jo Mas in 1958; they had four daughters. He visited the United States many times (one of his daughters was born there), teaching at Bryn Mawr and Middlebury colleges in 1960; this was followed by various terms at the universities of Buffalo, Northwestern, New Mexico (twice), Seattle, Middlebury again, and Louisville. In the meantime he had traveled all over Europe on lecture tours and had been to South America, Asia, and Australia. In 1964 he was in West Berlin on a Ford Foundation grant, and in 1981 he was the honoree of the Puterbaugh Conference at the University of Oklahoma.

For Butor and those in his generation, apparently no significant encounter with the texts of contemporary French creative writers could take place. Butor was too young to have read works such as Sartre's *La nausée* (*Nausea,* 1938) before the war, and by the time he did read them, they were no longer so strikingly live and new. In the late 1940's and early 1950's, when he was beginning to write, the most talked-about authors were not of the sort that could have done for him what Céline's *Voyage au bout de la nuit* (*Journey to the End of Night,* 1932) had done for Sartre in the 1930's. When Alain Robbe-Grillet's *Les gommes* (*The Erasers,* 1953) appeared, Butor had already written his first novel. Like many people, he read Nathalie Sarraute only when the second edition of her *Portrait d'un inconnu* (*Portrait of a Man Unknown*) came out in 1956; his own second novel was completed by then. The depressing moral climate of France in the 1940's may have encouraged him to read writers from other countries as well. In addition to Husserl and Heidegger, Butor was attracted to Sigmund Freud, whom he admired particularly as a writer and storyteller (in *Case Histories,* for instance), as well as to Kafka, Faulkner, and Joyce. He knew of Samuel Beckett because of their common interest in Joyce. Having read *Molloy* and, more practically, being acquainted with one of the editors of Les Éditions de Minuit, Butor was prompted to submit his first novel, *Passage de Milan,* to Beckett's publishers.

Ever since his student years Butor has returned to literature as a teacher and critic. He has written essays on many writers and on artists as well; these are in the five volumes of *Répertoire* (1960–1982), where his topics range from Donne and Racine to Joyce and Faulkner, from Holbein and Caravaggio to Piet Mondrian and Mark Rothko, and in a few separate publications (for instance, *Improvisations sur Flaubert,* 1984). What is noteworthy—and this applies to both French and non-French writers—is the stress he places on the innovative aspect of their art, the revolutionary nature of their thought. He is obviously fascinated with Rabelais's "gigantic indignation," Cervantes' "destructive truths," Châteaubriand's "outbursts of indignation"; he is pleased to observe that Pierre Alechinsky's painting "sometimes bares its teeth, too"; and so forth. To put it in a slightly different way, what interests Butor are the possibilities inherent in literature and what other writers have made of them; in the long run, while he is interested in teaching others to be better readers of Stendhal or Proust, he is perhaps even more interested in turning the latter's practice to his own profit. Everything is grist to a writer's mill.

While pursuing his studies in philosophy, Butor wrote a considerable amount of poetry, which he at one time termed irrationalistic and a mirror of his bewildered state of mind. Most of it remains unpublished, but a number of poems (those written in 1948 and 1951) appeared in French magazines in the early 1960's and in *Travaux d'approche* (Maneuverings, 1972). Later he returned to verse forms, often in texts related to the work of painters; some are in *Chantier* (Construction Site, 1985), for instance. He had at first detected a "hiatus" between his rational quest in the domain of philosophy and the nonrational pursuit of a parallel investigation in poetry. He was thus led to the novel as a meeting ground where the rational and the irrational might be brought into harmony.

Perhaps Butor conceived the novel as the receptacle into which he could pour his entire life, each successive novel constituting a more and more successful approximation of the ideal novel—one that might contain his whole being and one from which the reader, and the author as well, could eventually grasp the meaning of life. Most likely he did not set himself a goal in such crude and simplistic terms. Nevertheless, the ambition that can be detected in each one of his novels, and his acknowledged interest in Stéphane Mallarmé (who said that "the orphic explanation of the world" was "the poet's sole concern") certainly lend ample support to this theory—and so does, in a way, his breaking away from the genre after his fourth novel, *Degrés* (*Degrees,* 1960).

Poetry may be sought either by emphasizing framework—as Paul Valéry did—or by opening the doors to lyricism. Butor confessed to having been overwhelmed by Shelley's "Ode to the West Wind" when he was fourteen. His own lyricism seems instinctive; while he has never completely forsaken it (he repressed it for a time, and it came back after he started meditating on the works of artists), his main interest has been in the architectural approach. To him the framework of a work of art is not only that which distinguishes it from commonplace objects and appearances, it is also the means through which thought reflects upon itself and "reality in its totality becomes conscious of itself before it criticizes and transforms itself."

To put this in terms of the writer-reader relationship, poetry is the means a writer uses to impose upon readers an awareness of themselves, of their relationships with others, and of their situation—such an awareness being the necessary prelude to a desire to modify their own existence.

## *WORKS*

### Passage de Milan

*Passage de Milan,* Butor's first novel, is a fascinating book. Although not exemplifying his art in its most accomplished form, it reveals his aesthetic principles and ethical concerns. The title is characteristic in its ambiguity: in French, "Milan" is both an Italian city and a bird of prey (the kite), while "passage" refers to a small city street (mews or alley) as well as to the act of passing by or over. The rich associations that are evoked by the city of Milan—its material and artistic wealth, and its history of proud independence—are heightened by the repeated passing of what Butor has called a hieratic bird—also thought to be a cruel and bloodthirsty scavenger.

The initial sentence of *Passage de Milan,* unlike those of the novels that followed, is short, impersonal, and banal, and it can be translated without loss: "Father Ralon leaned out of the window." It is much like the beginning of any number of earlier twentieth-century novels that for the sake of realism attempt to plunge the reader *in medias res* without artificial or rational preparation. With the next few sentences, however, the particular tone that is Butor's slowly emerges out of the commonplace. What the priest sees when he looks out is a scene of Paris at dusk—a city enclosed by a wall of smog the color of iodine, chestnuts, and old wine. He looks out on a vacant lot featuring two scraggy trees and a pile of junk; the latter seems unchanging, but careful observation reveals that each day some objects are removed and others added, according to the needs of an unknown and mysterious owner—just as mysterious as the people who move into the lot by night, lighting small fires to keep themselves warm. Contrasting with the junk heap, but resembling it in several ways, masses of roofs, gutters, walls, balconies, and windows rise beyond it and briefly reflect the setting sun. Above it all, a kite is soaring; it is early spring.

The sentences rendering that scene are relatively long and complex; restrictive adverbs and clauses translate the difficulty there is in any attempt to apprehend reality ("any description is impossible" is a statement that obsesses a later work), while several qualifiers, partners in the same attempt, surround the important nouns. The priest enjoys watching the scene at this particular hour of the evening. When daylight wanes, he shuts the window and, sitting at his desk, watches the panes gradually cease being transparent and become reflective. As the story unfolds and the writer reveals the darker recesses of his being, the text, too, presumably, becomes less like an open window and more like a mirror.

Father Ralon is a scholar in Egyptology; his brother, Alexis Ralon, also a priest, is the chaplain of a lycée; they both live with their mother, a widow, on the second floor of an apartment building, 15 passage de Milan. On the third floor Frédéric Mogne, a mediocre bank employee, returns home about the same time as Father Alexis Ralon. At the age of fifty-five, sensing that he is near the end of a useless life, he goes through tired motions of a crowded existence with his wife, his father, his mother-in-law, and his five children (the two eldest boys sleep under the roof in rooms designed for the servants Mogne cannot afford). After putting on his slippers, Mogne fills his pipe in the living room, where his youngest son, Félix, pretends to do his homework. Mechanically, without any interest, he asks, "How did your work go today?" Looking for the newspaper, Mogne next enters his father's room, and the old man asks, as he has doubtless been asking every day as far back as anyone can remember, "How did your work go today?" Answers are unimportant because no one really cares.

On the fourth floor lives Samuel Léonard, a bachelor art collector, with his niece and two servants. On the fifth, a fairly prosperous couple, the Vertigues, who belong to the upper bourgeoisie, have organized a lavish coming-out party for their only daughter, Angèle, just turned twenty. A painter, Martin de Vere, his wife, their three small children, and a roomer live on the sixth floor. Servants, attached to three of these families, live on the top floor along with an older maid, out of work since her employers died in a plane crash, the two Mogne boys, a *métro* employee, a salesperson, and a younger cousin of the priests. Last is the then still inevitable Paris concierge couple (today they are called "gardiens") on the ground floor.

It soon becomes apparent that the fiction will deal primarily not with any of the characters who are being introduced one by one and almost, it would seem, ad infinitum but with the life of the apartment building as a whole. At this point the significance of what Father Ralon has seen from his window at the outset becomes clear: a microcosm of society, the building, with its numerous floors, inhabitants, and visitors, is analogous to the city; it is also analogous and reducible to the junk pile on the neighboring lot. One need not proceed very far before suspecting that the narrative, closely circumscribed in space, also will not extend over any great length of time. Indeed, *Passage de Milan* begins at seven on a Friday evening and ends, twelve chapters later, at exactly seven the following morning. The framework of the novel is thus provided by time, and time is hieratic: throughout the night bells of a nearby convent toll the hours; a priest opens the novel, another priest closes it. As priests of other religions relied on birds to foretell the future, so birds are linked to the Ralons; the kite, a bird of prey, casts a shadow of death on the house when Father Ralon looks out.

The families and their dependents, who occupy six floors of the building, represent many levels of society: scholars, educators, white-collar workers, engineers, artists, writers, businessmen, critics, laborers, and servants. Each lives in his or her own little realm, practically isolated from the others; even within each family there is little communion: like the Ralons they are all "solitary beings who occasionally visit one another and meet at mealtimes." Life is regulated by a complex series of rituals that inhibit communication. Some contact is made via the backstairs, but that hardly gives the building dwellers any sense of unity.

The novel, on the contrary, does have unity: it is provided by the tight limiting of time and, somewhat ironically, by ritual—that of the main party given on the fifth floor, supplemented by smaller parties given elsewhere. The entire building is fully conscious of, and affected by, the Vertigues' party. With the exception of the sponsors, however, the occupants of the building are affected as if by the presence of an exterior object; the participants themselves do not merge into the party: they merely contribute their own private worlds of ambition, hate, or desire. The ritual that provides aesthetic unity becomes the mirror that reveals the extent to which rituals may produce disunity and isolation.

Butor's handling of this situation in *Passage de Milan,* pointing to weaknesses as well as strengths, foreshadows an evolution that is shown in his two subsequent novels. Whenever he attempts a certain distance from his characters, he loses his grip on the reader. At one point, in presenting the Mogne dinner party, he describes the rites that are involved, rites that result in the complete mechanization of a reunion that should have brought warmth and joy to the participants. The description is successful, and the writing itself becomes cold and mechanical; but Butor fails to the extent that the reader tends to become as bored as the participants. Obviously Butor does not possess Flaubert's talent for destructive irony. When, on the other hand, he enters into a character's consciousness and uses his gifts for sympathy and empathy, the reader, too, is carried along.

The more promising part of the novel begins with chapter 6, during the midnight pause at the Vertigues' party, when a buffet supper is served and the solitary consciousness of each individual adds its melody to a counterpoint of interior monologues that nevertheless make some of the characters aware of the groups to which they belong elsewhere.

If *Passage de Milan* has plot (and subplots) and individualized characters, those traditional ingredients of fiction play only secondary roles. Architecture—that is, the manner in which such ingredients and other materials are combined into the framework—is of primary importance. Here all the ingredients are overwhelmingly oriented in the direction of failure, which, through the reflective process, may act as a warning. Rituals that should bind actually separate: the meeting of the art collector and his friends, which might have produced a common intellectual endeavor, proves to be a failure; the carefully laid plans of various characters eventually miscarry; Father Ralon realizes that he is, for practical purposes, an apostate; the crucial portion of a painting Martin de Vere is working on is ruined by fire and becomes a presage of the novel's climax; the party that was to signal the beginning of Angèle Vertigues' mature life, to mark her entry into society, and act as prelude to her wedding in reality signals her entry into the world of the dead. The promise of spring, however, is not completely broken. The young man who is an unwitting instrument of her death is given a new lease on life, away from the apartment building, from Paris, and even from France. Out of the dark recesses of night, winter, and death comes a chance for rebirth, probably in Egypt—as it was for Butor himself—at any rate within a different culture and civilization.

## L'Emploi du temps

Two years later *L'Emploi du temps* (*Passing Time,* 1956) fulfilled the promise implicit in *Passage de Milan.* In this novel poetry lies as much in the lyricism of the sentences as in the architecture; a spell-casting tone, intermittently noticeable in the earlier work, is maintained throughout, partly as a result of a first-person narrative technique; the very first words, Proustian in their evocative power, are like the opening chords of a symphony, setting the mood and penetrating the reader's unconscious mind: "Les lueurs se sont multipliées." Not lights but glimmers of lights, and quite possibly glimmers of understanding as well. The sentence, vague, harmonious, and tantalizing, stands out as a separate paragraph.

The second paragraph, consisting of a single ten-line sentence, introduces a physical setting from which precise topical references have been omitted. The event described is so commonplace, however, that such omissions facilitate the identification of reader with narrator and enable Butor to concentrate on the architecture that will give the action uncommon significance. Seven months previous to his telling the story, the narrator has arrived by train, at night, in a strange city whose faint lights, seen through the windowpanes, are those mentioned in the initial sentence. Alone in his compartment, his head numb from the train's noise, he has been dozing; as the noise abates, his full consciousness returns, and he looks out; it has been raining. At this point something happens that recalls the beginning of *Passage de Milan:* the windows are black and covered with droplets of rain—mirrors reflecting small fragments of the weak ceiling light inside the train.

Travel, darkness, solitude—the evocation of those three themes leads one to suspect that the novel will deal with a quest, and the reflecting raindrops point to an inner quest. The narrator, a young Frenchman named Jacques Revel, has been sent by his employers to spend a year with an English business firm in the mythical city of Bleston, where he arrives during that dreary night of 1 October. But his apprenticeship with Matthews & Sons will hardly attract our attention, for Revel soon senses that in Bleston he is not only a stranger but also an enemy and a potential victim; the true topic of the novel will be Revel's quest of himself in situation (to borrow a Sartrian phrase).

The weak ceiling light in the train matches Revel's inner weakness, which is thrown back at him by the events he is involved in, like the reflections in the raindrops. He seems a plaything to his environment: the inimical Bleston has cast a spell upon him. By 1 May too much has happened that he does not understand. Feeling he cannot go on unless he gives some order to his thoughts, he attempts to see through the "handful of ashes" that each day in the foreign city has accumulated before his eyes. He will keep a diary; he cannot, however, begin with the events of the first of May, for if those events are to be understood, they must be presented in the context of previous events. Unfortunately for him, the present does not stand still, and things keep occurring that throw a different light on what he has already told. Some things must then be retold, as past and present continuously interact; the pages of his diary become more and more confused from both the logical and the chronological point of view. Finally, on 30 September, his last day in Bleston, sitting in the railway coach that will take him away, he is still trying to recapture events of 29 February.

Butor's conjuring up an imaginary city rather than setting his story in Manchester, where he spent two years between 1951 and 1953 (Revel's diary dates coincide with those of the year 1951–1952), was probably intended to heighten symbolic values; by inventing monuments and names he was able to bring in mythical elements that underline his purpose. The arbitrary but plausible span of one year, which here allows for no individual future or past, restricting the fiction to those events that have taken place within that time, could well stand for the whole of a man's life. That it may also allude to the Christian myth of man is suggested by Revel's early fall on a muddy street, a fall caused by a woman, which indirectly and nonconsciously leads Revel to feel responsible for the attempt on the life of one George Burton, who has three personalities and has written mystery stories, for one of which he has adopted the pseudonymic initials J. C.

Allusions to classical myths also abound: their presence is adumbrated by the book's division into five parts—the five acts of French neoclassical tragedy, which drew so many of its themes, suitably distorted and assimilated, from Greek and Roman antiquity. Butor, of course, will provide his own purposeful distortions. These divisions, also corresponding to the five months during which Revel supposedly writes his journal, are superimposed on the twelve months of his stay and the twelve precincts of the city. Each part, in turn, is divided into five chapters, one for each week or portion of a week in a month; since he does not write during weekends, each week also comprises five days.

The architecture of the novel thus clarifies its title: an "emploi du temps" is a schedule, but it can also refer to the function of time, or to the use that is made of time. The critic Jean Roudaut suggested that Revel's quest has its source in a portion of Søren Kierkegaard's "A Quidam's Diary" (in *Stadier paa Livets vei* [*Stages on Life's Way*, 1845]), to which Butor had devoted a short essay. This is most plausible, especially when one considers Butor's comments on the Kierkegaardian hero, who is obsessed "not at all [by] a perpetual consciousness of the bygone event, but on the contrary [by] its absence, the feeling that a portion of himself has vanished, that a piece of the machine is missing, a part that prevents him from taking hold of real time" ("Un possibilité," in *Répertoire* I, pp. 113–114).[1]

As Revel is "born" into Bleston and received into his "family" at Matthews & Sons, the firm's first act is to have him registered at a hotel called L'Écrou—a word that in French refers to a commitment to jail (which I see as a significant echo of Sartre's concept of *engagement*). He automatically enters a given class of society and, although far from affluent, is assured of a

[1] Except as noted, all translations of Butor's works are by the present writer.

livelihood. During his first weekend in Bleston, Revel innocently wanders away from the section in which he belongs; and on the banks of a dark and frothy river with waters like "the sweat of peat" (the French word for "peat" is also used, in derogatory fashion, to refer to the masses) he meets a colored man who doubtless stands not only for the black in America and the North African in France but also for all the downtrodden and underprivileged of the earth. Ironically, he is the first man in Bleston to buy Revel a drink, treat him to dinner, and invite him into his home; it is he who conducts the ritual of welcome and makes the appropriate pronouncements, but he cannot help referring to "the magnificent city of Bleston" with a mixture of sarcasm and hatred. The man, named Horace Buck, reappears throughout the book, mysteriously linked with a series of spectacular fires that break out all over the city, disturbing its complacency.

Revel has also become a friend of one of his co-workers, James Jenkins, who could perhaps be called a member of the Bleston "establishment." Two weeks later he lunches with Jenkins and Jenkins' mother. One suspects that Butor knows the old coin-hiding game suggested by that surname, for Revel does "reveal" a number of things that Jenkins, whom he calls James the Secretive, has been concealing. The most curious of these comes out in the narration of a nightmare Jenkins has had, which turns out to be an exact account of the attempted murder of the novelist George Burton, an attempt of which he is legally innocent and in which he could not possibly have taken part, although the inner motivation was there.

Jenkins had introduced Revel earlier to a young woman named Ann Bailey, a clerk in a stationery store who had sold him maps of the city; one of these included a map of the city bus routes that looked like a mass of tangled thread—the thread that will guide him through the city of Bleston. In that occurrence we have an example of Butor's technique of gradually introducing mythical allusions: a few pages later, reference is made to the labyrinth that was built in one of the city parks, and we must wait another twenty pages before encountering the name of Theseus. Thus a partial analogy is established, buttressed by many other subsequent overt references, between Revel and Theseus, Ann and Ariadne, Ann's sister Rose and Phaedra, Bleston and the Cretan labyrinth, and so forth. There is no real identification, however, nor is *Passing Time* a retelling of that or any other myth.

Butor's starting point may well lie in the habit, not uncommon in schools and colleges, of tagging classmates and teachers with literary or historical names; in *Passage de Milan* he used the device fleetingly, and in a situation close to its source, when he had one of the Mogne boys, in an interior monologue, think of his eldest brother first as the Prince of Wales, next as Aeneas, then as Esau. Whatever the source, the literary value of this was most probably brought home to Butor by his study of the language of alchemy, where "symbols are variable terms, and their grouping clarifies their meaning." The process seems as much related to a poet's belief in the suggestive power of words as it is to a storyteller's delight in myths.

In an essay on Victor Hugo, Butor singled out for analysis the nineteenth-century writer's propensity for using lists of proper names in his verse. As he saw it, such listings were anything but displays of superficial erudition: they were the means "to establish between the nouns we know and those we do not a communication that allows them to swarm, to crawl, and to spread—continuously plunging back the famous ones into the mass of forgotten ones from which they emerge" ("Babel en creux," in *Repertoire* II, p. 204). In *Passing Time,* Revel constantly seems to shuttle between at least two respondents: at one moment he is a mole burrowing in the darkness of the city and a migrating bird looking down at the same city from above; he is a virus in a tissue and a man observing it through a microscope; he is Theseus, he is Cain, and he is Oedipus.

Like Oedipus, Revel is a man looking for a murderer. That aspect of the plot is, at the end of part 1, imposed upon the reader through the juxtaposition, within a few pages, of a newspaper headline concerning a murder in Bleston, of Revel's purchasing the thriller by George Burton entitled *Le meurtre de Bleston* (which might be rendered either as "The Bleston Murder" or "The Murder of Bleston"), and of a stained-glass window depicting Cain's murder of Abel. Revel, somewhat in spite of himself, assumes the part of a detective, whose role, precisely according to the author of the mystery story he has read, is "to unveil and to unmask."

Butor is concerned with Bleston not as a city in contrast with the country or the sea, but as a city among cities, as a microcosm of civilization, like Paris in *Passage de Milan.* The enmity of Bleston toward Revel—and the dangers it harbors—stems from its lulling, numbing, blinding powers. He is threatened with passively going through the comfortable motions of civilized life, just as characters in the previous novel went through the empty motions of their rituals. When he fights Bleston, Revel is undoubtedly a hero. He commits many errors, however, and the question that implicitly dominates the background of the narrative is what to accept or to reject and how to express a rejection of the contemporary world. Consciousness of himself and awareness of what, in the past, has molded his environment and himself will assist him, he hopes, in answering those questions. Like Butor he writes in order to give meaning to his life; his effort results in partial failure, not because he chose the wrong means but because he must preserve the reader's freedom in order to allow him or her, too, to seek a meaning for his or her life. The hero fails so that the novel may succeed.

## La modification

*La modification* (*A Change of Heart,* 1957), Butor's third novel, published one year after *Passing Time,* may well have been written to give expression to problems that were originally intended for development in that novel but had to be eliminated for aesthetic reasons. The kind of Joycean symbolism so characteristic of the first two works is almost completely absent from the third; instead, we focus on the single action of one individual, clearly circumscribed in time and space, actually and symbolically.

The framework is provided by the relatively long train trip from Paris to Rome; the book opens as the main character enters his compartment in Paris and closes as he leaves it in Rome. Léon Delmont is a successful businessman who has a wife and children in Paris and a mistress in Rome; he is making this particular trip to tell the latter that he has finally reached the decision she has been hoping for and urging upon him: he has found a job for her in Paris, and they will live together after he has abandoned his wife. During the trip he thinks of what he will do and how he will do it; he also thinks about his own life in general. The train itself, the same one on which he first met his mistress, brings back images of previous trips taken alone or with her or with his wife. Various objects and noises and the material components of the train compartment contribute to his thinking; other passengers also set off an abundant flow of ideas, especially a young couple (clearly on their honeymoon) who are at the outset of the kind of undertaking in which he has failed but in which he now thinks he can succeed if given a fresh start. Delmont, however, realizes the truth about himself. He is totally incapable of accomplishing what he has planned. He will not invite his mistress to join him in Paris; he will not even try to see her on this trip.

Basically this novel is about bad faith (in the Sartrian sense). Delmont's attitude is related to Revel's. Actually he is a Revel who fails to respond to the challenge of his situation—through the first part of the novel, at least. He is an obviously cultured person who, upon agreeing to run the Paris agency of an Italian typewriter firm, expressed the desire not to be contaminated by his job. He had no real interest in the typewriter business; he knew the machines he was supposed to promote were neither better nor worse than many others. Very soon, however, he became exactly like the men he associated with, and his entire life was changed. That is one of the "modifications" preceding the one that constitutes the main topic of the book. As the word implies, it is only a superficial change, for Delmont's expressed intention not to be contaminated by his position was merely a gesture in bad faith. His true project entailed the acceptance of the job and everything that went with it. He deeply wanted that kind of material success.

Delmont's bringing his mistress to Paris and his walking out on his wife and children might at first glance effect a real change in his life. This is the change the book seems to be about. During the trip, however, he realizes that it would represent no more than an additional gesture in bad faith; because "he wanted, for once, to be totally contained in his act," he is led to make the decision not to change. In fact such a decision, which does not show on the surface and thus is completely removed from the realm of gesture, is an authentic act. Through it Delmont assumes his weakness and raises the hope that he may be able to transcend it. Although his journey takes on the aspect of defeat, he has made a conscious, honest choice that sets him apart from the Sartrian category of *salauds* (smug, self-righteous bourgeois).

The handling of myth in *A Change of Heart* is comparable to that in the previous novels. Like the plot, it is also less complex; essentially it is limited to two recurring allusions. First, a careful reader might be led to suspect what will happen because of a number of references to Julian the Apostate. Like Julian, Delmont hates the Christian church (here, of course, more specifically the Roman Catholic church), and like him he lives in Paris as the representative of a Roman power. That this power, the typewriter firm, is but a perversion and a caricature of the Roman Empire is obviously a commentary on Delmont's life. Apostasy was already a theme in *Passage de Milan,* and Butor's fascination with it may also be detected in his account of the life of John Donne in an essay published in 1954, the year of that first novel. Second, and beginning about the middle of the book, allusions to the legend of the Master of the Hunt—"le Grand Veneur," who, clad in black, roamed the Fontainebleau forest on horseback—emphasize Delmont's guilt and desperation. Like the voice of conscience, the fabled huntsman's cries—"Do you hear me?" and "Are you expecting me?"—reverberate throughout the forest.

The impact of *A Change of Heart* is enhanced by the adoption of an effective device: the second-person narrative. While Butor might have found any number of precedents for such a technique, all quite limited in scope, he is likely to have been struck by its effectiveness in sections of Faulkner's *Absalom, Absalom!*—as W. M. Frohock suggested in his *Style and Temper* (pp. 135–136). Its generalized use here emphasizes the accusatory quality present in all four of Butor's novels. As a result this third novel reads somewhat as though it were spoken by a detective or a prosecuting attorney slowly building an airtight case against a suspect—who, indeed, is finally proven unworthy of his mistress' love. The second person also allows for an ambiguous writer-reader-character relationship, with the reader oscillating between identification with the prosecuting writer and with the guilty character. From that point of view, there is a definite analogy with what takes place in the reading of Camus's *La chute* (*The Fall,* 1956), except that the reader is given a greater freedom of choice: he is free to act either in good faith or in bad faith. Adopting the latter alternative, one identifies more and more with Delmont, especially in the final chapters, when the traveler is more like a victim than a guilty person; utterly exhausted by the trip and his introspective efforts, he goes through a combination of nightmares and hallucinations before arriving in Rome.

### Le génie du lieu

The title of a collection of essays published in 1958, *Le génie du lieu* (The Spirit of the Place, translated as *The Spirit of Mediterranean Places*), points to the near-surrealistic attitude Butor assumes in the presence of a locale. In *Passing Time,* Bleston's effectiveness as a symbol is due in no small part to the mysterious life the city exudes from its streets, stones, parks, rivers, monuments, and soot-laden atmosphere. In *A Change of Heart* the city of Rome casts a spell on Delmont's extramarital affair, helping to transform it into a myth, even undermining the reality of the city of Paris. What is so striking in those two works of fiction is also evident in the personal essays in *The Spirit of Mediterranean Places.* Córdoba, İstanbul, Delphi, Malia (in Crete), Mantua, and Ferrara—which Butor had visited—Salonika and Al-Minya—where he had lived—are the objects of lyrical essays often quite similar in tone to the prose of *Passing Time.* The significant omission of Manchester and Rome shows how much Butor poured into his novels. The whole spirit of Manchester (or Bleston) is presumably manifest in *Passing Time,* and a separate prose poem about the same city would be redundant. Butor must have visited Rome before writing *La modification,* but he did not go back during the summer of 1957, as he had first planned to do, in order to check a number of facts. This reveals how unimportant to him a certain category of details may be. The map of Bleston printed with *Passing Time* has many blank areas, many nameless streets; an attentive reading of the novels and *The Spirit of Mediterranean Places* discloses how much trivia has been omitted.

Places—and for Butor, especially in the 1950's and 1960's, places are often cities—are, to use his own metaphors, sources from which to drink and foreign texts from which selections are to be translated into his native language. Details, seemingly numerous, are chosen either to light a spark of recognition within the reader's mind or for their direct contribution to the architecture of the work. An object may be "like an emblem or a caption, none the less explanatory or enigmatic because it is a thing." Objects as explanatory captions filled the nineteenth-century novel; objects as enigmatic emblems are more characteristic of the contemporary one, and Butor suffuses them with what Louis Aragon, in his surrealist period, called "le merveilleux quotidien."

The publication of *The Spirit of Mediterranean Places* signals a turning point. For Butor to have written such poetic essays would indicate that he was no longer satisfied that everything could be made to fit into the architecture of a novel. In 1958 he probably reached the end of what might be termed a syncretic period. As of 1989, he had published only one additional novel.

### Degrés

From the standpoint of the contemporary novel, *Degrés* (*Degrees,* 1960) is a masterpiece; it is a "novel" Butor could not possibly transcend. It might be viewed as a sort of enlargement of the previous ones in that it strikes more chords that reverberate more deeply within the reader; it also evidences a stylistic refinement in that the verbal lyricism so noticeable in *Passing Time* has been toned down considerably.

The initial impetus to the narrative lies in an attempt to recapture the meaning and consciousness of a given hour in the life of a contemporary French lycée, its teachers, and its students at the beginning of the school year. On the surface such an undertaking seems even less portentous than the endeavors of Jacques Revel in Bleston or even, considering the effect on his personal life, the decision of Léon Delmont; in several ways it is more like that of *Passage de Milan.* A teacher, Pierre Vernier, decides to write the account of that school period for the benefit of his nephew, Pierre Eller, who happens to be a student in his class. Soon, however, a problem similar to that encountered by Revel comes to the surface: a tremendous amount of background will be necessary in order to make that hour intelligible. Vernier must know what the students have been doing during the summer, what other classes they had attended or would attend the same day, what was going on simultaneously in the other classrooms of the lycée, the family backgrounds and problems of teachers and students, and so on.

The narrative, told in the first person, is set in motion in solemn, ritualistic fashion but in plain, unadorned language: "I walk into the classroom, and I step up onto the platform." Restrained and often matter of fact, the tone, with few exceptions, does not perceptibly change as the story proceeds. The syntax, however, becoming increasingly complex, like that of *Passing Time* and *A Change of Heart,* mirrors the multiple interrelationships at hand. On the sixth page of the book there is a forty-three-line sentence that winds its way through ten paragraphs, two parentheses, one direct quotation, and several indirect ones—the whole sentence representing an interior flashback in the mind of the narrator. All the things that happen more or less simultaneously are inserted—by means of separate paragraphs and parentheses—within a sentence that apparently constitutes a unit of time. Quite possibly the train of thoughts described in the longer sentences flashes by within the same amount of time covered by the initial sentence. That, of course, is narrator's time and bears little relation to reader's time; but it does point to one of the many important themes of *Degrees:* the relationship between writer's truth and reader's truth. The writer is deceitful in order to permit the reader to reach authenticity.

Vernier soon realizes that he cannot learn by himself everything that goes on in the school. He therefore enlists the services of his nephew, who will report to him on the activities of other students. To give perspective to the events, the first part of the book is narrated by the uncle; the second part, describing identical activities, by the nephew. That, at least, is what the reader is led to believe for a while. But before long it is obvious that Vernier is only pretending to let the young Eller speak—just as Butor is only pretending that Vernier is the narrator. Tension between uncle and nephew increases as the latter is viewed with considerable suspicion and, eventually, animosity by his classmates, who resent his giving information to their teacher. The collaboration must cease, and Butor achieves a most striking effect when, intermixed with factual descriptions of classroom activities, he has Vernier accuse himself of lies and fraud, supposedly through Eller's mediation.

The whole process has completely exhausted Vernier both physically and mentally and he cannot finish the book. The third part is therefore narrated by Henri Jouret, another uncle of Eller and also a teacher in the same lycée. Things are not so simple as they may seem, however, for here again Vernier is, at first, only pretending to let Jouret speak; but there comes a moment when he "really" can no longer go on, and Jouret "really" speaks for himself and finishes the book. As Vernier lies on a hospital bed and Jouret, who has come to visit him, utters a word of greeting, he asks, without looking up, "Who speaks?"

That is the last sentence of the novel, and it reverberates back through the pages that have just been read. It is also echoed in the pages of other contemporary writers and critics—Roland Barthes, for instance—and suggests the difficulty of identifying the actual writing subject of any text. A haunting query, it has an analogue early in part 1 when a teacher of English asks for an explanation of Banquo's line "What, can the devil speak true?" In literature it is often difficult to tell who speaks; it is often a "devil" lurking in the writer's unconscious, and he does speak true. Or again, as Jean Cocteau has put it, the writer is a lie that tells the truth.

*Degrees* is, in part, the account of a sacrifice: that of Vernier, who accepts death so that Eller might live a better life. Vernier is writing a document for Eller to read later, when he is better able to understand what happened and also when he has forgotten what happened. But he is writing for others too: for anyone who might have been a student in a lycée or anyone who might have come into contact with such a person. While this has often been the purpose of the artist in general—to preserve for posterity the memory and the meaning of events that would otherwise be forgotten—two considerations qualify Butor's objective.

The first reflects ironically on the so-called universality of the work of art. André Malraux remarked that painters imitate not nature but other painters, and their works are judged in turn through confrontations with other paintings. The same is true of literature, and Butor acknowledges that books are written for people who have read many other books, that is, who have had what we would call a "liberal" education—a rather restricted universality. Hence the hopeful glance cast in the direction of those who might have dealings with the privileged group.

The second consideration derives from the nature of the events being recorded. What Vernier is transmitting to a hypothetical posterity is the description of the process through which, in the Western world, we acquire knowledge and consciousness of the past. In other words, he is describing the transmission and showing how flawed it is. Furthermore, his account is pointedly oriented toward recapturing the spirit of a particular period of the past, the Renaissance. The day that constitutes the focal point of the narrative is 12 October, Columbus Day, and what Vernier calls his pivotal lesson deals with the discovery and conquest of America.

Among the many texts that students read in his or other classes are a number of passages from Rabelais, beginning with those pertaining to reform in education—and there again the narrative reflects upon itself. As a result, description is once more transformed into accusation; what stands indicted is not only an educational system, for the lycée has a symbolic status similar to that of Bleston, but also a whole aspect of Western culture. Implicit in the indictment is a challenge and a hope that we will react against our past as the Renaissance reacted against the Middle Ages, and then proceed beyond the reforms (not fully carried out) that were instituted during the sixteenth century. The reaction that is called for is in many ways similar to that illustrated by Jacques Revel and Léon Delmont, but in *Degrees* illustration makes way for a kind of exhortation.

Butor, however, does not explicitly exhort, preach, or condemn. It is the reader who, through the juxtaposition of events, descriptions, and quotations, is led to make certain judgments. The devices used are common enough, but the confrontation of two common devices can produce forceful results. A teacher's demonstration of a simple law of physics, a student's boredom, and the inanity of a textbook illustration make an obvious point; so does the description of a wounded North African, his face covered with adhesive tape, sleeping on a bench in a subway station beneath a large poster advertising a food product. Combine the two on the same half page, and the inadequacy and futility of much of our educational process appears no longer silly but revolting.

The architecture of *Degrees* is one aspect of the novel of which most readers are not aware, and this in itself is an indication of how successfully it has been integrated into the work as a whole. The division into three parts does more than distinguish the supposed narratives told by members of a family group—two uncles and a nephew; for within the school there are many such trios, in which the relationships are not so close as in the first, decreasing with each successive group until the relationships become, so to speak, negative (a black student, the physical education teacher, and the Catholic chaplain). The three parts are divided into seven sections, new characters being introduced in each: three per section in the first part, two in the second, and one in the third, for a total of forty-two. The blood relationships of part 1 become neighborhood relationships in part 2 and solitudes in part 3—mirroring the deterioration of relationships in the main trio.

As the bonds between characters loosen, however, the unity and meaning of the novel become more evident; as accidental connections fade into the distance, *Degrees* affirms a truer human link between individuals. The breakups that occur are reminiscent of those noticed earlier in *Passage de Milan* but point toward a transcending of the failing relationships, a striving for the universal brotherhood of man. At the conclusion of *Passage de Milan* one of the characters escapes from Europe. In a loose but significant parallel to such an implied rejection of European values, *Degrees,* explicitly stressing the merits of non-European civilizations, derides "this exclusiveness of civilization that it [Europe] continues to arrogate to itself, despite all the proofs it has unearthed and continues to seek out and produce, thus nourishing this contradiction, this great fissure, this great lie that saps and undermines it." The antagonism between Europe and the rest of the world recalls, on a grander scale, the one between Revel and Bleston.

## *THE BOOK CONSIDERED AS AN OBJECT*

No other novel has appeared since 1960. Perhaps Butor expected too much from that literary genre; perhaps he sensed he was about to be swallowed up by his work, like Proust or Joyce—or worse yet, like Vernier; possibly he no longer wanted to be shackled within past norms. If he was to be constrained, let it be by rules of his own making. He told Madeleine Santschi, who conducted a remarkable set of interviews with him in 1980, that moving away from the novel form had "saved" him from a kind of success that might have come too easily; as it turned out, he felt challenged by other tasks that proved difficult for him but at the same time opened up the field of writing.

### Mobile

*Mobile* (1962), subtitled *Study for a Representation of the United States,* is clearly not a novel. Some critics even wondered if it was a "book." In order to determine what kind of work this is, instinctively applying the categorist's criterion, they compared it with the books they knew; they then decided that since it did not resemble any, it was not a book. They had, of course, forgotten Mallarmé's *Un coup de dés jamais n'abolira le hasard* (*A Throw of the Dice Will Never Abolish Chance,* 1897) but their conclusion begged the question anyway, for the criterion itself implies that any object its maker intended as a book contributes to the definition: an essentialist criterion might have avoided the logical impasse.

Butor himself, perhaps as a response to the critical reaction to *Mobile,* outlined a more fruitful approach in an essay entitled "Le livre considéré comme objet" (The Book Considered as an Object, in *Critique* 186 [1962]). His is a phenomenological approach whereby the book is examined in its attributes as a material object; the nature of this object entails obvious consequences for the reader and no less obvious although generally neglected possibilities for the writer. Indeed, if literature is an art, its effectiveness should depend in part on the use one makes of the physical means at one's disposal—in this instance the pages of a book: their size, shape, color, and the way they are bound, as well as the manner in which typographic characters are scattered upon them.

*Mobile* cannot really be forced into any of the conventional categories of novel, essay, or poem. Instead of imposing a label on it and on the works that followed, it might be better simply to keep the rather indefinite description of the subtitle and call it a study, bearing in mind the full artistic and musical connotations of the French word *étude.* A certain amount of virtuosity is implied, and that is surely present in *Mobile.* (Like the architecture of *Degrees,* however, it is unostentatious to the point that several critics have accused Butor of being too facile.)

The primary component of *Mobile*'s architecture is supplied by the many cities and towns bearing identical names—a use of homonymy Butor perhaps picked up from Raymond Roussel. In each state analogues are thus introduced, provided by such names as exist in other states that are either geographical neighbors or alphabetically contiguous. Butor has explained that he used those names as seminal words for the "cells" of his text. Corresponding to a sort of cytoplasm are the roman lines on the page, while italics constitute a nucleus; the position of the left-hand margin indicates whether we are dealing with an aspect of the topic state or with reverberations from other states. Various typographic dispositions throughout *Mobile* signal a number of recurrent themes; works and clauses are articulated through typography as they might be by syntactical connectives in more conventional prose. By putting together the themes that are evoked with each allusion to a particular state, one could paint its symbolic coat of arms: for North Carolina, the sea, Cherokee Indians, and blacks; on the escutcheon of Maine, birds, rocks, the sea, and dreams; and so forth.

Beginning in Alabama some time after midnight, when it is still pitch dark, where dark skins and dark minds abound, the reader's figurative tour of the United States ends in Wyoming some fifty hours later, at midnight, amid suggestions of deserts and extinct species, on the one hand, and slow nocturnal germinations, on the other, after every state of the union has been "visited" for various lengths of time. The visits, however, are anything but realistic. The chapter on New York is built around the five cities of Salem, Clayton, Franklin, Manchester, and Canton—Salem providing a link with New York's alphabetical predecessor, New Mexico, and the four others echoing the names of cities in a number of other states. In addition, each of those cities provides a shift of locale and a side trip to a nearby state: three to New Jersey, three to Pennsylvania, two to Connecticut, and so on. And while "in" Vermont or Massachusetts, the reader also makes several sorties into New York.

The representation of each state, made up of the total of such visits and side trips, unmistakably achieves poetic truth, for the importance of any state is less a consequence of its geographical size—or any other single characteristic—than of its role and influence in the life of all the other states. Likewise, the importance of a state is not reflected in the size of its chapter: Tennessee is given about 50 percent more space than New York. Rather, it is seen through the total number of entries devoted to that state throughout the book—in other words, through its impact on other sections of the country.

The United States is further unified by what might be called the Great Catalogue of American Objects as well as by common problems, attitudes, and habits. The Puritan background (which a Frenchman would emphasize) and the Salem trials; the Indian massacres and the establishment of reservations; the black problem and the minority groups; the cultivation of dreams and the obsession with taboos; the emulation of Western European sophistication; Americans continuously driving along highways, invariably above the speed limit—all those elements run through the book like additional threads binding it together. The Great Catalogue includes service stations, Howard Johnsons and their ice cream, Heinz soups, vitamin pills, Kleenex, marriage guides, health guides, do-it-yourself books, radios blaring out of cars and trucks, Sears Roebuck, Montgomery Ward, Coca-Cola, and Elizabeth Taylor.

Many other items figure in *Mobile,* but there are also interesting omissions: television, hard liquor, and teenagers, for instance are almost completely ignored. In other words, the picture we get has been taken at a given time (about 1960) by a visitor, albeit a perceptive one, part traveler and part reader, rather than by a resident immersed in the daily life of the country. Also, according to Butor, some of the missing themes were rejected by the book itself, so to speak, because they were organically incompatible with it.

Discontinuous accounts of the 1692 Salem trials and of writings by Benjamin Franklin and Thomas Jefferson, newspaper extracts, advertisements, signs, brief statements, and names of people, cities, counties, and states form a strange mosaic or, as the text suggests at one point, a patchwork quilt. The juxtaposition is not haphazard; as with the states themselves the basic order is alphabetical, and a number of complicated modifications are subsequently introduced in order to achieve maximum effect from various confrontations. The procedure is a generalization of the one followed in *Degrees,* one that is not unrelated to the surrealist image. Butor's juxtapositions are carefully planned (in contrast with Breton's supposedly fortuitous ones); they might also call to mind the baroque conceit. Mere confrontation, of course, is not enough; that had been done before, the most memorable example in French literature being Flaubert's orchestration in *Madame Bovary* of the duet between Emma and Rodolphe against the background of speeches at the agricultural fair. The symphonic effect aimed at by Flaubert is even more noteworthy when one considers Butor's interest in music; with him, however, the term "polyphonic" (also suggestive of baroque techniques) is favored over "symphonic."

Roland Barthes hailed *Mobile* as an outstanding illustration of what he calls the modern technique of "translation" (as in mechanics; for our purposes, "displacement" might do as a rough equivalent), in contrast to the traditional "variation," and he pointed to analogues in music (Anton von Webern) and painting (Piet Mondrian). Thus the continuous narratives concerning the Indians or the Salem trials (some of which originated in William Carlos Williams' *In the American Grain*) are, in their fragmented state, confronted with objects out of the Great Catalogue, brief descriptions, and the like. In that figurative displacement, seen each time in a different light, they are read, as it were, in a new key. The witchcraft trials also spread their puritanic note by means of the many towns called Salem that are scattered through the country. The name greets the reader as he leaves New Mexico and enters New York at noon on the second day, harmonizes with a glimpse into the conversion of the Seneca Indian Handsome Lake, clashes with the spirit of fun and entertainment of an amusement park, temporarily gets lost among the linguistic, ethnic, and traffic confusion of New York City, and then is echoed again. The bustle of the city, the noise of the subway, and statistics about the Empire State Building can silence the haunting memory from New England no more than they can obliterate that of the Indian reservations or deny the proximity of warblers, goldfinches, gulls, and terns.

As in previous writings by Frenchmen about America, *Mobile* strikes one by its stunning display of colors. A profusion of contrasting tints is found in the flora, the fauna, the human artifacts, and the people themselves—with the discredited phrase "for whites only" reverberating disturbingly in the reader's mind.

*Mobile* clearly opens up new vistas to the writer, who must keep seeking more effective ways of communicating a changing awareness of the world. America, indeed, is no longer viewed as the melting pot it was once imagined to be but, rather, as the constant juxtaposition and interaction of many different people and objects, struggling with the burden of a complicated past. In that respect it differs from other countries today only in numbers and kinds, and in the intensity of the differences. Likewise, at the other end of the scale, individuals do not grow in predetermined fashion, with their essence contained within a seed in the fashion of plants. Heredity is inescapable (as DNA and RNA attest), but people also become what they are when confrontation with other people, objects, or events releases this or that component in their potentialities. Given the proper stimulus or context, anyone might murder a brother, eliminate a monster, or kill the father; like Jacques Revel in *Passing Time,* anyone might be Cain, Theseus, or Oedipus. A person confronted with a given situation may either repress or release a latent trait, and that choice determines the kind of person he or she is. Life is thus seen as a series of confrontations or, possibly, a series of surrealist metaphors.

A certain resemblance may be detected here to the plot of André Gide's *Les faux-monnayeurs* (*Counterfeiters,* 1926), in which the main characters figuratively collide with one another while the reader listens, as when coins are dropped on a counter, for the ring of authenticity. Butor improves the device by matching a literary technique with the realities of psychology more accurately; the progress involved reflects, at least in part, the intervening presence of Sartre. Thanks to the more obvious manifestation of that technique in *Mobile,* we are better able to understand its subtle appearance in the previous novels. We can also detect the special kind of progression that leads from *Passage de Milan,* where the technique is used in a less sophisticated, and perhaps nonconscious, manner (a sort of shaking up of the contents of an apartment building on the occasion of a party), through a regression in *Passing Time* and *A Change of Heart,* caused perhaps by the relatively poor reception of the first novel, to a most successful use in *Degrees.*

### Description de San Marco

There is much in *Description de San Marco* (1963) to remind one of *Mobile.* But where *Mobile* provided us with only one of a number of possible displacements based on the same series of states, objects, and texts and was not intended as an account of actual travel in the fifty states, *San Marco,* evolving out of a detailed visit to St. Mark's basilica in Venice, stays very close to its object. On one level the book adequately mirrors its title and clamors for an accompanying album of photographs of the various parts of the church—or else it should be read shortly after returning from a visit to Venice. Mere description, however, could never satisfy Butor; relatively detailed as this one is, it is obviously not exhaustive, and the nature of the selections and quality of the commentaries serve to orient the work.

Three parallel texts make up the book, each typographically identified by the width of its left-hand margin. The first transcribes trivial snatches of conversation, exclamations, and greetings by tourists, which are overheard throughout the visit. Most noticeable and lengthy at the beginning and the end, they are momentarily hushed when the center of St. Mark's is reached. The second text gives subjective descriptions and commentaries; the third is devoted to factual description and quotations from the many inscriptions. All three texts alternate regularly, with variations in length—they are short at the outset, as we stand on the square with the inevitable pigeons; much longer when the mosaics are described; short again when we inspect the campanile. Through their confrontation and out of the wealth of descriptive praise, the ever-present element of denial, so characteristic of Butor, is impressed upon the reader; quite early one is reminded that the church owes its very existence to a theft (that of the evangelist's body), and in the last pages that butchers' stalls and wooden outhouses once confronted the Byzantine magnificence of the square.

### 6 810 000 litres d'eau par seconde

*6 810 000 litres d'eau par seconde* (1965) might be considered an outgrowth of *Mobile* because it is centered in Niagara Falls (and conveniently, if misleadingly, translated as *Niagara).* Typography and format recall those of the two previous books. Two texts from Châteaubriand's works, depicting the falls, play a role similar to that of biblical inscriptions in *San Marco* and to the various quotations in *Mobile.* The motifs of tourists visiting a famous monument are taken up again with different emphases. The technique of using a multiplicity of couples to express the recurring interests or obsessions of a few, and thus broadening them, is better integrated because of the honeymoon tradition associated with Niagara Falls. Disintegrating relationships make one think of *Degrees.* A complex architecture based on numbers and units of time is common to nearly all previous works.

*Niagara* is divided into twelve sections corresponding to the months of the year, from April to March. On another level the book encompasses a continuous time sequence of some seventy-six hours. Those, however, are not evenly divided among the twelve sections. As the waters of the Niagara River seem to increase their speed on approaching the precipice before the final downward rush, so the time of individual life appears to accelerate with the approach of death—hence the significance of the unwieldy French title. In Butor's text, too, hours slip by faster and faster, their number being regularly augmented until the final section includes twelve. Throughout the book an announcer provides a descriptive and thematic narrative; a second voice, not so strong in intensity (*Niagara* was originally designed for stereo radio broadcast), reads Châteaubriand's prose. At first there are two fairly continuous short excerpts that are soon broken up into isolated sentences and gradually rearranged so that words from one sentence are exchanged with words from another; both old and new sentences, along with single words or phrases, are inserted into a carefully chosen context—and this adds a touch of surrealism to the lines of the nineteenth-century writer.

The two voices are meant to originate at center stage, so to speak; the remaining voices—newlyweds, older married couples, unwed couples, divorced persons, widows, widowers, and single persons—are divided between right and left speakers for purposes of contrast and balance. With a broadcast performance in mind, Butor has provided what elsewhere he called "mobile structures"; one may choose among ten possible versions of varying lengths. The reader has the necessary instructions in order to select the version he or she deems most suitable; furthermore, "mobility of reading being greater than that of any kind of hearing situation," he or she should be able, "book in hands, [to] dream of all sorts of listening possibilities." The announcer's text, because of its intensity, appears in boldface type; Châteaubriand's text is in italics; time indications are in small capitals; conversations, thoughts, and dreams are in roman type; different margins approximate the separation between broadcast channels.

After the first section, which introduces the falls, mostly by means of Châteaubriand's words, two couples arrive at the site. We share their expectations, hopes, reactions, and memories among the profusion of flowers in the park and baubles in souvenir shops. The hint of deterioration heard in the initial section ("It goes without saying that the site has changed considerably") becomes a major theme in the third, its correlative being the appearance of a black couple along with references to the isolation into which blacks have been driven. Afterward, it gradually permeates all relationships.

At the core of the volume, "Bachelor's Invocation" conveys the lament of the contemporary individual alienated from so many things, especially from love. The theme of love (which a mere mention of Niagara Falls is bound to evoke), that of love's decline, and the pageant of seasons from spring to winter conjure up ancient myths of death and resurrection. Intimation of rebirth, however, such as could be detected in *Passage de Milan* or *Mobile,* is lacking here. The mood is more in keeping with that of *Passing Time.* The time of the final section is March, but there is no spring, nor does Adonis come to life again. Toward the end, the announcer speaks of tears and blood; the newlyweds fail to communicate, the older couple echoes the words of the opening section,

"We have changed." The text closes with Châteaubriand's description of badgers attempting to fish out of the whirlpool the shattered remains of other animals. The very last words are taken from the subtitle of Châteaubriand's *Atala:* "The Loves of Two Savages in the Desert." Once more Butor manifests his disillusionment with one aspect of human reality.

## *THE WRITER AND THE ARTIST*

Butor's interest in the material aspect of the printed page, his "composing" texts in unorthodox fashion, is surely linked to his interest in art, which in turn must have been nurtured by his father. Unlike Guillaume Apollinaire's rather mimetic *Calligrammes* (1918), which are conceptually similar to most of the examples (ranging from the fourth century to the present) given in Jérôme Peignot's *Du calligramme* (1978), the texts just described stress what might be called the poetics of typography. Mallarmé is at the source of this, and others, such as Filippo Marinetti and Lyonel Feininger, had, earlier in the twentieth century, experimented along the same lines in spectacular if abortive fashion.

Artists showed Butor how to organize shapes and lines on a surface; they also brought poetry back into his writing. Perhaps he viewed the works that appealed to him as graphic meditations that called for verbal meditations on his part. "A painting intrigues me," he wrote, "I return to it; I want to wrench away the secret of its power. . . . Thus it is my advantage that I seek." On another occasion he emphasized the role played by a Lucas Cranach painting (the diptych *Lucretia and Judith*) in the poet and ethnographer Michel Leiris's search for identity. Leiris had written *L'Age d'homme* (1939) not merely to record his past life but to try and find out who he was through the very process of writing. The painting allowed him, as Butor puts it, "to transform the image of himself that he had previously elaborated." Painting, like writing, is the mediating element that furnishes an awareness greater than that provided by direct personal experience.

### *Limited Editions*

Butor's first art book to be published was *Rencontre* (Meeting, 1962), an expensive, limited edition volume containing five etchings by Enrique Zañartu, each facing a text by Butor. Like a number of subsequent ones, it exemplifies a process whose sequence reverses the more usual one: Zañartu does not "illustrate" a pre-existing text by Butor; it is Butor who "illustrates" Zañartu's etchings. Beautifully printed in large type (the book is folio size), the page setting is conventional. *Litanie d'eau* (Ocean Litany, 1964), with ten prints by Gregory Masurovsky, and *Dialogue des règnes* (Dialogue of the Kingdoms, 1967), with fifteen copperplates by Jacques Hérold, are more innovative in at least two respects.

First, they represent a common undertaking on the part of artist and writer. Masurovsky worked on his engraving knowing that Butor would write a text to accompany them. Second, the words are disposed on the page in function of the artwork they accompany. The text is wrapped around the engravings, so to speak; as the latter have greater width than height, the text mass is similarly shaped, with inner blank spaces allowing the words to be spread out on the page regardless of their number.

The text is also meant to complement the engraving; for instance, Masurovsky's black-and-white work prompted Butor to pepper his prose with a profusion of color references. In *Dialogue des règnes* there is even greater interaction between artist and writer, since text and etchings appear on the same page; Butor and Hérold worked concurrently, the work of one inciting modifications in the work of the other. Eventually the typographic disposition on the page is determined by the position and shape of the graphics and vice versa. The resulting book is indeed a collaborative work of art.

Unfortunately, such items are not readily accessible—and Butor has produced many of them. One hundred and five copies of *Litanie d'eau* were published and ninety-five of *Dialogue des règnes;* there are only eight copies of *Signaux de fumée* (1982; with Alex Cassel) and three copies of *Imprécations contre la fourmi d'Argentine* (Curses Against the Argentine Ant, 1973; with Ania Staritsky), to mention just a few examples. There is, of course, only one *Mona Lisa,* but improved reproduction techniques have made Leonardo's painting relatively available. A limited edition book, practically by definition, is not supposed to be multiplied.

## Illustrations

Availability constitutes a problem for the reader who either cannot afford such expensive books or lives far from the libraries that own some of them. Butor's solution, a partial one, was to reproduce the texts alone in five volumes titled *Illustrations;* they are, however, printed in such fashion as to compensate, up to a point, for the absence of the original graphics. Although nothing can truly replace the art book, in which a text illustrates a graphic work and the two interact, the text alone, by means of typographic arrangement, may suggest the absent art as well as the kind of art it is. It may also, through textual modifications, have a different effect than it had in the earlier publication. Finally, through both typographic and textual manipulations, several texts may interact, thus enhancing one another. Needless to say, the more work these texts are subjected to, the greater the distance from the original.

The first two devices are already in evidence in *Illustrations I* (1964), and beginning with *Illustrations II* (1969) all three are strikingly present. Here, the first text is shattered and spread out over the entire length of the book; the second begins on page 2, but a few pages later its stanzas alternate with those of the third; the fourth text begins as the second one ends and, somewhat like the first, is spread over a large portion of the volume; the fifth begins immediately after the fourth and about halfway through the third, and it ends long after the sixth and seventh have started; the eighth begins after the end of the sixth; the ninth and final one, after the end of the seventh (a diagram would show that a remarkable symmetry is present).

Concurrent texts are never fewer than three, and there are as many as five in the central section of the book. Furthermore, words from one text are borrowed and inserted into another, and more than two dozen carefully selected lines from the Renaissance poet Pierre de Ronsard are fitted into appropriate spots throughout the entire composition. This amounts, in part, to a very sophisticated, controlled version of collage, and the effect is not unlike that produced by *Degrees*—a challenge of Western society, particularly noticeable because the Berlin Wall and the Vietnam war are among the topics involved. As the literary genre known as the novel was challenged in that earlier work, both maintained and transcended, so are literary codes challenged in *Illustrations II,* while a new concept of writing, fragmented and discontinuous, is affirmed—an outgrowth of *Mobile.*

Each of the subsequent volumes embodies its own specific pattern of transformations; translating their architecture into a diagram again would be quite revealing. In the third, texts are more meditative than collaborative. Paintings by Pierre Soulage, for instance, antedate Butor's texts, and their production was not affected by the latter, which are labeled "exploded meditations" and "captions"—a total of seventy-two short items. It is hard to find a link between those items and specific paintings by Soulage even though one senses a general conformity in affects. This was also the case with the first text of *Illustrations I,* based on several works by the early rococo painter Alessandro Magnasco. *Illustrations III* (1973) also provides a rare instance of Butor's interest in sculpture; the particular sculpture that inspired him, a rather unusual one, was Jacques Hérold's *Grand Transparent,* a surrealist work undertaken at the instigation of André Breton. It would seem that Butor is more at home shifting from the surface of a canvas to that of a page, less so entertaining the metaphor of the book as a spatial object—what Philippe Sollers, in *Writing and the Experience of Limits* (p. 9), called the "monumentality" of the text. Such a preference is in keeping with the proliferation of mirror and window images in his writings.

*Illustrations IV* (1976) is composed more like the second volume in the series: individual texts are mingled and shattered to a greater extent than in the third. The distance between graphic and textual items is considerable; someone not familiar with the former would be hard put to decide which lines of the text refer to the work of this or that artist—Gregory Masurovsky, Bernard Dufour, Victor Vasarely, and others. Here, however, we also have a text that refers not to an artist but to another writer, Georges Perros, a friend whose literary counsels Butor greatly respected. Aside from constituting a homage, such a text, by placing Perros on a par with Masurovsky and others, emphasizes the bonds that unite writers and artists.

Furthermore, by distancing any specific work, literary or artistic, from the reader, it places such works on the same level with what we call "reality." The buildings of Paris, the basilica of St. Mark, Niagara Falls, the paintings of Magnasco, the writings of Rabelais—all have the same degree of "reality"; as they become a "reference" in a particular text, they are given value to the extent that they are transformed and shaped by that text. Often, of course, the so-called "real" referents have already been mediated through earlier texts—Niagara Falls through the writings of Châteaubriand, for instance, or the Rouen cathedral through the paintings of Claude Monet. Eventually anything can be translated to the white surface of a page or canvas. As Butor wrote, "A city may well be viewed as a literary text."

## *DREAM NARRATIVES AND THEIR TRANSFORMATIONS*

The first public manifestation of Butor's interest in dreams was the appearance of *Histoire extraordinaire* (Extraordinary Tale, 1961), an essay on a dream of Baudelaire's. For a more creative use of dreams one had to wait for his *Portrait de l'artiste en jeune singe* (Portrait of the Artist as a Young Monkey, 1967), the title of which acknowledges both Joyce and Dylan Thomas. When one recalls Picasso's 1954 painting *Ape and Model,* one is also tempted to read the title as a discreet homage to the painter; Butor himself reminds us that in Egypt the ape was both "hieroglyphic for the artist and representation of the god of writing."

True, Butor had earlier attributed dreams to characters in his novels and narrated them—and he certainly was not the first writer to do so. In *Portrait,* however, the dream is central to a narrative that operates on two separate levels, in alternating chapters. "Realistic" chapters give an account of the visit paid by the narrator to a German nobleman shortly after the end of World War II, during which he explores his host's priceless library and his collection of precious stones and teaches him new games of solitaire. In other chapters Butor imagines a serialized dream that is adapted from the tale of the second Kalandar, begun by Scheherazade on the twelfth of her thousand and one nights. In that tale the Kalandar, who has been changed into an ape, is unwittingly responsible for the death of not one woman (as the young man was in *Passage de Milan*) but two—and the second one is literally turned into those ashes that were first introduced, metaphorically, in *Passing Time.*

In *Portrait* the Kalandar becomes a visitor to the German castle who narrates a dream that maintains the basic features of the Arabian story while shortening it and modifying some of its details. In adapting this story Butor possibly borrowed some aspects of Freud's dream narratives in order to make it sound like a dream. Actually the distance that separates a literary text from a dream narrative is not very great, with references to reality playing a part similar to that of the day's residues. Perhaps the most significant feature of the dream in *Portrait* is that its source has been erased from the text and the name of Scheherazade is not mentioned; neither is the reason for her telling her tales. Butor, however, could not repress that for long. In one of a series of interviews conducted by Georges Charbonnier, he elaborated on the myth of the writer as Scheherazade:

> Every writer is Scheherazade, every writer harbors within himself a threat of death . . . both within himself and about himself. The threat that lies outside of him corrodes him, so to speak, internally. . . . The writer, in speaking, will at once remove the death threat that weighs upon him and, of course, also weighs on the entire future of society.
>
> (Charbonnier, pp. 41–42)

In 1975 there appeared the first in a series of books titled or subtitled *Matière de rêves* (The Stuff of Dreams). It contained five "dreams" (with titles such as "Le rêve de l'huitre" [Dream of the Oyster]), and at first one might well harbor the impression that, in contrast to the night chapters of *Portrait,* these were indeed dream narratives later embellished to give them literary status. Then comes the back-cover statement stressing that these "dreams" are not an elaboration of notes jotted down upon awakening but a reworking of the dream-narrative form with the aim of exploiting new resources or deposits. The metaphor recalls a theme present in numerous texts by Butor—mining the earth for precious metals and stones; it also recalls a haunting sentence that appears early in *Passage de Milan* and is spoken by Father Ralon as night falls, just before he switches on the light: "Wasn't there a path, the path of nightfall, that one always abandoned too soon, that one would never have the courage to follow down to its major windings?" Some twenty years later Butor explicitly began to explore that downward path into the murky regions of being. Fittingly, later volumes of this series are called *Second sous-sol* (Second Basement, 1976), *Troisième dessous* (Third Floor Below Ground, 1977), *Quadruple fond* (Fourfold False Bottom, 1981), and *Mille et un plis* (A Thousand and One Folds, 1985).

Butor told Madeleine Santschi that a recurrent dream informed *Matière de rêves* and that many other dreams contributed bits and pieces to the narrative, imbuing it with a flavor of dreams. The narrative as a whole, however, does not read like a dream narrative; nor does it read exactly like any other kind of narrative.

Here it may be possible to isolate one of Butor's important aesthetic contributions, that is, the production of a new kind of text or genre. It is clear that *Degrees,* while it might still be termed a novel, was, like the "novels" of a number of contemporary writers (Maurice Roche and Philippe Sollers, for example), a book that made a number of readers uncomfortable—and *Mobile,* as we have seen, only made matters worse. Butor's dissatisfaction with conventional genres or texts led him to experiment with new forms, new textures.

Part of this experimentation involved bringing to the surface matters that novelists had previously kept hidden or repressed. Thus, in *Portrait* the narrator is specifically identified as a younger Butor; in *Matière de rêves,* his wife and daughters are mentioned by name on a par with fictional characters out of Stendhal and others. By way of contrast, Simone de Beauvoir conventionally disguised what made the main character of *L'Invitée* (*She Came to Stay,* 1943) a version of herself—revealing it only in her openly autobiographical *La force de l'âge* (*The Prime of Life,* 1960). On another level writers have always been affected by their unconscious, and in many instances this may be detected in their writings. To paraphrase Freud, writers and artists have blazed a trail for psychoanalysts, even though they were not aware of the process that was involved. Butor, however, had read Freud and he consciously seeks, in some of his writings, to give the unconscious a chance to emerge.

A link with *Illustrations I* now suggests itself, for the text that was inspired by Magnasco's paintings reads very much like a dream narrative. Indeed, in *Matière de rêves* one "dream" of the first volume and those of the two following volumes have their source in a kind of intense meditation before a set of paintings; needless to say, this produces neither art criticism nor even the narrative of any single dream but something like the stuff of dreams, the stuff the unconscious works with, now woven into a different sort of narrative, in which the paintings play a part similar to that of the day's residues in actual dreams. It evoked what Butor called "the medium in which the unconscious of each person breathes and develops."

To those strands of autobiography and dream narratives that contribute to the weaving of a new texture, I should add music (to which I shall come back shortly), commentary, paraphrase, and internal quotations. The latter refers to the device of quoting statements from one "dream" in all the other "dreams"; this gives the volume a textual coherence—in addition to the thematic coherence that might be found in a novel. I find this weaving process particularly significant in view of Julia Kristeva's theory on the origin of the novel as genre or text in medieval France; she viewed it as resulting from the interweaving of different kinds of texts belonging to recognized categories or genres, which in turn became less and less meaningful as such. Today's metamorphosis of the novel may well re-enact what took place at its origin.

## *MUSIC*

The artistic disposition of Butor's father was complemented by the musical proclivity of other members of the family. His mother and grandmother played the piano, as did his sisters. Michel, however, preferred the violin, which he began to play at age seven. Family lore has it that the full-size instrument he eventually played had been selected for one of his grandmother's grandfathers by Carl Maria von Weber in Vienna, and this added a prestigious aura to the instrument. He played for about ten years but had to stop when he went to the university because he no longer had enough time to practice; nevertheless, the experience sharpened his musical ear and made him learn the rudiments of music. His knowledge of music was soon far greater than that of the ordinary amateur, and his appreciation extended from Bach to such contemporaries as Karlheinz Stockhausen and Pierre Boulez and to folk music and jazz.

Hence it is hardly surprising to find music interacting with Butor's writing. As he himself was first to point out, the architecture of *Passing Time* is based on the canon form; devices used in a number of other works also have technical musical equivalents. As he has collaborated with painters, he also has worked with musicians; the most spectacular of such undertakings was *Votre Faust* (Your Faust), subtitled *Fantaisie variable genre opéra* (Variable Fantasy in the Operatic Mode).

It was written jointly with the musician Henri Pousseur at the latter's suggestion. Pousseur, a few years younger than Butor, studied under the organist Pierre Froidebisc and was a disciple of Anton von Webern, Pierre Boulez, and the Belgian surrealist André Souris. An early convert to serial composition, and also much interested in electronic music and the experiments of John Cage, he had composed, among other things, "Mobile" for two pianos (1958), and "Répons pour sept musiciens" (1960), for which Butor wrote a text later published in a limited edition as *Paysage de répons* (Landscape of Responses, 1968). Fascinated by some of the aesthetic ideas he found in Butor's critical essays, Pousseur proposed that the two of them collaborate on a "mobile opera," using the Faust theme as a point of departure. Butor agreed, and they started working on the project in June 1961 at a Belgian seaside resort. The result, a transposition of the legend to a contemporary setting, pictures the artist—in this instance a composer—as Faust, while Mephistopheles appears in the guise of a producer. It was many years in the making and was first performed in January 1969, at the Piccola Scala in Milan.

With characteristic ambiguity Butor conveys the impression that the producer is directing the performance we are witnessing. As in Goethe's version, the curtain rises on "Prologue in the Theater"; for theatrical atmosphere, however, this prologue is closer to the opening scenes of Paul Claudel's *Le soulier de satin* (*The Satin Slipper,* 1924). A calculated informality—a discussion of the show that is about to be put on—aims at a closer communion between actors and audience, stage and house, and (in *Votre Faust* more than in *The Satin Slipper*) forces the action to be a commentary upon itself. With the "Prologue in Heaven" irony creeps in: we are in almost total darkness, and the sound is produced not by the music of the spheres but by a small orchestra on stage, playing a traditional canon. The stage settings throughout are relatively simple, in the style of Jean Vilar: four raised platforms are disposed in a loose semicircle, and on them four singers (tenor, alto, soprano, and bass) are surrounded by a few musicians; above each platform rises a screen on which the scenery is projected; the actors, five in all, perform their parts on the portion of the stage in front of the platforms, with a bare minimum of props. No one leaves the stage during the performance: actors appear or disappear by means of lighting effects, just as projections indicate a change of locale.

The first part of the *fantaisie* is patterned in very general outline after the portion of Goethe's drama that precedes the Walpurgis Night, and the whole text is crammed with references to Goethe, Gérard de Nerval, and Christopher Marlowe. The music and the arias are also filled with quotations and allusions that mark a basic similarity with *Degrees* and *Mobile.* The Faust theme is further compounded by having the principal actors witness a strange puppet show (in which the puppets are impersonated by the singers on the platforms) dealing with "the frightful life of Dr. Faust." A somewhat similar device was used in Michel de Ghelderode's *La mort du Docteur Faust* (*The Death of Doctor Faust,* 1925), subtitled *Tragédie pour le music-hall,* with which a few other minor points of comparison could be made.

In the first prologue the producer suggests that Henri, the composer, who bears the name Goethe's Marguerite had given Faust, write an opera. He then comes to Henri's home, a room in a busy, noisy building, and sets the requirements: the story must be based on Faust, there will be no deadline for completing the opera, and all of Henri's material needs will be taken care of. After that, the signing of the pact with the devil takes place offstage. During the next sequences the composer meets a woman named Maggy, who gets thrown into jail through the producer's wiles, and an opera singer—the latter seemingly not in the Faustian tradition.

By now two familiar themes of Butor's early fiction have been stated again. The main character is trying to compose a work, and even though we already surmise that he will fail in his endeavor, it turns out to be the very one we are watching. Also, the temptation that faces him is that of complacency and inactivity: the conditions of his contract are such as to banish both care and conscience from his mind. Beyond the plot outline, however, and in a fashion that can only be alluded to here, the techniques used in the novels and in *Mobile* play a major role. Literary quotations and allusions are supplemented by musical ones, projection screens are added to traditional lighting effects, and liberal use is made of recorded tapes, along with instruments and voices singing or speaking in five different languages. All are viewed as basic units in the work, like words in a poem, and a number of displacements are effected that bring them in contact with one another to produce a series of neo-surrealist metaphors.

The conclusion of part 1 also marks for the spectator the end of the fixed portion of the operatic fantasy. Butor and Pousseur will not proceed on their own but, through the producer-director, request instructions from the audience. The word "variable" in the subtitle means that a number of versions are available. The performers, before the start of the show, have three slightly different renditions of the first part to choose from. Then, at five more or less predetermined moments, spectators must decide between two alternative plot developments; even after having made a basic choice (such as deciding whether Maggy is to be released from jail or allowed to be forgotten and die), they may alter that choice if they do not like the consequences. They do so either by a formal vote taken during the intermission or by less formal actions during the performance. At one point they are even encouraged to shout their disapproval, if so inclined, as children might do at a *guignol* show.

Such a procedure, a simplified version of which was later used in *The Mystery of Edwin Drood* (1985) on Broadway, brings into the open the necessary, tacit collaboration between writer and reader or spectator; suspension of disbelief is its indispensable premise. More than that, though, it serves to emphasize human freedom and responsibility. The manipulation of freedom by a writer is a complex and contradictory process, and no matter how well the reader's freedom has been preserved, no matter what illusions one might harbor concerning that of the characters, their fate has necessarily been sealed once the book has been written. Here, the solution to what may be an insoluble quandary is sought by playing upon the almost inevitable identification of the audience with the hero and, through that audience, by helping to restore his freedom of choice.

When a policeman arrests Maggy toward the end of part 1, and the composer's conscience has been numbed into indifference by the modern Mephistopheles, nothing irrevocable has yet taken place. Depending upon the audience, the show might well end with Henri's resounding "no" to the producer, his refusal to remain bound by the pact—and this would reinstate the condition he was in during the first prologue; it might also end with Henri's downfall and the producer's prophecy: "You will be dead before tonight. You are going to get drunk, you will stumble, you will drown. I shall be with you in spirit." From the tape recorder come the words ". . . things are settled now. . . ." Indeed, it is only then that his fate is sealed—perhaps against the wishes of Butor and Pousseur.

Different audiences might therefore see, or participate in, very different operas. Theoretically, twenty-five dissimilar endings are possible. Each version could serve as a psychological portrait of the audience. The implication, made in connection with *Degrees,* that the writer is the devil and that he speaks true finds a curious echo here. As the Mephistophelian producer implies at one point, this new writer-audience partnership involves sharing a certain amount of deviltry:

> I have among you all sorts of accomplices; I know them and I can see them. Now look, and listen to the outcome. Oh, don't worry, everything will be done according to the wishes of the most enterprising amongst you, but the disclosure could surprise you.
>
> (*Votre Faust,* p. 142, 144)

Deviltry covers a territory that encroaches upon the unconscious, and it includes chance as well. This was emphasized when a partial version of *Votre Faust* was recorded on a set of Harmonia Mundi disks in 1973, together with the instructions and paraphernalia needed for game playing. There are actually two different games, one devised by Butor (using a regular fifty-two-card pack) and the other by Pousseur (using a special thirty-six-card pack designed by Vera Vasarhelyi), allowing a number of players seated around a table to influence the operatic proceedings. As in the case of a live performance, one player may counter the wishes of another—provided he or she has the right cards.

Pousseur's music includes quotations from the works of Webern, Monteverdi, Gluck, Wagner, and Mozart, but not from those commonly associated with the Faust theme. What he borrowed from Mozart was the music accompanying the penultimate scene in *Don Giovanni,* in which the demons drag Don Juan into hell. In another version the complete scene with the Commandant is incorporated into the puppet show section of *Votre Faust.* While he had long been interested in the Don Juan myth, Butor has credited Pousseur with reviving that interest through his analysis of Mozart's opera. the significance should be obvious; just as Revel, in *Passing Time,* was Theseus, Cain, and Oedipus, Butor as a writer shares attributes of Scheherazade, Faust, and Don Juan. Somewhat like a polymorphously perverse child, he sees literature as a means of transforming the world and its objects into erogenous bodies (places as well as people) that give him pleasure.

Butor's contribution to the Don Juan mythology, so to speak, began with a text called *Une chanson pour Don Juan* (1973), a poem published in a limited edition volume done in collaboration with the painter Ania Staritsky. This poem, or song, turned out to be the matrix of a number of others; Butor has not, so far, written *mille e tre,* but the possibilities are there. The proliferation of the original text is based on a process that is imbued with a female connotation (the 1973 book was printed on handmade paper that featured a number of holes, other songs are produced by means of cards in which word spaces have been cut out and then superimposed in varying order), aleatory, and analogous to serial music composition. A most noteworthy version is entitled "Une chanson pour Don Albert," which was published in 1983 in a volume that included *Seize et une variations* (Sixteen and One Variations), a set of paintings by Albert Ayme, a text by Dominique Bosseur, and a musical score by Jean-Yves Bosseur. Butor wrote sixteen and one stanzas based on one of the original stanzas from *Une chanson pour Don Juan* and three others used as transformers; Jean-Yves Bosseur, starting with a series of thirteen notes separated by twelve different intervals, composed sixteen variations and a finale. Albert Ayme had completed his own sixteen and one variations twenty years earlier and viewed those paintings as homage to Raymond Roussel, Handel, and Paolo Uccello.

A third example of Michel Butor's collaboration with a musician is the libretto he wrote for René Koering, an Alsatian composer who was a great admirer of Gustav Mahler. Called *Elseneur* (1979), this text brings together four characters—Hans Christian Andersen, Dietrich Buxtehude, Tycho Brahe, and Hamlet—placing them in a dialectical relationship with four others—the "anti-ghost," Bach, Johannes Kepler, and Macbeth—a relationship that is mediated by four women. While the anti-ghost sounds a bit like the Don Juan of *Une chanson pour Don Juan,* the text as a whole reads very differently from that of *Votre Faust;* Butor stated that his writing is affected by the person he writes for—"for Koering, it has to be lyrical and somber."

As in the case of painters, Butor has based several texts on composers of the past. The most remarkable of these is *Dialogue avec 33 variations de Ludwig van Beethoven sur une valse de Diabelli* (1971). While parts of it might be termed meditations on the Beethoven work, it is a heterogeneous text comprising very different elements and written at the instigation of Henri Pousseur. Butor had first been asked to deliver a commentary after a performance of the variations at a festival in Liège; instead, he suggested a dialogue whereby sections of his text would be inserted between the variations. With Pousseur's enthusiastic approval this was done in September 1970, when pianist Marcelle Mercenier played the Beethoven variations.

The notion of a heterogeneous text brings us back to *Matière de rêves.* It was suggested earlier that one of the strands contributing to its texture was musical. What is involved here is not so much a general analogy of forms (for instance, the fugue for Gide's *The Counterfeiters* or the canon for Butor's *Passing Time*) but a very specific borrowing of techniques. Taking the first dream of the second volume, *Second sous-sol,* for instance, which is based on paintings by Paul Delvaux, one sees that it appears to be made up of a series of settings separated by additions of a different sort. After the end of the first such addition there is a repetition of the three-line sentence that preceded it (pp. 15–16, repeated on p. 16)—this constitutes the equivalent of a *ripresa.* The same happens about ten times in the "dream," with *ripresas* of varying length—a little over five lines at the most (p. 29, repeated on the same page) down to six words at the end (p. 50, repeated on p. 55). But within this final addition, which is over four pages long, the same short sentence is repeated twice (pp. 52 and 53); this brings the *ripresa* quite close to an ostinato. The same sentence reappears in the second "dream," with a change in verb tense (p. 87). Other repetitions with variations involving half a dozen lines with vocabulary changes occur in that "dream" (for instance, pp. 60, 67, 72–73, 77, 82, 89, and 97), but in spite of the changes they all convey the same impression or meaning; they echo a narrative in the first volume of *Matière de rêves* that may well have its source in an actual dream and reflect the nervousness of a traveler going through customs ("Le rêve de Prague," p. 99). This might be termed a motif.

Such variations are linked to a process of serial composition, as are the various versions of *Une chanson pour Don Juan.* There is a fairly fixed base made up of the syntactical frame of the statement, and within that framework an infinite number of variations may be effected. A grammatical category (noun or noun phrase, verb, and so on) is the equivalent of a note—but the equivalence is obviously not perfect.

Counterpoint is another musical technique of which Butor made use. Here, too, there are precedents—Dos Passos, Huxley, Gide, and Butor himself in a chapter in *Passage de Milan.* In those earlier examples, however, the similarity between literary practice and musical device was rather vague. Strictly speaking, one might even say that counterpoint is impossible in literature; if one grants that there is a similarity between melody and narrative, one would then have to posit that for writing to be contrapuntal it would need to include two superimposed narratives simultaneously perceived by the reader.

Now it would seem that Butor has taken a step in that direction in *Matière de rêves.* In "Le rêve de l'huitre," for instance, the following lines appear:

> A painting in which I see my face. Their hospital. Frayed texts. Floating. Cécile. On a lake. I love you. In the operating. Agnès. Room. Laminated texts. There is the same blue. Irène. Dazzling light. I love you. But there isn't. Mathilde. Any table. I love you. They stretch me out. Wire-drawn texts. On the tiled floor. I love you. And squat. Serpentine texts. Around me.
>
> (p. 16)

They comprise three different (nearly) simultaneous statements: a description of the writing itself, a fourfold declaration of love, and a quotation from another "dream," which, when put back together, reads as follows: "Their hospital, floating on a lake: in the operating room there is the same blue, dazzling light, but there is no table, they stretch me out on the tiled floor and squat around me." The image, which could be that of the writer about to be dissected by his critics, is given greater poignancy and tension by the presence of the two other statements. What we have here is music contributing its texture to the composition of a new kind of text.

## *PLACES*

The arbitrariness of categories, at least where Butor is concerned, should be getting more and more obvious. *Passage de Milan,* the first volumes of *Répertoire, Illustrations,* and even *Matière de rêves* all seemed quite distinct, belonging to separate categories; *Degrees,* on the other hand, along with *Mobile* and the later volumes of the series mentioned above, tend to come closer and closer together in their conception. The impact of painting, music, and dreams, an interest in the physical makeup of books—these might be detected in almost any of the many works he produced after 1960. The distinctive aura that radiates from a given place is something Butor is particularly attentive to, as noted earlier in connection with *The Spirit of Mediterranean Places.* Other texts might have been discussed in this section, except that those that Butor himself grouped under this rubric ("the spirit of places") convey a feeling of greater personal relationship, and this emerges from the text itself. Whatever feelings Butor had with respect to Manchester, they are placed behind a screen in *Passing Time,* since all the feelings that emerge from that novel are attributed to Revel, and Manchester has been mythified into Bleston. In *The Spirit of Mediterranean Places,* on the other hand, the narrator is unquestionably Michel Butor himself.

The second volume in the series, *Oŭ* (1971), bears an ambiguous title: the crossed-out accent enables one to read it as meaning both "Where" and "Or." The hesitation is similar to the one that informed *A Change of Heart*—Paris without the mistress or the mistress without Rome? But in the novel it was Delmont, not Butor, who traveled between Paris and Rome. In *Oŭ* the various narratives roughly correspond to episodes of Butor's travels or sojourns in the United States and Southeast Asia, and the "I" of the first-person narrative clearly refers to the writer himself.

To simplify matters, one could say that the two cultural poles between which the narrator is torn are Paris and Albuquerque—on the one hand a sophisticated French culture that impregnates the entire volume, and on the other the nearby presence of the alien, fascinating culture of the American Indians. From an architectural standpoint the book is put together like *Illustrations II* (and this implies a shattering and dissemination of individual components); other places interact with the "poles," with the weather giving each its particular aura: mud in Seoul, rain in Angkor, mist in Santa Barbara, snow between Bloomfield and Bernalillo (on a drive to Salt Lake City), and the cold in Zuni.

Quite often the writer's experience is mediated or assisted through a more familiar one. Thus, in the background of the trip to Brigham Young University there lies the text of Marcel Schwob's *Le livre de Monelle* (1894); and at the architectural and semantic center of the book, there are "35 vues du mont Sandia le soir l'hiver," into which "Neuf autres vues du mont Sandia" have been inserted. Although not widely known as such, Sandia is a sacred mountain; Butor enhances its status by means of an oblique reference to Hokusai's set of prints, *36 Views of Mount Fuji,* which, when he discusses them in an essay collected in *Repertoire IV,* are called "36 and ten" views. This makes the analogy with the 35 and nine views of Sandia even more obvious—also maintaining a superior status for Mount Fuji.

The other mediator for these views, perceived in the evening as the light changes fast, is Claude Monet; as the writer sat by "the rectangle of his window" in Albuquerque and attempted to describe what he saw, so the painter by his window in Rouen has left us twenty rectangular canvases depicting that city's cathedral as the light changed. In other words, one cannot escape one's culture; one needs it in order to interpret (and probably misinterpret) any other culture—fascinated as one might be by the aura or spirit of a given place.

Two texts emphasize the tension involved. At the beginning of *Oŭ,* "J'ai fui Paris" (I Fled Paris) serves as an introduction and describes, after a fashion, the plane trip from Paris to the United States. Americans returning home on the same plane serve to balance the adventure that lies ahead with the possible satisfaction of returning home. A quarter of the way through the book a new text begins: "Je hais Paris" (I Hate Paris). It is a tense, ironic one, in which words of hatred cannot fully hide the passionate emotion of love. Seven pages before the end, "J'ai fui Paris," which had been interrupted by the descriptions of Sandia Peak, starts again and affirms the inevitability of the narrator's return—in spite of everything. It also includes an acknowledgment that "this is not at all what I thought I was going to say" (p. 392). This echoes a statement repeated several times in the text of the "35 views" to the effect that "any description is impossible." What Butor is saying, beyond the recognition that reality is too complex to be fully accounted for in a description, is that any description is necessarily an interpretation.

Contrasts with the early *Passage de Milan* are striking. The coming-out ritual that gave unity to that novel but brought out the isolation of individual characters ended with Angèle's death. Here, while the text seems centered on Sandia Peak, the section called "Le froid à Zuni" (Zuni Winter) is devoted to the ceremony of the winter solstice at the Zuni reservation (witnessed in part by Butor and mediated through Matilda Coxe Stevenson's *The Zuni Indians* [1904]); even though viewed by an outsider, it is a ritual that unifies, ensures continuity, and ends with the hope of spring, "proclaiming the stability of space and particularly the perpetuation of the east, the site of the renascent sun." It will be recalled that *Mobile,* too, ended with a suggestion of hope. Rebirth is promised for everyone, not just one privileged individual as in *Passage de Milan.* Butor's one-year stay in Albuquerque could be said to parallel Revel's in Bleston (in *Passing Time*); but while Bleston was the enemy, Sandia is the impossible pole of desire and Paris the inescapable source of love and hatred.

The third *Génie du lieu, Boomerang* (1978), is a weighty tome: 460 pages, compared with 392 for *Où.* The title explicitly conveys what was implicit in the earlier book—the inevitability of coming back—and points to one of the text's referents, Australia, which Butor visited on several occasions. As in previous works, the Australian experience has been mediated by a number of texts, with the latter becoming perhaps more important than before. Seven strands (there were nine in *Où*) are interwoven in the texture of *Boomerang;* these strands or sections vary considerably, some written with the book in mind, others possibly called into it at a later moment—perhaps because the book needed them. One section, for instance, entitled "Courrier des Antipodes," includes numerous letters Butor wrote to his wife from Australia; he told Madeleine Santschi he knew before going there that he would write about that continent and took his portable typewriter along so he would have carbon copies of his letters, which he thought might constitute the backbone of his future text.

What cannot fail to strike the person who picks up and leafs through the book is that it is printed in inks of three different colors. Red is for "Courrier des Antipodes," blue for "Bicentenaire Kit" (which has its source in a text written on the occasion of the bicentennial of the United States and inserted, along with serigraphs by Jacques Monory and fifty objects and documents aiming to portray the American myth as seen by Frenchmen, in a blue plastic box inspired by Marcel Duchamp's green box), and black for "Jungle" (where Buffon's *Histoire naturelle* [Natural History, begun in 1749] is a mediator). The four other sections must borrow their colors from these three. One is led to wonder if, had it not been economically unfeasible, Butor might have liked to have his seven sections printed so as to correspond to the seven colors of the rainbow.

There is much that involves Australia in *Boomerang,* as there was much about the United States in *Où.* Both deal with the aura that emanates from that continent and that country, but no objective statement is made, nor could one ever be made. The writer brings his own myths along with him; the Australian texture, for instance, interacts with earlier texts (those by Bougainville, André Breton, and Jules Verne, among others) and modifies them but cannot erase them. He has visited other places and been affected by their auras, which in turn infiltrate the aura of the place he now visits (something similar, although less subjective, was at work in *Mobile*). In the final analysis Australia (like the United States, or Venice, or that lycée in Paris) is a pretext; it is no more than a part, albeit a distinctive one, of what we call the world of reality. What *Boomerang* is about is Michel Butor and his relationship to that reality. When he "explores" a new site, a new aspect of reality, all the texts previously written or read by him (and I give the word "text" its all-inclusive connotation) come back to him like a boomerang, forcing him to struggle with them, change them, reorganize them, so that he can take into account the new text he is deciphering. The same might be said of his other works; it may be, however, that Butor was more sensitive to the magnitude of the process at the time of his Australian journeys.

And when readers enter his texts, they soon discover that, like all first-rate poets, Butor is also writing about them.

## Selected Bibliography

### STANDARD EDITIONS


*Passage de Milan.* Paris, 1954.
*L' Emploi du temps.* Paris, 1956.
*La modification.* Paris, 1957.
*Le génie du lieu.* Paris, 1958.
*Degrés.* Paris, 1960.
*Répertoire,* 5 vols. Paris, 1960–1982.
*Histoire extraordinaire.* Paris, 1961.
*Mobile.* Paris, 1962.
*Réseau aérien.* Paris, 1962.
*Description de San Marco.* Paris, 1963.
*Illustrations I.* Paris, 1964.
*Jacques Hérold.* Paris, 1964.
*6 810 000 litres d'eau par seconde.* Paris, 1965.
*Portrait de l'artiste en jeune singe.* Paris, 1967.
*Essais sur "les Essais."* Paris, 1968.
*Rabelais et les hiéroglyphes.* Pisa, 1968.
*Illustrations II.* Paris, 1969.
*Les mots dans la peinture.* Geneva, 1969.
*La rose des vents.* Paris, 1970.
*Dialogue avec 33 variations de Ludwig van Beethoven sur une valse de Diabelli.* Paris, 1971.
*Où: Le génie du lieu 2.* Paris, 1971.
*Rabelais.* In collaboration with Denis Hollier. Paris, 1972.
*Les petits miroirs.* Illustrated by Gregory Masurovsky. Paris, 1972.
*Les sept femmes de Gilbert le Mauvais.* Illustrated by Cesare Peverelli. Montpellier, 1972.
*Travaux d'approche.* Paris, 1972.
*Illustrations III.* Paris, 1973.
*Intervalle.* Paris, 1973.
*Matière de rêves.* Paris, 1975.
*Les compagnons de Pantagruel.* Oxford, 1976.
*Illustrations IV.* Paris, 1976.
*Second sous-sol: Matière de rêves II.* Paris, 1976.
*Votre Faust.* Reggio Calabria, 1977. French text with Italian translation.
*Troisième dessous: Matière de rêves III.* Paris, 1977.
*Boomerang: Le génie du lieu 3.* Paris, 1978.
*Elseneur.* Yverdon, Switzerland, 1979.
*Envois.* Paris, 1980.
*Vanité.* In collaboration with Henri Maccheroni and Michel Launay. Paris, 1980.
*Quadruple fond: Matière de rêves IV.* Paris, 1981.
*Explorations.* Lausanne, 1981.
*Brassée d'avril.* Illustrated by Maria Helena Vieira da Silva. Paris, 1982.
*Naufragés de l'arche.* Photographs by Pierre Bérenger. Paris, 1982.
*Exprès: Envois 2.* Paris, 1983.
*Problèmes de l'art contemporain à partir des travaux d'Henri Maccheroni.* In collaboration with Michel Sicard. Paris, 1983.
*Résistances.* In collaboration with Michel Launay. Paris, 1983.
*Vieira da Silva.* Paris, 1983.
*Alechinsky dans le texte.* In collaboration with Michel Sicard.
*Alechinsky: Frontières et bordures.* In collaboration with Michel Sicard. Paris, 1984.
*Avant-goût.* Chavagne, 1984.
*Herbier lunaire.* Illustrations by Gochka Charewicz. Paris, 1984.
*Improvisations sur Flaubert.* Paris, 1984.
*Chantier.* Gourdon, France, 1985.
*Mille et un plis: Matière de rêves V.* Paris, 1985.
*Cartes et lettres.* Correspondence with Christian

Dotremont, 1966–1979. Preface by Pierre Alechinsky. Paris, 1986.

*Avant-goût II.* Chavagne, 1987.

*Dans les flammes: Chanson du moine à Madame Nhu.* Paris, 1988. From the 1965 limited edition that included watercolors by Ruth Franken.

*Le retour du boomerang.* Paris, 1988.

*Avant-goût III.* Chavagne, 1989.

*L'Embarquement de la reine de Saba.* Paris, 1989.

## LIMITED EDITIONS

This is a partial listing. Several hundred works belong in this category. No complete bibliography is in existence as of the date of this publication, although it is known that Michel Butor is supervising the compilation of one. Less than ten copies of a number of these limited editions were published, while others exist in sets of over one hundred copies. They are difficult to locate because of the small numbers that were made and the artisanal quality of their manufacture. Some may be found in the Bibliothèque Municipale in Nice, France; there are a few dozen in the library of Southwest Missouri State University, others are in various university libraries, galleries (such as La Hune, in Paris), and museums (there are a couple at the Museum of Modern Art in New York). The rest are still in Butor's possession or in private hands. I have tried to provide a representative list, showing the variety of artists with whom Michel Butor has worked in collaboration.

*Cycle.* With 9 gouaches by Alexander Calder. Paris, 1962. 500 copies.

*Rencontre.* With 5 etchings by Enrique Zañartu. Paris and Stockholm, 1962. 55 copies.

*Litanie d'eau.* With 10 prints by Gregory Masurovsky. Paris, 1964. 105 copies.

*Dialogue des règnes.* With 15 copperplates by Jacques Hérold. Paris, 1967. 95 copies.

*Paysage de répons* and *Dialogue des règnes.* With an etching by Gregory Masurovsky. Albeuve, Switzerland, 1968. 120 copies.

*La banlieue de l'aube à l'aurore* and *Mouvement brownien.* With 48 drawings and 1 etching by Bernard Dufour. Montpellier, 1968. 810 copies.

*Tourmente.* With drawings by Pierre Alechinsky, Bernard Dufour, and Jacques Hérold. Montpellier, 1968. 130 copies.

*Western Duo.* With 10 lithographs by Gregory Masurovsky. Los Angeles, 1969. 38 copies.

*Lettres écrites du Nouveau Mexique.* With 4 copperplates by Camille Bryen. Paris, 1970. 75 copies.

*Une chanson pour Don Juan.* With handmade paper by Georges Duchêne and copperplates by Ania Staritsky. Veilhes, 1972/1973. 50 copies.

*Octal.* With 9 (unsigned) chromolithographs by Victor Vasarely. Munich, 1972. 1,015 copies.

*L'Oeil des Sargasses.* With an etching by Gregory Masurovsky. Sint-Pieters-Kapelle, 1972. 70 copies.

*Petites liturgies intimes pour hâter la venue du grand transparent de Jacques Hérold.* With an etching by Jacques Hérold. Paris, 1972. 100 copies.

*Imprécations contre la fourmi d'Argentine.* With collages, calligraphy, and etchings by Ania Staritsky. Paris, 1973. 3 copies.

*L'Oreille de la lune: Voyage en compagnie de Jules Verne.* With prints by Robert Blanchet. Boulogne-sur-Seine, 1973. 220 copies.

*Bicentenaire Kit.* Text "USA 76" by Butor, serigraphs by Jacques Monory, 50 objects or facsimile documents, in blue plastic box. Paris, 1975. 300 copies.

*Saga.* With an etching by Gregory Masurovsky. Geneva, 1976. 30 copies.

*Pliages d'ombres.* Poem by Butor, 5 photographs and 1 pastel (in 20 of the copies) by André Villers. Mougins, 1977. 95 copies.

*Antisèche.* Graphics by Ania Staritsky. Paris and Nice, 1978. 250 copies.

*Lumière cendrée.* With 15 photographs by Annick Le Sidaner. Salignac Eyvigues, 1978. 300 copies.

*1/1.* With 81 aquatints by Roger Pfund. Geneva, 1979. 39 copies.

*Colloque des mouches.* With prints by Julius Baltazar. Nice, 1980. 70 copies.

*Jeux de boules.* Balls by Jean-Luc Parant photographed by André Villers, one actual ball attached by string. Mougins, 1980. 30 copies.

*Tableaux vivants.* Facsimile handwriting by Butor, 7 serigraphs and 1 copperplate by Jacques Hérold. Rome, 1980. 65 copies.

*Tarot.* With 21 serigraphs by Henri Maccheroni. Cannes, 1980. 64 copies.

*Les yeux perdus.* With 7 photographs by Cuchi White. Paris and Nice, 1980. 100 copies.

*Chronique des astéroïdes.* With 7 "graphisculptures" by Paolo Boni. Paris, 1981. 126 copies.

*Don Juan dans la propriété des souffles.* With 3 photographs by André Villers and 3 prints by Pierre Leloup. Nice, Chambéry, and Mougins, 1981. 45 copies.

*La face nord.* With 4 prints by Axel Cassel. Paris, 1981. 66 copies.

*Fenêtres sur le passage intérieur.* With 3 graphics by Julius Baltazar. Nice, 1981. 3 copies.

*Ferments d'agitation.* Handwriting by Butor, with 2 photographs by André Villers and 2 prints by Julius Baltazar. Nice, Mougins, and Ivry, 1981. 22 copies.

*Filaments sensibles.* With 11 dry-point engravings by Julius Baltazar. Paris, 1981. 67 copies.

*À fleur d'alentours.* Handwriting by Butor, watercolors, gouaches, and collages by Frédéric Appy. Aix-en-Provence and Nice, 1982. 10 copies.

*Brindilles du bout du monde.* Graphics by Jooao Frutos and André Villers. Vancouver Island, Le Creusot, and Mougins, 1982. 60 copies.

*Les complices.* Decoupage by Marti Pey, photographs by André Villers. Nice, Barcelona, and Mougins, 1982. 30 copies.

*Le déjeuner sur l'herbe.* With 17 photographs by André Villers, collages by Frédéric Appy, and a serigraph by André Dupertuis. Aix-en-Provence, 1982. 100 copies.

*Fenêtres sur le passage intérieur.* With prints by Jiří Kolář. Bois-de-Champ, 1982. 500 copies.

*Interventions pour le Pierrot lunaire.* With graphics by Pierre Leloup. Chambéry and Nice, 1982. 26 copies.

*Liminaires et préliminaires.* With a collage by Butor. Paris, 1982. 30 copies.

*La main sur le mur.* 1 print by Julius Baltazar. Paris, 1982. 60 copies.

*Reminiscences du corbeau.* With 5 prints by Alex Cassel. Luxembourg, 1982. 80 copies.

*Sifflets.* With 2 prints by Axel Cassel. Paris, 1982. 110 copies.

*Signaux de fumée.* Facsimile handwriting by Butor, prints by Alex Cassel. Paris and Nice, 1982. 8 copies.

*Entre-temps.* Facsimile handwriting by Butor, 4 photographs by Pierre Lacasta, and 6 by Pierre Canou. Gourdon, 1983. 25 copies.

*Offenbach Series.* Poem, "Les nourritures de la lumière," by Butor, prints by J. C. Prêtre. Basel, 1983. 37 copies.

*Seize et une variations d'Albert Ayme.* With graphics by Albert Ayme, Butor's "Une chanson pour Don Albert," and music by Jean-Yves Bosseur (printed score and audiocassette). Paris, 1983. 50 copies.

*Cinq rouleaux de printemps.* 5 scrolls in cardboard box, with facsimile handwriting by Butor. Oyonnax, 1984. Also same 5 scrolls in a wooden box with burnished title; includes a set of 5 colored "shapes" ["Cinq formes à combiner pour accompagner les rouleaux de printemps"]. Oyonnax, n.d.

*Le chien roi.* With etchings by Pierre Alechinsky. Paris, 1984. 95 copies.

*Dimanche matin.* Graphics by Gregory Masurovsky. Nice, 1984.

*Intempéries.* Facsimile handwriting by Butor, prints by Michel Sicard. Coutances, 1984. 40 copies.

*Loisirs et brouillons (1964–1984).* Graphics by Butor. Gourdon, 1984. 30 copies.

*Manhattan Flies.* Graphics by Baltazar. New York and Nice, 1984. 2 copies.

*Monologue du graveur de merveilles.* With gouaches by Pierre Leloup. Nice and Chambéry, 1984. 40 copies.

*Nuit blanche.* Handset poem. Harnoncourt, Belgium, 1984. 99 copies.

*L'Office des mouettes.* With etchings by Cesare Peverelli. Geneva, 1984. 115 copies. Also in smaller format with different etchings but same text. Geneva, 1984. 150 copies.

*Quatre versions de Saga.* With a collage by Butor. Bort, 1984. 20 copies.

*Le scribe.* With 4 prints by Alex Cassel. Spuren, 1984. 50 copies.

*Victor Hugo écartelé.* With 4 prints and one wash drawing by Julius Baltazar. Nice, 1984. 90 copies.

*Le Viking en partance pour l'Islande.* With a wash drawing by Patrice Pouperon. Vinon-sur-Verdon, 1984. 33 copies.

*Zodiaque de nuages.* Graphics by Julius Baltazar. Paris and Nice, 1984. 2 copies.

*À fleur de peau.* Five poems in facsimile handwriting by Butor. Paris, 1985. 150 copies.

*Cheminement.* With graphics by Bernard Dorny. Paris, 1985. 75 copies.

*L'Enfant satellite.* Engravings by Alex Cassel. Luxembourg, 1985. 60 copies.

*Les ephémères.* Graphics by Jean Miotte. Paris and Nice, 1985. 2 copies.

*Feuillets d'espace.* Paper made and "sculptured" by Michel Gérard. Paris, 1985. 7 copies.

*Hors-d'oeuvre.* With graphics by Jacques Hérold. Rouen, 1985. 500 copies.

*Malaria.* With prints by Alex Cassel. Spuren, 1985. 50 copies.

*Nuages.* Silkscreened handwritten text by Butor, 9 wrappings by Patrice Pouperon. Ginasservis, 1985. 35 copies. Also *Autres nuages.* Drawings by Patrice Pouperon. Ginasservis, 1985. 18 copies.

*Passages de fleurs.* With graphics by Jacques Hérold. Paris, 1985.

*Petits opéras fabuleux.* Graphics by Julius Baltazar. Vitry and Nice, 1985. 4 copies.

*Le train des fantômes.* Graphics by Julius Baltazar. Paris and Nice, 1985. 2 copies.

*Traitement de textes.* Graphics by Butor, texts by Jean-François Lyotard, Michel Sicard, Pierre Canou, and Patrick Stefanetto. Gourdon, 1985. 30 copies.

*Autour des mots.* Various reproductions. Avignon, 1986.

*Bouquet d'impressions.* Graphics by Seund Ja Rhee. Nice, 1986. 81 copies, of which 15 are printed on "Korean paper."

*Gîte.* With drawing and collage by Butor. Ginasservis, 1986. 99 copies.

*Menace intime.* 37 drawings by Jean Lecoultre reproduced by "photolitho" process. Denges-Lausanne, 1986. 275 copies, of which 12 include MS by Butor and an original drawing.

*Métropolitain.* Collages by Bernard Dorny. Paris and Nice, 1986. 15 copies.

*La prairie des éveils.* With 4 etchings by Mehdi Qotbi. Paris, 1986. 50 copies.

*Requête aux peintres, sculpteurs et cie.* With a wrapping by Patrice Pouperon. La Sétérée, 1986. 25 copies.

*Je salue ce qui me délivre.* Texts by Michel Butor and Michel Bohbot. Graphics by Julius Baltazar. N.p., n.d. 12 copies.

*Z.* Poem by Butor with calligraphic "diversions" by Roger Druet. Créar, n.d. [1986]. 30 copies, including 6 with original calligraphy.

*Demain ou les mondes.* 5 graphics by Patrice Pouperon, manuscript text by Butor. Ginasservis, 1986–1987. 4 copies.

*Ailes.* Poem by Butor, engravings by Guido Llinas. Paris, 1987. 125 copies.

*Apéritif.* Photographs by Maxime Godard. Gaillard and Saint-Denis, 1987. 66 copies, including 6 with MS page and additional photograph.

*Après San Marco.* Photographs by Jean-Michel Vecchiet. 3 folding sets of 9 color photos each, plus 1 initial and 1 concluding card; text on verso; boxed. N.p., 1987. 200 copies.

*L'Atelier de la Rogne Rousse.* Handwritten poem by Butor. Gaillard, n.d. [1987].

*Bientôt l'automne.* Silkscreened handwritten text by Butor, graphics by Michel Sicard. Paris and Gaillard, 1987. 75 copies.

*La danse des monstres marins.* Ten pages of text by Butor on light cardboard, unbound, each with graphic by Pierre Leloup either clipped or pinned to the page. In cardboard folder. Chambery and Gaillard, 1987. 30 copies.

*Luminy 87.* Graphics by Patrice Pouperon. Folding book (5 folds). Ginasservis, 1987. 27 copies.

*In memoriam Blaise Cendrars.* "Sculpture" by Patrice Pouperon. Gaillard and Ginasservis, 1987. 5 copies, of which the first 2 are handwritten.

*In memoriam Charles Baudelaire.* Poem by Butor, wood and metal sculpture by Patrice Pouperon. Gaillard and Ginasservis, 1987. 5 copies, 2 of which are handwritten.

*In memoriam Jacques Hérold.* "Sculpture" by Patrice Pouperon. Gaillard and Ginasservis, 1987. 5 copies, of which the first 2 are handwritten.

*In memoriam Michel Vachey.* "Sculpture" by Patrice Pouperon. Gaillard and Ginasservis, 1987. 5 copies, of which the first 2 are handwritten.

*Observatoire.* Collages by Bernard Dorny. Paris and Gaillard, 1987. 7 copies.

*Pousses de printemps.* 6 photographs by Maxime Godard. Edited by Gnêzi d'Marèla. N.p., 1987. 65 copies, including 5 with manuscript text and additional photograph.

*Le réveil des ours.* One-page poem by Butor on the occasion of a show around Butor's work in Bern, Switzerland. Ginasservis, 1987. 85 copies.

*Un soir à New York.* Serigraphs by Aljoscha Segard. Ginasservis, 1987. 27 copies, of which 9 include an original drawing by Segard.

*Le chuintement de la suie.* With graphics by Monique Toupin. Ginasservis, 1988. 36 copies.

*Douze fois le même galet.* With graphics by François Garnier. Nice, 1988. 67 copies.

*Enfouissement.* With graphics by Pierre Leloup. Gaillard and Chambéry, 1988. 50 copies.

*Haute tension.* With graphics by Dorny. Paris, 1988. 60 copies.

*7 & 6.* Text by Butor and Robert Creeley, graphics

by Robert Terrien. Albuquerque, N.M., 1988. 35 copies.

*Tornade légère.* With graphics by Jean Miotte. Nice, 1988. 60 copies.

## RECORDINGS

*Jeu de miroirs de Votre Faust.* Music by Henri Pousseur. Interpreted by Marcelle Mercenier, pianist; Basia Retchitzka, soprano; Cathy Berberian, alto; Louis Devos, tenor; and Jules Bastin, bass. Baden-Baden, n.d. [1968].

*Votre Faust.* Music by Henri Pousseur. Basia Retchitzka, soprano; Merete Beekkelund, alto; Louis Devos, tenor; Jules Bastin, bass; and the Ensemble Musiques Nouvelles (Brussels). Designed by Vera Vasarhelyi. With French and German libretto, instructions for playing the game, 2 packs of cards, and 2 playing panels. Freiburg, 1973.

*Fenêtre sur le passage intérieur.* Read by Butor. 1 audiocassette. Paris, 1988.

## TRANSLATIONS

*A Change of Heart.* Translated by Jean Stewart. New York, 1959.

*Degrees.* Translated by Richard Howard. New York, 1961.

*Description of San Marco.* Translated by Barbara Mason. Fredericton, New Brunswick, 1983.

*Extraordinary Tale.* Translated by Richard Howard. London, 1969.

*Frontiers.* Translated by Elinor S. Miller. Birmingham, Ala., 1989. Twelve short texts preceded by an interview with Butor by Christian Jacomino.

*Inventory.* Translated and edited by Richard Howard. New York, 1968. Selections from *Répertoire* and *Le génie du lieu.*

*Letters from the Antipodes.* Translated by Michael Spencer. Athens, Ohio, 1981. Extracts from *Boomerang.*

*Mobile.* Translated by Richard Howard. New York, 1963.

*Niagara.* Translated by Elinor S. Miller. Chicago, 1969.

*Passing Time.* Translated by Jean Stewart. New York, 1960.

*The Spirit of Mediterranean Places.* Translated by Lydia Davis. Marlboro, Vt., 1986.

## BIOGRAPHICAL AND CRITICAL STUDIES

### BOOKS

Albérès, R.-M. *Michel Butor.* Paris, 1964.

Aubral, François. *Michel Butor.* Paris, 1973.

Charbonnier, Georges. *Entretiens avec Michel Butor.* Paris, 1967.

Dällenbach, Lucien. *Le livre et ses miroirs dans l'oeuvre romanesque de Michel Butor.* Paris, 1972.

Helbo, André. *Michel Butor: Vers une littérature du signe.* Brussels, 1975.

Hirsch, Marianne. *Beyond the Single Vision: Henry James, Michel Butor, Uwe Johnson.* York, S.C., 1981.

Le Sidaner, Jean Marie. *Michel Butor: Voyageur à la roue.* Paris, 1979.

Lydon, Mary. *Perpetuum Mobile: A Study of the Novels and Aesthetics of Michel Butor.* Edmonton, Alberta, 1980.

McWilliams, Dean. *The Narratives of Michel Butor: The Writer as Janus.* Athens, Ohio, 1978.

Oppenheim, Lois. *Intentionality and Intersubjectivity: A Phenomenological Study of Butor's La Modification.* Lexington, Ky., 1980.

Raillard, Georges. *Butor.* Paris, 1968.

Raillard, Georges, ed. *Butor: Colloque de Cerisy.* Paris, 1974.

Roudaut, Jean. *Michel Butor, ou le livre futur.* Paris, 1964.

Roudiez, Leon S. *Michel Butor.* New York, 1965.

Santschi, Madeleine. *Voyage avec Michel Butor.* Lausanne, 1982.

Skimao and Bernard Teulon-Nouailles. *Michel Butor, qui êtes-vous?* Lyons, 1988.

Spencer, Michael. *Michel Butor.* New York, 1974.

Van Rossum-Guyon, Françoise. *Critique du roman: Essai sur "La modification" de Michel Butor.* Paris, 1970.

Waelti-Walters, Jennifer R. *Alchimie et littérature: À propos de "Portrait de l'artiste en jeune singe."* Paris, 1975.

———. *Butor: A Study of his View of the World and a Panorama of His Work (1954–1974).* Victoria, B.C., 1977.

Welch, Liliane, and Cyril Welch. *Address: Rimbaud, Mallarmé, Butor.* Victoria, B.C., 1979.

### SPECIAL ISSUES OF PERIODICALS

*L'Arc* (Aix-en-Provence). Number 39 (1969).

*Kentucky Romance Quarterly.* Volume 32, number 1 (1985).

*Magazine Littéraire* (Paris). Number 110 (March 1976).

*Musique en Jeu* (Paris). Number 4 (1971).

*Obliques* (Nyons). February 1976.

*Oeuvres et Critiques* (Paris and Tübingen). Volume 10, number 2 (1985).

*The Review of Contemporary Fiction.* Volume 5, number 3 (Fall 1985).

*Texte en Main* (Grenoble). Number 2 (Summer 1984).

*World Literature Today.* Volume 56, number 2 (Spring 1982).

## BIBLIOGRAPHIES

Mason, Barbara. *Michel Butor: A Checklist.* London, 1979.

St. Aubyn, F. C. "Michel Butor: A Bibliography of His Works, 1945–1972 (with Addenda: 1973–1975)." *West Coast Review,* 12 (June 1977, January 1978), 13 (June and October 1978).

———. "Butor's Rare and Limited Editions: 1956–1983." *The Review of Contemporary Fiction,* 5 (Fall 1985).

LEON S. ROUDIEZ

# MICHEL FOUCAULT

## *(1926–1984)*

> Nothing in his life
> Became him like the leaving it. He died
> As one that had been studied in his death
> To throw away the dearest thing he owed
> As 'twere a careless trifle.
>
> (*Macbeth,* I, 4)

### *THE DEATH OF THE AUTHOR*

According to a medical statement issued eighteen days later in the French newspaper *Le Monde,* on 9 June 1984

> Michel Foucault was admitted to the clinic for nervous disorders at La Salpetrière hospital in Paris to undergo examination for neurological symptoms complicating a case of septicemia. Examination revealed the existence of several areas of cerebral suppuration, and antibiotic treatment initially had a favorable effect. By the next week remission allowed Foucault to take cognizance of the first reviews of his last two books. A brutal aggravation wiped out all hope of effective treatment, and on 24 June 1984 at 1:15 P.M. Michel Foucault died.

He was fifty-seven years old.

It is somewhat more customary when introducing a body of writing or an intellectual career to begin with the life of the author rather than with his death. This custom reflects a widely held belief that the meaning or essence of a life's work is to be sought in the identity, intentions, and experience of the person known to be its author. Yet as a number of writers noticed at the time, it was Michel Foucault's death that seemed most aptly to epitomize the teachings of his career.

This is so for a number of reasons. Anyone familiar with Foucault's writings will instantly recognize in the impersonal, almost monotone violence of the medical report an instance of the kind of language—the anonymous, administrative, institutional discourse of the human sciences—he frequently analyzed in his own writing, which was a unique combination of history, philosophy, and polemic he called "archaeology" and which he once characterized—for reasons that will emerge in a moment—as "history of the present." Yet profounder affinities link death to language in Foucault's thought, and I would like to consider these as a way of introducing the central themes of his career.

It is not merely a play on words to suggest that Foucault's death evoked the perennial preoccupation of his work: the problem of authority in modern culture, or what has been called the death of the author. "The Author, when believed in," the French critic Roland Barthes once wrote, "is always conceived of as the past of his own book: book and author stand automatically on a single line divided into a *before* and an *after.* The Author is thought to *nourish* the book, which is to say that he exists before it, thinks, suffers, lives for it, is in the same relation of antecedence to his work as a father to his child." In other words, we start with the life of an author when attempting to understand the work because we tacitly believe that the former is somehow repeated or re-*presented* in the latter. Indeed, what Barthes points out is how closely bound up our conception of the author or authorship is with the idea of representation itself. Even the wildest fiction, we assume, or the most surreal flight of the imagination represents—at least in the minimal sense of registering the presence of—the subjective existence of the author who wrote it. As a child repeats the presence of the parent, so a text, we believe, repeats in some fashion the presence of its author.

What all such beliefs tacitly assume, however, is that writers in fact possess sufficient subjective authority and creative power to thus express themselves in discourse—to continue the truth of their being in linguistic and intellectual form. It is precisely such assumptions that Foucault sought to overthrow. An author for Foucault is in no sense the past or father or origin of his work. Indeed, far from the author begetting the work that then expresses him, to Foucault the work in a real sense begets the author—including the sense we have that the author is the originator of it.

Foucault was massively (if sometimes recklessly) learned, belonging, as he once said, to that "great warm and tender Freemasonry of useless erudition." The subject matter of his iconoclastic historico-philosophical writings ranged widely, from histories of madness and medicine to the changing structures of knowledge in philosophy and the human sciences; from the history of punishment to the history of sexuality and self-discipline; from painters, parricides, and pornographers to the links between knowledge and power and the modern state.

Across this remarkable range of books and essays, Foucault patiently documented how fragile and ephemeral human selfhood or subjectivity is, how highly contingent a by-product it is of stubbornly finite and transpersonal cultural structures and discourses—collective social forms that antecede and postdate the individual subject, and of which perhaps the best thing that can be said is that they have no permanent durability, and exist only to be one day haphazardly transformed. Against the optimism that words such as *author, authority,* and *representation* convey—a dream of potency and creativity, of continuity, meaning, and durable human presence—Foucault sought to document the implacable sway finitude holds over human existence. Hence the bleak pertinence death holds for his work. As the philosopher Jürgen Habermas wrote:

> Foucault's death came so unexpectedly and suddenly that one can scarcely resist thinking that its circumstantiality and brutality document the life and teaching of the philosopher. Even from a distance, [it] seems an untimely event affirming the merciless power of time—the power of facticity, which without sense or triumph prevails over the painstakingly constructed meaning of each human life. For Foucault the experience of finiteness became a philosophical incitement.
>
> ("Taking Aim at the Heart of the Present," p. 5)

A historian and philosopher of limits, Foucault was more impressed by what constrains and curtails human presence than by the pretensions human beings have to cause or to continue themselves, their histories, and their meanings.

Foucault once wrote of the avant-garde writer Georges Bataille: "He was perfectly conscious of the possibilities of thought that could be released by God's death, and of the impossibilities in which it entangled thought." He might just as aptly have been describing himself. More rigorously than any other writer since Nietzsche, Foucault sought to think out the implications of the dictum not only that God is dead but that God's murderer, man, necessarily died with him. For with God perished any point outside man's finitude capable of sustaining human claims to identity, continuity, and meaning. "By denying the limit of the

Limitless," Foucault wrote, "the death of God leads to an experience in which nothing may again announce the exteriority of being." He meant that God's death imprisoned man within the limits of his own existence; that with God's limitlessness perished any transcendental vantage point or source of authority outside of man's finite experience. With God's death human history fell subject to an "intrinsic finitude, the limitless reign of the Limit."

Foucault identified the experience of finitude with the most pressing questions of our modernity. Like many writers, he dated the advent of that modernity from about the time of the French Revolution—an event he took to be contemporary with (but in no simple sense the cause of) a mammoth upheaval in man's relation to authority, to tradition, to culture, and to himself. This upheaval, "which began in the eighteenth century, and from which we have not yet escaped, is bound up with a return to the forms of finitude, of which death is no doubt the most menacing, but also the fullest." As Foucault wrote in *Naissance de la clinique* (*The Birth of the Clinic,* 1963), what occurred in the late eighteenth century was "the death of the last mediator between mortals and Olympus, the end of the infinite on earth . . . after [which] the world is placed under the sign of finitude, in that irreconcilable, intermediate state in which reigns the Law, the harsh law of limit."

Less a metaphysical event than a transformation in the order of human culture and discourse, the "death of God" and the reign of finitude, for which the notion of God's death stands, defined for Foucault the horizon of our modernity, confining human actuality and any understanding of it to a present (and thus to a relativity) without recourse. Hence the terms Foucault adopted to describe his maverick historical project, which he variously called an "ontology of actuality," the "analytic of finitude," and "history of the present." Hence, too, his insistence that we abandon all conceptions of history that conceive of the past as the cause or origin of the present; all conceptions of meaning that conceive the "truth" of representations as lying in the objective reality they putatively reflect; and all conceptions of subjectivity as the expression of a fundamental identity underlying and legitimizing it.

In pressing these points, Foucault meant to apprehend unflinchingly the nature of power in modern society, which he took to be radically inhospitable to the ambitions of human subjectivity. In this respect, his work was an attempt to rethink the nature of knowlege, power, and human subjectivity in the harsh light of finitude and death. For the old Romantic themes of creativity, truth, and the self, Foucault substituted an analysis of the objective lineaments of power, discourse, and subjectivity. He had nothing but contempt for the authority of individual selves, dismissing "their capacity for creation" along with "their aptitude for inventing by themselves, for originating concepts, theories or scientific truths by themselves." As he wrote in the preface to the English translation of *Les mots et les choses* (*The Order of Things,* 1966), his best-selling study of the changing structures of knowledge in the human sciences, "I should like to know whether the subjects responsible for scientific discourse are not determined in their situation, their function, their perceptive capacity, and their practical possibilities by conditions that dominate and even overwhelm them."

In pursuing this inquiry, Foucault sought to describe the sheer power and order of discourse without reference to anything beyond the empirical space in which that order exists and has its effects. Above all, he insisted, the point is not where order comes from—an implicitly theological question, in Foucault's view—but precisely that "order *exists.*" Rejecting the notion of origins, Foucault's conception of the activity of culture might be likened to a gridlocked traffic jam: rigid configurations of mobilized constraint arising, contrary to any individual intention, as the unintended (but no less patterned and determining) structural consequence of specific arrangements of matter in motion. Power, in this view, as Foucault tirelessly pointed out, is no less constraining for lacking any point or foundation outside the system in which it has its immediate effects. On the contrary: in Foucault's view the fact that power in society is without transcendent or subjective foundation increases its ordering and oppressive reality—not least because man, being without a foundation, lacks serviceable access to the forces that make and bind (and unmake) him. Foucault thus conceives modern power, as Michael Ignatieff has noted, as "escaping the sovereignty of men's institutions and intentions."

These two themes, power and knowledge, meet most critically for Foucault in the question of the subject itself. "My objective," he said in 1982, "has been to create a history of the different modes by which, in our culture, human beings are made subjects." His term for that process was *assujetissement,* by which he meant not only how culture has subjugated man but also how it has done so by making him into a subject. *Assujetissement* is something culture accomplishes in a whole complex of psychological, moral, political, legal, and even philosophical and grammatical senses. Foucault sought, in other words, to understand man's subjugation as a consequence of his being constituted as a subject—a process he identified historically, in a further play on the word *sujet,* with man's emergence in the late eighteenth and early nineteenth centuries as the central subject of the human sciences.

At bottom, Foucault's ambition was to radically rethink the very nature and order of what an event in human thought and history is. If the themes of representation and the founding subject endow events with a spurious origin and purpose—in the process of creating what they claim to find, the great unities of history—Foucault sought to grasp events as irreducibly different and discontinuous singularities erupting and contending in a present without escape. Here, too, Nietzsche and death were Foucault's chief resources. Indeed, he took death to be a perfect example of what an event intrinsically is: singular, contingent, violent, material insofar as it implies an action of bodies, and incorporeal insofar as it is an irreducible and unrepeatable event. As Foucault notes, "the event—a wound, a victory-defeat, death—is always an effect produced entirely by bodies colliding, mingling, or separating," for which

> death supplies the best example, being both the event of events and meaning in its purest state. Its domain is the anonymous flow of speech; it is that of which we speak as always past or about to happen and yet it occurs at the extreme point of singularity
>
> ("Theatrum Philosophicum," in *Language, Counter-memory, Practice,* p. 174)

Grasped in their singularity, events speak of a reality very different from that evoked by the theme of representation, which implies continuity, sameness, and the unanimity of the common origin. To Foucault, the intrinsic hypocrisy of cultural institutions is that they mainly cover up this curt reality of human thought and deed. The transmission of a continuous human presence of which these institutions speak is in reality an (irrational) strategy for controlling the underlying disorder of the world. "I am supposing," Foucault asserted in 1970,

> that in every society the production of discourse is at once controlled, selected, organized and redistributed according to a certain number of procedures, whose role is to avert [discourse's] power and its dangers, to cope with chance events, to evade its ponderous, awesome materiality.
>
> (*L'Ordre du discours* [*The Discourse on Language*])

Foucault's purpose was to demonstrate how the human world is an irrationally *ordered* place—in part to show how human existence lacks not only rational point and purpose, but even the freedom of any overt disorder or randomness as well.

Foucault wished to incite culture to sense

the meaninglessness that is its essence, as if to help return it to its true patrimony, the abyss. "As the archaeology of our thought easily shows," he wrote at the end of *The Order of Things,*

> man is an invention of recent date. And one perhaps nearing its end.
>
> If those arrangements were to disappear as they appeared, if some event of which we can at the moment do no more than sense the possibility—without knowing either what its form will be or what it promises—were to cause them to crumble, as the ground of Classical thought did, at the end of the eighteenth century, then one can certainly wager that man would be erased, like a face drawn in sand at the edge of the sea.
>
> (p. 387)

"The essential task," Foucault wrote in *L'Archéologie du savoir* (*The Archaeology of Knowledge,* 1969), is "to free the history of thought from its subjection to transcendence." As he stated in an extraordinarily brilliant essay, "Qu'est-ce qu'un auteur?" ("What Is an Author?" 1969):

> The disappearance of the author—since [Stéphane] Mallarmé, an event of our time—is held in check by the transcendental. Is it not necessary to draw a line between those who believe that we can continue to situate our present discontinuities within the historical and transcendental tradition of the nineteenth century and those who are making a great effort to liberate themselves, once and for all, from this conceptual framework?
>
> (*Language, Counter-memory, Practice,* p. 120)

Foucault wished to eradicate from interpretations of human actuality the least remainder of what might be called the thought of the nonfinite, the extrafinite, the infinite; anything that seemed to provide a "privileged shelter for the sovereignty of consciousness" that man lost at the beginning of the nineteenth century, the dawn of the modern age. From within the ideal continuities of history, meaning, and identity that an anthropocentric culture and simple human hope seek to maintain, Foucault wished to elicit the corrosive power of the finite; to install, within the circle of human plans and ideas, the suzerainty of chance, materiality, and discontinuity as regnant forces and irreducible limits in the history of thought.

"I would like my books," he once said in an interview, "to be like daggers, Molotov cocktails, mine fields." Such a desire represents more than just an instinct, which Foucault had in abundance, for verbal shock tactics. For it issues from an ambition animating Foucault's entire career: to make of his own writing an intellectual event capable of resisting identification—and thus representation—by making explicit the historically specific rules and strategies through which the "identity" and "meaning" of a historical epoch or an individual author or a piece of writing is fabricated and forcibly maintained in and through the structures of discourse and society. An enemy of what he called the "thought of the Same," he once remarked:

> I am no doubt not the only one who writes in order to have no face. Do not ask who I am and do not ask me to remain the same: leave it to our bureaucrats and our police to see that our papers are in order. At least spare us their morality when we write.
>
> (*The Archaeology of Knowledge,* p. 17)

Foucault pursued his renegade projects with a kind of cheerfully bleak irreverence, enthusiastically reversing every shibboleth of humanism. In that spirit he not only conceived subjectivity to be a function of the discourse it purportedly creates but also claimed the body was the prisoner of the soul, and saw history not as progress or continuous unfolding but as a series of discontinuous and irrational transformations from one massive arrangement to another. Like many of his contemporaries, Foucault viewed authority and power as forces entirely on the side of society's structures, and not at all on the side of its subjects.

In expressing these views, Foucault took

to a new and rigorous extreme many of the main paradoxes and impulses of cultural modernism. Like Joyce, Kafka, Mann, Flaubert, Nietzsche (above all, like Nietzsche), he saw that man is caught remorselessly in a present that is little more than the accumulations of a past he cannot escape—except perhaps by chance, absurdity, anarchy, madness. Like them, too, Foucault energetically opposed all Romantic notions of the creative self—paradoxically, in the name of creativity or at least a kind of unbridled individual will. Like Rimbaud, he cultivated a ferocious antipathy to things as they are and yet was excruciatingly aware how little individuals can do to change them.

Along with T. S. Eliot, Foucault saw culture—what Foucault called the "archive" and Eliot called "tradition"—as an impersonal, internally coherent, and self-regulating system. Indeed, for both men the individual is less the agent of meaning in cultural production than its passive occasion, providing what Edward Said has called merely a "provisional start and finish" for an operation taking place elsewhere, at the level of a cultural order impervious to the claims of individuality. Eliot, of course, hailed this cultural edifice as the sole bastion of order in human history. Foucault, on the contrary, denounced what he saw to be the extraordinary deformations tradition wreaks upon the individual.

Like William Butler Yeats, Foucault seemed to yearn for a place where "body is not bruised to pleasure soul"—a place outside nature and culture he knew did not exist. At the center of his work was a perverse if archly rational hankering, not to "dissipate oblivion" but to accede without impediment to the abiding anonymity—to the *death*—that he took to be the truth of man's existence in discourse. For Foucault, as for Eliot, language does not express personality; it leaves personality behind. "I do not say things because I think them," Foucault once remarked, "I say them rather with the aim of self-destruction, so that I will not have to think any more, so that I can be certain that from now on, they will lead a life outside of me, or die the death, in which I will not have to recognize myself."

Discernible in all this is an ascetic reaching for personal oblivion in the production of discourse, and in this, too, he agreed with Eliot. Indeed, it was Eliot who wrote that "poetry is not a turning loose of emotion, but an escape from emotion; it is not the expression of personality, but an escape from personality." But then, as Eliot knew, "only those who have personality and emotion know what it means to want to escape from these things."

## *BEGINNINGS*

> I wish I could have slipped unnoticed into this lecture that I am supposed to be giving today—as into all those I shall be delivering here, perhaps over the years ahead. I would have preferred to be enveloped in words, borne way beyond all possible beginnings. At the moment of speaking, I would like to have perceived a nameless voice, long preceding me, leaving me merely to enmesh myself in it, taking up its cadence, and to lodge myself, when no one was looking, in its interstices as if it had paused an instant, in suspense, to beckon to me. There would have been no beginnings; instead of being him from whom discourse proceeds, I would stand in its path—a slender gap—the point of its possible disappearance.
>
> (*The Discourse on Language,* p. 214; translation rev. by E.B.)

Pressed once by in interviewer to provide a psychological account for one of his more troubling theories—the cultural emergence and subsequent demise of the figure of man—Foucault snapped that the question had nothing to do with the problem. When asked why he made such a problem of personal questions, he acidly replied, "I am not making a problem out of a personal question, I make of a personal question an absence of a problem."

Foucault was born on 15 October 1926 in Poitiers, France, the son of a doctor. There as yet exists nothing like a real biography, beyond brief sketches that have appeared in some of the longer studies of his work. If Foucault's own feelings on the matter are respected—especially his belief that discourses like biography (life-writing) largely fabricate the subjectivity they claim to express—none will ever appear. But then Foucault was the last to expect the order of discourse to respond to the wishes of an individual, which is why he felt it doesn't do much good to invoke personal experience as the origin of meaning in discourse. This is especially so when, as for Foucault, the suspicion has grown very great that discourse might cause the author more than any author author it.

"When I (no doubt wrongly) believe that I am saying something new," he explained to the hapless interviewer above, "I am nevertheless conscious that in my statement there are rules at work, not only linguistic rules, but also epistemological rules, and those rules characterize contemporary knowledge." Since most people believe that the individual has some impact on thought and shares some of the initiative in the creation of its order, Foucault's thinking presents some fairly impertinent difficulties right from the outset.

One of Foucault's most astute readers and critics, Edward Said, emphasized this troublesome aspect of Foucault's work by making him a central focus of his own 1975 book, *Beginnings,* a study devoted to the ironies and hazards of beginning intellectual and imaginative work in culture. As Said noted, Foucault "has become, in Roland Barthes's words, the very thing his works describe: a consciousness completely awakened to and possessed with the troubled conditions of modern knowledge." This tissue of citations—Said using Barthes on Foucault—may help to dramatize the nature of those troubled conditions, and particularly the undignified status of the biographical self in relation to its own thought.

Foucault starts from the perception that no absolute foundation or source (whether located in a transcendent deity, in tradition, in culture, or in the writer himself) exists to shore up the creative authority of the self, to ensure the inner identity and continuity (and hence meaning and purpose) of the thinking subject and its representations. The self is not a sufficient cause or origin of language. Any statement—like Said's, for example, concerning a writer and the nature of his work—derives its force and meaning not from the sovereign intentions embodied in the author's founding presence but, rather, from a colloquy of other statements and other voices that every statement inevitably repeats.

Here the chain of allusions, Said to Barthes to Foucault, is illustrative. For Foucault a statement does not express or invent an original thought: it is enmeshed involuntarily in systems of citation and reference, implicit or otherwise, whose own order and regularity subdue whatever initiative a statement's author may bring to it. The sheer fact and force of *the already said,* the existing pressure of words and ideas or discourse, as Foucault calls it, anticipating and organizing one's own thought and speech, work to overwhelm (rather than underwrite) the originating power of the self. Thus, to "begin" work in language is really to be taken up and worked over by so many other structures, forces, and rules as to render the dignity and creativity—the *originality*—typically associated with intellectual endeavor highly ironic and even untenable, not only from the start but *before* it as well.

Foucault was first educated in local state schools in Poitiers. He later attended Catholic school, where he passed his *baccalauréat* with distinction, and in 1945 was sent to board at the elite Lycée Henry IV in Paris, where he studied philosophy under the distinguished Hegel scholar Jean Hyppolite. In 1946 he was admitted to the École Normale Supérieure at the Sorbonne in Paris, the most elite institution in France for the study of philosophy, where he continued to study under Hyppolite as well as with the Marxist philosopher Louis Althusser. In 1948, Foucault took his *licence de philosophie.*

Philosophy enjoys enormous prestige in the

French educational system, and from the start Foucault was a student of extraordinary brilliance, by temperament passionate about the pursuit of truth, an *epistemophile.* Yet from fairly early on, he seems to have been shadowed by a doubt that the promises of philosophy would be kept. As reported by his English translator, Alan Sheridan, Foucault once described the French educational system

> as a form of initiation in which the secret knowledge promised was always postponed to a later date. In the primary school he learned that the really important things would be revealed when he went to the *lycée;* at the *lycée* he found that he would have to wait until the "*classe de philo*" (the final year). There he was told that the secret of secrets was indeed to be found in the study of philosophy, but that this would only be revealed at the university stage, that the best place to find it was at the Sorbonne and that the holy of holies was the École Normale Supérieure.
>
> (*Michel Foucault,* p. 2)

Foucault's education ironically taught him, as Sheridan remarks, that "there is no secret knowledge." What Foucault is describing here is the uneasy perception that even as one pursues philosophical truth—a truth always deferred in time and place—one is being held in the grips of a discursive and institutional order whose own organization and mode of being, at once tritely self-evident but almost never observed, is where the *real* action is. This perception would become the abiding theme of Foucault's career: how under the seductively reasonable guise of leading us to the "truth," our discursive habits, the self-possessed language of reason, together with the institutions that support them and that they in turn support, coercively constrain and shape not only what we think (the subject of our thoughts) but also what we are (ourselves as thinking subjects).

Philosophy and the whole edifice of the human sciences are important to Foucault, then, not for what they represent about reality but for what they do to man in the process. It is the desire to grasp this active shaping character of discourse, its intrinsic relation less to truth than to power, that underlies Foucault's express intent "to return to discourse its character as an event." "The real political task of society," as he saw it, "is to criticize the workings of institutions, which appear to be both neutral and independent; to criticize and attack them in such a manner that the political violence which has always exercised itself obscurely through them will be unmasked, so that one can fight against them." From early on, Foucault seems to have been interested less in truth than in the reality of the will to power behind it.

Restless with the academic study of philosophy, less certain that it was the road to truth, Foucault moved toward the study of psychiatry. In 1950 he received a *licence de psychologie,* and two years later the *diplôme de psycho-pathologie.* For two years he taught at the École Normale Supérieure and observed mental patients in local Parisian hospitals. This research resulted in a small book published in 1954, *Maladie mentale et personnalité* (Mental Illness and Personality, translated as *Mental Illness and Psychology*), a fairly conventional analysis informed by both Marxist theory and physiological observation, of the origin and variety of mental disorders. More dissatisfied than ever with the consolations of philosophy and science, Foucault left France in 1954 to take up a position in the French department at the University of Uppsala in Sweden.

In 1954, as Foucault began his self-exile in Uppsala, the outlines of *Folie et déraison: Histoire de la folie à l'âge classique* (Madness and Unreason: A History of Madness in the Age of Reason, 1961; translated as *Madness and Civilization: A History of Insanity in the Age of Reason*) began to emerge. The book constituted a radical break with most contemporary ideas about history, the history of ideas, and the nature of reason and truth itself. To understand the nature of that break, it is necessary to understand something more of the tradition in which Foucault intervened.

## *SUBJECT AND STRUCTURE*

The 1930's and 1940's, the period of Foucault's philosophical training, saw the emergence or transformation of a number of intellectual and cultural currents in France. Phenomenology, existentialism, surrealism, Marxism, socialism, and the cultural criticism of the Frankfurt School all vied for predominance on the Paris scene. Disparate as these currents often were, they were united by a shared sense of social and political urgency, by the possibilities of Soviet Communism, and above all by the threat of fascism. "Beginning with Hitler's takeover" in 1933, the historian John Heckman said, "the interest in social questions among [French] philosophers began to be more explicit."

Slanted to the experiences of everyday life and seemingly responsive to the urgent questions of the day, phenomenology and existentialism in particular (the "philosophies of existence") offered philosophical acuity and political relevance. In tandem with the iconoclastic political and literary ambitions of the surrealists, they represented the "perfect alternative to French academic philosophy and [Henri] Bergsonian idealism"—quietistic intellectual trends regnant in France in the 1920's. This new wave of critical thinking came to one kind of zenith in the postwar ascendancy of the philosophers Jean-Paul Sartre and Maurice Merleau-Ponty, who injected the phenomenological and existential analyses of Edmund Husserl and Martin Heidegger with a new vitality and direction.

Summarizing the French cultural situation at the time Foucault came to maturity, the critic Michael Clark remarked that while "no single ideological perspective dominated [the French] scene . . . many of the groups did share at least one general philosophical assumption." As he states in *Michel Foucault, An Annotated Bibliography,* this was

> the belief that political action, social organization, and cultural forms are the expression of independent, creative individuals acting within their moment in history. The most sophisticated expression of this common point was Jean-Paul Sartre's *Critique de la raison dialectique* (1960), which tried to effect a synthesis between two different relations between the individual and history: the Marxist perspective of history in its objective dimension as viewed from the outside, and the existential focus on the subjective experience of the individual. Sartre's aim, he said, was to construct a "historical anthropology" that would reveal Man in history and history in Man. (p. xxii)

Sartre's historical anthropology, his image of man as a complex but finally viable historical actor, was indebted first and foremost to the philosophy of the nineteenth-century German thinker Georg Wilhelm Friedrich Hegel. If it was the devastating experiences of fascism that gave political impetus to the intellectual trends of the 1930's and 1940's, it was the influence of Hegel that connected and presided over the new historical urgencies of French intellectual life. Foucault's teacher and mentor, Jean Hyppolite, himself sponsored much of the new interest in Hegel through his magisterial translations in 1939 and 1941—the first ever into French—of Hegel's dialectical masterpiece, *Phänomenologie des Geistes* (*The Phenomenology of Mind,* 1807); through his teaching in the lycées and at the École Normale Supérieure, and through his commentary on Hegel's *Phenomenology, Genesis and Structure* (1946), which appeared immediately after the war. It would be impossible to overstate the importance of Hyppolite's work on Hegel to French intellectual culture during this period.

What united the new interest in Hegel to the intellectual and political trends of the period—what made Hegel compelling as he had never been before, at least in France—was a characteristic stance they all shared toward what the historian Perry Anderson has called the "master problem" of postwar French intellectual culture: "the nature of the relationships between the structure and subject in human history and society." This problem, which has both a cognitive and a social dimension, has constituted a central crux for much of modern academic culture. On the one hand, it concerns the relationship between the subjects of knowledge (both who knows and what is known) and the structures of knowledge (the way knowledge is known, the discursive forms through which objects of knowledge are represented to subjects that know). On the other hand, it concerns the nature of the authority of the individual self or subject in relation to the transpersonal institutional structures of society.

Many writers and thinkers in the modern period, Foucault included, have perceived that a whole host of factors since the French Revolution (the breakdown of traditional social and political forms under the weight of the Industrial Revolution, the death of God, the advent of new forms of knowledge) have worked to erode the authority of the subject, mainly by rendering questionable any foundation outside the circumstances of history itself upon which such authority might be based. With the French Revolution, as Edmund Burke perceived, the present erupted furiously into history. Since then the question of man's authority has been stark, the "master problem" of modern culture has become this: What kind of authority can the subject—of language, knowledge, history—have in modern culture? What is the relation of knowledge to power, and of both to human subjectivity, in the circumstances of modern culture? Do the subjects of history and knowledge have any leverage over the structures in which they are embodied, or is their authority completely overwhelmed by those structures?

Hegel, writing in the early nineteenth century in response to the new social and philosophical conditions the French Revolution seemed to pose, located the authority of the subject in the very movement of history itself, conceiving the process as a dynamic transaction: subjects positing, struggling with, and superseding their own objective structures. His conception of the "present movement" of the temporal spirit embodying and recognizing itself historically held out the promise of an eventual reconciliation between man's subjective hopes and the objective historical and structural conditions he finds himself in—between his ideals, in short, and his reality.

In the period immediately preceding, during, and after World War II, there was a very great energy in Europe, an anxious enthusiasm, to believe somehow in the capacities of subjects to master the objective structures that dominate them. Hegel's writings seemed to provide a foothold for such belief, and Jean Hyppolite's translation and teaching of Hegel's *Phenomenology* proved to be one of the central intellectual events of the 1940's. At a time when history seemed more menacing and inescapable than ever before, Hegel's philosophy combined historical engagement with a promise that the subjects of history could overcome their subjugation. This Hegelian social and political optimism found an epistemological correlative in the belief that the subjects of knowledge, through the action of self-consciousness, could provide an adequately authoritative foundation for truth.

This is not the place to discuss Hegel's massive historico-philosophical system in any greater detail. Suffice it to say that it was against the entire Hegelian tradition that Foucault came to rebel. For Hegel, it was the figure of man himself in the progress of his own history that formed the meeting place of subject and object, the difficult and active reconciliation of these opposites. Foucault asks us to forget man, insisting that we replace "the Hegelian [theme] of present movement," which stitches man's aspirations and his historical reality into a coherent anthropological whole, with the "theme of the foundations of discourse and its formal structure," in which the figure of man is contingently constituted and dispersed.

Foucault's conception of man has less in common with Hegel's anthropological ideal than with another very different response to the French Revolution—Mary Shelley's monster, the bastard construction of a reason gone mad. Frankenstein's invention is the very image of aborted man—of a reason not only unsuccessful in its attempt to embody itself objectively but also finally destroyed by the lurching construction it is incapable of controlling.

Point by point, Foucault's project sought to demonstrate not only the discrepancies dividing each side of the Hegelian equation (subject and object) one from the other, but also the enormous hegemony the latter wields over the former. In Foucault's view, as in Nietzsche's before him, Hegel dissolved everything most oppressive and difficult about culture and history into an abstraction, which he then called, with great philosophical audacity, "experience." For the Hegelian theme of the implicit origin of thought and history, Foucault substituted the theme of present beginnings, rough transformations in the present. For the theme of history as knowledge progressively elaborating itself toward truth, he substituted an archaeology of the will to truth. For the theme of the dialectic of history, marvelously bridging past and future, self and other, things and words—"the force," as Dylan Thomas once put it in an exquisitely Hegelian poem, "that through the green fuse drives the flower"—Foucault substituted the analysis of discourse: a stubborn and menacing presence straddling human actuality, a reality governed by its own materiality, discontinuity, and chance.

Whence this devastatingly bleak picture of human reality? For Foucault, as for a number of other writers who came of intellectual age during and just after the dark period of World War II, the tragedies that fascism and the moral failure of communism represented seemed to shatter any hope that the integrity of the human subject could withstand the withering domination of social structures. "I have very early memories," Foucault remarked in a 1981 interview in *Time* magazine, "of an absolutely threatening world, which could crush us. To have lived as an adolescent in a situation that had to end, that had to lead to another world, for better or for worse, was to have the impression of spending one's entire childhood in the night, waiting for dawn. That prospect of another world marked the people of my generation, and we have carried with us, perhaps to excess, a dream of Apocalypse."

Foucault's thought was formed in direct opposition to the (frail) social and epistemological optimism of his teachers, which he took—in whatever form it came, whether it was Marxism, Hegel, phenomenology, hermeneutics, or science—to be a species of wishful thinking with pernicious consequences. Foucault dabbled briefly in French Communism, then left the party in 1951, even more certain that the philosophical and political movements of the day were built on sand. He had come by the early 1950's radically to doubt that subjects of knowledge could ever generate adequate structures of thought and thus confirm truth as the universal ideal of knowledge, as well as the idea that the subjects of history could sooner or later overthrow the objective structures of society and thus confirm freedom as the normative condition of society. The Hegelian tradition in which Foucault was raised had purported to establish salutary continuities between the subjects of language and language itself, between language and the reality it supposedly represents, and between the subjective desires of individuals and the objective structures of society. These traditions, in Foucault's view, not only mask the oppressive hold culture maintains over individuals but also tighten it. If for Hegel the image of the activity of man in society was the difficult but organic growth of an oak tree, for Foucault it became that of man in prison.

## THE MADNESS OF REASON

From the new waves of phenomenology and existentialism, through Hyppolite's Hegel, down to Sartre's gigantic philosophical and biographical labors, the immediate postwar period saw a renewed epistemological exaltation of the experience and figure of man. In Foucault's view this whole tendency combined philosophical naïveté with a deluded political optimism in the ability of human beings to master and direct their fates. In this respect, his work was part of a general intellectual movement in French and European culture, known in its first waves during the 1950's and 1960's as structuralism and in its more exacerbated and self-conscious phases thereafter as poststructuralism, which saw the structure, and not the subject of society and knowledge, as decisive. "The ultimate goal of the human sciences," the anthropologist Claude Lévi-Strauss wrote in *La pensée sauvage* (*The Savage Mind,* 1962), "is not to constitute man but to dissolve him."

A half-century before, Sigmund Freud had displaced the sovereignty of man's consciousness. Now the new French structuralists, such as the psychoanalyst Jacques Lacan—who with Foucault and Lévi-Strauss had studied with Jean Hyppolite and whose work was likewise in part a continual rethinking of Hegel's thought—were displacing consciousness once again, proclaiming not only that consciousness is structured by the unconscious but that the unconscious itself is structured like a language. Borrowing the insights of the Swiss linguist Ferdinand de Saussure, especially as they were elaborated in the work of Émile Benveniste and Roman Jakobson, structuralism was an attempt to formalize analysis of language and human culture without reference to the *cogito*—the thinking subject—and hence without the conceptual baggage that since before Descartes had gone with it: origins, identity, progress, purpose, and so on.

This emphasis on structure over subject, on language over thought, is what Perry Anderson has called the "exhorbitation of language" and Edward Said, "linguicity." It came to a zenith in the writings of Lévi-Strauss, Roland Barthes, Jacques Lacan, the Marxist philosopher Louis Althusser, Jacques Derrida, Foucault, and many others.

But while Foucault shared the structuralist interest in the way radically determining formations of knowledge and culture exist independently from the intentions of subjects, he did not, or did not for long, share what he saw as their tendency to build hypothetical structures into new absolutes, in the light of which the entire content of a particular area of human reality could be understood. Indeed, structuralism itself became, as Foucault's work progressed, one of the discursive objects he was most interested in analyzing and repudiating. He saw it as a symptom and discursive offshoot of the central phenomenon of contemporary thought, one of the "impossibilities" (and indeed hypocrisies) in which modern thought had become entangled: the imperative to rethink transcendence in relation to the reality of a finite world. In exalting—often in highly sophisticated and subtle forms—one aspect or another of human, and especially verbal, reality into a new absolute, the structuralists, in Foucault's view, tended to elide the specific reality and concrete effects of the phenomena they attempted to analyze. (Lévi-Strauss thus elevates structure into a new absolute; the philosopher Jacques Derrida elevated *écriture,* or writing; and so on.) The consequence of that elision, moreover, was almost invariably a tendency to overlook the specific functioning and discursive effects of power.

"When I think back now," Foucault remarked in a 1977 interview, "I ask myself what else it was that I was talking about, in *Madness and Civilization* or *The Birth of the Clinic* but power?" Yet the problems treated by Foucault's first two major works were not explicitly formulated in these terms—insofar as he lacked, in his own words, a "field of analyses at my disposal" capable of adequately treating the issue of power. Nevertheless, as Foucault stated in an interview published in *Power/Knowledge,* "When I was studying during the early 1950's, one of the great problems that arose was that of the political status of science and the ideological functions which it could serve."

It was above all the notorious Lysenko affair of the 1950's that broached the question of the relation between science and politics, knowledge and power. Trofim Denisovich Lysenko was a Soviet geneticist whose thoroughly discredited theory—that environmentally acquired characteristics could be passed on genetically—nevertheless became official party and Soviet state dogma in the late 1940's and early 1950's. The uproar over Lysenko led Foucault to question the relationship between science and knowledge, on the one hand, and politics and economics, on the other. The Lysenko affair posed a theoretical question concerning the way power dominates through "rationality" that was raised in a more practical way by the relationship between doctors and mental patients that Foucault was observing in psychiatric wards at the time. To ask such a question of a "hard" science like physics, Foucault speculated, would be impossibly difficult to answer; but

> couldn't the interweaving of effects of power and knowledge be grasped with greater certainty in the case of a science as "dubious" as psychiatry? It was this same question which I wanted to pose concerning medicine in *The Birth of the Clinic:* medicine certainly has a much more solid scientific armature than psychiatry, but it too is profoundly enmeshed in social structures.
>
> (*Power/Knowledge,* p. 109)

*Folie et déraison* was first published in 1961. This was followed in 1963 by a much shorter paper edition and, two years later, by an English translation, *Madness and Civilization,* based more or less on the shorter version. Given that less than half of the original text is available in English and that a number of crucial debates (notably that between Jacques Derrida and Foucault) have centered on untranslated portions of the book, one difficulty for American readers is that no complete translation of Foucault's classic first work exists in English.

Another difficulty is that it is not really a book about madness as such. Foucault did not set out to isolate a more or less definable fact—madness—and then chart its history over the course of a few hundred years. Indeed, the claim that such a history could be written implies belief in the sovereign powers of reason to classify, order, and accurately represent the world—and this possibility Foucault rejected. *Madness and Civilization* is not a record of the inner experience of madness but, rather, an attempt to understand the ways in which the discursive and extradiscursive institutions of Western culture have objectified and historically constructed something called "madness."

Indeed, as Foucault wrote, "We have yet to write the history of that other form of madness by which men, in an act of sovereign reason, confine their neighbors, and communicate and recognize each other through the merciless language of nonmadness." Implicit is Foucault's belief that what we call reason has no particular claim to reasonableness or rationality at all. Indeed, what separates reason from madness, Foucault insists, is not any intrinsic property of nonmadness the former may possess, but simply the nonrational and epistemologically indefensible division that Western society instituted between the two around the time of the Renaissance and still maintains. "Madness," as Michael Ignatieff has put it, is thus "not initially a fact, but a judgment—even if that judgment becomes itself a fact."

*Madness and Civilization* begins at the close of the Middle Ages with a consideration of the cultural phenomenon of leprosy. For most of the Middle Ages leprosy played a crucially ambiguous symbolic role in European culture. Driven out of cities and yet at the same time rigidly confined within spaces attached to them, lepers confronted medieval life with the reality of man's moral corruption and the inevitability of his death. Through affliction, the leper drew closer to God's truth: illness made him holy. In symbolic but also frankly concrete ways, lepers were thus located at the threshold of human reality, occupying a critical liminal position between this world and the other, life and death, sin and punishment, damnation and redemption—a position confirmed and maintained by the social ritual of exclusion.

At the end of the Middle Ages the incidence of leprosy dramatically declined in Europe, leaving behind it the physical structures of exclusion, now empty of their tragic human cargo. In the course of the next two centuries madness would come to replace leprosy as the ultimate "limit" experience in Renaissance culture; in Christian terms, madness offered an even more complete access than leprosy to the truth of man's fallen world, to its reality as corruption, death-in-life.

> The substitution of the theme of madness for that of death does not mark a break, but rather a torsion within the same anxiety. What is in question is still the nothingness of existence, but this nothingness is no longer considered an external, final term, both threat and conclusion; it is experienced from within as the continuous and constant form of existence.
>
> (p. 16)

Cast adrift in the Renaissance on ships of fools, madmen circulated, imaginatively and in fact, as that excluded but still communicating middle, an otherness "at the heart of things and of men."

Emerging in the fifteenth century as a differentiated experience—in reality, as the cultural experience of differentiation—madness became in the Renaissance a theme of ubiquitous, even obsessive, concern. Seized on by the cultural imagination, it was represented in two principal forms, one pictorial, the other literary. Both through painters (most notably Hieronymous Bosch, Albrecht Dürer, and Pieter Breughel the Elder) and through writers such as Shakespeare, the Renaissance continued to express a vertiginous sense of madness as a special form of access to that *other* world that founds (and also confounds) man's world.

But increasingly this theme circulated side by side with literary representations of a crucially different kind. This was the humanist image of madness as folly, vice, disorder, and excess—all the general forms of man's essential un-reason. It is here, in works such as Erasmus' *Moriae encomium* (*In Praise of Folly,* 1509), that Foucault detects a divergence of emphasis heralding a profound transformation in the way madness will thenceforth be represented and embodied in Western culture—a "great line of cleavage in the Western experience of madness."

The cleavage is this: Madness for Erasmus is part of the "critical consciousness of man," existing not as a negation of his reason (as it had in Shakespeare) but in a sense for it. Madness, for Erasmus, is the instrument of a rational rebuke to the excesses and abuses of reason—and thus is finally only an extension of the sovereignty of reason itself. This new characterization marks the beginning of a tactical appropriation of madness by reason, an appropriation that is really a refusal. Madness is no longer

> linked to the world and its subterranean forms, but rather to man, to his weaknesses, dreams and illusions. Whatever obscure cosmic manifestation there was in madness as seen by Bosch is wiped out in Erasmus; madness no longer lies in wait for mankind at the four corners of the earth; it insinuates itself within man, or rather it is a subtle rapport that man maintains with himself.
>
> (*Madness and Civilization,* p. 26)

Madness, in short, has now been aggressively subsumed within a humanistic tradition, "seized in the universe of discourse," and made the ironic knowledge of man himself. No longer connecting humanity to its profoundly other cosmic foundation through intimations of an invasive annihilating force, as in Bosch or Dürer, it is instead a way of confirming the identity of nonmadness. It is already half excluded from man's world by a sovereign reason.

Total exclusion follows. The next age, which

Foucault calls the Classical period, begins in the mid seventeenth century and stretches to the end of the eighteenth. Foucault identifies the onset of this period above all with the Great Confinement, when the Hôpital Générale was created by royal decree in Paris in 1656. All the mad were now rounded up and confined, more or less indiscriminately, with all the other socially and economically useless classes—the poor, the criminal, the diseased, the infirm—in hospitals, prisons, and madhouses. We can rightfully think of this period as the *ancien régime* of reason—that period, from the early seventeenth century to the French Revolution, when reason enjoyed absolute and undiluted sovereignty—as if (like kings) by divine right. The Hôpital Générale, a "structure proper to the monarchical and bourgeois order of France, contemporary with its organization in absolutist forms, soon extended its network over the whole of France." From being the intimate of reason, madness now became its radical other: a sort of pure absence that no longer held reason's truth, but simply defined a space absolutely outside the cool sovereignty of the cogito. We had entered the age of Descartes, the beginning of the Enlightenment, a period of clear and distinct reason without shadow. All that was unreason would now be secluded in the great hospitals, out of sight if not entirely out of mind.

It would remain there until the time of the French Revolution, when the hospitals and madhouses, symbolically and in fact, were thrown open and the mad allowed to walk abroad openly again. Simultaneously, madness was no longer grouped in the cultural mind with the dangers of crime and depravity, but was seen itself as the separate and distinct affliction of the madman himself. The third period, the modern age proper, had begun. Once again, as in the Renaissance, madness was in contact with nonmadness, but now as the object of a unilateral moral (and soon scientific) discourse that seeks to see in insanity the secret illness of an individual soul, substituting "for the free terror of madness the stifling anguish of responsibility." Visible once again, madness became the object of a medical, juridical, and proto-psychiatric gaze or examination that, in claiming tacit mastery over madness as its medical and normative opposite, ironically perpetuated and indeed accentuated the constraints of the Great Confinement, only now as a "gigantic moral imprisonment."

If the mad were derided and beaten during the Classical period, this new moral regime was to Foucault a worse form of torture, because it was subtler and more detailed. Madness was now no longer the truth of the world, telling man what he really is, as it was in the Renaissance, or a pure aberration to be shunned and ignored, as in the Classical period. Instead, madness had become a failing of the soul and soon would be a disease of the psyche, requiring detailed observation, diagnosis, treatment, and rehabilitation—along with the complete submission of the madman, now a "patient," to the paternal authority of the doctor. This would become the entire modern orthopedic regimen of the soul.

Yet as insanity was increasingly defined by and confined within a new medical discourse, the actual experience of madness itself became ever more mute. Indeed, "the language of psychiatry," as Foucault puts it—"a monologue of reason *about* madness"—is "established only on the basis of such a silence." Indeed, so silenced has madness become in our own period, according to Foucault, that the "sovereign language of unreason" is legible only in the infrequent "lightning flash" of the great mad writers like the Marquis de Sade and Nietzsche, and the mad painter van Gogh.

"Madness," in Foucault's history of its objectification by reason, goes through a series of abrupt changes in the course of its cultural manhandling. Part of Foucault's point in showing this is to demonstrate that the history of reason has nothing to do with the progressive march of science toward truth. But cutting across this tale of the irrational transformations of the discourse of reason on madness is, as Hubert L. Dreyfus and Paul Rabinow have noted, a "description of a rather more continuous story of confinement and exclusion." At the end of the Middle Ages, "madness" emerged as the object of a rigorous social division, a way of articulating the identity and thus consolidating the power of the social body. The Classical period and the Great Confinement continued in a more brutal and physical form this dynamic of objectification and consolidation, a process that has been extended even further in the modern period "if we are willing to admit," with Foucault, "that what was formerly a visible fortress of order has now become the castle of our conscience."

Discontinuous at the level of discursive forms and knowledge, however, history is rather more continuous in the progressive development of forms of power that, from the Middle Ages down to our own time, have shown an insidious increase in subtlety and control. These two apparently contrasting historical developments—continually increasing power and abrupt changes in knowledge—are in fact two aspects of the same phenomenon: the increasing differentiation of madness, and its final separation from all other forms of "unreason" only in the modern age. Moreover, in binding the madman to an increasingly normative idea of a human soul or psyche, psychology, psychiatry, and medicine exert an ultimately much more binding kind of control on the mad than ever before. This control is part of what Foucault later described in his study of penal practices as the disciplinary regime of the body—the body made prisoner of the soul. Thus the "humanitarian" improvements in the treatment of the insane that came with the nineteenth century represent to Foucault a dubious achievement at best.

*Madness and Civilization* sought to demonstrate, as Foucault would later put it in "Nietzsche, la généalogie, l'histoire" ("Nietzsche, Genealogy, History," 1971), that "what is found at the historical beginning of things is not the inviolable identity of their origin; it is the dissension of other things. It is disparity." History does not uncover identities and then trace them as they develop continuously through time. It finds arenas of discrepancy, places where what seems to be the "identity" of something (reason, for example) is shown in fact to be contingently constituted in the conflict and dissension of different things rather than in the stability of an underlying essence.

Yet Foucault does essentialize one element in his book, if only negatively, and that is madness itself; and here we touch upon the central methodological contradiction of his first work. It is true that his refusal to talk about madness as an experience allows him to trace the history of its cultural objectification without perpetuating the repression that culture's "rational" discourses on madness have only served to augment. Yet if studying culture's way of representing madness allows him to devalue reason, Foucault confers upon madness itself a transcendental value. Madness—not what reason constructs, but the experience itself—hovers on the margins of his book, a transcendental force very like an absolute identity and origin. It is as if Foucault secretly believed in the foundational forces (albeit in the devastating and ironic form that madness brings) his book otherwise explicitly denies. This backhanded methodological reinsertion of cosmic forces is discernible in the apocalyptic potential he thinks madness might soon unleash in the modern world: "Madness has become man's possibility of abolishing both man and the world."

Many of Foucault's early essays betray this tension between an explicit denial of transcendental foundation and something like a dream of its possible reappearance—if only in the annihilating forms of madness and death. Foucault would soon move away from this somewhat incongruous desire to communicate with a force or being that founds history. Yet the powerful desire for an absolute of some kind, even the absolute of death, remains palpable in all his work.

In his next work, *The Birth of the Clinic,* Foucault once again focused on a major transformation. As Michael Clark writes, "Having displaced the notion of an object of knowledge in *Folie et déraison* [*Madness and Civilization*], Foucault turned to the role of the subject in *La naissance de la clinique* [*The Birth of the Clinic*]. There he showed that the function of the doctor—that is, the "knower" of medical knowledge—was just as variable and contingent upon specific conditions of a particular society as is the subject of knowledge." And once again the transformation that served as Foucault's subject took place in the late eighteenth and early nineteenth century; "one of those periods," as Foucault wrote in *The Birth of the Clinic,* "that mark an ineradicable chronological threshold: the period in which illness, counter-nature, death, in short, the whole dark underside of disease came to light, at the same time illuminating and eliminating itself like night, in the deep, visible, solid, enclosed space of the human body."

The interplay of illumination and elimination in Foucault's formulation is crucial. For the distinctive feature of the emerging mode of medical discourse will be the way it disclaims its reality as discourse in the very gesture of opening up a new domain of knowledge. This will be a recurrent theme of Foucault's analysis of knowledge in the modern period: its tendency to disguise the relevant historical and epistemological contingencies that make it possible.

According to Foucault, before the end of the eighteenth century medical knowledge was based upon the authority of a kind of ideal truth. That is, its authority rested on an encyclopedic corpus of knowledge contained and codified in tables and books, a knowledge "prior to and separate from the perception of symptoms." With the work of the anatomist and physiologist Xavier Bichat and others, however, medicine suddenly began to base its authority on the visible, finite volume of the body itself, on the etiology and trajectory of the observable symptom. This transformation is of the profoundest importance to Foucault, for with it man becomes defined in relation to his own finitude, not in relation to any transcendent powers. Indeed, in defining the individual as a medical object in relation to his finite body, medicine began, according to Foucault, to constitute man himself, as we now know and think of him: that unique entity and complex being who is at once the subject and the object of his own thought. This is something that Foucault would continue to explore, in relation not just to medicine but to all the sciences of man, which together would comprise the topic of his next major book, *The Order of Things.* Only when the knowledge of those phenomena we now think of as pertaining most intimately to man—his physical body, his social body, and language, the body of his thought—began to be defined not in relation to a transcendent, transhistorical order but in relation to the stubborn and recalcitrant order of his concrete historical existence—only then did the figure of man as we know him really emerge:

> The possibility for the individual of being both subject and object of his own knowledge implies an inversion in the structure of finitude. For Classical [i.e., eighteenth century] thought, finitude had no other content than the negation of the infinite, while the thought that was formed at the end of the eighteenth century gave it the powers of the positive: the anthropological structure that then appeared played both the critical role of limit and the founding role of origin. It was this reversal that served as the philosophical condition for the organization of a positive medicine; inversely, this positive medicine marked, at the empirical level, the beginning of that fundamental relation that binds modern man to his original finitude. Hence the fundamental place of medicine in the over-all architecture of the human sciences: it is closer than any of them to the anthropological structure that sustains them all.
>
> (*The Birth of the Clinic,* pp. 197–198)

At the concrete level of discourse, this transformation involved a fundamental change, indeed a reversal, in the relation between words and things, the speakable and the visible—that is, between the transcendental and the finite—as these are held together in discourse.

Knowledge and the word no longer precede the concrete embodiment of a symptom: they now proceed from it. "What has changed," Foucault writes, is nothing less than "the silent configuration in which language finds support: the relation of situation and attitude to what is speaking and what is spoken about":

> At the beginning of the nineteenth century, doctors described what for centuries had remained below the threshold of the visible and the expressible, but this did not mean that, after over-indulging in speculation, they had begun to perceive once again, or that they listened to reason rather than imagination; it meant that the relation between the visible and the invisible—which is necessary to all concrete knowledge—changed its structure, revealing through gaze and language what had previously been below and beyond their domain. A new alliance was forged between words and things, enabling one *to see* and *to say.*
>
> (*The Birth of the Clinic,* p. xii)

Since this alliance is, according to Foucault, prerational, the transformation in medical perception it represents cannot be described as scientific progress. Rather, it is a radical, subrational translocation of what counts for truth in medicine from language to vision, from speaking to seeing, from the mouth to the eye.

But what really distinguishes the modern order of medical discourse—this is the chief effect of the new alliance of words and things—is the disappearance of discourse itself, its seeming demotion in ontological and epistemological status in favor of a new scheme of visibility, overseen by the doctor's supposedly "neutral regard": the medical gaze. Things are no longer subordinate to a language that seems to express their essence; rather, they stand out with a new and dense quiddity, or thingness, of their own. In substituting for the mere word of an ideal discourse the tangible proof of an empirical science, medicine—"the first scientific discourse concerning the individual"—seemed to displace the arbitrary and deluded pronouncements of a merely discursive knowledge with the transparent techniques of a true one.

But in fact, Foucault argues, discourse did not actually vanish at the end of the eighteenth century: it simply became invisible. Sometime around the French Revolution, discourse seemed to lose authority; knowledge apparently fell out of direct contact with power; discourse, no longer the sovereign instrument of man's kingly reason, appeared to become meekly subordinate to the empirical, demonstrably visible, and seemingly incontrovertible world of facts and things. But what actually happened was that discourse, disguised now in the neutrally veridical language of the human sciences, increased the specificity and the concrete mobility of its grasp on individuals. Invisible but just as real and arbitrary as ever, the discourses of man's finitude augmented the tactical and political hold that knowledge and the social institutions that accompany them exert over individuals, even as it removes the authority over knowledge from them, all in the name of a will to truth. What begins to emerge in Foucault's histories of modern culture, then—and this will be even more explicit in later works such as *The Order of Things* and *Surveiller et punir* (*Discipline and Punish,* 1975)—is a picture of the coercive duplicity of discursive power.

"Foucault's greatest intellectual contribution," Edward Said has written in "Criticism Between System and Culture," "is to an understanding of how the will to exercise dominant control in society and history has also discovered a way to clothe, disguise, rarefy, and wrap itself systematically in the language of truth, discipline, rationality, utilitarian value, and knowledge." What distinguishes modern discourse is the intrinsic distinction it both masks and maintains between what language seems to be and what it is. And what it is, moreover, does not involve something deeper about discourse, but something right on the surface: the disguise is part of the surface effect of discourse itself. Indeed, our attempt to read a deeper reality into discourse, one of the cognitive illusions to which discourse invites us to succumb, is part of the political containment that discourse imposes on us. Thus, for example, while we may believe it is ourselves whose voice is expressed in discourse or that there is an objective reality represented by it, the real truth is that discourse is tying us to positions it, and only it, has sanctioned or made possible for "subject" and "object" positions. The truth of discourse, in short, is not its fidelity as a representation but its reality as event. And since this is true of the discourse that describes as much as of the discourse that is described, in attempting to describe discourse as an event, Foucault's own work is necessarily intended to be not only epistemologically corrective—that is, to show us what the world really is—but politically insurrectionary insofar as it seeks to change the world.

In charting the course of culture's construction, first of madness as an object of knowledge and then of medical perception as a subject of knowledge, Foucault defined three broad periods separated by two abrupt transformations, one in the mid seventeenth century, the other at the end of the eighteenth and beginning of the nineteenth centuries. With some variations, this chronological structure organizes all of his historical works. The crucial event in this periodization, around which virtually all his later works turn, is the latter transformation: an epistemological, discursive, and social upheaval of overwhelming importance to Foucault's entire view of culture, with consequences for everything from psychology and medicine to the human sciences that study man's physical body, his social body, and language; the body of his thought (the central discourses analyzed in *The Order of Things*); from the methodology of history and the history of ideas (*The Archaeology of Knowledge*) to the nature of the law and penal practices (*Discipline and Punish*) and to sexuality (*Histoire de la sexualité* [*The History of Sexuality*, 1976–1985]).

What Foucault charts, and what the late eighteenth century above all seems to represent, is the secularization of cultural power and the fundamental change in the way authority inheres in discourse. Foucault invites us to think of this as a shift in the provenance and embodiment of power and authority from the subjective being of God in the Renaissance (the heyday, as it were, of infinity) to the objective structures of discourse in the nineteenth century (the heyday of the finite), via the transcendent reign of an infinite and sovereign reason during the Classical period. According to this scheme, power flowed from God in the Renaissance; then became internalized in man's reason in the Classical period; and finally, in the late eighteenth century—when, as Foucault writes in *The Order of Things*, "being has fallen outside representation"—fell outside subjective grasp. Looked at in this way, Foucault's work is a tale of diminishing authority: God, king, man, will. But the diminution of authority is on the subjective side of history, as it were: objectively what we see is a steady increase in the efficiency of power. Thus, with a decrease in the subjective basis or transcendent authority of power comes an increase in its secular and objective efficiency.

What Foucault invites us to see, under the duplicity of human cultural history, is a relentless transaction, the historical transfer of power from the subject to the object of history, from word to thing, a transfer that enhances the range and effectiveness of power even as it places it outside the compass of subjective intentions and human institutions. This transaction takes place in a special element that is not quite subject and not quite object, neither word precisely nor thing. It is this element that Foucault calls discourse.

In December 1970 Foucault gave his inaugural lecture to the Collège de France, *L'Ordre du discours* (*The Discourse on Language*, also translated as "The Order of Discourse"). Here, at what turned out to be the exact midpoint of his career, he looked back over his previous work, summarizing the theoretical and historical positions he accepted and rejected and laying out a program of work to come. The lecture, more than a summary and plan of work, was a brilliant verbal performance in which Foucault dramatized the encounter of past and present as it is embodied in the intellectual, discursive, social, and institutional circumstances of his own career. These included the rhetorical and personal circumstances in which Foucault, onetime enfant terrible, found himself addressing the distinguished institutional body to which he had recently been elevated. I would like to consider the historical perspective that Foucault vehemently rejected in some detail and then turn, using *The Discourse on Language* as a main reference, to the nature of discourse and the historical encounter of present and past as Foucault understands it. I will then turn briefly to three works—*The Order of Things, Discipline and Punish,* and *The History of Sexuality*—in which Foucault gave his most sustained historical account of the three great axes of this encounter, always separate but always intertwined: discourse, power, and subjectivity.

## *COMMENTARY*

> Must we admit that the time of discourse is not the time of consciousness extrapolated to the dimension of history, or the time of history present in the form of consciousness? Must I suppose that in my discourse I can have no survival? And that in speaking I am not banishing my death, but actually establishing it; or rather that I am abolishing all interiority in that exterior that is so indifferent to my life, and so *neutral,* that it makes no distinction between my life and my death?
>
> (*The Archaeology of Knowledge,* p. 210)

In *The Archaeology of Knowledge,* Foucault essayed a theoretical exploration of the methods of analysis used and implied by his previous works. In it, he laid out a protocol of study, "archaeology," free from all "transcendental narcissism": that is, a method of historical description that does not attribute quasi-divine powers to the thinking, performing subject as the putative origin and cause of thought and action. Since the themes of historical causality, continuity, progress, and identity depend upon the myth of man as the sovereign author of his consciousness, this rejection of transcendence opens up research to previously hidden historical discontinuities and differences in discourse and thought that can now be seized in all their specificity and concrete detail. It also allows one to describe the nonrational, historically specific conditions of possibility that govern the arrangements and the order of knowledge and language as material human practices: conditions of possibility that are not the origin of those practices, but their present material basis.

Cultures tend to resist interpreting their mental and linguistic habits as concrete material practices. In fact, Foucault says, societies tend to think of language as almost anything but what it really is. "Each culture," he wrote in his 1967 essay "Nietzsche, Marx, Freud," "has had its own system of interpretation, its techniques, its methods, its own manner of suspecting that language means something other than what it says, and of suspecting that there is language elsewhere than *in* language." These two suspicions, that there is a being underneath language that *gets into it* and that the beings of the world *speak,* imply each other and imply something else: a distinctly Christian view, which is also a hope, that word and thing are intimately bound together by some authoritative force that makes it reasonable to read from one to the other, from words to things and back. Foucault lumped all such methods of interpretation under the rubric *commentary.*

It is Foucault's feeling that the *something other* of which language allegedly speaks, that quality of things which makes them seem to speak or mean things, are beliefs more properly associated with the discourse of another age. In any case, they represent ways of connecting words and things, past and present, other and self, no longer viable in our own time. Commentary in the Renaissance, Foucault writes in *The Order of Things,* was a way of reading God's underlying being in the surface prose of the world: in the resemblances things maintained with each other and with words was legible a deep self-sameness, God. Since the nineteenth century, however, Western man has found himself rather too distant from such a transcendent being, and rather too close to his own finitude, to make commentary anything but a piece of abandoned cultural baggage—something Foucault rather urgently wishes to dump.

And yet interpretations of discourse (and by implication interpretations of the interaction between human presence and the cultural past) have, according to Foucault, for over 150 years remained anachronistically governed by the habits of commentary. In *The Birth of the Clinic,* Foucault provided a graphic analysis of the way commentary posits an ideal origin to words and language. The interpretive protocol of commentary, according to Foucault, "questions discourse as to what it says and intended to say; it tries to uncover that deeper meaning of speech that enables it to achieve an identity with itself, supposedly nearer to its essential truth; in other words, in stating what has been said, commentary has to state what has never been said."

Commentary garrulously struggles to raise the silent but rich semantic potentiality latent in another text to the brilliant surface of its own language. Commentary is thus simultaneously more archaic and more contemporary than what it comments upon. It is more archaic because it realizes or releases more completely and explicitly deep meanings only latent in the primary text (commentary, that is, becomes more like the original text than the original text itself). At the same time it is more contemporary because the very meaning of this development is that the potentiality of a text or the past comes to fruition only by progressively and continuously being unfolded into the present. As Foucault says in *The Discourse on Language,* commentary "must—and the paradox is ever-changing yet inescapable—say, for the first time, what has already been said, and repeat tirelessly what was, nevertheless, never said."

Commentary thus seems to be both less and more than the original text it translates. By the same token, the notion of history it implies suggests that the present is both less and more than the past that underwrites it, and that the continuity between them is sustained in this dialectical tension. Crucially, however, whether less or more, the present or the secondary text in this scheme of things is necessarily dominated by the past, which is conceived along the lines of a primary text from which it takes its definition. For "commentary's only role is to say *finally,* what has silently been articulated deep down." We can test this assertion by pointing out that when a commentary is *less* than an original, this is because it is conceived as being derived from it, while when it is *more* than the original, it is because it has repeated its essence.

"To comment is to admit by definition the excess of the signified [that is, what a word refers to, here a primary text] over the signifier [the word itself, here the commenting, secondary text]." This excess is

> a necessary, unformulable remainder of thought that language has left in the shade—a remainder that is the very essence of that thought, driven outside its secret—but to comment also presupposes that this unspoken element slumbers within speech [*parole*] and that, by a superabundance proper to the signifier, one may, in questioning it, give voice to a content that was not explicitly signified.
>
> (*The Birth of the Clinic,* p. xvi)

Commentary for Foucault ignores the surface reality of language and writing in favor of a mythical, semioccult entity alleged to have originated speech and a semioccult one said to interpret it. As a mode of interpretation, this implies a whole system of beliefs concerning the way authority underlies and inhabits human history, subjectivity, and discourse. In the first place, the authority that validates commentary always resides in a "supposed space": commentary always invokes a hypothetical origin or essence that cannot be demonstrated. The signified or origin, silent and "supposed," finds expression only in the verbose excess of signifier or commentary—which contains its own supposed latency waiting to be construed by another commentary into explicit verbality.

"Commentary," says Foucault, conceals "a strange attitude toward language"—and, we might add, history. To see language as the commentary of one text on an original, the new signifier giving voice to a signified, is to ignore the tangible reality of words, to compel attention away from discourse toward a supposed drama taking place just before language and just after it, a drama in which creative subjects allegedly originate and attempt to recuperate meanings. Commentary inserts a distance, however slight, between the phenomenon under consideration—discourse—and what is thought to cause it. This distance renews, in Foucault's view, the entire false theme of transcendence. A whole series of continuities emerges from this arrangement that would otherwise have none: between an author and a text, between one text and another, between the past and the present—a whole fabricated web of genetic origins and semantic relations.

What does all this accomplish in Foucault's view? Insofar as it suppresses all that is singular, random, unrepeatable, and new, commentary brings about the discursive domination of chance. Everything different about the present, anything various and new, all the "open multiplicity, the fortuitousness" of discourse, is ignored and read back into the primary text and made to repeat the presence of its past. "Commentary averts the chance element of discourse by giving it its due: it gives us the opportunity to say something other than the text itself, but on the condition that it is the text itself which is uttered and, in some ways, finalized." The point of commentary is to prevent the present from being different from the past, which is what it above all is. Commentary is thus the normative or normalizing agency in textual and historical interpretation.

"Is it inevitable," Foucault asks, "that we should know of no other function for speech [*parole*] than that of commentary?":

> To speak about the thought of others, to try to say what they have said has, by tradition, been to analyse the signified. But must things said, elsewhere and by others, be treated exclusively in accordance with the play of signifier and signified, as a series of themes present more or less implicitly to one another? Is it not possible to make a structural analysis of discourses that would evade the fate of commentary *by supposing no remainder, nothing in excess of what has been said, but only the fact of its historical appearance*?
>
> (*The Birth of the Clinic*, p. xvii)

Foucault wants to examine things that are said, as Edward Said has put it, "as they happen before him," without reference to any depth they may sustain. Like Nietzsche's, Foucault's work will be a "critique of ideal depths, of the depth of conscience, which [Nietzsche] denounced as an invention of philosophers." Transcendental notions like origin, truth, and subject, and activities like commentary that invoke them, are precisely what hold the reality of discourse at a distance. All of these things are part of a whole ensemble of procedures every society, Foucault thinks, exploits to avoid the scandalously material, different, and random substance that is discourse.

Situating the order and force of language at once too far above and too far below the actual existence and performance of words themselves, commentary thus involves an "elision of the events produced" in discursive practices; the "invention of voices behind texts to avoid having to analyse the modes of implication of the subject in discourse; [and] the assigning of the originary as said and unsaid in the text to avoid replacing discursive practices in the field of transformations where they are carried out." Foucault's rejection of commentary, then, is a way of addressing more directly the severe reality of discursive and cultural events, along with the transformed nature of human authority within them. Indeed, for Foucault we can grasp the common concrete and historical relations holding discursive and extradiscursive institutions together only if we abandon the belief, which commentary upholds, that discourse is the product of subjects accurately describing an objective world.

Commentary, we can see, is thus the textual protocol of Hegelianism. Under the guise of finding the present in the past, of seeing the present representing the past, it subdues the surface differences of the present by redefining them as repetitions of the deep interiority of the past. Commentary thus tends to homogenize the space of a text (or of history) into the uniform expression of sameness. This, to Foucault, is a form of conceptual totalitarianism.

Commentary, Foucault thinks, is just one of a whole set of procedures and rules according to which the production of discourse in society is policed so as to avert everything risky, different, and scandalously physical about it. In *The Discourse on Language,* Foucault anatomizes these procedures as society deploys them to keep the dangers of discourse at bay. In one of the turnabouts characteristic of Foucault's thought, of course, these procedures are themselves a heightened form of what they attempt to dissipate; that is, the rules governing discourse are no less arbitrary, specific, and physical than the qualities of chance, discontinuity, and materiality they attempt to dispel.

## *ARCHAEOLOGY*

The order of discourse arises, for Foucault, not according to the creativity or ingenuity of discoursers, or to the unfolding of a science bent on grasping reality and marching toward truth, but according to what he calls the historical a priori governing discourse. These a priori are conditions specific to the existence of any verbal act. They govern in a positive way what an utterance is and can be as a discursive object and event. Discourse is a web of relations, concrete and transpersonal, holding around and between words and things, subjects and objects, with a specific density and being of its own. Foucault is at pains to distinguish this substance from anything yielding transcendence:

> Instead of seeing, on the great mythical book of history, lines of words that translate in visible characters thoughts that were formed in some other time and place, we have in the density of discursive practices, systems that establish statements as events (with their own conditions and domain of appearance) and things (with their own possibility and field of use). They are all these systems of statements (whether events or things) that I propose to call *archive.*
>
> (*The Archaeology of Knowledge,* p. 128)

In *The Order of Things* Foucault calls all this the positive unconscious of knowledge, the specific organization of which in a given period is an *episteme.* Whether as positive unconscious, episteme, or archive, this a priori does not "elude historicity: it does not constitute, above events, and in an unmoving heaven, an atemporal structure; it is defined as the group of rules that characterise a discursive practice: but these rules are not imposed from the outside on the elements that they relate together; they are caught up in the very things that they connect."

The order of discourse is immanent in the material practice and events that embody discourse itself. Discourse takes shape in practice, and in relation, not to an anterior and interior authority that engenders it, but to the exterior shape of the discursive environment with which it interacts and in which it is immersed. For this reason

> archaeology tries to define not the thoughts, representations, images, themes, preoccupations that are concealed or revealed in discourses; but

> those discourses themselves, those discourses as practices obeying certain rules. It does not treat discourse as *document,* as a sign of something else, as an element that ought to be transparent, but whose unfortunate opacity must often be pierced if one is to reach at last the depth of the essential in the place in which it is held in reserve; it is concerned with discourse in its own volume, as a *monument.* It is not an interpretative discipline: it does not seek another, better-hidden discourse. . . . It is nothing more than a rewriting: that is, in the preserved form of [discourse's] exteriority, a regulated transformation of what has already been written. It is not a return to the innermost secret of the origin; it is the systematic description of a discourse-object.
>
> (*The Archaeology of Knowledge,* pp. 138–140)

As the very name implies, archaeology "is an attempt to define a particular site by the exteriority of its vicinity." The effect of commentary is to produce a false materialization of something that isn't there, while at the same time rendering invisible something that is. Put simply, Foucault's method is to reverse this: to make what isn't there go away and make what is there more apparent. The something that isn't there is an underlying cause, a being, an origin, a creative force. The something that is there is discourse. On its own terms, commentary finds unities under discourse. Viewed as a discursive practice, commentary is a procedure that imposes unities on language.

Seen archaeologically, the difference commentary maintains between a primary text and a secondary text is not proof of the fund of meaning the former has to endow the latter. It is a surface phenomenon, part of the discursive function of commentary that, as such, "plays two interdependent roles." On the one hand, "it permits us to create new discourses ad infinitum"; on the other, it controls the multiplicity of these inventions by subduing them to the primacy of the original text. Of course an original text is always a highly relative thing with no intrinsic claim to superiority. But historically contingent though it is, the "original" still performs a critical function. This is what Foucault calls the rarefaction it imposes upon discourse: literally, the way the profusion of differences discourse invariably contains are restricted to a drastically limited set of themes by a limited set of functions that together work to tame differences.

Rarefaction is a key notion for Foucault, and it describes an activity or principle of which not only commentary but also the author is an aspect. The author, as an ensemble of discursive themes carried along by a text rather than the hypothetical origin of it, is a "unifying principle in a particular group of writings or statements, lying at the origins of their significance, as the seat of their coherence." Seen from the point of view of discourse, "the author is he who implants, into the troublesome language of fiction, its unities, its coherence, its links with reality." Foucault's point is that while every verbal act is performed by someone ("it would be ridiculous to deny the existence of individuals who write, and invent"), this function of providing coherence and a link with a creative external reality is not something that all verbal performances have or need. Laundry lists, technical prescriptions, and mundane remarks quickly forgotten: such things may have been written or spoken by someone, but they don't have an author, in Foucault's view. The attribution of identity and coherence to one or a set of verbal performances is something controlled by the cultural system of discourse in which the particular utterance in question takes place.

Foucault's point is that there is a difference between what the individual who writes a text is and what that text's author is: the identity of the latter cannot be reduced to the former. The "author-function" is "not formed spontaneously through the simple attribution of a discourse to an individual; it results from a complex operation whose purpose is to construct the rational entity we call an author." And far from implying the potent individuality of one individual, the author-function "gives rise . . . to a series of subjective positions that individuals of any class may come to occupy."

Nor is the author-function a "universal or constant in all discourse"; rather, it varies according to the period and the form of discourse concerned. In our own day, scientific discourse has almost become anonymous, authorless. This would have been unthinkable, Foucault points out, in the Middle Ages, when the identity of the promulgator of a scientific discourse was the chief source of its authority.

"Commentary limited the hazards of discourse through the action of an *identity* taking the form of *repetition* and *sameness.* The author principle limits this same chance element through the action of an *identity* whose form is that of *individuality* and the *I.*" According to Foucault, a third form of limitation is the field of research, the discipline. In certain respects, the discipline functions somewhat differently from the way commentary and author function, which are ways of reducing the voluminous detail of verbal performances to unities underlying them. By contrast, "for a discipline to exist there must be the possibility of formulating—and of doing so ad infinitum—fresh propositions."

"But there is more," Foucault says, "in order that there may be less. A discipline is not the sum total of all the truths that may be uttered concerning something." This is not just because any discipline rejects erroneous statements, but because historically specific and fluctuating rules—governing what counts as a valid object of knowledge, what counts as a valid perception, what kind of causal explanation can validly be invoked in a particular field like botany or medicine or literary criticism—stand guard over what can be counted as a proposition at any given field at any given time.

Foucault does not mean that truths do not exist nor that the propositions of intellect are completely chimerical. Indeed, counter to positions frequently ascribed to him, he does believe that at some level there is something like transhistorical truth. "It is always possible," he says, that "one could speak the truth in a void," as the geneticist Gregor Mendel did, enunciating truths of genetics long before the historical circumstances were such as to allow his propositions to be incorporated into biological discourse. But this is precisely Foucault's point: abstractly true or not, a statement is, as he phrases it, *dans le vrai* (*in* the truth) only "if one [obeys] the rules of some discursive 'policy' which . . . have to be reactivated every time one [speaks]." "In short, a proposition must fulfil [*sic*] . . . onerous and complex conditions before it can be admitted within a discipline; before it can be pronounced . . . 'within the true.'"

Discipline, commentary, author: these function in various ways to reduce the element of chance in discourse. They constitute internal rules or operations carried out within discourse and concern its "principles of classification, ordering and distribution." A second rather different set of procedures is what Foucault calls rules of exclusion. These rules operate on the exterior of discourse, patrolling the relation between discourse and nondiscourse and working to modulate the power of discourse. Foucault identifies three basic kinds of exclusion. First are prohibitions. These are rules governing what can be said, where things can be said, and who can say them. In our own society, politics and sexuality are the main areas where prohibitions operate.

A second kind of exclusion involves a principle of division. This is the procedure that divides madness from reason and that, as we saw in *Madness and Civilization,* has no fundamentally rational basis. Rationality is the consequence rather than the origin of this primary division.

A third rule of exclusion opposes truth to falsehood, and here, Foucault acknowledges, the terrain is somewhat more slippery. "As a proposition," he admits, the "division between true and false is neither arbitrary, nor modifiable, nor violent," the way prohibitions and the rejection of madness are. Yet the will to truth, which Foucault calls the "master discourse" in our society, is always based upon specific and historically constituted divisions. To support this contention Foucault cites the way true discourse in ancient Greece underwent a mutation between the sixth and fifth centuries, when suddenly the truth of a statement was no longer identified with the power of its enunciator but with what it said. Both the subject and the object of truth have their abstract claims to truth, but Foucault's point is that historically one was accorded more authority at one time than at the other.

And this is not all, for in addition the will to truth always "relies on institutional support: it is reinforced and accompanied by whole strata of practices such as pedagogy . . . the book-system, publishing, libraries," and so on, and these, too, fluctuate historically. And again, truth always has a specific political affiliation. Foucault cites somewhat whimsically, the Greek adage "that arithmetic should be taught in democracies, for it teaches relations of equality, but that geometry alone should be reserved for oligarchies, as it demonstrates the proportions within inequality."

But for Foucault the real point about the will to truth is the way it "tends to exercise a sort of pressure, a power of constraint upon other forms of discourse"—at least in our own society and in the last 150 years. Thus trends like realism or naturalism in literature; or the necessary reference, in fields such as economics, biology and philology, to demonstrable historical data; or the justification of the law and the penal code in relation to the propositions of medicine, psychiatry, sociology, psychology—all testify to the pressure the will to truth has exerted on discourse in the modern period. Much more powerful than the rules prohibiting words and dividing madness, the will to truth, Foucault believes, has invaded, and continues to invade, every discourse and facet of human reality, and "daily grows in strength, in depth and implacability." All the while, what makes this aspect of discourse so difficult to resist is the pretense it maintains that it is not discourse but truth. As Foucault writes in *The Discourse on Language,* "True discourse, liberated by the nature of its form from desire and power, is incapable of recognizing the will to truth which pervades it; and the will to truth, having imposed itself upon us for so long, is such that the truth it seeks to reveal cannot fail to mask it." Blinded by truth's self-evidence, we cannot see, Foucault says, "its vocation of exclusion."

Yet a third group of rules, in Foucault's view, serves to control discourse. These rules determine "the conditions under which it may be employed" and impose "a certain number of rules upon those individuals who employ it, thus denying access to everyone else. This amounts to a rarefaction among speaking subjects: none may enter into discourse on a specific subject unless he has satisfied certain conditions or if he is not, from the outset, qualified to do so." Like all the others, these forces or rules are historically and culturally specific, and can be divided into four distinct types: (1) rituals defining the qualifications required of the speaker; (2) corporate guild pressures that encourage speakers of discourse to affirm the exclusive identity of the discursive community; (3) doctrinal adherence, which "links individuals to certain types of utterance while consequently barring them from all others"; and (4) the great force exerted by the "social appropriation of discourse": the fact that speaking is always dependent upon (or heavily influenced by) considerations of educational, social, and class affiliation. As Foucault points out, these rules and pressures usually act in concert, not alone.

Acting with all of these specific discursive procedures are the great philosophical themes—of a founding subject, of originating experience, of universal mediation—that in Foucault's view effectively "conform to this activity of limitation and exclusion" by "denying the specific reality of discourse in general." These are the themes that reduce discourse to everything but what it is: philosophical habits that subdue discourse to the status of a sign always betokening something else. Together with the system of taboos, barriers, thresholds, and limits itemized above, these themes betray a "profound logophobia, a sort of dumb fear of these events, of this mass of spoken things, of everything that could possibly be violent, discontinuous, querulous, disordered even and perilous in it, of the incessant, disorderly buzzing of discourse itself."

"To abolish the sovereignty of the signifier" and thus "restore to discourse its character as an event," Foucault proposes four methodological imperatives. First, a principle of reversal:

> Where, according to tradition, we think we recognize the source of discourse, the principles behind its flourishing and continuity, in those factors which seem to play a positive role, such as the author, discipline, will to truth, we must rather recognize the negative activity of the cutting-out and rarefaction of discourse.
>
> (*The Discourse on Language,* p. 229)

An author, or anything else conceived as originating discourse, is not a potent source. Instead, the author-function designates sites in discourse where a particularly great number of limitations and exclusions are in effect—social, doctrinal, attributive, and so forth. Discourse prepares places for authors to occupy according to collective rules that, as Said has noted in *Beginnings,* "antedate the speaker's appearance and postdate his disappearance." Discourse, in other words, does not exist for the use of an author; an author exists for the use of discourse.

Second, a principle of discontinuity:

> The existence of systems of rarefaction does not imply that, over and beyond them lie great vistas of limitless discourse, continuous and silent, repressed and driven back by them, making it our task to abolish them and at last to restore it to speech. Whether talking in terms of speaking or thinking, we must not imagine some unsaid thing, or an unthought, floating about the world, interlacing with all its forms and events. Discourse must be treated as a discontinuous activity, its different manifestations sometimes coming together, but just as easily unaware of, or excluding each other.
>
> (p. 229)

Once we view discourse from the point of view of the archive, as a formation whose shape is a function of collective practice and not the invention of consciousness, the idea of order no longer entails seamlessness. Moreover, lacking the continuity of a creative source, it's not as if discourse is then itself an unbroken, anonymous field. Defined not by an author's "interiority" but "by the exteriority of its vicinity," the order of discourse is compatible with all the stops and starts and discontinuities of the site that forms it.

Third, a principle of specificity:

> The principle of *specificity* declares that a particular discourse cannot be resolved by a prior system of significations; that we should not imagine that the world presents us with a legible face, leaving us merely to decipher it; it does not work hand in glove with what we already know; there is no prediscursive fate disposing the word in our favor. We must conceive discourse as a violence that we do to things, or at all events, as a practice we impose upon them; it is in this practice that the events of discourse find the principle of their regularity.
>
> (p. 229)

Discourse is nothing but what it is: not representation, it is an event. As such its effect, its "meaning"—though by this point in Foucault's analysis the philosophical apparatus supporting such a notion is no longer intact—is indistinguishable from what it is as an event.

Finally, a principle of exteriority. This

> holds that we are not to burrow to the hidden core of discourse, to the heart of the thought or meaning manifested in it; instead, taking the discourse itself, its appearance and its regularity, that we should look for its external conditions of existence, for that which gives rise to the chance series of these events and fixes its limits.
>
> (p. 229)

Discourse is there for us to see and to face it if we will. It is really nothing but the outer face it confronts us with—in all its "particular, fearsome, and even devlish features."

Foucault's four principles collectively define not only a method of analysis but also the nature of what is being studied. Where themes of authorial power present discourse to us as a form of expression, reversal forces us to see discourse—our own and another's—not as an expression of something else but as event. Similarly, discontinuity forces us to see discourse in series, not as continuous foundation. Specificity forces us to see discourse as possessing regularities, not unities. And exteriority substitutes a discourse's conditions of existence for any notion of the creative force that invents or sustains it.

All four of these principles and attributes of discourse imply what Foucault calls a philosophy of the event, which he juxtaposes to all philosophies of representation. An event is the characteristic of something (be it a word, a thought, or a deed) in its way of happening. It is not the substance of a thing or a quality it possesses: it is not its body or some attribute of it. Yet it is supremely material: an event is a collision, an emergence, an act of violence. Neither corporeal like a body nor immaterial like an idea, an event partakes of what Foucault calls an incorporeal materialism, the paradox he employs to express the simultaneous evanescence, physicality, and singularity of an event. It is at the level of the event that the stuff of discourse and history has its greatest reality for Foucault, and whatever order language and action in a human world have for him emerge from events taking place at this level. Methodologically, the idea of the event, as Foucault says, is like an insidious wedge in all our dreams of a human order: a "tiny device permitting the introduction, into the very roots of thought, of notions of *chance, discontinuity,* and *materiality.*" Step by step, term by term, Foucault's notion of the discourse-event dismantles the Hegelian dream: history and meaning as necessarily progressing toward an ideal.

Rarity, discontinuity, specificity, exteriority: these are the tools of Foucault's escape from Hegel, for whom the corresponding trademarks of discourse and history were plenitude, continuity, generality, and interiority. Yet, as Foucault remarks, "truly to escape Hegel involves an exact appreciation of the price we have to pay to detach ourselves from him." To detach ourselves, Foucault knew, is to tear ourselves away from the ruses of representation that so dominate thought and history, and to do that is to discard all the habits by which identities, including our own, are maintained. It means that the confrontation we provoke with our past cannot be a question of defining the contents of our own identity, but a rather more difficult task: to define the exteriority of our own position in relation to that which it is not. This is what makes archaeology a much better metaphor than representation for understanding the way the present engages the past. "It is an attempt," as Foucault put it in *The Archaeology of Knowledge,* "to define a particular site by the exteriority of its vicinity; rather than trying to reduce others to silence, by claiming that what they say is worthless, I have tried to define this blank space from which I speak, and which is slowly taking shape in a discourse that I still feel to be so precarious and unsure."

## *DISCOURSE*

*Madness and Civilization* and *The Birth of the Clinic* earned Foucault a reputation for iconoclastic brilliance and extraordinary erudition in academic circles, but were restricted to a fairly limited audience. *The Order of Things* made him famous overnight. It sold three thousand copies in its first week, fifty thousand more in the months thereafter, and was quickly translated into every major European language. "As a cultural phenomenon," Michael Clark has said, "Foucault's popularity in the mid 1960's surpassed even that of Jean-Paul Sartre in the decades following World War II, and his stature in the academic community was formally confirmed in 1970 by his election to the Collège de France," the most distinguished academic body in France.

By then he had also published many shorter works on a wide range of authors, topics, and issues—all of which concerned, in one way or another, the themes of finitude and nontranscendence as these affected human knowledge, power, and subjectivity.

*The Order of Things* takes up this theme in relation to the history of man's knowledge of himself. In this massive work, Foucault painstakingly charts the history of the way words and things have been ordered in relation to each other from the Middle Ages through the modern era in the discourses that have had most to do with the knowledge of man. Two major upheavals in the cultural configuration of knowledge, two great discontinuities, one in the early seventeenth century and the other at the time of the French Revolution, divide the period into three distinct epochs—the Renaissance, the Classical period, and the modern era—each with its own structure or "episteme" governing the "the order of things" and the relation between words and things. The object of Foucault's analysis in each period is discourse, those concrete discursive practices through which, at any given period, words and things are held together in an epistemological substance of their own.

The episteme of an age is "the order on the basis of which we think." It is the historical a priori of knowledge during an age, the implicit concrete space of thought on the basis of which knowledge is possible. In some complex sense Foucault doesn't specify, these epistemes are the cause and effect of specific discursive configurations in a culture at a particular time, something like the "pure experience of order and its mode of being" at a specific point in time. A major part of Foucault's point is that these epistemes, which form the conditions of rationality of a culture, are stubbornly prerational; while they function as the basis of reason, they have no reason themselves. Thus changes from one episteme to another represent the abrupt supersedure of one empirical space of knowledge by another rather than any progression of knowledge. We may, Foucault clearly hopes, be on the verge of another cataclysmic epistemic transformation, when man as the object and subject of knowledge will disappear entirely.

The first period Foucault treats is the Renaissance. Up to the end of the sixteenth century, he argues, words and things shared a common mode of being: resemblance. Organized into one great "book of nature," the discursive order of things—the "prose of the world"—holds words and things together according to the vast system of resemblances and similarities they exhibit. Ultimately these resemblances are sustained by the presence of God's being, which underwrites everything. This episteme abruptly gives way in the early seventeenth century to an entirely different order of things in which resemblance plays no part. The density of words and things in the earlier period, along with the system of resemblances that made them significant, vanish. The implicit discursive order now governing the arrangement of words and things is that of representation: the bright order of things in the Classical episteme is guaranteed by the capacity things have to be precisely distinguished from each other and represented in a transparent language.

The center of Foucault's story, densely argued and extremely complex, is that man as we understand him—a hybrid who is partly the object of knowledge and partly the subject who knows—is a figure of relatively recent historical origin, arising from a radical shift in the relationship of words and things that took place at the end of the eighteenth century. During the Classical period, discourse had perfectly mapped things, superimposing language in the form of representation upon beings fully represented by it. In Foucault's words, "the fundamental task of Classical 'discourse' is *to ascribe a name to things, and in that name to name their being.*" Identical with the representational powers of thought, this transparent language perfectly ordered and represented the table of similarities and differences through which the true identity of things could be securely known. Yet while theoretically capable of perfectly representing the world of things, man himself is not one of the things reason represented during the Classical age. As long as he was fully identified with his sovereign power of reason, Foucault says, "man" as such was not really a possible subject of knowledge. Only when the sovereign power to reason and represent the world was entirely broken did man appear and the modern age begin.

When this occurs, around the time of the French Revolution, "the very being of that which is represented is now going to fall outside representation itself." Things as they now appear in discourse no longer offer themselves up to language with an orderliness susceptible to complete representation. They become denser, more opaque, heavy with being again, somewhat as in the Renaissance, but no longer sustained by any play of resemblances or by God. Indeed, beings no longer have *any* foundation, and existence is characterized by the irremedial differences between things. At the same time words lose their ability to represent, and language, acquiring a specific weight of its own, loses its transparency. Words and things no longer hold together; language only imperfectly and incompletely recovers a reality too dense and impenetrable to be exhaustively represented and known. Man now appears where representation and being, words and things, no longer meet; he is at once a stubbornly finite object of thought and a thinking subject no longer assured of its transcendent reason—a walking paradox Foucault calls an "empirico-transcendental doublet."

Most of *The Order of Things* is devoted to a detailed analysis of the discursive changes that took place at the end of the eighteenth century in the three disciplines or areas of study most intimately related to man: those which study life (in which man's physical body is objectified), wealth (in which man's social body is objectified), and language (in which the body of man's thought is objectified). In the Classical period, these studies existed as natural history, the analysis of wealth, and general grammar. What these discourses studied were all ideally orderable entities, theoretically susceptible to perfect representation by thought. At the end of the eighteenth century, these disciplines were abruptly transformed (without progress) into the modern disciplines of biology, economics, and philology. Each of the new disciplines, which have more in common with each other than they do with the disciplines they supplant, now redefines its object in relation to the dense, specific, and mysteriously finite history its objects possess, now conceived to be the substratum and origin of knowledge.

One example of this radical shift will suffice. It pertains to the transformation from what in the eighteenth century was the Classical analysis of wealth to what in the nineteenth century became economics. Value in the Classical period, Foucault says, was determined on the basis of the total system of equivalences that could be established among all commodities—as if each commodity contained a measurable fraction of an ideally measurable (and hence knowable and representable) quality. In the writings of Adam Smith, this whole paradigm is subtly (but radically) transformed. For in *The Wealth of Nations* Smith for the first time makes labor, as the fact of production, the basis of value. And the human qualities involved in labor—physical, stubborn, historically concrete, and different from case to case—cannot be ideally measured and represented. What Adam Smith formulates is "a principle of order that is irreducible to the analysis of representation: he unearths labour, that is, toil and time, the working-day that at once patterns and uses up man's life."

With Adam Smith, in other words, finitude erupts into the realm of economic discourse. And as in economics, so in philology, biology, and—although Foucault is unclear about this—apparently in the rest of the human sciences (Foucault sometimes pointedly restricts his analysis to these disciplines, at other times seems to imply that *all* knowledge underwent a mammoth sea change):

> The threshold between Classicism and modernity (though the terms themselves have no importance—let us say between our prehistory and what is still contemporary) had been definitively crossed when words ceased to intersect with representations and to provide a spontaneous grid for the knowledge of things. At the beginning of the nineteenth century they recovered their ancient, enigmatic density; though not in order to restore the curve of the world which had harboured them during the Renaissance, nor in order to mingle with things in a circular system of signs [as they had then]. Once detached from representation, language has existed, right up to our own day, only in a dispersed way: for philologists, words are like so many objects formed and deposited by history . . .
>
> (*The Order of Things,* p. 304)

It is not possible here to do justice to the breadth and brilliance of Foucault's arguments in the book. But a few points can be made. Since discourse is his central topic in the book, the status of language has a special pertinence for him, over and above the disciplinary changes that affected the study of words along with the study of life and wealth. Language, that is, is not simply one of the objects of analysis he dissects in the Classical age. Indeed language, which during that episteme is fully identified with a power to represent beings, provides the discursive basis for all knowledge. All knowledge is based on the order of representation, and thus discourse is predicated during the Classical period on the ability of thought, through its transparent language, fully to represent being—without there being, as it were, any more "being" than representation can represent. The event that occurs at the end of the eighteenth century is something like a massive upwelling of being over and above the capacity of language to represent it.

With that event "the being of that which is represented falls outside of the representation itself." Henceforth language will be doomed to lag behind things, discontinuous with the objects it still *attempts* to express, but which in their new density can no longer be adequately represented. When language loses this power to represent being, Foucault says, a dramatic thing transpires in and for discourse, language, and culture. On the one hand, there is the discursive change we saw in philology, of a kind analogous to what happens in the other sciences: the finitude and dense history of the object (rather than some ideal identity) becomes the focus of the human sciences. But since language in its role as pure representation during the Classical period itself provided the basis of all discursive knowledge, when it loses its power to represent, the common denominator holding the entire edifice of knowledge together in one transcendent order "topples and falls." The very essence of that which holds all knowledge together—language—is fragmented in its very being, Foucault says, when it loses its power to represent. Thus, now that language is not representation, the human sciences have lost a common basis in transcendence. Since the eighteenth century each has wandered off in the direction of the particular finitude—production (economics), the body (biology), specific linguistic objects (philology)—that is its object.

But what, then, of the being of language itself? Beyond the antique forms the philologist studies, what ontological basis does it have now that its very presence—representation—has been shattered? Since the beginning of the nineteenth century, according to Foucault, the great question has been what language *is* if it is not representation. And here he notes two distinct replies, which he associates with the work of Nietzsche and Stéphane Mallarmé, respectively.

First Nietzsche. When at the end of the eighteenth century the sign loses its power to represent, when the depth of the sign—its ability to anchor itself securely in things—is dispelled, two important things happen. Without a stable interior reference to check or clearly identify what a thing is and what a word can mean, the production of meaning and interpretation becomes an endless, infinite process. More important, as Foucault wrote in "Nietzsche,

Marx, Freud," "interpretation will henceforth be always [the] interpretation of 'who'?: one will not interpret what there is in the signified, but at bottom, *who* has posed the interpretation." Put another way, when "the thing being represented falls outside of the representation itself," as it does at the end of the eighteenth century, the emphasis of interpretation shifts from a set of themes associated with the signified (the past, the father, the origin) to a set associated with the signifier (the son, the beginning, above all the present). Thus for Nietzsche, the important thing about any statement is not what is said but the question of who is speaking. Language and discourse must be interrogated constantly to locate the wills that motivate it.

In the Nietzschean view, language is fragmented, dispelled, and reduced to the myriad extralinguistic forces traversing it. If language is no longer representation, it has become an empty field for a battle of wills. Mallarmé answers the question somewhat differently, supplying in the process the other characteristic theme of modernity. For Mallarmé, language, no longer representation, has its own being in and of itself. As Foucault phrases it in *The Order of Things,* "to the Nietzschean question: 'Who is speaking?', Mallarmé replies—and constantly reverts to that reply—by saying that what is speaking is, in its solitude, in its fragile vibration, in its nothingness, the word itself—not the meaning of the word, but its enigmatic and precarious being."

This is the characteristic response of literature in the modern period, claiming an autonomy and fragile sufficiency for the word over against any impossibly diminished act of representation it may be asked to perform. Between Nietzsche and Mallarmé, we see divided and posed the great questions that the end of representation holds for culture: Is discourse anything in and of itself (Mallarmé's query) or is it entirely *something else* (as Nietzsche thought)? Is it a way of doing something, as Nietzsche held, or is it a thing in its own right (as Mallarmé believed)? These are questions that address more than just the status of language, according to Foucault, since in doing so, they address the very status of man's authority in modernity. Can man *be* anything with autonomy in the modern period? Or is his presence always a specific contest, a battle, an event, a rivalry with other wills for precedence?

For all its evident complexities, the arguments of *The Order of Things* reside upon an instructively simple contrast Foucault establishes between the Classical age of representation and the modern age of man. It is a contrast based essentially, I think, upon what Foucault sees as the equation (which Classical discourse *did* make, but which modern discourse does not) of man's transcendental reason with man himself. The irony of all this is that so long as the equation was discursively maintained, "man" himself could not appear in the field of human knowledge—as if, identified with the sovereignty of his own reason, man was not enough of a problem to be an object of thought. There is thus an inverse relation for Foucault between the power to represent and the appearance of man. That power is present in the Classical age of reason, and hence knowledge comprises an integrated representational whole from which man as an object is absent. This power is absent in the modern age and thus knowledge is now diminished, divided, and fragmented into different disciplines—and man himself, who constitutes a problem, appears.

Man's authority, put another way, is parasitic upon his ability to represent, which is why he does not appear in the Classical period and does in the modern. In the eighteenth century, man is that figure who—gifted with a transcendent power, the sovereign power of reason with which he is identified—cannot be represented. Man's very essence during the period is inseparable from his being the representer, an inseparability that Descartes's cogito—"I think, therefore I am"—nicely summarizes.

This equation or identity between man's sovereignty as a representing subject and man himself is precisely something that cannot be represented. It is for this reason that man as such does not appear during the period, an absence Foucault dramatizes in a dazzling analysis of Velázquez' painting *Las Meninas,* which acts as a presiding image for the book as a whole. The painting depicts the artist in the act of pausing as he paints the king and queen of Spain. Indeed, the painting is painted from the point of view of the king and queen as they watch themselves being painted. Their position (shown in the painting by their reflection in a mirror) is also the one Velázquez actually stood in to paint the painting and where the spectator stands when viewing it. According to Foucault, what *Las Meninas* represents is everything about the function of representation—the scene, the tools, the court figures in attendance, the light from the window, and so on—except the subjectivity of the representer himself. This is evident from the fact that the subjects whose subjectivity is crucial to the creation and maintenance of the representation are all actually absent from it: the king and queen who are the subjects of the painting; Velázquez himself, who as the painter is shown pausing and not actually in the process of representing; and the spectator, whose subjectivity is equally alluded to by the painting but excluded from it. Each of these—the painter, the spectator, the royal couple—stands in the implied foreground of the painting, looking on at the scene being depicted, but neither painter, spectator, nor model is actually seen painting, spectating, or posing.

"There exists, in this painting by Velázquez," Foucault says, "the representation . . . of Classical representation." As long as man's subjectivity is tied to his sovereign power to represent—represented in Velázquez' painting by a series of triple analogies linking the political, the artistic, and the spectatorial aspects of representation and subjectivity—man himself cannot be a subject of representation. Indeed "man" as such—both the object of knowledge and the subject who knows—did not yet exist. Discursively, man at this point is still all subject. But when the discursive mirror of the Classical age is shattered, and man and his ideal reason are no longer fully identified, discourse is invaded, as it were, by the reality of man's finite objective being—and hence man per se appears on the scene as an object of knowledge.

It is this link between the breakdown of representation and the advent of an inescapably finite human cultural world that ties Foucault's local analyses of the disciplinary changes in the study of life, wealth, and, above all, language to his obsessive concern with the problem of representation:

> When natural history becomes biology, when the analysis of wealth becomes economics, when, above all, reflection upon language becomes philology, and Classical *discourse,* in which being and representation found their common locus, is eclipsed, *then,* in the profound upheaval of such an archaeological mutation, man appears in his ambiguous position as an object of knowledge and as subject that knows: enslaved sovereign, observed spectator, he appears in the place belonging to the king, which was assigned to him in advance by *Las Meninas,* but from which his real presence has for so long been excluded.
>
> (*The Order of Things,* p. 312)

The underlying structure of *The Order of Things* is a great deal neater than its sprawling volume might at first make it seem. Nevertheless, we have barely touched here a set of arguments that Foucault follows out with surpassing brilliance in an effort to transcribe the twists and turns, the ironies and pitfalls, of man's attempt to come to grips with the discursive and epistemological conditions of knowledge in modernity.

## *POWER*

From the early works on madness and medicine, Foucault displayed an extraordinary sensitivity to the forms of power that knowledge enforces and, reciprocally, to the forms of knowledge that power exploits. This sensitivity derived, as we saw, from a perception that power and knowledge in the modern world are sustained by no transcendent source in God or man; that, deprived of that source, reason is without reason, and must be seen first and foremost as the creature of will; and that power, no longer flowing from anything like a sovereign authority, has slipped the leash of man's subjectivity and turned on man.

Starting from these perceptions, Foucault's early work opened up two related lines of inquiry. One sought to create a description of discourse that ascribed no transcendental foundation to thought. This new method of discursive analysis would aspire, he wrote in *The Archaeology of Knowledge,* to the "intrinsic description of the monument" that is discourse. The other line sought to grasp the relation between power and knowledge and the connections between discursive and extradiscursive institutions in society.

Both lines emerge from Foucault's perception of how bereft man is of the authority to know or to do, and yet, ironically, how powerfully shaping and ordering are the cultural systems in which he is enmeshed. Both lines were clearly apparent in *Madness and Civilization.* Yet under the extraordinary predominance of structuralism in France in the late 1950's and 1960's—an influence Foucault frequently (if not always persuasively) played down in his own work—Foucault's research and writing were for some time after *Madness and Civilization* intent more on the intrinsic analysis of discursive structures than on the institutional affiliations of discourse with power. Both projects were centrally concerned with the status of the modern form of subjectivity and with the way the subject is constituted and oppressed by powerful, transpersonal cultural structures. But the work of the first half of Foucault's career was devoted mainly to describing the intrinsically discursive transmutations of an essentially epistemological subject. It was this line of inquiry that culminated in 1966 with *The Order of Things,* which argues that "man" is a function of historically specific arrangements of discourse, and three years later with *The Archaeology of Knowledge,* an attempt to describe the theoretical underpinnings of his antifoundational method.

By then, a new political activism had come to a crescendo in France with the riots and student revolts (especially those of May 1968), and Foucault's interest began swinging back to the directly political power of knowledge. In examining discourse as a self-inaugurating and self-deposing system, Foucault had ignored the appurtenances that knowledge might provide for a less purely discursive and more directly institutional and corporeal administration of power. When he turned to this topic in the early 1970's in *Discipline and Punish,* it was again to the figure of the king that he turned. This time, however, it was to provide an account of the social utility and function of systems of punishment as they have changed over the last 250 years. If the 1960's for Foucault was the decade of discourse, the 1970's would be the decade of power.

The atmosphere of this study is less philosophically portentous than that of his earlier works and a good deal more attentive to the transactions between knowledge, discourse, and power. Foucault is still concerned with discourse. But now it is those discourses which, in tandem with the physical structures, daily schedules, and corporal regimens of modern penal techniques, finely enmesh man's body in a powerful web of compulsions and constraints. The chief constraint in which Foucault is interested here is at first blush a novel one: the way the modern conception of psychological individuality—man's psyche, the modern soul—was discursively constructed and socially deployed as a political object in the early nineteenth century through a mesh of penal, legal, scientific, and cultural practices. What he calls the disciplinary model of penal technique is a form of power and constraint continuing down to our own day to imprison the body. If formerly Foucault was interested in weighing the discursive proportions of word to thing and subject to object in man's knowledge of himself, in *Discipline and Punish* he attempts to understand the relation of the body to its soul and the way the latter—a real discursive construct in modern penal practice—has facilitated the intimacy (and thus the insidiousness) with which power can be exerted and maintained over the individual and social body.

Foucault begins his study with a simple and gruesome juxtaposition: the public torture and execution of an attempted regicide in Paris in 1757 and, eighty years later, the minutely detailed schedule of a prisoner's daily disciplinary regime. Each defines a certain penal style, a unique mode of investing the legal, political, and jurisprudential power of society in the individual's body. Foucault is interested in charting the cultural change that in a relatively short period of time substituted the timetable of the prison for public executions.

Up until the mid eighteenth century, public torture and ritual execution were common public spectacles in Europe. These performances applied the most extreme varieties and gradations of pain to the body of the condemned man, culminating in death. A theater of pain, public "penal torture" was, Foucault says, an "organized ritual for the marking of victims and the expression of the power that punishes. . . . In the 'excesses' of torture, a whole economy of power is invested."

In part, this economy was a judicial ritual: it superimposed through torture the "ritual that produced the truth" (the condemned man was tortured until he reconfessed) upon "the ritual that imposed the punishment." But it was also a political investment and part of the monarch's right to maintain absolute power over life and death. This special surplus power of the sovereign, ultimately divine in provenance, was what was affronted by the criminal in the eighteenth century, and the elaborate and excruciating public tortures were a way of reinstating the indisputable, absolute nature of that power. Penal torture "made the body of the condemned man the place where the vengeance of the sovereign was applied, the anchoring point for a manifestation of power, an opportunity of affirming the dissymmetry of forces" operant in society.

Between this old form of acceptably atrocious public torture and the form of disciplinary punishment characterizing our own day—which Foucault finds morally worse—Foucault identifies a brief intermediary moment in the history of punishment. This was the ideological project instituted by judicial reformers in the latter part of the eighteenth century that sought to create what Foucault terms a "semio-technique of punishments." This program, never fully implemented, was intended to serve as a way of representing the relationship between crime and punishment to the body politic at large by transforming the criminal's body into a sign of the crime he had committed. This marked an important shift in the economy of punishment. It involved some humanization of penalties but, more important to Foucault, it also involved the standardization of criminal penalties *for* the awareness of the body politic. The immediate object of this form of middle-class, nonmonarchical penal power, the real point of its application, "is no longer the body, with the ritual play of excessive pains, spectacular brandings in the ritual of the public execution; it is the mind or rather a play of representations and signs circulating discreetly but necessarily and evidently in the minds of all. It is no longer the body, but the soul." Discourse, law, and penal practice have begun to constitute the modern soul. Or almost.

For the modern form of punishment to emerge, a whole complex of ideologies, discursive regimes, politico-economic exigencies, architectural forms, and medical and jurisprudential practices must merge. This they do at the end of the eighteenth and the beginning of the nineteenth century. What these cultural practices effectively construct are the modern forms of subjectivity as we know it; and it is through such constructions, Foucault wants us to see, that power in modern society is chiefly exerted. In this respect, *Discipline and Punish* is part of Foucault's larger project to "grasp subjection," as he remarked in a lecture in 1976, "in its material instance as a constitution of subjects."

Thus the second half of *Discipline and Punish* charts the way a complex apparatus of disciplinary techniques, normative conceptions of individuality, and a new "panopticism" in the sphere of knowledge and surveillance of individual behavior comes together in the nineteenth century to constitute a novel political investment of the body. This investment is no longer based—or, rather, no longer based *explicitly*—on the flesh that must be mortified, but on the soul that must be corrected, retrained, and disciplined into normalcy. In the regimens of prisons, armies, schools, and hospitals; in Jeremy Bentham's Panopticon, an architectural scheme that provided an all-seeing vantage for supervising prisoners from a central, unseen, "panoptic" point; in the emerging medical ideas of normalcy Foucault charts the emergence of a new disciplinary strategy of punishment whose effect, if not intent, is to reach into the interior of the individual to correct his "soul"—a supposed psychic undergirding to each individual that Foucault believes to be the creation of the very discourses that claim to discipline it. The point of this regime of surveillance and discipline—or at least its effect—is to produce "docile bodies": self-regulating individual members of society who have internalized the psyche that discourse constructs. Orthopedically conforming themselves to their own soul, individuals thus voluntarily comply with the infinitely detailed and skillful power of knowledge exerted upon them. In this fashion, Foucault argues, they make themselves more readily available to the routines of capitalism and modern culture.

Foucault describes the new penal apparatus as bound up in a "microphysics of power," in which individual subjectivity, social "scientific" discourses, and political arrangements of power converge, minutely constituting and reinforcing one another:

> The history of this "micro-physics" of the punitive power would then be a genealogy or an element in a genealogy of the modern "soul." Rather than seeing this soul as the reactivated remnants of a [Christian] ideology, one would see it as the present correlative of a certain technology of power over the body. It would be wrong to say that the soul is an illusion. . . . On the contrary, it exists, it has a reality, it is produced permanently around, on, within the body by the functioning of a power that is exercised on those punished—and, in a more general way, on those one supervises, trains and corrects, over madmen, children at home and at school, the colonized, over those who are stuck at a machine and supervised for the rest of their lives. This is the historical reality of this soul, which, unlike the soul represented by Christian theology, is not born in sin and subject to punishment, but is born rather out of methods of punishment, supervision and constraint. . . . But let there be no misunderstanding: it is not that a real man, the object of knowledge, philosophical reflection or technical intervention, has been substituted for the soul, the illusion of the theologians. The man described for us, whom we are invited to free, is already in himself the effect of a subjection much more profound than himself. A "soul" inhabits him and brings him to existence, which is itself a factor in the mastery that power exercises over the body.
>
> (*Discipline and Punish,* pp. 29–30)

"The soul," Foucault concludes, "is the effect and instrument of a political anatomy; the soul is the prisoner of the body."

In rendering this genealogy of the modern soul, in registering the complex intersections of power and knowledge that form human subjectivity and that human subjectivity in turn embodies and implies, Foucault specified a new set of rules for understanding the modern deployments of power. First, he sought to see modern punishment as a constitutive and productive practice, not as a repressive and limiting injunction. Power, in Foucault's view, is a collective social function that molds and shapes and enables more than it suppresses, limits, or constrains. Second, he sought to see punitive methods not as reflections or consequences of other forces—legislation or social structure—but as an ensemble of specific techniques and practices with a coercive power of their own. Third, he sought to see the two broad domains analyzed in his book—penal law, on the one side, and the human sciences, on the other—not as separate domains that happen to overlap in the modern prison. Rather, he sought to "make the technology of power the very principle both of the humanization of the penal system and of the knowledge of man."

## *SEXUALITY*

From the middle 1970's on, Foucault focused on the concrete ways in which individuality in modern culture is constructed at once as an "object for a branch of knowledge and a hold for a branch of power." The project he embarked upon after *Discipline and Punish,* and that absorbed him until the time of his death, was a history of sexuality.

*The History of Sexuality* is not a history of sexual conduct, sexual practices, religious or scientific ideas about sexuality, or sexual manners. The books instead sought to understand a somewhat different phenomenon, something more discursive and more intimately connected in modern society with forms of subjectivity and power. He set out to describe the way what we call sexuality has come to be constituted as the central concern and truth of our innermost selves—to the point that sex in our own day has come to be seen as the self-evident hub around which our experience of ourselves and our bodies inevitably seems to turn.

Sexuality, Foucault takes pains to note, is not the innate human force to reproduce or take pleasure. As he points out, it is possible to do these things without talking obsessively about sex the way modern culture does, and without tying the "truth" of personality to a secret sexuality that discloses to us the most hidden (because the deepest) secrets of our selves. Sexuality for Foucault is, rather, a historically contingent ensemble of discourses, themes, and practices that, since the dawn of the modern period, have come with increasing sophistication to hold individuals within certain social and discursive relations of power. Sexuality is how we administer, produce, and oversee our bodies, our actions, and our social relations in modern society. It has been the dominant thematic of our personal will to truth in the nineteenth and twentieth centuries, and as such it is the main strut in culture's systematic subjugation of the social and individual body.

To reinterpret sexuality in this way, Foucault rejects "the repressive hypothesis" about sexuality: the commonly held view maintains that sex has been the object of social repression in the modern period—at least until fairly recently. The heyday of sexual repression, under this hypothesis, was the Victorian period when sexuality was so harshly constrained and policed by social, political, and moral custom that sex was driven almost completely underground—only to burst forth again, as if under hydraulic pressure, on the margins of culture in the form of sexual perversions, outbreaks of venereal disease, a marked rise in prostitution, and so on. This scenario of a repressed sexuality undergoing constraint, perversion, and re-emergence finds its modern sequel, according to Foucault, in contemporary ideologies of sexual liberation. Thus, since Freud, it is believed the immoderately moral closed door to sexuality has been reopened, and we are slowly regaining more direct access to the secret center of our drives and lives.

Foucault overturned this scenario. Instead of seeing sexuality as something first repressed and then liberated by social forces and discourses, he wishes to consider the relations of sexuality to power and knowledge as more entwined and more reciprocally and mutually reinforcing and reproductive. Victorian society was not, Foucault asserts in the first place, particularly repressed. Indeed, sexuality, far from being less frequently talked about or made the object of concern in nineteenth-century culture, was in fact forced relentlessly into the public spotlight. If the Victorians spoke prudishly of sexual behavior, they nevertheless spoke of it continuously. Meanwhile, prostitution, pornography, and an immense medicalization of sex in studies of venereal disease, masturbation, and the proper regulation of sexual appetite bore witness to an unprecedented sexualizing of culture—all in the name of not talking about sex at all. In manuals, medical texts, legal arguments, primers for correcting and adjusting sexual behavior in children, Foucault argues, the nineteenth century spoke urgently about sex, producing a thematic and a culture of sexuality in the process.

The advent of Freud and psychoanalysis, in Foucault's view, represented not the liberation of sexuality but an exacerbation of the same Victorian trend to sexualize more and more aspects of life, to talk more and more garrulously about sex in relation to more and different kinds of knowledge and experience. Thus with Freud, sexuality becomes the centerpiece and truth of every aspect of our lives: we speak sex in our slips of the tongue, in our dreams, in our postures, habits, and clothes. Freud made sure, in other words, that we can escape sexuality nowhere in our experience of ourselves. Foucault saw this pervasive, discursive sexualizing of experience as continuing in contemporary culture with legal, moralistic, medical, homiletic, psychological, therapeutic, and popular ramifications. "What is peculiar to modern societies," he concludes, "is not that they consigned sex to a shadow existence, but that they dedicated themselves to speaking of it *ad infinitum,* while exploiting it as *the* secret."

Sexuality for Foucault is, in the end, only the most complex and insidiously intimate discursive attempt to reimpose the old illusory thematic of depth: the notion of a hidden meaning, beckoning from beyond or encoded within the surface signs and symptoms of everyday life. Foucault's intent in his analysis of the modern discourse of sexuality is to turn attention from false depths to actual surfaces—where, in his view, the shape of modern subjectivity is fashioned and maintained.

Rather than seeing sex and power as opposed, Foucault's method in *The History of Sexuality* is to grasp the modes through which sex and power coexist both discursively and in the social behavior of men and women, in "perpetual spirals of power and pleasure" that constantly reinforce and multiply the positions, situations, topics, and themes in which sexuality as a discursive entity, the "secret truth" of our lives, is produced. When linked with the moralizing and normalizing institutional pressures of the confession—according to Foucault, the discursive form in which most of us speak the "truth" of our sexuality—sexuality emerges as one of the dominant cultural forms through which subjectivity is produced and reproduced, to be fretted about and normalized. Foucault's project in *The History of Sexuality* is to "define the strategies of power that are immanent in this will to knowledge" that is sexuality.

Linked via pleasure to the body, via discourse to knowledge, and via the relations both are enmeshed in to power, sexuality, in the complex positive pathways through which it moves with discourse and power, is the central forming element of our subjectivity.

The vast project on sexuality that Foucault outlined in this first volume would finally go astray. After the first volume, he shifted his focus from the modern period to classical and premodern writings on sexuality, and from an overtly political critique of the relations of power, pleasure, and knowledge in modern culture to a more ascetic consideration of the techniques of self-mastery in sexual relations. Foucault had completed four volumes of the *History of Sexuality* when he died in 1984, a victim of acquired immune deficiency syndrome (AIDS). The ironies of such a death for an author who was himself so exquisitely sensitive to the interplay of power, knowledge, and pleasure in the political construction and maintenance of our sexualized, subjective selves have been lost on few of Foucault's readers.

## *CONCLUSION*

In all of his writing, Foucault was primarily interested in the way thought and language take their order from collective systems rather than individual sources. Much of this interest derived from his angry perception of just how perniciously ordered any individual is by that collectivity, and from a temperamental sympathy with all that is outcast and deviant.

Yet Foucault was in no simple sense a revolutionary, and indeed here again (as everywhere in his writing) paradoxes multiply. In 1961 Roland Barthes first characterized Foucault's writing as *inquiète* (uneasy). Since then it has become habitual to describe him as a supremely elusive and troubling writer. A historian—but of what: Ideas? Language? Discourse? Power? A philosopher, so alert to the duplicitous conditions of modern thought as to be himself almost ungraspably paradoxical: a sort of intellectual Möbius strip, always impossibly twisting back on itself or, in an analogy the anthropologist Clifford Geertz has used, an M. C. Escher drawing. Geertz aptly described Foucault's mercurial slipperiness as a writer when he noted in 1978 that Foucault had become "a kind of impossible object: a nonhistorical historian, an anti-humanist human scientist, and a counter-structuralist structuralist."

Foucault sought throughout his career to embody a principle of resistance to the cultural and political establishment, to be sure, but to its established opposition as well. A historian of vast, transpersonal systems of discourse and power, he himself discoursed with a supple and imperiously idiosyncratic authority not easily reconciled with his insistence upon the frailty, indeed the impotence, of individual human agency. Studying the history of Western thought about madness, disease, language, punishment, power, subjectivity, and sexuality, he wished to uncouple thought from what he took to be an intimate complicity with power. Yet the force of his writing suggested that complicity is inevitable; that the rhetoric of liberation is itself as enslaving as the domination it seeks to overturn; that change, if not impossible, is at least unspeakable, and hence seriously unpredictable. One of his English translators once remarked that the "prospect of Marxist critics trying to get a grip on *Les mots et les choses* was rather like that of a policeman attempting to arrest a particularly outrageous drag-queen."

For all that, Foucault acceded in 1970 to the most prestigious academic chair in French letters. Somewhat like Roland Barthes, and a great deal more than such illustrious French (near-) contemporaries as psychoanalyst Jacques Lacan, anthropologist Claude Lévi-Strauss, and philosopher Jacques Derrida (with whom Foucault shared a common intellectual patrimony and an instinct for iconoclastic overstatement), Foucault resisted intellectual categorization and especially discipleship. That has not stopped—indeed, it has probably incited—a vast outpouring of books and articles on his work. So refractory, and yet so massively influential has Foucault's writing already proved, that it is tempting to conclude that he wished to achieve the very thing his work so fiercely militated against: the continuity, even after death, of a human identity in language.

# Selected Bibliography

## EDITIONS

*Maladie mentale et personnalité.* Paris, 1954. Revised and reissued as *Maladie mentale et psychologie.* Paris, 1962.

*Folie et déraison: Histoire de la folie à l'âge classique.* Paris, 1961.

*Naissance de la clinique: Une archéologie du regard médical.* Paris, 1963.

*Raymond Roussel.* Paris, 1963.

*Les mots et les choses: Une archéologie des sciences humaines.* Paris, 1966.

*L'Archéologie du savoir.* Paris, 1969.

*L'Ordre du discours: Leçon inaugurale au Collège de France prononcé le 2 décembre 1970.* Paris, 1971.

*Ceci n'est pas une pipe: Deux lettres et quartre dessins de René Magritte.* Montpellier, 1973.

*Surveiller et punir: Naissance de la prison.* Paris, 1975.

*Histoire de la sexualité.* 4 vols. Vol. 1, *La volonté de savoir;* vol. 2, *L'Usage des plaisirs;* vol. 3, *La souci de soi;* vol. 4, *Les aveux de la chair.* Paris, 1976–1985.

## ESSAYS

"Introduction." In Ludwig Binswanger, *Le rêve et l'existence.* Paris, 1954.

"Le 'non' du père." *Critique* 18:195–209 (1962).

"Le langage à l'infini." *Tel quel* 15:44–53 (1963).

"Préface à la transgression." *Critique* 19:751–769 (1963).

"La folie, l'absence d'oeuvre." *Table ronde* 196:11–21 (1964).

"Le langage de l'espace." *Critique* 20:378–382 (1964).

"Le prose d'Actéon." *Nouvelle revue française* 12:444–459 (January–March 1964).

"La pensée du dehors." *Critique* 22:523–546 (1966).

"Un 'fantastique' de bibliothèque." *Cahiers de la compagnie Madeleine Renaud-Jean Louis Barrault* 59:7–30 (1967).

"Nietzsche, Marx, Freud." *Cahiers de Royaumont—Philosophie* 6:183–192 (1967).

"Sur l'archéologie des sciences: Réponse au cercle d'épistémologie." *Généalogie des sciences: Cahiers pour l'analyse* 9:5–44 (1968).

"Qu'est-ce qu'un auteur?" *Bulletin de la Société française de philosophie* 63:73–104 (1969).

"Theatrum Philosophicum." *Critique* 26:885–908 (1970).

"Mon corps, ce papier, ce feu." *Paideia* (September 1971).

"Nietzsche, la généalogie, l'histoire." In *Hommage à Jean Hyppolite.* Edited by Michel Foucault. Paris, 1971.

"La politique de la santé au XVIII^e^ siècle." In Michel Foucault et al., *Les machines à guérir (aux origines de l'hôpital moderne).* Paris, 1976.

## INTERVIEWS

"Foucault répond à Sartre." *Quinzaine littéraire* 46:20–22 (March 1968).

"Réponse à une question." *Esprit* 36:850–874 (1968).

" 'Sur le sellette': Michel Foucault." *Nouvelles littéraires* 17:3 (March 1975).

"Pouvoir et corps." *Quel corps?* 2 (1975).

"Questions à Michel Foucault sur la géographie." *Hérodote* 1 (1976).

"Pouvoirs et stratégies." *Les révoltes logiques* 4:89–97 (1977).

"Entretien avec Michel Foucault: 'Les rapports de pouvoir passent à l'intérieur des corps.' " *Quinzaine littéraire* 247:1–15 (January 1977).

"Le jeu de Michel Foucault." *Ornicar?* 10 (July 1977).

## WORKS EDITED BY FOUCAULT

*Hommage à Jean Hyppolite.* Paris, 1971.

*Moi, Pierre Rivière, ayant égorgé ma mère, ma soeur et mon frère . . . : Un cas de parricide au XIX^e^ siècle.* Paris, 1973. Includes an essay by Foucault.

*Herculine Barbin, dite Alexina B.* Paris, 1978.

## TRANSLATIONS

"Afterword." In Hubert L. Dreyfus and Paul Rabinow, *Michel Foucault: Beyond Structuralism and Hermeneutics.* 2d ed. Chicago, 1983. Also contains an interview with Foucault.

*The Archaeology of Knowledge.* Translated by A. M. Sheridan Smith. New York, 1972.

*The Birth of the Clinic: An Archaeology of Medical Perception.* Translated by A. M. Sheridan Smith. New York, 1973.

*Discipline and Punish: The Birth of the Prison.* Translated by Alan Sheridan. New York, 1977.

*The Discourse on Language.* Appendix to *The Archaeology of Knowledge.* Translated by Rupert Sawyer. New York, 1972.

"Final Interview." *Raritan* 5:1–13 (Summer 1985).

*The Foucault Reader.* Edited by Paul Rabinow. New York, 1984. Includes excerpts from *Madness and Civilization* ("The Great Confinement" and "The Birth of the Asylum"), *Discipline and Punish*

("The Body of the Condemned," "Docile Bodies," "The Means of Correct Training," "Panopticism," "Complete and Austere Institutions," "Illegalities and Delinquency," and "The Carceral"), and *The History of Sexuality,* vols. 1 and 2 ("Right of Death and Power over Life," "We 'Other Victorians,' " "The Repressive Hypothesis," and "Preface to *The History of Sexuality,* Volume II"), essays ("What Is Enlightenment?" "Truth and Power," "Nietzsche, Genealogy, History," "What Is an Author?" and "The Politics of Health in the Eighteenth Century"), and interviews ("Space, Knowledge, and Power," "On the Genealogy of Ethics: An Overview of Work in Progress," "Politics and Ethics," and "Polemics, Politics, and Problematizations: An Interview with Michel Foucault").

*Herculine Barbin: Being the Recently Discovered Memoirs of a Nineteenth-Century French Hermaphrodite.* Edited by Michel Foucault. Translated by Richard McDougall. New York, 1980. The English edition includes an introduction by Foucault.

"History, Discourse, and Discontinuity." Translated by Anthony M. Nazzaro. *Salmagundi* 20:225–248 (1972). Translation of "Réponse à une question."

*The History of Sexuality.* 3 vols. to date. Translated by Robert Hurley. Vol. 1, *An Introduction;* vol. 2, *The Use of Pleasure;* vol. 3, *The Care of the Self.* New York, 1978–1985. Volume 4 is forthcoming.

"Human Nature: Justice Versus Power." In A. J. Ayer et al., *Reflexive Water: The Basic Concerns of Mankind.* Edited by Fons Elder. London, 1974. An interview with Foucault and Noam Chomsky on Dutch television, transcribed by Fons Elders.

*I, Pierre Rivière, Having Slaughtered My Mother, My Sister, and My Brother . . . : A Case of Parricide in the Nineteenth Century.* Edited by Michel Foucault. Translated by Frank Jellineck. New York, 1975.

*Language, Counter-memory, Practice: Selected Essays and Interviews.* Edited by Donald F. Bouchard. Translated by Donald F. Bouchard and Sherry Simon. Ithaca, N.Y., 1977. Includes "A Preface to Transgression, Language to Infinity," "The Father's 'No,' " "Fantasia of the Library," "What Is an Author?" "Counter-memory: The Philosophy of Difference," "Nietzsche, Genealogy, History," "Theatrum Philosophicum," "History of Systems of Thought," "Intellectuals and Power," and "Revolutionary Action: 'Until Now.' "

*Madness and Civilization: A History of Insanity in the Age of Reason.* Translated by Richard Howard. New York, 1965.

*Mental Illness and Psychology.* Translated by Alan Sheridan. New York, 1976. Translation of the revised 1962 edition.

"My Body, This Paper, This Fire." *Oxford Literary Review* 4:5–28 (1979).

*The Order of Things: An Archaeology of the Human Sciences.* Translated anonymously. New York, 1970.

*Power/Knowledge: Selected Interviews and Other Writings, 1972–1977.* Edited by Colin Gordon. Translated by Colin Gordon et al. New York, 1980. Includes "On Popular Justice: A Discussion with Maoists," "Prison Talk," "Body/Power," "Questions on Geography," "Two Lectures," "Truth and Power," "Power and Strategies," "The Eye of Power," "The Politics of Health in the Eighteenth Century," "The History of Sexuality," and "The Confession of the Flesh."

"Preface." In Gilles Deleuze and Felix Guattari, *Anti-Oedipus: Capitalism and Schizophrenia.* New York, 1977.

## BIOGRAPHICAL AND CRITICAL STUDIES

Anderson, Perry. *In the Tracks of Historical Materialism.* London, 1983.

Arac, Jonathan. "The Function of Foucault at the Present Time." *Humanities in Society* 3:73–86 (1980). Special number on Foucault.

Barthes, Roland. "Savoir et folie." *Critique* 17:915–922 (1961). Translated as "Taking Sides" in his *Critical Essays.* New York, 1972.

Baudrillard, Jean. *Oublier Foucault.* Paris, 1970. Translated as "Forgetting Foucault" in *Humanities in Society* 3:87–111 (Winter 1980). Special number on Foucault.

Bersani, Leo. "Pedagogy and Pederasty." *Raritan* 5:14–21 (Summer 1985).

Bové, Paul A. "The End of Humanism: Michel Foucault and the Power of Disciplines." *Humanities in Society* 3:23–40 (Winter 1980). Special number on Foucault.

Donato, Eugenio. "Structuralism: The Aftermath." *Sub-Stance* 7:9–26 (1973).

Derrida, Jacques. "Cogito and the History of Madness." In his *Writing and Difference.* Translated by Alan Bass. Chicago, 1978.

Dreyfus, Hubert L., and Paul Rabinow. *Michel Foucault: Beyond Structuralism and Hermeneutics.* 2d ed. Chicago, 1983.

Elders, Fons. "Postscript." In A. J. Ayer et al., *Reflexive Water: The Basic Concerns of Mankind.* Edited by Fons Elder. London, 1974.

Fraser, Nancy. "Foucault's Body-Language: A Post-Humanist Political Rhetoric?" *Salmagundi* 61:54–70 (Fall 1983).

Friedrich, Otto. "France's Philosopher of Power." *Time,* 16 November 1981.

Habermas, Jürgen. "Taking Aim at the Heart of the Present." *University Publishing,* no. 13 (Summer 1984).

Hegel, G. W. F. *The Phenomenology of Spirit.* Translated by A. V. Miller. London, 1977.

Hyppolite, Jean. *Genesis and Structure of Hegel's Phenomenology of Spirit.* Translated by Samuel Cherniak and John Heckman. Evanston, Ill., 1974. Includes an introduction by John Heckman.

Ignatieff, Michael. "Michel Foucault." *University Publishing,* no. 13 (Summer 1984).

Jameson, Frederic. *The Prison-House of Language: A Critical Account of Structuralism and Russian Formalism.* Princeton, N.J., 1972.

———. *The Political Unconscious: Narrative as a Socially Symbolic Act.* Ithaca, N.Y., 1981.

Lemert, Charles C., and Garth Gillan. *Michel Foucault: Social Theory and Transgression.* New York, 1982.

Lentricchia, Frank. *After the New Criticism.* Chicago, 1980.

———. "Reading Foucault (Punishment, Labor, Resistance)," parts 1 and 2. *Raritan* 1:5–32 (Spring 1982) and 2:41–70 (Summer 1982).

Marcus, Steven. "Madness, Literature, and Society." In his *Representations: Essays on Literature and Society.* New York, 1975.

Megill, Allan. "Foucault, Structuralism, and the Ends of History." *Journal of Modern History* 51:451–503 (1979).

Meisel, Perry. "What Foucault Knows." *Salmagundi* 44/45:235–241 (1979).

Major-Poetzl, Pamela R. *Michel Foucault's "Archeology" of Western Culture; Toward a New Science of History.* Chapel Hill, N.C., 1983.

Poirier, Richard. "Writing off the Shelf." *Raritan* 1:106–133 (1981).

Racevskis, Karlis. "The Discourse of Michel Foucault: A Case of an Absent and Forgettable Subject." *Humanities in Society* 3:41–53 (Winter 1980). Special number on Foucault.

———. *Michel Foucault and the Subversion of Intellect.* Ithaca, N.Y., 1983.

Said, Edward. "An Ethics of Language." *Diacritics* 4:28–37 (Summer 1974).

———. "Abecedearium Culturae." In his *Beginnings: Intention and Method.* New York, 1975.

———. "Criticism Between System and Culture" and "Traveling Theory." In his *The World, the Text, and the Critic.* Cambridge, Mass., 1983.

Sartre, Jean-Paul. "Jean-Paul Sartre répond." *L'Arc* 30:87–96 (1966).

Sheridan, Alan. *Michel Foucault: The Will to Truth.* New York, 1980.

Sprinkler, Michael. "The Use and Abuse of Foucault." *Humanities in Society* 3:1–21 (Winter 1980). Special number on Foucault.

Thompson, E. P. *The Poverty of Theory and Other Essays.* New York, 1978.

White, Hayden. "Foucault Decoded: Notes from Underground." *History and Theory* 12:23–54 (1975). Reprinted in his *Tropics of Discourse.* Baltimore, 1978.

———. "Michel Foucault." In *Structuralism and Since: From Lévi-Strauss to Derrida.* Edited by John Sturrock. New York, 1979.

## BIBLIOGRAPHY

Clark, Michael. *Michel Foucault, an Annotated Bibliography: Toolkit for a New Age.* New York, 1982. An excellent analytic bibliography and an indispensable guide to Foucault that includes an introduction by Clark.

ERIC BURNS

# GÜNTER GRASS

## (b. 1927)

GÜNTER GRASS BEGAN his writing career modestly with grotesque, uncomfortable poems and short plays (1956–1958), but it was the *Danzig Trilogy* (as it was later called) of 1959–1963 that captured international attention. The first novel of the trilogy, *Die Blechtrommel* (*The Tin Drum,* 1959), won the 1958 prize of the prestigious Gruppe 47. In the opinion of many, Grass had, through his depiction of provincial life, discovered a telling approach to recent German history, an approach that conveyed the horror of historical events without glorifying them, that combined parodistic grotesqueness with realism, that expressed regret for a lost world without denying its atrocities. Grass also made his mark as an active member of the Socialist party and as a graphic artist.

The *Danzig Trilogy* evokes Grass's birthplace and source of inspiration, the Baltic city of Danzig. Once the capital of the German province of West Prussia, from 1920 Danzig was designated as a free city under the League of Nations in order to give Poland access to the sea. Grass was born here on 16 October 1927 in the ugly, highly provincial working-class suburb of Langfuhr, now Wrzeszcz (in *The Tin Drum,* Oskar does not spare us the obvious joke about this Polish, unpronounceable name). Grass's father was a grocer; his mother was of Cassubian origin. In the trilogy and elsewhere in his works the world of his childhood is recalled with a loving eye and a nose for often repellent detail. The underlying nostalgia for a childhood milieu that vanished with unusual completeness is, however, in a sense unjustified, for the region's wealth of tradition degenerated into the horrors of recent history. Beguiling folklore becomes entangled, in its modern context, with mass murder in the regional concentration camp and finds a fitting climax in the destruction of the old city. The strain thus created finds expression in grotesque imagery that, combined with powers of detailed observation, yields an overwhelming sense of the absurdity of human activities and history.

After the war, as a discharged prisoner of war, Grass for a time led the wandering life not unusual for a man of his generation in Germany, working as a farmhand, a miner, and a monumental mason's assistant (a flourishing trade in that era). He also studied sculpture in Berlin.

Grass entered the literary world by being awarded a third prize for a lyric poem submitted for a competition organized by South West German Radio in 1955. This humble beginning attracted the attention of the members of Gruppe 47, a group of writers founded by Hans Werner Richter in 1947 to encourage a fresh start in German writing. Poems published in *Akzente,* the group's periodical, led to Grass's first volume of poetry, which was published with the surrealist title *Die Vorzüge der Windhühner* (The Advantages of Windfowl, 1956).

The volume contains ten pen-and-ink drawings, evidence of Grass's artistic training in Düsseldorf (1948–1951) and Berlin (1953). The "windfowl," frail creatures of the poet's imagination, illustrate Grass's poetic principles by embodying simultaneously both the object described in the world of experienced reality and the description itself.

The poems accordingly present a disturbing world dominated by self-expressive objects in which, to give a simple example, the air is not simply "cutting" but full of scissors, duly shown in a drawing. In this way humble, domestic objects that surround the poet—a chair, a wardrobe, or a crumpled bed sheet—open directly onto a terrifying world, as they might for a child. Other poems suggest childhood and traditional ways brutally threatened: poems on street organ-grinders or autumnal North German bean-and-pear dishes overwhelmed by images of winter and disaster. The final poem of the forty-one included in the volume, "Blechmusik" ("Music for Brass")—the title and theme suggest *Die Blechtrommel*—has the poet's refuge in an idyllic past destroyed by a military trumpet blast. One poem, "Polnische Fahne" (Polish Flag), with its play on red and white images is, as Grass later stated, filled with motifs from *The Tin Drum.*

The early plays, too, written or drafted between 1954 and 1957, show affinities to the first novel. The absurdist refusal to regard dramatic situations as significant, the deliberate withholding of the respectful attention that our teachers, leaders, and world-historical figures would wish, is the essence of much of Grass's dramatic work and of the two amusing one-act plays *Noch zehn Minuten bis Buffalo* (*Only Ten Minutes to Buffalo,* premiere 1959) and *Beritten hin und zurück: Ein Vorspiel auf dem Theater* (*Rocking Back and Forth,* 1958). In the first play, the gripping tale of a Lake Erie steamer imperiled by a fire that broke out on board, known to German schoolchildren through the nineteenth-century ballad "John Maynard" by Theodor Fontane, is transferred, with all its sweating urgency and nautical terminology, to a rusty locomotive immobile in an Alpine meadow. In the second play, a rocking-horse obstinately marks time on the stage while directors, actors, and critics declaim, denounce, quote Goethe, and bring on love triangles and low comedy.

A similar comic stasis marks Grass's first full-length play, *Hochwasser* (*Flood,* premiere 1957), which insists that all climaxes are anticlimaxes. At the height of the flood, which threatens Noah's house, an aunt is seen stitching sunshades, for catastrophes come and go in the senseless cycle of history. The adventurer Kongo, washed up by the flood, has a brief fling with the daughter of the house, who finally returns to her boring fiancé. Two rats make amusing choric comment; as the waters recede, they prepare to leave, demonstrating that Noah's house has become a sinking ship. There is a plain parallel to the coming "New Biedermeier," a period of stuffy, bourgeois comfort, anticipated by Kitty during the war in *The Tin Drum.*

The same earnest striving to arrive nowhere creates the structure of *Onkel, Onkel* (*Mister, Mister,* 1965), during which the mass murderer Bollin, addressed affectionately by the children as *Onkel,* systematically fails to find another victim. The prospective victims simply fail to respond appropriately. The girl under whose bed he lurks treats his sudden appearance in a matter-of-fact way, while he has to stave off the advances of her widowed mother. The forester in the second act falls into the pit prepared for him, but seems unaffected in thought or in his habitual sententious language. The voice of an officer, imitated by Bollin, praising him for his murders, suggests that the play is a parable of historic changes that make murder praiseworthy at some periods, unthinkable at others. In the absence of other guidance, events are left to the revolver, an imperious object that, in the hands of the children, kills Bollin in the last act.

In *Die bösen Köche* (*The Wicked Cooks,* 1961) a secret recipe for a gray soup provides an absurd central motif. The Count, who possesses the secret, appeared in the final scene of the premiere wearing a mask depicting Grass's face, thus making the incommunicable secret recipe correspond to the meaning of the play and of numerous other passages in Grass's works in which repulsive food appears. As one commentator remarked, in *The Wicked Cooks* a single image is expanded to a five-act play with the help of choreography.

Grass wisely turned to the novel. At the 1958 meeting of the influential Gruppe 47 he read the first two chapters of *The Tin Drum.* According to anecdote, Grass was down to his last twenty marks, and the prize won at the meeting enabled him to visit Poland for research and to finish his novel, which was published in 1959. Much of it had been written in Paris, where Grass and his first wife, a ballet dancer, lived from 1956 to 1959. According to his account of those years, three versions of the novel were consigned to the flames of his stove, and he spent much time scribbling in bistros, as writers do in bad movies.

This first, lengthy novel covers the history of the Third Reich, which it parodies by descending to a grotesquely dwarfish, vivid, provincial perspective, that of the narrator, Oskar Matzerath, born in 1925 in lower middle-class surroundings in the disputed city of Danzig. Oskar's mixed German-Slav origins, his fairy-tale suggestiveness, his vitality (somewhat reduced after the war), his fate as a subject of Hitler and subsequently as a refugee in the West provide parodistic parallels to modern German history, parallels that descend to absurd, even obscene, detail.

The opening of the novel bristles with puzzling, fragmentary statements, for Oskar is an inmate of a mental hospital. As such, however, he is in tune with the events he recalls, and the fragments fall into place on further reading. Among the visitors, for example, there is a lawyer who appears some 400 pages later when the narrative returns to West Germany and we learn that Oskar wishes for a trial and release from the institution in which he is confined on a charge of murder (although Oskar is somewhat reticent about this). The complicated and absurd opening postures of the work, with Oskar looking out, observed by his attendant Bruno looking in, corresponds, we come to see, to the perspective of the novel, in which the author is observing himself as a child who in turn is observing the adult world. It has become a commonplace that the subjective cannot authentically be separated from the objective, and so it is appropriate that Oskar, the observer of recent German history, should be a fairy-tale dwarf, talented and full of misplaced energy, guilt-ridden in his present confinement.

The title of the first chapter, "The Wide Skirt," is explained when Oskar begins his autobiography in October 1899, long before his birth, with the five skirts of his grandmother. In this scene the grandmother, Anna Bronski, is sitting in a West Prussian potato field, its location exactly designated by long-vanished village names. Her skirts, which Oskar's grandfather, a fugitive from the police, hides beneath to escape his pursuers in a scene at once improbable and earthily realistic, represent the refuge and security that Oskar craves all his life. Not that life was dull in those distant days. The grandfather's adventures after the conception of Oskar's mother, which took place under the grandmother's skirts, take him deep into Russia and back to Danzig on a raft before he vanishes, to reappear, perhaps, in America as a businessman. This spacious and colorful life contrasts with Oskar's hygienic hospital ward in postwar West Germany, adorned with Oskar's obscene scribbles, of which this novel is perhaps an example.

The skirts are a first example of the grotesque *chosisme* of this novel, of the objects that steer events and behavior in the absence of other guidance. To Oskar's grandfather, the skirts mean security and promise, but they lead Oskar to an unhealthy and restrictive hiding place and finally to his hospital bed. Another enigmatic but powerful object, red and white like the Polish and the Nazi flags, that emerges at the beginning of the second chapter is Oskar's tin drum, which helps him to drum up the past. Its magic is bound up with Oskar's young, malicious vitality and the militarism of the Third Reich, though it is not tied to any human categories or organizations and can work against the Nazi movement. This is seen on the occasion (prominent in the film version) when the drum breaks up a Nazi party meeting with waltz and jazz rhythms. Oskar's birth, of which he is farcically aware in all its detail, takes place in circumstances and surroundings that mark him indelibly as lower middle class. A forty-watt light bulb is a powerful object here, and recurs throughout the novel to remind Oskar of his humble origins, although Oskar likes at times to claim that it was a sixty-watt bulb.

Oskar's birth seems to be absurdly and inextricably entangled with the equally absurd history of Danzig. Oskar has two fathers, a Pole (Jan Bronski) and a German (Alfred Matzerath). He shares his mother's preference for the sickly, romantic Pole over the stolid German, but later admits that the German (who saved Oskar from euthanasia at the hands of the authorities) is probably his true father.

In his disjointed fashion Oskar introduces another object, the photo album that recalls the vanished past to him, a refugee. We learn how Oskar and his friend, Klepp, as refugees in West Germany, childishly cut up photographs, reflecting the fragmented methods that Grass uses to relate postwar and prewar events. Another piece of grotesquerie emerges that is relevant to the novelist's perspective. Oskar resolved to cease growth at the age of three. He contrives an accident with a trapdoor (for which the German Matzerath receives the blame) and goes through life as a bright three-year-old, militarily equipped with a drum, a worthy representative of his era. The events around him, including the "great" historical events, are viewed from this dwarf's perspective.

What makes Oskar even more representative of his era is his absurd but sinister power of being able to shatter glass with his voice, a feat that foreshadows the destruction of Danzig in the war. When they take him to school and try to remove his drum, gently at first, Oskar responds by shattering the teacher's spectacles with a deadly yell, a grotesque scene in the context of the everyday ordinariness of the school. Thus little Oskar's first day at school is also his last, a comic scene not without pathos. He is forced to seek his education among the vividly drawn characters of his Danzig world, for example, the eccentric greengrocer Greff, who has a taste for Boy Scouts and scouting. Oskar's reading includes a life of Rasputin and Goethe, and the reader can perceive that this insane chronicle is, in addition to many other things, a parody of the German bildungsroman, which traces with respectful attention the hero's spiritual development in the manner of Goethe's chronicles of Wilhelm Meister. Oskar later joins a traveling theater company, an essential part of Wilhelm Meister's education. At times he feels elevated to the rank of a messiah, yet he is always threatened by the Black Cook of children's rhymes and remains a dwarf.

The other children in the tenement block are part of the ever-present threat. They force Oskar to eat a soup of brick dust and urine, for in Grass's work the eating of repulsive food is integral to being alive. As if to further illustrate this gross side of life, Oskar's mother continues her obsessive affair with Bronski, leaving Oskar with the Jewish toyshop owner Markus each time she goes to meet her lover. With sad prescience, Markus perceives that her position, caught between Germany and Poland, resembles that of Danzig and advises her to flee with him to London or at least to avoid identification with the fated Polish cause. Private lives and historical events are seemingly subject to the same ill-starred, absurd governance, a fact that is emphasized when Oskar, a perverse prophet of the coming war, climbs a tower and calls doom on the old city, shattering windows.

The arrival of the Third Reich in 1933 is

signaled at the local level by Oskar's visit to an open-air Wagner performance. Thus the all-important theatrical aspect of young Oskar's education is honored, suitably continued by a circus visit in 1934. It is here that Oskar meets fellow dwarves, above all the Goebbels-like Bebra. At home Beethoven and Hitler, the opposite poles of German culture, glare at each other across the Matzeraths' parlor. It is during this period that Matzerath, an eager Nazi party member and an object of some sympathy, starts to attend Nazi meetings, leaving his wife to Bronski. Oskar, beating his drum under the platform, causes a meeting to break up in chaos: the destructive principle inherent in the drum is even stronger than its incidental manifestation. The church, too, plays its due part in Oskar's education when he tries unsuccessfully to foist his drum on a statue of the infant Jesus. The cluster of religious themes reaches a kind of climax in the notorious Good Friday scene. This episode opens with an old man on the beach fishing for eels, using a horse's head as bait. Oskar's mother is sickened, especially when "the longshoreman . . . plunged both hands into the horse's maw and pulled out two eels as long and thick as your arm." But Matzerath, after initial hesitation, buys eels for supper with a show of heartiness suitable for a Nazi party member. Oskar's mother, first driven to a feverish frenzy of excess that manifests itself in a craving for fish and for Jan's embraces, sickens and dies, overcome by the repulsiveness of existence.

With two many-faceted anecdotes, Oskar's narrative slides down into World War II. One tells of Herbert Truczinski, the type of the honest, suffering workingman (he works in a bar that betrays Grass's admiration for *Moby Dick*) who falls victim to a figurehead of Niobe, a fateful object with roots deep in German history. The other anecdote tells of a certain Meyn. Once a Communist and now a trumpeter in the Brownshirts, he kills his four cats and is expelled from the Nazi party for cruelty to animals, despite his zeal in destroying a synagogue. The repugnant atrocity of this action against Jews is represented at Oskar's level by the destruction of Markus' toyshop.

In book 2, the war is similarly reduced in scale. Its outbreak is depicted through the absurd attack on the Polish Post Office in Danzig that took place on 1 September 1939. As the war looms, Bronski and Matzerath cease to play cards together and Oskar contrives to lure Bronski to the post office, where he is caught up in the deadly skirmish being expressed in the letters and postcards exchanged between Germany and Poland. He comes under command of the janitor Kobyella, a typical minor character in Grass, a courageous war veteran who is contemptuous of Bronski's faintheartedness. The last defenders take refuge in cards, the familiar game of skat, until matters take their weary course and the German attackers burst in with the usual cries of "Rauss." Oskar, as a seeming three-year-old and a victim of Polish vileness, gets off scot-free with a new drum, but is nonetheless haunted by the bad conscience endemic to his time and place: he confesses to denouncing Bronski, his kind uncle, to the Germans who eventually shoot him (the notification is signed by one Zelewski).

At this point, while the radio is trumpeting the further course of the war, Oskar is preoccupied with his first love, Matzerath's new assistant, Maria. Their love finds its objective correlative in fizzy lemonade powder that is poured into her hand and brought to effervescence by means of his saliva. Adolescent love (for Oskar is now sixteen), chemical fizz, and the era itself, with its artificially excited masses, are plainly related. In his West German present, Oskar recalls his lemonade powder nostalgically. Maria, no longer a country girl, claims to remember nothing of these disgusting crudities. Yet Oskar persists in recalling the war in terms of sexual encounters. The Russian campaign is thus represented by an unenlightening pornographic scene between Maria and the forty-seven-year-old widower

Matzerath, in which Oskar enviously intervenes. As the special reports on the war pour from the radio, Maria's son is born; Oskar improbably insists of thinking of him as his own son. When the German campaign in Russia finally bogs down, Oskar is found wallowing with the sluttish Frau Greff, neglected wife of the greengrocer and former scoutmaster.

Oskar is at this point understandably dissatisfied with his education, restricted as it has been to lower-middle-class circles. He enters the theatrical sphere by joining a troupe of midgets touring the Western front with Bebra and the ageless Roswitha. A cabaret song on the concrete bunkers of the Atlantic wall anticipates the "New Biedermeier" of postwar prosperity and underlines the senseless cycle of history.

His education complete after a conventional wartime romance with Roswitha (followed by the tragedy of her death), Oskar, inspired by another visit to the church on his return to Danzig, aspires to an even loftier role—that of Christ's successor, a figure of satanic stature. As always, Oskar is dragged down to his own level. Maria is no longer interested in him since the birth of her son Kurt (whom Oskar vainly claims as his own). After Matzerath saves him from euthanasia, Oskar falls in with a gang of a type that flourished during the late stages of the war.

The story offers vivid glimpses of Danzig during this period, but the events do not bring about any change in the pattern of Oskar's life. He allows his band, which has adopted him as a leader, to be captured while he is treated like a misused three-year-old. The gang members have to dare a "high jump"; this phrase, which also suggests the scaffold, is transposed literally, as is Grass's manner, into a nightmare scene in which each jumps from the diving platform of an empty swimming pool, in analogy to the trials of traitors that took place during the closing stages of the war. Oskar does not jump, and this refusal and the accompanying sense of guilt characterize his existence. Indeed, Oskar betrays Matzerath, sheltering in his cellar, to the Russians when they enter Danzig. Oskar prevents Matzerath from hiding his Nazi party badge, forcing him to conceal it from the Russians by swallowing it—"swallow his words" is thereby transposed into concrete fact—so that he painfully chokes to death. This significant grotesqueness mingles unobtrusively with the reality of the time: the main road lined with hanged deserters while expelled Poles move in. Matzerath's grocer's shop is taken over by Fajngold (who had been sent to the Treblinka concentration camp), a man crazed by his experiences, portrayed through a tactful mixture of the grotesque and the real.

Oskar's education proceeds; he is now twenty-one and grows to his present 1.21 meters in the refugee train from Danzig, a growth that is accompanied by a loss of vitality, a parallel to the development of Germany.

Oskar's postwar life in book 3 of *The Tin Drum* draws extensively on Grass's own experiences as an apprentice stone carver and a student at the Düsseldorf Kunstakademie. The period atmosphere of hasty repairs and of black market deals with American cigarettes as currency is captured—but above all Grass follows his teacher Alfred Döblin in presenting history as a senseless cycle. After the currency reform of 1949 has put Germany on its feet again, Oskar resumes his tentative Jesus role and his drums; there is even a nostalgic visit to old haunts on the Atlantic wall. Here Corporal Lankes re-enacts offstage (reported by Oskar in a parody of Greek drama) the shooting of nuns who had strayed onto the beach. This was an atrocity forced on Lankes by an insane officer; the highly competent ex-corporal is not proud of it, but he is not prepared to make dramatic amends. Atonement seems a dubious proposition as it is attempted in the Onion Cellar, a fashionable night club in which onions held by the West German clientele induce tears of repentance.

The past continues to haunt Oskar and his prosperous West Germany. Late at night the last streetcar bears its freight of recent history, and Oskar's last ride on it repeats the events at the Polish Post Office. In a desolate industrial landscape in which history has left behind its dead, Oskar's dog finds a woman's finger. As a result Oskar is wanted for the murder of the nurse Dorothea. The reader has already heard of his attempt to seduce her; the finger seems to be connected with an earlier and equally unsuccessful attempt to pose as Hamlet. Oskar's education is concluded on an escalator in Paris, ascending to heaven, where he is captured; thereafter, at the significant age of thirty, he finds refuge in his secure hospital bed in West Germany, still haunted by the ever-present Black Cook.

Grass's second volume of poetry, *Gleisdreieck* (Triangle Junction, 1960), with its eccentric format of a child's picture book with eighteen charcoal drawings, clarifies Grass's imagery. His fascination with Berlin, where he was then living, is apparent in the title (designating a Berlin subway station where lines from East and West meet) and in a poem devoted to the "Trümmerfrau" (Rubble Woman). The poem "Adebar" links the myth of babies being delivered by storks with concentration camps (by focusing on the centrality of chimneys to both). Through this linkage Grass seeks to demonstrate the ability of fairy stories and folktales, apparently timeless and gracious, to lend their irrational powers to modern atrocities. In a similar fashion Grass links certain persons and objects of his world—nuns, cooks, birds, dolls, and children's verses—to sadism. Notable are the staccato "Kinderlied" (Children's Song) and "Diana—oder die Gegenstände" ("Diana—or the Objects"); the latter work expresses Grass's principle of not allowing his body to be injured by a "shadowless idea." Above all, the poem "Askese" ("Askesis")—the title means self-denial, asceticism—clarifies Grass's distrust of bright, dramatic events, insisting that

> The cat speaks
> What does the cat say then?
> Thou shalt strike out the navy blue
> the cherries, poppies, bloody noses,
> that flag too thou shalt strike out
> and scatter ashes on geraniums.
> (*Selected Poems*, p. 49)

At the 1960 meeting of Gruppe 47, Grass read a chapter from a new novel. Part of this material was diverted to *Katz und Maus* (*Cat and Mouse*, 1961), the second part of the trilogy; this short work is full of motifs from the long novels, yet concentrates on a single incident, the theft of a medal, in the approved manner for the German *Novelle.*

The first-person narrator is reluctant to introduce himself, possibly because he has failed to understand his subject, the central figure, Mahlke. It is a failure that the narrator Pilenz seems to share with the world at large, and in the opening scene it is presumably he who demonstrates this failure by setting a cat on Mahlke's "mouse"—the prominent Adam's apple that signalizes Mahlke's virility, courage, and vulnerability. It is the summer of 1940, a year after the outbreak of war, and the setting is workaday Danzig, seen in anything but a nostalgic light: an airplane and a crematorium figure prominently as emblems of war and the concentration camps and the close ties between technology and death. We also learn a detail that acquires significance in due course—that Mahlke had only recently learned how to swim.

The swimming, we understand, indicates physical courage and Mahlke's readiness for war. Mahlke was a sickly child who had his first swimming lessons late in 1939, at the age of fourteen. Then he joined a group of classmates who spent their free time on a sunken Polish minesweeper. In spite of his late start, he soon excels all the others in feats of diving, during which he brings up objects like an English screwdriver and a Polish medallion from the wreck. These objects, forerunners of the Knight's Cross, the medal that is later stolen, testify to his prowess as a warrior; they are, so to speak, trophies captured from the enemy, duly hung round his neck next to the virile Adam's apple.

Physical courage, however, is only the basis of Mahlke's character, which (as the reader discovers) is admirable if one can make allowances for the distorting lens of the narrator. Thus, his courage is placed at the service of his religion, particularly of the Virgin Mary, a knightly cult. Mahlke's piety is genuine; he attends early mass in St. Mary's Chapel, where Pilenz serves as an acolyte. In rescuing a boy from drowning in 1942, after what appears to be a period of self-communing and inactivity in readiness for greater feats, he discovers the entrance to the minesweeper's radio cabin, accessible only to him, and here he establishes a chapel to Mary, adorning it with a medal to the Black Madonna of Częstochowa—a "Polish object" that the school principal Klohse has forbidden him to wear—and a phonograph on which he plays "Ave Maria." He also plays secular music, including the popular songs of the day. He is knightly, too, in his learning (which embraces liturgical texts and the naval matters that naturally fascinated wartime schoolboys), in his tolerance (his refusal to gossip about Pilenz's mother's loose life), and in setting fashions (the woolen pompoms worn as neck ornaments that were, as a matter of historical fact, a wartime fashion in Germany).

The pompoms are, in their way, an admirable fashion, a gentlemanly gesture against the exaggerated martial spirit of wartime. They are also ridiculous and condemned by the authorities; all too often it is only this ridiculous aspect of Mahlke that Pilenz observes. Yet to the imperceptive an undignified appearance often conceals something admirable. Thus it is with Mahlke's contentment with an obscure position in the Hitler Youth (which his fellows can appreciate) or his ability to protect an elderly schoolteacher from an obscene, adolescent practical joke (which they cannot). In the sexual realm Mahlke shows (under an absurd surface) an effortless prowess. This is demonstrated when Tulla, the temptress, joins the boys on the wreck (an incident in the novella that earned the displeasure of real-life educational authorities). It is also shown in another absurd incident in the winter of 1941–1942, whereby Mahlke so impresses Pilenz's girl cousins from Berlin that they are willing to urinate in the ice at his request, so that he can bore a hole down to the wreck. Here the absurd may outweigh the heroic even to Mahlke's staunchest supporter.

But then there is Mahlke's outspoken admiration for his father, who died in heroic circumstances while working as a civilian for the Polish Railways; such admiration can be considered absurd only by the biased. Above all, Mahlke passes the test that in Grass we must all submit to: eating repulsive foods. Here again he excels by eating something that the others dare not touch—a can of frogs' legs salvaged from the wreck and other unwholesome substances.

Undoubtedly Mahlke has some of the characteristics of the Holy Fool, depicted in the novel through a caricature with a halo drawn on the blackboard by the Latvian baron's son. Even more, certain aspects of Mahlke (most prominently his upbringing as a fatherless innocent who dresses fantastically) recall Parzival, the hero of Wolfram von Eschenbach's Middle High German epic. Both Dostoevsky and Parzival appear in a conversation with the narrator just before Mahlke deserts from the army.

Thus it is only appropriate that Mahlke should be fascinated by the Knight's Cross worn by a fighter pilot who is invited to lecture at the school. By the time the second Knight's Cross wearer arrives, this time a U-boat commander with a flowery turn of phrase (Mahlke's language is always plain, sober, and incisive), Mahlke's longing for this supreme neck ornament, for which he has been unconsciously preparing, gets the better of him. He steals the medal while the hero is taking part, with showy condescension, in a gymnastics lesson. When the hero discovers his loss, there is a comic flurry—an innocent bystander is slapped because of his cheerful smile—and the hero departs in a huff. Naturally Mahlke finally confesses and is relegated to an inferior school;

demotion to an inferior status seems to be the natural reaction of the authorities to Mahlke's qualities.

At this point Pilenz loses sight of Mahlke, except for a brief Advent visit during which Mahlke shows commendable pride in his father's Polish and civilian heroism. Pilenz suffers the usual fate of his generation and is conscripted. It is then, in 1944, that he hears of Mahlke's exploits as a soldier. As always, the absurd partially conceals knightly achievements. For one thing, Mahlke has dealt with a bullying superior officer of a type that flourishes in all armies by cuckolding him, fulfilling every recruit's dream of revenge. He has also discovered an arms cache hidden by the partisans, for which feat his commanding officer is forced to congratulate him in public, and there is talk of awarding him a medal. Pilenz sees (and obliterates) Mahlke's name (which dominates the obscene scrawls in the camp latrine) together with the opening of the hymn to Mary that Mahlke knows by heart: "Stabat mater . . ." Mahlke is now on active duty, serving on the Russian front where, needless to say, he comports himself heroically. But even this news comes to Pilenz in a distorted, comic form: Mahlke's aunt cannot quite understand a letter reporting the number of enemy tanks that Mahlke has destroyed. Nonetheless, for his achievements at the front he is awarded the Knight's Cross and would seem thus to be in harmony with the authorities.

Mahlke then wishes to give a speech in his old school, as the others had done. But his old enemy Klohse, with his pompous official rhetoric, refuses permission, instinctively recognizing in Mahlke a principle alien to his type of authority. Klohse may be said to win the contest, for Mahlke, provoked by the refusal, strikes his old principal, and this departure from the knightly code seems to mark Mahlke's recognition that he does not belong to this society in spite of his military prowess, and brings on his downfall. After wandering through the night with Pilenz, Mahlke announces his intention of deserting. On Pilenz's advice, Mahlke takes refuge in the wreck, thus literally "going under." To this very day Pilenz, now secretary of a Catholic organization in Düsseldorf, searches in vain for Mahlke, but has to be content with recording his adventures, plagued, much like Oskar, by memories and a bad conscience. Mahlke can perhaps be summed up as a "hero against absurdity" as Grass, in the essay "Über meinen Lehrer Döblin" ("Döblin, My Teacher," 1967), describes the heroes of Döblin's novels.

It would seem that Mahlke had to "go under" because he was at odds with everyday existence. For all his warrior's qualities, he did not fit in with the world of the Third Reich; for all his genuine piety, he was at odds with the church. He was greatly misunderstood by those around him, even by the conscientious narrator.

*Hundejahre* (*Dog Years,* 1963), the final part of the trilogy, has the three-part structure of *The Tin Drum,* but goes far back into the history of Danzig, even embracing the mythic past. Ancient lore is linked to recent horrors by a constant shift in time. There are three narrators who are not always sure of their facts (but this is true of all Grass's narrators) and whose accounts overlap and fail to agree. The first member of the "authors' collective" to tell his tale is Brauxel (variously spelled), who functions as a general editor within the text and who, in addition, turns out to be identical with three Jewish characters of the novel (Amsel, Haseloff, and Goldmäulchen). Brauxel emerges as the manager of a former potash mine in which scarecrows that absurdly reenact all human activities are now manufactured; personal and historical planes are indistinguishable. This process exemplifies Grass's absurd view of history, and the narrators' mining endeavors correspond to a descent into the author's subconscious for their material, where they find much that is common to all humanity:

> The present writer bears the name of Brauxel at the moment and runs a mine which produces nei-

> ther potash, iron, nor coal, yet employs, from one shift to the next, a hundred and thirty-four workers and office help in galleries and drifts, in stalls and crosscuts, in the payroll office and packing house.
>
> (Ralph Manheim trans., p. 3)

Brauxel's early "shift" or "stratum" (the German *Schicht* means both) opens with the river Vistula, which carries along all the debris of Danzig history from Old Prussian heathen gods to Napoleonic uniforms (and a hidden acknowledgment, in the name of a Polish robber, to the East German poet Johannes Bobrowski). The banks of the river are undermined by burrowing rats, history threatens to overflow, and two boys are grubbing in the flotsam. One of them, Matern, throws a knife (a present from the other boy, Amsel) into the water. Amsel, who later turns out to be identical with Brauxel, is an artist and observer of Jewish descent; with this action, which recurs throughout the novel, his persecution at the hands of the active, ideologically motivated Matern begins. The relationship is ambivalent, for Matern sometimes protects his friend and is a victim, too, of his own difficult, not insensitive nature. In the fifth chapter, "Fifth Morning Shift," the motif of the dog appears. The ancestors of Hitler's favorite dog come from the Danzig region, so that dogs, particularly the carpenter's dog Harras (who lives in a lumberyard in industrial Danzig), enact great historical events. We can especially note how Harras' sterling character deteriorates as the Nazi era takes its course. Indeed, the "dog years" of the title, a dog's lifetime, correspond to the duration of Hitler's Third Reich (1933–1945). The grotesque story of Matern's christening, which follows, and in which Grass's beloved Danzig dialect is heard, is also a tale of malice. Matern's grandmother, chairbound for years in a windmill, takes advantage of her miraculous recovery to beat the servant maid.

We read of Amsel's father, a converted Jewish general dealer who strives to demonstrate the falsity of anti-Semitic clichés, especially those of Otto Weininger, a well-known racial theoretician who held that the Jews were effeminate; the father ends by dying for his country at Verdun. Amsel emerges as a maker of scarecrows, and his christening procession is threatened, grotesquely, by a flock of birds. Amsel hopes that his scarecrows, by laying bare human motives, will lead to improvements (the hope of the creative artist), and these hopes seem justified when Matern protects his friend after seeing the scarecrows enact persecution. But the effect is temporary. In 1927 the two friends attend school in the city. They explore a medieval passageway that leads under the Trinity Church. Here they find a skeleton, and Matern, overcome by the ingrained spirit of history, turns on his friend and abuses him as a Jew. When the boys go to summer school in the country, another picturesque aspect of the region is added to myth and legend: the lore and rogue's argot of the forest gypsies. It is here that the schoolmaster Brunies adopts a daughter, Jenny, a mild-mannered counter to the brutal (if beguiling) Tulla. With this book 1 ends and Brauxel introduces Harry Liebenau, the son of a carpenter and the author of book 2.

Young Harry's first-person chronicle takes the form of love letters to his cousin Tulla and parodies the epistolary novel form. His love has its foundations in the very origins of her family, for the name *Tulla* recalls to Harry that of a mythical water creature described in local fairy tales. There is a sense of continuity here, of an unbroken link with the past, for Tulla's family, the Pokriefkes, originally moved into the city (where her father works in the yard owned by Harry's father) to become part of the urban proletariat. Yet this continuity also entails the weakening of tradition, illustrated in the deterioration of the epistolary form in Harry's chronicle.

The same can be said of other aspects of Harry's childhood; the watchdog Harras, for example, turns into a bully and comes to be the father of Hitler's dog. Tulla's father is fit only for unskilled labor with the glue pot, and his daughter Tulla exists in a concentration-camp odor of boiling bones. Skinny and irate, in 1933 she torments the plump Jenny at the seaside, so that Harry has to intervene, calling off Harras who is Tulla's willing assistant. The same fateful year is marked by the drowning of Tulla's little brother; water portends a new era, the age of Aquarius. Tulla's mourning takes the form of sharing the dog's offal; again the motif of repulsive food as a test and condition of existence appears. It is at this time that Harras is taken to the police kennels for breeding purposes, a comically portentous episode that links the details of Harry's lower-middle-class Danzig to "great" historical events, for the result of Harras' union is a new beginning in the form of Hitler's future dog. Harry's report to his school class on this episode naturally omits coarse details and is adjusted to fit the reigning ideology. Tulla and Jenny do not fit into any symbolism. Tulla is malicious and yet attractive in comparison with her victim, the plump Jenny. Harras, too, remains attractive, even though he attacks Jenny's music teacher three times while the innocent Harry is blamed for these incidents and is punished.

Harry's letters lose their form as events turn brutally grotesque. Amsel, expelled from the sports club, rents a villa and builds scarecrows. Matern joins the Brownshirts and becomes an actor (suitable occupations for one born under the sign of Aries). Language itself breaks up in the formless bellows of a beer-hall fight ("Ei wei, schalle machei!"). Snatches of Heidegger are also heard in the tumult.

In January 1937 matters take a long-threatened turn when storm troopers beat up Amsel and Matern knocks out his teeth. Amsel leaves Danzig and returns as Haseloff, an old-fashioned Central European impresario with a mouthful of gold teeth. He engages Jenny as a dancer after Tulla has marked her as a victim, burying her in snow near the fateful Gutenberg memorial. Matern goes to pieces, is expelled from the Brownshirts as a drunk, and walks around Danzig reciting Heidegger and (unacknowledged) Gottfried Benn, intellectuals attracted by the Nazi movement in its early days. On the eve of the war, Matern, an unbalanced opponent of the regime, poisons the dog Harras before joining the army; his revenge seems doomed to take such unsatisfactory forms. Harry's father, a coarse, brutal man but not a true Nazi, weeps for his dog while Tulla, genuinely pitiless, is unworried. As consolation, the father is invited to meet Hitler on his way to the Polish campaign, but has to be content with seeing the Führer's dog. This is history at a local level with a vengeance.

With the outbreak of war, Tulla resumes her role as persecutor, which centers about the brewery. She traps Jenny and Harry in the icehouse, where they are forced to spend the night. The path descends to Stutthof concentration camp, to which the schoolmaster Brunies is confined after he has been reported for stealing the children's vitamin tablets (he has a sweet tooth). The camp is marked by a pile of bones that people conveniently ignore with Heideggerian powers of evasion; only Tulla identifies them for what they are.

Signs of the end are visible. In a bleak landscape Tulla, who has been boasting of her pregnant condition, aborts her child, a horrifying event covered up in a flood of parodied Heidegger. Harry's father demolishes Harras' empty doghouse on Hitler's fifty-fifth birthday (20 April 1945). The dog metaphor is retained to the end, when the action moves to Hitler's headquarters, from which the dog Prinz runs off to what is to become West Germany, in spite of Russian barking countermeasures. Thus are historical events reduced to absurd trivialities.

In book 3, where Matern takes over, the dog represents the Nazi past that Matern cannot shake off in postwar Germany. At first he is in a British "Antifa" (antifascist) camp, where he stylizes himself into a Communist resistance fighter and protector of his Jewish friend Amsel. From the men's toilet in the Cologne railway station, he sets out on his "Materniads" to punish former Nazis. The attempts are obscene and ridiculous. He infects their womenfolk with syphilis and ends, exhausted and encumbered with a wife and child, by strangling a pensioner's canary. A final attempt to force Heidegger to account for his past ends with Matern damaging the philosopher's front gate. Nobody takes him seriously, as West Germany is prospering. Eminent figures from postwar West Germany consult the old miller Matern, whose mealworms foretell a bright future. There is little that Matern can do against the repetitive flow of history or private life.

In 1955 special spectacles are available for those aged seven to twenty-one that grant their wearers an insight into their parents (those over thirty). Above all they see their fathers as murderers, but theirs is no revolt. Matern's daughter, looking at him through a pair, is horrified. Matern gives up his futile retaliatory mission and takes employment reading children's stories on the radio. He agrees to become the object of a youth discussion led by Harry Liebenau, in which Matern's guilt is once more laid bare, including the opening incident of the knife thrown into the Vistula. Yet discussion destroys the urge to act. Matern decides to move to East Germany and sees Hitler's dog following him through the fields. Leaving the train in West Berlin, Matern meets Jenny and her impresario. The tableau is repeated, the knife thrown into the murky, history-laden waters of the Landwehr Canal. Finally, the friends fly to Hanover and enter Brauxel's mine, in which the scarecrows act out their parody.

Grass did not allow his sense of absurd or his dislike of clichés and slogans to deter him from political activity. His distrust of the Adenauer regime is amply apparent in the Danzig novels, and after his return to Germany from Paris in 1960, he became politically active on behalf of the Social Democrats. He met Willy Brandt, then mayor of West Berlin, and the first part of *Über das Selbstverständliche* (translated in part as *Speak Out!,* 1968) contains cheerful pamphlets that Grass wrote for the 1965 election. One early pamphlet proposes the founding of a new Danzig in the West, complete with dialect; his aim was to reconcile the inhabitants of West Germany with the postwar Polish boundaries. But the main drift of Grass's political statements, contained here and in *Der Bürger und seine Stimme* (*The Citizen and His Voice,* 1974) is a sober, un-Hegelian skepticism about the grandiose goals of history. He rejects claims to possess absolute truths or to have discovered an inherent revolutionary dynamism. Grass's socialism means a deliberate sobriety, attention to details close to home rather than dramatic calls for revolution. The Western radical Left should be concerned with the Prague Spring of 1968, not with gestures by Che Guevara.

The evasiveness of the intellectual Left in matters close to home is the theme of the play *Die Plebejer proben den Aufstand* (*The Plebeians Rehearse the Uprising,* 1966), in which Grass contrives simply to confront Bertolt Brecht (called "the Boss") with the workers' uprising in East Germany of 17 June 1953.

Grass had already touched upon this theme in a lecture he gave to the Berlin Academy of Arts in 1964 on the occasion of the 400th anniversary of Shakespeare's birth. In the lecture Grass criticizes Brecht's distortion of Shakespeare's *Coriolanus* for political ends, whereby cowardly tribunes are made into fighters in the class struggle and Coriolanus is coarsened into a brutal warrior. Grass proposes an idea for a play in which Brecht, rehearsing *Coriolanus* in Berlin, is confronted with a delegate from the construction workers' uprising.

In *The Plebeians Rehearse the Uprising* we encounter Brecht in act 1 rehearsing his version of *Coriolanus,* and yet, ironically, revealing his contempt for the inability of the German working classes to make a proper revolution. Brecht's play will show how it should be done. Two assistants discuss the Boss's (Brecht's) principles:

> LITTHENNER: The Boss's idea is to upgrade the plebeians and tribunes, give Coriolanus class-conscious enemies.
>
> PODULLA: He himself is enemy enough. Coriolanus defeats Coriolanus.
>
> LITTHENNER: With us the plebeians win out.
>
> PODULLA: I know his thesis. No muddleheaded insurrectionists—conscious revolutionaries. Can it be done?
>
> (Ralph Manheim trans., p. 6)

The actress who is playing Volumnia, Coriolanus' mother, enters with news of a real revolt. Brecht is not impressed. Then a delegation of workers shuffles on, requesting a written statement from the great man. Brecht treats their modest complaints that work norms have been set too high by calling them tame revolutionaries who are afraid to walk on the grass. When Volumnia (that is, Helene Weigel) urges Brecht to show sympathy, he reveals that a certain caution lurks behind the contempt.

Act 2 reveals another aspect of Brecht's evasiveness: his aestheticism. In a remarkably unconvincing scene, we find him staging, with the help of the workers, a parody of the uprising. The workers are not pleased and say that Brecht is letting down the shutters, just as was done at the university. Another event occurs to prevent Grass's static play from coming to a halt: the official "people's poet," Kosanke (based on one Kurt Bartels, otherwise known Kuba), confronts Brecht and the workers with the strict party line. In act 3 the workers discuss the indifference to their revolt that the West displays. When messages arrive announcing the spread of the movement, the workers, in a strangely listless scene, start to hang the Boss and his assistant, Erwin, but are dissuaded when the latter tells the old tale of the belly and the limbs used by Shakespeare.

Russian tanks are heard, and drama intrudes onto Brecht's stage from the outside. A wounded man who has torn the Russian flag from the Brandenburg Gate enters, followed by a hairdresser, who, inspired by Kathrin in Brecht's play *Mother Courage,* tries to tempt the Boss out onto the street. For a brief second he nearly yields. But a state of emergency has been declared, and the turning point finds Brecht delivering a soliloquy.

In the fourth and final act, Erwin announces the failure of the uprising. The actors return from outside and report on how the populace attacked Russian tanks. The official poet returns to gloat, while the Boss retires to the interior world of Brecht's late poetry. The sober, sensible demands for adjusted work norms have been falsely despised by the arrogant intellectuals, represented by Brecht with his Coriolanus-like attitude of disparagement, and the whole affair has been distorted into false drama.

Grass's distrust of dramatic activism emerges clearly in the thirteen scenes of the play *Davor* (*Max,* 1969) in which five figures hold a discussion (as in Goethe's *Tasso*) on the propriety and legitimacy of action. Two forty-year-old schoolteachers confront two seventeen-year-old students, one of whom proposes burning his dachshund in public to protest the Vietnam War (it is January 1967) and the coalition government in West Germany. An unnamed dentist is also present to represent the advantages and absurdities of matter-of-factness. The student finally refrains from the cruel and absurd drama of activism.

The third volume of poetry, *Ausgefragt* (Cross-examined, 1967), strikes a political note, although reminiscences of prewar Danzig are still present. In this latter category are poems about Grass's childhood in Langfuhr and later visits to Gdansk. Filling out a hotel registration form, the poet recalls that the house where he was born is still standing, with the number plate in the same position, though the stucco has crumbled. These are simple, direct reminiscences, not traditional "literary" images, as in the earlier poetry. There are poems about cooking and smoking, and ten restrained but threatening pencil drawings among the sixty poems (some of which are translated in *New Poems*).

But it is the political poems in the section "Zorn, Ärger, Wut" (Anger, Vexation, Rage) that aroused indignation by their attacks on the fashionable protesters of 1966. In "Platzangst" ("Claustrophobia") the poet complains of the oppressive presence of middle-class ideologues, "sons of too good homes." Other poems attack the student habit of hissing at uncongenial opinions and the "new mysticism" of some socialist circles and "spiritualist Leninists." Right-wing politicians are attacked, and the reader is urged to vote for the Socialist party (SPD).

The plot of the play *Max* corresponds to the central section of Grass's next novel, *örtlich betäubt* (*Local Anaesthetic,* 1969), which turns to postwar Germany as a central concern. It is set in 1967, a period marked by student unrest, and deals with "hard, sober, peacetime problems." Störtebeker, the leader of a gang of youths who plundered a Danzig church in *The Tin Drum,* is now a forty-year-old high school teacher called Starusch.

In the first and the third sections of the novel, Starusch is at the dentist, the beneficiary of two types of anesthetic that modern society provides. There is the Novocain that precedes treatment and the television screen that humanely distracts the patient from the prick of the injection. The comforting effect is enhanced by advertisements for freezers and vulgar displays of luxury foods. The dentist himself offers up Stoic doctrine, complete with quotations from Seneca and a demonstratively undramatic belief in hygiene and technology.

The dentist and his elaborate equipment embody to some extent the anesthetizing of revolutionary impulses that Herbert Marcuse so loudly condemned in the 1960's. Yet the violent activism that he and other intellectuals commended in that period (with the working classes conspicuously absent) is no solution, as we can see in the example of Starusch's most intelligent and enterprising pupil, Scherbaum, who develops a plan to burn his dog in front of comfortable bourgeois ladies eating cream cakes; the action is intended as a protest against the use of napalm in Vietnam. Revolutionary theory—to which Scherbaum is slowly converted by his girlfriend and fellow student, the fanatical Maoist Vero Lewand—can only turn out, in practice, to be cruel, absurd, and ineffective. Scherbaum slowly abandons the plan rather than pose as a man of decision, a conversion brought about by his awareness of the need for compromise. This awareness, too, passes through an absurd stage in his request to the dentist to anesthetize the dog. But he ends by scrapping the whole plan and parting from Vero.

Starusch, with memories of being seventeen years old and in revolt against the authorities, is tempted by the political dynamism of the times: "When I was seventeen, I could, too." He cannot give his pupil guidance, especially when the latter recalls a certain seventeen-year-old Bartholdy who, in 1797, tried to proclaim a republic in Danzig (he is referred to in *Der Butt* [*The Flounder,* 1977]) and suffered long imprisonment. Even more disturbing is Scherbaum's discovery of an apprentice, Helmut Hübener, executed in 1942 at the age of seventeen. The latter, unlike the anarchistic Störtebeker, proceeded pragmatically against the Nazi regime. At times, in the dentist's chair, Starusch has enticing visions of "bulldozers clearing the way in a revolutionary gesture." But a vision of student protesters with their ritual chant of "Burn, warehouse, burn" is abruptly terminated by a real burning sensation when the dentist's forceps slip. When Vero Lewand, with her loose revolutionary jargon, insists that the teacher should not "tranquilize" Scherbaum, she is arrogantly overlooking the inevitability of pain, a matter on which the dentist is tediously insistent.

Vero is egged on by Starusch's colleague Irmgard Seifert, who had, confusingly enough, been fanatical at the age of seventeen in her hatred of the official enemies: Jews and Bolsheviks. Now she is a fervent partisan of the radical cause. Moreover, she bears a burden of guilt from the past. As an obedient member of a Nazi party youth organization, she had denounced a backslider to the authorities. Scherbaum finds her rhetoric merely bewildering. On the other hand, to use an expression that rouses radical ire, Irmgard's tropical fish seem to demonstrate, in a comic manner, that social ills cannot be solved by welfare and prophylaxis. The fish are carefully tended, yet every morning one is found floating belly-up.

Starusch, too, is deformed by the past, and his lengthy course of dental treatment is to improve his brutal appearance caused by prognathous malformation. The reader is told of Starusch's past. In the early 1950's he had studied mechanical engineering and had prospects of marriage into a well-to-do family in the cement industry whose works were spreading a layer of dust as Germany registered a postwar recovery. But Starusch had abandoned the promising career open to him when the father of the family, a field marshal with a murderous record, returned from Russian captivity, neatly avoiding protesters, and engaged his daughter in war games.

Starusch turned to teaching German and history, thus (feebly?) removing himself from active participation in the economic miracle and yielding his bride to another (he is still subject to absurd fantasies about murdering the family). By the same token, Starusch now stands aloof from the activism of the young middle-class revolutionaries. His values provide no certainties and are open to criticism. He reduces Scherbaum to conformity. The dentist's chair of hygiene and rationalism in which Starusch's prognathism has already been treated has been presented with tedious attention to detail. Now Scherbaum, too, will be subjected to "local anesthetic." Vero Lewand marries a Canadian linguist. To add to the uncertainty, at the end of the novel the central figure is still in need of dental treatment.

Although *Local Anaesthetic* is haunted by doubt, the need for a snail's pace rather than self-indulgent revolutionary arrogance is the theme of *Aus dem Tagebuch einer Schnecke* (*From the Diary of a Snail,* 1972), which appeared in time for the 1972 elections and tells, among much else, of Grass's political activities during the 1969 elections in which Willy Brandt, the socialist, won a narrow victory. Grass toured the country in a Volkswagen van and gave more than a hundred speeches for the Social Democrats. The *Diary* is faithful to the inconclusiveness of lived experience—and hence to the honesty of Brandt's variety of socialism—by utilizing a multiplicity of forms: documentary autobiography, a novelistic plot with narrator's and narrated time, personal anecdotes, history, reflection, and memory. A consistent narrative is never allowed to develop; instead, it is constantly interrupted by association and events from disparate periods.

In the first place, an account of the day-to-day campaigning gets mixed with the grotesque life of one Hermann Ott, known as "Doubt," who collected snails and tried to help the Jewish community in prewar Danzig. Then there are Grass's apologetic remarks to his children to justify his absences ("still the same old SPD"). Much of the Ott story concerns the past and Danzig, a romantic lost province with half-timbered warehouses in the Mausegasse "where silent in their overcoats, aged Jews went on waiting." Contained in the story are some experiences of the critic Reich-Ranicki, and this in its turn arouses speculations as to how he will receive the *Diary.* Ott is forced to take refuge in a cellar, where he continues his study of snails and encounters the inarticulateness of Lisbeth Stomma. Ott, then, roughly embodies the boredom of the political campaign and the honesty of its aims. The approach of the Dürer year 1971 (Albrecht Dürer was born in 1471) leads to consideration of the engraving *Melencolia I* and another strand in the pattern of the diary. Thus we have the account of the campaign, with Grass's belief in a snail's patience and progress; the story of the anti-Hegelian Ott with his passion for snails, whose story takes him from 1933 to the collapse of Danzig in 1945; and the figure of Dürer, who represents the melancholy skepticism shared by Ott, Grass, Willy Brandt, and Schopenhauer, the Danzig philosopher and corrective to Hegel. *Melencolia*'s choler and depression illustrate the boredom of political campaigning in modern, democratic elections, in which trite speeches, the shaking of hands, and a succession of hotel rooms play a necessary part. Yet such mundane matters are not to be despised. The theme of domesticity constantly intrudes in the book, generally in the form of a chorus of disrespectful children and descriptions of cooking (to show the virtues of slow simmering). They are depicted in the author's stream of consciousness, at the same level as historical events and newsworthy items.

Self-criticism is present in the children's lack of appreciation of their father's oblique approach. When he shows them a postcard of the Dürer engraving on a dull Sunday at home, or tries to tell them tales of Ott and his snails in Danzig long ago, they are disappointed that their father provides speculative models instead of the truth.

Nonetheless, Grass persists with his eccentric snail imagery to convey that progress is slow and tedious, that children learn slowly, and that adults change their habits slowly. Yet snails achieve much and are even recommended in the context of lovemaking—Grass's customary scurrility serves to bring politics to the level of the everyday. Thus, too, with the petty squabbles and mishaps of domestic life, for they are to be encountered everywhere. Willy Brandt is in the snail tradition, an unromantic leader, anxious and taciturn before his campaign appearances, fidgeting with matches and retiring into his shell in the manner of Grass and Ott. His political victory, with which the *Diary* concludes, is no radical new beginning but (and this is ultimately its strength) part of a policy of small steps, of a problematical, plodding progress.

With his long novel *Der Butt* (*The Flounder,* 1977) Grass turned to feminist questions in an approach that is concerned with food (in all its phases), sex, and unofficial (often downright eccentric) history. As in the *Diary,* scurrility and eccentricity prevent Grass from indulging in the resounding clichés, attitudinizing, and false drama to which political themes are prone. As in the *Diary,* too, the narrator is close to the author. In the novel, the narrator constantly slips into historical realms from the Stone Age to the mid 1970's, although the historical costume is always slipping, with humorous effect. Autobiographical elements are openly present to an extent unthinkable in the earlier novels.

The elements of the novel are held together by the fairy tale "The Fisherman and His Wife," one of those collected by the Grimm brothers. In this tale, a fisherman good-naturedly releases a talking fish and is rewarded, on his wife's insistence, by being granted several wishes. The first wish, for a neat house in place of a tumbledown cottage, is duly granted. But the wife, Ilsebill, is still not content. She sends her apologetic husband back to the beach to make further demands for a mansion, a palace, and royal crowns, demands that culminate in the wish for divine status. The fish then withdraws what he has granted, and the disgruntled woman has to return to the original cottage.

The sensibility expressed in this ancient tale is akin to that of a cat among pigeons: comic, irreverent, unjust, yet not without insight into human nature. Furthermore, the tale is calculated to provoke the ideologically minded. The narrator's wife, Ilsebill (her name is the first word of the novel), has the same restless insistence as her prototype, though her demands (for a dishwasher and other items) are not exorbitant. The novel is also held together by another age-old element unamenable to ideology, yet not to be overlooked: that of childbirth. The book opens with conception and ends with a (cesarean) birth, with nine chapters in between. Each bears the name of the wife of the narrator concerned for each of the nine ages from the Stone Age to the present. To prevent excess and unnatural neatness, there are actually three women in the first age (Aua, Wigga, and Mestwina, born in 997). The last woman and cook is Maria Kuczorra, born in 1949, who works in a canteen in Gdansk.

The whole is a vivid yet grotesque history of the human race (with emphasis on the Danzig region) in which the role of women is at last acknowledged. The first phase, set in Stone Age Danzig, parodies modern anthropology of the type that fills gaps left by orthodoxy, in the manner of Lévi-Strauss. Thus the first woman, Aua, a female Prometheus, is a matriarch whose three breasts (Grass makes much of this) enable her to subjugate the men in her society. She is transformed into two other matriarchs and then into a succession of women living in the Danzig region: Dorothea von Montau (fourteenth century), Margarete Rusch (1498–1585), Agnes Kurbiella (1619–1689), Amanda Woyke (1734–1806), Sophie Rotzoll (1784–1849), Lena Stubbe (1848–1942), Dr. Sibylle Miehlau (1929–1963), and, finally, Maria. They are all cooks, and each woman demonstrates her era in a farcical, exaggerated way; Margarete Rusch, for example, is a feminist Rabelaisian, an abbess with drastic ways in bed and at table. Amanda, an eighteenth-century rationalist, plays a worldly role—unacknowledged, of course—as the inventor of potato soup. Lena, in the nineteenth century, writes a proletarian cookbook and meets August Bebel and Rosa Luxemburg. It is also characteristic of this chronicle that Lena should have married two dockyard workers who regularly beat her before she is finally murdered in the Stutthof concentration camp at the age of ninety-three. And so it is with the other women. Agnes is raped at the age of thirteen during the Thirty Years' War and ends her days by being burned as a witch. Toward the end of the novel the girl Billy (Sibylla) is raped and murdered by a motorcycle gang who run her over on Father's Day in 1963. Briefly, the brutal violence of history seems to be especially concentrated in the relations between men and women, however preposterous this history may be.

The urge to find a cure brings us to another strand of Grass's novel, which begins when the flounder allows himself to be caught by three hard-bitten feminists (using improvised tackle) in a Baltic Sea hopelessly polluted by the masculine spirit of enterprise. The fish speaks to them, a startling event that the women discuss in a parody of student revolutionary jargon. The flounder, when finally allowed to speak, explains that he has come to the conclusion that the male principle, which has ruled for so long, has turned merely destructive. He wants the women to set him free to build a better world, eliminating the old, antifeminist version of the ancient tale. But the women wish first to investigate the flounder's part in the history of male domination. Accordingly, they hold a trial in a Berlin movie theater, where the fish holds forth from a specially constructed tank before a gathering of feminists who are increasingly inclined to hostility. It is from the preposterous trial that the narrator obtains the material for the version of history given here.

Although the oppression is real enough, the trouble is that what emerges is merely an antithetical version of male-biased history. Perhaps the distortion arises from the nature of historical narration, which imposes coherent, logical structures by rearranging fragments. This narration is no exception. It sets out to prove a point: the feminist theory that the disasters of history spring from the psychic disorders of the male. Cast out from the womb and the contentment of Aua's matriarchal society, men vainly seek substitutes, engaging in killing as a continuation of sexuality by other means. The women's histories reveal a tale of male violence. Many of the men are engaged in armament production, and their violence gets worse as the weapons get more dangerous.

There is some truth in all this, and male oppression is a real enough phenomenon. Yet this history is a mirror version resembling the suppressed version of the Grimms' tale revealed in this novel. Here Ilsebill is entirely reasonable, and it is the fisherman's Faustian urge to dominate nature that spoils everything. He finally wishes to reach the stars, so that the fish has to recall him and the new Ice Age sets in.

Indeed, the whole novel sets out to show that no improvement is to be expected from mere reversal. Certainly the relentless bureaucratic formality with which the flounder's trial is conducted seems to promise little improvement from the government of women. It is true that the flounder is released, but this incident is greeted by a shower of stones from the radicals. The disjunctive structure of the novel and the multitude of styles suggest that a solution lies in a refusal to accept any single model or authority. Accordingly, the novel has three conclusions, corresponding to the last three months in which a living birth can take place. In the seventh month there is the conclusion suggested by the flounder, in which the man stands resigned before his history that now has the timeless form of a fairy tale: "Once upon a time . . . " The conclusion of the eighth month is completely pessimistic: the women rule in the old masculine way and repeat male failures. It is the ninth month that brings the open conclusion that Grass prefers. A girl is born, and we see the flounder in consultation with Maria, the last cook.

The next novel, *Das Treffen in Telgte* (*The Meeting at Telgte,* 1979), is derived from the fourth chapter of *The Flounder,* which tells of Martin Opitz, an important literary arbiter in seventeenth-century Germany, and his part in the Thirty Years' War. Grass professed to be surprised that foreigners should be interested in the intensely German events recorded in *The Danzig Trilogy,* but this novel is the most German of all, dealing as it does with literary and historical figures and events that are not well known outside German-speaking countries. Who, for example, outside of Germany has heard of the literary societies of the baroque period, the Kürbishütte and the Aufrichtige Tannengesellschaft? Even within Germany the younger generation is apt to be less familiar with, say, Martin Opitz or Andreas Gryphius than is Grass's generation.

Undeterred by such obvious considerations, Grass has his narrator report, from the standpoint of the twentieth century, on a meeting of writers said to have taken place in 1647, at the end of the Thirty Years' War. The meeting is imaginary, and its depiction represents an admiring parody of the meetings of the Gruppe 47 that Grass first began to attend in 1955. The writers meet at a time when their country has been torn apart by war and devastated by invaders. Nonetheless, they converge at an inn near Osnabrück in Westphalia, to the north of what today is the Ruhr district.

The writers and poets come from distant places, many of them now outside Germany; names and routes are given in detail. There is a hitch when the inn reserved by Simon Dach (a leading figure in Königsberg literary circles) is found to be occupied by Swedish troops attending the peace negotiations at Osnabrück (Protestant) and Münster (Catholic), two towns thirty miles apart. Fortunately, the enterprising young Grimmelshausen, one of the literary figures in attendance, recalls that Mother Courage (an imposing figure in one of his novels, later taken up by Brecht) keeps an inn at Telgte, situated between the two factions, so that the poets can represent a third force. In fact such a meeting never took place; it can be shown that the participants were somewhere else (Weckherlin, for example, was in London, working for Oliver Cromwell). Grimmelshausen obtains rooms for his party by a novelistic ruse; he drives off the occupying merchants by a rumor of plague. Some Protestant delegates have misgivings, but Dach (who represents Richter) addresses them and there is general conversation in a variety of dialects. This question of the use of dialects instead of High German is (among many other matters) a subject of debate, and manuscripts are read as they were at the meetings of Gruppe 47. The variety of points of view corresponds to Grass's conviction of the complexity of reality. Wild-eyed theoreticians and idealists encounter the self-taught, experienced, and sometimes rather coarse Grimmelshausen (a figure for Grass) or the diplomatic, commonsense Dach (Richter).

Grass's self-criticism is perhaps present in an incident in which, after a long evening of entertaining anecdotes, Dach wonders whether they have been guilty of "verbal whoring." Grass's abhorrence of cliché is reflected in Grimmelshausen, who expresses the unorthodox view that old folks are often childish and children are wise, noble ladies are coarse and peasants are refined, and states that brave heroes of his acquaintance have blasphemed even at the hour of their death. This is confirmed in the novel, for Mother Courage tells a better tale than the professional men of letters, and Gryphius cultivates a style of despair, proclaiming the end of poetry, but in fact is prosperous and well fed (a thrust at Heinrich Böll?). The poet Philipp von Zesen, out walking in the twilight, sees corpses in the river (in particular a pair of entwined lovers) and uses them as poetic metaphors. For him, in any case, the war is the consequence of the degeneration of language resulting from the neglect of Opitz. Here is a case of literature being used as a means of evasion in the manner of the bugbear Heidegger or, more recently, Jacques Lacan.

The composer Heinrich Schütz (Hans Werner Henze?) arrives in time for the second day's readings, looking for a text to set to music. He is highly critical of some passages. A lavish banquet is prepared, but here, too, Schütz turns out to be an uncomfortable companion. Instead of showing suitable gratitude, he accuses Grimmelshausen of having taken the supplies from foraging Swedes. He then departs, leaving behind the poets, who enjoy the meat provided and yet are troubled by the persistent guilt characteristic of the postwar German literary scene. The festive board becomes a picture of desolation. Only Dach will have none of this universal guilt, which is expressed so forcibly by Gryphius. Finally Grimmelshausen is put on trial, rather like the flounder before him, and is acquitted, but his character is stained. Poets are difficult people, and Grimmelshausen has already created an untoward incident by punching Mother Courage in the face for taunting him for his lack of education (something that Grass has made a matter for self-criticism). She therefore ignores Grimmelshausen when he takes his leave by throwing down a purse full of silver that he found, he claims, in Mother Courage's bed as he prepares to depart. Old Weckherlin claims the purse quietly and without loss of dignity; nobody laughs. In spite of his principles, Grimmelshausen has relied on the conventions of literary clichés, and they have turned out to be as invalid as political slogans.

Through all these upsets, accompanied by internecine hatred (old Weckherlin has always loathed the Swabians with their greed, their narrowness, their mania for cleanliness, and their prevarication—all increasingly thought of as German qualities)—the poets manage to compose an appeal for peace. The appeal creates much bad feeling. Accusations of "bourgeois niggling" and "flowery rhetoric" are flung about. Nonetheless something gets hammered out.

Unfortunately the appeal is lost when the inn goes up in flames, and the poets wend their various ways. The voice of the third force of tolerance and humanity is, all the same, admirable for all its querulous self-contradictoriness and ineffectiveness. Critics praised Grass for his skilled use of literary and historical seminar material. The German edition ends with a short anthology of poems by the principal figures in the novel.

The narrative essay with fictional elements and time-shifts, the form of the *Diary*, is also the form of the next work, *Kopfgeburten; oder, Die Deutschen sterben aus* (*Headbirths; or, The Germans Are Dying Out*, 1980). As the narrative opens, Grass, now a celebrity, has been invited to make an Asian tour and lecture at Goethe Institutes together with Volker Schlöndorf, the director of the film version of *The Tin Drum* (1979). Also in 1979 Grass married Ute Grunert, having separated from Anna the previous year. Ute is mentioned in the text, which has a strong autobiographical element. The problem of overpopulation, which inevitably strikes Grass when he and his wife are among the teeming bicyclists of Shanghai, arouses in him the fantasy of imagining that the Germans were as numerous as the Chinese, 950 million Germans, predicted to multiply to over 1 billion by the year 2000. Is it not strange that he should lecture to 200 patient Chinese on the division of Germany, a matter that hardly seems to interest the Germans? Nevertheless, the narrator continues to think about the German past and the German elections in this Asiatic context, where the Chinese have had more recent troubles of their own in the form of the counterrevolutionary era under the Gang of Four, during which the nation was stultified.

For the sake of the population problem, Grass invents a married couple, Dortë and Harm Peters, schoolteachers worried about the state of the world, who undertake an Asian tour. They are driven to distraction by the question of whether or not they should have a baby. What answer will the sight of Asian slums provide? Will the wife conclude that there are already too many people starving on a small planet? Or will they choose an alternative cliché and compare the joyful fecundity of these simple people to the distressing fact that the Germans are dying out? (This is shouted by a girl student of Dörte Peters, who daily makes a show of swallowing a birth-control pill before adressing her class.) They return home as confused as ever by ideas that are contradictory, illogical, and disturbing, the "headbirths" of the title starting up like hares.

Is childlessness a passing social trend, or is there cause here for dismay? In a primitive fishing village near Bombay, Dörte is seized by the wish to have a child until the couple notice the village children, who, although unspoiled by TV compulsion, are "just quietly too many." Only Grass and Schlöndorf try to pull these random thoughts into shape in the script for a film to be called *Headbirths*—a film that is not, it is to be feared, very promising. Again home in Germany, in a town ruined by modernization, the schoolteachers nearly run over the child of a Turkish guest worker and do not know what to say in German.

In this novel Grass has once more demonstrated, through a variety of perspectives (including his own as author and writer of film scripts), his disbelief in dramatic revelations. The solution to the world population problem lies neither in the scrupulosity of the Peterses (whose vacation includes slum visits), nor in the bureaucracy of the Chinese (who limit each couple to one child), nor in the careless fecundity of India. The guide to the Peterses' imaginary tour (which to some extent resembles the real journey undertaken by Grass and his wife), a master of all languages, points in a superior fashion to the drawbacks of all solutions offered and earns the dislike of his little flock. The German question, which obsesses Grass during many digressions from the main plot, is equally elusive. There is also a subplot involving a liver sausage from Germany that is carried about the world by the schoolteacher couple. Even this, we are told, is autobiographical. The real-life sausage was a present for the German ambassador in China, a reminder that Grass is now a celebrity who is received in such circles.

If history can be said to have solutions, they emerge from an accumulation of doubts (as in *Headbirths*) or of detritus (as in the opening of *Dog Years*). In the earlier work the opening narrator, Brauxel, dabbling in the mud of the Vistula, assembles his chronicle from the deposits of history. In all its absurdity history is all-pervasive; even the trees outside the windows of Amsel's villa are full of squirrels and Prussian history. Stutthof concentration camp has a history that is duly recalled in *Dog Years*, and, when we have descended to these nether regions, the very rats that haunt this desolate area of bones have a history, beginning with Noah: "The same old song since the days of Noah. Rat stories, true and made up. And when Paris was besieged. And when the rat sat in the tabernacle . . . When they disemboweled the clocks and confuted time . . . When they were sanctified in Hamelin" (*Dog Years,* p. 328).

It is this history that Grass has chosen for his 1986 novel with the strange title *Die Rättin* (*The Rat,* 1986; perhaps better translated as *The Ratess,* a similarly made-up word meaning a female rat). The rat in question, a Christmas present to the narrator, is not without the appeal that animals possess (the reader is invited to notice her little five-fingered paws), but nonetheless she pronounces doom over all humankind, choking in its own garbage. Rats were excluded from Noah's ark as unclean, yet when Noah sent the dove out, it returned with an olive branch and reports of having seen fresh rat droppings. The creatures had survived in God's hand (even having a litter) to plague mankind. In the late twentieth century, when valleys are choked with depressing filth, when poisons furtively jettisoned and myriad plastic bottles and wrecked autos are strewn about, the rat alone seems capable of survival.

A poem on Grass's beloved Baltic Sea tells of the jellyfish that fill those polluted waters so that the sea threatens to turn into one big jellyfish. It is true that research is being undertaken. We read of a crew of women who have restored a romantic old Baltic lighter for this purpose, a vessel that has survived two world wars and the terrible closing stages of the second, when the Baltic was full of the corpses of drowned refugees. But the rat is not disconcerted by this activity or by this evidence of enlightenment. She points out that human beings create filth and garbage even when they are seeking the truth. Rats have grown fat on folios, parchments, and encyclopedias. The solution offered is even more dubious than usual. In chapter 7 the narrator finds himself, dreaming of the rat and of Danzig, addressing the Bundestag. He is recommending use of the neutron bomb, which preserves artworks while allowing mankind to perish through evaporation of body fluids. There are, it is true, technical difficulties (e.g., a layer of soot that would form on the artworks concerned), but these could surely be overcome by means of research. The women's research vessel, the *New Ilsebill,* then sets out for the lost city of Vineta and the interesting discovery of singing jellyfish (culture will survive catastrophe).

From the standpoint of the present, often strangely inhabited by Grass characters, further developments are suggested. For example, in chapter 6, the figure of Matzerath from *The Tin Drum,* now the owner of a Mercedes with chauffeur, has a vision of a sort of crossbred human rat achieved by manipulation of genes. The idea is based on the forgeries of the painter Malskat, whose mention brings out reminiscences of the late war and postwar period when he adorned Lübeck churches with medieval wall paintings. By chapter 11, with the aid of the Grimm brothers, Malskat, and modern gene technology, these new creatures replace the rats already occupying the historic city of Danzig (Gdansk). Grass does not miss the opportunity to compare this invasion with previous ones by the Goths and the Teutonic Knights, to name but two. The rat people are blue-eyed, handsome, with a touch of pig. Swedish influences seem to have been at work. They mark their conquests in the usual rat manner, with their droppings. Then the observers—Grass and the female rat—notice that the young are undergoing military drills. Dragonlike bulldozers appear from underground concrete silos, clearing away the greenery that has grown on the autobahns since mankind vanished. The bulldozers proceed to destroy all the figures from the Grimms' fairy tales (the vehicles are also equipped with old-fashioned flamethrowers from the attack on the Polish Post Office in *The Tin Drum*).

A brief hope is offered in the last chapter that these new rat people will bring back some form of civilization, especially as Matzerath, who by now is identical with the author himself, is celebrating his sixtieth birthday and producing videos for public entertainment. The new rat people even have a museum of objects from the human period (including the concentration camp Stutthof). There is a rat person playing Bach or Buxtehude on the organ, and the rat people have established a just society. It could be claimed that it represents the Polish Solidarity movement, which had its beginnings in Gdansk. But there follows a sad, strange confession from Matzerath-Grass that Oskar's drum was a vain attempt to summon up the past merely for entertainment in an era of increasing prosperity. He allows the rats to return at the conclusion of the novel. He tries to shake off the vision, but the female rat maliciously informs him that the rats are far more real than the first dream of a peaceful mankind living natural lives. On this note the elaborate, often comic, fantasy ends.

A professor at Matzerath-Grass's sixtieth birthday party describes his host as a typical phenomenon of the 1950's. Grass's opposition to all ideologies, so clearly expressed in his first novel, is certainly characteristic of his generation. His rejection of the false guidance of doctrinal convictions, associated with the evils of the recent past, places Grass among the humanist existentialists of the 1950's and early 1960's. His ingrained distrust of ideologies was less popular with a later generation in the 1970's, which found his liberalism and gradualism ineffective or even a disguise for something more sinister.

According to Grass, it is incumbent upon each of us to face reality in all its absurdity without the false props of ideological beliefs or, what is related, the belief in sudden revelations or dramatic conversions. Drama represents an inauthentic attempt to reduce an absurd world to a state of artificial order. The individual is isolated in this contingent world, though this idea, too, can be overdramatized (indeed, this is the source of Oskar's irony); this realization does not exclude individual commitment and responsibility, especially within the context of German history.

Thus, for all its irreducibility, history should be studied; it is also entertaining. *Dog Years* opens with an extended image of history in which the accumulations of the past, the detritus of the river Vistula, build up to the present: "What had long been forgotten then rose to the memory, floating face up or face down on the Vistula." The list that follows is full of exotic names: Adalbert, the martyr who came to convert the Prussians; Swantopolk, who was baptized; fiery-red Perkunos and pale Pikollos, the heathen gods; Kynstute, who resisted the Teutonic Knights; the knights who drove the heathen Prussians into the forests of Lithuania; and the Napoleonic Wars. The tale of violence continues unbroken to the present, and in the last novel is projected into the future; the centuries are mingled with private lives and historical events. Comically grim metaphors have their origin in the intertwining of the trivial and quotidian with historical forces. Thus the dogs of *Dog Years* have a pedigree akin to that of their human companions. In fact, this heritage stretches back to the myths of heathen Prussia, in which the grandson of a Lithuanian she-wolf, the black dog Perkun, sired the bitch Senta. We descend eventually to the police barracks in Danzig and Harry's father, as proud as if he had been chosen for stud purposes. On the wall are photographs of twenty-four dogs and one of Hindenburg.

The absurdist approach to history and to human activities means that colors, with their random and contradictory associations, are often important; the color black is linked to the dogs. Even more prominent is Grass's often obscene and comic insistence on basic matters that official history prefers to ignore, especially questions of food and sex. Grass will not allow us to forget our limitations. All these aspects of Grass's work—ranging from his stylistic variety to the perspectives of his narrators—go back to his postwar hostility to ideology. There are no universal laws, and events do not obey the constructs of human logic or philosophy: class struggles, Hegel's *Weltgeist*, or historical turning points. Thus the soothsayer Matern, the miller in *Dog Years* who listens to mealworms, is the only guide through the exciting years of the "economic miracle," and *The Diary of a Snail* recommends patience, humility, and Brandt's policy of little steps.

In the matter of literary influences, no commentator on Grass should fail to mention Alfred Döblin, acknowledged by Grass in the essay "On My Teacher Döblin" (1968). Döblin is best known as the author of *Berlin-Alexanderplatz,* but Grass devotes his attention to another novel, *Wallenstein* (1920). Schiller's play *Wallenstein* created order and logic, made sense of an incoherent series of events. Grass praises Döblin for consciously shattering this neat order so that reality might emerge. A related refusal to draw any distinctions between the real and the grotesque is the basis of Grass's style and imagery, and of his peculiar power as a writer.

## Selected Bibliography


### EDITIONS

#### INDIVIDUAL WORKS

NOVELS

*Die Blechtrommel.* Neuwied, 1959.
*Katz und Maus.* Neuwied, 1961.
*Hundejahre.* Neuwied, 1963.
*örtlich betäubt.* Neuwied, 1969.
*Aus dem Tagebuch einer Schnecke.* Neuwied, 1972.
*Der Butt.* Neuwied, 1977.
*Das Treffen in Telgte.* Neuwied, 1979.
*Kopfgeburten; oder, Die Deutschen sterben aus.* Neuwied, 1980.
*Die Rättin.* Neuwied, 1986.

POETRY

*Die Vorzüge der Windhühner.* Neuwied, 1956.
*Gleisdreieck.* Neuwied, 1960.
*Ausgefragt.* Neuwied, 1967.
*Mariazuehren. Hommageàmarie. Inmarypraise.* Munich, 1973.
*Liebe geprüft.* Bremen, 1974.
*"Ach Butt, dein Märchen geht böse aus": Gedichte und Radierungen.* Darmstadt and Neuwied, 1983.

PLAYS

*Beritten hin und zurück: Ein Vorspiel auf dem Theater.* In *Akzente* 5:399–409 (1958).
*Theaterspiele.* Neuwied, 1970. Contains *Hochwasser, Onkel, Onkel, Noch zehn Minuten bis Buffalo, Die bösen Köche, Die Plebejer proben den Aufstand,* and *Davor.*

POLITICAL WRITINGS

*Über das Selbstverständliche.* Neuwied, 1968.
*Briefe über die Grenze: Versuch eines Ost-West-Dialogs.* Hamburg, 1968. With Pavel Kohout.
*Gunter Grass: Dokumente zur politischen Wirkung.* Edited by Heinz Ludwig Arnold and Franz Josef Görtz. Munich, 1971.
*Der Bürger und seine Stimme.* Neuwied, 1974.
*Denkzettel: Politische Reden und Aufsätze 1965–1976.* Darmstadt and Neuwied, 1978.
*Widerstand lerner: Politische Gegenreden 1980–1983.* Darmstadt and Neuwied, 1984.

LITERARY CRITICISM

*Über meinen Lehrer Döblin und andere Vorträge.* Berlin, 1968.

#### COLLECTED WORKS

*Gesammelte Gedichte.* Neuwied, 1971. Contains poems from his first three books of poetry, plus others drawn from his journals and novels.
*Werkausgabe in zehn Banden.* 10 vols. Edited by Volker Neuhaus. Neuwied, 1987.

### TRANSLATIONS

*Cat and Mouse.* Translated by Ralph Manheim. New York, 1963.
*Dog Years.* Translated by Ralph Manheim. New York, 1965.
*The Flounder.* Translated by Ralph Manheim. New York, 1978.
*Four Plays.* Translated by A. Leslie Willson and Ralph Manheim. New York, 1967. Includes *Flood, Mister, Mister, Only Ten Minutes to Buffalo,* and *The Wicked Cooks.*
*From the Diary of a Snail.* Translated by Ralph Manheim. New York, 1973.
*Headbirths; or, The Germans Are Dying Out.* Translated by Ralph Manheim. New York, 1982.
*In the Egg and Other Poems.* Translated by Michael

Hamburger and Christopher Middleton. New York and London, 1977.

*Local Anaesthetic.* Translated by Ralph Manheim. New York, 1969.

*Max.* Translated by Ralph Manheim and A. Leslie Willson. New York, 1972.

*The Meeting at Telgte.* Translated by Ralph Manheim. New York, 1969.

*New Poems.* Translated by Michael Hamburger. New York, 1968.

*On Writing and Politics, 1967–1983.* Translated by Ralph Manheim. San Diego, 1985.

*The Plebeians Rehearse the Uprising: A German Tragedy.* Translated by Ralph Manheim. New York, 1966.

*The Rat.* Translated by Ralph Manheim. San Diego, 1987.

*Selected Poems.* Translated by Michael Hamburger and Christopher Middleton. New York, 1966.

*Show Your Tongue.* Translated by John E. Woods. San Diego, 1989.

*Speak Out! Speeches, Open Letters, Commentaries.* Translated by Ralph Manheim. New York, 1969.

*The Tin Drum.* Translated by Ralph Manheim. New York, 1962.

## BIOGRAPHICAL AND CRITICAL STUDIES

Brode, Hanspeter. *Günter Grass.* Munich, 1979.

Cunliffe, W. Gordon. *Günter Grass.* New York, 1969.

Durzak, Manfred. *Der deutsch Roman der Gegenwart.* Berlin, 1979. See especially pp. 247–327.

———, ed. *Zu Günter Grass: Geschichte auf dem poetischen Prüfstand.* Stuttgart, 1985.

Geissler, Rolf, ed. *Günter Grass: Ein Materialienbuch.* Neuwied, 1976.

Hayman, Ronald. *Günter Grass.* London, 1985.

Hollington, Michael. *Günter Grass: The Writer in a Pluralist Society.* London, 1980.

Jurgensen, Manfred. *Über Günter Grass: Untersuchungen zur sprachbildlichen Rollenfunktion.* Berne and Munich, 1974.

Just, Georg. *Darstellung und Appell in der "Blechtrommel" von Günter Grass: Darstellungsästhetik versus Wirkungsästhetik.* Frankfurt, 1972.

Kaiser, Gerhard. *Günter Grass: Katz und Maus.* Munich, 1971.

Lawson, Richard H. *Günter Grass.* New York, 1985.

Leonard, Irène. *Günter Grass.* Edinburgh, 1974.

Loschütz, Gert, ed. *Von Buch zu Buch–Günter Grass in der Kritik: Eine Dokumentation.* Neuwied, 1968.

Miles, Keith. *Günter Grass.* New York, 1975.

O'Neill, Patrick, ed. *Critical Essays on Günter Grass.* Boston, 1987.

Reddick, John. *The 'Danzig Trilogy' of Günter Grass: A Study of The Tin Drum, Cat and Mouse, and Dog Years.* New York, 1975.

Rölleke, Heinz. *Der wahre Butt.* Düsseldorf, 1978.

Schwarz, Wilhelm Johannes. *Der Erzähler Günter Grass.* Bern and Munich, 1969.

Tank, Kurt Lothar. *Günter Grass.* Translated by John Conway. New York, 1969.

Thomas, Noel. *The Narrative Works of Günter Grass: A Critical Interpretation.* Amsterdam and Philadelphia, 1982.

Wagenbach, Klaus. "Günter Grass." In Klaus Nonnemann, ed., *Schriftsteller der Gegenwart.* Olten, 1963.

Wieser, Theodor. *Günter Grass.* Neuwied, 1968.

Willson, A. Leslie, ed. *A Günter Grass Symposium.* Austin, Tex., 1971.

Yates, Norris W. *Günter Grass: A Critical Essay.* Grand Rapids, Mich., 1967.

## BIBLIOGRAPHIES

Cepl-Kaufmann, Gertrude. *Günter Grass: Eine Analyse des Gesamtwerkes unter dem Aspekt von Literatur und Politik.* Kronberg, 1975.

Everett, George A. *A Select Bibliography of Günter Grass.* New York, 1974.

Görtz, Franz Josef. "Kommentierte Auswahl-Bibliographie." *Text + Kritik* 1/1a: 97–113 (1971).

Neuhaus, Volker. *Günter Grass.* Stuttgart, 1979.

O'Neill, Patrick. *Günter Grass: A Bibliography, 1955–1975.* Toronto, 1976.

W. GORDON CUNLIFFE

# MILAN KUNDERA

## *(b. 1929)*

MILAN KUNDERA WAS born in Brno, the capital city of Moravia, on 1 April 1929—almost exactly ten years before the Nazi tanks put an end, with a quiet consensus of Europe, to the young Czechoslovak republic. The writer's official literary career in his own country ended in 1968, when tanks, this time rolling from the east, ended the Prague Spring, an effort to reform the Communist system from inside. His life in Czechoslovakia, like that of many of his colleagues from Central Europe, was erratic and difficult, and he was constantly engaged in a struggle to protect his art from the confines so crudely drawn by historical events. In an interview conducted shortly before the Soviet invasion in 1968, he remarked:

> The events we have lived through in the last thirty years were no milk and honey, but they gave us a tremendous working capital for artistic exploitation. . . . Our experience may thus enable us to ask more basic questions and to create more meaningful myths than those who have not lived through the whole political anabasis.
>
> (*The Politics of Culture*, p. 148)

And indeed, the literature of Central Europe, mostly forced into exile or underground before the late 1980's, did create a number of lasting myths that established themselves in the mainstream of contemporary Western culture.

Kundera's own life resembled the typical path of a Central European intellectual, developing according to sudden, often painful turns of history. His early years were spent in an atmosphere of culture, national pride, and tradition. His father was a musician and a rector of the Brno Janáček Academy of Music, where he had been a pupil as well as one of the first interpreters of the great composer. As a boy Kundera studied music, later calling it his life's first great revelation of art. Yet he never considered choosing the musical profession because he was disappointed by the pretentiousness and pettiness of the musical community. Music did remain his lifetime fascination, though, and appears as a motif in much of his fiction.

Kundera spent his early youth in occupied Czechoslovakia, witnessing the undoing of what had been one of the most democratic countries in Europe. While in high school, he was forced to learn German, but as an act of rebellion he started secretly to study Russian. At the age of fourteen he began to write poetry, following the example of his older cousin who was a member of a group of wartime surrealists that included poets, artists, and sculptors. Surrealism was the main influence on the Czech avant-garde of that time and was associated there, as it was in Western Europe, with modern, rebellious lifestyles and progressive, radical politics. None of Kundera's poems written in that period survived, yet the author later recalled that they had a strong surrealist cast and in his opinion were better than many that he published after the war.

In 1947, at the age of eighteen, Kundera joined the Communist Party. As was often the case in his generation, the decision was more a spontaneous act of rebellion, a rite of passage into adulthood, than a conscious ideological choice. Communists in Czechoslovakia enjoyed genuine support in the first years after the war. There was a considerable tradition of left-wing politics practiced in the interwar period within the framework of parliamentary democracy, and, unlike in neighboring Poland, the Czechs never saw Marxism as something totally alien to their national tradition.

Unaware of the Stalinist atrocities, Czechoslovakia in 1945 greeted the Russians as liberators. At the same time, there was a lingering widespread disappointment in the country with Czechoslovakia's prewar allies, England and France, who had proved unable to protect it against Nazi Germany's territorial claims. On 29 September 1938 British Prime Minister Neville Chamberlain and French Premier Edouard Daladier had met with Hitler and Mussolini in Munich and had agreed to Nazi demands for cession of Czechoslovak regions with large German minorities. The Munich Conference thus initiated the dismemberment of Czechoslovakia, and consequently the German expansion throughout Central Europe. After the war the memory of Munich evoked profound skepticism among the population of the region about the moral validity of Western democracies, and in some cases paved the road for Communist propaganda.

In the first years of what seemed at that time a new era in the history of Europe, Communism was perceived by a large number of Czechoslovaks as the most radical, daring, and uncompromising manifestation of the spirit of the future, and as such it attracted the restless and the rebellious. Joining the Communists, claimed Kundera in one of his interviews, was seen as the utmost expression of nonconformity and freedom—a path followed by almost all Czech avant-garde artists and poets of the war generation. The new converts, however, soon discovered that in aesthetics, as in everything else, the party did not particularly care for the spirit of adventure, individualism, and liberty. After 1948 Czechoslovakia turned into a small replica of the Soviet Union, as did all the countries that had been recently incorporated into the Soviet bloc.

The new political dogmatism, which engulfed all walks of life, reached also the domain of art, in the form of "socialist realism" as the only officially approved style. Art was required to be realistic in method, romantic in spirit, optimistic, and always reflecting the party line. Artists who embraced the new movement soon woke up in the nightmare of kitsch. The party required them to follow the same petit-bourgeois aesthetics they had been rebelling against.

In the first years after the war the authorities courted artists and writers—always an important and useful elite section of every Central European society. Even after the Stalinization of culture had become quite obvious, some of those who accepted the initial offer displayed a curious though not uncommon tendency to look the other way and to humble themselves in the face of the country's new rulers. Not all of this was motivated exclusively by conformity and fear, as Kundera explained:

> An intellectual is a doubter. Above all he doubts himself, with great persistence and brilliance. Crisis, alienation, impotence, isolation—these supposed characteristics of intellectuals were actually invented by intellectuals themselves and turned into the great literary theme of the twentieth century. Intellectuals constitute the only segment of society capable of unmasking and analysing itself. Thus, there exists a certain masochism among intellectuals. To understand truths unfavorable to oneself requires great mental effort, and such an effort flatters the intellectual.
>
> (*The Politics of Culture,* pp. 136–137)

In the 1960's, when Kundera traveled to the West, he discovered the same taste for self-flagellation among many left-wing Western intellectuals. In time the same mechanism of self-doubt, even self-punishment, among Czech and other Central European intellectuals made them the vanguard of de-Stalinization. In the 1940's and 1950's, however, Kundera and most of his generation were more than ready to limit, and even to debase, their talents and ambitions in order to "serve" the new proletarian culture as envisioned by the party leadership.

In 1948 the author temporarily abandoned poetry and joined the FAMU, the Prague Film and Music School, which in the following years produced a whole group of outstanding film directors such as Miloš Forman, Jiří Menzel, and others. Despite the widespread excitement about the range and potentials of the cinematic art that was evident throughout Central Europe in those years, Kundera presented his decision as an act of sacrifice. Recalling his thoughts on that occasion, he said:

> I'll give up music and poetry precisely because these are too close to my heart, and I will make films because cinema doesn't have any special attraction for me. In this way I will get rid of personal consideration and I will take part in the only art which is just, the "art which serves people."
>
> (*The Politics of Culture,* p. 137)

A little thereafter, however, he was expelled both from the Communist party and from the school—an expulsion probably provoked by his taste for paradox and his lively imagination. He was accused of a lack of seriousness and of "hostile thoughts," which he apparently shared with some of his friends. Thus he learned one of the basic tenets of the totalitarian world: anything professed by those in power has to be taken with absolute seriousness. The system cannot tolerate any trace of humor or irony, which inevitably introduce an element of doubt and relativism. Much later the experience provided the material for Kundera's first novel, *Žert* (*The Joke,* 1967), in which the main character also falls victim to his own lack of respect for the solemnity of the new creed.

After 1950 the author worked for some time as a manual laborer and occasional jazz musician. In 1953 he managed to publish his first book of verse, *Člověk zahrada širá* (Man, the Vast Garden). As he admits, the book did not transcend the possibilities and limitations of the political and aesthetic atmosphere of the period, although at the time he saw it as an attempt to polemicize both with the narrow politicized vision of man, and with the restrictive requirements of "socialist realism." Even this timid departure from what the Communists considered a proper "proletarian" approach to poetry was enough to provoke attacks from the literary guardians of the party line.

In 1955 Kundera published his second book of poems, *Poslední máj* (The Last May), probably the most conventional and inconsequential of his works. In the meantime he managed to rejoin FAMU, this time as a member of its faculty teaching world literature. In 1956 he was reinstated in the Communist party and in the same year became a member of the editorial board of *Literární noviny* (Literary News), a weekly organ of the Czechoslovak Writers' Union. Throughout Central Europe, 1956 was a turbulent year. It witnessed the anti-Communist uprising in Hungary and a series of workers' unrests and party infighting in Poland. In Czechoslovakia the struggle for liberalization was slower and more cautious. The new party echelon, under the first secretary and president Antonín Novotný, tried to contain the intellectual and labor ferment while at the same time introducing a slightly modernized version of the Communist rule.

The growing demands from the Prague intelligentsia for more open policy were suppressed, however. The suppression culminated in the frontal attack on the Czechoslovak Writers' Union and its literary journal, although its victims were also Czechoslovak scholars, philosophers, and filmmakers. There was a series of dismissals from the party, as well as from teaching and editorial jobs, and the Communist authorities used a whole array of disciplinary measures and economic pressures to remove the undesirable elements from positions of influence. For those in the cultural forefront it was a time of struggle. Yet those who envy the Central European intellectuals the excitement of their campaigns should remember that apart from the more immediate risks they had to take, the continuous debate with the narrow-minded, anticultural politicians was for many of them a stifling and frustrating experience. Kundera compares it to putting a full-grown, adult culture back into the nursery, asking it in good will to start from the elements—to invest most of its energies into learning, or pretending to learn, the alphabet.

The author's third book of poetry, *Monology* (Monologues, 1957), is ostensibly apolitical. It is a sequence of confessional monologues of lovelorn, frustrated women, in which Kundera established one of his most pervasive themes—the erotic passion seen as one of the extreme situations that reveal what is unstable, irrational, and paradoxical in life. The book was sold out soon after its publication but could not be reprinted for eight years. Like *Člověk zahrada širá,* it became a target of violent criticism from official quarters, this time on moral rather than political grounds. It was claimed to be too blatant, pessimistic, and cynical in the treatment of its subject.

After the publication of *Monology,* probably his best poetic achievement, Kundera renounced poetry and turned to literary theory, drama, and especially to fiction. The reason, as he explained in his interviews, was a sudden distaste for any form of lyricism, a view he later developed into his own theory of literary genres, which became of great consequence for his writing as well as his view of the modern world. At that time he experienced certain problems with the "practice of literature," which made him devote more time to his literary theory. The fruit of this theoretical interest was the long essay, *Umění románu* (The Art of the Novel, 1960), a study of the work of a Czech novelist, Vladislav Vančura.

In 1962 Kundera wrote his first drama, *Majitelé klíčů* (The Owners of the Keys), which enjoyed considerable success and was staged in fourteen countries, among them Britain and the United States. Set in the era of the Nazi occupation of Czechoslovakia, it portrays the vacillations of a young, idealistic student who has to choose between his meditative detachment and involvement in the violent struggle of the Czech resistance.

Since the play gained some attention in the West after 1968, Western critics have tended to interpret it anachronistically as a veiled political work with references to the Soviet occupation. Nicholas Howey, who produced the drama at the American University in Washington, D.C., wrote in his introductory note that "an anti-Nazi play written in 1962 is not necessarily about the Nazis. A Czech play produced in the United States is not necessarily about the Czechs." Richard L. Coe, writing in *The Washington Post* (12 March 1970), remarked: "Setting his play in Nazi-occupied Czechoslovakia and using swastika armbands for an officer, Kundera employs one of the gambits he and others of the Czech Writers' Union use to try to keep alive the liberalization program of only two years ago."

At the time when the play was written, however, the moral option that faced most people was a choice between private decency and public conformity rather than the 1968 choice between private decency and public heroism. It is more plausible that Kundera used the classical home-versus-society theme to explore what happens when a choice is made that can affect one's whole life. The play, written in a simple, realistic mode, is interrupted by "visions" that portray the hypothetical consequences of the hero's decisions. Kundera seems to be interested chiefly in the very mechanism of choosing: How much of it results from our projection of the future, the pressure of the environment, the public demand, and the awareness that we are what we choose?

The 1960's were the most prolific and creative period in Kundera's career in Czechoslovakia. During this time he published three consecutive books of short stories under the common title *Směšné lásky* (*Laughable Loves,* 1963, 1965, 1968) and his first novel, *The Joke,* generally considered one of his major achievements. This period was also a time of growing tensions and divisions both within the Czechoslovak intellectual circles and in the political leadership. The weekly *Literární noviny* became the main forum for the supporters of a far-reaching liberalization in culture and politics. Along with two other cultural weeklies, *Kulturní život* and *Kulturní tvorba,* it enjoyed great popularity. According to some estimates the combined circulation of the three periodicals reached 300,000 in a country whose population did not exceed fourteen million.

The camp of the party conservatives, however, was becoming increasingly aggressive and in 1967 *Literární noviny,* after the rebellious Fourth Writers' Congress, was taken over by the Ministry of Culture. The year also witnessed the considerable activization of university students and younger faculty. In October 1967 a group of students housed in one of the dormitory complexes near Prague staged a peaceful demonstration demanding the improvement of their living conditions. The police brutality with which the demonstrators were met was one of the factors that changed their dissatisfaction into a political force that in turn enlarged the social base of the liberalization movement and produced a younger, and in many cases more radical generation of dissidents.

Simultaneously, anti-Stalinist sentiments started to mount in Slovakia, which until then had been relatively dormant and complacent. In the 1950's many Slovak leaders were purged on the accusations of "bourgeois nationalism." In 1960 they were rehabilitated by Novotný, but their position remained precarious. By the late 1960's, led by a relatively young first secretary of the Slovak Communist Party, Alexander Dubček, they demanded more autonomy for Slovakia within the bi-national Czechoslovak state. In October 1967, during a session of the Central Committee of the Czechoslovak Party, a clash occurred between Novotný and the Slovaks. Novotný tried to use the old argument about the alleged Slovak nationalism, but the move proved a major political mistake. At that time Novotný was isolated both internally and on the international arena. According to some reports he appealed for help to the Soviet leader Leonid Brezhnev, who, however, refused to get involved. On 19 December Novotný was forced to resign from the position of the first secretary, and on 5 January 1968 he himself recommended Dubček as his successor.

What followed is widely known to the world as the "Prague Spring," a short-lived yet explosive period of freedom in almost all walks of the public life. The reformist group within the party, led by a somewhat disoriented Dubček and supported by the intellectual elite, was frantically trying to win as much liberty and plurality as seemed possible within the framework of the socialist system. (It was at this time that Kundera joined *Literární listy,* the successor of the renowned *Literární noviny.*)

This unique situation in the history of the Soviet bloc was terminated on 20 August 1968, when more than 200,000 Soviet troops, supplemented by forces from East Germany, Poland, Bulgaria, and Hungary, invaded Czechoslovakia with tanks and paratroops. Faced with massive street demonstrations, the invading forces were subsequently increased to 650,000. Czechoslovak leaders—among them Alexander Dubček—were flown to Moscow where they were made to sign a document abandoning the democratizing reforms as well as accepting an indefinite Soviet military presence in their country.

During the Fourth Writers' Congress, held in June 1967, Kundera had delivered the opening address calling for greater artistic freedom. In a transparent allusion to the politicians in power he criticized those who "live purely in their own immediate present tense . . . quite capable of turning their country into a wasteland with no history, no memory, no echo of beauty." His words expressed one of the dominant themes of his writing, as well as a prophecy fulfilled in the 1970's and 1980's.

After the Soviet invasion Kundera, like thousands of writers, artists, intellectuals, and political leaders, was accused of counterrevolutionary sympathies and dismissed from his position at the Academy of Music and Dramatic Arts. His second play, however, *Ptákovina, čili Dvoje uši—dvoje svadba* (Double Wedding, 1968), was staged by a young experimental company in Prague as late as 1969. The fact that this drama, interpreted as a disguised attack on conformists, informers, doublethink, and the Russian occupation, could reach the stage under the Russian occupation testifies to the strength of the resistance and the sense of solidarity and defiance in the Czechoslovak society, which tried to salvage as much as possible of the brief period of freedom. These efforts, however, proved futile.

By 1969 the new Soviet-supported regime was firmly in power, and the purges intensified. Kundera was banned from publication and was forced out of his job at *Literární listy,* which was closed down. In 1970 he was offered the opportunity to "rehabilitate himself" through public self-criticism. Having refused, he was stripped of any possibility of earning his living as a writer. His works were removed from libraries, and he was forbidden to travel to the West. His foreign royalties were taxed at a rate of 90 percent. The author returned temporarily to Brno, where, under a pseudonym, he started to write an astrology column for a local magazine. But even this source of income was denied him when his authorship was discovered in 1974. One year later he received an invitation from the University of Rennes in France, offering him an assistant professorship in literature. For the first time since 1968 he obtained permission to leave his country and thus assumed his new position. The moment of departure—a mixture of lightness, relief, and remorse—returns as a motif in many of his works.

France proved especially hospitable to Kundera's writing. After the appearance of the French translation of *The Joke,* with an introduction by Louis Aragon, all his subsequent works were published first in France, by Gallimard, and then were put out in the Czech original by the Sixty-Eight Publishers in Toronto. Kundera's second novel, *Život je jinde* (*Life Is Elsewhere,* 1973), won the prestigious Prix Medicis for the best foreign novel published in France, gaining him the friendship and support of many French intellectuals. His subsequent novels—*Valčík na rozloučenou* (*The Farewell Party,* 1976), *Kniha smíchu a zapomnění* (*The Book of Laughter and Forgetting,* 1979), and *Nesnesitelná lehkost bytí* (*The Unbearable Lightness of Being,* 1984)—were equally well received.

With his wife, Vera, Kundera settled permanently in Paris, where they quickly became familiar figures in the French intellectual circles. He continued to write his fiction in Czech but wrote his essays in French. Until 1979 Kundera remained a Czechoslovak citizen, but when *The Book of Laughter and Forgetting* was published, the Czechoslovak authorities stripped him of his citizenship.

Even before this mostly symbolic final separation from his country, however, the author had to define for himself his new situation. The need for such definition, especially important for a writer, appeared in the form of a question faced by many exiles: whether to live like an émigré, a person whose consciousness and imagination still reside in the "old country," or to become "a Frenchman among the French." Kundera chose the second option and became a curious, yet not uncommon phenomenon—a French writer writing in a foreign language. As he said to Olga Carlisle in one of his interviews:

> My stay in France is final, and therefore I am not an émigré. France is my only real homeland now. Nor do I feel uprooted. For a thousand years Czechoslovakia was part of the West. Today, it is part of the empire to the east. I would feel a great deal more uprooted in Prague than in Paris.
> (*New York Times Magazine,* 19 May 1985)

Kundera's literary reputation is based primarily on his achievements as a novelist. For the author of *The Joke* the novel has a special significance both as a set of artistic possibilities and as a certain philosophy shaping our attitudes toward the surrounding world. "Lyricism, the epic, the drama," he says, "are not simply artistic genres from which an author is free to choose as he pleases; they are also existential categories" (*The Politics of Culture,* p. 146). Thus Kundera's decision to abandon poetry in the late 1950's and devote himself to narrative prose deserves our attention, since it illuminates both the aesthetic and moral aspects of the author's vision of the condition of modern man and his culture.

The negative part of this decision, according to Kundera, was connected with the discovery of certain dangers inherent in the lyrical mode of perception. A "lyrical state," as the author understands it, is one in which the self turns the objective, visible world into a hall of mirrors and a vehicle for self-contemplation. Lyricism derives its energy from emotion and the uncompromising yearning of the self for something larger and more perfect than the world known through everyday experience. Emotion is elevated to the rank of supreme value and the only criterion of truth. Persistent lyricism, for Kundera, is a kind of permanent adolescence, a one-man vendetta against everything that is imperfect, relative, and contingent. A lyrical state excludes what he sees as the basic feature of the mature mentality: disciplined reflection, skepticism, and wit. It is also a state especially prone to seduction and manipulation by all systems of thought that purport to provide a vision of a new, perfect reality free of relativism and accidentality.

> We cannot do without feelings, but the moment they are considered values in themselves, criteria of truth, justifications for kinds of behavior, they become frightening. The noblest of national sentiments stand ready to justify the greatest of horrors, and man, his breast swelling with lyric fervor, commits atrocities in the sacred name of love. When feelings supplant rational thought, they become the basis for an absence of understanding, for intolerance; they become, as Carl Jung has put it, "the superstructure of brutality."
>
> (*Jacques and His Master,* pp. 2–3)

Kundera saw this process exemplified in the times of Stalinist terror in Czechoslovakia—times that coincided with his own "lyrical age." A period of political trials, cruel persecutions, and invasion of privacy, this was also, however, a time of veneration of poetry, when people thronged poetic readings by the thousands and when most of the country's poets gave wholehearted or hypocritical—but always vocal—support to the new political order. "I am still able to remember vividly," says Kundera, "this state of passionate lyrical enthusiasm which, getting drunk on its frenzy, is unable to see the real world through its own grandiose haze." Then he continues:

> On the other side of the wall behind which people were jailed and tormented, Gullibility, Ignorance, Childishness, and Enthusiasm blithely promenaded in the sun. And so in periods of angry bias it seems to me that among the accused standing before the court—somewhere between Enthusiasm and Gullibility—I recognize the face of Seduced Lyricism.
>
> (*The Politics of Culture,* pp. 145–146)

Kundera's definition of lyricism as an adolescent excess of emotionalism and his equation of lyricism with poetry in general, may strike us as narrow and simplistic. It does not take into account the numerous possibilities modern poetry has developed in order to express doubt, irony, and reflection. It overlooks a whole chapter of highly developed poetry that derived from the same Central European experience and managed to provide some of the most truthful and clear insights into the condition of people living under the reign of Terror and Lie. Yet Kundera's "angry bias" points toward a quite real possibility of literary abuse that he wanted to avoid and to which he tried to find an antidote. He found it in the long tradition of the European novel, which came to signify for him the artistic and philosophical ideals he cherished most.

From his Central European observatory Kundera saw the fates of people and nations crushed by seemingly uncontrollable forces and governed by ideologies claiming to be the only repositories of truth. Like many of his colleagues from this part of the world, he sensed something more than a period of brutality and lies; he apprehended a feeling of decline of a certain civilization that in the Central European capitals had been taken for granted until World War II. Such moments demanded clear definitions of what was being lost and reassesments of the most rudimentary values. For Kundera this reassesment meant a search for a definition of European identity and culture, which he found in the tradition of the European novel, the most ambiguous and paradoxical of literary genres. In the novel he also discovered a model of the European character.

Kundera declared himself deeply attached to the idea of modernity—the secular, rationalistic, skeptical culture that emerged with the great intellectual breakthroughs of the eighteenth century. He also saw the subjection of his part of Europe to Stalinism as a radical negation of the modern spirit. It should be noted that the Czech author's affinity for the modern heritage is contrary to some intellectual tendencies that appeared in the same area in response to the totalitarian experience. It suffices to recall only the names of Alexander Solzhenitsyn or the Polish poet Czeslaw Milosz, who tended to see totalitaranism as the direct, perhaps inevitable, result of the same modern tradition that Kundera cherished. For them the seeds of the totalitarian utopias were planted in the age of reason, which they considered to be the source of narrow determinism and materialism. Kundera took issue with their arguments and proposed a different, more complex definition of modernity:

> Lately it has become a habit to speak ill of the eighteenth century to the point that we hear this cliché: the misfortune of Russian totalitarianism is the product of Europe, particularly of the atheist rationalism of the Enlightment, of its belief in all-powerful reason. I do not feel myself qualified to debate with those who blame Voltaire for the gulag. But I do feel qualified to say: the eighteenth century is not only the century of Rousseau, of Voltaire, of Holbach; it is also (perhaps above all!) the age of Fielding, of Sterne, of Goethe, of Laclos.
>
> (*New York Review of Books,* 13 June 1985)

In "The Novel and Europe" (1984) Kundera noted that the novel, both as a literary genre and as a particular mode of perception, emerged exactly at the time when the new science was reducing the world to an object of technical and mathematical analysis, pushing philosophy into the tunnels of specialized knowledge. The more specialized science became, the less clearly man could see either the world as a whole or his place in it. To describe this process the German philosopher Martin Heidegger used the phrase "forgetting about being," which returns in Kundera's fiction in numerous variations.

At the moment when Europe started to forget about her being, however, there appeared a great European art that was nothing less than an eruption, in a myriad of individual manifestations, of curiosity about being. This art, created by Cervantes, Sterne, and Diderot, took up the investigation into the nature of time, psychology, and emotion that was being abandoned by philosophy. The passion for knowing, the essence of the European spirit, says Kundera, "seized the novel and led it to observe man's concrete life closely and to protect him from the 'forgetting of being'" (*New York Review of Books,* 19 July 1984).

The rise of the novel, in Kundera's view, coincided with yet another feature of modernity: the sense of relativity of values in the secularized culture. In "The Novel and Europe" the author writes:

> As God slowly departed from the seat whence he had controlled the universe and its order of values, told good from evil, and given a sense to each

> thing, then Don Quixote came out of his mansion and was no longer able to recognize the world. In the absence of the supreme arbiter, the world suddenly acquired a fearsome ambiguity. The single divine truth decomposed into myriad relative truths shared among men. Thus was born the world of the Modern Era and with it the novel—the image and model of that world—sprang to life.
>
> (*New York Review of Books,* 19 July 1984)

In his address on receiving the Jerusalem Prize for Literature and the Freedom of Man in Society in May 1985, Kundera expressed the same thought even more figuratively, referring to the Jewish saying "Man thinks, God laughs." Why does God laugh at human intellectual exercises? asks the author. It is because "man thinks and the truth escapes him. Man's thoughts diverge from one another. Man is never what he thinks he is, nor is the world. The dawn of modern times revealed this fundamental situation of man as he emerged from the Middle Ages" (*New York Review of Books,* 13 June 1985).

The loss of certainty of values can lead to confusion and despair, but it can also become the foundation of salutary skepticism and tolerance. "It is precisely in losing the certainty of truth and the unanimous agreement of others that man becomes an individual." The domain of individual freedom, according to Kundera, is constantly threatened by two opposite tendencies: total nihilism and decomposition of all values and craving for one indivisible and undeniable truth. The novel, says Kundera, took the challenge to defend that uncertain territory and to become "the imaginary paradise of individuals . . . where no one possesses the truth, but where everyone has the right to be understood" (*New York Review of Books,* 13 July 1984). In order to do so it had to incorporate the divine laughter at human intellectual and moral inadequacy, the irony and skepticism that refuses to take the world seriously and to believe what the world would like us to believe. Kundera heard that laughter in the works of Cervantes and Rabelais, but most of all in his two great masters—Diderot and Sterne. He saw *Tristram Shandy* as "unserious throughout, since it does not make us believe in anything, not in the truth of its characters, nor in the truth of its author, nor in the truth of the novel as a literary genre. Everything is called into question, everything is entertainment" (Introduction to *Jacques and His Master,* p. 6).

The novel, at least in the early stage of its development, was seen by Kundera as a double invitation: to a journey and to a play. It offered a journey of newly liberated minds into a vast, still unmapped universe. It was also a play in which everything could turn out to be different from our expectations, where theoretical constructions could reveal their relativity, and where a thinking self could try on innumerable costumes. It provided a stage on which partial, individual truths could clash with each other, producing moments of joy, laughter, or pain, and where only such momentary sensations warranted the approval or rejection of these truths.

In the claustrophobic atmosphere of Central Europe, Kundera tried to recreate in his own writing the lightness and adventure of the modern spirit expressed in the novel form. His characters, besieged by powerful forces and circumstances beyond their control, seek routes of escape through skepticism and irony, through irresponsibility and unseriousness. Yet at the same time the author is aware that a recreation of the free space in which the modern spirit of humanity used to move is impossible. In his own writing the pursuit of adventure often turns into a painful grotesque, and a joke becomes a trap that confines the joker instead of liberating him. Something irreversible happened to our culture, narrowing our choices and silencing laughter. After four centuries of wandering, Kundera points out in his essay, Don Quixote returns to his village as K., the hero of Kafka's *The Castle,* his quest reduced to the squabble with the administration about a mistake in his dossier. Diderot's Jacques and his master turn into Vladimir and his servant, immobilized forever in Beckett's *Waiting for*

*Godot.* Kundera's works are nostalgic recollections of their journey and meditations on its possible end.

Kundera's first book of fiction, published in 1963, was the collection of short stories, *Směšné lásky* (*Laughable Loves*), which was followed by *Druhý sešit směšných lásek* (*The Second Book of Laughable Loves*) in 1965 and *Třetí sešit směšných lásek* (*The Third Book of Laughable Loves*) in 1968. The author considered the whole sequence one of his favorite achievements and the product of his happiest, most carefree years—a surprising statement, since amidst comic situations and brilliant, ironic dialogue, one often discovers underlying melancholy and pessimism. Most of the stories are built around the theme of a seduction, or an erotic adventure, although for their predominantly male protagonists sensuality and desire play suprisingly insignificant roles. Some of them, like the heroes of the story "Zlaté jablko věčné touhy" ("The Golden Apple of Eternal Desire"), do not even care to consummate the relationship with the women they relentlessly pursue. Womanizing, with its inevitable deceptions and role playing, is for them a statement of radical "unseriousness" through which they try to escape their narrow everyday existence. Kundera apparently follows the steps of W. H. Auden, who defines Don Juanism as "a mood of distaste for everything that is to any degree a bore, that is, for all forms of passionate attachment, whether to persons, things, actions or beliefs."[1] Such passionate attachments in Kundera's fiction are always suspicious and tend to bring disastrous results. "When you believe in something literally," says one of the characters in *Laughable Loves,* "through your faith you'll turn it into something absurd" (p. 111). Having discovered that life is an arbitrary, often absurd game, the heroes of the stories try to master it by becoming conscious, unrepentant players. "I can invent anything, make a fool of someone, carry out hoaxes and practical jokes," says a young art historian in "Nikdo se nebude smát" ("Nobody Will Laugh"), "and I don't feel like a liar and I don't have a bad conscience. These lies, if you want to call them that, represent myself as I really am. With such lies I am not simulating anything, with such lies I am in fact speaking the truth" (p. 86). And a young protagonist of one of the most interesting and complex of these stories, "Eduard a Bůh" ("Edward and God"), involved through an absurd accident in an affair with an aging, unattractive headmistress, proclaims to his older brother:

> Why in fact should one tell the truth? What obliges us to do it? And why do we consider telling the truth a virtue? Imagine that you meet a madman, who claims that he is a fish, and that we are all fish. Are you going to argue with him? Are you going to undress in front of him and show him that you don't have fins? . . . If you told him the whole truth and nothing but the truth, only what you really thought, you would enter into a serious conversation with a madman and you yourself would become mad. And it is the same way with the world that surrounds us. If I obstinately told a man the truth to his face, it would mean that I was taking him seriously. And to take something as unimportant seriously means to become less than serious oneself. I, you see, *must* lie, if I don't want to take madmen seriously and become one of them myself.
>
> (pp. 238–239)

Yet there is a darker, more upsetting side to this seemingly lighthearted philosophy of lies that brings Kundera's stories closer to Kafka than to Diderot. To say that life is a game of appearances does not imply that it is free of suffering. If every attempt at seriousness inevitably ends as a joke, a joke often turns into a tragedy; a carefree game of impersonations can suddenly reveal hidden brutality and hatred. In "Symposion" (originally entitled "Symposium"), among elegantly detached and ironic debates about life, sex, and death, a rejected girl tries to commit suicide. The young, ambi-

[1] "Don Juan," in *The Dyer's Hand and Other Essays* (New York: Vintage, 1968), p. 387.

tious teacher of art in "Nobody Will Laugh" devises an intrigue to ridicule and humiliate an impertinent autodidact but ends up losing his job, his career, and his girlfriend. In "Falešný autostop" ("The Hitchhiking Game"), a vacation prank of two happy lovers who decide to play total strangers to each other leads to mutual humiliation and distaste.

The most frightening and depressing aspect of the games in which the characters of *Laughable Loves* become involved is the fact that all human relations gradually lose their substance. Even people blur, lose contours, become interchangeable and insignificant. The title hero of "Edward and God," having finally possessed the girl he desired, discovers that his conquest is in fact a result of a misunderstanding, an illogical conclusion drawn from a wrong premise. In consequence he starts to see the object of his desire as

> an accidental conjunction of a body, thoughts, and a life's course; an inorganic conjunction, arbitrary and unstable. He visualized Alice . . . and saw her body separately from her thoughts. He liked this body but the thoughts struck him as ridiculous, and together they did not form a whole being. He saw her as an ink line spreading on blotting paper, without contours, without shape.
>
> (p. 237)

The hidden longing for some essence, stability, or "seriousness of being" that could reach beyond all appearances can be detected in many stories from *Laughable Loves.* Edward, who is an atheist and whose affairs both with the headmistress and with Alice culminate in mockery of religion, starts to visit churches. As the narrator of the story says,

> God is essence itself, whereas Edward had never found (and since the incident with the directress and with Alice, a number of years had passed) anything essential in his love affairs, or in his teaching, or in his thoughts. . . . And that is why Edward longed for God, for God alone is relieved of the distracting obligation of *appearing* and can merely *be.* For He solely constitutes (He Himself, alone and nonexistent) the essential opposite of this unessential (but so much existent) world.
>
> (p. 242)

The skeptic, the joker, and the blasphemer, unrepentant and unfulfilled, returns to the imaginary source of essence only to discover, like so many of his predecessors since the eighteenth century, that the source is dry.

Even a master of the game cannot put himself above the pain of such awareness. But the game itself, though bringing no liberation, has to go on, if only for the sake of the memory of the lightness and adventures of the past. One of the heroes of "The Golden Apple of Eternal Desire" meditates after a frustrated romantic escapade:

> Does perhaps some magnet not attract me to lead expeditions back to the time of freedom and wandering, of choice and searching, to the time of lack of commitment and initial choice? . . . What does it matter that it's all a futile game? What does it matter that I *know* it. Will I stop playing the game just because it is futile?
>
> (p.116)

The first novel by Kundera, *The Joke,* was published in Czechoslovakia in 1967. It brought the author international recognition when it appeared next year in French translation and when it was made into a film presented at Cannes in 1969. Yet it also revealed the peculiar situation of a writer from Central Europe when he reaches the Western literary market. Owing to political circumstances, the novel was received primarily as a political pamphlet. In his preface to the second English translation (of 1982) Kundera recalls how during a television discussion in 1980 someone called *The Joke* "a major indictment of Stalinism," to which the author interjected: "Spare me your Stalinism, please. *The Joke* is a love story" (p. vii). And in one of his interviews he explains the matter further:

> When, in my novel *The Joke,* I returned momentarily to the 1950's, I wasn't interested in some sort of sensational revelation of new facts, nor in painting a so-called portrait of the times. Rather, I was drawn to the 1950's because during that period history was making all sorts of experiments with Man; the unique historical circumstances showed Man from unusual angles and thus enriched my knowledge and my doubts about human nature and human fate.
>
> (*The Politics of Culture,* p. 147)

Apart from being a love story—or rather a story about a misuse and debasement of love—*The Joke* is a parable of the futility of revenge and an investigation into various ways in which people try to cope with failure. The novel has an intricate "musical" structure. Its characters—Ludvik Jahn, the main hero; Helena, his lover and victim; and his friends Jaroslav and Kostka—appear first as voices speaking out of darkness, then slowly assume human shape, history, and a place in one or more of the book's several plots. Different in tone and mood, they are all variations on the same theme of disillusionment and loss, each concentrating on a single moment that changed the course of the protagonists' lives.

A long time ago, in his student years, Ludvik had sent a postcard to his girlfriend, whom he considered too serious about her political commitments. "Optimism is the opium of the people," the note said. "A healthy atmosphere stinks of stupidity! Long live Trotsky!" The card, however, fell into the hands of the party apparatchiks, and Ludvik, unable to treat his prank with adequate seriousness, was removed from the party and from his university. Subsequently he was drafted into a penal military battalion and after serving his time, was forced to do menial jobs until his rehabilitation and return to his career as a scientist. Disgusted with all ideologies and people, Ludvik conceives a plan to revenge himself on his onetime friend Zemanek, who played a chief role in his demise. When the occasion comes, he seduces Zemanek's wife, Helena, concentrating all the hatred he had accumulated into one act disguised as love. The plan, however, backfires miserably and turns into a joke. Ludvik discovers that Zemanek, once a party doctrinaire, has turned into a famous liberal and an idol of his students. Helena, estranged from her husband, falls hopelessly in love with Ludvik and, learning the truth about his real motives, tries to commit suicide. Even this attempt, however, turns into its own parody when, instead of a vial of sedatives, Helena takes a dose of laxative. Zemanek, having discovered his wife's infidelity, feels free to divorce her and live with his young lover. Ludvik thus ponders his frustrated plans:

> When vengeance is tabled, it turns into an illusion, a personal religion, a myth which recedes day by day from its cast of characters, who remain the same in the myth of vengeance, while in reality (the walk-way never stops moving) they have changed radically: today another Jahn stands before another Zemanek, and the blow I still owe him is beyond resurrection or reconstruction, is lost once and for all.
>
> (pp. 243–244)

Ludvik is one of Kundera's heroes who get trapped in their own jokes. The victim first of his lightheartedness and then of his "private religion" of revenge, he witnesses his joke turn into a drama, and a drama into a joke. His tragedy, comments the author in the introduction, "lies in the fact that the joke has deprived him of the right to tragedy. He is condemned to triviality" (p. xi).

Apart from Ludvik's story, however, there are two important subplots in the novel that strike a tone of real tragedy. One of them concerns Lucie, a silent, mysterious girl Ludvik meets while still serving in the army. They fall in love, and their relationship almost frees Ludvik from his bitterness and disenchantment. Although the girl declares her love, she stubbornly resists Ludvik's sexual advances. Finally they part, both equally confused and hurt. Ludvik learns Lucie's true story years later from his friend Kostka, who had known her in a different time and under different circumstances. As a young girl she had fallen victim to brutal sexual abuse by a gang of her colleagues. As a result, love and sexuality became for her two different, mutually exclusive things.

The protagonist of the second subplot is Jaroslav, a folk musician and a one-time idealistic Communist. We see him as an aging man, desperately trying to maintain his youthful idealism and his jovial, simple optimism. As the paradise of future brotherhood promised him by his ideology disintegrates in the triviality and arrogance of the present, Jaroslav withdraws into his private paradise of the past—Moravian history and folklore. He is especially fascinated by a custom called the Ride of the Kings, whose meaning and origin has been forgotten. Jaroslav imagines that its mystery reaches back to the pagan rites of passage or to Dionysian festivities of antiquity. "The folk song and the rite," he says, "are a tunnel beneath history, the tunnel that keeps alive much of what wars, revolutions, and brutal civilization have long since destroyed above ground, and allow us to look far into our past." Jaroslav lives by his memories of the time when he was the King of the Ride and dreams of the day when this honor will be bestowed on his son. At the end, however, he sees the ritual debased and ridiculed during a party-organized festival, and his son rejects the honor in order to watch a motorcycle race.

The three themes of the novel converge at the end, when Ludvik suddenly discovers the symmetry of his, Jaroslav's, and Lucie's fates:

> And suddenly Lucie appeared before my eyes, and I decided I finally knew why she'd turned up first at the barbershop and then in Kostka's story, his amalgam of truth and legend; it was because she wanted to tell me that her fate, (the fate of a rape victim) was very much like mine; that even though we'd failed to understand each other and were lost to each other, our life stories were twinned, intertwined, ran parallel, because they were both *stories of devastation;* much as Lucie was devastated by physical love and therefore deprived of life's most elemental value, so I was robbed of values I had originally meant to live by, values pure and innocent in origin; yes innocent: physical love, devastating though it may have been in Lucie's case, is still innocent, just as the songs of my region and the ensemble playing them are innocent, and the region itself, much as I'd grown to hate it, and Fubik, whose portrait I couldn't stomach, and the word "comrade," though I always heard a threat in it, and the word "future," and many other words. The blame lay elsewhere and was so great that its shadow had fallen over a vast area, over the world of innocent things (and words) and was devastating them. We lived, Lucie and I, in a world of devastation; and because we lacked the ability to commiserate with the things thus devastated, we turned our backs on them, offending both them and ourselves in the process.
>
> (p. 262)

Ludvik, Lucie, and to a certain extent Jaroslav, who almost abandons his music, are victims of circumstances, but also of their own narrowness of vision. They fail to distinguish between "pure and innocent things"—such as love, friendship, art, the idea of the brotherhood of men—and the external forces that corrupt and debase them. Yet they live in a world in which devastation and corruption are a rule rather than exception. Kundera never clearly explains the source of evil that destroys his protagonists' lives. It is possible to interpret it both as a result of particular political circumstances, and as a general condition of modern life. What is more important to the heroes of his story, and what adds to their helplessness, is the fact that the world they live in is not only the world of devastation, but also the world of forgetting that reduces their pain, anger, and longing to a set of gestures incomprehensible even to themselves. After his encounter with Zemanek, Ludvik meditates:

> By now history is nothing more than the thin thread of what is remembered stretched out over the ocean of what has been forgotten; but time moves on, and new eras will arise, eras the limited memory of the individual will be unable

> to grasp; centuries, millennia, will therefore fall away, centuries of painting and music, centuries of discoveries, battles, books, and the consequences will be dire: man will lose all insight into himself, and his history—unfathomable, inscrutable—will shrink into a handful of senseless schematic signs. Thousands of deaf and dumb Rides will set out to deliver their messages to those far-off descendants of ours and none of them will have time to listen.
>
> (p. 244)

In Kundera's fiction a personal drama or a misadventure often reveals some striking parallelism with the general condition of the world in which his heroes move, and their introspections usually lead to meditations on the state of history. "I have alvays been convinced," writes the author in the introduction to the American edition of *The Joke,* "that the paradoxes of history and private life have the same basic properties" (p. xii). This correspondence is also the main theme of his second novel, *Life Is Elsewhere.* Since for more than twenty years after 1968 no works by Kundera (with the exception of *Ptákovina*) were made officially available in Czechoslovakia, the book appeared first in France as *La vie est ailleurs* in 1973. Its main plot is the perennial drama of adolescence, and the novel uses the structure of a classical bildungsroman. In fact it is Kundera's bitter pamphlet on the "lyrical age" and its moral and political consequences.

The author uses a rather predictable theme of a torturous relationship between a mother and her son. The mother, Maman, unable to cope with the frustration of her marriage, her petit-bourgeois inhibitions, and her suppressed sensuality, uses her son, Jaromil, as a weapon against the world and a justification of her failures. Kundera takes a clearly skeptical view of motherly love, revealing its more doubtful and selfish side. Jaromil, as a young boy, discovers the power of his casual, mostly thoughtless verbal inventions and later, encouraged by his mother, begins to think of himself as a poet, despite lack of evidence that he has real talent. His life becomes that of continuous "lyrical" self-consciousness, which for Kundera represents immaturity in its most condensed form. Maman, afraid that her son will grow up and "run away" into the adult world, thus depriving her life of its only justification, wholeheartedly encourages his pseudopoetic aspirations. As long as his mostly unfortunate encounters with the "mature" world of adventure, sex, and politics result in self-pity and lyrical self-examination, she feels secure in her dominant role.

The story of Jaromil's struggle to grow up is depicted against the backdrop of the postwar years in Czechoslovakia, when the Communists were consolidating their power and trying to win over the younger generation. Jaromil joins the movement with fanatical zeal, seeing it as a route into the "real" world of action and adulthood. His involvement, however, ends in moral degradation when, in trying to prove his manhood, he deliberately causes the arrest of the woman who loves him. Rejected and humiliated by his colleagues, he dies of pneumonia after a theatrical suicide attempt.

Jaromil's torments serve as a diagnosis of a more general "lyrical sickness" that the author saw corroding Czechoslovak society. He asks in *Life Is Elsewhere:*

> What actually remains of that distant time? Today people regard those days as an era of political trials, persecutions, forbidden books, and legalized murder. But we, who remember, must bear witness. It was not only a terrible epoch but a lyrical one as well! It was ruled by the hangman—but by the poet, too.
>
> The wall behind which people were imprisoned was made of verse. There was dancing on both sides of it. No, not a danse macabre! A dance of innocence. Innocence with a bloody smile.
>
> (p. 255)

The assumption of the natural collusion between poet and executioner seems to be one of the most ambiguous and questionable of

Kundera's propositions. After all, nowhere else than in Central Europe did poetry prove to be the most powerful antidote to the poison of ideologies and the paralysis of fear. Poland's Czeslaw Milosz and Zbigniew Herbert and Bohemia's Vladimir Holan and Jaroslav Seifert are only a few examples of poets who preserved the antitotalitarian sensibility in verse. For Kundera, however, the equation serves as a way of focusing our attention on the lyrical aspect of the revolutionary mentality. Like some kinds of poetry, says the author, revolutions require a measure of adolescent disagreement not only with a particular kind of political or social reality but also with reality as such. A mature person, in Kundera's view, is aware of the imperfection and relativity of the world. He knows that "the absolute is an illusion, that nothing human is either great or eternal." The immature man, on the other hand, believes that perfection is possible, although it constantly eludes him as if through a conspiracy of malicious forces. The life he is striving for is always "elsewhere," and this evokes both self-pity and anger, as the narrator of *Life Is Elsewhere* explains:

> In immature man the longing persists for the safety and unity of his universe inside his mother's body. Anxiety (or anger) persists as well—toward the adult world of relativity in which he is lost like a drop in an alien sea. That's why young people are such passionate monists, emissaries of the absolute; that's why the poet weaves his private world of verse; that's why the young revolutionary (in whom anger is stronger than anxiety) insists on an absolutely new world forged from a single idea.
>
> (p. 206)

*Life Is Elsewhere* is a novel about disappointment with youth, which the author associates with the Stalinist era. Kundera's next novel, *The Farewell Party* (published in France in 1976 as *La valse aux adieu*), bears, by contrast, the mark of a more immediate and perhaps more devastating experience—the shock of the sudden suppression of the Prague Spring. Though it does not mention the Soviet invasion, and direct political references are even more scarce than in *The Joke* and *Life Is Elsewhere,* it is by far the gloomiest book Kundera ever wrote. The author once remarked that the novel was meant to be his farewell to his literary profession, to a whole way of life, and to an era in the history of his country. Like Thomas Mann's *The Magic Mountain,* it is set in the stifling, claustrophobic environment of a spa, where even the most trivial dramas assume almost tragic finality. Like Kafka's *The Trial,* it starts with an unexpected accusation that sets in motion a bizarre sequence of events leading to a real death and a universal sense of guilt that paradoxically spares only the murderer.

One of the novel's antiheroes, the jazz musician Klima who visits the spa to entertain its patients—middle-aged women suffering from infertility—receives a phone call from the spa's nurse, Ruzena, who claims that he is the father of her would-be child. It is never clear whether her pregnancy is real or imaginary, but it is clear that Ruzena is using her condition, and Klima, in order to escape her hopeless, small-town life. Klima, married to a beautiful though sickly woman, is one of Kundera's compulsive womanizers for whom the game has lost its excitement but who continue their pursuits out of fear of boredom and stasis. Although he knows that his fatherhood is scarcely likely, he takes Ruzena's revelation with surprising seriousness. Acting upon the advice of his cynical friends, he decides to pretend to be passionately in love with the girl in order to persuade her to have an abortion.

Their mutual intrigues bring them in contact with an assortment of other grotesque and frustrated characters populating the spa. Ruzena's local boyfriend pursues the nurse desperately, trying to convince her that the child is his. The spa doctor, Skreta, secretly inseminates his female patients with his own sperm, apparently attempting to create a whole generation of true brothers and sisters. Ruzena's psychopathic father, who has a taste for policing, organizes his fellow retirees into a squad of volunteer dogcatchers. There is also a mysterious foreigner, Bancroft, who has a seemingly endless supply of silver dollars and who is also, the novel suggests, a superhuman messenger with a halo around his head and a mission to fulfill in the decrepit world of the spa. Even his powers, however, fail in the face of some dark, ominous force that hangs over Kundera's protagonists. They all try to move beyond their limited destinies and devise plans of escape. Ruzena dreams about the elegant world at Klima's side. Klima wants to revive his past power over women. Skreta begs Bancroft to adopt him and take him to America. These fantastic attempts, however, only push them all deeper into the quagmires of their lives.

The most fascinating of the background characters is Jakub, a one-time Communist imprisoned during the Stalinist purges, who after his release plans to emigrate from Czechoslovakia. He is the only link between the limited, oppressive world of the spa and the larger though no less oppressive world outside. He is the only person who would cross the border of which the others only dream. More important, he is the bearer of death—literally, since he keeps a poison pill his friend Skreta gave him during his stay in prison. Acting on an irrational impulse, he places the pill in a vial of similar pills used by Ruzena. After some half-hearted attempts to recover it, he lets events run their course. Ruzena actually takes the pill and dies, but only after Jakub had left the town, and thus the terrifying, gratuitous murder remains to him purely hypothetical.

On his way toward the border Jakub tries to compare himself to Raskolnikov, yet he discovers that unlike Feodor Dostoevsky's character, he sees his deed as "weightless, easy to bear, light as air" (p. 195). He also realizes that his seemingly unmotivated act is a logical consequence of his whole life, a "crevice" where "all his disgust with people could be lodged and gain leverage" (p. 194). Like Ludvik from *The Joke,* Jakub seems to live by his "private religion" of contempt. He considers himself a victim yet notices that he is not different from his tormentors.

> Jakub loved nobility and refinement, but he had learned that these were not human qualities. He knew people well, and for that reason he did not like them. Jakub was noble, and thus gave them poison.
>
> I am a murderer through nobility of soul, he said to himself, and it seemed comical and sad.
>
> (p. 194)

*The Farewell Party* occasionally reads like a parable or metaphysical puzzle whose terms are not spelled out clearly enough. On a more immediate level, however, it is a powerful evocation of a world at the moment of its dissolution. The border toward which Jakub is driving, as well as the border he crosses when he places the poisonous pill in Ruzena's vial, become the symbol of an ultimate failure of hope and humanity. Kundera makes clear that beyond these borders there is no liberation, no new beginning. When Jakub takes a last look at his past life and his country, the narrator says:

> The day before he had thought that this would be a moment of relief. That he would be glad to leave. That he would be leaving a place where he had been born by mistake, and where he didn't really belong. But now he knew that he was leaving his only homeland, and that he had no other.
>
> (p. 205)

Crossing borders in both the geographical and moral sense is also the subject of Kundera's next novel, *The Book of Laughter and Forgetting* (1979), probably the first written specifically with the Western reader in mind. It is possible to read this book as a collection of short stories, since it consists of seven parts with different sets of characters and independent plots. Yet the author calls the book "a novel in the form of variations . . . leading toward a theme, a thought, a single situation, the sense of which fades in the distance" (p. 165). *The Book of Laughter and Forgetting* contains a whole passage devoted to Beethoven's sonatas in which the author sees the art of variation as an invitation to a voyage, which is one of Kundera's favorite terms to describe the spirit of European culture. The novel itself is Kundera's invitation, addressed to the Eastern European as well as the Western public, to a journey through the darkest areas of the contemporary Central European experience. Its main theme is the process of forgetting as it affects equally the lives of individual people and of whole nations.

One of the novel's characters is Tamina, a Czech girl who had to leave her country after 1968 and now earns her living as a bartender in a small French town. She is obsessed by the memory of her late husband and the chronology of their life together. This obsession has probably as much to do with their love as with her desire to maintain a degree of unity and continuity in her uprooted existence. Trying to recover the letters she used to exchange with her husband, which were left in Prague, she is pushed into an affair with a self-important French intellectual who promises to make a trip to Czechoslovakia. Yet the liaison eventually robs her of the memories she tried to preserve. Tamina surrounds herself with an impenetrable wall of silence that divides her as much from her new environment as from her past life, which has been irretrievably lost.

Kundera contrasts Tamina's story with that of Mirek, a Czech dissident with police on his heels who desperately wants to forget a one-time love affair he considers a discordant note in his life. Like Tamina he tries to recover his old love letters, but only in order to destroy them and obliterate the affair from memory. Other characters of the novel are involved in equally obsessive and frustrated pursuits. A young couple receives a surprise visit from the husband's mother just at a time when they plan to enjoy a *ménage à trois* with their mutual female friend. A young, self-pitying student resembling Jaromil from *Life Is Elsewhere* falls hopelessly in love with an older, primitive woman from the provinces. A bored womanizer, Jan, seeks in vain for "the long, mysterious, inscrutable, wonder-working arousal of a man over the body of a woman" (p. 227). Their often comic stories and their individual struggles with memory and forgetting seem to be mysterious emanations of Prague, the city of Kafka, whom the author calls "the prophet of the world without memory." Prague, a Central European capital haunted by the ghosts of destroyed monuments and the buried past, becomes the main and the most tragic hero of the novel.

"The struggle of man against power," says Mirek shortly before his arrest, "is the struggle of memory against forgetting" (p. 3). For Kundera the problem of Czechoslovakia, of Communism, and of the whole of Central Europe was less that of physical oppression than of institutionalized, forced forgetting. The totalitarian rule requires the world to be without memory, and it usually directs its sharpest criticism toward those who are the custodians of memory: writers, artists, and intellectuals.

One of the most striking illustrations of the bitter struggle between political power and memory is the anecdote told at the beginning of the novel. The first Communist leader of Czechoslovakia, Klement Gottwald, and his close friend and comrade, Foreign Minister Vladimir Clementis, posed for a photograph on a balcony of a baroque Prague palace during the Communist takeover in 1948. Four years later Clementis was charged with treason and executed together with ten other high party officials. His image was carefully removed from the photograph, which had been reproduced in thousands of copies. All that remained of him was the fur cap he had lent his friend Gottwald moments before the picture was taken. "On that balcony the history of Communist Czechoslovakia was born," writes Kundera ironically about the double takeover: the seizure of political power and the amputation of historical memory.

In *The Book of Laughter and Forgetting* the act of forgetting figures as an inevitable aspect of our existence in time. It can also result from an accidental break in the continuity of life or from a systematic destruction of a culture by external forces. Yet there is also another, more pervasive and dangerous kind of forgetting to which the Czech author wants to direct our attention. Memory, for Kundera, is synonymous with maturity and complexity. It is what makes men separate, independent individuals. Yet it is also a burden, and in order to bear it one has to be motivated by a strong conviction about its ultimate value. The author seems to suggest that there is a powerful yearning, embedded in each individual and each culture, to cast this burden away, to go beyond one's self and to disappear in some kind of amorphous community in which nobody possesses any memories, and therefore nobody is different. It is the Arcadian dream of Innocence Regained and of naive, primordial delight in existence in which an individual "loses all memory, all desire, cries out to the immediate present of the world, and needs no other knowledge" (p. 58). In Kundera's novel the chief expression of this state is ecstatic, mindless laughter and its visual image—a dance in a circle.

It is in this romantic and naive dream that Kundera sees the deepest psychological roots of the totalitarian utopia. In *The Book of Laughter and Forgetting* he recalls one of numerous Communist festivities, a celebration of youth and innocence staged a day after the Czech surrealist Záviš Kalandra, a friend of André Breton and Paul Éluard, was executed for allegedly "plotting against the people." The streets full of young, dancing people seemed to him like a unanimous verdict condemning not only Kalandra but anyone who dared to break the circle.

The paradise without memory and the magic dance in a circle appear in the novel as the most alluring and most misleading myth of humanity. It seems to offer radical solutions both to the burden of remembering and the pain of forgetting. Yet in the end it only destroys all the defenses man has against political and nonpolitical powers conspiring against his fragile, often difficult freedom. European civilization, says Kundera, is based on memory. The only liberty it knows is the liberty that results from free interactions between mature, sometimes lonely individuals—each of them carrying his or her private universe and private truth. The circle of dancers joined by a simple, common rhythm, he says, is the most closed of all figures. One cannot leave it and return at will. One can only stay in it forever or become its enemy.

Tamina's story ends with a fable. Tired by the pain of forgetting about her husband, she is magically transposed to an island of children who live in what seems a carefree, innocent anarchy. She is invited to join their games and to "forget about forgetting." She accepts, only to discover that the paradise is in fact a totalitarian nightmare in which no one is allowed to be different from the others, the rules of the games are brutally enforced, and privacy is constantly invaded. At the end of the story Tamina drowns during an attempted escape, watched by hostile and scornful children.

If the world in *The Book of Laughter and Forgetting* can be seen as a struggle between memory and forgetting, maturity and innocence, skepticism and utopia, there is little doubt which side the author takes. Yet on a higher, more abstract plane of the novel, each of the testing ideas appears as inseparable from its opposite, and the only desirable state is that of balance. In a passage "On Two Kinds of Laughter" Kundera introduces yet another opposition, this time between "angels," the advocates of rationality and meaning, and "demons," the skeptics, ironists, and iconoclasts:

> World domination, as everyone knows, is divided between demons and angels. But the good of the world does not require the latter to gain precedence over the former (as I thought when I was young); all it needs is a certain equilibrium of power. If there is too much uncontested meaning on earth (the reign of the angels), man collapses under the burden; if the world loses all its meaning (the reign of the demons), life is every bit as impossible.
>
> (p. 61)

Kundera focuses on moments in which this balance is unsettled and the fates of his characters, as well as the world around them, swing dangerously toward the nightmare of total harmony or of total chaos. Jan, the disenchanted, skeptical émigré who lives an "empty, unstructured life" and loses himself in sexual excesses, feels the proximity of a border "beyond which everything loses meaning: love, convictions, faith, history. . . . Yes, cross the border and you can hear the fateful laughter. And if you go on farther, *beyond* laughter?" (pp. 206, 217).

The delicate balance of oppositions is also the subject of *The Unbearable Lightness of Being.* The novel opens with a long passage on Nietzsche's concept of the "eternal return." If we assume that life is a sequence of transitory events that disappear without a trace, then every thing or emotion seems to us "a shadow, without weight, dead in advance, and whether it was horrible, beautiful, or sublime, its horror, sublimity and beauty mean nothing" (p. 3). If, on the other hand, we try to see every single act and every moment as recurring ad infinitum, everything becomes "a solid mass, permanently protuberant, its inanity irreparable" (p. 4). In the world of eternal return every choice and every move is burdened with unbearable responsibility. To see things as transitory or as eternally present is a choice that introduces one of two contradictory moral perspectives battling each other in the life of the modern man. These two perspectives, which Kundera associates with the notions of "lightness" and "weight," constitute the main dichotomy governing the lives of the characters in *The Unbearable Lightness of Being.* If the feeling of lightness can be pleasant and liberating, it also makes man "soar into the heights, take leave of the earth and his earthly being, and become only half real, his movements as free as they are insignificant." It reveals "the profound moral perversity of a world that rests essentially on the nonexistence of return, for in this world everything is pardoned in advance, and therefore everything is cynically permitted." In the hypothetical world of eternal return, which Nietzsche called "the heaviest of burdens," the responsibility connected with even the most trivial act "crushes us, we sink beneath it, it pins us to the ground." Yet at the same time "the heavier the burden, the closer our lives come to earth, the more real and truthful they become" (p. 5).

The three main characters of the novel—Tomas, a famous Prague surgeon, his wife, Tereza, and his lover, Sabina—illustrate various human consequences of the central dichotomy. Sabina is a personification of lightness. She walks away from all commitments, abandoning her father, her numerous lovers, and her country. She leads a life of betrayal and programmatic irresponsibility. Yet her lightness has its own center of gravity. As an artist she is trying to escape what she calls "the kitsch of existence." An exhibition of her works is arranged in the West after 1968, but when she reads in the catalog that her paintings express the political struggle of her country, she reacts by saying that she does not really care for politics. Her only enemy is kitsch.

Kitsch, as Kundera explains in *The Unbearable Lightness of Being,* is "the aesthetic ideal of the categorical agreement with being," which leaves out everything that is accidental, ambiguous, or individual. It is a realm ruled by sentiments shared by multitudes. "Kitsch causes two tears to flow in quick succession. The first tear says: How nice to see children running on the grass! The second tear says: How nice to be moved, together with all mankind, by children running on the grass!" (p. 251). The kitsch that Sabina is struggling with is similar to the dance in the circle from *The Book of Laughter and Forgetting.* They both originate in the dream of false brotherhood, and both find their fullest realization in the totalitarian utopia.

In a totalitarian world everything that infringes on kitsch must be banished for life, says Kundera; every display of individualism, every doubt, and every trace of irony must be done away with. "In this light, we can regard the gulag as a septic tank used by totalitarian kitsch to dispose of its refuse" (p. 252). Thus Sabina's outburst against the political interpretation of her art is only partly justified. In her life as in her art, irony and surrealist imagination are in fact a form of political statement. She is reacting to kitsch, but primarily in its Communist version—the official optimism and idyllic imagery that are "folding screens that curtain death." Her paintings are canvases sliced with a knife to reveal a true, more disturbing picture. In her escape from kitsch, commitment, and responsibility, however, Sabina reaches a point at which everything becomes doubtful and meaningless, and even her protest loses all significance.

If Sabina represents the element of lightness, Tereza, at least in Tomas' eyes, is her direct opposite. She appears in his life as an emanation of necessity. Through her love and vulnerability she demands from her husband total devotion and fidelity and becomes a crushing burden he has to bear until the end of his life. After the meeting with Tereza, Tomas' existence seems to be guided by the principle of weight. His life fills with fortuities that inevitably push him toward "heavy" decisions. After 1968 he stays briefly in the West, where he is offered an interesting and lucrative job, yet he decides to follow Tereza back to Czechoslovakia. He refuses to recant his article on the corruption of power written during the times of liberalization and loses his job. Yet he also refuses to join a group of dissidents, because he sees little rationality in their methods of resistance. He allows himself to be reduced to the position of a window washer and then a truck driver on a state farm. Even his death has symbolic meaning; he dies with Tereza, crushed by the weight of his truck.

Tomas acts as if guided by some categorical imperative, though there is a strange ambiguity in all his choices. He himself cannot find any clear motivation for his decisions. An ironist and skeptic, temperamentally inclined toward lightness, he seems to be much closer to Sabina than to Tereza. He knows that nothing in his life is a result of necessity and that everything is chance. Even his meeting with his future wife, which sets in motion all his fateful decisions, is an accident that did not have to occur. Had he decided not to accept her love or to stay in the West, they would both have found different partners and nothing would have excluded the possibility that their lives would be as happy as, or happier, than their life together. In fact, Tomas sees all human choices as purely accidental, since their psychological motives are always ambiguous and their consequences unknown.

> There is no means of testing which decision is better, because there is no basis for comparison. We live everything as it comes, without warning, like an actor going on cold. And what can life be worth if the first rehearsal for life is life itself? That is why life is always like a sketch. No, "sketch" is not quite the word, because a sketch is an outline of something, the groundwork for a picture, whereas the sketch that is our life is a sketch for nothing, an outline with no picture.
>
> (p. 8)

This perspective resembles the principle of "nonexistence of return" from the dichotomy proposed at the beginning of the novel. And yet, despite this awareness, Tomas acts as if his deeds were "a solid mass, permanently protuberant." In his meditations on Beethoven's music, which is one of the recurrent motifs of the novel and accompanies Tomas' relationship with Tereza, the author points out the almost universal association between the notions of necessity, weight, and value, which tells us that "only necessity is heavy, and only what is heavy has value." There is nothing, however, in the novel itself which would indicate that Tomas' life assumes any value it would otherwise lack. "Which is better, lightness or weight?" asks the author at the beginning of the book, yet he leaves the question without any decisive answer. We are in fact made to believe that both qualities have an important function in life and that the victory of one over the other, like the final victory of "angels" or "demons" in *The Book of Laughter and Forgetting,* could bring about disastrous consequences.

The novel ends on a note of sorrow but also of reconciliation, which comes at the end of the road when the opposite poles of human existence are finally allowed to meet. Shortly before their death Tereza reflects on her life with Tomas, which has been reduced to a set of simple gestures of tenderness and resignation:

> On they danced to the strains of the piano and violin. Tereza leaned her head on Tomas's shoulder. Just as she had when they flew together in the airplane through the storm clouds. She was experiencing the same odd happiness and odd sadness as then. . . . The sadness was form, the happiness content. Happiness filled the space of sadness.
>
> (pp. 313–314)

The mood of sadness rewarded by a new clarity of vision also appears in *Jacques et son maître* (*Jacques and His Master,* 1981), Kundera's dramatic variation on Diderot. Its publication in the West followed that of *The Unbearable Lightness of Being,* but the play was completed approximately at the same time as *The Farewell Party.* In one of his interviews Kundera said that the play, written in the darkest period of his marginal existence after 1968, was meant, like the novel, to be his farewell to his life as a writer. If *The Farewell Party,* however, is a gloomy, even apocalyptic good-bye, the play is, in the author's words, a "farewell in the form of an entertainment." It is a nostalgic yet humorous look at the European values most cherished by Kundera: the spirit of liberty, adventure, individualism, and tolerance, but most of all the salutary laughter that tells us that nothing in the world should be taken too seriously, since nothing is what the world would like us to believe.

In his essay "Introduction to a Variation," published as a foreword to the play, Kundera says that *Jacques* was his private defense against the ideological and cultural abuses resulting from the Soviet invasion: "When the weight of rational irrationality fell on my country, I felt an instinctive need to breathe deeply of the spirit of the post-Renaissance West. And that spirit seemed nowhere more concentrated than in the feast of intelligence, humor, and fantasy that is *Jacques le fataliste*" (pp. 3–4). In the times of rigid dogmatism Kundera was looking for an intellectual space where "*everything* is called into question, *everything* exposed to doubt; *everything* is entertainment" (p. 6). Diderot's novel appeared to the Czech author as a model of the "imaginative realm where no one is the possessor of the truth and where everyone has the right to be understood" (*New York Review of Books,* 13 June 1985).

Kundera's version of the story of Jacques, his aristocratic master, and their amorous adventures imitates the digressive form of the original. Four main characters—Jacques, his master, the Innkeeper, and the Marquis des Arcis—tell their stories, which are in fact variations on the same simple theme of love, betrayal, and illusion. Their narratives are repeatedly interrupted by questions, anecdotes, and fragments of other stories. Kundera saw Diderot's novel as "a big noisy conversation" in which all possibility of melodramatic identification is thwarted by changing perspectives and unexpected conclusions. His own "variation," as he calls *Jacques and His Master,* seeks the same effect. The characters of the play change roles enacting their own tales and the tales of their partners. At one point, when the Innkeeper tells the story of Madame de Pommeraye, who punishes her unfaithful lover by tricking him into marrying a young prostitute, Jacques assumes the role of the unhappy husband in order to forgive both Madame de Pommeraye and his fictitious spouse, and change the moral of the story. There is no reason to accept only one interpretation of events, he claims,

> because nothing on earth is certain, and the meaning of things changes as the wind blows. And the wind blows constantly, whether you know it or not. And the wind blows, and joy turns to sorrow, revenge to reward, and a loose woman becomes a faithful wife with whom none can compare.
>
> (pp. 65–66)

With *Jacques and His Master* Kundera returns to the moment when modern man discovered the relativity of his judgments and the limitations of his reason and learned that his condition can be seen both as tragic and liberating. He evokes the laughter that led modern culture into its intellectual journey, where nothing was as it seemed to be and every truth was breaking up into fragments of relative truths. Yet with the passing of ages the travelers have become weary and confused. The final reunion between Jacques and his master, when the servant is miraculously saved from the gallows, is strangely melancholic and sad, and the author suggests that their departure from the empty stage may be final. "Servant and master have made their way across all the modern history of the West," says Kundera in his introduction. "In Prague, city of the grand farewell, I heard their fading laughter. With love and anguish, I clung to that laughter as one clings to fragile, perishable things, things that have been condemned" (p. 12).

The fascination with the process of forgetting, a mixture of irony and sentiment for fragile things in the moment of their disappearance, informs Kundera's writing no matter whether its subject is the paradoxes of human relations or the paradoxes of history. Tracing the source of this particular mood, the author himself pointed toward Central Europe, his native realm and a frequent point of reference. Central Europe, as Kundera stressed both in his works of fiction and in his essays, belongs to the West. It is the West in the most condensed, though often anachronistic form. In his essay "The Tragedy of Central Europe," the author defined this domain as "a small arch-European Europe, a reduced model of Europe conceived according to one rule: the greatest variety within the smallest space." Since the nineteenth century, however, it had also been an "uncertain zone of small nations" aware that their very existence can be put in question at any time. The sense of fragility caused by the permanently unstable political situation resulted, according to Kundera, in a typically Central European ironic and mistrustful attitude toward history. Small nations do not create history, he says, and more often than not they find themselves on its wrong side, as outcasts and victims. Thus they can hardly take history seriously, as Hegel and Marx did, treating it as an incarnation of reason and a judge of collective fate. In Central European eyes history appears more often as a farce and a mockery of its own supposed grandiosity. "Never forget that only in opposing History as such can we resist the history of our own day." This quotation from the Polish writer Witold Gombrowicz should, in Kundera's opinion, be engraved above the gate to Central Europe.

At the end of the nineteenth and the beginning of the twentieth century, noted Kundera in his essay, Central Europe was one of the most important cultural centers. It gave Europe the music of Arnold Schönberg, Gustav Mahler, and Béla Bartók, the literary works of Franz Kafka, Jaroslav Hašek, Robert Musil, Hermann Broch, and Stanislaw Ignacy Witkiewicz, and comparable achievements in visual arts and theater. It witnessed the birth of serial music, structuralism, the new linguistics, psychoanalysis, and a special kind of modernist sensitivity that was much more painful and prophetic than its Western counterpart. Kundera attributed this unprecedented eruption of creativity partly to the mixture of ideas, national cultures, and traditions that had become the mark of that region and partly to its particular disabused view of history—a sense of decline more acute there than in other parts of the continent. For Kundera, the significance of Central European culture derived from the fact that it was aware of its vulnerability and made this vulnerability its primary subject:

> It's enough to read the greatest Central European novels: in Herman Broch's *The Sleepwalkers* History appears as a process of gradual degradation of values; Robert Musil's *The Man Without Qualities* paints a euphoric society which doesn't realize that tomorrow it will disappear; in Jaroslav Hašek's *The Good Soldier Schveik* pretending to be an idiot becomes the last possible method for preserving one's freedom; the novelistic vision of Kafka speaks to us of a world without memory, of a world that comes after historic time. All of this century's great Central European works of art, even up to our day, can be understood as long meditations on the possible end of European humanity.
>
> (*New York Review of Books,* 26 April 1984)

Milan Kundera's own novels and short stories present us with a world in which the prophecy of Europe's decline has been fulfilled, but the meditation goes on. The fates of his characters, their misguided pursuits and confused desires, intermingle with the fate of their part of Europe. In his essay on Kafka, "Somewhere Beyond," the author remarked that the private and the public spheres constantly reflect upon each other, and the "psychological mechanisms set in motion by great historical events (seemingly incredible and inhuman) are the same as those which control even the most private situations (quite common and deeply human)" (*Formations,* p. 126).

In fact the private situations in which Kundera's heroes become entangled often resemble minuscule models of the totalitarian system, where privacy is brutally destroyed in the name of love, false accusations invite real crimes, and lyrical frenzy turns into institutionalized brutality. We are often reminded that Central Europe, whose condition Kundera evokes with great accuracy, is only a laboratory of something that stretches far beyond its borders. The Czech author is clearly not satisfied with merely political interpretations of the tragedy of his world. Coercive doctrines and repressive political systems, hostile to the spirit of European plurality and tolerance, appear as effects rather than causes. The primary source of the decline is man and his cultural self-image.

The world in which Kundera's heroes move is built around sharp dichotomies: reason and skepticism, freedom and necessity, sentiment and irony, lightness and weight. Between these poles, as he suggests, stretches modern European culture. It has survived by maintaining a delicate balance between extremities, yet it is becoming increasingly difficult to maintain this balance. The human universe portrayed by Kundera seems to be constantly threatened by a fall into one of two forms of immaturity: an adolescent romanticism and lyric dream of perfection or an equally adolescent nihilism and anarchy.

Kundera admits that the modern era contained in its birth the seed of its demise. Yet he seems reluctant to reject the modern tradition with its fragile rationalism, skepticism, and plurality of values. As in *Jacques and His Master,* the journey must continue. In the meantime the author refers once more to his favorite Central European writers, Kafka, Musil, and Broch: "Distrustful of the illusions concerning progress, distrustful of the kitsch of hope, I share their sorrow about the Western twilight. Not a sentimental sorrow. An ironic one" (*New York Times Magazine,* 19 May 1985).

## Selected Bibliography

### CZECH EDITIONS

#### POETRY

*Člověk zahrada širá.* Prague, 1953.
*Poslední máj.* Prague, 1955.
*Monology.* Prague, 1957.

#### FICTION

For the last four titles the dates in brackets represent the original French publication by Gallimard.

*Směšné lásky.* Prague, 1963.
*Druhý sešit směšných lásek.* Prague, 1965.
*Žert.* Prague, 1967.
*Třetí sešit směšných lásek.* Prague, 1968.
*Život je jinde.* Toronto, 1979 [1973].
*Valčík na rozloučenou.* Toronto, 1979 [1976].
*Kniha smíchu a zapomnění.* Toronto, 1981 [1979].
*Nesnesitelná lehkost bytí.* Toronto, 1985 [1984].

PLAYS

*Majitelé klíčů.* Prague, 1962.
*Ptákovina, čili Dvoje uši—dvoje svadba.* Prague, 1968.

LITERARY CRITICISM

*Umění románu.* Prague, 1960.

## FRENCH EDITIONS

*Jacques et son maître.* Paris, 1981. The only book originally written in French.

## ENGLISH TRANSLATIONS OF KUNDERA'S FICTION

*The Book of Laughter and Forgetting.* Translated by Michael Henry Heim. New York, 1980.
*The Farewell Party.* Translated by Peter Kussi. New York, 1976.
*Jacques and His Master.* Translated by Michael Henry Heim. New York, 1985.
*The Joke.* Translated by Michael Henry Heim. New York, 1982.
*Laughable Loves.* Translated by Suzanne Rappaport. New York, 1974.
*Life Is Elsewhere.* Translated by Peter Kussi. New York, 1974.
*The Unbearable Lightness of Being.* Translated by Michael Henry Heim. New York, 1985.

## ESSAYS, ARTICLES, AND ADDRESSES

"1968: Prague, Paris, and Josef Škvorecký." Translated by Anne-Marie La Traverse. *World Literature Today* 54, no. 4:558–560 (Autumn 1980).
"The Czech Wager." *The New York Review of Books,* 22 January 1981.
"All I Cared About Was Women and Art." *The New York Times Book Review,* 24 October 1982.
"On Kafka and Chaos." *Vogue,* February 1982.
"A Little History Lesson." Translated from the French by Linda Asher. *The New York Review of Books,* 22 November 1984.
"The Novel and Europe." Translated from the French by David Bellos. *The New York Review of Books,* 19 July 1984.
"Somewhere Beyond." Translated from the Czech by Jaroslav Schejbal. *Formations* 1:122–129 (Spring 1984).
"The Tragedy of Central Europe." Translated from the French by Edmund White. *The New York Review of Books,* 26 April 1984.
"The Legacy of The *Sleepwalkers.*" *Partisan Review,* 51, (4)–52, (1) (1984–1985).
"Man Thinks, God Laughs." Translated from the French by Linda Asher. *The New York Review of Books,* 13 June 1985.
"Prague: A Disappearing Poem." Translated from the French by Edmund White. *Granta* 17 (Autumn 1985).
*The Art of the Novel.* Translated by Linda Asher. New York, 1988. A collection of previously published essays.

## INTERVIEWS

"Milan Kundera." In Antonin J. Liehm, *The Politics of Culture.* Translated from the Czech by Peter Kussi. New York, 1970. Pp. 130–150.
"Kundera: Comedy Is Elsewhere." George Theiner. *Index on Censorship,* 6, no. 6:3–7 (November–December, 1977).
"Journey into the Maze." Francine du Plessix Gray. *Vogue,* February 1982.
"When There Is No Word for 'Home'." Jane Kramer. *The New York Times Book Review,* 29 April 1984, 46–47.
"A Talk with Milan Kundera." Olga Carlisle. *The New York Times Magazine,* 19 May 1985.

## CRITICAL STUDIES

Brodsky, Joseph. "Why Milan Kundera Is Wrong About Dostoyevsky." *The New York Times Book Review.* 17 February 1985.
Fuentes, Carlos. "The Other." *Triquarterly* 51:256–275 (Spring 1981).
Kussi, Peter. "Milan Kundera: Dialogues with Fiction." *World Literature Today,* 57, no. 2:206–209 (Spring 1983).
Misurella, Fred. "Not Silent, but in Exile and with

Cunning." *Partisan Review,* 52, no. 2:87–98 (1985).

Nadeau, Maurice. "Contre l'indifférence et l'oubli." *La Quinzaine Littéraire* 302, 16–31 May 1979, 4–6.

Podhoretz, Norman. "An Open Letter to Milan Kundera." *Commentary* 78:34–39 (October 1984).

Roth, Philip. "Milan Kundera the Joker." *Esquire,* April 1974.

Sturdivant, Mark. "Milan Kundera's Use of Sexuality." *Critique* 26, no 3:131–140 (Spring 1980).

White, Edmund. "Kundera à la mode." *Nation,* 12 May 1984.

JAROSŁAW ANDERS